Management
and Organization

A critical text

Stephen Linstead
*Director of Research and Professor of
Organizational Analysis, University of Durham*

Liz Fulop
*Professor of Management in the School of
Marketing and Management,
Griffith University, Queensland*

Simon Lilley
*Reader in Information and Organization
at the Management Centre,
University of Leicester*

with contributions from

Bobby Banerjee
Joanna Brewis
Michael Browne
Rodney J. Clarke
Richard Dunford
Jonathan Gosling
Ann-marie Greene
Harold Hayward
Alison Linstead
Frank Mueller
Stephen Procter
David S. Richards
William D. Rifkin
Graham Sewell
Robin Stanley Snell
Edward Wray-Bliss

palgrave
macmillan

First published 2004 by
PALGRAVE MACMILLAN
Houndmills, Basingstoke, Hampshire RG21 6XS and
175 Fifth Avenue, New York, N.Y. 10010
Companies and representatives throughout the world

PALGRAVE MACMILLAN is the global academic imprint of the Palgrave
Macmillan division of St. Martin's Press, LLC and of Palgrave Macmillan Ltd.
Macmillan® is a registered trademark in the United States, United Kingdom
and other countries. Palgrave is a registered trademark in the European
Union and other countries.

ISBN 0–333–94750–9

This book is printed on paper suitable for recycling and made from fully
managed and sustained forest sources.

A catalogue record for this book is available from the British Library.

Library of Congress Cataloging-in-Publication Data

Linstead, Stephen, 1952–
    Management and organization : a critical text / Stephen Linstead, Liz
Fulop, Simon Lilley ; with contributions from Bobby Banerjee ... [et al.].
      p. cm.
    Rev. ed. of: Management / Liz Fulop and Stephen Linstead. 1999.
    Includes bibliographical references and index.
    ISBN 0-333-94750-9 (pbk.)
     1. Management. 2. Organization. 3. Management–Australia. I. Fulop, Liz.
II. Lilley, Simon. III. Fulop, Liz. Management. IV. Title.

HD31.F853 2004
658—dc21   2003054921

Editing and origination by
Aardvark Editorial, Mendham, Suffolk

10 9   8   7   6   5   4   3
13 12 11 10 09 08 07 06 05 04

Printed and bound in China

EMENT
ANIZATION

Contents

List of figures

List of exhibits

List of case studies

Preface

Stephen Linstead, Liz Fulop and Simon Lilley

In 1992, Liz Fulop, Faye Frith and Harold Hayward from Australia collaboratively edited a book called *Management for Australian Business: A Critical Text.* This was the first management textbook in the world to use 'critical' in its title. It was a bestseller in Australia despite the sceptical views of many academics who thought that critical and management did not go together! Back then it was the stock market collapse of the late 1980s, and the associated management issues this upheaval caused, that made it imperative to look more critically at management than was occurring in many mainstream textbooks and management programmes. In the original preface to the 1992 book, the editors said:

It goes without saying that there is nothing simple about management. There never was; nor should there be. Too much is at stake. This book is written with the firm conviction that to become a successful and clever manager involves mastering much more than a few simple 'recipes' or 'easy steps' for performing management functions ... the function of a management textbook should be to equip managers with enduring skills and knowledge that will help them cope with the complexity and ambiguity that await them in their daily endeavours. The book places a premium on developing critical thinking and analytical capacities that can be successfully applied to any management situation ... an understanding of management is not enhanced by uncritical 'one best way' approaches (Fulop et al. 1992: vi).

A second text was written in 1999 by Liz Fulop and Stephen Linstead in an attempt to update the content of the first book for students of the next century. The book, called *Management: A Critical Text*, was adopted not only in Australia but elsewhere, including the UK and Canada, and it became the benchmark for a truly critical management textbook that did not ape other more traditional texts, or confine itself to organizational theory or organizational behaviour alone.

As we looked at the ideas that had animated the first book, what became strikingly obvious was, first, that taking such a critical approach to management was more important than ever and, second, that the market was no better served in this regard than it had been when the first book was written. But things had changed, and changed considerably. A focus on Australian business seemed parochial to the point of absurdity in the context of internationalization and globalization. What managers of the future would need was an early exposure to ideas

and cases from a number of cultures and contexts – the USA, Europe and Asia-Pacific in particular. Similarly, learning had moved so much to centre stage in the consideration of how organizations and managers could remain effective that it demanded more extensive and upfront consideration. Diversity as a topic had become more significant than it had ever been, and although all the material in the book needed to be revisited in this light, the issue of gender could no longer be marginalized but demanded focused treatment. In addition, the growth of a concern with ethics, which was once an optional feature of most business programmes, was increasingly being recognized as a foundational element of a critical approach to management. Sadly, the corporate collapses of the late 1990s and early 2000s, and the unethical and illegal management practices associated with many of these, suggest that more than ever management *must* be taught from a critical perspective and across all business programmes.

As we reviewed what needed to be done for the second revision, we came to realize that the first book, which we had felt was quite radical in its time, was looking more and more conservative – and we were more critical than ever! What was needed was a rethinking of many of our assumptions and a reframing of some of the core issues – such as power, leadership, motivation – that remain at the heart of studies of management. Some topics, such as interorganizational relations and teamworking, were so clearly a part of ways of working of the future, and could no longer be dismissed as transitory fashions, that they required proper treatment in their own right, and not as part of a broader and more synoptic consideration.

Our new text grew out of the need to expand the topics that were covered in the 1999 text and to address an even greater range of issues that are now pressing on managers and their organizations. To this end, Simon Lilley was brought into the editorial team and our range of associates expanded. We have included topics on structure, control, conflict, change, sustainability and the virtual world. The title reflects what was already a goal of the 1992 book, which was *to bring organization and management studies together*. Managing is an organizationally situated and context-specific activity, and driven by the need to organize work around complex relationships that are constrained by structural arrange-ments, be they teams, hierarchy, job titles, an organ-ization chart or the layout of an office. Management and organization must be thought through together.

Who is this book for?

This book is an *advanced introduction* to the topics in it. This means that you don't have to have familiarity with the topics themselves in order to use it effectively, as the introductory basics that we consider relevant are included, but we do move on further and faster than an introductory text would. If you've studied introductory management before, you might find you have to unlearn some of the approaches you are familiar with, which is why we have provided a good deal of our own introductions to topics. We don't cover everything, but we do cover all we think you'll need. The book can be used effectively on final-year undergraduate courses and second-year specialist options, obviously with students of business and management, sociology, politics, history, geography and even English in our experience. However, the book will be most valuable to masters students – core courses on masters in management or MBA, or courses on critical management as part of programmes across the social sciences. PhD students in management and organization will find it invaluable in getting quickly up to date in current critical research across a range of areas.

Each of us, in fact, has taught the material differently as we have developed it. Liz has used the text in undergraduate teaching and selective chapters in postgraduate masters subjects. Simon has used one chapter to teach a whole subject while Steve has used the book as the basis for a core course, both at masters and MBA levels. What we have also found is that our colleagues, in addition to our using the book for our own specialist courses, have used the chapters individually to support and provide a critical dimension to their own courses such as strategy. In these cases the book has been adopted as a *programme text,* which students carry with them throughout their whole masters or final-year studies to provide a different perspective to conventional approaches. The text lends itself to creative use and interpretation and we have tried not to constrain its users.

We provide the textbook not primarily as a course book to be worked through chapter by chapter, week by week, although this can be done, but as the first and most comprehensive resource for people *teaching management critically.* We also have some additional support materials available on the book's website for adopters, and we welcome your suggestions for ways in which we can enhance this.

How this book is organized

We have followed the *collaborative approach* developed in the original book, expanding the range of specialist international contributors and this has helped produce a book which is far more original in its approach than any other in the marketplace, and far more up to date, with cutting-edge research in each area. We hope that readers will also recognize the benefits of collaboration in the consistency of approach throughout the book achieved through our co-authoring of many of the chapters.

We have deliberately chosen *not* to develop this book according to a model which we then work laboriously through section by section. Management and organizational behaviour (OB) texts often break the subject down into three areas – the individual, the group and the organization. Sometimes a text will add a fourth area, the environment. The drawback with this approach is that it separates out processes which in reality are not so easily separated – gender, for example, is a property of individuals, is defined by groups, is an important way in which organizations work and are divided, implicitly and explicitly, and is the subject of environmental regulation, legislation, demographics, ethics and ideological debate which varies dramatically across cultures. We have tried to capture this *multilayered nature of each topic* within its chapters.

We also recognise that the conventional division of organization and management into these areas is useful, but we see it as a little more complex than commonly presented. So we present our underlying conception of management as the *management of relationships*, and in the Introduction we outline a model of how these relationships can be thought of. This model can function as a broad map of the terrain, and shows how the topics in this book relate to some topics, such as quantitative analysis and techniques, which may be part of management as a whole but which are not covered in this book.

The book features *substantial cases* within each chapter, which is connected with the fact that we chose *to exemplify our approach to case analysis* in the text rather than in the instructor's guide accompanying it. However, we have chosen cases on the basis of how well they illustrate our arguments and encourage reflection on the part of students. We have not chosen them on some contrived notion of similar style or uniform length. To do otherwise would make a mockery of the real-life situations that cases are meant to represent. We begin the chapters with *questions about the topic* – but not questions from the point of view of the academic lecturer. We have used questions which *our students* have told us were in their minds when they asked themselves, what do I really want to know about this topic? What puzzles me about it? Many of the chapters give some outline answers to these questions at the end of each chapter. We also ask questions about each case and give answers at the end, but don't expect there to be the same number of questions in each chapter or the length of the answers to be the same. The questions are chosen more on the basis of how much they make you think and the amount of class discussion they usually provoke.

Each chapter is *a substantive piece of work in its own right* and contains some original material related to the topic. Unlike most textbooks, it is not simply a representation of work done by others but an introduction to the state of work on the topic at the present time. The research we draw on is as up to date as we could make it – in some cases we draw on unpublished work if we consider it sufficiently important.

The book is structured simply. The first part we call 'Core Concepts', and this contains the basic concepts which we consider underpin all the other chapters in the book. We take a different view to most other books, in that we think, in a book which is supposed to help its readers to learn, *learning* should be the first concept addressed; *gender* and *culture,* as two fundamental dimensions which affect the way theory itself is constructed should be addressed next; that *structure* is best addressed alongside culture, with which it is often confused; and *nature,* in the form of managing sustainably, is equally fundamental to the way we think about organizing, not an afterthought to strategy which is how it is often regarded. *Power* is fundamental to shaping organizations and cannot meaningfully be dealt with without considering *control.* Finally, *ethics* now more urgently than ever needs to be a foundation for what we do rather than a way in which we reflect on it. All the topics in the first part can be read into the topics in the second part.

In the second part, we look at 'Management Processes', moving from those more personal ones like *motivation* and *leading,* to the management of *teams,* and the issues that arise such as *conflict, change* and *decision making.* The last two chapters in this section take a more macro-view, looking at *strategy* and beyond, the ways in which organizations themselves work together collectively in *networks.* Our conclusion offers some reflections and speculation on what it will be like to manage in a *virtual world.*

As you read through the new book, you will see that we have retained much of the original content but have updated where necessary as well as venturing into new, exciting areas. We have deliberately not written to the formulae and format of standard texts – we see little virtue in artificially contrived chapter lengths and format. We do not assume that students think in neat compartmentalized ways or that they are incapable of dealing with differences in style and format. To do so would be to contradict and destroy the meaning of critique as we understand and profess it.

We remain committed to developing an understanding of critical management that draws not only on more traditional ideas of critique but one that emphasizes the micro-practices of managers. It is vital that managers are able to make sense of their multifaceted roles and relationships, the forces and processes that either enable or impede them in doing their jobs, and the rich pastiche of ideas and theories that can enrich their thinking and practice. All managers have complex workplace relationships to deal with and we want to help them do this. Our text offers a scholarly and highly challenging way to study management but it has practice firmly in mind. As we have repeatedly said in past texts, this book is not for those managers or students seeking simple 'truths' and 'rules' by which to manage. Rather, it is for those who want to be challenged and transformed by what they read and learn. We would love to hear what you think of the book, how you've used it, what you love or hate about it, how we could or should improve it, and how we ourselves could learn more about what we are achieving as authors and how we could better serve you, our readers.

Thanks are due to all our co-authors, for the hard work they put in, for the critical scrutiny they endured and, in some cases, for putting up with phone calls that arrived in the middle of the night – one of the perils of collaborating to meet deadlines across time zones! Thanks are also due to our current and past students in MBA, masters of management and international management and undergraduate business degrees at Durham, Essex, Keele, Griffith, Sunderland and Wollongong for their responses to the material in this book. We owe thanks to Sarah Brown, formerly commissioning editor for Palgrave Macmillan (UK), who initially urged us to pursue a third revision of the textbook, and then courageously accepted our proposal to produce a quite different one in content. We also want to thank Ruth Lake who took over from Sarah and kept the project on track. Ursula Gavin took over the responsibility for the project around the time the deadlines had to be met and, despite coming into the project so late, got to grips with it very quickly and professionally. She was able to give us constructive and valuable advice on revising the manuscript yet allowed us to maintain the integrity of the text as a unique product in the marketplace.

Finally, at the end of a project which has spanned three years and several thousand miles, a period in which we have all separately had to cope with both tragic and joyful events, we are delighted to find we are still talking to each other! In the end though, what counts most to us is our passionate commitment to changing how managers learn about management, our faith that others share this commitment and the gratitude of past students who were challenged by our texts. These are the things that made the writing of this book so important to us, and we hope you will find it equally rewarding.

Acknowledgements

The authors would like to thank the following:

Alison Linstead for material on the 24-hour society in Chapter 17; Troy Thompson for his contribution to writing the section on Scenario Planning in Chapter 15; Faye Frith and Harold Hayward for contributions to Chapter 14 from the earlier (1992) text; Dennis Mortimer for contributions to Chapter 9 from the earlier (1992) text; Faye Frith for her contributions to Chapter 12 from the earlier (1992) text and to Chapter 6 from the earlier (1992 and 1999) texts; Richard Dunford as a co-author of Chapter 10 on the basis of the use of selected material from R. Dunford, 'Leadership and the manager' in L. Fulop, F. Frith and H. Hayward (eds) *Management for Australian Business: A Critical Text*, Melbourne, Macmillan Education, 1992, also reproduced in Chapter 5 of Liz Fulop and Stephen Linstead *Management: A Critical Text*, Melbourne and Basingstoke, Macmillan 1999. All new material contained in Chapter 10 has been written by Liz Fulop and Stephen Linstead who remain responsible for the content and design of the chapter. Liz Fulop would like to thank Ewa and Alan Buttery for their contributions to Chapter 16 from the earlier (1999) text. Their contributions are also separately acknowledged in the chapter.

Robin Snell, author of Chapter 8, would like to thank a number of others for their valuable help for material used from the 1999 text: Anthony Wai-kei Cheng, who at the time was a PhD student at City University of Hong Kong (CUHK), for providing some useful initial review notes on ethical philosophy and codes of conduct; May Yu, Alice Pang and Richard Wong, former research assistants, also at CUHK, who helped to compile preliminary case material on 'green' issues; Almaz Chak, a colleague of the author's at CUHK, conducted the ethical dilemma interview that is still used in the current text; Faye Frith for some material on whistle-blowing based on an article written by her entitled 'Crime and punishment: Whistleblowing and intimidation rituals' in *Employment Relations: Theory and Practice*, **3**: 651–2. The interpretations and arguments (and all their faults) are the responsibility of the author.

The authors and publishers are grateful to the following for permission to reproduce copyright material:

Harvard Business Review for Figures 1.2, 3.4, and 13.4;

for Exhibits 10.2 and 15.2; Table 13.5 and the cases on p. 66 and p. 347. Copyright © by Harvard Business School Publishing Corporation, all rights reserved.

Figures 3.1 and 14.1 reprinted by permission of John Wiley & Sons, Inc.

Tables 11.3 and 12.3 and Figures 1.1, 1.3 and 1.4 reprinted by permission of Pearson Education, Inc.

Table 16.1 copyright © 1993 Alter and Hage. Reprinted by permission of Sage Publications, CA.

Human Relations for Table 1.1 and the 'Culture in Company T' case study on p. 93. Reprinted by permission of Sage Publications Ltd, copyright © The Tavistock Institute 1990 and 1997.

Organization Studies for Table 16.2. Reprinted by permission of Sage Publications Ltd, copyright © Sage Publications 1998.

Figures 7.4 and 13.6, Table 3.3 and the 'Sherwoods' case study on p. 111 reprinted by permission of Sage Publications Ltd. Copyright © Sage Publications 1999, 1994, 1995 and 1996.

Figure 12.4 reprinted by permission of The Grubb Institute. Copyright © The Grubb Institute 1988.

Exhibit 6.1, Figure 3.5 and Table 14.2 reprinted by permission of The Penguin Group.

Figure 10.3 reprinted by permission of HarperCollins Publishers Ltd. Copyright © Kenneth Blanchard, Patricia Zigarmi and Drea Zigarmi.

Figure 12.1 reprinted with permission of John Wiley & Sons (UK). Copyright © John Wiley & Sons 1992.

Figures 13.3, 15.8 and 15.9 reprinted with permission from Elsevier.

Figures 7.1, 7.3 and 7.5, Table 2.2. and the cases on p. 108, p. 110 and p. 280 reprinted by permission of Thomson Learning.

Jennifer Hewett for the case study on p. 603, reprinted with permission. Copyright © Jennifer Hewett 2000.

Maureen Freely for the 'She who must be vilified' case study on p. 31, reprinted with permission. Copyright © Maureen Freely 2000.

Anne-Marie O'Connor for the 'Elvira Ruiz' case study on p. 29. Copyright © 1997 *Los Angeles Times*. Reprinted with permission.

Jonathan Turner and the American Sociological Association for Table 9.1.

McGraw Hill Australia for Figures 13.8 and 13.9.

TIME Inc. for Exhibit 15.3 and the case study on p. 604, © TIME Inc., all rights reserved.

The *Guardian* for the case study on p. 595, © The *Guardian*.

Professor Prem Sikka for the case study on p. 598.

Pearson Education Limited for Exhibits 3.1 and 3.2; Figures 3.2 and 3.3. © Andrew Brown 1995, 1998, reprinted by permission of Pearson Education Limited.

The Free Press, a Division of Simon & Schuster Adult Publishing Group, for Figures 15.4, 15.5 and Exhibit 15.1.

Gower Publishing, Aldershot, UK, for Table 3.1.

Marillion (www.marillion.co.uk) for the case study on p. 592.

California Management Review for Figure 9.2, copyright © The Regents of the University of California.

A critical approach to management and organization

Liz Fulop and Stephen Linstead

Management is a fascinating topic for more than just managers. Airport bookshops are bulging with popular management bestsellers, which attests to the level of interest in the subject, and perhaps to the level of anxiety which managers feel about how they go about their task. After all, while the middle levels of management have been shrinking, in what Gibson Burrell (1997) has called 'corporate liposuction', arising from the downsizing and outsourcing of the 1990s, managers are constantly asked to work both smarter and harder and ensure that those who work for them do the same. In the early 2000s globalization continues to force many 'branch offices' to close or move elsewhere; mergers are on the rise again; shareholder value dominates corporate decisions; stock markets increasingly dictate that businesses operate in very short time frames; and e-commerce is changing how businesses connect to each other and customers. On the other hand, lifestyle changes have increased the demands for flexibility, choice and lifelong learning opportunities at work. By the same token, employees in many organizations are being asked to take some managerial responsibility for their work through what is sometimes called 'empowerment', while the rewards for those at the very top of the managerial tree have been increasing dramatically. In fact, Warren Bennis (p. 75, cited in Hodgetts 1996), a highly regarded management academic, quoted average salaries of chief executive officers (CEOs) as being 187 times greater than their employees – a trend he described as obscene. Whether it is obscene or not, the trend continues today, with ever larger payouts being made to CEOs of the largest corporate failures in the world such as Enron in the US. The trend is also replicated in the UK – while employees' pay remained relatively static and other directors' pay rose moderately, CEO pay leapt dramatically between 1992 and 2002 (see Ezzamel and Watson 2002; data on CEO pay on Datastream). No wonder managers wait anxiously for their flights and thumb the pages of the next panacea with some agitation. The favoured few might become very wealthy, but most managers work long and hard under the shadow of retrenchment or the next performance review, while consultants and top management argue for the dissipation of management functions throughout the organization, in flatter organizations, which offer fewer opportunities for advancement while posing greater challenges for motivating others to perform. Given this scenario, we might well ask the question: 'Who would want to be a manager?' Or more to the point, 'who would want to manage for someone else?'

One thing this book does not do is take the 'faddish' approach that offers a new salvation in the latest tools or techniques, or even the latest mantra for managing (see Collins 2000 for an extended critique). We don't think that there are a few basic principles down to which management can be distilled. We do, however, think that those who practise management can do it better by taking a critical approach to their own practice and the contexts in which they practise. We also believe that they can learn valuable lessons that they can take into other situations from the *learning process*. The key skill that is needed to practise management is to learn how to undertake *critical inquiry*, to learn how to learn, and to be able to do this not just from books, but also from practice and inspire this in others. It is the objective of this book, therefore, while placing emphasis on the contribution which good critical scholarship can make to the understanding and practice of management, not to neglect the importance of applying knowledge, and even good old common sense, to managerial problems. But what we do need is the ability to tell the difference between them, and to know when each is necessary and appropriate.

For us, being *critical* does not mean standing outside management and exposing its flaws and weaknesses. It entails an active and passionate commitment to improving the abilities of those practising management to manage better. This involves both sustained investigation at the practical level and equally sustained critical activity at the level of theory and analysis; it also entails a requirement of both managers and academics to be self-critical. A critical capacity then is not something that is outside and opposed to management – on the contrary, it is the very condition for management to be able to learn, adapt and influence the rapidly changing world conditions of this new century.

We acknowledge that there are different ways of presenting a critical approach to management to what is proposed here. However, one of the aims of this book is to be relevant to those who have to practise management and help them to navigate the rich panoply of ideas, theories, approaches and models that they may find useful. Many of the models and approaches we examine are those that management practitioners are likely to come across in the management and organizational behaviour (OB) literature, including the fads, fashions and bestsellers. Our aim is to deal with whatever forms of knowledge managers may need to engage with and use and present these through a critical lens that helps them in managing both in and beyond the workplace. Our focus then is on management as a set of practices that can be performed by a variety of people and is not confined to a particular group of people called 'managers'. Indeed one of the challenges in the new millenium might well be to consider the possibility of the 'end of management' in many organizations and the rise of new practices that are 'beyond' management. Perhaps some intimation of this was heralded by the rise (and fall of many) of the dot.coms and the Internet revolution in the late 1990s.

We are also aware that management is no longer simply an organizational activity, but even for those organizations not involved in international activities, it is nevertheless a global issue. This is because globalization does not just occur at the level of the brand, product or service; or at the level of material resourcing, human resourcing or financing; or even in terms of markets and spheres of operation. It is a complex process which is cultural, social, economic, political and informational – and through it we come to recognize that even our theories as well as our practices are culturally shaped and relative. Even so, globalization is so widely touted as the justification for all manner of changes – in public administration as well as private enterprise – that much of the globalization discourse, as presented in both the popular and some of the academic media, has the status of mythology. In this book, we take seriously the facts of global enterprise, organization and management, but are critical of its fictions.

The approach of this book

This book takes a very different view of organization theory and management from that found in many mainstream texts. Along with Roy Jacques (1996: 166), we see management as a set of practices that

fundamentally entail the power to influence the flow of information and resources and the authority and power relationships through which work is organized and rewarded. This 'flow', as Jacques describes it, is embodied in different individuals at different points of time, but does not reside in a distinct body or group called the 'managers'. Mere positions or titles in a hierarchy are no guarantee that influence will be embodied in such positions or that others with less status will not be more powerful at some time. Management, and the act of managing, is increasingly embedded in complex and fluid relationships, where the old notions of managing employees or their behaviour is giving way to the emphasis on *relational management*. The reason why relational management has come to the fore is due in large part to the rise of knowledge work and knowledge workers who are seen by many as being very different from employees who work in the factory system dominated by manufacturing (Jacques 1996: 182–91). The very notion of 'knowledge workers', and the rise of the 'new economy', presents a significant challenge to how we think and theorize about organizations and their workings.

Knowledge work is popularly characterized as the dawning of a new age, as exemplified in works such as Thomas A. Stewart's book, *Intellectual Capital*, (1997a). In an excerpt from the book published in *Fortune*, the popular business magazine, Stewart (1997b) describes two worlds of work – the old factory system and the new world of intellectual capitalism. He argues that the factory flourished under a system of management that is no longer seen as relevant, at least not in affluent Western economies. Stewart believes that in the future industries will be built on intellectual capital and will no longer need the huge factories of the past that required massive outlays of capital on buildings, machinery and equipment. He goes on to say:

The logic of capitalism was simple. Mr Moneybags got an idea for a business. He turned his money, plus some from a bank, into fixed assets – a factory, machines, offices. He hired a Man in a Gray Flannel Suit to manage the assets. The manager, in turn, hired workers to operate the machines. Moneybags paid them – hourly wages to the easily replaceable workers, annual salaries to the managers, a reflection of their longer-term value. Moneybags kept all the profits; he was also responsible for paying the bank, maintaining the machines and buying new ones. He might offer the public a chance to share ownership with him; occasionally he gave managers the option to buy a piece too. He almost never let the workers in on the action, though in good years he gave them a goose for Christmas. (Stewart 1997b: 71)

Stewart's crude depiction of capitalism seems to capture some of the key elements of the old system, particularly the relationship between managers, workers and owners of the firm. Over the years, 'Mr Moneybags', who used to be the owner and the main risk taker in the business, increasingly shared the profits and risks of running the business with his managers, but never with his employees. Stewart's description of the decline of the factory system is only one of a number of such predictions. Paul Thompson and David McHugh (1990: 94) have also divided the organization of work into two distinct eras. They use the term 'the first industrial divide' to describe the era of mass production, when large-scale businesses (factories) first flourished and intense specialization and division of labour were introduced. Others use terms such as 'modernity' or 'modern management' to describe the old factory system that was the pillar of manufacturing in Western economies (Clegg 1990: 203). Thompson and McHugh use the term 'second industrial divide' to describe the decline of manufacturing and the rise of a new economy.

The decline of manufacturing has been a recognized worldwide trend. In 1995, for example, *Fortune* published figures citing what were then considered to be the worst industries in the US in terms of job losses or downsizing. The list was headed by aircraft and parts manufacturers at the top while steel mills were at the bottom. The study did not suggest that these industries would disappear, but rather that they were shrinking in terms of the job opportunities they would provide in the future. Indeed, even Stewart (1997b: 71) argued that many jobs still, and always will, require big, expensive machines for large-scale production but not the labour. Steel mills, for example, continue to be built in many countries but these are now designed as 'mini mills', using sophisticated technologies as opposed to being labour intensive as in the past and require a much more lean and skilled workforce.

Fortune also identified where it thought the best jobs will be in the future. These were to be found in industry sectors dominated by knowledge workers and predominantly in services. Many of the jobs in these sectors are more difficult to automate (that is, substitute with technology) and require greater flexibility, unavailable under mass production. It was not surprising, for example, given the ageing population in many Western societies, to find home healthcare highest on *Fortune*'s list of expanding industry sectors. Industries associated with media, home entertainment, Internet technology and virtual reality technologies and communication were also high on the list. The image of the worker in many of these industries is different from the old factory system. According to Stewart:

Intellectual capitalism is different. In knowledge-intensive companies, it's not clear who owns the company, its tools, or its products. Moneybags' modern-day descendant starts with seed money from a Silicon Valley venture capitalist. He leases office space in some Edge City corporate village and doesn't own a factory; a company in Taiwan manufactures his products. The only plant and equipment the company owns are computers, desks and a 1950s Coke machine someone picked up at auction. Whereas Moneybags bought the assets of his company, it is unclear who makes the investments on which intellectual capitalism depends, the investments in people. The manager – the Man in the Ralph Lauren Polo Shirt – paid his own way through business school. The worker is shelling out for an electronics course she takes at night, though the company will reimburse her for half the cost when she completes it. Every manager and worker receives stock options – as a group they may own as much stock as the capitalists. (Stewart 1997b: 71)

Jacques (1996: 182–3) puts knowledge management into a different perspective, arguing that it dates back to the early 1900s, the factory system of production. He says what distinguished the industrial era was the need to capitalize on knowledge management through formalization (rules, procedures and so on), professional training and development, and the design of machines and jobs to match them. In the post-industrial era (or intellectual capitalism), the challenge is to capitalize on learning, both at the individual and organizational level. In what he terms a 'knowledge theory of value', Jacques contends that the ability to learn represents not knowledge management per se, but the capacity to change knowledge. He coins the term 'learning worker' to describe one whose value lies not in what he or she knows, but the combination of discretion and skill that permits such a person to change what he or she knows (1996: 181). He goes on to say:

Perhaps, instead of imagining the knowledge worker to be newly emergent as a *post*-industrial worker, we should imagine him/her as a worker who has been there all along and who is now in the spotlight due to the confluence of certain socio-economic accidents – new technologies, redefined market boundaries, global redistribution of classes of work … which place this worker at critical confluences of power … Perhaps what is changing today is not the *importance* of the worker knowledge, but the *kind* of knowledge that is important. For three generations, systems have been refined to produce worker knowledge leading to *compliance* with decisions made by a specialized sub-group of employees ('management'). Increasingly, post-industrial organizations are seeking systems producing worker knowledge leading to *initiative*. This is not simply a different goal; it is one that conflicts with every element of disciplinary work practices. (Jacques 1996: 143)

As Jacques goes on to say, 'the central problem of "managing" the "employee" has been one of knowledge' (1996: 181). The central problem for managing the learning worker is very different. This leads us to the rationale of this book.

Each of the chapters addresses a core topic that is generic to what might be seen as traditional areas of organization and management, but it is framed in terms of the challenges of *relational management*. The content of the chapters is designed to reflect the current state of critical scholarly activity in the field, which of course reflects the state of the practice of management in this new century. The chapters build on existing knowledge in various fields, highlighting some enduring theories and approaches, but then pushing the boundaries of management beyond these ideas. So you will find chapters on *teams, managing change, conflict, control, leadership, culture, power, motivation, strategy, structure, decision making* and *sustainability*, which, as we said, are familiar topics in most managerial and organizational behaviour texts. A difference in our focus is how we use traditional approaches in many of these areas as the basis of examining these topics. We then go on to reframe them in the light of a critical appraisal of the current emphasis, in both academic and popular literature, surrounding each topic. Our approach differs most noticeably, however, when we come to consider *knowledge* and *learning, gender, ethics, networking* and *virtuality*. These topics are no longer marginal notes on the practice of management, but are at the heart of what those who practise management have to address every day, from their own personal development, through their relations with colleagues, and even to the point where organizational boundaries dissolve into networks and virtual organizations. We have brought these topics into the mainstream of this text because we believe that they have already established their intellectual and practical significance in the world of management and they represent a realistic agenda for the study of both for the next 10 years.

However we have also taken an approach in which each chapter, as far as possible and appropriate, addresses a group of key themes related to its content. These themes are:

- sources and uses, including abuses, of *knowledge* and *information*
- *learning in organizations*, both its oppressive and liberating forms
- *reflective practice* and *self-reflexivity*
- *diversity*, including but not limited to race, gender, ethnicity and cross-cultural issues
- *power* in its many and varied forms.

We begin each chapter with some questions which you might like to keep in mind when you consider the topic of the chapter; don't jump ahead at this point, but be reassured that in most cases we do attempt to answer those questions at the end of the chapter! Of course, by the time you reach the end of the chapter, you will have your own answers, which might not be quite the same as ours. But there is more than one way to respond to these complex questions and, as we shall see, management is not a simple question of right and wrong, but of using both reasoned judgement and feeling to make sense of complicated situations. Accordingly, we also begin each chapter with a short case study and some questions on it, which we ask you to think about before you read the chapter and reflect on as you progress through the chapter. By the end of the chapter you should be able to make a thorough response to these questions, but to help you along we address them ourselves in Revisiting the Case Study – but not in the sense of our having the final word. We would also expect you to challenge our assumptions, based on your reading of the chapters and your interpretations of the materials. We have chosen the case study method because it is a way of framing problems that can be shared in common and from which some lessons and insights can be drawn. Ideally, we would have left the questions out and left it up to you, the reader, to formulate them. However, we have to pose and answer these questions because we want to expose our own limitations and imperfections and open ourselves to scrutiny and challenge. There is no 'one best way' to deal with a case study. There are only better questions than others!

Why study management?

There are many sides to management, no simple and clear answers, and no 'one best way' to do it. Management is a complex field of activity and one that requires enormous effort and will to do well. It is not something that comes naturally to many of us, yet it is something that almost all of us might be called upon to do, not only through involvement in formal organizations, but in our private lives as well. Our focus in this book, however, is primarily on formal organizations, but we do consider public, private and voluntary organizations to be within our compass.

There are two main reasons for studying management. The first is to gain knowledge and understanding of management and what it is and, in the process, learn how to be a better and more effective manager. There is no simple way to do this. There is also no guarantee that what will be learnt in the theory of management will be easily translated into the practice of management. This raises the second reason why it is important to study management. When we study management we need a framework that will allow us to develop reflective practice, which is at the heart of critical thinking as we see it. In this textbook, the notion of 'critical thinking' remains a core idea, considered essential to the development of the manager and, more importantly, to the better practice of management (Fulop 1992; Thomas 1993). There are of course a number of different ways in which critical thinking and a critical approach can be developed. We consider some of these shortly.

We can develop reflective practice by adopting perspectives that help us to see familiar situations in new ways, and by considering things that challenge our perceptions about people, organizations and ourselves. Adopting a questioning, quizzical attitude can help us to recognize and solve problems, identify opportunities and think creatively (Thomas 1993). Robert Chia and Stuart Morgan (1996: 58) state:

The purpose of management education is not so much knowledge acquisition and accumulation as it is sensitizing students to our own peculiar culturally based (and often idiosyncratic) ways of ordering the world. It is about inculcating an intimate understanding of the way … management knowledge … is organized, produced and legitimized … In other words, the priority of *education* is quintessentially about gaining an understanding of [how we organize and represent knowledge from various sources].

In a nutshell, learning about management requires a critical perspective that is guided by four key processes of inquiry:

1. identifying and challenging assumptions
2. developing an awareness of the context in which management ideas have evolved historically, culturally and socially
3. always seeking alternative ways of seeing situations, interpreting what is going on, understanding why an organization is configured the way it is, and speculating about the way the organization could be managed differently and in ways that disrupt routines and established order;
4. being appropriately sceptical about what one hears and reads about management (Thomas 1993: 11 Brookfield 1987, cited in Alvesson and Deetz 2000: 8).

Much as these processes sound like work, the essence of managing is learning about managing in a way that brings 'the connection between *knowledge*, *imagination* and the zest for life' to the fore (Chia and Morgan 1996: 57).

The critical approach

This introduction outlines a *critical approach to management* that enables us to reflect on how we learn about management. It is designed to help us to develop the intellectual rigour and knowledge to deal with the complex and multifaceted issues that arise every day in work situations. Managers need to know how to analyse problems, how to use the knowledge they have acquired in a questioning manner, and how to employ their creative capacities to see things in new ways in order to resolve dilemmas. A vast body of knowledge and research can be drawn upon to help analyse and respond to what is happening or unfolding in organizational situations.

What *sources of knowledge* about managers and organizations are most useful, and how does a manager use or adapt them in a meaningful and constructive manner? Most of what is found in the management, organizational behaviour (OB) and organizational literature is based on theories, research or studies that have been undertaken in various organizations, sometimes even in laboratories, under different sets of constraints, some more scientific than others, often in different countries and within different time frames. This means that most ideas or suggestions have to be adapted to take account of the peculiarities and uniqueness of the manager's own situation or context.

In Chapter 1, we discuss some of the complexities and problems associated with learning, both from the vantage point of the individual and the organization. Enhancing individual and organizational learning (or collective learning) is perhaps the hardest thing any manager will ever have to do, and it requires the art or skill of *reflective practice*. Reflective practice has been popularized in the organizational learning literature (for example Senge 1990), but draws heavily on the work of the late Donald Schön (1977). Some theorists argue that this type of learning cannot occur unless organizational members are able to identify new knowledge, transfer and interpret new knowledge, use the knowledge to adjust behaviour or practices and pass on this knowledge to others (Levinson and Asahi 1995: 59–60). Others present different views of what it is to be a reflective practitioner (Golding and Currie 1999).

Others argue that *self-reflexive practice* is a further development of reflective practice. Questions such as 'who am I and who am I becoming?' are ones that self-reflexive practitioners will ask of themselves. Questions such as 'what *really* happened, why, and what can I do about it?' are typically posed by the reflective practitioner. To engage in self-reflexive practice is something akin to trying to rethink and rework one's own identity, values and assumptions, to such an extent that self-reflexive practice has been regarded as being tantamount to trying to 'jump over one's shadow' (Limerick and Cunnington 1993: 221). Our use of the term 'reflective practice' in this book includes the important, more postmodern sense of self-reflexivity. This form of reflective practice adds another dimension to the education of managers. Typically, management has been taught or thought of as something that is achieved by imparting particular forms of knowledge and know-how. Often it is taught as a skills-based activity or set of practices. In contrast, reflective practice emphasizes the need for all managers to develop abilities to critique and to be creative (Chia and Morgan 1996). Or, as Mats Alvesson and Stanley Deetz (2000: 8) suggest, critique allows a person to recognize if and how certain ways of organizing, reasoning and representing the world constrains imagination, autonomy and decision making. The very idea of reflective practice also raises the perennial question: what is good management? How do I know when I've done well?

As stated above, we take the approach that management is the management of relationships and, as such, is a *relational practice*, so the answer to these questions will not be fixed and final but will change as the relationships between the elements of management change. However, before we take a look at the nature of these relationships, we need to address our fourth theme, that of diversity.

Diversity is an issue which managers are being forced to confront both in the workplace and increasingly outside it in terms of relationships with, for example, overseas suppliers and overseas manufacturing facilities, investors or joint venture partners. The recognition of the existence of diversity and, in some cases, the desire to increase or create it have led to a more intense focus on managing relationships in the workplace and managing differences more effectively (see Chapter 2). Differences are based on age, race, gender, sexuality, ethnicity, beliefs, experience, disability and so on, although often gender and race receive most attention. These differences have to be accommodated, or even celebrated, in managing. For example, whether or not managers are male or female, the fact remains that they have to understand and accommodate better a broader range of differences than in the past. In addition, they need to do their part in providing genuine opportunities for meaningful, equitable and rewarding careers for those whom they manage. By using diversity as a lens through which we examine the content and issues of management, we can begin to become aware of a much broader set of consequences, questions, challenges and potential sources of creative solutions to organizational problems, besides uncovering a few more of these problems to which we were previously oblivious. Certainly the consideration of diversity can change the nature of relationships in the workplace and what we see as the management task – as we shall see in Chapter 2 – and in particular the way we theorize management.

While it is important for managers to learn about and confront issues of diversity, changing the nature of relationships in the workplace will not be achieved unless issues relating to power and control are also addressed. We explore the complex ways in which power becomes embedded in relationships, both in its more obvious and less obvious forms. Power is integral to explaining how relationships are formed, but also why they often fail or are difficult to sustain over longer periods. In considering issues of power, we do not wish to identify ourselves with any particular one of the various 'critical' positions which have emerged over the past two decades – among them critiques grounded in the critical theory of the Frankfurt School, notably Jürgen Habermas (Alvesson and Willmott 1992, 1996); varieties of postmodernism, influenced by Michel Foucault and Jacques Derrida in particular, although their work has often been poorly understood, which have sometimes sought to lay claim to the field of critical management studies (Fournier and Grey 2000); critical postmodernism, which has attempted to bridge the distance between postmodernism, critical theory and Marxism, often inspired by Theodore Adorno (Boje et al. 1992; Alvesson and Deetz 1996); and critical realism, a position which is sometimes guilty of producing an absurd and poorly understood version of those perspectives to which it seeks – with frequent immodesty – to offer an alternative (Ackroyd and Fleetwood 2000). Critical realism rejects the extremes of positivism, which treats social phenomena as though they were things (reification), and radical relativism, which takes the approach that 'anything goes' and people have free and unfettered choice over how they act (voluntarism). Critical realists try to recognize that the social world may have objective qualities independent of the discursive and conceptual constructions of its members, or the ways they make sense of it. Nevertheless they recognize that the world ultimately depends on these sense-making practices for its reproduction and transformation, maintenance and change. Accordingly they try to follow an empirical strategy which claims both an active reflexivity (critique of its own practice) and an acceptance of causality in method and analysis. We will have more to say about some of these perspectives but we all have our preferences and arguments in defence of those preferences, and ours will emerge during the course of this book, but we are not attempting to sell a particular perspective here or engage in internecine warfare over the 'critical' high ground. What we hope to do is utilize work from a variety of traditions that we consider to be critical, in order to introduce our readers to the richness of these approaches and the range of insights that they can offer to the inquiring and questioning manager.

Management is the management of relationships

Management is often presented as the management of

things, which includes resources (and people are treated as *human* resources). This reification (literally, 'thing-making') reinforces the artificial separation between the component disciplines through which management is defined and taught. However, the separate disciplines of management – accounting, organizational behaviour, information systems, operations management, marketing and so on – cannot easily be separated in practice, as each interlocks with the other (see also Jacques 1996: x). Real-life problems are overlapping and interconnected, rather than self-contained, and even when a management problem is solved successfully, the process is never finished. Relationships are constantly changing and the process of managing, and perhaps improving, them is continuous. It is not surprising to hear managers often refer to their daily work as largely one of 'putting out fires'.

Management is a relational, differential activity, involving criteria that shift and environments that change at different rates. Because management is a relational activity, managers have to deal with multiple realities, roles and identities, and multiple loyalties of individuals. It is the recognition that individuals have multiple realities, roles, identities and loyalties that is so central to managing diversity in organizations. Whether it involves dealing with the natural environment, with other colleagues, with customers/clients and competitors, with communities, networks or alliances, the managing of 'relationships' will be paramount. How is the relational view different from more traditional approaches to management?

Traditional approaches to management tend to emphasize (implicitly and often explicitly) management as the *control of relationships*. Scientific management, as we shall see in Chapters 2, 6 and 11, constructs the supervisor–employee relationship as that between the head and the hands, with the head (manager/supervisor) firmly in control, giving the instructions, and the hands (employees) carrying them out. Yet studies of business pioneers and entrepreneurs emphasize the role of the entrepreneur in bringing people and things together, the literal meaning of the word 'entrepreneur'. Here the important role of the entrepreneur/manager is the *bringing of relationships into being* for mutual advantage. Some that are more focused on the power of management as a group than on the individual manager, such as labour process theory, emphasize *inequality or asymmetry in relationships*. They focus on relationships where one group becomes powerful and remains dominant over another for long periods of time (see Chapters 6, 7 and 11). Systems thinking, which developed in the 1940s and has enjoyed a resurgence of popularity in the learning literature (see Chapter 1), takes a particular view of the *process of relationships*, looking for functional and dysfunctional elements and emphasizing the relationship of *fitting in* with the

environment in order to survive and grow. Strategic management approaches (which we discuss in Chapter 15) build on this and increasingly view business failure in terms of failure to stay in touch with changes in the competitive environment, in terms of *interrupted* or *distorted relationships*, where something is wrong with the conversion of system inputs into the right sort of system outputs. Developing as far back as the Hawthorne Studies (see Chapters 2 and 11), but changing as the field of psychoanalysis changed with each decade, psychodynamic approaches have emphasized *problematic relationships* – organizational pathology as the result of a failure to maintain psychological balance in relations, resulting, for example, in group conflict. In Chapter 10 we discuss the concept of 'narcissism', which is an example of how such distorted relationships can profoundly affect organizational practice. In short, existing studies suggest that, at a basic practical level, without building, maintaining and developing relationships a manager cannot manage. We also extend this argument into managing the environment and finding ways in which control and mastery can give way to sustainable and manageable relationships in this highly sensitive and political area of global development in which managers are pivotal figures.

Two things, however, are important to the perspective we are taking here. First, these relationships are in a *dynamic field*, in constant (although not necessarily profound or radical) change, and, second, they embody *flows* of energy and power through the field. The manager then has to be able to monitor how these changes are occurring, and has to be able to channel these flows of energy, interest, knowledge and power in order to get things done in the organization. What becomes of particular interest to studies of these networks or webs of relations is:

- *what* is related, *how,* and how this in turn changes
- how *changes in one part of the web affect other parts* or are prevented from doing so
- how managers act in establishing, *maintaining* and *changing relationships*
- how *existing patterns of relationships pose constraints* and how these can be addressed by managers.

What also emerges from these considerations are the skills and qualities which managing these relationships demands:

- sensitivity to a *wide variety of types of information* and forms of *knowledge* – technical, cultural, emotional – as well as different narrative forms such as stories or workplace myths

- the ability to visualize and perceive *new patterns* of relationships
- the ability to tolerate *ambiguity* and *uncertainty*
- the ability to be *persuasive*
- the confidence to *take risks and intervene*, to exercise judgement in the absence of authoritative prescriptions such as rules, policies, procedures
- the capacity to be *self-critical*, learn from mistakes and *develop continuously*.

If we take the individual manager as our focus, these relationships could rather crudely be said to fall into two groups (see Figure 0.1). One group of relationships is that which is related to the job, the organization and *the demands of the manager's formal role* in relation to the organization's 'rational-purposive' dimension: goals such as making a profit, meeting production targets, retaining customers and so on. The other group is that related to the manager's *personal desires*, ambitions, social demands, familial relations and so on. In the practising manager's world, these fields are in tension and may from time to time be in overt conflict – such as

when the managing director calls an 'away day' meeting to discuss changes in the company strategy on your wedding anniversary or your partner's 30th birthday party. Let's look at this division more closely, with the help of the summary overview provided by Figure 0.1.

Role-focused, goal-oriented relationships

At their simplest, these roles are all about what it is that managers do that differentiates management from any other activity. Lots of writers, for example Henry Mintzberg (1975) and Rosemary Stewart (1988), have focused on this. At this level it is those features of the job and the role in the organization that exert demands and create tensions in the manager's life. Most relevant are practical problems that confront managers in their formal role, such as how to do the job, how to do it better, how to change it, how to get others to cooperate and so on.

Henry Mintzberg (1975) undertook a groundbreaking study that challenged much of the received wisdom

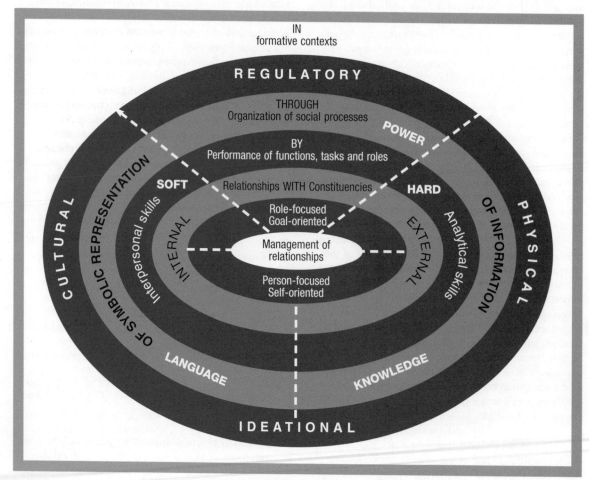

Figure 0.1 The management of relationships

about management. In a blatant challenge to classical management theories, which argued that there was 'one best way' to manage, that management was simply the application of a set of principles or that management was the collective term for a group of functions, such as planning, coordinating, leading and controlling, Mintzberg instead argued that it was an evolving process. Classical theories of management were poor descriptors of the interactive and complex reality of

what managers actually do. Indeed, while it is tempting to think of management in terms of these functions of organizing it is also dangerous, as it leads us to try to make the reality of the task fit its image – as Burrell (1997) and Collins (2000) argue, it de-forms reality rather than informs us about it. After observing and recording the activities of a number of senior managers, Mintzberg identified three groups of roles, shown in Figure 0.2, and described here:

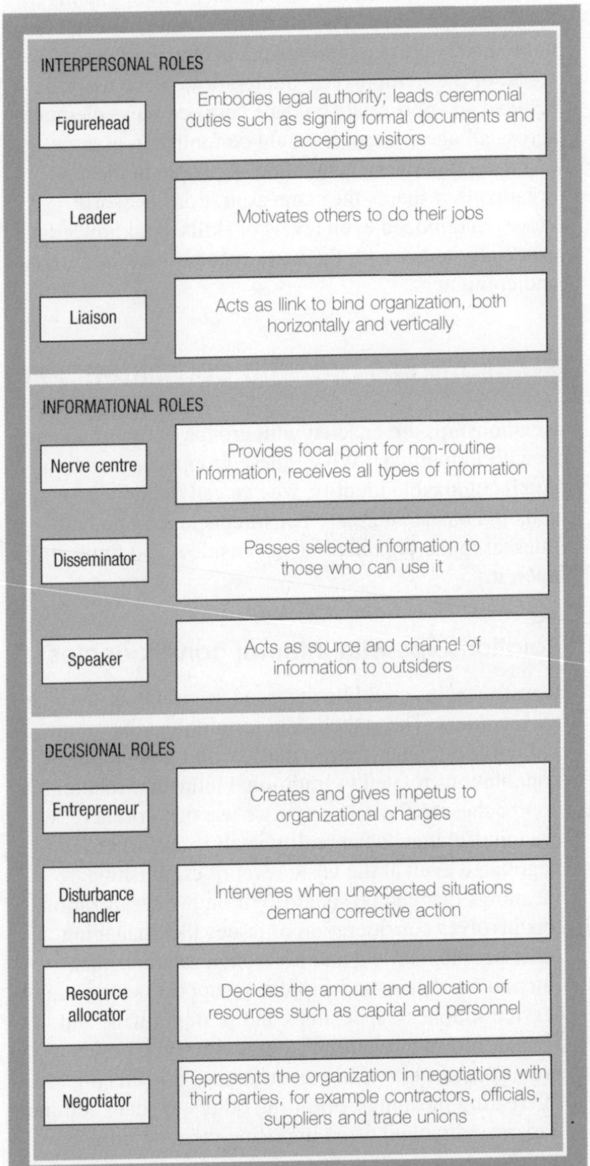

1. *Interpersonal roles* – Most people in organizations engage in a good deal of interpersonal contact. When one is acting as a manager, these interactions increase emphatically and have three differing aspects, whether the manager is performing as figurehead (representing to other bodies), leader (managing internal relations) or liaison (bridging with other groups).

2. *Informational roles* – All managers act as focal points for information, and accordingly they enhance their understanding of the organization and its environment by being caught up in this flow of information. As nerve centres and disseminators, they facilitate the achievement of organizational objectives by channelling information to the most appropriate points. They often act as spokespersons to channel and control information to outside bodies.

3. *Decisional roles* – Managers are engaged in change, where they act as entrepreneurs, stimulating and driving it through, and also in 'running the business', keeping activities going smoothly by handling disturbances, allocating resources and negotiating.

Figure 0.2 Mintzberg's managerial roles

Source: Adapted and reprinted by permission of *Harvard Business Review*. From 'The manager's job: folklore and fact' by Henry Mintzberg, March/April 1990, p. 168. Copyright © 1990 by Harvard Business School of Publishing Corporation. All rights reserved.

Critics of Mintzberg say, in particular, that he generalizes about all managers from a small sample of those at or near the top of the organization. While Mintzberg has suggested that the roles can and do apply to other managers, he has also welcomed the work of other researchers who have narrowed their focus to look at the roles of those managing in specific functions, such as HRM, R&D or marketing, or managing at different levels, where middle management has received particular attention (see Thomas and Linstead 2002; Linstead and Thomas 2002). 'Downsizing' processes intended to cut costs in making organizations 'lean' during the recessionary times of the late 1980s and early 1990s were subsequently found to have left organizations lacking an often critical resource by removing middle managers. Middle managers did far more than simply link decisions at the top with actions at the bottom (Naylor 1999: 11–13).

The managerial task may therefore have changed and be changing since Mintzberg's research. Although his critique of classical management theory was trenchant, it could be argued that his own model no longer fits the reality of managing in the postmodern world. It has been suggested, for example, that for middle managers in information technology-enabled organizations, the tasks of communication and coordination have been ceded to information and knowledge management systems, while other roles have come to the fore. Dauphinais (1996, cited in Naylor 1999: 13) identifies four of these roles:

1. *Creators and implementers of strategy* – making quick responses to developments within the framework of organizational goals, largely enabled because middle managers, in particular, gain early knowledge of internal problems and shifts in the marketplace.
2. *Influencers* – middle managers' roles are at junctions of vertical and horizontal communication. Their key responsibilities require them to manage key tasks or functions yet their position enables them to influence people above, below and at the same level.
3. *Key sources of stability* – middle managers may be a source of resistance to change, but may on the other hand use their experience to consolidate and integrate the improvements that may result from change.
4. *Drivers of continual change* – middle managers have an important role in, and may control the outcomes of, project and teamwork, which have grown as forms of work organization to match the need for flexibility in changing environments.

So although Mintzberg's work pioneered the view of management as a relational process, it also emphasized the need to monitor continually the changing nature of management over time, and to question its own conclusions by comparing them against everyday reality.

Person-focused, self-oriented relationships

This area of concern focuses on managers as individuals, and the impact that the role may have on them. It covers effects on the manager's personality, including emotions and stress (see Chapters 2 and 9). It can also include: the consideration of ethical and moral issues that might arise as personal dilemmas during the course of doing business (see Chapter 8); and the consideration of learning, learning styles, levels and types of learning, self-management and self-development (see Chapter 1). Diversity in the workplace puts emphasis on people, differentiates their perspectives, views and mindsets and stresses that these differences have to be managed to ensure organizations gain the maximum benefit from potential sources of knowledge. Relational management also recognizes that people bring their 'whole self' to

work, not just a 'work self', that is, they also bring their sexuality, spirit, emotions and connections to family and friends with them every day. These aspects of people's identity need to be taken into account to enrich the meaning and context of work (Zangari and Cavaleri 1996: 338–9). Commitment and attachment to work and the organization can diminish as people find meaning, identity and the whole self beyond work (Handy, cited in Ettore 1996: 15). It is naive to expect that people will centre their lives entirely around their employment, as we discuss in Chapter 9. The managerial challenge is not to annex and incorporate the personal and social world of their employees, but to allow space for and achieve an appropriate balance between these elements across all age groups. It would be foolish to assume, for example, that every generation of people in the organization shares the same aspirations or world views, and indeed even levels of skills and knowledge, especially today with the widespread use of the Internet and computers.

Relationships are with constituencies

Relationships are enacted with groups of others as well as with individuals. Where these groups have a strong and recognizable identity, we can call them *constituencies*, and these constituencies can be both internal to the organization or outside it and impacting upon it.

Relationships with internal constituencies

Constituencies could be regarded as groups of *stakeholders*. The stakeholder terminology has some rather unfortunate 'representative' and 'bargaining' connotations related to traditional industrial relations approaches. In the sense that we use the term here, we are mindful that social reality itself is constructed and negotiated even at the basic level of establishing meanings that can be shared. Within the organization, this involves consideration of issues like managing other people, vertical and horizontal relationships, internal customers and suppliers, support systems and service suppliers, specialists and professionals, and formal/informal relations, along with some basic principles of organizational structure. It is this process of creating meanings, enrolling others to share common understanding and often imposing them on others, which gives people their 'stake' in something.

Relationships with external constituencies

From the organization's point of view, these are the *external stakeholders* – customers, clients, suppliers, investors, those involved in the micro-legal environment, the public in terms of public image, competitors, collaborators, cooperators, coexistors, collectives, agents/distributors/franchisees, potential recruits/suppliers/customers and so on, and former members of the organization in some cases. This also involves the manager's own community, family, partner and friends who are the core of other networks whose interests and influence may cut across those of the organization and produce tension for the manager. The home, for example, is perhaps the most powerful external constituency for most people.

However, the notion of the external stakeholder changed in the 1990s and this change challenged managers' capacities to deal with the relational dimensions of their work. As Warren Bennis (cited in Hodgetts 1996: 75) argued, organizations have responsibilities not only to internal stakeholders (that is, employees) but to customers and the community. Yet many companies are increasingly focused on serving the needs of shareholders more than their other constituents. Institutional investors (banks, finance companies and so on) that constitute the most powerful group of shareholders often pursue short-term strategies to maximize shareholder returns. Bennis and others (for example Peter Drucker, cited in Caulkin 1993: 42) believe that these trends have produced CEOs who benefit from the 'bottom-line', market-driven, hard-nosed, hard-driving image that reaps them millions through stock options and pleasing stock markets. This focus or shareholder mindset (Bennis 1996: 75, cited in Hodgetts 1996) leaves little room for managing or building long-term relationships, when the personal wealth of CEOs can increase substantially when they downsize or opt for short-term gains. These trends have raised concerns about how organizations can build trust and commitment and create the intellectual capital they need to compete.

Relationships are managed by performance

If we now turn to consider how relationships are managed, it is not too difficult to see that they must be managed by *action* or *performance* of some sort. There are three different objects of performance:

1. *The performance of functions, tasks and roles* This involves looking at what managers do in terms of specific tasks, including the functions of marketing, operations management, human resource management (HRM), finance and so on, and how these specialized areas relate to the general properties of management – in other words, what is common or overlapping across these functions. Much work has been done in this area in regard to

classical studies of management principles. Colin Hales (1993), in a review of various historical formulations of 'management principles', identified a staggering variety, yet pointed out that this was only a small sample of the existing work.

2. *The performance of interpersonal skills* This is where task performance intersects with the skills of interaction with others – leadership in a personal sense, presentation skills, negotiation skills, group dynamics and facilitation, decision making, competencies, critical thinking, change management and even managing emotions. In this mode the manager may come close to the performance artist, employing complex skills, rehearsing and changing roles where necessary (see Chapters 9 and 13).

3. *The performance of analytical techniques* Managers do need some quantitative or analytic skills, albeit in varying degrees, and at the very least they need to understand enough to know how to use technical specialists in the best ways or interpret quantitative data provided by 'experts' in the course of their work. Quantitative analysis, just-in-time (JIT) knowledge, quality measurement and benchmarking, information technology, especially in support of statistical process control, economic analysis, financial and accounting skills, market analysis and research all relate to the general conceptualization of management at this level.

The combination of functional task skills as an accountant, marketer or other specialist, combined with interpersonal skills and the ability to understand and use quantitative data, all enable managers to manage their key relationships flexibly and effectively. But to what ends do they apply these skills?

Relationships are managed through organization

The managers' performance skills are realized through applying them to organize specific arenas of action to their advantage. This means the organization of:

1. *Social processes* In this area the influence of sociological thinking is most clearly felt in studies of management, and particularly in the critical linkage of language, knowledge and *power*. The performance of tasks and functions takes place through social processes that can constrain or enable different forms of action. Through focusing on power, social processes involving political action, such as network and coalition building and establishing and leveraging power bases, are

emphasized. Critical views also emphasize structural inequality, control, hegemony and domination in relations. They also regard ideology as a mystification that enables power to become the rule of the powerful – to create domination, subordination and hegemony (the perpetuation of one group in domination over another). The labour process perspective is also important here, including issues of exploitation and extraction of surplus value and the manager's role in the process, as are issues of class, race and gender differences and discrimination (see Chapter 6, but also Chapters 2, 7, 11 and 12).

2. *Symbolic representation* An important part of management is what has been called the 'management of meaning'. Thus 'symbolic' management, or the attempt to create corporate cultures, teams, new forms of motivational tools, 'transformational' or visionary leadership (and of course other styles), is significant here (see Chapters 3 and 10). In addition, the dramaturgical view of management as a performance, staged in a theatrical sense, or the acting of scripts and storylines is relevant. The focus here is on verbal and visual *language* used to create meanings that literally define for people the 'rules' of membership in an organization (even down to the appropriate language to use) and the communicative methods by which they are sustained (see Chapters 1, 2 and 3).

3. *Knowledge and information* One of the key influences and drivers of change in organizations is the increasing speed of the flow of information. The ways in which 'knowledge' is formed from information are important to some companies, but critical for 'knowledge-intensive firms', a rapidly growing area of commercial activity and study (Microsoft is an example). Networks and virtual organizations all depend on knowledge and information flow, and issues of copyright secrecy, confidentiality, privacy, theft and robbery, viruses, corruption and fraud have assumed new dimensions. Information is at the heart of the 'deal' which produced the spectacular successes on paper, and the equally spectacular collapses of the highly leveraged entrepreneurs and corporate raiders of the 1980s. Similarly, many of the dot.com failures in the late 1990s and early 2000s were also created through inflated paper values and stock market perceptions and misinformation. In addition to learning to master information technology, the information superhighway, cyberspace, the Internet and a range of relevant databases, there is still the pervasive and important traditional form of information flow – the grapevine, the rumour mill, gossip, stories, talk and so on – which has not diminished in its significance.

Knowledge and power have a close relationship, and language could be seen as the glue which holds them together (see Chapters 7, 13, 14 and 15).

The manager then exercises performance skills by building and changing relationships based on *managing power*, *meaning* and *knowledge*. But these processes also have broader social contexts which inform them. Managers do not act in a vacuum – their behaviours are always subject to some constraints due to the complex web of relationships in which they operate.

Relationships are managed in formative contexts

Taking a look at the broader canvas, we could use Brazilian critical legal and social theorist Roberto Unger's (1975, 1987) idea of 'formative contexts' to express the sense in which action is shaped but not necessarily determined by wider sociocultural influences. These contexts, it should be emphasized here, are historically situated (time, cycles), regionally or globally located (place, cyberspace), and discursively formed and sustained (through specific combinations of customs, languages, cultural knowledge and power relations). In other words, managing is always tailored to considerations of time, place and discourse (see Chapters 8, 12 and 14). These contexts could be divided into four broad subdivisions that we will call 'environments' which impinge upon and shape the manager's actions:

1. *Regulatory environment* The regulatory context is the formal background of the law, regulations and restrictions against which businesses and managers must operate. The significance of the regulatory environment becomes glaringly obvious to even the most superficial consideration of British economy and society during nearly two decades of Thatcherism; as it does, for example, in any consideration of Hong Kong's future development as a capitalist city in a communist country. Political influence, policies and initiatives, economic factors like interest and exchange rates and tariff control, trade agreements and common market agreements all shape the ground on which business is conducted (see Chapters 5, 8 and 11).

   At the organizational level, rules and structures act as frameworks for managerial action, and organizational design options open up choices and facilitate some practices rather than others, although ultimately, like the broader regulatory environment, they are subject to challenge, subversion and change. Alternatives in organizational structures and new forms, global corporations and multinational corporations (MNCs) and strategic alliances, the virtual corporation, and even the question of 'modern' or 'postmodern' organizations affect what management is becoming here. This also articulates consideration of the competitive environment that is the specific focus of strategy and marketing (see Chapters 15 and 16).

2. *Cultural environment* Here the impact of cultural diversity is recognized. Culture can of course be studied at several levels, and here it is those things which extend beyond organizational boundaries that are most significant. While professional, local and industrial subcultures are important, perhaps the most important are national/ethnic and cross-national cultural features. The increasing need to manage across cultures in terms of marketing, procurement and manufacturing combines with the increasing ethnic diversity and mobility of work-forces to pose highly significant challenges. Gender issues too are very important at this level (see Chapters 2 and 3, and also parts of each chapter).

3. *Physical environment* The rise of 'green management' is one of the best examples of how the physical environment has become central to the study of management. The need to operate in a way which sustains rather than exploits natural resources, limits pollution and cares for the com-munities in which facilities are located is perhaps the most important new emphasis in global manage-ment. An increased concern with risk and reliability as demands for products and services and the speed at which they are delivered increases also raises concerns about managing the physical environment. Recent research and emphases on disaster avoidance and management have led to a very substantial new multidisciplinary field emerging in management and engineering studies. Concerns about the physical environment have spread beyond disciplinary boundaries. This area also covers more traditional issues of climate and geography, and the logistics of infrastructure (see Chapters 5, 8 and 15).

4. *Ideational environment* This is the world of ideas which account for, legitimate, question and make possible certain lines of argument and action, dividing the world up in characteristic ways. This is still shaped by the classic ideas of management, particularly scientific management and Fordism (see Chapter 11). Indeed, Jacques (1996: Chapter 1) argues that many of the so-called 'new' manage-ment ideas, such as knowledge management and learning organizations, can be dated back to the early nineteenth century. Many ideas that have come to form a corpus of contemporary ideas about managing need to be carefully interrogated to ensure that outmoded ideas and world views are not continually informing contemporary practice, when such practice was faulty or flawed all along. It is therefore important to consider *why* management seems so peculiarly vulnerable to 'fads and fashions' that are often really not new at all (see Chapter 1). At this level, too, broader sociological studies of morals and ethics are important beyond the consideration of individual moral dilemmas (see Chapters 8, 9 and 15).

These different levels of consideration can of course be related across their boundaries. For example, if we wanted to consider the management issues relating to the space shuttle Challenger disaster, which occurred in 1986, and in which all lives aboard were lost including that of a civilian, we would find that it has been analysed from every possible angle from engineering to psycho-analysis! NASA, the US space agency, was blamed for this accident – on grounds which ranged from neglect of engineering safety issues, to an arrogant organizational culture. Technology failure – the disintegration of the 'O' rings, which caused the fire on board – was a major contributor to the accident. But technology operates as a mediator beneath all three circles described in Figure 0.1 (mostly down the right-hand side) as it mediates analysis and task performance, the physical environment and the circulation or otherwise of information. If we look at information, and the circle in which it appears in Figure 0.1, the management of information is the management of knowledge and is part of the triadic interaction of power/knowledge/language. Managers need to see the relations between language and symbolic representation, knowledge and information, and power and social processes and the broader contexts in which they are embedded. What has made the Challenger disaster a classic case for managers to study is that such cases, incorporating diverse perspectives, are rare. With the Discovery shuttle disaster in 2003, which disintegrated on re-entry to the earth's atmosphere killing all seven crew including Indian and Israeli astronauts, NASA's activities were again put under the microscope and the investigations were as wide-ranging and thorough. In the Challenger case, however, the point was repeatedly emphasized: managers are trained to deal with management problems in a fragmented fashion, often with a narrow view. But if you look closely enough and range widely enough, the full range of connections can be made from only a small amount of information. The management of relationships means management as a process in whatever circumstances it occurs, and our final argument is that the challenge of *relational management* is threefold:

1. To be able to 'surf' the waves of changing relationships and maintain a sense of balance.

2. To be able to sense the immense interconnectedness of things through these relationships, without being overcome by the vertigo of possibilities (a kind of 'analysis paralysis'), and still be able to *act effectively*.

3. Not to look for simplicity where it cannot be found, but rather to see the complexity of managing relationships as a distinct advantage, which is vital to learning about oneself and one's organization.

References

Ackroyd, S. and Fleetwood, S. (eds) (2000) *Realist Perspectives on Management and Organizations*, London: Routledge.

Alvesson, M. and Deetz, S. (1996) 'Critical theory and postmodern approaches to organization studies' in S. Clegg, C. Hardy and W. Nord (eds) *Handbook of Organization Studies*, London: Sage, pp. 191–217.

Alvesson, M. and Deetz, S. (2000) *Doing Critical Management Research*, London: Sage.

Alvesson, M. and Willmott, H. (eds) (1992) *Critical Management Studies*, London: Sage.

Alvesson, M. and Willmott, H. (1996) *Making Sense of Management: A Critical Introduction*, London: Sage.

Boje, D., Gephart, R. and Thachenkery, T. (1992) *Postmodern Management and Organization Theory*, Thousand Oaks, CA: Sage.

Burrell, G. (1997) *Pandemonium: Towards a Retro-Organization Theory*, London: Sage.

Caulkin, S. (1993) 'The lust for leadership', *Management Today* November, 38: 40–3.

Chia, R. and Morgan, S. (1996) 'Educating the philosopher manager', *Management Learning* 27(1): 37–64.

Clegg, S.R. (1990) *Modern Organizations*, London: Sage.

Collins, D. (2000) *Management Fads, Fashions and Buzzwords: Critical-Practical Perspectives*, London: Routledge.

Dauphinais, G.W. (1996) 'Who's minding the middle managers?' *HR Focus* 73(10):12–13.

Ettore, B. (1996) 'A conversation with Charles Handy on the future of work and an end to the "century of organization"', *Organizational Dynamics* summer: 15–26.

Ezzamel, M. and Watson, R. (2002) 'Pay comparability across and within UK boards: An empirical analysis of the cash pay awards to CEOs and other board members', *Journal of Management Studies*, 39(2): 207–32.

Fournier, V. and Grey, C. (2000) 'At the critical moment: Conditions and prospects for critical mangement studies' *Human Relations* 35(1): 7–32.

Fulop, L. (1992) 'Management and critical thinking', in L. Fulop, F. Frith and H. Hayward (eds), *Management for Australian Business: A Critical Text*, Melbourne: Macmillan.

Golding, D. and Currie, D. (1999) *Thinking about Management: A Reflective Practice Approach*, London: Routledge.

Hales, C. (1993) *Managing Through Organisation*, London: Routledge.

Hodgetts, R.M. (1996) 'A conversation with Warren Bennis on leadership in the midst of downsizing', *Organizational Dynamics* summer: 72–8.

Jacques, R. (1996) *Manufacturing the Employee: Management Knowledge from the 19th to 21st Centuries*, London: Sage.

Levinson, N. and Asahi, M. (1995) 'Cross national alliances and interorganizational learning', *Organizational Dynamics* autumn: 13–31.

Limerick, D. and Cunnington, B. (1993) *Managing the New Organisation: A Blueprint for Networks and Strategic Alliances*, Sydney: Business and Professional Publishing.

Linstead, A. and Thomas, R. (2002) 'What do you want from me?: A poststructuralist feminist reading of middle managers' identities', *Culture and Organization* 8(1): 1–20.

Mintzberg, H. (1975) 'The manager's job: Folklore and fact', *Harvard Business Review* July–August: 49–61.

Naylor, J. (1999) *Management* London: Financial Times/Pitman Publishing.

Schön, D.A. (1983) *The Reflective Practitioner*, New York: Basic Books.

Senge, P. (1990) *The Fifth Discipline: The Art and Practice of the Learning Organization*, New York: Doubleday/Currency.

Stewart, R. (1988) *Managers and their Jobs*, London: Macmillan.

Stewart, T.A. (1997a) *Intellectual Capital*, New York: Doubleday/Currency.

Stewart, T.A. (1997b) 'Brain power: Who owns it … how they profit from it', *Fortune* 17 March: 70–4.

Thomas, A.B. (1993) *Controversies in Management*, London: Routledge.

Thomas, R. and Linstead, A. (2002) 'Losing the plot? Middle managers and identity' *Organization* 9(1): 71–93.

Thompson, P. and McHugh, D. (1990) *Work Organizations: A Critical Introduction*, London: Macmillan.

Unger, R.M. (1975) *Knowledge and Politics*, Illinois: Free Press.

Unger, R.M. (1987) *Social Theory: Its Situation and its Task,* Cambridge: Cambridge University Press.

Zangari, N.J. and Cavaleri, S.A. (1996) 'Relational management', in S. Cavaleri and D. Fearon (eds), *Managing in Organizations that Learn*, Oxford: Blackwell Business.

Part I

Core
Concepts

Management know-ledge and learning

Liz Fulop and William D. Rifkin

1

Questions about management knowledge and learning

1 What sorts of knowledge do managers need?
2 How do managers learn about management?
3 What forms of knowledge are likely to be easier for managers to grasp than others?
4 What role(s) do managers play in helping their organizations to learn?

CHRIS'S DILEMMA

Silence. No one was volunteering for the project. 'Why not?' thought Chris Stefano.

Five people had gathered in the meeting room. They exchanged pleasantries and a few jokes. Chris had entered the room late, knocking over a chair and spilling the cup of tea perched precariously on top of a pile of computer print-outs Chris was carrying. Chris had thanked everyone for coming – it was their lunch break – and outlined the urgency of the situation facing the organization. A detailed description was given of the outstanding work needed to complete the project and meet the project deadline, and Chris finished the presentation by asking for a volunteer. Then there was this silence. No one had come forward. Chris had felt stunned and embarrassed and had a flashback to university days when a team project had been due, and none of the other team members would help on the night before it was to be submitted. The project had been given a fail grade!

Chris was facing a difficult and frustrating situation and was under immense pressure to complete a project of major importance to the organization. The project had been stalled for some weeks, and the deadline for completion was now becoming almost impossible to meet. Critical information had been difficult to extract from the organization's information system, and what data there were had been presented in a cumbersome form, requiring hours of rework. Whoever volunteered for the project would have a difficult and time-consuming task ahead of him or her. Chris could not employ extra staff to help as there was a freeze on hiring casual staff. The project had to be completed, no matter what. Chris had called a meeting of staff to progress the project, specifically to find a volunteer.

Roderick Cage had cleared his throat and mumbled that his workload had doubled since Lou Chan went on paternity leave, with no immediate replacement for him. Looking somewhat annoyed, Rebecca Spalding had quickly interjected, saying that since the new accounts system had changed her workload was now the heaviest of all present. Phil Bosevic, who had recently missed out on promotion, just shrugged his shoulders and said he was understaffed and could not take on any new work. Wasim Shan, who had only been in the job for four months, said he believed he was being transferred in the next fortnight. Merilyn Hue simply smirked at Chris, somewhat nonchalantly, and said that she was going on special leave next week.

Chris had looked around the room and had fixed a nervous gaze on Phil and then as pleasantly as possible had said to him: 'I'd appreciate it if you would complete the data for the project and ...' Before Chris could finish the sentence, Phil had swung out of his chair, snatched up his papers and stormed out of the room, slamming the door behind him. Chris followed him, but by the time Chris reached the door, Phil had disappeared.

Chris had then rushed down the hall into the managing director's office, slammed the door and glared at Dr Cora Harvey. In utter despair and rage, Chris had banged a fist on Cora's table and said: 'None of them would help me! Can you believe it? I had to order Phil to do it.' Cora had stared at Chris with a piercing gaze and had said sternly: 'If I were you Chris ...', but just then the phone had rung, cutting her off in mid-sentence. She had signalled Chris to leave the room, but as Chris walked out she had shouted: 'Sort it out Chris and get the damn project finished. I don't care how you do it! Just do it!'

Chris had shouted back at her: 'If I have to, I will do it myself and then there goes the new defence contract!' Chris thought, just like at university, having to finish the project alone the night before it is due.

QUESTIONS ABOUT THE CASE

1 What advice would you give to the manager in this incident?
2 What knowledge or experiences have you drawn on to give your advice?
3 How would you judge it to be good advice?

Introduction

The incident selected for this chapter presents a common management dilemma. It might not be judged by many as a spectacular event, in the sense that it is not related to a programme of major change, a corporate takeover or the removal of a chief executive officer (CEO). Rather, it concerns the typical struggle of a manager, who is also a colleague, co-worker, employee, probably a professional of some sort, possibly a shareholder, trying to achieve outcomes under intense pressures to perform in a highly specific situation. Although the individuals in the incident are fictitious, the incident is based on observations and experiences that the authors have had in their own organizations – universities that strive to work under various notions of collegiality. Whether it is collegiality or some other form of peer group pressure or value system, it is certainly an experience that many of us could relate to – trying to get someone to volunteer for an unpleasant, but necessary task. In this instance, the manager might appear to be facing a relatively simple problem, but nothing could be further from the truth. As we go through the chapter, the answers to all the questions should be revealed. But be warned, the answers are not revealed in terms of 'rights' and 'wrongs' or 'truth' and 'falsity', but in terms of how well you engage in *reflective practice* – practice informed by theory and theory that challenges our thinking about workplace practices and common-sense assumptions.

In this chapter, we examine how managers find out and learn about management. Certain forms of management know-how are easier to come by, and learn from, than others. There are different types of knowledge from which managers can draw insight: learning about management very much depends on where the manager or the would-be manager searches for knowledge, and where this search stops. Managers can gain an appreciation and understanding of the difficulties that confront them by learning more about management and, in the process, help others in their organizations to learn. We are not, however, treating knowledge in the way that many conventional approaches to the topic might. Rather we are interested in how knowledge is presented to managers, how knowledge is conditioned by the perspective of the knower, and how management knowledge is legitimated in different forms of discourse (Jacques 1996: 187). This chapter is particularly interested in identifying different sources of knowledge that managers are likely to come across in their careers and studies. These sources of knowledge are based on particular genres of managerial writing and, in a sense, each form represents a particular *managerial discourse*. Following Roy Jacques (1996: 19), we view management discourse or discourses as presenting particular ways to frame problems, to present ideas and arguments and impart them to others. The management talk that arises from engaging in particular discourses affects how information is represented and what can or cannot be said to, and about, the subjects of a discourse. Such discourses shape particular values and ways of seeing and carving up the world of work so that either the status quo is maintained or it is challenged.

Many come to the study of management equipped with assumptions, experiences and certain levels of practicality or 'hands-on' knowledge and information that are all likely to affect their views of what management is all about. Most often a manager wants to learn about management quickly so that he or she can solve an immediate problem with a successful outcome guaranteed. This can be described as an *instrumental orientation* (Dehler 1998: 72–4) that sees as its goal the pursuit of knowledge or know-how that will lead to some action or end result to solve the problem. The consumers of management knowledge and know-how (what has been tested through practice) often seek out books and courses on management that will give them 'answers' to their immediate and pressing problems and offer solutions or guides on how to manage certain situations, with accompanying steps or recipes to follow to attain success or some outcome. This has also been described elsewhere, and by a number of management writers, as the quest for the 'one best way' to manage (Fulop 1992: 18; Shapiro 1995: xvi). Management practitioners are usually action-oriented and always seeking to improve their work situations (at least good managers are) and they are often bemused and overwhelmed by what they see in the academic studies on management.

Academics who have developed the study of management have also attempted to determine and disseminate 'best practice', but they require evidence which is capable of more rigorous interrogation from a 'scientific' point of view with regard to validity and generalizability than do practitioners. Often they are interested in developing knowledge that questions the practice of apparently successful companies, seeking to disconfirm what their managers are claiming about their organizations unless it can be backed up with carefully obtained and objectively analysed data. Many management scholars produce knowledge that is *conceptual* in nature to help them better understand what it entails to manage across many settings rather than necessarily solving specific problems for any one organization. It is our view it is not a matter of choosing between these two different aspects of management, but one of realizing that both instrumental and conceptual forms of knowledge have to occur and that defining and understanding a problem is as important as solving it (Dehler 1998: 74, 84). While managers will continually focus on a finite world in which they define their problems in terms of a specific symptom, such as a high level of absence from work, academics will more likely focus on classes of interesting problems (for example the general characteristics of absenteeism) and try to generate information that applies beyond a single setting (Dehler 1998: 76). For managers who are looking for definitive answers or prescriptions, the formal study of management brings them into a rich world of knowledge in which utilization of both instrumental and conceptual knowledge is brought together: many academics enhance their work by drawing on the knowledge and experience of their students and other managers (Dehler 1998: 84). Management, by its very nature, focuses on many issues and practices that are dynamic, ambiguous, complex, contradictory, often political in nature, highly gendered and deeply embedded in specific situations and contexts. No one form of knowledge can claim to provide the sole answer to how these aspects of management should be studied or researched. Rather, there must be room for both and for learning from both.

Even highly accomplished technical experts and professionals often comment on how difficult they find the management part of their jobs, and that their accomplishments, even at the highest levels of their specialist fields, leave them ill-equipped for the task of managing. As Gordon Dehler comments (1998: 85), unlike other professional fields, such as medicine and law, where expertise and knowledge are highly prescribed and the framework of practice is externally regulated and subject to peer review and penalties, in management those who practise it come from various functional areas and can assume the job of a manager with little or no formal qualifications or training in management itself, attaining the position through promotion, seniority, merit, possessing functional expertise (Dehler 1998: 65) or other less salutary means. In many large organizations credentialism is now essential in management but much of this is based on specialized technical training, such as that in accountancy or marketing which often involves studies that have little room for management as a process or organization studies. Moreover, unlike other professionals, who are compelled to keep abreast of new knowledge through certification and accreditation, the same does not generally apply to managers or management, except perhaps in their narrow disciplinary areas such as accountancy or engineering. Often managers want to have their practices rationalized and legitimated through the management education system rather than have them criticized and questioned by academics, who are often dismissed in some quarters as not working in the 'real world' or as living in 'ivory towers' and being irrelevant to the practising manager (Dehler 1998: 85). We suggest that this is simply a popular myth propagated to 'dumb

down' and disguise the need for greater intellectual engagement by managers with theories and abstract conceptualization.

Graeme Salaman and Jim Butler (1994: 36–9) contend that many management consultants and trainers, and many business school lecturers, have tended to propagate a view that managers learn best through experience and doing and value most practical techniques or methods that have direct or immediate application. These same people suggest that highly theoretical knowledge, such as abstract theory, is not often valued or sought after by managers. There is almost a mantra in many business programmes and schools to 'dumb down' management theory to accommodate the needs of practitioners, to make it a saleable and attractive product that can be exported anywhere in the world. This has led to a highly lucrative market for particular styles of texts and knowledge production, typified by the US management industry (Jacques 1996: xiv) which has mass produced texts offering prescriptions or 'one best way' techniques and tools for the manager (Fulop 1992: 8–9). A number of top journals in the field of management, for example the *Harvard Business Review*, are specifically focused on the practitioner level, and many of their articles use arbitrarily selected examples to illustrate complex ideas. This approach appeals to those seeking quick and easy solutions to problems (Dehler 1998: 77). As we discuss below, there are different sources of know-how and knowledge available to the practitioner, ranging from common sense to the conceptualization end of the spectrum. This text is at the latter end of this spectrum! We also argue that to move along this spectrum is both necessary and challenging and requires a critical and reflective posture on the part of managers, because the translation of ideas from one domain or context to another is not without its problems (Czarniawska and Sévon 1996). Rather than being slaves to instrumental orientations, we hope that managers can be more enlightened thinkers who are capable and comfortable with complexity, paradox and ambiguity. As Dehler notes (1998, citing Astley and Zammuto 1992: 455): 'Complicated understandings are important because many of the problems managers face … are complex … [and] can be framed in many different ways, have many possible answers, and are rarely definitely resolved.' We will illustrate what we mean by this different framing when we look at some popular theories in management.

Management is a contested or controversial concept. Alan Thomas (1993) points out that all major areas of management – leadership, teamwork, motivation, quality, best practice, knowledge management – are subject to disagreement by academics and practitioners and capable of being treated from a number of different perspectives. There is no shortage of declared 'experts' in both the academic and practitioner camps who profess to have 'authoritative' views on managing, and as many opinions on how to do it well. The manager needs to understand how know-how and knowledge are manufactured and packaged by these various experts, and what claims they make about solving particular management problems and how these claims will impact in the work setting of the manager. All managerial practices proceed on the basis of some theoretical assumptions, frames of reference or models of action. All managers need to think of themselves as having to always question assumptions and the ways problems are defined and solutions offered for them.

So an important question to ask is: where *should* I start the search for management knowledge or know-how? Should I read a bestseller, emulate the practices of so-called successful CEOs, such as Rupert Murdoch (second-generation media magnate), Richard Branson (founder of Virgin Airlines and the Virgin Group of companies) or Anita Roddick (founder of the cosmetics company, The Body Shop)? Should I buy a management textbook, enrol in a university business course or is it just as easy to 'fly by the seat of my pants'? After all some of the wealthiest and most successful business-people have never completed a university education, let alone management education – a case in point being Branson. The discussion above and what follows give the manager strong reasons to doubt that there is an easy route to gaining management knowledge.

Sources of management know-how and knowledge

There are three main sources of management know-how and three of knowledge. Each represents a genre as described above centred around instrumental and conceptual orientations and these are outlined in Exhibit 1.1. Some of these sources of know-how and knowledge are often not examined in books about management. Their relevance is often trivialized or misunderstood by commentators on management, such as journalists, consultants and managers themselves, who point out that management is mundane, relies heavily on common sense or is just plain jargon-ridden and meaningless. Other critics, such as academics in non-management areas, would argue that management is not theoretical or scientific enough, lacks rigour, universal laws and is unable to produce infallible truths that one might expect in scientific disciplines such as physics. They go on to argue that managers deal with many things that are obvious or amount to just plain common sense so a field of study or discipline of management is not needed. These critics contend that managing a business or organization is obvious to all and sundry and can be learnt 'on the job' and through practice alone (see James 1997: 56). Managers actually

either overvalue common sense or seriously undervalue it (Linstead and Harris 1983: 10, citing Burgoyne 1981). Business schools tend to encourage the undervaluing of common sense, while critics of management draw attention to its overvaluing aspect. We suggest that one of the things a manager needs to learn is that common sense is only one source of knowledge among many and has its place.

Managers who undertake formal business studies in universities will discover that in many courses, such as accounting and marketing, high value is placed on developing the calculative or rational capacities of managers, relying heavily on quantitative methods that draw on the natural sciences to define and solve problems. The manager might be taught that there are preferred ways to solve problems, ones that are superior to others and that simple but effective answers found in different forms of shared experiences are not a rigorous way of creating useable knowledge. The business or management education industry, and particularly many examples of the master of business administration (MBA) degree, depend on marketing products that offer a certain form of mastery and control over the environment, workplace and its employees. The need for mastery and control is a strong driver in much of modern management thinking and has privileged certain forms of knowledge over others. However, what makes management such an interesting area of study today is that, more than ever, there is widespread questioning and challenging of the foundations of modern management thought. There is a greater acknowledgement of and tolerance for different forms of management knowledge, and this has made it more exciting and challenging to teach and learn about management. Along with this shift has come a greater tolerance and recognition of the different sources of knowledge that can influence how one learns about management as well as the virtues and vices of each form of knowledge generation. In Exhibit 1.1 we explore a number of sources of management know-how and knowledge, and touch upon some of the forms of ideas one might discover therein, offering important critiques of each.

In the discussion that follows, considerable attention will be paid to the first three methods of acquiring management know-how and knowledge because these are the most accessible to managers and more tempting in the sense of offering what appear to be solutions to management problems. *Learning by doing*, *local accounts* and *popular accounts* need to be addressed in terms of how they affect reflective practice and critical thinking in managers, often impeding these capacities. The *fads and fashions approaches* tend to dominate the consultancy marketplace, particular management programmes and the mass media, and it is here that most managers source their information and knowledge

Exhibit 1.1 Six sources of management knowledge

1. **Learning by doing** Much of managing involves talking to people to get tasks done; much informal learning about managing occurs during these 'first-order' conversations.

2. **Hearing local accounts** Ordinary everyday talk or stories about work that has been done; these stories are either first- or second-hand accounts of events.

3. **Reading popular accounts** Published, electronically transmitted or publicly recounted (for example at management seminars) accounts of management stories or sagas with 'lessons' or tales of hands-on experiences for other managers to benefit from.

4. **Reading the fads and fashions approaches or theories** The bestsellers or fads and fashions in management magazines and workshops; dominated by works and training methods that

contain recipes or prescriptions for management actions derived from a variety of approaches.

5. **Studying 'soft' academic theory or middle-range theories** Textbooks that attempt to link theory and practice, but the manager reading or hearing this material might sense that it has less emphasis on prescription than popular theory and is more analytically demanding.

6. **Deciphering 'hard' academic theory** Emphasis on theory building and testing or discovering new principles or fundamentals of organization theory, work, technology, personality, society and so on. This is very analytically demanding and rigorous, with a lot less emphasis placed on directly applying knowledge to the day-to-day practice of the manager. Emphasis is placed on managers extrapolating what they see as important for them.

---

about management. The power and attraction of this form of knowledge generation is that it blends the instrumental orientation or the know-how of successful managers with theories that are neither deeply conceptual and intellectually challenging nor rigorous in terms of the research undertaken. The fads and fashions marketplace is dominated by gurus or aspiring gurus who, as David James (1997: 53) says, 'command worldwide audiences, often have a more far-reaching effect on industry policy than politicians and have developed one of the most influential dialogues [discourses or ways of talking] in world economics'. These gurus, he says, are also 'laying down the law, reshaping institutions, refashioning our language and, above all, reorganizing people's lives' (James 1997: 53). Supporting the fads and fashions market is a vast consultancy market in which many businesses trade on selling and repackaging the fads and fashions for individual customers or clients. Many professional associations, formed to serve particular management groups, are also major transmitters of the fads and fashions through their journals and activities (also Dehler 1998: 77). Trying to unravel the appeal of the fads and fashions, and the guru industry behind it, has become a field of study in itself. Academics want to understand why, if the prescriptions and solutions offered by the gurus almost always fall short of expectations, the industry continues to flourish (Collins 2000; Jackson 2001).

By contrast, almost all textbooks, and more mainstream management or organizational books, tend

to contain *soft* or *hard* academic theory. As discussed above, research in management, and hence the field of study, is in tension. There is a need to study problems that are often interesting and not directly relevant to the day-to-day concerns of managers on the one hand, and on the other, with identifying significant emerging problems that can only come from working closely with practitioners (Dehler 1998: 83). As Stephen Linstead (1996: 7) has pointed out, soft theories are more concerned with the quest for theoretical understanding of practical problems, and hard theories more with the development of knowledge for its own sake – to build new theories and break new ground on how we think about organizations and management. This textbook is devoted to developing and exposing managers to 'hard' theories and breaking new ground. The fads and fashions also draw on soft theories but package them in certain ways to appeal to the marketplace. The pursuit of knowledge for its own sake is as important as knowledge that has practical application as its only focus. Through conceptualizing, new theories or paradigms can be developed, but these might not be seen as immediately relevant by business practitioners in terms of how they see their organization's problems (Jacques 1996: x). It is often difficult for those outside the academic or scientific community to understand the debates about what constitutes knowledge and how knowledge can be best developed within the boundaries of a discipline. However, it would be wrong to assume that all management research ought to be there to serve the interests of practitioners (Dehler 1998: 83–4).

Academics are judged for much more than serving the interests of business and have to satisfy the demands of promotions, publications and other pressures that come with such careers. For the practising manager, it might appear to be a matter of academic arrogance and even 'navel gazing' that university researchers focus on problems they cannot understand or comprehend. And there is a downside to how knowledge is generated in most disciplines. As Jacques (1996: 8) points out, 'scientific rigour dictates that knowledge be developed cumulatively, based on prior knowledge presumably about a stable system. Business needs for knowledge are based on an already turbulent world where the pace of change is increasing'. Jacques concludes that the more the quests for rigour and relevance diverge, the pressures of trying to create a scientific base for knowledge pushes theorists endlessly to defend their knowledge on the basis of rigour. This leads to old knowledge being recycled in a Procrustean fashion and applied to new problems which, in turn, increases the likelihood of its irrelevance (Jacques 1996: 8–9). As Dehler notes (1998: 83, citing Schön 1983): 'Uniform principles in the form of standardized knowledge cannot be produced in inherently unstable conditions. Focusing on problem definition rather than solutions preserves academic integrity while supporting practitioner needs.'

Dehler (1998: 86) also suggests that if complicated understanding is to develop in management, then new partnerships or relations have to be forged between practitioners and academics, where relevant research that is informed by practice will lead to new forms of questioning and problematizing 'answers' so that critique and reflexivity become the centrepiece of management studies. As we go through this chapter, we will be endeavouring to show how critique and reflexivity work to problematize how managers might see their worlds.

Learning by doing

The type of dialogue that occurs when Chris Stefano rushes into Dr Cora Harvey's office and starts to recount what went on in the meeting goes on in millions of organizations every day. Their conversation represents a *first-order account* because it is the actual spoken 'text' between two people from which one or both can learn. Much of what goes on in workplaces is in the form of direct conversations, such as that between Chris and Cora, or conversations that recount events such as the incident involving Chris and the others at the meeting. What gets talked about in everyday practice tends to be concerned with survival, getting through the day, determining those things that are important or that demand immediate attention, and

identifying those things that can safely be ignored (Linstead 1996: 7). Most of what gets said or done, even in the heat of the moment, is fundamental to how we cope with complexity and uncertainty, and how we deal with things on the basis of their relevance to the task at hand. In one respect, this is why we all tend to operate for a large part of our day in what is anonymously termed 'the mire of immediacy'.

What gets said or often recounted in everyday practice tends to be based on knowledge that draws heavily on common sense. Thus, in terms of the dilemma described earlier, it seems to be common sense for Chris to call a meeting, outline the task at hand, ask for a volunteer and then expect someone to come forward. There are probably millions like 'Chris Stefano' around the world trying to execute similar management manoeuvres each day. Common sense operates through determining, in a fairly ad hoc fashion, what can be taken for granted, assumed and unquestioned, what is accepted as commonly known, what is left implicit or tacit, and what remains unconsciously 'known' and almost a 'rule of thumb' (Linstead 1996: 7). However, one of the great ironies of organizational life is that common-sense or taken-for-granted knowledge is highly problematic as the basis for getting things done.

Whereas in everyday life we do many things unquestioningly (for example answering the phone, taking a coffee break, organizing an outing), in workplaces almost everything we do has to be accounted for, justified and rationalized to someone else and not always to our 'superiors' (Weick 1995: 63, citing Czarniawska-Joerges 1992). When we answer the phone at work, we might be very careful about how we introduce ourselves, the title we give ourselves, the tone of our voice and the information we disclose about the organization. Karl Weick points out that there is a lot of controlled processing and negotiation that has to occur before individuals can begin to address dilemmas and take actions that signal a willingness on their part to take responsibility for those actions (Weick 1995: 63–4). Chris Stefano, like many other managers, was operating on the premise that individuals will attend a meeting if a crisis faces the organization and, because of their status as employees, these same individuals will carry out assigned tasks, and that certain things, such as deadlines, will be met. Common sense dictates that these assumptions about taking responsibility should be implicitly understood and shared by all, but in fact in the workplace this is not always the case.

Common-sense knowledge (or its application) supports an 'action first' mentality that tends to force individuals to operate through abstractions, simplifications, contractions and abbreviations of events and circumstances (Linstead 1996: 7). These short cuts mean that when it comes to management practice, there is a tendency to avoid testing assumptions or taking the time just to rethink how one operates day to day. As a result, we often get annoyed when our assumptions are challenged or we cannot even understand why anyone would want to question our assumptions. The challenge slows things down, causes 'hiccups' in the system, gets in the way of what we might believe is an otherwise smooth-running group, unit or organization. In the interests of 'getting by' and 'getting the job done' or taking action, we tend to resort to common-sense knowledge and expect others readily to see and agree with us over what needs to be done. This 'action first' culture dominates many organizations, and managers often feel that they should be out there doing something rather than taking the time to sit, question and discuss issues and problems (Lawson 1997: 3). Jacques (1996: xiv) identifies this action first mindset as part of the American mythical management hero successfully exported abroad who encapsulates virtues such as 'the endlessly self-actualizing Protestant perfectionist, … the pioneer, the "man of action" who scorns reflection as impractical'.

It is often difficult for us to see our common-sense constructs of the world as mere constructs that need to be tested, modified and challenged. The way in which we see things is how we think things actually are. We are often afraid to test our common-sense assumptions because we know that these assumptions are not properly formalized and we do not want to appear ignorant or foolish by admitting that we might be in error or have misjudged a situation. Alternatively, we can come to believe so strongly in the 'truth' of our assumptions that we see no reason to question them. The importance of understanding how management knowledge and know-how in particular is acquired is fundamental to our being able to evaluate critically both what we learn formally and our own common-sense assumptions about management. The important thing is not to lose confidence in either form of knowledge acquisition. Managers should have the courage to make assumptions, but they should also have the courage to allow them to be debated, criticized and modified by practice and through discussion (Linstead and Harris 1983: 10). Formal studies of management (that is, studying 'soft' and 'hard' theories) are important in this respect for challenging common-sense assumptions (Fulop 1992: 8–12).

Common-sense assumptions, which remain unquestioned, are highly vulnerable to being influenced by myths, stereotypes, biases and prejudices that can misguide the manager (Fulop 1992: 12–15). In *Imaginization*, Gareth Morgan (1993) recounts how he asked employees to describe their bosses by using animal or storybook characters. He recounts a female employee using the image of Beatrix Potter's *Tale of Jemima Puddle-Duck* to describe the behaviour of her boss; a boss seemingly helpful like the fox in the story, but not to be trusted because he was out for himself alone and was capable of eating employees alive. In recounting the story, Morgan's intention was to illustrate how we use metaphors to deal with many intangible feelings and images to convey meanings that invoke similarities, such as the one between a manager and a fox. Metaphors are used for dramatic effect and to achieve an impact on the listener. The images they convey are usually biased, in that they selectively focus on some behaviours to the exclusion of others. Images are in fact distortions that allow individuals to imagine something as if it were something familiar (Bolman and Deal 1984: 15). However, images, such as metaphors, are powerful constructs that grasp the essentials of how, in the case of the *Tale of Jemima Puddle-Duck*, one individual feels about her boss (Morgan 1993: 24–5; also Fiol 1994: 405). Stereotypes and metaphors narrow and restrict our interpretations of, and responses to, what others do. Yet we all resort to them and use them every day to convey meanings and get our message across to our audience. They are deeply ingrained in our common-sense assumptions.

The more we take for granted or operate from common sense, the less anxiety we might seem to have in our lives (Downing 1997: 33). Reducing anxiety seems to make it easier for us to get on with the job at hand and learn other things, and it might even lead to our letting go of or questioning some of our common-sense assumptions. Yet many stereotypes, such as those about foreigners, gender and social class (that is, based on education, income), are particularly resistant to change or reframing. The stereotypes we carry around with us provide simple guidelines for interactions with diverse groups of people, and we habitually fall back on them to get by, especially when under pressure. Most of our frames of reference also contain rules relating to how we should handle our emotions, and these rules are important in getting by on a day-to-day basis (Downing 1997: 33). Just to get through the day often means leaving many of our common-sense, everyday stock of knowledge and underlying frames of reference unchallenged. The problem is that this can breed complacency, ignorance and dogma. Why question or challenge something that appears to give security, ease and, often, even a sense of superiority?

This leads us to another point. Rather than merely focusing on the common-sense, taken-for-granted knowledge that individuals draw on to make sense of their workplaces, it is also important to ask why individuals do what they do in the first place (Fineman 1993: 23). In other words, what emotions – fear, anxiety, confidence, aggression, jealousy – also contribute to situations arising, such as the one described above with Chris? Emotional games or subtexts are played out in every organizational encounter (Fineman 1997, 2000; Fulop and Rifkin 1997; Höpfl and Linstead 1997). Perhaps Chris is insecure, feeling threatened by work colleagues or has an annual review coming up and is anxious about it. Chris's anxiety may result in the tension or lack of compliance of the group as a whole. Alternatively, perhaps Phil is just plain upset about his failure to get promoted and this has coloured his outlook. In other words, Phil might be venting anger and frustration about his non-promotion at Chris, who in Phil's mind represents the authority that denied him his promotion (presuming Chris is Phil's boss). There are two interesting points about emotions: the first is that we are all prisoners of our personal histories (however 'good' or 'bad' these might be), and the second is that most of us are unaware of our most basic motivations and feelings, although we inflict them on others every day (Fineman 1993: 24). In other words, our histories permit events to catalyse a wide array of emotions and yet we are often not introspective about them. Nor do many management courses or textbooks deal with these topics, preferring either to put them in the 'too hard basket' or seeing them as irrelevant (see, for example, Bedeian 1995).

Stories, which we will address next, result from events at work and help to make sense of the practice of managers. The manager's practices, as we saw above, are most often based on and rationalized in terms of common sense rather than being the result of a deep questioning of assumptions. Common sense and rules of thumb save us time and effort and may have a certain attraction as being safe and familiar. Unfortunately, they can leave us open to many misguided actions and decisions because they might well be constrained by the very metaphors that also help us to make sense of, for example, an untrustworthy (fox-like) boss.

Local accounts

Local accounts abound in organizations and often take the form of stories you hear in corridors, lunchrooms, toilets, car parks, on the golf course and in meeting rooms before meetings start (Fineman and Gabriel 1996: 1). Stephen Fineman (1993: 21) suggests that one of the reasons individuals choose to tell their stories or have conversations in these places is because these are places where emotional control can be relaxed and people can feel safe to speak away from the scrutiny of those who are their 'superiors' or likely to be judging their performance. Stories can also be transmitted electronically on the Internet – they need not be face to face. We all participate in telling stories. Gossiping, telling jokes and sharing anecdotes are all examples of the story-like or narrative form. Weick (1995: 127)

suggests that individuals think in narratives and make sense of organizations in a narrative form. Yet many things that are done or processed in organizations are not based on this easy to digest narrative or story form, but rather on argumentation and rational discourse. Because of this diversity of discursive forms, and the dominance of one form, organizations can be very difficult places for many individuals to negotiate and make sense of. For people from different cultural backgrounds, it is even more difficult; for example, the story of Chris's meeting when told from the perspective of Phil might seem absurd to people from another culture because they are used to a narrative form different from the one that Phil might use. They would tell the story differently with different meanings attached to events. In many Southeast Asian countries, it would be unacceptable to volunteer for a task – one could lose face by appearing to be inconsiderate of fellow employees. The expectation would be that a senior person would assign the task and would not ask for a volunteer. Even certain facial expressions might be considered irreverent as well as expressions of emotion or feelings.

The story format is used because it is such an easy one in which to capture the essence of our experiences. So, one might see half of one's life in an organization spent making decisions and acting on commands and orders, and the other half spent trying to make sense of the actions of others. We cram what we perceive into a story's plot but neglect or ignore those aspects that do not fit our preferred version of events. Although these tendencies have their inherent dangers, our words and actions, and the accounts told about them, can be seen as the most accessible and rich reservoir of management know-how and general knowledge we must contend with.

Both accounts in practice and local accounts, and indeed accounts of any kind, depend on the understanding and meanings of those sharing a conversation. When an account is given, there are usually two and often three simultaneous forms of knowledge being imparted to the listener. The first relates to the *content of the communication* (Fiol 1994: 405), which refers to the categories or labels (for example stereotypes or metaphors) being used. So, in the Chris Stefano story, these might relate to what is said later about other people in the meeting. Chris could be described as behaving like a 'headless chicken'; Roderick Cage criticized for being sexist; Rebecca Spalding for always whingeing; Wasim Shan for being lazy; or Merilyn Hue for being 'bitchy'. These are all filtered perceptions of reality, and thus are unlikely to be accurate ones. But they might, nonetheless, become a significant part of the content of the communication about the meeting or subsequent local accounts.

Meaning also resides in a second form of

knowledge, *frameworks* or *ways of framing communication*. '"Framing" refers to the way people construct their arguments or viewpoint, regardless of its content' (Fiol 1994: 405). Thus for some the meeting might be a monumental disaster, for others a typical event in a typical day, and for others a great opportunity to improve something in the organization. A third form of knowledge that conveys meaning is a *relationship component* (Austin 1962; Watzlawick et al. 1967; Bateson 1975; Garko 1994; Rifkin 1994). The importance given to a story may depend on who tells it and what that person's relationship is to a listener. If Wasim Shan tells the story of the meeting to a colleague who works for him, the colleague might try to remember the events for future reference in order to impress Wasim. If Rebecca Spalding tells the story to a co-worker, it may sound to the co-worker like more whingeing from Rebecca. Such relationships are influenced by power including those based on gender, ethnicity, age, professional affiliation, status and so on. Given these different dimensions of meaning or forms of knowledge – content, framing and relationships – individuals can be understood to need to agree on a broad frame of reference about events and with the people they might be listening to in order to solve a problem collectively or come up with a brilliant new innovation that many are willing to adopt (Fiol 1994: 406).

One of the greatest paradoxes facing any group, and those trying to manage it, is to work out how members of the group can learn collectively and develop a broad frame of reference they can all share. For collective learning to occur, there has to be some consensus or unity of interpretations about certain things or events, and there has to be public confirmation of these interpretations for the sharing of knowledge (Fiol 1994: 404). Then there also has to be a diversity of interpretations for new knowledge to develop and progress to occur in organizations (Fiol 1994: 404). Progress embraces more than just innovations because not all innovations spell improvements for an organization or society (Abrahamson 1996a: 5). Thus both consensus and diversity have to coexist, and neither can be subordinated to the other. This means that collective learning is built upon the sharing of common understandings, but also the development of new understandings, and this often entails exploring and finding new frames of reference. Managers need to understand the ways in which knowledge is shaped and shared in everyday practice, in learning by doing and through local accounts, which create and sustain the frames of reference that individuals draw upon to make sense of their organizations and the actions of those in them.

Managers will have to learn more than just how meanings are communicated. All social practices, such as communicating, also involve two other elements:

power and the use of normative sanctions (Salaman and Butler 1994: 39; Coopey 1995: 198). All forms of communication are situated within structures (for example a hierarchy) and organizational processes (for example bargaining and negotiating) of power and are underscored by potential normative sanctions, such as rewards and punishments or 'carrots and sticks'. Members of organizations usually seek to control their work lives and conditions, that is, to maximize their opportunities and rewards. Yet organizations or at least managers in them create dependency relations in which many tasks and jobs can only be done through collective effort. Collective effort is constrained by unequal personal access to resources, such as finances, promotions, information, opportunities to occupy positions of authority (that is, give orders to others) and so on that affect how tasks or work are accomplished (Coopey 1995: 197; see also Chapter 6). Having to depend on others involves a risk because failure or success at completing tasks usually carries negative and positive sanctions respectively; the former refers to coercion (punishment) and the latter to inducements (rewards) that are endorsed by top managers and broadly accepted by others in the organization (Coopey 1995: 198). Controlling one's work life or conditions is very much a political process fraught with risks that sometimes are worth it and at other times can cause chaos and havoc which can seriously harm one's career.

As Salaman and Butler (1994) also point out, since managers exist in structures of power, reward and evaluation (that is, sanctions), they will often learn only what is seen as legitimate (that is, involves positive inducements or rewards) and helps them get ahead. To do otherwise would be considered mad and managers who did so would probably be made redundant or dismissed (1994: 38–9). In other words, managers often have a vested interest or priorities in *not* learning or adopting new frames of reference, the very source of creativity, innovation and learning. These vested interests can come in the form of, say, departmental loyalty, professional affiliations, different levels of skills, knowledge, expertise and even gender exclusion strategies. All these can breed differences in perspectives that can get in the way of cooperation and collective action (Salaman and Butler 1994: 39; also Chapter 6).

Popular accounts

Stories that attract or hold our attention tend to be about remarkable experiences that often relate to something unexpected or out of the ordinary (Weick 1995: 127–8). A remarkable enough story gets published – it becomes a popular account. Such stories have particular forms or genres that are derived from quite surprising sources.

Exhibit 1.2 Dominant plots

1. **The quest** A progressive ('nice') hero or heroine adventurer, who challenges the status quo or conventional wisdom, experiences setbacks, but ultimately succeeds and becomes rich and famous. The 'quest' plot is linked to the high adventure novel or the romance genre of the great love affair or story.

2. **The contest** A polarized struggle between two heroes or heroines characterized as representing the forces of good and evil in which there is a climactic battle, and good prevails over evil. The plot is melodramatic.

3. **The conquest** A hero or heroine who succeeds by way of force, plunder or bullying, but achieves his or her ultimate goal and succeeds in the face of opposition and attack. Unlike the contest, the conqueror comes to be seen as good once he or she has 'saved the day' or achieved fame and fortune. This type of storyline can invite loathsome or begrudging admiration of the feats of the hero or heroine.

4. **The downfall** A hero or heroine slips from success and must face danger and humiliation,

primarily as a result of wrongdoing or some weakness of personality. They usually have to confront fear and suffering and are likely not to prevail or survive. Fear and pity are strong emotions evoked by this plot, which is essentially the modern-day tragedy in which we keep saying: 'if only'.

5. **The disaster** A hero or heroine falls from success and must face danger, humiliation and great loss. Unlike the 'downfall', this loss is likely to be the result of events outside the control of the hero or heroine. They suffer a great deal, but always hold out the hope of a 'comeback'! Pity and disbelief are strong emotions associated with this plot, which is essentially a drama of epic proportions.

6. **The scam** A hero or heroine is exposed as incompetent, corrupt or foolish; what were past heroic actions are reinterpreted to reveal a scam to defraud or fool others. This type of plot is riddled with irony as people and events turn out to be not what they seem, and there is a sense of being cheated or let down.

To explain what we mean by these forms or genres, we need to look beyond learning by doing and local accounts to what we have termed 'popular accounts'.

A popular account is usually a noteworthy story that is circulated outside the organization. It can be a newsletter story of a boost in production; a newspaper profile of a manager receiving a promotion; a revelation on email about new products; a manager's report in a magazine of 20 per cent growth in productivity due to re-engineering; an in-depth television documentary on reductions in the workforce at a local factory; or a 'leak' from an internal policy meeting about changes. It has usually been reproduced in the media in some form or another as a *second-* or *third-order account* of an organizational event or state of affairs, usually in a sensationalized form.

Both the person who recounts a story about an exceptional event, person or experience and the person about whom it is told are involved in and affected by a particular storyline. The storylines of popular accounts are likely to revolve around six main plots that can be interwoven into one storyline, or one plot might dominate a storyline. Storylines, particularly those that draw on legends and fairy tales, function as powerful frames of reference by which individuals come to rationalize or legitimize what goes on in their

organizations, including their successes and failures. These storylines become the lessons that others might learn from someone else's experiences. The six dominant plots that are most likely to be represented in popular accounts in Western businesses are ones that we (at least in Anglo-Saxon cultures) have grown up with and learnt about in fairy tales and stories. Following Stephen Downing (1997: 37–9), but with the inclusion of the 'disaster' and 'conquest' plots, and some other modifications, the six dominant plots are shown in Exhibit 1.2.

Examples of popular accounts are reproduced in the six case examples below. Try to make out why these accounts have appeal, and then see if you can identify the main plots in each storyline. The first one presents a less common or flattering account of Branson's rise to fame and fortune.

The main storyline involving Branson is the *quest*, but some omitted sections, such as his battle with British Airways, also reveal the *contest* plot. The excerpt does not describe his daredevil stunts, but it does allude to the fact that he courts death with his adventures, such as hot-air ballooning (in pursuit of world records). He flouts tradition, rejects the status quo with his dress, is flamboyant, fun, wealthy, powerful, sought after, breaks the rules of business

CASE EXAMPLE

RICHARD BRANSON

Let's examine a hypothetical situation, a sort of elaborate role-playing fantasy. Prepare to assume the mindset of a character. To begin with, you're a self-made billionaire. You have a parkside mansion in one of the world's great cities, a manor in the countryside and your own island paradise in the Caribbean where you've installed a first-rate chef. You own a record label, an airline that flies to four continents, a national radio station, a pan-European train service, a worldwide chain of music stores, a jeans and casual clothing company, a string of hotels and a message service. You even own the brand of vodka you drink. You have hundreds of millions of dollars of capital readily available, and yet you don't really need it because other people are willing to put up all the money for your daring business ventures, taking all the risk while you hold majority ownership in the new companies and retain control – such is your track record, professional reputation and intangible aura of X-factor.

You're still young (46), handsome, slender and leonine; your hair is as thick as a mane. You're a symbol of the baby-boomers who came of age in the 1960s and later brought their progressive values to their entrepreneurial ventures. You're happily married to the beautiful woman you've lived with for 21 years, and together you're raising two adorable kids. Your wife, a former hippie, apparently doesn't mind when you stay out until 3 am on week nights at your nightclub, flirting shamelessly with the prowling temptresses who surround you wherever you go.

This entire scenario has been taken from the life of Richard Branson, the chairman of the Virgin Group of companies – that sweater-wearing icon of British business – a man who makes a bizarre hobby out of courting and cheating his own death. Branson explains that he likes to finance new companies as a way of helping other people pursue their dreams. Virgin Bride was the brainchild of Virgin Atlantic flight attendant, Alisa Percy, who is now the top executive at the start-up. The launch event for the first Virgin Bride store was held on site, in a grand limestone building near London's Trafalgar Square. A legion of impossibly cheerful waitresses buzzed about, pouring champagne. They wore the spiffy scarlet suits and pumps of Virgin Atlantic flight attendants because that's what they were: cabin crew on a layover. Branson never uses pretentious jargon like synergy, but that's exactly what he was creating with this endeavour, and it wasn't just that employees were handling other jobs. The new store will help brides book their honeymoons, pushing Virgin flights and Virgin hotels. Synergy!

But wait: that's just the beginning of the cross-pollination. Next there was a fashion show, and a procession of models strutted out to show off some of the wedding dresses the store would carry. The catwalkers came from Branson's modelling agency, Storm, which represents the likes of Elle McPherson and Kate Moss. For the show's finale, Branson himself appeared, the Virgin king pretending to be the Virgin bride. He wore a white gown with white fishnet stockings and big white bow in the back atop a long, fluffy train. Branson had even shaved off the rakish beard he had sported since his teenage years. He threw red roses to the frenzied crowd as the paparazzi shouted, 'Show us your garter!' There's almost always some kind of big stunt when Branson opens a new store or inaugurates an airline route or launches a company.

Branson is being sued for sexual harassment by one of his American employees, who claims he fondled her breasts at a company party. He denies the allegations, although it's not hard to see how his style of good-natured partying would be treated with less tolerance in the US. He's unabashedly flirtatious, but his lasciviousness goes only so far. The British tabloids have never accused him of marital infidelity.

Branson makes a habit of lavishing his people with recognition and hospitality. Every summer he invites all of Virgin Atlantic's 3500 employees and their kids to his country house near Oxford for a five-day party. Virgin Atlantic workers aren't paid as much as their counterparts in airlines such as British Airways, but Branson has other, more creative approaches to motivation.

Branson hosts an award dinner for Virgin Atlantic's flight attendants-of-the-month from the previous year, crew members who were mentioned by passengers on survey forms or singled out by their bosses for exceptional work. For the finale, Branson picks one name out of a hat: the chosen crewmate wins a vacation to Neckar, Branson's own Virgin Island. The winner is a woman in a black cocktail dress, and she's exuberant. All of a sudden, Branson picks her up by the waist and turns her upside down, exposing her black underwear. The audience cheers wildly, the woman laughs with them. It's Branson's favourite party stunt.

At 16, Branson dropped out of school to go into business. He started a magazine called, ironically, *Student* and fearlessly solicited articles from such counter-culture icons as Jean-Paul Sartre and James Baldwin. The venture was short-lived and morphed into a discount mail-order record business and then a record label. Branson didn't have much sense about trends in music, but his colleagues did. His own contributions were vital though: charismatic leadership, prodigious energy, unbounded and reckless ambition, shrewd deal making and negotiating, and a knack for charming bankers and eluding creditors.

Source: Abridged from Alan Deutschman (1997) 'Heavens above', Good Weekend, *The Sydney Morning Herald*, 23 August, pp. 16–19.

protocol, has temptresses chasing him and has the so-called 'X-factor'. He is the modern corporate hero providing the dream of all, a 'rags to riches' story. The image of the hero is so strong that many of Branson's faults or shortcomings are overlooked or 'forgiven'. For example, the sexual harassment case against him is represented by the male writer as a clear misinterpretation of the antics of a 'harmless' prankster. Branson is depicted as anarchic non-conformist and after all it should not be expected that he conform to all the rules, in this case, a rather trivial mistake.

The quest plot influences the ways in which people talk and think about management. For example, leadership theories have been dominated for years by a heroic masculine image (Huey 1994) based on the pursuit of the quest, particularly of self-made entrepreneurs such as the likes of Branson. The dream for many managers might be represented by the Branson-type storyline – quest and contest. Many senior managers, when they talk about such things as strategic planning and creating a mission, purpose and vision, also try to engage others in a type of quest or bold adventure with a promise of a better, wealthier and happier workplace (Downing 1997: 29). The storyline, and its plots, are a way of trying to get others to share a particular frame of reference to legitimize what is being done and how it is being done, and in the process also helping to build commitment and understanding. These storylines become a part of the corporate myth or a way of reinforcing that this is how 'things work around here' (Schwartz 1996: 41). Thus the fact that Branson might do a lot of peculiar things is legitimated through the storyline that becomes the representation of Branson's quest. Branson would hope that all in Virgin subscribe to his storyline and adopt it as their own. It fuels or satisfies the employees' dreams of a 'fairy tale' land, where the dashing and cavalier 'Prince Charming', that is, Branson, wants to make everyone's dreams come true. He wants everyone to have common behaviours, beliefs and perceptions or share common myths about being a Virgin employee (Schwartz 1996: 41).

Liz Fulop and Fran Laneyrie (1995), reviewing a study by Amanda Sinclair (1994) of top male CEOs in Australia, noted that the public tales told by these CEOs centred on heroic images of the sort described above in the Branson story. These heroic images were invariably cast in a narrow, masculine storyline. The CEOs' quests described in Sinclair's study drew on mythical images,

such as that of Ulysses, the hero who must overcome obstacle after obstacle in a journey that some CEOs might say would inevitably lead them to the top. Along the way, the story of Ulysses depicts temptresses trying to avert the hero from the path to success. Such temptress images reflect what the authors contend is a problematic aspect of success stories, and stories in general in our Western cultures. Almost all mythical images of powerful women, except for the 'mother figure', generally represent evil. Fulop and Laneyrie contend that such constraints in the mythical imagery, from which public tales of success are told, reinforce the stereotypes and biases that work against women climbing to the top of organizations. They support a movement of 'remythologizing' whereby, for example, Ulysses can be recast as 'a sadistic bully, whose joy in plundering and raping and pillaging others is far from heroic' (Fulop and Laneyrie 1995: 64; also Laneyrie 1995). This would be akin to adopting the conquest plot. The Australian CEOs in Sinclair's study also represented women with some positive images, however, portraying some in their organizations as 'good mothers' (the proverbial 'Oedipal myth', the story of Oedipus who loved his mother) or 'good virgins' who were focused, knowledgeable and direct. The women's main virtue is portrayed as being that they are not out solely for their own gain. Such virtue or goodness is even captured in company names, such as Branson's own use of 'Virgin'.

The Ruiz story, by contrast, with its feminine 'hero', is a representation of the *contest*. Her ethics and *feminista* ideals, her willingness to face danger head on, and being the first at any shoot-out, cast her as 'the good' challenging 'the bad'. All decent or honest people would want to see her win and beat the 'baddies'. This makes her a particular type of heroine in the management domain in which she operates. The contest plot is often the one used to make sense of organizational power and politics, both of which are prevalent in the Ruiz story. The interesting thing to note in this storyline is that the so-called 'baddies' in the story – the drug dealers and cartel members – would probably prefer to present the Ruiz story from the conquest storyline, pointing to her unreasonable aggression and harassment of them as being out of step with the spirit of the law.

Storylines, and their plots, are in one form or another 'vocabularies of motives' in which the descriptions of

CASE EXAMPLE

ELVIRA RUIZ

[The place]: Playas de Tijuana: When Elvira Ruiz took charge of this seaside district's municipal police, she faced a legion of drug punks and street criminals determined to show her who was boss. She was shot at, run off the highway and threatened with death.

Inside the dusty precinct, a different war was being waged. Ruiz's subordinate officers, all male, bristled at the idea of a woman in command. They withheld information. They emptied petrol tanks of patrol cars and disconnected their starter cables. They employed time-honoured gender warfare tactics, smearing her with unsavoury locker room lies. They spearheaded a lobby to oust her.

How Ruiz won her battle on both fronts is a testimony to character over circumstances, Ruiz's image as a clean cop and sheer stubbornness. Her honest reputation, if merited, remains a risky distinction in a city where authorities are forced to choose between *plata o plomo* – bribes or bullets – by the Tijuana drug cartel, an empire backed by an array of well-connected gunmen and millions of dollars in cash. Eight ranking Baja law enforcement officers have been killed in the past year. Some victims, according to US court documents, were corrupt collaborators who got bribes *and* bullets.

US anti-drug experts say it is only a matter of time before reform-minded officers are transferred, intimidated, demoted, bought off – or worse. The most pessimistic believe institutional corruption is so pervasive it is extremely difficult for any honest officers to rise to command.

'Elvira does not steal,' said Baja California Superior Court Magistrate Victor Manuel Vasquez. 'She works night and day. She cannot be intimidated because she knows she is doing the right thing. If there were more Elviras in the police force, we would be much better off.' Ruiz commands an 80-officer division within the 1200-strong city police force. She is one of five district chiefs who report to Tijuana's police commander. Said Ricardo Arenas, spokesman for the municipal police: 'If there's an emergency call, she answers it herself. If there's a gunfight, she's first at the scene. Our only complaint is she should stop working when she's sick.'

Just shy of 1.5m tall, Ruiz is a soft-spoken, articulate, divorced workaholic who looks younger than her 38 years. When not in uniform, she prefers black designer jeans, blue eye shadow, fuchsia lipstick and maroon nail polish. She does not hide her disregard for machismo, the masculine expression of the Mexican gender balance of power, or shrink from the 'F' word. Ruiz is an unabashed feminista.

Ruiz's new command, Playas de Tijuana, was a one-time beach resort that had once been virtually crime-free. But by the time Ruiz arrived, the district was becoming a battleground for control of the local trade in methamphetamines and other drugs. When Ruiz arrived on the scene, street punks who thought of themselves as untouchable were startled to find themselves being photographed for the arrest scrapbook she keeps on her desk. Even car thieves, small-time drug dealers, burglars and drunk drivers began to insinuate that if she didn't leave them alone, she was playing with fire. The death threats began not long after she arrived, and in August 1994 a car sped alongside her and forced her to skid off the road. Like many law enforcers, Ruiz preaches a fatalistic stoicism.' If I were afraid, I wouldn't do this.'

Source: Abridged from Anne-Marie O'Connor (1997) 'Woman shakes up Tijuana police brass', *The Sydney Morning Herald*, 1 March, p. 24 (report from *The Los Angeles Times*).

human conduct, such as those of Ruiz or Branson, are not normally derived from the individuals being described, but are imputed to them by the media or those producing the accounts. Ruiz might or might not be pleased with being described as an 'unabashed *feminista*'. What is also often missing from the stories or popular accounts are 'the diverse objects, resources, events, and social relations' (Silverman 1985: 10) that are part and parcel of the representations being made. In other words, the stories are always incomplete and often one-sided, particularly when they are abridged as they have been for this chapter. Moreover, as David Silverman argues, 'social relations specify who is obliged to describe whom and the form and consequences of these descriptions' (1985: 10). Storylines or plots are also 'vocabularies of power'. This means that the description of Ruiz, for example, proffered by magistrate Vasquez is one that is appropriate for consumption in the public domain and, as would be expected, is cast in terms of law and order issues. Privately, he might well say very different things. For Ruiz, the public account has enormous personal and professional consequences as it reflects on her honesty, accountability and performance. In other words, considerable power is accorded to those such as Vasquez who are seen as being legitimately positioned to present their views of others – their opinions and views get listened to and are far harder to dismiss than those of others. Their descriptions become a discursive resource or capability that helps to ensure that managers, such as Ruiz, perform as expected, or risk a potentially less flattering storyline being circulated about them. Yet the storyline cannot escape casting her as other than a manager. The author insists on describing her clothes,

looks and make-up almost to highlight a weak, feminine side or a sexual object easier to relate to and understand than an accomplished police chief. How would the story be written if Ruiz were not a woman? The title would probably be something along the lines of 'Tough new chief shakes up Tijuana police brass'.

CASE EXAMPLE

THE RISE OF JACQUES NASSER

Meet Jac the Knife, executive vice-president of the Ford Motor Company, a man hell-bent on reinventing the world's wheels. In the quiet of the cellar, Jacques Albert Nasser sounds not at all like a Jacques. When he responds to a good natured interjection, the accent is more … Bruce [means a real Australian bloke]. 'Don't take the piss too much,' he grins, the delivery as broad and flat as a mulga wood ashtray. The Lebanese-born kid from Melbourne's suburban Northcote, the one they called a wog at school, is running Ford's global operations in Detroit. In his spare time, he's also mounting a rescue of the company's European theatre, amid strikes and saturation media coverage.

Wall Street says Jac Nasser, 49, shapes as the heir apparent to the chairman's office at Ford Motor. Tonight, he's doing one of the many things he does well: laying on the personal charm. Deftly he moves from Grange Hermitage fine wine to computer technology, a rust belt revival and, finally, to Detroit's fondness for overstatement.

Jacques Nasser is less a trimmer of corporate fat than a one-man guillotine. His blade removes arms and legs, but his surgery has returned many Ford businesses to robust health. The word 'ruthless' is often used. 'You can't ask a customer in the marketplace to pay for waste, inefficiency and a lack of focus,' he counters.

Wall Street has IOUs from Nasser amounting to $US11 billion, the promised savings from a dramatic restructuring of the way Ford develops and builds its new cars and trucks – his version of reinventing the wheel. Under a plan called Ford 2000, he has promised to freeze the company's huge new model costs, delivering more profits for the company's Dearborn headquarters and cheaper cars and trucks for customers. He has shown Wall Street the minutiae: how reducing the variety of cigarette lighters in Ford vehicles from 14 to just one will save a million dollars a year. And the big picture: that 6000 fewer engineers will be needed when he cuts by a quarter the number of Ford's vehicle 'platforms', the building blocks for every new model, while doubling the number of parts they share.

A shrinker of head counts and a slasher of costs,

Nasser also has the flair to create successful, exciting new models which just happen to be very profitable. He is an enthusiast, more than comfortable coaxing young designers into creating his current pet project, a 21st-century version of the 1955 Ford Thunderbird.

For grimy, time-worn Detroit, he is a one-man culture shock. A graduate in business studies from Royal Melbourne Institute of Technology, where he returned this week to collect an honorary doctorate, he is a rare blend of hard-nosed human abacus, astute politician and old-fashioned petrolhead. He speaks five languages and often eschews a chauffeur, driving a giant red pick-up truck. He's the antithesis of the insular, Detroit WASP high-roller, and his relentless, sometimes colourful, approach has Ivy League colleagues sniffily suggesting he lacks a certain … polish. 'The old Detroit had a narrow focus on the US,' says Nasser dismissively. 'What we're seeing with the new Detroit is a focus on what's right globally and that's right down my alley.'

As president of Ford Automotive Operations (FAO), Nasser has huge worldwide clout. With more than a tinge of sarcasm, FAO has become known in Detroit as Foreign Accents Only as Nasser strives to break an all-American culture, with wave after wave of offshore executives, enough from his homeland to give rise to another testy label: For Australians Only.

As a Ford executive, you either believed in the Nasser doctrine or you were out of a job. 'He was a bit like that Monty Python sketch with the black knight,' a close colleague remembers. 'He'd cut off an arm, then a leg, but fully expect the knight to continue giving its best.'

Now Nasser is but one step removed from the chairman's office and the ultimate power to steer that 'world beater' vision into reality. His rise has been meteoric since taking the chairman's role at Ford of Europe in 1993. He'd wagered his career by turning down the lesser role of president. 'There's satisfaction in knowing you are ultimately responsible for the livelihoods of thousands of people,' he explains. 'They blame you or they praise you, no one else. That has a certain energising value for me.'

In Europe, as in Australia, Nasser's hands were deep in the clay of new model development, championing among other designs a new small car, the groundbreaking Ka, introduced last year to rapturous response.

'The standard Jac line,' says a former close colleague,

'is always the same. How can we do better? How can we take this and improve it?' Nasser is a talker, a great persuader with infectious enthusiasm and a direct style the media love. Hard as nails but smooth as oiled glass when there's something he wants, he is totally without side when the business is done. Nasser's social skills are extraordinary. He never seems to forget a name or a face and has the happy knack of making those around him comfortable. 'To me, almost everything you do has to be people-related. You can't get away from it. Relationships matter. Emotions are important. Friendships are important. If you start to lose a feeling of loyalty and trust and confidence in your own friends and community you're

gone. What's left for you to fight for?'

That legendary patience is sorely tested by the inevitable question. 'So how do you feel about sacking your mates, Jac?' He doesn't miss a beat, but is clearly displeased. 'Yes, I've done that. I've done it when I've really felt that the loyalty wasn't there, that they didn't share common views. When that happens you've really got to separate. I like people who are passionate about what they are doing and I don't suffer fools.'

Source: Abridged from Phil Scott (1997) 'Jac the Knife', *The Sydney Morning Herald*, The Spectrum Features, 8 March, p. 3.

In the 'Jac the Knife' storyline we see the dominant plot being that of the *conquest*. This is the classic American 'captain of industry', Rockefeller story who, incidentally, wrote his storyline through autobiography. Such 'captains of industry' were notorious for being hard on employees, often unpopular, but highly focused commercially. It is difficult to see how the quest or contest plots would apply to this story. There is no visible high adventure or romance being depicted or, for that matter, good prevailing over bad. The image that prevails is that of the ruthless manager who conquers all in his path and 'takes no prisoners'. In the end, the success of the individual and his or her organization invokes admiration for his or her achievements. The conquest plot was prevalent in the 1990s with the spread of downsizing and re-engineering of many large organizations, both in the private and public sectors. Those who have masterminded huge labour-shedding and cost-cutting exercises became the corporate heroes of the 1990s, and they were identified with and revered for their extreme toughness and grit. It is the ultimate macho storyline. The 'Jac the Knife' storyline has had many similar counterparts across the international business world which is dominated by the above three plots and

the media do much to disseminate these stories. However, there are other stories – the downfall, the disaster and the scam – which provide counter-stories or lessons about those who fail to make the corporate grade or make it and then 'fail'. They provide powerful imagery and stereotypes of the fall from grace and the loss of power. Indeed one story can mutate into another, as appears to have been Nasser's fate – although he went on to become president and CEO of Ford, and the world's highest paid auto-executive, in 1999, after a troubled tenure marked by loss of market share, two recalls of Firestone tyres fitted to Ford Explorer four-wheel drive vehicles for safety reasons, a loss of market share, a cash crisis and a rift with Chairman William Clay Ford Jnr, whose family own 40 per cent of the company, he lost his position after 33 years with Ford in 2001. Quite a downfall. Below we provide an excerpt from a newspaper article which appeared in the *Observer* that looks at how a number of prominent women, who have 'failed' in their career, have inevitably been cast in the downfall genre but in a highly negative way. The author compares their downfall to those of their male counterparts and finds a huge difference in the representations being adopted in the media.

CASE EXAMPLE

SHE WHO MUST BE VILIFIED

When Peter Mandelson [the British Cabinet minister who masterminded the return to power of New Labour in 1997] resigned last year, after remembering that he had forgotten about the funding arrangements of his mortgage, no one passed comment on the colour of his shoes. When Geoffrey Robinson [the former paymaster-general in the Cabinet who had loaned Mandelson the

money] went on the *Today* programme last month to defend his reputation, no one complained about his tone of voice. When Tony Blair makes a blunder during Prime Minister's Question Time, no one would dream of suggesting that the trouble might have something to do with the fact that he was a father-of-three 'with another on the way' [now of course four]. But if it is a woman in the hot seat, you can expect to hear about nothing else.

If it's not her credentials as a mother that are found wanting, it's her selfish decision not to have any children. If it's not her selfish decision to forgo children, it's her shoes. If it's not her shoes, it's her dress size, her taste in wallpaper, and the state of her hair. If she has a high voice, she's too silly. If she has a low voice, she's too much like a man. The higher her profile, the pettier the complaints. No matter how big her job is, it will be her personality that people argue about.

And when she fails? It's more of the same, as we saw in the press post mortem of Jennie Page's career at the Dome [former chief executive of the high-profile, government-backed Millennium Dome project in London]. For some, Page had failed because she didn't have children, and so didn't know how to make the Dome a place they liked. For others, it was her management style: she was 'awkward, rude and impossible to deal with'. For Stephen Bayley, the Dome's original interior designer, her tragic flaw was that she lacked the 'bravery and style' to stand up for her own ideas.

In his poison-pen portrait in the *Mail on Sunday*, he portrayed her as a toady run amok: 'There was never any doubt that Jennie Page, a driven, focused, frenetic woman, would do everything necessary to get the Dome finished on time and budget. This "everything" included an astonishing disdain of other people which took the form of (a) ignoring expert advice and (b) an unreflective willingness to chew up and dispose of individuals who got in the way.'

The headline for this article was 'A Noisy Mouse Who Presided Over a Disgrace.' Page, says Bayley, was 'a noisy mouse, no slave to fitness or fashion'. But other papers gave her a glossier image. In the *Daily Telegraph*, she is the 'Empress of the Dome'. It is hard to imagine a real-life woman who could come across as an empress and a mouse. But it is very rare to read a news report about a very important sacked or about-to-be-sacked woman in which she is not portrayed as an unstable marriage of unhappy opposites. Consider Clare Spottiswoode, who stepped down as Ofgas [government regulator of the gas industry] boss when news broke of an extramarital affair, and was called Boadicea, Annie Oakley, Mumsy, and 'Ingrid Bergman on a bad hair day'. To say that one woman could be all of these things, is to suggest that she is suffering from multiple personality disorder.

The press gave a similar moral to the Nicola Horlick story. She became a celebrity not because she lost a power struggle at Morgan Grenfell, the merchant bank, but because her high-powered career had not stopped her having five children. The tabloids dubbed her the female Icarus. She failed because she had flown too close to the sun, overestimating her abilities. 'We never called her Superwoman,' a former colleague told the *Daily Mail*, 'we called her Brenda like the Queen.' But now that she had been shown to be an emotional toddler, her career was doomed.

At no point during these 'so farewell then' rituals does anyone say: 'This woman cannot be trusted with power because she is a woman.' Instead, her critics seek to disqualify her by saying she is muddled, spineless, childish, wishy-washy. This is not to say that men in disgrace don't face caricature and harsh criticism, too. But there is a big difference between the sort of coverage Geoffrey Robinson has had and the coverage Mo Mowlam [former Cabinet minister responsible for Northern Ireland] has been getting since her return from Northern Ireland. The question marks around Robinson concern his performance and his conduct, Mowlam's concern the very quality of her mind. Robinson's story is grounded in events; Mowlam's is grounded in a Westminster whispering campaign.

In 1997, *Women in Journalism* did a research project in which it compared the coverage given to Alan Howarth MP when he left the Tories for New Labour, with the coverage given to Emma Nicholson MP when she left the Tories for the Lib Dems only a few weeks later. The differences were stark. While Howarth was portrayed as a man of vision acting on his conscience, Nicholson was described as witch-like and menopausal. Even in straight news stories, her decision was described as vengeful, petty and petulant. These same stories described her appearance and her family connections in many column inches before they bothered to mention what she had achieved in her own career.

All these criticisms suggest critics who are deeply ambivalent about women with power, not to mention a future in which more women might have more of it.

Source: Abridged and adapted from Maureen Freely (2000) 'She who must be vilified', *Observer*, Sunday, 13 February, p. 3.

In the above article, the *downfall* is couched in different forms of language and imagery for men and women. In the case of women there are strong references to physicality (what clothes they wear, hairstyles and make-up and how they look), negative and popular stereotypes reinforced by popular binaries of being good or bad something (for example bad working mother, not being a mother), employing symbolic devices that are contradictory and demeaning (for example 'toady', 'empress', 'infantile toddler') and using metaphors to colourfully discredit, such as, 'cold, steely' or 'empress of the Dome'. There are other aspects to this reading that we will not explore here, but the interesting thing to note is how the downfall story is not the same for men and women. For example, in the case of males, the fatal flaws in personality are related to performance and conduct, whereas for women, it is such things as the colour of their shoes, their hairstyles, how many children they do or do not have and if they look after them or not that matter. It is not even that women are judged in terms of male standards but rather standards that strongly reinforce the notion that women ought not to be in the workplace at all and should be relegated back to the domestic sphere where their downfall is not imminent!

CASE EXAMPLE

THE MAN PASSENGERS LOVED TO HATE

When Gerald Corbett agreed in 1997 to become chief executive of Railtrack, the company set up to run the UK rail infrastructure when rail services were privatized, overnight he became one of the UK's most high-profile businessmen. Three years into the job, even the combative and direct Corbett admitted it was more difficult than he had expected. With an appalling punctuality and safety record including fatalities and major track closures, he resigned in November 2000. By late 2001, the government had placed Railtrack into administration (receivership) with massive debts.

Corbett was not a rail or even a transport specialist. He studied history at Cambridge and attended London and Harvard business schools, before joining Boston Consulting Group, the international management consulting firm, where he stayed until 1982. Prior to joining Railtrack, he had been finance director at Grand Metropolitan (hotel, leisure conglomerate); he held senior positions at Dixons (electrical retailing) between 1982 and 1987 before becoming group finance director at Redlands, the building materials company. Many critics of Railtrack felt that it would be difficult for a CEO with this background to send the right messages through the company about the importance of safety and punctuality. At best, Corbett was on a steep learning curve; at worst he wasn't even on the curve and left those matters to others.

After privatization, Railtrack became the focus for passenger complaints about overcrowding, delays, expense and, most serious of all, their fears about safety. In 1997, 7 passengers were killed and 150 injured when a train run by Great Western Trains (GWT) ploughed into a freight train at Southall when a driver failed to notice a red light. GWT were subsequently fined £1.5 million, and although Railtrack were not culpable, public safety fears were heightened. The company, however, failed to respond and ignored reports criticizing its own safety practices, even from government inspectors. One of its own directors noted that the culture went downhill rapidly. It seemed only a matter of time before a disaster occurred, but financial specialist Mr Corbett argued that privatization of the industry left Railtrack in a tricky position. 'It's not possible to reconcile the needs of shareholders with our public service obligations and that's because the incentives we were set up with do not encourage investment. They've done it the wrong way,' he said. 'We want to be directly incentivized to deliver on our service obligations so that as punctuality improves, investment in safety improves and profits go up.'

In October 1999 31 people were killed when two trains collided after one went through a malfunctioning stop signal at Ladbroke Grove, near Paddington. The Cullen Report was subsequently highly critical of the company. That year, Mr Corbett waived his bonus in light of the events of the year and his position in the industry saying 'The work we have done has not been good enough ... it has been truly dreadful and it's largely down to us and our contractors. We are trying to do a hell of a lot of work and the way we have been doing it has not been good enough. I'm very sorry about that.'

In October 2000, after the Hatfield crash, where a train was derailed by faulty track as a result of delayed maintenance, killing 4 people and injuring 30, he offered his resignation to the Railtrack board. After a show of support by the rail industry and even the newspapers, the board rejected his offer and asked him to stay on to tackle the company's problems. The media were full of Mr Corbett's and Railtrack's apologies for the situation, some of them in paid advertisements addressing travellers. But ten days later the pressure proved too much and he resigned. It was subsequently revealed – to considerable public outcry – that he received a payoff of £1.3 million.

Source: This version of the case was written by Stephen Linstead in 2003, using data sourced from a variety of reports from BBCi (www.bbc.co.uk/news). It is for classroom discussion and should not be taken to reflect the true nature of BBCi.

Corbett's tenure was undoubtedly a *disaster* for passengers and ultimately for the company, although until the collapse shareholders had reaped benefits which critics argued should have been spent on safety. The wrong man in the wrong job, he did not have the experience or skills to manage a complex technical operation or the interpersonal qualities to keep public confidence, and he concentrated on seeking financial solutions first and hoping the rest would follow. Yet it was not a career disaster for Gerald – the Kingfisher Group snapped him up as chairman of Woolworths on a salary of £400,000, and after a subsequent demerger he moved into a non-executive role with another substantial payout. Incompetent he may have been, in some areas at least, and the rewards he received some critics may have regarded as immoral to the point of being criminal, but it is doubtful that Corbett fits the bill in any other way. A perfect *scam* storyline, however, in which it is difficult to know how many of the protagonists were in fact criminally involved, is the story of Robert Maxwell and the Mirror Group.

There are other storylines that are more mundane,

CASE EXAMPLE

THE ROBERT MAXWELL STORY

Jan Ludvik Hoch was born in extreme poverty in the Carpathian mountains in then Czechslovakia in 1923 and did not have a pair of shoes until he was seven. Yet he succeeded in building a publishing empire that spanned the world. In 1991, his name by now Robert Maxwell, his body was recovered from the sea off the Canary Islands after he had been reported missing from his private yacht, but no one has yet cleared up the mystery of his death. His drowning initially prompted a series of eulogies for his achievements, but as more news emerged of the true state of his company's finances he was damned by press and public alike for the way he ran his businesses. In 1996, two of his sons Kevin and Ian were cleared of criminal conspiracy to defraud, in aiding their father to rob his own companies' pension funds of £400m to buy shares in his ailing empire and artificially prop up their share prices. But in 2001 after a nine-year Department of Trade and Industry (DTI) investigation, Kevin was found to bear 'heavy responsibility' with conduct that was 'inexcusable', and city investment bank Goldman Sachs and Coopers & Lybrand, now part of PricewaterhouseCoopers (PWC) were castigated for 'substantial responsibility' for allowing Robert Maxwell to manipulate the stock market. 'We, and doubtless many other firms in the city and elsewhere, were intentionally and successfully deceived' pleaded the bank.

Maxwell's orthodox Jewish parents were victims of the Nazis, and he only just managed to escape the concentration camps to arrive in Britain in 1940. Describing himself as 'self-educated', he spoke several languages and by the end of war, he had emerged as a British army officer with commendations for bravery. After the war, he was located in Berlin, where he decided to publish scientific journals and set up Pergamon Press in 1949. Pergamon was quickly and hugely profitable and the now-married Maxwell decided to turn his attentions to politics. As one of the few businessmen who liked to proclaim his socialism, Maxwell stood for the Labour Party in Buckinghamshire in 1964 and held his seat until 1970. His relationship with the Labour Party was an uneasy one, with the political party wary of angering the man who owned newspapers sympathetic to Labour principles. Many people cowered from criticising him, not least because of his readiness to confront his critics in the libel courts.

Even when he was a Labour MP, signs were emerging of his dishonesty. In 1969, Maxwell agreed to a takeover bid for Pergamon from Leasco, an American financial and data processing group. However, when Leasco questioned Pergamon profits, the talks fell apart and Maxwell was subjected to a DTI enquiry. The inspectors found that Pergamon's profits depended on transactions with Maxwell family private companies. The DTI report said: 'We regret having to conclude that, notwithstanding Mr Maxwell's acknowledged abilities and energy, he is not in our opinion a person who can be relied on to exercise proper stewardship of a publicly quoted company.'

Few businesspeople could recover their career after such comments, let alone carry on to build a global publishing company, yet dust had gathered on the DTI report by the time Maxwell came to take over the troubled British Printing Corporation in 1980, renaming it Maxwell Communications Corporation, and his troubles seemed to be forgotten. He had long hoped he would be able to take over a national newspaper, but had twice lost out to News Corporation's Rupert Murdoch, who succeeded in taking over the *Sun*, the *News of the World* and Times Newspapers. But he got his chance to run a national newspaper when he bought Mirror Group Newspapers (MGN) in 1984 from Reed International, which proved a drain on resources. His 1988 purchase of America's (formerly British) Macmillan publishers dragged his company further into debt. In 1991, he floated MGN as a public company, desperate to raise cash because the rest of the company was veering towards bankruptcy with debts of over £2bn.

Maxwell plundered pension funds to help his ailing companies, but it was also to finance a lifestyle for which he had long since stopped counting the pennies. He was one of the last of the post-war tycoons and the kind of life he enjoyed belonged to another era, one of excess, ridiculous extravagance and outrageous behaviour. Flying around the world by helicopter or private jet, seeking meetings with heads of state, throwing lavish parties in his own honour, splashing his exploits across the *Mirror* newspaper, Maxwell's behaviour was showy and brash. Indeed, Tony Delano, a Mirror group director until 1985, recalls: 'One of the charming things about Bob was that he did not know how to behave.' BBC economics editor and former Maxwell Chief of Staff Peter Jay contends that Maxwell only understood two relationships, buyer and seller and master and slave.

'Where he thought he was a seller and someone else was a buyer, he could be positively obsequious. He treated anyone who he thought was a buyer with reverence and flattery,' he said. But those who weren't holding a cheque book were treated slightly differently. 'The Maxwell technique depended very heavily on bullying and intimidation, almost of a physical kind. He was a very large man, he had a way of approaching people, and nudging them with his belly and breathing into their nostrils,' Delano described.

His sons were among those bullied, dismissed and humiliated. His employees were at his beck and call, night and day. But for bullies to get what they want, they need cowards and Maxwell did succeed in surrounding himself with people prepared to do as he said. 'He had a very high level of low cunning, he learnt about

British ways, and British values, he saw how eminently corruptible the British were and how cheap they were to corrupt,' Delano said. 'You didn't have to spend a great deal of money buying their consent or their presence on a board, you simply had to give them a job or a salary … he never had any difficulty in attracting these kind of people.'

'He didn't talk about his childhood very much. You had a very strong sense that no one could have been as gross as he was, were he not running away from some hideous poverty,' Jay said. But the desperate Maxwell's war experience of violence, corruption and clandestine operations seems also to have left its mark on a scandalous legacy of unprecedented proportions.

Source: This version of the case was written by Stephen Linstead in 2003, using data sourced from a variety of reports from BBCi (www.bbc.co.uk/news). It is for classroom discussion and should not be taken to reflect the true nature of BBCi.

such as the bureaucratic blunder storyline; the boss who always messes up; union versus management (or the 'them versus us' stories); the crisis one where everything is so badly managed that only a crisis creates action; or the reorganization story where every new manager has to change the organization. The Chris Stefano story, being more mundane and certainly not qualifying as an extraordinary story, could be typified as one of these storylines.

The six dominant plots, and their associated storylines, become particularly appealing in periods of rapid change and turbulence in organizations, such as Ford with the 'Jac the Knife' storyline. Each of the three success storylines – quest, contest and conquest – is particularly effective for managers trying to clinch others' support for management's values and beliefs. Each of these plots offers a way of explaining collective experiences, and as such has emergent elements of an organizational ideology (Coopey 1995: 209). Authors of texts can often exert enormous control over the ways in which frames of reference either are allowed to be challenged or become sacrosanct. This sacrosanct element is particularly evident in the 'Jac the Knife' tale, where it is so important to Nasser, and the future security of employees, that employees share and subscribe to his views. However, texts that are sacrosanct for one audience may be considered heretical by another, and an audience whose support is taken for granted may over time become recalcitrant. Nasser appears to have neglected the need to sustain consensus with the Ford family and the powerful independent board of directors – which eventually, in large part, cost him his job. The need for adherence to a public

storyline is less obvious in Branson's case because his antics and 'games' tend to distract attention from how he might deal with recalcitrance or those who do not go along with the Virgin storyline. Such stories, when propagated by managers, are in discursive forms that are often familiar and comfortable because we have all grown up with fairy tales, storytelling and homilies and much of our world is constructed through this medium.

Fads and fashions

In the late 1990s, the management consultancy market was one of the fastest growing in the world and, as an industry, the top 25 firms in the market had earned between them around $US25.9 billion annually (James 1997: 53; Macken 1997: 46). It continues to grow at rapid rate. The world's top management gurus, mainly from the USA and male, were earning at the top end of the scale about $US90,000 per day and at the lower end, about $US20,000 per day (James 1997: 56). Book sales in the popular management market were worth around $US930.4 million annually, 'despite 70 per cent of managers saying management tools don't deliver and four out of five failing to finish the books' (Macken 1997: 46). We were not told who or where the 70 per cent of managers come from, but the comment highlights the power and influence, nevertheless, of management gurus, their fads and the industry that is behind their success. In Exhibit 1.3 we have reproduced some of the fads and fashions that have been popular in the 1990s and early 2000s and some of the 'buzz-words' that have been generated in the bestselling books often, although not always, written by management gurus. Some highly successful managers, such as Ricardo Semler in Brazil, who wrote a bestseller called *Maverick* (1993), went on to enjoy guru status. Many famous CEOs write their stories or autobiographies but not all of them will become part of the guru market, as in the case of Roddick (2000).

The fads and fashions marketplace is divided into several segments, but the two main ones are the consultancy market, dominated by management techniques and tools, and the guru marketplace dominated by trend-setting books and ideas about management. Both markets tap into an important area of management knowledge, that is, professional practice where managers or would-be managers are usually preoccupied with improving the running of their units or operations and trying to learn quickly from others who have succeeded at management and made a lot of money (see above and Dehler 1998). They are looking for role models and others to follow and this marketplace fills this niche. It seems common sense for managers to look to successful corporations, other successful managers and their successful advisers/consultants for advice or help.

In contrast to the consultancy market, management gurus invent new ways of talking about management and heavily influence what become the new buzz-words in management (for example Exhibit 1.3). These gurus are very adept at making surprising and accurate observations of future trends in management. They almost promise the future as a successful one. Their buzz-words become part of the management discourse, often expressed in catchphrases, clichés and rhetoric, such as 'best practice', and their ideas are used by businesses around the world to gain a competitive edge or claim to be doing so (James 1997: 53–4, 57). The gurus do not make their reputations from solving individual organizational problems, but from being seen to be at the leading edge of organizational and management developments and 'revolutions'.

Exhibit 1.3 Buzz-words

❏ **'Old' and 'new' economy** Used to describe the differences between organizations that are based in the manufacturing sector (and have high physical infrastructure or 'bricks and mortar') compared to the new rapidly expanding economy of Internet-based services and providers (the 'clicks').

❏ **'Post-'** Implies a break with many of the ideas that were popular in the 1980s. A plethora of 'post-' terms are in currency; post-heroic leadership and postmodern organization. No doubt there will be a plethora of post dot.com organizations that incorporate old and new economy strategies (see Introduction).

❏ **Balanced scorecard** Replaces the emphasis on total quality management in the 1990s and focuses on managers using a balanced set of measures to assess the performance of their organizations such as financial measures, customer satisfaction, operational performance and innovation and learning.

❏ **Business re-engineering and downsizing** Suggests you can start from scratch and make big changes to your processes (via technology/management information systems enhancements). Reinventing the organization by shedding labour and then when the upturn comes re-employing them as casuals and contract workers. Trend associated with outsourcing.

❏ **Dot.coms** Businesses that were at the leading edge of Internet and Web-based technology and communication developments and were floated at high share prices on the IT stock market in the US, called the NASDAQ, for billions of dollars. These companies were heralded as the new age organizations until they went through major stock crashes in the early 2000s. Many grew through debt and borrowings as opposed to self-funding through profits. Many founders of dot.coms were called 'geeks' because they were often strong in technical expertise but lacked management skills, preferring to buy this in to their new start-up companies.

❏ **E-commerce and e-business** Can describe a 'bricks-and-mortar' company that goes online and starts to use the Internet in business-to-business (B2B) transactions such as with suppliers or business-to-customer (B2C) transactions such as providing online shopping. Can apply to a wide range of uses of Internet technology and telecommunications but suggests that this is an inevitable part of businesses of the future. IBM prefers to use the term 'e-business'.

❏ **Emotional intelligence (EQ)** Refers to how someone handles themselves and their relationships to good effect. There are drivers, enablers and constrainers of emotional intelligence and these can be measured. EQ is claimed to be a source of competitive advantage to organizations by enhancing how people work together and something that can be fostered in people through training. Women are claimed to have higher EQs than do men.

Exhibit 1.3 **continued**

❏ **Knowledge management and intellectual capital** Involves organizations developing practices and policies that reward, recognize and harness the storehouse of knowledge of its people to continually innovate and remain creative using this brainpower as a source of competitive advantage. Much of this knowledge is thought to be tacit and is not codified or routinized and is very difficult to develop in any collective form. Some organizations are valuing their intellectual capital along with such things as market value, sales and other tangible assets.

❏ **Learning organization** A term still in currency but more commonly associated with ideas relating to the intellectual capital and knowledge management of organizations and the relentless pursuit of improvements and innovations (see above).

❏ **Strategic alliances** Usually refers to external relationships with customers, suppliers, distributors and even competitors and is seen as part of the pressures of globalization that makes it more important for organizations to reduce costs by outsourcing, re-engineering and becoming more focused on core competence.

❏ **Virtual corporation** Usually highly flexible organizations, often associated with Internet businesses or the use of technology to limit the importance of physical space and location in favour of cyberspace. This organizational form typically encourages very flexible work arrangements, often with team members interacting mainly through the Internet and other modes of electronic and telecommunication.

Management consultants, by contrast, generally make their living from inventing, packaging, interpreting, translating or tailoring the fads and fashions to suit a client's management and organizational problems. Some consultants make their living from helping organizations to solve their problems once the organization has failed to achieve results based on the fads and fashions (Lawson 1997: 3).

From the point of view of the manager, the appeal of fads and fashions is understandable. They have strong rhetorical (persuasive) appeal. As Eric Abrahamson says, 'Rhetorics must not only create the belief that the techniques they champion are rational, but also that they are at the forefront of management progress' (1996a: 10; also Collins 2000; Jackson 2001). This belief is achieved in several ways. Examples are cited of companies that have had success using the technique or method, and it

is implied that the same performance outcomes can be achieved in all companies. Various quasi-theories are produced in order to support claims for improved performance, or scientific studies are produced in order to support claims of success (Abrahamson 1996a: 10). Fads and fashions hold out the promise to managers that they will be at the leading edge and are doing something to get there. Managers are given an 'assurance' that they are not being left behind and are up there with the best companies in the world (Shapiro 1995: xv–xvi; the editor, *World Executive's Digest* 1997: 19). They promise significant improvements or results. The following is an example of the types of fads or techniques that are likely to attract managers, the prime rhetorical appeal being the uptake by top companies of the 'bizarre activities' described below, based on pseudo-theories of child development.

Fads and fashions can be packaged in many different ways and some approaches appear more bizarre than others. A very interesting one reported in *Fortune* magazine in 1997 (see Grant, 1997; Fulop and Rifkin, 1999, pp. 34–5) described how an IT company in Boston sent 200 of its employees running around the city streets dressed up in animal costumes such as lions, dogs and even weasels. Other employees were set different tasks aimed at bringing out the 'kid in them'. The whole idea of this exercise was to break down barriers to teamwork, remove inhibitions (for example shyness, fear and so on) and, hopefully, to ignite the creative potential of the organization. The programme was developed by an IT executive and was used in organizations such as Hewlett-Packard and PricewaterhouseCoopers. There

are numerous variations of these sorts of exercises – many companies employ adventure-type weekends and activities (such as white water rafting, bungy jumping and so on) to change learned behaviour and draw on pseudo-theories of child development to reinvent the employee. In a less extreme form, companies, such as Microsoft for example, allowed employees to decorate their offices with toys and other homely objects to rekindle the creativity and fun-loving ways of childhood in order to tap the creative potential of these prized employees.

Source: Fulop, L. and Rifkin, W.D. (1999) 'Management knowledge and learning'. In L. Fulop and S. Linstead (eds), Management: A Critical Text, Melbourne: Macmillan Education Australia Pty Ltd.

Fads and fashions fulfil other apparent purposes as well. The language and jargon they extol can be used to establish expertise, impress, influence, exclude, baffle, establish ('expert') status or cover up ignorance or fear (Rifkin 1994; Rifkin with Martin 1997). Managers can use fads and fashions recognized by employees and shareholders to make change seem inevitable and foolish to avoid – to make management look highly competent and rational (Abrahamson 1996a: 3–4). When urgent and pressing problems need quick and tried solutions, when the problem seems insurmountable, the temptation is to reach for one of these panaceas, which are usually presented as a universal solution to any organization's problems (Fulop 1992: 15–17; Huczynski 1996).

Importantly, the gurus in particular have a way of giving the manager a 'manifesto' or 'message' of self-improvement and organizational renewal – a 'born again' credo (James 1997: 57). The gurus have also helped glamorize the manager and transform him into a hero stereotype (rarely are they women). The gurus provide an identity for the manager, a masculine one almost akin to a megastar or at least a super sports star. The material that the gurus draw on to illustrate their theories or ideas are drawn from the wealthiest companies in the world, such as the Fortune 500 companies. And the success stories, which are usually memorable ones, are told from the vantage point of top managers or CEOs who command salaries of millions of dollars per annum. The gurus also use these CEO voices to articulate what are often very appealing 'theories of action' that seem simple for other managers to follow or learn from.

Theories of action describe how people in organizations respond to challenges and problems, often through trial and error, as they try to operate both defensively and offensively to deal with changes in their organizations (Weick 1995: 121). Theories of action are used to guide behaviour and make sense of it in ways that appear to make problems more manageable and that allow for new rules to be developed to guide future behaviours. Thus many theories of action are based on 'if – then' types of arguments: 'If' you find

yourself in this situation, 'then' do this next time or try this (Weick 1995: 122, citing Argyris 1976; see also Argyris and Schön 1978).

One important observation to make about the managers who become the gurus' models is that often the theories of action these managers espouse are inconsistent with the theories they actually use in practice (Weick 1995: 123, citing Argyris 1976 and Silverman 1970; see also Argyris and Schön 1978). For example, Rupert Murdoch is quoted as saying about management: 'Most of it is fairly obvious, you know' (Macken 1997: 46). It is likely Murdoch would qualify this with a number of very complex 'if – then' type statements about how he, and his large team of highly competent managers, run Newscorp. Murdoch's empire would not be run on a theory of action that works from the principle that most of management is fairly obvious. Thus gurus and their CEO informants often present crude maps of what goes on in organizations (Weick 1995: 123), and these maps are not easy to copy or follow in practice. Yet, these theories of action are sold widely as a commodified (that is, marketed and sold) version of what some would claim is merely hyped up common sense, which is what Murdoch is trying to say.

With possibly a few exceptions, the fads and fashions in management have come predominantly from the US and rely heavily on US business experiences. There are problems with this trend. One problem is that cultural bias inevitably creeps into the models contained in these works. As the following extract reveals, for managers in countries outside the USA, the fads and fashions have their limitations. Even though some of the fads and fashions mentioned in the article might not be adopted everywhere, it shows that cultural differences do not allow for universal approaches to management and the fads and fashions prevent the emergence of regional forms of knowledge (Jacques 1996: xv). Although events have changed in Asia, the problems associated with exporting culturally embedded management techniques and approaches remain the same even today, including the arrogant assumptions that underpin such an enterprise.

CASE EXAMPLE

ASIA'S ANTIDOTES: WHY FADS ARE DOUBLY DANGEROUS FOR THE REGION'S MANAGERS, AND HOW TO MAKE THEM LESS SO

In fashionable boutiques across the region, Asian con-sumers are snapping up ready-to-wear designer clothes. By flexing their increasing purchasing power,

they can instantly acquire a global sense of style.

In many of the region's boardrooms, managers are treating management fashions in the same way. They take the latest fads, apply the generic models that come with them, and expect instant competitiveness. Management approaches, however, are much too complicated for the formula to work.

For one, the impetus for change is different. Re-engineering, for instance, was born in a slow-growth

US economic environment. Its appeal there came from the promise of realizing higher profits without large increases in sales. In high-growth Asia [up to mid-1997], the cost-cutting aspect isn't as important as the need to raise customer service and operational efficiency to world-class levels. Dr Michael Loh, *World Executive's Digest* contributing editor in Singapore, says Asian CEOs 'despair they cannot change their organizations fast enough to cope with high growth,' and hence, become interested in re-engineering.

The cultures are also different. Dr John Romanga, managing director of QSA Mortiboys in Hong Kong, says that many family-controlled groups quickly spin off new companies to deal with different sets of customers.

'They don't need to create a new commercial culture to replace a bureaucratic outlook,' he says. These cultural differences with the West create inherent problems. Concepts like self-managed teams, total quality management and re-engineering [see Exhibit 1.3] require a high level of participative management. That is not easy to expect from generations of Asian workers used to following the father-figure at the top. Says one CEO in Thailand, 'Chief executives may be ready for re-engineering, but it is not that easy to enhance decision making at lower levels.'

Source: Adapted from The Editor (1997) 'The threat of fads', *World Executive's Digest*', July, p. 20.

But managers around the world are attracted to books written by the gurus. That is why these books become bestsellers! They tend to be easy to read, entertaining and even fun! They are written to be as engaging as a novel, with the aim of simplifying the complex. The knowledge they impart, and how they impart it, is affected by the need for mass marketing and commercial appeal (Abrahamson 1996a: 7). Humour, wit, good storylines and the latest technology are the hallmarks of these bestsellers. Even being against fads and fashions can give someone guru status. Scott Adams, one of these gurus, who also has a website, created the cartoon character Dilbert to actually ridicule management fads and quick fixes. He had two targets – the inept boss (who oversees Dilbert, an electrical engineer working in an aimless company that is forever adopting new management fads) and the abused employees, Dilbert's co-workers. Through Dilbert, humour is used to reveal what Adams sees as the perennial lies of management. The irony though is that the *targets* of the humour, the managers, are also the ones who embrace Dilbert as an icon (Ackroyd and Thompson, 1999).

A number of anti-fads and fashion books seek to expose the sham of these approaches (for example Hilmer and Donaldson 1996; Micklethwait and Wooldridge 1996; Spitzer and Evans 1997; Collins 2000; Jackson 2001). Along with academics who spend considerable time critiquing the fads and fashions, these books seek to reveal the enduring problems of management, which the fads and fashions might also address but never adequately. These enduring problems have been represented as, for example: putting economic performance first; having direction or some shared view of what the problems are of the organization; organizing so that the organization does not impede effective action; and leadership involving developing direction, having people trust you, and delivering on results (The Editor, *World Executive's*

Digest 1997: 20). Some writers proffer other perennial problems, such as Roger Allen, who in his book *Winnie-the-Pooh on Management* (1995) suggests the following: establishing objectives, organizing, motivating, developing people, communicating, and measurement and analysis. One can readily see that even these so-called enduring problems are not easily defined or agreed to (see Pfeffer 1993).

Academics raise a number of major concerns about fads and fashions, beside the fact that the gurus, who are often academics themselves, earn a lot more money than most of their counterparts in academia:

■ Management fads or fashions that are truly innovative and progressive (that is, critique, supplant or refine what has come before) deserve to be popularized, but not many of them fit this category.

■ Sometimes fads and fashions do revive what are discredited ideas or those that are incorrect and should be exposed as such.

■ Fads and fashions are often packaged as new ideas, but in fact are often old ideas that have been revamped and might not have relevance to current problems (Fulop 1992: 15–17, 23; Shapiro 1995; Abrahamson 1996a, 1996b: 618; Jacques 1996: 2–3).

The above criticisms become more meaningful if we look at how one particular fad, the learning organization, squares off when subjected to critique that draws on knowledge that goes beyond the fads and fashions texts.

Soft and hard academic theory

The Fifth Discipline is a very successful and influential fad book written by Peter Senge (1990) that popularized the term 'learning organization' (LO) (see Exhibit 1.3). Were managers to use this book as a basis for trying to introduce or experiment with organization learning, they might be surprised to find that the ideas come from a theoretical approach or paradigm that was developed in 1969 (Jacques 1996: 9; also Jackson 2001) and has been widely criticized in the academic literature for its flaws. The same could be said of the term 'knowledge management' that Jacques has traced back to the works of US theorists writing as early as 1909! The balanced scorecard is also a revamp of ideas from the quality movement dating back to the turn of the nineteenth century and the scientific management movement (Jacques 1996: 9). A paradigm is like a frame of reference with implicit assumptions or beliefs about 'what sorts of things make up the world, how they act, how they hang together, and how they may be known' (Weick 1995: 118). It represents a big set of theories or assumptions that are clustered around some central idea, such as the realization that the earth circles the sun and not the other way around. Around these paradigms have been built particular disciplines and theoretical traditions. In management the most recent challenge posed to the major paradigms comes from postmodern thinkers, who question the validity of the term 'learning' as it is currently used. They argue that knowledge as we currently construct it is seen as bounded and framed, and learning is a process of reframing or frame expansion. However, this framing process still sets knowledge out as though it is a picture within our field of vision – sometimes called *frontal knowledge*. Postmodern learning, on the other hand, is seen more as a 360° process, such as listening, where knowledge flows around us and learning comes from relations and connections constantly being made and remade, without being stable, linear or incremental – *lateral knowledge*. The full impact of such challenges has not yet been felt, but the editor of the leading academic journal *Management Learning* has argued that we need to be *against* learning in the current senses of the term (Grey 2001).

Over the last 13 years the idea of the *learning organization* has gained much prominence in the management and organizational literature. The LO is today's label for an organization that improves somehow and builds its knowledge base – it delivers packages more quickly, its hamburgers taste better, the staff at the customer service counter seem more helpful, it is more innovative and creative, and profits are healthy if not increasing. Somebody, or some bodies, figured out something to make things work 'better', and the organization continues to innovate. Senge, along with several other academics (for example Pedler et al. 1988) has popularized the idea of the LO and *The Fifth Discipline* became the blueprint for many different versions of it.

From the point of view of disciplines, a number have been particularly influential in the learning in organization literature. Table 1.1 gives a brief summary of these disciplinary approaches, illustrating the fields of knowledge that exist in soft and hard academic theory from which fads and fashions draw. There is a distinct body of knowledge that explores the process of learning in organizations but the fads market has been dominated by attempts to build models of the product of such learning – the LO. Many of these disciplinary orientations belong to eras that have since passed in relevance as have their specific problems. However, the recycling of ideas to meet pressing problems is a hallmark of fads and fashions and the quest to be relevant to managers.

In developing his approach to the LO, Senge adopted principally what is termed a 'systems paradigm', in which he extolled harmony, stability and consensus as the prime logic of a healthy learning system. The book devotes considerable space to developing tools and techniques that are also influenced by the author's incorporation of organization development (OD) strategies that were popular in the 1960s and 70s (see Table 1.1). So in terms of paradigms there is nothing new here but what is new is how Senge tries to apply this knowledge to new problems in organizations. His treatment of issues such as teamwork, power and leadership are limited by the theories he draws on. Some of these limitations are quite serious for the manager trying to work with Senge's ideas. For example, the idea of power and politics presented in *The Fifth Discipline* is one that favours the eradication of organizational politics, portraying it as aberrant or deviant and a source of unnecessary distraction and dysfunction. It does not see politics as an inevitable feature of organizations (see earlier discussion and Table 1.1), as endemic to social practice and structures within organizations. Nor does it view power and politics as a likely source of creative tension and innovation (see Chapter 6). Senge wants to get rid of it, as though this is possible in the world of work.

Teamwork is also presented as a strong tool for creating consensus. According to Senge it can be used to create unity in vision, purpose and direction and help overcome impediments to group behaviour, with conformity of members being the ultimate aim. Teams are not viewed by Senge as potentially problematic because issues of diversity and power are not included in his analysis, or in those of other organization learning theorists (Coopey 1995; Easterby-Smith 1997: 1095; Rifkin and Fulop 1997: 140). Senge's view of leadership suffers similar limitations. While he is not in favour of propagating the heroic leader model of the lone CEO or head of the organization, such as Branson and Nasser, and instead proffers the idea of followership and a sharing of the leadership role, his

Table 1.1 Disciplinary approaches in organization learning			
Discipline	Main focus	Key ideas, contributions	Key problems it addresses
Psychology and organization development (OD)	Human development	Importance of context, cognitive maps, underlying values, learning styles, dialogue, hierarchies of learning and experiential learning	Why and how people learn, and how to transfer individual to collective learning
Management science (systems approach)	Information processing	Building knowledge, memory, error correction, holism (understanding how a whole system works), informating (how technology can free up people and help with tasks, but also control people and tasks), creating feedback systems – simple to complex	Non-rational behaviour, information overload, long- versus short-term views, and how to unlearn from mistakes or discard old knowledge
Sociology and organization theory	Social structures and interaction	Effects of power structures and hierarchy, conflict as normal, ideology and rhetoric, interests of actors, meanings and understandings	Conflicts of interests, organizational politics, influence, and discourses of power
Strategy	Competitiveness and core competence	Organization – environment interface, levels of learning, networks and strategic alliances, learning in, across and between groups and nations, exploiting tacit knowledge	Environmental alignment and turbulence, competitive pressures (for example globalization) and general versus technical learning
Production management	Efficiency/productivity	Productivity, learning curves (for example cost reduction trends), internal and external sources of learning, links of learning to production design and analysis	Limits of measurement, especially single-dimension measures (for example output), uncertainty about outcomes
Cultural anthropology	Meaning systems	Culture as cause and effect of organizational learning, beliefs and values, norms, customs, ritual, problems with cultural superiority views	Culture as a barrier to transferring or learning new ideas, whose ideas dominate?

Source: Adapted from Mark Easterby-Smith (1997) 'Disciplines of organization learning: Contributions and critiques', *Human Relations*, **50**(9): 1087. Reprinted by permission of Sage Publications Ltd. Copyright © The Tavistock Institute 1997.

analysis does not address leadership in terms of power and control. Thus his recommendations for developing leaders among different layers of management seem unrealistic when examined against the common trend that many in power seem to want to hold onto it and amass it rather than give it up (Coopey 1995: 207). Senge's discussion of leadership leaves the reader unable to examine it in the context of managing diversity, which we mentioned as being a key issue for managers, paying little attention to the differences in the workplace based on gender, ethnicity or race (see Rifkin and Fulop 1997: 139–42).

The consequences for management practice of adopting a particular approach to learning in organizations and the learning organization can be illustrated by describing four different ways to approach the topic (see Rifkin and Fulop 1997):

1. *Learning organization* (LO) – a prescriptive model using predominantly systems theory as popularized in the fads and fashions by Peter Senge.
2. *Organizational learning methods* (OLM) – emphasizing training strategies, tools and techniques to promote learning and knowledge sharing, also popularized in fads and fashions and drawing mainly from OD strategies.
3. *Learning environment* (LE) – emphasizing the importance of meanings, understandings and actions

and the managerial policies and practices that are directed at creating more disruptive and unorthodox opportunities for learning. The LE is derived mainly from sociology and organization theory.

4. *Learning space* (LS) – focusing on framing ideas, understanding relationships and interactions, and how these shape or produce effects such as an organization, power relations and agency (that is, the ability to think, choose, question and act). These ideas are derived mainly from sociology, social anthropology and organization theory.

The LO/OLM approaches tend to originate from popular theory and popular accounts; the LE approaches are characteristic of soft academic theory, the orientations of which are critical and interpretive; and insights into LS are found in what the manager would view as being hard academic theory, drawing on postmodernist ideas. Each presents a different role for the manager and each develops a specific approach for what an organization, or its learning processes, should look like. Each also differs in respect of the mode of learning being championed, ranging from specific prescriptions, such as do X and achieve Y, as in the popular accounts, to consideration of the extent to which learning reflects processes that a manager should not, or cannot, control, as in the LS. The LO approach tends to refer to both organizations designed to enable learning (that is, have the capabilities to learn) and those within which learning is already occurring (Steingard and Fitzgibbons 1993: 37; Mirvis 1996).

The OLM theme overlaps conceptually with the LO theme. The OLM theme, as discussed in Table 1.1, usually encompasses measures or methods that a manager can implement to create 'organizational learning', and work towards having a 'learning organization'. OLM popularly refers to a set of processes that result from management practices and training that will help to create the LO (Jones and Hendry 1994; Addleson 1996: 34). This dual use of the terms 'LO' and 'OLM' has created confusion, and a number of authors have stated that there is no consensus on what OLM is, how organizations learn and what an LO might look like (Crossan et al. 1993: 229; Mirvis 1996: 21). Some critics have suggested that the altruistic, ethical assumptions of the learning organization are at odds with the performative values and interests of modern organizations (Snell 2001) or the multiple realities of organizational life and are hence an idealization that is extremely problematic in relation to practice (Salaman 2001). Even more sceptical critics such as Armstrong argue that the learning organization and all its variants are merely more elaborate and subtle extensions of forms of control that dominated twentieth-century

industrialization, ultimately deriving from classical approaches to management (Armstrong 2001: 359).

These critiques notwithstanding, some approaches to learning in organizations and LOs are more responsive and organic than others and not all views are based on tools or models. The LE departs from this view and instead focuses on learning that does not occur in direct response to particular measures that a manager undertakes. The term 'LE' is used here to refer to an approach where primary importance is placed on meanings, actions and understanding or the interpretive capacities of individuals as the building blocks for learning (for example Addleson 1996; Mirvis 1996). Attention is focused on conditions that might enable and support what have been variously termed 'communities of understanding', 'organizational renaissance', 'systems of self-correction and creativity', or 'self-organizing systems' (McWhinney 1992; Stacey 1993; Addleson 1996: 38; Mirvis 1996: 25, respectively). Associated with these are such ideas as 'liminal learning' or learning from mistakes or trying to anticipate the unintended effects of policies and actions (Turner 1992).

There is even less managerial control of learning in the LS than in the LE. The LS is a 'space' (window of opportunity) opened by a conscious and/or unconscious release of control by management. This 'space' is transitory – an opportunity to learn occurs as a kind of momentary and creative collusion between people. In the LS, people have freedom to think, explore and engage in uninhibited questioning of such things as managerial control. In the LS, difference and diversity, multiple meanings and multiple realities are the central ideas associated with how people construct their identities and use them to enact their daily lives in the organization (Heterick and Boje 1992: 54; Boje and Rosile 1994; Chia 1995; Watson 1995). In the LS, managers are meant to reflect on, and engage in, practices that are not controlling or 'managing' per se. The uncertainty in outcomes and the difficulty of surrendering control makes the LS, for many, difficult if not impossible to entertain. The fundamental issue in the LS is who sets directions for learning and whose knowledge should be privileged in the process – is it a particular level or group of managers or is everyone equal? (See Easterby-Smith 1997: 1095, citing Coopey 1995; Fulop and Rifkin 1997: 59.) The LS reflects a far more disorganized, disaggregated concept of learning than the LO, OLM and LE approaches and may offer a potential response to the criticisms of Snell, Salaman and Armstrong noted above.

The struggle will continue among academics, and others no doubt, to make sense of the broad literature on organizational learning (Tsang 1997; Hong 1998; Gherardi 1999). Our own breakdown in terms of LO, OLM, LE and LS is a conceptualization and can be understood as a means for managers, and aspiring managers, to recognize different types of approaches for working towards achieving learning in organizations. That is, they can identify managerial strategies recommended for undertaking learning and begin to ascertain their strengths and weaknesses. How effective such strategies are remains a question as we are still left with a knowledge gap about what actually happens as organizational learning occurs. There are precious few, if any, in-depth studies of organizational learning in process that point decisively to a constellation of strategies that any one of us as managers can employ. We wish to illustrate these points.

In the case study below, in which one of the authors of this chapter took part (Rifkin 1998), observation suggests that when a manager attempts to stimulate organizational learning, a number of things occur: several modes of learning may be attempted at once; there is not always an organization-wide effort in each mode; and often enough results may be barely tangible or at best transitory in their effect in the face of other forces impacting the organization. The notion of organizational learning itself seems redundant. In the case observed, efforts were made to employ practices of user-centred design by getting steel mill operators to help guide research engineers in upgrading technology in their plant. This effort was quite small in relation to issues of running the plant in general, but it aligned with the more 'empowering' approach towards shop-floor workers taken by the mill's manager. The manager had gone through the parent firm's intensive, personal development programmme and was trying to implement its lessons. In this context, this technology project can be referred to as a site for 'project-based organizational learning'. Within the microcosm of the one project, the observer can see indications of a range of larger organizational processes that are underway. Unfortunately, it would be hard to define the impact of any one organizational learning strategem due to the mixed threads of the various factors involved, such as changing technology, individual development and the history of worker–manager relations.

CASE EXAMPLE

ORGANIZATIONAL LEARNING IN A STEEL MILL

Measures undertaken to change the way that new technology is developed and installed in a steel mill can be readily sorted by our framework of OLM, LE, and LS. The mill was taking part in a project, of the research division of the parent company, to use computer modelling in real time to optimize plant control settings ('real time' means that the computer reads what is happening now, calculates some answers very quickly and tells the operator what to do next). The computers would assist human operators to adjust the speed that the steel being processed is moved through the plant, determine hydraulic pressure on wheels used to turn the hot steel strands into round bars, and set flow rates of water that cools the formed steel into a bar of specific strength and quality. The aim of the computerization was to avert deviations from what operational data indicate are ideal settings, settings that both minimize the production of low-quality steel bars and reduce stoppages and the losses and damage that might result. Such stoppages include 'cobbles', chinks in the hot steel strands causing them to jump from their guides and snake across the shop floor at high speed. Strategies for getting operator input into the design and testing of the research equipment were observed and assisted by a university research team.

- At the OLM level, the university research team co-facilitated and observed the use of an operator-centred design method imported from overseas, noted stories on the project written in the mill's newsletter, and recorded technical briefings for operators by the research engineer prior to installing the test equipment (such early orientation briefings were a first, the engineer said). In these instances, straight technical information was the main content of the communication and intended learning, that is, information about what to do and how to do it.
- At the LE level, there were briefings for mill employees on the overarching research programme into computer control (where workers noted concerns about losing jobs), the concept of holding such a pilot test at a plant, and a workshop for operators to determine what they wished to see on the TV monitors that were to display suggested control settings as part of the research testing. These measures seemed to focus on issues related to reconsidering who to rely on for information and determining what operators, managers and research engineers needed to learn beyond the day-to-day menu of control settings.
- At the LS level, the invited presence of the university researchers introduced indeterminacy into the organization (albeit a minor amount), as it was not clear beforehand, to people in the plant, what questions the researchers might ask or stimulate in the minds of

operators and managers. Also introducing indeterminacy was a plant-sponsored trip by some operators to the corporate laboratory, 1200 kilometres away, in order to see the laboratory test apparatus that was modelling what might happen in the steel mill's pilot test. Mill management noted how the trip gave workers the intended morale boost as well as reassurance about the new technology. The trip also yielded for the corporate research engineers new insights into how the plant actually worked as seen by the operators, an unexpected insight that was then employed to make the laboratory testing more realistic.

After these and other 'learning measures' were undertaken by the plant manager, results in terms of lessons learned and bottom-line improvements seemed mixed. The plant manager was moved on to a dead-end assignment and subsequently left the company; the project implementation team of operators and supervisors, it was revealed, met only when the university researchers attended and asked them to; the new technology researcher stated that he genuinely learned new, operator-centred approaches to testing equipment in various plants; and this particular plant remained open while others nearby in related industries closed.

This case suggests that macro-factors, such as the economics of an industry, and mezzo- (middle-level) factors, such as corporate decisions about the careers of key managers, seemed to influence the outcomes of the micro-learning measures.

One can conclude from the case study that there is a huge gap between theory and practice in organizational learning strategies. The middle manager can act day to day at the micro-level to stimulate learning, but manager and employees will be buffeted in unpredictable ways by middle-level corporate issues and macro-level market forces.

Learning about learning

On face value and with very clever packaging and marketing, many managers will be attracted to the idea of the LO as depicted by Senge. There is also a glossy toolkit that goes with the book, making it all the more appealing in terms of implementing its ideas. However, our brief exposé of some of the conceptual problems with how the LO has been developed should sound a warning. Is it the case that the sum of the learning of individuals in an organization is what makes up the LO, or is it the case that individual learning can never make up a collective learning experience or strategy as proposed by Senge's notion of the LO? We will explore this problem further to illustrate how theories are invaluable in unravelling these sorts of issues, although not necessarily solving it at the moment. We also want to focus on how learning itself is a very complex idea and one that any manager will have to understand before entertaining the idea of using Senge's prescriptions. We are reinforcing our earlier argument that it is vitally important to understand the nature of a problem and define it properly before setting about resolving it.

The differentiation of levels of learning has caught the attention of learning theorists, particularly in terms of the relationship between organizational learning and individual learning (Coopey et al. 1998). Some argue for distinguishing different kinds of learning at individual, group and organizational levels (Crossan et al. 1999). Management theorist Sylvia Gherardi suggests that these three levels, plus interorganizational learning (see Chapter 16), are inextricable from one another as a form of 'learning-in-organizing' (Gherardi 1999, 2001). Learning-in-organizing is not simply for problem solving but is oriented towards improving the relationships that are needed whenever people endeavour to act in an organized way. This process of learning to relate occurs as a form of 'situated learning' within 'communities of practice' (Brown and Duguid 1991) rather than as isolated, individual learning. Communities of practice are defined as collections of individuals with varying degrees of expertise in a particular area, who share insight and a sense of identity. They are an elaborated concept of an occupational community, one that decides what counts as legitimate knowledge and appropriate behaviour for their profession, be it Mexican midwives or African tailors (Lave and Wenger 1991), or, as in the example above, steel mill operators.

With the help of notions such as communities of practice, a growth in popularity of organizational learning concepts has turned the attention of management writers and some practising managers to issues of individual learning, long the purview of human resource trainers, psychologists and schoolteachers. Knowledge of individual learning processes and styles is useful for the manager or aspiring manager, to the extent that limitations of common theories in use are understood. If properly used, this knowledge can prove useful in providing insights into processes such as conflict resolution and cultural melding during mergers and takeovers. That is, individual learning can be seen as the process by which people change and grow as their careers progress and as they come to terms with new operational and strategic challenges.

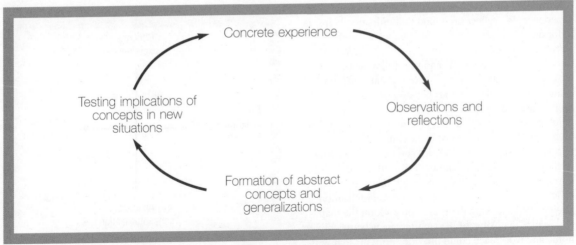

Figure 1.1 The Kolb experiential learning cycle (1)

Source: Organizational Psychology: An Experiential Approach, 1976 (2nd edn) (pp. 26–34) by Kolb/ Rubin/McIntyre, ©. Adapted by permission of Pearson Education, Inc., Upper Saddle River, NJ.

For those in the management field, 'learning styles' are often the entry into understanding individual learning. OB texts typically approach this topic in a very uncritical fashion. To begin with, a learning style, as a concept, usually describes the personal preferences for learning situations, which may be how someone learns best, be it by reading, watching, analysing, theorizing, feeling, walking through or trying out, listening, or whatever. For example, if you think about a situation in which you want to learn how to do something you cannot currently do, for example play a musical instrument (for the sake of this example, let us say it is a saxophone), how would you begin? Some people might head for the library and take out as many books as they could on the instrument and read all the theory about it so they could understand exactly what was happening when they eventually came to pick it up. Others might go straight to the nearest jazz club and immerse themselves in the playing of others for inspiration before learning to play. Some would work out specific objectives for learning, such as to play a particular tune, and would get the required music and instructions to meet the objective. Yet others would just pick up the instrument and blow, and see what sounds came out, and keep trying till they made music. They would be displaying a learning style that favoured theory, experience, practical application or experimentation, or, from another point of view, would place different emphasis on the eyes, ears, mind or hands. While some 'know your learning style' popularizations of learning style theory might present them as relatively fixed and enduring, research evidence is at best inconclusive, and studies over time suggest that learning styles may mature and become more rounded as people widen their behavioural repertoire –

with experience we can learn how to learn in ways that do not come naturally.

We might then ask: where do learning styles come from? Psychological studies vary in their emphasis, but most concur that it is partly from personality and partly from experience, especially educational experience. It is argued that when we are in our twenties, the influence of previous education is strongest and styles tend to be most extreme, while the older we get the more our styles mellow as we acquire a different range of experiences. We can choose to avoid new situations and thus enhance the dominance of one learning style, or we can actively seek situations with which we are less comfortable in order to broaden our learning abilities. Because it is experiential in its focus, the learning style taxonomy referred to most often in management is David A. Kolb's classification of experiential learning styles (Kolb 1994; Kolb et al. 1971). Kolb draws his typology from a characterization of the experiential learning cycle depicted in Figure 1.1. Tests to measure one's style along Kolb's typology are available online and in many texts and it is widely cited in areas of problem solving, creativity and innovation.

This cycle has four moments, which can occur in any order. A learning style can be understood as the point on the cycle in which an individual is likely to spend most time. That is, we dwell on those areas we are most comfortable with and try to skip through those with which we are least comfortable, like dodging out of a maths lesson. It can also indicate the point on the cycle where an individual is most likely to begin learning, theorists with theory, practitioners with practice, as we suggested above. The four moments all must be present for the learning cycle to be complete, whatever order they occur in and even if there may be some backtracking.

A learning cycle can be seen to begin with an experience. We reflect on it, and that reflection helps us to formulate explanations of what happened and possible rules for action in similar situations. We test those out in new situations and see if they work – if so we consolidate the learning, if not we start reflecting again. For example, a detour because of road repairs might cause you to take a new route to work, one that involves trips down side streets that you had not driven on before. This detour constitutes your 'concrete experience' (see Figure 1.2). As you drive, you might 'reflectively observe' the amount of traffic, the things you see along the way and the time it takes to reach the office. You then do some 'abstract conceptualisation' – maybe even checking the route you took on the map – and realize that some of the smaller roads between your home and workplace could provide shortcuts that will reduce your travel time and/or be more pleasant and relaxing. Active experimentation follows when you decide on the way home that evening to turn down some unfamiliar streets in search of quicker routes. This experimentation produces a new concrete experience and the learning cycle begins again, although the steps of the cycle might not necessarily proceed in the same order. Kolb suggests that some people are stronger through habit, personality or practice in one or another phase of this cyclical learning process – some people might prefer to begin by reading the map, others would never consult one. Kolb identifies four learning styles according to the phase or quadrant of the process in which the style tends to be best. These are shown in Figure 1.3 and described in Table 1.2.

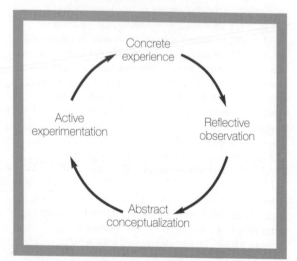

Figure 1.2 The Kolb experiential learning cycle (2)

Source: Adapted from D.A. Kolb, I.M.Rubin and J.M. McIntyre (1971) Organizational Psychology: An Experiential Approach, Englewood Cliffs, NJ: Prentice Hall, p. 28.

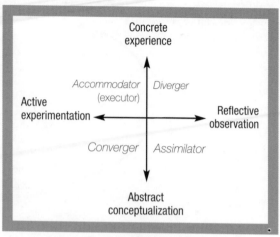

Figure 1.3 Kolb's learning style preferences

Source: Organizational Psychology: An Experiential Approach, 1976 (2nd edn) (pp. 26–34) by Kolb/ Rubin/McIntyre, ©. Adapted by permission of Pearson Education, Inc., Upper Saddle River, NJ.

Kolb's learning styles can be related to the organizational problem-solving process, with some styles excelling in problem finding, others in problem solving as shown in Figure 1.4. Kolb's methodology for determining styles, which entailed expressing preferences for individual words as characteristic of one's learning style, has attracted some criticism. Subsequently Peter Honey and Alan Mumford (1982) developed a more discursive method, based on agreement or disagreement with statements rather than words, a slightly modified version of the learning styles taxonomy which has been popular in management practice, especially in Europe.

Alongside styles of learning, there are also fields of learning. In terms of management, the taxonomy most often referred to is the seven 'intelligences' of the Harvard educational psychologist, Howard Gardner (1983). These are:

- linguistic – ability with words and language
- logical-mathematical – numerical and deductive ability
- bodily-kinesthetic – sport, craft, and artistic skill
- spatial – visual insight into how physical objects fit together
- musical – composing, playing and listening critically
- interpersonal – insight into how people interact
- intrapersonal – self-knowledge.

These last two categories can be recognized as the basis of 'emotional intelligence' (EQ), as popularized by Daniel Goleman (1995) (see Exhibit 1.3). Tests to

Table 1.2 Kolb's learning styles and their characteristics

Style	Dominant learning abilities	Characteristics
Converger	Abstract conceptualization Active experimentation	Greatest strength lies in the practical application of ideas. Called the converger because a person with this style seems to do best in those situations where there is a single correct answer or solution to a question or problem. His or her knowledge is organized in such a way that it can be focused on specific problems. Research shows that convergers tend to be relatively unemotional, preferring to deal with things rather than people. They tend to have narrow interests, and often choose to specialize in the physical sciences. The style is characteristic of many engineers.
Diverger	Concrete experience Observation	The diverger has the opposite strengths of the converger and his or her greatest *reflective* strength lies in his or her imaginative ability. Divergers excel in the ability to view concrete situations from many perspectives and to organize many relationships into a meaningful pattern or structure. Called diverger because this type performs better in situations that call for the generation of ideas, such as brainstorming sessions. Divergers are interested in people and tend to be imaginative and emotional. They have broad cultural interests and tend to specialise in the arts. Research shows that the style is characteristic of persons with humanities and liberal arts backgrounds. The style is often found in personnel managers, organization development consultants and counsellors.
Assimilator	Abstract conceptualization Reflective observation	The assimilator's greatest strength is the ability to create theoretical models. He or she excels in inductive reasoning and in assimilating disparate observations into an integrated explanation. Like the converger, he or she is less interested in people and more concerned with abstract concepts, but less concerned with the practical use of theories. It is more important that the theory be logically sound and precise. As a result, this style is more characteristic of basic sciences and mathematics than the applied sciences. In organizations, the style is found most often in the research and planning departments.
Accommodator	Concrete experience Active experimentation	The accommodator has the opposite strengths of the assimilator. His or her greatest strength lies in doing things, in carrying out plans and involving himself or herself in new experiences. Accommodators tend to be more risk takers than people with the other styles. Called accommodators because they tend to excel in situations where they must adapt to specific immediate circumstances. In situations where theory or plans do not fit the facts, the accommodator will be likely to discard the theory. Solves problems in an intuitive, trial and error manner, relying heavily on other people for information rather than his or her analytic ability. At ease with people, but sometimes seen as impatient and 'pushing'. Educational background is often in technical or practical fields like business, and accommodators are often found in organisations in action-oriented jobs, often marketing and sales, or as entrepreneurs.

gauge your learning style, or the relative strengths of your seven intelligences or your EQ, are available on the Web and are readily found by using a search engine. However, consultants often build some of their credibility around having a 'better' and more accurate test for determining these styles and guard their intellectual property carefully. While the idea of testing people for their styles of problem solving (and this is only the tip of the iceberg) was less fashionable in the past, extensive psychological testing is now a standard practice in most search companies or head-hunting firms. These tests can be used for any number of reasons relating to recruitment and promotion, and not always in ethical ways. The concept of learning styles, theories of individual learning, the methodologies from which these are derived, the connections between them and the uses to which they are put are problematic and therefore cannot be approached uncritically.

One of the major assumptions in learning theories is that just as children and adults are said to have different

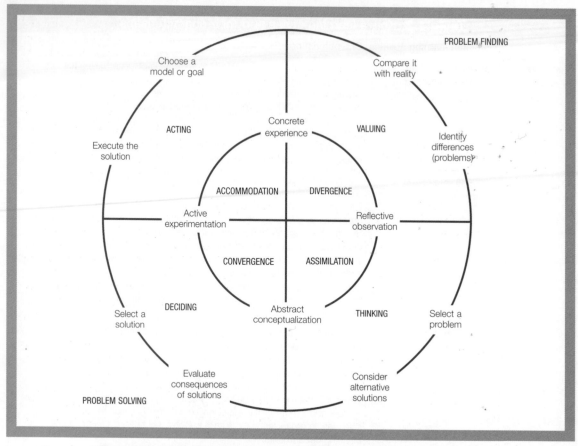

Figure 1.4 Comparison of experiential learning styles and
the problem-solving process (after D.A. Kolb)

Source: Organizational Psychology: An Experiential Approach, 1991 (7th edn) (p. 256) by Kolb/Rubin/
Osland, ©. Reprinted by permission of Pearson Education, Inc., Upper Saddle River, NJ.

approaches to learning, so are women and men. To
oversimplify, men are said to be capable of evolving
from being driven to find a single right answer to
becoming more tolerant of – and eventually
appreciative of – a diversity of opinion (Perry 1970).
Women are said initially to feel silenced by a classroom
or parental authority figure but then evolve to a stage
where they openly question authority and finally
acknowledge that they can state their own 'truths',
integrating objective insight with subjective,
empathetic understanding (Belenky et al. 1986). These
sorts of assumptions are now being challenged as
creating artificial distinctions that fail to recognize the
feminine and masculine in both men and women and
neglect socialization processes (see Chapter 2). In
addition to distinctions in learning styles between
individuals, there are also theories about differences
within individuals as well as between cultures. There is

popular literature that grew in the 1980s and 90s on
differences between left brain, logical thinking, and
right brain, visual and creative thinking. Exercises have
been developed to stimulate one's right brain and get
one thinking 'outside the box'. A difference between
routine, 'single-loop' learning, where one improves on
a standard operation, and 'double-loop' learning, where
one questions underlying assumptions in order to
develop new and more effective routines, has been
popularized by Chris Argyris and Donald Schön (1978)
and subsequently by Senge (1990). They are following
theories of multidisciplinary anthropologist, biologist,
philosopher, psychologist and systems theorist Gregory
Bateson (1975) (although Bateson's more advanced
work prefigures postmodern learning approaches). In a
search for ways to improve learning, some have
ventured into the traditions of non-Western cultures,
exploring methods including storytelling and bodily

and spiritual experiences. As a result, some organizations have their employees engage in adventure learning outdoors (for example 'ropes courses') or undertake literally walking on hot coals or various forms of meditation or group bonding. Data on the long-term impacts of such 'alternative' forms of learning range from unsubstantiated sales pitches to encouraging, but selective, anecdotes. It might be best to defer any conclusions.

The academic and popular psychological literature on learning styles seems to have both practical and ideological areas of vulnerability. Firstly, it tends to focus on the individual out of context, outside the organization and unconnected to the 'community of practice' engaged in the skill or knowledge that the individual seeks to learn. Secondly, the literature on learning styles may be taken to offer schemes for classifying employees, which may be seen as a form of control. Learning style tests can be understood to be what Foucault called 'technologies of the self' and forms of 'confession' (Foucault 1981; Townley 1993). Such tests may yield analytical insight into one's self, but they also cause one's unique characteristics to be minimized and one's character to be captured by a limited set of variables (Townley 1993; Newton 1994). This narrowing process opens possibilities for choice and advancement for some, but it closes those opportunities for many others through stereotyping and 'pigeonholing'. There is an attempt to explore exactly how such classification schemes – whether for learning styles or other abilities or personality characteristics – are also used by employees to resist the controlling influences of their organization and its culture (Garrety et al. 2000). Evidence to date suggests, as Foucault (1980) theorized about other modes of power, that such 'technologies of the self' can indeed be double-edged swords, giving some power to management but also some to employees.

It seems that the more we read and observe about learning and learning styles, the more we realize how little we know about how exactly an individual does learn *in the context of a particular organization*. The plethora of literature about learning styles suggests that diversity in approaches is the norm. In addition, each individual might have not only a preference in *how* they prefer to learn but *what* they prefer to learn about doing their work and managing. Learning styles and preferences must be acknowledged and appreciated, much as any sort of difference must be, so that everyone's learning needs can be addressed. Experience suggests, though, that it is well-nigh impossible to satisfy all.

Conclusive research fieldwork that links theories of individual and organizational learning to practice is lacking. Yet, as we have noted earlier, certain academics argue in favour of carefully thought through prescriptions for what may be an unachievable, ideal form of learning organization (Snell 2001; Salaman 2001). They contend that such idealizations can help in achieving not only a more functionally desirable organization, in terms of innovativeness and profitablity, but a more morally and politically desirable one as well. At the very least, the very notion of the LO carries within it the ideals of an openness of communication and acceptance and appreciation of diverse viewpoints. It follows that aspiring to an LO means addressing differences in perspective through collective dialogue that, in turn, stimulates critical thinking by individuals and furthers individual and organizational learning in some form.

This attention to the ties between processes occurring to individuals and those that occur collectively in the organization are among practical concerns now beginning to earn attention from management theorists addressing notions of unlearning, mistakes and learning, and emotions and learning. These concepts have been explored theoretically from a psychological perspective focusing on the individual's fears related to learning and unlearning in an organization (for example Schein 1993). Similarly, emotions in organizations are increasingly a recognized area of sociological study (for example Fineman 1993, 2000). There is also an emerging focus on how your individual, emotional well-being in the organization impacts on the organization's function (Kets de Vries 2001) and, by implication, its learning. A synthesis of these lines of thought, and some practical strategies, are things to look for in the coming decade.

Unlearning occurs when you give up a tried and tested pattern of behaviour, something that we have all experienced. What remains unclear, though, are what conditions are needed for a whole organization to make that shift and abandon an old way of operating. These conditions are critical because, before such a shift occurs, alternatives to traditional approaches will need to be explored by individuals and made public within the organization. This process constitutes what some will label as 'deviance', behaviour that may be condoned by the disaffected but rarely seems supported by management (Ackroyd and Thompson 1999). Such deviance from norms attracts attention particularly when the alternatives undertaken fail, as some are bound to do. A new computer program has problems, or a new arrangement of shift work results in short-term increases in absenteeism. A learning process, though, requires failure on a limited scale to be 'okay'. In many places, in their organizational myths as well as in their reality, a blaming mentality makes such failure something to be avoided at all costs. For failure during learning to be okay, an organization would need to abandon a blaming mentality in favour of an experimental one.

An organizational culture that supports experimentation can be seen as a prescription in recent popular writings on 'chaos' in organizations, particularly in the US (for example Brown and Eisenhardt 1999; Wheatley 2001). Experimentation constitutes the uncontrollable, 'chaotic' activity that managers are not only supposed to permit, but should cultivate in order to foster innovation. The term 'experiment' has been traced etymologically to the concept of 'to undertake without peril' – 'ex' corresponding to 'without' and 'per' coming from the root of the term 'peril'. The term 'experimentation' can then be understood to refer to a low-risk way of trying new approaches that might otherwise present some danger to one's career, status or operating budget. Risk taking brings along with it emotional dimensions, such as fear and courage. Thus, the emotional environment of an organization should play a role in the degree and ease of experimentation and learning that are possible. It is not unlikely that this realization drove the father of the total quality management (TQM) movement, William Edwards Deming (1988), to place 'drive fear out of the workplace' in his classic 14 points for creating 'total quality' organizations (Fulop and Rifkin 1997). Practical strategies and initial theoretical understanding are only just emerging to show how an emotionally safe environment in an organization can be created, one that fosters organizational learning and the necessary unlearning.

As this discussion reveals, as a source of learning for managers, popularly published approaches to managing have their attractions but also their pitfalls, as with local accounts – the stories and conversations in the workplace. The popular and fads approaches promise success. They are conveyed in an engaging way and are easy to understand. They contain enough jargon to give devotees a sense of belonging – devotees recognize one another by their use of the same jargon. Use of the jargon is also a way to legitimate choices by referring to ideas whose wide acceptance is signalled by the jargon's popularity. Popular and fad approaches, because of these attractions, are traps, too. They can address issues that are only transitory or local, which can make such an approach susceptible to being applied unreflectively in inappropriate situations. Even in those instances where such approaches are meant to be applied, a manager needs to know whether they actually work. Important factors, such as diversity or power, are not addressed at all by many of the popular and fad approaches, which is why academics warn against adopting fashions without an understanding of their paradigm-based biases and assumptions. Our excursions into the discussions of OL, OLM, LE and LS are attempts to show how complex the issues are and that popular, fad books are not designed to deal with the complexity we have unearthed – bestsellers are such because they artfully simplify the complex and, in turn, give managers false hope of control and mastery over events and people.

Conclusion

When managers start to look at knowledge as residing in the six general areas described in this chapter, they are probably moving away from a purely 'foundational' approach to management knowledge and practice (Morgan 1993: 286). A foundational approach to knowledge is dominated by a search for the one best way of doing things or authoritative approaches that tell the manager 'this is the way it is', or 'this is how you should do it'. By contrast, making sense of such things as local and popular accounts forces the manager to recognize that any situation might have multiple dimensions and meanings. It challenges the manager to try to see situations or problems from a number of perspectives or be able to reframe problems and issues so that they can be tackled from a number of different directions (Bolman and Deal 1984, 1991; Morgan 1993: 286). Being able to reframe problems and see them in novel ways is an important part of developing reflective practice and complex understanding, as discussed above (Morgan 1993: 286).

What is implicit in this sentiment is that we need to come to terms with the six sources of management knowledge and how knowledge is represented in theories, fads, popular stories, myths, metaphors and so on. Consider again the stories of the

Conclusion continued

corporate hero Branson and police maverick Ruiz. They engage. As Robert Chia and Stuart Morgan contend: 'Education entails not just information acquisition but an "awakening" of the senses' (1996: 57). The education of the manager cannot advance with exposure to only a select few ways of gaining knowledge. Although it might seem odd, there will be times when, in the interests of practice, managers will need to develop some useful formulae or theories of action at the common-sense level. There will be times when managers will need to delve into theory to enhance their understanding of complex issues, and at times these learning experiences might not seem very closely related to day-to-day practice (Linstead 1996: 9). This suggests that if managers are to develop understanding and the potential to act and change their circumstances, then they have to have a perspective from which to judge knowledge claims such as 'the LO is the only way for an organization to learn'.

Answers to questions about management knowledge and learning

1 What sorts of knowledge do managers need? There are at least six forms of management knowledge and know-how.

2 How do managers learn about management? Managers learn by doing, as well as from local and popular accounts told by colleagues and management gurus. They can also study soft and hard theory in universities or on their own.

3 What forms of knowledge are likely to be easier for managers to grasp than others? This whole chapter indicates that things that are most familiar and most organizationally legitimate are easiest to learn but are not necessarily the most insightful or effective.

4 What role(s) do managers play in helping their organizations to learn? Managers help organizations to learn by surveying varied sources of knowledge and reflectively questioning assumptions and biases that might be contained in stories, theories and paradigms. This reflection is done with colleagues and other organizational stakeholders. Thus, Chris Stefano, the manager having problems with the team at the beginning of this chapter, might learn to recognize that Roderick Cage likes to learn procedures and needs a checklist to learn from, which he will enlarge and place prominently on the wall in front of his desk. Rebecca Spalding will work best by having a team of co-workers walk her through a new procedure a couple of times with the radio playing top 40 songs quietly in the background. Wasim Shan likes to take home a book on the topic and absorb the basic concepts over a cup of black tea by an open window before having a long lunch with Chris the next day to discuss the general approach. Phil Bosevic prefers to watch how others work, all the while pacing back and forth simulating the undertaking with hand motions in order to gain a better understanding of his subordinates' jobs. To Chris, these 'learning styles' or learning preferences are not hidden. Chris just needs to look and ask.

REVISITING
THE CASE STUDY

Based on these conclusions, which constitute soft theory making that undoubtedly contains its own biases, you now need to address Chris Stefano's situation. To what degree can the advice you give stand up to scrutiny involving critical thinking and reflective practice? Were myths, stereotypes or metaphors invoked and if so what were the consequences of this? Was there an underlying dominant storyline being pushed? More importantly, was account taken of the politics of the situation and the issues of diversity, and was some attempt made to offer advice from a number of perspectives, with some clarity of the underlying assumptions upon which the various perspectives operate? To get to the point:

1 What advice would you give to Chris Stefano, or Dr Cora Harvey?

How does that advice differ from what you might have said initially, before reading this chapter? Would you go to fads, academic literature or just ask around? If you do, what are the problems with doing each of these things?

2 What knowledge or experiences have you drawn on?

Which types of know-how or knowledge do you rely on more and which types do you rely on less? Why are you comfortable with one form more than another? How can you learn to behave or act differently?

3 How might you use our analysis here of sources of managerial knowledge to evaluate the potential effectiveness of your advice?

Are your recommendations just tips, or are they based on information that has proven to be a reliable approach to difficult situations?

The message of this chapter, and of this book as a whole, is that you need to reframe what you observe and hear from others. People with a variety of different roles, experiences and value sets are looking at exactly the same problem as you. You need to understand their perspectives in order to manage your relationships with them. A good way to gain this insight is to engage in a more critical study of management.

References

Abrahamson, E. (1996a) 'Management fashion, academic fashion, and enduring truths', *Academy of Management Review* **12**(1): 254–85.

Abrahamson, E. (1996b) 'Management fashion, academic fashion, and enduring truths', *Academy of Management Review* **21**(3): 616–18 (Abrahamson responds to critiques of his 1996 article).

Ackroyd, S. and Thompson, P. (1999) *Organizational Misbehavior*, London: Corwin Press.

Addleson, M. (1996) 'Resolving the spirit and substance of organizational learning', *Journal of Organizational Change Management* **9**(1): 32–41.

Allen, R.E. (1995) *Winnie-the-Pooh on Management*, New York: Methuen.

Argyris, C. (1976) *Increasing Leadership Effectiveness*, New York: John Wiley.

Argyris, C. and Schön, D.A. (1978) *Organizational Learning: A Theory of Action Perspective*, Reading, MA: Addison-Wesley.

Armstrong, H. (2000) 'The learning organization: Changed means to an unchanged end', *Organization* **7**(2): 355–61.

Astley, W.G. and Zammuto, R.F. (1992) 'Organization science, managers, and language games', *Organization Science* **3**: 443–60.

Austin, J.L. (1962) *How To Do Things with Words*, Oxford: Clarendon Press.

Bateson, G. (1975) *Steps to an Ecology of Mind*, New York: Ballantine.

Bedeian, A.G. (1995) 'Workplace envy', *Organizational Dynamics* **23**(4): 49–56.

Belenky, M.F., Clinchy, B.V., Goldberger, N.R. and Tarule, J.M. (1986) *Women's Ways of Knowing: The Development of Self, Voice and Mind*, New York: Basic Books.

Boje, D. and Rosile, G. (1994) 'Diversities, differences and authors' voices', *Journal of Organizational Change Management,* **7**(16): 8–17.

Bolman, L.G. and Deal, T.E. (1984) *Modern Approaches to Understanding and Managing Organizations*, San Francisco: Jossey-Bass.

Bolman, L.G. and Deal, T.E. (1991) *Reframing Organizations: Artistry, Choice and Leadership*, San Francisco: Jossey-Bass.

Brown, J.S. and Duguid, P. (1991) 'Organizational learning and communities of practice: Toward a unified view of working, learning, and innovation,' *Organization Science* **2**: 40–57.

Brown, S.L. and Eisenhardt, K.M. (1999) *Competing on the Edge: Strategy as Structured Chaos*, Boston: Harvard Business School Press.

Burgoyne, J.G. (1981) 'Approaches to integration in management education', in C.L. Cooper (ed.), *Developing Managers for the 1980s*, Basingstoke: Macmillan – now Palgrave Macmillan.

Chia, R. (1995) 'From modern to postmodern organizational analysis', *Organization Studies* **16**(4): 508–604.

Chia, R. and Morgan, S. (1996) 'Educating the philosopher manager', *Management Learning* **27**(1): 37–64.

Collins, D. (2000) *Management Fads and Buzzwords*, London: Routledge.

Coopey, J. (1995) 'The learning organization, power, politics and ideology', *Management Learning* **26**(2): 193–213.

Coopey, J., Keegan, O. and Emler, N. (1998) 'Managers' innovations and the structuration of organizations,' *Journal of Management Studies* **35**(3): 263–84.

Crossan, M.M., Lane, H.W. and Hildebrand, T. (1993) 'Organization learning: Theory to practice', in J. Hendry, G. Johnson and J. Newton (eds), *Strategic Thinking: Leadership and the Management of Change*, Chichester, New York.

Crossan, M.M., Lane, H.W., and White, R. (1999) 'An organizational learning framework: From intuition to institution,' *The Academy of Management Review* **24**(3): 522–37.

Czarniawska, B. and Sévon, G. (eds) (1996) *Translating Organizational Change,* Berlin: deGruyter.

Czarniawska-Joerges, B. (1992) *Exploring Complex Organizations: A Cultural Perspective*, Newbury Park, CA: Sage.

Dehler, G.E. (1998) '"Relevance" in management research: A critical reappraisal', *Management Learning* **29**(1): 69–89.

Deming, W.E. (1988) *Out of the Crisis: Quality, Productivity, and Competitive Position*, Cambridge, Cambridge University Press.

Deutschman, A. (1997) 'Heavens above', Good Weekend, *The Sydney Morning Herald*, 23 August: 16–19.

Downing, S.J. (1997) 'Learning the plot: Emotional momentum in search of dramatic logic', *Management Learning* **28**(1): 27–44.

Easterby-Smith, M. (1997) 'Disciplines of organizational learning: Contributions and critiques', *Human Relations* **50**(9): 1085–113.

Fineman, S. (ed.) (1993) *Emotion in Organizations*, London: Sage.

Fineman, S. (1997) 'Emotion and Management Learning', *Management Learning* **28**(1): 13–26.

Fineman, S. (ed.) (2000) *Emotions in Organizations* (2nd edn), London: Sage.

Fineman, S. and Gabriel, Y. (1996) *Experiencing Organizations*, London: Sage.

Fiol, M. (1994) 'Consensus, diversity, and learning in organizations', *Organization Science* **5**(3): 403–20.

Foucault, M. (1980) *Power/Knowledge: Selected Interviews and Other Writings by Michel Foucault, 1972-1977*, (C. Gordon, ed.), Brighton: Harvester.

Foucault, M. (1981) *The History of Sexuality: Vol. 1, The Will to Knowledge*, London: Penguin.

Freely, M. (2000) 'She who must be vilified', *The Observer*, Sunday, February 13: 3.

Fulop, L. (1992) 'Management and critical thinking', in Fulop, L., Frith, F. and Hayward, H. (eds), *Management for Australian Business: A Critical Text*, Melbourne: Macmillan.

Fulop, L. and Laneyrie, F. (1995) Commentary: 'Trials at the top: Chief executives talk about men, women and the Australian executive culture, by Amanda Sinclair', *International Review of Women and Leadership* **1**(2): 61–7.

Fulop, L. and Rifkin, W.P. (1997) 'Representing fear in learning in organizations', *Management Learning* **28**(1): 45–64.

Gardner, H. (1983) *Frames of Mind: The Theory of Multiple Intelligences*, New York: Basic Books.

Garko, D.M. (1994) 'Communicator styles of powerful physician-executives in upward-influence situations', *Health Communication* **6**(2): 159–72.

Garrety, K., Badham, R., Rifkin, W.D. and Zanko, M. (2000) 'A "Dickhead" or an INTJ? Talk about Personality Type as a Vehicle for Emotion-Work in a Male-Dominated Heavy Industry,' European Group on Organization Studies Conference.

Gherardi, S. (1999) 'Learning as problem-driven or learning in the face of mystery?, *Organization Studies* **20**: 101–24.

Gherardi, S. (2001) 'From organizational learning to practice-based knowing,' *Human Relations*, **54**(1): 131–9.

Goleman, D. (1995) *Emotional Intelligence*, New York: Bantam Books.

Grant, L. (1997) 'First get a weasel costume – Do people get together better after wearing diapers on their heads and dressing up like animals?', *Fortune* 17 March: 90.

Grey, C. (2001) *Against Learning*, Judge Institute of Management Studies, University of Cambridge – Research Papers in Management Studies WP4/2001.

Heterick, W.P. and Boje, D.M. (1992) 'Organization and the body: Post-Fordist dimensions', *Journal of Organizational Change Management* **5**(1): 48–57.

Hilmer, F. and Donaldson, L. (1996) *Management Redeemed: Debunking the Fads that Undermine our Corporate Performance*, Sydney: Free Press.

Honey, P. and Mumford, A. (1982) *The Manual of Learning Styles,* London: Peter Honey Publications.

Hong, J. (1998) 'Organizational Learning and the

Knowledge Creation Practices of Japanese Companies,' *Management Japan* **31**(2): 17–24.

Höpfl, H. and Linstead, S. (1997) 'Introduction: Learning to feel and feeling to learn: Emotion and learning in organizations', *Management Learning* **28**(1): 5–12.

Huczynski, A. (1996) *Management Gurus: What Makes Them and How to Become One*, London: Thomas.

Huey, J. (1994) 'The new post-heroic leadership', *Fortune* 21 February: 24–38.

Jackson, B. (2001) *Management Gurus and Management Fashions*, London: Routledge.

Jacques, R. (1996) *Manufacturing the Employee: Management Knowledge from the 19th to 21st Centuries*, London: Sage.

James, D. (1997) 'High priests of the corporate world', *Business Review Weekly* 23 June: 52–7.

Jones, A.M. and Hendry, C. (1994) 'The learning organization: Adult learning and organizational transformation', *British Journal of Management* **5**: 153–62.

Kets de Vries, M.F.R. (2001) 'Creating authentizoic organizations: well-functioning individuals in vibrant companies', *Human Relations* **54**(1): 101–11.

Kolb, D.A. (1994) *Experiential Learning: Experience as the Source of Knowledge and Development*, New Jersey: Prentice Hall.

Kolb, D.A., Rubin, I.M. and McIntyre, J.M. (1976) *Organizational Psychology: An Experiential Approach,* (2nd edn), Upper Saddle River, NJ: Pearson Education.

Kolb, D.A., Rubin, I.M. and Osland, J.M. (1991) *Organizational Psychology: An Experiential Approach,* (7th edn) Upper Saddle River, NJ: Pearson Education.

Laneyrie, F. (1995) 'Images of women in management: Archetypes – a new dimension?', paper presented to Australian and New Zealand Academy of Management Conference, 3–6 December, Townsville, Australia.

Lave, J. and Wenger, E. (1991) *Situated Learning: Legitimate Peripheral Participation*, Cambridge: Cambridge University Press.

Lawson, M. (1997) 'The fad busters', *The Australian Financial Review* 11 April: 3.

Linstead, S. (1990) 'Developing Management Meta-Competences: Can Distance Learning Help?', *Journal of European Industrial Training* **14**(6): 18–27.

Linstead, S. (1996) 'An introduction to management – week 1', in PAGE *Distance Education Package for Management 906*, Wollongong: Department of Management, University of Wollongong.

Linstead, S. and Harris, B. (1983) 'Reality and role of playing: The use of a 'living case study' in management education', *Personnel Review* **12**(1): 9–16.

Macken, D. (1997) 'How did we ever manage?', Good Weekend, *The Sydney Morning Herald Magazine* 5 April: 46.

McWhinney, W. (1992) *Paths of Change: Strategic Choices for Organizations and Society*, London: Sage.

Micklethwait, J. and Wooldridge, A. (1996) *The Witch Doctors: What Management Gurus Are Saying, Why It Matters, and How to Make Sense of It*, London: William Heinemann.

Mirvis, P. (1996) 'Historical foundations of organization learning', *Journal of Organizational Change Management* **9**(1): 13–31.

Morgan, G. (1993) *Imaginization: The Art of Creative Management*, Los Angeles: Sage.

Newton, T.J. (1994) 'Discourse and agency: The example of personnel psychology,' *Organization Studies* **15**(6): 879–911.

O'Connor, A.-M. (1997) 'Woman shakes up Tijuana police brass, *The Sydney Morning Herald* 1 March: 24 (report from *The Los Angeles Times*).

Pedler, M., Boydell, T. and Burgoyne, J. (1988) *Learning Company Project: A Report on Work Undertaken – October 1987 to April 1988*, Sheffield: The Training Agency.

Perry, W.G. (and associates) (1970) *Forms of Intellectual and Ethical Development in the College Years*, New York: Holt, Rinehart & Winston.

Pfeffer, J. (1993) 'Barriers to the advance of organizational science: Paradigm development as a dependent variable', *Academy of Management Review* **18**(4): 599–620.

Rifkin, W.D. (1994) 'Who need not be heard: Deciding who is not an expert', *Technology Studies* **1**(1): 60–96.

Rifkin, W.D. (1998) *BHP Human Factors in IMS – Organisational Learning: Preliminary Report: Project-Based Organisational Learning*, New South Wales, Australia: University of Wollongong, BHP Steel Institute Management Research Program.

Rifkin, W. and Fulop, L. (1997) 'A review and case study on learning organizations', *The Learning Organization* **4**(4): 135–48.

Rifkin, W.D. with Martin, B. (1997) 'Negotiating expert status: Who gets taken seriously', *IEEE Technology and Society Magazine* Spring **15**(1): 30–9.

Roddick, A. (2000) *Business as Usual: the Triumph of Anita Roddick*, London: Thorsons.

Salaman, G. (2001) 'A response to Snell: The learning organization: Fact or fiction?', *Human Relations* **54**(3): 343–60.

Salaman, G. and Butler, J. (1994) 'Why managers won't learn', in Mabey, C. and Iles, P. (eds), *Managing Learning*, London: Routledge.

Schein, E.H. (1993) 'How can organizations learn faster? The challenge of entering the green room,' *Sloan Management Review* **34**(2): 85–97.

Schön, D.A. (1983) *The Reflective Practitioner*, New York: Basic Books.

Schwartz, P. (1996) *The Art of the Long View*, NSW: Australian Business Network (first published in 1991, New York: Doubleday Currency).

Scott, P. (1997) 'Jac the Knife', *The Sydney Morning Herald*, Spectrum Features 8 March: 3s.

Semler, R. (1993) *Maverick! The Success Behind the World's Most Unusual Workplace*, London: Century.

Senge, P. (1990) *The Fifth Discipline: The Art and Practice of the Learning Organization*, New York: Doubleday/Currency.

Shapiro, E.C. (1995) *Fad Surfing in the Boardroom*, Reading, MA: Addison-Wesley.

Silverman, D. (1970) *The Theory of Organizations*, New York: Basic Books.

Silverman, D. (1985) 'Telling convincing stories: a plea for cautious positivism in case studies', revised version of a talk given to the plenary session of the BSA Sociology of Medicine Conference, University of York, September.

Sinclair, A. (1994) *Trials at the Top: Chief Executives Talk about Men, Women and Australian Executive Culture*, Melbourne: The Australian Centre at the University of Melbourne.

Snell, R.S. (2001) 'Moral Foundations of the Learning Organization,' *Human Relations* 54(3): 319–42.

Spitzer, Q. and Evans, R. (1997) *Heads You Win – How the Best Companies Think*, New York: Simon & Schuster.

Stacey, R.D. (1993) *Strategic Management and Organizational Dynamics*, London: Pitman.

Steingard, D.S. and Fitzgibbons, D.E. (1993) 'A postmodern deconstruction of total quality management (TQM)', *Journal of Organizational Change Management* 6(5): 27–42.

The Editor (1997) 'The Threat of Fads', *World Executive's Digest* July: 19–21.

Thomas, A.B. (1993) *Controversies in Management*, London: Routledge.

Townley, B. (1993) 'Foucault, power/knowledge, and its relevance for human resource management,' *Academy of Management Review* 18(3): 518–44.

Tsang, E.W.K. (1997) 'Organizational learning and the learning organization: A dichotomy between descriptive and prescriptive research,' *Human Relations* 50(1): 73–89.

Turner, B.A. (1992) 'Organizational learning and the management of risk', paper presented to the British Academy of Management Conference, 14–16 September, Bradford Management School, Bradford, UK.

Watson, T.J. (1995) 'Rhetoric, discourse and argument in organizational sense making: A reflexive tale', *Organization Studies* 16(5): 805–21.

Watzlawick, P., Beavin, J.H. and Jackson, D.D. (1967) *Pragmatics of Human Communication: A Study of Interactional Patterns, Pathologies, and Paradoxes*, New York: Norton.

Weick, K.E. (1995) *Sensemaking in Organizations*, Los Angeles: Sage.

Wheatley, M.J. (2001) *Leadership and the New Science: Discovering Order in a Chaotic World* (revised and expanded edn), San Francisco: Berrett-Koehler.

2

Gender and management

Joanna Brewis and Stephen Linstead

Questions about gender

1 What *is* expected of managers in modern Western organizations? What should be expected? How does this relate to gender?
2 To what extent has management theory made room for gender?
3 Is gender a profit issue or a moral issue?
4 Are you more likely to attain a management position if you are male?
5 Are men and women concentrated in different occupations?
6 What is positive discrimination?
7 Are women equal to or different from men?
8 Is globalization creating more opportunities for women or perpetuating their subordination?
9 Does being male or female make a difference to the way you manage?
10 Do men experience gender-related problems too?
11 Would a 'feminization' of organizations represent a desirable alternative?
12 What is the relationship between gender and management?

TRANSCORP

Matthew looked at his watch as he locked his car and began to hurry across the car park. '7.15,' he thought, 'I really should have got in earlier today.' Slightly breathless, he pushed open the doors of TransCorp, pausing only briefly to nod to the caretaker, and ran up the stairs to his office two steps at a time. The office looked less than welcoming – desk positioned strategically to face the door, filing cabinets gleaming, the only personal touch a small cactus on his window sill – as he removed his jacket and sat down at his PC. It seemed only minutes later when there was a knock at the door and his boss David entered. He began immediately: 'Matt, there's a problem on the floor. Some of the morning shift haven't arrived yet and you know we've got a rush on with that order for InterMotor. Can you go down there and wait for the latecomers? They need talking to. We really need to get this sorted out today – they've been goofing off down there recently and it's not good enough.'

Without further ado, David left. Matthew stared at his screen, willing himself to descend to the shop floor and reprimand the stragglers. He did not enjoy this particular aspect of his work, but in his position as deputy production manager he knew it was his responsibility. Sighing, he donned his jacket once again and made his way down to the floor.

Half an hour later, Matthew returned to the office, feeling wrung out and upset. There had been the predictable angry scenes on the floor, with staff complaining that the revised shift start times were inconvenient for them and that it was not fair to expect them to come to work an hour earlier than usual. He had had to reiterate that it was only a temporary measure, the order was important and the staff had to arrive on time so as to be able to meet their targets. However, secretly he sympathized with them. He was also growing increasingly tired of the long hours expected of him, the way he had to behave towards his staff, a style set by David and his other seniors, and the continual effort he had to make to suppress his own emotions, which surfaced particularly when he was feeling tired – and he certainly was today. It was now 8 am and Matthew reflected that people working for other companies, in other positions, were only now arriving at work, knowing that they could leave at 5 pm, or 6 at the latest. He himself faced at least another twelve hours, and that was only if the remainder of the day's production went according to TransCorp's carefully laid plans. Otherwise he could be at work until midnight or later.

Matthew spent the rest of the morning, in between dealing with constant calls from the floor and interruptions at the door, drafting a plan for the plant's summer shut-down. This year was going to be especially difficult, as machinery needed to be replaced and moved around the floor as well as the usual repairs and maintenance being carried out, but budgets had been cut to the extent that only a very limited number of personnel could be retained during the two weeks that the plant was officially shut. Because of the considerable overtime available, he was only relieved that the responsibility for deciding who these staff were to be belonged to human resources and not his own department. David had made it clear to Matthew that his plan needed to be as radical as possible – the minimum possible number of staff working the maximum possible number of hours. It was 2.30 pm before he looked at his watch and realized that he had not eaten or drunk anything that day. At this point, his phone shrilled again – his partner Sarah wanting to know if he could get home by 7.30 that evening to look after the children, as she wanted to attend her evening class. He told her that it would be impossible, they began to argue and he eventually hung up the phone cursing her. 'She just doesn't understand,' he told himself. 'Here I am struggling to keep it all together at work, in a crucial period for the company, and all she can do is complain about how I'm never at home.'

Later that day, some time towards 7 pm, Matthew walked down to the snack machine at the end of his corridor and began to punch in his request, when Julie, a production colleague, appeared from her own office, looking furious. She began to reel off her own list of complaints:

'You'll never guess what that git of a boss of yours has just said to me. "Nice legs, Jules!" Can you believe it? God knows, they look at me like I've just landed from Mars if I turn up in trousers and then I have to put up with that kind of rubbish when I wear a skirt. And even then they expect me to walk, talk and behave like a man. I hate this place sometimes.'

Matthew remembered Julie's outburst when he was driving home. He thought to himself that while he found his job exciting and challenging on the whole and it gave him immense satisfaction when an order was completed to the correct standards and went out by the deadline, there were times when he really resented having to be 'one of the boys' and join in with the sexist jokes and chat. When he arrived home he found Sarah in bed, lights extinguished all over the house and a note on the kitchen table telling him how furious she was. He wearily walked upstairs, undressed and got gingerly into bed beside her, only managing to set the alarm for 5.30 am before falling into an exhausted sleep.

QUESTIONS ABOUT THE CASE

1 What are your impressions of TransCorp as an organization?
2 What does the description of Matthew's day tell you about what it means and how it feels to manage in TransCorp? What do you think is expected of managers in this organization?
3 Given Matthew's feelings about his work, does it seem to suit his preferred managerial style?
4 What does this suggest about Matthew's view of himself as a manager and/or as a man?
5 What are the consequences of Matthew's behaviour as a manager
    (a) for him as an individual?
    (b) for his staff?
    (c) for Sarah and his children?
6 Julie tells Matthew that she is disgusted by the comment that David makes about her legs. What other problems might you expect a female manager in TransCorp to encounter?

Introduction

Gender is a powerful principle in the organization of our lives. An individual's identity as either male or female, possessing masculine or feminine qualities, makes a difference to the way in which he or she experiences his or her social world. It is therefore significant to consider the influence of gender when examining what managers do and how they do it.

Although this was not historically the case, there is now a large body of organizational literature which insists that gender is taken into account when examining managerial work. Within this body of work we can identify several competing perspectives on

gender, although it is also true to say that some (for example liberal feminism, diversity) are much better represented than others (for example radical feminism). In this chapter we discuss five of these perspectives – the *liberal feminist*, *radical feminist*, *diversity*, *gender in management* and *gendering management* approaches. The key characteristics of each are summarized in Table 2.1.

Where the first three approaches place different emphases on the impact of gender on management *practice*, the gender *in* management and the gender*ing* management approaches insist on introducing the concept of gender into management *theory*. This reveals the extremely significant neglect of gender in the foundational theories of management, and inspires us to take a look at how some of the main theories about management and organization have failed to take gender issues into account – especially classical management theory, human relations theory and the work of Abraham Maslow on motivation. In fact, in contrast to commentators such as Fiona Wilson (1996) and Frances Tomlinson, Anne Brockbank and Joanne Traves (1997), we find that these theories were not gender *blind*, but on the contrary very gender *aware* in their active efforts to *suppress gender difference*. Later theories, on the other hand, which built on their predecessors, did in fact fail to take gender into account. We then look in more detail at the more contemporary attempts to bring gender and management together, two of which fall under the gender in management heading – these are the *feminine in management* approach and the *gender globalization* approach. Finally, after identifying certain key problems with these viewpoints, we outline the characteristics of our preferred alternative, building on the gendering management approach and focusing on management *processes*, that is, regarding gender as fluid, and carefully examining the ways in which gender and management interact and *mutually* shape each other.

Table 2.1 Perspectives on gender		
Perspective	**Key concepts**	**Typical writers**
Liberal feminism	Women not naturally inferior to men Importance of social justice/equality Vertical segregation (glass ceiling) Horizontal segregation Long agenda of equality of opportunity	*Historical:* Mary Astell Mary Wollstonecraft Hannah Woolley *Contemporary:* Marilyn Davidson and Cary Cooper Betty Friedan Rosabeth Moss Kanter Barbara White
Radical feminism	Women naturally superior to men Importance of social emancipation/change Radical reversal/inversion of contemporary social structures Separatism	Mary Daly Shulamith Firestone Marilyn French Susan Griffin Kate Millett Valerie Solonas
Diversity	Diversity, including gender difference, should be recognized in organizations Individualist focus Improve productivity through a widening of organizational access and participation Strong business case MOSAIC	Patricia Arredondo Rajvinder Kandola and Johanna Fullerton Stella Nkomo R. Roosevelt Thomas
Gender *in* management	Management relational Women and men socialized differently, manage differently Male transactional versus female transformational leadership Transformational leadership most effective in current socioeconomic climate Globalization of gender	Beverly Alimo-Metcalfe Helen Brown Marta Calás Linda Smircich Sally Helgesen Judy Rosener
Gender*ing* management	Interaction of management and gender Foucauldian – gender identity produced by discourse Masculinist organizational discourse sustains masculine managerial identity Successful managers (whether male or female) therefore masculine Problems of this emphasis on masculinity	Mats Alvesson Yvonne Due Billing David Collinson Margaret Collinson Silvia Gherardi Jeff Hearn Deborah Kerfoot David Knights Albert Mills Peta Tancred Stephen Whitehead

Liberal feminism

Liberal feminism can be traced back to eighteenth-century writers such as Mary Wollstonecraft (1970 [1792]) and further. It argues that men and women are equal in all important respects and, more specifically, that women are as capable as men of the reasoned behaviour required in the modern workplace. An important strand of the liberal feminist literature identifies the existence of a 'glass ceiling' in modern organizations. This refers to an invisible, implicit but impenetrable attitudinal barrier which prevents women from reaching senior management positions. Marilyn Davidson and Cary Cooper (1992), for example, claim that women find it difficult to break through this ceiling because of the ways in which they are viewed and view themselves in both wider society and individual organizations. In a similar vein, Richard Anker (1997: 325) points to the common preconception that women are assumed to be less than happy supervising others and more comfortable taking orders – and the resultant belief that they are unsuitable for management and supervisory work. Moreover, Davidson (1997) has augmented her analysis of the glass ceiling by publishing her findings from research into the problems and challenges faced by black and ethnic minority women managers. According to her argument, this group of managers faces a double bind – of gender *and* race – when seeking career development. Davidson suggests that this double bind manifests itself as a *concrete* ceiling, which is not only more difficult to pass through but also blocks these women's view of the top jobs, thus sapping their motivation to achieve them.

Work like Davidson's and Cooper and Anker's claims that the historically influential definition of women as somehow irrevocably feminine, congenitally subordinate, emotional and irrational, and therefore ill-equipped for work at the top of the organizational 'tree', results in *vertical segregation* – the situation in organizations where men predominate in the ranks of the most senior. This phenomenon is neatly illustrated by a series of articles published in the British newspaper the *Independent on Sunday* reporting data from extensive research into the FTSE 100 company index. This index lists the biggest hundred publicly quoted companies in the UK, using market worth as its measure. Between them these companies employ two million workers and generate 80 per cent of the UK's GNP. They include Vodafone Airtouch, BP Amoco, Tesco, Whitbread and BSkyB. John Quelch (2000) argues that those running the FTSE companies probably have more impact on the life of the average British citizen than many government ministers. However, perhaps unsurprisingly, of the 1048 FTSE 100 directors, only 58 – less than 7 per cent – are women (*Independent on Sunday* 2000b; Nisse 2000). Out of these 58 women, only 7 are executive directors, that is, directly involved in day-to-day operations at their respective firms. This is despite the fact that Marjorie Scardino, chief executive of the publishing giant Pearson since January 1997, has turned the company around so that it is now worth more than £13 billion; this following several significant investment mistakes made by her predecessors, including the sale of BSkyB shares which subsequently doubled in value. Although Ms Scardino has categorically proved on behalf of her gender that women can and do make extremely astute senior managers, it is hard to disagree with the *Independent on Sunday*'s (2000b) assertion that the representation of women in the highest echelons of these powerful companies is little more than window dressing to convince onlookers of the attention paid to the equality ideal. It is also worth noting that the situation described above has altered very little since the FTSE 100 was set up in 1984 (*Independent on Sunday* 2000a).

Furthermore, even in European countries with a better reputation than the UK for forward thinking regarding gender equality, such as Sweden:

> [the] gender division of labour … is as pronounced as in most other Western countries. In most high level jobs, male over-representation is very strong. Only about 10–15 per cent of higher middle and senior managers and seven per cent of all professors are women. (Alvesson and Billing 1997: 4)

In Finland, which has a similarly progressive image, 'managerial labour markets continue to be vertically segregated according to gender' (Tienari 1999: 6). Elsewhere in Europe, in the post-communist Czech Republic for example, patterns of vertical segregation are similar; Rosemary Crompton (1997: 139) suggests that women here 'predominate … in lower-level occupations'. Indeed Crompton concludes that, in banking in particular, despite the general expansion in employment positions following privatization of this sector after the 'velvet revolution', Czech women seem to be stuck at the level of middle management and experience considerable difficulty ascending to the most senior jobs. This, she says, mirrors the situation in the same industry in the West (Crompton 1997: 140). Indeed, banking might be more widely seen as an example of men 'riding the glass elevator' (Williams 1995, cited in Teigen 1999: 103), that is, although it is dominated overall by women, it is men who fill most of the senior management positions. So men benefit from what Williams refers to as their 'token' status in this occupation, whereas the same is scarcely true of women in male-dominated jobs. Indeed Janne Tienari (1999: 3) suggests that, even where women are relatively successful in achieving senior positions in the banking industry, in France for example, this occurs because the

Table 2.2 Gender changes in occupational orders, 1981–1991

		% increase in men	% increase in women
1	Professional and related supporting management; senior national and local government managers	33	155
2	Professional and related in education, welfare and health	3	22
3	Literary, artistic and sports	12	54
4	Professional and related in science, engineering, technology and similar fields	4	72
5	Managerial	9	61
6	Clerical and related	−19	2
7	Selling	−9	6
8	Security and protective services	−12	6
9	Catering, cleaning, hairdressing and other personal services	0	−1
10	Farming, fishing and related	−24	4
11	Materials processing; making and repairing (excluding metal and electrical)	−20	−27
12	Processing, making, repairing and related (metal and electrical)	−31	−31
13	Painting, repetitive assembling, product inspecting, packaging and related	−25	−26
14	Construction, mining and related not identified elsewhere	−20	43
15	Transport operating, materials moving and storing and related	−23	−9
16	Miscellaneous (general labourers and foremen)	−61	−45
17	Inadequately described and not stated	−74	−79
	Total	−15	5

Source: Data calculated from 1981 census and 1991 census, 10 per cent sample, coded using 1980 occupational classification by Sylvia Walby (1997) *Gender Transformations*, London: Routledge, Table 2.9, p. 37.

women involved are willing to work full time, even if they have young families, and take the minimum time off for maternity leave and so on, if indeed they choose to have children at all. That is, female managers in French banking adopt an approach to work which could be argued to emphasize their 'sameness' with their male colleagues, but which probably involves 'personal difficulties and sacrifice'.

Habib Zafarullah agrees that in 'advanced' countries the 'brick wall' blocking women's *entry* into the workplace has largely disappeared, but the glass ceiling still poses a problem. For women in the developing world, however, she argues that *both* of these barriers are still very much in place. For example, she cites figures from Bangladesh suggesting that only 5.1 per cent of administrative and managerial jobs, 23.1 per cent of professional and technical jobs, 4.2 per cent of clerical jobs and 6 per cent of government jobs are filled by women (Zafarullah 2000: 197, 201).

Furthermore, the available figures about women in management are often contradictory. Fiona Wilson (1995: 17–18) and Frances Tomlinson et al. (1997: 219)

claim that numbers of women at management level are *falling* both in the USA and the UK, whereas Mats Alvesson and Yvonne Due Billing (1997: 3) suggest that in most Western countries they are increasing, albeit at a somewhat gradual pace. Still, as Alvesson and Billing (2000: 145) assert elsewhere:

Of course, statistics are always unreliable and frequently say more about norms of classification than about reality 'out there', but it is still clear that men have close to a monopoly on the most senior positions and greatly outnumber women in middle-level managerial jobs in virtually every country.

However, it would be wrong to underestimate the radical changes that *have* taken place in the gender composition of management in recent years. Table 2.2 illustrates comparative census data for 1981–1991 which suggest that, while British men increased their absolute presence in professional and managerial positions in national and local government (33 per cent) and general management (9 per cent), the numbers of women in these categories increased respectively by

155 per cent and 61 per cent (Walby 1997: 37). On the basis of data such as these, Sylvia Walby notes that 'the massive changes which are taking place in women's employment and education are transforming gender relations' (Walby 1997: 64).

Despite the fact that there might be *some* room for optimism as regards women's progression into management, liberal feminism also points to the substantial evidence suggesting that they are perceived to be more or less suited to particular *occupations* on the basis of their gender. Richard Anker (1997: 325) offers a helpful summary of these employment-related clichés which describe women as having: caring natures; skills in domestic work; greater manual dexterity; greater honesty; a more attractive appearance; less physical strength; less ability in science and maths; less motivation to travel; more motivation to work at home; less willingness to face danger or to employ force; more docility; less willingness to join trade unions; more tolerance of mundane and repetitive work; more acceptance of lower wages; and less need for income.

Illustrating the operation of these clichés in the labour market is also fairly straightforward. In the UK, for example, Labour Force Survey statistics showing employment by occupation for spring 1998 demonstrate that women made up 89 per cent of nurses, 86 per cent of primary and nursery teachers, 81 per cent of cleaners and domestics and 92 per cent of care assistants and attendants, but only 3 per cent of drivers, 8 per cent of production, works and maintenance managers and 21 per cent of computer analysts and programmers (Equal Opportunities Commission 1999: 10). Similarly, Rosemary Crompton, drawing on 1994 statistics, points out that in the Czech Republic, women doctors are overrepresented in 'the more caring aspects of medicine' such as paediatrics, neonatology and general practice (1997: 139, 145). There is also evidence that assumptions about 'women's skills' underpin recruitment patterns in UK service industries (see Brewis and Kerfoot 1994, for example). That is, it seems that women are often preferred over men for customer liaison positions in, for example, the financial services, because women are assumed to be more socially adept, more welcoming and less threatening than men. Indeed, and unusually in comparison to other industries, it is *older* women in particular who employers appear to favour for front-desk positions such as these; the assumption being that they are maternal, sympathetic characters to whom the public can relate easily and with whom they can communicate.

This *horizontal segregation* also occurs at managerial levels. Evidence suggests that certain management functions represent 'female ghettos', in the sense that (i) they are less well paid than other functions; (ii) they are less well regarded and less likely to be represented at board level than other functions; and (iii) they are overpopulated by women. One particularly pertinent example is human resource management, an area which, we would suggest, is again assumed to require a specific kind of people-related skills base, to demand sensitivity, intuition and a certain gentleness. In the UK, for instance, 1 in 2 HR managers are women, despite the fact that only 33 per cent of British managers and administrators overall are female (Vine 1997; Equal Opportunities Commission 1999). Moreover, women managers tend to be located in staff or support management functions per se as opposed to what could be seen as the 'front line' or 'battle zone' of line management (Tienari 1999: 1).

It is this evidence of horizontal and vertical segregation which compels liberal feminists to demand that steps be taken to address gendered inequality of opportunity in the workplace. They demand that gender be managed in organizations in such a way as to minimize any differences between the employment chances available to men and those available to women. Thus they espouse what is often described as the *long agenda* of equal opportunities (EO). A *short agenda*, as defined by David Goss (1994: 158), focuses solely on staying within the parameters established by anti-discrimination law (for example the Sex Discrimination Act in the UK). As Exhibits 2.1 and 2.2 demonstrate, however, this legislation is frequently insufficient to provide for genuine equality between working men and women – in this instance in the area of pay.

A *long agenda* of equality of opportunity, on the other hand, aims at what is known as 'equal share', that is, allowing women the same level of access to and participation within every level and area of the organization. The long agenda implies a more concerted attack on gendered inequalities, and often incorporates so-called *positive discrimination*, which deliberately favours women over men in an effort to 'level the [organizational] playing field' (Goss 1994: 160). Measures might include: equal opportunities policies; gender sensitization training; family-friendly provisions like flexitime, job share or subsidized workplace crèches to accommodate domestic responsibilities; tracking of recruitment, retention, promotion and job movement rates to identify any problem areas; performance management systems that reward those managers who achieve equal opportunities objectives in terms of recruitment, development and promotion, and penalize those who do not; succession planning; feeder groups at local educational institutions; and group-based selection processes to minimize bias. Some employers may even choose to introduce quota systems, mentors and management and leadership training especially for women to build confidence, although these approaches have to be carefully managed so that they don't in fact break the existing legislation by

Exhibit 2.1 Pay inequalities in the entertainment industry

❏ It is now three decades since the Equal Pay Act 1970 was passed in Britain. This legislation requires that men and women working for the same employer and doing the same or similar work be paid the same wages. However, data from a study published in September 2000 by the Industrial Society, conducted as part of a government-led consultation on equal pay, suggest that British women working full time still earn only *73.8 per cent* of what their male counterparts command. Moreover, many women are actually *worse off than this* in comparison to men, as we can see in the recent revelation that the three female members of bestselling band Steps, Claire, Lisa and Faye, earn only 50 per cent of what the two boys, H and Lee, make. During the six months up to November 1999, Lee was reported to have raked in some £100,000, whereas Lisa earned £50,000 during the same period. While their manager Tim Burn had nothing to say on the matter, Steps' record company Jive pointed out that different contracts could have been signed by the individual members of the band, although apparently when Steps was formed in 1995 all five started out on equal royalty payments. Moreover, although it is accepted practice in the music industry for those with the most creative input into a band's success to receive the greater share of royalty monies, no such justification applies to Steps, for Claire, Lisa, Faye, H and Lee all do exactly the same job, singing the same songs and performing the same dance routines.

❏ A similar situation apparently occurred on the set of the hit BBC television series *Men Behaving Badly*, when Caroline Quentin (who plays Dorothy) and Leslie Ash (who plays Deborah) threatened to quit when they found out that Neil Morrissey (Tony) and Martin Clunes (Gary) earned £25,000 more per series than they did. *Blue Peter* and the radio programme *Today* have attracted criticism from their female presenters for the same kind of gender-based disparities in wages.

❏ Such cases are arguably even more invidious given that these women do *exactly the same* jobs as their male co-workers; the British legislation after all only requires that a woman do *equivalent work* or *work of equal value* to a male colleague to be able to claim the same remuneration as him, since the passing of the Equal Pay Regulations in 1983 at least. However, the public sector workers' union Unison and the Equal Opportunities Commission are both solidly behind the fight to narrow the earnings differential. This has also emerged as a key issue from the government's Listening to Women initiative, as their recent instigation of the consultation referred to above implies. The Industrial Society, moreover, has publicly challenged the existing legislation, describing the procedures for bringing a claim of unequal pay as cumbersome and difficult to follow; it also urges employees to discuss their salaries openly so that gender-based pay differentials are more easily exposed.

❏ Given this current interest in pay (in)equality, perhaps Claire, Lisa and Faye will follow in the footsteps of Quentin, Ash, Konnie Huq from *Blue Peter* and Sue MacGregor from *Today*. Whatever happens, they are probably relieved not to be tennis players, given Tim Henman's recent outburst on the subject of his female colleagues' greed for (horrors!) wanting to be paid the same as the men.

Source: Based on Libby Brooks (1999) 'Some are more equal than others', *Guardian*, G2 section, 11 November, pp. 2–3 and Cherry Norton (2000) 'Men 'prolong low pay for women', *Independent*, 15 September, p. 9.

Author's note: The members of Steps dissolved their association to pursue other projects on 26.12.2001.

Exhibit 2.2 Similar job, more responsibility, different gender

❏ Kate Bornstein describes leaving a job at an American IBM subsidiary for a post at Ford Aerospace following her gender reassignment surgery. The jobs were similar, except that the Ford position carried more responsibility, but Bornstein took a 30 per cent pay cut when she moved to Ford. As she points out: 'The only thing that had changed in my life was the gender I was presenting'. At IBM she had been hired as a man, at Ford as a woman.

Source: Based on Kate Bornstein (1998) *My Gender Workbook: How to Become A Real Man, A Real Woman, The Real You, or Something Else Entirely*, New York: Routledge, p. 152.

discriminating against men – as the all-women Labour Party shortlist of prospective general election candidates was ruled to do by the European Court in 1996 (Whitehead 1999: 23, 30–n2).

The case for gender sensitization training in particular can be made by reference to prevailing stereotypes which tend to delay the progress of women into senior management positions, even where EO policies and legislation are in place. Amanda Sinclair (1998) firstly identifies what she calls the 'pipeline effect' stereotype; that is, the belief that over time more women are obtaining degrees, gaining access to businesses and acquiring relevant experience, so that all we have to do now is wait for them to progress into management, having made sure that enough are coming in at entry level and providing the right kind of training and development. She also points to the stereotype which suggests that women don't make it into management because there is a lack of suitable candidates for the positions falling vacant, which therefore constructs women as undereducated, less committed, insufficiently mobile and ill-equipped to stand the organizational 'heat'. This second argument has it that the problem lies with women, and that it is one which no amount of equal opportunities labour will change (Sinclair 1998: 18–24). Moreover, although much of the available evidence actually contradicts such beliefs – suggesting that women in reality are more committed to career, organization and staff, and harder working than their male colleagues, or at least that there is very little difference between the genders in this regard (see, for example, White 1995; Wilson 1995: 26–32) – *both* stereotypes were found to be alive and well among male *and* female managers in British retailing (Tomlinson et al. 1997: 224–5).

Rosie Cunningham, Anita Lord and Lesa Delaney (1999) also argue that the attitudes of senior managers are central to making sure that equal opportunities initiatives endure. In particular, they claim that restructuring in the British Civil Service has had a detrimental impact on gains that its women have made in areas such as breaking through the glass ceiling, in the main because the Next Steps project, established in 1988 to improve service and increase efficiency, has led to a fragmentation of the organization into semi-autonomous agencies. This in its turn has created greater autonomy for those managers who might not be sympathetic to the equal opportunities cause. The specific agency that Cunningham et al. examined had several laudable initiatives in place, yet greater managerial freedom as a result of Next Steps had also increased workload and concomitantly reduced individual managers' desire to promote equal opportunities. Budget constraints on the new agencies also meant less commitment to 'intangibles' of this kind. Less central control translated into less

accountability, for example in terms of equal opportunities monitoring. Moreover, the marketization of the Civil Service saw it having to compete to retain its contracts and, as a result, equal opportunity initiatives like flexiwork and job share were often seen as being at odds with the need to keep costs as low as possible when submitting contractual bids.

In sum, the main impetus behind liberal feminist arguments is *social justice*, the *moral* case for equality of opportunity, organizationally and elsewhere. As Sally Holtermann (1995: 105) argues, if employers choose to pursue the long agenda:

Employees gain the benefits of increased equality of opportunity for men and women in the workplace (and at home). All family members gain from an easing of the strain of juggling work and caring responsibilities, and some children will gain the social and development benefits of quality childcare facilities.

However, as Holtermann (1995: 104–5) also points out, there are distinctive advantages in *business-related, quantitative* terms to those employers who choose to adopt an equal opportunities stance. For example, corporate image should be enhanced, employee productivity may rise and labour relations improve as a result of greater respect for the employer, and cost savings may also be generated by greater retention of female labour and lower absence rates. Holtermann also notes that other employers benefit from efforts in this area, for example from an enlarged pool of skilled and experienced labour, and that national productivity may rise, thus benefiting the country as a whole. Nonetheless, she also asserts that there are certain dangers in promoting this *business case* – not least because equality of opportunity may become seen not 'primarily as a matter of social justice, desirable in its own right, but merely as something that can be pursued if, and only if, it coincides with the employing organization's own self-interest' (Holtermann 1995: 110–11).

Radical feminism

The liberal feminist stance can be compared to the particular radical feminist position taken, for example, by Susan Griffin (1980) and Mary Daly (1984a, 1984b). This suggests that women are in fact naturally different from men – that they possess certain characteristics which render them closer to nature, closer to their passions and emotions, more intuitive and instinctive, and therefore superior to men. Radical feminism may therefore advocate that women be deliberately introduced into the higher echelons of management so as to counterbalance the narrow masculinist thinking evident at these levels. This kind of thinking produces supposedly rational outcomes such as nuclear weapons. These are, their supporters would have it, intended as deterrents, as guarantors of continued peace. However, if such weapons are used, as they were by the US in August 1945 on Hiroshima and Nagasaki, they make for the long-term erosion of genetic health and the environment across a huge geographical area, quite apart from their immediate capacity for annihilation. It is this kind of objection which radical feminists identify women as uniquely equipped to make (see, for example, the discussion of the women's peace movement in McNeil 1987: 40–56).

In a slightly different vein, but one which also extols the virtues of women over men, the Australian Master Builders Association (AMBA) claimed that, now technological change has removed much of the heavy labour from the industry, women are to be preferred for construction jobs over men because they are highly motivated, diligent, conscientious, neater, cleaner, better communicators and good negotiators. Thus, say the AMBA, women construction workers will improve standards, management practices, safety records and customer relations (Vincent 1998). Other writers in the radical feminist tradition, however, would see the entry of women into traditionally male fields as a form of collaboration with the enemy. They advocate instead a form of separatism where women live and work separately from men, so as to allow them to run their lives according to feminine principles. An example is the tendency for women-only organizations to be flatter in structure and more cooperative in ethos than those employing both men and women (Oerton 1996). The extreme separatist case is made by Valerie Solonas (1983), who calls for women to destroy men altogether as otherwise, she counsels, they can never achieve genuine freedom.

However, Sarah Oerton (1996) also suggests that women-only organizations face pronounced viability problems, given that they tend to attract fewer customers and resources than their mixed-sex counterparts. This is not simply, Oerton argues, because these organizations are categorized as inefficient, utopian, downmarket, radically left wing and operating in the 'wholefood … (and) woolly jumpers' sectors of the economy (1996: 30). She points out the widespread assumption that those working in such organizations must also be feminists, lesbians, and therefore man-haters who are beyond heterosexual control. The consequent threat constructed around these women is effectively neutralized via their economic marginalization. This, as Oerton also states, happens regardless of the sexuality of the people involved (and in some cases regardless of their political orientation).

Diversity

Again in contrast to the equal opportunities stance, of which organizational liberal feminism forms an important strand, there is also a growing body of work around the need to manage what has become known as *diversity* in the workplace – to be responsible for and sensitive to the different types of individual who make up an organization. Anna Lorbiecki and Gavin Jack (2000: S18) suggest that diversity management is now 'common practice' in the US and is increasingly being implemented in the UK and Canada. This interest in diversity has arguably received a considerable fillip from the current furore around *globalization*. There are many definitions of this phenomenon, but the one offered by Barbara Parker is useful for our purposes here:

[the] increased permeability of traditional boundaries of almost every kind, including physical borders such as time and space, nation-states and economies, industries and organizations and less tangible borders such as cultural norms or assumptions about 'how we do things around here'. (Parker 1998: 6–7)

These economic, sociocultural, political and technological developments mean that people are generally moving more freely across the surface of the globe, and they translate into increasingly diverse workforces in many organizations worldwide. The department in which we work (in a university located in southeast England) is a case in point – at the time of writing, its various members hailed from countries as diverse as Singapore, Scotland, Greece, India, Rumania, Ireland, England, Belgium, Egypt, Syria and China. Moreover, with labour shortages of the order of 75 million workers predicted for the European Union in years to come, it seems that such movements, leading to more diversity within member states' workforces, are set to continue – this despite current controversies about immigration in the same geographical region.

Gender is an important topic in diversity, as are race, ethnicity, class, (dis)ability and HIV status, as well as other issues less prominent in the equal opportunities literature, such as personality, value systems, working style, religion, lifestyle, education level and so on. As Patricia Arredondo points out, the idea of managing diversity refers to:

a strategic organizational approach to workforce diversity development, organizational culture change, and empowerment of the workforce. It represents a shift away from the activities and assumptions defined by affirmative action [an equal opportunities tactic involving positive discrimination] to management practices that are inclusive, reflecting the workforce diversity and its potential. Ideally it is

---

Exhibit 2.3 Problems with equal opportunities approaches

❏ Those who are the recipients of supposedly preferential treatment being stigmatized.

❏ The development of a culture of tokenism, within which 'getting the numbers right', that is, achieving a target number of disadvantaged employees, is the main issue.

❏ An 'assimilation' or 'melting pot' culture being established, where differences are minimized and not developed to their full potential and individuals are expected to fit into a predetermined mould, the consequences of which are seen to be a 'play it safe' approach to work and a reluctance to be creative or take the initiative.

❏ Targeting the disadvantaged on a permanent basis rather than making efforts to ensure that an organization naturally encourages equality of opportunity for *all*.

❏ The outdated idea that organizations still need to focus on recruiting the disadvantaged, rather than ensuring that they are present at all levels of the organization.

❏ The incorrect assumption that overt and blatant prejudice is still an issue in organizations.

❏ The creation of poor role models for aspiring members of disadvantaged groups; and so on.

Source: Based on Rajvinder Kandola and Johanna Fullerton (1998) *Managing the Mosaic: Diversity in Action*, London: Institute of Personnel and Development; and Roosevelt Thomas (1991) *Beyond Race and Gender: Unleashing the Power of Your Workforce by Managing Diversity*, New York: AMACOM.

---

a pragmatic approach, in which participants anticipate and plan for change, do not fear human differences or perceive them as a threat, and view the workplace as a forum for individuals' growth and change in skills and performance *with direct cost benefits to the organization.* (Arredondo 1996: 17, cited in Lorbiecki and Jack 2000: S19, emphasis added)

The main issue for proponents of diversity management is that managers need to empower *all staff* to 'realize their full potential – with 'all staff' explicitly including white men. In fact, Kandola and Fullerton and US writer R. Roosevelt Thomas argue that equal opportunity approaches such as liberal feminism are aimed only at the disadvantaged and therefore potentially create problems in organizations. Exhibit 2.3 outlines some of the key difficulties which diversity writers associate with claims for equal employment opportunity.

As a result of these identified deficiencies of equal opportunity approaches, the managing diversity camp suggests that an alternative is to focus on individual development needs, to allow all members of the organization the opportunity to develop as they need to in order to become fully productive employees. Kandola and Fullerton (1998), for example, propose MOSAIC as the paradigm for managing diversity. Exhibit 2.4 outlines key components of the MOSAIC approach.

Of course many of these techniques can also be identified as forming part of the long agenda of equality of opportunity, described earlier on. The difference is that diversity initiatives supposedly target *everyone* within an organization, as opposed to focusing simply on less well-represented groups such as women or people of colour.

According to Lorbiecki and Jack (2000: S20–1), although the US diversity initiative initially gained momentum as a result of late 1980 and early 1990 claims about changing workforce demographics and the consequent need for employers to turn their attention to 'non-traditional' sources of labour, a more political turn in the literature occurred when it became clear that diversity connected with prevailing New Right standpoints and their emphasis on the individual. That is, diversity began to be seen as an alternative to affirmative action, a new and more appealing way for employers to demonstrate their social and moral commitments. Diversity, quite simply, was easier to market to American and, by this stage, European employers. It then took on a third dimension – that of economics – when writers began to counsel that diversity was the only means of ensuring corporate survival, preserving company image and enhancing the bottom line. The highly variegated global market, such commentators claimed, simply could not be served by 'eight white guys at the top of the organization making decisions for 40,000 people around the world' (*Sloan Management Review* 1995: 16, cited in Lorbiecki and Jack 2000: S21).

Nonetheless, and in contrast to the liberal feminist and radical feminist projects, because the main objective of diversity is to improve business performance, such projects arguably have little moral or social strength (Lorbiecki and Jack 2000: S21). Any such benefits could even be regarded as incidental. As a consequence, a company pragmatically following gender-sensitive policies as a result of diversity initiatives to increase productivity might find itself following research and development or marketing practices which ignore and

Exhibit 2.4 **Managing diversity via the MOSAIC acronym**

❑ **M**ission and value A set of values which supports and justifies diversity management and encourages the expression of differences.

❑ **O**bjective and fair processes All organizational processes (for example recruitment) must be regularly audited in order to ensure that they are fair to *everyone*.

❑ **S**killed workforce Managers and workforce alike must be skilled in 'fairness and awareness', they must understand the principles of diversity management, know why it is important and work to ensure that diversity is respected. Managers should adopt an approach of continuous development of self and others, asking for feedback on their own performance and continually working to improve that performance, as well as ensuring that others' progress is not left to chance.

❑ **A**ctive flexibility This also needs to be implemented, not only in the organization of work (for example flexitime), but also in benefits. A 'cafeteria' of benefits can enable each employee to choose the benefits that most suit them. For example, if an individual does not have children, he or she will not have need of an organizational crèche, but may be keen to own company shares.

❑ **I**ndividual focus Individual employees are the focus of diversity management, *not* groups of employees such as women.

❑ **C**ulture that empowers The culture must be empowering, encouraging employees to experiment with ways of respecting and managing diversity themselves.

Source: Based on Rajvinder Kandola and Johanna Fullerton (1998) *Managing the Mosaic: Diversity in Action*, London: Institute of Personnel and Development, pp. 144–66.

CASE EXAMPLE

MANAGING DIVERSITY IN THE WORKPLACE: CORNING USA

When James Houghton took over as chief executive officer of Corning in 1983, he apparently made diversity management a key principle. This was primarily because Houghton had identified that turnover rates for women and blacks were higher than for white men, with the consequence that Corning's investment in these groups in terms of recruitment and selection costs, and training and development, was being wasted. He also felt that the make-up of Corning's workforce should become more reflective of its customer base, so as to ensure better consumer relations. To address these issues, Houghton firstly implemented two quality improvement teams – one for blacks and one for women. Awareness training was made mandatory throughout the organization so as to identify which unconscious organizational values were working against these groups. One issue identified as a result of this training was the importance that the Corning culture placed on working late and the way in which this disadvantaged women, who were more likely than men to have pressing domestic responsibilities. There was also a general improvement in communication about diversity – for example, the publication of stories in the company newspaper about Corning's diverse workforce and successful organizational projects involving diverse groups of people. Further, career planning was introduced for everyone. Corning also began to offer educational grants in exchange for students working summers at a plant within the corporation. Many of the participants in this programme then came to work for the organization upon graduating. Corning's summer internship programme also expanded, with a particular emphasis on offering places to women and blacks, and, finally, contacts with university groups such as the Society of Women Engineers were instigated. Significantly, given the overall thrust of the managing diversity argument, while James Houghton acknowledges the social and moral benefits of the approach that he has implemented, he also states that: 'It simply makes good business sense' (Houghton, cited in Thomas 1990: 10).

Source: Adapted and reprinted by permission of *Harvard Business Review*. From 'From affirmative action to affirming diversity' by R. Roosevelt Thomas, March/April 1990, p. 110. Copyright © 1990 by Harvard Business School of Publishing Corporation. All rights reserved.

Authors' note: Ironically, in 1997, Dow Corning, a Corning subsidiary, was forced to pay several million dollars in damages to thousands of women who had been damaged by its faulty silicone breast implants. The alleged cause was that the product was insufficiently tested; that is, women did not take sufficient part in its development and their needs were not properly monitored.

ultimately damage the interests of women – as Dow Corning did with the breast implant scandal.

Also in this vein, David Thomas and Robin Ely (1996) suggest that approaches to managing diversity in practice fall into two main categories, one of which (the 'learning paradigm') is much more far-reaching than the other ('access legitimacy'). These approaches are summarized in Exhibit 2.5.

It would scarcely be controversial to argue that those organizations fitting within the learning paradigm are likely to be few and far between. Fully developed diversity, it seems, is a difficult goal to achieve, although Thomas and Ely (1996: 89) also warn that simply seeing its benefits in business terms (the access legitimacy approach) may prevent problems such as racism, sexism, homophobia and sexual harassment being addressed as part of any such initiative.

The three approaches to gender and management which we have examined so far identify gender as properly having a certain kind of impact on management *practice*. Liberal feminism, for example, argues that managers should make every effort to minimize gendered differences in terms and conditions, whereas radical feminism suggests that differences between men and women should be recognized, either so as to make the most of women's 'special

contribution' to organizations, or via some form of economic separatism. Diversity, on the other hand, counsels that, although gender difference needs to be recognized, celebrated and exploited in organizations, it should receive no more attention than any other kind of difference.

However, there is another way to conceive of the relationship between gender and management which involves introducing the concept of gender into management *theory*, and understanding how gender affects the way managers think and act. With this in mind, we now move to consider the theory of managerial work, which attempts to conceptualize what management is (and, more often than not, what it should be), with particular attention to the presence and positioning of gender within that analysis. It quickly becomes apparent from our discussion that such theorizing traditionally has sought either to deny the significance of gender for an understanding of managers and managing, or has simply not taken it into account. It fails to recognize the relationship between management and gender: first, because it makes little or no room for any analysis of the actual individuals who occupy the management role, treating management as an abstract set of functions, principles or processes (see Chapter 10); and, second, because it fails to recognize

---

Exhibit 2.5 Two approaches to managing diversity

Access legitimacy

❑ Accepts and celebrates differences and emphasizes equality for everyone.

❑ Main aim is to ensure that external market (customers) matches internal market (workforce), so emphasis is on hiring staff of an appropriate gender, ethnic and cultural mix.

❑ Benefits include the hiring of minority groups who were previously disadvantaged in the labour market.

❑ More of a marketing/PR strategy, no real attention given to developing capacities which the diverse workforce might have.

❑ Global companies might use this approach to interact with external markets and different cultures.

❑ No strategies in place to incorporate differences across the board so may remain dominated at management level by white, Anglo-Saxon men.

Learning paradigm

❑ Differences to be incorporated at *all* organizational levels but equality for everyone is also stressed.

❑ Changes market, products, strategies and organizational culture, for example the legal firm Deway-Levin, after recruiting a female Hispanic lawyer, changed the type of case that it pursued.

❑ Seeks to learn from its diverse staff group and develop their capabilities, which may uncover unforeseen opportunities.

❑ Organization may change its core business or identify new business possibilities.

Source: Adapted from David A. Thomas and Robin J. Ely (1996) 'Making differences matter: a new paradigm for managing diversity', *Harvard Business Review*, September–October: 79–90.

gender as a significant variable in organizational life even in the face of overwhelming empirical evidence. Indeed, it has been widely suggested that *main*stream management theory is actually more accurately labelled '*male*stream'. Management in this kind of theory is typically presented as gender*less*, either because it consists solely of a collection of functions (classical management theory) or because it can be explained as a more or less appropriate relationship to one's workforce (theories of human relations or management 'style'). However, management is an inescapably *embodied* and therefore also a *gendered* experience, an experience which is different for men and women whether they are the managers or the managed. The omission of gender by mainstream/malestream theories of management means that such theories cannot account for the complexity of the management experience; they cannot capture *how it feels* and *what it means* to manage (or indeed to be managed) in a modern organization. We assert, therefore, that gender and management connect with each other in significant and highly visible ways and go on to review two bodies of work presenting exactly this argument.

Nevertheless, at this juncture it is also important that we remember the point made by Chris Grey (1995) and Mats Alvesson and Yvonne Due Billing (1997), who warn against *over*gendering management theory. As Alvesson and Billing have it:

Any perspective runs the risk of being used in a one-eyed fashion, reducing all phenomena to issues of men and women or masculinity and femininity. Gender over-sensitivity … means not considering or too quickly disregarding other aspects or possible interpretations. It means an over-privileging of gender and a neglect of alternative standpoints. (1997: 12)

So the 'gender' lens is *not* the only way to look at management, any more than the lenses of structure, functions, culture or quality are. It does not reveal any ultimate or privileged truth about management, although it is an important, and practically useful, means of understanding how management gets 'done' in modern organizations. This caveat established, the discussion which follows concerns the ways in which gender has been constructed in management and organization theory.

Classical management theory

For classical management theory, as exemplified in the work of Frederick Winslow Taylor (1947 [1911]), Henri Fayol (1949 [1916]) and Colonel Lyndall Urwick (1969 [1937]) in the early twentieth century, management consists simply of the execution of a series of *functions*. It is these functions, suggest such theorists, which

ensure the smooth and effective running of the organization. Management here is presented as a depersonalized activity; it is manage*ment* that is the focus rather than the real-life *process* or *performance* of manag*ing* (Hayward 1992: 186–8). Indeed, the inclusion of the adjective 'classical' in the name of this body of thinking offers a clue to its preoccupations. Richard Baker (1972, cited in Buchanan and Huczynski 1997: 393) tells us that classical management theory is so-called because it is above all else concerned with the generation of *straightforward* recommendations for the design and administration of organizations *across the world*, and is characterized by its emphasis on formality, rigidity and symmetry. Urwick, for example, claims that the study of the human experience of organizing can yield up principles which can govern *any form* of human organization. For him, regardless of the organization's type (it could be a local church, hospital, government agency, army regiment, supermarket, newspaper), purpose, people (manual workers, knowledge workers, men or women) or the political and social theory behind its creation (capitalism or socialism), these principles were technical and universal; they applied to *all* managerial situations (Urwick 1969 [1937]: 49). An excellent example of the supposedly global character of the principles put forward by the classical management theorists is the fact that Lenin was keen to apply the four key tenets of Taylor's capitalist scientific management methods in Communist Russia! However, it is worth noting at this stage that commentators did not agree with each other on what the 'universal' principles were, and that many of these writers have sought variously to retain, restate, narrow or refute the original formulations such as those offered by Fayol, as discussed below (Hales 2001: 2). Nonetheless, such tensions notwithstanding, the belief in universality held firm for several decades.

As we might expect from its insistence on formality, there is also an overall emphasis within classical management theory on the application of science to the study of management, in order – through observation, hypothesis development and experimentation – to arrive at the 'one best way' to manage. Fayol (1949 [1916]), for instance, on the basis of his own management experience, suggested that management (which he referred to as administration) consisted of:

- *organizing* (dividing tasks to be done between workers, and ensuring that this division of labour is efficient and effective)
- *coordinating* (overseeing division of labour in terms of ensuring that the parts support each other)
- *controlling* (monitoring the activities of workers within the division of labour, including discipline if necessary)

■ *purveyance* (forecasting and planning future workforce activity).

In a similar vein, Taylor's (1947 [1911]) key ideas were, firstly, that every individual's labour should be designed using a scientific analysis of that work. Furthermore, Taylor stated that managers must coordinate their workers' activities in order that the tasks to be done are in fact completed. He also believed in a strict separation of conception and execution. That is, Taylor stated that managers should manage and workers work; he counselled that workers should not themselves have any control over the way in which they work or over what they do (also see Chapter 11). Fourthly, scientific management does not ignore the fact that individuals have different abilities – far from it. Taylor was at pains to point out that not everyone was capable of working in a scientifically determined 'one best way', and that individuals needed to be carefully selected according to their abilities to work hard and in accordance with instructions. He also emphasized that rates were to be negotiated with individuals only and not with the collective or group, although, as Chris Nyland (1989) has pointed out, Taylor came to embrace the necessity, and arguably the positive features, of collective bargaining with trade unions in his later years. Similarly, he was aware that there were women in the workforce. In fact a review of the role of women in scientific management by Sue Ainslie Clark and Edith Wyatt was welcomed by Taylor. The recent republication of this review includes correspondence between Taylor and Wyatt, who later gave very supportive evidence to a US congressional committee addressing scientific management (Nyland 2000). Moreover, although within this approach the gender of managers has no relationship to the way that they *should* manage, Taylor implicitly acknowledged that in reality, and in most circumstances, it will have some relationship to the way that they *do* manage. This is why he argued that the principles of scientific management need to be fully enunciated and understood. Scientific management would, it can be inferred, thereby enable women and men to overcome any differences in their 'innate' styles of managing and manage in the most efficient way.

Yet, despite Taylor's awareness of and interest in the effects of scientific management on women, including his suggestion that they should be given two days off a month with no questions asked, the implication being that this was to accommodate the menstrual cycle, for him individual or gender characteristics were not the *defining* features of either work or management. Other underlying and objectively observable principles determined what work and management were, and could be measured. Here, then, the main emphasis is on the manager as a functionary, as an individual who works for the benefit of the whole organization – and therefore of all of those within it (the last assumption is especially apparent in Taylor's work) – but who has no especial identity or contribution which is unique to him or her *as an individual* as far as the organization is concerned. Management for Taylor and his fellow classical management theorists was *normative*; any managerial work on relationships was just a matter of aligning people with the correct abstract principles (*norms*), adherence to which was the overall function of management (also see Chapter 11). Difference and diversity were not just to be ignored, they were to be *suppressed* and rationality, traditionally regarded as a male/masculine trait, was to dominate in the workplace (Linstead 2000).

Max Weber, whose theory of bureaucracy was as theoretically influential as were Taylor's recommendations for practice, had a similar view of the association between women and emotion and the need to banish emotion (and consequently women) from the organizational stage in favour of objective institutional rationality (Bologh 1990: 28–9; Burrell 1997: 244). But it was in the reform of office work, and particularly through the efforts of Frank and Lilian Gilbreth (see, for example, Gilbreth 1911), that the labour process became most obviously gendered, where (rational) men managed (emotional) women and order was maintained thereby – as immortalized in the film *Cheaper by the Dozen*. Here the Gilbreths' insistence on the routinization of the workplace was extended into the home and even the womb (they had 12 children), and the story turned into an ironic romp about the way they reputedly lived family life according to work study principles. The 'one best way' to do things was gently 'sent up'. However, despite some glimpses of gender in the principles put forward by classical management theory, it is also true to say that it was never directly addressed as an issue for managers, or for the managed.

Human relations theory

What is sometimes viewed as a 'softer' turn in management and organization theory, away from the emphasis on measurement and timing in classical management, was primarily associated with the Hawthorne Studies, and their development under the influence of Elton Mayo. It is also associated with the later theoretical influence of Abraham Maslow and his theory of the hierarchy of human needs. Both Mayo and Maslow conducted research in which women played a significant part, yet subsequently produced theories which ignored gender as a factor. The reasons for this are different in each case, but had a considerable effect on later studies.

The Hawthorne Studies were initiated in 1924 by managers of the Hawthorne Plant of the Western

Electric Company in Chicago. They had originally been ergonomic studies of the effects of the physical surroundings of work on productivity – especially that of lighting. After all, as an electricity producer, Western had an obvious interest in demonstrating that using more electricity could increase companies' profits – an approach which is currently being rediscovered as managing your customers' value-added. There had been clinical studies of fatigue and monotony since the First World War, and the methodologies used by Hawthorne were an extension of these. The apocryphal account of how Mayo, an Australian philosopher/ psychologist working at Harvard University, came to be involved has it that the managers involved in the early days of the studies had no idea how to interpret the data and asked him to help them with their analysis because of similar workplace studies he had conducted and his connections with the prestigious Rockefeller Foundation. In actual fact, the managers had plenty of ideas – what they wanted was an expert to help *mediate* their interpretations. Mayo, however, had ideas of his own and when he eventually came to write on the studies he treated the data rather selectively and as a platform for his own theories (Mayo 1945, 1960 [1933]; Trahair 1984; Gillespie 1991).

One of these theories was based on the fact that as a young man he had had bad experiences of political demagogues in Adelaide who had swayed the local unions and caused considerable industrial and social unrest and political damage. He was, as a result, deeply mistrustful of collective sentiment. He had also failed twice, in Adelaide and Edinburgh, to become a doctor of medicine, and had subsequently channelled his energies into psychology, particularly counselling and psychiatry. As a consequence, Mayo's approach to organizations was to treat their problems as symptoms of a malaise which might be collective, but was probably individual. Its source, he felt, was the disruption of traditional community occasioned by urban concentration; for Mayo, work organizations therefore had to fulfil some of the functions of community for their workers in order to prevent tensions manifesting themselves in lowered output, absenteeism, fatigue, boredom, sickness and what he called 'pessimistic reveries'. A third factor might be added, which was that Mayo had never fitted neatly into any particular academic discipline himself – he also read widely if not always wisely in many genres. This emerged in his methodology as multidisciplinarity; one of the most distinctive features of the Hawthorne Studies was the inclusion of psychologists, social anthropologists, statisticians and representatives from a range of other disciplines in the research programme.

Mayo liked to build 'big picture' social arguments, and his perspective was not too dissimilar from that of Taylor, as critical commentators like Harry Braverman

(1974) have pointed out. Yet it is still remarkable that, although the empirical phase of the Hawthorne experiments was conducted on two groups, one of which was entirely male and the other entirely female, this gender segregation was not treated as an object of analysis. The female group was initially coerced into taking part in the experiments and was separated from the main body of the shop floor by being put in a separate room, with a male supervisor. They were closely supervised and monitored, involved in the distribution of activities and the organization of work, given incentives and manipulated in other ways, and were also medically monitored for changes in their condition which might lead to fatigue. Such was the intrusiveness of the management in fact that two of the workers who had become difficult and vocal in their argumentation for improvements in conditions were removed from the group against their will.

In discussing the accounts of the experiments, Richard Gillespie (1991: 204) points out that both Mayo (1945, 1960 [1933]) and later Fritz Roethlisberger and William Dickson (1939) ignored the possibility of collective action by workers. The only dimension that mattered was the individual, and any economic arguments – even where, as with the male group in the bank wiring room, these seemed to have considerable merit – were regarded as 'simply an unconvincing rationalization of behaviour actually driven by sentiments' (Gillespie 1991: 204). This is despite the fact that output by the women increased and output by the men decreased! As Jeff Hearn and Wendy Parkin (1994) point out, the absence of gender and sexuality from the consideration of 'human relations', 'interpersonal relations' and 'emotional relations' calls into question what these terms can possibly mean. They argue that gaps like these are in fact attempts by male theorists not just to reorganize social relations, but to incorporate gendered and sexual relations into organizational analysis in a non-gendered and asexual way (Wilson 1996: 829). However, this was not 'gender *blindness*', as Wilson (1996) and Tomlinson et al. (1997: 219) argue, but a conscious and active *suppression* of gender difference, arising from an intellectual commitment to abstract generalizations, disembodied reasoning and a basically Freudian view which saw women, despite their surface differences, essentially as men without penises (Linstead 2000).

Maslow's hierarchy of needs

Another theorist whose work, although not directly related to organizations, was incorporated into the human relations approach was the psychologist Abraham Maslow. Maslow had similar views about the fundamental nature of human beings to those of Mayo, and his theory of motivation is said to treat men and women as if gender were inconsequential. Maslow argued that human beings are 'driven' by needs which can be classified according to a hierarchy, ranging from basic physiological survival at the bottom, through safety/security, social/affiliative and esteem/recognition, to self-actualization at the top. For Maslow, self-actualization was the ultimate need, but his critics assert that, although his studies of self-actualizing people included women, his definition of self-actualization itself reflects stereotypically *male* experiences and traits (Kasten 1972; Cullen 1994; Wilson 1996). Thus, self-actualization becomes an expression of the male self which *denies* relatedness rather than the female self which *defines* itself in relation to others (Chodorow 1989). Maslow, it is claimed, also privileged the notion of a need hierarchy rather than seeing these needs as webs of interrelated emotional and physical needs (Gilligan 1982; Wilson 1996).

Interestingly, Maslow's starting point for the hierarchy was in fact research on captive primates with regard to dominance behaviour. Human behaviour was at the time (the 1930s) widely held to be predominantly determined by sex (Freud) or dominance/power (Adler). Maslow focused on the latter issue and worked with primates at first in order to develop a basic understanding of dominance behaviour. Nonetheless (and quite apart from the questionable value of extrapolating conclusions based on animal behaviour to human behaviour), his research was deeply flawed. This is particularly evident in the fact that, as later field studies demonstrated, apes behave differently in their wild communities, where social skills rather than physiological traits were more important in the emergence of certain apes in dominant roles, from the way they do in an experimental setting (Cullen 1997). Moreover, recent work has indicated that the reproductive strategies of female primates are far more complex than was hitherto assumed. Females will deliberately mate during their most fertile period with males outside their community, thus adding variety to the gene pool, while continuing to mate with males from the tribe during infertile periods. Hidden subversive behaviour, then, seems to have greater consequence than more obvious dominance behaviour (Weiss 1997).

Based on this somewhat problematic study, then, Maslow concluded that the apes that were less aggressive and most relaxed about their dominance (and consequently most *worthy* of their positions) had greater confidence in themselves. He carried this idea through into his research on sexuality, which focused on women and what he called 'dominance-feeling' (later 'self-esteem'), which was an essential underpinning for self-actualization. However, when giving examples of self-actualizers, he came up with a sample which was predominantly male. This has been variously held to be a result of restricted opportunities for women in society at the time (Friedan 1963: 310), or a consequence of the fact that the ways in which Maslow believed women self-actualized (for example motherhood) are not publicly recognized (Maslow 1954: 92; Cullen 1994: 130). But the gender bias in the hierarchy actually came from the aforementioned conflation of dominance behaviour with self-esteem, which led Maslow to conclude that high-dominance women, who displayed more masculine traits, had more in common with high-dominance men than low-dominance women. He therefore suggested that any gender distinction could be *dropped altogether* as it was so misleading (Maslow 1939: 18; Cullen 1994: 134).

As is also the case with Taylor, Mayo and others, Maslow here is not *unaware* of gender, but instead chooses to deny observable differences between men and women for theoretical reasons. As Cullen points out, his low-dominance women had many qualities which were indicative of high self-esteem if viewed from a more relational perspective, but for Maslow they could not be self-actualizers. The high-dominance women, we would add, conversely display many behaviours which could be regarded as narcissistic or self-centred. Furthermore, we already know from Dallas Cullen's work that Maslow's primate research was notable for its methodological problems, and she (1994: 134–5) makes the same observation of his later studies. Especially disturbing is his 1963 assertion that, on the basis of his knowledge of high-dominance women, and in contrast to men, 'women generally were not destroyed by being raped because fear makes women more feminine and rape represents a woman's desirability and power since the rapist has an erection' (Lowry 1982: 90, cited in Cullen 1994: 136). Yet the hierarchy built on flawed primate research and even more flawed sexuality research, and displaying a very significant gender bias, has been so influential in management and organization theory as to have been regarded as a 'classic among classics' (Matteson and Ivancevich 1989: 369, cited in Cullen 1994: 127). As Robert Rosenfeld and David Wilson (1999: 85) suggest: 'Maslow has permeated at all levels from health and safety at work to the self-actualizing need of creative leaders, currently fashionable in management literature.'

Later management theories

It is true to say that later management theories do become more sophisticated in their greater recognition of the fundamentally *relational* nature of the management task (Wilson 1996), paying greater attention to the fact that managing not only involves the persuasion and cooption of others, but also itself evolves as an activity in response to the outcomes of these negotiations. The developing relationship between workforce and management, leaders and followers, emerges as important. Such theories also recognize that management is a process rather than a function, it involves undertaking the task of manag*ing*, there are various different ways to manage and some of these are more appropriate or effective in certain circumstances than others. So these theories retain the emphasis on the organizational efficiency and effectiveness characteristic of classical management and human relations theory, but also emphasize that management is relational, stylistic and processual. Much of this work has concentrated on leadership styles, and often blurs the boundary between leadership and management, which is discussed in Chapter 10.

However, all these more relational (and more recent) theories – here we would include the work of theorists such as Fred Fiedler (1967, 1974), Robert House (1971) and Paul Hersey and Kenneth Blanchard (1996), fuller details of which are presented in Chapter 10 – can also be criticized for their gender blindness. Indeed we would claim here that this *is* a blindness rather than a suppression, because none of these theorists seem to be following such a grand social mission or theoretical plan as Taylor, Mayo or Maslow – they are arguably mere technicians when considered alongside the pervasive influence of these giants. Although managing in this later work is more modestly acknowledged to be temporally located, there is greater emphasis on the *relationship* between the manager and the workers than on the specific characteristics, background and extrinsic factors (for example gender) which affect the *individual* involved in managing. The manager is a shadowy figure, someone who remains anonymous, a non-reflective practitioner who simply needs to choose or be assigned to manage in suitable ways in specific situations. There is no discussion of what we referred to earlier as the 'embodied' experience of managing, how it feels and what it means to be a manager, and therefore no discussion of the individual manager's gender. But if we continually speak and write about management as a series of functions, principles, processes, relationships and/or styles, we cannot begin to understand how it is practised in different contexts or why.

Gender *in* management

Despite this absence of gender from mainstream/ malestream management theory, some organizational analysts have sought to establish the interrelation between gender and management. That is, they consider the embodied nature of managerial work, management as performed by gendered subjects, by individuals who identify as male or female, and the consequences that

this may have for organizational and managerial practice. In other words, how male and female managers *actually* manage becomes the focus. This work tends to retain the relational theorists' emphasis on management as process and the differences between managerial styles, as well as often relying on the classical management theory notion of a 'one best way' to manage as regards organizational effectiveness – if perhaps seeking to reverse it. However, the real contribution of this more contemporary theory is arguably its acknowledgement that it *matters* what *kind* of person is doing the managing.

This *gender in management* approach argues that, because men and women are socialized differently, they manage differently. Researchers in this area have therefore concentrated on identifying the key characteristics of 'masculine' and 'feminine' managerial styles. Judy Rosener (1990, 1997), for example, argues for an emphasis on the *feminine in management* because feminine styles, she claims, are most effective in the current socioeconomic climate. Critics of the feminine in management school, however, adopt a *gender globalization* approach, which insists that specific management styles are relatively insignificant except that they facilitate the globalization of masculinized organization (for example Calás and Smircich 1995). Women are introduced into the domestic workforce as having the most appropriate managerial styles because this allows males to strut the international stage and be more globally mobile. Let us look more closely at these approaches.

The feminine in management approach

Judy Rosener's (1990) research asked male and female managers to describe their own managerial style. She discovered that male managers, by their own account at least, adopted what she refers to as a *transactional* leadership style. This style uses the principle of exchange in managing – giving rewards or punishment for work done well or badly. Rosener's male respondents also said that they relied a good deal on their positional authority – the status conferred upon them by the organization – in order to manage others. Women, on the other hand, reportedly used a style that Rosener calls *transformational* leadership. This places the emphasis on motivating staff by: persuading them to commit to group/organizational goals; encouraging them to participate in decision making; managing through personal qualities rather than by using one's position; and trying to make staff feel good about themselves (see Chapter 10 for other, slightly different definitions of transactional and transformational leadership). Rosener attributes these differences between men and women to gender socialization in early childhood. She also has it that the feminine model of leadership is likely to be more apposite and more successful in economically turbulent times than the command-and-control style preferred by her male respondents. Rosener's more recent work continues to extol the virtues of women managers. *America's Competitive Secret: Women Managers* (1997), for example, argues that the key to maintaining America's corporate success and ability to compete in global markets is having women in senior positions in organizations, because their management style increases productivity, innovation and thereby profits through women's aptitude for ambiguity and their willingness to empower others.

Sally Helgesen (1995) echoes Rosener's sentiments, firstly in her suggestion that gendered management styles develop as a result of differential socialization, and that women are consequently better at developing creativity, cooperation and intuition in others than men. She goes on to emphasize their preference for managing via relationships as opposed to hierarchical position, to claim that they listen and empathize much more than their male counterparts and to assert that feminine leadership 'principles' are becoming more influential because they simply suit today's public realm better than the 'warrior values' espoused by men. Helen Brown's suggestion that *women-only* organizations tend to be characterized by flat structures with diffused leadership (as also claimed by Sarah Oerton) is relevant here too, especially given her argument that women have the right social skills to create and manage such non-hierarchical organizations (Brown 1992, cited in Gherardi 1995: 91).

Indeed similar evidence emerges from at least two meta-reviews of the literature on management styles and gender. Alice Hendrickson Eagly and Blair T. Johnson (1990) reviewed a total of 370 studies using varying methods, concluding that the evidence does point overall to women adopting a more democratic and people-centred approach to managing others, and men tending to be more autocratic and task/production oriented, although these gender differences, apart from democracy versus autocracy, were found to be strongest in *artificial* environments such as laboratories or assessment centres. Studies undertaken in *real* workplaces did not indicate such pronounced differences. Ellen Fagenson (1993, cited in Alvesson and Billing 2000: 147–8) also summarizes the available research and suggests that women err towards the transformational, web-based, interdependent style of leadership, instead of using their status as men would tend to do.

Taking a rather different approach to the exploration of gender and management style, the British researcher Beverley Alimo-Metcalfe theorizes that the way in which decisions are made in organizations about managerial selection and promotion is at least part of the reason why there are relatively few women in senior management positions. Given that men make up the majority of those involved in formulating choices of this kind, she focuses on discovering whether men and women see leadership qualities differently, so as to be able to ascertain if, 'by excluding a significant or matched proportion of women from this sample, one is likely to end up with male-biased criteria of leadership qualities' (Alimo-Metcalfe 1995: 4). In fact, from Alimo-Metcalfe's research, it appears that male and female managers *do* define effective management differently. Her female managers perceived an effective manager to be someone who relates to others as equals and is sensitive and aware of the effects that they have on others. Alimo-Metcalfe's male managers, on the other hand, valued influence and self-confidence as being particularly important among managerial interpersonal skills. Furthermore, the women spoke positively of a working style which is supportive and which empowers and builds teams, whereas the men placed the emphasis on drive, direction and the transmission of a clear purpose to staff. Alimo-Metcalfe borrows from Rosener in designating these differences of style as transformational and transactional. She then proposes that transformational qualities are undervalued when managerial assessment takes place because, as we already know, it is men who dominate in these situations, and it is also men who would tend to favour transactional characteristics, as displayed by other men, across the board. Moreover, this general preference for promoting men is evident despite the fact that much of the available research, as we have seen, emphasizes the importance and relevance of the transformational leadership approach in a complex and diverse world, and the fact that quality management and leadership is deemed to be central to our collective success and well-being in the future (Rosenbach and Taylor, cited in Alimo-Metcalfe 1995: 8; see also Chapter 10). In sum, then, Alimo-Metcalfe's conclusions – that men and women managers value different kinds of managerial style, and the style valued by women may be more apposite in today's organizational world, whatever the stance taken by those who select for and promote to managerial positions – are very similar to those emerging from the research undertaken by Rosener, Helgesen and others.

Finally, although Mats Alvesson and Yvonne Due Billing (1997: Chapter 6) point out that there are two 'camps' of researchers in the gender in management school – one asserting that there are *no* significant differences between the genders in this regard – they also suggest that the 'differences' camp has come to the fore in recent years, despite the fact that 'the majority of the academic empirical work supports the no-or-little-difference thesis' (p. 145).

Gender globalization

While also belonging to the gender in management school, a radical critique of the feminine in management approach comes from Marta Calás and Linda Smircich (1995). They argue that this approach combines with the emphasis on globalization to perpetuate the second-class status of women in the workforce. At the risk of oversimplifying their subtle argument, they point out that, as globalization takes an increasing hold, American male managers are forced to become 'global managers' and spend long periods of time overseas. As a result, there is a need for them to be replaced back on the 'home front'. Couple this to the argument that the new flexible organizations, which employ team-based work and expect high commitment from their members, need softer, more relational, 'feminine' skills rather than the controlling hard-driving style of traditional management (an viewpoint also espoused by the feminine in management theorists). The result? A greater 'domestication' of US home industry, women becoming the 'reserve army' of labour, while the global scene becomes more of a battlefield. Women are brought into the workforce and increasingly into management positions to care for the home-based workforce, while the promotable males are sent overseas to grow and develop the business – to do battle with the competition in the global marketplace, or develop strategy in the rarefied air of the boardroom. Men are after all much less encumbered with domestic duties and childcare and so are generally more mobile, women's 'special' interpersonal skills notwithstanding (see, for example, Thomas 1999). Women, as we have already seen, may also be constructed as less willing to undertake occupations which necessitate considerable travel, indeed as more motivated to work at home per se, that is, actually in the domestic environment (Anker 1997: 325).

Nick Forster, writing on the subject of those women who *do* achieve international careers, echoes Calás and Smircich in his claim that 'they still represent only a tiny proportion of the total worldwide expatriate population' (Forster 1999: 79), despite the fact that women appear to be just as keen as men on working overseas and are as successful as their male counterparts when they are given the chance to do so. Nonetheless, their selection is much less likely due to assumptions about their domestic commitments. They also face adaptation difficulties in more patriarchal cultures like those of the Middle East or Asia and often do not receive any organizational support for their partners if they choose to travel as well. In fact, of Forster's own sample of British managers and professionals on international assignments (IAs), 89 per cent of the women were single, compared to only 27 per cent of the men. Moreover, Forster's data suggest that the women involved on IAs were more junior than the men, such that there is a glass ceiling in the international context just as there is domestically, and that women were less likely to be given significant projects to oversee. He finishes by arguing that 'if companies are really committed to turning the dual mantras of "internationalization" and "equal opportunities" into strategic and HRM realities, then many will have to take a critical look at their current expatriate management policies' (1999: 89), not least because of the competitive realities of attracting and utilizing the best human resource, regardless of gender. Others writers agree with Calás and Smircich and Forster that the building blocks of the international order are gendered, and the personal is not only political but also international (see, for example, Enloe 1990, 1993; Walby 1997: 185–7).

The changing role that women are playing in the economy (which, it should be noted, is also highly variable across the global market – see, for example, Brewis and Linstead 2000: 248) is therefore inextricably connected to global developments which the feminine in management approach tends to ignore. However, what is also of relevance is the way in which Calás and Smircich in particular make an implicit connection between women and the transformational approach to management, and men and the transactional approach, as do the feminine in management researchers.

Assessing the gender in management argument

The varying cases made by Rosener, Helgesen, Alimo-Metcalfe, Calás and Smircich and others then, seem to rest on the assumption that women are socialized to manage in certain ways and therefore to value a particular kind of managerial approach. However, although these studies represent an advance on traditional management theory in acknowledging the importance of gender, we suggest they do not take sufficient cognizance of important processes *within* the organization –they place too much emphasis on life 'outside the factory gates'. It is implied that male and female managers arrive at work fully socialized, that the workplace itself has little effect on the ways in which they behave. Thus the gender in management researchers perhaps fail to recognize the *interplay* of gender and management, the ways in which gender works to shape managerial work *and vice versa*. Rather, they seem to adhere to an 'add gender and stir' approach.

In criticizing Judy Rosener in particular, Cynthia Fuchs Epstein (*Harvard Business Review* 1991: 151), for example, places more emphasis on work context than pre-work gender socialization in shaping individuals' behaviour at work. Epstein also cites her research among lawyers and her own experience as demonstrating that women frequently engage in 'combative', 'punitive' and 'authoritarian' (that is, 'masculine') behaviour. *In*-work variables, then, such as the size and culture of the organization, should not be underplayed as influencing and in turn being influenced by management style. Additionally, age, class and ethnic differences as non-work variables *apart* from gender may also shape/interact with managerial behaviour. Gender is perhaps perceived as being too 'sexy' in contemporary management theorizing, attracting so much analytical attention that the exploration of other important factors which influence the way management is done are neglected (Mansbridge, *Harvard Business Review* 1991: 154–6). This is what Mats Alvesson and Yvonne Due Billing (1997) refer to as gender oversensitivity. Moreover, women managers' preference for the transformational style of leadership, if it exists at all, may actually be a function of *those whom they manage*. Allan Cohen argues that Rosener, for example, overlooks the fact that many of her female managers were responsible for professionals who may well not have taken kindly to a more directive managerial approach. Like Epstein, he also criticizes her for overestimating the influence of pre-work gender socialization (Cohen, *Harvard Business Review* 1991: 158).

Indeed, it is important that we do not overplay the *differences* between men and women's socialization per se. The socializing of women to work outside the home does not occur in a context separate to the one in which men are socialized. Neither does their socialization into the essentially private world of caring and nurturing. Women do not learn to be women in isolation from men and then bring these values into the workplace – they are socialized in interaction with men (Gherardi 1995: 91). And if we overemphasize gender differences in management theorizing, asks Silvia Gherardi, how can we then account for those men who prefer to work within a more democratic organizational framework and manage in more democratic ways – like the 52 per cent of male managers who said they preferred to use teamwork and a participative management style when surveyed by the British Institute of Management (Vine 1997)? Gherardi suggests that some accounts of gender and managerial work overvalorize the 'either/or' of the gender framework, and points instead to the concept of *dual presence*, as developed by Italian feminists in the 1970s. This represents the mindset of women at this time who self-identified in a 'cross-wise' manner. These women saw themselves as subverting *but not abandoning* conventional feminine role models by operating in *many* arenas *across* the social spectrum. They did not allow the world to be symbolically divided up into 'men's business' and 'women's business' – they continually transgressed, did things they were not supposed to do and caused men's and women's

activities to merge until the gender divide, at the level of action at least, became more fluid (Gherardi 1995: 94–5). In a similar vein, Mats Alvesson and Yvonne Due Billing, in their critique of the feminine in management literature in particular, agree with Gherardi that it makes 'no distinctions … between different groups of women (or men) or historical and culturally different settings' (2000: 148) and Judy White's (1995) research into female executives concludes that these women were more different in their approach to leadership than they were similar. She suggests that these differences derived from their varying ages, experiences and expectations.

Other key problems with approaches which connect gender and management style include the fact that their conclusions might be seen only to reinforce the stereotypical recruitment patterns which are already apparent in management practice. We already know that management functions like human resources are female ghettos, and that women predominate in such areas because they are widely understood to have particularly well-developed people skills, to be more intuitive, more sympathetic and more effective communicators than men. Such gender-based segregation at work limits women's opportunities in management, as well as those of their male counterparts, who may be considered insufficiently masculine if they undertake positions which are seen to fall under the heading of 'women's work'; indeed they may experience difficulties in gaining access to these kinds of jobs per se. By way of contrast, Epstein argues that:

Women ought to be in management because they are intelligent, adaptable, practical, and efficient – *and* because they are capable of compassion, as are other human beings … men also can (and do) express [humanitarian values] if they are not made to feel embarrassed about showing them. And those categories of toughness and drive that many men are made to feel comfortable with should be prized in women who wish to express them when they are appropriate. The category is 'people', not 'men and women'. (Epstein, *Harvard Business Review* 1991: 151, emphasis added)

Moreover, as Diane Meehan (1999: 39) notes:

In many ways, women cannot win. They are criticized for adopting the masculine model of management, but they are also likely to be criticized for displaying an overtly feminine approach, which may be perceived as weakness by others or, in its extreme form, as betrayal of other women. It is difficult to know what is more irritating to other women: a woman manager operating within the masculine model or one who flutters her eyelashes.

Meehan here suggests that 'feminine' approaches to managing others, especially if they are pronounced, may be interpreted by others, not least other women, as inappropriate for the cut and thrust of organizational life, the tough realities of the global marketplace. We know already that at least one of the feminine in management theorists, Beverley Alimo-Metcalfe, concurs with this, although she sees such judgements as misguided in the face of the particular economic challenges that we currently face. However, Meehan then develops the point to claim that women managers who adopt exaggeratedly feminine styles may be despised by female colleagues *in particular* for trading on their sexuality at work. In a similar vein, Paula Nicolson (1996: 124) claims that 'Women who achieve at work frequently are seen as having "used" their sexuality, while men are seen as being "natural" or as having been "used" by the woman'. An apposite example of Nicolson's claim is the controversy surrounding the notorious tabloid the *News of the World*'s 'snaring' of England rugby captain Lawrence Dallaglio.

> After having been fraudulently offered £500,000 for his involvement in a Gillette advertising campaign, Dallaglio twice ended up drinking and talking about sex and drugs with undercover *News of the World* journalists Phil Taylor and Louise Oswald, who he thought were Gillette UK's managing director and a Gillette public relations representative respectively. It seems that the champagne, Taylor and Oswald's stories of their drug use and the promise of the money encouraged Dallaglio to tell some lurid (albeit invented) tales of his own regarding taking and dealing in ecstasy and cocaine. When the *News of the World* was published the day after the trio's second meeting, the resultant furore led to Dallaglio's resignation as England captain, his withdrawal from the English squad for some three months, and his being fined £15,000 by the Rugby Football Union for bringing the game into disrepute (Ackford 1999; Graves 1999; Cleary 1999). The subsequent and widespread media use of the term 'honeytrap' to describe the tactics used by Louise Oswald to get Dallaglio to talk indicates the belief that her feminine 'wiles' were the cause of the hapless player's downfall. Indeed Oswald later hit back, arguing that the same judgements would not have been made if she had been male, and that Taylor's part in the exposé had been largely ignored.

Assessments like those made of Oswald imply prevailing processes of 'feminization' which firstly construct women as inescapably and irrevocably feminine and secondly construct the feminine as damaging, even pathological, in organizational contexts.

Equally, however, as Meehan also recognizes, women face problems in adopting a more masculine approach to management. Epithets like the 'Iron Lady' as applied to Margaret Thatcher, underlining her cool, emotionless demeanour and unerring ability to make the toughest of decisions, but at the same time intended as a criticism of these qualities in a *woman*, demonstrate how discomfiting it can be for others to see women transgressing the gender boundary. Such vilification is also evident in the media's sniping at Jennie Page, former chief executive of London's Millennium Dome. Page was forced to resign from her £150,000 a year position in February 2000, following disappointing ticket sales and a threatened revolt by six of the Dome's biggest corporate sponsors (Arlidge 2000). But as Maureen Freely (2000) also points out in her discussion of Page and prominent women of her ilk, as we discussed in Chapter 1:

If it's not her credentials as a mother that are found wanting, it's her selfish decision not to have any children. If it's not her selfish decision to forgo children, it's her shoes. If it's not her shoes, it's her dress size, her taste in wallpaper, and the state of her hair. If she has a high voice, she's too silly. If she has a low voice, she's too much like a man. The higher her profile, the pettier the complaints. No matter how big her job is, it will be her personality that people argue about. And when she fails? It's more of the same.

Freely asserts that what happened to Page – variously described as lacking an understanding of children and so unable to design the Dome accordingly, being awkward and rude, cowardly, uncreative and unassertive, but also bossy, contemptuous, domineering, unreflexive and unwilling to listen to others, as well as dowdy and overweight – would probably not have happened to a man in the same position. She suggests that the attacks on Page and other well-known women who have 'slipped up' in the public eye (including British MPs Harriet Harman, criticized for her 'heartless' benefit cuts for single parents, and Mo Mowlam, said to have lost her intellectual abilities as the result of radiotherapy to treat a brain tumour) are the result (i) of the notoriety of powerful women, because there are so few of them, and (ii) of widespread ambivalence about their power. Stephen Whitehead (1999: 21) observes, in a similar vein, that those women who became British MPs in May 1997 found fairly quickly that the media were far more concerned with their private lives and what they looked like than any of their political opinions. Many withdrew from the public spotlight as a result.

Carlene Boucher (1997: 154) also acknowledges that women managers face a double bind. She quotes one of her respondents as saying that 'influencing' as a style of management is, she feels, 'more condoned for women' than the direct (and masculine) approach of simply telling someone to do something. Boucher goes on to suggest that a woman who 'tells' as opposed to 'selling' may well attract derogatory nicknames like 'bossyboots' – a term which, she also remarks, would never be used to describe a man (also see Sheppard 1989). Mari Teigen (1999: 97) echoes Boucher's point in her analysis of the case of a woman who failed to secure an administrative position at the Norwegian Directorate of the Coast, and was rejected because she was defined as 'domineering and arrogant'. However, as Teigen also points out: 'If we think about gender differences in terms of binary oppositions, identical behaviour from a decisive and self-confident man might appear as dominating and arrogant coming from a woman.' Mats Alvesson and Yvonne Due Billing (1997: 183) agree that any deviation on the part of women managers from the transformational style often leads to unfair evaluations of their performance, and Tomlinson et al. point to these sorts of judgements being made about women managers by their *female* colleagues, quoting, for example, a store manager who says that 'there is a tendency among some women [managers] to over-react, try to be too hard and too severe to prove that they're not a weak-kneed woman' (1997: 222). Judy Wajcman (1998), in a study of companies which had been recognized as having exemplary equal opportunities policies, found that despite this those policies could not reach to the heart of such prejudices, and that women wanting to achieve corporate success were forced to 'manage like a man' or suffer the consequences.

A picture therefore emerges of female managers continually having to work to prove their 'gender competence' (Gherardi 1995: 135–6), whereby they are permitted to achieve at work, so long as they also and simultaneously do all the things and have all the feelings that 'proper' women do and have – wanting and having husbands and children, sustaining close and intimate relationships with others, seeking to placate and persuade as opposed to asserting themselves etcetera. The massive global success of the Fox Television series *Ally McBeal* neatly demonstrates what modern Western society expects of its 'career women', and can be at least partly explained by Ally's combining workplace ability and hankerings for hearth and home. The connections made between gender and management style by the feminine in management literature in particular can be seen only to reinforce such problematic stereotypes.

It is also worth reminding ourselves that the same literature tends to claim that women's 'special' approach derives from the division of domestic labour and the consequent socialization of women to be nurturing, caring and comforting so that they are later able to care adequately for children and run welcoming and functional homes. A celebration of the skills that result from such socialization runs perilously close to reinforcing the patriarchal positioning of women as *properly* in charge in the private sphere. We could add, of course, that expectations of women with regard to domestic labour already make it difficult for them to accede to and succeed in management, given the challenges of combining organizational demands with a full load of household duties. Moreover, women managers could end up being exploited as peacemakers or as troubleshooters, being called upon to resolve conflicts, make cuts and carry out dismissals, as a result of the assumed connection between their gendered socialization and their particular repertoire of management skills. Finally, it is also true to say that women can be caring and loving parents at home and demanding, transactional managers at work, which blows the key assumption behind most gender in management claims out of the theoretical water (Alvesson and Billing 2000: 149–50, 151, 153–4; also see Brewis 1996: 108, 133 – n28).

To summarize, in asserting women's 'preference' for a transformational approach, commentators like Rosener fail to question the gender divide and thus end up being complicit with it. Indeed, as long as they continue to label women's managerial behaviour as typically different from men's, they reinforce the assumed connection between women and femininity and thus continue to ensure that women who do not conform will always be subject to assessments which derogate them. As Alvesson and Billing argue, 'In this way "knowledge" of female managers creates its own truth effects – it does not so much mirror as produce socially constructed "reality"' (Alvesson and Billing 1997: 146; also see Alvesson and Billing 2000: 150–1). As an alternative to this kind of argument, we would argue that any analysis of gender and managerial work must take into account not only the orientation to work that gender socialization *outside* the organization might produce, but also how the experience of work *in itself* produces and maintains particular forms of gender identity. Relatedly, we would contend that gender identity is much more dynamic and much less rooted in biological sex than the analyses provided by the gender in management school might imply. That is, we would argue that the process of becoming gendered continues *and changes* through life. How then does this process happen in the organization? How are our subjective experiences of gender informed and moulded by what happens in our workplaces? The final part of our discussion in this chapter, which deals with the gendering management perspective, seeks to answer these questions.

Gender*ing* management

This approach has it that not only is one's identity as male or female, masculine or feminine, something separate from one's biological sex, but that the development of one's sense of oneself as gendered is the powerful result of discourse. Masculinity and femininity in this analysis are clusters of textual roles created by the operations of contemporary discourse around gender difference, roles which individuals must strive to live up to. The discourse of gender difference therefore shapes and delimits the possibilities open to us as men and women (Brewis et al. 1997: 1277). Most men, it is true, never reach the fantasized ideal of masculinity, the kind of image popular heroes like actors George Clooney and Brad Pitt or sportsmen Michael Johnson and Jonah Lomu project, just as few women look like model Giselle Bundchen, actress Jennifer Aniston (who is married to Pitt) or singer Andrea Corr. As Pat Nivins (quoted in Bornstein 1998: 23) argues:

being a woman (or a man for that matter) is a lot like being an Aryan superman – a myth. Gender is a continuum with very few people at either extreme, and everybody else in the middle. At some point you just have enough characteristics of one or the other where society sees you as being of a particular gender.

Deborah Kerfoot (2000: 238) agrees that it is crucial to recognize the difference between real women (/men) as individuals, and 'Woman' (/'Man') as discursive category. However, it is also true to say that such images of the Real Man and the Real Woman, of the Perfect Genders, and the degree to which they are valued, certainly inspire ordinary people to work towards them; in fact Kate Bornstein (1998: 41) argues that it is precisely the impossibility of these standards that means most of us continue to be motivated to achieve them. As a result, they may be experienced as oppressive, for example through anorexia or bulimia nervosa, or the condition known as body dysmorphic disorder. Moreover, the fact that actors, sports stars and singers are rarely anything much like their images does not matter – the images may not be real, but they have effects in the real world, on real men and women.

This suggests that we as human individuals come to know who we are through being exposed to particular interpretations of what it is to be human, in this case, either male or female, masculine or feminine. Because we are expected to be either/or, we create and reinforce these stereotypes in our everyday acts and interactions with others. Moreover, gender identity here is not the *inevitable* product of biological sex, as Mats Alvesson and Yvonne Due Billing have it, 'there is not an automatic relationship between body, specific processes of social construction and a set of characteristics/orientations' (1997: 218). How we understand ourselves and how we work to present those selves to the world may in fact be the diametric opposite of our physiological sex. There is considerable evidence, for example, that women managers labour to distract their colleagues from their female bodies, in order to emphasize that they are just as capable of the masculine behaviours and demeanour which we have already identified as desirable in the modern organization. Formal kinds of office dress such as suits and blouses, which avoid any hint of sexuality and lend their wearer a professional, almost asexual image are an example of this labour (Brewis et al. 1997: 1287–8; Brewis 1999: 90–1; Brewis and Sinclair 2000: 200). Indeed, we could even argue that sex itself is less a matter of biological reality than of social construction, given the medical profession's insistence on labelling even newborns with the most ambiguous of sex organs as boys *or* girls (O'Donovan 1985). And as Kate Bornstein (1998: 26) asks: 'who says that penises are male and vulvas are female?' She also points out that, although many cultures across the globe give babies a fixed and immutable gender at birth, dependent on the presence or absence of a penis, some allow or even encourage gender changes later in life (1998: 28). An example of the latter case would be the general acceptance (although not absolute tolerance) extended to *katoey* (biological males who display some degree of transgendered behaviour) in Thailand. Nonetheless, we would also acknowledge that the powerful discursive connection between sexed body and gender identity (Whitehead and Moodley 1999: 2; Kerfoot 1999: 186; Alvesson and Billing 2000: 146) means that it is men who are more likely to identify with the masculine and women with the feminine.

The upshot of this analysis, though, is that women may strive to project a masculine identity just as men tend to. Masculinity therefore is *not* what men do and what they are without thinking much about it; men have problems being men, and they certainly do not have exclusive property rights on masculinity (Kerfoot and Knights 1993: 660; Kerfoot 1999: 186). Neither is being male definitive or exhaustive of all that men are or can be (Kerfoot and Knights 1996: 85). The masculine subject is, rather, 'that person who invests a sense of being in masculine discourses; those languages, practices and symbols that speak to stereotypical ways of being a man, and which are subsequently dominant or hegemonic in various sites across the social field' (Kerfoot and Knights 1999: 201).

Masculine values

As implied in our discussions of the transactional management style, the prevailing form of contemporary

Western masculinity revolves around being rational, objective, sure of oneself, logical, decisive, unemotional, tough and competitive. This masculinity centres on control. It means being explicit and assertive, saying what you think and speaking your mind plainly; being outer-focused, possibly aggressive; valuing work, sports and organized activities; being action-oriented, liking to get things done, a doer; being analytical or calculating about situations, rather than intuitive, relying on hunches or gut feelings; being dualistic, or tending to see things as black or white, either/or; preferring quantitative solutions which involve numbers to qualitative ones which involve opinion; linear thinking (for example X causes Y, making predictive connections) rather than lateral thinking (making unusual connections, being creative); being rationalist, valuing reason more than emotion or playfulness; being reductionist, liking to reduce things to their simplest terms and principles, rather than relishing subtle differences; being materialist, with a constant eye on resources, costs and benefits; being constantly aware of one's position in a hierarchy, engaging in one-upmanship with colleagues, striving to maintain the upper hand and protect oneself from challenges; and isolating oneself from others and rejecting dependence on them (Hines 1992: 328; Tannen 1993: 24–5, cited in Nicolson 1996: 146). Not all men will exhibit all these features of masculinity, because the whole taken together is a stereotype, but it is one which still resonates powerfully in Western society, even at the level of myth.

Nonetheless, there is a hidden fear at the heart of this version of masculinity. In taking a position in the world which emphasizes being active and assertive over others rather than yielding, listening and being gentle, men reject intimate relations and achieve social status and esteem by means which glorify force – in war or sport – or by force expressed as power in business and politics. Men then typically have difficulty handling their feelings because feelings make them vulnerable and womanly. Emotion is dangerous not only because it is impossible to fully control, but also because it represents everything that is anathema to masculinity (Glaser and Frosh 1994: 24). Only certain feelings, like anger, which may be channelled towards competitive organizational goals, may be legitimately expressed (Reynolds 1992). Moreover, because masculinity revolves around control, sustaining this way of being in the world compels those who subscribe to it to look for constant reassurance that they are actually in control. Any evidence of weakness is simultaneously evidence of personal failure. And because social relations are far from being predictable or stable, control is only rendered all the more desirable for being impossible to attain/maintain. Consequently, those who seek to be masculine find their identities continually threatened;

the masculine, far from being a seat of contentment and complacency, is a particularly worrisome place; an identity on which one must work continually to gain, assert and retain control (Hines 1992; Kerfoot and Knights 1993, 1996; Kerfoot 1999, 2000).

Despite its anxiety-generating tendencies, striving to identify with this form of masculinity is nonetheless likely to make the individual a successful organizational participant, someone deemed suitable to manage others, because modern management itself is largely a masculine activity. As Kerfoot (2000: 241–2) points out, employment security and material success, as well as the 'psychic kick' of sensations of mastery, are therefore two good reasons why people continue to work at being masculine, even though it is fraught with never-ending challenges. That is, masculinity is as seductive as it is anxiety making. Men *and women* who aim towards success at work, or who already belong to the ranks of management, are therefore likely to be *particularly* driven to identify with masculinity, or, as regards the women at least, to achieve an acceptable *balance* of masculine and feminine attributes. In other words, as we have argued above, women just as much as men might be 'seduced by a masculinist way of being' (Whitehead 1999: 27) and the organizational advantages it seems to offer, which at the very least derive from not standing out against a masculinist backdrop (also see Sheppard 1989; McDowell and Court 1994; Collinson and Hearn 1996; Brewis et al. 1997; Collinson and Collinson 1997; Kerfoot and Knights 1998; Kerfoot 1999, 2000; Alvesson and Billing 2000).

Masculine modern management, as we would expect, requires its incumbents to remain in control, of themselves, others and the environment, by virtue of level-headed decision making, undertaken without anger, emotion or bias. Modern management is therefore, as Ian Lennie (2000: 130–5) claims, predicated on a Cartesian separation of mind and body, on metaphorical disembodiment, within which the manager knows the world through detached, objective, cerebral observation and is therefore able to change it, by virtue of directing others' bodies in the execution of particular kinds of labour. As he argues, the management 'order' understands 'the sensual world as manageable, in the sense that it stands waiting to be shaped by the vision of a knowing subject' (Lennie 2000: 134). Being able to exercise managerial prerogative, carrying out the 'right to manage' others in contemporary organizations, also depends on instrumental control, on sustaining output through imposing targets that are quantifiable and often highly abstract, but which carry penalties if not achieved and are coercively policed, through the threat of discipline or dismissal, for example (Kerfoot and Knights 1996: 90). Managers therefore need to demonstrate their ability to take command, to show that they are capable of 'being "on top of" things … to appear always in control of situations, even where circumstances dictate that this could not possibly be the case' (Kerfoot 2000: 232).

Unsurprisingly, those who identify as feminine (arguably mainly women, although this category can include those men who either choose not to or cannot perform masculinity) are uncomfortable with or marginalized by management's masculinity. They find its competitiveness, bureaucratic impersonality, emotional coldness and lack of intimacy alien. This may result in their distancing themselves from the content and the context of their work, appearing detached and uncommitted, valuing home, friends and family above their job; but at the very least it will translate into a constant sense of dissonance at work, a feeling of not fitting into the organizational environment (Kerfoot 1999: 188). Indeed there is empirical evidence to the effect that even women who have reached the organizational peak may opt out. Judi Marshall (1995), for example, talks of how her middle and senior management respondents paused to assess their careers, which for many then led to a period of unemployment as a result of their disassociation from the male organizational cultures in which they were employed. In a similar vein, Michelle Martinez (1997) quotes Judy Rosener's (1997) claim that 'Most women [managers] don't want to fit into a male-dominated company mold', as well as citing research data from the US consultancy Catalyst which suggest that 'The women [managers, all of whom had quit their jobs] … surveyed were either moving to companies who provided a more level playing field, or starting their own businesses'. In fact Catalyst (1998) have produced a manual which they suggest will enable organizations to retain their female human resource, based on 'best practices from the corporate leaders'. Organizations cited include Motorola, Deloitte and Touche, IBM, Avon, American Airlines, McDonald's and Texas Instruments. Another category of 'female escapee' is the woman achiever who gives up work because she finds juggling work and domestic commitments impossible, and wants to put her family first. Former barrister Naomi Rose, for example, who has a school-age daughter and a baby son, gave up her job when she realized that her devotion to her children far exceeded any commitment to her clients, and that hiring someone suitable to care for them while she worked would in fact cost as much as she was earning. As Maureen Freely points out, Naomi is also a woman who was 'raised to think that all able-bodied adults were meant to work and that work was the only route to a secure and dignified life' (1999: 1). In a similar vein, Brenda Barnes, former president/chief executive of Pepsi-Cola North America, left her £1-million-plus-a-year

position so that she could spend more time with her three offspring. As she herself puts it:

After years of hectic travel, dinner meetings, missing children's birthday parties and even living in separate cities from my husband as we both pursued careers, I decided I had made enough trade-offs for Pepsi. Now I need to give my family more time. I want to be like any other housewife. (quoted in Gordon 1997: 7)

However, it isn't just women who 'bail out' – consider, for example, Daniel Petrie, former vice-president of Microsoft. Petrie was very attracted in the first instance by working for Bill Gates, despite the lengthy working days required. Many employees slept at the office or worked around the clock; at the very least a 12-hour day was expected. However tiring the work was, Petrie also states that he wanted to be a part of the energy and buzz which such high levels of commitment engendered. Nonetheless, he hadn't worked at Redmond Campus (the Microsoft HQ in Seattle) very long when the work started to take its toll. The trigger was the birth of his first child, but the feelings got worse when Petrie's sister was killed in a car accident. He started to absent himself from meetings held at unsocial hours, and told his staff to go home when he felt they had worked too hard or for too long. The upshot was that Petrie quit his job and went home to Australia to build a lifestyle which allowed for a shorter working week and more time with his kids – despite the disbelief of his Microsoft colleagues, who couldn't believe what he was giving up (Swan 1996).

The crucial point here is that modern work environments encourage and nurture masculine ways of relating to self and behaving. However, organizations are not the only social site where this takes place, and masculinity is not uniform. Amanda Sinclair (1998: 61, citing Maddock and Parkin 1993: 76, and Collinson and Hearn 1994), for example, lists the various kinds of masculine managerial subcultures that may exist in modern organizations:

■ traditional authoritarianism (maintained via bullying and a culture of fear)
■ gentleman's club (protectionism, paternalism, based on the assumption that men are born to rule)
■ entrepreneurialism (task-oriented, a workaholic culture)
■ informalism (schoolboyish, 'larky', attached to sporting and sexual rituals)
■ careerism (values expertise and bureaucratic career progression)
■ gender-blind (everyone, regardless of gender, is 'one of the boys')
■ feminist pretenders (supportive of equality but the onus is on women to make the necessary changes,

that is, take the responsibility for developing equality)
■ smart macho (highly competitive, driven by performance, discriminates against those who cannot work at the desired pace or who question the competitive ethos).

Neither is masculinity static. Deborah Kerfoot (1999, 2000; also see Kerfoot and Knights 1999) asserts that demands on managers are changing as organizations become increasingly concerned with flexibility and quality in order to ensure responsiveness to customers and therefore continued profitability in a highly charged business environment. Kerfoot argues that managers now find themselves responsible for getting the best out of their staff, fully exploiting the creativity and potential of their organization's human resource and extracting the optimum levels of productivity and service, as opposed to simply seeing workers as a 'necessary evil' (Kerfoot 1999: 191). She suggests that managers now have to 'communicate with, rather than dictate to, subordinates. This in a manner that demands more sophisticated means of control and direction than through the traditional impersonal hierarchical chain of command' (2000: 232). That is, Kerfoot has it that a certain 'feminization' of management is taking place within which managers must display both 'social skills' and 'emotional awareness', and build at least a degree of intimacy with their staff. This, she also claims, creates difficulties for managers because intimacy of any kind equates to a certain vulnerability, a revealing of aspects of oneself that self-estranged forms of masculinity insist are hidden away. Secondly, developing relationships with staff is both time consuming and unpredictable in terms of quantifiable outcomes, and therefore 'troubling to masculinity' for these reasons (Kerfoot 1999: 194).

Perhaps, then, as Kerfoot and Knights (1999) suggest, new forms of management are challenging dominant forms of organizational masculinity. Do those identifying with 'old' masculinity – controlling, detached, impersonal, hierarchical – risk having their carefully honed traits and behaviours deemed unproductive in current organizational environments, even to the extent that these men and women lose their jobs? Can we speculate that:

an unintended consequence of such [new management] practices would lead to a fundamental questioning of masculinity in management, organization and subjectivity? Does such critical reflection on the business of management itself [hold] the key to creating the conditions within which an alternative means of managing can emerge – one that is grounded in non-instrumental modes of relating to others? (Kerfoot and Knights 1999: 212)

In fact we would argue that such changes in management techniques and approaches can be seen very differently; the required shift towards a more open and engaged form of communication on the part of managers could be understood as a colonization of the feminine with the result of *reinforcing* the edifice of masculinism. This may well make management/ masculinity *easier* to perform in the sense that it becomes less anxious and less obsessed with control in its 'trying on' of feminine intimacy. As Arthur Brittan has it, 'hegemonic masculinity is able to defuse crisis tendencies in the gender order by using counter and oppositional discourse for its own purposes' (1989: 187).

The above analysis supports the view that masculinity is historical *in itself*, existing in different forms in different times, in different cultures and in different locations within the same culture (also see Connell 1995; Alvesson and Billing 2000). However, while organizational masculinity itself might shift in emphasis, or exist in multiple forms in the same cultural site, or even in multiple forms in the same organization, this is unlikely to mean that men relinquish any of their privilege; although what is also clear is that the requirement to do masculine behaviour, of whatever sort, is a social challenge, not a natural expression of the essence of being male. In the workplace, behaving in this way in order to succeed as a 'manager' is *problematic*; the demands of masculine management are potentially damaging, not just to male (and female) managers themselves, but also to their staff, colleagues, customers, families and the community at large. Norman Jackson and Pippa Carter (2000: 197; also see Hales 2001: 70–1) offer an especially evocative example of the ways in which an emphasis on quantifiability, neutrality and the bottom line require almost inhuman responses to very human problems. They cite the case of a flaw in the Ford Pinto which meant that in certain conditions the fuel tank would rupture, the vehicle catch fire and the occupants burn to death, or at the very least sustain serious injuries. Ford decided it was *more efficient* simply to pay out on the resultant insurance claims than to work on redesigning the car, or even call in the existing model for repair. Would, ask Jackson and Carter, the victims and their families have agreed with this assessment of the best way to proceed?

In contrast to arguments discussed above, the diversity approach in particular, our emphasis here is therefore much less on the connection between gender and management as a route to business efficiency. We are interested in the fact that, in the quest to become a 'real manager', people may come to depersonalize others, turn them into objects and resources rather than see them as fellow human beings. At the same time, sacrificing a whole range of one's own experience causes managers to become desensitized, further diminishing their capacities to empathize with and care about others, even themselves, suppressing 'a range of emotions, needs, and possibilities, such as nurturing, receptivity, empathy, and compassion … because they might restrict [the] ability and desire to control [them]selves or dominate [other] human beings' (Kaufman 1994: 148). Macho managers who are hard on their employees are often even harder on themselves, and this self-sacrifice is another important element of masculine experience (Donaldson 1991). At the end of this process of stifling emotion, thwarting impulses, suppressing spontaneity for the sake of control, concealing true feelings and intentions – the process of *self*-discipline – managers come to regard their selves as just another resource, just another commodity to be 'downsized' if necessary (Jackall 1988). Management is predicated on particular forms of masculine identity work which limit the range of possibilities for managerial subjects to interact with others, and thus make for alienation and self-estrangement, but which simultaneously devalue other, more engaged forms of interaction (Kerfoot and Knights 1996; Kerfoot 1999, 2000). Thus managers may do things, but they do not necessarily feel that it was them*selves* who acted – they often see themselves as playing a role. Similarly, they may endure a great deal of stress as a result of the alienating and disembodying effects of the management role, becoming unable to assess the effects that the labour of management is having on their physical and emotional well-being. It may be others who have to inform such an individual of the damage that he or she is sustaining as a result (Lennie 2000: 135–6).

Furthermore, as Mike Donaldson (1991: 21–2) sees it, this form of masculinity turns on the man sacrificing himself for his family through submitting himself to the challenges of the working day, so that even though the role of breadwinner affords him a certain level of power, it is not without its costs. Indeed, there are data which suggest that fatherhood can impel men to spend *more* time at work for the sake of the child; new fathers feel driven to work *harder and longer* in order to provide better for their progeny, especially if the child is a boy (Kettle 2000). It may also be that men (and women) build their reputations as managers by spending as much time at work as possible. David Collinson and Margaret Collinson (1997), for instance, quote one male senior manager who jokes about making 'guest appearances at home' (p. 391), and his female colleague who works a 70-hour week but has a full-time live-in nanny for her children (p. 392). In a similar vein, research carried out at Edinburgh University suggests that high-flying men, who view a 10-hour working day as normal, spend as little as 15 minutes a day with their children. Many, suggests this study, 'are enslaved by an office culture that regards pleas of wanting to spend more time with their children as professional vulnerability' (Harlow 1999: 5).

> British Prime Minister Tony Blair, a self-identified 'family man', was emphatic that he would not be taking leave following the birth of his fourth child. Blair in fact insisted until immediately after the birth that he would simply be scaling down his workload, because being prime minister was not the kind of job that one could simply abandon in order to spend more time with new arrival Leo (born 20.5.00) and his mother Cherie. This was in spite of Cherie's previous public announcement that she was very impressed by the decision of Finnish Prime Minister Paavo Lipponen to take six days off following the birth of his second child in March 2000, and that she expected her husband to follow suit. In the event, it was announced three days after Leo's birth that Deputy Prime Minister John Prescott would take over Blair's duties temporarily while the family decamped to Chequers, although Blair still remained in overall charge of the country (Jones 2000; Jones and Barwick 2000; Ward and Black 2000).

It is not just the (male) Labour leader who finds that the demands of his job potentially compromise his home life. Stephen Whitehead (1999: 22) quotes one of Blair's female MPs on her obsession with her work:

Politics takes over and dominates your life. It shapes the rest of your life and time with the family … politics imposes tremendous sacrifices in people's families. The sacrifice is mainly made by our partners and children … I'm conscious that in pursuing politics in the way I have done I haven't spent time with the family.

Feminine values

In the light of the above, the question we must now ask is: Would feminine values provide an alternative to the dominance of masculine identities in workplaces? Ruth Hines says yes, feminine values should be reintroduced into organizations to balance out the values of controlling, competitive, aggressive masculinity. She claims that the existing imbalance is damaging to personal survival, growth and wholeness, psychologically, physically and spiritually. This argument says that what is at stake is not just the suppression of *women*, individually or as a group, but the suppression of ways of thinking, feeling and acting that are considered *feminine*. These possibilities for thinking, feeling and acting become unavailable to women *or men* (Hines 1992: 314–15, 317). The wide-ranging taboo on the feminine at work is seen to be problematic because organizational subjects come to relate to themselves and others in highly restricted and restrictive ways. They can neither be fully themselves nor fully *human*. A better balance of organizational values would therefore ensure a healthier workplace. Carol Frenier (1996) agrees. Writing from a perspective informed by the psychology of Jung, Frenier asserts that we all have masculine and feminine aspects to our characters, whether we are male or female. She goes on to claim that an injection of feminine values into modern organizations, to complement the existing emphasis on the masculine, will make our progress towards genuinely sustainable lifestyles (a goal she sees as particularly important) more straightforward. Frenier claims that the feminine turns on dialogue, reflection and the development of community, the better to challenge some of the maxims we organize by, for example 'growth is the name of the game'. Her theme is one of encouraging not only our continued well-being but also our commercial success. In a similar vein, Carlene Boucher (1997) suggests that the women managers she spoke to about leadership sought to actively 'reject the stereotypical (male) values of a leader (emotional distance, objectivity, unconditional confidence, and so on) and develop a clear sense of their own values'. This, she argues, *tempers* 'some of the more potentially self-destructive aspects of this social construction of leadership' (Boucher 1997: 155) through its emphasis on connectedness and relatedness (with oneself and others), integrity and honesty.

The kind of argument presented by Hines, Frenier and Boucher does not *necessarily* privilege the feminine *over* the masculine but, rather, catalogues the problems which an *im*balance of values can generate in the organization. It claims that organizations should be informed by a consideration of what they presently do not welcome, the values of the feminine, or at least by a critical examination of the masculine character of modern organizational values/managerial practice and its consequences. As Mats Alvesson and Yvonne Due Billing (2000: 149) suggest, although there are undoubtedly problems with some of the available constructions of feminine values, as well as with certain suggestions about how they can benefit organizations, as we have already established in our discussion of the gender in management literature, feminine leadership could 'be seen as a constructive counterfoil to prevailing or older ideas about leadership, a counterfoil making it easier for a number of females – and progressive men – to identify with leadership and get some guidelines and legitimation'. They continue by pointing out that men and women who manage using the *range* of gendered behaviours may well be more effective because of their ability to care and share *as well as* to direct and control (p. 152).

However, the problem with the 'imbalance of values' position is that in some of its forms it remains attached to its liberal feminist origins. It tends to be written in a paradoxical combination of demands for political action and gentle new age spirituality, the idea of 'balance' in particular implies inertia. As a view of gender, this is, as we have implied above, too *static*. Gender emerges and changes in a *dynamic* between a variety of features and forms of masculinity and femininity, which grow alongside each other. Indeed Kate Bornstein (1998: 8–9) argues that our gender identity might change hour by hour, minute by minute, even second by second:

In response to each interaction we have with a new or different person, we subtly shift the *kind* of man or woman, boy or girl, or whatever gender we're being at the moment. We're usually not the same *kind* of man or woman with our lover as we are with our boss or a parent. When we're introduced for the first time to someone we find attractive, we shift into being a different *kind* of man or woman than we are with our childhood friends. We all change our genders.

This argument is not new. In the 1850s Engels remarked that within the working class the men were the bourgeoisie and the women the proletariat, in an internal relation of domination in which the oppressed *supported* the oppressors (Campbell 1984). Beatrix Campbell provides a detailed discussion of how this relationship continued to work in the north of England during the depression of the early 1980s. As she points out, in establishing such relations detail is everything. Ongoing studies of the organizational micropractices by which gendered subjectivity is shaped, the actual relations of power, knowledge and gender in talk, myth, image and action, need to be produced as a matter of course if we are to understand better how gendered identity emerges, is changed by and itself affects management practice over time.

Moreover, we should perhaps point out that, even in those studies which do not seek to assert the superiority of femininity over masculinity, there is perhaps a tendency at least to downplay what masculine values have to offer us in organizational terms. Straightforward derogation of masculinity, and a call for a feminization of organizations (as evident in much of the gender in management literature), is obviously problematic, not least because it argues for a reversal of the relations between the norm and the margins, such that the feminine moves to centre stage and the masculine takes over her inferior position (Brewis et al. 1997: 1294–7). But even where this does not happen, there is a notable absence of analysis which acknowledges that masculine ways of doing things in organizations have afforded us considerable benefit over time, masculinity is integral to scientific, economic and technological progress, masculinity gets things done because it is task-focused and *beneficial* forms of production and development (for example medical innovations) can be attributed to masculine behaviours and orientations (Alvesson and Billing 1997: 202). Furthermore, if we accept the proposition that most capitalistic organizations are instrumentally driven, being premised upon an efficient use of resources and a strong orientation to results which may necessitate cost cutting and an exploitation of available labour, then we can begin to see that perhaps the feminine is not 'fully transferable to all or most [existing] organizations'; that it may in fact be of most relevance in '"family-like" organizational contexts' such as nurseries, rest homes, daycare centres and their ilk (Alvesson and Billing 2000: 150).

Conclusion

In sum, then, 'gendering management' identifies the ways in which gender and management actually interact. It does not focus on management as a process which needs to result in organizational effectiveness (at least not the kind of effectiveness which many commentaries take as their benchmark, where enhancement of the bottom line appears as the be all and end all), nor does it measure its value in accordance with its contribution to that process. Rather, it suggests that the most interesting and socially valuable material that can be gained from a study of management is a focus on how and why it happens in the way that it does.

Finally, to return to our set of opening questions. By now you should be able to come up with some answers to these for yourself so, rather than answer them for you, we will finish with a guide to where we discuss the issues in the text.

Answers to questions about gender

1 **What *is* expected of managers in modern Western organizations? What *should* be expected? How does this relate to gender?** The feminine in management approach: page 72; Masculine values: page 78.

2 **To what extent has management theory made room for gender?** Classical management theory: page 68; Human relations theory: page 69; Maslow's hierarchy of needs: page 70; Later management theories: page 71; Gender *in* management: page 72; The feminine in management approach: page 72; Gender globalization: page 74; Gender*ing* management: page 78; Masculine values: page 78; Feminine values: page 82.

3 **Is gender a profit issue or a moral issue?** Liberal feminism: page 59; Radical feminism: page 63; Diversity: page 64; Masculine values: page 78.

4 **Are you more likely to attain a management position if you are male?** Liberal feminism: page 59.

5 **Are men and women concentrated in different occupations?** Liberal feminism: page 59.

6 **What is positive discrimination?** Liberal feminism: page 59.

7 **Are women equal to or different from men?** Liberal feminism: page 59; Radical feminism: page 63.

8 **Is globalization creating more opportunities for women or perpetuating their subordination?** Gender globalization: page 74.

Answers continued

9 Does being male or female make a difference to the way you manage? Gender *in* management: page 72; Assessing the gender in management argument: page 74; Gender*ing* management: page 78; Masculine values: page 78.

10 Do men experience gender-related problems too? Masculine values: page 78.

11 Would a 'feminization' of organizations represent a desirable alternative? Feminine values: page 82.

12 What is the relationship between gender and management? Gender and management – the whole chapter.

And one final question. Thinking back to the case of Chris Stefano in Chapter 1, what gender is Chris? We deliberately did not give any clues, but you probably gave Chris a gender anyway. Thinking about how you came to ascribe to Chris the gender you did might give some clues as to your own potential gender bias.

REVISITING
THE CASE STUDY

So, having discussed gender and management in theory at some length, let us try to apply some of our ideas in practice by returning to our case study questions. The case is fictionalized, but is drawn from our research – the problems of Matthew and Julie are real ones.

1 What are your impressions of TransCorp as an organization?

To begin with, it seems from the case that TransCorp is an organization which expects its employees to work long hours – Matthew, as deputy production manager, routinely works at least a 12-hour day, and his staff are also expected to work beyond the confines of 9 to 5 if the organization requires it. TransCorp's culture also appears to emphasize a very impersonal mode of interaction – staff are expected to leave their personal feelings at home. This is evident in the symbolism of Matthew's office, a shrine to efficiency and lack of distraction. TransCorp is also an organization which values hardheadedness, logic and the bottom line in decision making. Matthew is relieved that he does not have to make the difficult choice as to who will work during the summer shutdown, but

he is expected to come up with a staffing plan to cover that period, which focuses on minimum cost and maximum output and seemingly pays little attention to the effects on the staff involved (and indeed those who aren't involved). Finally, it seems that TransCorp does not value its staff sufficiently to listen carefully to their opinions and needs. The layout of Matthew's office, with its desk positioned to provide both a physical vantage point (others can't sneak up on him) and a symbolic barrier between himself and visitors, is testimony to this. As is, perhaps more evocatively, David's insistence that the production staff are simply 'goofing off' when they fail to turn up on time for an earlier-than-usual shift start.

2 What does the description of Matthew's day tell you about what it means and how it feels to manage in TransCorp? What do you think is expected of managers in this organization?

TransCorp can be seen as a very masculine organization, conforming to Ruth Hines' (1992: 328) description of the prevailing form of Western masculinity as 'hard, dry, impersonal, objective, explicit, outer-focused, action-oriented, analytic, dualistic, quantitative, linear, rationalist, reductionist and materialist'. Its culture emphasizes formal rationality, which is instrumental, calculative and directed at the efficient achievement of goals, at the expense of substantive rationality, which has more to do with reflecting on goals themselves, assessing whether or not these goals, if achieved, will lead to fulfilment and satisfaction for those involved. This is evident, as we might anticipate, in what TransCorp requires from its managers. Matthew is expected to keep his staff in line, to control them (David's insistence that he talks to the latecomers on the early shift); to appear formally dressed at all times (having to put his jacket back on to visit the shop floor); to put organizational targets above the needs of his team (reiterating the requirement for them to start their shift early to meet a particular deadline); and to approach his managerial work with the bottom line always in mind (the 'radical' plan required for the shutdown).

3 Given Matthew's feelings about his work, does it seem to suit his preferred managerial style?

It is clear that Matthew resents having to be one of the boys, or at least having to align himself with the prevailing definition of masculinity/ management at TransCorp. One might surmise from his objection to having to work long hours, behave in a dictatorial manner with his staff and suppress emotion in dealing with others that his personal preference might lean more towards what Judy Rosener (1990) and others call a transformational leadership style: encouraging staff participation in goal setting; relating to staff as equals; interacting with and leading staff by virtue of his personal qualities rather than his managerial position; having some measure of intimacy with his staff; and being sensitive to the effect his actions have on his staff and others in the organization. So we might suggest that Matthew's image of himself as a manager conflicts, at least to some extent, with what TransCorp actually requires of him and, furthermore, that he perhaps resists the discourse of masculinity which prevails in the wider society. It seems that he does not necessarily conceive of himself as masculine in terms of being rational, objective, sure of himself, logical, decisive, aggressive and competitive, nor yet does he fear the expression of emotion. Thus to a degree Matthew is the kind of man that Silvia Gherardi (1995) acknowledges as (ideally) preferring to work within a more democratic organizational framework and manage in a more democratic way, like the majority of male managers surveyed by the British Institute of Management (Vine 1997). He therefore subverts either/or assumptions about the gender framework.

4 What does this suggest about Matthew's view of himself as a manager and/or as a man?

However, Matthew also identifies with the prevailing managerial discourse at TransCorp because, it is implied, he will not make the grade at work if he does not – and we know from Deborah Kerfoot's (2000) work that making the grade in this kind of management affords not only employment security and material success, but also the thrill associated with feelings of mastery. Matthew has not, therefore, rejected the masculine identity that life in TransCorp creates, sustains and reinforces, to the extent that he finds himself marginalized by it or he has to opt out, as Judi Marshall (1995), Judy Rosener (1997) and Deborah Kerfoot (1999) suggest might happen to those who find such values alien. He does find his work exciting and challenging, and also satisfying (although at the same time he resents it for what it forces him to do). Thus Matthew has not reached the stage where his 'experience of managerial … work is one of dislocation, and a continual sense of being at odds with [his] environment and the working practices that surround [him]' (Kerfoot 1999: 188). It is arguably this ambiguity in his life as a manager and as a man which creates specific problems for him. He obviously finds his work stressful and entirely too demanding at times. He does not eat properly during the day, he wakes up tired and goes to bed exhausted. He anticipates with anxiety any confrontations during the day, like the one with the personnel on the morning shift, and any negative consequences of the decisions he makes, like his plan for the summer shutdown. However, he is not sufficiently disaffected to withdraw from TransCorp, as is made clear when he reacts angrily to Sarah's request for him to come home early and look after their children. This in itself reveals an enduring commitment to TransCorp on Matthew's part – he mutters to himself that he is struggling to keep it all together at work, in a crucial period for the company.

5 **What are the consequences of Matthew's behaviour as a manager**
   (a) for him as an individual?
   (b) for his staff?
   (c) for Sarah and his children?

(a) What does managing mean for Matthew, working within an organization which values a particular kind of masculinity as being the most appropriate way to interact with others and relate to oneself and one's managerial work? As we have seen, this form of masculinity is not necessarily one to which Matthew himself fully aspires, which causes him not inconsiderable difficulty, but, at the same time, he is also able to lose himself in it, to the extent that he does not always acknowledge the impact that this identification has on him as an individual. His constant fatigue is just one of the ways in which managing takes its toll, although he also berates himself for not having arrived at work earlier on the day with which the case study deals, and he goes to bed that night having set the alarm for 5.30 am the following morning. As Ian Lennie (2000) points out, it may well be others who bring to a manager's attention just how much damage they are doing to themselves through their constant efforts to 'play the organizational game'. Managing, then, is partly a trap, yet it is also rewarding and frequently exciting – it represents a paradox.

(b) Matthew's approach to management, conforming as it does to the prevailing culture at TransCorp, also has ramifications for his staff, as he is rendered unable to listen to their complaints or suggestions, and instead exercises managerial prerogative in any situation of conflict. He is disengaged from their concerns and only permits himself to care about them in his more depressed moments. That is, Matthew for the most part has to suppress any tendencies to empathize with and feel compassion for his staff. His managerial labour means that he must be largely dismissive of their needs (Kaufman 1994; Kerfoot and Knights 1996; Kerfoot 1999, 2000), except on the odd occasion where, for example, he relates to them having to work longer hours than usual, or feels concern for those who will be denied overtime for working the summer shutdown.

(c) Finally, Matthew spends very little time at home with his family, which Sarah clearly resents, and which he himself is dimly aware of. However, one might surmise that he also has a nagging sense that he is doing the right thing by his family by acting as the breadwinner (which might be argued to be a component of the prevailing form of masculinity, as Mike Donaldson (1991) has suggested), and therefore perhaps fails to realize what he may be doing to them by allowing work to take over his life. Certainly, as David Collinson and Margaret Collinson (1997), John Harlow (1999), Stephen Whitehead (1999) and Martin Kettle (2000) all point out, it is by no means unusual for men (and women) in senior positions to work extremely long hours, even when they have young children.

6 **Julie tells Matthew that she is disgusted by the comment that David makes about her legs. What other problems might you expect a female manager in TransCorp to encounter?**

Expectations of managers at TransCorp mean that women within the organization are also subject to the demands of masculinity if they aspire to success, as Stephen Whitehead (1999) and others suggest is commonly the case. Indeed, Julie complains to Matthew that she is expected to walk, talk and behave like a man by TransCorp in order to prove herself as a manager. However, Julie's other complaint is that TransCorp also expects her to retain some measure of femininity, for example she says that her colleagues 'look at me like I've just landed from Mars if I turn up in trousers'. This bears testimony to the particular problems experienced by women managers, or by those women who aspire to managerial positions, in organizations like TransCorp. On the one hand, they have to relate to themselves and behave in a very masculine way, which may be difficult because of the particular way that women are socialized to be feminine within modern Western cultures (Rosener 1990, 1997; Alimo-Metcalfe 1995; Helgesen 1995). On the other hand, they must not appear to be too masculine, as they will be punished in equal measure if they step too far beyond their prescribed societal gender role, that is, femininity, which Deborah Kerfoot and David Knights (1996: 87) describe as 'not instrumentally attached to securing itself through projects and goals, and … more engaged with, rather than detached from, the world'. The balance can be difficult to achieve, as researchers such as Deborah Sheppard (1989), Silvia Gherardi (1995), Mats Alvesson and Yvonne Due Billing (1997, 2000), Carlene Boucher (1997), Frances Tomlinson et al. (1997), Diane Meehan (1999) and

Mari Teigen (1999) have suggested, and Julie's disgust at David's sexism is evocative of this. The advantage that men like Matthew have over women like Julie, then, as implied by Stephen Whitehead and Roy Moodley (1999), Deborah Kerfoot (1999) and Mats Alvesson and Yvonne Due Billing (2000), is that the strong cultural link between biology and gender behaviour makes it more acceptable for male managers to identify with the masculine discourse of management than it is for female managers.

In short, we can see from the case that management is a process and a set of practices which can be usefully understood by reference to discourses of gender difference. Any exploration and analysis of gender in this context, as we suggested earlier, provides examples of the ways in which it intersects with, informs and is informed by managerial behaviour. In particular, this suggests that the predominance of masculinist discourses of management in organizations bears examination in terms of the particular challenges and demands that it presents for real managerial subjects. It would, however, be foolish, not to say inaccurate, to overestimate the power of gender as an organizing principle of management work; it is important to remember what Chris Grey and others have to say regarding the perils of gender oversensitivity, as well as the need to acknowledge the other differences which 'criss-cross' our gender identities and render generalizations on the basis of 'all men' or 'all women' virtually impossible. While a consideration of the interaction between gender and management is a fruitful one through which to arrive at an understanding of what it means and how it feels to manage, there is also room for applying a similar analysis to issues of ethnicity, class, (dis)ability and the limitless other features of diversity which form important components of our relationship with ourselves as individuals and as managers. Recalling one of the major objectives of this book, what is important is that these things about which we tend to make assumptions are subjected to critical thinking. This is the only way in which we can guard against blindness – gender blindness, race blindness, disability blindness – in all its forms. We can then challenge suppression where it is found, and as a result we can learn, personally and organizationally, so as to be able to manage with our eyes wide open.

References

Ackford, P. (1999) 'Bright lights, champagne nights and the fall of a sporting hero', Electronic Telegraph, 30 May, issue 1465. Online. Available at: http://www. telegraph.co.uk (accessed 1 August 2000).

Alimo-Metcalfe, B. (1995) 'An investigation of female and male constructs of leadership and empowerment', Women in Management Review 10(2): 3–8.

Alvesson, M. and Billing, Y.D. (1997) Understanding Gender and Organizations, London: Sage.

Alvesson, M. and Billing, Y.D. (2000) 'Questioning the notion of feminine leadership: a critical perspective on the gender labelling of leadership', Gender, Work and Organization 7(3): 144–57.

Anker, R. (1997) 'Theories of occupational segregation by sex: an overview', International Labour Review, 136(3): 315–37.

Arlidge, J. (2000) 'Dome chief resigns as sponsors revolt', Guardian Unlimited, 6 February. Online. Available at http://www.guardian.co.uk (accessed 4 August 2000).

Arredondo, P. (1996) Successful Diversity Management Initiatives, Thousand Oaks: Sage.

Baker, R.J.S. (1972) Administrative Theory and Public Administration, London: Hutchinson.

Bologh, R. (1990) Love or Greatness: Max Weber and Masculine Thinking – A Feminist Inquiry, London: Unwin Hyman.

Bornstein, K. (1998) My Gender Workbook: How to Become A Real Man, A Real Woman, The Real You, or Something Else Entirely, New York: Routledge.

Boucher, C. (1997) 'How women socially construct leadership in organizations: a study using memory work', Gender, Work and Organization 4(3): 149–58.

Braverman, H. (1974) Labour and Monopoly Capital: The Degradation of Work in the Twentieth Century, New York: Monthly Review Press.

Brewis, J. (1996) Sex, Work and Sex at Work: A Foucauldian Analysis, unpublished PhD thesis, Manchester: UMIST.

Brewis, J. (1999) 'How does it feel? Women managers, embodiment and changing public sector cultures', in Whitehead, S. and Moodley, R. (eds), Transforming Management: Gendering Change in the Public Sector, London: UCL Press, 84–106.

Brewis, J. and Kerfoot, D. (1994) 'Selling our "selves"? Sexual harassment and the intimate violations of the workplace', paper presented to the British Sociological Association Annual Conference, 'Sexualities in Social Context', 28–31 March, University of Central Lancashire, Preston, UK.

Brewis, J. and Linstead, S. (2000) *Sex, Work and Sex Work: Eroticizing Organization*, London: Routledge.

Brewis, J. and Sinclair, J. (2000) 'Exploring embodiment: women, biology and work', in Hassard, J., Holliday, R. and Willmott, H. (eds), *Body and Organization*, London: Sage, 192–214.

Brewis, J., Hampton, M. and Linstead, S. (1997) 'Unpacking Priscilla: subjectivity and identity in the organisation of gendered appearance', *Human Relations* 50(10): 1275–304.

Brittan, A. (1989) *Masculinity and Power*, Oxford: Blackwell.

Brooks, L. (1999) 'Some are more equal than others', *Guardian* (G2 section), 11 November: 2–3.

Brown, H. (1992) *Women Organising*, London: Routledge.

Buchanan, D. and Huczynski, A. (1997) *Organizational Behaviour: An Introductory Text* (3rd edn), Hemel Hempstead: Prentice Hall.

Burrell, G. (1997) *Pandemonium: Towards a Retro-Organisation Theory*, London: Sage.

Calás, M. and Smircich, L. (1995) 'Dangerous liaisons: the "feminine-in-management" meets "globalization"', in Frost, P., Mitchell, V. and Nord, W. (eds), *Managerial Reality*, New York: HarperCollins, 164–80.

Campbell, B. (1984) *Wigan Pier Revisited: Poverty and Politics in the Eighties*, London: Virago.

Catalyst (1998) *Advancing Women in Business – The Catalyst Guide: Best Practices from the Corporate Leaders*, San Francisco, CA: Jossey-Bass.

Chodorow, N. (1989) *Feminism and Psychoanalytic Theory*, New Haven, CT: Yale University Press.

Cleary, M. (1999) 'Dallaglio fined but not banned', Electronic Telegraph, 26 August, issue 1553. Online. Available at: http://www.telegraph.co.uk (accessed 1 August 2000).

Collinson, D.L. and Collinson, M. (1997) '"Delayering managers": time-space surveillance and its gendered effects' *Organization* 4(3): 375–407.

Collinson, D.L. and Hearn, J. (1994) 'Naming men as men: implications for work, organization and management', *Gender, Work and Organization* 1(1): 2–22.

Collinson, D.L. and Hearn, J. (eds) (1996) *Men as Managers, Managers as Men: Critical Perspectives on Men, Masculinities and Management*, London: Sage.

Connell, R.W. (1995) *Masculinities*, Sydney: Allen & Unwin.

Crompton, R. (1997) 'Women, employment and feminism in the Czech Republic', *Gender, Work and Organization* 4(3): 137–48.

Cullen, D. (1994) 'Feminism, management and self-actualization', *Gender, Work and Organization* 1(3): 123–37.

Cullen, D. (1997) 'Maslow, monkeys and motivation theory', *Organisation* 4(3): 355–73.

Cunningham, R., Lord, A. and Delaney, L. (1999) '"Next Steps" for equality? The impact of organizational change on opportunities for women in the Civil Service', *Gender, Work and Organization* 6(2): 67–78.

Daly, M. (1984a) *Gyn/Ecology: The Metaethics of Radical Feminism*, London: The Women's Press.

Daly, M. (1984b) *Pure Lust: Elemental Feminist Philosophy*, London: The Women's Press.

Davidson, M.J. (1997) *The Black and Ethnic Minority Woman Manager: Cracking the Concrete Ceiling*, London: Paul Chapman.

Davidson, M.J. and Cooper, C.L. (1992) *Shattering the Glass Ceiling: The Woman Manager*, London: Paul Chapman.

Donaldson, M. (1991) *Time of Our Lives: Labour and Love in the Working Class*, Sydney: Allen & Unwin.

Eagly, A.H. and Johnson, B.T. (1990) 'Gender and leadership style: a meta-analysis', *Psychological Bulletin* 108(2): 233–56.

Enloe, C. (1990) *Bananas, Bases and Beaches: Making Feminist Sense of International Politics*, London: Pandora.

Enloe, C. (1993) *The Morning After: Sexual Politics at the End of the Cold War*, Berkeley, CA: University of California Press.

Equal Opportunities Commission (1999) *Facts About Women and Men in Great Britain 1999*, Manchester: EOC.

Fagenson, E.A. (1993) 'Diversity in management: introduction and the importance of women in management' in Fagenson, E.A. (ed.), *Women in Management: Trends, Issues and Challenges in Managerial Diversity*, London: Sage.

Fayol, H. (1949 [1916]) *General and Industrial Administration* (translated by C. Storrs), London: Sir Isaac Pitman.

Fiedler, F. (1967) *A Theory of Leadership Effectiveness*, New York: McGraw-Hill.

Fiedler, F. (1974) 'The contingency model – new directions for leadership utilization', *Journal of Contemporary Business* 3: 65–79.

Forster, N. (1999) 'Another "glass ceiling"? The experiences of women professionals and managers on international assignments', *Gender, Work and Organization* 6(2): 79–90.

Freely, M. (1999) 'Nice work if you can get it', *Observer* (Review section), 4 July: 1–2.

Freely, M. (2000) 'She who must be vilified', Guardian Unlimited, 13 February. Online. Available at: http://www.guardian.co.uk (accessed 26 June 2000).

French, M. (1993) *The Women's Room*, New York: Abacus.

Frenier, C. (1996) *Business and the Feminine Principle:*

The Untapped Resource, Oxford: Butterworth Heinemann.

Friedan, B. (1963) *The Feminine Mystique*, New York: Dell.

Gherardi, S. (1995) *Gender, Symbolism and Organisational Cultures*, London: Sage.

Gilbreth, F.B. (1911) *Motion Study*, New York: Van Nostrand.

Gillespie, R. (1991) *Manufacturing Knowledge: A History of the Hawthorne Experiments*, Cambridge: Cambridge University Press.

Gilligan, C. (1982) *In a Different Voice*, Cambridge, MA: Harvard University Press.

Glaser, D. and Frosh, S. (1994) *Child Sexual Abuse*, London: Macmillan – now Palgrave Macmillan.

Gordon, G. (1997) 'I gave up £1m a year for my three babies', *Daily Express*, 25 September: 7.

Goss, D. (1994) *Principles of Human Resource Management*, London: Routledge.

Graves, D. (1999) 'Dallaglio quits over "set-up"', Electronic Telegraph, 25 May, issue 1460. Online. Available at: http://www.telegraph.co.uk (accessed 1 August 2000).

Grey, C. (1995) 'Review article: Gender as a grid of intelligibility', *Gender, Work and Organization* **2**(1): 46–50.

Griffin, S. (1980) *Woman and Nature: The Roaring Inside Her*, New York: Harper & Row.

Hales, C. (2001) *Managing Through Organization: The Management Process, Forms of Organization and the Work of Managers* (2nd edn), London: Thomson Learning Business Press.

Harlow, J. (1999) 'Men give 15 minutes a day to children', *Sunday Times*, 23 May: 5.

Harvard Business Review (1991) 'Debate: ways men and women lead', January–February: 151–60. It incorporates: Cohen, A.R. (p. 158); Epstein, C.F. (pp. 150–1); Goldberg, C.R. (p. 160); Mansbridge, J. (pp. 154–6).

Hayward, H. (1992) 'Management: theory and practice', in Fulop, L. with Frith, F. and Hayward, H. (eds), *Management for Australian Business: A Critical Text*, Melbourne: Macmillan 186–212.

Hearn, J. and Parkin, W. (1994) 'Sexuality, gender and organisations: acknowledging complex contentions', British Sociological Association Annual Conference, 'Sexualities in Social Context', 28–31 March, University of Central Lancashire, Preston, UK.

Helgesen, S. (1995) *The Female Advantage: Women's Ways of Leadership*, New York: Currency/Doubleday.

Hersey, P. and Blanchard, K.H. (1996) *Management of Organizational Behavior: Utilizing Human Resources*, Englewood Cliffs, NJ: Prentice Hall.

Hines, R. (1992) 'Accounting: filling the negative space', *Accounting, Organizations and Society* **17**(3): 314–41.

Holtermann, S. (1995) 'The costs and benefits to British employers of measures to promote equality of opportunity', *Gender, Work and Organization* **2**(3): 102–12.

House, R.J. (1971) 'A path-goal theory of leader effectiveness', *Administrative Science Quarterly* **16**: 321–38.

Independent on Sunday (2000a) 'For 1984 read 2000: boardrooms are dominated by white males ... ', 5 March. Online. Available at: http://www.independent.co.uk/www (accessed 28 July 2000).

Independent on Sunday (2000b) 'The glass ceiling', 5 March. Online. Available at: http://www.independent.co.uk/www (accessed 28 July 2000).

Jackall, R. (1988) *Moral Mazes*, Oxford: Oxford University Press.

Jackson, N. and Carter, P. (2000) *Rethinking Organisational Behaviour*, Harlow: Financial Times/Prentice Hall.

Jones, G. (2000) 'Blair will not take full birth leave', Electronic Telegraph, 15 May, issue 1816. Online. Available at: http://www.telegraph.co.uk (accessed 4 August 2000).

Jones, G. and Barwick, S. (2000) 'Leo takes a firm grip on power', Electronic Telegraph, 23 May, issue 1824. Online. Available at: http://www.telegraph.co.uk (accessed 4 August 2000).

Kandola, R. and Fullerton, J. (1998) *Managing the Mosaic: Diversity in Action* (2nd edn), London: Institute of Personnel and Development.

Kasten, K. (1972) 'Toward a psychology of being: a masculine mystique', *Journal of Humanistic Psychology* **12**(2): 23–4.

Kaufman, M. (1994) 'Men, feminism, and men's contradictory experiences of power', in Brod, H. and Kaufman, M. (eds), *Theorizing Masculinities*, Thousand Oaks, CA: Sage, 142–63.

Kerfoot, D. (1999) 'The organization of intimacy: managerialism, masculinity and the masculine subject', in Whitehead, S. and Moodley, R. (eds), *Transforming Management: Gendering Change in the Public Sector*, London: UCL Press, 184–99.

Kerfoot, D. (2000) 'Body work: estrangement, disembodiment and the organizational "other"', in Hassard, J., Holliday, R. and Willmott, H. (eds), *Body and Organization*, London: Sage, 230–46.

Kerfoot, D. and Knights, D. (1993) 'Management, masculinity and manipulation: from paternalism to corporate strategy in financial services', *Journal of Management Studies* **30**(4): 659–77.

Kerfoot, D. and Knights, D. (1996) '"The best is yet to come?": the quest for embodiment in managerial work', in Collinson, D.L. and Hearn, J. (eds), *Men as Managers, Managers as Men: Critical Perspectives* on Men, Masculinities and Managements, London: Sage, 78–98.

Kerfoot, D. and Knights, D. (1998) 'Managing managerialism in contemporary organizational life: a "man"agerial project', Organization 5(1): 7–26.

Kerfoot, D. and Knights, D. (1999) '"Man" management: ironies of modern management in an "old" university', in Whitehead, S. and Moodley, R. (eds), Transforming Management: Gendering Change in the Public Sector, London: UCL Press, 200–13.

Kettle, M. (2000) 'Blair "defies dad's instincts"', Guardian Unlimited, 17 June. Online. Available at: http://www.guardian.co.uk (accessed 4 August 2000).

Lennie, I. (2000) 'Embodying management', in Hassard, J., Holliday, R. and Willmott, H. (eds) Body and Organization, London: Sage, 130–46.

Linstead, S.A. (2000) 'Gender blindness or gender suppression? A comment on Fiona Wilson's research note.' Organisation Studies 21(1): 1–7.

Lorbiecki, A. and Jack, G. (2000) 'Critical turns in the evolution of diversity management', British Journal of Management, Special Issue, 11(s1): S17–31.

Lowry, R. (ed.) (1982) The Journals of Abraham Maslow, Brattleboro, VT: Lewis Publishing.

McDowell, L. and Court, G. (1994) 'Performing work: bodily representations in merchant banks', Environment and Planning D: Society and Space 12: 727–50.

McNeil, M. (1987) 'Being reasonable feminists', in McNeil, M. (ed.), Gender and Expertise, London: Free Association Books, 13–61.

Maddock, S. and Parkin, S. (1993) 'Gender cultures: women's choices and strategies at work', Women in Management Review 8(2): 3–9.

Marshall, J. (1995) Women Managers Moving On: Exploring Career and Life Choices, London: Routledge.

Martinez, M. (1997) 'Prepared for the future: training women for corporate leadership', HRMagazine, April. Online. Available at: http://www.shrm.org/hrmagazine/articles/0497cov.htm (accessed 7 February 1998).

Maslow, A. (1939) 'Dominance personality and social behaviour in women', Journal of Social Psychology 10(1): 3–39.

Maslow, A. (1954) Motivation and Personality, New York: Harper.

Matteson, M.T. and Ivancevich, J.M. (eds) (1989) Management and Organizational Behavior Classics, Homewood, Ill: BPI, Irwin.

Mayo, E. (1945) The Social Problems of an Industrial Civilization, Boston, MA: Division of Research, Graduate School of Business Administration, Harvard University.

Mayo, E. (1960 [1933]) The Human Problems of an Industrial Civilization, New York: Viking Press.

Meehan, D. (1999) 'The under-representation of women managers in higher education: are there issues other than style?', in Whitehead, S. and Moodley, R. (eds), Transforming Management: Gendering Change in the Public Sector, London: UCL Press, 33–49.

Nicolson, P. (1996) Gender, Power and Organisation: A Psychological Perspective, London: Routledge.

Nisse, J. (2000) 'Such great power, so few hands', Independent on Sunday, 5 March. Online. Available at: http://www.independent.co.uk/www (accessed 28 July 2000).

Norton, C. (2000) 'Men "prolong low pay for women"', Independent, 15 September: 9.

Nyland, C. (1989) Reduced Worktime and the Management of Production, Cambridge: Cambridge University Press.

Nyland, C. (2000) 'An early account of scientific management as applied to women's work with a comment by Frederick W. Taylor', Journal of Management History 6(6): 248–71.

O'Donovan, K. (1985) Sexual Divisions in Law, London: Weidenfeld & Nicolson.

Oerton, S. (1996) 'Sexualizing the organization, lesbianizing the women: gender, sexuality and flat organizations', Gender, Work and Organization 3(1): 26–37.

Parker, B. (1998) Globalization and Business Practice: Managing Across Boundaries, London: Sage.

Quelch, J. (2000) 'Meet Britain's real rulers: the first men of the Footsie', Independent on Sunday, 5 March. Online. Available at: http://www.independent.co.uk/www (accessed 28 July 2000).

Reynolds, L. (1992) 'Translate fury into action', Management Review 81(3): 36–8.

Roethlisberger, F.J. and Dickson, W. (1939) Management and the Worker: An Account of a Research Program, Conducted by the Western Electric Company, Hawthorne Works, Chicago, Cambridge, MA: Harvard University Press.

Rosener, J.B. (1990) 'Ways women lead', Harvard Business Review November–December: 119–25.

Rosener, J.B. (1997) America's Competitive Secret : Women Managers, Oxford: Oxford University Press.

Rosenfeld, R.H. and Wilson, D.C. (1999) Managing Organizations: Text, Readings and Cases, London: McGraw-Hill.

Sheppard, D.L. (1989) 'Organisations, power and sexuality: the image and self-image of women managers', in Hearn, J., Sheppard, D.L., Tancred-Sheriff, P. and Burrell, G. (eds), The Sexuality of Organisation, London: Sage, 139–57.

Sinclair, A. (1998) Doing Leadership Differently: Gender,

Power and Sexuality in a Changing Business Culture, Melbourne: Melbourne University Press.

Sloan Management Review (1995) 'CEO Thought Summit', **36**(3): 13–21.

Solonas, V. (1983) *SCUM Manifesto*, AIM/Phoenix Press.

Swan, N. (1996) 'Interview with Daniel Petrie', Radio National (Australia), 26 September.

Tannen, D. (1993) *You Just Don't Understand: Women and Men in Conversation*, London: Virago.

Taylor, F.W. (1947 [1911]) *Scientific Management*, New York: Harper & Row.

Teigen, M. (1999) 'Documenting discrimination: a study of recruitment cases brought to the Norwegian Gender Equality Ombudsman', *Gender, Work and Organization* **6**(2): 91–105.

Thomas, D.A. and Ely, R.J. (1996) 'Making differences matter: a new paradigm for managing diversity', *Harvard Business Review* September-October: 79–90.

Thomas, R. (1999) 'Who's wearing the apron?' *Observer*, 31 January: 18.

Thomas, R.R. Jr (1990) 'From affirmative action to affirming diversity', *Harvard Business Review* March–April: 107–17.

Thomas, R.R. Jr (1991) *Beyond Race and Gender: Unleashing the Power of Your Workforce By Managing Diversity*, New York: AMACOM.

Tienari, J. (1999) 'The first wave washed up on shore: reform, feminization and gender segregation', *Gender, Work and Organization* **6**(1): 1–19.

Tomlinson, F., Brockbank, A. and Traves, J. (1997) 'The "feminization" of management? Issues of "sameness" and "difference" in the roles and experiences of female and male retail managers', *Gender, Work and Organization* **4**(4): 218–29.

Trahair, R.C.S. (1984) *The Humanist Temper: The Life and Work of Elton Mayo*, New Brunswick, NJ: Transaction Books.

Urwick, L. (1969 [1937]) 'Organization as a technical problem', in Gulick, L. and Urwick, L. (eds), *Papers on the Science of Administration*, New York: Augustus M. Kelley, 49–88.

Vincent, P. (1998) 'She'll be right mate', *Sydney Morning Herald*, 2E. Saturday, 5th September, page 1 (Employment Section).

Vine, P. (1997) 'Battling the myth of superwoman', *British Journal of Administrative Management* November–December: 12–13.

Wajcman, J. (1998) *Managing Like a Man : Women and Men in Corporate Management* University Park, PA: Penn State University Press.

Walby, S. (1997) *Gender Transformations*, London: Routledge.

Ward, L. and Black, I. (2000) 'The big question: will this woman's husband take paternity leave?', *Guardian*, 24 March: 3.

Weiss, R. (1997) 'Evolving view of chimp communities: dominant females' reproductive success suggests new hierarchy model', *The Washington Post*, 8 August: A03.

White, J. (1995) 'Leading in their own ways: women chief executives in local government', in Itzin, C. and Newman, J. (eds), *Gender, Culture and Organizational Change: Putting Theory into Practice*, London: Routledge, 193–210.

Whitehead, S. (1999) 'New women, new Labour? Gendered transformations in the House', in Whitehead, S. and Moodley, R. (eds), *Transforming Managers: Gendering Change in the Public Sector*, London: UCL Press, 19–32.

Whitehead, S. and Moodley. R. (1999) 'Introduction: locating personal and political transformations', in Whitehead, S. and Moodley, R. (eds), *Transforming Managers: Gendering Change in the Public Sector*, London: UCL Press, 1–15.

Williams, C.L. (1995) *Still A Man's World: Men Who Do 'Women's Work'*, Berkeley, CA: University of California Press.

Wilson, F.M. (1995) *Organisational Behaviour and Gender*, London: McGraw-Hill.

Wilson, F.M. (1996) 'Research note: Organisation theory: blind and deaf to gender?', *Organisation Studies* **17**(5): 825–42.

Wollstonecraft, M. (1970 [1792]) *A Vindication of the Rights of Woman* (2nd edn), Farnborough, Hampshire: Gregg.

Zafarullah, H. (2000) 'Through the brick wall and the glass ceiling: women in the civil service in Bangladesh', *Gender, Work and Organization* **7**(3): 197–209.

Managing culture

Stephen Linstead

Questions about culture

1 What is organizational culture? What is it good for?
2 Are companies with strong cultures always successful?
3 What are the dysfunctions of culture?
4 What are subcultures, and are they healthy?
5 How is organizational culture related to national culture?

CULTURE AT COMPANY T

Company T is a Canadian automobile assembly plant employing some 1300 people. In response to increased foreign competition, the corporation decided to implement a participative management programme focused on quality. In 1980, the plant hired consultants to help implement a quality of working life programme. The union refused to participate, but approved a participative management programme and the plant management decided to go ahead.

The plant was functionally organized, with a plant manager, assistant plant manager and six department managers, including industrial relations, controller, quality, operations, manufacturing engineering and materials. The plant ran two shifts a day and in addition to the operations manager, there were 2 production managers (one responsible for each shift), 8 superintendents, 22 general supervisors, 7 utility supervisors and 66 foremen, each of whom supervised up to 50 hourly workers.

As a result of problems encountered in the implementation of the QWL programme after two years, it soon became clear that while both consultants and managers had originally engaged in a process with social and technical redesign goals, the real challenge was one of cultural change and personal transformation. They were up against a distinctive and extremely strong company culture, whose assumptions were working a kind of sea change with their interventions, distorting their purpose and twisting their outcomes.

Aggression: 2 x 4 management

The culture of Company T was distinctive even by the estimation of company members. It positively sanctioned an aggressive macho management style, termed 2 x 4 management, which consisted of reprimands in the form of intensive verbal abuse ('yelling and screaming'), dramatic confrontations, and generally, figuratively, 'beating up' on offenders. Extreme examples of this behaviour had become myth in the organization and perpetrators were spoken of as something of folk heroes:

In the old days here, there used to be a lot of grandstanding, but a lot of it was for show. I can remember one day, 'X' came out onto the floor and he saw a piece that he did not like, and he started jumping up and down on it and he bashed it all in and yelling and screaming and then he said, 'Now throw it out, because it is not good for anything' and when he turned around, he winked at me. It was a show, it was fun, it was a game. It was just like a John Wayne movie, as soon as the movie was over with, they became human again.

The perception was that those who were good at 2 x 4 management got promoted at Company T:

If your boss catches you out, catches something wrong with the product in your area, you can respond in one of two ways. You can say, 'OK, I'll find out what's wrong,' or you can say, 'God dammit, it's John Smith. I'm going to call him in here and chew him out.' The second way looks much better, more glory in it.

This macho style was seen by many as being quite anachronistic, as representing a culture very distinct from the 'larger' culture in which managers spent their family, civic and recreational lives. Some experienced embarrassment when describing their work environment to their friends and families:

My brother, who is an accountant, says he cannot believe this place, that it is like a game instead of a workplace, but he thinks everything about this place is ridiculous.

And even the worst 2 x 4 managers were recognized as being quite different away from work:

Mind you, he was a fine fellow outside. He used to tell me that he kept his leopard skin suit in the guard house and would put it on when he came in. In the past, if you wanted to get ahead, you had to do a little more of the 2 x 4. The idea was, if you did not beat, you got beaten.

Managers referred to the company culture as a jungle, the workers as 'animals', the extreme 2 x 4 type managers as 'monsters', and yet, while many expressed aversion to the harsh style, others found it tough, 'honest', and, hence, appealing:

> I prefer the straightforward approach. I don't like the foul language. But I do not think people listen to you if you are a nice guy. I don't think people listen to [the assistant plant manager] as much as they used to. People are scared of someone who chews them out.

Competitiveness: 'shiftitus' and empire building

If the tough macho management style was one of the salient values underlying the Company T culture, the other was an intense competitiveness which manifested itself in two forms of behaviour: competition between shifts ('shiftitus') and lack of cooperation between functions ('empire building'). Both these forms of competition were highly valued. 'Shiftitus', with its disease-like connotations, was defined by one manager as 'we do not like to see the other shift run as well as we do'. It was intense in Company T. As mentioned earlier, there were two shifts, A and B. The two shifts were constantly compared and invited to compete in order to encourage people to work hard. At times, however, it got out of hand:

> It is a big game, to get the other guy. There is a lot of resentment and competition. We base everything on results and so people will resort to things like counting back on the line [including items made on the production line but not packed or despatched as shift output] to get a better count for their shift. Sometimes the foreman will lock up his tools so that the other people on the next shift will not get them. We have to do process books, to make sure things like tools and materials are exchanged, otherwise people start breaking into each others lockers. Rivalry is good but you have to keep the lid on.

Despite the recognized damage and waste incurred by the competition, it had some defenders. These fell into two categories. There were those who felt that, in general, it was healthy because it fostered 'good, clean competition'. Others felt that it was part of the fun of working at Company T. It was a macho, competitive, street-fighting world:

> I knew everything about the machines in my area and I used to turn up the speed on the line for brief periods of time so that my boys could produce more units than the other shift. Sometimes the foreman from the other shift would sneak in early to make sure I was not going on overtime. But I just knew to regulate the line and get things done faster and I had everyone behind me, my boys loved to do it that way. They loved to shove it in their [the other shift's] face.

Similarly, functional loyalty was very strong in Company T. This was sometimes referred to as 'empire building' and

permeated all levels of the organization from the operating committee down:

> It is really incredible how one unit pits itself against another in this place. It is as if there is a wall at the end of each unit, and anything that passes through that wall is no longer a problem for that unit. People pass things along because there is always pressure, there is always pressure to deliver the numbers. Despite all the lip service about quality being most important, if you do not get the numbers, you get nothing.

Lying, cheating and stealing culture

While the two values of 2 x 4 management and competitiveness formed the basis of the company culture, pursuit of these values on the individual level was commonly recognized as resulting in a set of interconnected assumptions about behaviour which were widely recognized as dysfunctional. On an individual level, the 2 x 4 management led to considerable fear of being exposed and humiliated and forced people into a secretive, self-defensive, mode termed 'covering ass':

> I've had it solid, with that 2 x 4 style, it nullifies you. You just start covering ass and playing your cards close to the vest. You collect a lot of excuses and you are ready to hand them out if anything comes up. So the problems never get solved.

The competitiveness, on the other hand, meant that functions and shifts worked actively to pass the buck, passing poor quality products from one department to another, failing to take responsibility for product defects, and rushing faulty products out the door in an effort to 'beat' the other production shift in a race for numbers. This activity was known in the culture as 'shipping shit':

> The biggest problem around here is that there is no trust, no one wants to get blamed for anything. So say the sealer goes bad and you know how to fix it, but you do not fix it, what you do is to call maintenance or to call industrial engineering. That way they get stuck with the problem and you do not get chewed up for it. It could be that it was your fault, that your guys screwed up the gun, but you try to cover that up and get it pinned on maintenance and engineering. For example, if you had a big hole, it might be something you could fix, but if you fixed it too many times, then it would become your responsibility, you would pick up the job and you can't hold that job.

The need to hide personal and functional problems and failures, fuelled by the desire to be competitive and to win, combined with the fear of retaliation resulted in tacit acceptance of all kinds of rule breaking which managers in Company T called 'lying, cheating, and stealing'. Essentially, these terms referred to the concealing of information, parts and personnel and was viewed as a 'survival tactic':

> This culture [lying, cheating, and stealing] is still important, this is how they survive. If someone gets on their back, they say 'we know how to fix that: lie, cheat, and steal'. There is not real progress there. There is a recognition that it is a problem, but to tell

you the truth I think [the assistant plant manager] does it as well. He lies, cheats and steals to get the plant manager off his ass.

'Lying, cheating and stealing' also involved concealing (stockpiling) parts, hiding personnel and falsifying reports concerning injuries, defects and manpower:

The book records say that we have a million dollars of obsolete material. But before the last launch, we shipped it out and it turned out to be 2 million dollars worth. There are kitties all over the place. Foremen squirrel things away that they think they need. Foremen get hit over the head all the time for scrap, so it is better to hide it away and call it lost stock. I think I would do the same thing. But it makes for a lot of waste in the system.

Another example is, if you are running rough on certain parts of the line and defects come up, someone will stamp it off so that it does not show up as a loss for our department. That is dangerous, it is just bad for the company. We are more concerned about covering ass than quality or quantity. We would rather run with one man less than we need to do the job properly. We expect the repairmen to pick up the slack. If the repair does not get it, it goes out and the warranty gets it.

Again, as with competition and the macho style, lying, cheating and stealing, while felt by some to be dysfunctional, were seen by others as simple flexibility, with the goal of getting the job done. This perspective is not unusual and often forms an important aspect of the informal value system of organizations:

We all fight to keep down costs, but ... costs are still way out of control. But you know, it is mostly the new supervisors whose budgets are way over. If they understood the old system better, they maybe would lie, cheat, and steal a little and would be better off. Old supervisors who know the ropes, his budget will always be under ... lying, cheating, and stealing is a system which has worked. Everyone watched what they spent and they stayed on their toes ... Most seasoned supervisors can keep it within limits.

Finally, of course, there were those who perceived the lying, cheating and stealing as part of the fun of Company T culture. It represented a kind of freedom to wheel and deal, to live by your wits. It was perceived as a game with its own challenges and satisfactions, a healthy environment for those that survived. Part of the difficulty in introducing change was that many managers liked the excitement and the subterfuge. They had survived in Company T because they were good at playing a game and holding a job which required considerable skill, knowledge and personal toughness.

Source: Adapted from Frances Westley (1990) 'The eye of the needle: Cultural and personal transformation in a traditional organization', *Human Relations*, 43(3): 273–93. Reprinted by permission of Sage Publications Ltd. Copyright © The Tavistock Institute 1990.

QUESTIONS ABOUT THE CASE

1 Does company T have a shared culture?
2 Is company T a 'strong' culture?
3 What are the problems of the culture?
4 Do you think the company can be changed?

Introduction

Organizational culture has become an essential element in our understanding of organizations. There is an interrelatedness between this and other concepts such as leadership, organizational structure, motivation, power and strategy. The rise of the popularity of the organizational culture concept in the 1970s and 80s, offering as it did to secure employee commitment, coincided with the relative decline in both the popularity of and research interest in the field of motivation. Although culture was often presented as the 'answer' to the problems of failing companies, Peter Anthony (1994: 6), in discussing one of the few longitudinal studies of organizational change, notes that 'the attempt to change corporate culture was accompanied by complex political processes and structural adjustment' and later comments 'the case for culture cannot win; if change is confined to culture it will not work, if accompanied by structural change it

cannot be isolated as crucial to success' (Anthony 1994: 15). More recently, there has been a growing recognition that it is impossible to extricate culture as a 'variable' from other elements of the organizational context. Nevertheless, one of the main reasons for the rise in interest in organizational culture was to understand how it impacts on organizational change; for a time it was seen as the hidden obstacle to success.

The growing concern with the economic ascendancy of Japanese companies and the need to dismantle the crumbling industrial bureaucracies of the West at the end of the 1970s fuelled the dramatic rise of the organizational culture or 'excellence' literature (see Pascale and Athos 1980; Deal and Kennedy 1982; Peters and Waterman 1982). Old structures and the old-fashioned values associated with them needed to be replaced, but with what? Thomas Peters and Robert Waterman and Terrence Deal and Allen Kennedy were in no doubt that 'strong' cultures were the key to prosperity. The suggestion was simple, timely, flattering and inspiring in its concern with success, and comforting in its implication that for a company to become successful it simply had to change its core values (Guest 1992; Anthony 1994: 16).

Unfortunately, most of the major culture changes of the 1980s were accompanied by major downsizing or divestment and depended significantly on size and growth strategies (see Chapter 15). This is not to deny that culture is an important dimension of organization, although it does seem to be easier to argue for culture as a barrier to change (Johnson 1992) than as a guarantor of success. Steven Feldman (1996) argues that culture is neither one thing nor the other, and is simultaneously both an obstacle to change and a ground for creative development – it forms the *context* for action. Frances Westley (1990), as we have seen above, provides an example of a culture with which no one was happy but to which almost everyone subscribed, in an organization that was committed to conflict, violent and abusive management and internal competition. Company T, as Westley calls it, was proud of its '2 × 4' management, which dealt with people verbally as though they were hitting them with a 2 × 4 inch plank of wood; 'shiftitus' where shifts doing the same job would strive to better each other to the extent of damaging overall performance; and 'lying, cheating and stealing', which was basically do or say anything to make yourself and your group look good and everyone else look bad. The people who worked in this system did not like it, nevertheless it was powerful and they felt unable to change it; as a culture it was just as 'strong' and pervasive as McDonald's or IBM but worked against organizational effectiveness.

The origins of organizational culture

The idea of culture in relation to organizations has a long, but tortuous history (Chan and Clegg 2002). The initiatives of nineteenth-century work reformers such as Robert Owen were foundational in setting an agenda for industrial organization in cultural as much as organizational terms, and ethical capitalists such as Joseph Rowntree and Edward Cadbury saw their mission in sociocultural as well as business terms. Indeed even Taylor's scientific management had important cultural objectives, which threatened the subcultural influences of both organized labour and management. From the 1920s, at least, it was overtly recognized that the social dimensions of work are important elements of effectiveness through the Hawthorne Studies, which also identified the critical function of the supervisor or shop-floor leadership (see Chapter 10). But it was Elliott Jaques (1952) who perhaps first coined the term 'culture' in relation to work organization in *The Changing Culture of a*

Factory, which was part of a series of accounts of participatory management in the Glacier metal company, although structure (that is, size and design of the organization), reward systems and the use of hierarchy (that is, different layers of authority from top management to shop-floor supervisors) were also important to the success of the project.

During the following years, organizational psychologists such as Chris Argyris (1964) were beginning to note the importance of the subconscious dimensions of organization and its psychological health. In the 1950s Alvin Gouldner, a sociologist, also identified the importance of the implicit dimensions of working life that were taken for granted, in two books, *Wildcat Strike* (1955) and *Patterns of Industrial Bureaucracy* (1954). In the first he tells the story of a gypsum mine in which the local managers had been accustomed to letting the men have little favours – borrowing equipment, leaving early, taking breaks and so on – in return for working committedly when necessary. The mine was taken over by new management from outside the area – 'cosmopolitans' – who did not understand the implicit system of concessions and obligations (which Gouldner called the *indulgency pattern*) and immediately tightened up discipline and rules. The workforce did not like this and performance dropped, culminating in a 'wildcat strike' when one of the workforce was dismissed for an infringement which had been normal practice under the old regime (see also Chapter 6).

Another related development in the 1960s was the discovery of *negotiated order theory*, which was based on work done in psychiatric hospitals by Anselm Strauss and his colleagues (1963). What Strauss et al. argued was that hospitals are composed of different groups or 'congeries' of professionals and non-professionals. Each of these groups has an interest in how, for example, a patient is managed, treated by drugs, given occupational therapy or cared for on the ward, and each has an influence over how the actual treatment happens in practice (think of a time you may have spent in hospital: Did you prefer it when one doctor saw you rather than another? When one shift of nursing staff was working rather than another? How about the cleaners or voluntary workers? How did the presence and behaviour of the other patients affect your treatment? Did you ever notice any tensions between groups of staff?). Strauss et al. argued that each of these groups had a view about what made their job easier, what should be their responsibility and into what decisions they should have an input; each also had a view about what was morally and ethically desirable behaviour. In addition, individuals within groups developed relationships with particular patients and shared these perceptions over time, individuals have careers and even patients can have 'sick careers', and there were always issues of power and resource allocation in the background. Strauss et al. argued that the way things were done was constantly shifting and realigned from time to time, there were implicit rules as well as explicit ones, and groups customarily *negotiated the order* of how things happened, consciously and unconsciously. A good film to watch, which relates to negotiated order, power and culture, is *One Flew Over the Cuckoo's Nest* (1975) starring Jack Nicholson and directed by Milos Forman (see also Chapter 6).

Around the same time, Harold Garfinkel (1984 [1967]) was developing *ethnomethodology*, a form of sociology which concentrated on the ways in which people make sense of their social situations, that stressed the importance of unspoken rules, talk, common sense and the taken-for-granted aspects of social life. The idea of *membership* was also important to Garfinkel, and particularly the things people had to learn to become a 'member' of a social group. Much of Garfinkel's work overlapped with the work of anthropologists, who customarily studied exotic societies, and in 1971 Barry Turner (who was influenced by the work of Garfinkel and the philosopher Alfred Schütz, on whose work Garfinkel based many of his ideas) published the first book, *Exploring the Industrial Sub-Culture*, to bring the two disciplines together in looking at the way stories, rites, rituals and humour shaped behaviour in organizations. Turner's book did not have immediate impact but is recognized as having been pioneering some 25 years later.

Related to the emphasis of this work on the non-obvious, and the importance of the implicit and taken-for-granted in forming our experience of organizations, some social psychologists involved in organizational change, who called themselves organizational development (OD) specialists, began to recognize the significance of the unsaid as a barrier to transformation. They often argued that their work was to bring out the unconscious obstacles to organizational change, as a form of cultural intervention. So ideas of culture, in relation to organization and organizational change, had been around for quite a while before the 'excellence' literature picked them up, but in contrast to that literature they emphasized *the implicit and unconscious* elements of experience and *the processes of sense making and meaning making* rather than the content of communication and the explicitly expressed values (see Chapter 1).

Jim Olila (1995) argues that in the tradition of the study of the non-obvious, anthropologists who study organizations are interested in the tensions that people experience as a series of 'gaps' in their organizational experience. Not exactly creating a definition of culture, he suggests that in practical terms cultural tension as the object of investigation can be seen as 'gaps'. These gaps are described as:

- the *ideal/real* culture gap (the tension between what ought to be done and what actually takes place)
- the *formal/informal* culture gap (the tension between the official, often written description of who, what, why and when in an organization versus the unofficial, unwritten, yet frequently the most comfortable, traditional or successful ways of getting things done by those who are deemed best, most fun or most compatible for the job or task regardless of their official position, title or duties)
- the *overt/covert* culture gap (the tension between known and publicly acknowledged ways of thinking, feeling and doing and those known ways which are never spoken about, the shadowed or occluded areas of the culture)
- the *conscious/unconscious* gap (the tension between ways of thinking, feeling and doing in which we are aware we participate and those in which we engage but are not aware are taking place).

He also argues that this approach recognizes the complexity of everyday life: rather than having *single* identities, loyalties and experiencing the *same* reality, we all have *multiple* identities, loyalties and experiences of reality, and the exciting thing about investigating organizational cultures is teasing out this tissue of differences and seeing how it works or can work better. In a management sense, we are talking about the *management of diversity*.

Charles Hampden-Turner (1990) also draws on anthropological sources and argues similarly that culture is a response to human *dilemmas*, a means of problem solving. Human beings are faced with alternatives in living their lives in a very fundamental way: how to develop communities; how or whether to cultivate the land; whether to be dominating or cooperative as a society; how to arrange for procreation and succession of the race; how to manage time and adapt to the climate; whether to be individualistic or group-oriented. Some of these things, through mutual interaction over time, become shared and common; others become more elaborated and differentiated, a result of the difference that Olila identifies. In organizational terms, these dilemmas become formulated in such terms as 'the need to adapt the organization to a changing environment' versus 'the need to integrate members of the organization internally'; or 'the need for periodic change' versus 'the need to preserve key continuities'. Culture is what evolves to bridge these gaps.

Defining culture

Myriad attempts have been made to define culture, but this does not necessarily mean that the concept is elusive – on the contrary, the manifestations of culture are often very concrete in buildings and behaviours. Andrew Brown (1998) gives a list of what he calls *definitions* of culture, but in actuality, taken out of the context of the pieces of which they were originally part, most of them are just partial descriptions of culture, and all of them make some sense (see Exhibit 3.1). Brown also attempts to classify these into a rather crude structured hierarchy, but this is a confused and confusing exercise, as is his account of the development of theories of culture.

A useful collection of definitions can also be found in Martin (2002: 57–8) and Alvesson (2002) is also helpful. Paul Bate (1994: 20) seeks to examine what other writers have tried to define culture *as*, and also comes up with a wide variety of types of definition. But

his approach is both more subtle and theoretically alert than is Brown's. What Bate argues is that culture and strategy are not just related, or similar, but that strategy is a cultural phenomenon (an outcome of cultural processes) and culture is strategy (a way of dealing with problems so that living becomes easier). This does not mean that the culture of a company and its strategy will be seamless and supportive, but that work needs to take place in both areas simultaneously if either is to change. The issue of culture and strategy is explored further in Chapter 15. However, given Peter Anthony's argument that every culture change process has taken place at the same time as a structural change, so its effects are hard to measure, there is little wonder that the many attempts to isolate and measure 'culture' as a variable (from the early 'climate' studies onward) have tended to founder.

Exhibit 3.1 Some definitions of organizational culture

❏ The culture of the factory is its *customary and traditional way of thinking and doing things, which is shared to a greater or lesser degree by all its members*, and which new members must learn, and at least partially accept, in order to be accepted into service in the firm. Culture in this sense covers a wide range of behaviour: the methods of production; job skills and technical knowledge; attitudes towards discipline and punishment; the customs and habits of managerial behaviour; the objectives of the concern; its way of doing business; the methods of payment; the values placed on different types of work; beliefs in democratic living and joint consultation; and the less conscious conventions and taboos (Jaques 1952: 251).

❏ The culture of an organization refers to the *unique configuration of norms, values, beliefs, ways of behaving and so on* that characterize the manner in which groups and individuals combine to get things done. The distinctiveness of a particular organization is intimately bound up with its history and the character-building effects of past decisions and past leaders. It is manifested in the folklore, mores and the ideology to which members defer, as well as in the strategic choices made by the organization as a whole (Eldridge and Crombie 1974: 89).

❏ A set of *understandings or meanings shared by a group of people*. The meanings are largely tacit among members, clearly relevant to the particular group and distinctive to the group. Meanings are passed on to new group members (Louis 1980).

❏ Culture is *a pattern of beliefs and expectations shared by the organization's members*. These beliefs and expectations produce norms that powerfully shape the behaviour of individuals and groups in the organization (Schwartz and Davis 1981: 33).

❏ Organizational culture is not just another piece of the puzzle, it is the puzzle. From our point of view, a culture is not something an organization has; a culture is something an organization is (Pacanowsky and O'Donnell-Trujillo 1982: 126).

❏ A pattern of *basic assumptions* – invented, discovered or developed by a given group as it learns to cope with its problems of external adaptation and internal integration – that has worked well enough to be considered valid and, therefore, to be taught to new members as the correct way to perceive, think and feel in relation to those problems (Schein 1985: 9).

❏ The *shared beliefs* that top managers in a company have about how they should manage themselves and other employees, and how they should conduct their business(es). These beliefs are often invisible to top managers but have a major impact on their thoughts and actions (Lorsch 1986: 95).

❏ Culture is 'how things are done around here'. It is *what is typical of the organization*, the habits, prevailing attitudes and grown-up pattern of accepted and expected behaviour (Drennan 1992: 3).

Source: Adapted from Andrew Brown (1998) *Organizational Culture*, London: Pearson Education Limited, p. 6.

Exhibit 3.2 The sources of an organization's culture

According to David Drennan the twelve key causal factors which shape a company's culture are:

1 Influence of a dominant leader

2 Company history and tradition

3 Technology, products and services

4 The industry and its competition

5 Customers

6 Company expectations

7 Information and control systems

8 Legislation and company environment

9 Procedures and policies

10 Rewards systems and measurement

11 Organization and resources

12 Goals,values and beliefs

Source: Andrew Brown (1998) *Organizational Culture*, London: Pearson Education Limited, p. 42. Adapted from D. Drennan (1992) *Transforming Company Culture*, London: McGraw-Hill.

This empirical confusion has given rise to some theoretical confusion as well, as can be seen in Exhibit 3.2. Here Drennan identifies causal factors which determine culture, but of these several are structural factors, and some environmental. Items 1 and 6 might be components of corporate culture, but only item 12 would be considered to be part of organizational culture. Culture is not, as in Drennan's functionalist approach, about the content of causal chains; on the contrary it is about how factors that may or may not occur within causal chains are interpreted and become meaningful in the context of social action by members of the organization.

The question then remains: Is culture a factor for success? Despite the views of managers and consultants, research has been unable to demonstrate it, although there does seem to be some evidence that it has impact in particular combinations of factors, including economic climate, and that it can be a *barrier* to success (Barney 1986).

Culture is a means of finding a way to resolve differences, of helping people work together, often through symbols which work effectively without our having to think about them (see also Johnson 1992). We 'know' what things mean, without having to be too specific – in other words, symbols work best as an umbrella which is sufficiently general to contain a diversity of orientations (like the national flag of a country; the Union Jack of the UK actually combines elements of the national flags of England, Scotland and Ireland within it) rather than having a great deal of specificity. Ed Young (1989) and Stephen Linstead and Robert Grafton Small (1992) also argue that rather than culture being an exclusive expression of shared values, where it is most strongly expressed it is an attempt to contain potentially divisive difference and conflict. In short, if we all think the same we do not need to express it, we tend to accept it. In fact, we are not even aware that we do all think the same, because we accept our views as reality and don't positively choose to accept or reject alternatives. The historian Edward Gibbon once observed that the one feature that indicates that the Koran was written by an Arab is the complete absence of camels in the text. A Westerner trying to write a Middle Eastern document would think that camels were an important symbol of authenticity and would remark on them repeatedly; an Arab who saw them constantly, however, would take them for granted and think them not worthy of remark. This raises a major question about 'strong' visible cultures – to what unspoken problems are they a response, and what conflicts are being avoided or suppressed? Paradoxically, perhaps where cultures are most visible is where we should expect the deepest conflict and divergence of opinions.

Of course, *organizational culture* still relates in many ways to a system of shared meaning held by members that distinguishes the organization from other organizations, but this may not always be easy to articulate for the members. In fact, the concept of 'culture' relates to something that most of us can recognize from our experience of organizations, but is rather elusive when we attempt to define it. For Deal and Kennedy (1982) and Peters and Waterman (1982), culture is 'the way we do things around here' or 'the rules of the game for getting along in the organization'. For Linda Smircich (1983), culture is 'not something an organisation *has*, but something an organisation *is*'. In other words, an organization is a place where cultural processes happen, but it is also an outcome of those processes working in society. The organization itself is both a product and a producer of culture. This dual dimension is often missed by the more managerialist of commentators who seem to see culture as an object. But we can go further to suggest that cultural processes do not operate in a unified way – they are fragmentary, incomplete, contradictory, disrupted and neither stop nor start when we want them to. Although culture cannot be completely controlled, it can still be open to some manipulation.

Edgar Schein (1985) defines culture as 'the deeper level of basic assumptions and beliefs that are shared by members of an organisation, that operate unconsciously, and that define in a basic, 'taken-for-granted' fashion, an organisation's view of itself and its environment'. Schein has a model which identifies three levels of culture (as described in Figure 3.1). The three levels comprise: *artefacts* and *creations* (objects, buildings, uniforms, technology and so on); underpinned by *values* which are not visible, but of which we are or can be made aware; and *basic assumptions*, which are taken for granted, invisible, preconscious and hard to access. Furthermore, he argues that the culture reveals itself when it is most stressed, when presented with problems, rather than in its routine, which is similar to Hampden-Turner's dilemma-centred view of culture. This has an important consequence: to observe what a culture does when faced by problems, you have to be there, you cannot rely on questionnaires. Further, if culture is unconscious, it cannot be easily articulated; therefore questionnaires can only access the known, visible and pretty unremarkable aspects of culture. Nevertheless, many 'culture investigations', both academic and commercial, rely on such instruments. Whatever it is that these instruments elicit, Schein and others (especially social anthropologists) would argue, it is not culture.

Linstead and Grafton Small (1992: 333) argue that a distinction can be made between 'corporate culture' and 'organizational culture'. The former is:

devised by management and transmitted, marketed, sold or imposed on the rest of the organisation, with both internal and external images yet also including action and belief – the rites, rituals, stories and values which are *offered* to organizational members as part of the seductive process of achieving membership and gaining commitment.

The latter, however, is that which 'grows or emerges within the organization and which emphasizes the creativity of organizational members as culture-makers, perhaps resisting the dominant culture'. In other words, the organizational culture may consist of subcultures, it may be fragmented, but it will be the outcome of cultural processes which take place wherever human beings attempt to achieve a collective understanding of their everyday world by making it meaningful.

Joanne Martin (2002: 111–14) notes that there are distinctions that need to be made between the related concepts of organizational culture – organizational climate, organizational identity and organizational image (Ashkanasy et al. 2000). Organizational climate (Denison 1990) tends to take a psychological approach to the measurement of content themes (beliefs, values, basic assumptions) or informal practices (behavioural norms) while neglecting the cultural and symbolic forms – stories, physical arrangements, rituals, jargon – which are the core of organizational culture research. Climate studies therefore tend to take a narrow approach to cultural issues, and, insofar as they assume consistency of culture and climate, assume that the manifestations of culture in symbolic forms would be consistent with and predicted by the key measures upon

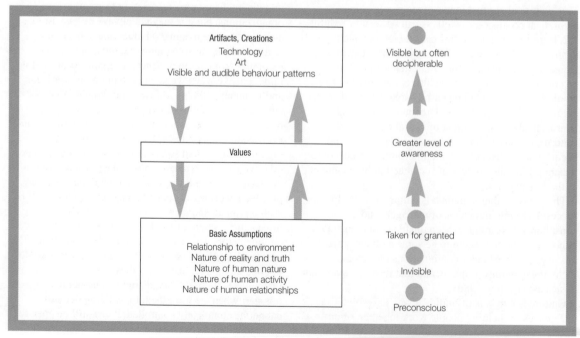

Figure 3.1 Schein's three levels of culture

Source: Edgar Schein (1985) *Organizational Culture and Leadership*, p. 14. Copyright © Edgar Schein 1985. Reprinted by permission of John Wiley & Sons, Inc.

which they concentrate their attention. Many culture researchers would disagree, and would argue that the distinction between the two lies in how they define *meaning* and what phenomena they consider to be significantly *meaningful*. *Organizational identity* (Hatch and Schultz 1997) refers broadly to what *members* perceive, feel and think *about their organization* and is thus less broad than culture. *Organizational image* is what the organization's *audiences* – customers, shareholders, regulators, key publics – believe to be its values and beliefs and their values and beliefs about the company. These images are projected outward and may then be absorbed back into the company's meaning system to affect its identity, that is, who we are and who we think we are is always in interaction with who others think we are. In this chapter, we will concentrate on the idea of culture only, but there will inevitably be points at which questions of image overlap.

Basic dimensions of culture

Organizational cultures, viewed as a whole, may vary along different dimensions. Brown (1998: 58) argues that the key dimensions are transparency/opaqueness and simplicity/complexity (see Figure 3.2). The first dimension relates to whether the culture is easily understood in terms of clarity, whether things are what they appear to be, whether the 'ropes' and rules of the culture are immediately accessible or whether they need to be discerned through experience and insight. This varies according to how tightly or loosely coupled the various elements of the culture are, and whether the actual culture corresponds to the espoused culture. The simplicity/complexity dimension refers to the quantity

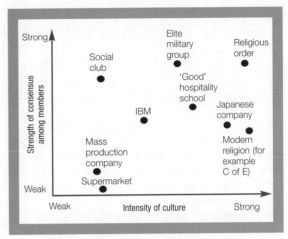

Figure 3.3 Examples of strong and weak cultures

Source: Andrew Brown (1998) *Organizational Culture*, London: Pearson Education Limited, p. 76. Adapted from Roy Payne (1990) 'The Concepts of Culture and Climate', *Working Paper 202*, Manchester Business School.

of cultural artefacts, beliefs and assumptions; the diversity of such items; and the number of embedded subcultures and their relationships to the dominant culture. Where a culture is both complex and opaque, it will take a newcomer considerably more time to learn how to 'fit in'.

Another commonly mentioned measure of organizational culture is strength or weakness. Brown adapts a formulation by Payne which regards strength as a production of the interaction of the widespread distribution of beliefs, or strength of consensus, and the intensity with which beliefs are held, or strength of feeling. These dimensions are illustrated in a range of organizations from supermarkets to religious organizations as shown in Figure 3.3. Taken in combination with the dimensions of transparency/ opacity and simplicity/complexity, the textural variety of cultures is readily apparent, although such schematic treatments of culture inevitably sacrifice subtlety and detail for the ability to contain a broad picture of cultural possibilities.

Strong cultures

Despite the variations to be observed in cultural strength, the literature has not been obsessed with cultural processes but with 'strong cultures' and how they can be created. Traditional control processes in organizations tend to operate through direct orders or programmes and procedures. Cultural control strategies tend, however, to operate by generating the consent of

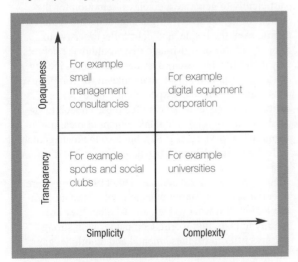

Figure 3.2 Culture and socialization

Source: Andrew Brown (1998) *Organizational Culture*, London: Pearson Education Limited, p. 59.

Exhibit 3.3 **Supervisory culture in Algiers and Montreal: managers' views**

The **good employee** *(who has the potential to become a foreman) is:*

- ❏ *submissive:* ever consenting, obedient and disciplined;
- ❏ *punctual:* doesn't lose a half-minute of production time;
- ❏ *serious:* 'doesn't talk', totally absorbed in his task;
- ❏ *malleable:* lets himself be 'formed', acquires the 'right' bent;
- ❏ *ambitious:* 'wants it', 'works his guts out' to succeed, gives 'his maximum'.

Foremen *should (in order of importance):*

- ❏ *achieve their assigned objectives:* quotas are first and foremost, everything else comes 'after';
- ❏ *set an example:* particularly concerning the points listed above;
- ❏ *be 'firm':* never yield on any issue, do not be 'soft', output before all else;
- ❏ *be a policeman with 'velvet gloves':* supervise and obtain productivity without problems;

- ❏ *'have a grip':* able to boss the men, the inflexible and uncompromising;
- ❏ *not 'try to please':* 'to please' the employees is 'playing their game';
- ❏ *know how to be tough:* 'deal severely with', 'sanction' and 'make an example of offenders to avoid shirking' on the part of the employees;
- ❏ *be 'able to solve his own problems':* 'to show initiative';
- ❏ but all the same, know how to 'communicate' while 'maintaining discipline' and 'not going further than he's asked'.

Formal criteria for the evaluation of foremen *in Montreal:*

- ❏ Production per line
- ❏ Production per machine
- ❏ Production per job
- ❏ Number of breakdowns
- ❏ Number of conflicts.

Source: Omar Aktouf (1996) 'Competence, symbolic activity and profitability', in Stephen Linstead, Robert Grafton Small and Paul Jeffcutt (eds) *Understanding Management*, London: Sage, pp. 66–77.

the workforce through the diffusion and popularization of either the culture of the senior management, or a culture which senior management popularize without actually sharing (Bate 1994: 39). The values and norms are first disseminated; then there may be some denial and censorship of alternate or oppositional views; finally there will be some attempt to define and limit the parameters of what is able to be discussed, and eventually people will internalize this and just avoid certain topics and lines of critique (Kirkbride 1983: 238). Interestingly, people tend to leave organizations when this happens. However, control is increasingly being exercised over sensory, aesthetic and emotional responses – people are being told what to feel as well as what to think, and these feelings are played on by culture manipulators. Omar Aktouf (1996), in Exhibit 3.3, outlines some of the characteristics which managers seek to disseminate among the brewery workers he studied.

Strong cultures are intended to engender commitment, dedication and devotion, enthusiasm, passion and even love in employees. And they can work, at least they can have great impact. If employees 'feel' for the company, if it touches them in some way, they will follow its leaders anywhere because they

value, even idolize, everything it stands for. Or so the argument runs. Arlie Hochschild's book *The Managed Heart* (1983) looks at the issue of emotional labour, where employees are required to manage their *selves* sufficiently to generate a display of emotion for the benefit of the company. Flight attendants are required to 'smile from the inside' and debt collectors have to project the sort of self-image that would make debtors pay their bills. Hochschild argues that human feeling has been commercialized, manipulated for competitive advantage. Companies expect their employees artificially to generate sincere feelings. The job of the leader then is not just the management of meaning (Smircich and Morgan 1982), but also the management of feeling (Bate 1994; Hancock and Tyler 2001: 125–49).

Employees, as Deal and Kennedy (1982) argue, are uncertain not only about what to think in the modern world, but also what to feel, and whether they are worthy to be in that world. Companies with strong cultures offer to fill these mental and emotional gaps; 'think this', 'feel this' and act accordingly and you will be worthy, they say (Schwartz 1990). Dedicate yourself to the company, constantly go the extra mile, love its products and services – Ray Kroc of McDonald's constantly urged his employees to love the beauty of a burger, an aesthetic which still escapes many of us – and success is virtually ensured.

Bate (1994) goes on to look at how order is maintained in strong cultures. He identifies six processes:

1. *Taking care of people* – making them feel safe, valued, comfortable and secure, fully employed and protected. But it also means, as Deal and Kennedy (1982: 56) put it, 'not permitting them to fail'. This is sometimes known as 'tough love'.

2. *Giving people their head* – people are given freedom, responsibility and considerable autonomy in how the task is achieved. But this freedom depends entirely on whether they 'deliver'. It requires the employee to take the corporate mission personally, to literally take it to heart. This is referred to as 'loose–tight' control (Peters and Waterman 1982: 318).

3. *Having fun* – criticism and resistance to control can be disarmed by encouraging an atmosphere of playfulness and a sense of fun. In many companies with strong cultures, joking is common, parties frequent, fancy dress, pranks and humorous gifts and spoof awards habitual. Everyone joins in; affection, loyalty and community are developed; having a good time and laughing at oneself are encouraged, while questioning the point of the event is discouraged. Not that employees do not see through the hokum – they acknowledge it *and* value it for its playfulness, its non-seriousness. In this way, criticism is neutralized (Willmott 1991: 10).

4. *Giving personal gifts* – companies can reward employees with personal gifts direct from the CEO after good performance. Scandinavian Airline Systems in Sweden (SAS) did this in 1982 with Jan Carlzon, the managing director, himself sending each employee a gold watch after a year in which the company returned to profitability (Carlzon 1987: 113). The range of gifts, being direct and personal, is supposed to have more impact than a mere monetary bonus. Bate argues that this affects the individual *cognitively*, that is, accepting the gift from the leader is tantamount to accepting the leader's definition of the corporate mission, and *emotionally*, as such a gift can physically trigger positive emotions about the company which can be recalled for a long period.

5. *Spelling it out* – the vagueness of feelings is always grounded in specific rules which define standards. Even if these rules are informal and implicit, violation of them can be serious to the point of termination.

6. *Getting heavy* – strong cultures, in short, need their 'bastards' to make them stick (Deal and Kennedy 1982: 56). Making visible public examples of people – one executive at National Cash Register (NCR) in the USA returned from lunch to find his desk and chair on the pavement and in flames – reminds everyone what the rules are and who has the power.

Finally, not only do strong cultures have to manage the positive, softer emotions like love and affection, but fear, anger and jealousy can be powerfully manipulated too. These issues are explored further in Chapter 9. They might not produce the apparent degree of unity behind the corporate mission or the sense of dedication and loyalty that the celebratory cultures do, but they are deeply ingrained and hard to dislodge. Both types of culture 'trap' people. Company T is an example of such a culture, as were many of the big engineering-based industrial bureaucracies that dominated Western smokestack industry for most of the twentieth century. Some of these companies have become dramatically smaller since the 1980s, but little seems to have changed in their cultures. Organizations with strong cultures not only seek complete loyalty and compliance from members but also try to become the dominant basis for a member's identity. Some regard these organizations as 'greedy institutions' that make extraordinary demands on individuals (Flam 1993: 62). Nevertheless, as Thompson and McHugh (2002: 207) note, because the vast majority of organizations have varieties of weak culture, and strong cultures remain comparatively rare, we should be cautious in employing approaches which may lead to 'underestimating both the fragility of corporate culture and the creative appropriation, modification and resistance to such programmes'.

Cultural heterogeneity

Organizational cultures, even when they do represent a common perception held by the organization's members, or a system of shared meaning, are not uniform cultures. Large organizations, like British Airways, might have one *dominant culture* expressing the core values of the corporation, which in a very general way are shared by most of the organization's members. They also have sets of *subcultures* typically, but not exclusively, defined by department designations and geographical separation (see Parker 2000 for a through discussion of the importance of subcultures supported by empirical evidence). However, as Hampden-Turner (1990) argues, the corporate response to tension between subcultures, as in that between the service elements and the operational elements in British

Exhibit 3.4 **Supervisory culture in Algiers and Montreal: the workers' view**

The workers' profile of an ideal foreman:

❏ 'competent', firstly;

❏ has confidence in us, doesn't feel obliged to be incessantly on the workers' backs;

❏ we can trust him, isn't 'two-faced';

❏ a man of his word, dignified, a 'true example';

❏ talks to the employees, listens, 'has a heart';

❏ 'respects' the employees, treats them like 'people';

❏ is fair;

❏ is not 'tense' (obsessed with output, and who transfers obsession to everybody).

The profile of the typical real foreman:

❏ 'Most of the guys are chosen (to become foremen) not because they're competent hard

workers, but because they're 'two-faced' or 'hard-headed'; these are guys who climb over the backs of their colleagues, I don't like that'.

❏ 'They don't know anything, don't do anything except try to catch you out just to shame you! Those are the types that are encouraged'.

❏ 'Good or bad, they're all the same. A dog doesn't eat dog, so they close ranks against us'.

❏ 'There are some here who only want to crush you, crush you with work and filth'.

❏ 'They never stop pushing. One might think they're only here to make trouble'.

❏ 'One time I injured my hand, blood was pissing out of me, and all the boss was interested in was that I fill out a report before going to the hospital! And they come around every year to shake your hand!'

Source: Omar Aktouf (1996) 'Competence, symbolic activity and profitability', in Stephen Linstead, Robert Grafton Small and Paul Jeffcutt (eds) *Understanding Management*, London: Sage, pp. 66–77.

Airways (BA), is what shapes the culture itself. His approach to culture seeks to identify key dilemmas. In BA, despite the undoubted success of the airline in turning itself round from public loss maker to private profit maker, there were divergences between the rhetoric of the corporate culture and its professed values, and what people reported as the reality. Aktouf (1996), in his ethnographic study of breweries in Algiers and Montreal, noted the same thing at an empirical level. There was a strongly articulated idealized view by the managers as to what their criteria for promoting supervisors were, as we saw in Exhibit 3.3, yet the workers' more realistic view of what it was necessary to actually do in order to get promoted diverged strongly from this, as we see in Exhibit 3.4.

Basic cultural types

Some commentators have attempted to identify basic types of culture found in organizations. These typologies are necessarily crude and general, but may nevertheless have value in broadly characterizing organizations. Perhaps the earliest such attempt was by Roger Harrison (1972) and later developed by Charles Handy (1993: Chapter 7). Harrison uses dimensions of centralization and formalization to identify four cultures – role culture, task culture, power culture and atomistic culture (which Handy calls a person culture)

as shown in Figure 3.4. *Formalization* refers to the extent to which rules, policies and procedures dominate organizational activities, while *centralization* refers to how much power and authority is concentrated at the top levels of an organization. Centralization is most evident in terms of what types of decision are allowed at various levels of an organization, particularly in authorizing and giving rewards to employees.

Ironically, Harrison's dimensions are in fact *structural* dimensions rather than cognitive or behavioural ones and are certainly not symbolic ones! However, what he is saying is that there are typical sets of behaviours, and associated mindsets, that tend to go along with particular structures, examples being project teams, big bureaucracies, small entrepreneurial companies or chambers of lawyers. Andrew Kakabadse, Ron Ludlow and Susan Vinnicombe (1988: 225–37) took the same framework but looked at what they called *power levers*, that is, the characteristic and different types of influence which work best in each culture. Again, in this example culture is difficult to separate from power and structure (see also Chapter 6). Their framework is described in Table 3.1.

Another typology was also attempted by Deal and Kennedy (1982) as shown in Figure 3.5. They related the amount of *risk* involved in the core activities of the company to the speed of *feedback on performance* to assess the organization's culture, which enabled them to categorize four main cultural types.

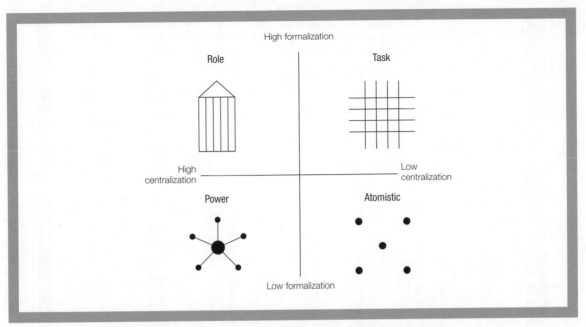

Figure 3.4 Culture quadrant by Roger Harrison

Deal and Kennedy's cultures are characterized as follows:

- The *tough-guy macho culture* A world of individualists who regularly take high risks and get quick feedback on whether their actions were right or wrong.
- The *work hard, play hard culture* Fun and action are the rule here, and employees take few risks, all with quick feedback; to succeed the culture encourages them to maintain a high level of low-risk activity.
- The *bet-your-company culture* Cultures with big-stakes decisions, where years pass before employees know whether decisions have paid off. A high-risk, slow-feedback environment.
- The *process culture* A world of little or no feedback where employees find it hard to measure what they do; instead they concentrate on how it's done. We have another name for this culture when the processes get out of control – bureaucracy!

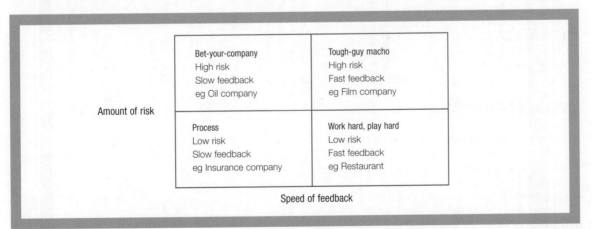

Figure 3.5 Simple quadrant by Deal and Kennedy

Table 3.1 Relationships between power-related behaviours and cultures

Types of power lever	Power culture	Role culture	Task culture	Person culture
Reward levers	Rewards offered for supporting key power figures	Rewards offered for following existing rules, regulations and procedures	Rewards for high task performance, project leadership, etc.	Acceptance by peers
Coercive levers	Mistakes, misdemeanours and actions punished if they threaten key power figures	Punishment for working outside role requirements or breaking rules, procedures or communication patterns	Focuses on low task performances or differences of expert opinion. Rejection from elite group or cancellation of project possible	Threatened by/with group expulsion
Legitimate levers	Rules and regulations can be broken by key power figures	Behaviour in keeping with defined authority, relationships, rules, procedures, job outlines and descriptions	Problem-solving ability through technical expertise. Senior management can be challenged on technical grounds	Behaviour according to needs of individuals in situation. Loyalty to those with whom one interacts, with allegiance to organization as a whole
Personal levers	Strong, decisive, uncompromising, charismatic behaviour. Manipulation by leaders. Low support for those who are not key power figures	Personal power from perceived rightful issuing, observance and interpretation of rules, procedures and allocation of work. Personal support offered only to fulfil role requirements	Status and charisma derived from problem-solving skills	Personal power through sharing and partnership. Personal growth, developing supportive environment
Expert levers	Knowledge and performance standards based not on professional criteria but on influence over others – political	Working solely within one's specialist role – not crossing boundaries or disturbing existing role structure	Constant skills development to solve new and more complex problems. Driving standards higher	Behaviour and work standards developed by group members at any one time. Individuals expected to adhere to current informal standards
Information levers	Information valued only if it helps achieve personal ends	Information flows according to role prescriptives and established patterns and procedures	Driving to acquire and share new information for better problem solving	Any relevant information to be shared among the group
Connection levers	Making numerous contacts and connections is vital, within and without the organization. Generates a closed shop culture	Contacts and connections only required to fulfil role demands according to regulations – e.g. health and safety advisers	Extensive network of experts inside and outside the organization. Loyalty to experts (profession, discipline) rather than organization	A personal sympathetic/ emotional link with others. Satisfy a need to be with people one likes

Source: Adapted from Andrew Kakabadse, Ron Ludlow and Susan Vinnicombe (1988) *Working in Organizations*, Aldershot: Gower, pp. 228, 229, 232, 234.

In Deal and Kennedy's scheme, the major influencing factor on the culture seems to be the *task* of the organization, coupled with the financial consequences of its operations. But feedback about task performance also affects the identity of employees, their sense of who they are in these companies. Collectively, groups develop patterns of behaviour which may become ritualistic; symbols and symbolic behaviours (or meanings associated with particular behaviours) which are peculiar to them; their own language and jargon; and stories, legends and traditions. These features help to establish meanings and beliefs and they are transmitted – as culture is a communicative phenomenon – through formal and informal socialization processes. The formal processes emphasized in much of the culture literature include:

- education and training
- selection and appraisal
- role modelling by superiors and peers
- leadership.

Culture and leadership

In particular, leaders can exert a powerful influence on the culture of their organization, especially if they are the founder. Organizations are replete with stories and myths about founders, and significant leaders who came after the founder. Leaders can shape the culture of their organizations by:

- what they pay attention to and notice
- their reactions to problems and crises
- role modelling, coaching, mentoring and teaching
- their criteria for selection, reward, promotion and punishment/sanction
- their influence on organizational structure and policy.

This is in general reinforced, or may be undermined, by its consistency of fit with:

- mechanisms of control in the organization (for example meetings, budgets, peer surveillance)
- organizational structure (for example size of subunits, levels of hierarchy, number of sites, distance of divisions from headquarters)
- organizational systems (for example types of production technology, operating procedures)
- formal statements (for example policies, reports, manuals, press releases).

We might think of the leader's actions (the first list) as the reality and the more formal arrangements (the second list) as the rhetoric or the difference between doing and saying. Sometimes bringing policy and practice into alignment is referred to as the need to 'walk the talk', which is not always easy to achieve. The study by Aktouf cited earlier revealed a glaring dichotomy, as he says:

the organization (i.e., its members) does the utmost to maintain an official discourse, and then acts in direct opposition to that discourse. When asked about the reasons for the systematic promotions of foremen whose behaviour and attitude are a blatant contradiction with the organization's official position, managers inevitably answer that it was 'because the workers did not want to be promoted'!

When companies are small and leaders can be visible and lead by example, the influence they can have over the development of the company can be much more directly felt than when they are CEOs of a large multidivisional company. Communication then becomes critical, but it is often seen as being one-way, the problem being defined as spreading the CEO's word to get people to follow, rather than increasing upward and lateral flows of communication to improve sharing, if shared meaning is really what culture is about. Two examples of this are illustrated below.

In 1988, at a management development seminar held at the Basingstoke Hilton in the UK, the arrival of the company's human resources director was preceded by a flurry of activity to present a well-ordered reception. He had masterminded the company's much vaunted and very successful culture change over the previous three years. The great man arrived, his acolytes running before him to announce his coming. The conference room was hushed. 'Now,' he began, 'the first thing I'd like to see is you all holding up your mission cards!' A forest of small cards rustled across the room as hands were raised in the apparent expression of a common faith. Within a year, the company and the great man parted abruptly at the chief executive's instigation.

On another occasion, at the end of a management development course, managers gathered at the company's country house management development centre. The chief executive was to arrive en route to the airport to take a flight to the Far East. He would interrupt his progress to present awards to the assembled managers. The morning was spent in preparation, scripting, the preparation of the ceremonials, the formal dressing, the arrangement of the setting, the rehearsal of the presentations, the preparation of the appropriate frame of mind. The chairman arrived. His limousine pulled up outside the centre and course participants, tutors and staff of the centre alike mentally came to attention. His hand was raised, the signal given and the ceremony began. The course participants went forward one at a time to shake hands with the incarnate author of their corporate performance. It was a dignified and solemn moment. He exchanged a few words with each of the managers in turn and many commented afterwards that he seemed 'quite human'. The performance completed, he gestured his valediction. A chauffeur ushered him to his waiting car, to the airport and to other incarnations, other performances.

Source: Adapted from Heather Höpfl (1996) 'Authority and the pursuit of order in organizational performance', in Paul Jeffcutt, Robert Grafton Small and Stephen Linstead (eds) *Organization and Theatre*, special issue of *Studies in Cultures, Organizations, and Societies*, 2(1), pp. 73–4.

The above quite empty incidents demonstrate how difficult it is for the CEO to change anything so 'deep' as culture with the customary methods in use. Much of the culture literature recognizes that meaning and common-sense understanding are the bedrock of culture, and that they are transmitted in some circumstances by stories, myths, rites and rituals (see Chapter 1). But primarily they are imparted by experience, especially shared experience, and the everyday occurrence of events which may be weakly and metaphorically described as rites, or storytelling. These rites have the advantage of being living and organic, changing and developing, rather than having the dead quality of the contrived stories which most companies now construct or stage-manage about their senior managers. For example, Michael Levin, the consultant who helped BA to change its culture in the 1980s, tells this story of the first day of the relaunched Super Shuttle service from London to Manchester, which provided hot breakfasts and newspapers for the first time:

We then had 96 people lined up in front of the BA desks. I was frantic. We were not clearing them fast enough. I tried to get some four-stripers [supervisors] to help but they said 'We are four-stripers, we can't do that'. But then I happened to see out of the corner of my eye that one of the managers was helping. Guess who it was – Marshall [the CEO]. They were in horror, they were aghast. (Young, D. 1989: 3)

While one might wonder what the CEO was doing at the check-in desks, and who on earth had trained him to

use the computer system, it makes a good story. BA modelled its changes on those at SAS, which had been described in the bestselling book *Moments of Truth* by Jan Carlzon (1987), its managing director. In the book, Carlzon tells an almost identical story of himself helping with the baggage on a flight, saying that he did it to emphasize to the workers that everyone at every level is responsible to the customer and if necessary should help out. BA and Marshall must have not only copied this example, with the slight change to check-in desks, and also contrived it, as Marshall had no skills and no experience in the airline industry, so if he was not to make things worse he must have been trained beforehand. If the incident ever happened, of course (other than Levin, neither the author nor his colleagues in several years of working and researching in BA was ever able to find anyone who actually witnessed the incident). Ironically, in June 1997, while BA was negotiating with the unions on a pay cuts and redundancy package, it was revealed that it was training its managers to operate flights and check-in procedures in preparation for a strike. It was widely felt that BA engineered the strike to break the union, and it completely backfired on management and the high-profile CEO Bob Ayling, who no doubt was planning a similar publicity stunt himself. However, by the time of the strike he was so unpopular with the customers he would have found it difficult to show his face in the check-in area. BA has since tried strenuously to rebuild both its public image and its culture, by reaffirming the importance of people (Walsh 1997).

Additionally, no matter how hard the CEO might try to motivate with corporate symbolism and ritual, and the issuing of mission statement cards to everyone, and even if the message is successfully bought by the shop floor, the level where culture hits a problem is the level where organizational politics is most keenly felt. Sometimes this is in senior management, sometimes at supervisory level, as in this short example.

Sometimes, workers find that managerial politics get in the way of their motivation to perform well in accordance with the 'mission' of the organization. Meeting production targets and delivering a quality product or service often conflict, and 'culture' is supposed to resolve these kinds of dilemmas. In a bakery in the north of England, where the workers in question were making mince pies for the early Christmas market, the workforce frequently showed considerable concern for their product's quality. They would often fail to pack pies which they considered to be substandard. Once a pie was made, the policy according to supervision was 'pack as much as we

It was very difficult for workers in this organization, with an understanding of the organization's mission and what the customer (who could easily be themselves) would want, to find that these considerations were overridden by internecine warfare between the plant manager and quality control. This is also difficult for CEOs to understand and hear about: people generally will not tell them; it will not appear as a response in a survey; and generally employees will be reluctant to reveal it to inquirers. Middle managers also experience difficulties with corporate culture initiatives, according to Anthony (1994: 64–77), because top management often engineers its culture change with staged performances, such as we have discussed, with the only real objective being to improve financial performance, not to change values. But they sell it to middle management as the great new initiative, and expect them to sell it to supervision and the shop floor. Supervision and the shop-floor workers have, of course, seen it all before and are typically cynical, they go along with change for a while but expect that top management will eventually show its 'true colours' with dismissals, redundancies, savage cuts, disciplinary measures or just plain heartlessness. Eventually this might happen, especially if top management never believed in the 'new order', but got their efficiency gains; the shop floor expected to be sold out and they were; and the middle managers who believed in and worked for the new cultural changes often feel deeply betrayed and cheated. It is now quite common to find managers still working long hours effectively, but who claim to have lower morale than ever. They work because of their professionalism, they say, not because of their 'commitment'.

Symbolic action

Jeffrey Pfeffer (1981) introduced the distinction between *symbolic management* and *substantive management* in the early 1980s, to distinguish between those acts of a manager which were done deliberately to carry extra meaning, and those which were part of the normal run of things. This distinction has been widely propagated, mostly by writers who have little understanding of the symbolic process. The corollary of this is that managers often believe that anything can become symbolic, but just because they think it *ought* to be does not make it symbolic. Neither does it make it inevitable that if it does become symbolic, the manager's preferred meaning will be the one that is taken (Feldman 1996). Of course, if you are the CEO and have the power, you are more likely to be able to make your meaning stick, at least in public. The stories about Marshall and Carlzon above were of 'symbolic' management, yet there is little *evidence* as to how these stories were received, although they were widely retold. But they were powerful images, and as such would be likely to circulate and have impact. Jack's rebuttal of the workers on the quality issue was no less symbolic, and delivered a powerful message to those involved, but it was not a memorable image.

Sometimes humour will be used to undermine the intended symbolic message. Acting symbolically is more a matter of acting publicly, in ways that give off powerful images which can easily be associated with the other more content-laden messages that are being given out. Ralph Halpern, for example, chairman of the UK Burton Group, a menswear manufacturer and retailer, always wore the group's clothes and insisted from the start that the companies' employees would 'wear the strategy' – actually wear the clothes which they were selling to the public. This gave a powerful message to the employees. Some years later, when the fifty-something Halpern, now Sir Ralph, was exposed for having an affair with an 18-year-old topless model, she revealed that he still insisted that she wear the group's products during their erotic assignations (luckily the group had by that time diversified into sexy lingerie!). The shareholders found this consistency symbolically reassuring, perhaps additionally consoled by his reported demands for sex 'up to five times a night'. Four days after his exposure they voted him Britain's best CEO remuneration package of £2 million p.a. and called him 'the greatest Englishman since Churchill'. Halpern was clearly no novice in the art of symbolic management as Gerry Johnson (1989: 547) points out. Back in 1977 when the Burton Group was in crisis, he obtained a reduction in capacity, which could have just as easily been obtained by closing several small plants, by closing the main headquarters plant in Leeds. He did this because the headquarters 'castle' symbolized the stability and complacency he wanted to challenge, and closing it down signalled that manufacturing was not the heart of the company, giving a much-needed boost to the retail section. The Burton turnaround was spectacular, with it becoming Britain's most profitable retailing group less than 10 years after posting a £13 million loss.

So although the idea of symbolic management is theoretically flawed and practically difficult to control, acts with strong symbolic associations and high image quality do seem to have an impact upon and help to change people's minds about a company, often without them knowing it, because symbols are effective, to the extent that they mean something without the 'reader' having to think about it. Some companies then fall into the trap of contriving images and events and symbolic performances, while others do not. The example below illustrates one extended metaphor that in the end had the opposite effect to what was intended.

CASE EXAMPLE

WHAT WERE YOU DOING THE DAY THE WAR ENDED?

The British Airways UK Sales Conference: September 1989

The following account of a piece of organisational theatre was provided by a participant. It demonstrates how meanings are invested in performance and what happens when the performance becomes insupportable.

That Autumn the airline business was buoyant. The company was achieving most of its revenue targets and people in the Sales Department were charged with anticipation. Every September, all members of the Sales Department, some three hundred people, are invited to participate in the Annual Sales Conference and this particular year everyone felt they really had something to celebrate.

The location and theme of the conference is always a fairly well kept secret. This adds to the general air of expectancy. Stories and anecdotes concerning previous conferences were rife. Rumours, predictions and theories about who, where and what were put forward by just about everybody in the weeks before the event.

The suspense was eased yet stimulated by the arrival of 'The Invitation'. The location was Gatwick or rather a four star hotel very close to it. The theme was announced as, 'What were you doing the day the War ended?' The Invitation itself came from the Allied HQ and was printed in a 1940s style. All those attending the conference were requested to dress in the attire which they felt best fitted in with the theme of the conference.

The conference itself started on a warm Saturday afternoon in September. It was to run through to Monday morning. A large majority of the participants had requested a day off for the Monday aware that alcohol and sheer exhaustion would necessitate at least 18 hours sleep after a 'good sales conference'.

The next thing to do was to hire a costume. This turned out to be quite costly despite sales teams using the same fancy dress hire shop and getting a bulk order discount. The cost of hiring the costumes, £35 for the weekend (washing, if necessary, was extra) promised to be well worth it. The first opportunity to 'dress up' came on Sunday morning. The scene at breakfast was extraordinary. Italian generals ate cornflakes with women from the French Resistance. An American five star general with foot long epaulettes on each shoulder politely ordered bacon, sausage and tomato. The Field Sales Manager, Adolf Hitler, swapped jokes with two young London evacuees who were fully kitted out with gas masks and name labels. The feeling of excitement continued as everyone boarded coaches taking them to the venue for the main conference seminar. Here an introduction to the proceedings was given by the Field Marshall, General Manager UK Sales. His role was to explain the campaign strategy, to identify the location of enemy action. He prowled up and down, pointing with his swagger stick to the battle lines drawn up on a wall chart.

And so the day went on. All the presentations contained innumerable references to war. The evacuees, French Resistance, Gestapo, American Generals, The Home Guard and the Medical Corps all listened dutifully. Lunchtime continued with the war-time theme. Wooden trestle tables, benches, masking tape crosses on the windows and a catering company's idea of what 1940s army rations might have been kept 'the troops' in the mood. Indeed, all the day's events were planned to keep people 'in the mood' but by 4.30 in the afternoon the proceedings began to drag. The novelty of being dressed as a Japanese Admiral or a Desert Rat began to wear off. The team from Northern England Sales who were all dressed as clowns began to have trouble with their face make-up. The Japanese Admiral finally discarded his heavy overcoat with a sigh of relief.

The presentations ran on. The event should have finished by 6.00pm but it was 6.30pm when the Field Marshall rose to give his final address. It was too late. He was confronted by a weary and lack-lustre assembly of ridiculously over-dressed, tired and irritated individuals who had enough of the 'performance'. As their leader tried to rouse them with exhortations to future performance targets their own performance and participation had become unbearable. They had thrown off their roles and the props which supported them.

Source: Heather Höpfl (1996) 'Authority and the pursuit of order in organizational performance', in Paul Jeffcutt, Robert Grafton Small and Stephen Linstead (eds) *Organization and Theatre*, special issue of *Studies in Cultures, Organizations, and Societies*, 2(1), pp. 74–5.

Culture and control

One of the earliest writers to publish a sociological critique of organizational culture, utilizing the work of Durkheim, Carol Axtell Ray (1986) argues that in the early years of the twentieth century, scientific management and associated techniques established what Weber (1964) termed *bureaucratic control*. In essence, the *manipulation of rewards* established, or rather bought, the workers' *loyalty*, which led to the organization's ultimate objective, *increased productivity*. After the impact of the Hawthorne Studies (see Chapter 2), recognition of the social needs of the workforce was increasingly taken into account. In this model of *humanistic control*, it was the provision of a *satisfying task or work group life* that produced worker *loyalty*, which in turn led to *increased productivity*. In more recent times, *culture control* has been achieved. By a *manipulation of culture*, including myth and ritual, the workforce comes to *love the firm and its goals* and as a result, we find *increased productivity*. Of course, reality is rather more complex than this, but the critique does have substance. For some commentators, cultural management is just the latest control strategy, a direct descendant of Taylorism, except that human control replaces technical control (see Boje and Winsor 1993: 66–7; see also Chapters 2 and 11).

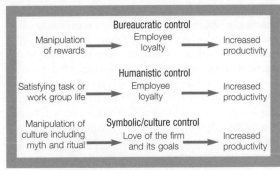

Figure 3.6 From bureaucratic to symbolic control

Source: Adapted from Carol Axtell Ray (1986) 'Corporate culture: The last frontier of control?' *Journal of Management Studies,* **23**(3), pp. 287–98.

In a similar vein, Smith and Wilkinson (1996) offer an unusual account of what they call a *totalitarian* culture. Sherwoods, the company they studied, is a progressive, non-hierarchical company, a very successful part of a hugely successful multinational. Pursuing 'furious interaction' and 'knocking the corners off politics' with a religious fervour that places everyone, even top management, in an open-plan office, they produce a self-policing conformity. Managers can

CASE EXAMPLE

SHERWOODS

The central feature of this organization is that it is both an open system and yet achieves unusually complete control. There is little scope for privacy. Managers have been active in bringing this about. 'We are our *own* policemen.' They are not passive 'cogs in a machine'. The family who own the company would not want them to behave mechanically. Anti-bureaucratic, relatively undifferentiated, this organization is *not an organization*. Yet its reach is very complete. This degree of control is exceptional: the institutionalization of cooperation; the exorcism of politics through the 'cleansing' effect of 'free speech'; job rotation between functions for managers – 'safer promotions'; and through keeping the characteristics of new recruits within known and agreed parameters – the 'sheep dip'. Sherwoods is a somewhat totalitarian system not in a fascist, violent sense, but because, research scientists excepted, who work in a separate building, it is *total*. It is full of methods for creating consent. Several of its officers reported that when they first came, they thought Sherwoods 'a bit funny', but they can 'see it as natural now'.

This lack of privacy precludes serious dissent. Criticism

is encouraged, but only within bounds. Excepting the unchallenged, strategic rules of ROTA (the accounting system – return on total assets), open management and FAN (social responsibility, lobbying and supplier control policy – friends and neighbours), day-to-day restrictions are set by the evolving collective conscience of the organization itself. Control is not imposed by *officers*. Control does not have a specific location. 'Everybody is at the heart of things', but everybody also has several others within their gaze, and everybody is clearly observed by others. Everybody is *central* both as a necessary agent and in terms of the encircling attention of co-agents.

Attentiveness is probably the best approximation of the way Sherwoods works. In any organization there are dividing lines and points of censure. But few would devote the attention that Sherwoods gives to happy 'separations', nor the obsessive degree of quality control, for which Sherwoods is well known. In this attentive organization, members are also held to attention. They are their own policemen.

Source: Adapted from Steve Smith and Barry Wilkinson (1996) 'No doors on offices, no secrets: We are our own policemen: Capitalism without conflict?', in Stephen Linstead, Robert Grafton Small and Paul Jeffcutt (eds) *Understanding Management*, London: Sage, pp. 130–44. Reprinted by permission of Sage Publications Ltd. Copyright © Sage Publications 1996.

be demoted by their subordinates if they are not performing, and they are paid well in excess of the industry norms in order to keep them – the 'golden handcuffs'. Smith and Wilkinson raise some disturbing questions about how conflict is apparently obliterated in this company, arguing that 'Sherwoods takes on a nightmarish quality because tight control co-exists with a high degree of autonomy and an almost citizen status for members. If there is an analogy with penal institutions, it is the open prison.'

Drawing on these critiques and examples, we can pick up two lines of critique which are essentially postmodern, that culture can be seen either in terms of *surveillance*, where control is exercised through peer observation and self-discipline, a view which will be explored further in Chapter 11 in relation to teams, or *seduction*, where people 'buy into' a version of their organization, which is in fact a fantasy, a blueprint copy of a supposedly successful original that never existed. In fact, many companies nowadays maintain control through a combination of both these strategies, as can be illustrated in Disneyland or McDonald's, where fantasy images of the company are used to sell the product, surface pleasantry is vital, but behind the smile are two very Tayloristic and disciplinarian corporations (see Ritzer 1990, 1999; Van Maanen 1991; Boje 1995).

The move from bureaucratic to symbolic control is in fact difficult for most organizations, but particularly those in which there are concentrations of professionals, such as hospitals, universities and other areas of public service. A number of studies have drawn attention to how public sector employees tend to have stronger union affiliations, strong client-based relations, weak identification with the employing organization, stronger identification with professional bodies and peers, considerable expert power (see Chapter 6), and are more likely to be oriented to ethical as opposed to commercial values (Sinclair 1991: 326–7). In recent cases, such as Enron (see further discussion in Chapter 17), a group of professionals within an organization may develop unethical values. Research from which these observations are made supports the view that professional public sector employees, such as clinicians, nurses, academics, welfare workers and engineers, are less likely to tolerate management-imposed constraints, will treat the organization as a means to an end and as a place to do the work they have chosen as a vocation or career. These professionals tend to strive for high levels of autonomy or freedom and generally have high expectations of achieving intrinsic self-fulfilment without strong identification with the organizations in which they work. Strong beliefs about public service, dedication or almost a 'calling' to the job, especially where there

are heavily client-based relations, such as with clinicians, strengthens the view that strong subcultures or multicultures flourish in these types of organizations (Eastman and Fulop 1997, citing Bovens 1992 and Sinclair 1991). As Amanda Sinclair comments, control through a dominant culture, especially one based on private sector models, such as McDonald's, might not be an appropriate management approach to integrate, accommodate or exploit the differences in organizations with strong multicultures (1991: 328–9). Moreover, many public sector organizations are recognized as having a range of governance or control structures, including collegial, bureaucratic and professional ones – the typical *knowledge organization* with a high concentration of experts – that defy one all-embracing culture (Sinclair 1991: 328, citing Benveniste 1987).

In many organizations there might also be different operational demands that encourage a 'culture' that is not easily brought under any group or individual's control. Members of the University of California, Berkeley, have been studying organizations that they describe as 'high-reliability organizations'. They have studied aircraft carriers, nuclear power plants, air traffic control systems and the operation of large electric power grids – organizations all likely to be involved in major crises, needing rapid response capacities and even having to deal with major catastrophes (Pool 1997: 44). In high-reliability organizations there is no one permanent structure or pattern of activity, in the sense that some groups operate bureaucratically and in a hierarchical manner, others in a professional and collegial way (as described above), while others operate in an emergency mode. The high-reliability organization, or the ones that seem to outperform others in their industry, has the capacity to have *everyone* switch between these modes of operating, depending on the situation. At any one time, all members might be operating in an emergency or crisis mode for a period of time. Communication in these organizations is intense, frequent and encouraged, as is the practice of challenging rules and procedures or looking for what can go wrong before it happens. Mistakes are not punished when someone is trying to do the 'right' thing. An inbuilt tolerance or expectation of ambiguity and uncertainty in management practices is the norm, which the researchers noted was one of the most unsettling aspects of these organizations. Often managers and employees alike struggle with this ambiguity because they believe that a well-functioning organization always knows what it is doing next and how (Pool 1997: 44–5). To sustain 'high reliability' literally means working with and encouraging multicultures as the basis of encouraging a 'culture' of learning (see also Pauchant and Mitroff 1988).

The cultural relativity of management

Another reason why values might be difficult to change could be the extent to which they are connected to wider cultural values which support them. Workforce diversity is increasingly a worldwide phenomenon. Many cultures still hold or have held parochial attitudes and ethnocentric views, even when their society is multicultural in its composition. Whether these biases translate into a predominantly monolingual society or an intolerance towards other cultural norms, it does prevent a country or organization from taking full advantage of the new global opportunities in faster growing regions like China and Asia-Pacific. That companies need to 'Think Global: Act Local', or practise globalization in the new world markets, has now become something of a cliché (see Torrington 1994). However, some writers have examined the consequences of the developing global–local dilemma (Humes 1993) and found that despite the visionary rhetoric, the practice is anything but simple. Hari Bedi (1991) provides an insightful analysis of globalization from the practising Asian manager's point of view, critiquing the extension of Western practices (ersatz capitalism) into other cultures, which themselves have long histories of civilization and their own complex social arrangements and values.

However, as Edward Hall (1959) argues, cultures are communicated by more languages than simply the verbal. Consider the following questions:

1. You arrive for a meeting with a business client at the scheduled time of 10:00. By 10:45 the client is still not ready to see you. What do you think?
2. You arrive for a meeting with an agent whose performance is likely to be very important to your operations. The agent's office is small, crowded and cluttered and in a seedy part of town. How is your confidence affected?
3. You arrive at the offices of a major supplier who has told you how well the business is doing. However, the managing director's office is almost bare, with simple furniture and little decoration. Do you still believe the company is doing well?
4. Your company asks you to review the restaurant of a friend as a venue for entertaining clients. The food is awful. Your friend tells you that he really needs the business and is relying on you for a good review. What do you do?
5. You have clinched the deal and shaken hands on it, but when you try to set a date to meet and sign formal contracts, the other party is reluctant to commit. What do you do?

Each of these questions would normally be interpreted as a warning signal in Australia, the UK or the USA.

But they would be answered quite differently in other cultures, such as South America, East Africa or Japan (where the Western haste to do business is often a disadvantage); the Middle East (where a crowded office is a good sign that the agent is busy and in touch with the action); Japan (where minimalist furnishing is a sign of great discernment and can even be more expensive than opulence); various parts of Southeast Asia, the Middle East and South America where personal relationships incur obligations (that is, you would give the good public review but tell the friend in private that the food required improvement); and parts of Asia and Africa where a 'gentleman's agreement' is considered more binding than a written contract. Hall identifies five non-verbal languages which communicate information to us without anyone speaking, and they correspond to each of the five questions above: *time*, *space*, *things*, *relationships* and *agreements*. Hall's point is that we all have a characteristic way of 'reading' these things according to our cultural background, and we do this without thinking. When we go into other cultures, however, we may be making the wrong reading, and we need to be on our guard against this.

Two other major frameworks have also been developed to help identify the differences in cross-cultural understanding. Robert Westwood (1992) gives a useful outline of the theory behind the concept of culture, including the framework developed by Kluckhohn and Strodtbeck (1961; see also Adler 1991). These two frameworks identify five basic orientations or core dimensions of culture as responses to questions which all societies must answer:

1. What is the essence of *human nature*?
2. How do/should people relate to their *environment*?
3. What is the basic *time orientation* of people?
4. What state of *being and action* are people basically predisposed to?
5. What is the basis for a *relationship* between people?

The frameworks then identify three states of possible cultural responses – positive, negative and neutral – which are tabulated horizontally against the five vertical dimensions, as shown in Table 3.2. Although the columns in Table 3.2 may be vertically related, the orientations may also vary horizontally between questions. In other words, because you believe that people are basically evil does not *necessarily* mean that you think they are subservient to nature – a negative response to one item does not automatically entail a negative response to all. So, any culture may not necessarily have all its scores in one column, and may have items of value in all three as part of its basic cultural matrix. Understanding this cultural underpinning can often help to make inexplicable actions – like the Arab car mechanic who refuses to

Table 3.2 Dimensions of basic cultural assumptions

Core dimensions	Cultural assumptions		
	1	2	3
What is the essence of human nature?	People are basically evil	People are a mixture of good and evil	People are basically good
How do/should people relate to the environment?	People are subservient to nature	People are in harmony with nature	People should be masters of nature
What is the basic time orientation of people?	To the past	To the present	To the future
What state of being and action are people basically predisposed to?	The desirable state is simply to 'be'; to act spontaneously and without long-term expectations	People should act and strive towards their own self-development and actualisation	People should act so as to achieve measurable accomplishments
What is the basis for a relationship between people?	Lineal – orientation is towards the group – is based on family ties; continuance of family line is a prime goal	Collateral – orientation towards a group – less emphasis on blood-ties. Continuance through time	Individual – the individual person is the focus. Individual interests take precedence over group interests

Source: Robert Westwood (1992) *Organizational Behaviour*, Hong Kong: Longmans, p. 43, adapted from Kluckhohn and Strodtbeck (1961).

commit to a time for having your car repaired – explicable (Arab cultures would score in column 1 in Table 3.2 across the dimensions of 'time', 'being' and 'relationships', a common phrase being 'inshallah' or 'if Allah wills'). Having respect for the past, they value traditional obligations highly, and lineal obligations can at any time take precedence over work-related ones. This also poses problems for the introduction of quality initiatives which require the statement in advance of performance standards, service standards and benchmarks (see Chapter 11). In Chapter 1, we also gave the example where many management fads were difficult to copy in Asia and one reason for this was the strong basis of family ties in businesses (that is, scoring in column 1 on 'relationships').

The oft-quoted studies by Geert Hofstede (1980) saw the development of a framework of cultural differentiation along four continuums, to which Hofstede and Michael Bond (1988) added a fifth:

- *Individualism–collectivism* (is it more important to stand out as an individual, or to be established as a member of a group?)
- *Power distance* (tall societies with the very poor and very rich, and authority structures in which those in authority do not respond to the wishes of those below, are distinct from those egalitarian societies in which many voices are heard and taken into account)
- *Uncertainty avoidance* (the need for certainty, risk avoidance, caution)
- *Masculinity–femininity* (quantity, measurement, regulation and order as against quality of life,

caring, concern with feelings and expression)
- *Long-term–short-term orientation* (Confucian dynamism – the ability to pursue long-term and general goals as against short-term gain and advantage).

These dimensions, when related to each other, produced cultural maps of the world which enabled countries to be located relative to each other. This classification has not been without its critics and controversies. Cultural assumptions are very deep, and are expressed in a variety of ways, of which verbal language is just one. Learning to read the other non-verbal languages of culture is an important skill, which international managers of the future must acquire.

For Hofstede, these five continuums are the assumptions, shared meanings and relativities which underpin social and organizational life in different national cultures and inevitably shape behaviour. In terms of the power distance dimension, we would appreciate power differently, for example, according to whether we lived in a society in which a few people had wealth and influence and many people had little wealth and no influence, or whether we lived in a society in which most people had a good standard of living and a chance to participate in decision making. Similarly, our view of knowledge, in terms of what we may know and how we may know it, could vary: high power distance societies often restrict the flow of information from the few to the many, regarding most people as not worthy of knowledge; while low power distance societies are more open and communicative about a variety of matters, regarding most people as having great ability to learn and improve themselves. So the concepts of organizational learning and the learning organization are likely to be highly culturally relative: in Hong Kong, for example, it has been difficult for researchers to gain access to companies and gather evidence. Cultural differences, especially as argued by Hofstede (1980, 1991), are associated with these forms of power and knowledge and traditional justifications such as membership of certain clans or castes, religious rituals, veneration of ancestors and so on and are often used to maintain the exclusion of the many from access to knowledge and power. Patriarchs in societies who encourage headship not leadership (see Chapter 10) do not want their employees to learn too much. Similarly, in certain collective cultures with high power distance, where members of certain family groups or tribes have job security, such as parts of the Middle East, there is often little incentive for managers to develop themselves, and initiatives such as total quality management (TQM) have had great difficulty in getting a foothold. Many of the concepts that Western businesses use to talk about 'competitiveness', 'efficiency' and 'profitability' are technique-driven and ignore the harder aspects of culture, both national and organizational (Negandhi 1986).

These cultural substructures have *expressive forms* in social and organizational institutions like the education system, the property system or the tax system, and are represented in language and symbol. Thinking again of *institutions* in terms of the power distance idea, high power distance societies would tend to have an elitist education system for the children of the wealthy, whereas more egalitarian societies would tend to provide education for all those who were able to benefit. Political systems would usually offer at best a restricted participation in high power distance societies and would more often be dictatorships, even if paternal ones. Low power distance societies would tend to have more participatory, democratic systems. In terms of specific *practices* and behaviours, high power distance societies would have more rules of exclusion restricting individual freedom, more initiation rituals and more taboos, while low power distance societies would have rules conferring individual rights and guaranteeing access to information. Privately, individuals in high power distance societies would tend to have more topics which they would discuss in open conversation, such as religion or politics, whereas in low power distance societies these would often be the subject of popular debate and satirical humour.

Non-verbal artefacts (things, objects, social and organizational arrangements) can carry cultural meaning as well as verbal ones. Hierarchy, as a structure, is a highly significant symbol of life in high power distance societies, and in some societies such as Japan it is necessary for a person to know the exact social level of another before they can determine the correct way to address them. Position in the hierarchy here carries privilege and respect and requires others to act in a deferential way. In low power distance societies, such as the USA and the UK, hierarchy is regarded more loosely, and in terms of function in the organization not in terms of personal worth, and is less meaningful. To be the managing director of a company in Hong Kong is far more socially significant than being the managing director of a similar company in Huddersfield, Houston, Helsinki or Hyderabad. Societies where place, time, body language, buildings, dress, property and other non-verbal symbols are regarded as important are known as *high-context* societies, where the primary focus is on who is speaking rather than the content, and many Asian and Middle Eastern societies fit this description. Western societies, where what people say tends to be taken at face value, are known as *low-context* societies, and here the focus is on *what* is being said rather than on who said it. In a high-context culture, criticism of a speech is seen as criticism of the speaker and as disrespectful; in a low-context culture it is seen as criticism of the words only, and no disrespect is implied. It is very difficult for low-status managers from a low-context culture, where they may have been used to speaking freely in front of the managing director and having their opinions listened to, to move into a high-context culture where they will find themselves ignored and will run the risk of giving great offence to the senior managers there.

Nonetheless, the notion that a unified, homogeneous national culture can adequately explain all patterns of behaviour at the organizational level is subject to questioning. Many studies do not differentiate between national and organizational culture and often treat organizational culture as homogeneous because it exists in a particular country (Tayeb 1988: 41). Even though perceptions of power are heavily influenced by wider cultural influences, Monir Tayeb (1988) suggests that such things as education, age and the seniority of a manager are also likely to affect perceptions of power and these demographics might explain differences found in organizations in similar cultures. National culture does impact strongly at the organizational level in areas such as autonomy and freedom, economic rewards, job expectations and management approaches (Tayeb 1988: Chapters 8 and 9). Attitudes, values and norms relating to autonomy and freedom influence expectations about delegation and hence authority within organizations as well as devolution or the decentralization of such things as decision making. Thus, as previously stated, the extent to which participatory and democratic practices are possible in organizations is largely culture-specific. As a result, many management approaches are, according to Tayeb, also strongly related to the national culture. Thus, whether or not egalitarian and democratic management approaches, as opposed to inegalitarian, paternalistic and autocratic ones, are considered appropriate in an organization is largely a byproduct of national culture and extremely difficult to change. Formalization, or the degree to which people accept rules, policies and procedures, is also determined to a large extent by national culture and thus impacts more directly on organizational culture. Values relating to privacy and independence of the individual over the group are the key determinants of how much formalization is tolerated in workplaces.

A range of other *societal factors*, such as the labour market composition (for example level of skills, levels of employment, degree of unionization, extent of casual versus full-time employees), the industrial relations system (laws covering employment and work conditions, conciliation and arbitration of disputes and union and employer rights) and the class system of a country (for example how wealth and opportunities for social mobility are distributed) also affect how organizations operate and the cultures within them. These are often referred to as *institutional factors*. Commitment and trust of employees by management, for example, are two particularly important aspects of organizations that can also be heavily influenced by such things as the labour market and industrial relations systems within countries (Tayeb 1988: Chapters 8 and 9). Other *national factors*, such as the economic system (for example capitalist, socialist, mixed economy, closed economy), systems of government (for example elected, dictatorship) and the legal system (for example nature of civil and commercial law) also affect certain work practices and the cultures of organizations. Both the social and national factors are embedded in national cultures, but they are often more easily changed or manipulated than widely held attitudes and values (see Fulop 1992: 361–9). For many years Japanese companies offered such things as lifetime employment, which many observers attributed to something paternal or clan-like in the culture of Japan, and hence its organizations. Yet when hard economic times arose these practices were quickly questioned and ceased in many large companies (Fulop 1992: 367).

At the organizational level, a number of other factors called *contingency variables* also influence the type of organizational structure and culture that might emerge. Thus the size of an organization might mean that larger organizations tend to be more bureaucratic and therefore centralized, no matter where they might be located. The markets that organizations enter are likely to influence how they practise management; for example, many Japanese 'transplant' companies in the car industry have had to modify their management practices to operate in countries such as Australia, the USA and the UK. Technologies can also influence how organizations develop their management practices, for

example certain computer technologies, mass production and assembly methods produce similar problems across a range of countries irrespective of national culture. It is no surprise to realize that core aspects of scientific management were adopted in many parts of the world. The ownership of the company or business (for example shareholders versus owner managers) can affect the degree of centralization and hierarchy in organizations, probably more than national culture (Tayeb 1988: Chapters 8 and 9).

The culture of one organization may be a weave of subcultures or multicultures, overcrossed by a variety of external cultural, social, national and contingency factors. Culture, structure and strategy are not separate 'variables', as some theorists might wish to argue, but rather need to be seen as inseparable and treated holistically as suggested by Bate and Anthony. Because culture is not an 'independent' variable, you cannot change structure or strategy without affecting culture.

Gender and culture

Talk is an important part of culture. Therefore, if men and women communicate differently we might anticipate differences in the kinds of cultures which develop where one or the other is dominant. We might also expect that the way people are customarily required to communicate will make it easier for one or the other gender to become successful in that culture. Men and women have never been viewed as, or treated as, equals in the workplace. Jobs have been differentiated and even whole occupations, especially those in service industries, have been designated 'women's work'. As we saw in Chapter 2, fewer than 20 per cent of all managerial posts are held by women, and at more senior levels this falls to 10 per cent. Men are often seen to be rational, calculating and resilient whereas women are seen as being emotional, changeable and lacking resolution. This forms the background to what men and women do in any real organization, but Deborah Tannen (1990) indicates that men and women actually talk differently and thus communicate different things when they speak. As Tannen (1990) argues, women tend to learn styles of speaking which make them appear less confident and self-assured than they really are, and as a result they lose out on those organizational issues, like promotion, that depend on appearing confident. Women tend to say 'we' rather than 'I' when discussing work, and as a result get less credit for what they do. They tend to boast less and ask more questions, which can often make them seem less sure of themselves. Women downplay their certainty while men minimize their doubts. Men are more likely to save their own face in a problem situation. Above all, powerful people, which

	Table 3.3 Gherardi's classification of women's cultural positioning		
	Women's reciprocal positioning		
Male positioning	*Accepted*	*Contested*	*Imposed*
Friendly	*The guest* A cooperative position	*The holidaymaker* A mismatched position	*The newcomer* An open-ended position
Hostile	*The marginal* A stigmatized position	*The snake in the grass* A contested position	*The intruder* A unilaterally imposed position

Source: Silvia Gherardi (1995) *Gender, Symbolism and Organizational Cultures*, London: Sage, p. 109. Reprinted by permission of Sage Publications Ltd. Copyright © Sage Publications 1995.

usually means men, are more likely to reward people with similar language styles to their own.

To give another example, a New York psychiatrist in the mid-1980s joined one of the earliest Internet chat groups in order to try to develop a new way of counselling and helping people. He chose as his name 'Doctor', which he had not fully realized was gender-neutral. One day he was chatting in a side room with a woman and he realized that she had thought that he too was female. He was astonished by the richness and openness of the communication that he was receiving and assumed that this was the way women talked to each other. As a result, he created a false identity for himself, an easy thing to do on the Internet, as a woman. He was able to build some very loyal friendships in this way and helped many people, but he wearied of the strain of constantly having to be someone else, and so he joined the group under his own identity, his female alter ego introducing him as a great guy and a lovely person, a fine doctor and so on. He hoped that he would build relationships with all his friends and the female alter ego could disappear from the picture. Unfortunately, none of his friends from his other identity could get along with him when he was being himself, and they found him stiff and a bit cold! As a man, he could not communicate in the same way – they did not expect it and were unreceptive to it – and they did not communicate with him in the same manner either (Stone 1995: 63–87).

So what you say and how you say it are different depending on your gender, and this may both open and close doors to you depending on your gender's position within the organization's culture. Of course an organization which only rewards one communicative style is losing its ability to hear a wide range of information and increase the flexibility of its actions, but it does not stop there. As Silvia Gherardi (1995) notes, organizations tend to write stories for their participants, with gendered roles for women to play. She identifies six discursive positions that were offered to or imposed on women in her studies, in which men were basically either friendly or hostile and women's positions were either accepted, contested or imposed (see Table 3.3). Women could be accepted in a friendly manner, as a guest, treated pleasantly, but politely circumscribed and not allowed to be a 'real' member of the culture like the men were. Gherardi's respondent Giovanna tells us:

I felt as if I was a guest. Just as a guest is placed at the head of a table, treated politely, and never allowed to wash the dishes, so I was surrounded by a web of polite but invisible restraints. I began to suspect something when I saw the other women when they arrived and were, so to speak, 'integrated'. For example, I almost never go into the production department to talk with the workers. My older male colleagues go because they like it. They go and see their friends, and then they pretend that they are protecting me from the 'uncouthness of the working class'. So I find myself constantly on the phone dealing with the editorial office, the commercial office, the administration. I'm almost always in the office. *It's as if I'm at home and they're always out.* It's true that they are better at what they do, and I'm better at what I do, or we women are, but constantly being their guest is getting me down. (Gherardi 1995: 110–11, emphasis added)

We might recall the argument of Marta Calás and Linda Smircich in the last chapter on how women are being used to domesticate the workforce and free up males for international assignments, apparently because of women's greater interpersonal and caring skills. It is part of the permanent guest role that women are being asked to play. However, things could be more unpleasant if the males were hostile. Gherardi's respondent Fiorella tells of her experience of being marginalized:

I felt I'd become invisible, I thought I was transparent. There's no point in recounting individual episodes or blaming things on hostility. Formally, everything was as it should be, and they treated me politely, like gentlemen, but I counted for nothing. I discovered this little by little and it was tough admitting it to myself. What had I got to complain about? The situations were quite clear, the solutions were reasonable, indeed they were the only ones feasible. Everything was already decided and all I had to do was agree and implement. There was no need to open my mouth at meetings. I realised I had been pushed to one side even though my expertise was publicly praised. (Gherardi 1995: 112)

These kinds of examples show how limited by organizational culture the equal opportunities and positive discrimination approaches can be. Nothing was done wrong in either of these situations and the men were reasonable, polite and even gentlemanly. However, the women were 'second-class citizens' and powerless.

In Gherardi's other examples, the positions are more uncomfortable. If the woman is in the *holidaymaker* position, then everyone else is just waiting for her to move on, nothing really changes, and they all make contingency plans behind her back; if seen as a *snake in the grass*, then they plot to get rid of her and make her fail; if seen as a *newcomer*, then they reserve judgement,

for long periods of time, are anxious and make it hard to get commitments to projects and participation in processes; and if seen as an *intruder*, she will be constantly openly challenged. Many of these categories could apply to men in some situations, but the question is clearly one of degree; women start off by being *other*, whereas men at the very least receive the benefit of the doubt and the 'testing' of a new male appointee is not likely to last for years but to be resolved fairly quickly. The feeling of being trapped by invisible nets is a typical indicator that the problem is cultural, and making these invisible nets visible is difficult, particularly when the 'nets' are often constructed and enacted by those with the power to change the situation.

Conclusion

Despite the fact that it is difficult to define, the idea of culture captures some dimensions of human social organizing that other strictly psychological, sociological or economic approaches cannot adequately address. It is about interaction, sharedness, distinctiveness, similarity and difference, meaning and significance, signs and symbols, rituals and tokens, leadership, common-sense and the taken-for-granted. It is also about problem-solving, thinking strategically, devising and operating within structures and, perhaps surprisingly, change. It is not entirely separable from these activities, and is affected by power relations, gender, ethnicity, time and place. In the late 1970s and 1980s the main concern of studies of culture was with creating new cultures of excellence in performance; in the late 1980s and 1990s the concern developed into changing cultures which were a drag on performance and perception of the environment. As we move into a new century, the focus has shifted as a result of such cases as Enron (see Chapter 17) to address how and whether cultures which are excellent in terms of performance can also excel morally. Culture has so many facets that as research on culture and the application of ideas of managing culture are put into practice, new emphases continually emerge. Although it became something of a fad in the 1980s, as this chapter has shown, culture has a firm basis in a range of underlying theories across disciplines and remains one of the most important concepts we have in management and organization theory.

Let us now revisit our questions on culture at the beginning of the chapter.

 ## Answers to questions about culture

1 **What is organizational culture? What is it good for?** Organizational culture is a complex phenomenon, usually related to shared values and shared meanings in an organization, but also related to common ways of dealing with, or ignoring, commonly experienced problems. It is a form of common sense, an outcome of cultural processes at work in a particular setting. The benefits of paying attention to culture are that it focuses on people but in particular on the symbolic significance of almost every aspect of organizational life. It emphasizes shared meanings, even if implicit, and alerts

Answers continued

us to the influencing potential of values, beliefs, ideology, language, norms, ceremonies, rituals, myths and stories. It constructs leaders as shapers of meaning. It also emphasizes the importance of communication and learning; it emphasizes the importance of how others perceive us; and it alerts us to the fact that organizational environments are also socially constructed.

2 Are companies with strong cultures always successful? No! Strong cultures can be a barrier to change if they are negative cultures, but, even so, with the happiest, most creative culture there are still other factors that can frustrate performance, such as the economic climate and competitive situation, that are out of the organization's control.

3 What are the dysfunctions of culture? Culture tends to select and socialize people who are alike, and so often there is a lack of diversity and critical thinking in strong cultures, and the tendency to stick to old recipes even when things change. There can be a focus on the emotional and non-rational, to the extent that simple but important technicalities, like structural arrangements, inventory control or quantitative analysis of the market, can be neglected.

4 What are subcultures and are they healthy? Subcultures are groups of people who are part of a wider group, subscribing to the overall culture but with some distinctly different values of their own. Large companies will certainly have many of these; sometimes they will be associated with functions – marketing, maintenance and so on – or with professions – engineering, legal, accounting. But they can occur even in small companies and may not be related to any company features. They can be a source of creativity or division and destructive conflict, depending on the nature of their values and how they differ from those of the rest of the company.

5 How is organizational culture related to national culture? Organizational culture is often influenced by the background culture in which it is located, sometimes explicitly. Indeed, in the 1990s BA removed the British flag from the tailplanes of its jets and replaced it with a variety of different ethnic tailplane designs to reflect the diversity of its business and its increasingly global culture, or at least give that impression. There are several underlying assumptions about the world, which are characteristic of different national cultures and affect the ways in which people habitually think and orient them towards particular organizational preferences. However, these assumptions are not intractable, although it should not be assumed that they can be easily changed or set aside. Culture is a complex concept and other variables such as national and contingency ones need to be considered when trying to make sense of organizational cultures and subcultures.

REVISITING
THE CASE STUDY

Let us take a look at the questions we raised on the case study in the light of our discussion.

1 Does company T have a *shared culture*?

The answer here is broadly 'yes'. Although many people declare themselves unhappy with it, because of the 'sink or swim' nature of the culture, they go along with it and play the game.

One feature of culture is that if a culture is shared this does not mean it is shared equally; not everyone will believe in it to the same extent, some may be enthusiastic, some may hate it, some just comply. The culture, however, is not one which unites them behind a collective objective – the shared culture is a divisive one of every shift/department for itself.

2 Is company T a 'strong' culture?

The answer here is again 'yes'. It is not a positive one in the sense that the literature talks about companies like McDonald's, Hewlett-Packard, Marks & Spencer, Ben and Jerry's, of which commitment, dedication and love of the company are hallmarks and few people seem to be having fun, but it is one which quickly sanctions those who are not part of it. You suffer if you do not play the game. It is also very explicit and dramatic, but the performances are not formally staged on occasions; people do the 'staging' on an everyday basis, which suggests that the behaviour is habitual and ingrained and will consequently be hard to shift.

3 What are the *problems of the culture*?

Well first of all, it is divisive and defensive. It sets sections up against each other and produces senseless internal competition. Managers try to look good and cover up problems, and no one is working towards a mutual goal or goals. The lying, cheating and stealing means that the organization has systems and procedures that do not work and those new managers who try to follow them end up failing. The organization is not getting the information it needs passed up the hierarchy, and as a result it cannot be a learning organization. Development will be difficult, if not impossible. At an individual level, the 2 x 4 culture makes people anxious, perhaps bitter, but certainly risk averse. Fear is the worst climate for creativity and problem solving. In addition, although there is no evidence on the gender balance of the company, it would appear to have a masculinist culture, which would affect the potential benefits to be gained from a greater diversity of approaches.

4 Can the company be changed?

Well, any culture can be changed given time. The consultants in this case worked with key managers at an interpersonal level, exploring with them the problems they were facing and the effects of the culture, and tried to get them to change their behaviour. This was not always easy for them – people who have been 'beaten up' every day have a tendency to miss the beatings when they stop and crave the structure that the old ways gave them. Additionally, any change produces a period of mourning for the old way before the new behaviour is internalized, and so plenty of support and reinforcement is necessary. However, managers involved in this type of individual change can provide mutual support for each other. It is also essential in opening up channels of communication. At the right time, top-down support will also be an important reinforcement, especially if changes in structure and procedure are complementary to and require changes in behaviour. So change will be difficult, but it is possible, given effort across a range of mutually supporting areas.

References

Adler, N. (1991) *International Dimensions of Organizational Behaviour*, Boston: PWS-Kent.

Aktouf, O. (1996) 'Competence, symbolic activity and promotability', in Linstead, S., Grafton Small, R. and Jeffcutt, P. (eds) *Understanding Management*, London: Sage.

Alvesson, M. (2002) *Understanding Organizational Culture*, London: Sage

Anthony, P. (1994) *Managing Culture*, Buckingham: Open University Press.

Argyris, C. (1964) *Integrating the Individual and the Organization*, New York: John Wiley.

Ashkanasy, N.M., Wilderom, C.P.M. and Peterson, M.F. (2000) *Handbook of Organizational Culture and Climate*, Thousand Oaks: Sage.

Barney, J. (1986) 'Organizational culture: Can it be a source of sustained competitive advantage?', *Academy of Management Review* **2**(3): 656–65.

Bate, S.P. (1994) *Strategies for Cultural Change*, London: Butterworth Heinemann.

Bedi, H. (1991) *Understanding the Asian Manager*, Sydney: Allen & Unwin.

Benveniste, G. (1987) *Professionalizing the Organization*, San Francisco: Jossey-Bass.

Boje, D.M. (1995) 'Stories of the storytelling organization: A postmodern analysis of Disney as "Tamara-Land"' *Academy of Management Journal* **38**(4): 997–1035.

Boje, D.M. and Winsor, R.D. (1993) 'The resurrection of Taylorism: Total quality management's hidden agenda', *Journal of Organizational Change Management* **6**(4): 57–70.

Bovens, M. (1992) 'Conflicting loyalties: Ethical pluralism in administrative life', paper presented at the First International Productivity Network Conference, 21–24 July, Canberra, Australia.

Brown, A. (1998) *Organizational Culture* (2nd edn), London: Financial Times/Pitman.

Carlzon, J. (1987) *Moments of Truth,* New York: Harper & Row.

Chan, A. and Clegg, S. (2002) History, Culture and Organization Studies *Culture and Organization,* **8**(4): 259–73.

Deal, T.E. and Kennedy, A.A. (1982) *Corporate Cultures: The Rites and Rituals of Corporate Life*, New York: Addison-Wesley.

Deal, T.E. and Kennedy, A.A. (1988) *Corporate Cultures: The Rites and Rituals of Corporate Life*, London: Penguin.

Denison, D. (1990) *Corporate Culture and Organizational Effectiveness,* New York: John Wiley.

Drennan, D. (1992) *Transforming Company Culture,* London: McGraw-Hill.

Eastman, C. and Fulop, L. (1997) 'Management for clinicians or the case of "bringing the mountain to Mohammed"', *International Journal of Production Economics,* **52**: 15–30.

Eldridge, J.E.T. and Crombie, A.D. (1974) *A Sociology of Organizations,* London: Allen & Unwin.

Feldman, S. (1996) 'Management in context: Culture and organizational change', in Linstead, S., Grafton Small, R. and Jeffcutt, P. (eds) *Understanding Management,* London: Sage.

Flam, H. (1993) 'Fear, loyalty and greedy organizations', in Fineman, S. (ed.) *Emotion in Organizations*, London: Sage.

Fulop, L. (1992) 'Management in the international context', in Fulop, L., Frith, F. and Hayward, H. (eds) *Management for Australian Business: A Critical Text*, Melbourne: Macmillan.

Garfinkel, H. (1984 [1967]) *Studies in Ethnomethodology,* Cambridge: Polity Press.

Gherardi, S. (1995) *Gender, Symbolism and Organizational Cultures,* London: Sage.

Gouldner, A. (1954) *Patterns of Industrial Bureaucracy,* New York: The Free Press.

Gouldner, A. (1955) *Wildcat Strike,* London: Routledge & Kegan Paul.

Graves, D. (1986) *Corporate Culture: Diagnosis and Change,* New York: St Martins Press.

Guest, D. (1992) 'Right enough to be dangerously wrong: An analysis of the "In Search of Excellence" phenomenon', in Salaman, G. (ed.) *Human Resource Strategies,* London: Sage.

Hall, E. (1959) *The Silent Language,* New York: Doubleday.

Hampden-Turner, C. (1990) *Corporate Culture: From Vicious to Virtuous Circles,* London: Economist Books/Hutchinson.

Hancock, P. and Tyler M. (2001) *Work, Postmodernism and Organization* London: Sage

Handy, C. (1993) *Understanding Organizations,* London: Penguin.

Harrison, R. (1972) 'How to describe your organization', *Harvard Business Review* **50**(3): 119–28.

Hatch, M. J. and Schultz, M. (1997) 'Relations between organizational culture, identity and image' *European Journal of Marketing* **31**, 356–65.

Hochschild, A.R. (1983) *The Managed Heart,* Berkeley: University of California Press.

Hofstede, G. (1980) *Culture's Consequences: International Differences in Work-Related Values,* London: Sage.

Hofstede, G. (1991) *Cultures and Organizations,* London: HarperCollins.

Hofstede, G. and Bond, M.H. (1988) 'The Confucian connection: From cultural roots to economic growth', *Organizational Dynamics* **16**(4): 4–21.

Höpfl, H. (1996) 'Authority and the pursuit of order in organizational performance', in Jeffcutt, P., Grafton Small, R. and Linstead, S. (eds) *Organization and Theatre,* special issue of *Studies in Cultures, Organizations, and Societies* **2**(1): 67–80.

Humes, S. (1993) *Managing the Multinational: Confronting the Global–Local Dilemma,* New York: Prentice Hall.

Jaques, E. (1952) *The Changing Culture of a Factory,* New York: Dryden Press.

Johnson, G. (1989) 'The Burton Group (B)', in Johnson, G. and Scholes, K. (eds) *Exploring Corporate Strategy,* London: Prentice Hall.

Johnson, G. (1992) 'Managing strategic change – strategy, culture and action', *Long Range Planning* **25**(1): 28–36.

Kakabadse, A., Ludlow, R. and Vinnicombe, S. (1988) *Working in Organizations,* London: Penguin.

Kirkbride, P.S. (1983) 'Power in the workplace', unpublished PhD thesis, University of Bath, UK.

Kluckhohn, F.R. and Strodtbeck, F.L. (1961) *Variations in Value Orientations,* Evanston, IL: Row, Peterson.

Linstead, S.A. and Grafton Small, R. (1992) 'On reading organizational culture', *Organization Studies* **13**(3): 331–55.

Lorsch, J. (1986) 'Managing culture: The invisible barrier to strategic change', *California Management Review* **28**(2): 95–109.

Louis, M.R. (1980) 'Organizations as culture-bearing milieux', in Pondy, L.R., Frost, P.J., Morgan, G. and Dandridge, T.C. (eds) *Organizational Symbolism,* Greenwich, CO: JAI Press.

Martin, J. (2002) *Organizational Culture: Mapping the Terrain,* Thousand Oaks, CA: Sage.

Negandhi, A.R. (1986) 'Three decades of cross-cultural management research', in Clegg, S.R., Dunphy, D.C. and Redding, S.G. (eds) *The Enterprise and Management in South-East Asia*, Hong Kong: Centre for Asian Studies, University of Hong Kong.

Olila, J. (1995) 'Corporate anthropology and organizational change', unpublished working paper, Erasmus University, Rotterdam.

Pacanowsky, M.E. and O'Donnell-Trujillo, N. (1982) 'Communication and organizational culture', *The Western Journal of Speech and Communication* **46** (Spring): 115–30.

Parker, M. (2000) *Organizational Culture and Identity,* London: Sage.

Pascale, R.T. and Athos, A.G. (1980) *The Art of Japanese Management,* London: Penguin.

Pauchant, T. and Mitroff, I. (1988) 'Crisis prone versus crisis avoiding organizations: Is your company's culture its own worst enemy in creating crisis?', *Industrial Crisis Quarterly* **2**: 53–63.

Payne, R. (1990) The Concepts of Culture and Climate, Working Paper 202, Manchester Business School.

Peters, T. and Waterman, R.H. (1982) *In Search of Excellence,* New York: Harper & Row.

Pfeffer, J. (1981) 'Management as symbolic action: The creation and maintenance of organizational paradigms', in Cummings, L.L. and Staw, B. (eds) *Research in Organizational Behaviour* **3**(1): 1–52.

Pool, R. (1997) 'When failure is not an option', *Technology Review* July: 38–45.

Ray, C.A. (1986) 'Corporate culture: The last frontier of control?', *Journal of Management Studies* **23**(3): 287–98.

Ritzer, G. (1990) *The McDonaldization of Society,* Thousand Oaks, CA: Pine Forge Press.

Ritzer, G. (1999) *Enchanting a Disenchanted World: Revolutionizing the Means of Consumption,* Thousand Oaks, CA: Pine Forge Press.

Schein, E. (1985) *Organizational Culture and Leadership,* San Francisco: Jossey-Bass.

Schwartz, H. (1990) *Narcissistic Process and Corporate Decay,* New York: NYU Press.

Schwartz, H. and Davis, S.M. (1981) 'Matching corporate culture and business strategy', *Organizational Dynamics,* **10**: 30–48.

Sinclair, A. (1991) 'After excellence: Models of organisational culture for the public sector', *Australian Journal of Public Administration* **50**(3): 321–32.

Smircich, L. (1983) 'Concepts of culture and organizational analysis', *Administrative Science Quarterly,* **28**(3): 339–58.

Smircich, L. and Morgan, G. (1982) 'Leadership: the management of meaning', *Journal of Applied Behavioural Science,* **18**(2): 257–73.

Smith, S. and Wilkinson, B. (1996) ' No doors on offices, no secrets: We are our own policemen: Capitalism without conflict?', in Linstead, S., Grafton Small, R. and Jeffcutt, P. (eds) *Understanding Management,* London: Sage.

Stone, A.R. (1995) *The War of Desire and Technology at the Close of the Mechanical Age,* Boston: MIT Press.

Strauss, A., Schatzman, L., Ehrlich, D., Bucher, R. and Sabshin, M. (1963) 'The hospital and its negotiated order', in Friedson, E. (ed.) *The Hospital in Modern Society*, New York: Macmillan.

Tannen, D. (1990) *You Just Don't Understand: Men and Women in Conversation,* New York: William Morrow.

Tayeb, M.H. (1988) *Organisations and National Culture*, London: Sage.

Thompson, P. and McHugh, D. (2002) *Work Organisations: A Critical Introduction* London: Palgrave Macmillan.

Torrington, D. (1994) *International Human Resource Management,* New York: Prentice Hall.

Turner, B.A. (1971) *Exploring the Industrial Sub-Culture,* London: Macmillan – now Palgrave Macmillan.

Van Maanen, J. (1991) 'The Smile Factory: Work at Disneyland', in Frost, P., Moore, L.F., Louis, M.R., Lundberg, C.C. and Martin, J. (eds) *Reframing Organizational Culture,* Newbury Park, CA: Sage.

Walsh, J. (1997) 'BA hopes to clear air with top-flight moves', *People Management* **23** (October): 11.

Weber, M. (1964) *The Theory of Social Economic Organizations*, London: Heinemann.

Westley, F.R. (1990) 'The eye of the needle: Cultural and personal transformation in a traditional organization', *Human Relations* **43**(3): 273–93.

Westwood, R. (1992) *Organizational Behaviour,* Hong Kong: Longmans.

Willmott, H. (1991) 'Strength is ignorance; slavery is freedom: Managing culture in modern organizations', *Journal of Management Studies* **30**(4): 515–52.

Young, D. (1989) 'British Airways: Putting the customer first', unpublished paper, Ashridge Strategic Management Centre, Ashridge Management College, UK.

Young, E. (1989) 'On the Naming of the Rose: Interests and multiple meanings as elements of organizational culture', *Organization Studies* **10**(2): 187–206.

Managing structure

CHAPTER

Liz Fulop, Harold Hayward and Simon Lilley

4

Questions about managing structure

1 What is organizational structure?

2 Is there 'one best way' to structure organizations?

3 Are non-hierarchical structures viable?

4 Should bureaucracy be abandoned?

TIME TO CHANGE THE WAY WE WORK?

Wall Street traders went back to work this week with flags in their hands and a sense of purpose that might in the normal course of events have been missing in their lives. They were out to make money, as always, but also to make a point – that work and life would go on. Old habits die hard and restoring the familiar routine is an important part of the catharsis for those who live and work in New York. This is unsurprising in a workforce suffused with a serious work ethic. It is far too early to gauge whether the attack on the World Trade Center will transform attitudes in the workplace at one time, but there may be a greater willingness among employers to look at alternative ways of working. How many survivors, for example, will entertain the prospect of working again in a tower block? How many will look for alternatives when once they would have flown to meetings without a second thought? Massing tens of thousands of people together in multitiered boxes the size of a town is no longer necessary for many types of work, including trading on the financial markets. Licensed software applications exist that could allow people to trade from their living rooms if they wished. Putting people together in offices has become a habit but many of the supposed efficiencies of this have disappeared with the arrival of the modem and the internet. Richard Arkwright, the 18th century English cotton spinner and one of the pioneers of mass production, brought workers together in large mills, partly to make economies of scale – he could use a single power source to run his machines – and partly to prevent scrutiny of his machines by those who would copy them in defiance of his patent. Most significantly perhaps, it allowed him to control and to profit from this concentration of production.

The factory system that characterised the industrial revolution was expanded on a grand scale by those, such as Henry Ford, who introduced moving assembly. At the same time, office systems proliferated to handle the masses of paperwork demanded by trading and accounting systems. Factories remain a necessary constituent of manufacturing – but the office in its traditional sense is surely becoming obsolete. Its main function today appears to be to maintain a sense of workforce cohesion.

Various studies in the past few years have highlighted the importance of communications and maintaining relationships among workforces, yet relatively few employers have been bold enough to design workplaces to take account of such needs. Close working relationships are unlikely to develop among people sitting at their desks, staring at screens eight hours a day, yet this is the reality of much desk-bound working.

New ergonomics research and legislation in Scandinavia is transforming the office. Most of the new desks bought for workplaces in Denmark today allow people the choice of standing or sitting at their workstation. Peter Kurstein, an ergonomics expert working with the Office Institute in Denmark, says: 'People need variety in their work. They want to chat to their colleagues near the coffee machines and they like to stand in groups as they would in the street or in a bar.'

Massing tens of thousands in multitiered boxes is unnecessary

This is the way relationships are forged in an organization but static desk work, where a colleague may email a simple request from a few yards rather than speaking, erodes such relationships. If people need variety at work, why can they not mix their jobs so that they do some work at home and other work – such as essential meetings and social encounters for the trading of gossip in the workplace? Some people need the hubbub of the office to do their best work, others need to be more detached. But people should have more choice, where possible, over where and when they work. Too often such flexibility is opposed by control-hungry managers who want staff where they can see them. The need for a shared experience in response to the events of last week may underline the gregarious nature of work. People were talking this week of the need to get back into work. But some are likely to harbour deep reservations about tower block working, high above the ground.

If the loss of the World Trade Center leads to changes in workplace design or working conditions, it will not be unprecedented. Ninety years ago, in 1911, a fire broke out in the Triangle Shirtwaist company in Lower Manhattan, New York. Women were packed into overcrowded workshops in the top three storeys of the high-rise Asch building. Fire spread so quickly that avenues of escape were blocked. Many women, some with their clothes alight, jumped to their deaths rather than face the fire. Some 146 died. The tragedy led to new workplace arrangements, regulations and safety laws that still exist today.

Unlike the case of the 1911 disaster no one is saying after last week's catastrophe that employers were negligent or that people worked in poor conditions. But, in spite of being designed to withstand the impact of a large aircraft, the World Trade Center could not survive the explosive impact of fuel-laden jets.

Many newer workplaces, particularly call centres, have been created in single-storey, shed-like structures on the outskirts of towns and cities. The high-rise phenomenon has prevailed where space is limited and city authorities have been convinced that financial businesses need to be in close proximity. How much of this need, I wonder, is born of habit and the herd instinct?

Workers in specific occupations historically have always chosen to congregate, sometimes for safety, sometimes to find new work if one source of work disappears. Networking is still an important feature of the job market so it may be unrealistic to expect any widespread dissipation of companies in the financial markets. The need to stay in touch is evident, even among the more solitary professions. In trading houses it is vital. But much of the contact is telephone-based, following the rhythm of the international markets.

Fear of losing out to the competition has stimulated the latest generation of high-rise plans. It may be that different fears – for human safety particularly – must be considered if the high-rise office is to overcome phobias arising from the terrorist threat.

When the understandable gestures of defiance displayed by New York's financial workers give way to some sober reflection, the slavish attachment to the office may begin to evaporate. If so, companies already concerned to keep their best people may need to be increasingly inventive in their definitions of the workplace. Greater choice and imagination about workplace flexibility would be a step in the right direction.

Source: Richard Donkin, 'Time to change the way we work: one outcome of the appalling events in New York may be to allow greater diversity of workplace choices', *Financial Times*, 21/09/01, p. VII.

QUESTIONS ABOUT THE CASE

1 Why are large numbers of people placed together in tower blocks?
2 How closely is organizational structure connected with architecture and technology?

Introduction

The structuring of organizational activity is as old as organizational activity itself. The Roman Empire developed a well-disciplined and organized army and evolved a hierarchical system of public administration, based on caesars, prefects, vicars and governors, a system later taken over by the Church when the Empire collapsed. Metaphors deriving from the army and the Church are still used in explanations of business organization. The word *hierarchy* derives from a Greek word meaning 'sacred rule' and referred at one stage to levels in the priesthood. The term *chain of command* clearly derives from military organizations. These metaphors still influence our thinking about organizational arrangements even in situations where hierarchies and chains of command may not be appropriate (Watson 1986: 40; Shafritz and Ott 1987: 10–18). The notion of the *structure* of an organization also clearly resonates with geometric and particularly architectural notions, as the case indicates. And there are obviously enduring links between the physical structure of an organization, the way in which its buildings are arranged, and the *organizational structure* which seeks to govern the relationships between those employees who inhabit these buildings. But the latter does not flow automatically from the former, and indeed, the nature of physical structure chosen will likely reflect the nature of relationships imagined by those who have designed the organization. The twofold question remains then: How are organizational structures conceived and what are their consequences? This is the question we set out to answer in the rest of this chapter.

We do this by firstly outlining the ideas of a couple of, what might be termed, the father figures of modern organizational structuring: Henri Fayol and Max Weber. Because the latter's pioneering work on articulating the nature of bureaucracy has arguably had a much more significant, if often unacknowledged, impact on the structuring of modern organizations, we devote most of our attention to Weber. Having dealt with the ideas of these two influential theorists, we go on to outline some of the work that has attempted to produce integrative structures of organization in order to overcome some of the problems of rigidity associated with traditional structure. We also look at work considering the relationship of structure to contingencies such as the environment of the firm and the technology it employs. Next we consider ways in which the organizational excellence literature of the 1980s led not only to something of a reassertion of the 'one best way' approach to structuring, but also seemingly questioned the value of any form of rigid, centralizing structure. However, we go on to argue that the seeming radicalness of this literature represents something of a chimera and articulate the ways in which a fundamental rejection of hierarchical structuring is almost unthinkable for us. These thoughts lead us to consider both the gendered dimensions of organizational structuring and cross-cultural views on the theme, which themselves allow us to consider the ways in which structures derived from a bureaucratic base involve a curious denial of emotionality and a privileging of rationality. Finally, to come full circle, we close our chapter with an attempt to defend bureaucratic principles from some of the criticisms that have been levelled at it – in some circumstances, for some purposes, it may indeed be seen to be the very best form of structuring available to us! We discuss newer forms of organizing, such as the virtual organization, in Chapter 17.

Early approaches to structuring organizations

As we note throughout this text, the founder of classical management theory is generally regarded as being Henri Fayol (1841–1925), a French mining engineer, whose success in managing a large mining and metallurgical combine inspired him to commit his ideas on management to paper. His book, *General and Industrial Management*, was not printed in English until 1949, after which it was widely used. However, it was accessed and popularized by management writers like the Englishman Lyndall Urwick (1943) and the American Luther Gulick (1937), who adapted many of Fayol's 'principles'. It is important to note, however, that Fayol himself never used the word *principle* in a universal or dogmatic way. In fact, he quite clearly stated that there were no absolute rules or principles in management:

The soundness and good working order of the body corporate depends on a certain number of conditions termed indiscriminately principles, laws, rules. For preference I shall adopt the term principle while dissociating it from any

---

Exhibit 4.1 Fayol's 14 principles of management and organization

1. *Division of work:* Specialization allows the individual to build up expertise and thereby be more productive.

2. *Authority:* The right to issue commands, along with which must go the equivalent responsibility for its exercise.

3. *Discipline:* The importance of employees obeying orders, but orders will only be obeyed if managers are good leaders.

4. *Unity of command:* Employees should have only one boss; there should be no conflicting lines of command.

5. *Unity of direction:* People engaged in the same kind of activities must have the same objectives of a single plan.

6. *Subordination of individual interest to general interest:* Management must see that the goals of the firm are always paramount.

7. *Remuneration:* Payment is an important motivator so remuneration must be adequate.

8. *Centralization or decentralization:* Operations will be centralized or decentralized depending upon

the condition of the business and the quality of its personnel.

9. *Scalar chain:* A hierarchy is necessary for unity of direction but lateral communication is also fundamental as long as supervisors know that such communication is taking place.

10. *Order:* Both material and social order are necessary. The former minimizes lost time and useless handling of materials, and the latter is achieved through organization and selection.

11. *Equity:* In running a business, a 'combination of kindliness and justice' is needed in treating employees if equity is to be achieved.

12. *Stability of tenure:* This is essential, due to the time and expense involved in training good management.

13. *Initiative:* Allowing all personnel to show their initiative in some way is a source of strength for the organization, even though it may well involve a sacrifice of 'personal vanity' on the part of managers.

14. *Esprit de corps:* Management fosters the morale of its employees.

Source: Adapted from D.S. Pugh and D.J. Hickson (1989) *Writers on Organisations*, Harmondsworth: Penguin pp. 87, 88.

suggestion of rigidity, for there is nothing absolute or resolute in management affairs, it is all a question of proportion. Seldom do we have to apply the same principle twice in identical conditions; allowance must be made for different changing circumstances. (Fayol, cited in Pugh 1990: 181)

On the basis of this quotation, one could argue that Fayol was really the founder of the contingency (that is, situational) approach to management and organization which had wide currency in the 1970s and 80s and is discussed later in this chapter. However, in the hands of many popularizers, Fayol's ideas hardened into the fixed and universal principles of classical management. For Fayol, management consisted of five elements: forecasting and planning, organizing, commanding, coordinating and controlling.

According to Fayol, organizing referred to 'the building up of the structure, material and human, of the undertaking' and related to this, coordinating referred to 'binding together, unifying and harmonising all activity and effort' (Pugh and Hickson 1989: 86). Linked to these elements, Fayol evolved 14 principles of management and organization. These are set out in Exhibit 4.1.

These principles have been criticized at various times but together they do at least provide a starting point from which to examine organizational structure and design by giving us a language and concepts that

we can employ in this task. The other dominant father figure when considering the structuring of organization is Max Weber who conducted extensive studies on the emergence of bureaucracy. The word *bureaucracy* has suffered from a wide variety of uses and misuses. Many people have misconceptions about what it means. It is often used to describe or criticize situations such as the rigid application of rules or procedures, bottlenecks, 'buck passing', red tape, laziness, empire building, exaggerated secrecy and so on. Probably one of the most common forms of bias or tunnel vision surrounding the idea of bureaucracy is the popular image of the bureaucrat or public servant: the descriptions in Figure 4.1 portray these stereotypes in a humorous way. Political or Civil Service bureaucracy was best captured in the popular BBC series *Yes Minister* and *Yes Prime Minister*, in which Sir Humphrey Appleby enshrined the bureaucratic personality par excellence. Videos of the series are worth viewing to appreciate fully the complexity of bureaucratic conduct. However, the bureaucratic personality is as common as the form of organization that gives rise to it. Public service bureaucracy has its counterpart in industrial bureaucracy and the characteristics found in Figure 4.1 and *Yes Minister* are shared by many workers, not just those in public service organizations. Much of the common usage of the term skirts around the quite

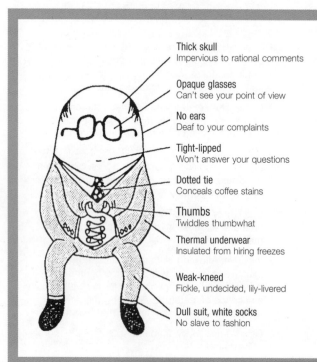

Thick skull
Impervious to rational comments

Opaque glasses
Can't see your point of view

No ears
Deaf to your complaints

Tight-lipped
Won't answer your questions

Dotted tie
Conceals coffee stains

Thumbs
Twiddles thumbwhat

Thermal underwear
Insulated from hiring freezes

Weak-kneed
Fickle, undecided, lily-livered

Dull suit, white socks
No slave to fashion

PHYSICAL CHARACTERISTICS

1. *Blank look.* Bureaucrats treasure anonymity and by evolution have gradually lost distinguishing facial characteristics. For this reason, they are often called 'faceless bureaucrats'.
2. *Large hands.* Accommodates his remarkable facility to pass the buck.
3. *Streamlined and double-jointed thumbs.* Allows for proficient twiddling.
4. *Elevated shoulder blades.* Enables him to respond rapidly to all questions with an emphatic shrug.
5. *Unusually thick skull.* Makes him virtually impervious to rational thought or comment.
6. *Weak knees.* Stems from always having feet propped up on his desk.

Figure 4.1 Anatomy of the bureaucrat

Source (adapted): 1981 © Dots Okay, 4437 Stark Place, Annandale, Virginia 2003.

complex reasons why an understanding of the bureaucratic phenomenon is important.

Bureaucracy affects everyone as it is a pervasive form of organizing and its elements are endemic to many organizations. The study of bureaucracy will help managers to understand the nature of this type of organization and its enormous influence on management practices. The simple fact is that many large organizations are designed along bureaucratic lines, and even though managers might experiment with other forms of structure, it is generally difficult to eliminate *bureaucratic tendencies*. However, before delving too deeply into Weber's work, we first outline some of the key dimensions of structure using Fayol's ideas as a starting point.

Dimensions of structure

The main organizational building block is the division of labour and it is interesting that this principle heads Fayol's list. It provides the rationale for job specialization (both horizontal and vertical), departmentalization and divisionalization. Arising out of the division of labour are the organizing concepts of *span of control*, *chain of command* (or to use Fayol's term, *scalar chain*) and *centralization/decentralization*. Each of these principles is discussed in the following sections. It will be shown that they can be combined in different ways to produce different organizational configurations or profiles. We then go on to discuss the ways in which Weber utilizes many of these self-same notions in his somewhat more profound delineation of the bureaucratic ideal type.

Job specialization

In many large organizations, written job descriptions exist to specify the tasks attached to jobs and nominate the person to whom the job holder is accountable for performance. Job descriptions are therefore part of the organizing and control functions of management. Despite its advantages, job specialization can create problems at all levels of the organization. Job specialization has three major advantages:

- efficiency, through job holders developing expertise in a narrow range of tasks
- control of employees, through the precise definition of tasks and responsibilities
- ease of training and replacement of employees.

On the other hand, the disadvantages of job specialization are:

- boredom and lack of motivation through task repetition

- difficulty in replacing highly skilled specialists
- lack of organizational flexibility, that is, workers unable or unwilling to act outside their areas of specialization
- unresponsiveness to situations of environmental change because of reluctance or inability of employees to work outside an area of specialization (that is, trained incapacity)
- lack of appreciation of the total job, product or service.

Job specialization is related to increasing size in organizations, the design of technical and productive systems and managers' need for control. When organizations are small, and tasks relatively straightforward (for example not technically sophisticated or requiring expert knowledge), it is relatively easy for a group of people to work interchangeably on tasks and jobs. Indeed there are many advantages in this: it allows flexibility in the use of staff (work does not stop if someone is away); it improves communication (everybody knows what's going on); and it may be motivating through the existence of task variety, identity, significance, responsibility and feedback. However, as organizations become larger and some areas of work become more difficult, job specialization inevitably occurs. For example, a small manufacturing business may operate initially as a sole trader but gradually acquire a bookkeeper, a salesperson and a production assistant. With further expansion and job specialization, it is necessary to appoint managers to coordinate departments of finance, marketing and production. Thus vertical job specialization is linked to horizontal job specialization.

Departmentalization

Departmentalization is also based on the division of labour principle and involves the grouping together of related jobs into administrative units typically called *departments*. Basically, there are two broad types of departmentalization used in business operations: *functional/process* and *market*.

Functional departmentalization is based on business functions such as marketing, production or accounting. A variation is departmentation based on the processes through which products pass during manufacture, for example casting, moulding and finishing. Another variation of this is departmentalization based on the knowledge and skills required for the work. For example, a university might have faculties, schools or departments dealing with law, medicine, science, engineering and the arts.

Market departmentalization focuses more on the needs of the user. There are three types of market departmentalization: *product*, *client* and *location*. With product departmentalization, the basis for grouping is the products being produced, for example a pharmaceutical company might have separate administrative units dealing with pharmaceutical, cosmetics, hygiene and surgical products. Client departmentation segments the organization on the basis of the clients to be served, for example retailing, wholesaling and government or customers A–E, customers F–K, customers L–Q and customers R–Z. In the final type, jobs are grouped on the basis of region served, for example Europe, North America or Asia, or, on a smaller scale, city, metropolitan and country.

The advantages and disadvantages of the two main types of departmentation have been much debated. The functional/process form is very widely used and encourages a high level of skill and knowledge development within the particular functions or processes. However, it may lead an organization to be unresponsive to market (customer) needs. Market-oriented structures, however, are much more likely to be responsive to client or regional needs but may not develop the specialist expertise to be found in functional structures. In practice, many large organizations use both forms of departmentation. There is no absolutely right or wrong structure, only what is best for a particular organization in its special circumstances (Stoner et al. 1985: 305–13).

Problems may arise in organizations through the attempt to embrace in a single structure departments or subsystems with radically different professional or functional orientations. The tension that sometimes exists between marketing and production departments may be explained by the dependence of the former upon the latter and the adaptive role of marketing (meeting customer needs) and the maintenance role of production (keeping existing operations going). Another aspect of this is the tension between professional subsystems and administrative ones in organizations such as universities and hospitals. The professional requirements, skills and modes of professionals may bring them into conflict with bureaucrats whose work is both more regulated and regulating. The term *professional bureaucracy* is sometimes applied to these dual hierarchy organizations.

Divisionalization

Divisionalization represents a still higher level of the principle of departmentation. A division consists of a whole group of departments or units related to a product, service or market. For example, CSR Ltd – a major international organization founded in Sydney, Australia in 1855 as a sugar refiner, became a public company in 1887 and began manufacturing building materials in 1936 – has operational divisions for 'sugar', 'aluminium', 'construction materials (USA)', 'construction materials (Australia and Asia)' and 'building materials (Australia, New Zealand and Asia)'.

It will be noted that this is a mixture of a divisionalization based on product and location. The divisional form, sometimes called the *conglomerate*, has its origins in the United States, and is based on the principle that profit responsibility is assigned to general managers of divisions, which in effect operate as separate business units. Head office is the strategic centre and has overall control of strategic planning, policy, special projects and financial control, including resource allocation to the divisions. Corporate headquarters remain committed to the profit of the whole organization and not any one division. This form became popular throughout the world and is now a model for many multinational corporations (Child 1984: 193–5). However, in recent years major corporations such as ABB Hyatt have sought to revitalize this structure, with more more entrepreneurial or intrapreneurial elements such as service webs and and internal markets, as we discuss in Chapter 11.

Divisionalization frequently arises as a result of takeovers or amalgamations. When a company acquires another profitable one, it often makes sense to allow the acquired company to continue with its way of operating if successful, and divisionalization is a way of permitting this. The advantages of divisionalization are that it:

■ provides accountability and focus on outcomes within the division which operates as a small company
■ frees corporate headquarters from the concern of day-to-day operations
■ provides an excellent training ground for general managers through divisional autonomy
■ encourages the accumulation of technical and production expertise
■ means that poorly performing divisions can be lopped off with minimum disruption to the organization
■ allows 'buying' or sharing services and resources
■ allows better alignment with market characteristics.

The problems or weaknesses of the divisional form are many. These include (Child 1984: 94–5; Robbins and Barnwell 1989: 196–7):

■ duplication of resources between head office and the division (for example both have marketing and production departments) which increases costs and makes it difficult to locate the source of poor performance (for example was it a head office decision or a divisional one that caused a major failure?)

- divisions become highly competitive for corporate resources, and poor results can be posted in order to secure more resources at the expense of other apparently efficient divisions
- autonomy is exercised within constraints, for example uniform policies and procedures approved by head office usually apply to divisions. Sometimes these policies can affect a division's performance, for example the purchase of raw materials from a particular supplier and so on. Information systems and bonus schemes and so on are also controlled by head office
- divisions create coordination problems because they rarely cooperate and often compete with each other if they are in the same industry. The extent of autonomy between divisions raises serious problems because economies of scale or joint ventures can be affected by rampant competition among divisional staff and managers
- divisions can often lose sight of corporate goals and formulate their own goals.

Span of control

As organizations become larger and jobs become more specialized, the need for jobs to be coordinated is increased. This coordination is regarded as a management function by classical theorists and gives rise to the *span of control*, which is defined as the number of positions that can be satisfactorily coordinated by one person. Early writers on management believed that the ideal span of control was six (Child 1984: 68). It was thought that this supervisory ratio would enhance control by allowing for adequate supervision, communication and coordination of tasks between individuals. However, it is now recognized that the actual size of a span of control is dependent upon a number of factors, such as the complexity of the task, the skill of subordinates and the supervisor, motivation, technology and so on. Highly complex tasks might require narrow spans of control but tasks employing relatively simple technologies might permit broad spans of control (Child 1984: 69–75).

Chain of command

The linking together of employees into spans of control by supervisors coordinated by spans of control at a higher level, is what gives an organization its typical pyramidal structure or configuration. The network of reporting relationships that flows from this is referred to as the *chain of command*, or *scalar chain* in Fayol's term. In theory, commands or directives flow down through the chain of command from senior management through middle management to first-line managers and subordinates, and reporting relationships flow upwards through the same channel. These management levels in the organization are sometimes referred to as the *hierarchy*. The combination of spans of control and number of levels in the hierarchy determine the final shape of the organizational *pyramid*. An organization with narrow spans of control and many levels in the hierarchy will be a *tall* structure. An organization with wide spans of control and few levels in the hierarchy will be a *flat* one (Mullins 1985: 88–90).). Even though many organizations claim to be more devolved, many still produce conventional organization charts to capture the flow of power and influence in the organization, which is invariably from top to the bottom.

Line and staff functions

An aspect of departmentalization is the distinction between *line* and *staff functions*. Line functions are those which carry out the primary purpose of the business; staff functions are ancillary to these and serve the organization's purposes indirectly by the provision of support services (see Table 4.1). In strategic terms, these distinctions have become quite political, in terms of determining which areas add value to the core business and customers and which are support and basically back-room functions that can often be outsourced (see Chapter 15).

Staff-type departments exercise responsibility for their particular function throughout the entire organization. This is sometimes referred to as *functional authority*. Conflict sometimes arises in organizations because of the staff/line distinction. For example, a production manager may be working to achieve certain production targets. He or she may feel hampered in doing this because of, say, a shortage of staff or a lack of finance to buy essential equipment. These concerns may lead to friction with the personnel manager, who is responsible for staffing, and with the finance controller who is responsible for finance. This situation simply

Table 4.1 Line and staff distinctions

LINE	STAFF
Manufacturing business	
Production	Accounting
Selling	Personnel
	Purchasing
Retail business	
Buying	Accounting
Selling	Personnel
Hospital	
Doctors	Administration
Nurses	Maintenance

points to the difficulty of designing structures that do not have the potential for conflict.

In the preceding discussion, the staff concept was applied to certain functional departments. The word *staff* is also applied to individuals who constitute the personal staff of a manager. These positions are usually of the 'assistant to' variety. Personal staff of this type do not hold any line responsibility. They have no authority over any of the position holders shown beneath them on an organizational chart (Mullins 1985: 95–7; Stoner et al. 1985: 360–4).

Centralization, decentralization and formalization

Organizations which maintain tight control of authority at or near the top of the organization are said to be centralized. Those which delegate decision making closer to where the work is performed are said to be decentralized. Historically, organizations moved into decentralized modes because of factors such as size, market demands and geographical dispersion, where the referral of matters to *head office* or a central administration might mean costly delays and poor customer service. Centralized organizations are deemed to have the following advantages:

- greater overall control and hence more consistency in policy implementation
- greater expertise and hence better decisions
- benefits of economies of scale and hence a saving in equipment and labour costs.

Decentralization has been deemed to have the following advantages (Mullins 1985: 94):

- it enables decisions to be made closer to where the work is performed, which may mean better and quicker decisions
- it provides opportunities for training and development
- it is likely to be more motivational
- there is greater responsiveness to environmental change.

It might be noted that the need to decentralize, based on increasing size or geographical dispersion, has diminished because of online computing and improved telecommunications (think back to the case). However, it remains true that large organizations with diverse operations have great difficulty with completely centralized control. Rather than relying on structure, control is exercised through policies, budgets and profit centres. Within these policies and budgets, a great deal of local discretion may be allowed. So in practice a large organization (for example a divisionalized structure) might use a combination of centralization and decentralization.

Formalization is also related to control. Formalization refers to the extent to which rules, policies and procedures dominate activities in an organization and is considered at much greater length below in our discussion of Weber's work on bureaucracy. Formalization may allow an organization to be decentralized operationally while a measure of centralized control is retained.

Weber and bureaucracy

As we noted above, most of the early management theorists either offered universal prescriptions on how to organize and manage the shop floor in 'one best way', or, in the case of Fayol, have been read as so doing despite their own assertions that they should not be so read! Max Weber's early study of bureaucracy, however, broke from this tradition much more clearly because it sought to develop a historical and sociological account of the rise of modern organizations. Weber's theory of bureaucracy was not translated into English until the late 1940s, and by then the methods associated with scientific management and human relations had already established themselves as the dominant management and organizational theories. What Weber offers that is particularly distinctive is an account of ways in which formalized organization can work, by delineating how and why its imperatives are accepted by those who are subject to them. He was able to achieve this by carefully delineating the bureaucratic, formalized organization from other types and by noting the way in which each type was associated with a different sort of belief system, which acted to legitimate its imperatives.

Weber's studies of the German state bureaucracy became the foundation for a very detailed analysis of the bureaucratic form. His theory of bureaucracy contained one of the most complex descriptions of organizational administration that has emerged in the literature. Some believe that there are three ways to treat Weber's works on bureaucracy: as a *benchmark* by which to judge the development of modern organizations; as an *explanation* for social change suggesting all organizations undergo some form of bureaucratization; and as a way of *identifying* the problems of modern, large organizations (Rogers and McIntire 1983: 9). Most of the management literature has concentrated on the last aspect (Leivesley et al. 1990: 370–6).

One of the reasons Weber is considered complex is because of the way he studied the bureaucratic phenomenon. He used an ideal type construct to analyse the emergence of the bureaucratic form of organization. The ideal type, as devised by Weber, is a construct or a device used to identify the salient characteristics of social phenomena such as bureaucracies. Weber used this ideal type to distinguish it from other forms of organization, which the emerging bureaucratic form was replacing in the Prussia (northeast Germany) of his time. Weber stated that a pure form of bureaucracy would not be found in real life, that is, the totality of characteristics will not always be present in a specific case. The ideal type is a type, made up of ideas, useful for identification and sensitizing purposes (Lamond 1990: 468–72; Leivesley et al. 1990: 369–70). Weber identified the Prussian Church, army and Civil Service as instances of this newly emerging bureaucratic form. However, there is no sense in which he was prescribing an organizational form. He did, however, recognize bureaucracy as a technically efficient device for relating organization means to ends, for example modern accounting systems relate the resources of the enterprise to the achievement of the organization's goals in a precise and calculable way. In this emerging form of organization, Weber saw a power instrument of the first order. He saw bureaucracy as embodying a powerful combination of knowledgeable officials ruling by law and regulations on a precisely calculable basis. He believed this power phenomenon would challenge the very bases of democracy (Gerth and Mills 1967: 196–244).

Power and authority

Weber suggested that one of the ways of understanding how organizations evolved was to examine the nature of authority in these organizations. He started from the proposition that the exercise of authority was different from the exercise of power:

'Power' (macht) is the probability that one actor within a social relationship will be in a position to carry out his own will despite resistance. (Weber 1964: 152)

Authority (or *imperative control*) was defined in terms of the probability of certain commands or orders being obeyed by a group. There had to be a certain degree of voluntary submission on the group's part to these commands and an acceptance of the need to obey. Weber uses the term *legitimate order* to describe how the exercise of authority is based on groups' or individuals' beliefs that commands or orders are binding on them and, in fact, desirable to imitate. These commands or orders are ultimately obeyed automatically and promptly (Weber 1964: 124, 152–3, 324–9). He believed that organizations or leaders seek legitimacy of their actions in different ways through the exercise of authority.

Weber identified three organizational types, which he differentiated on the basis of the type of authority that was being exercised in them. He labelled these three ideal types: *charismatic*, *traditional* and *rational-legal* (Weber 1964: 328–67; Weber, cited in Pugh 1984: 15–19). Each of these ideal types was represented by a distinctive form of organization (see Table 4.2). For Weber, the notion of *authority* was always inextricably bound up with the idea of a legitimate order. He contended that, for the continual exercise of authority in any organization, there had to be a willingness on the part of members to conform to and accept a leader's rules and orders, that is, to see them as legitimate. If a person had authority, then he or she had a right to expect total obedience and compliance from subordinates. Force or coercion was not used by those in charge because that would involve the costly and ineffective use of threats and force, that is, power. Table 4.2 outlines Weber's three ideal types of authority, based on the type of leadership required, the beliefs that reinforce obedience or compliance, and the types of obedience that are generally considered acceptable.

Charismatic authority rests on devotion to an outstanding individual who is a leader by virtue of certain special qualities (for example heroic, prophetic) that appeal to his or her followers. This form of authority is most clearly seen in sectarian groups. Political leaders have been able to elicit this kind of

Types of authority	Organizational form (example)	Type of leadership	Types of belief	Basis of obedience
Charismatic	Movement or sect	Supernatural or special gift	Affective: spiritual or personal renewal, worship and subservience	Unquestioning obedience to a person
Traditional	Monarchy, Church, tribe	Figurehead by birth or ordination	Affective: duty, obligation, custom, ritual	Reciprocal obligations but in favour of figurehead
Rational-legal	Bureaucracy or modern organization	Individuals appointed to a position	Instrumental: money/ material ends valued and the means to secure them	Impersonal, calculable rules and so on govern everyone's conduct, even senior members

Table 4.2 Ideal types of authority and organization

Source: Liz Fulop (1992) 'Bureaucracy and the modern manager', in Fulop et al. (1992), p. 137.

response as well. Former US President Bill Clinton has often been referred to as having charisma. Entrepreneurs such as Richard Branson and hero managers such as Lee Iaccoca have also been said to have this quality, although, as we argue in Chapter 10, there is a fine line between charisma and narcissism. One of the problems with the pure charismatic organization (that is, a sect) is that its continuation is dependent on the survival of the charismatic leader. Moreover, such leaders must continually demonstrate their special qualities so that there is a constant sense of extraordinary events occurring within the organization. They may have to perform outstanding deeds or deliver on a prophecy. Weber saw charismatic organizations as highly unstable because of the need to renew faith, belief and extraordinary experiences in order to sustain legitimacy.

Traditional authority is based on precedent and custom. The leader holds authority by virtue of the status he or she has been granted or inherited. Examples here would be the Church, the monarchy and chiefs in various tribal systems. In the case of traditional authority, leaders cannot offend their members or break with the images expected of them, for example monarchs must behave as monarchs are expected to. Although the British royal family has no political authority these days, it has always been expected to behave in ways accordant with its respect and influence. The 'young royals', Prince Andrew and Sarah Ferguson, Princess Diana, Prince Edward and Sophie, have all been criticized since the 1980s for failing to preserve the authoritative image of the monarchy. However, as with charismatic authority, traditional authority alone does not provide a continuous basis for the management of large businesses.

In Weber's work, *rational-legal authority* is a term that is virtually interchangeable with bureaucracy. In bureaucracies, authority is legal because it is exercised through formalized laws and regulations, which govern all activities and people. Conformity is expected to the laws and rules of the organization rather than to a particular person or the cult of charisma. It does not require sentiment or loyalty on the part of members to some figurehead or charismatic leader. It is an impersonal system devoid of a strong identification with exceptional leadership.

The three ideal types can be briefly summarized as:

1. Under charismatic authority, the personality of the leader is the governing factor in relationships.
2. Under traditional authority, relations are governed by custom and usage.
3. Under legal-rational authority, relationships are governed by the rules and laws of an organization and the recognized competence of officials.

Even though Weber described these ideal types of authority, he never discounted the fact that in many organizations there could be elements of charismatic and traditional authority coexisting with the rational-legal type. Certainly, many charismatic leaders have also been traditional leaders, such as the Ayatollah Khomeini, who ruled Iran until 1990. However, Weber did argue that, because of the superior qualities of bureaucratic organizations, this form would spread and become the most dominant way in which modern organizations were structured (Miner 1982: 389–90).

Modern approaches to bureaucracy

Many of Weber's ideas have been lost either in translation or in the application of his work to solving modern organizational and management problems. Exhibit 4.2 lists the characteristics considered to be typical of a modern bureaucracy. These bear only a vague resemblance to Weber's own ideal type construct (Weber 1964: 329–41). Nonetheless, Weber's work remains relevant to the modern manager because of the wealth of research and ideas that it has generated in the past, continuing to the present. Here we examine four aspects of Weber's study of bureaucracy and authority. Many more could be added. What is intended is to demonstrate the relevance of Weber's ideas to the modern manager.

Beliefs and meaning systems

The notion of *belief systems* was central to Weber's theory of bureaucracy and rational-legal authority. Occupying a particular position in the hierarchy of an organization, even the top one, did not automatically mean that the person could exercise authority. Power, and even more subtle uses of influence, could be brought to bear on organizational members to make them carry out an order, but this did not mean that the order or command had legitimacy. Weber's observations on authority are remarkably relevant. He maintained that the beliefs, meanings and self-interest of individuals had to be bound into the fabric of the organization, so that authority could be exercised. He argued that an individual's propensity to accept authority was conditional upon a number of expectations being met. In a bureaucracy, an individual's self-interest had to be in harmony with the commands (rules and policies) operating within the organization. Weber believed that most individuals worked for instrumental reasons (as a means to an end) and as long as administrative conditions allowed for attainment of these ends, then there would be relative trust and acceptance of authority. For reasons not too dissimilar to Taylor, Weber believed that the spread of capitalism and the Protestant work ethic would

Exhibit 4.2 Characteristics of a modern bureaucracy

- ❏ Work rules and regulations established by management
- ❏ Job results evaluated by superiors or senior management
- ❏ Pay levels based on seniority
- ❏ Freedom of action heavily limited by organizational guidelines, rules and procedures
- ❏ Policies established by management
- ❏ Screening and selecting new employees accomplished by a computerized system
- ❏ Policies, rules and guidelines have to be based on methods that allow accurate calculation of outcomes (for example performance reviews)

- ❏ Hierarchy prevails
- ❏ Senior managers take risk and responsibility for failures
- ❏ Resources for carrying out work are allocated by management
- ❏ Many decisions and activities are centralized
- ❏ People recruited on the bases of merit and qualifications
- ❏ No one is irreplaceable
- ❏ Following the rules is what counts most
- ❏ Rules are portrayed as being impartial and equitable

Source: Adapted from J.B. Miner (1982) *Theories of Organizational Structure and Process*, New York: Dryden Press, p. 423.

encourage individuals to seek material and economic rewards. However, unlike Taylor, Weber did not view this as necessarily a good thing, but rather as an inevitable 'fact' of progress (Clegg 1990: 29–30).

Some of the ways in which Weber's concepts of meaning systems and self-interest might be applied to modern organizations include the following (Albrow 1970: 43–5; Thompson 1980: 9; Weber, cited in Pugh 1984: 16–17):

1. Individuals must believe that the organization has established laws and policies that apply to all members (junior and senior) so that they are willing to accept and follow the rules (*impartiality*).
2. Individuals must also believe that the policies and laws of the organization comprise a system of fairly general rules that can deal with individual cases (*generalizable*).
3. There must be assurances that those involved in the administration of policies and laws are not arbitrarily or wantonly able to reinterpret them to suit specific situations or persons (*equity*).
4. There has to be a belief that senior staff members exercising authority are also bound to comply with the policies or laws. Nobody is above this impersonal system or able to act outside it without penalty (*uniformity*).
5. Individuals are likely to accept the policies and laws because they only apply while they are members of a particular organization; they do not bind them outside this context (they are *restrictive* with regards to their legitimate site(s) of application).
6. It is the overall legal framework (policies, rules,

regulations) which is obeyed rather than a specific individual (*impersonal*).

It is difficult to imagine that a manager who rejects these principles could achieve wide acceptance of his or her authority. Most individuals would subscribe to all the principles listed above and judge those in authority as less than legitimate if the latter sought to manipulate or neglect the spirit and intent of such things as equity, uniformity and impartiality. In Weber's mind, it was clear that the impressions individuals gained of those in authority were heavily influenced by the meanings attached to their actions, and the standards of conduct they engendered.

The impersonal nature of bureaucracies, and the fact that they continue to operate long after their leaders and members depart, led Weber to the conclusion that this type of organization overcame the problems of succession that riddled charismatic and traditional ones: for example the head of a university or large corporation is obviously more easily replaced than an unsuitable monarch or religious guru. It is common to see an advertisement in a paper for a managing director or vice-chancellor but not for a queen, king or a charismatic leader! But other elements were also important for the exercise of authority and control. These related to the structural and procedural features covered in the three areas below.

Specialization and centralization

Echoing what we noted above in our consideration of Fayol's work, the division of labour played a central part in Weber's account of the bureaucratic organization and many of the particularities of its form are attributable to this basic phenomenon. Bureaucratic organizations are seen to be hierarchical and structured so that order, discipline and command are understood by all. According to Weber, members of bureaucracies enter with special skills and knowledge acquired through some form of external training or examination. The system is supposed to see that those with superior qualifications rise to the top positions, while those with fewer qualifications are ranked below them. This means that there will be specialized functions based on training and credentials. Moreover, those at the top make the important strategic decisions while those ranked below them implement their orders or commands. Weber believed that bureaucracies would be highly centralized, which logically implied that all major decisions would be issued through a chain of command, from the top down to the bottom. These general observations of Weber's led the Aston School researchers in the UK to conduct research into the trends towards centralization and specialization in large organizations. Most studies on bureaucracy use these two dimensions to measure variations in structure (Albrow 1970: 43–5; Salaman 1979: 130–2; Miner 1982: 390; Weber, cited in Pugh 1984: 20–1).

Rules and procedures

According to Weber, a legitimate order based on rational-legal authority was premised on a minimum voluntary level of compliance and obedience of members in carrying out commands or orders. Legitimacy of an order, as already mentioned, can be based on several different types of belief, but in bureaucracies they depend on the legality of the system: 'the readiness to conform with rules which are formally correct and have been imposed by accepted procedure' (Weber 1964: 131–2). Weber went to great lengths to outline the rules of conduct and the procedures that would lend legitimacy to the position of officials in bureaucracies. In fact, he outlined the rules of conduct that he thought should govern all members' actions in every position or office to ensure the honesty and integrity of the system. Many practices based on ritual, custom, favouritism and nepotism were meant to decline and be replaced by impartial and uniform procedures. These have been summarized (Weber 1964: 333–4; Gerth and Mills 1967: 198–204; Weber, cited in Pugh 1984: 20–1) as:

1. Recruitment based on ability and technical knowledge. The selection criteria must be objective, with each position carrying appropriate rewards based on merit and seniority.
2. The selection and attainment of a position is based

on a free contractual relationship; no one can be forced or coerced into membership.
3. Members are personally free (are not 'owned' by the bureaucracy) and only subject to legal contractual obligations in relation to their specified duties.
4. Salaries must be fixed and retirement pensions provided so that those who devote themselves to the organization are rewarded for loyalty and service (that is, for sole, lifelong employment).
5. The scope for termination of employment is limited, although an employee is free to resign at will.
6. A member's work in the bureaucracy forms his or her main occupation and career.
7. A member cannot personally own or have a property interest in the organization.
8. Strict discipline and conduct is required in one's position. There is a code of conduct.
9. There is a career path and opportunities for promotion, and movement up the hierarchy through gaining qualifications or training.

These features of bureaucracy are the more commonly known ones. In the hands of the Aston School, they were translated into terms such as *formalization* and *standardization*. Undoubtedly, formalization (setting rules) and standardization (making practices uniform) relate to processes found in many private and public sector organizations, as we noted above. That is why it can be said that many organizations display bureaucratic tendencies. Formalization and standardization are often touted as the real benefits of bureaucracy. They support such things as credentialism, contractual obligations, impersonality and equity (Clegg 1990: 39–40).

Weber contended that as long as members believed that the rules controlling them were fair and applied to everyone uniformly, then equity and fairness would prevail. Bureaucracy was, after all, becoming depersonalized, objective and increasingly governed by impartial rules (Weber 1964: 340). It was developing into a system devoid of passion and hence without affection or enthusiasm. In Weber's ideal type, senior staff could only exercise authority within the rules set down in written policies and laws; these constrained them as they did subordinates. It was a system of mutual control and supposed benefits:

the position of the bureaucrat, his relation to the ruler, the ruled and his colleagues are strictly defined by impersonal rules. These rules delineate in a rational way the hierarchy ... rights and duties of every position [and] the methods of recruitment and promotion. (Gerth and Mills 1967: 229)

Good examples of what is meant by formalization and standardization, apart from the conditions and methods of employment mentioned above, are university admission policies. When students apply for entrance into particular courses, they must comply with rules (formalization) and meet certain minimum criteria for entry (standardization). The selection procedures for admitting students are difficult to alter or adjust to unique cases. However, the 'system' attempts to provide impartiality and fairness in its procedures. Imagine how upset a student would be to discover that he or she had been denied a place in a university course because someone with lower marks, who did not meet the relevant criteria, had been granted entry because a family member 'pulled strings'. In other words, nepotism and favouritism are not expected or tolerated. Most organizations strive to formalize and standardize their procedures and practices to rid themselves of favouritism and its consequences, including corruption and nepotism.

Technical rationality and expertise

Belief in legal statutes and rationally created rules were part of the explanation Weber used to describe the *pervasiveness* of bureaucracy. He was convinced that it was its *rational* aspect that ensured its spread as an organizational form. Weber wrote:

Bureaucratic administration means fundamentally the exercise of control on the basis of knowledge. This is the feature of it which makes it specifically rational. (cited in Pugh 1984: 26)

For Weber, it is not the number of rules that make an organization more or less bureaucratic, but rather the extent to which these are based on objective principles of calculation or scientific/technical *know-how*. This means that the more an organization's management can quantify and measure activities in terms of means and ends, the more they eliminate the potential for favouritism or whimsical decisions. In Weber's view, calculation, precision, order and predictability were the distinctive features of *technical rationality*.

In the business context, the development of modern business methods, such as accounting and information systems, are examples of what Weber means by technical rationality (Weber, cited in Pugh 1984: 24). Technical rationality involves adopting particular business methods or systems based on scientific/technically based knowledge, sometimes called *expert systems*. Today, there is ever-greater pressure for organizations to adopt this form of rationality in all areas of their activities, leading to the formalization and standardization of all sorts of inputs and outputs. Developing computer-based technologies in areas such as marketing, personnel, accounting, corporate strategy and computer-based decision making all reflect this trend. Within the framework of technical rationality, organizational problems or processes are treated as inputs into the system or factors which can be manipulated in a highly impersonal and neutral fashion: for example manpower planning done by computer software is supposed to eliminate human error and biases. Most modern concepts of budgeting, corporate planning and programme evaluation, for example, derive from the application of systems based on technical rationality (Wilenski 1988: 215–17). Modern technology simply enhances it.

Weber considered technical rationality as the crucial feature of modern organizations, differentiating them from traditional or charismatic forms: technical or instrumental rationality was pervasive (Albrow 1970: 89). Weber concluded, however, that in bureaucracies knowledge was always of two kinds: *expert* and *procedural* (rules and policies) and that those who mastered these areas would maintain control. He agonized over the potential power of experts or highly trained bureaucrats to subvert the influence of the political leaders they were meant to serve. However, the growth of different groups of professionals and experts was a phenomenon beyond Weber's experience (Weber, cited in Pugh 1984: 26).

Weber predicted that within both modern capitalist and socialist societies, bureaucracy would develop because it provided the most specialized and technically sophisticated form of administration. Weber saw the spread of bureaucracy as neither evolutionary nor totally predictable. He believed that the continual growth and incorporation of all levels of society into the bureaucratic form (the growth of the characteristics identified under the ideal type) would lead to the bureaucratization and rationalization of society (Gerth and Mills 1967: 204; Albrow 1970: 45; Aron 1970: 246).

Dysfunctions and problems with bureaucracy

Many studies have highlighted both positive and negative aspects of bureaucracies. Byrt, for example, considers the following advantages of the bureaucratic form (Byrt 1973: 49):

1. Impersonality
2. Impartiality
3. Professionalism of management
4. Suitability for large organizations and those involving complex administrative tasks
5. Provision of careers.

Some of the negative or dysfunctional aspects of bureaucratic organizations, sometimes termed *bureaupathic behaviour*, he summarizes as follows (Byrt 1973: 60):

1. Minimal acceptable, or get-by performance
2. Rigidity of behaviour and inadequate search for alternative courses of action
3. Defensiveness and/or aggression on the part of groups towards superiors, other groups, and clients
4. Overemphasis on operational or measurable objectives
5. Cynicism, dissatisfaction and pessimism towards the organization on the part of its members
6. The taking of decisions at a point remote from the work situation
7. Weakening of the formal lines of authority, with concentration of power at the top
8. Strong resistance to change
9. The development of the informal organization
10. Overconformity in behaviour
11. Parkinson's law: work expands to fill the time available for its completion
12. The Peter Principle: in a hierarchy every employee tends to rise to the level of his or her incompetence.

We interrogate some of these criticisms in significantly more detail in later sections of the chapter, but it is a worth saying a little more about some of them even at this juncture. We can delineate a number of possible reasons why Weber's concept of bureaucracy has been seen as problematical and has created difficulties for those using the ideal type. Firstly, Weber is often criticized for *not being aware of the types of influence which may halt the spread of instrumental rationality* (Luhmann 1982: 24). Weber could not foresee all the pressures that have given rise to industrial democracy, worker participation, professionalism, quality of work life and other demands of modern workers that have changed the nature of loyalty and commitment, and hence the acceptance of authority. However, it would be a mistake to think that Weber was not aware of the partial and limited allegiances people have to bureaucracies, and he noted that unlike charismatic and traditional organizations, loyalty is not absolute or all-encompassing for members of bureaucracies. Few people attach the same meaning to work as they do to activities based on custom or ritual of some kind. Bureaucracies provided a system of imperative coordination that was uniquely modern and suited to the instrumental orientations of workers (Georgiou 1975: 293–95; Thompson 1980: 12; Miner 1982: 418). This having been said, modern commentators such as George Ritzer (2000) (see Chapter 9) argue that Weberian bureaucracy has spread even more rapidly than Weber could have predicted, due to its combination with Fordism and Taylorism in *McDonaldization* – the spread of the principles of the fast-food industry to other types of commercial and non-commercial activity.

Secondly, many critics have used Weber's ideal type of bureaucracy as though it was prescribing how to establish a *perfect or efficient form of organization*, a 'one best way' (for example Rickards 1985: 65). According to some observers, Weber's intention was not to create a model but rather a conceptual construct that would identify characteristics of a bureaucracy. Weber never intended the ideal type to be proved or disproved. More importantly, it is unwise to treat it as a prescriptive model for establishing a perfect or efficient bureaucracy (Mouzelis 1967: 38–44; Blau and Meyer 1971: 24–5; Rogers and McIntire 1983: 8).

However, the ideal type has been useful in guiding research into the problems of complex organizations and its value in this regard is immeasurable. Research using Weber's ideal type has not supported some of the relationships Weber considered as 'typical' of bureaucratic development. It would seem that the more bureaucratic an organization becomes (greater standardization, formalization, specialization and technical rationality), the more likely it is that certain practices become decentralised. Once organizations establish standards and rules and introduce mechanisms such as computer-aided decision making, top management tends to delegate certain decisions and activities to middle and junior managers. As we noted above, the growth of these indirect control mechanisms has enhanced decentralization in many large organizations. Even in public service ones, people now talk of a preference for delegation and accountability rather than direct methods of control (Radbone 1987: 119–21). It seems the only decisions that remain highly centralized are strategic ones relating to finance, markets and the selection of key personnel (Miner 1982: 403, 407, 418–19). Ironically, while Weber did not specify that the ideal type was a prescriptive model for success, research has also found that organizations which can implement some of the core elements such as formalization, standardization, specialization and technical rationality are likely to perform quite well under certain conditions (Miner 1982: 403–7). We consider what these conditions might be in our later account of the contingency approach to organizational design.

Thirdly, Weber's definition of legal authority concentrated on *the enforcement of rules*. For Weber, legal authority was most 'pervasive' when 'the spirit of formalistic impersonality' (or rules) dominated all decisions and choices (Salaman 1979: 130). Some researchers, however, have questioned the degree to which rules are so easily enforced. Gouldner (1954), for example, conducted research into the effects of rules and concluded that the way they were introduced influenced their effectiveness (see also Chapter 6). His work focused on three different types of bureaucratic patterns which can exist in the workplace, depending on how rules are established in the first place: *punishment-centred*, *mock* and *representative rules*. In the mock pattern, rules exist but are ignored by both staff and management (for example no smoking rules, particularly in certain European countries). In the representative pattern, rules are mutually agreed to and are accepted as fair by all (for example using safety clothing in a toxic industry). In the punishment-centred pattern, one party imposes rules against the others' wishes, generating conflict and power struggles (for example abolishing tea breaks to save money). Gouldner's research in a gypsum mine in the US highlighted how difficult it was for management to eliminate perks and privileges and change mock rules. Changing rules against pilfering eventually led to bitter industrial conflicts and the final closure of the mine. According to Gouldner, bureaucracy is man-made and 'is a function of human striving; it is the outcome of a contest between those who want it and those who do not' (quoted in Salaman 1979: 147). To simply presume that all rules could be agreed to and exercised by those at the top of the hierarchy ignores manipulation, dissent and rejection of them (Gouldner 1954: 20; Byrt 1973: 49; Gouldner, cited in Pugh et al. 1983: 20–4).

Gouldner's study was a descriptive piece of research that attempted to draw attention to the manner in which rules could be interpreted and acted upon differently by all within organizations. It was a study that did not adopt a managerial perspective (or myth of the true description) and tried to show that rules had significantly different meanings for workers than for managers. The more management tried to institute more bureaucratic procedures (stricter rules, regulations and disciplinary measures), the more workers resented the abolition of practices that were based on nepotism and favouritism, even though these were detrimental to improving productivity. Gouldner's study was one of the earliest to approach the problem of control and authority from an action approach, by focusing on the importance of meaning systems, as pointed out by Weber (Silverman 1970). However, his work was based on shop-floor practices and a very narrow definition of rules and thus largely applies Weber's theory outside its original intent or purpose.

Lastly, while Gouldner's work highlighted the problem of rules and authority, a study by the French sociologist Crozier (1964) created even more doubts about Weber's theory of authority. Crozier set out to study how authority was actually exercised in large organizations, especially in areas in which it was not always easy to replace people or eliminate their tasks. He did not start from the premise that people's actions were oriented to rule following and complicity, but rather from the assumption that:

through the organisation's effort to eliminate the discretion of employees, some area of uncertainty will remain, and such uncertainty is the breeding ground for efforts to achieve some, however slight, self-control ... The final structure of an organisation ... is the result of these negotiations, interpretations in which organisational members actively strive to resist some directions and control. (Salaman 1979: 146)

Crozier's study of maintenance men in the French tobacco industry is instructive. He found that through their union, these workers controlled the repair of machines and could potentially disrupt the work and halt all major activities in the factory. The maintenance men were specialists or experts who controlled an area of uncertainty and upon whom management depended for the work to progress. This dependency relationship gave these workers enormous power over executives of the company and other workers. They enjoyed immense freedom and discretion. This won them control. Studies such as Crozier's led many to ponder the problem of power and dependency in organizations and their implications for Weber's theory of authority (Crozier 1964: 160; Byrt 1973: 52–3; Salaman 1979: 146, 167–8). It also reminds us that not all of the structuring of an organization is the result of deliberate efforts on the part of management. Managers do not have a blank sheet of paper on which to draw up the way in which the organization is structured. Since any formal structure seeks to manage or legitimize the use of power, structure will inevitably be a site of conflict, and a conflict in which, as Crozier reminds us, management will not always have the upper hand.

One area that has attracted a lot of attention as a result was the study of the power of experts or professionals in organizations. According to some writers, it is difficult to coordinate or control experts through bureaucratic procedures and structures (Mintzberg 1983a: 163–70). Specialized knowledge attained outside the organization through lengthy training is difficult to control or eliminate by rules or procedures alone. Many managers cannot afford the costs of training professionals or experts but must face the problem of integrating them into the routine practices and authority systems of their organizations. According to Mintzberg, the professional training of experts often conflicts with the rules and expectations in most workplaces. Furthermore, many experts achieve discretion in their work roles because of the complexity of the tasks they master which other senior staff may not understand, forcing the latter to defer to experts. In Mintzberg's view, legal-rational authority systems are eroded by professional expertise and associated professional systems. This has been particularly noted in places such as research and development (R&D) departments, where managers find it difficult to control staff who, through their expertise over small areas of knowledge, can increasingly influence decision making. Establishing staff departments, such as data processing

> ### *Exhibit 4.3* Characteristics of professional systems
>
> - ❏ Work rules and regulations established by professional group
> - ❏ Job results only validly judged by other professionals
> - ❏ Pay levels based on nature and extent of professional training and education
> - ❏ Actions heavily influenced by professional standards, rules and regulations
> - ❏ Punishment or discipline accepted as part of self-regulation by other professionals
> - ❏ Screening and selecting of professionals seen largely as responsibility of other professionals; leaders must be professionals
> - ❏ Performance standards judged against those set by the profession
> - ❏ Hierarchy based on professional qualifications and experience
>
> - ❏ Risk and responsibility for failure come down to professional judgement
> - ❏ Resources allocated and determined by other experts
> - ❏ Decisions decentralized to professional/expert groups
> - ❏ Staff recruited only on the basis of merit and qualifications
> - ❏ Some individuals are not easily replaced because of high level of expertise
> - ❏ Following professional judgement and standards is what counts most
> - ❏ Professional knowledge is valued over procedural knowledge (policies, rules and so on)
> - ❏ Impartiality determined by professional standards of conduct; equity via professional competence and credentials
>
> *Source:* Adapted from J.B. Miner (1982) *Theories of Organizational Structure and Process*, New York: Dryden Press, p. 423.

and personnel, may be seen as a sign of attempts by management to integrate experts into the organization (Chatterjee and McDonald 1981: 38; Miner 1982: 395). Compare Exhibit 4.2 with Exhibit 4.3: the latter illustrates the professional or expert-based system. Note that significant differences occur in the beliefs and structural arrangements favoured by professionals and experts, although some are compatible with bureaucracy. It would seem that professionals and experts can diminish the cohesiveness of organizations and small groups can erode the characteristic unity of an organization, especially when they exercise control and power through expertise (Mintzberg 1983a: 165). Nobody has yet found a definitive solution to this problem, although many believe bureaucratic organizations must come to terms with these developments. In fact, some theorists suggest that bureaucracy was the first modern form of organization, but now it must give way to a postmodern one that can deal with the changes in society, such as the rise of professionals and experts (Clegg 1990: 176–81). Many of these issues are taken up below, as we begin to consider the ways in which various integrative mechanisms have been employed in an attempt to maintain the benefits of structural arrangements, while avoiding the various rigidities and conflicts which can afflict them.

Integrative structures

The preceding discussion identified the following potential problems or areas of difficulty with traditional structures and particularly the bureaucratic form:

- the effect of structure on communication: problems of horizontal communication in broad flat structures, problems of vertical communication in tall structures
- staff/line conflict, especially professionals and experts versus line managers
- centralization versus decentralization.

Attempts to deal with such problems have led to the development of *integrative* or mixed structures such as committees, task forces and matrix structures (Child 1984: 97–103; Stoner et al. 1985: 313–17; Dawson 1986: 118–19; Robbins and Barnwell 1989: 222–7).

The *committee* is a time-hallowed method of attempting coordination between disparate areas of work, improving communication and achieving consensus. Committees of various kinds exist in organizations: standing or permanent, temporary and ad hoc. An example of a standing committee might be a finance committee. A temporary or ad hoc committee might be called together to resolve some short-term problem, for example the allocation of spaces in a car park.

Task forces or *project teams* are really temporary committees with responsibility for the investigation, recommendation and perhaps resolution of a problem or problems affecting a number of subunits. For example, a task force consisting of potential users might be set up by a company to investigate and recommend on the type of computing system to be introduced.

Committees and task forces will not necessarily resolve the problems of power and conflict in organizations. Politics becomes involved whenever vested interests are affected and committees are prone to agenda manipulation, compromise and tunnel vision. Their success depends upon the adequacy of the representation, the information available to them, the willingness of members to cooperate and whether committees are executive or advisory in nature.

Matrix structures aim at handling more effectively situations where a regular intermeshing occurs between two or more lines of accountability. The matrix structure was developed in the aerospace industry in the US, where workers had dual accountability both to a project leader for a specific project and a functional or process head in relation to a function or process. In the simplified matrix structure shown in Figure 4.2, the engineer (E1) is simultaneously a member of the engineering department and accountable to its head, and

of the Project A group and accountable to its head for engineering work associated with that particular project.

It will be clear from Figure 4.2 that a matrix structure is a way of simultaneously handling a number of projects that may have different requirements and different completion dates. Matrix structures can also be used to resolve the staff/line tension and the functional versus marketing departmentalization problem previously discussed. In Figure 4.2 functions are represented along the horizontal axis, and the products (in this case three projects) along the vertical axis. The matrix structure may be used for an entire organization or just some aspects of its activities. The claimed advantages of matrix structures are (Stoner et al. 1985: 317; Robbins and Barnwell 1989: 226):

- flexibility in both the use of people and material resources
- relatively easy to expand to take on other projects
- encouragement of interdisciplinary/functional cooperation
- excellent training ground.

The potential disadvantages are:

- weakening of accountability through duality of command

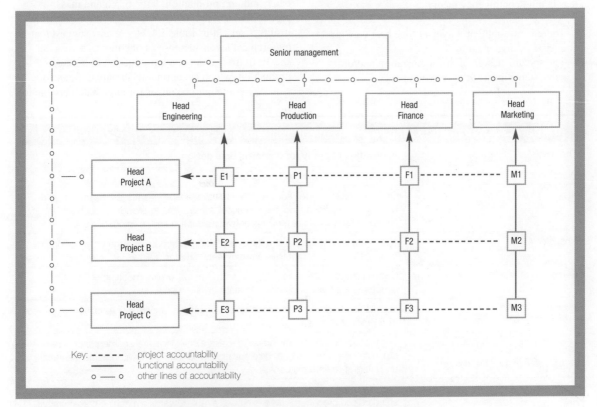

Figure 4.2 Simplified matrix structure

Source: Harold Hayward (1992) 'Organising and organisation', in Fulop et al. (1992), p. 169.

- possibility of role conflict among members because of duality of command
- matrix members may lose their career paths in the mainstream.

Mintzberg (1983b) borrowed Toffler's (1970) term *adhocracy* to describe what he saw as the increasing use of an almost unstructured structure, to enable sophisticated innovation in organizational activity and its outputs. We will return to this at some length later in the chapter. For the moment, we note merely Mintzberg's assertion that certain structures are better for certain things, a theme that is the central issue for the so-called contingency approach that we consider in the next section.

Contingency factors in organizational design

The contingency approach argues that the structure of an organization is influenced by certain *contingencies*, or *situational* factors, with the most commonly identified ones in this literature being *technology*, *size* and *environment*. An appropriate structure is one which 'fits' the demands of these contingencies. The main ideas behind contingency theory are:

- There is no single or universal 'one best way' to design an organization.
- The specific design of the organization and/or its subsystems must 'fit' its environment.

- The better the 'fit' between the subsystems of an organization, and between the organization and the environment, the more effective the organization.
- The needs of organizational members are better satisfied when the organization is properly designed and the management style is appropriate to the requirements of the tasks and the maturity of the work group.

A summary of the main writings and research studies that support the contingency approach is set out in Table 4.3. A review of the research results of three seminal studies that bear upon contingency theory – those of Woodward, Burns and Stalker, and Lawrence and Lorsch – follows.

Woodward and the technological imperative

Contingency theory became very fashionable in the 1960s and 70s, given impetus by the work of Joan Woodward, whose studies of manufacturing organizations in Essex between 1953 and 1957 led her to the conclusion that there was a connection between production technology and organizational structure. In her study, she isolated three technology types: small batch and unit production; large batch and mass production; and process production. A summary of her results is set out in Table 4.4. Her results suggest that hierarchical levels increase as one moves across the spectrum from small batch production to process production, which is continuous in nature. Spans of control were seen to be wider for large batch production

---

Table 4.3 Contingency factors in organizational design (summary of research studies)

Theorist(s)	Implication of study for organizational design
Woodward (1965)	Structure is influenced by type of technology.
Katz and Kahn (1978)	Organizations as 'open social systems', have 'adaptive' subsystems to deal with boundary conditions, and 'maintenance' subsystems to provide throughput stability. (The possibility exists of tensions between adaptive and maintenance subsystems.)
Chandler (1962)	A decentralized divisional structure results from attempts by large organizations to cope with a more competitive environment: 'structure follows strategy'.
Burns and Stalker (1968)	Organic (flexible) structures fit better with dynamic environments; mechanistic structures are more appropriate to static environments.
Thompson (1967)	In changing environments, organizations engage in 'uncertainty reduction' to protect their productive cores.
Lawrence and Lorsch (1967)	Organizational subsystems adapt to relevant environmental segments. Effective organizations combine both differentiation (resulting from environmental demands) and integration (internal cohesion).
Pugh and the Aston Group (1976)	The larger the organization, the more likelihood of task specialization and standardized procedures (size exercises a 'pull' towards a machine bureaucracy).

Source: Harold Hayward (1992) 'Organising and organisation', in Fulop et al. (1992), p. 171.

Table 4.4 Summary of the results obtained by Woodward

Organizational characteristics	Small batch and unit	Large batch and mass	Process production
Number of levels of authority	Few	Medium	Many
Supervisor's span of control	Narrow	Wide	Narrow
Ratio of managers to total personnel	High	Medium	Low
Labour costs	High	Medium	Low
Ratio of indirect labour to hourly workers	Low	Medium	High
Proportion of graduate supervisors	Low	Medium	High
Chief executive's span of control	Narrow	Medium	Wide
Organizational flexibility	High	Low	High
Primary communication mode	Verbal	Written	Verbal
Number of specialists	Few	Many	Few
Separation of production planning from supervisors	No	Yes	No
Industrial relations	Good	Poor	Good
Organizational size[1]	No relationship	No relationship	No relationship
Organizational success[2]	No relationship	No relationship	No relationship

Notes: The terms in this table are relative

1 A relationship was found within each production type

2 Within each production type the most successful firms were found at the median score on each characteristic

Source: R.D. Lansbury and R.P.Gilmour (1977) *Organizations: An Australian Perspective,* Melbourne: Longman Cheshire, p. 39.

than for both process production and small batch (unit) production. Woodward also noted that those organizations that generally conformed to the seemingly optimal pattern tended to be the most efficient.

These results caused considerable consternation among the classical theorists of the 1960s who were still preaching the concept of fixed principles of organization. Woodward claimed, however, that her results did not destroy classical theory, but rather validated it for the mass production (Taylorist) model on which it was based (Tosi 1984: 160–6).

Woodward's study can be criticized on the grounds of her sampling, her definition of 'efficiency' and her inability to deal adequately with the possible interfering effects of other contingencies, particularly size. However, her results do have intuitive appeal. It is not difficult to appreciate, for example, that a mass production manufacturer using non-complex technologies would have a 'flattish' organizational structure, with fairly wide spans of control.

Organization and environment

In the early 1960s Professor Tom Burns of the University of Edinburgh and G. M. Stalker undertook a study of Scottish firms seeking to cope with the introduction of electronics technologies and changing market conditions. The study led Burns and Stalker to propose two 'ideal' organizational types, the *mechanistic* and the *organic*. The mechanistic type corresponds closely with the traditional classical model and the archetypal bureaucracy: clear task specialization, hierarchical with centralized decision making. This type was seen to be well adapted to stable environments.

The organic type was characterized by informality, network-type relationships and decision making related to knowledge/expertise rather than to position in a hierarchy. This type of organization was more suited to environmental conditions of instability and change. A summary of the main characteristics of the two organizational types is set out in Table 4.5.

Burns and Stalker found that the traditionally structured Scottish firms did not adapt well to new technologies and changing market conditions. In their efforts to deal with these changes, certain *pathologies* were identified. These were (Pugh 1990: 71–3):

■ *ambiguous figure system:* a tendency for subordinates to delegate upwards and for superordinates to bypass the chain of command and begin dealing on a person-to-person basis with key subordinates

■ *mechanistic jungle:* the creation of new jobs and

Table 4.5 Characteristics of mechanistic and organic forms of organization

Organizational characteristics	Organizational form	
	Organic	Mechanistic
Span of control	Wide	Narrow
Levels of authority	Few	Many
Centralization of decision making	Low	High
Number of formal rules	Few	Many
Specificity of job goals	Low	High
Content of communications	Advice	Instructions
Range of skill levels	Narrow	Wide
Knowledge-based authority	High	Low
Position-based authority	Low	High

Source: T. Burns and G.W. Stalker (1968) *The Management of Innovation*, London: Tavistock Publications.

even new departments to resolve problems the existing systems couldn't handle, arguably aggravating the situation and creating subsystems with a vested interest in ensuring problems didn't disappear

■ *committee system:* a proliferation of committees as a way of solving structural problems.

During the 1960s, Paul Lawrence and Jay Lorsch (1967) also sought to relate organizational structure to environmental conditions. Their study involved 10 American firms in three industries: plastics, food and containers, and examined the way that three subsystems in each of these organizations, sales, manufacturing and research and development (R&D), related to their respective environmental contexts.

The first industry studied was one manufacturing and selling speciality plastics to customers in the automobile industry, toy manufacturing, textiles and paper manufacturing. The viability of the product depended heavily on product development in what was

---

Exhibit 4.4 Summary of the contingency approach

TECHNOLOGY (Mintzberg 1979: 249–66)

1. Highly regulatory technologies, which make work routine and predictable, will tend to encourage formalized structures and bureaucracy.

2. Mass production technologies tend to be associated with 'flat' structures.

3. Process technologies encourage 'tall' structures.

4. The more sophisticated the technical system, the more elaborate the administrative structure. Specifically, there is likely to be a higher proportion of professional staff, greater decentralization of decision making and greater use of liaison devices, for example committees.

5. Automation of technologies creates possibilities for more organic structures by the elimination of routine jobs and supervisory levels, and as a result of the increasing proportion of professionals.

SIZE (Mintzberg 1979: 227–48)

With increasing size (more employees), the following are likely to occur:

1. Jobs become more specialized.

2. Unit size and spans of control increase (partly a function of increasing job specialization).

3. Behaviour and structure become more formalized.

4. Problems of red tape and communication breakdown become more apparent.

5. There is decentralization.

ENVIRONMENTS (Mintzberg 1979: 267–87)

1. The more dynamic the environment, the more organic the structure.

2. The more complex the environment, the more decentralized the structure.

3. The more diversified the organisation's markets, the greater the propensity to split into market-based units.

4. Extreme hostility in its environment drives an organization to centralize its structure temporarily.

5. The greater the external control of the organization, the more centralized and formalized its structure.

a highly competitive market. Executives in these companies viewed their environment as turbulent or uncertain, and the development of new or revamped products as crucial to the success of the business. Both technical knowledge and customer demands were always uncertain. However, Lawrence and Lorsch found that while the R&D areas in the organizations experienced this flux and uncertainty, the production side operated in a stable environment because of automation and computerization. Staff in the various departments had different attitudes, values and priorities, for example production staff concentrated on cost reduction and efficiency while sales focused on customer demand and trends in the marketplace. Thus, different departments responded differently to the circumstances of their external environments (Hall 1972: 166).

Consistent with the work of Burns and Stalker, Lawrence and Lorsch found that under conditions of environmental change, successful firms differentiated their structures, that is, the three subsystems responded in a decentralized, semi-autonomous way to the relevant segments of the firms' environment. However, the danger of such differentiation was loss of control or direction for the enterprise as a whole. Thus successful firms also found a way of integrating (bringing together) their subsystems so that the organization could act cohesively, for example using committees and liaison people (Lupton 1978: 129–32; Pugh and Hickson 1989: 46). The greater the differentiation (suggesting high environmental uncertainty), the more elaborate the integrative mechanisms employed. The container firm, operating in a less turbulent environment, relied on traditional methods of integration, for example hierarchy and written communications.

Arising out of the work of Woodward, Burns and Stalker, Lawrence and Lorsch and other contingency theorists, Henry Mintzberg (1979) has offered a number of general propositions about the effect of contingencies on organizational structure. These propositions are summarized in Exhibit 4.4.

Some criticisms of contingency theory

Contingency theory has been widely criticized, but for present purposes, only some of the major criticisms will be discussed. Some contingency theorists, in their reaction to the 'one best way' of classical management, have been guilty of determinism, that is, of seeing organizational structures as being determined or pushed by contingencies. However, as Child has pointed out, decisions about technology are a matter of strategic choice on the part of management. Managers are not obliged to implement particular technologies or adopt

any special kind of structure in relation to that technology (Child 1972: 1–22).

With regard to environments, Weick (1979) argues that organizations through their managers 'enact' them, that is, environments are to some extent a creation of the markets that managers choose to influence. Consider the example below of the Mexaco organization, studied by Simon Lilley (1995).

CASE EXAMPLE

MEXACO

Mexaco invested significant sums of money in the late 1980s and early 1990s in information systems that sought to enable managers of refineries to regain effective control of the assets for which they were responsible. However, much of the complexity that these managers faced, and was the cause of much of their difficulties, was itself the result of previous decisions taken by Mexaco managers. For example, at some refineries, the need to service markets for intermediary refined products created a great deal of turbulence in refinery operations that made the refinery difficult to manage. But these intermediary markets were themselves produced by the actions of major oil companies, who continued to run their refineries in the absence of demand from their own distribution networks during the early 1980s. They had sought to ensure some contribution to the massive fixed costs associated with refining by running their assets when overcapacity in the industry meant that demand had not grown in line with earlier expectations. They thus in part 'enacted' the problematic environment to which the refinery information systems were seen as a potential solution. The environment to which they were supposedly 'responding' was largely a product of their own making.

More generally, contingency theory (and classical theory, for that matter) tends to reify organizations (and indeed environments), that is, give them a 'life' or existence which is independent of organizational participants and organizing processes. The approach suggests that managers rationally and purposively design organizations as responses to environmental changes or threats. It ignores the fact that organizational structures can be created or changed because managers are acting politically or pursuing agendas which have nothing to do with environmental turbulence or the constraints of other contingencies such as technology or size (Silverman 1970: 111–25; Clegg and Dunkerley

1980: 251–84; Honour and Mainwaring 1982: 187–90; Mullins 1985: 109–10; Dawson 1986: 122–32).

In the light of these criticisms, should contingency theory be abandoned? Clearly, once a new technology has been introduced it will have implications for the way people interact, and structure will almost certainly be involved. This is not to say, however, that technology is an imperative which 'necessitates' certain structural arrangements, since this involves a denial of human choice and agency. It is also likely to be true that increasing size may trigger managerial responses for greater control, hence bureaucratization. Similarly, it is undoubtedly true that some structural arrangements are likely to fit better with some environmental contexts than others. However, this is quite different from the determinism suggested by contingency theorists. In the circumstances, it is best to regard the contingency propositions outlined above as tendencies or 'pulls', not inevitabilities.

Organizational excellence

Contingency theory has made a major contribution to the elimination of the myth of 'one best way' in designing organizations. In turn, criticisms of contingency theory have discouraged the view that effective organizational design is a matter of 'best fit' between its structure and its contingencies (Dawson 1986: 128). But the notion contained within contingency theory that different environments make different demands on organizations, demands that are

likely in some way to be reflected in their structures, took a strange twist in the mid-1980s. Following the shocks of the oil crises of the 1970s, there seemed a general feeling abroad that from now on all environments were turbulent and that this turbulence had to be responded to with increased innovation on the part of organizations. Much of this re-emergence of a subtly transformed 'one best way' philosophy may be associated with the 'excellence' literature that stemmed from Tom Peters and Robert Waterman's bestselling book *In Search of Excellence* (1982). Based on research into 62 companies, Peters and Waterman deduced a list of eight attributes that were characteristic of 'excellent' companies. These are described in Exhibit 4.5.

These eight attributes have been presented as a 'one best way' to achieve innovation and entrepreneurship in any organization in the face of the seemingly endlessly challenging and changing markets of contemporary business life. Of the eight attributes, numbers 1, 3, 7 and 8 relate to structure. It is not difficult to see reflected in them some of the conclusions of the contingency theorists previously discussed. Burns and Stalker's organic model, for example, has similarities to Peters and Waterman's simple form, lean staff (attribute 7). Lawrence and Lorsch's integration/differentiation criterion resembles Peters and Waterman's simultaneous loose–tight properties (attribute 8). Productivity through people (attribute 4) would have a familiar ring to human resource theorists. The need to 'stay close to the customer' (attribute 2) is an aim of market departmentalization (previously discussed), and

---

Exhibit 4.5 Back to basics: Eight 'attributes of excellence'

1. **Bias for action:** a preference for doing something, anything, rather than sending an idea through endless cycles of analyses and committee reports

2. **Staying close to the customer:** learning his or her preferences and catering to them

3. **Autonomy and entrepreneurship:** breaking the corporation into small companies and encouraging them to think independently and competitively

4. **Productivity through people:** creating in all employees the awareness that their best efforts are essential and that they will share in the rewards of the company's success

5. **Hands-on, value-driven:** insisting that executives keep in touch with the firm's

essential business and promoting a strong corporate culture

6. **Stick to the knitting:** remaining with the businesses the company knows best; decide what the company stands for and go for that

7. **Simple form, lean staff:** few administrative layers, few people at the upper levels, one structural dimension, product or function or geography should have clear primacy

8. **Simultaneous loose–tight properties:** fostering a climate where there is dedication to the central values of the company combined with tolerance for the idiosyncrasies of employees who accept these values; a paradoxical combination of central direction and individual autonomy.

Source: Adapted from S. Dawson (1986) *Analysing Organisations*, London: Macmillan – now Palgrave Macmillan, p. 134, based on T. Peters and R. Waterman (1982) *In Search of Excellence*, New York: Harper & Row.

decentralization (also previously discussed) is not unrelated to a bias for action (attribute 1). Indeed, taken individually, there is little very original about the excellence attributes. What is of interest is the way the package has been put together and the revivalist zeal with which the philosophy of excellence has been taken up and promoted (Maidique 1983: 157; Soeters 1986: 299–311).

The excellence model has been criticized on a number of grounds. Joseph Soeters has pointed out that the 62 companies chosen by Peters and Waterman were not representative of American industry as a whole. It appears that companies in slow growth industries had little chance of making it to the sample list. Of the 43 companies identified by Peters and Waterman as 'excellent', only 14 were subsequently discussed in the book (Soeters 1986: 299–303), and it appears that some are no longer regarded as such. Moreover, the so-called excellent companies studied do not seem to have dispensed with rigidity, merely moved that rigidity from the structural to the cultural realm. And replacing structural control with cultural control is far from simple. As Modesto Maidique (1983) notes, the values deemed to lie at the core of excellent companies had often been established by one or two leaders, over a long period of time. His conclusion was that 'if you have a good leader, buy him a book'. If you don't, find a leader with vision and in 'ten or twenty years you may have an excellent company about which people could write books about management' (Maidique 1983: 157). And although the rather thin structures of excellence are seemingly aimed at encouraging entrepreneurship at all levels, the extent to which all can behave entrepreneurially, while *an* organization persists, is questionable. Indeed, as we have already hinted, the loosening of structure in excellent companies may be something of a distraction, for the control that the structure used to deliver is now offered by the 'strong' culture of the organization. And the climate and nature of cultural control in such companies seems antithetical to the independence of spirit characteristic of genuine entrepreneurs (Miner 1982: 423; Willmott, 1993; see also Chapter 7). Generally, the approach glosses over the realities of politics in organizations and its assumptions of ultimate harmony among organizational stakeholders places it within a unitary frame of reference, a frame of reference that we have criticized for its naivety throughout this text.

Radical decentralization?

Peters and Waterman's structural principles have provided the basis for what has become known as *radical decentralization*. Radical decentralization aims at creating flatter structures for the purpose of improving communication, human cooperation and responsiveness to the environment. In divisionalized structures it goes beyond ordinary decentralization to the extent of devolving corporate functions such as personnel/human resource management, marketing, computing services and aspects of strategic planning to operational divisions. Corporate structures contract to little more than a small executive body. What supposedly results are virtually autonomous divisions (which may well be competitive), where encouragement is given to teamwork and the breaking down of rigid departmentalization and staff/line dichotomies (Dawson 1986: 134–41; Dunphy and Stace 1990: 46–7). Transformational leadership, envisioning and empowering are seen as the main means of bringing about the change of climate seemingly necessary to allow the emergence of radical decentralization (Dunphy and Stace 1990: 154–72).

And despite the theoretical objections to the excellence model, Rosabeth Kanter, among others, has observed a move by American organizations 'to adopt new flexible strategies and structures'. She has noted a tendency towards 'acquisitions and divestitures aimed at a more focused combination of business activities' ('stick to the knitting'?), reductions in management staff and levels of hierarchy, and an increased use of performance-based rewards (Kanter 1989: 85). She further notes that in a growing number of companies, horizontal ties are replacing vertical ones as channels of activity and communication. She claims that some companies are 'turning themselves inside out' by buying services externally that were previously supplied internally, and by forming strategic alliances with customers and suppliers which bring them 'inside', where their practices can be influenced. Such corporations she calls 'post-entrepreneurial' because they involve 'the application of entrepreneurial creativity and flexibility to established businesses' (Kanter 1989: 85). This trend is a further development of radical decentralization. Other work in this area has focused upon the setting up of novel structural arrangements that encourage learning (see, for example, Senge, 1990; and Chapter 1) and radically increasing the ad hoc nature, the flexibility and changeability, of Mintzberg's (1983b) *adhocracies*. However, one could legitimately ask how radical such 'radical' changes really are. For, as Mintzberg himself notes (1983b: 265, emphasis added):

the Administrative Adhocracy structures itself as a system of work constellations, each located *at the level of the hierarchy* commensurate with the kinds of functional decisions it must make.

What is important to note here is the persistence of hierarchy, albeit somewhat shifting, and thus, also, the persistence of the centring and structuring of organizational relationships and the privileging of certain positions. A really radical decentralization of organization would not be a restructuring but a destructuring and it would not entail merely the removal of a few organizational layers. For, as David Knights and Darren McCabe (2001: 640), as well as inumerable others, have noted:

Taking out some layers in the hierarchy through downsizing does not necessarily make organizations less status conscious. Indeed, the fewer the levels, the stronger the demarcations and boundaries between them.

Structure and centralization, however minimalist, while they remain, remain about control and distinction, about allowing the few to decide for the many, whether what they decide are the detailed rules (as in a typical bureaucracy) or the core values of the culture (as in an empowered 'adhocracy'). Arrangements other than this do exist in the world around us, but we have to look hard to find them. As Ricardo Blaug (1999; see also, Kavanagh, forthcoming) in particular has noted, because such arrangements and their associated actions seem somehow *dis*organized, they are very difficult to see. He contends that when we bother to pay attention to 'anti-institutional, non-hierarchical forms of organization, at radical, local, grassroots … groups', along with other 'spontaneous' forms of 'micro-politics', what we tend to see is not effective organization, but rather 'parochialism, irrelevance and idealism'. We tend to assume intuitively that such (temporary) arrangements are 'hopelessly inefficient, quite incapable of running complex activities, quite unable to coordinate action' (Blaug, 1999: 35). But as Blaug goes on to note, such a set of assumptions involves a particular interpretation of the concept of organization, one that he terms *hierarchism*. Hierarchism has much in common with the modes of organizational structuring that we have considered in this chapter so far (Blaug 1999: 35):

- Hierarchism assumes that 'to act together successfully in the world necessarily entails a hierarchy of command, centralized control and the institutionalization of roles of expertise and leadership'.
- It assumes that this requires the sorts of structuring that epitomizes bureaucracy: 'the division of labour, the systematization of tasks and the immunization of elite decision-makers against input from those defined as lacking expertise'.
- It is strictly instrumental in orientation. It sees organized structure as the route to success in any endeavour, and 'success' as defined by such reasoning as the only factor to be considered.
- It substitutes 'written rules and impartial,

formalized procedures' for judgements arrived at through discussion and 'deliberative argumentation'.

Blaug links our fascination with hierarchism and our assumption that it alone constitutes effective organization to what he terms 'the tyranny of the visible'. Since it is easier to see (particularly the persistence of) forms of organization that correspond to the hierarchism model, it is this model that we take to be the exemplar of organization. It is 'the way we understand the problematic of organization' (1999: 35). In essence, what Blaug seeks to achieve is not to point out ways in which the hierarchical model of organizational structuring might be improved by making it less rigid or more decentralized. Instead he wants us to see that there may be *totally other ways* of organizing that do not rely upon fixed structuring of any sort. And, moreover, that many of these ways may be just as effective, if not more so, than their more visible cousins. They are just not so good at enabling a perpetuation of the status quo in terms of the maintenance of existing inequality and privilege. Obviously, Blaug faces a difficult task, if we are to accept any of his claims, for if we only see hierarchism as organization, how are we to see other forms of, albeit temporary, ordering as organization? To do so we have to overcome the perceptual blindness of our current assumptions, to look in different ways. To help us to do this, Blaug provides both a number of examples of successful non-hierarchic organizations and a reconsideration of our fascination with or fetishization of order. For example, we could see, from Blaug's perspective, that our discussion above of the contingency approach represents a particular way of robbing the notion of *contingency* of its power and unpredictability. In the account of the contingency theorists, the contingent becomes that which is 'dependent upon or conditioned by something else' rather than that which 'is not logically necessary' or is 'subject to chance or unseen effects' (definitions from *Webster's Ninth New Collegiate Dictionary*). Similarly, managerialist versions of radical decentralization seem to be not too radical and look a lot more like recentralization than decentralization, while delayering is clearly a form of restructuring rather than a destructuring.

The central example that Blaug runs through his paper to illustrate his case for the power and the possibility of modes of organization that are not based on hierarchism is that of the comprehensive defeat of the XXth Legion of Rome in the Teutoberg Forest in AD 9. 'Rome saw itself as the champion of organization' (Blaug 1999: 37) and this defeat of one of the key instruments of its power, seemingly at the hands of disorganized Germanic tribes, 'sent shock waves throughout the empire' (p. 48). According to Blaug (1999: 43) this victory was the result of swift, seemingly unpredictable, dispersed action by small semi-independent units of the tribes, action that was invisible to the hierarchically blinded Romans until it was too late. For they could see no centre of power, no command and control, to subdue in order to prevent their demise. The actions of the tribes were nevertheless 'co-ordinated', for the participants were 'brought together… by a common hatred'. Such a description could seemingly easily be applied in our present circumstances to understand the amorphous and potentially endless 'war against terror' in which the West is currently engaged. It also characterizes much resistance in the workplace and beyond, even when such resistance has little immediate and visible effect. According to Blaug (1999: 43–4) such 'cultures of resistance' have:

their own ways of communicating, their own spaces where they can interact freely, beyond the eyes of the elite. These are disorganized networks, horizontal and largely bereft of hierarchical structure, along which information passes with tremendous speed.

Once beyond the surveillance of their masters, slaves grumble and ridicule, workers start rumours and carry out anonymous acts of vandalism, students feign stupidity and drag their feet.

This form of organizational structuring and the action it gives rise to, or perhaps better, organization in the absence of structure or coordination in the absence of organization, which Blaug sees as invisible to those wearing hierarchic lenses, he terms, following Deleuze and Guattari (1987), *rhizomatic*. It is a form in which 'intensities circulate along neural networks', challenging formal power structures 'with viral micro-operations':

These are rhizomatic activities, flat networks of communication, lacking centralized guidance yet somehow with the capacity to co-ordinate effectively collective action. (Blaug 1999: 45)

Other examples provided by Blaug of these phenomena include the mass mobilizations that brought down the puppet regimes of Eastern Europe at the end of the 1980s, the success of guerilla forces against seemingly stronger states in a number of twentieth-century wars and the French Revolution. These examples alert us to the fact that rhizomatic action can indeed be very effective, for its dispersed nature enables the exploitation of local knowledge, and quickly, without the need to wait for the say so of any centre. But it is also effective because it is a form of action that feels liberating, tremendous energy can be released as the alienating nature of (imposed) structure is overcome. Its effectiveness is *different* from that of hierarchism (Blaug 1999: 48, bold added):

■ The effectiveness of hierarchism turns on its capacity for **simplification**. By institutionalizing conduits for information collection and dissemination, by concentrating decision-making power on centralized nodes, processes of communication and command are *limited* in such a way as to enable the delivery of efficiency.

■ The effectiveness of rhizomatic action derives from its **complexity**. Information, here passing along a myriad of everyday passages: face-to-face discussion, non-verbal communication, and, indeed, every available medium, travels *exponentially* through a network of individuals.

It is clearly just such attributes that the gurus of excellence and managerialist radical decentralization seek from their prescriptions for organizational restructuring. But as Blaug reminds us, such individuals are extremely unlikely to get what they want from these changes, for they cannot allow the true potential of rhizomatic action to be expressed. To do so would fatally imperil those structures that managers and the elite require to perpetuate their privileges and their (albeit partial) control. Rhizomatic action, truly *radical* decentralization and destructuring, remains the preserve of resistance, not power. And while it is clear that 'rhizomatic action can coordinate' and 'defeat hierarchism in the field', 'it cannot run states' (Blaug, 1999: 51) or indeed, large capitalist organizations. It can certainly organize, but it cannot manage the predictability and hierarchical control that executives and financial markets demand.

In the next section we explore this last point a little further. We consider the ways in which our common-sense notions of structure are intensely masculine, providing us with a lens to look at organizational structure, but also a set of blinkers to prevent us from seeing alternatives to that which we expect to find. And we also glimpse a way out of the seeming impasse between rigid structure and the status quo, and radical structure and the impossibility of the maintenance of an organized form.

Gender and the structure of organizations

Feminist scholars of organization have found it relatively easy to unmask the gendered nature of organizational structuring, particularly that form of structuring that derives from bureaucratic principles. In its fixation upon control and its fetishization of rationality, they see a form of organization that is perhaps best described as 'a structural manifestation of male domination' (Ashcraft 2001: 1302). The defining features of the bureaucratic form – rationality, professionalism, the exclusion of emotionality, the suppression of private needs and the legitimation of hierarchy – are all intensely masculine. They reflect and privilege the imperatives of control and order over the private, sexual, intimate and unpredictable aspects of life (Ferguson 1984; Pringle 1989; Acker 1990; Knights and McCabe 2001). Nevertheless, it must be noted that despite the best efforts of masculinization, the feminine is always likely to exist within organizations, for, as we have noted throughout this text, rules alone can never get the job done (Collin 1987). Management is, after all, a relational business and intimacy is required to oil the wheels of the bureaucratic machine.

The indictment of traditional forms of organization as masculinist has predictably led feminist scholars to seek out organizational forms and structures that are better able to promote real rather than superficial empowerment. The keys to the realization of such empowerment have primarily been seen to be through structures that encourage and reward personal development and self-reliance and support more egalitarian relations between individuals and groups within the organization and beyond (Reinelt 1994). As Karen Lee Ashcraft (2001: 1302) notes:

Typically, feminist organization is found in women-centred missions, feminist healthcare agencies, rape crisis centres, domestic violence shelters, bookstores, banks and other smaller non- and for-profit organizations.

Unfortunately however, such organizations tend to suffer much the same fate as the rhizomatic ones discussed by Blaug (1999). They are either not seen at all by mainstream organization theorists and practising managers or are seen as some sort of quaint, inefficient experiment, reactions which clearly reflect the dominance of the masculinist approach to organizations. Alternatives appear, when they appear at all, as somehow deficient or inadequate, not quite up to the job. And indeed, this latter view is not without some empirical support, for many feminist organizations do seem to have some difficulty in persisting over time. Of course, this is partly because they receive less support than more 'normal' arrangements and consequently must endlessly struggle to maintain the flow of resources upon which they depend. They may also change radically in form in the course of their existence, as an organization, formed to meet a particular set of concerns, splits to form two new organizations dealing with particular aspects of these concerns, or as original staff move on to other projects. But these reasons alone might not be enough to account for why feminist organizations do not seem to have the same persistence as bureaucracies. As Linda Putnam (1997: 131) has observed, while feminist organizations clearly do 'differ from bureaucratic structures, the verdict is still

out' as to whether they constitute viable, 'genuine alternatives'. The viability of such organizational forms seems to be threatened by the contradictions between the ideals they seek to embody and the demands of practice – practice that must be conducted in a world in which they must interact and often compete with masculinist modes of organization that may indeed be more 'efficient', in a narrow sense. It also seems to be very difficult to prevent the emergence of informal power structures, even within communities of practice seemingly committed to preventing them emerging (see, for example, Ristock 1990). However, for many scholars this focus upon the purity of a feminist organizational form and its problems seems somewhat self-defeating. Rather than giving up entirely on the laudable ends of feminist organizational structuring, they content themselves with constructing and conceiving of organizations that can partially further feminist aims but are 'not premised on a principled hostility to all aspects of bureaucracy or market exchange' (Sirianni 1984: 484). One such form is the somewhat strange notion of the 'feminist bureaucracy' (Ashcraft 2001). Such hybrids try to live with the complexities and ironies of the pursuit of ideals in an imperfect world. They accept that hierarchically sanctioned action by the nominally powerful may be able to enhance egalitarianism in the workplace, if the wielder of the power of the position is sufficiently committed to such aims. Indeed, in many situations it may be the only way to further such aims. Hybrids such as the feminist bureaucracy also note that structure is not the sole determining feature of life in an organization, it is merely one resource among many that can be drawn upon in action. Indeed, such a perspective privileges the flow of action over the static picture offered by an overemphasis upon structure. Finally, such a perspective is alive to the ways in which structure can be ridiculed and downplayed in the context of action, as well as the ways in which it can be buttressed and supported. In short, it accepts that incongruity and conflict are not only not inevitably detrimental to effective action, they are probably endemic features of organized life and as such should perhaps be celebrated and exploited rather than hidden or denied. Such 'dissonance' (Ashcraft 2001) in ideal and form may provide a potent resource for feminist organizations and a viable alternative to fatalistic inaction or demise. In Table 4.6 we reproduce Ashcraft's contrast between the ideal types of bureaucracy, feminist organization and the hybrid of the two that she terms 'organized dissonance'. In the next section we continue our exploration of the masculine nature of bureaucracy along a slightly different path, by considering the relations between bureaucracy and emotion.

Table 4.6 Comparison of bureaucracy, feminist organization and organized dissonance as ideal types			
Feature	Bureaucracy	Feminist organization	Organized dissonance as embodied in feminist bureaucracy
■ Primary goal/rationality	■ Organization as means to an end: efficient standardization in the service of productivity	■ Organization as end: women's empowerment	■ Organization as means and end: efficient, productive, gender-conscious empowerment
■ Power structure	■ Hierarchical; authority centralized at the top of the chain of command	■ Egalitarian and/or hierarchical; authority decentralized and grounded in the collective via consensual decision making	■ Formal hierarchical structure, undermined by [quasi]egalitarian practices; *centralization/ decentralization* and *inequality/ equality* dialectics
■ Rules	■ Formal, exhaustive rules; objective universalism (standardized application across situations)	■ Few, informal rules; subjective particularism (situational application and negotiation), control via shared belief preferable	■ Formal 'living' rules generated by affected members and subject to situational context; *universalism/ contextualism* dialectic
■ Division of labor	■ Formal: specialized	■ Informal: nonspecialized; task rotation preferable	■ Formal and informal: *task stability/ flexibility* dialectic
■ Status of/qualific- ations for hiring and promotion	■ Formal, technical criteria: control via internalized design for individual advancement	■ Informal criteria such as life experience and skill or feminist beliefs valued over professional credentials; goal of individual advancement replaced by that of building community	■ Multiple measures of education and merit: personal advancement tempered by collective good; *formal/informal sources of expertise* and *individual/ community development* dialectics
■ Ideal member relations	■ 'Professional' defined as rational and impersonal: public and private separated	■ Emotional and personal; work selves, embrace and accommodate private needs	■ 'Professional' expanded to include emotion and private needs; rationality–emotionality balance preferable; *impersonal/ personal* and *public/private* dialectics

Source: Karen Lee Ashcraft (2001) 'Organized dissonance; feminist bureaucracy as hybrid form', *Academy of Management Review*, **44**(6): 1301–22.

Conclusion

In defence of bureaucracy

Much of the preceding material has been critical of bureaucratic structuring, but in closing we want to make some attempt to defend the form against some of the more virulent attacks that have been levelled against it. We do so because we believe that the bureaucratic organization has been unfairly caricatured. This caricaturing is most obvious in the work of Peters and Waterman (1982) and their derivatives, which, as we noted, slyly reintroduces a 'one best way' approach to consideration of organizational structure. As Paul du Gay (1994), most prominently has noted, this ennoblement of the entrepreneurial view of structure propagated by the excellence school, and the simultaneous denigration of the bureaucratic model, entails something of a 'just so' story. In this story, as we noted above, all 'environments' are seen to have changed in the direction of more uncertainty and complexity, and such environments can only be responded to with increased innovation and entrepreneurialism. But that is not all that the proponents of this model proclaim; they also suggest that these changes are 'cause

Conclusion continued

for celebration' since they offer 'hopeful ways of living with difference and promoting pluralism in contrast to the bureaucratic practice of excluding or nullifying difference and suppressing pluralism' (du Gay 1994: 125).

In contrast to this view, du Gay contends that the entrepreneurialist model and its extension to many areas of modern life, including huge tranches of the public sector, represents a 'colossal immodesty', in which a form of organization that *may* be appropriate for certain businesses in certain circumstances is seen to be the only legitimate mode of structuring organized life. To make his argument, du Gay draws upon Michael Walzer's (1984) conception of the liberal 'art of separation'. Walzer suggests that in any complex modern society, the idea of 'simple equality' – where everybody gets the same amount of the same things in the same forms – is not only undesirable, it is also not achievable. It would require excessive constraints being placed upon individual liberty and would unduly constrict change and innovation; it would produce a static and rather tedious world. In its place, Walzer advocates a 'complex equality' (1983: 8–9) in which 'different goods are distributed for different reasons, in accordance with different procedures, by different agents and all these differences derive from different understandings of the social goods themselves' (du Gay 1994: 128). For example, while we might believe that luxury goods should be allocated on the basis of one's ability to pay for them, we might also believe that higher educational opportunity ought to be distributed on the basis of ability.

According to Walzer and indeed du Gay, the way to defend pluralism is not, therefore, to ensure that everything gets allocated by a market, in the name of its sovereign consumer, to whom all other activities must be in thrall. Rather, we should 'vigilantly patrol the borders between different distributive spheres' (du Gay 1994: 128) to ensure that success or worthiness in one sphere is not illicitly or automatically converted to success or worthiness in another. If we do not engage in such patrolling, then it is likely that only economic interests will be respected, which seems a curious thing to do if what one wants to do is defend, maintain and enhance pluralism and difference. For such patrolling to be possible, and the different forms of justice that each sphere demands to be defended, strong impartial administration is required. To do this, structure needs to be maintained and the distinctions between public and private supported rather than broken down. This will mean accepting some hierarchy, inequality, domination and subordination, in order to ensure that the systems of administration of social life as a whole can function adequately to safeguard the rights of all and not only those who meet market demands. In short, du Gay suggests that the circumstances under which bureaucracy was an appropriate form of organization have not disappeared entirely, nor are they likely to in any future in which the legitimacy of power is, at least in part, determined by factors other than one's ability to serve a market. The ethos of office, so carefully articulated by Weber as involving the ability and will to act in the way demanded by the office and not according to one's 'private political, moral, regional and other commitments' (du Gay 1994: 141), should not be regarded as obsolete. Bureaucracy has its place and its role in that place should be stoutly defended. That place is outside the market and its rules and prerogatives, regulating it and smoothing its greater excesses. It is the realm of public administration

Conclusion cont'd

in which a little 'economic inefficiency' might be seen as a small price to pay for the maintenance of 'impartiality, complex equality' and 'pluralism' (du Gay 1994: 144). Certain bureaucracies should clearly be made more responsive to the publics they should seek to serve, of that there is little doubt. But if we extend this argument to all examples of the bureaucratic form, we lose more than we gain. For while the free market may be dynamic and energizing and encourage commitment to customer service, when its rules and moralities dominate everything, it becomes tyrannical like any other actor to whom no checks and balances apply. Both bureaucratic and entrepreneurial organizations are essential if our demands as both consumers and citizens are to be heard, let alone met.

Answers to questions about managing structure

1 **What is organizational structure?** Organizational structure is the more or less permanent specification of relationships and legitimate power within an organization. Perhaps the archetypal organizational structure is the bureaucracy delineated by Max Weber. Although many aspects of a pure expression of this organizational form have been criticized by theorists and modified by practitioners, the fact remains that much of the essence of the bureaucratic model continues to exist in the majority of organizations that populate our world.

2 **Is there 'one best way' to structure organizations?** No. Certain structures seem to be better suited to dealing with particular contingencies pertaining to the organization. These contingencies include the technology employed in the organization, its size and the type of environment(s) in which it operates. The goals of the organization are also important factors to consider when designing organizational structure. Certain organizational missions may be incompatible with certain forms of organizational structure.

3 **Are non-hierarchical structures viable?** Non-hierarchical structures can not only be viable, they can be superior in terms of performance to hierarchical organizations in certain circumstances. They are also much more consonant with some organizational missions, such as those of feminist organizations. However, such structures are difficult to see and take seriously due to our intuitive sense that structure is inherently hierarchical. They also tend to last for short periods of time, until the 'normal service' of hierarchy is reimposed. Finally, and relatedly, although non-hierarchical structures may indeed be able to get things done, they cannot effectively support and maintain the privileges of elite members over those of ordinary participants. As such, they face many powerful, conservative forces that seek to tramel and curtail their existence when they do come into being.

4 **Should bureaucracy be abandoned?** While bureaucracy may be the bedrock of hierarchical organization and anathema to feminist approaches to organizational life, it may also have its virtues in certain circumstances. Just as there is no 'one best' structure for organizations in all circumstances, so

Answers cont'd

too is there no 'one worst'. The impersonal virtues of bureaucratic office appear to be extremely viable and useful in certain circumstances, particularly those where production, distribution and allocation needs to be carried out on the basis of either equality or any other basis not derived from the laws of the market. Indeed, it may be the case that bureaucratic structures are those best suited to engage in the regulation of markets in an attempt to ensure that they function to serve the interests of the many rather than the few.

REVISITING
THE CASE STUDY

1 Why are large numbers of people placed together in tower blocks?

Firstly, for control. It is much easier to control large numbers of people if you get them in one place. However, most tower blocks contain many different corporations, so the next important factor has to be networking and proximity of significant players in the same industry. This may be driven by the urge to collaborate, or simply the need to keep an eye on the competition. In businesses where the product is not visible, such as finance, the sense of the reality of the industry is given to participants by 'herding' and to investors and customers by the symbolic messages given by the huge solid buildings, which suggest reliability and permanency. It is no accident that most of the large tower blocks, from the earliest days, have been developed for and by finance houses. Another reason is communication, and a further one job mobility or the provision of a pool of skilled and experienced professional labour.

2 How closely is organizational structure connected with architecture and technology?

A lot more closely than most organization theory would acknowledge, with the notable exception of Hatch (1997). Technology throughout the nineteenth and twentieth centuries, along with the limitations imposed by the building materials available and their cost, has affected the development of hierarchical organizational structures and departmentalization in particular. The technologies now available in the twenty-first century mean that networking, communication and control can be accomplished without the need to keep people in the same place physically. This places new requirements on architecture, which can mean that workplaces need to become more like social centres if workers are to attend them less frequently, and for different purposes to the traditional day at the office. Symbolically, however, there is little substitute for the imposing edifice – an impressive Web presence may enhance short-term identity but the dot.com collapses have underlined that the Web may be virtual in more than one respect. The means to work differently are available, but whether the business world will put them fully into practice remains to be seen.

References

Acker, J. (1990) 'Hierarchies, jobs, bodies: A theory of gendered organizations', *Gender and Society*, **4**: 139–58.

Albrow, M. (1970) *Bureaucracy*, London: Pall Mall.

Aron, R. (1970) *Main Currents in Sociological Thought*, Gretna, LA: Pelican.

Ashcraft, K.L. (2001) 'Organized dissonance: Feminist bureaucracy as hybrid form', *Academy of Management Review*, **44**(6): 1301–22.

Blau, P.M. and Meyer, M. (1971) *Bureaucracy in Modern Society*, New York: Random House.

Blaug, R. (1999) 'The tyranny of the visible: Problems in the evaluation of anti-institutional radicalism', *Organization*, **6**(1): 33–56.

Burns, T. and Stalker, G.M. (1968) *The Management of Innovation*, London: Tavistock Publications.

Byrt, W.J. (1973) *Theories of Organisation*, Sydney: McGraw-Hill.

Chatterjee, S.R. and McDonald, C. (1981) 'Some aspects of expert power in work organisations', *Human Resource Management Australia*, Autumn: 37–44.

Child, J. (1972) 'Organisational structure, environment and performance: The role of strategic choice', *Sociology* **6**: 1–22.

Child, J. (1984) *Organisation*, London: Harper & Row.

Clegg, S.R. (1990) *Modern Organizations: Organization Studies in the Postmodern World*, London: Sage.

Clegg, S.R. and Dunkerly, D. (1980) *Organisations, Class and Control*, London: Routledge & Kegan Paul.

Collins, H.M. (1987) 'Expert systems, artificial intelligence and the behavioural coordinates of skill', in B.P. Bloomfield (ed.) *The Question of Artificial Intelligence*, pp. 258–83.

Crozier, M. (1964) *The Bureaucratic Phenomenon*, Chicago: University of Chicago Press.

Dawson, S. (1986) *Analysing Organisations*, London: Macmillan – now Palgrave Macmillan.

Deleuze, G. and Guattari, F. (1987) *A Thousand Plateaus: Capitalism and Schizophrenia*, Minneapolis: University of Minnesota Press.

Donkin R. 'Time to Change the Way We Work : One outcome of the appalling events in New York may be to allow greater diversity of workplace choices' *Financial Times* 21/09/01, p VII.

du Gay, P. (1994) 'Colossal immodesties and hopeful monsters', *Organization*, **1**(1): 125–48.

Dunphy, D. and Stace, D. (1990) *Under New Management: Australian Organisations in Transition*, Sydney: McGraw-Hill.

Fayol, H. (1948) *General and Industrial Management*, London: Pitman.

Ferguson, K. (1984) *The Feminist Case Against Bureaucracy*, Philadelphia: Temple University Press.

Fulop, L. with Frith, F. and Hayward, H. (eds) (1992) *Management for Australian Business: A Critical Text*, Melbourne: Macmillan.

Georgiou, P. (1975) 'Weber's ideal type of bureaucracy', in R.N. Spann and G.R. Curnow (eds) *Public Policy and Administration in Australia*, Sydney: John Wiley.

Gerth, H.H. and Mills, C. Wright (1967) *From Max Weber: Essays in Sociology*, London: Routledge & Kegan Paul.

Gouldner, A.W. (1954) *Patterns of Industrial Bureaucracy*, New York: Free Press.

Gulick, L. (1937) 'Notes on the theory of organisation', in L. Gulick and L. Urwick (eds) *Papers in the Science of Administration*, New York: Institute of Pubic Administration, Columbia University.

Hall, R.H. (1972) *Organisation Structure and Process*, London: Prentice Hall.

Hatch, M.J. (1997) *Organization Theory: Modern, Symbolic and Postmodern Perspectives* Oxford: Oxford University Press.

Honour, T.F. and Mainwaring, R.M. (1982) *Business and Sociology*, London: Croom Helm.

Kanter, R.M. (1989) 'The new managerial work', *Harvard Business Review*, November–December: 85–91.

Kavanagh, D. (forthcoming) 'Can the Celt Speak? Voices from Beyond the Pale', *Organization*.

Knights, D. and McCabe, D. (2001) '"A different world": Shifting masculinities in the transition to call centres', *Organization*, **8**(4): 619–45.

Lamond, D.A. (1990) 'The irrational use of Weber's ideal types', *Australian Journal of Public Administration*, **49**(4): 464–73.

Lansbury, R.D. and Gilmour, R.P. (1977) *Organizations: An Australian Perspective*, Melbourne: Longman Cheshire p. 39.

Lawrence, P.R. and Lorsch, J.W. (1967) *Organisation and Environment*, Boston: Harvard University Press.

Leivesley, R., Scott, N. and Kouzmin, A. (1990) 'Australian organisation theory: A garbage can?' in A. Kouzmin and N. Scott (eds) *Dynamics in Australian Public Management: Selected Essays*, Melbourne: Macmillan.

Lilley, S. (1995) 'Disintegrating chronology', *Studies in Cultures, Organizations and Societies*, **2**(1): 1–33.

Luhmann, N. (1982) *The Differentiation of Society*, Cambridge: Polity.

Lupton, I. (1978) *Management and the Social Sciences*, Harmondsworth: Penguin.

Maidique, M.A. (1983) 'The New Management Thinkers', *California Management Review*, **26**(1): 151–61.

Miner, J.B. (1982) *Theories of Organizational Structure and Process*, New York: Dryden Press.

Mintzberg, H. (1979) *The Structuring of Organizations: A Synthesis of the Research*, Englewood Cliffs, NJ: Prentice Hall.

Mintzberg, H. (1983a) *Power In and Around Organizations*, Englewood Cliffs, NJ: Prentice Hall.

Mintzberg, H. (1983b) *Structure in Fives: Designing Effective Organizations*, Englewood Cliffs, NJ: Prentice Hall.

Mouzelis, N.P. (1967) *Organisation and Bureaucracy*, London: Routledge & Kegan Paul.

Mullins, L.J. (1985) *Management: Organisational Behaviour*, London: Pitman.

Peters, T.J. and Waterman, R.H. (1982) *In Search of Excellence*, New York: Harper & Row.

Pringle, R. (1989) 'Bureaucracy, rationality and sexuality: The case of secretaries', in J. Hearn, D. Sheppard, P. Tacred-Sheriff and G. Burrell (eds) *The Sexuality of Organizations*, London: Sage, pp. 158–77.

Pugh, D.S. (ed.) (1984) *Organization Theory, Selected Readings*, Harmondsworth: Penguin.

Pugh, D.S. (ed.) (1990) *Organisation Theory: Selected Readings*, Harmondsworth: Penguin.

Pugh, D.S. and Hickson, D.J. (1989) (eds) *Writers on Organizations*, Harmondsworth: Penguin.

Pugh, D.S., Hickson, D.J. and Hinings, C.R. (eds) (1983) *Writers on Organizations*, Harmondsworth: Penguin.

Putnam, L.L. (1997) 'Organizational communication in the 21st century: Informal discussion with M. Scott Poole, L.L. Putnam, and D.R. Seibold, *Management Communication Quarterly*, **11**: 127–38.

Radbone, I. (1987) 'Innovation and the Bureaucrat', *Australian Journal of Public Administration*, **66**(2) June.

Reinelt, C. (1994) 'Fostering empowerment, building community: The challenge for state-funded feminist organizations', *Human Relations*, **47**: 685–705.

Rickards, T. (1985) *Stimulating Innovation, A Systems Approach*, New York: St Martins Press.

Ristock, J.L. (1990) 'Canadian feminist social service collectives: Caring and contradictions', in L. Albrecht and R.M. Brewer (eds) *Bridges of power: Women's multicultural alliances*, Philadelphia: New Society Publishers, pp. 172–81.

Ritzer, G. (2000) *The McDonaldization of Society,* 2nd edn, Thousand Oaks, CA: Pine Forge Press.

Robbins, S.R. and Barnwell, N.S. (1989) *Organisation Theory in Australia*, Sydney: Prentice Hall.

Rogers, R.E. and McIntire, R.H. (1983) *Organisation and Management Theory*, New York: John Wiley.

Salaman, G. (1979) *Work Organisations, Resistance and Control*, London: Longman.

Senge, P.M. (1990) *The Fifth Discipline: the Art and Practice of the Learning Organization*, New York: Doubleday.

Shafritz, J.M. and Ott, J.S. (1987) *Classics of Organisation Theory*, Chicago: Dorsey Press.

Silverman, D. (1970) *The Theory of Organisations*, London: Heinemann.

Sirianni, C. (1984) 'Participation, opportunity and equality: Toward a pluralist organizational model', in F. Fischer and C. Sirriani (eds) *Critical Studies in Organization and Bureaucracy*, Philadelphia: Temple University Press, pp. 482–503.

Soeters, J.L. (1986) 'Excellent companies as social movements', *Journal of Management Studies*, **23**(3): 299–311.

Stoner, J.A.F., Collins, R.R. and Yetton, P.W. (1985) *Management in Australia*, Sydney: Prentice Hall.

Thompson, K. (1980) 'The Organizational Society', in G. Salaman, K. Thompson (eds) *Control and Ideology in Organizations*, London: The Open University.

Toffler, A. (1970) *Future Shock*, New York: Bantam Books.

Tosi, H.L. (1984) *Theories of Organisation*, New York: John Wiley.

Urwick, L. (1943) *The Elements of Administration*, New York: Harper & Row.

Walzer, M. (1983) *Spheres of Justice*, Oxford: Basil Blackwell.

Walzer, M. (1984) 'Liberalism and the art of separation', *Political Theory*, **12**(3): 315–30.

Watson, T.J. (1986) *Management Organisation and Employment Strategy*, London: Routledge and Kegan Paul.

Weber, M. (1964) *The Theory of Social and Economic Organization*, A.M. Henderson and T. Parsons (translators) New York, The Free Press.

Weick, K.E. (1979) *The Social Psychology of Organising*, New York: Addison-Wesley.

Wilenski, P. (1988) 'Social change as a source of competing values in public administration', *Australian Journal of Public Administration*, **67**(3): 213–22.

Willmott, H. (1993) 'Strength is ignorance; Slavery is freedom: Managing culture in modern organizations', *Journal of Management Studies*, **30**(4): 515–31.

Managing sustainability

CHAPTER 5

Bobby Banerjee

Questions about managing sustainability

1 How does the natural environment impact a company's business?
2 What are the social impacts of a business?
3 What factors influence a company's environmental strategy?
4 How does a company integrate environmental and social considerations into its strategy?
5 What are the consequences of a corporate environmental strategy?

THE CALVERT CORPORATION

Rana Bose was angry. His email and voicemail were overflowing with dozens of messages, all marked urgent. There was a terse handwritten note from his boss asking to see him immediately. And he was still jet lagged after returning from a tiring conference in Europe with EU officials, outlining new environmental legislation that threatened his entire European market. As marketing manager of the metal products division of Calvert Corporation, a large, transnational corporation with interests in mining and metal products, Rana was responsible for overseeing marketing operations in North America as well as their export business in Europe, where the company maintained sales offices in the UK, France, Germany, Sweden, Italy, and Spain. The EU was setting up a comprehensive environmental legislative framework to regulate and standardize environmental legislation in emissions, waste production, packaging, recycling and materials usage. Almost all the division's products in the region would be affected by the new legislation and Rana, along with a number of other North American business executives, had spent the past week lobbying EU officials trying to delay implementation of the new regulations. Without much success, thought Rana sourly, because the damn greenies in Europe seem to lobby their governments more strongly than they do here. As he walked down the corridor to the marketing director's office, he knew there was going to be more trouble.

Marianella Jobim, the marketing director, was on the phone and greeted Rana with a glare as she motioned him to sit down. 'Don't worry, I'll look into it,' she said into the phone before she hung up. 'That was Mario Gonzalves from BS&T. Yesterday they returned our last consignment, all $1.4 million worth.' Rana was shocked; they had never had a quality problem with BS&T, their biggest customer, before. 'And you want to know why?' continued Marianella. 'Excess packaging. Can you believe it? They say we have too much styrofoam and plastic. And they now have a new system

that all suppliers have to follow. They want all sorts of information on recycled content of the plastic, papers and cardboard we use, where we get our raw materials, who our subcontractors are, even what wood our damn crates are made of. They're faxing me this new proforma we need to complete before they can place any more orders with us.' Looking out of the window at a cold, wet and gloomy Chicago afternoon, Rana grimaced as he prepared to tell Marianella the bad news from his European trip.

A continent away, in the blistering heat of the Western Australian desert, John Phillips, general manager of Calvert's copper mine in Pilbara, was equally gloomy as he put the finishing touches on his quarterly report to the vice-president of mining operations. Low metal prices and rising operational costs had seen a steady decline in the copper mine's profitability and projections for the next three quarters indicated a loss in earnings. And now the government, with heavy lobbying from green groups and Aboriginal communities living near the mine site, had just passed legislation outlawing the discharge of effluents from mining operations into the Pilbara River. Treating and storing the effluents would cost the company close to half a million dollars a year. To make matters worse, their licence application for exploration work for another mine site was tied up in court with three Aboriginal tribes laying claim to the land, two of whom were opposed to mining. Costs because of delays and legal fees were mounting. How the hell was he going to justify this to headquarters when earnings had more or less disappeared? He made a mental note to recommend temporary sourcing of copper from their mine in the Philippines instead, where the environmental laws were less draconian and the natives were friendlier.

Back in the company's Chicago headquarters, Lee Morgan, CEO of Calvert Corporation, was reflecting on his just concluded fortnightly meeting with all the divisional heads. A forty-year veteran of the mining industry, Lee

Morgan was surprised to hear the same environmental concerns voiced by almost all his divisional heads, with problems in manufacturing, raw material purchase, waste management, emissions control, even marketing. It was clear that the company needed to develop a consistent approach to environmental issues. There was no doubt that environmental issues were becoming a key factor impacting the industry. Environmental groups had been targeting the mining industry for years and their voices were increasingly being heard at policy level. The company had several mine sites in Papua New Guinea, the Philippines, Australia and South America located near indigenous communities. While no major environmental disaster had occurred as a result of the company's mining activity, complaints from communities living near their mine sites were on the rise. A campaign by an indigenous community near one of their Australian mines, claiming irreversible water pollution due to the company's mine, was receiving a lot of international atten- tion and the company board had received several 'please explain' letters from shareholders. Future mining activity in the region was in doubt, as the campaign called for a halt to all mining and exploration activity in the area until a comprehensive environmental assessment was undertaken.

Lee Morgan decided a company-wide response was needed. Several divisional heads commented that a senior person was required, who would be responsible for managing the company's environmental strategy. He would talk to his people tomorrow about creating a new senior position in the company, maybe a vice-president – environ- mental issues.

Note: This fictitious case was developed by Bobby Banerjee, but examples of environmental concerns described in the case are based on experiences of two US corporations in the mining and chemical industry.

QUESTIONS ABOUT THE CASE

1 What external and internal forces have influenced Calvert Corporation's relationship with the natural environment?
2 What strategies can the company develop to address environmental issues?
3 Should the company engage with its stakeholders to develop an environmental policy? Why? Who are these stakeholders?
4 What social impacts do the operations of the company have? How can it address the social issues relating to its business?
5 How will environmental and social issues affect the competitiveness and profitability of the company in the long term?
6 How will the company ensure that all its employees are aware of the company's environmental policies?
7 How can the company develop a triple bottom-line policy for its business? What would be the elements of such a policy?

Introduction

As the above story illustrates, environmental issues can influence all aspects of an organization's activities, from manufacturing to raw material procurement, product development to marketing. Traditionally, environmental issues were addressed at the manufacturing level and the focus was limited to pollution control. Governments enacted laws regulating the production of hazardous wastes and companies that did not adhere to these laws were fined. In the past 20 years the focus has expanded to encompass a wider range of corporate strategies that deal with environmental concerns. Stricter environmental regulation, rising public environmental concern and increasing costs of environmental compliance have seen the focus shift from pollution control to pollution prevention. Companies are also aggressively pursuing environmentally concerned consumers: The Body Shop and Ben & Jerry's are examples of companies that came into existence because of environmental concerns. Many products that we use every day have been modified or developed to reduce their environmental impact, from washing machines to television sets, cars, soaps, detergents, processed foods, furniture and household goods. Environmentalism as it relates to organizations today is no longer a manufacturing or marketing issue: it pervades all levels of an organization and marks a strategic shift, where many companies are reframing environmental issues as an opportunity instead of a threat.

In this chapter, we will describe how corporations integrate environmental concerns into their decision making, the internal and external forces that drive these corporations to respond to environmental issues, the consequences for corporations and society and the relation of corporate environmentalism to the larger debate on sustainable development. The conceptual framework of corporate environmentalism, its driving forces, relationship with organizational strategy and its consequences will be identified and each element will be discussed in detail in this chapter. In concluding, we critique the 'win–win' rhetoric of corporate environmentalism employed by corporations and governments, by taking a critical look at some of the assumptions underlying corporate environmentalism and discussing its limits.

The emergence of corporate environmentalism

The modern environmental movement in the West can be traced back to 1962 with the publication of Rachel Carson's book *Silent Spring*. Carson documented the harmful effects of chemicals and pesticides and described how dangerous toxins were introduced into the food chain. Her book served as a 'wake up call' to US government officials, consumer advocates and citizens, resulting in a series of environmental laws such as the Clean Air Act, the Clean Water Act, the Resource Conservation and Recovery Act. The US's Environmental Protection Authority (EPA) was created in 1970 to monitor the extent of industrial pollution. Similar government agencies and environmental laws were created in Europe as well. The counterculture movement of the 1960s also saw the emergence of what were then called *ecology action groups*, the first environmental activists in the US. It must be remembered that the modern environmental movement is rooted in Western concepts of nature, concepts that are very different from several indigenous views of nature. In that sense, the countless battles over land use and natural resources fought by indigenous communities like Native Americans and Aboriginal Australians with European settlers over the past 300 years are also examples of indigenous environmental activism.

The first Earth Day was celebrated on 22 April 1970, as a day for reflection and discussion of environmental problems and to demonstrate North America's growing consciousness of the environment. In an interview with *Time* magazine, one of the organizers, then Wisconsin Senator Gaylord Nelson, commented that '[the growing consciousness of ecology] could kick off one of the toughest – and most expensive – political fights this country has ever seen'. Thirty years later, the fight is far from over, although battle lines have been redrawn and roles and interrelations of major protagonists have changed over the years as well. Politicians (with very few exceptions) and corporate representatives were conspicuous by their absence in the many nationwide events marking the first Earth Day. In fact, several large corporations were the targets of protests due to their polluting activities. One of the most noticeable changes at the 20th anniversary of Earth Day in 1990 was that protesters, on arrival at the various events, were greeted by leading business executives from some of the world's biggest polluters, appropriately attired in 'Save the Whale' or 'Save our Planet' T-shirts and handing out glossy brochures describing how their corporations were protecting the environment.

The grass roots, anti-business environmental movement of the 1960s and 70s has undergone a dramatic transformation: today it is the large transnational corporations that are setting the global environmental agenda. After nearly a decade-long hiatus in the 1980s (except for the public furore after the 1984 Bhopal tragedy in India, the worst environmental disaster caused by a corporation in which the accidental release of methyl isocyanate, a highly toxic gas, resulted in the deaths of more than 30,000 people) environmentalism re-emerged in the late 1980s with a major difference: it became an important issue for business, with the potential to affect a company's profitability.

Corporate environmentalism

'Corporate environmentalism' is the organization-wide recognition of the legitimacy and importance of the biophysical environment in the formulation of organizational strategy and the integration of environmental issues into the strategic planning process (Banerjee 1999). It involves the recognition by firms that environmental problems arise from the development, manufacture, distribution, consumption and disposal of their products and services. Integrating environmental issues in the strategic planning process is another theme of corporate environmentalism. The importance placed on environmental concerns and the extent of their integration into organizational strategy largely determine a company's approach to environmental issues leading to a wide range of activities and outcomes.

Examples abound in the business press of corporate environmental initiatives worldwide (Ottman 1993; DeSimone and Popoff 1997), as shown in Exhibit 5. 1.

Business firms have not always paid attention to environmental issues. Following the logic of neoclassical economics, which still underpins business strategy, pollution and other environmental problems were considered to be 'externalities' and not taken into account as an organizational cost of business. It was left to governments to address these issues. In cases where manufacturing facilities, emissions or waste produced were potentially dangerous, corporations focused on issues of health and safety of their employees and neighbouring communities. With rising public concern about environmental problems and increased governmental scrutiny of industrial pollution, many companies attempted to address environmental issues by developing an integrated environment, health and safety policy (see Exhibit 5. 2 for an example of an

---

Exhibit 5.1 **Examples of corporate environmentalism**

❏ After years of complaints by environmentalists, McDonald's, one of the world's biggest producers of waste, launched a major recycling and waste reduction programme in 1990 in alliance with the Environmental Defense Fund, a major non-governmental organization. McDonald's released a public statement that year outlining its environmental strategy, which included the aim of 'becoming one of the world's leading educators about environmental issues'.

❏ 3M invested in a comprehensive range of pollution controls in its manufacturing facilities, in several cases exceeding what the law required.

❏ Procter & Gamble pledged to spend more than $20 million annually to develop composting facilities for disposable nappies.

❏ Xerox initiated a programme with its suppliers to reuse containers and pallets for shipping, reducing 10,000 tons of waste and saving up to $15 million annually.

❏ Saturn, a division of General Motors, regularly collects used and damaged plastic materials from its cars for reprocessing and reuse in new vehicles.

❏ In developing their compact green TV, Philips eliminated almost all hazardous materials, used recycled materials, 30 per cent fewer components and increased energy efficiency of the product.

❏ Manufacturers are also developing products targeted specifically at environmentally conscious consumers. The number of new *green* product introductions in the US increased from 60 in 1986 to 810 in 1991. The share of green products of all new product introductions rose from 1.1 per cent in 1986 to 13.4 per cent in 1991.

---

environmental policy developed by the consumer products corporation Church & Dwight, one of the world's largest manufacturers of baking soda). Environmental policies often focus on compliance with existing laws on environmental pollution as well as health and safety requirements, and are generally limited to a firm's manufacturing facilities. In recent years, some corporations have taken a more proactive approach to environmental issues and are attempting to reframe environmental costs as environmental opportunities with revenue-generating potential.

It is no coincidence that the biggest polluters in the

Exhibit 5.2 **Church & Dwight's environmental policy**

Our corporate environmental policy is to produce quality products which, in the totality of their lifecycles, have minimum impact on the environment. We will be a model of corporate environmental responsibility in this regard. Our carbonate-based technologies and products enable us to be a leader in toxic reduction and source reduction programmes especially as they relate to our nation's air and water resources.

To fulfill this policy, we make the following commitments:

1. We will understand the environmental impact of our technologies and products, and take scientifically sound steps to minimize them.

2. We will implement, as part of our Quality Improvement Process, an Environmental Improvement Process which will help ensure that minimization of environmental impact continues to be part of our corporate culture.

3. We will develop products and processes which can be demonstrated to have a more favorable impact on air and water quality than most existing products and processes by focusing on the toxic reduction and source reduction capabilities of carbonates.

4. We will help educate our consumers and customers on environmental issues and the environmentally responsible distribution, use, and disposal of our products and packaging.

5. We will assist environmental stakeholders in the development of environmentally responsible policies, programmes and communications.

6. We will measure and regularly review our environmental performance against these commitments.

world, large transnational corporations in a variety of industry sectors, such as chemicals, energy, oil, automobiles and mining, all have environmental policies in place. As we will see in a later section, these corporations faced similar internal and external pressures that forced them to respond to environmental issues. Critics maintain that these policies are merely window dressing and corporations are not really making any radical attempt to minimize their environmental impact.

In the next few sections, we will discuss the different ways in which corporate environmentalism has been conceptualized. An examination of the academic literature on the topic as well as policy documents of governments and international environmental agencies, case studies from industry and environmental organizations reveal three main themes, where corporate environmentalism is described as a:

1. *paradigm shift* involving a different way of looking at the world
2. *stakeholder issue* involving an organization's social responsibility to a wide range of stakeholders
3. *corporate and business strategy* that provides long-term competitive advantage.

Corporate environmentalism as a paradigm shift

Environmentalists have always been critical of the way neoclassical economics treats environmental costs. They argue that pollution should not be treated as an 'externality' arising from economic activity and advocate including all environmental costs in market transactions. Public policy actions frequently attempt to internalize these externalities by estimating the external cost of pollution and applying pollution taxes. The misleading nature of current economic indicators of 'progress' is another example of the inappropriateness of the neoclassical paradigm. For instance, measurement of gross national product (GNP) does not reflect any environmental damage caused by economic activity. Even worse, it counts environmental destruction as a positive contribution to a nation's economy as long as it is a market transaction. For instance, one of the world's major environmental disasters, the 1989 Exxon-Valdez oil spill in Alaska actually showed up as an *increase* in the US's GNP because of the goods and services required to clean up the spill. Destroying old forests for their timber contributes positively to a country's GNP; however, the permanent and irreversible effects of deforestation are not counted.

The conventional paradigm or world view is *technocentric* (Gladwin et al. 1995). It makes a conceptual distinction between humanity and the natural environment, where the human role is the domination of nature through technology. This paradigm assumes a world of limitless resources (or the availability of technology to create new resources when natural resources run out) where the primary economic objective is the efficient allocation of resources through the exploitation of natural capital. In contrast, the *ecocentric* paradigm takes a different view of nature and recognizes that there are limits to the growth and carrying capacity of the planet. This paradigm does not recognize that humans occupy a privileged position in nature and values non-human nature for its intrinsic value. It places less faith on technological fixes to environmental problems.

Since all human activity is performed within the biophysical environment, any relationship between humanity, society, or institutions cannot ignore the effects on the biophysical environment. *Ecological theory* or *ecosystem theory* examines how humans, plants, soils, microorganisms, water and air function together as an integrated community. All constituents of the natural system are functionally interdependent and their relationships can be analysed in terms of energy transfer, food chains, diversity patterns and feedback systems (Petulla 1980). Human, social, technological and economic systems all interact with the ecosystem and consequently are subject to the same laws that govern the ecosystem (Odum 1971; Gray 1992). The fundamental premise underlying the laws of ecology is the interrelatedness of all processes within the ecosystem, including human activity. Commoner (1972) summarized the four basic principles of ecology:

1. Every separate entity is connected to all the rest.
2. Everything has to go somewhere.
3. You cannot get something for nothing.
4. Nature knows best.

While some of the above principles may seem facetious, the next case example (The Parachuting Cats) will highlight the interrelatedness of all components of an ecosystem.

This story illustrates the dangers of following a classical technocentric problem-solving approach with a narrow and static view of the environment. The technocentric and ecocentric paradigms take two opposing, conflicting and apparently irreconcilable approaches to the preservation of the planet. Obviously, the technocentric paradigm has always informed business activity and continues to do so. For-profit organizations do not see the ecocentric paradigm as being relevant to their needs. However, a few of the more radical environmental organizations promote this view.

In recent years, the emergence of a new paradigm, the *sustainability* paradigm, offers a way to synthesize the opposing positions of the other two paradigms,

CASE EXAMPLE

THE PARACHUTING CATS

In Borneo in the early 1950's, the World Health Organization (WHO) was faced with the problem of malaria among the Dayak people in Borneo. They had an answer that was short, simple, and wrong, which was to spray DDT all over the place to kill the mosquitoes that carried malaria. The mosquito population declined, the incidence of malaria declined, and everybody declared the program a success.

They discovered, however, that the roofs of people's houses were falling in on their heads. It seemed that the DDT had poisoned wasps which parasitized thatch-eating caterpillars. Without the wasps the caterpillars proliferated, they ate the thatch in the roofs, and the roofs fell in.

WHO found it had a worse problem, which was that the DDT had built up in the food chain – it got into the insects, which were eaten by little lizard-like creatures called geckos, which were eaten by the cats. The cats died, the rats flourished, and the WHO was faced with an outbreak of sylvatic plague and typhus, which it itself had created. It was then obliged to parachute live cats into Borneo.

Source: A. Lovins (1977) *Soft Energy Paths*, Cambridge, MA: Ballinger.

---

representing a compromise between unbridled growth and no growth. Rather than take the opposing positions of dominating nature for human welfare or being just another species found in nature, the role of humans in the sustainability paradigm is one of planetary stewardship involving the conservation and maintenance of natural capital (Gladwin et al. 1995). We will discuss concepts of sustainability and sustainable development later on in the chapter.

Corporate environmentalism as a stakeholder issue

Corporate environmentalism also involves the integration of stakeholder needs (see Chapter 8). The traditional view that the social responsibility of a firm means maximizing profits for shareholders (Friedman 1962) is being challenged by the stakeholder perspective (Freeman 1984; Bowie 1991). Stakeholder theory sees a business as comprising a constellation of different stakeholders, including shareholders, employees, customers, the local community, government agencies, public interest groups, trade associations and competitors. This implies that since all stakeholders are legitimate partners in a business, a business must consider the impact of its actions on all stakeholder groups and prioritize actions to meet stakeholder needs. Including the planet as a stakeholder (arguably the ultimate stakeholder) in this framework implies that firms need to be accountable for environmental damage.

Increasing concern about environmental issues has resulted in the emergence of *green stakeholders*, environmentally concerned citizens and groups demanding that organizations be made more accountable for their environmental impact. In many cases these stakeholders work on specific environmental projects in collaboration with organizations. Government environmental protection agencies in Australia, Europe and the US have many ongoing projects with chemical, mining and manufacturing corporations that focus on reducing emissions, eliminating the use of hazardous substances in the manufacturing process, and increasing both recycling of waste and the use of recycled products in the manufacturing process. Several non-governmental organizations (NGOs) are also working with corporations on a range of environmental initiatives. For example, the World Wide Fund for Nature helped Western Mining Company develop a public environmental reporting system. McDonald's and the Environmental Defense Fund are collaborating on several recycling projects. The North American utility giant, Pacific Gas & Electric has teamed up with environmental groups, some of whom the company fought in courts during the 1970s and 80s, to conduct a $10 million study on energy efficiency.

However, a stakeholder perspective does tend to complicate managerial decision making even further. There is no universal agreement on who or what constitutes a legitimate stakeholder (Donaldson and Preston 1995). The vast majority of the work in this field tends to be descriptive or prescriptive, with a few empirical studies of organization–stakeholder interactions. Research has focused on defining and refining the concept of stakeholder management, developing frameworks to analyse stakeholder relationships, and describing organization–stakeholder relationships (Freeman 1984; Preston and Sapienza 1990; Westley and Vredenburg 1991; Clarkson 1995; Mitchell et al. 1997).

Related to the stakeholder concept is another stream of literature that examines the social performance of corporations. Environmental issues are often framed as social issues and some researchers argue that firms should not only be evaluated by their economic performance, but also by their social performance. Since environmental issues are part of a firm's social responsibility, environmental criteria should also be used to assess a firm's performance. One problem with this approach is the normative dimension underlying these theories: the focus of theorizing is on 'what should be done' by organizations to address environmental problems and how organizations should be socially responsible and take into account the needs of all their stakeholders. The normative justification is based on moral grounds and researchers argue that managers should recognize stakeholder needs in an ethical and moral fashion (Clarkson 1995; Donaldson and Preston 1995; and Chapter 8). Thus, from an environmental perspective, the focus is on developing an 'environmental ethic' in firms.

While these are undoubtedly important issues, there are pragmatic difficulties in working with stakeholder theory in real-world business decisions. Different groups can have differing interests, and balancing competing interests to satisfy the needs of all stakeholders can be a difficult task (Mitchell et al. 1997). Some even take the extreme view that stakeholder theory is simply incompatible with business and that balancing stakeholder benefits is an unworkable objective (Sternberg 1996). In fact, some firms (The Body Shop and Ben & Jerry's come readily to mind) that attempted to position their operating strategy as ethical, environmentally and socially responsible are coming under increasing scrutiny by the public, media and government. False advertising claims about environmental attributes of products and services and attempts to *greenwash* the public are some criticisms directed at these firms (Entine 1995; Rosen 1995).

The stakeholder approach to corporate environmentalism involves some degree of recognition of the importance of environmental issues as well as efforts to develop strategies for stakeholder integration. Several firms have ongoing cooperative alliances with environmental organizations, consumer groups or government agencies in order to develop initiatives that minimize their environmental impact (Banerjee 1999). Thus, the stakeholder perspective of corporate environmentalism involves recognizing stakeholders' environmental concerns, which are translated into strategic actions designed to improve a firm's environmental performance as well as its relations with key external stakeholders.

Corporate environmentalism as a strategic issue

In conventional strategic planning, *environmental scanning* refers to an analysis of the external environment of the firm, for example the social, political, economic and cultural environment (see Chapter 15). The natural or biophysical environment did not play much of a role in corporate strategic planning until recently. However, since the 1980s, there has been increasing recognition that environmental issues can affect a firm's competitiveness and profitability. Much of this research focuses on the strategic implications of environmental issues for the firm. Thus, environmental strategies are developed and implemented in order to enhance competitiveness, increase market share, increase efficiency, decrease waste generation, create and enter new markets and enhance additional revenue-generating capabilities.

The resource-based view

The underlying assumption in the environment as strategy theme is that corporate environmentalism can provide sustained competitive advantage. In an attempt to incorporate environmental considerations into management theory, Stuart Hart (1995: 986) proposed a 'natural-resource-based view of the firm'. We will see in Chapter 15 how the traditional *resource-based theory of the firm* links available resources to the firm's capabilities and competitive advantage. A firm's capabilities are based on the nature of its internal and external resources: the less imitable the resources are, the more unique the capabilities they can provide. These unique capabilities create competitive advantage. Thus, managing *core competencies* is a key strategic task for achieving competitive advantage (Prahalad and Hamel 1990).

From a resource-based perspective, focusing solely on product/market decisions is too restrictive; instead it is argued that sustained competitive advantage can be gained by leveraging competencies that arise from resource characteristics. Hart (1995) takes this argument a step further by stating that the constraints imposed by the biophysical environment will provide new capabilities for firms and recognizing, managing and leveraging these (natural) resource constraints will ultimately lead to sustained competitive advantage. Thus, pollution prevention (rather than 'end-of-the-pipe' pollution controls involving clean-up technologies and processes) becomes a strategic capability that can lead to competitive advantage by lowering the costs of compliance.

For example, in a study of the Canadian oil and gas industry, Sanjay Sharma and Harrie Vredenburg (1998) found that companies which were environmentally proactive developed unique organizational capabilities. In particular, the proactive firms in their sample demonstrated capabilities for stakeholder integration, higher order learning and continuous innovation. These capabilities were also associated with self-reported managerial perceptions of competitive advantage. However, the link between corporate environmentalism and financial performance is yet to be fully explored. A few studies show there is a positive relationship. Using stock prices as firms' performance measure and environmental awards and crises as proxy variables for corporate environmentalism, Robert Klassen and Curtis McLaughlin (1996) found that the market valuation of firms rose significantly in the period following the announcement of an environmental award. The converse was also true: significant negative returns were demonstrated for firms that faced environmental crises. Michael Russo and Paul Fouts (1997) used return on assets as a measure of firms' performance and environmental ratings of firms by an external agency as a measure of environmental performance and found that environmental performance and economic performance were positively related. However, this was true only for high-growth industries.

Another study by Thomas Dean and Robert Brown (1995) indicated that high levels of environmental regulation actually conferred an advantage on firms in a variety of manufacturing industries, as these regulations served as entry barriers to new firms. Environmental legislation is typically framed as a threat to corporate competitiveness and profitability. However, some researchers, such as Michael Porter for example, argue that strict environmental standards make business more competitive in international markets because tough standards trigger innovation and quality improvement. Porter (1995) cites the case of Germany, which has one of the world's toughest environmental regulations and, consequently, is a world leader in developing and exporting technologies dealing with air pollution and other environmental issues. By developing new products that are less environmentally damaging, businesses can also take advantage of the growing market for environmental goods and services, which the US Environmental Protection Agency (1990) estimates to be worth $200 billion.

Environmental performance

While the ability successfully to integrate environmental concerns becomes a strategic capability that can confer competitive advantage, caution must be used to advocate the 'it pays to be green' maxim to all firms and industries. Although significant cost advantages can accrue due to corporate environmentalism, the relationship between corporate environmentalism and economic performance is more complex and not always a win–win strategy (Walley and Whitehead 1994; Hart and Ahuja 1996). There is also the problem of measurement: while measuring the financial performance of a firm is easy, developing comparable indicators of environmental performance of different firms in a variety of industries is a complex and difficult task. How do we define environmental

---

Exhibit 5.3 **Measures of environmental performance**

❏ **Capability studies:** What capabilities relating to environmental issues does the company have? How does it deploy these capabilities and prepare to develop new environmental capabilities?

❏ **Environmental audits:** Does the company conduct regular audits that assess its environmental impact? Are these audits conducted or ratified by external bodies? Does the company communicate the results of its environmental audit to all its stakeholders?

❏ **Environmental policy statements:** Does the company have a detailed environmental policy? Does it set environmental goals and targets and regularly evaluate its performance against them?

❏ **Future activity analysis:** Does the company address environmental issues in its diversification and expansion planning decisions? Are environmental issues integrated into new product development?

❏ **Risk analysis and management:** Does the company have a clear understanding of the environmental risks posed by all its activities? Does it develop plans and commit resources and people to actively manage these risks?

❏ **Continuous improvement in emission levels:** Does the company regularly monitor its emission levels? Does it have goals and strategies to reduce hazardous emissions? Is it an industry leader in setting emission standards?

❏ **Input measures:** Does the company assess the environmental impact of its inputs? Does it evaluate its suppliers on environmental performance? Does it use recycled products as inputs and can its products be recycled?

❏ **Efficiency measures:** How efficiently does the company use its resources? How much waste does it produce? How efficient is its energy consumption and does it use renewable energy sources?

performance and how can we assess it? William Judge and Thomas Douglas (1998: 245) defined environmental performance 'as a firm's effectiveness in meeting and exceeding society's expectations with respect to concern for the natural environment'. However, this definition is fairly broad and difficult to operationalize. In the studies described earlier, environmental performance was measured in a number of ways: self-reports, proxy measures (for example environmental awards) or environmental ratings provided by external agencies. The following have been suggested as measures for environmental performance as shown in Exhibit 5.3.

While 'objective' environmental performance measures are needed to assess a firm's actual environmental impact, universal indicators can be quite difficult to develop, as there is considerable disagreement among the scientific community on what constitutes environmental impact and how this is to be measured.

If integration of environmental concerns is the key to developing a strategic capability, how is this to be done? How can a company develop a more proactive environmental strategy that can leverage competitive advantage instead of merely reacting to environmental concerns by complying with existing legislation? Research indicates that companies that integrate environmental concerns at the corporate level develop more capabilities than those who follow a more functional approach to environmental strategy (Banerjee 1998, 2001).

Strategic levels of corporate environmentalism

Enterprise strategy

Organizational strategy can be created at four hierarchical levels: enterprise, corporate, business and functional (Schendel and Hofer 1979; also see Chapter 15). An organization's *enterprise strategy* integrates the total organization into its total environment. The focus of an enterprise strategy is on the role of an organization in society and its fundamental mission and licence to operate in society. A business exists because it provides goods and services needed by society; it is the ability of a firm to fulfil this need that determines its legitimacy. Thus, providing value to customers, developing quality products and services and creating shareholder wealth are all legitimate goals of a business. However, a firm is also a social entity producing social and environmental impacts. Environmental concerns can lead to the development of new societal norms that determine the legitimacy of the business enterprise, and integrating environmental concerns at the enterprise strategy level is one way by which a firm can seek institutional legitimacy in society.

Corporate strategy

Corporate strategy involves identifying the kind of businesses that a firm should enter in order to meet its enterprise strategy goals. Product/market decisions are made at this level, as are decisions on technology development and use. Strategic options arising from the integration of environmental concerns at the corporate level include entering environmental protection businesses such as the manufacture of pollution control equipment. Environmental protection markets are one of the fastest growing markets internationally, with the focus on clean production and waste minimization. Several small and medium-sized enterprises (SMEs) specializing in environmental technology have emerged over the past decade. These firms offer technical expertise and equipment, pollution control and waste management systems. The corporate strategy of these firms is to provide technology and services related to environmental management: this defines their market and choice of decisions. Diversification decisions are also made at this level and environmental issues can influence the direction of these decisions. The Boston Park Plaza is one of the environmental leaders in the hotel industry, with an international reputation for innovative strategies to reduce the environmental impact of its hotel properties. The success of these strategies led to the creation of a consultancy arm that provided environmental expertise to a range of service industries, resulting in new growth opportunities for the organization.

Business strategy

Business strategy involves the optimum allocation of its resources to achieve competitive advantage. Environmental issues can influence business strategies by providing cost advantages in recycling and reduced materials usage. Competitive strategies are created at this level and corporate environmentalism offers opportunities for cost reductions, product differentiation based on environmental criteria and niche marketing. For example, Paul Shrivastava (1995) describes three types of environmental business strategies: *ecologically sustainable least-cost strategy*, *ecologically sustainable product differentiation strategy* and *ecologically sustainable niche strategy*. Ecologically sustainable least-cost strategy involves standardizing *green* product designs while reducing manufacturing and disposal costs. 3M's Pollution Prevention Pays programme (3P Plus) was based on a strategy to reduce pollution at source rather than clean it up later. This source reduction strategy has generated cost savings of more than a $1 billion since 1975. For example, 3M generated savings of more than $125,000 a year on a $45,000 investment in equipment involving redesigning a resin spray booth that had been producing large amounts of overspray requiring special incineration disposal. Organic pesticides and biodegradable detergents are examples of a product differentiation strategy. Exploiting 'green' markets, something that The Body Shop and Ben & Jerry's do very well, is an example of a niche strategy. Dow Chemical, 3M and Philips have all developed new products catering to the niche of environmentally concerned consumers.

Functional strategy

Coordination is the key to a functional strategy: for example, the advertising strategy for a new product launch is coordinated with personal selling and sales promotions. *Green marketing* is an example of a functional strategy where environmental concerns can influence some or all the elements of a firm's marketing mix. Apart from product development (biodegradable detergents are an example), environmental issues can affect pricing decisions (most natural and organic brands of foods, cosmetics, soaps and detergents are priced at a premium), distribution decisions (reverse

channels of distribution where a firm takes its products back from the customer for recycling) and promotion decisions (*green advertising* where a firm advertises the environmental benefits of its products and services). Thus, the greening of the marketing mix can be the basis of an environmental functional strategy.

Because the levels of strategy are hierarchical, each level of strategy is constrained by the one above it. If environmental issues are integrated at higher levels of strategy, a wider range of outcomes will result. Firms with an environmental strategy focused at the functional level may tend to have more ad hoc programmes. For instance, the main environmental efforts of several manufacturing SMEs are geared towards complying with emission laws and are limited to manufacturing and waste management. The major emphasis is on complying with federal and local environmental legislation and to 'get the EPA off our backs' as one manager put it. In the case of a local food products firm, packaging was a major environmental initiative, in response to an imminent law requiring the use of recycled content in packaging. A functional strategy was also followed in this case: the marketing personnel

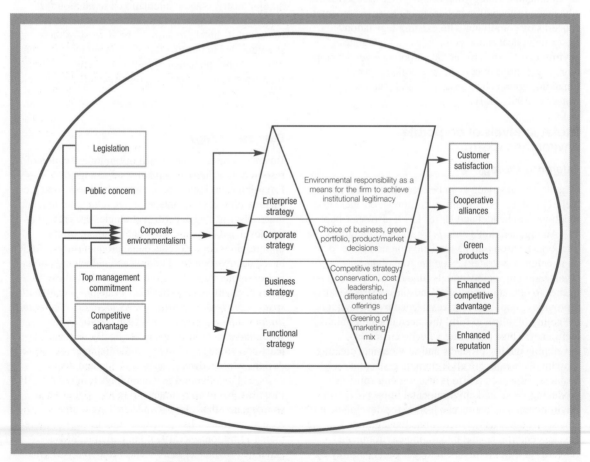

Figure 5.1 The biophysical environment

designed a new package that incorporated more recycled content. The strategy focus was on complying with legislation and was developed and implemented at a lower level of strategy, the functional level. There was no conscious overhauling of strategic planning to integrate environmental concerns at the corporate or business strategy level.

This difference in the levels also indicates the reactive or proactive nature of the firm's environmental strategies: functional environmental strategy often focuses on issues of compliance, whereas corporate environmental strategy treats the environment as a market where competitive advantage can be leveraged. The range of corporate responses to environmental issues is determined by the emergence of market opportunities, the level of environmental risk faced by a firm, public environmental concern and the regulatory climate. Figure 5. 1 shows how a range of environmental strategies emerges from integrating environmental issues at different levels of strategy. The range of environmental strategies moves from reactive to proactive, from compliance to innovation, as we go up the levels.

Integrating environmental issues into strategy

If environmental issues can be integrated at different levels, how does a company go about doing this? What mechanisms facilitate the process of integration? In this section I will discuss three methods by which a company can integrate environmental concerns into its strategy: total quality environmental management, lifecycle analysis and design for environment.

The role of total quality environmental management

A common tool used by many corporations to integrate environmental issues is *total quality environmental management* (TQEM). Just as total quality management focuses on 'zero defects', the aim of TQEM is *zero emissions*. Although the aim of zero emissions is scientifically impossible (it contradicts the second law of thermodynamics), it provides a direction for managers to develop environmental strategy using zero emissions as a goal. In TQEM the conventional notion of quality is expanded to include environmental quality and is a process that examines all environmental costs involved in every stage of manufacturing, distribution, consumption and disposal of products (GEMI, 1992). Managers prefer using TQEM to determine environmental impacts because it results in a quality improvement in the process or product and often delivers a measurable economic benefit to the

organization. The basic elements of TQEM are derived from TQM practices, with its focus on customer identification, continuous environmental improvement and employing a systems approach. For many corporations, TQEM has helped to shift environmental strategies from the functional level to the corporate level and a move away from a regulatory-driven, compliance-based strategy to a market and customer-based strategy (Piasecki et al. 1999). TQEM is the basis for most corporate environmental policies that set objectives and implementation plans. The entire operation of a corporation is reviewed using a systems-based approach to identify current or potential problems with environmental management systems and develop appropriate solutions.

TQEM provides a way to integrate environmental issues into all levels of strategy. As the CEO of a large, transnational computer manufacturer put it, 'the environment is every employee's business. We don't separate our business projects from our environmental projects. Our business policy is our environmental policy and vice versa.' TQEM is popular among managers because it delivers economic and environmental benefits to firms and it is easier to justify an investment if it improves the environment, enhances quality and reduces costs. Strategies that do all three are normally selected. Environmental improvements may or may not improve product quality. Procter & Gamble developed a pump action hairspray to avoid using aerosol propellants. While the product had a lower environmental impact, its sales were poor. Procter & Gamble's executives felt this was because customers felt that hand pumping was inconvenient and did not think the environmental tradeoff was worthwhile. A win–win situation in this case would involve redesigning the product or developing a less harmful substitute for aerosol that avoids trading off environmental protection for convenience.

In other cases environmental improvements led to quality improvements, often inadvertently. A transnational computer equipment manufacturer changed its packaging from plastic to cardboard as an environmental improvement strategy. Apart from saving costs, it also led to quality improvements because damage to the product was reduced since the plastic package had higher breakage rates than cardboard. It was an environmental improvement as well, since it reduced material usage, was recyclable and was made from recycled materials to begin with. Polaroid Corporation had a similar experience. New environmental legislation in Germany required less material to be used in packing its cameras. Trials of the new package showed that product breakage rates were higher due to the resulting diminished protective capacity of the new package. The TQEM process Polaroid had in place led to a shift in its approach to problem solving from the package to the product. Polaroid scientists increased the durability of their cameras to withstand damage during shipping with the lighter package and, as a result, breakage rates not only went down, but were better than they had been in the older, heavier package (McCrea 1993).

Lifecycle assessment

Lifecycle assessment (LCA) considers the environmental impact of a firm's upstream and downstream activities, from raw material procurement (including assessing the environmental performance of suppliers and the environmental impact of raw materials used to make other raw materials), manufacturing process design, product and package design, and the environmental impact of transporting, consuming and disposing of the product. The LCA process involves three stages: a *lifecycle inventory*, where environmental inputs and outputs are quantified; *impact analysis*, where the environmental impacts of each element are assessed; and *improvement analysis*, which is a systematic evaluation of strategies to reduce environmental impacts (Frankel, 1998). While not yet an exact science, lifecycle assessment attempts to quantify as many areas of environmental impact as possible and sometimes throws up interesting results. For example, after conducting a lifecycle assessment of its dishwashers, the German appliance maker Bosch-Siemens Hausergäte found that the manufacture of dishwashers accounted for only 2 per cent of the product's lifetime energy and material utilization. Product use accounted for 96 per cent of energy and material use. Designing dishwashers that use less energy and water would be an obvious environmental strategy for manufacturers and these products would have a lower environmental impact than existing products. The total systems approach used in LCA also found that carbon dioxide emissions from *daily* car trips to work by its employees was 10 per cent greater than from the *lifetime* energy consumption of *one* dishwasher (DeSimone and Popoff 1997). Car pooling and using public transport to reduce the environmental impact of a dishwasher is not a connection managers would normally make. A similar analysis conducted by Procter & Gamble of their compact powdered detergents found that the product used less energy, less material and produced less waste than traditional powders. If a product uses fewer raw materials and less packaging, there are significant upstream effects, involving fewer raw materials being mined, processed and transported, resulting in less energy use and less waste.

Design for environment (DFE)

The other tool that is gaining increasing acceptance is *design for environment* (DFE). As the name suggests, DFE aims to integrate environmental concerns into the product design process. As the practice of recycling increased in a variety of industries, products were designed to make their dismantling easier for recycling. Automobile manufacturers, appliance manufacturers, electronics manufacturers, computer manufacturers and consumer product firms regularly use DFE principles in designing new products or modifying existing ones. IBM's PS/2E (the 'E' stands for environment) was designed with the environment in mind: it had more recycled components, was more energy efficient and was designed for easier disassembly so that parts could be reused or recycled. The Dutch electronics giant Philips developed a range of products, ranging from TV sets to imaging systems, lighting tubes and packages, based on DFE principles of energy efficiency in the manufacture and lifetime use of the product, recyclability, hazardous waste production, durability and repairability (DeSimone and Popoff 1997). Both lifecycle assessment and design for environment converge in corporate environmental strategies of new product development.

International environmental standards: the ISO 14001 series

In an attempt to make environmental management systems consistent worldwide, the International Standards Organization established the ISO 14001 series as international standards for environmental management systems. Based on the philosophy of TQEM and the international standards on quality management (the ISO 9000 series), ISO 14001 is aimed at implementing a total environmental management and control system designed to measure, manage and improve a firm's environmental performance. To gain ISO certification, every manufacturing facility of a company is assessed on several key areas:

- policy setting (developing a company environmental policy)
- environmental impact assessment
- setting specific and measurable objectives and targets
- implementing the total environmental management system
- environmental monitoring and auditing
- conducting regular management reviews of the system.

While certification does not come cheap (estimated certification costs for large firms range from $100,000 to $1 million per plant and between $100,000 to $200,000 for smaller firms), there is potential for cost and energy savings as well as enhanced environmental education of employees, customers and suppliers. Some transnational corporations require their suppliers to be ISO 14001 certified so the certification system could produce a ripple effect in different industries.

However, it is important to note that the ISO standards are process standards not performance standards. They do not prescribe acceptable levels of pollution or industry standards. A simple statement such as 'we will comply with all relevant environmental legislation' is adequate as a goal and a system is set up accordingly. The environmental benefits of these standards are therefore limited, given the varying degrees of legislation that exist across the world. A firm can relocate to a country that has much weaker environmental legislation, set up a plant and apply for certification without making any significant environmental improvement, instead taking advantage of a friendlier regulatory climate.

We have seen a number of ways in which companies can integrate environmental issues into their strategy. Companies carry out a range of activities depending on the extent of integration. The question is, what are the forces that drive corporate environmentalism? Why do some firms pay more attention to environmental issues than others? Why are strategies of some firms compliance-based and reactive and those of others

market-based and proactive? In the following section, we will discuss some forces that drive corporate environmentalism.

Driving forces of corporate environmentalism

Two types of forces can influence a firm's response to environmental issues. *External* forces like the threat of legislation and public concern can lead to changes in a firm's strategies. The need for competitive advantage and top management commitment are *internal* forces that can influence a firm's strategies (Banerjee et al. 2003). The forces influencing corporate environmentalism and the potential outcomes are listed in Table 5.1.

How these forces influence the level of corporate environmentalism depends on a number of things: industry characteristics, company characteristics and market forces to name a few. For instance, environmental legislation is more of a threat in certain industries, such as chemicals, engineering and utilities, than others. Public concern for the environment may

Table 5.1 Corporate environmentalism and outcomes	
Driving forces	**Outcomes**
Legislation	Higher levels of corporate environmentalism in firms operating in industries facing stricter legislation than firms in other industries. Corporate environmentalism integrated at higher levels of strategy (corporate or business strategy) leading to:
Corporate strategy	Greater levels of investment in environmental protection when corporate environmentalism is integrated at higher levels (corporate or business strategy).
	Green product positioning.
	Cost advantages arising from environmental considerations, such as energy and resource conservation.
Public concern	Higher levels of corporate environmentalism when organizational decision-makers perceive their customers to be environmentally conscious.
	Negative public perceptions of a particular industry imply higher levels of corporate environmentalism among firms in these industries.
	Increased expenditure on green advertising emphasizing the environmental benefits of products/services and promoting a green corporate image.
Top management commitment	Higher levels of corporate environmentalism in firms where top management team is supportive of environmental initiatives.
	Members of the top management team will coordinate corporate environmental policies and programs.
Competitive advantage	Higher levels of corporate environmentalism in firms that have experienced cost savings due to environmental initiatives.
	New product development based on environmental considerations.
	Developing new markets for environmental goods and services.

Source: Bobby Banerjee (1999) 'Corporate environmentalism and the greening of strategic marketing'. In M. Charter and M.J. Polonsky (eds) *Greener Marketing: A Global Perspective to Greening Marketing Practice,* 2nd edn, Sheffield: Greenleaf Publishing, pp. 16–40.

have a greater effect on strategic decision making in certain visibly polluting industries, such as chemicals and oil. Firms in these industries tend to have a poor public image on environmental issues. Many such industries currently use environmental responsibility as a theme in their corporate advertising campaigns (Banerjee et al. 1995). Thus, both internal and external forces influencing corporate environmentalism have varying effects on the level of corporate environmentalism depending on the type of industry.

External forces

Legislation

The threat of tougher legislation and the rising costs of complying with environmental regulations are possible motivating factors for firms to incorporate environmental concerns in their strategies.

Pollution standards are becoming stricter: the 1995 Clean Air Act has higher standards for air pollution and acid rain emissions that are expected to cost US business $21 billion annually. Tougher legislation can affect a firm in two ways: first, the cost of compliance can become prohibitive. It is estimated that companies spend over $350 billion each year on environmental compliance. Given these legislative forces, many senior managers of firms perceive that a more effective strategy is to reduce emissions at the start instead of complying with clean-up and pollution control regulations.

Second, legislation can require substantial changes in product or package design or distribution channels. For example, several leading automobile manufacturers are incorporating the DFE process to include disassembly as a factor in their product design process. Another example is the reformulation of perfumes and colognes that is required to comply with new regulations proposed by the California Air Resources Board. In Germany regulation requires manufacturers of electronics to take back used equipment and EU directives regarding the recyclability of automobiles and electronic equipment are already in place.

Another rising concern for firms is the increase in environmental liabilities and risks incurred. Investors consistently rank liabilities and litigation as the most important type of environmental information required for their investment decisions. The US Securities and Exchange Commission has also mandated that corporations must disclose estimates of current and future environmental expenditures and liabilities. Companies are liable for not only any present damage to the environment but also all future damage and they must disclose any environmental risks known to be potentially significant. Moreover, environment-related litigation, estimated to be growing at over 5400 per cent between 1970 and 1993, is not uniformly distributed

across industries, largely because environmental risks and liabilities vary. For firms in industries with high environmental impact (chemicals, utilities, mining), environmental legislation is the most important incentive for developing pollution prevention strategies (Ochsner 1998). Generally strategies of pollution prevention or source reduction, as opposed to pollution control and waste clean-up, were more common in industries subject to strict environmental legislation.

Thus, corporate environmentalism can stem from a perception that environmental legislation will increase and that the firm should not only respond to these pressures, but also attempt to anticipate future legislation. Legislation can lead to different degrees of corporate environmentalism depending upon the level of strategy in which the firm includes environmental concerns. At a purely functional level, responses to legislative pressures can mean complying with existing regulations. At a higher corporate level of strategy, threat of environmental legislation and liability could influence decisions on new business opportunities.

Public concern

Another important reason for firms to develop an environmental orientation and strategy is increasing public concern for the environment. There are literally hundreds of opinions polls on the environment conducted in Europe, Asia and the US indicating that environmental concern is a high-priority issue in both industrialized as well as developing countries. Research indicates that besides the traditional reputational elements of a firm such as dependability, ethics and honesty, environmental attributes are becoming an integral part of corporate reputation. This includes corporate policies that demonstrate a concern for the environment, the degree of responsiveness to public concerns about the environment, environmental self-regulation and programmes to minimize the generation of waste.

The results of many national polls tracking environmental concern among the general public indicate that environmental protection remains high on the agenda of the American public despite escalating economic woes. Three separate national surveys conducted by the Yankelovich Organization, the Roper Organization and Simmons Market Research Bureau indicate that between 25 per cent and 43 per cent of the American population constitute the 'green' segment: consumers who are concerned about the environment.

The need to maintain a good public image and respond to public concerns can lead to firms adopting corporate environmentalism. Many industries, such as the chemical or oil industry, by the very nature of their products and processes, have a negative environmental image among the public. This probably explains why the most visible polluters like the chemical and oil industries are the ones that are publicly and privately paying the most attention to the environmental impact of their operations. A negative public image can influence firms in this industry to adopt corporate environmentalism as a strategy to survive and grow in the marketplace. All the large chemical corporations publicly affirm their commitment to environmental protection and have developed environmental mission statements or policy statements. Given the nature of their business, however, they continue to remain one of the most polluting industries. Significant reductions in environmental impact will probably take some time, although declining levels of emissions in some cases are the direct result of integrating environmental concerns into business strategy.

In some cases public perceptions of a company's environmental impact can lead to a direct change in strategy, as the case example highlights.

For years, McDonald's was the target of environmentalists as a large producer of solid waste and user of environmentally unsafe packaging. As environmental awareness grew, so did the negative public image of McDonald's. McDonald's abandoned their 'clamshell' polystyrene box after years of constant complaints by their customers and lobbying by environmental groups. Their initial response was to set up a recycling programme for polystyrene. However, due to operational problems and the public's negative perception of polystyrene, the recycling programme did not prove to be effective. In an effort to alleviate consumer concerns, McDonald's entered into an alliance with the Environmental Defense Fund, hoping to influence public perception of its waste reduction activities. Despite investing in recycling programmes for polystyrene, McDonald's decided to replace the clamshell box with a paper wrap, due to continued consumer pressure and the advice of its environmental partner.

Responding to public concerns goes beyond understanding and anticipating the needs of consumers and the market. Influences from customers, suppliers, regulatory agencies, environmental organizations, employees and shareholders can play a major role in developing corporate environmentalism. Company environmental concerns are influencing purchasing procedures in business-to-business (B2B) marketing. Major industrial customers of computer manufacturers are insisting on CFC-free products and other pro-environmental initiatives. This sets up a chain reaction wherein computer manufacturers now have to change their raw material requirements and insist on environmentally friendly products from their suppliers. This greening of the supply chain results in environmental concerns being addressed not only by manufacturers but also by their suppliers (and, in turn, influences their suppliers as well). Business-to-business purchase decisions are being increasingly influenced by the environmental quality of the product, as corporate customers find their environmental performance is closely linked to that of their suppliers.

Internal forces

Top management commitment

Top management's role in fostering and promoting corporate environmentalism has been discussed in numerous studies (Taylor and Welford 1993; Drumwright 1994; Starik and Rands 1995). Generally top management's direct involvement in environmental issues is more prevalent in firms that perceive regulations to be a major threat or whose dominant customer segment comprises the environmentally conscious (Banerjee 1998). Environmental problems associated with a firm's business activities can provide the stimulus for changing existing organizational patterns of behaviour. Environmental issues can challenge existing ways of thinking within a firm, and corporate environmentalism requires the support of top management for promoting an environmental ethic throughout the organization. The development of new ways of thinking and efforts to develop an environmental orientation throughout the firm are possible when all organizational members share the vision of top management or vice versa. The total quality environmental management approach discussed earlier, for example, requires the support of top management in implementing environmental strategies.

One way by which top management can manifest its public commitment to environmental protection is by developing an environmental mission or vision statement. Many corporations already have environmental mission statements and are making efforts to align environmental strategy with corporate strategy. Eastman Kodak Company has a 'vision of environmental responsibility' that includes a formal programme to guide managers in integrating environmental responsibility into their business operations (Poduska et al. 1992). Kodak's CEO chairs a special management committee on environmental responsibility that sets environmental goals and periodically reviews the company's progress on achieving these goals. Activities performed by this committee include educational and training programmes, communication of environmental practices and goals within the organization and environmental assessment programmes.

Commitment to corporate environmentalism is often

demonstrated by appointing senior managers responsible for overseeing the environmental orientation and strategies of their firm. These managers tend to have specialized job titles, for example director of environmental affairs or environmental marketing manager, and are responsible for developing and implementing environmental strategies at the business or corporate levels (Banerjee 1998). In other cases, for example Dupont, Digital Equipment Corporation, Kodak, 3M, members of the top management team are directly involved in environmental issues facing their firms by crafting appropriate corporate policies. Such direct involvement promotes a corporate atmosphere conducive to policy implementation which, when backed with adequate rewards and incentives for employees, leads to improved environmental performance of the whole organization.

The managing partner of Boston Park Plaza, a hotel chain that has won numerous environmental awards, sees himself as an environmental crusader. Describing his concern for the environment as a 'personal passion', the managing partner created an environmental task force, which he personally headed. As a result, the hotel implemented a range of environmental initiatives including introducing double-glazed windows in all rooms thus reducing the hotel's energy bills, buying recycled containers, reducing waste and expanding its recycling activities. Environmental education (of both customers and its own employees) was a key component of its environmental programme and, probably as a result of its leader's enthusiasm, the company's environmental strategies received enthusiastic support from all levels of employees. An incentive scheme for innovative ideas to reduce the hotel's environmental impact proved very popular, with the managing partner receiving emails from cooks, waiters, limo drivers as well as accountants and managers discussing their ideas for environmental improvement.

Need for competitive advantage

Competitive strategy, involving the business and corporate strategy levels, has been the major focus in strategic management research. A long-term competitive advantage can be obtained by having lower costs than competitors or having differentiated offerings and being able to command a premium price. Corporate environmentalism can provide both these sources of advantage.

For instance, there are numerous cases where the installation of new environmentally friendly

technologies has reduced costs for firms. New production processes and manufacturing changes in several firms (AT&T, Carrier, 3M, to name a few) have resulted in unexpected cost savings while meeting environmental protection goals. A strategy of source reduction instead of pollution prevention has proven to be more advantageous for firms. Procter & Gamble used a dual source reduction strategy for the product (Downy softener) and the package (refillable pouch). The refillable package was found to be more cost effective than the recycling option and led to a 95 per cent reduction in waste. Energy efficient initiatives have resulted in huge cost savings for firms in a variety of sectors.

Constant innovation in cleaner technologies and products can enable firms to differentiate their product based on their environmental friendliness. This may allow the firm to command a premium price for its products and thus provide the competitive advantage. New marketing opportunities have and will continue to emerge due to recognition of environmental problems. For instance, the US firm Pacific Gas & Electric dropped their proposed expansion plans for new nuclear power plants and decided that energy conservation was a more profitable investment. Environmental concerns were key issues driving this strategy. Also, Dupont used its technical knowledge derived from its in-house pollution prevention programme to set up a consulting operation that generated additional revenue for the company.

New strategic markets that have emerged due to environmental concerns are growing rapidly. A study conducted on 16 firms (Roy 1999) concluded that designing a 'greener' product that performed better helped to create new markets and increase or maintain market share as the following example illustrates.

Boston Park Plaza Hotel, by redesigning its facilities in an environmentally friendly manner, provides a good illustration of how to gain competitive advantage. As part of a comprehensive environmental marketing strategy, the hotel embarked upon many programmes that simultaneously reduced costs and attracted newer customers. One programme involved changing the shampoo and soap delivery systems from the traditional and wasteful small disposable vials to cheaper and larger wall-mounted units. Another example involved changing all windowpanes to ones more thermally efficient. These and other such strategies not only reduced costs but also attracted new customers by creating an environmentally friendly image for the business.

The Body Shop and Patagonia Inc. are two highly publicized examples of a successful 'green' strategic market positioning; both companies derive their competitive advantage from this positioning. These examples suggest that corporate environmentalism can lead to competitive advantage and unique market positions.

Consequences of corporate environmentalism

The preceding section has discussed conditions that can lead to a corporate environmental strategy. Corporate environmentalism has far-reaching consequences affecting the firm, customers, suppliers and employees, as well as society in general. Some possible consequences of corporate environmentalism will be discussed next.

Customer satisfaction

If one motivation for firms is to respond to the changing needs of their customers, a corporate environmental strategic focus should lead to enhanced customer satisfaction. The concept of customer satisfaction needs to be broadened beyond traditional criteria like quality, service and value to include environmental quality. Communication of company environmental activities to customer groups and company efforts to educate consumers about environmental issues are some important activities for an effective implementation of an environmental strategy. Environmentally concerned consumers are a significant niche market, and firms targeting this segment can increase customer satisfaction by offering minimum environmental impact products and services.

Enhanced reputation

Organizational commitment to environmental protection can also lead to an enhanced corporate image and reputation. A majority of 'green' advertisements focus on corporate environmental activities, and many firms are clearly attempting to portray an image of environmental responsibility. Underlying themes in these ads include social responsibility, consumer and employee health and safety, and support for environmental causes. A positive corporate identity on the environmental dimension has real value in the market and on a company's share price. However, there is a danger of the positive image of a 'green' firm not living up to its environmental performance, as has been the case with Ben & Jerry's and The Body Shop. This might lead to a consumer backlash. Thus, it is important for a firm to appear credible in its green image campaigns.

Cooperative alliances

In an attempt to enhance the effectiveness of their environmental strategies, firms may develop cooperative alliances with various groups: policy makers, public environmental groups and even with competitors. Some firms that have recognized the importance of environmental issues have already begun this process. The Irvine Company has an ongoing alliance with the Nature Conservancy to manage 17,000 acres of habitat in southern California. The Dow Chemical Company has formed alliances with the Nature Conservancy and the National Fish and Wildlife Foundation to protect wetlands. The Buy Recycled Business Alliance is a consortium of 25 major corporations, many of them direct competitors, that is involved in increasing demand for recycled products. These alliances go beyond conventional cause-related marketing and include specific activities, like waste reduction and wetland preservation as well as financial contributions. Consumer education is also a major theme of these alliances. Household recycling and composting, promoting use of recycled products and energy conservation are some programmes that have been conducted as a result of the alliances. These alliances result in new markets for member firms as well as marketing opportunities for new firms capable of meeting the new demand. As firms increasingly integrate environmental issues into their strategic planning process, such cooperative alliances with other stakeholders will become more common.

Green product launches

An environmental strategic focus can influence the new product development process and lead to the launching of environmentally positioned products such as phosphate-free detergents, recyclable and recycled packages, catalytic converters and 'natural' pesticides. Retailers are also attempting to environmentally position their outlets: Eco-Mart, the first Wal-Mart 'green' prototype store carrying environmentally positioned products, opened in 1993. Environmental influences are not limited to merchandise: the store itself has been constructed using environmentally friendly building materials and uses less energy than conventional stores Some retailers have even launched their own brand of environmentally positioned products.

Research and development

Corporate environmentalism represents an ongoing process, and not a one-shot strategy. Firms attempting to link environmentalism with company strategies are investing substantial resources in R&D of environmentally friendly technologies, products and processes. For instance, 3M's environmental strategy goes beyond compliance with legislation, as a result the company invests $100 million a year on environmentally related R&D and an estimated $200 million on environmental operations worldwide.

Enhanced competitive advantage

Positive impacts on traditional strategic performance measures like profitability and market share are also possible consequences of corporate environmentalism. Although it may take some years before environmental investments yield the expected payoffs, many firms have already realized significant cost savings as a result of implementing environmental programmes. Apart from cost advantages, environmental product positioning can also lead to product differentiation and gains in market share. Source reduction strategies, the emergence of new markets for environmentally friendly products and technologies, and environmental influences on buyer preferences are some sources of competitive advantage. Corporate environmentalism also enhances a firm's risk management skills by creating a proactive framework to deal with environmental liabilities and regulations, thus decreasing the costs of compliance.

Until now the focus of the chapter has been at the organizational and industry level. Corporate environmentalism refers to strategies and actions at the level of the individual firm. How does it relate to the broader picture of economic growth and global sustainability? Environmental problems such as pollution or climate change do not recognize national boundaries and have detrimental effects for the entire planet. Environmental problems also do not operate in isolation but have social and cultural impacts that are particularly severe for the rural poor who depend on the natural environment for their survival. A century of economic growth has not reduced the world's social and economic inequalities; in fact, in most cases the disparity between the rich and poor has widened in recent years. At the global level, the debate is about changing the way development proceeded during most of the last century where, despite phenomenal economic growth and advances in science and technology, 25 per cent of the world's population still live in poverty, without adequate food, clothing and shelter. Deforestation and the resulting loss in biodiversity puts more pressure on resources, creating more poverty among the rural poor. These problems have been debated at the policy level in international institutions such as the United Nations and the World Bank, resulting in calls for a systematic reappraisal of current trends in economic growth to include social and environmental concerns more explicitly. The notion of sustainable development emerged from this debate and

in the next section we will explore themes of sustainable development and its relationship to corporate environmentalism.

Sustainable development and corporate environmentalism

The concept of *sustainable development* emerged in the 1980s in an attempt to explore the relationship between development and the environment. While there are over 100 current definitions of sustainable development, the one most commonly used is that of the Brundtland Commission, which defines sustainable development as:

a process of change in which the exploitation of resources, direction of investments, orientation of technological development, and institutional change are made consistent with future as well as present needs. (World Commission on Environment and Development 1987: 9)

This broad definition is at the root of several controversies and there is considerable disagreement on how this definition should be operationalized and how sustainability should be measured. The Brundtland definition does not elaborate on the notion of human needs and wants and the concern for future generations is problematic in its operationalization. Given the scenario of limited resources, this assumption becomes a contradiction, as most potential consumers, the yet unborn future generations, face a few technical difficulties in accessing the present market for exhaustible resources.

Despite these problems, the Brundtland definition continues to be widely used as scholars and policy makers all over the world continue their efforts in refining the concept of sustainable development. The Brundtland definition of sustainable development attempts to balance economic growth with environmental protection and equity. It aims to achieve economic growth, environmental maintenance and equity simultaneously. Thus, sustainable development attempts to reconcile apparently irreconcilable positions of economic growth versus environmental protection and growth versus equity. While such a goal is laudable, there are serious concerns about whether it is achievable (Kirkby et al. 1995). The major proposals of the Brundtland agenda include changing the quality of growth, ensuring a sustainable level of population, conserving and enhancing the resource base, managing technology and environmental risks, and incorporating the environment and economics into decision making. While some scholars feel that sustainable development is the new paradigm for the 1990s and beyond, others take a more critical stance.

For instance, Arturo Escobar (1995) argues that sustainable development does not represent a major theoretical breakthrough, in the sense that it is very much subsumed under the dominant economic paradigm. Major assumptions of the neoclassical paradigm remain unchallenged and economic growth remains unquestioned: it is recast as sustainable growth. There is an underlying assumption that market forces can be relied upon to achieve sustainability. Political interventions, international agreements and national environmental regulations are other ways to promote the concept of sustainable development. However, as Michael Redclift (1987) has pointed out, most environmental initiatives carried out by governments and international organizations attempt to minimize 'externalities' of economic growth rather than outline ways in which development should proceed. As recent events, such as the international agreements at Rio, Kyoto and Oslo, have shown, environmental considerations do not take top priority when they clash with strategic economic, political or national interests. In other words, when there is a clash between economic and environmental interests, the former is preferred. Sustainable development attempts to reconcile these opposing interests and aims to simultaneously maximize economic and environmental benefits. Exactly how this is to be achieved is a matter of considerable debate all over the world.

Redclift (1987) points out another contradiction of sustainable development. This concerns the differing environmental objectives in developed and developing countries. The rural poor directly depend on the biophysical environment for survival, and notions of conservation and protection that are common in developed countries are contestable in developing countries. While poverty and environmental degradation are often linked in the literature, the role of 'development' in diminishing access to natural resources for the rural population is not frequently discussed.

Apart from attempting to reconcile economic growth with environmental maintenance, the sustainable development agenda of Brundtland also focuses on social justice and human development, within the framework of social equity and the equitable distribution and utilization of resources. In a content analysis of different definitions of sustainable development, (Gladwin et al. 1995) several themes were identified including human development, inclusiveness (of ecological, economic, political, technological and social systems), connectivity (of sociopolitical, economic and environmental goals), equity (fair distribution of resources and property rights), prudence (avoiding irreversibilities and recognizing carrying capacities) and security (achieving a safe, health and high quality of life).

A more specific concept was developed by Pearce et al. (1989: 27) who emphasized 'constancy of natural capital stock' as a necessary condition for sustainability. According to Pearce et al. (1989), changes in the stock of natural resources should be 'non-negative' and man-made capital (products and services as measured by traditional economics and accounting) should not be created at the expense of natural capital (including both renewable and non-renewable natural resources). Thus, growth or wealth must be created without resource depletion. 'Doing more with less' is a laudable goal and at the corporate level provides efficient use of resources but how this can achieve global sustainability remains unclear, given the gross inequalities in access to resources and technologies.

Conditions for sustainability

In a more recent attempt to operationalize the notion of sustainability, Karl-Henrik Robrt described four 'system conditions' of global sustainability (Frankel 1998). These include:

1. no systematic increase of substances from the earth's crust in the ecosphere
2. no systematic increase of substances produced by society in the ecosphere
3. no systematic diminishing of the physical basis for productivity and diversity of nature
4. fair and efficient use of resources and social justice.

While this may be a more precise definition than Brundtland's, problems of operationalizing remain: there is still considerable disagreement among the scientific community on the evaluation of environmental impact of products and processes. There are also other practical issues: what is the baseline from which we can measure 'systematic increases?' Are goals of 'zero-emissions' as stated in environmental policy statements of several transnational firms mere feel-good statements or are they achievable? While it is important for all stakeholders to agree on what sustainability means and examine the consequences of such a definition, more research is needed on the ways and means to achieve such an end.

The above components of sustainable development are fairly abstract concepts and are difficult to operationalize even at the macro-level. These concepts become even more challenging to address at the organizational level when assessing the activity of a business. As societal goals shift from growth to sustainable development, organizations need to change as well. Environmental management, industrial ecology, pollution prevention, optimum resource utilization and energy conservation are some ways that firms are beginning to address environmental issues within the larger framework of sustainable development.

However, there is some disagreement among

researchers about the relationship between sustainable development and corporate environmental practice. That corporations play a significant role in the path to sustainability is not in doubt. The question is, are current environmental practices compatible with notions of sustainability? Or are they mere *greenwashing* exercises designed to ensure that the corporation maintains a positive public image? Some researchers caution that the greening of industry should not be confused with the notion of sustainable development (Pearce et al. 1989; Schot et al. 1997). While there have been significant advances in pollution control and emission reduction, this does not mean that current modes of development are sustainable for the planet as a whole (Hart 1997). As the rate of international transactions continues to increase in today's global market economy, environmental degradation in developing countries also continues to increase steadily. As several researchers have pointed out, the greening of industry in developed countries has, in many cases, been achieved at the expense of Third World environments through the relocation of polluting industries to the developing countries (Redclift 1987; Escobar 1995; Hart 1997).

There is also a gap between sustainability and current environmental management practices. Very few companies address concepts of sustainability in their annual environmental reports. The few companies that do tend to focus on vague and general issues around their goals of becoming a 'sustainable' corporation, without much specific information on how these goals are to be reached. So-called 'socially responsible' companies like The Body Shop and Ben & Jerry's have faced problems about the veracity of their claims of 'environmentally sustainable' business operations (Entine 1995). Most companies focus on operational issues when it comes to greening and lack a vision of sustainability (Hart 1997). This narrow focus is often blamed on limited conceptualizations of 'organizational environment' and the fact that strategic management either ignores the role of the natural environment or treats it as an 'externality'.

Corporate environmentalism in the new millennium: the triple bottom-line approach to sustainability

Corporate environmentalism in the twenty-first century has become part of a broader strategy to integrate economic, social and environmental issues into organizational decision making. This is designed to broaden the parameters that measure organizational performance and reflect the 'triple bottom line of 21st century business' (Elkington 1997: 4). According to John Elkington, the interactions between the three themes of sustainability, economy, environment and

society, create three 'shear zones'. Corporate environmentalism is an outcome of the economic-environmental shear zone where companies try to become more 'eco-efficient', reducing environmental impacts while increasing production efficiency. Organizational efforts in environmental education is one outcome of the social-environmental shear zone, involving environmental literacy and training for employees, customers, shareholders and other stakeholders. Tensions between the social and environmental create new problems such as environmental refugees, communities that are forced to find other means of existence because they have lost their livelihood due to air or water pollution, deforestation or soil erosion. The intersection of the economic and the social results in a re-examination of corporate social responsibility, business ethics, human rights, diversity and the social impact of investments.

However, on closer scrutiny, a few cracks can be seen in the new 'green' face of corporations. While we have seen several examples of corporate environmentalism, there are an equal if not greater number of cases of corporate 'anti-environmentalism'. Some critics dismiss the corporate hype of becoming cleaner and greener as greenwashing, at best a set of practices with very limited pro-environmental impact and, at worst, outright lies and deception to fool the public and regulators and create a good image. Behind the glossy environmental reports of many companies lie some grim realities. There are many examples of this in the business world as shown below.

Until recently, the engineering giant Asea Brown Boveri (ABB), one of the 'founding fathers of corporate environmentalism', was involved in a controversial hydroelectric project in Malaysia that almost every international environmental agency described as a social and environmental disaster, despite ABB's environmental policy of 'promoting sustainable development, and playing its part in the transfer of environmentally sound technologies and methods to developing countries' (Frankel 1998: 97). Obviously, the company did not see any inconsistencies between its environmental policy and a project that will flood 1000 sq km of rainforest, increase greenhouse emissions and forcibly relocate over 10,000 indigenous people. The company's argument that it simply intended to carry out the wishes of the Malaysian government is also a bit hollow, given the power of transnational corporations and their interests in economic, political and legal affairs of developing countries.

There are similar contradictions in many such organizations that are 'environmental leaders', as shown below.

General Motors, which has come up with several environmental innovations, has been criticized for making exaggerated claims about its environmental record and attempting to defeat electric vehicle incentives in the US. For many years the company was the automobile industry's leader in opposing environmental controls for cars. Its strategy of aggressively marketing light trucks that are less fuel efficient than cars and its opposition to governmental interest in reducing greenhouse gas emissions are not the hallmarks of a leader in environmental responsibility. The US automobile industry's history on environmental and social issues is not particularly distinguished. US car makers in Detroit spent a lot of money in the 1930s, 40s and 50s buying up public transport companies in order to shut them down so that consumers would be more dependent on cars. The industry has consistently fought regulators, community and environmental groups on a significant number of safety and environmental initiatives.

Wal-Mart's much-publicized 'eco-store' is another case in point where the line between enlightened self-interest and genuine environmental responsibility begins to get blurred, as the following shows.

Wal-Mart stores have several environmental innovations that minimize energy consumption, use recycled materials and promote recycling behaviour. However, the relative environmental impacts do not address the broader effects on communities. The environmental costs of building these gigantic stores are high, no matter how 'green' the construction is. More people now need to shop in one place, which increases driving distances. Community leaders and non-profit institutes agree that the Wal-Mart strategy of selecting a small town that can only economically sustain one megastore tends to undermine community. With the company's financial and retail muscle, these megastores drive out small local businesses and it is doubtful that the attraction of lower prices makes up for the social and environmental costs (Frankel 1998).

However, it is important to point out that becoming environmentally sustainable is a very complex task and environmental problems can rarely be laid out as a series of neatly packaged alternatives. At the same time, there is a need to separate green hype from grim reality in corporate environmentalism. Environmental issues, like many other things in life, are not all win–win situations despite corporate rhetoric to the contrary. There is some evidence to suggest that the cost savings resulting from environmental improvements may be levelling off. The initial high-return/low-investment period of environmental improvement has come to an end for most industries and managers are finding that additional environmental improvements often involve significant investment and, as a result, the company's environmental strategies hit a *green wall* (Piasecki et al. 1999). Not all environmental strategies can be justified based on benefits to the environment and costs (and benefits) to the company. For instance, Apple Computers recently disbanded its award-winning Advanced Environmental Technology Group as part of its corporate downsizing. Warner Lambert is in the process of divesting from environmental packaging. Techniques such as lifecycle assessment and design for the environment discussed earlier require significant amounts of time and money. Convincing product and marketing managers that these expensive and time-consuming processes will contribute to higher sales of their products is also not an easy task.

While current corporate environmental practices might not be sustainable in the long term, the question is whether environmental management practices *could* be made sustainable. Several large transnational corporations are trying to define what sustainability means for them as individual corporations. The focus in all the discussions about sustainability, whether at the corporate or governmental level, is on win–win situations. However, this presents only a part of the solution, and restricts environmental problems to only those that can be solved by increasing corporate profit or competitiveness. Any radical notions of environmentalism or alternative theoretical viewpoints are dismissed as 'philosophical' or 'impractical', raising serious doubts about the limited efficacy of solutions that emerge from this problem misspecification. Environmental problem solving involves working with existing systems and providing technical solutions to problems with little chance of an alternative emerging from the outside or dismantling current systems. Thus, as David Harvey (1996: 148) points out, the debate about resource scarcity, sustainability, biodiversity, population and ecological limits is ultimately a debate about the 'preservation of a particular social order rather than a debate about the preservation of nature per se'.

Discourses of sustainability

This explains the popularity of win–win situations in

government and corporate rhetoric on sustainability. Discourses of sustainable development are becoming increasingly corporatized. For instance, the Dow Jones recently launched a Sustainability Group Index after a survey of Fortune 500 companies. A sustainable corporation was defined as one 'that aims at increasing long-term shareholder value by integrating economic, environmental and social growth opportunities into its corporate and business strategies' (Dow Jones Sustainability Group Index 2000). The rationale behind creating this index for investors is that environmentally and socially responsible corporations will provide long-term shareholder value and outperform corporations that do not address these issues. 'Green' investment funds have been around for more than a decade, and some of these funds such as the Environmental Value Fund or the Dow Jones Sustainability Group rate companies on a sustainability index.

It is interesting to observe how notions of sustainability are constructed, manipulated and represented in both the business press and academic literature. Corporate discourses on sustainability displace the focus from global planetary sustainability to sustaining the corporation through 'growth opportunities'. What happens if environmental and social issues do not result in growth opportunities remains unclear, the assumption being that global sustainability can be achieved only through market exchanges. This form of corporate social responsibility is not dissimilar to Milton Friedman's (1962) concept of corporate social responsibility involving the maximization of shareholder value, despite the rhetoric of 'stakeholders' and 'corporate citizenship' (Banerjee 2000). Despite framing sustainable development as a 'strategic discontinuity' that will change 'today's fundamental economics', corporate discourses on sustainable development, not surprisingly, promote the business-as-usual (except greener) line and do not describe any radical change in world views.

The problem of 'global' sustainability

Since the late 1980s there has been increasing recognition that environmental problems can no longer be solved at the national level and that a global effort is required. While the first Earth Summit in 1992 at Rio de Janeiro promised a global agenda for environmental protection, the complete breakdown at Oslo during the last round of meetings on carbon emissions demonstrates how contentious global environmental protection measures can be.

Third World countries

Espoused as a solution to the environmental ills facing the planet, 'global' environmentalism remains firmly rooted in the tradition of Western economic thought and, despite their rhetoric of inclusiveness, global environmental policy regimes do little to address the concerns of indigenous peoples and peasant populations who constitute the majority of the world's population. Differing environmental objectives in industrialized and Third World countries pose another contradiction for sustainable development. Environmental concerns in industrialized countries revolve around conserving rural spaces, valuing the aesthetics of nature, keeping beaches clean and providing the opportunity to acquire suntans without the risk of cancer. Environmentalism in the Third World, especially in rural areas, is a matter of survival, keeping control over natural resources and control over technology that transforms the environment (Redclift 1987). While 'the environment is everybody's problem' might be a good slogan for a bumper sticker, it not only obscures gross inequalities of resource access but is silent on how the problem was created in the first place.

Images of polluted Third World cities abound in the media, without acknowledgment of the corresponding responsibility of industrialized countries who consume (Renner 1997):

- 80 per cent of the world's aluminum, paper, iron and steel
- 75 per cent of the world's energy
- 75 per cent of its fish resources
- 70 per cent of its ozone-destroying CFCs
- 61 per cent of its meat.

The US:
- has 5 per cent of the world's population
- uses 25 per cent of the world's energy
- emits 22 per cent of all carbon dioxide produced
- accounts for 25 per cent of the world's GNP.

India:
- has 16 per cent of the world's population
- uses 3 per cent of the world's energy
- emits 3 per cent of all carbon dioxide produced
- accounts for 1 per cent of the world's GNP.

What will happen to the environment once all Third World countries 'develop' (however 'sustainably') to reach First World standards of living is not a pleasant prospect to consider.

The poorer regions of the world destroy or export their natural resources to meet the demands of the richer nations or meet debt-servicing needs arising from the 'austerity' measures dictated by the World Bank. It is ironic to the point of absurdity that the poorer countries of the world have to be 'austere' in their development while the richer nations continue to enjoy standards of living that are dependent on the austerity measures of the poorer nations. Neither the dangers of environmental destruction nor the benefits of environmental protection are equally distributed: protection measures continue to be dictated by the industrialized countries, often at the expense of local rural communities. This perverse logic pervades notions of 'sustainable' growth. Consumer spending and 'confidence' are essential in order to sustain the socioeconomic system, while welfare policies for the poor are dismantled because they are a 'pernicious drain on growth' (Harvey 1996: 144). Thus, the 'teeming millions' in the Third World are responsible for damage to the biosphere, whereas conspicuous consumption in the First World is a necessary condition for 'sustainable growth'.

Critics of sustainable development also argue that it can colonize areas of Third World social life that are not yet ruled by the logic of the market or the consumer, areas such as forests, water rights and sacred sites (Visvanathan 1991; Escobar 1995). The rural poor directly depend on the biophysical environment for survival and notions of conservation and protection that are common in developed countries are contestable in developing countries. While poverty and environmental degradation are often linked in the literature, the role of 'development' in diminishing access to natural resources for the rural population is not frequently discussed. Rather, the tendency is to blame the victim: farmers and peasants who engage in industrialized farming using fertilizers and pesticides are blamed without examining the role of the chemical industry or market-based institutions that are responsible for promoting their use. 'Slash-and-burn' peasants are blamed for the destruction of the forests while logging and timber companies, which have a far greater impact, are given tax incentives for following 'sustainable' practices (Banerjee 2003).

'Green' incentives are provided for corporations and policy measures put in place to evaluate and minimize the ecological impacts of logging. There are no indicators that can measure the devastating impact on local communities. Even the construction of a single road has multiplier effects: it reduces the transaction costs of the logging company (at public expense) while increasing land alienation of local communities, converting a hitherto knowledgeable and resourceful community into a pool of 'unskilled labor' (Gupta 1997). This 'sustainable' process is praised by corporations and governments for creating employment opportunities for local communities, without recognizing the disempowerment and poverty it created due to dispossession of land and natural resources.

Conclusion

If sustainable development is indeed about social, economic and environmental sustainability, we need to rethink current notions of progress and development. These concepts not only limit but represent a failure of the Western technocentric approach that serves to empower corporate and national economic interests and prevents communities from preserving their rights to control their resources. An unpacking of the notion of development is required and concepts of sustainability must go beyond seeking a compromise between environmental protection and economic growth. Sustainable development is not just about managerial efficiency (although that has a part to play); it is about rethinking human–nature relationships, re-examining current doctrines of progress and modernity and coming up with alternate visions of the world.

REVISITING THE CASE STUDY

1 What external and internal forces have influenced Calvert Corporation's relationship with the natural environment?

It is clear that the company needs to develop a comprehensive environmental policy. Some of the driving forces of corporate environmentalism discussed earlier have affected Calvert Corporation. The company is facing pressure from customers, regulators and the community to improve its environmental performance. Internally, key senior managers in the company have been faced with a range of environmental challenges that can negatively impact their operations. The company needs to engage with its various stakeholders to fully understand the range of environmental and social impacts its operations have all over the world in order to develop a policy that manages these impacts.

2 What strategies can the company develop to address environmental issues?

In setting up an environmental management system, the company needs to review its entire operating system, from its raw material sourcing, to processing, manufacturing operations, transportation, energy usage at all points of activity, product usage, disposal and recycling. The company does not seem to have a comprehensive environmental strategy and its approach appears to be compliance-based and at the functional level of strategy. A comprehensive environmental strategy requires that environmental issues be integrated at the corporate level. Top management commitment is a key factor that can make this happen. The Calvert case presents an ideal example of how an organization learns to integrate environmental and social issues. An organization as a system learns when it interacts with its environment in a manner that results in the translation of new knowledge into new goals, norms, expectations and roles. By recognizing the importance of environmental issues, top management can act as facilitators of the learning process and provide a climate for the organization as a whole to learn. Integrating social sustainability issues is even more complex.

The company needs to develop and implement a number of strategies. First, it needs a comprehensive environmental policy that informs strategy at the functional, business, corporate and enterprise level. The broad policy has to be translated into specific measurable objectives that are reviewed periodically. Second, the company needs to develop a community and stakeholder integration strategy. This involves building coalitions with different community and environmental groups and regulators. A system of publicly reporting environmental and social performance also needs to be developed. Third, the company needs to develop education and training programmes for its employees, suppliers, customers and other stakeholders in order to implement its environmental and social policies.

3 Should the company engage with its stakeholders to develop an environmental policy? Why? Who are these stakeholders?

Apart from the technological investments that need to be made to clean up manufacturing facilities and reduce overall environmental impact, there is considerable education that needs to be done inside and outside the company. If Lee Morgan is serious about transforming the environmental culture within the company, its efforts need to be more than greenwashing. The company should enter into dialogue with regulators, environmental groups, suppliers, customers, community members and other stakeholders in developing its environmental policy. The company can build credibility by being transparent in its dealing with stakeholders and should be willing to disclose publicly the extent of its environmental impact. Establishing and maintaining cooperative alliances with regulators, environmental agencies and community groups for specific projects is one way by which this can be done.

4 What social impacts do the operations of the company have? How can it address the social issues relating to its business?

Addressing social concerns, such as the needs of indigenous communities who live around its mine sites, is a more complex problem. Obviously, the company's relations with the indigenous communities that live near mine sites are far from cordial. Building trust will not happen overnight, especially given the long and often violent histories of the relations between indigenous peoples and mining companies. Dealing with communities that are actively opposed to mining, given the damaging environmental, social and cultural consequences of mining for these communities, is an enormous challenge. Some mining companies have taken the stance of not proceeding with mining if the community was opposed to it and exploring alternative sites instead, rather than trying to force the issue legally or politically. The company needs to develop a consistent policy in its communications and dealings with indigenous communities. Its idea of relocating supplies to its Philippine site because of a weaker regulatory climate is inconsistent with a responsible social and environmental policy.

5 How will environmental and social issues affect the competitiveness and profitability of the company in the long term?

Developing and implementing environmental and social policies while keeping an eye on dwindling profit margins is a major challenge. If the market and investors take a short-term view on immediate profits, it is likely that the market value of Calvert Corporation could weaken in the short term. However, the company might be better prepared to face even more difficult environmental and social challenges in the future. New environmental legislation in their European markets can threaten the company's market share and competitiveness in the region. Depending on the vision and risk-taking ability of its senior management the company can either develop a reactive or proactive strategy. The former approach focuses on compliance with existing environmental legislation. A more proactive approach would ensure that the company becomes a leader in integrating environmental and social issues in their industry. A stakeholder approach to these issues would promote a more cooperative and collaborative relationship with the company's key stakeholders that could enhance the company's image and reputation and have positive effects on its future growth strategies.

6 How will the company ensure that all its employees are aware of the company's environmental policies?

In terms of its environmental policy, appointing a senior manager with specific organization-wide environmental responsibilities is a first step. However, the importance of environmental issues needs to be recognized by all managers and employees to effectively implement an environmental strategy. The company needs to develop ongoing environmental education programmes for its employees, customers, suppliers and community members. Periodic newsletters describing the company's environmental activities should be circulated to all employees and key stakeholders. Senior management should play a prominent role in disseminating information about corporate environmental strategies and actions.

7 How can the company develop a triple bottom-line policy for its business? What would be the elements of such a policy?

Developing a comprehensive triple bottom-line policy is a challenging and difficult task for the company. While there are several ways to assess a company's environmental impact using a variety of indicators that measure these impacts, evaluating the social impact of a company's operations is more difficult. The social and environmental impacts of mining in remote indigenous communities have to be explicitly addressed if the company is serious about its triple bottom-line philosophy. Developing education and training programmes for indigenous communities, promoting long-term employment opportunities for these communities and health and safety issues are some areas that the company can consider. Specific measurable goals and performance indicators need to be developed to address these areas and the company should be transparent and accountable in all its dealings with its stakeholders. How far can the company go to determine the parameters of its triple bottom-line performance? What would an environmental and social strategy at the enterprise level look like for a mining company? Can environmental and social issues become sustainable growth opportunities for the company? Or will it hit the 'green wall' after reaping the initial payoffs? To whom is the company ultimately accountable? How will shareholders react if a representative from Greenpeace, an official from the Environment Protection Agency and the leader of an Aboriginal tribe are invited to join the board of directors? It is difficult to address these questions in isolation and at the level of an individual firm. Radical political and economic changes need to occur at industry and government levels to ensure that the economic system does not penalize firms trying to operate on triple bottom-line principles.

References

Banerjee, S.B. (1998) 'Corporate environmentalism: Perspectives from organizational learning'. *Management Learning*, **29**(2): 147–64.

Banerjee, S.B. (1999) Corporate environmentalism and the greening of strategic marketing, in M. Charter and M.J. Polonsky (eds) *Greener Marketing: A Global Perspective to Greening Marketing Practice*, 2nd edn, Sheffield: Greenleaf Publishing, pp. 16–40.

Banerjee, S.B. (2000) 'Whose land is it anyway? National interest, indigenous stakeholders and colonial discourses: the case of the Jabiluka uranium mine'. *Organization and Environment*, **13**(1): 3–38.

Banerjee, S.B. (2001) 'Managerial perceptions of corporate environmentalism: Interpretations from industry and strategic implications for organizations'. *Journal of Management Studies*, **38**(4): 467–91.

Banerjee, S.B. (2003) 'Who sustains whose development? Sustainable development and the reinvention of nature'. *Organization Studies*, **24**(1): 143–80.

Banerjee, S.B., Gulas C.C. and Iyer, E. (1995) 'Shades of green: A multidimensional analysis of environmental advertising'. *Journal of Advertising*, **24**(2): 21–31.

Banerjee, S.B., Iyer, E. and Kashyap, R. (2003) 'Corporate environmentalism and its antecedents: Influence of industry type'. *Journal of Marketing*, **67**(2): 106–22.

Bowie, N. (1991) 'New directions in corporate social responsibility'. *Business Horizons*, **34**(4): 56–65.

Carson, R. (1962) *Silent Spring*. Boston: Houghton Mifflin.

Clarkson, M.B.E. (1995) 'A stakeholder framework for analysing and evaluating corporate social performance'. *Academy of Management Review*, **20**: 92–117.

Commoner, B. (1972) *The Closing Circle*. New York: Bantam Books.

Dean, T.J. and Brown, R.L. (1995) 'Pollution regulation as a barrier to new firm entry: initial evidence and implications for future research'. *Academy of Management Journal*, **38**: 288–303.

DeSimone, L.D. and Popoff, F. (1997) *Eco-efficiency: The Business Link to Sustainable Development*. Cambridge: MIT Press.

Donaldson, T. and Preston, L.E. (1995) 'The stakeholder theory of the corporation: Concepts, evidence, and implications'. *Academy of Management Review*, **20**: 65–91.

Dow Jones Sustainability Group Index (2000) http://www.dowjones.com/djsgi/index/concept.html. Accessed January 15, 2001.

Drumwright, M.E. (1994) 'Socially responsible organizational buying: environmental concern as a noneconomic buying criterion'. *Journal of Marketing*, **58**(3): 1–19.

Elkington, J. (1997) *Cannibals with Forks: The Triple Bottom Line of 21st Century Business*. Oxford: Capstone.

Entine, J. (1995) 'Rain-forest Chic'. *Toronto Globe & Mail Report on Business*, 41–52.

Environmental Protection Agency (1990) *Environmental Investments: The Cost of a Clean Environment*. US Government Printing Office, Washington DC.

Escobar, A. (1995) *Encountering Development: The Making and Unmaking of the Third World, 1945-1992*. Princeton, NJ: Princeton University Press.

Frankel, C. (1998) *In Earth's Company: Business, Environment and the Challenge of Sustainability*. Gabrieola Island, BC: New Society Publishers.

Freeman, R.E. (1984) *Strategic Management: A Stakeholder Approach*. Marshfield: Pitman.

Friedman, M. (1962) *Capitalism and Freedom*. Chicago: University of Chicago Press.

GEMI (1992) *Total Quality Environmental Management: The Primer*. Global Environmental Management Initiative, Washington, DC.

Gladwin, T.N., Kennelly, J.J. and Krause, T.S. (1995) 'Shifting paradigms for sustainable development: Implications for management theory and research'. *Academy of Management Review*, **20**(4): 874–907.

Gray, R. (1992) 'Accounting and environmentalism: An exploration of the challenge of gently accounting for accountability, transparency, and sustainability'. *Accounting, Organizations and Society*, **17**(5): 399–425.

Gupta, A. and the Honey Bee Network (1997) Linking grassroots innovations, enterprise, investments, incentives and institutions: democratizing knowledge through Honey Bee network. Paper presented at the World Bank for Global Knowledge Conference, Toronto.

Hart, S.L. (1995) 'A natural-resource-based view of the firm'. *Academy of Management Review*, **20**(4): 986–1014.

Hart, S.L. (1997) 'Beyond greening: strategies for a sustainable world'. *Harvard Business Review*, January/February: 6–76.

Hart, S.L. and Ahuja, G. (1996) 'Does it pay to be green? An empirical examination of the relationship between emission reduction and firm performance'. *Business Strategy and the Environment*, **5**: 30–7.

Harvey, D. (1996) *Justice, Nature and the Geography of Difference*. Oxford: Blackwell.

Judge, W.Q. and Douglas, T.J. (1998) 'Performance implications of incorporating natural environment issues into the strategic planning process: An empirical assessment'. *Journal of Management Studies*, **35**: 241–62.

Kirkby, J., O'Keefe, P. and Timberlake, L. (1995) *Sustainable Development*. London: Earthscan.

Klassen, R.D. and McLaughlin, C.P. (1996) 'The impact of environmental management on firm performance'. *Management Science*, **42**: 1199–1214.

Lovins, A. (1977) *Soft Energy Paths*. Cambridge, MA: Ballinger.

McCrea, C.D. (1993) Environmental packaging and product design. Paper presented at Professional Development Series: American Marketing Association (Boston Chapter).

Mitchell, R.K., Agle, B.R. and Wood, D.J. (1997) 'Toward a theory of stakeholder identification and salience: defining the principle of who and what really counts'. *Academy of Management Review*, **22**: 853–86.

Ochsner, M. (1998) 'Pollution prevention: An overview of regulatory incentives and barriers'. *NYU Environmental Law Journal*, **6**: 586–617.

Odum, E.P. (1971) *Fundamentals of Ecology*, 3rd edn. Philadelphia: W.P. Saunders.

Ottman, J.A. (1993) *Green Marketing: Challenges And Opportunities For The New Marketing Age.* Lincolnwood: NTC Business Books.

Pearce, D.W., Markandya, A. and Barbier, E.B. (1989) *Blueprint for a Green Economy.* London: Earthscan.

Petulla, J.M. (1980) *American Environmentalism: Values, Tactics, Priorities.* Texas: A & M University Press.

Piasecki, B.W., Fletcher, K.A. and Mendelson, F.J. (1999) *Environmental Management and Business Strategy: Leadership Skills for the 21st Century.* New York: John Wiley.

Poduska, R., Forbes R.H. and Bober M.A. (1992) 'The challenge of sustainable development', *The Columbia Journal of World Business,* **27**(3&4): 287–91.

Porter, M.E. (1995) 'Green and competitive: Ending the stalemate'. *Harvard Business Review,* **73**(5): 120–34.

Prahalad, C.K. and Hamel, G. (1990) 'The core competence of the corporation'. *Harvard Business Review,* **68**(3): 79–91.

Preston, L.E. and Sapienza, H.J. (1990) 'Stakeholder management and corporate performance'. *Journal of Behavioral Economics,* **19**: 361–75.

Redclift, M. (1987) *Sustainable Development: Exploring the Contradictions.* London: Methuen.

Renner, M. (1997) *Fighting for Survival: Environmental Decline, Social Conflict and the New Age of Insecurity.* London: Earthscan.

Rosen, H. (1995) 'The evil empire: The real scoop on Ben & Jerry's crunchy capitalism'. *The New Republic,* 22–5.

Roy, R. (1999) 'Designing and marketing greener products: The Hoover case', in Charter, M. and Polonsky, M.J. (eds) *Greener Marketing: A Global Perspective to Greening Marketing Practice,* 2nd edn, Sheffield: Greenleaf Publishing, pp. 126–42.

Russo, M.V. and Fouts, P.A. (1997) 'A resource-based perspective on corporate environmental performance and profitability'. *Academy of Management Journal,* **40**: 534–59.

Schendel, D.E. and Hofer, C.W. (1979) *Strategic Management: A New View of Business Policy and Planning.* Boston: Little, Brown.

Schot, J., Brand, E. and Fischer, K. (1997) 'The greening of industry or a sustainable future: Building an international research agenda.' *Business Strategy and the Environment* **6**: 153–62.

Sharma, S. and Vredenburg, H. (1998) 'Proactive corporate environmental strategy and the development of competitively valuable organizational capabilities'. *Strategic Management Journal* **19**: 729–53.

Shrivastava, P. (1995) 'The role of corporations in achieving ecological sustainability'. *Academy of Management Review,* **20**(4): 936–60.

Starik, M. and Rands, G.P. (1995) 'Weaving an integrated web: Multilevel and multisystem perspectives of ecologically sustainable organizations'. *Academy of Management Review,* **20**(4): 908–35.

Sternberg, E. (1996) 'Stakeholder theory exposed'. *The Corporate Governance Quarterly,* **2**: 4–8.

Taylor, G. and Welford, R. (1993) 'An integrated systems approach to environmental management: a case study of IBM (UK)'. *Business Strategy and the Environment,* **2**(3): 1–11.

Visvanathan, S. (1991) 'Mrs Brundtland's disenchanted cosmos'. *Alternatives,* **16**(3): 377–84.

Walley, N. and Whitehead, B. (1994) 'It's not easy being green'. *Harvard Business Review,* **72**(3): 46–52.

Westley, F. and Vredenburg, H. (1991) 'Strategic bridging: The collaboration between environmentalists and business in the marketing of green products'. *Journal of Applied Behavioral Science,* **27**: 65–90.

World Commission on Environment and Development (1987) *Our Common Future.* London: Oxford University Press.

6

Power and politics in organizations

Liz Fulop and Stephen Linstead

Questions about organizational power and politics

1 Are power and politics generic to all organizations?
2 Do some circumstances more than others give rise to power struggles and politics in organizations?
3 Why is power such a difficult thing to deal with in organizations?
4 Is everyone able to gain or exercise power in organizations?

FAWLEY RIDGE

In the UK in the late 1980s, many polytechnics were about to become universities, of which Fairisle Polytechnic was one. At this time, however, they were still under the control of local authorities and they still provided non-advanced further education (NAFE) courses – work of sub-degree standard. It was becoming clear that this level of work was regarded by government as the province of local authority institutions. It would only be left in the hands of the new universities if there was no alternative local provider, and in Fairisle there were several competent others. It followed that any site which was designated a NAFE site by the Asset Commission would revert to the local authority when they decided on the terms of separation, that is, 'divorce and alimony'. Fairisle currently occupied as one of its many sites a campus at Fawley Ridge, an area of prime residential land, rapidly appreciating in value and conservatively estimated to be worth at contemporary prices around £1.5 million as a piece of land alone. The new university would need such an asset given its desperate need for building space, but the site was almost exclusively NAFE, being devoted to evening classes in a huge range of languages and providing daytime courses for local businesspeople. Only the highest level of linguistic qualification offered was regarded officially as being 'advanced' for funding purposes, and this was only 5 per cent of the total workload.

In that period, a new director, Paul Kost, had taken over the reins of the polytechnic, which held some very specific challenges. Kost was considered an outstanding candidate for the directorship: he had contacts in government on all sides, a thorough understanding of parliamentary procedure and committee work and an almost uncanny ability to pre-empt ministers and government policy. Personally, he was a brilliant public speaker, an erudite, charming host and chairman, but also blunt and ruthless once he made a decision. Kost inherited a structure of what was basically 16 baronial fiefdoms or empires with several scandalous situations – financial and academic – ready to explode.

Fairisle Polytechnic, on Kost's accession, was an inappropriate organizational structure with inadequate financial accountability, inadequate monitoring of quality, inappropriate physical accommodation, underperformance in research, and staff who were highly unionized and politicized and who had tried to resist the squeezing of resources.

Kost set about structural change by grouping departments into faculties, combining some of them, removing many of the 16 heads and forcing others to reapply for their posts. Deans were created by external and internal appointments. The new heads were charged with two missions: to scour out the corruption of the old guard and identify any slack or underperformance in teaching commitments, supervision, research or quality monitoring. They were required to suspect everything and trust no one. Kost removed some deputy directors, created new heads who were his political affiliates and, with no constituency in the academic community, were entirely accountable to the director.

Derek Elliott was appointed as head of the department of continental management. He was relatively young at 35 to be a head, but he was experienced in course administration and also had a good publications record. The department was a product of Kost's restructuring efforts. Elliott was politically astute, but also had a personal commitment to managing in an open way, with a 'light hand on the tiller'.

Early in his tenure at Fawley Ridge, the director told Derek that the site was out of financial control, with earnings not being properly accounted for to the centre, and the only way to get on top of this was to remove Cyril Lancashire, the lecturer in charge, to whom many of the staff felt a strong allegiance. Cyril was close to retirement age and it was not difficult for Derek to persuade him to accept the director's offer of leaving early, but Derek felt uneasy about the rationale. He had found the affairs of the centre to be entirely proper, Cyril to be honest and well intentioned and staff to be dedicated. The director did not see it that way and needed to be clearly in control of Fawley Ridge and therefore Cyril Lancashire had to be removed. The staff were, however, devoted to Cyril and were hurt by the way they perceived him being treated.

Despite his feelings about this incident, Derek intended to try to manage according to his principles. As part of his policy of openness and involvement in strategic planning, Derek had begun to discuss possible futures and priorities with his staff on all three sites on which the department operated. After talking to his six full-time staff at Fawley Ridge, however, a disaster occurred. Derek had asked them to consider several 'what if' scenarios, including possible closure of some courses; by the time this leaked 'along the grapevine', it became a story that the polytechnic was to close the site. One of the students, a newspaper reporter, published this story and Derek found himself sitting facing an angry public meeting with the dean, the director and 300 irate students.

Kost was brilliant in his handling of an explosive situation and chose not to deny that closure was a possibility and suggested that it was a threat because of government policy. He suggested that the students should organize a political lobby, and the polytechnic would support them. He was cheered to the echo at the end of the meeting.

However, there was a groundswell of resentment building up. Shortly after this incident, Kost attempted to acquire a building from the Textile Industry Association (TIA), which would mean students would have to move to a different site for classes. The students, who had not been consulted, mounted a very effective campaign of demonstrations, slogans and leaflets and eventually the TIA pulled out of the deal.

At this point, Derek, the head of the department which occupied the site as one of its three subdivisions, was called in to the director's office with William Fisher, the deputy director. The position was outlined. Space in the polytechnic was at a premium. Fawley Ridge was a valuable property which under present usage the new university would lose after vesting day. It was imperative that the property be safeguarded by bringing its usage for advanced (degree or equivalent level) work up to over 60 per cent. The only viable proposition would be to transfer the languages and business degrees (for which Derek's department was responsible), library holdings, support staff and language labs over to the Fawley site. Students would have to be bused six miles for their classes, after a three-mile journey for most of them to reach the present departmental HQ site, Shaw's Park, from which they would have to leave, Fawley being so inaccessible. Derek looked glum. The director reassured him somewhat hollowly, 'We haven't made the decision yet. If anything emerges that clearly indicates that this will damage the quality of education of the students we won't – we daren't – do it. The whole situation is very delicate as I'm sure you appreciate. But everything else is negotiable. Work closely with William and see what you can do; at this point it's our only option.'

Source: Adapted from Stephen Linstead (1997) 'Resistance and return: Power, command and change management', *Studies in Cultures, Organizations and Societies,* **3**(1): 67–89.

Note: The second part of this case study appears later in the chapter.

QUESTIONS ABOUT THE CASE

1 Who has power in this situation?
2 What are the sources of their power?
3 What kind of power is it?
4 What are the obvious conflicts of interest, and how would you expect people to behave as a result?

Attempt to answer these questions before you read on. They are discussed later in the chapter under Analyses.

Introduction

Power is an indisputable part of everyday life, every social relationship imaginable and one of the most controversial aspects of organizations. Nothing is more certain than that every individual will have to deal with power in some way or another, will be subjected to the politics of others, and engage in it themselves. By virtue of how organizations are designed or managed, individuals are automatically placed in potential power struggles whether they like it or not. There are many examples of such power struggles: strikes over redundancy payments; problems enforcing equal employment opportunity policies; disputes over noisy or dirty facilities; fights over the size of offices or titles given to positions; conflicts over patronage and preferential treatment, nepotism (jobs for family members) and favouritism (preferential treatment for one's friends); clashes over closures and relocations; and mismanagement by senior management and boards. Power is experienced, interpreted and dealt with differently by each individual or group as well as across cultural contexts, as we discussed in Chapter 3.

Power is an extremely complex and important phenomenon for managers to understand. In fact, we believe it is one of the most enduring aspects of human relationships. Power and influence are sought-after 'prizes', and this in itself is not a problem. What is problematical and of concern is how power can be used for purely self-interest and the exploitation of others. Managers are often reluctant to admit that they operate politically or crave power, and feel that to do so would automatically qualify them as being 'Machiavellian' or a highly instrumental and ruthless person. Suffice it to say, understanding how one operates politically is essential to managing and grasping the importance of the relational nature of management.

Organizations, or at least managers in them, tend to establish a structure of command, although not absolute command, that creates many sources of discontent and resistance. Hierarchical organizations, such as many large public and private sector organizations, are structures of difference, where those at the top speak both *for* and *to* those below them. Organizations are also structures of desire or aspirations, as those below seek to rise in the hierarchy in order to receive deference and respect themselves in various ways. All too often, those who rise in the hierarchy pass on the unpleasantnesses and resentments associated with being exclusively subjected to command without having anyone to whom they can give command. Indeed, it is our contention that it is the deference relationship that produces the key relational problems in organizations and gives rise to power struggles and organizational politicking.

The chapter reviews a number of approaches to power popularly referred to as the *behavioural*, *political*, *radical* and *relational* approaches. Diverse ideas and perspectives are apparent in each approach, but by far the most popular in the management discourse have been those that are aligned with the behavioural and political views. We will also examine a number of other approaches that do not necessarily fit neatly into the four-way typology described above but have had significant influence on the topic.

Approaches to power

Max Weber, whose theory of bureaucracy contained a very complex view of authority, left no doubt that power was a pervasive force in organizations (see Chapter 4). Weber's notion of rational-legal authority stated that authority was not automatically accepted by individuals but had to be earned and legitimated in order for systems of domination to exist (Weber 1964: 124, 152–3, 324–9). By legitimation, he meant the execution of rules or orders in such a way that people believed that the orders or commands issued were binding on them and desirable to imitate or follow. Weber was not advocating that those in command had automatic authority, but rather that there were conditions and rules that had to be adhered to in order to maintain authority. Once a leader legitimated his or

her authority, Weber believed that this would be mirrored in the followers' willingness to carry out the leader's orders or commands with compliance. Weber clearly recognized the potential for power struggles in his own theory of bureaucracy, especially in the role of professional experts and seasoned bureaucrats acting in self-interested ways. Weber was principally concerned with how public sector organizations (bureaucracies) created and maintained the authority relations between politicians and bureaucrats and what the consequences were of not acting with integrity and legitimacy (see Fulop 1992: Chapter 6). Weber's theories are more widely recognized in organization theory and organizational behaviour (OB), particularly in Europe and Australia, but less so for many years in the US.

Even so, the dominant approaches to power in many OB and management texts, especially those emanating from the US, have all emphasized behaviour, and its outcomes, as the key to understanding power. These approaches have struggled to preserve the notions of authority that Weber proposed, taking a much narrower view of authority and often simply calling it 'positional power'. Weber was not the only one to see authority as critical to understanding power. Steven Lukes' (1974) book *Power: A Radical View*, which became one of the most widely cited books on the topic, was heavily influenced by political sociology and political science and a desire to move beyond rigid class-based views of power to understand social and political issues. His work has also been incorporated into organization theory, OB and management per se with varying modifications (for example Dunford 1992; Frith and Fulop 1992). Others in the organizational studies field (for example Clegg 1989) have also theorized on power, drawing on Lukes and others, to develop more complex, sociologically informed accounts of power. In fact, Lukes (1974) identified three 'dimensions' of power, to which other theorists (for example Burrell 1988; Clegg 1989; Knights and Vurdubakis 1994) added, de facto, a fourth. Cynthia Hardy (1994) was one of the first explicitly to develop a fourth dimension that we have described as the *relational view of power*. Lukes integrated three dominant views of power and he termed these the *one-*, *two-* and *three-dimensional views of power*. Table 6.1 provides a summary of these three dimensions as well as the fourth.

Following Lukes, a *one-dimensional* view of power, the *behavioural view* (exemplified by Robert Dahl 1957), takes a focus on behaviour in the making of decisions over which there is overt conflict of interests. In other words, A has the power to get B to do something B would not otherwise do. A *two-dimensional* perspective, incorporating the *non-decision-making* view, as taken by Peter Bacharach and Morton Baratz (1962), involves the consideration of ways in which decisions are prevented from being taken

Table 6.1 Four views of power

	Description	Focus	Critique	Theorists	Image
One-dimensional	Behavioural view	Decision-making behaviour. Overt conflict (observable). Subjective (perceived) interests seen as policy preferences revealed in political participation.	Of 'grand theories' of power in political economy – focuses on overt action. Power is exercised.	Dahl	Power is like a hammer hitting a nail.
Two-dimensional	Political view	Includes non-decision making. How potential issues are avoided. How conflict is avoided. Interests manifest as grievances and are manipulated through policy.	Qualified critique of behaviour adds focus on inaction. Negative behaviour and resistance are the focus. Power can be felt although not exercised.	Bacharach and Baratz	It is possible to hide the nails or the hammer and still 'hit' the nail.
Three-dimensional	Radical structural view	The dominant are in control of socialization processes and political agendas. This is a universal 'fact'. They control how issues are defined because of common ideology and beliefs. Conflict can be latent because unconscious real interests differ from subjective ones – manipulation and influence used to control and suppress interests of certain groups.	Of behavioural focus, insists on importance of social structure and ideology, or powerful ideas. False consciousness, management of meaning, unobtrusive control.	Lukes	Power is like a dark building through which we must move.
Four-dimensional	Relational view	Power is involved in everything we do – always implies resistance. Not only the dominant are powerful, it is relational. Conflict is relative. Issues are defined by discourses that shape knowledge. 'Discourse' includes locally variable contexts, practices, institutions, techniques, and so on. Nothing is universal.	Of structure – looks at how power depends on knowledge, but also influences how knowledge is formed. Power is a capillary force, moving everywhere and not the property of so-called dominant groups.	Foucault	Power is everywhere, moving through a crowd – sometimes chaotic, like a carnival, sometimes coordinated, like the Mexican wave at a sports ground.

Source: Modified from Liz Fulop, Stephen Linstead and Faye Frith (1999), 'Power and politics in organizations', in Fulop, L. and Linstead, S. (eds) *Management: A Critical Text*, Melbourne: Macmillan Business, p. 126.

on potential issues of public concern over which there is observable conflict of interests. In other words, A prevents B from realizing that B has a problem, through deception, trickery and other illegitimate tactics, and thus B continues or begins to do what he or she would not otherwise do. If B had been given the information or the opportunity to raise issues and be party to discussions, instead of being duped, B might act differently. The second dimension of power is considered more fully in Chapter 14, in which we consider non-decision making and the mobilization of bias by powerful people in order to structure agendas to protect their interests and quell opposition.

The third of these dimensions, the *radical structural view* of Lukes, is that power includes the capacity to determine decisive socialization processes, and therefore the power to produce reality. In other words, A educates and persuades B to accept their role in the order of things, and not to perceive any conflict of interest. In organizations, and in a much reduced form, this is close to the 'management of meaning' approach to leadership and organizational culture (Anthony 1994) mentioned in Chapter 3. In criticizing the behavioural and political approaches in general, the radical or *three-dimensional* view of power draws attention to the unobtrusive, but nonetheless insidious methods of manipulation and influence used in organizations to ensure that power, authority and control remain in the hands of managerial groups who represent dominant interests, such as capital (Clegg and Dunkerley 1980: 197–8).

Extending Lukes's analysis, the fourth view of power could be called the *relational view*. Power in this view exists not as a property of A or B, but as a quality of the relationship between them and in particular contexts. Each is empowered in some ways and limited in others, by the relationship. Both master and slave, for example, are constrained to behave in particular ways by the roles assigned to them and the fact that they exist in the 'institution' of slavery. Neither can escape these encumbrances without difficulty nor afford to take them lightly. Thus, rather than seeing power as held by the powerful and exercised to enforce conformity among the powerless, it is more instructive to attend to 'those contextually specific practices, techniques, procedures, forms of knowledge routinely developed in attempts to shape the conduct of others' (Knights and Vurdubakis 1994: 174; see also Gergen 1989, 1992; Hardy 1994; Buchanan and Badham 1999: 173–5). Whereas the third dimension of power is still seeking to identify who holds power, the relational view sees power as implicated in many micropractices of daily life, such as surveillance and monitoring of employees through seemingly benign technologies and techniques and various discourses.

While the above present very specific sociological views of power, other perspectives have been put forward in OB and management theory, such as the *unitary* and *pluralist views of power*, and the notion of *empowerment*. The notion of a unitary and pluralist view of power was initially derived from the work of Alan Fox (1974) and was developed by Gibson Burrell and Gareth Morgan (1979: 204, 388) to differentiate the radical view of power from others and also align it with studies of conflict (see Chapter 12 for a fuller discussion). The unitary and pluralist distinction was common in the industrial relations literature, where it provided a useful taxonomy for understanding conflict in workplaces (Hall 1972: 237–40; Child 1973: 186; Fox 1974: 250; Nightingale 1974; Lupton 1978: 81–8; Farnham and Pimlott 1979: 53; Honour and Mainwaring 1982: 115; Kelly 1982: 173–88; Dawson 1986: 18–36). OB and management also incorporated this typology at an early stage (for example Robbins 1974). The unitary approach generally treats power as an aberration and threat to the organization, reinforcing the idea of managerial prerogative and authority. Pluralists focus on identifying various sources of power in order to explain the nature of organizational politics. They champion the idea that power is available to all in organizations and it is up to individuals to take advantage of the opportunities afforded them to move up the hierarchy and secure the status and prestige associated with career mobility. This highly individualistic and masculinist view of power stands in stark contrast to more critical views of power, such as those offered by Lukes' third dimension.

It would, however, be difficult to suggest that Lukes' first dimension of power (Hardy and Leiba-O'Sullivan 1998: 461) completely encompasses the unitary and pluralists views of power. Lukes' theory was derived from a very different theoretical tradition to that found in many OB and management texts. Indeed, the third dimension of power offers a critique of the unitary and pluralist assumptions found in many of these texts, and certainly the second dimension is rarely recognized in mainstream texts. Furthermore, consideration of the fourth dimension of power introduces a more reflexive view of power, which focuses on its relational aspects and how discursive practices, such as talking, writing, arguing (Gergen 1989, 1992), and disciplinary practices, such as tools of surveillance and assessment (for example performance measurement), shape people's identities and 'the field of force relations' (Buchanan and Badham 1999: 173; also Clegg 1998; Chan 2001: Part III). For the sake of clarity, we will use the typology developed by Lukes in the remainder of the chapter, but extend it to include some studies that do not neatly fit into it and are better seen as part of the pluralist tradition.

The behavioural view of power and authority

The behavioural view of power has many diverse interpretations. In Robert Dahl's (1957) work, and that of Lukes, the concept was used to explain how policy making affected interest group politics and the decision-making practices of politicians and drew heavily on political science to explain how power and politics intersect. The concept of power crept into the OB and management literature under the aegis of the *unitary view of power*. This approach presents management's authority as being relatively automatic, its legitimacy sanctioned through hierarchical relations, rules and procedures within an organization and exemplified by their leadership roles. In the unitary approach, the exercise of power is seen negatively and is associated with the illegal use of force, coercion and threats. The unitary (or rational) organization is one in which managers emphasize the importance of common goals and purposes. It is presumed that those at the top of the hierarchy have the right to make all the critical decisions and that the authority to do this is vested in the position and office of senior management. Contractual agreements bind everyone to the principle of 'a fair day's work for a fair day's pay'. The goals of profitability and efficiency are the same for all, and the contract of employment binds subordinates to a common managerial purpose. Titles, formal lines of communication, organizational charts, contracts, rules and policies all vest authority in management and its prerogative flows from these systems of command. Power has no place in the unitary or rational organization. Authority prevails. Overt power struggles, hence visible conflict, are symptoms of a breakdown of authority relationships and the stability that the organization is designed to achieve (Velasquez 1988: 303–5). They signal a potential challenge to management's authority and their right to exercise absolute control in the interest of maintaining concerted action(s) to achieve organizational goals (Forster and Browne 1996: 139).

The concept of authority, as subscribed to in the unitary approach, is strongly bound up with notions of obedience, trust, mutual respect, paternalism, discipline, command and control. Many approaches to leadership even today have unitary assumptions. For example, Douglas McGregor's (1960) famous Theory X model of leadership (described in Chapter 10) captures one dimension of the unitary view of authority: its coercive, disciplinary, forcing, policing and punishment aspects. His Theory Y model, by contrast, focuses on the manipulative and cajoling approach to leadership. Even though McGregor advocated participatory practices under Theory Y, the use of more subtle forms of control

and a more 'velvet glove' approach to authority, he still maintained that the exercise of authority was the absolute prerogative of management. Other leadership theorists (for example Blake and Mouton 1978; also see Chapter 10) also share a unitary perspective, because they advocate supportive and participative leadership styles in which authority must be accepted by subordinates and imbalances in power or power issues will not arise. Unitary views of power see power as being dysfunctional because it is usually associated with conflict and is thus defined as being divergent from good management practice (Forster and Browne 1996: 139). There was indeed a major stream of literature in the US and UK that developed the unitary and pluralist views of conflict from which much of the view of power was also derived (see Frith and Fulop 1992; Chapter 9).

The *pluralist approaches* championed in the US shifted attention from authority to a focus on position power and the broader access to influence available to all in organizations. These approaches emphasize the dynamics of power and influence in social interactions. According to one view of pluralism, any partner to an exchange (that is, where someone does something for another person) enters into a *dependency relationship*. All interactions are considered to involve exchange, and hence dependency. Thus to gain acceptance into any group usually involves giving up some freedom or rights in order to belong. According to some pluralists, exchange involves questions about the types of influence that will be tolerated or rejected, and how dependencies might be created or neutralized. For some pluralists, *influence* means the use of power, which is associated with acquiring certain resources that help create dependencies. Dependency is the obverse of power: dependency can weaken or strengthen power (Pfeffer 1981: 99–115; Handy 1985: 118–19; Dawson 1986: 159). There are many versions of the exchange model of power that assume people are conscious of the power plays going on around them. They usually involve individuals (as per Dahl's one-dimensional view of power, often referred to as A and B) or groups (for example departments or subunits) doing something they would not otherwise have done had influence been absent. Pluralists generally concentrate on explaining overt forms of influence (that is, influence that most parties are aware of) and the power resources used to create unequal dependency relationships. The approach presumes individuals are generally aware of the influence being exerted over them because it is usually associated with some form of overt conflict. There are many different versions of how influence can work, and in much of the literature there is a differentiation between managing power up, down and across the hierarchy.

Power of lower participants

Early pluralist studies in the US focused attention on the exercise of power among groups who were described as lower participants. David Mechanic's (1962) famous study described how lower participants in various organizations gained influence over their superiors by using power resources such as information, persons and instrumentalities to build up dependency relationships. Mechanic defined these resources as follows: *information* refers to knowledge of organizational procedures, rules and resources; *persons* means having access to experts or important individuals; *instrumentalities* relates to control over physical resources such as equipment, machines or facilities. He argued that access to these resources was not solely dependent on a person's position in the hierarchy and that lower participants could, through such things as *effort*, *interest* and even *attractiveness*, increase their access to these resources, thereby making others dependent upon them. These 'others' can and did include senior staff (Mechanic 1962).

Mechanic's study showed how hospital attendants were able to create a dependency relationship between themselves and doctors through resolving problems associated with the administration of wards. Attendants assumed the administrative responsibilities of the ward in exchange for having an increased say in decisions affecting patients, for example scheduling of the operating theatre. Doctors disliked doing administrative work and gladly 'traded' these duties with the attendants, but in so doing helped build a dependency relationship. This was a quid pro quo arrangement in which attendants gained some influence through their efforts and interest in routine administration. This also increased their access to information (power) resources and made them indispensable to the doctors, who came to defer to the attendants on matters of routine ward administration. The price of limiting the influence of attendants (lower participants) would have meant extra work and effort on the part of doctors in an area of hospital administration that did not interest them. Doctors had discretionary control over these tasks and were able to unofficially delegate these responsibilities. Had hospital rules and procedures prevented this, attendants might not have been able to create the dependency relationship. If a ward person, for instance, had objected to these informal practices, then power struggles and conflicts would inevitably have arisen.

Pluralists from within the US tradition, with its strong anti-union and collective bargaining orientations, argue that lower participants in any organization can gain some control over power resources and thus exert some influence over their superiors. Mechanic gives the example of prison guards bending rules or allowing violations of regulations (for example possession of certain illegal items) in order to extract cooperation from inmates. Logically, guards should try to enforce sanctions and punishment against inmates who break rules and regulations, but at the risk of appearing to lack authority and the ability to command obedience should prisoners riot or simply refuse to comply. So informal practices avoid the types of confrontation and conflict associated with the win–lose situations that warders might be anxious to circumvent. The study of the power of lower participants highlights the generic nature of dependency and exchange relationships in organizations. Translated into everyday practice, pluralists suggest that managers or supervisors who have nothing of relevance or value to trade with their employees or subordinates might encounter resistance and be unable to extract cooperation or satisfactory performance from lower participants. Supervisors who have no input, for example, into the promotion or salary review of their staff will probably lack influence and be heavily dependent upon subordinates to get things done (Dawson 1986: 161).

Power resources and strategies among managers

None of the studies mentioned so far has directly examined the methods of influence used by supervisory or managerial groups. Table 6.2 describes some of the pluralist theorists who have dealt with this aspect of power. John French and Bertram Raven's (1959) typology of power attempted to explain how subordinates react to managers' power (they did not differentiate power from influence). Thus *coercive power* is reflected in a subordinate's fear of punishment or negative consequences of his or her actions. *Reward power* is associated with a belief that benefits will flow from complying with management's orders. *Referent power* is similar to charisma, invoking strong identification with a manager; it is one of the most effective ways of gaining compliance. *Expert power* means that a subordinate accepts the superior knowledge of a manager. *Legitimate power* is probably similar to authority or the acceptance of a manager's position and the rights and responsibilities associated with it. This typology of power identifies the individual power resources of managers and their effects on subordinates, and does not explain how or when these resources can be used.

A more complex model emerged in Charles Handy's famous typology of power, which still, however, concentrated on explaining individual sources of power, but adding the dimension of *influence* (Handy 1985: 118–36). Handy's typology advanced the pluralist argument by separating power resources from methods of influence. He also pointed out that power is not an absolute factor in a social relationship, but can vary

Table 6.2	Development of power perspectives in management		
French and Raven (1959)	Handy (1976–85)	Kotter (1977)	Mintzberg (1983)
All managers	*All managers*	*Middle managers*	*Middle managers*
Types of power Reward power Coercive power Legitimate power Referent power Expert power	*Power resources* Physical Resource Position Expert Negative Personal *Influence* Force Rules and procedures Exchange Persuasion Ecology Magnetism	*Influence* Creation of sense of obligation Building of reputation as expert; fostering identification Creating dependence by making others believe the manager has resources Using formal authority (that is, position)	*Political games* Games to resist authority Games to counter resistance Games to build power base Games to change the organization

Source: Modified from Faye Frith and Liz Fulop (1992) 'Conflict and power in organisations', in Fulop, L. with Frith, F. and Hayward, H., *Management for Australian Business: A Critical Text*, Melbourne: Macmillan, p. 225.

depending on its salience or relevance to another individual, the balance of power between two individuals (remember even prisoners have power) and the limits placed on power (for example managers can most affect their direct subordinates, but not others) (Handy 1985: 121). Exhibit 6.1 outlines Handy's typology. All the resources can be used positively (that is, to gain promotions, support peers, achieve results) or negatively (to obstruct, hinder or disrupt). Handy contends that not every manager can hope to succeed in acquiring all power resources (hence methods of influence). The most common ones are resource and position power, although in Chapter 10 on leadership, it is argued that expert and personal power are becoming more important as people move away from hierarchical forms of organization (see below as well).

According to Handy, the choice of various methods of influence will also depend on the type of environment in which a manager works. For example, in a consultancy firm, expert power and persuasive influence are thought to be the most potent. In fact, Handy (1985: 152) believes that these are the preferred or most effective combinations in many modern organizations. He has a number of other dimensions to his typology dealing with how subordinates react and cope with influence.

John Kotter (1977) and Henry Mintzberg (1989) have also presented interpretations of the more overt forms of power and influence available to managers. Mintzberg's *political games* model contains a number of common tactics or strategies that are considered effective in protecting one's position, while

simultaneously coping with potential threats and uncertainty from various stakeholders. *Games to build power bases* involve such things as: securing a powerful sponsor or 'star'; building an 'empire' with subordinates; securing control of resources; and flaunting one's expertise or authority. Mintzberg advocates that, played in moderation, these games are healthy; in excess they are considered destructive to the survival of the organization (Kotter 1977: 128–43; Mintzberg 1983: 188–217; Mintzberg 1989: 238; Keys and Case 1990).

Both Table 6.2 and Exhibit 6.1 represent some of the classics in the pluralist view of power but they are by no means exhaustive and new ones continue to emerge (see Buchanan and Badham 1999 for an excellent summary). For example, in 1992 Jeffrey Pfeffer was advocating a seven-point plan to get things done through the use of power and influence including: decide your goals; diagnose patterns of dependence and interdependence, including which individuals are influential; establish their views of your goals; identify their power bases and your own; determine effective strategies and choose a course of action (cited in Buchanan and Badham 1999: 148). Others have developed similar or more elaborate approaches, such as the one described by Bristol Voss (1992, cited in Buchanan and Badham 1999: 178) who included the following:

- focus on the job to build your credit
- skills of observation and listening
- skills to identify opinion leaders and fence sitters

Exhibit 6.1 **Handy's typology of power**

1. **Power resources** Physical, resources, position, expert, personal
2. **Method of influence** Force, exchange, ecology, rules and procedures, persuasion, magnetism

Match of power and influence

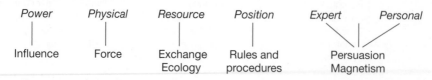

1. Power resources		2. Method of influence	
Physical force	Bullying, stand over person, shouting	Force	Threats, bullying, physical punishment, boss who loses his or her temper
Resource power	Benefits others, usually contained in job contracts and so on. Need not be material, for example giving status or recognition or invited to exclusive clubs	Exchange	Bargaining and negotiating or even cajoling or bribing, for example incentive systems or motivation schemes
Position	Entitlements and rights of one's position affect resource power, for example control over information, right of access, right to organize	Ecology	Environmental constraints, such as noise, size, organizational structure, climate and so on.
Expert power	Knowledge, specialist training or education, sought-after resource	Rule and procedures	Institute rules and procedures, and most likely to be used by those with position power
Personal power	Charisma, as described by Weber	Persuasion	Logic, power of argument and evidence of facts
		Magnetism	Attraction, popularity, charm (personal or expert power is usual source)

Source: Adapted from Figure 3.1, page 133 of Charles Handy *Understanding Organizations* (Penguin Books, 1976, 4th edn 1993). Copyright © Charles Handy 1976, 1981, 1985, 1993, 1999.

(and, we would add, the 'brown nosers' or those seeking approval and patronage from their seniors);

- judge personalities and interests
- ability to develop unobtrusive partnerships and use reciprocity
- avoid blatant use of power
- negotiation skills and knowing when to push and when to pull back or concede
- ability to make the boss look good
- not alienating superiors by saying 'no'
- developing loyal and competent subordinates who make you look good
- patience.

David Buchanan and Richard Badham (1999), having reviewed all the major theories of power, came up with their own in respect of how change agents could use power to affect major organizational changes. Their findings raise another dimension to the study of power that we will consider in Chapter 13: that is, how is power related to or used during organizational change events. The issue of change, as well as the identification of power resources and tactics and their deployment, raises the question of how power can be beneficial to an organization. The notion of empowerment did much to lend legitimacy to the idea that power is an integral and vital part of organizations and their management and, far from being a negative thing, is essential for change and innovation.

Empowerment

The concept of *empowerment* owes much to the work of Rosabeth Moss Kanter (1977a, 1977b, 1979, 1982, 1983, 1989a, 1989b) who initially made the term *power* (which she referred to as the 'last dirty word in management') synonymous with entrepreneurship and innovation, and later with empowerment. In her early definition of entrepreneurs or *change masters*, she referred to middle managers who successfully used power resources to change and innovate, so that new strategies, products, work methods and structures could be created. There was no doubt in Kanter's mind that organizations can only survive if they empower their middle managers. For Kanter, managers who occupy positions that do not give them access to vital power resources, hence making them highly visible and successful, were more likely to become 'stuckers' who were unable to innovate or promote change. Many bureaucratically structured positions, she argued, bred powerlessness because they provided few opportunities to act or work other than in a routine way.

For Kanter three important power resources were needed and these consisted of three 'lines' or methods of access:

- *Lines of supply* Managers have the capacity to bring in the things that their own departments need, for example materials, money or resources, to distribute as rewards.
- *Lines of information* To be effective, managers need to be 'in the know' in both the informal and the formal sense.
- *Lines of support* In a formal framework, a manager's job parameters need to allow for non-ordinary action, for a show of discretion or exercise of judgement. And, informally, managers need the backing of other important figures in the organization whose tacit approval becomes another resource they bring to their own work unit (Kanter 1983: 134).

In many respects Kanter's empowering strategies are more or less a hybrid of those mentioned in Table 6.2. She identified four key empowering strategies available to middle managers. The first of these was *ride the right coat-tails* which meant working with someone who has clout and was successful. This also relates to gaining sponsorship (or mentoring) and succeeding by being associated with other successful managers in the organization. *Monument building* was about creating or rearranging departments or divisions to promote uncertainties and provide new rewards for loyal subordinates (for example a new position). *High visibility* was associated with risk taking and solving critical problems or coping with uncertainties. *Peer alliances* related to building networks and establishing supportive relationships with those moving up the ladder. Kanter (1977b) identified these strategies as masculine ones, not readily available to women. Kanter was one of the first theorists to consider and analyse diversity as a dimension of power relations. We will return to this point shortly.

Kanter's approach was also different from other pluralists because she recognized structure as an important factor in empowering managers. She acknowledged that empowering was not solely dependent on individual initiatives or actions, but was limited or hampered by inappropriate structures that have to be changed by senior management. As already stated, powerlessness was identified by her with bureaucratic structures and values. Kanter maintained that power resources must circulate and if they did not then the more negative and destructive aspects of conflict and powerlessness would engulf an organization.

Kanter (1989c, cited in Ragins 1997: 487) pointed out that mentoring relationships help protégés to develop power resources in and across the organization and provide 'training' for protégés in developing their political skills and influence. As Kanter noted, mentors can also provide challenging assignments and place their protégés in highly visible positions where they can develop expert power and be noticed by those who count in terms of career development. Moreover, mentors provide 'reflected power' to protégés and the mentor's influence can augment that of protégés, both in terms of the resources they get and the protection they receive from adverse organizational events or forces. Mentors provide career development and advancement opportunities (Kanter 1977b, 1989c, cited in Ragins 1997: 487).

Kanter's work marked a watershed in the theorizing about power and did much to attenuate the negatives associated with the Machiavellian view of power. According to Buchanan and Badham (1999: 132, 138), one of the difficulties of confronting the issue of power is to engage with both its dark or negative sides as well as its beneficial and necessary aspects. In their view, Kanter tried to overcome the negative and destructive effects of powerlessness by presenting empowerment as a highly integrative, almost unitary concept (see also Fulop 1991). In Kanter's approach, empowerment, with its focus on open communication, counselling and appeals to rationality, suggests the end of dirty dealings, back stabbing and other forms of political manoeuvrings. Moreover, the political tactics she suggests are always underscored by participative styles involved with persuasion, team building and consensus. However, Buchanan and Badham suggest that this utopian view fails to acknowledge that different approaches are needed in organizations to deal with change and innovation and sometimes this might require autocratic action. They go on to develop their own approach to the 'political entrepreneur' (Buchanan and Badham 1999: 161–4), which explicitly acknowledges the Machiavellian elements of power as well as relational and ethical views of power. Perhaps where Kanter's work has been most revealing is in its focus on the gendered nature of power.

Gender and empowerment

One of the key propositions of empowerment relates to mentoring. Mentoring is a highly gendered relationship, although the literature seeks to obscure this. As Wajcman (1998:126) notes 'a mentoring relationship is essentially about a powerful older man identifying with a younger version of himself' (see also Kanter 1977b: 184). Belle Rose Ragins' (1997) research into mentoring, especially the impact of diversity on mentoring relationships and hence empowerment, found that gender was a major factor in successful and unsuccessful mentoring outcomes. Ragins drew mainly on pluralist perspectives to examine how diversified mentoring relationships in selected US organizations were working. All the approaches mentioned in Table 6.2 are essentially blind or neutral to diversity issues as indeed is the literature in general (exceptions being Hatch 1997; Buchanan and Badham 1999).

Informal mentoring relationships are the main types of mentoring found by Ragins, but she did acknowledge that some organizations did establish formal mentoring programmes as well. Ragins argues that informal mentoring relationships are not easy to form among people from diverse backgrounds. *Diversified mentoring relationships* are those involving people from different power and status-related groups (based on gender, sexuality, race, disability or ethnicity) (Ragins 1997: 499). People in these relationships usually find it more difficult to identify and relate to each other. Mentoring relationships with people of similar characteristics or social status (that is, more homogeneous relationships), create potentially greater comfort and ease for those involved. Ragins points to research that has found that cross-gender or cross-race mentoring relationships face particular problems. In one US study cited by Ragins (1997: 499), women reported being reluctant to form mentoring relationships with men for fear that this approach by them could be construed as a sexual advance by the male mentor or others in the organization. Similarly, social activities outside work (for example playing golf) are far more limited in diversified mentoring relations than those involving persons of the same gender.

A 1996 study of 461 women executives in the USA (Ragins 1997: 497, citing Catalyst 1996) found that even women who attributed their success to having a mentor also claimed that they had consistently to exceed performance expectations and present themselves in ways that made male co-workers feel comfortable with them. Joan Margretta (1997: 19) has coined the term *comfort syndrome* to describe a range of implicit, often subtle codes of feeling that are likely to affect mentoring between men and women. The comfort syndrome covers feelings and emotions and gender stereotypes such as fear, prejudice, envy, greed and aggressiveness in women.

Ragins (1997: 492) also indicates that diversity for any individual or group usually comprises multiple identities (for example an ethnic male, a woman who is also a lesbian, a male who also has a disability) and therefore the split into homogeneous and diversified mentoring relationships is in some ways an artificial construct which simplifies what are often extremely complex relationships. Ragins also cites research in the USA (Ely 1995) which found that private sector organizations with few women in positions of power were more likely to support and foster stereotypical gender roles as opposed to firms with more balanced representation.

Ruth Simpson (1997: S122) lends support to Ragins' findings by citing research in the UK which found that women who typically form a minority (20 per cent or less of the total workforce for any minority makes them token members) find themselves being marginalized and excluded through stereotypes. Stereotypes can be polarized or exaggerated to create boundaries between groups, assimilated into a group's subculture or even more widely adopted in the organization. Women tend to be isolated in these cultures, but are nonetheless still highly visible (Simpson, citing Kanter 1977b). Some of the stereotypical *role traps* can include: 'mother role (comfortable and caring), the seductress (sexy and dangerous), the pet (sweet but incompetent)', and for those who do not conform to these, the 'iron maiden (asexual and strident)' (Simpson 1997: S122). Simpson cites research by Marshall (1995) confirming evidence of role traps being used in corporations to marginalize and exclude women from power and influence through these informal processes. In her study of 100 women managers who were MBA graduates, Simpson found no evidence of role traps but rather strenuous efforts being made by women to avoid these role traps by overperforming or performing well above expectations. Moreover, people with a higher socioeconomic status or background receive more career development support from mentors than do people with a lower socioeconomic background (Ragins 1997: 507, citing Whitley et al. 1991). This is covered by the old adage 'it's not what you know but who you know'. As Ragins (1997: 507) also points out, even groups that have similar demographic characteristics can experience differences in values, attitudes and beliefs among their members.

Paul Gollam (1997: 25–6), writing on staff selection

in Australia, notes how the apparent undervaluing of women in Australian businesses means that it would probably take another 170 years to achieve equal representation between the sexes in management. He quotes research showing that between 1995 and 1996 the proportion of women in management positions had declined. This trend continues in most OECD countries. He also cited research showing that 73 per cent of Australian women managers leave their jobs because of limited career opportunities. In other words, not only is the pool of mentors available to other women not expanding, but the problems with diverse mentoring relationships are probably also taking their toll. Gollam (1997: 25) suggests that when one looks at management in Australia, one is still confronted with an image of the 'old boy network'. It is likely that this image manifests across many countries.

Similar trends are apparent in the UK (see also Chapter 2) where a national study in 1995 found only 5 per cent of women were at the senior levels and only 3 per cent directors of boards (Simpson 1997: S121). In Simpson's study (mentioned earlier), the single greatest barrier that women experienced in their careers was the presence of the 'men's club'. In her study, *token* women (women in the minority) recorded a much higher incidence of having experienced the men's club as a barrier to career advancement than those women in organizations with a greater gender balance (non-token women). Simpson (1997: S122, citing Coe 1992; Maddock and Parkin 1994) says the men's club can operate to separate and exclude women through sexual innuendo (sexist jokes) and conversations dominated by such things as sport. These tactics, which are often ritualized, act to exclude women from informal encounters where important information is exchanged, often affecting decisions and, ultimately, careers (Simpson 1997: S127).

Empowerment became one of the buzz-words of the 1990s in many areas of management and business. Yet Cynthia Hardy and Sharon Leiba-O'Sullivan (1998: 463) suggest that management rarely introduces empowerment strategies in order to share power or create a more democratic workplace. This applies equally to men and women. Rather, empowerment programmes are usually associated with management's goals of improving productivity, lowering costs or increasing customer satisfaction. In fact they argue that there are two main approaches to empowerment adopted in business. The first entails *delegating power and authority* to those employees who thrive on stress and challenges and can be trusted to use power for the benefit of the organization.

Empowerment can also be used by management as a *motivational strategy* and not to share power. This entails using open communication, inspirational goal setting and leadership to increase the commitment and

involvement of people to their organization's success (Hardy and Leiba-O'Sullivan 1998: 464). Instead of focusing on the delegation and sharing of power, this motivational approach to empowerment seeks to give people encouragement and feedback, help them to learn, provide them with emotional support to alleviate stress and anxiety, and create positive emotional responses to organizational goals. This is a very unitary view of power because its main aim is to address the *feelings* of powerlessness among people and imbalances in power and certainly neglects the problems women may face. As one of Buchanan and Badham's respondents notes, should those groups and individuals empowered start to come up with solutions not acceptable to management, then the organization 'would have … to deal with that problem' (Badham and Buchanan 1999: 122).

David Collins (2000: 213–49) develops an argument based on the work of the late Harvie Ramsay (1977) that participation and empowerment initiatives are part of longer wave historical fluctuations in economic and social conditions, which mean that management periodically needs to tighten and relax its methods of control in order to maintain effectiveness and hence its long-term objective of securing and remaining in control. Similar arguments are made by Grint (1997a, 1997b) and Barley and Kunda (1992). For Collins, empowerment then is neither simply a product of management initiative, nor a passing fad, but part of the historical unfolding of cycles of control and is occasioned by, in response to or anticipation of, subordinate action rather than being a cause of subordinate action.

Collins does not consider gender in his discussion of empowerment, and there have been no other attempts to our knowledge to consider gender, equal opportunity or diversity initiatives as cyclical. But over the time of a career there is some evidence that women experience empowerment differently. Wajcman (1998) notes that women, in particular, run out of mentors as they rise up the organization. Not only is this because there are fewer women at this level, but also because those men who are comfortable with women and less involved with the men's club networks also tend to have a limit to their progress. As one of her respondents observes:

My first role models were not women, they were men who nurtured me in my career… who were definitely not threatened by me, who I found to be liberated men. When you get to the top those kind of men seem to have fallen by the wayside somewhere, and quite frankly many of the men at the top are not that appealing. (Wajcman 1998: 129)

In one of the companies Wajcman studied, a formal women's network was set up to compensate for the lack of informal networking opportunities which males had,

Exhibit 6.2 **The unwritten rules of success**

Rule 1: Work comes first, above any personal or family concern.

Rule 1a: If you are a man and a father, you can break Rule 1 and be a great guy; if you're a woman and you break Rule 1, you're not serious about your future.

Rule 2: Long hours are a requirement. If your boss wants you and you're not there, he or she will learn quickly to want someone who is.

Rule 3: Take credit for what works (no matter how tangential your role) and run from what doesn't.

Rule 3a: If you're a man and you break Rule 3 because you gave credit to a woman, you immediately get more credit for yourself because of your fairness and magnanimity. If you're a woman and you think that Rule 3a behaviour is disgusting, the resulting failure to follow Rule 3 results in perpetual middle management and the possibility that the words *good old*

might eventually precede your name. On the other hand, too much exercise of this rule gets you the hard-to-lose epithet 'aggressive' and it's not a compliment.

Rule 4: There is only one career in your life and only one path. If you step off it, you're out of luck.

Rule 4a: If you are a man and you break Rule 4, you were probably downsized: tough luck, it won't hurt you. If you broke Rule 4 because you are a woman who stayed home with your children for a while, you are a swell person, but a bad bet for future employment, to say nothing of advancement.

Rule 5: This is about hierarchy. Your job is to make your boss look good and your boss's job is to make his or her boss look good.

Rule 6: The goal is to get as close to the top as possible. There is no end to what you are supposed to achieve or want.

Source: E.P. McKenna (1997) *When Work Doesn't Work Any More: Women, Work and Identity,* New York: Hodder & Stoughton, pp. 189–213.

---

yet it suffered from friction because the needs of junior and senior women appeared to be different. As one of her respondents observed:

Women ... who've been incredibly competitive ... have not wanted to help anybody along the way until they felt that *they* had hit the glass ceiling. And then they trade off the support for other women by using their support [ie the support of other women] to get them through [the glass ceiling]. Suddenly it's 'oh what can I do for you?' And you know that the hidden agenda in this is, 'what I want you to do for me.' (Wajcman 1998: 130)

Such a self-serving attitude of manipulative politics, using others to one's own ends, competing by other means and promoting one's own interests at all times even when ostensibly promoting those of others is merely conforming to what McKenna (1997) calls the 'unwritten rules of success', in which success has little to do with loyalty, dedication, excellence or hard work. McKenna, discussed by Buchanan and Badham (1999: 123–5) spells out, somewhat cynically, these unwritten rules.

McKenna perhaps overstates the case, but puts forward a strong argument that women need to feminize work by challenging these unwritten rules and, rather than managing like a man as many of Wajcman's respondents feel they have to do, reward collaboration, share information and redefine success in terms of the value of what is produced rather than conformance to the existing system's requirements. For McKenna, empowerment, which means simply being given permission to behave like a man, is not the way forward; empowerment needs to be regendered.

Political view of power

Bacharach and Baratz's (1962) work grew out of political science and public policy and dealt with issues related to community politics and struggle and the mobilization of interests in rather sinister ways by powerful groups. The political view of power helped shift focus away from individual accounts of power to look more broadly at institutional practices that change the bases of power in organizations and create different forms of politics and power relationships. Once the focus shifted to subunit power, the explanations and dynamics involved in power also changed.

Strategic contingency view of power

Sociologists and organizational theorists sought to identify the types of influence used by departments or subunits in organizations to counter control and establish patterns of resistance. This type of collective influence is considered to be different in many respects from individual methods of influence. Michel Crozier's famous study, *The Bureaucratic Phenomenon* (1964), examined a group of maintenance men in the French tobacco industry and provided important insights into subunit power and the role of unions and other social forces in shaping power relations. In the US, the concern with subunit power paved the way for a *strategic contingency view of power*. Drawing on Crozier's work, the strategic contingency theorists argued that the maintenance men controlled and authorized the repair and maintenance of machines. Speedy repair of breakdowns and proper maintenance helped to reduce uncertainties for management and other workers, for a number of interrelated reasons. The plant used technologies and work processes that were interdependent, so that if a machine broke down the whole plant would grind to a halt. The maintenance men also successfully resisted attempts to routinize their work through planned or preventive maintenance and used their union to forestall the introduction of alternative or substitute methods to carry out maintenance. Thus they were very influential because they remained central to work flows, coped with uncertainties and were able to prevent substitute methods or activities being introduced. Their jobs were non-routine and the dependence on them was very strong. All levels within the plant had to defer to their decisions and demands, while they remained strategically important or were able to cope with critical uncertainties (Hickson et al. 1971; also see below).

Subsequent studies have supported the argument that for subunits the important power resources are *centrality*, *coping with uncertainty* and *non-substitutability* (Hickson and McCullough 1980). However, as Hickson et al. (1971) suggest, these power resources or strategic contingencies are always susceptible to erosion, especially through routinization and the introduction of new technology. A sales department, for example, which attracts a high volume of orders during an economic recession is likely to have increased influence and power. It acts to reduce uncertainty in the organization by guaranteeing future growth and profits. By the same token, if the department secures a number of long-term orders, then it might become strategically less important. Subunit

power is variable (contingent) and managers will always have to deal with subunits or departments that have strategic importance to the organization. The strategic contingency approach to power gives ample clues as to how subunit members foster dependencies and the strategies managers can use to deal with these dependency or power relationships. Where it lacks some sense of cross-cultural relevance is its failure to recognize the importance of unions and industrial relations systems that can curtail the power of managers in order to minimize the salience of certain contingencies, a view not strongly put in the US literature.

The political organization

The political perspective views organizations as coalitions of individuals or groups who are by and large pursuing their own agendas and interpretations of what constitute appropriate or valid goals (Bailey 1970: 19–22; Child 1973: 192; Burrell and Morgan 1979: 202–5). Conflicts of interest arise in predictable ways because of the interdependencies and power differentials that are structured or built into organizations through such things as the division of labour and task specialization. These help to create horizontal and vertical dependencies. Interdependence is also fostered by the technologies adopted in organizations, particularly the extent to which they can be either substituted or routinized or used to skill or deskill organizational members.

Organizations also have limited resources or operate under conditions of scarcity. This means that rewards and opportunities are never adequate to meet everyone's expectations, thus conflict and power struggles remain endemic. Through centralization or decentralization, power resources can be either concentrated at the top of the organization or allowed to flow down the hierarchy. Organizational members will react to either situation, with the probability of conflict being greater in decentralized structures. Figure 6.1 summarizes some of the common sources of conflict and power struggles in political organizations. As Figure 6.1 shows, conflict derives from both internal and external influences on organizational members.

The concept of the seminal political organization was also evident in Alvin Gouldner's (1954) and Crozier's (1964) works. Both of these works emphasize the ways in which structures (for example division of labour, rules, technology) both constrain and enable certain strategies or tactics of organizational members.

Gouldner conducted research into the effects of rules and his work identified three different types of bureaucratic pattern which can exist in the workplace, depending on how rules are established in the first place: *punishment-centred*, *mock* and *representative*

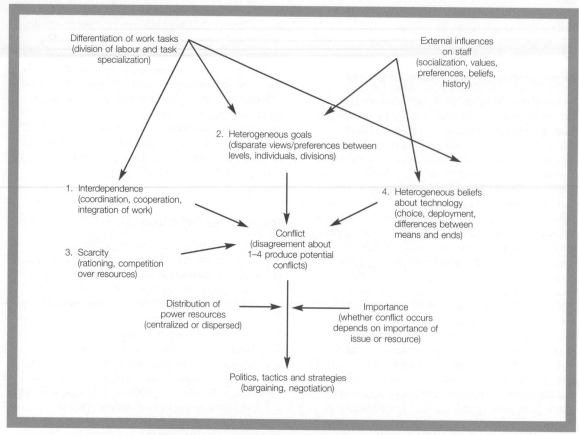

Figure 6.1 Conditions for the use of power

Source: Adapted from Jeffrey Pfeffer (1981) *Power in Organisations*, London: Pitman, p. 69, developed by Graeme Sheather, University of Technology, Kuring-gai, New South Wales.

rules. In the mock pattern, rules exist but are ignored by both staff and management (for example no smoking rules were breached). In the representative pattern, rules are mutually agreed to and accepted as fair by all (for example using safety clothing in a toxic industry). In the punishment-centred pattern, one party imposes rules against the others' wishes, generating conflict and power struggles (for example abolishing tea breaks to save money). Gouldner's research in a gypsum mine in the USA highlighted how difficult it was for management to eliminate perks and privileges and change mock rules. Changing rules against pilfering eventually led to bitter industrial conflicts and the final closure of the mine. According to Gouldner, bureaucracy is man-made and 'is a function of human striving; it is the outcome of a contest between those who want it and those who do not' (quoted in Salaman 1979: 147). To simply presume that all rules could be agreed to and exercised by those at the top of the hierarchy ignores manipulation, dissent and rejection of them (Gouldner 1954: 20; Byrt 1973: 49; Lansbury and Spillane 1983: 105–6; Pugh et al. 1983: 20–4).

Gouldner's study was a descriptive piece of research that attempted to draw attention to the manner in which rules could be interpreted and acted upon differently by all within organizations. It did not adopt a managerial perspective and tried to show that rules had significantly different meanings for workers and managers. The more management tried to institute bureaucratic procedures (stricter rules, regulations and disciplinary measures), the more workers resented the abolition of practices that were based on nepotism and favouritism, even though these were detrimental to improving productivity. Gouldner's study was one of the first to approach the problem of control and authority from an action approach, by focusing on the importance of meaning systems, as also pointed out by Weber (Silverman 1970).

While Gouldner's work highlighted the problem of rules and authority, the study by Crozier (1964) created even more doubts about the nature of authority and power. Crozier set out to study how authority was actually exercised in large organizations, especially in areas in which it was not always easy to replace people or eliminate their tasks. He did not start from the premise that people's actions were oriented to rule following or complying with authority, but rather from the assumption that through the organization's effort to eliminate the discretion of employees, some area of uncertainty will remain, and such uncertainty is the breeding ground for efforts to achieve some, however slight, self-control. It supported the view that 'the final structure of an organization … is the result of these negotiations, interpretations in which organizational members actively strive to resist some directions and control' (Salaman 1979: 146).

In the case of Crozier's maintenance men, their expertise and ability to repair machines enabled them to avoid the otherwise tight regulatory system that applied to other areas of production and, through their union, resist routinization of maintenance procedures. Power struggles ensued between the maintenance men and management, with the latter attempting to regain control through increasing the rules and regulations affecting the work of the maintenance men. However, Crozier noted that even these actions of senior management were partially constrained by cultural norms in French society, which frowned upon such things as open exercise of authority or face-to-face conflict (Reed 1985: 159–61).

In the political organization, human agency or actions give shape and meaning to structure. The interests of organizational participants are implicated in some way in the social relations and structures that they experience as either enabling or constraining them. In such an organization, the rules of the game, the 'prizes' and conduct expected of participants are very much a negotiated process in which the struggle for power, to limit, resist or escape it, is an endemic feature (Reed 1985: 141–6; Clegg 1989: 207). The political organization, whether labelled 'innovative', 'entrepreneurial' or 'divisionalized', is infused with power relations and the politics that ensue.

Mintzberg has argued that politicized organizations must include both internal and external coalitions, such as shareholders, unions, governments, banks, suppliers and customers. To be a politicized organization, in Mintzberg's view, means enduring or experiencing conflicts between internal and external coalitions. He says a 'complete political arena' exists when an organization experiences severe and uncontrollable conflicts between internal and external coalitions. He argues that conflicts have predictable forms, depending on their intensity (level of hostilities), pervasiveness (how widespread) and duration (brief or lasting). According to Mintzberg, few organizations can survive very intense, highly pervasive and lasting conflicts: they self-destruct. Political arenas (or politicized organizations) are enduring configurations and emerge wherever organizations are wholly or partially captured or invaded by obvious and visible conflicts. By this definition, every organization is a political arena (Pfeffer 1981: 154–76; Mintzberg 1983: 420–66, 497–502).

Theorists, such as Kanter, have proposed that the successful political organization must institutionalize power by developing empowering strategies and structures (Kanter 1983, 1989a, b; Mintzberg 1989: 237–302). Kanter argued that in the post-entrepreneurial organization, traditional concepts of hierarchy, task specialization and even departments would give way to more complex and fluid structures in which interdependence would take on new forms. Power, she felt, was becoming more decentralized in these organizations. Kanter identified four trends as indicative of a new form of political organization which emerged in the 1990s:

1. Relationships of influence or power were shifting from the traditional hierarchies to fluid structures such as peer networks, cross-functional projects, business units, joint ventures with other companies, labour management forums and strategic partnerships with suppliers or customers. These were creating new centres of power that cut across the chain of command in quite diverse ways. Middle managers and supervisors were becoming involved in many more cross-boundary relationships, that is, across departments, companies, suppliers and so on (see also Chapters 11, 14 and 17 for discussion of the virtual organization concept).
2. The developments mentioned in point 1 created a greater variety of channels for taking action and exerting influence through agenda setting. Cross-functional relationships placed managers in more diverse coalitions and as a result the scope to redefine assignments, tasks, jobs and interdependencies increased. Delegation and responsibility for more strategically important decisions were becoming more dispersed since senior management was unable to maintain tight control over these more complex, messy and fluid arrangements. Reputations inside and outside organizations were becoming an important source of power and influence.
3. Political skills associated with networking, bargaining, negotiating and building alliances were becoming as important for success as technical expertise or qualifications (see Bolman and Deal 1991: 207–19).
4. External relationships were becoming as important and vital to success as internal ones for developing a career and gaining power and influence. Informal networks and coalitions were essential to the empowered manager.

Kanter's model of the political organization proposes

the institutionalization of power and interests so that politics becomes a normal part of management strategies and daily practices. This view has been criticized above for its unitarist leanings and its lack of attention to other forms of power that remain unexplored.

The radical view of power and domination

Behaviourists, pluralists and empowerment theorists have been criticized on a number of counts, but primarily for their assumption that power is widely dispersed and not concentrated in the hands of an elite group. They propagate the view that there are diverse spheres of influence (for example networks or coalitions) that are generally accessible to all who wish to participate in power games (Burrell and Morgan 1979: 216), they fail to deal with power disparities between groups. For example, in the pluralist model, the bargaining or negotiating processes are seen as 'tools' for restoring equality in the power bases between various stakeholders, including management. It is argued that having balanced power bases between the various groups creates checks and counterchecks that lead to the stability of the power system within organizations.

In more direct terms, the one- and two-dimensional views of power, and other similar approaches, do not focus adequately on the fact that in organizations disparities exist between the power of the managed and those who manage them. Particularly in the pluralist approaches popular in the US, the dominant group, be they owners/managers, are seen as just another power group whose power can be contested just as easily as anyone else. In this vein, such approaches are said to be ideological tools of subordination and legitimation, used semi-purposely to condition subordinates into accepting the status quo and believing that power is a resource circulating for all to use (Kirkbride 1985: 277).

The issue of *domination* is a critical one because it raises the problem of the relationship between authority and power, and the different types of influence that flow from each. Pluralists in general are weak in their analysis of authority and hence fail to address the deeper and more complex aspects of domination and control in organizations. Clegg and Dunkerley (1980: 444) suggest that all organizations have hegemonic systems or identifiable power groups that are strategically positioned not only to play power games but define the very rules of such games. To put this into context, Clegg argues that in any game of chess, the queen is more powerful by virtue of the rules of the game: she has more moves and options than a pawn or a castle. Anyone positioned this way has more power to interpret the rules by which to play the game or make

more strategic moves (Clegg 1989: 210). From this view, every organization represents a system (or systems) of domination. Domination is another way of describing the basis of legitimacy and acceptance of authority within organizations. It is argued that any system of domination is sustained by often unobtrusive or unquestioned methods of control that are accepted as legitimate. 'Legitimacy derives from internalized norms which provide a broad base for compliance' (Dawson 1986: 150). These internalized norms can lead to unquestioning compliance with such things as recruitment procedures and job descriptions, even though these may be discriminatory in nature and consistently disadvantage particular groups. They can be parts of the storylines used in organizations, especially by senior management, to justify why things are as they are.

Pluralists, and those who operate from the one- and two-dimensional views of power, make no reference to systems of domination. In fact, because many pluralists treat power and authority as two different things, collapsing or ignoring authority altogether, they create the impression that bargaining, negotiating and developing dependency relationships afford ambitious and astute individuals some real gains and advantages. In the case of lower participants, for example, effort and interest are said to increase power resources (control over information, persons and instrumentalities) and hence lead to influence. The question has to be asked, however: influence to do what? Lower participants, such as ward attendants, may indeed gain discretionary control over ward administration but doctors continue to have the authority to change the rules, procedures, policies and technologies (for example computerize jobs) and control appointment and review procedures. Doctors can circumvent the influence of the ward attendants if they choose. If a dependency relationship becomes a problematical one, then authority and power can crush the endeavours of lower participants. Mechanic in fact presented his theory to show how managers could enhance their control over aspiring lower participants. The same could be said of the subunit power perspective. In this vein, pluralists reinforce power differentials in organizations, often keeping lower participants in their places (Clegg and Dunkerley 1980: 438–44; Ryan 1984: 37).

Following on from the previous point, the one- and two-dimensional views emphasize overt methods of influence (strategies and resources) while ignoring covert forms of influence. They suggest that power struggles usually follow from the efforts of individuals or groups to secure scarce resources and maximize their advantage against other groups. While organizations are continually subject to conflicts, upheavals and change, they are also subject to constraints that are often so entrenched that they are taken for granted and not questioned. From the radical point of view, constraints act to reinforce the status quo and maintain systems of domination. Constraints come mainly in the form of technology, administrative rules and procedures, structure (hierarchy, division of labour) and ideologies (Clegg and Dunkerley 1980: 444–51; Hickson and McCullough 1980: 27–55; Pfeffer 1981: 179–225; Ryan 1984: 29–40; Dawson 1986: 145–65).

Take the example of rules. For many years rules and policies relating to recruitment based on seniority were accepted and unchallenged in many organizations, even though these policies discouraged the merit principle and rapid promotion among young and talented employees. The individuals most likely to change these rules were usually those in senior positions who most benefited from them. In other words, actions can be constrained by seemingly entrenched policies. Many structures, procedures and rules reflect the interests of those who have a stake in maintaining the status quo.

Similarly, according to the radical view, ideological constraints can act to preserve the status quo and maintain the balance of power and authority within an organization. Ideological constraints partly refer to the critical forms of meaning that are sanctioned or legitimated in the language, symbols, rituals and practices of an organization. Kanter alludes to this when she refers to the 'rites of passage' to senior management being essentially a masculine ritual (sponsorship, patronage) from which women are generally excluded. Similarly, from a radical perspective, sexist categorizations in the workplace also act as an ideological constraint ensuring that gender relationships mirror female subordination. It is now generally accepted that labelling jobs as masculine and using male standards for job descriptions have kept women from participating in certain occupations and devalue the work they perform (Burton 1987, 1991). As Erving Goffman says of female subordination:

The expression of subordination and domination through this swarm of institutional means is more than a mere tracing or symbol or ritualistic affirmation of the hierarchy. These expressions considerably constitute the hierarchy; they are [its] shadow and substance. (Goffman 1979: 6)

Lastly, pluralists have argued that power and influence are associated with overt forms of conflict. The extent of such conflict or knowledge of the critical issues affecting an individual varies. However, pluralists would contend that if there is no visible conflict between parties, then power is not normally involved or being exercised. In the case of Crozier's maintenance men, conflict and power occurred in tandem; the men knew the critical issues and the actions that were in their best interests. They sought and used influence and power to secure a strategic advantage;

however, without their collective power (union strength) they might have had to accept the decisions of managers and defer to their authority.

According to the radical view, pluralists cannot explain how more covert forms of influence are used to manipulate individuals, so they are unable to identify the critical issues that may gravely affect them. Suppose employees at a chemical plant are offered higher salaries and bonuses in exchange for increased productivity so that backlogs on new orders and contracts can be met. These orders and contracts require handling and processing highly toxic substances. To increase productivity and profitability, the company decides to continue with its current safety standards even though more toxic substances are being handled. The company advises workers that current safety standards are adequate and appropriate even though some information available to management raises some serious doubts about one of the substances. In this case, the best interest of workers (health and so on) does not become an issue, it has been suppressed. The best interests that are put forward in these situations are management's. Power has been exercised but conflict is unlikely to arise. The decision of the managers is not likely to be challenged. They have used influence to minimize conflict and potential disruptions to work. This form of influence (manipulation) has depended on both the exercise of authority and power (Lukes 1974).

It is sometimes difficult to establish what is in the best interest of workers or managers. However, Clegg (1989) points out that in most power situations, 'organizational outflanking' is likely to occur. This means the outflanked (usually those with limited power) either have an absence of knowledge (they are ignorant) or they have sufficient knowledge of a kind that consistently discourages resistance, allowing systems of domination to prevail. In terms of ignorance or absence of knowledge, this can extend to the outflanked not even knowing that a power game is in play. By contrast, sufficient knowledge of the outcome of courses of action (its probable outcome and benefits) can ensure that power games are 'won' without the game even being played (Clegg 1989: 221–3). When whistle-blowers are publicly condemned and sacked for their purported disloyalty and clandestine actions, this provides sufficient knowledge for other would-be whistle-blowers of the costs of resistance and the limited likelihood of success (Glazer and Glazer 1989; see Chapter 8).

How would the questions raised at the beginning of the chapter be answered from the radical perspective?

The relational view of power

At this point it is important to address the distinction

between conscious and unconscious resistance as, following from the radical view, it appears that subjective circumstances themselves prove resistant to certain types of change in ways that are not fully understood by the subjects themselves. Clegg (1994: 295) observes that 'organizational outflanking' (the sort of moves which occur in the second and particularly the third dimensions of power to prevent resistance arising) is something that occurs prior to resistance because resistance requires consciousness. This is only partially true, as Clegg implicitly acknowledges. He observes that 'people can exercise power without knowing that they are doing so', but fails to link this with the Foucauldian view of power and resistance as a continuity or force ever present in social situations (Barbalet 1986: 531; Clegg 1994: 308).

The fourth view of power distinguishes *frictional* resistance (imposing limits on power through an absence of positive interest in the goals of power) from intended or direct resistance (noted by Clegg 1994: 286). This at least leaves the door ajar for the conceptualization of an unawareness that one's actions are affecting the interests of power in any way. Indeed, often the interests of power are thwarted precisely because the powerless would need more information in order to perform more effectively, which would entail the revelation of motives the powerful would rather suppress. If power is a relational flow, then the medium through which it flows may be more or less conductive, and that medium is subjective consciousness shaped by the history of past actions and past decisions, patterned practices and previous instances of making sense of how things fit together. Power in this view does not exist as a property of A or B, but is a quality of the relationship between them. Each person is empowered in certain ways, each limited in others by the relationship (Linstead 1997: 69). Thus the fourth view of power can be called the *relational view*, which attempts to explain sites of differences and sites of resistance and steps outside the hegemonic view of power (see Gergen 1989, 1992). Although conscious resistance is perhaps the most important type of resistance, every day change agents face the reality of unconscious resistance in assessing readiness for change by all sorts of individuals in organizations. Even when the subject (be this a manager or someone else) is consciously resisting, they themselves may not be aware of the motivational sources of that resistance. Often the discussions that take place during the planning and negotiation of change are ambiguous – questions which are apparently commonplace are interpreted as resistant, managers' routine activities are interpreted as power plays. Change itself is often messy, confused and paradoxical, to the extent that members do not really know whether they are resisting it or not, and find it difficult to articulate their positions. Part of

this is reflected in the diverse local accounts that people have of a change situation, and the storylines they adopt (see Chapter 1).

How individual resistance becomes collective resistance is a perennial problem. However, the work of Elias Canetti, the Nobel Prizewinner, on crowds and revolutions offers a breakthrough in understanding. Power can be defined, Canetti urges, *as the expression of order through command*. A command consists of two dimensions, *momentum* and *sting*. The momentum forces the recipient to act, in accordance with the command. The sting remains behind, mute, invisible, unsuspected 'and may only reveal its existence by some faint scarcely perceptible recalcitrance before the command is obeyed' (Canetti 1987: 354). The sting sinks deeper into the person who has carried out the command, and even though they might feel uneasy or unhappy about the command, no immediate action is taken to avenge it. The effect of the sting might remain hidden for years before it comes to light, waiting for the chance to be avenged. Freedom from control, in this sense, is not being able to rid oneself of commands by carrying them out then passing them on, but of avoiding them altogether in the first place (in Clegg's organizational sense, outflanking rather than resistance). The longer it takes to rid oneself of the command, if at all, the less free that person is (Canetti 1987: 355). This drive to reproduce previous situations, but in reverse, 'is one of the chief sources of energy' in human activity, Canetti argues. Robert Cooper (1990: 49) notes that this desire for reversal can play an explanatory role in human motivation, which transforms it from an individual characteristic to a social product, such as avenging a command.

The reversal of the sting is in most cases deferred, often for years or decades, even, Canetti argues, generations. The sting is the objection to an *obeyed* command or occasioned *act of deference*, but organizations are *structures* of deference. Often a command is experienced without having a clear source, it is dispersed among several people, a group appears to give the command, or the command is not crisply defined. Even when a clear command from a single commander is discernible, it may be possible for the recipient to avoid carrying it out, or carry it out in such a way as to subvert it (Collinson 1994). If the recipient is forced to carry out the command against his or her will, and feels this 'sting', the drive to reversal of the sting is inevitably deferred although not indefinitely; sometimes it can even be immediate.

Organizations are a particularly effective way of domesticating commands (Canetti 1987: 355–7) and perpetuating deference over time. In a sense, organizations operate on the basis that instead of killing the faithful dog, the master feeds it, as he or she also does with the faithful servant or worker. Nevertheless, even when this return in kind becomes transformed into salaries, rewards and pension schemes, even membership of exclusive clubs, 'every command contains the same threat. It is a modified threat, but there are stated penalties for non-compliance and these can be very heavy' (Canetti 1987: 357). Of course, the fact that the command is given and the sting invoked, and the 'victim' remains alive, means that there can be recoil or pain to the giver of the command, which Canetti calls 'the anxiety of command'. This is an interesting dimension to the understanding of stress (and leader burnout), which goes beyond seeing it as a byproduct of unhealthy practices, to be remedied by counselling or therapy. It is an inevitable condition of one's position in the deference structure, the tension produced by the chronically deferred sting and the giving of commands.

If we look at the ways in which corporate cultures are allegedly established and transmitted, a great deal of the success of these 'cultures' is not cultured behaviour in the sense of shared understanding and problem solving established over time, but *crowd* behaviour associated with the alleviation of the fear of the sting. In fact, the cultural dimensions of organizations are importantly shaped by the myriad of acts that invoke the deferred return of a sting. Every organization's culture is implanted and dispersed with deferred stings that can be released as collective grievances if circumstances permit. Sites of resistance might not emerge for some time, hidden in the corporate memory of many people's different experiences of a deferred sting.

Finally, we should also consider the dimension of *reciprocation* implicit in the sting, because reciprocation implies a *relationship*, giving each participant some kind of power over the other. Reciprocation also defines acts of deference. Marcel Mauss (1990) argues that there are three aspects to gift giving that create reciprocation: *the obligation to give*, *the obligation to receive*, and *the obligation to reciprocate*. Thus on gift giving occasions, one is not able to refuse to give, and, depending on the particular society or setting, gift giving is often a necessary way to explore and build relationships. If a gift is offered, it must be received in the appropriate manner, and the recipient cannot refuse it without giving great offence both socially and personally. Then, having received the gift, the recipient is placed in debt and is thus in a *state of deference* created by the apparent kindness of the other. But as Mauss emphasizes, this ritualized giving is not a kindly or voluntary act but an obligatory one and hence there must be reciprocation on the part of the recipient. This obligatory form of reciprocation is intended to restore the imbalance created by the asymmetrical situation between the giver and recipient, and reverses the *sting of the deferential burden* placed on the recipient. It could be logically inferred that if the gift is not received appropriately, the potential recipient

escapes deference and the sting of a deferential burden. They escape indebtedness to another and the need to deal with a potentially asymmetrical power relation.

The notion of reciprocation is a very complex one and is revisited in Chapter 9 when we discuss commitment and trust. However, an illustration will help explain how reciprocation can become a source of a deferred sting. In many organizations people often feel that they not only contribute their labour, as defined in job contracts, agreements and various packages, but also give a 'gift' to the organization in the form of such things as loyalty, trust, commitment, dedication, long hours (above what is paid for or expected), personal sacrifices (such as time away from family or other valued relationships) and so on. If there is no adequate recompense for these 'gifts of labour', this can cause people over time to feel the *sting of an improperly reciprocated deference* relationship. Persons who are not being adequately recompensed (appreciated, rewarded or given some recognition they seek) can develop an unconscious desire for reversal (as mentioned earlier), and this might motivate them or others to avenge the situation, even if this occurs some years down the line. This can happen in many ways, but the end result is an act of resistance or retaliation by an individual or group who seeks to bring the asymmetrical power relationship into some temporary or permanent balance – to return the sting.

The failure on the part of the employer, in this example, to recognize that they have this added debt to the employee – that the employer is being perceived by the employee to be in a state of deference to them – sows the seeds of future resistance. The sting of the deferential burden is not being accepted or even recognized by employers, who might fall back on the employment contract, awards and agreements to define the basis of their reciprocal relationship or obligation to their employees. Employees, on the other hand, might struggle many years with an unconscious sense that they are not receiving adequate or just recompense for the gift they have offered in the workplace. Subconsciously they want reciprocation for the gift, but the relationship might well be defined by one party (the employer) as not being a gift giving situation at all. The problem is that organizations operate both formally and informally with the idea of reciprocation which underpins such things as trust and commitment.

In the fourth dimension, many instances of political behaviour on the part of individuals and groups occur either in retaliation to the sting associated with an 'unwelcome' command or to imbalances arising from the reciprocation of the deferred sting. The case study below goes on to explain how Derek and the deputy director, William Fisher, sought to handle the transfer of students and courses to Fawley Ridge. It raises issues particularly sensitive to the fourth dimension of power.

FAWLEY RIDGE – THE MOVE

Derek, with William's approval, immediately called the president of the Students' Union, Ed Grimley. Ed agreed to come with representatives of the committee to an open meeting to be held with William and Derek, and David Burland, the dean. Ed warned them that this move would be unpopular and the union would fight it. 'All we ask you to do is come along and keep an open mind', he said, 'and unless you agree to it we won't do anything.' The staff were also invited, as were students likely to be affected. The understanding was that Students' Union representatives and staff (academic and non-academic) had priority of admission, then any available space could be taken up by students. In the three days before the meeting the students mounted a virulent campaign. Anti-move stickers were printed and appeared all over the campus. On the day of the meeting there was a large demonstration outside the meeting room with banners and chants of over 200 students. The meeting room was packed, and William and Derek faced the crowd, resolving to relax despite the dryness of their throats. William outlined the pressure on the Shaw's Park site where the meeting took place and the problems of finding alternative accommodation. He also pointed out that Fawley had lots of daytime space and plenty of complementary resources. He added that the purpose was to help to support the move but not to push it through regardless, and that it could not go through without the support of everyone – technicians, secretaries, academics and students.

What they needed to know was: How would people be affected by such a move? What did they need to overcome the difficulties such a move would impose? What would absolutely stop such a move being viable? Derek took over to propose that the meeting determine a working party from within each of the groups. Each group would look at its own position and requirements, staff relocations, resources, transport, equipment and so on and decide on its criteria for evaluation of the move. Then the group representatives would meet together and gain an overview of the move as a whole. At this point, if the group could say that educational quality would be affected badly, the move would not take place. Otherwise, the group was left to its own professional judgement to decide what things were required to make the move a success and William and Derek would negotiate the resources with the institution.

Questions followed. The working party went away, came up with recommendations and William and Derek followed up what they could. They then held another question and answer session. Individual staff were encouraged to come to see Derek if they had concerns. Derek visited the site frequently to talk to staff there. Gradually the opposition to the change, despite continuing demonstrations, evaporated – no one group, not even the students, would say that it could not go ahead. Then Derek set up a change planning group to manage the change. A site head was appointed, being one of the members of staff who had been most opposed to the move, and other parts of the move down to scheduling the buses and negotiating the contracts with the bus company were all delegated and weekly question and answer sessions continued. Requests for resources and follow-up plans were constantly refined, until the physical move took place over the summer recess. Derek claimed he had done very little, but such was the commitment of the staff that one Saturday when the language labs were to be relocated, the academic staff started to dismantle and remove the equipment when the removal men were late, despite the fact that they were on holiday. The move went smoothly, and Derek's job became to respond to and relay requests from the site head and others to deal with any problems arising connected with the move. Follow-up meetings were held and were institutionalized as part of the course review and evaluation procedures. The site was secured as an asset, and Ed Grimley, the Students' Union president, called Derek to congratulate him on his handling of the move. 'That's how it should have been done', he said, 'with consultation right from the word go.' The dean, David Burland, remarked on how impressive he had found the hands-off approach to change, and how difficult he felt it must have been for Derek and William not to be directive. Nevertheless, despite the success, Derek still felt some uneasiness and within six months he had left the institution for another job.

Source: Adapted from Stephen Linstead (1997) 'Resistance and return: Power, command and change management', *Studies in Cultures, Organizations and Societies*, 3(1): 67–89.

MORE QUESTIONS ABOUT THE CASE

5 How well do you think the change was managed?
6 How was conflict anticipated and dealt with?
7 What forms of power were at work here, and who used them?
8 Why was Derek uneasy?

Analyses

Let us take a look at how each of the views of power we have discussed would make sense of the Fawley Ridge case and the questions asked about the case at the beginning of the chapter. The questions would be answered differently depending on the approach one adopts.

Unitary view

From a unitary view it could be concluded from the case study that as communication was widely used in open meetings, interpersonal problems were overcome and unions were included, all was well. There was a common strategic focus, with all members working in a coherent and coordinated fashion to reach a common objective, and consensus over those common objectives prevails because of the notion of a common set of norms and values. Kost's earlier actions were entirely justifiable as the exercise of management's right to manage, bringing the organization back under control in *everyone's* interest. Politics and power struggles would be seen as dysfunctional, detracting from achieving the goals of management – the move to Fawley Ridge.

Pluralist view

In a pluralist view, power is seen to be diffused throughout the organization and all groups or coalitions have power and no one group is wholly sovereign. In the case study a pluralist analysis would contend that all the key parties were known, the issues were clear and visible and all groups were potentially able to influence the decision-making processes. Conflict was overt as interest groups bargained over the decision-making processes, vis-à-vis scarce resources. In the case study we can see how organizational politics involves effort by various actors to mobilize interest groups and coalitions. The case study also highlights how organizational change can threaten the existing power bases and resource allocation and thus political action will occur. Kost demonstrated the importance of using *external* pressure groups.

The pluralist view would also incorporate Lukes' two-dimensional view of power, which would emphasize such things as non-decision making. An example of this in the case is where Kost does not bring into the public arena the reasons why he intends to move students to the Fawley Ridge site. Once Kost has 'made' this decision, everything else becomes 'academic', so to speak, to justify the decision.

Kanter would focus on how Kost does or does not provide adequate power resources (for example lines of information) to his heads of department. She would focus on how managers at Fawley Ridge might develop strategies to get ahead such as gaining high visibility and being seen to be solving problems for the organization. This is clearly what Derek is doing in trying to solve problems for Kost, such as 'removing' Cyril. Kanter would also focus on the structures at Fawley Ridge and she would see the bureaucratic structure, with its hierarchy and command structure (Kost's new direct reports who were political appointees), as problematic and bound to create powerlessness for some of the 'old guard' managers.

Kanter says this sort of 'monument building' – creating or rearranging departments – ensures uncertainty and builds loyalty (and fear) among subordinates.

Radical view

In this view, Lukes would argue invisible power is used and exercised in such a way that the best interests of a group or groups are not being served, in that they are unable to form conscious preferences or choices around issues, and thus they are never consciously able to formulate or understand their real interests.

In the case study, a radical view would argue that Kost was able to hide the 'real' issues by using arguments apparently based on uncontestable educational principles and not allowing them to come to the surface; consequently the *real* interests of the groups were never discussed. Choices were made and accepted as a result of the use of invisible power and the domination and control of outcomes orchestrated by Kost. Kost, by setting up a system of domination, was able to create a set of values to advantage some individuals or groups over others. Derek and the new heads of department are 'coopted' in Kost's new system, and are asked repeatedly to accept his rationalizations and the government's to save Fairisle Polytechnic. Kost does not encourage open debate but creates a 'climate' for all to mistrust each other and accept no one from the 'old guard' as an ally.

The relational view

This view would argue that there is resistance present, and Fairisle Polytechnic shows examples of the sting working at different levels. The deference relationship, underscored emphatically by the government's approach to academic staff, being seen as the source of commands, which led to depressed salaries, larger classes, fewer resources and deteriorating buildings, was the source of the stings experienced by individuals. Academic staff had been complying with specific commands with which they were not in agreement for some time, but Kost's accession and his hardline approach to dealing with perceived problems was seen to be qualitatively much more severe. A sense of injustice and unrest was prevalent, coupled with a sense of dislocation as the hierarchy seemed to engineer a split between deans and the directorate – influence was not moving upwards, only command was moving downwards. In this situation, a specific command does not have to be directly given as long as the recipient perceives what is said to be a command, or to rest on a command which is veiled behind rhetoric. Kost's policies were turning the staff into a *crowd*.

The director, in apparently asking Derek to talk to Cyril about early retirement, was giving a command.

Derek felt it, did not want to carry it out, but nevertheless complied with the deference order and performed persuasively. Cyril, for his part, could see that he was being made an offer he could not refuse, he would be removed from his position in some other way if he stayed and his present situation was untenable. Cyril was, in effect, being given the command 'Go!' and he knew it. So did the rest of his staff, and Derek, through the hierarchy, was seen as the commander. The episode involving Cyril and his staff would not be lost from the corporate memory; it would be remembered by many others who over time might feel the same sting of an improperly reciprocated deference relationship. Cyril and his staff's gift of labour (long service, loyalty, dedication) were not being seen by Kost as valuable or worthwhile. Derek's position in talking to and trying to incorporate the staff into his strategic thinking was something that was difficult for them to appreciate, given their history and the particular past actions, past decisions and patterns of practices that had characterized their response to being managed. They almost instinctively interpreted this intervention as yet another piece of command hiding behind fine words, and some of them at least decided to lash back – they would not mildly carry out this perceived command to plan for their own demise. The stings of recent events would be returned in a demand for accountability – not of them to their managers, but of the managers to the body public.

Kost handled this perfectly in two ways. One was that he deflected the returned sting onto a wider body. Just as a sting can be passed on down the hierarchy, so return, in some circumstances, can be deflected up the hierarchy. This restored the balance of constraints under which he was labouring. Second, as Canetti emphasizes, he perceived the large gathering's need to become a crowd, and by skilful use of rhetoric he made them one. The perceived sting was thus generalized and dispersed, its specificity and focus and hence its returnability dissipated.

Unfortunately, for reasons which certainly included the need to try to come to a quick decision, Kost was unable to avoid this in the Textile Industry Association (TIA) episode. The sting of his recent commands was being felt by the students, the atmosphere of suspicion was rife, and the apparent command to move to the TIA building, which was presented as non-negotiable, produced a challenge which built on the cumulated stings (many of them reaching back beyond the time) and produced the drive to become a crowd. The students formed themselves into a crowd through slogans, and were able to focus on a closely defined issue, which resulted in their success.

Kost wisely chose to stay out of the Fawley Ridge negotiations. He realized that he had been seen to be the architect of the TIA defeat and that the students, flushed with success, would relish another confrontation. He also intuitively knew that it was wise to seek consensus before a decision was presented or perceived to have been made. Although there was opposition, the consistent refusal of Derek and William to commit themselves to a decision until the participants had thought through all the aspects and gathered the relevant information was successful in removing the sting – *without command there can be no sting*, and without a focus for reversal, sting cannot be returned. The decision was removed from the command structure which was reversed – the criteria, once jointly set, became the authority, and as the working group translated the criteria into imperatives, the 'commanders' facilitated those imperatives by taking upward or horizontal action.

Why then was Derek uneasy? Was this not a successful example of avoiding the sting and return? Substantially yes, but Derek knew that the situation was more complex. No one knew that the site was likely to be a valuable asset. That possibility had never been put forward as one of the criteria at issue as, if it had become public knowledge, the local council would have cried 'foul' on the move as a subterfuge. Once the move was established and the process seen to be thorough, it could be defended along with the site. Derek knew that despite the fact that there was a real need for space at Shaw's Park, the real estate value of Fawley was the main reason. If it ever became apparent that this had been the case, and that in fact there had been a veiled command behind the process, it would be seen as nothing more than a piece of successful brinkmanship. If any attempt was made to decommission and dispose of the site soon after vesting day, or other deals were done with the same effect, this would retrospectively evoke the sting and possibly its immediate return. The consequences for staff relations, especially given the way in which morale had been positively affected by the move, could have been disastrous. So Derek really reserved his judgement to see if the follow-up procedures were maintained, the promised resources materialized, and the style of change management was embedded as a characteristic feature of the institution rather than a happy bit of expediency.

One interesting question to ponder is: Why are all the key players in the case male? Fawley Ridge is a real case study although pseudonyms have been used. Given the discussion in Chapter 3 on gender, what do you think would have happened if Derek had been a woman manager?

Conclusion

It is generally true that pluralists offer a more comprehensive way of dealing with organizational problems than do unitary approaches. Through adopting such an approach to power, managers have a wider range of understandings and techniques by which to deal with the diverse problems confronting them. Clearly, a pluralist manager is still better equipped to deal with conflict and power than is a unitary one. The unitary approach belonged to an era of management in which conformity and authority were seen as mutually self-reinforcing and unchallengeable. That era no longer exists, although managers may act as though it does.

Even though the political perspective allows for a deeper understanding of interests and power, it is still only a partial account of organizational politics. The pluralist view of power tends to blur or conceal practices of domination found in organizations, thereby often distorting sources of real power. Issues of domination and control are not readily dealt with in a pluralist or behaviourist framework. The pluralist presentation of the political organization, in its various forms, rests on the premise that there is relatively equal access by all to the power resources and strategies that ultimately account for who succeeds, wins or gets ahead. The discussion on mentoring and diversity suggests the latter view is subject to criticism. The more deeply entrenched and pervasive systems of domination that are structured into many organizational systems and processes are denied or neglected by pluralists.

The radical view of power attempts to redress the naive pluralist and behaviourist assumptions that organizations are 'level playing fields' in which power struggles are contested on relatively equal footings. Instead, the radical view argues that much of what happens in organizations is about sustaining managerial dominance and control over the workforce. Thus, many of the techniques and methods of conflict resolution offered by pluralists are considered to be manipulative strategies used by management to weaken the collective power of labour (unions). Radical theorists would be looking to push for significant changes in power relationships between management and workers through the creation of more democratic work organizations.

The fourth dimension argues that power is dispersed, that everyone has some power, that resistance is born alongside power, and that power is relational. Although the 'playing field' is not level, and the advantage is to the powerful, this is not a static and unchanging situation of domination. What is necessary is to understand how discourse and argument come together with power to define *knowledge*, and on the basis of knowledge people act. So rather than looking at how action is controlled, this view looks at how knowledge is produced, how the powerful are advantaged in shaping knowledge through discourse, and how resistance can begin from insignificant origins – even to topple the Berlin Wall. Of course, the critical analysis of discourse, and the production of knowledge, also lead to more open and democratic organizations, but also emphasize how *learning* needs to occur in an awareness of the relationship between knowledge and power.

We will now go back to the questions raised at the beginning of the chapter.

Answers to questions about organizational power and politics

1 **Are power and politics generic to all organizations?** The answer is 'yes', at least in the pluralist, radical and relational views of power and politics. Each of these approaches offers different accounts of why this might be the case, and all of them suggest different strategies or ways of addressing power issues. Only the unitary approach implies that the 'normal' state of events is to have no politics or power struggles. The pluralist view is somewhat ambivalent on this point, preferring to see the power and politics managed for the good of the organization. Notwithstanding the insights drawn from the radical and relational views of power and politics, most management strategies are dominated by the unitary approach, even more so than the pluralist one. The latter is often the rhetoric managers use when they talk of power and politics, while their theories in use are often unitary. Both the unitary and pluralist views provide a 'comfort zone' for dealing with power and politics, suggesting that there are practices or activities that managers can ultimately control and remedy. This is not the case with the radical view, which implies that management is an agent of capital (or capitalism) and as a collective group is responsible for the power imbalances and exploitations that give rise to power struggles and organizational politics. Organizations are deeply embedded structures of domination. The relational view presents power and resistance as generic to social relations within command structures and never totally controllable or solvable by management alone. Managers would need to be highly skilled in reflective practice and critical thinking (see the Introduction) if they wish to understand the relational view of power and act from its assumptions. People engage in various discursive practices (for example local and popular accounts) that can become the basis for questioning assumptions and ways of thinking that often appear entrenched and highly resistant to change.

2 **Do some circumstances more than others give rise to power struggles and politics in organizations?** The answer again is a qualified 'yes'. The case study analysis under each perspective addresses this question. The circumstances that are identified are based on value assumptions and particular frames of reference peculiar to each approach. However, the relational view of power presents the most complex and subtle perspective on the circumstances that might give rise to power and the resistance to it, particularly the notions of the command, the sting and reciprocation.

3 **Why is power such a difficult thing to deal with in organizations?** This derives from the fact that managers often favour the unitary or pluralist views of power as their preferred 'stock of knowledge' on the topic. As Kanter says, many managers also treat 'power' as a 'dirty word', something to be denied, decried and discarded (Kanter 1979: 65). Furthermore, managers are often reluctant to analyse or deal with the more complex sources of power and resistance identified in the radical and relational views of power. Many are unable to create a learning environment (LE) or learning space (LS) (see

Answers continued

Chapter 1) that would help them to raise debate, discussion and dialogue relating to power issues. Ultimately, managers who believe they have power (and authority) do not often feel compelled to question it, share it or surrender the prestige and status often used to embellish their positions, particularly at the senior levels (see Chapter 10).

4 Is everyone able to gain or exercise power in organizations? Three of the approaches are circumspect on this point. Only the unitary approach is clearly against this idea, seeing it as deviant or aberrant for individuals to pursue their interests through power and politics. The pluralists are likely to present the organization as a level playing field with checks and balances in place to ensure that smart or clever managers can advance themselves or their careers through power and politics. The radical view does not see a level playing field at all and fears that the less powerful are always outflanked or outmanoeuvred by dominant groups and interests. The relational view does not suggest that there is necessarily a level playing field, but that there are opportunities to enter power relations that can effect certain wins to groups that the radical view would normally view as powerless. The radical or three-dimensional view is more concerned with aggregated or collective power of groups, such as management, organizations, government, the state and unions to whom it attributes a form of collective consciousness or ideology. The fourth view is more focused on the pressure points within these relations and does not accept a monolithic or aggregated view of power. It does acknowledge that people can act collectively to avenge a grievance (or deferred sting) if circumstances permit. One such circumstance can be the imbalance in reciprocation.

It would be a very unwise manager who did not seriously contemplate the answers to these questions, and who did not, as a result, start to reflect on his or her own assumptions and practices in relation to organizational power and politics.

References

Anthony, P. (1994) *Managing Culture*, Buckingham: Open University Press.

Bacharach, S. and Baratz, M.S. (1962) 'Two faces of power', *American Political Science Review* **56**(4): 947–52.

Bailey, F.G. (1970) *Strategems and Spoils*, Oxford: Blackwell.

Barbalet, J.M. (1986) 'Power and resistance', *British Journal of Sociology* **36**(1): 521–48.

Barley, S. and Kunda, G. (1992) 'Design and Devotion' *Administrative Science Quarterly* **37**(2): 363–99.

Blake, R. and Mouton, J. (1978) *The New Managerial Grid*, Houston: Gulf.

Bolman, L.G. and Deal, T.E. (1991) *Reframing Organizations: Artistry, Choice and Leadership*, San Francisco: Jossey-Bass.

Buchanan, D. and Badham, R. (1999) *Power, Politics, and Organizational Change*, London: Paul Chapman.

Burrell, G. (1988) 'Modernism, postmodernism and organization studies 2: The contribution of Michel Foucault', *Organization Studies* **9**(2): 221–35.

Burrell, G. and Morgan, G. (1979) *Sociological Paradigms and Organisational Analysis*, London: Gower.

Burton, C. (1987) 'Merit and gender: Organisations and mobilisations of masculine bias', *Australian Journal of Social Issues* **22**(2): 424–49.

Burton, C. (1991) *The Promise and the Price: The Struggle for Equal Opportunity in Women's Employment,* Sydney: Allen & Unwin.

Byrt, W.J. (1973) *Theories of Organisation*, Sydney: McGraw-Hill.

Canetti, E. (1987) *Crowds and Power*, Harmondsworth: Penguin.

Catalyst (1996) *Women in Corporate Leadership: Progress and Prospects*, New York: Catalyst.

Chan, A. (2001) *Critically Constituting Organization,* Amsterdam: John Benjamins.

Child, J. (ed.) (1973) *Man and Organizations: The Search for Explanation and Social Relevance*, London: Allen & Unwin.

Clegg, S.R. (1989) *Frameworks of Power*, London: Sage.

Clegg, S.R. (1990) *Modern Organizations: Organization Studies in the Postmodern World*, London: Sage.

Clegg, S.R. (1994) 'Power relations and the constitution of the resistant subject' in Jermier, J., Nord, W. and Knights, D. (eds), *Resistance and Power in Organizations: Agency, Subjectivity and the Labour Process,* London: Routledge.

Clegg, S. (1998) 'Foucault, power and organizations', in McKinlay, A. and Starkey, K. (eds), *Foucault, Management and Organization,* London: Sage.

Clegg, S.R. and Dunkerley, D. (1980) *Organizations, Class and Control*, London: Routledge & Kegan Paul.

Coe, T. (1992) *The Key to the Men's Club*, London: Institute of Management.

Collins, D. (2000) *Management Fads and Buzzwords: Critical-Practical Perspectives* London: Routledge.

Collinson, D. (1994) 'Strategies of resistance: Power, knowledge and subjectivity in the workplace', in Jermier, J., Nord, W. Knights, D. (eds), *Resistance and Power in Organizations: Agency, Subjectivity and the Labour Process*, London: Routledge.

Cooper, R.C. (1990) 'Canetti's sting', *SCOS Notework* **9**(2/3): 45–53.

Crozier, M. (1964) *The Bureaucratic Phenomenon*, Chicago: University of Chicago Press.

Dahl, R. (1957) 'The concept of power', *Behavioural Science* 2 July: 201–15.

Dawson, S. (1986) *Analysing Organisations*, London: Macmillan – now Palgrave Macmillan.

Dunford, R.W. (1992) *Organisational Behaviour: An Organisational Analysis Perspective*, Sydney: Addison-Wesley.

Ely, R.J. (1995) 'The power in demography: Women's social construction of gender identity at work', *Academy of Management Journal,* **38**: 589–634.

Farnham, D. and Pimlott, J. (1979) *Understanding Industrial Relations*, London: Cassell.

Forster, J. and Browne, M. (1996) *Principles of Strategic Management*, Melbourne: Macmillan.

Fox, A. (1974) *Beyond Contract: Work, Power and Trust Relations*, London: Faber and Faber.

French, J.R.P. and Raven, B. (1959) 'The bases of social power', in Cartwright, L. and Zander, A. (eds), *Group Dynamics, Research and Theory*, London: Tavistock.

Frith, F. and Fulop, L. (1992) 'Conflict and power in organisations', in Fulop, L. with Frith, F. and Hayward, H., *Management for Australian Business: A Critical Text*, Melbourne: Macmillan.

Fulop, L. (1991) 'Middle managers: victims or vanguards of the enterpreneurial movement', *Journal of Management Studies* **28**(1): 25–44.

Fulop, L. (1992) 'Bureaucracy and the modern manager', in Fulop, L. with Frith, F. and Hayward, H., *Management for Australian Business: A Critical Text*, Melbourne: Macmillan.

Gergen, K. (1989) 'Organisation theory in the postmodern era', paper presented at the Rethinking Organisation Conference, University of Lancaster.

Gergen, K. (1992) 'Organization theory in the postmodern era', in Reed, M. and Hughes, M. (eds), *Rethinking Organizations: New Directions in Organization Theory and Analysis,* London: Sage.

Glazer, M.P. and Glazer, P.M. (1989) *Whistle-Blowers: Exposing Corruption in Government and Industry*, New York: Basic Books.

Goffman, E. (1979) *Gender Advertisements*, New York: Harper & Row.

Gollam, P. (1997) 'Successful staff selection: The value of acknowledging women', *Management* October: 25–6.

Gouldner, A.W. (1954) *Patterns of Industrial Bureaucracy*, New York: Free Press.

Grint, K. (1997a) 'TQM, BPR, JIT, BSCs and TLAs: Managerial waves or drownings' *Management Decision* **35**(10): 731–8.

Grint, K. (1997b) *Fuzzy Management,* Oxford: Oxford University Press.

Hall, R.H. (1972) *Organizations, Structure and Process*, London: Prentice Hall.

Handy, C. (1985) *Understanding Organizations* (3rd edn), Harmondsworth: Penguin.

Hardy, C. (1994) 'Power and politics in organisations', in Hardy, C. (ed.), *Managing Strategic Action: Mobilizing Change,* London: Sage.

Hardy, C. and Leiba-O'Sullivan, S. (1998) 'The power behind empowerment: implications for research and practice', *Human Relations* **15**(4): 451–83.

Hatch, M.J. (1997) *Organization Theory: Modern, Symbolic and Postmodern Perspectives*, Oxford: Oxford University Press.

Hickson, D.J. and McCullough, A.F. (1980) 'Power in organizations' in Salaman, G. and Thompson, K. (eds), *Control and Ideology in Organizations*, Milton Keynes: Open University Press.

Hickson, D.J., Hinings, C.R., Lee, C.A., Schneck, R.E. and Pennings, J.M. (1971) 'The strategic contingencies theory of intraorganisational power', *Administrative Science Quarterly* **16**(2): 216–29.

Honour, T.F. and Mainwaring, R.M. (1982) *Business and Sociology*, London; Croom Helm.

Kanter, R.M. (1977a) 'Power games in the corporation', *Psychology Today* July: 48–53.

Kanter, R.M. (1977b) *Men and Women of the Corporation*, New York: Basic Books.

Kanter, R.M. (1979) 'Power failure in management circuits', *Harvard Business Review* **57**(4): 65–75.

Kanter, R.M. (1982) 'The middle manager as innovator', *Harvard Business Review* **60**(4): 95–105.

Kanter, R.M. (1983) *The Change Masters: Innovation and Entrepreneurship in the American Corporation*, New York: Simon & Schuster.

Kanter, R.M. (1989a) 'Swimming in newstreams: Mastering innovation dilemmas', *California Management Review* **31**(4): 45–69.

Kanter, R.M. (1989b) 'The new managerial work', *Harvard Business Review* **67**(6): 85–92.

Kanter, R.M. (1989c) *When Giants Learn to Dance: Mastering the Challenge of Strategy, Management and Careers in the 1990s*, New York: Simon & Schuster.

Kelly, J.E. (1982) *Scientific Management, Job Redesign and Work Performance*, London: Academic Press.

Keys, B. and Case, T. (1990) 'How to become an influential manager', *Academy of Management Executive* **4**: 38–51.

Kirkbride, P.S. (1985) 'The concept of power: A lacuna in industrial relations theory?', *Journal of Industrial Relations* **27**(3): 265–82.

Knights, D. and Vurdubakis, T. (1994) 'Power, resistance and all that', in Jermier, J.M., Nord, W.R. and Knights, D. (eds), *Resistance and Power in Organizations: Agency, Subjectivity and the Labour Process*, London: Routledge.

Kotter, J. (1977) 'Power, dependence, and effective management', *Harvard Business Review* **55**(4): 125–36.

Lansbury, R.K. and Spillane, R. (1983) *Organisational Behaviour in the Australian Context*, Melbourne: Longman Cheshire.

Linstead, S. (1997) 'Resistance and return: Power, command and change management', *Studies in Cultures Organizations and Societies* **3**(1): 67–89.

Lukes, S. (1974) *Power: A Radical View*, London: Macmillan – now Palgrave Macmillan.

Lupton, T. (1978) *Management and the Social Sciences*, Harmondsworth: Penguin.

McGregor, D. (1960) *The Human Side of Enterprise*, New York: McGraw-Hill.

McKenna, E.P. (1997) *When Work Doesn't Work Any More: Women, Work and Identity* New York: Hodder & Stoughton.

Maddock, S. and Parkin, D. (1994) 'Gender cultures: How they affect men and women at work', in Davidson, M. and Burke, R. (eds), *Women in Management: Current Research Issues*, London: Paul Chapman.

Margretta, J. (1997) 'Will she fit in?', *Harvard Business Review* March–April: 18–32.

Marshall, J. (1995) *Women Managers Moving On: Exploring Career and Life Choices*, London: Routledge.

Mauss, M. (1990) *The Gift*, London: Routledge.

Mechanic, D. (1962) 'Sources of power of lower participants in complex organisations', *Administrative Science Quarterly* **7**: 349–64.

Mintzberg, H. (1983) *Power in and around Organisations*, Englewood Cliffs, NJ: Prentice Hall.

Mintzberg, H. (1989) *Mintzberg on Management: Inside Our Strange World of Organisations*, New York: Free Press.

Nightingale, D. (1974) 'Conflict and conflict resolution', in Strauss, G., Miles, R.E., Snow, C.C. and Tannebaum, A.S. (eds), *Organizational Behavior: Research and Issues*, California: Wadsworth.

Pfeffer, J. (1981) *Power in Organisations*, London: Pitman.

Pfeffer, J. (1992) *Managing with Power: Politics and Influence in Organization* (2nd edn), Boston: Harvard Business School Press.

Pugh, D.S., Hickson, D.J. and Hinings, C.R. (1983) *Writers on Organizations*, Harmondsworth: Penguin.

Ragins, B.R. (1997) 'Diversified mentoring relationships in organizations: A power perspective', *Academy of Management Review* **22**(2): 482–521.

Ramsay, H. (1977) 'Cycles of control', *Sociology* **11**(3): 481–506.

Reed, M. (1985) *Redirections in Organisational Analysis*, New York: Tavistock.

Robbins, S. (1974) *Managing Organisational Conflict: A Non-traditional Approach*, Englewood Cliffs, NJ: Prentice Hall.

Ryan, M. (1984) 'Theories of power', in Kakabadse, A. and Parker, C. (eds), *Power, Politics, and Organisations: A Behavioural Science View*, London: John Wiley.

Salaman, G. (1979) *Work Organisations, Resistance and Control*, London: Heinemann.

Silverman, D. (1970) *The Theory of Organisations*, London: Open University.

Simpson, R. (1997) 'Have times changed? Career barriers and the token woman manager', *British Journal of Management* (Special Issue) **8**: S121–30.

Velasquez, M. (1988) *Business Ethics*, Englewood Cliffs, NJ: Prentice Hall.

Voss, B. (1992) 'Office politics: a player's guide', *Sales and Marketing Management,* **44**(12): 46–52.

Wajcman, J. (1998) *Managing Like a Man: Women and Men in Corporate Management*, University Park, PA: Penn State University Press.

Weber, M. (1964) *The Theory of Social Economic Organization*, London: Heinemann.

Whitley, W., Dougherty, T.W. and Dreher, G.F. (1991) 'Relationship of career mentoring and socioeconomic origins to managers' and professionals' early career progress', *Academy of Management Journal*, **34**: 331–51.

7 Organizational control

Simon Lilley, Edward Wray-Bliss and Stephen Linstead

Questions about control

1 What is control?
2 What are its sources in organizations?
3 Why is it necessary for management?
4 Can control ever be complete?

BANKING ON CONTROL

Viewed from the outside, Telebank plc's telephone banking call centre at Fordsal in the north of England looks less like a building belonging to a commercial bank and more like a correctional institution. It is a large, squat, grey building, located in an anonymous industrial estate with some 20 other similarly anonymous buildings in a traditional working-class area with a reputation for being 'rough'. An impenetrable ten-foot fence of steel posts, topped in places with vicious looking barbed wire surrounds the building. To enter you have to go through two reinforced glass security doors. An electronic swipe card opens the first door, the second is opened by the security guard on the inside. Once inside, confronted by the guard behind his chest-high 'reception' desk, you have to complete the security log. You will give your name, business, organization and the person you have come to see, who the guard then telephones to escort you. You will be issued with a temporary identity card that you will wear at all times in the building. As you pass the guard, now that you are safely escorted, you will see the array of security monitors by which the guard constantly watches the perimeter. These pictures are relayed and recorded by the remote-controlled security cameras that ring the outside of the building. Several of these cameras will have captured you a few moments ago. Such security provisions, designed to prevent the disruptive influence of those who do not share the bank's definitions of order or their claims to monopoly of control over the resources inside the building, do not end with this separation and segregation of the 'dangerous' outside from the 'safe' inside. Those reinforced glass doors may be read not as the exit from the world-that-must-be-watched into a world-of-freedom, but as an entrance into a space saturated with and structured around control.

Nowhere is this control more sophisticated, and more proudly regarded by the manager, than in the department called 'customer line'. Customer line is the department through which all of Telebank's business customers' contacts with the branch are routed. Customer line's answering of customers' calls may be understood as the central function of the centralized telephone banking building. The majority of calls to customer line are routine and will be dealt with by the first clerk who takes the call. Sixty-three per cent of calls are requests for balance information and the movements of recent items on customers' accounts. Other routine tasks conducted by clerks on customer line include transferring money between accounts, stopping cheques, and ordering cheque books, standing orders or copies of statements. The customer line department is open continually between the hours of 8 am and 8 pm Monday to Friday and 8 am until 12 pm Saturdays. Depending on the time of day it is staffed by between five and twenty clerks, predominantly women, and answers upwards of 1100 customer calls each day.

To enable so few remotely located Telebank staff to deal with so many calls from the bank's business customers all around the UK, Telebank has installed sophisticated information and communication technologies (ICTs) to control calls, bank services and staff. Surveillance of clerks is facilitated via the linking of the telephone communication system with the information processing system. This enables each individual clerk's work to be minutely and constantly scrutinized. Statistics on all clerks' performance (broken down by individual clerk) are continually generated and displayed on a computer next to the team leader. Locating this information next to the team leader, at the edge of the team's space, enables all clerks to check up on their own, and others', performance figures. The physical movement to the screens that this entails also means that such self/peer surveillance is itself open to others' surveillance. The main information displayed on these screens shows number of calls, number of times 'wrap up' has been used (a temporary break from the call queue initiated by the clerk by pressing a button on the telephone, so that a task arising from the last call can be completed), number of calls transferred and details of average time durations. Further, the computer summarizes this information to produce daily and weekly statistics, tables and graphs for managerial use containing more detailed breakdown of timings, by clerk and by team. Clerks are individually evaluated and rewarded according to the number of calls they answer. Pressure to answer more calls is reinforced further through the design of clerks' telephones. A red light on each clerk's telephone flashes when a call is waiting to be answered. The more calls waiting, the faster the light flashes. Mounted on the walls and situated on two sides of the department are metre-long LED displays of number of calls waiting for each cell and length of time they had been waiting. These act as a constant visible reminder to work faster, to keep the customer from waiting. Actions performed by clerks are also open to surveillance by senior team members and the team leader. All of a clerk's actions upon a customer's account can be checked at any time by accessing the account on screen. As well as enabling surveillance, the ICT system serves to individualize clerks' jobs. Clerks are literally tied to the phone through wearing headsets rather than using telephone handsets. This, combined with the automatic call feeding system, means that control over receiving a call is removed from clerks and vested in the ICT system. Rather than allowing the clerks the control of picking up a telephone handset when they are ready, the computerized system merely emits a 'beep' in the clerk's headset a fraction of a second before the customer's voice is heard. The organization of the ICT system thus binds clerks to their desks preventing them, for instance, from moving around the office and returning when they hear the phone ring. This individualization is combined with competition. All clerks have individually 'agreed' targets detailing number of calls that a clerk must answer a day. To achieve their target, clerks must organize the work so that the automatic call feeding system feeds them the next call in preference to their colleague. This requires that clerks finish calls quickly, so that they are logged by the computer as waiting the longest – the criterion upon which call allocation was based.

Gary, the departmental manager, is very proud to be in charge of a department that yields such possibilities for sophisticated technological control. 'This machine is wonderful,' he said in a training session for new staff, 'it tells me when you're breathing, eating, sleeping ... some people look on this as a version of 1984 and Big Brother ... if you think this is bad, wait till the future, stuff is being developed that will make this seem like heaven.' Perhaps unsurprisingly, staff on the department tended to be less enthusiastic. The high-pressure, fast-paced, target-driven work, the constant surveillance by the computer system and constant reminders of calls that need answering, and the endlessly repetitive requests by customers for balances and other routine services – all of which must be answered ever faster if the computer-controlled targets are to be met – means that frustration and dissatisfaction with the job are common. Department member Steve summarized the views of many. 'It's like more or less working in a factory and most people didn't come here to work in a factory. They could get paid more by going and working for Kellogg's putting plastic toys in a box. How can you be into taking 100 balances a day? How can you enjoy that?' For the staff, meeting or beating targets yields only fleeting satisfaction, a too brief respite until the next day of work. There has to be more to their life at work than this stressful, pressured, routine pursuit of targets.

So the clerks add more to their work life. As the computerized, quantified targets construct their work as an unsatisfying, stressful and ultimately meaningless activity, akin to putting plastic toys in a box of cereal, clerks shift territory. They redefine their work on the telephones as caring for the customer. In stolen conversations between calls, at breaks or lunch and after work, they talk up and create a mutual understanding that their job was to help the human beings that use the bank's services. For the clerks, their job becomes a meaningful, socially useful activity. They aren't engaged in the mindless pursuit of targets, but rather in the mindful activity of caring for and servicing others. They come to understand and talk openly about the manager Gary's emphasis upon quantified targets and speed of calls as holding back the proper nature of the job they are employed to do. Management's targets are seen as being in opposition to the quality of care or service that they, the clerks, should be offering. As department member Pam put it, 'before the targets I must admit I enjoyed it more because the quality of service you can give is a lot better when you've not got the pressure on that today you've got to do 81 calls and you've only done 50 and you've got one hour to go, you know it's a case of getting everybody off the phone. Gary would come back and say 'yeah but you can do that' and I would say 'I don't dispute I can do it, I know I can do it, but what quality am I going to be giving?'

Gary, the departmental manager, generally didn't seem particularly concerned about this kind of 'resistance'. He had faith that the computerized control system would keep each clerk working at or above target pace – after all, any change in the clerks' behaviour, any more time spent on calls or lessening of call-answering pace would be automatically recorded by the computer. In such a tight system of control and surveillance, he explained in conversation with others, the clerks could think what they liked as long as they kept meeting the number and speed of call targets that he was set by his senior managers. In fact, as far as he was concerned, clerks talking about 'customer service' and 'customer care' could be seen as a good thing. The banking world has long traded upon an image of good customer service, and by valuing these aspects of their work clerks would be concerned to provide the necessary 'human' or 'caring' touch in their calls, thus helping to avoid an impersonal dehumanized service that customers don't like. All this talk then of 'customer service' was no real threat to the bank's targets because it could only benefit the bank and it actually made controlling a telephone banking service easier.

For the clerks, though, defining their job as customer service was in opposition to Gary's and the bank's demands for an ever faster and cheaper service. Customer service meant more time on the phones, following up queries that customers had, chatting with the customers if that is what they wanted. In short, it meant longer, more involved calls and therefore fewer of them per day per clerk. Customer care was also in opposition to what they experienced as the bank's cheapening of their work. Clerks valued the sense of themselves as occupying the historically responsible, relatively high status and socially useful role of being bank clerks. They passionately rejected being viewed by others as 'glorified switchboard operators' or worse still, as 'cogs in a machine'. Defining their work as customer care gave the clerks a way to resist what they understood as the bank's attempts to alienate them from the useful, meaningful and responsible nature of their jobs.

At times, this opposition to the bank's definition of their work – as meeting targets – spilled over into overt acts of resistance. Christine, for instance, a clerk who worked on the department in particularly busy times, took the clerks' shared language of customer care one small step further and used it to refuse to meet the targets that she was given. Explaining this she said: 'If you pick up the phone 100 times a day and cut them off that's OK with Gary. I'm at odds with Gary over targets, it's not good customer service. I've got a target of 40 calls but I don't care, I do the job as I think it should be done, we're here to help people.' For Christine, the bank could have all the sophisticated computerized control systems it wanted, but if it didn't match her understanding of what constituted proper customer care she wasn't going to let it control her.

Source: Prepared by Ed Wray-Bliss on the basis of his extensive research on call centres in the UK.

QUESTIONS ABOUT THE CASE

1 What is the bank trying to control?

2 What are the mechanisms used by the bank to control the customer line department?

3 Does this control succeed?

4 How do clerks experience this control?

5 Should the clerks' redefinition of their work as 'customer care' be viewed as resistance? If so, resistance to what? If not, why not?

6 What do you think will happen in the future in the customer line department?

Introduction

Participation in organized human activity inevitably involves constraints on individual action, if the whole of organized action is to exceed the sum of its parts. Control, therefore, seems an essential feature of organizations. Within classical management theory, control was viewed simplistically as a series of techniques for measuring the effectiveness of other management functions such as planning, organizing and leading, and as the basis for taking appropriate corrective action when that effectiveness was seen to be lacking. However, it is not only managers who exercise control, control is also exercised by non-managerial groups, whether in the form of resisting rules, restricting output or through blatant conflict. Realizing that attempts to exercise control are not the exclusive preserve of managers forces us to reconsider the position of control within the list of functions delineated by classical management theory. For while we may all plan, organize, lead and control our *own* activities, managers seem to have the special status of being *legitimately* allowed to exercise these functions *over* the activities of *others*. In which case, we might say that management is essentially about control, that the so-called *managerial prerogative* – 'management's right to manage' – is dependent upon management's ability to secure the ability to control others. In short, control is the *primary* managerial function but it is rarely exercised without some form of resistance.

Noting that managerial control does not go uncontested, and that it does not emanate from only one site, should also alert us to the existence of a multitude of modes of control, which we can expect to find in a complex and dynamic mix in any particular situation. It is the aim of this chapter to try to separate this mix, so that we can analyse each of its constituents, in order that we can subsequently better understand the ways in which they interrelate in practice. We will see that control may be exercised within, between and over organizations and their members and that it may be resisted in myriad ways at its points of application. Control is thus intimately related to power and influence.

A distinction frequently utilized in discussions of control is that between the *formal* and *informal* dimensions of the phenomenon. Formal controls tend to be those associated with the rights and responsibilities delineated for a bureaucratic office, the clearly spelt out, often written, rules and procedures intended to govern individuals' conduct and their interrelations at, and between, particular places in an organizational hierarchy (see Chapter 4). Informal controls are those associated with custom and practice and the cultural norms that pertain in a particular location. However, such a distinction becomes increasingly difficult to sustain in the face of the deliberately designed, so-called *cultural change* programmes, much beloved of corporations of the 1980s and 90s. Within such practices, managers are enjoined also to manage the informal dimensions of organizational life, to utilize nuanced manipulation of the informal as another source of control. Nevertheless, consideration of the ways in which formal controls combine into *control systems* does provide a useful way in to analysis of how control is exercised in organizations. Thus we delineate the key aspects of a formal control system in some detail, outlining both the likely elements of successful formal control systems and the potential dysfunctions that may emerge from the application of such systems. We then briefly examine the emergence of the profession of management as both cause and consequence of the changing dynamics of control in organizations. Following this, we consider one particularly important constituent of the internal organizational control system: *management accounting*. We do so because it allows us to open up our discussion of control in a number of different directions. Firstly, we try to provide an answer to the question of why so many directorial positions in the English-speaking business world are filled by accountants. The answer to this question allows us to delineate further the importance of *professions*, and indeed of contests between different professions, in consideration of control in organizations, and also to introduce the virtue of labour process analysis to consideration of organizational control. Labour process analysis sees the shape of technology adopted within and over production as a crucial source of control in the workplace, and accounting is not just a profession, it is also a *technology*. It is a technology that labour process analysis allows us to apprehend as a crucial component in the control of labour in capitalist enterprises in the Anglo-Saxon world. A critical analysis of control requires that we examine this more materially based account of control before we look at other forms of explanation that align more with the relational view of management presented in this text.

Technology also often facilitates what has, following analyses building on the work of the French historian, philosopher and social theorist, Michel Foucault, become known as *disciplinary* control – a key subject in our next section. Accounts in this tradition outline the key role played by *self-discipline* in the maintenance of control. Here we are seen not only as coerced into control by others, but also as *seduced* into assuming control of ourselves. Many explicitly designed corporate cultures can be best conceptualized in this light. Culture appears here as means to enable a relaxing of formal rules to overcome their dysfunctional aspects and allow the release of initiative, while this initiative is itself controlled by employees identifying, through seduction, with the aims of engineered culture as their conduct is monitored through technologically mediated surveillance.

We then utilize a short account of cross-cultural dimensions of control as a bridge to consider the increasing role played by globalization in controlling and disciplining both organizations and their members. We then briefly consider the gender dimension of the modes of control we have been considering before concluding by considering what our analyses of control mean for the conceptualization and practice of *resistance* and a relational view of management. Before all this, however, we need to delineate the key aspects of a formal control system in some detail

Formal control and cybernetics

Perhaps the most basic conceivable view of control is one based on the notion of feedback. According to Vincent Luchsinger and Thomas Dock ([1976]1988: 35):

Feedback is a *control mechanism* which measures output, compares output to a standard, and adjusts new inputs and operations based on this information. (emphasis added)

Such a view is derived from the ideas of *cybernetics*, which Gordon Pask (1961, cited in Emmanuel et al. 1990: 8) defines as the study of 'how systems regulate themselves, reproduce themselves, evolve and learn'. The simplest common cybernetic systems are things like a steam engine controlled by Watt's governor or a heating system controlled by a thermostat. According to David Otley and Anthony Berry (1980) there are four necessary conditions that must be met if a process is to be said to be formally controlled:

1. Objectives for the process being controlled must exist, for without an aim or purpose control has no meaning.
2. The output of the process must be measurable in terms of the dimensions defined by the objectives. That is, the degree to which the process is attaining its objectives must be assessed.
3. A predictive model of the process is required so that causes for the non-attainment of objectives can be determined and proposed corrective actions evaluated.
4. There must be a capability of taking action so that deviations of attainment from objectives can be reduced. If any of these conditions … fail to be met, the process can no longer be said to be 'in control' (Emmanuel et al. 1990: 8–9).

The key essential elements of such a system and its control are represented schematically in Figure 7.1.

Although control can be applied to the inputs, throughputs and indeed the people involved in a system, the ultimate aim of such interventionary mechanisms is always, in a cybernetic view, the control of the outputs of the system. Examples of control systems founded

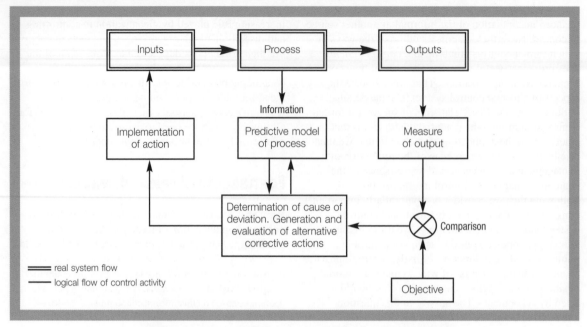

Figure 7.1 Necessary conditions for control

Source: Emmanuel, C., Otley, D. and Merchant, K. (1990) *Accounting for Management Control* (2nd edn), London: Chapman & Hall: 9.

upon cybernetic principles, in common use in organizations, are:

- budgets (cash, sales, financial and so on)
- quality controls (purchases and production)
- inventory controls
- production controls

It is important to note that the objective of the system to be controlled is not necessarily static. It may be revised in the light of experience. The process of control is often described as *cyclical*. The system goes through cycles in which performance is compared to expectation and if expectation is not being met, then corrective action is taken. Changes with regard to what is expected would then be seen as a 'meta-cycle' of the system in which its objective itself would come under scrutiny and action taken to revise it, what Chris Argyris and Donald Schön (1978) have termed 'double-loop' learning.

These elements of a controlled system at work are seen in budgeting. As part of the planning process, for example, an income and expenditure budget may be prepared for a forthcoming financial year. Such a budget would seek to estimate income deriving from sales and other sources, and also the expenses relating to the operation of the organization. Such estimates provide a guide to profitability, pricing and permissible expenditure. In this sense a budget is also a control. To the extent that a budget defines operating agendas and

affects the allocation of resources, the process of budget formulation is likely to be political.

Generally, yearly budget periods are broken down into smaller ones, like months or quarters, in order to more closely monitor performance. Variance reports measuring results against estimates, and sometimes providing a comparison with previous years and periods, are supplied to managers in order to indicate any areas that may be deviating from standard. Being 'over budget' on expenditure during one month, for example, may signal a need for tighter control over expenditure in a subsequent one. Certainly, the deviation would need to be justified. Similarly, a shortfall in income would need to be identified quickly, the reason for it considered and corrective action, if necessary, taken. From a management perspective, one benefit of regular performance reports is the early identification of trends likely to damage the financial viability of the organization.

Management by objectives (MbO) is similarly both a planning and a control technique. This approach to management, originally suggested by Peter Drucker in 1954 (Mullins 1985: 154), was popularized in the 1960s and 70s and applied to a variety of public and private enterprises. It is based on the 'goals as a means–end chain' concept of classical management theory, where strategic goals are broken down into intermediate and operational ones, such that the achievement of lower level goals ensures reaching higher ones. MbO involves the translation of such organizational goals into goals for key personnel at all levels of the organization.

In theory, this is a cooperative effort, with superiors and subordinates reaching agreement on key result areas for each job, the objectives to be obtained and the resources required to achieve them. These arrangements establish responsibilities and accountabilities against which the performance of personnel can be assessed. Claimed advantages are that MbO identifies key performance areas, clarifies roles, improves communication, provides a basis for performance appraisal and facilitates personnel training and development (Mullins 1985: 159). The process of MbO clearly involves the control system elements outlined above.

Characteristics of effective formal control systems

The preceding model, although simplistic, raises some important questions about control systems. For example: what is the basis for the establishment of standards; who should make evaluations; to whom should the results be reported; and what consequences flow from reported deviations? The answers to these questions depend largely on the wider climate of control within the organization, which we discuss in the rest of the chapter. Nevertheless, even at this point, the following generalizations (adapted from Stoner et al. 1985: 740) can be offered about the effectiveness of control systems:

1. The system must draw attention to key organization processes. While this seems an obvious suggestion, firms sometimes measure inconsequential factors because the critical processes do not easily lend themselves to measurement. (Controls can be a means by which some organizational actors justify their roles.)
2. Standards must be realistic, achievable and understood by those responsible for meeting them. Ideally, those affected by controls should be consulted in their establishment.
3. The performance areas measured should be within the control of those being monitored. To hold someone responsible for performance outside his or her sphere of control is not only pointless in terms of achieving control of an overall system, it is also likely to be distressing, demotivating and distracting.
4. Feedback should be provided as soon as possible and should be made direct to the persons concerned. This allows corrective action to be taken as soon as possible and potentially allows the control mechanism to be seen in a positive light by those subject to it, as an aid to improving their performance rather than merely a stick to beat them with.

5. The timing of performance checks must be such that early identification of deviations is possible.
6. The system should be flexible and provide insight into the cause of deviations.
7. The benefits of the system should exceed the costs.

Some dysfunctions of formal control systems

Apologists for formal control systems have stressed their motivational advantages. While it is true that they can convey a sense of achievement and direction, they can also be demotivating, as we hinted above. Often, a feature of the design of these systems is that they draw attention to operator failure rather than operator success. In such circumstances, what gets noticed is not the number of successes associated with a particular person, position or role, but the number of failures or shortfalls associated with it. Obviously, this can be demotivating to those subject to such an ethos and system of control. Some specific potential problematic outcomes of applying formal control systems include the following (adapted from Lawler and Rhode 1976: 83–94 by Hayward 1992):

1. *Rigid bureaucratic behaviour:* for example reluctance to work outside one's area of responsibility; the concentration on subunit goals rather than the goals of the organization as a whole; acceptance of minimum standards; more effort devoted to controls rather than what they are supposed to measure.
2. *Strategic behaviour:* for example deferring essential expenditure in order to meet a budget requirement; 'slipshod' work in order to meet a target; 'patchy' scheduling such as working harder later in the period of evaluation in order to meet a target.
3. *Invalid reporting data:* for example provision of misleading data in order to influence the setting of standards, or to appear to justify standards.
4. *Resistance:* both to feeling excessively controlled, and thus lacking in freedom to act, and also to the particular effects of specific control systems – for example controls may create new subsystems in organizations thus changing the power and structural configurations, or they may lead to threats of redundancy in an attempt to control costs.

The foregoing does not suggest that control systems are unnecessary in organizations, but rather that great care should be used in their design, implementation and use. One of the ironies of control is that the dysfunctions arising *because of control* may actually *aggravate the need for greater control*. For example, when inadequate performance is seen as an occasion for the imposition of a control, such action draws attention to the power superiority of management and aggravates the feelings of subordination and dependence on the part of operatives. One of the ways that workers can resist their feelings of powerlessness and subvert the power of their controllers is through adaptive or strategic behaviour. This might then lead to further tightening of existing controls or, indeed, the introduction of new ones, creating a vicious circle in which the costs of controls increase as their effectiveness diminishes.

Such an example highlights the symbolic implications of control systems. Workers' reactions to control systems are often not just the consequence of what the control means to them practically, but also of what it says to them about the way they are viewed in the organization. Also the ways in which specific controls are 'read' will vary from situation to situation. In a friendly, collegiate-style organization, a particular control might be well received. A similar control in an oppressive, authoritarian organization may be received with suspicion and concern. Or, just as likely, a formal control introduced into a friendly collegiate-style organization might be automatically rejected, merely because it is seen as 'a control', while the same intervention may pass virtually unnoticed in the oppressive, authoritarian organization, as just a little more 'business as usual'. Hence, despite the inevitability of some form of control, the question of specific controls and their acceptability and effectiveness cannot be separated from the overall climate, context and history of control that exists in an organization.

But why are managers seen as the ones who should exercise control? And, perhaps more fundamentally, how is management control different from the forms of control previously exercised in the direction of the production of goods?

The profession of management

In a text of exceptional breadth and depth, Roy Jacques (1996) tries to answer just these questions (along with innumerable others that are usually neglected yet are of equally great import for understanding contemporary managerial practices). With admirable dedication to the detailed historical record, Jacques outlines the interrelated emergence of the two key bodies of modern organizational life: the employee and the manager. His primary focus is upon the emergence of these entities in the US at the beginning of the twentieth century. And while this may limit the applicability of his insights, the fact that American managerial thought is the de facto market leader, and is 'exported round the world as objective science' (Jacques 1996, back cover), significantly mitigates this problem. For it is American managerial sense that is naively seen to be common sense by most of the managerial world.

As Jacques notes, with the emergence of American industrialism at the end of the nineteenth century, a series of changes were wrought upon American society. The federalism which had characterized the previous history of (white) America, and had succeeded the early colonial history of the continent, imagined and, indeed, largely constructed a society made up of self-determining citizens who came together in small communities. The key players in this world were farmers, small merchants and craftsmen. What these different types of people shared was a reliance upon a small community in which they were known and in which their good 'character' was the key to their trustworthiness in affairs of business and government. Much production was not carried out in the commercial sector, with citizens working to meet many of their own needs for food and housing from the land and resources that surrounded them. Citizens were action-oriented, believed in progress, could turn their hands to most tasks without special training and tended share a set of traditional middle-class values which buttressed their limited mutual dependency (Jacques, 1996: 39–40).

However, with the advent of industrialism, this previously largely unified character of the citizen was broken up. The employee came to replace the citizen as the role of social action for the majority. Others took on specialist roles as either business leaders or governors, or indeed split their activities between the two, as the public sector became more formally split from the private. The role of the average citizen was divided, with the producer working outside the home as employee while the consumer shopped, rather than worked, to meet other needs of the home. But these were not the only splits at work. The category of the employee was itself further split. While the arrangements of the US federal system had generally allowed the combination of the operational and financial control of enterprises in the body of the owner, the emergence of larger scale, industrial organizations encouraged a separation of ownership and control. This separation mirrored that which had previously occurred in Europe (although there it was largely the result of the aristocracy's view of work as a socially tainted activity). Within this separation, operational control becomes the remit of a new set of organizational bodies: managers. And, according to Jacques (1996: 87), the role of the manager is not best considered as representing a set of changes to the roles of employer or foreman that preceded it. Rather the manager must be seen as a special case of the employee, an employee who is 'formally charged with representing the interests of ownership' to other employees.

With employees working to produce goods, while profits from the sale of those goods would be enjoyed, in large part, not by them but by the owner of the enterprise and the increasing scale of production preventing the owner from personally ensuring maximum effort from those employees, the embodiment of the interests of the owner in a number of managerial employees, who could be dispersed throughout the enterprise, presented a potential solution to the new problems of control and increased productivity. To emphasize this point, Jacques (1996: 88) notes that Frederick Taylor claimed that the owner of the Midvale Steel works 'believed that he had the interests of the works more at heart than the other workmen' because he 'happened not to be of working parents' (Taylor 1911: 50–1). Jacques (1996: 87) also provides evidence for this claim in the approving citation given to the comments of a senior railway official by James Fagan (1909: 62). The official candidly told a Harvard audience that, due to increasing competition between company and union loyalty, his organization was being 'compelled to abandon' its policy of internal promotion of staff to managerial positions 'and to look elsewhere, particularly to the colleges, for our material'. Such comments indicate both 'the increasing status of technical knowledge' (hence the knowledge worker is born!) in matters of organization and an attempt by employers to answer 'the labour question' by constructing a special group of managerial employees, 'not sharing the sympathies of the production worker – as, apparently, did the traditional foreman' (Jacques 1996: 88). But what of the sort of control that these new managers were expected to exert?

Coercive control of generic labour has been practised successfully for at least several millennia. Physical punishment was not yet dead. Monetary fines for tardiness, carelessness and inappropriate behaviors were common from the earliest industrial environments and are mentioned as a technique by Taylor (1911). Systematic compensation policies did not yet exist to protect workers from income reductions. Firing could be done more or less at will. If all one needed was to boss the factory 'hand' one did not need a manager.

It is the *insufficiency* of these traditional forms of control that produces the manager. (1996: 88)

Having solved many of the original basic questions about how to organize work efficiently, a new conception of the notion of control emerges, one in which 'coaxing and persuading' take centre stage (Jacques 1996: 88). Barnard has argued that among the conditions on which organizational participants will accept orders in an organization (that is, authority) is that such orders are consistent with the participants' view of the purpose of the organization, and that the participants see it as in their interests to comply (Barnard 1970: 165). Consistent with this view, Barnard saw the formulation

of purpose in organizations as an essential executive function (Barnard 1970: 231) and recognized the use of persuasion and propaganda to this end. As Jacques and innumerable others note, no matter how much we 'deskill' the production environment, the knowledge and discretion of workers remain necessary for (profitable) operation. Human 'hands' are present because they carry such knowledge and discretion with them, in ways that the callipers of robotic claws do not (see also Collins 1987). And if men (and we are talking predominantly about men in this historical context) had to be present, they had to be 'handled' – coaxed and persuaded into appropriate performance. Those that were to do the handling needed a new name to convey the specificity of their organizational role and hence the term *management* entered the business lexicon – the word itself being 'derived from the Italian verb *Il maneggiare*, meaning "to handle", especially to handle horses' (Jacques 1996: 88).

As the profession of management has divided itself into numerous functions, a much older profession has been encouraged to join the fold, a profession that has, at least in the English-speaking world, arguably become the dominant one in terms of organizational control. That profession is, of course, accounting and its relation to organizational control is the subject of our next section.

Management accounting and control

As even the most cursory review of a collection of annual reports from the Anglo-Saxon world of business reveals, individuals holding some form of accountancy qualification predominate at executive board level. Such a preponderance of accountants is not observed, however, if one looks to the top of German or Japanese enterprises (see for example Hutton et al. 1977; Lawrence 1980; Coke 1983, all in Armstrong 1985), which, incidentally, are among those deemed to have performed best in the contemporary corporate world. The predominance of accounting at the top of the organizational hierarchy in the English-speaking world cannot therefore be explained solely by reference to the meeting of a narrowly defined functional need, perhaps one relating to reporting requirements, or broader relations to a universal 'outside world'. Rather, we must, as Peter Armstrong (1985: 129) does, relate this phenomena to the accounting profession's 'characteristic strategy for controlling labour' in the Anglo-Saxon world and, indeed, to competition between it and other professions to secure the dominant position with regard to the control of labour. *Control of the means to control labour* is, as Armstrong argues, the key to understanding the rise of accounting in Anglo-Saxon business hierarchies.

Although accountants in capitalist enterprises perform other functions ... their importance in management hierarchies depends on the adoption of their particular approach to the control of the 'labour process' (the conversion of labour power into particular forms of labour so as to yield a surplus). (Armstrong 1985: 130)

Armstrong attempts to provide a historical account of how accountants have come to dominate the approaches favoured in the Anglo-Saxon world to the control of labour, and how, as a result, they have come to dominate the higher echelons of organizational hierarchies in that world. Here we will attempt to follow the key moves he deploys to produce this account, as by doing so we can consider:

1. The ways in which professions control their members
2. The ways in which different professions compete for pre-eminence in organizational hierarchies
3. The ways in which competition between professions is related to the ability to maintain control of the key technologies to which each of those professions lay claim.

Professions, control, technique and the labour process

Professions may be seen to represent something of a pact, mediated by a governing body, between the members of the profession and society at large. Members of a profession agree to adopt certain standards of work – standards of collegially governed technical proficiency – and agree to do that work in an independent and ethical manner (notions that are, themselves, also collegially defined in practice). In short, they agree to submit to (collegiate) control by their profession. In return, members are granted both exclusionary rights over certain fields of activity and an unusually high degree of autonomy within those fields of activity. The key to achieving such a privileged position clearly lies in an ability to lay exclusive claim to a particular body of knowledge and/or set of technological competencies that can be employed to provide some sort of service valued by society at large. In order to lay such an *exclusionary* claim, the 'knowledge base' or set of technological competencies must be both 'sufficiently codifiable to be transmitted as a professional culture' and of 'sufficient indeterminacy to debar outsiders from professional practice' (Armstrong 1985: 132, drawing on Larson 1977).

However, as Armstrong notes, professions are not only granted special status because they independently and ethically apply an exclusive and objective body of knowledge and skills. To think otherwise would be to

accept 'at face value the professionals' own account of the reasons behind their exclusionary practices and demands for autonomy' (1985: 133, drawing on Roth 1974; but see also Haber 1991). He further notes that demands for professional autonomy have as much to do with a wish for independence as they do with the desire to be a controller of one's job rather than being controlled. Child et al. (1983, cited in Armstrong 1985: 133) argue that demands by professionals in staff positions in British industry to be allowed to work according their own conception of professional standards are also part of a concerted effort to impose these standards on other managers and hence exert control over the production function.

From a perspective on the activities of a capitalist society grounded in labour process theory, securing a position among 'the controllers' is likely to depend upon one's capacity to fulfil part of the function of capital, that is, the extraction of surplus value from labour. Such a perspective, deriving its main impetus from Braverman's (1974) somewhat narrow interpretation of the work of Karl Marx, begins its analysis from a recognition of the deeply ingrained social divisions of ownership and control, particularly of the means of production, that characterize our world. In such circumstances, conflicts over control of organizational activity, between the labour that operates the means of production and the capital that owns it, are seen to be both inevitable and endemic. As John Child (1984: 16) has remarked, organizational design and development can only go so far in helping to eliminate conflicts of interest in organizations, because the existence of those conflicts is related to tensions between ownership and control that beset capitalist organizations.

Armstrong (1985: 132) notes that although one of the key mechanisms utilized to control labour in the Anglo-Saxon world – scientific management (see Chapter 11) – was originally developed by engineers, this professional group was not able to exploit its benefits to move its members up the organizational hierarchy to join the ranks of the controllers. The methods proved too easy for others to understand and implement, despite Taylor's insistence that they should be implemented as part of a total system.

Accountancy and financial control

Instead, as we noted, it is accountants who command the peaks of organizational hierarchies in the English-speaking world. But why them? Just because engineers failed to exploit what should have been a key advantage, we cannot say that control was thus automatically given to accountants. What was it that accounting could offer capitalism in terms of control of labour that other professions could not? Firstly, it is important to realize that accountants had always had a firm foothold within the key structures of capitalism in the UK and USA as a result of the incorporation into law of audit requirements within those countries. But, prior to the mid-1920s, they were seen as neither particularly important for profitability nor sufficiently valuable to warrant their holding of leading positions within organizations (Armstrong 1985). With profit margins suitably high, there was little need to know the details of internal costs as a precursor for their strict control. However, the economic crisis of the depression of the mid-1930s increased the need for information on internal costs and, according to Armstrong (1985: 135), it was the evolution of management accountancy in response to this need which allowed accountancy to consolidate itself as a major profession within the capitalist world. This seems to have occurred despite the fact that 'it was early industrial engineers who pioneered the techniques of cost accountancy in America' (Chandler 1977: 464, quoted in Armstrong 1985: 139). Indeed Armstrong cites the work of the historian David Noble (1977), who claims that it was industrial engineers who were responsible for creating the 'rationalized' modern corporation on the basis of their scientific expertise and thus is was they who 'generated modern management' (Armstrong 1985: 139).

So how did accountants manage to utilize their foothold in auditing not only to break the de facto monopoly that engineers would have held on the techniques of cost accounting, but to use these techniques to claim for the members of their profession the senior positions within Anglo-Saxon organizational hierarchies? This would seem to be a position to which, by virtue of their expertise in the control of labour – in scientific management and associated rational

organizational design and in cost accounting – engineers were surely entitled? But, as we have already noted, the techniques of cost accounting and scientific management were simply too lucid for engineers to retain exclusive rights over them. Other explanations require us to turn to the business context of the Anglo-Saxon world, where two key aspects are important. The first is the major reconstruction of US enterprises, exemplified and prototyped by Alfred P. Sloan Jr's restructuring of General Motors in response to the economic crisis of 1920–22. The following describes the key principles behind these restructurings (see also Jacques 1996: 106–10), on the importance of 'rationality' for wide-scope organizations and financial capitalism; and Chapter 4.

The audit and control

While this shift occurred later within the UK, Armstrong does note the existence of an early exemplar of a similar set of changes within Unilever. Nevertheless, the second factor that may be used to explain the rise of accountants in English-speaking organizational hierarchies is certainly common to both countries. That is, that the major source of finance for manufacturing firms in these countries is capital markets, which require the provision of audited accounts by the firms they support, in order to function. We can witness what happens when audit breaks down in terms of the guarantees it seems to offer investors in the Enron and World.com scandals which recently gripped the US. Exhibit 7.1 shows ten questions that non-executive directors should ask of their auditors in the wake of this fiasco.

In Germany and Japan similar shifts in organization to

Exhibit 7.1 Ten questions non-execs should ask the auditors

1. When did you last validate the relationship between our subsidiaries' real transactions and their own local records?

2. When did you last confirm that our consolidation system correctly reflects subsidiaries' locally recorded performance?

3. How often do you perform a diagnostic review of the contents of our consolidation system?

4. Do you apply automated tests to detect unusual subsidiary performance?

5. Have you identified any turning points in business indicators, such as orders or sales?

6. Do you check our smallest subsidiaries (since while they may never make much profit they could record huge losses)?

7. Does our board report contain the results of tests 4, 5 and 6 above, or is this information presented only to divisional management?

8. How much of this information are we disclosing to our bankers and shareholders?

9. Are we as non-executive directors able to access the underlying trends in any of our subsidiaries?

10. If this were your business, what would keep you awake at night?

Source: 'When it all adds up to disaster', Robert Bittlestone, *Observer*, Sunday April 14, 2002.

that exemplified by General Motors have occurred but, crucially, accountants did not have a toehold in the organizational hierarchy provided by audit requirements, since in these two countries the major sources of industrial finance were, respectively, the banks and government. Accountants were thus not in the same position to utilize the change in circumstances to engage in upward movement for their profession and its members. Indeed, in Germany in particular, techniques of cost accounting are still practised but such techniques are far from the sole preserve of accountants, and managerial hierarchies are dominated by those with an engineering background. In this context, key techniques of cost management are taught to engineering students at under- and postgraduate level.

But things are not entirely rosy for accountants or indeed bleak for engineers within the Anglo-Saxon world. Engineers who are willing and able to become general managers, through their mastering of the techniques and language of accountancy (for example cost allocation techniques, discounted cash flows, net present value and so on), often through participation on MBA programmes, can and do take on senior organizational roles, significant positions in the global function of capital. And not all accountants enjoy control over themselves and others as a result of their profession's success. Many find themselves in a similar position to that of the majority of engineers, doing fairly repetitive and unrewarding work, in both the financial and psychological senses, as they fulfil roles that have come to be defined as merely 'technical'.

These fissions within professions, dividing mere technical workers or specialists from more senior and general managers (Johnson 1980; Armstrong 1985), neatly illustrate the endlessly ramifying battles for control in organizations: battles which occur between and within professions and involve the deployment of all manner of potentially available resources. Similar games are played out most visibly in the current organizational world within and between the new professions of IT and business analysis and the older ones that surround them. Two points are particularly worthy of note here, and both concern the ways in which professions are able to garner control through their pact with wider society. As we have already noted, professions gain most control in relation to their clients in the wider society when they are able to monopolize not only the competence to perform tasks within their professional arena, but also the ability to judge that performance. To maintain control, ideally one wants to place oneself in a position where it is difficult for others who do not share one's profession to exercise judgement over one's activities. Since engineering activity, which may in itself be 'esoteric and inaccessible to lay judgement' (Armstrong 1985: 140), results in a product which can be judged by outsiders,

the maintenance of control positions by engineers often requires that they partially give up their engineering credentials to take on more general managerial, financial concerns. This is obviously less of a problem for accountants, whose work ends as a balance sheet or other set of accounts which they both draw up and can claim monopolistic expertise in the interpretation and judgement of. Indeed, it is this notion of 'interpretation' that explains the fission within accounting.

Accounting expertise has been divided into two parts: the codifiable technical aspects which are taught in basic training and form the stock in trade of those who merely produce accounts (a relatively low status occupation); and the more esoteric and experientially based interpretation of and acting upon those accounts which is seen to be the preserve of more senior individuals. This delegation of routine tasks on the part of the elite has the rather neat effect of preserving the sense of 'indetermination' of those activities that the elite retains, and thus helps to reinforce its monopoly of them (Armstrong 1985: 137). Such shifts have led some more junior accountants, with the support of key senior colleagues, to engage in new attempts at colonizing more general managerial control functions, through, for example, specifying the costs of quality and reasserting finance's role as the lingua franca that can enable the conversations across functions seen to be required in dynamic, contemporary circumstances (see for example Ezzamel et al. 1997, forthcoming). They have done so in the face of a renewed professional challenge for the position of organizational top dog, one that has been mounted by a reformed and renamed group of personnel specialists. The personnel profession, the managerial profession with historically the greatest representation of women and, perhaps consequently, in the sexist world of organizations, for long the mere handmaiden of real professional control, has finally made a big push for power. Rebranded as human resource management, this newly hungry profession has a new weapon in its armoury, that of culture. And culture is seen to form a key component of today's organizational control kit.

Discipline and seduction: the technologies of the self

The work of the historian, social theorist and philosopher Michel Foucault has provided a major impetus to consideration and theorization of control in organizations. Particularly important has been work building upon his 1977 book, *Discipline and Punish: the Birth of the Prison*. Here Foucault provides not only an account of the emergence of the modern prison, but also delineates a historical shift in the form of control employed in European societies. Through this shift the spectacular exercise of power by the sovereign, exemplified in acts of public torture, is replaced by the more detailed and continuous disciplining of the body throughout society, exemplified in its most extreme form by the total institution of the reformatory prison. At the centre of Foucault's argument is an account of the English philosopher Jeremy Bentham's putative model for an ideal prison: the panopticon. The panopticon design featured a central tower, occupied by the prison warders into which, through careful usage of lighting and blinds, it was impossible for prisoners to see. The prisoners themselves were to occupy largely open cells, organized in a concentric ring around the tower, in which they would always be potentially visible to those who occupied the tower.

Foucault builds upon Bentham's understanding of the functioning of this architectural arrangement to delineate how self-control of, by and through the individual is constructed through the action of an intermittent, but potentially omnipresent, surveillance acting upon that individual. According to Smart (1985: 88), the panopticon constitutes a method for 'the efficient exercise of power'. This efficiency is achieved by arranging those subject to power in such a way that at any moment they may be exposed to 'invisible' observation. Power works through the distribution of knowledge that the architectural arrangement determines. Prisoners 'know' they may be watched, but they don't know when. They know that if they transgress the rules, they will probably be caught (as a result of their visibility). But they must also know that the power that views them has available to it certain unpleasant sanctions that can be applied to punish and correct their behaviour; that misbehaviour will be apprehended and disciplined. The application of sanctions is only likely to be required in the early stages of the adoption of the panoptical mechanism and in the socialization of new members/inmates, because of the efficient functioning of the relationship between power and knowledge that is established within the set-up. This is because:

- If you know that you are always potentially visible, but don't know when you are being watched, the 'rational' thing to do is to control yourself, to act in the ways in which you think your overseer wants you to
- When this happens, the overseer is largely relieved of his or her responsibility, since you yourself assume 'responsibility for the constraints of power'
- In effect, you play both roles in the relationship of control – the controller and the controlled. You become the source of your own subjection (adapted from Foucault, 1982: 221–2).

Bentham did not see the potential uses of the panopticon as limited to the prison alone, but envisaged

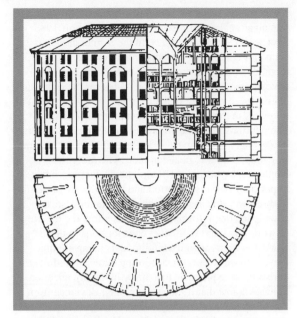

Figure 7.2 Bentham's panopticon
Source: http://is.gseis.ucla.edu/impact/f96/
Projects/dengberg.

its application in any arena in which a large number of subjects needed to be controlled by a small number of guards or overseers. Foucault uses the image of the panopticon to describe the forms of control increasingly adopted throughout modern society, forms of control in which direct confrontation with brute force seemingly becomes rarer and rarer. Instead, subjects assume responsibility for their own control: they control themselves in the knowledge that if they do not their inappropriate conduct will immediately be seen and corrected. They accept and enact discipline on and of themselves. Such an account of control differs from the notion of 'negative conditioning' offered by a Pavlovian or Skinnerian behaviourism (see for example Brown 1982). This is because it does not see the compliance on the part of the subject as an automatic response, a simple conditioned reflex to avoid pain. Rather it conceives of control as operating through the consciousness of the subject. This is control of the self by the self that results from the combination of reasoning and knowledge of the situation. The self, on the basis of the knowledge available to it, calculates the action most likely to result in reward and least likely to result in punishment (see for example, Miller and O'Leary 1987; Barnes 1988; Rose 1990).

These ideas have been deployed to account for control in organizations in a number of different ways. The two most prominent strands of this work are those which employ the ideas to make sense of contemporary human resource management (see for example Townley

1993) and the role of information systems in organizational control (see for example Zuboff 1988; Sewell and Wilkinson 1992). In the former case, decisions concerning the appropriate modes and methods of recruitment, selection, appraisal, development and compensation to deliver the right sort of employee working in the right sort of way are seen as exercises in the construction of appropriate 'selves'. The relationship of the employee to the organization is increasingly individualized, in the employment and the so-called 'psychological contract'. The individual employee, by 'reading' HRM systems, learns what is important to the organization and thus how to garner the best rewards that are available. In the latter case, the knowledge that information systems allow the tracking of work flows and individual contributions to those work flows is seen to lead individuals to ensure that they are always working according to, or exceeding, the norms of 'best practice' that apply in the organization. For they know that if they do not, their deviance from this ideal will immediately be identified and unpleasant consequences are likely to follow. However, such a distinction is somewhat unfounded. What both sets of work do is illustrate the interconnectedness of the collection and management of information on the individual with management of the individual: a process which works because individuals know that information on their conduct is being collected and assessed (see for example the various contributions to McKinlay and Starkey 1998; also Chapter 9). Graham Sewell and Barry Wilkinson build upon Zuboff's work to suggest

that the use of computer technologies can allow the construction of a panoptical mechanism that exceeds the limitations of visibility associated with the architectural version of the arrangement. What they term the *electronic panopticon* can enable control through the collection, storage and instantaneous display of data on individual performance on a scale that would be impossible if one were to rely on the extent of vision of a single human eye and the storage capacity of a single human memory. As long as information on each individual's performance can be delineated as an account of that individual's performance, that individual will discipline his or her own conduct to avoid being called to account.

It is crucial to note, however, that the applicability of Foucault's ideas is in no way limited to understanding the ways in which control operates within organizations. It also enables us to understand the operation of control in liberal-democratic societies more generally, as the work of writers such as Rose (1988, 1990), Miller and O'Leary (1987) and Foucault himself suggest. To illustrate this point and the role of computers in realizing the electronic panopticon, take a look at Exhibit 7.2, which is derived from promotional literature provided by Safeway's supermarket in the UK to introduce its customer-operated, bar-coded scanning device to its shoppers (see Bateson 1999: 40 and Kanter et al. 1990 for accounts of the origins of this innovation).

The ability to use the scanning device comes as part of a package. The customer receives an Added Bonus Card (ABC) on completion of a relatively detailed 'joining form'. This loyalty card is used to store accumulated discount and/or entitlements to 'free gifts' based upon prior spending, but it is also the key that allows the shopper access to 'the revolutionary *Self*Scan system' – the card is inserted into a unit housing a number of the scanners, one of which will flash to indicate that it is the one to be used. The ensemble is completed with the addition of the 'Safeway Green Box'. Four 'Green Boxes' sit snugly in the shopping trolley, and can be lifted straight from here to the boot of one's car, allowing a quick and easy exit once one's shopping is complete. One scans the bar codes of one's groceries by passing the head of the hand-held scanning device over the parallel lines of the item's bar code, while holding down a plus key. The price of the item is displayed on a LCD panel on the device and added to one's total shopping bill. If one decides to return an item to the shelves, its trace can be eliminated by repeating the above procedure while holding down the minus key. Pressing the equals key reveals a current subtotal and a count of the items scanned so far. At the end of one's shop, one simply returns the handset to any available housing in the dispenser unit and a summary of activities emerges, in the form of a bar-coded 'total' slip, to be read at the checkout and translated into a

---

Exhibit 7.2 Instructions on how to use '*Self*Scan'

Shopping has never been so easy!

The revolutionary *Self*Scan™ system, putting you in control

What is Self*Scan*™?

*Self*Scan™ is a unique hand held bar code scanner that you operate yourself. It allows you to scan your purchases as you shop. It tells you the price of every item, enabling you to monitor your total spend. It is a totally flexible system, that allows you to add or delete any item at any time during your shop …

Source: Safeway [UK] promotional leaflet.

For both your benefit and ours, the computer system will randomly select shopping to be re-checked for accuracy. The procedure is as follows. The first few times you self scan, you may have your shopping re-scanned at the checkout to ensure you have fully understood how to use the system. Further random checks will then occur on future shopping trips – determined solely by the computer system. No-one decides when to check you or knows the result of the check, however, the more accurate you are the less frequently you are likely to be checked. Equally, if you are inaccurate every time, your shopping is likely to be checked every time. Customer Service Staff can help you find out why if you ask them. After an accuracy check you will always be asked to pay the total shown by the till.

standard supermarket till receipt. Here, accumulated discount on one's ABC card is updated while payment is made. And, all being well, one leaves the store unhindered by any rechecking.

But how does Safeway ensure that the system is not abused? How does it make sure that one does scan all one's groceries? That one does not attempt to use the system to steal? Well, the store uses its computer system to operate a panoptical surveillance system, as the promotional leaflet goes on to note, under the neutral sounding title of 'accuracy' (see Exhibit 7.3).

The tying of the future 'randomness' of checks to past observation – 'the more accurate you are, the less frequently you are likely to be checked' – is just the sort of mechanism required for the 'internalization' of control on the part of the shopping subject. Safeway doesn't have to check everybody, every time they shop: by not allowing the customer to know when their shopping will be checked and by ensuring that sanctions follow from inappropriate conduct – being checked frequently and being asked to pay a till total different from that arrived at on one's own scanner are likely to be both annoying and embarrassing occurrences – Safeway can ensure that its customers take responsibility for disciplining themselves. Here, Safeway relies upon its customers' dislike of inconvenience and embarrassment in order to make them comply. Customers value less inconvenience and less embarrassment and thus, in the presence of the panoptical scheme, moderate their actions to ensure a minimum of both.

Controlling culture

In the world of work, however, management increasingly seeks to manipulate what employees value by various attempts to manage organizational culture (see Chapter 3). Such culture management can be seen as a key control technology and when arrayed next to consideration of the panopticon, it can be seen that what is being attempted here is control of the basis upon which the calculating selves of employees will do the calculation of their interests. That is, culture management attempts to ensure that the 'ends' against which employees will calculate the relative merit of various 'means' of action are those favoured by managers.

As we note in Chapter 3, the management of culture and ideology has been a major theme in the literature of management and organization during the 1980s and 90s, strongly reflected in the Peters and Waterman bestseller *In Search of Excellence* (1982). The fifth attribute of the excellence formula, 'hands-on, value-driven' is essentially about belief systems. The two authors identify seven beliefs held by excellent companies, as shown in Exhibit 7.4.

Socialization plays a huge role in the inculcation of such beliefs, as Chester Barnard was only too aware (see the section above 'The profession of management'). Applicants to excellent companies are chosen to ensure that they fit with the existing organizational culture. Peters and Waterman claim that many of the companies they talked to were 'known for bringing potential recruits back seven or eight times for

Exhibit 7.4 **Excellence culture**

1. A belief in being the best

2. A belief in the importance of the details of execution, the nuts and bolts of doing the job well

3. A belief in the importance of people as individuals

4. A belief in superior quality and service

5. A belief that most members of the organization should be innovators, and its corollary, the willingness to support failure

6. A belief in the importance of informality to enhance communication, and

7. Explicit belief in and recognition of the importance of economic growth and profit

Source: T.J. Peters and R.H. Waterman (1982) *In Search of Excellence*, New York: Harper & Row, p. 285.

interviews' (1982: 265). Expected ways of behaving are inculcated through myths, particularly founder stories, rituals (for example management talks every morning), behavioural reinforcement and 'new languages' (for example 'boot-legging', 'unjustified variations') (Peters and Waterman 1982: 106–7, 264, 280–1). Transformational leadership plays an important part in the philosophy of excellence. In this regard, Peters and Waterman approvingly offer a supporting quotation from Pettigrew:

The [leader] not only creates the rational and tangible aspects of organisations, such as structure and technology, but is also the creator of symbols, ideologies, language, beliefs, rituals and myths. (Peters and Waterman 1982: 104)

Joseph Soeters has drawn attention to the uncanny parallel between the attributes of the excellence philosophy and the characteristics of social movements (Soeters 1986: 299–311). Indeed, many of Peters and Waterman's management heroes appear to behave like religious evangelists. Control by corporate culture views people as 'emotional, symbol-loving and needing to belong to a superior entity of collectivity [the organization]' (Ray 1986: 295). But by meeting this need by providing a culture to which people can 'belong', control is also enabled by managing what people 'value' and thus what they will consider as important when engaging in self-calculation of the best course of action to follow.

Attitudes and values also appear to play a major part in the rhetoric of total quality control (or total quality management (TQM) as it is sometimes called), the other significant management movement of the 1980s which shows little signs of going away in the new millennium. As we note in Chapter 11, TQM 'sought to transform the entire work culture or ethic of Western business to mirror the values, norms and attitudes (that is, culture) of Japanese workplaces … through a strong collective orientation to continuous improvement'. Its apparent aim is to design goods and services to customer specification with zero defects. Various control techniques are applied to monitor input and throughput processes but the key to the successful use of such techniques is seen as the prior development of 'quality awareness' at all levels in the organization (Dale and Plunkett 1990: 15). Collard (1990) stresses that quality management has less to do with economic or technological considerations than with people and management factors, as we also note in Chapters 9 and 11. The assumption seems to be that the manipulation of culture can increase collective loyalty and even love of the firm, so that increased productivity follows (Ray 1986: 294). The other assumption is that this 'love' will translate into appropriate things being valued – in this case managerially defined notions of what constitutes

'good' quality – when one calculates what is the right thing to do in any given situation. This is the seductive counterpart of disciplinary control – the management of the ideals in the image of which one will seek to discipline one's self. Thus, although proponents of corporate cultural management often render their activities as morally worthwhile, since they seem to promote autonomy in the workplace (see for example Ouchi 1981: 84–5), this moral claim is a chimera, as Hugh Willmott (1993: 515) has eloquently demonstrated. For real autonomy *cannot possibly be realized* 'in monocultural conditions that systematically constrain opportunities to wrestle with competing values, standpoints and their associate life projects'.

If what one values has been decided for one, by somebody else, in advance, and it is on the basis of what one values that one decides what is best to do, one is exercising self-control only in a fairly empty sense. Control is passing through the self, but the self is not the origin of the basis of control, merely its relay in a wider system, a system which itself is centred elsewhere.

Emotional control

While we will discuss ideas of emotional labour in relation to motivation in greater detail in Chapter 9, it is important here for us to note that although organizational structure has been strongly associated

---

Exhibit 7.5 Bureaucracy and emotion

The peculiarity of modern culture, and specifically of its technical and economic basis, demands this very 'calculability' of results. When fully developed, bureaucracy also stands, in a specific sense, under the principle of *sine ira et studio*. Bureaucracy develops the more perfectly, the more it is 'dehumanised', the more completely it succeeds in eliminating from official business love, hatred and all purely personal, irrational and emotional elements which escape calculation (Max Weber 1978: 975).

In general bureaucratic domination has the following general consequences:

The dominance of a spirit of formalistic impersonality: *Sine ira et studio*, without hatred or passion, and hence without affection or enthusiasm (Max Weber 1978: 225)

Source: Adapted from Max Weber (1978) *Economy and Society,* trans. G. Roth and C. Wittich, Berkeley, CA: University of California Press, extracted in Martin Albrow (1997) *Do Organizations Have Feelings?* London: Routledge.

with rationality, especially in Weber's theory of bureaucracy, as we discussed in Chapter 4, this has stemmed from a rather lazy reading of Weber. From Exhibit 7.5, we can see that bureaucracy is in fact *centred* around emotion, but from the point of view of controlling or eradicating it. Emotion is not something banished by bureaucracy: on the contrary it is so prevalent in organizational life that it is the very *raison d'être* of bureaucracy. Organizations develop rules not just to govern the actions of their members, but to control their feelings – or at least, how far those feelings may be allowed to intrude into their everyday working lives. In some cases, as we discuss in Chapter 9, there are formal prescriptions of the sort of emotion which employees are allowed or expected to display, especially in customer contact roles. Yet in most organizations, there are also informal 'rules', or strong expectations, that people will not regularly display certain types of emotion, and this may be gendered. For example, male managers may be allowed or even expected to display anger regularly, but not to burst into tears. On the other hand, for a female manager, the occasional display of tearful emotionality may pass unremarked. The point, for Weber as well as for us, is that organizations are fields where reason and emotion meet and the ground where they struggle. Reason without emotion would be unthinkable, emotion without reason intolerable. Control is necessary to maintain a sensible balance between the two, which may vary from situation to situation, but it should be precisely that – control of the balance between the two, not the control of emotion by reason, which is all too often how the problem of emotionality is interpreted.

Culture, context and control

We have already touched upon cross-cultural notions of control in our discussion of the relative status of the profession of accounting in the organizational hierarchies of different countries. Here we briefly return to this theme of difference in control techniques in different geographical regions, as a means to link our preceding discussion on the use of culture as a control technology with the increasing importance of 'globalization' within the discourses of organizational control. The salience attributed to culture, as a key part of the means of organizational control in businesses of the West, arose at a particular time, the 1980s, and in a particular context, that of growing fears in the West about the rise of the Japanese challenge (see for example Halberstam 1987; Chapter 3). Thus we can 'read' the rise of corporate culture *in the West*, as a response to the rise of Japan as a key source of business competition for the organizations *of the West*. This response may be seen as one in which an attempt is made to mimic those aspects of Japanese organizational practice that are seen to be the source of Japanese business success. Indeed, the subtitle of Bill Ouchi's (1981) *Theory Z*, an account of how culturally bonded 'clan' organizations can offer a new recipe for business success, is *How American Business Can Meet the Japanese Challenge!* As Phil Hancock (1997) argues, and our preceding discussion intimates, much of the corporate culture literature can be seen as an attempt to return to feudal forms of organization in which loyalty to one's Lord was enacted through obedience expressed by rituals and ceremonies of a symbolic nature. In such a world, one does not follow rationally constructed rules, as one would in a Weberian bureaucracy (see Chapter 4). Rather one devotes oneself to the corporation as a cultural entity and source of meaning.

As Hugh Willmott (1993: 531) notes, it is no accident that 'Japan, the spiritual home of corporate culturism' is one of the places in world in which the European 'Enlightenment break with feudal values is less advanced'. Feudal-like aspects of Japanese organizational life, strongly imbued with Confucian values, include practices within the financial institutions which fund business activity, the closeness of the industry–government relationship (Eccleston 1989) and the expectation, which held until relatively recently, that one would 'serve' the same organization for the whole of one's working life while, reciprocally, the organization fulfilled various relatively extensive (by Western standards) obligations to its employees. In such circumstances, organizational control enacted through cultural means is not a new invention, an add-on to extant techniques, rather it forms part of the essence of the ordinary and entirely natural – for members of Japanese society – way in which things get done.

Japan did not experience the Enlightenment. The Japanese society that underwent industrialization in the nineteenth and twentieth century did so with feudal values that expressed a Confucian ethic … The Japanese worker does not think of himself as engaged in an economic function (being an electrical engineer, a production engineer, lathe operator, accountant and so on) which is divorced from the firm, an occupational function that can be done anywhere. He is a Hitachi man, a Honda man, and so on, a member of a community. It is a profoundly different way of looking at work. (Locke 1989: 50–1, in Willmott 1993: 545)

As the quote makes clear, this profound difference in the way of looking at work is related to other profound differences in the wider context of work. Thus any attempt to transplant and exploit this way of looking at work in a different context is likely to succeed only to the extent that the salient aspects of the original context can be transplanted as well (see also the example of NUMMI, discussed in Chapter 11). Nevertheless, in the contemporary climate, the relative rise (and fall) of the fortunes of nations such as Japan has been reinscribed within a homogenizing discourse of everything: the discourse of globalization. It is to this discourse that we now turn because it frequently functions as the justification for all manner of organizational impositions and thus as a key rhetorical resource in organizational control.

Globalization and the rhetoric of necessity

As we have intimated throughout our account, persuasion of one sort or another has been seen as an increasingly important ingredient of success in the achievement of control, since the inception of 'management' as a separate occupation. And the current trump term in matters of persuasion is the dictates of 'globalization' – the new, world brand of the profession of marketing (see for example Naomi Klein's (2000) *No Logo*). The discourse of globalization works on those who are subjected to it through its positing of an increasingly liberated and demanding customer – the embodiment of freedom – who will always take the best that the world can offer. And one can only garner the right to continue to survive by being one of the best, by accepting the controls that customers, mediated by markets, demand. In their unmasking of the rhetorical power of the globalization discourse. Bobby Banerjee and Stephen Linstead (2001) note the myriad ways in which this discourse, which operates in the name of us all, as consumers, has taken hold over the last 20 years. Statements about living in a 'global village', where national boundaries and cultures melt into one, are frequently made and taken for granted, consuming 'global' brands, such as NIKE, lends power to the discourse, corporations continually talk about having to be competitive in the 'global marketplace', and governments push the rhetoric of having to respond to the 'global' economy (Banerjee and Linstead 2001: 684). Today of course, it is 'global terrorism'.

Globalization appears here as an unstoppable force of progress, the collective outcome of our individual free choices as consumers, an unalloyed good. But, as Bannerjee and Linstead also note, there is much here that we can argue with: that the power of this rhetoric can be muted by asking some uncomfortable questions, that there is much in globalization that, far from being progressive, perpetuates colonialism. Globalization may be considered as a means of control precisely because its rhetoric renders it as inevitable, a force of nature that must be accommodated. To stand against globalization is to be seen to adopt the position of Canute, the king who vainly sought to test his powers by standing on the beach commanding the tide not to come in! It is used by governments to justify the dismantling of costly social institutions, in order to maintain a country's global competitiveness, and by managers who demand plant closures, redundancies and/or low wages to ensure similar competitiveness for their organizations. But beneath the rhetoric sits an uncomfortable reality. For example, there is little that is new or indeed even radical about the internationalization of the economy. Banerjee and Linstead suggest that changes in the international economy have been taking place since the nineteenth century but this does not mean that the world is global. In fact they state that: 'international penetration of financial markets in OECD countries was actually greater between 1900 and 1914 than in the 1980s, as was the ratio of foreign trade and GDP' (Banerjee and Linstead 2001: 688, drawing on Hirst and Thompson 1998).

What is new is how internationalization is talked about, how it appears as outside of choice, as just the way in which things are and increasingly will be. What this masks are the decisions and actions taken by individuals, organizations and governments to enact this state of affairs, and the recognition that 'the socio-cultural impacts of globalization are not the result of free and self-regulating market economies but the result of coordinated political and economic management' (Banerjee and Linstead 2001: 689). In other words, managers and governors use power, particularly the power of the rhetoric of globalization, 'to force people to participate in the economy in a certain way' (Haddon 1971: 23, cited in Banerjee and Linstead 2001: 689). This alerts us to the fact that despite its universalizing rhetoric, the impact of globalization is far from even.

Certain people, countries, institutions and organizations benefit from the operation of globalization while many others do not. Indeed Banerjee and Linstead draw on the work of both Bauman (1998) and Castells (1998) to suggest that the reality of globalization is better captured as a remapping and restructuring of the inequalities of the system of economic exchanges that the world supports. In this process, different rights and responsibilities are handed out to different people in different positions in the world order. Indeed, the position of some seems to be to stay in (an increasingly impoverished) place, while others get to go where they please. These lucky few have little time, they are always in demand as they jet between the centres of decision making in the globalized world. They receive handsome material rewards, as the supply of the sort of competent managers and governors that the world demands is seemingly limited. For many, with the resources to consume, travel is also a possibility while their other desires are recognized by the system, collectively, in an endless supply of new goods. For the majority, however, the only resource at their disposal is their

Exhibit 7.6 From global migration to global trafficking

It cannot be repeated too often that the issue of migration cannot be separated from the workings of the global economy (Skrobanek et al. 1997: 20). As the global economy becomes more integrated, we see more and more people working far from their place of origin; and since the trajectory of such displacement is usually from poor countries to rich, it is only to be expected that the wealthy countries seek to exclude people they now refer to as 'economic migrants'. People will naturally seek to circumvent such arbitrary restrictions and will find a way of crossing boundaries. This leads to more and more people living in conditions of secrecy, as hidden or clandestine inhabitants of the countries in which they labour; which in turn exposes them to greater levels of exploitation and ill-treatment (Skrobanek et al. 1997: 12).

The trafficking of human beings is a complicated subject. Migrant labourers, especially illegal migrant labourers, frequently find themselves forced into exploitative working conditions. In this sense they are just like the victims of trafficking. But migrant labourers have not necessarily been tricked or deceived during the migration process. Trafficking, on the other hand, refers to the transportation of people within countries or across international borders using force, trickery or the abuse of power.

People, men, women and children, are trafficked in order to channel them into exploitative forms of labour. There is a massive trade in these people because they are relatively poor to start with and they will accept lower wages and tolerate worse working conditions than local labourers – trafficked people are easy to manipulate and exploit because they are made to be dependent on others. Some trafficking victims are employed in sweatshops or on building sites. Sometimes they are trafficked to work as domestic servants, as beggars and sometimes as prostitutes (Brown 2000: 21–2).

Source: Adapted from Siriporn Skrobanek, Nattaya Boonpakdi and Chutima Janthakeero (1997) *The Traffic in Women: Human Realities of the Sex Trade,* London and New York: Zed Books; and Louise Brown (2000) *Sex Slaves: The Trafficking of Women in Asia,* London: Virago.

poverty, which enables them to sell their labour cheaply. For them, travel, if it occurs, is a necessity that must be undertaken in order to find work (see Exhibit 7.6). Indeed, for a truly unfortunate few it may be an imposition, as they are sold and moved to meet the needs of consumers in an increasingly 'globalized' sex industry, as Exhibit 7.7 illustrates (Banerjee and Linstead 2001: 713).

Exhibit 7.7 Hierarchy and networks in the traffic in women

An international trafficking hierarchy parallels Asia's economic pecking order. At the bottom are the poorest nations. These are the 'sending' countries that export their women. They are typified by Bangladesh, Vietnam and Nepal. These countries do not import women because there is no one else poor enough to consider it financially worthwhile to sell sex in these desperately poor societies. At the top of the pecking order are 'receiving' countries: those rich societies that host sex workers from the poorer sending countries. The best example of a receiving country is Japan, which imports women from just about everywhere.

In the middle of the international trafficking networks are countries that have multiple functions: they are transit countries acting as brokers in the trafficking process and they can also be both receiving and sending countries. India and Thailand are the prime examples and both run an incredibly busy trade in women. To give just a few examples of the way trafficking networks operate, there are thought to be well over a hundred thousand Nepali prostitutes in India, hundreds of thousands of Burmese women in Thai brothels and over a hundred thousand Thais and Filipinas in Japan. The existence of 'Little Bangkoks' and 'Little Manilas' in Japan is well known. And now there are also 'Little Colombias', 'Little Russias' and 'Little Romanias' too. The list goes on. Name a country with economic problems, limited opportunities for females and a flourishing criminal underworld and you can guarantee that at least some of its women will be recruited for Japan's vast and very demanding sex industry.

Source: Adapted from Louise Brown (2000) *Sex Slaves: The Trafficking of Women in Asia,* London: Virago, p. 23.

Gender and control

Our last point above highlights the ways in which gender is also embroiled in the processes and practices of control. As Bannerjee and Linstead (2001: 713) note:

The number of women involved in, sold into, trapped into or indentured by the global sex industry dwarfs the number of male providers of similar services.

But it is not only at such margins that we can witness the interrelationship of gender and control. For example, Patricia Yancey Martin (2001) examines accounts from a number of women concerning their experiences of the ways in which men 'mobilize masculinities' at work, in ways that are often associated with their exercise of control. She noted the ways in which her female informants were able to see much of their male colleagues' activity at work as unrelated to the formal tasks at hand, despite being rendered by those men as part of their normal work activity. Sometimes this behaviour could be interpreted as being concerned with competing with other men, both inside and outside the organization: men would 'peacock' as they 'vie[d] with each other for attention'; 'self-promote', through gregariously aggrandizing their personal contribution; 'dominate' or subordinate female colleagues; and 'expropriate' the labour and efforts of others, either by not acknowledging the contribution or indeed by passing it off as their own (Martin 2001: 601). But they could not seem to see themselves as doing anything other than ordinary work. At other times they mobilized and displayed their masculinities to other men in an effort to affiliate with them, to form alliances. These alliances could be for self and/or mutual benefit or to protect a fellow man, for example from the consequences of their poor job performance. Such activities could involve 'visiting' other men, 'sucking up' to them, 'supporting' them or 'expressing fondness' for them (Martin 2001: 602–3) and, consequently, decisions could be based upon 'liking or disliking' rather than 'official/organizational' criteria (Martin 2001: 602). Needless to say, such practices meant that women often found themselves out of the loop of organizational control. Once again, although such behaviours were seen, by Martin's female informants, as being particularly masculine and unrelated to the 'real' job at hand, the men involved seemed unable to see them as anything other than the routine, genderless enactment of organizational life. Nevertheless, these behaviours were felt to be unpleasant and distracting by the women who witnessed them. As she notes, they marginalize women and serve to keep them outside the key circuits of power:

When men mobilize masculinity/ies in meetings or interactions at or in work, they conflate masculinity/ies processes with working processes. Conflation consists of a fusing of masculinities and working, with the result that *work fosters masculinity/ies.*

The women's accounts indicate that conflated work and masculinity dynamics sap energy, waste time; communicate that men are concerned with something other than work; show that men and women are 'different'; and make them feel excluded. It is perhaps noteworthy that men are able to conflate working and masculinities because they predominate in the powerful positions and because men and masculinity have more legitimacy (than do women and femininity) in work contexts. (Martin 2001: 605)

Masculinity and control fixation

A number of points are worth pursuing here. Through their mobilization of masculinity, men make work a masculine place, a place in which women always appear as different and to which they find themselves, to some extent, excluded. But it is not just masculinity in the singular that Martin (2001) draws attention to. As she carefully notes, there are different ways of doing 'masculine' within organizations, a theme which we take up by considering a paper by David Knights and Darren McCabe (2001) that looks at the masculinities associated with a set of organizational changes in a UK financial services organization. Although they delineate two particular types of masculinity in their paper, Knights and McCabe note that the thing that links them, that justifies the label of masculinity being applied to both, *is their abiding concern with control*:

The relationship between modern management and masculinity is the association of the former with engineering and other technological skills that are explicitly instrumental in controlling the objects of their domain ... Masculine discourses ... are uncomfortable with that (e.g. the social) which is beyond control. (Knights and McCabe 2001: 622–3)

What distinguishes the two masculinities that Knight and McCabe discuss – a macho masculinity associated with a new, business process re-engineering discourse and an older, more 'gentlemanly' paternalistic one – is the way in which each seeks, in its own way, to control intimacy, to marshal and order the unpredictable elements of the social. The paternalist discourse they identify is associated with an older, formal, hierarchical arrangement of the organization in which individual bank branches were central players. This paternalism 'clearly has resonance with patriarchal, father–child relationships' but it also 'facilitates the development and legitimacy of hierarchy by giving the appearance of 'softening' the inequality through fatherly and even communal intimacy' (Knights and McCabe 2001: 627–8). However, any intimacy that is expressed within such an organization is 'feigned' and/or very strictly circumscribed. In a paternalistic atmosphere, there is a general discomfort with social relations, and particularly that most potent form of social relations, that charged with sexuality. By managing the way in which intimacy is displayed, by minimizing its expression, the paternalist can protect himself 'from what is ordinarily uncertain, unpredictable and uncontrollable in social relations – namely sexuality' (Knights and McCabe 2001: 628; see also Kerfoot and Knights 1993).

Although often 'caring', the hierarchy of paternalism is one in which formality is the order of the day, the messiness of real intimacy is kept at bay and is clearly ruled and decided upon by the father figure at the top of the tree. Such structures bestow power and prestige on those who sit on top of them, both inside and outside the organization. But they are also essentially about preventing the eruption of the uncertainty and unpredictability associated with a freely social environment, about keeping the social and the sexual strictly in its place (which, for that latter particularly, means outside the borders of the organization!). And it is important to note here that although (a particular form) of masculinity is dominant here, and it is one that supports the placing of men in positions of superiority, men are not immune either from its control or the more damaging aspects of its reach. Much of this has to do with the invisibility of the discourse, particularly for those who are privileged by it (cf. Martin, above) and for Knights and McCabe (2001: 641) that is perhaps the 'greatest tragedy of masculinity'. Those managers who express it most profoundly and who are consequently rewarded for such expression with passage up the organizational hierarchy, seem those most 'oblivious to its embrace' (Knights and McCabe 2001: 641).

This problem is particularly clear in the second masculinity that Knights and McCabe consider, the more macho form of the discourse that they saw as particularly associated with the bank's efforts to engage in a re-engineering of its processes. As a result of this change, branches were significantly diminished in importance as more and more work was conducted in and through call centres and extensive, centralized back office processing sites. Consonant with much of the language of business process re-engineering (BPR) (see Grint 1994; Case and Grint 2001; Knights and McCabe 2001, particularly: 623–6), tough managers were seen to be making tough decisions, imposing a new process-oriented organization on often unwilling employees, in the name of the good of the organization as a whole. 'BPR is nothing if not aggressive, rationalist and control fixated' (Knights and McCabe 2001: 625). But in order for the new structures to work, a different strand of the BPR message was called upon, one focusing upon 'teamworking and a concern with employee creativity' (Knights and McCabe 2001: 625;

but see also Chapter 9 in this volume). Such a focus entailed regular team meetings in which not only functional issues were discussed, but broader feedback was encouraged. Meetings 'were designed specifically to "open up" one's emotions' (Knights and McCabe: 641) to enable the intimacy that real teamwork and creativity were seen to depend upon. However, our macho managers, in their 'quest for control, power and status ... recoil from emotional displays, which call into question their claim to objectivity, rationality, omniscience and omnipotence' (Knights and McCabe: 640). For 'emotions are difficult to control; they are unpredictable and render those who express them vulnerable to charges of irrationality and instability and ultimately incompetence' (Knights and McCabe: 640). As a result, the toughness and single-mindedness they adopted in order to push through the macho demands of the BPR initiative look likely to themselves prevent the complete success of the programme:

If a team spirit is to develop, and managers are to become 'mentors', encouraging 'invention and discovery, creativity and synthesis', it will be necessary for them to go beyond simply dictating orders in a cold, impersonal and disembodied manner. (Knights and McCabe 2001: 640)

By buying one side of the BPR package, managers, through the form of masculinity they had adopted, found themselves almost obliged to reject and resist the other side. And it is to the possibilities for resistance more generally that we turn in our concluding section.

Resistance and control

Foucault's conception of power has often been read as leaving no place for resistance. He has suggested that 'power is "always already there", that one is never outside it, and there are no margins for those who break with the system to gambol in' (Foucault 1980: 141). But to make such a claim does not foreclose on the possibility of resistance. Resistance in this rendering merely appears as productive of and for 'power', not as something outside, standing against it. As David Knights and Theo Vurdubakis (1994: 180) note:

Resistance ... plays the role of continuously provoking extensions, revisions and refinements of those same practices it confronts.

To illustrate their point, Knights and Vurdubakis provide the example of IT consultants who utilize the notion of sites of ' "resistance to change" ... as [a] crucial vehicle ... through which the services and expertise of consultants are sold, and spaces of intervention carved out in client organizations' (Knights and Vurdubakis 1994; Bloomfield and Vurdubakis 1994). The existence of 'resistance' serves here to legitimate the instigation and extension of practices that seek to combat it. And this extension of practices will probably provoke further resistance, providing further grounds for further 'extensions, revisions and refinements'. This gaming is endless. Indeed, for Foucault 'there are no relations of power without resistance' (1980: 142, cited in Knights and Vurdubakis 1994). But this does not mean that, to use the old Hollywood war film phrase, 'resistance is futile'. Rather it shows that power and resistance have much in common and the latter is likely to be more effective and substantial precisely because it emerges at precisely those locations where power is exercised.

A similar case may be made about the power relations surrounding the self-scanning regime we considered earlier and the 'resistance' to it that may take the form of exploiting the extended opportunities for shoplifting that the system potentially offers. It is the possibility for resistance through theft, provided by the system, that necessitates the computerized 'accuracy' checks. It is the possibility of resistance that calls power to control. All of which takes us back to our initial points concerning the emergence of the profession of management. Management is required because we employ *people* who carry with them particular skills, knowledge and aptitudes that are necessary for the smooth running of organizations. Because they are people they will always resist, because when they give up resisting they give up the ingenuity and rational abilities that make them people and that made them attractive as employees in the first place. As Foucault notes:

power is only exercised over free subjects and only insofar as they are free … for where the determining factors saturate the

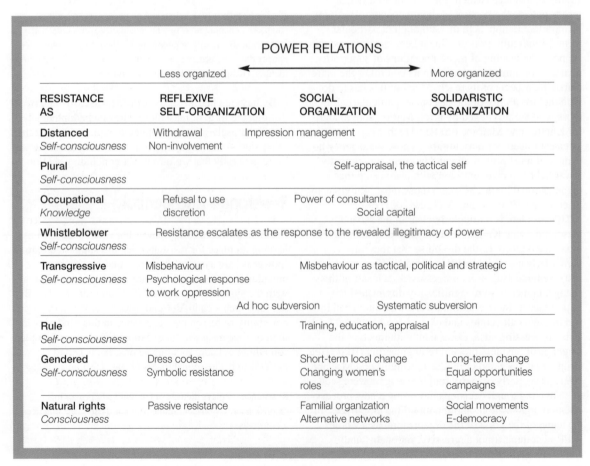

Figure 7.3 Power/resistance matrix

Source: Adapted by Stephen Linstead from Stewart Clegg 'Power relations and the constitution of the resistant subject' in John M. Jermier, David Knights and Walter R. Nord (eds) (1994) *Resistance and Power in Organizations,* London: Routledge, p. 298.

whole there is no relationship of power. (Foucault 1982: 225, cited in Knights and Vurdubakis 1994: 179)

Clegg argues that who the 'subject' is in any context of power relations will vary along a continuum from less extensive organization to more extensive organization, with self-aware self-organization at one end of the continuum, social organization in the middle, and solidaristic organization (for example trade union militancy) at the other. The type of resistance will also be affected by the psychological consciousness of the subject, that is to say, who individuals think they are in this relational context. He argues that as a result of this interaction there are a variety of possible types of resistance which can be represented, as in Figure 7.3:

- *Distanced self-consciousness* – where the individual is isolated or disengaged from organizational practice, or alienated from other workers, may be seen in such strategies as impression management, where the idea is to appear to be doing what the organization wants superficially but without commitment or investment. Resistance here is to psychological incorporation, allowing the organization to have one's body but not the heart and mind, and may be little more than the symbolic reclamation of individuality. In a bakery factory where Stephen Linstead (1985a) did fieldwork, a typically desensitizing and authoritarian production line environment where everyone had to wear the same white overalls and hats, the workers found ways to express their individuality by folding the hats in different ways, wearing them at different angles or subtly decorating them with small, almost imperceptible designs and mottoes.
- *Plural self-consciousness* – this is where the recognition that selves may be plural offers another possibility for resistance. Here the self-aware individual may operationalize different organizational selves for different contexts, and may express this in manipulating such organizational devices as self-appraisal schemes. It may also be seen in the ways in which individuals tactically decide who they will present themselves as from different organizational situation to situation, and even in the separation of work self from 'real' self.
- *Professional self-consciousness* – occupational knowledge is another dimension of consciousness which individuals may exploit. This may extend from the realization of the need for operator discretion in some of the smallest tasks, and its withdrawal, to the political consciousness of consultants using their specialist knowledge for power purposes (Buchanan and Badham 2000). It also contains the idea of social capital, where, particularly but not exclusively in the cases of

professionals, networks of educational and social contacts enable them to move between organizations, often taking customers or clients with them (see Chapter 16).
- *Whistleblower self-consciousness* – often starts with an individual making an ethical stand on an issue, without knowing what broader support may be necessary. The strength of this consciousness grows as the organization makes its responses and the social mobilization of resistance into collective resistance may be a function of the repressive nature of such a response and the effectiveness of communication.
- *Transgressive self-consciousness* – seems to have a different and somewhat disjointed dynamic – at one end of the continuum it contains acts which are psychological responses to frustration or oppression; at the other end it contains acts which are deliberate, premeditated and part of organized campaigns to disrupt the functioning of the organization. Sometimes they may fall somewhere between the two, as in the case of shift rivalries discussed in the Company T case in Chapter 3, and in Linstead (1985b). Clegg calls this 'saboteur behaviour'.
- *Rule consciousness* – indicates the degree to which individuals are trained, educated and informally socialized into workplace practices. Knowing how formal and informal rules are to be applied and when is key to the proper functioning of an organization, and resistance may be found in overrigid application of the rules, when exceptions would normally be made, and deliberate bending of the rules. In Linstead's research, the unions effected a 'work-to-rule' by exploiting a loophole in the company's training rules, which said that anyone who worked with a piece of equipment needed to follow a training course and be 'passed out' after a test by the training officer and supervisor. The union insisted, during a period of particularly tense pay and terms negotiations – that this meant any piece of equipment, including buckets, brooms and squeegees (Linstead 1984). This was, temporarily, extremely disruptive to the normal functioning of the factory.
- *Gendered self-consciousness* – involves the recognition that the individual is not just a worker but also a man or a woman in the workplace, however that recognition arises. This may encompass symbolic resistance, as in the manipulation of dress codes or the personalization of work stations in call centres, through the coordination of action to achieve both short and long agendas for change in the workplace and beyond, as discussed in Chapter 2.
- *Natural rights consciousness* – may be both the most basic form of resistance in the form of a passive

refusal to do something which violates either one's own or another's basic rights, through to the development of alternative networks to represent, lobby or embody different sets of values in the workplace (for example, The Body Shop's initial attempts to structure itself around the values of the family) through to the use of new technologies by trade unions, social movements and other activists to campaign and promote forms of e-democracy.

Organizational misbehaviour

Ackroyd and Thompson (1999) in Figure 7.4 argue that there are some forms of behaviour which, while disruptive to organizational functioning, are not sufficiently directed or sustained to be accurately termed 'resistance', and are more appropriately understood as *organizational misbehaviour*. These forms of behaviour vary from the committed and engaged to the detached and hostile on the one hand, and involve different types of appropriation (or reappropriation) of time, work, product and identity from the organization's control, all of which have a

tendency to become rendered as organizational commodities. At the most integrated with the organization's functioning, these may involve the manipulation of time perks, breaks and time off; the appropriation and use of the product for personal purposes; or the manipulation of activity to serve personal goals as well as organizational ones, including the reprioritization of goals. At the most hostile end, this could include turnover, destructiveness and sabotage, theft, or the achievement of a class or group solidarity which may be militant against organizational practices and ends.

Clegg (1994: 294) also considers the ways in which resistance may be 'outflanked', that is, anticipated by the powerful and defused even before it occurs. Indeed, Clegg argues that consideration of this needs to come *before* consideration of resistance, as resistance can only occur when people are conscious that issues exists. Clegg identifies that outflanking can be achieved through keeping people in ignorance of the true nature of their situation, secrecy and operation behind closed doors; keeping people isolated from each other and in a state of frustration, so that they fail to see events which are strategically related as being connected; keeping

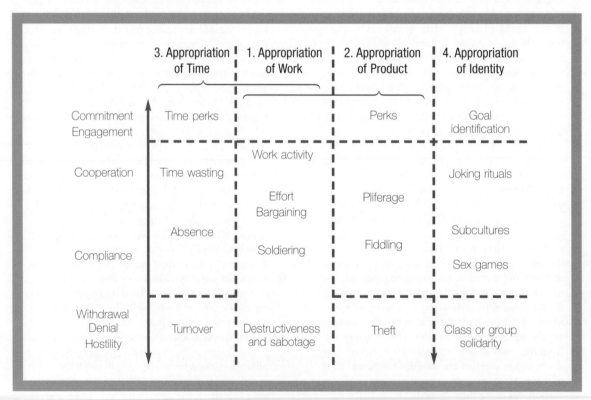

Figure 7.4 Dimensions of misbehaviour

Source: from Stephen Ackroyd and Paul Thompson (1999) *Organizational Misbehaviour,* London: Sage. Reprinted by permission of Sage Publications Ltd. Copyright © Sage Publications 1999.

them divided and focused upon their own interests and problems, either through inter-sectional conflict or personal instrumentality; or by providing a heavily biased form of knowledge, which weights the negative consequences of resistance or even alternative forms of behaviour so that the odds against success are perceived as being overwhelming. Clegg notes that effective resistance depends on differing degrees of contact and cooperation possible with others, overcoming isolation, diverting knowledge flows and sharing experiences.

Finally, he argues that resistance in a situation where knowledge is distributed widely, if unevenly, characterizes employment relations in most of the advanced economies, where power and resistance share the same space and do not play 'winner-takes-all' or 'win–lose' games, but play out their respective roles in an ongoing drama in which both will continue to exist. This view has an interesting consistency with the approach that we will take to conflict and negotiation in Chapter 12.

POWER RELATIONS

Less organized ⟵⟶ More organized

OUTFLANKING OF RESISTANCE THROUGH	REFLEXIVE SELF-ORGANIZATION	SOCIAL ORGANIZATION	SOLIDARISTIC ORGANIZATION
Ignorance	Individuals kept in ignorance of others in similar situations *Resistance* by 'coming out'	Ignorance of the cultural networks of power *Resistance* through culture and culture clash	Ignorance of potential groups of organizational allies *Resistance* through defiance, strikes
Isolation	Events and actions not connected Strategically – viewed with fatalism *Resistance* through frustration, alienation Anomie	Active searches begin for allies who will help to combat isolation – begin to connect individual resistances which can then be less easily regarded as examples of individual deviance	
Division	Divided life worlds lead to compartmentalization of life and work, department or division *Resistance* may happen through creation of psychic compartments e.g. the instrumental worker seeking to maximize reward for every effort	The powerful in organizations play a game of divide and rule, thinking strategically and using perspective *Resistance* can only occur through communication, coordination and the perception of common interest or common cause – and this may extend internationally	
Knowledge	Costs of resistance made very clear to those who might resist *Resistance* to overwhelming odds may be more symbolic than real People may be more bound up with everyday life issues of survival, doing something will make a difference rather than support lost causes	Knowledge exists and is distributed on both sides, but formal arenas for organization and formal resources of organization (e.g. collective bargaining agreements and closed shop trade union membership) are necessary for meaningful resistance to occur *Resistance* may become ritualistic (e.g. collective bargaining in some industries) Power and resistance coexist in a drama where neither threatens the continuance and reproduction of the other	

Figure 7.5 Outflanking resistance

Source: Adapted from Stewart Clegg 'Power relations and the constitution of the resistant subject' in John M. Jermier, David Knights and Walter R. Nord (eds) (1994) *Resistance and Power in Organizations,* London: Routledge, p. 294.

Conclusion

In conclusion then, we have seen that control has many dimensions. It is of course necessary for the effective functioning of any organization, but the problem is that it can often become an end in itself. Control is usually accomplished through measures, and often those measures themselves can displace the real objectives of the organization. As Goldratt (1984), in common with most cybernetic theorists, would argue, the argument that we should seek to measure *everything* just creates more distraction. The idea that if it can't be measured it doesn't count is far too extreme to the point of silliness. A few key measures, as long as they are the right ones, should ensure that organizations remain creative and flexible but sufficiently aware of the consequences of their actions to maintain success.

Of course, control is not only functional, it is always political and may even be psychological, as we will see in Chapter 10 on leadership and managing. Some people will find that exercising control is emotionally demanding and draining; some may relish the power they have and may even exercise control viciously and spitefully. Everyone, from the very top to the bottom, is subject to some form of control, and some may find the controls placed upon them to be soul-destroying, while others will find their very lack of discretion to be emotionally and psychologically liberating. Control will always be resisted and may be subverted; just as management will always be about the exercise of power. Its control will never be complete, until that is the employees who are managed have ceased to be people at all. This entails an awareness, then, not only that resistance exists and the variety of its forms, but that power and resistance will always coexist, there will always be alternatives, and that the object of control is to keep these alternatives in a workable relationship in order to sustain the survival of the organization, respecting diversity and plurality and occasionally recognizing incommensurable goals, but finding a way to go on and keep talking to each other.

Answers to questions about control

1 What is control? Control is the activity that seeks to bring order to other activities. In many ways it is the essence of organization. It may be involved in ensuring the compliance of action to that which was planned or it may be more dispersed, and necessitate decision making and planning in situ, in the face of a changing situation. It may be applied to the inputs to a process, the outputs of the process or indeed the process itself. In the latter case it is most likely to be explicitly concerned with the control of the conduct of those involved in the process.

2 What are its sources? Control is intimately related to power. And power may come from a number of different sources. These include those of: 'the profession'; the formal rules of a control system or the built-in rigidities of technology; persuasion, as in the example of the discourse of globalization; association with other sources of power, for example that of the relative societal hegemony of masculinity. Control may also be seductive, as witnessed in the case of culture. But, in any particular context, a multitude of

Answers continued

controls are likely to be in play. Often these controls will work together, but this need not necessarily be the case, as we saw with the problems associated with the masculinity engendered and supported by BPR.

3 **Why is it necessary for management?** Control is necessary for management since the primary role of management is to ensure the perpetuation of order and organization, to keep an organization in existence by keeping it under control. However, management control is a particular form of control, that associated with maintaining a *social* order, since management involves getting things done through other people. These people cannot be told, in advance, how to do every single thing or how to respond to every particular situation that may confront them in their organizational lives – the list of instructions required would be infinite. Instead, management control must work by engaging employees in such a way that they are still willing and able to deploy their initiative to ensure that the job gets done successfully.

4 **Can control ever be complete?** As our answer to **3**, above, makes clear, the answer to this question is obviously a resounding 'no'. The embodied judgmental abilities of human beings that make them successful employees are precisely the same abilities that allow and ensure that human beings will always resist controls. A completely compliant employee does not represent the dream of management, rather it represents a nightmare. Not only would the completely compliant mean the end of management, it would also mean the end of the creativity upon which successful organization depends.

REVISITING
THE CASE STUDY

1 What is the bank trying to control?

There are numerous things the bank is trying to control in this case study. From the physical description of the building, we can see that the bank is trying to control who has access to the premises and, therefore who has access to the bank's records, systems and procedures. More widely this control of physical access also highlights the broader issue of control of resources. The impenetrable appearance of the bank, combined with its location within, but secure separation from, a historically working-class and poverty-stricken area in the north of England, could be understood as a metaphor of the unequal access to capital and resources in modern capitalist society. The bank is also trying to control the labour of those who enter the premises. When, how and how hard clerks will

work is a prime target of the bank's control. The bank is trying to get the clerks to work as fast as possible, to answer as many calls as possible in each shift. This is also part of a broader attempt to control costs, to minimize the labour costs associated with maintaining customers' accounts and thereby to maximize the accumulation of profit or capital. As we shall see below, the bank is also concerned to try to control the clerks' understandings of, and relationship to, their labour. More effective than getting people to reluctantly behave as you want them to, is to have people want to behave as you want them to!

2 What are the mechanisms used by the bank to control the customer line department?

The primary mechanism of control on the department is the use of a sophisticated information and communication technology system. This system monitors and records many aspects of the clerks' work. Every call, every pause between calls and every break is monitored in seconds and recorded for ongoing and cumulative comparison with individual and team targets set by the department manager and his senior managers. These targets are linked to performance appraisal and pay. Control over the pace of work is also facilitated through the flashing lights on telephones warning of calls waiting, and the use of large wall-mounted LED display screens signalling calls waiting and the length of time they have been waiting. Clerks' actions on customers' accounts are also monitored, entries on customers' accounts can be called up at any time and in most cases traced back to individual clerks. These computerized systems of control do not just focus upon clerks' behaviour however. Gary, the manager, supplements these technological systems with his own watchful managerial presence. Gary is instrumental in attempting to get clerks to internalize an understanding that their work is primarily about meeting number of call targets. Thus the bank can be seen as trying to control both clerks' behaviour at work and their thoughts and feelings about that work.

3 Does this control succeed?

It depends on what is your measure of success. For the time being at least, most of the clerks seem to be meeting their targets. So the bank could be seen as successfully controlling clerks' labour (their behaviour at work). However, dissatisfaction among the clerks is rife. There is open and widespread dissent from, and disagreement with, the bank's practices. More fundamentally, Telebank's commitment to the banking industry's long-espoused values of customer service is being questioned by the clerks. And some clerks (for example Christine) have started to refuse to work to target pace, legitimizing their actions in terms of the values of customer care. Appeal by clerks to these values to legitimize their dissent is troublesome for managers; because to discipline the staff member for not meeting targets might then be read as an admission by management that they do not really care about customer service – an admission that few businesses wish to be seen to make. If businesses can no longer justify their existence in terms of appeals to 'fulfilling customers' needs', how can they justify their extraction of profit from their activities to the public?

4 How do clerks experience this control?

It is clear from the case study that the clerks negatively experience some of the controls to which they are subjected. Clerks experience the attempts to control the pace of their work (management attempts to use the computer system to enforce targets that necessitate a high number of calls, shorter time on calls and lower quality of service) as an attack upon the quality of the service that they can offer. But, arguably, clerks' negative experience of the target-driven control goes further than this. The clerks can be understood (as perhaps most of us can) as valuing a sense of themselves as helpful, moral or useful people. At work this valued sense of self is reinforced by helping customers with their banking needs. However, when high targets for the number of calls are imposed and clerks consequently have less time to help and relate to customers, clerks feel that they are now able to help the customer less. This diminishes the quality of service that customers may receive, but it also diminishes their sense of the value of their labour and of themselves. In Marxist terms, clerks experience working at target pace as more 'alienating', in that it feels to them less like a personally and socially meaningful activity and more like an alien or meaningless activity like 'putting plastic toys in a box of cereal'.

5 Should the clerks' redefinition of their work as 'customer care' be viewed as resistance? If so, resistance to what? If not, why not?

This question is more difficult. Gary, the departmental manager, tends to view clerks' appeal to 'customer care' not as resistance but as evidence that the clerks have internalized the bank's and the business world's customer service discourse. He sees clerks' use of 'customer care' discourses as benefiting the bank, in that clerks will still meet call targets but now will also be concerned to make customers feel valued even while they are being rushed off the phone. Gary might also be happy that clerks are talking about 'customer care' and not organizing in other ways, through unions for instance, to resist the pressure and stresses of their work. In short Gary feels that clerks' appeal to 'customer care' is not a troubling form of resistance but rather sees this as a marker that clerks are more effectively controlled by the bank than perhaps even the clerks themselves realize.

Gary's view is not shared by the clerks, however. They clearly understand the values of customer care as in opposition to Gary and the bank's management of the department in terms of speed and quantity of calls. Drawing upon these ideas we could read into clerks' appeal to 'customer care' several forms of resistance. First, clerks may be understood as resisting what they experience as management's attempts to render meaningless the work that they do. As discussed above, clerks value the sense of themselves as caring, useful people that helping customers reinforces. By using the language of customer care to dissent from management's privileging of targets, clerks can maintain some sense of themselves as caring people who do not agree with treating customers as if they were on a production line. In a sense the clerks are using 'customer care' as a way of refusing to be reduced to the status of uncaring automatons by the work that they do. Second, at times, as in the case of Christine, 'customer care' can inform more explicit acts of resistance and refusal to work at target pace – this is clearly a direct challenge to managerial control. Third, although the overt resistance that Christine engages in was not (yet) widespread, it was informed by Christine's initial challenge to the value base (that is, the privileging of targets, speed and low-cost service) upon which managerial control in the department is built. It is this managerial value base that all clerks on the department can be seen to be resisting – they simply do not identify with Gary, or share the bank's definitions of what constitutes their work and customer service. In a sense, the clerks can be understood to be repudiating the moral basis of the bank's management, seeing the bank as more interested in profit than its ultimate legitimatory source, customers.

So, given these quite contrasting views of clerks use of 'customer care', should we view it as resistance or not? The difficulty is that both the interpretations above are plausible, and academics and academic knowledge is good at making the plausible sound true. The problem is, however, that to definitely decide between these positions seems to require the ability to tell the future of the department. For instance, if more clerks behave like Christine and refuse to meet the targets because it is bad 'customer care', then perhaps we could categorically say that it is resistance. If targets keep being met, if they keep being raised and clerks just keep on working as management desire them to, then perhaps we could say control is not being threatened by this. This leads us to the final question.

6 What do you think will happen in the future in the customer line department?

Each of us can probably imagine several plausible narratives for the department; these futures will probably be built upon our own individual ethical/political desires for how we would like this tension at Telebank to resolve itself. However, academic study and academic knowledge gives us no certain ability to predict the future. As the sociologist Bauman (1988: 89) writes: 'the competence of sociology ends where the future begins'. Both the clerks and Gary are likely to act upon their own understandings of 'customer care', but we cannot definitively say what clerks' use of a discourse of 'customer care' might mean for the future of the department. One thing that perhaps we can say is that control and resistance in a multitude of different forms are certain to remain at the centre of the Telebank call centre studied here, and arguably all other workplaces.

References

Ackroyd, S. and Thompson, P. (1999) *Organizational Misbehaviour,* London: Sage

Argyris, C. and Schön, D.A. (1978) *Organisational Learning: A Theory of Action Perspective*, Reading, MA: Addison-Wesley.

Armstrong, P. (1985) 'Changing management control strategies: The role of competition between accountancy and other organisational professions', *Accounting, Organizations and Society,* **10**(2): 129–48.

Banerjee, S.B. and Linstead, S. (2001) 'Globalization, multiculturalism and other fictions: Colonialism for the new millennium?', *Organization,* **8**(4): 683–722.

Barnard, C.I. (1970) *The Functions of the Executive*, Cambridge, MA: Harvard University Press.

Barnes, B. (1988) *The Nature of Power*, Cambridge: Polity Press.

Bateson, J.E.G. (1999) *Managing Services Marketing*, London: Dryden Press.

Bauman, Z. (1988) *Freedom*, Milton Keynes: Open University Press.

Bauman, Z. (1998) *Globalization: The Human Consequences*, Cambridge: Polity Press.

Bloomfield, B. and Vurdubakis, T. (1994) 'Re-presenting technology: IT consultancy reports as texual reality constructions', *Sociology*, **28**(2): 123–46

Braverman, H. (1974) *Labor and Monopoly Capitalism*: New York: Monthly Review Press.

Brown, L. (2000) *Sex Slaves: The Trafficking of Women in Asia,* London, Virago.

Brown, P.L. (1982) *Managing Behavior on the Job*, New York: Wiley.

Buchanan, D. and Badham, R. (2000) *Power, Politics and Organizational Change,* London: Sage.

Case, P. and Grint, K. (2001) 'Now where were we?: BPR lotus eaters and corporate amnesia', in Knights, D. and Willmott, H. (eds) *The Reengineering Revolution: Critical Studies of Corporate Change*, London: Sage.

Castells, M. (1998) *End of Millennium*, Oxford: Blackwell.

Chandler, A.D. Jr (1997) The Visible Hand: The Managerial Revolution in American Business, Boston: Harvard University Press.

Child, J. (1984) *Organisation: A Guide to Problems and Practice*, London: Harper & Row.

Child, J., Fores, M., Glover, I. and Lawrence, P. (1983) 'A price to pay professionalism and work organisation in Britain and West Germany', *Sociology*: 63–78.

Clegg, S.R. (1994) 'Power relations and the constitution of the resistant subject', in J.M. Jermier, D. Knights and W.R. Nord (eds) *Resistance and Power in Organizations* London: Routledge.

Coke, S. (1983) 'Putting professionalism in its place', *Personnel Review*: 44–5.

Collard, R. (1990) *Total Quality*, London: Institute of Personnel Management.

Collins, H.M. (1987) 'Expert systems, artificial intelligence and the behavioural co-ordinates of skill', in B.P. Bloomfield (ed.) *The Question of Artificial Intelligence: Philosophical and Sociological Perspectives,* London: Croom Helm.

Dale, B.G. and Plunkett, J.J. (eds) (1990) *Managing Quality*, New York: Philip Alan.

Eccleston, B. (1989) *State and Society in Post-War Japan*, Cambridge: Polity Press.

Emmanuel, C., Otley, D. and Merchant, K. (1990) *Accounting for Management Control* (2nd edn), London: Chapman & Hall.

Ezzamel, M., Lilley, S. and Willmott, H. (forthcoming) 'Accounting, representation and the road to commercial salvation', *Accounting, Organizations and Society*.

Ezzamel, M., Willmott, H. and Lilley, S. (1997) 'Accounting for management and managing accounting: Reflections on recent changes in the UK', *Journal of Management Studies*, **34**(3): 439–64.

Fagan, J.O. (1909) *Labor and the Railroads*, New York: Houghton Mifflin.

Foucault, M. (1977) *Discipline and Punish: The Birth of the Prison*, London: Allen Lane.

Foucault, M. (1980) *Power/Knowledge: Selected Interviews and Other Writings 1972–1977*, C. Gordon (ed.), Brighton: Harvester Press.

Foucault, M. (1982) 'The subject and the power', in H. Dreyfus and P. Rabinow, *Michel Foucault: Beyond Structuralism and Hermeneutics*, Brighton: Harvester Press.

Goldratt, E. (1984) *The Goal,* London: Gower.

Grint, K. (1994) 'Reengineering history: Social resonances and business process reengineering', *Organization*, **1**(1): 179–201.

Haber, S. (1991) *The Quest for Authority and Honor in the American Professions, 1750–1900*, Chicago: University of Chicago Press.

Haddon, R. (1971) 'Foreword', in C. Kerr, J.T. Dunlap, F. Harbison and C.A. Myers, *Industrialism and Industrial Man*, Harmondsworth: Penguin.

Halberstam, D. (1987) *The Reckoning*, London: Bantam.

Hancock, P. (1997) 'Citizenship or vassalage? Organizational membership in the age of unreason' *Organization*, **4**(1): 93–111.

Hirst, P. and Thompson, G. (1998) *Globalization in Question*, Cambridge: Polity Press.

Hutton, S.P., Lawrence, P.A. and Smith, J.H. (1977) *The Recruitment, Deployment and Status of the Mechanical Engineer in the German Federal Republic*, University of Southampton, Department of Mechanical Engineering.

Jacques, R. (1996) *Manufacturing the Employee: Management Knowledge from the 19th to 21st Centuries*, London: Sage.

Johnson, T. (1980) 'Work and power' Chapter 1 (pp. 35–71) in G. Esland and G. Salaman (eds) *The Politics of Work and Occupations*, Buckingham: Open University Press.

Kanter, J., Schiffman, S. and Faye Horn, J. (1990) 'Let the customer do it', *Computerworld*, August 27: 75–8.

Kerfoot, D. and Knights, D. (1993) 'Management, masculinity and manipulation: From paternalism to corporate strategy in financial services in Britain', *Journal of Management Studies*, **30**(4): 659–77.

Klein, N. (2000) *No Logo: No Space, No Choice, No Jobs, Taking Aim at the Brand Bullies*, London: Flamingo.

Knights, D. and McCabe, D. (2001) '"A different world": Shifting masculinities in the transition to call centres', *Organization*, **8**(4): 619–45.

Knights, D. and Vurdubakis, T. (1994) 'Foucault, power, resistance and all that', in J. Jermier, D. Knights and W. Nord (eds), *Resistance and Power in Organizations*, London: Routledge.

Larson, M.S. (1977) *The Rise of Professionalism: A Sociological Analysis*, University of California Press.

Lawler, E.E. and Rhode, J.G. (1976) *Information and Control in Organisations*, Santa Monica: Goodyear.

Lawrence, P. (1980) *Managers and Management in West Germany*, London: Croom Helm.

Linstead, S.A. (1984) Ambiguity in the Workplace unpublished PhD thesis CNAA/Sheffield City Polytechnic.

Linstead, S.A. (1985a) 'Organizational induction: The re-creation of order and the re-reading of discourse', *Personnel Review*, **14**(1): 3–11.

Linstead, S.A. (1985b) 'Breaking the purity rule: Industrial sabotage and the symbolic process', *Personnel Review*, **14**(3): 12–19.

Locke, R. (1989) *Management and Higher Education Since 1944: The Influence of America and Japan on West Germany, Great Britain and France*, Cambridge: University Press.

Luschinger, V.P. and Dock, V.T. ([1976]1988) 'Reading 4: Organizational Systems', in J.C. Wetherbe, V.T. Dock and S.L. Mandel (eds), *Readings in Information Systems: A Managerial Perspective*, orginally published in V.P. Luschinger and V.T. Dock, *The Systems Approach: A Primer*.

McKinlay, A. and Starkey, K. (1998) *Foucault, Management and Organization Theory*, London: Sage.

Martin, P.Y. (2001) '"Mobilizing masculinities": Women's experiences of men at work', *Organization*, **8**(4): 587–618.

Miller, P. and O'Leary, T. (1987) 'Accounting and the construction of the governable person', *Accounting, Organizations and Society*, **12**(3): 235–65.

Mullins, L.J. (1985) *Management and Organisational Behaviour*, London: Pitman.

Noble, D.F. (1977) *America by Design*, Oxford: Oxford University Press.

Otley, D.T. and Berry, A.J. (1980) 'Control, organization and accounting', *Accounting, Organizations and Society*, **5**: 231–46.

Ouchi, W.G. (1981) *Theory Z: How American Business Can Meet the Japanese Challenge*, New York: Addison-Wesley.

Pask, G. (1961) *An Approach to Cybernetics*, London: Hutchinson.

Peters, T.J. and Waterman, R.H. (1982) *In Search of Excellence*, New York: Harper & Row.

Ray, C.A. (1986) 'Corporate culture: The last frontier of control', *Journal of Management Studies*, **23**(3): 287–97.

Rose, N. (1988) 'Calculable minds and manageable individuals', *History of the Human Sciences*, **1**(2): 179–200.

Rose, N. (1990) *Governing the Soul: The Shaping of the Private Self*, London: Routledge.

Roth, J. (1974) 'Professionalism: The sociologist's decoy', *Sociology of Work and Occupations*: 6–23.

Sewell, G. and Wilkinson, B. (1992) '"Someone to watch over me": Surveillance, discipline and the just-in-time labour process', *Sociology*, **26**(2): 271–89.

Skrobanek, S. Boonpakdi, N. and Janthakeero, C. (1997) *The Traffic in Women: Human Realities of the Sex Trade*, London and New York: Zed Books.

Smart, B. (1985) *Michel Foucault*, London: Tavistock.

Soeters, J.L. (1986) 'Excellent companies as social movements,' *Journal of Management Studies*, **23**(3): 299–312.

Stoner, J.A.F., Collins, R.R. and Yetton, P.W. (1985) *Management in Australia*, Sydney: Prentice Hall.

Taylor, F.W. (1911) *The Principles of Scientific Management*, New York: Norton.

Townley, B. (1993) 'Foucault, power/knowledge and its relevance for Human Resource Management', *Academy of Management Review*, **18**(3): 518–45.

Weber, M. (1978) *Economy and Society* trans. G. Roth and C. Wittich, Berkeley, CA: University of California Press, extracted in Martin Albrow (1997) *Do Organizations Have Feelings?* London: Routledge.

Willmott, H. (1993) 'Strength is ignorance; Slavery is freedom: Managing culture in modern organizations', *Journal of Management Studies*, **30**(4): 515–31.

Zuboff, S. (1988) *In the Age of the Smart Machine: The Future of Power and Work*, Oxford: Heinemann.

8 Managing ethically

Robin Stanley Snell

Questions about business ethics

1 Does ethics have anything to do with business?
2 Should business decisions be governed by profitability alone?
3 Does there always have to be a conflict for business between serving the needs of staff members (that is, personal gain) and pursuing corporate profitability (that is, the interests of the shareholders)?
4 Should managers conform to local rules, customs and etiquette, or are there universal standards to follow?
5 What are the options for managers facing moral dilemmas?
6 What aspects of an organization's culture help managers to make ethical decisions?
7 How valuable are codes of ethical conduct in business?
8 To whom should managers look for moral leadership?
9 Is it possible to change a manager's ethical predisposition?

Consider the following case from a Hong Kong-based research project (Snell et al. 1996). It concerned an ethical dilemma faced by Simon, a 35-year-old deputy accounting manager with eight years' service at 'Sunny', a Japanese-owned trading company with a branch in Hong Kong. Sunny is managed by expatriate Japanese, but employs mainly local Hong Kong Chinese staff – Simon is one of the latter. This is Simon's account of his ethical dilemma.

SIMON'S STORY

My boss regularly asks me to act as translator (English–Chinese) in meetings with other Chinese staff. He can speak only Japanese and English, whereas the junior staff can only speak Cantonese. It was very difficult for me at one meeting, because my boss was going to dismiss a cleaning lady who had worked for the company for 20 years. I understood that the staff member was the breadwinner of her family, and that such a decision would surely be a shock to the staff member. Therefore, during the translation, I changed the tone and the content of my boss's remarks a little bit. Instead of letting her know that she was to be fired because of her age, I told her that the company wanted her to take her retirement a little earlier. (At the time of writing, July 2000, there still is no old age pension as such in Hong Kong, and many companies such as Sunny have no pension scheme of their own.) I also tried to add some further beautiful explanations. Despite my efforts, she felt very distressed and surprised at the management's decision. To behave professionally, I understood that my duty was to translate exactly what the boss told me. However, I could not do that, as it would have hurt the staff member. In addition, I was myself ambivalent about the decision. In the company's interest, it was better to dismiss the staff member as she was quite old and she was not physically strong enough to complete all the cleaning jobs here. Therefore, in the end, I didn't discuss the decision with other staff. In fact, I was not sure whether that would secure any better arrangement for the dismissed staff member. However, I kept on thinking that this company does not care very much. She had worked so long for the company. However, I didn't take any action to voice my feelings and did not disclose the decision to others.

QUESTIONS ABOUT THE CASE

Before proceeding with the rest of the chapter, ponder or ask yourself the following:

1 What else might Simon do, and why might or should he do it?
2 What would you, the reader, do in a similar situation?
3 What would your actions reveal about your ethical behaviour or predisposition?

Introduction

Simon's story illustrates the type of moral dilemma to which there is no single, final answer, but for which we can identify some solutions that are better than others. It is also typical of the type of situation we might all face in the workplace, irrespective of the cultural context. However, before I go any further, I want to explore what it might mean to have an ethical and moral dilemma. Many texts use the terms *ethics* and *morals* interchangeably, and this lack of clear differentiation between ethics and morals/morality is built into our language. I don't see any difference in what I mean by 'moral development' and 'ethical development'. Nonetheless, one can also differentiate between the two terms. 'Moral/morality' comes from the Latin *more*, meaning 'custom'. Morals/morality refer to sets of personal and/or social values about what is good/bad in an action or life space. Morals/morality refer to phenomena that are more embedded in wider social structures, traditions, or social norms. Ethics comes from the Greek *ethos*, which also means 'custom'. However, possibly because the Greeks were more philosophically inclined, the term 'ethics' often refers to 'moral philosophy', the critical or analytical study of morals/morality, or stances derived from or bound up with such analytical/critical study. So ethics has also come to acquire more of a technical, specialist, perhaps even 'objective' flavour, the individual agent working out what to do, and we talk about 'legal ethics', 'medical ethics' and even 'corporate codes of ethics' rather than 'legal morality', 'medical morality' or 'corporate codes of morality'.

In this chapter I will consider some major *objections to business ethics*. As one writer has noted, a common view in the community is that business ethics is an 'oxymoron' (McKenna 1999: 138), meaning that it is contradictory and incongruous to speak of business and ethics in the same breath. Richard McKenna (1999) goes on to say that our everyday experiences of business might well confirm this negative view, but that a more objective and academic study of the subject is likely to convince us otherwise. A good starting point for developing a more objective view is to examine the bases of *modern business ethics* and the major ethical systems that have developed which might inform business practices. As you will see, various strands of business ethics have emerged from within particular discourses relating to the conduct of business and, ultimately, the role of business in society. Within these discourses, ethics is presented as an immanent struggle over choice and the rights of individuals over collective interests. As we have pointed out elsewhere, the privileging of individualism is part of the dominant discourse of modern management in Western societies (see also McKenna 1999: 141), and is predominantly masculinist in its view of the ideal individual. In the study of ethics there is a distinct history of privileging masculinist world views over feminist ones. I explore the implications of this more fully in the discussion of the moral development of the manager.

In the global context, business ethics raises many perplexing issues that are extremely difficult to resolve. For example, most breaches of ethical behaviour reported in the media entail examples of *corruption*, and deal with such things as *bribes*, *commissions* and *gifts* and, to a lesser extent, *nepotism*. In a cross-cultural context, what might constitute a bribe, commission or gift can be difficult to understand and deal with. Cultural relativists, who subscribe to what is termed cultural relativism, argue that we should respect other cultures and go along with how businesses operate in the 'host' culture. If bribes are a part of doing business, then that is not really being corrupt, but merely accepting another set of cultural norms. However, critics of this view argue that no one society's norms and practices can determine alone what should be accepted as the benchmark for what is ethically right or wrong. I will discuss how these differing points of view might be reconciled, and how accepting bribes, commissions and gifts can cause businesses untold problems.

Other global issues are also impacting on how we treat the topic of business ethics. Human rights issues and violations, especially in the newly industrializing economies (NIEs), such as Asia and Southeast Asia, the Middle East, Africa, Latin America and parts of Eastern Europe, are becoming problematical for many multinationals, especially in marketing their products. The perceived exploitation of the NIE's workforce, popularized in the notion of *sweatshops*, is an inescapable reality that managers will have to deal with. However, as I show in this chapter, the notion of the sweatshop is not confined to the NIEs, but is also a feature in Western businesses, raising serious concerns about the conduct of managers in this part of the world, especially in terms of how they breach labour laws and human rights in the name of profit. *Green issues* or the environment, and the ethical dilemmas they pose in the global context, are also raised, although this topic is taken up in more detail in Chapter 5.

In the remainder of the chapter I look at how managers can improve their own moral behaviour or motivation as well as the ethical standards and practices within their organizations. My approach to moral development draws on the work of Lawrence Kolhberg and his model of the stages of moral reasoning. However, drawing on feminist critiques of this model, I emphasize that moral behaviour is very much about personal character ('what sort of person should I be') and the balancing of 'ethics of justice' with 'ethics of care' (also Maclagan 1998; Pataki

2000). In other words, moral behaviour is as much about 'character virtue' as it is about learning to make ethical decisions using detached ethical reasoning. Using detached ethical reasoning (that is, the 'what should I do' approach) does not demand of managers that they look long and hard at themselves and reflect on how morally credible or trustworthy they are in the eyes of others. Character virtue also emphasizes the importance of developing moral intuition and judgement so that managers can act morally in a variety of settings and circumstances. However, I also argue that organizations, as a collectivity, have to take responsibility for the moral or ethical behaviour of their members. I describe what happens when organizations fail to do this by discussing the problem of *whistle-blowing*. I conclude the chapter by offering ideas for how Simon (and, of course, all managers) might draw upon everyday experience as a means of moral development.

Objections to business ethics

The five main objections to business ethics are: *psychological egotism*; *Machiavellian*; *legal-moral*; *agency arguments*; and *cultural relativism* and these are summarized in Exhibit 8.1. Cultural relativism will be covered later in the chapter as it directly impacts on discussions relating to corruption, human rights and 'green issues'.

Psychological egotism

The first objection to business ethics is that urging managers to take other people's best interests into account runs contrary to the spirit of human enterprise. For example, Ivan Boesky's maxim that 'greed is good' became established in the acquisitive business climate that developed in the 1980s (Walker 1992). The objection thus stems from the world view of *psychological egotism*, which holds that people only ever follow their own immediate interest, looking out for 'number one' (Beauchamp 1988: 16), and pursuing 'self-interested, outcome-oriented individualism' (Mitchell and Scott 1990: 23).

There are two fundamental problems with the psychological egotism view of ethical behaviour. Firstly, it is refuted by any action of genuine altruism, benevolence, service or citizenship by a successful businessperson (Kanungo and Conger 1993). Secondly, if indeed some adults are permanently locked into this mentality, then according to cognitive sociomoral development theory (for example Kohlberg 1981, 1984, 1986; Kohlberg et al. 1983) they belong to a minority who are 'retarded' in their moral development. This is not to deny that certain strong

---

Exhibit 8.1　Five main objections to business ethics

- ❏ **Psychological egotism:** taking other people's interest into account runs contrary to good business and acting morally is only justified if it promotes the manager's or organization's best interest.

- ❏ **Machiavellian:** 'the means justify the ends', even if you have to be the arch 'political animal' to avoid being a corporate or organizational 'loser'.

- ❏ **Legal-moral:** this implies that if it is legal, then that's all you have to worry about and the rest will look after itself. So long as you comply with the 'spirit of the law', organizations do not need to worry about ethical codes and so on.

- ❏ **Agency arguments:** profit maximization is the rule of business and the 'market is the key arbitrator' of what is 'right' or 'good' for business. Just keep shareholders happy, make sure that the stock market and management interests are looked after and the rest will look after itself. Social responsibility for business is an oxymoron.

- ❏ **Cultural relativism:** we should respect other cultures and go along with how businesses operate in the 'host' culture.

---

feelings such as anger, fear, guilt or passion can, in particular contexts or situations, drive otherwise altruistic or ethically sensitive people to 'look out' only for 'number one' (Flam 1993: 59, citing Frank 1988: 53–4). Thus a person, who has been repeatedly overlooked for promotion for reasons that are unjust, such as on racist or sexist grounds, might well decide that looking out for 'number one' is the best possible thing to do under the circumstances, until perhaps a new job is found. The implication is that while egotism is a typical response to injustice, it may not help to build fairer business communities.

Machiavellian

The second objection to business ethics is based on *Machiavellian* analyses of power, and claims that rising to the top of the organization necessitates games of manipulation, blaming and attacking rivals, controlling and massaging information, lobbying, image building, ingratiation, 'bootlicking', forming coalitions and allies, creating obligations and indebtedness among followers, gaining control of scarce resources and so on. It evidently follows that attending to business ethics means surrendering these power tactics and resources, thereby condemning oneself to a 'loser's life' among the lower echelons of the organization. Another version of this argument is that business has its special brand of ethics, rather like those applying to the card game called poker (Carr 1993). This view is problematic. The office and the boardroom, unlike the poker table, are complex, interconnected sets of actions that have influence way beyond anything so fleeting as a card game. Employment consumes our most active years (Schor 1992). Since industrial and commercial endeavour has a major impact on all other human (and animal) activity, how it is carried out is therefore a matter of wider ethical concern. To simply say that it is OK for businesses to develop their own brand of ethics – Machiavellian or otherwise – implies that business does not impact on wider society.

Legal–moral

The third objection is that business ethics is unnecessary since 'if it's legal, then it's morally OK' (Bowie 1988). It implies belief (whether naive or pragmatic) that the letter of the law is an adequate and complete *substitute* for ethical sensitivity and moral reasoning. As I shall mention again in the section on 'Moral reasoning, moral motivations and care', seeing beyond the limits, however reassuring they may be, of 'law and order mentality', reveals laws to be human artefacts, not divine truths. How they are formulated and interpreted by authorities falls inescapably short of complete objectivity and justice.

Granted, there is emerging East–West consensus that the rule of law tends to help economic development and reduce corruption, and is an essential foundation for ethical conduct in modern market economies (Hao 1999). Where the legal system is relatively undeveloped, as in the former Soviet bloc (Bohatá 1997), what is permissible may depend on the self-serving decisions of corrupt officials or Mafia-like groups (Filatov 1994), and Europe may have something to learn from Hong Kong regarding the effective use of law to stamp out misconduct. Hong Kong's highly regarded Independent Commission Against Corruption (ICAC) helped to reduce corruption in business and government (including the police force), by strictly enforcing anti-bribery legislation within the borders of Hong Kong (McDonald 1994).

However, as Gael McDonald points out, the ICAC does not merely enforce a particular set of laws. It engages extensively in community relations work, offers advice and training in corruption prevention, develops public education videos and much besides. This is because many ethical issues and dilemmas in management remain out of the law's reach. Much can go on at work that is questionable, such as unjustly pressurizing, intimidating or reprimanding subordinates and 'padding' or 'fiddling' expense accounts, but is not normally under legal scrutiny (Boatright 1993: 13–14). Some limitations in the law result from the choices made by lawmakers, who may decide not to enact comprehensive legislation on topics such as product safety, race or sex discrimination, and share dealing, preferring the subsidiarity of self-regulation and voluntary codes of practice. Indeed, in many countries, powerful vested interests in the business world strive to prevent laws from being enacted or changed, by directly or indirectly lobbying governments and sponsoring political campaigns. Abiding by the law can become a game of minimal conformity, with companies hiring lawyers to fight their cause on technical grounds, as has occurred within the tobacco industry for many years. Legislation may not keep up with fresh moral challenges revealed and produced by advances in science and technology, such as genetic engineering, environmental protection and data privacy. The domain of ethics covers large and inevitable gaps between legal compliance and what is thought and felt to be morally right, socially beneficial, fair, just and compassionate.

Agency arguments

The fourth objection is the *agency* argument of Milton Friedman (1970), who condemns what he calls 'the doctrine of social responsibility'. From this perspective, a corporate executive is legally the agent of the firm's owners or principals, and is thus contractually obliged to serve only their interests, while keeping within the law and avoiding deliberate deception. Friedman claims that using corporate resources for anything other than profit maximization amounts to stealing from the principals. It would follow that managers should invest no more in serving the wider community interest than can be justified by the payoffs in corporate image, consumer loyalty, less governmental interference and healthy share prices. Friedman cites Hong Kong as a free-market model for the world to learn from. We can learn much from Hong Kong, and I include cases from the Special Administrative Zone in this chapter, but not all the lessons are in concordance with Friedman's ideological beliefs.

Larue Hosmer (1987: 34–48) offers a succinct analysis of the microeconomic theory behind the agency argument. In an ideal economy, goods and services are distributed by competitive markets so effectively that it would be impossible to make anyone better off without harming someone else. Hosmer exposes the flaws of this argument: the exclusion of segments of society (for example the poor and unskilled); its self-serving ideological nature; and its low regard for the worth of human beings (Hosmer 1987: 51). When a company is sued for damages, or goes broke, shareholders stand to lose only the value of their shares because they enjoy the privilege of limited liability. Others affected may lose their livelihood, all their savings, even their lives. If business decisions can inflict harm or loss on individuals or communities which have no legal means of redress, other than claiming government compensation or benefits, it follows that managers need to take account of wider community interests, not just the needs of the shareholders. This point justifies the *stakeholder* approach discussed later in this chapter, although the law in many countries has not caught up with this point yet (see also Hosmer 1987: 51) and, in any case, as argued above, would not yield a complete solution. Charles Handy (1995: 15) reminds us that Adam Smith, the founding father of free-market economic theory, argued in *A Theory of Moral Sentiments* that a stable society depends on everyone's moral duty to have regard and sympathy for fellow human beings. This principle is absent from microeconomic theory but without it, Smith's 'invisible hand', promoting the ends of society as a whole (Smith 1937: 423), cannot work to the benefit of all. The fifth objection, that of cultural relativism, which suggests that there is no universal measure of 'the good', only culturally sustained 'local agreements' on such matters, will be considered in more detail later in the chapter.

Modern business ethics

This part of the chapter sketches out five bodies of thought which represent much, although not the entirety, of the substance of ethical thought and argument. These are: *utilitarianism, deontology, justice, stakeholder* and *character virtue* perspectives, as summarized in Exhibit 8.2.

Utilitarianism

Utilitarianism is based on the ideas of the English philosophers Jeremy Bentham (1748–1832) and John Stuart Mill (1806–73). It is a rule-based system of ethics that weighs the worth of all that is achieved, produced, delivered or dumped. Bentham assumed that the most ethical policy or course of action was that which gave rise to 'the greatest good for the greatest number' of those affected. Mill (1998: 28) similarly advocated the 'greatest happiness principle', which holds that 'actions are right in proportion as they tend to promote happiness; wrong as they tend to produce the reverse of happiness'.

> ### Exhibit 8.2 Foundations of modern business ethics
>
> ❑ **Utilitarianism:** basically means going along with those actions that give the greatest net benefit for the greatest number of people or meet intrinsic human needs.
>
> ❑ **Deontology:** has two rather powerful ethical precepts built around the notion of the 'categorical imperative': 'do unto others as you would have done unto yourself' and, never treat others as a means to an end.
>
> ❑ **Justice:** this assumes notions of rights and principles of fairness and while overlapping with deontology, has a much stronger emotional basis and the view of positive rights.
>
> ❑ **The stakeholder view of justice:** debunks the agency argument saying that businesses have a wide constituency of interests to look after and protect other than shareholders.
>
> ❑ **Character virtue:** shifts emphasis away from the content of decision making to a focus on the manager's conduct and his/her credibility and trustworthiness.

However, while Bentham held that all pleasures were of equivalent worth, Mill argued that the 'higher pleasures' arising from 'healthy pursuits' were qualitatively superior to mere 'sensual indulgences'. Mill claimed that the capacity to enjoy the former distinguishes people from beasts, and that 'the general cultivation of nobleness of character' was the best foundation for a good society, where the greatest happiness would arise from one another's mutually uplifting presence and noble deeds (Mill 1998: 31). The contemporary ambitions of the Chinese Communist Party for 'socialist spiritual civilization construction' (Dirlik 1989: 35–6; Ding 1999) resemble Mill's aspirations, but are similarly challenged by the lures of material civilization. *Rule utilitarianism*, an approach that some commentators attribute to Mill, seeks to identify a small set of rules of behavioural conduct which, if everyone followed them, would in theory lead to the greatest good for the greatest number affected (*Internet Encyclopedia of Philosophy*, 2000b).

Utilitarian thought in the developed capitalist world has tended to follow Bentham rather than Mill, perhaps because it is easier to calculate the 'greater good' if all pleasures are reduced to a single unit. Thus, according to Manuel Velasquez (1992), utilitarianism judges the moral worth of actions by the utility (surfeit or excess

CASE EXAMPLE

FORD PINTO

In the 1970s, the Ford Motor Company in the US performed cost–benefit analysis (for example one life = $200,725, of which $10,000 represented the victim's pain and suffering) to determine whether to change the design of the Ford Pinto, which located the fuel tank behind the rear axle, a position vulnerable to rear-end collision. There had already been fatal collisions in which the fuel tank had punctured and the car's interior had burst into flames, but the company, after deliberation, decided not to proceed with design changes that would have cost $11 per model (total costs = $137 million, total benefits $49.5 million). The case outraged many commentators (see Hartman 1998: 340–55). Ford might have arrived at a more socially acceptable assessment had they drawn upon prospect theory (Whysall 2000: 26), which weighs pains, dissatisfactions and distresses more heavily than pleasures and satisfactions in utilitarian assessments.

of benefits over costs) of their foreseeable consequences for each and every person affected by a certain set of actions. Manufacturers of vacuum cleaners (helping to keep houses cleaner by their labour-saving devices) would probably do better in a Benthamite moral assessment than manufacturers of landmines (which were maiming and killing civilians in Cambodia long after hostilities had ceased). Markets, for all their imperfections, sometimes serve up reasonable utilitarian assessments: a company that is seen to deliver little or nothing of value to anyone is likely to go bust. After Gerald Ratner, heir to a popular British chain of gift and jewellery retail outlets, joked once too often, in a 1991 speech to the UK's Institute of Directors, that a Ratner's decanter set was cheap because it was 'total crap', and that a Marks & Spencer prawn sandwich would last longer than a pair of Ratner's gold earrings, the business nose-dived (*Wall Street Journal* 1993; Whysall 2000: 22–3).

In contemporary utilitarian cost–benefit analysis, a legacy of Bentham, the impact of policy decisions on national economies, labour markets, healthcare systems and so on are translated into dollar (or euro) values, a convenient aggregate proxy measure of human pain and gain. Such assessments, however, often require some tough-minded and controversial valuations of human life, a fact that can make the existence and operation of such systems appear extremely problematic. The short case study on the Ford Pinto illustrates this point.

However, as Alasdair MacIntyre (1977) points out, cost-benefit analysis leaves several questions unanswered. These include: What is the range of alternatives to be considered? Who decides what counts as the benefits and costs that are to be measured? How can we arrive at standard measures of incommensurable items (for example apples and oranges, profits and human lives)? What counts as a consequence? How far into the future should we calculate consequences and repercussions?

On the surface, the evident cold-heartedness of the Ford Pinto case makes it appear exceptional, yet the weighing of safety and well-being risks against cost, inconvenience and profit are endemic in industries such as energy, transportation, drugs, construction, agriculture and insurance. Indeed, it is difficult to imagine an industry where utilitarian assessments are not pervasive.

There are other alternatives to utilitarianism. Buddhism, which predates utilitarianism by two millennia, holds that the seeds of unhappiness reside within ourselves – pain, suffering, unhappiness and dissatisfaction stem from unwholesome desires, temptations, materialistic illusions and obsessions. We might attain profound inner peace by learning to remove these unwanted 'needs' through the quiet practice of meditation (Lim 1994). Deontology is another.

Deontology

Deontology, or duty-based ethics, is based on the idea that we are morally obliged to follow fundamental rules and principles regardless of the consequences (Frankena 1963). It focuses on the manner and spirit in which we interact with other individuals, groups, organizations and collectives. Utilitarians are preoccupied with actual results and outcomes, but for deontologists, correct intentions and means of going about one's activities are all-important. The German philosopher Immanuel Kant (1724–1804) proposed a basic set of deontological 'categorical imperatives', that is, moral obligations or commandments, which he claimed we must always follow, regardless of our own feelings, special needs or circumstances. He expressed these imperatives as four formulae (*Internet Encyclopedia of Philosophy*, 2000a), and claimed that they are based on 'pure reason'. They may be simplified into the following three axioms (Raphael 1994: 56; Maclagan 1998: 27):

1. Act as if, through your actions, you were making universal law for everyone to follow. This formula

instructs us only to do the things that we would tolerate anyone else doing, and not to give ourselves special privileges or excuses. When applied, it could mean, for example, resisting the temptation to spy on competitors, bribe contractors, delay payment to suppliers or mislead customers, if we do not wish these practices to become the norm.

2. Always treat any human being (self included) as an end in himself or herself, never merely as a means to an end. This may mean, for example, not taking advantage of others' gullibility, incapacity, naiveté, oversight or lack of information; not exploiting, scapegoating, victimizing, or objectifying people (treating them as 'things'); and respecting the safety and dignity of employees and customers

3. Act as if you were a member of a community of fellow moral legislators who are ends in themselves (for example don't force your will upon another).

Kenneth Goodpaster (1984) considered how deontological ethics of this kind would apply to business and management, arguing that businesspeople are morally obliged to keep to the following, not quite complete, list of general 'common-sense' (but, taken together, utopian) principles:

1. Avoid and prevent harming others
2. Help those in need
3. Do not lie or cheat
4. Respect the rights of others
5. Keep promises or contracts
6. Obey the law
7. Be fair
8. Encourage others to follow these principles.

Deontology, in prescribing how we should do things (the means), complements utilitarianism, which focuses on what we actually bring about (the ends). There is, however, an overlap. Deontology is rule-based, and its prescriptions correspond with those of rule utilitarianism, mentioned earlier. Arguably, if everyone held to the principles of deontology, the world, overall, would be a better place for all.

To see the correspondence, imagine that Goodpaster's moral obligations had already 'come true', that is, had been established as standard, everyday norms of business behaviour. Leading economies might, in relation to his first principle, have cooperated promptly to prevent further radioactive leaks at the Chernobyl nuclear reactor site in the USSR. In 1986 the reactor caused the world's greatest nuclear accident, killing all near it and damaging food and crops worldwide. In relation to the second principle, the education, prophylactics and medications now provided in relation to HIV and AIDS in wealthier Western countries might have been made widely available and affordable in AIDS-ravaged Eastern Europe, Africa and Asia. In relation to the third principle, had the business world become a lie-free and fraud-free zone, we could transact business freely on the Internet without fear of fraud. If the fourth and fifth principles were consistently adopted and applied, less time and money would be spent on litigation. And so on. From this perspective, consistently following Goodpaster's principles would result in much good. But are we sufficiently self-aware and morally sensitive to know whether or not we are following them?

I find a tension within deontology, between aspirations for pure, absolute logicality and concern to respect people's feelings and dignity. While many readings of Kant emphasize our supposed duty to conform to absolutely logical moral rules, a grain of subjectivity that rubs against this rational fortress may (*pace* Kant) also be an important ingredient. To consider the Gerald Ratner case again, while the company may have long been breaching Kant's second formula, it is not immediately obvious that Ratner, in admitting to this, consciously breached any of Goodpaster's eight principles. His evident disdain for and lack of empathy with customers' feelings clearly caused grave offence, however.

Justice, in its many forms

Another great school of ethical thought and practice, once again rule-based, relates to *justice*, which in modern Western societies assumes the notion of rights and the principle of fairness (note the overlaps with deontology). Compared with deontology, the underlying emotional basis of justice ethics is much stronger and is potentially explosive and perhaps implosive. People typically become distraught by perceived injustice (Batson et al. 2000). To appreciate this, think back to the last time you felt that your rights were violated. An assertive or aggressive response to injustice entails attempting to eliminate distress by revenge, or redress. A passive response allows the hurt inside to fester. What might ethical analysis offer?

The English philosopher John Locke (1632–1704) argued for justice in his *Second Treatise of Government*, claiming that the basis of our natural rights was that 'no one ought to harm another in his life, health, liberty, or possessions' (1986). More recent ideas recognize 'positive' human rights (or entitlements) to basic necessities such as food, clothing, shelter and emergency medical treatment, and 'negative' human rights to free movement and non-interference. To those, one can add the positive right to equal opportunity and the negative right to anti-discrimination and fair treatment. The Universal Declaration of Human Rights, adopted on 10 December, 1948 by the General Assembly of the

United Nations, promised more than any governments have been willing or able to deliver in full (*Internet Encyclopedia of Philosophy* 2000c). At least five kinds of justice, often interwoven, may be identified:

- *compensatory:* atoning for prior harm or breaches of promise or contracts and so on
- *retributive or punitive:* punishment for bad deeds, for example, corporate theft
- *procedural:* establishing mechanisms, protocols and rules for developing agreements and so on for example, grievance procedures
- *distributive:* handing out benefits and burdens, for example, compensation packages, salary packages, recruitment policies
- *interactional:* quality of face-to-face interaction and how far decisions are seen to be justly made and executed.

Compensatory justice

This concerns the making good of rights, violations and, related to this, the rectification of contract or psychological contract violations. A customer has a right to a product or service that works in the manner implied or promised, meets safety requirements and is delivered in a timely manner. Typically, customers buying consumer durable goods in Western Europe expect to return faulty goods within a reasonable time period and receive a replacement or their money back. Further compensation, in proportion to additional consequential losses, may also be warranted. The following case example illustrates the complexities of extracting compensatory justice.

Retributive justice

This entails punishment for inflicting harm, wrongdoing, indeed for any form of perceived injustice, including unfair prior retribution. Occasions for retribution typically invoke primal emotions. The ancient maxim 'a life for an eye, two lives for one', represents *escalated retribution* (Batson et al. 2000: 36), more severe even than the Old Testament's 'eye for eye, tooth for tooth, hand for hand' (Exodus 21: 24), which advocates *matched retribution*. The right to retribution, therefore, may best be restricted to formally constituted legal or professional authorities, on condition that they mete out punishments less severe than the initial offence, de-escalating violence (Batson et al. 2000: 36), and thus serving the utilitarian greatest good for the greatest number. Except perhaps in the case of wars, which could be regarded as state-sponsored cruelty (Bauman 1993), an orderly system of retributive justice is better than having angry individuals or gangs taking the law into their own hands, engaging in spirals of violent retaliation, fuelled by self-serving or ego-defensive bias.

In mainland China, however, where there is no tradition of human rights, managements have eagerly claimed the 'right' (as in 'might is right') to administer arbitrary fines and penalties as instruments to instil and maintain work discipline (Lee 1999). Several cases of the violation of workers' rights through 'rough justice', even corporal punishment, administered by management have been reported (Chan and Senser 1997; Boje 1998; Chan 1998).

In cultures where workers' rights have more support in law, managers may be less inclined to dispense retributive justice. As noted earlier, however, the law does not replace ethics, so the responsibility for dealing with many cases of alleged employee misconduct at work tends to remain within companies rather than being passed to the courts. In such cases, management's moral responsibility entails administering compensatory, rather than retributive justice, and doing so in a fair and even-handed manner, in accordance with procedural justice and interactional justice (see below), so that cases are considered on the

CASE EXAMPLE

Someone buys a hammer from a DIY store. The next day, after a few minutes usage, the hammer head flies off and breaks the glass of a picture frame. The customer brings the glassless picture frame to the store, along with the broken hammer, and perhaps succeeds in negotiating a free replacement piece of glass as well as a new hammer (or money back for the old one). Much would depend on the experience of the store manager and on whether she or he believes the customer's story. If instead the customer demands £2000 damages or threatens to use connections to get a critical story published in the local press or TV station, the demand would probably be seen as extortionate, rather than a sincere attempt to obtain justice. At that point, the store manager might employ emotional intelligence to help the customer calm down and try to resolve the problem in an amicable manner. (Most wars are fought in the name of justice, but, as Zygmunt Bauman (1993: 228) observes, 'injustice tends to be compensated for by injustice with role-reversal'.) As a final recourse, the store manager may advise the customer to contact the company's legal department.

basis of sound evidence and the relationship between misdeeds and punishments remains consistent. Codes of conduct (discussed later in the chapter) and disciplinary procedures that have been developed in a consensual manner are helpful in this respect. It is important that justice is seen to be done. The hurt feelings of being unfairly sacked or laid off, too harshly disciplined or even unfairly criticized can trigger verbal or physical retributive violence by aggrieved employees or former employees (Allen and Lucero 1998). The ready availability of firearms in the USA has permitted fatal shootings of former superiors (Allen and Lucero 1996).

Procedural justice

This requires that decision makers operate decision procedures fairly and consistently, with reference to clearly agreed and relevant decisional criteria, and in accordance with due process, without bending to the distorting influence of private self-interest and prejudice, for such matters as job appointments, promotions, competitive tendering and disciplinary cases. Procedural justice is its own justification, but rule utilitarianism lends support to it. For example, procedural fairness in recruitment and selection is likely to achieve a better match between people and positions, to the ultimate benefit of the great majority. Curiously, Kant's version of deontology, as I read it, does not logically rule out procedural injustice, so that, for example, a homogeneous group of decision makers could will and wish that everyone shared their own particular brand of bias or bigotry. This may have happened in the former West Germany during the 1970s. People suspected of involvement in political parties to the left of the Social Democratic Party were subjected to *Berufsverbot* ('job ban'), and could not enter careers in the civil service or teaching. Goodpaster (1984) and other contemporary deontologists would be eager to stamp out such threats to procedural justice, along with bribery (discussed later in this chapter), intimidation, harassment, favouritism, nepotism and unfair discrimination on the grounds of ethnicity, gender, family status, sexual preference and age.

In many jurisdictions, such as Hong Kong, Australia and the UK, Equal Opportunity Commissions support the adoption and implementation of codes of practice promoting anti-discrimination and anti-harassment at work. However, much unfair discrimination in organizations arises unconsciously and unintentionally, and is perpetuated by systemic arrangements rather than deliberate actions and decisions (see Maclagan 1998: 90–4). Patrick Maclagan (1998) gives the example of rigid 9 to 5 working hours, which can exclude those with particular domestic circumstances and family obligations. 'Macho' norms for turning up at the office

on Saturdays and Sundays are similarly discriminatory. Becoming aware of threats to procedural justice requires that managers critically examine and question everyday organizational norms and practices, rather than taking them for granted.

Distributive justice

This concerns the handing out of benefits and burdens (De George 1995: 105). John Rawls (1971), addressing both procedural and distributive justice, argued that the architects of an imagined society would, under the 'veil of ignorance', that is, not knowing what position they themselves would occupy in that society, resolve to establish basic equality of human rights, opportunity and dignity. If every leader took the view that he or she might wake up tomorrow in the shoes of the lowliest clerk or cleaner, there might be more emphasis on procedural and distributive justice at work. Inequalities of wealth, income, influence and prestige would be allowed, only to the extent that the least advantaged group would ultimately become better off as a result, and would not be left impossibly far behind. In other words, 'any inequalities in a social system must benefit the least well off under conditions of equal opportunity for all' (Maclagan 1998: 97).

Arguably, if merit-based systems of salary and bonus determination were carefully designed to reflect the dynamics of wide-open labour markets and real value-added by a person's work, while motivating high-level performance in the future, then the relatively high remuneration received at the top end would be morally justified. What people get would then be based both on their real needs and equity – the effort put in and the merit of their contribution (Steidlmeier 1992: 69–70). It is, however, difficult to reconcile the salaries and bonuses of some company directors with principles of distributive justice. For example, in July 2000, mobile telephone company Vodaphone Airtouch announced a controversial £10 million bonus payment to Chief Executive Chris Gent. Such cases may serve to keep alive the debate about distributive injustice in relation to corporate 'fat (Tom) cats', who allegedly benefit from small circle decisions that disturb but are tolerated by shareholders, but which outrage the wider public.

Another important principle in distributive justice is that of 'equal pay for work of equal value'. Once again, typical practice appears not to accord with the principle, so that in the USA, jobs held predominantly by men pay significantly more than those held predominantly by women (Ehrenberg 1989; Hartman 1998: 415), a situation also reflected in the UK (Storey 1999: 7) and across the rest of Europe (Plantenga and Hansen 1999). Pincus (1998) argues that the 'free' labour market has arrived at this pattern of salary differentials, because women players have tended to settle for it: it's up to individual women to bargain for more! Against this individualistic argument, I would note that the market makers for the labour market are those at the strategic apex (traditionally male), whose decisions govern the anchor point for labour price (Hultin and Szulkin 1999). In these circles, there is considerable inertia and an inclination to benchmark with, and perhaps be nostalgic about, a past epoch when women were thought to belong at home. Collective political action may be required in order to rectify such injustices. In the UK, for example, the mainly female speech therapy profession has acted collectively in pursuit of the rectification of pay inequality in relation to other, male-dominated professions within the National Health Service (Overell 1998).

Interactional justice

This refers to the quality of face-to-face treatment received from a decision maker, and how far formal decision procedures are seen to be properly applied by those who have to implement them (Bies and Moag 1986). Administering justice as a manager thus requires all-round political skill: self-awareness and control of one's own feelings and biases; sensitivity to the feelings of others; and the ability to demonstrate to others that justice is being done. Simon Baddeley and Kim James (1987) note that ethically inclined managers need to use political skill in order to continue to operate justly, while, of course, some managers may employ political skill for egotistic ends, without intrinsic concern about the justice of their actions.

Stakeholder approaches

The idea that it is appropriate for businesses to serve *stakeholders* and not only shareholders (Weiss 1994) goes against the notion of business as a self-contained 'game' (see Carr 1993), and against Friedman's maxim that social responsibility equals profit maximization plus legal compliance. Stakeholder perspectives hold that corporations are obliged to evaluate and balance the far-reaching economic, political, environmental and ethical consequences of their decisions for those individuals, groups and institutions upon whom a company depends for its survival and success. According to Freeman (1998), the company is morally bound by a set of implicit social contracts with each of these stakeholder groups, and is thus governed by distributive justice, under which the interests and welfare of all stakeholder groups are coordinated and balanced, so that no single group (such as the shareholders) is consistently favoured over the others, and no group is persistently neglected. Distributive justice thus 'trumps' utilitarianism which, by pursuing only majority needs, might neglect minority interests. Under a stakeholder approach, shareholders, bondholders and lenders would nevertheless get *fair* returns on their financial investment. The nature of other social contracts in and around the stakeholder organization is sketched out below.

Suppliers who may tailor many of their systems to the focal company's needs, offer special help in servicing peaks of demand, join in a cooperative relationship with the focal company and work to reduce and resolve supply problems, would expect loyalty in return. They would feel betrayed if opportunistically discarded in favour of a competing supplier, promising a cheaper deal, having benchmarked services and systems on the original supplier. Customers who are not respected or cared about will take their custom elsewhere, as in the Ratner case. Neighbourhood communities and government agencies provide infrastructure (roads, networking forums, police protection, waste disposal and so on) and in return expect employment openings for local residents, prompt tax or rates payments and cooperation with environmental protection laws and codes of practice.

As the 'new economy' comes to emphasize knowledge generation and enhancement, the social contract between companies and their managers and other employees becomes increasingly oriented towards learning and development (Hall and Moss 1998). Employees are expected to engage in lifelong individual learning so as to avoid obsolescence, share individual know-how, contribute to collective knowledge development, invest psychological energy in meeting the demands of the various stakeholder groups, and balance the competing claims of other stakeholders. In return for all this, the stakeholder-oriented company (a learning organization) allows time for, and supports, their growth and competence enhancement, gives access to environments rich in know-how, information and learning support, and encourages developmental relationships and networks between colleagues, which may outlast a person's membership of the company.

On some definitions, there is a wider set of stakeholder relationships than this, involving all those who affect or are affected by an organization's decisions and actions. One might, accordingly, add to this already very complex picture. Communities of practice extending beyond the formal boundaries of the organization, competitor organizations, trade associations, regulatory bodies, environmental pressure groups, schools, universities and healthcare agencies each make contributions, and each have corresponding needs. Then there are stakeholders, such as unborn generations and wider ecological systems, who have rights because they are affected in some way by a company's operations.

Balancing stakeholder interests

In balancing stakeholder interests, an ideal is to build and maintain relationships of trust and cooperation among all the stakeholders, not just some of them (Green 1994). Kantian deontology would command a company to treat every human stakeholder entity as an end in itself, never merely as a resource to use or obstacle to remove. One type of stakeholder imbalance is the neglect of social contracts with, or deontological moral obligations to, particular stakeholder groups. That exposes a company to the risk of losing moral legitimacy, something that may have been happening for example, to Microsoft in 2001 with the anti-competitive case in 2000 brought against it by the American Justice Department, exposing some extremely coercive company practices. Another type of stakeholder imbalance is the overemphasis of particular relationships, for example cartel conspiracy, overclose cooperation (for example price-fixing) with competitors. Both kinds of imbalance may lead to governmental intervention and/or legal action.

Some companies conduct social audits of their performance in relation to their various stakeholders on various indices (Weiss 1994). John Burgoyne (1994) notes, however, that understanding and balancing contrasting motives, perceptions, feelings and values among different stakeholder groups is not an exact science, but requires critical political sensitivity and analysis, and respect for qualitative differences, such as those arising from diverse ethnic and social class backgrounds. Hosmer (1991) recognizes the difficulty and complexity of the stakeholder approach, but argues that it should have a central place in business education.

Many stakeholder theorists tend to fall into two mutually supporting camps (see Donaldson 1999). The first camp justifies a stakeholder approach on the grounds of instrumental reasons, that is, that stakeholder-oriented companies perform better financially in the long run than other companies – an assertion that has received substantial empirical support (Jones 1995). The second camp emphasizes the normative aspects, that is, that it is 'right' for companies to adopt the stakeholder approach, period. Both camps reject psychological egotism and the agency arguments of Friedman, and express concern for others' needs and welfare. Both camps assume that capitalism is compatible with ethical principles, and that it works more effectively when decision makers embrace morality of a reasonably high standard.

If, in future, empirical evidence were to turn the other way, that is, show that stakeholder-oriented companies achieve consistently *worse* financial results than non-stakeholder-oriented companies, then the comfortable consensus among stakeholder theories and theorists would break down. Stakeholder companies might then face crisis and questioning of the legitimacy of economic systems would intensify.

Stakeholder enabling

Jerry Carlton and Nancy Kurland (1996) argue that stakeholder approaches place the manager at the centre of the nexus of stakeholders, adjudicating between stakeholder differences by exercising their discretion within a fairly defined and constrained organizational space. They suggest a form of stakeholder enabling as a means of giving greater voice to stakeholders, stressing firm and stakeholder mutual interdependence. They argue that their model replaces privileged managerial monologues with multilateral stakeholder dialogues, and takes a more postmodern view of stakeholder ethics and social responsibility. Calton and Kurland argue that multilateral models depend on the creation and building of trust, which they achieve via communication and collective action in 'collaborative governance. In the process, they recast managerial discretion, as exercised in judging between stakeholder differences, with management as moral agency, taking part in dialogues without having the 'casting vote'. The model thus moves away from individualism as the core of ethics to an 'ethic of care' position that is also found in Kohlberg's work, although by a different route. A similar critique is made by Ten Bos (1997) in discussing Bauman's postmodern ethics. Ten Bos argues, with Bauman (1993), that business ethicists, consultants and managers who claim to be able to do the moral thinking for others need to reconsider the idea of the moral autonomy of those who work in organizations. In a voice which echoes Richard Sennett's arguments about the corrosion of character, he argues that as far as business ethics 'does not enhance this moral autonomy but instead proffers a rationalized and rule-governed ethics, it may very well undermine the moral nature of people working in organizations' (Ten Bos 1997: 997). For each of these postmodern commentators then, moral agency is important, and stakeholder dialogue significant in re-empowering individual organizational members in the processes of organizational governance.

Character virtue

The fifth approach to business ethics shifts attention away from the content of ethical decision making, towards a manager's social manner and conduct; the ideal ethical manager being someone of good character and sound personal integrity. Virtue ethics has a long history in both East and West. Confucius (c. 551–479 BC) and a long line of subsequent Chinese philosophers advocated a self-disciplined approach to life that emphasized traditional etiquette, the honouring of properly developed and diligently maintained social ties and obligations, humility, moderation, self-restraint, respect for others and moral self-cultivation (Ivanhoe 2000). The Greek philosopher Aristotle (384–322 BC) emphasized a not-dissimilar set of qualities of good leaders, including 'honesty, reasonableness, kindness, hopefulness, love of home and of friends and comrades and guests, and of one's fellow-men, and love of what is noble' (Aristotle 1952). Tom Morris (1997) notes also that 'magnificence' was a key Aristotelian virtue, charisma that made a leader stand out. He suggests that contemporary team players be loyal, sincere, reliable, trustworthy, benevolent, sensitive, helpful, empathic, modest, open, tolerant, faithful, committed, dignified and self-disciplined.

No single set of characteristics, however, defines the 'good person'. Character adjectives are less useful than role models, something that Mao Zedong, in lionizing model workers, realized (Mao 1990; Ebrey 1993). Virtue ethics may nevertheless help to counterbalance psychological egotism. While partners, close friends and perhaps colleagues will remind us of our unique faults, we can also cultivate our own virtues. There are several everyday opportunities for ongoing moral self-development, including handling adversity, detecting and avoiding hubris (overconfidence and arrogance) and noticing and appreciating others' virtue (see Snell 1993a: 222–8). I will take up this theme again, in the section on 'Lifelong learning and business ethics'.

However, the character virtue argument raises one of the most important questions in ethics: who is responsible for injustices, oppressions and unfairness – the system or the individual? Maclagan (1998), who is one of the strongest proponents of the character virtue approach, would argue that it is the manager's responsibility because he or she always has leeway to act and make choices. He contends that managers are the moral agents of an organization and not vice versa. What Maclagan (1998: 48) believes organizations need to do is develop a dialogic mode of dealing with ethical dilemmas, in which dilemmas are shared and dealt with by proceeding in a judgmental mode, collectively. This argument assumes that moral character will prevail because people have the potential for critical reflection and deliberation and will act responsibly or rise to the occasion (Pataki 2000: 839). The problem with this view is that it fails to address the need for organizations to deal with system problems, as in the case of healthcare, where medical errors that cause deaths can be prevented, not by pressuring doctors to take greater care and responsibility, but by altering how, for example, certain drugs are administered (Herman 2000). In other words, there are areas in which institutional responsibility for certain risks and adverse events requires protocols, routines and standards of care, and should not be left to 'moral heroes' to right

such wrongs (Pataki 2000: 839). I will return to these arguments in the sections on 'Whistle-blowing' and Corporate codes of conduct.

Cultural relativism, global ethics or dialogue?

There remains a fifth objection to business ethics, to which I now turn. It stems from the discovery that business customs and moral standards vary from culture to culture, as do feelings and perceptions about what is fair and just (Leung 1988). *Cultural relativism* assumes that such variations mean that moral obligations stem from the customs, mores, laws and rules of a particular culture or society and that conduct is ethically appropriate and legitimate if it conforms to predominant local norms and practices (Frederick 1995; Williams 1992: 14–16). A related claim would be that family upbringing and wider socialization through formal and informal education combine to form the moral principles which 'good citizens' within a particular culture share. It would follow from these assumptions that we should operate as 'cogs' in whatever moral machinery we happen to find ourselves caught up in.

Doing cross-cultural business in an ethical manner would, according to cultural relativism, entail learning the norms of the host culture and following them, even if they violate standards at home. Cultural relativist advice to ethically minded managers travelling abroad, and suffering 'culture shock', is to close their eyes and visualize a placard bearing the words: JUST KNOW THE CUSTOMS AND CONFORM! To become a cultural relativist, the manager, although familiar with deontology and other ideas discussed above, while travelling abroad, leaves the dynamic play of these various theories locked in the suitcase, and instead follows the expectations, whatever they are, of those, whoever they are, who 'own' the territory, wherever it is. On returning home, she or he still keeps the homeless ideas of deontology and so on locked in the suitcase, and adopts the homespun morality expressed in newspaper editorials, at the local club or by the boss. Cultural relativism has no satisfactory answer (see also Wellman 1963). It decommissions critical thinking and considered moral judgement (Midegely 1984: 71; Hauserman 1999: 215).

That said, the crux of the cultural relativist argument – that there are no a priori and 'culture-free' moral values and therefore supposedly 'universal' standards may in reality merely be 'might is right' impositions by the powerful – is difficult to categorically refute. However, cultural relativism fails to resolve this problem and can itself be used to excuse questionable practices, while failing to provide guidance on the production of 'better' ones. In any case, morality in any one locality is rarely monolithic; even 'strong' corporate cultures allow organizationally committed managers to have their own private reservations and antagonisms (Höpfl 1992; Chapter 3). Mutually contradictory moral traditions coexist in Western countries (MacIntyre 1988), and a different set, also characterized by eclectic richness and inconsistency, operates in China (Hua 1995: 33–4). Some 'customs', such as bribery (see below) ... and nepotism (see below) by officials to those connected to them by family or gift-giving ties, known as *guanxi* in China (Steidlmeier 1999), may represent the entanglements of traditions that have become corrupted as modernity has outflanked them, and serve narrow, special interests only. Or they may be expedient ways, tolerated but not welcomed by most local citizens, of coping with the absence of distributive justice.

In polar opposition to cultural relativism, the idea that there is a single set of universal or objective standards for judging moral conduct has gained momentum. Peter Singer (1991) predicts that moral traditions around the world are likely to converge. Such ideas are encouraged by the discovery that every major religion (Judaism, Christianity, Confucianism, Hinduism, Buddhism and Islam) teaches the golden rule: do as you would be done by (see Allinson 1995: 30; Treviño and Nelson 1995: 277; Marcic 1997). The Caux Round Table principles, a global code of business conduct, was published in 1986 in Switzerland by senior business leaders from Europe, Japan and North America (*Business Ethics Magazine* 1995). Such codes are potentially helpful guides, but, as noted above, they risk unilaterally imposing the values of the strong onto the weak in a totalizing manner, similar to the way the International Monetary Fund (IMF) has been stamping economic rationalism onto developing nations, particularly in the wake of the Asian financial crisis of the late 1990s.

Integrative social contracts theory (ISCT)

The ISCT (Donaldson and Dunfee 1999) is a partial attempt to steer a course between the 'reef of relativism' on one side and the 'reef of colonial morality' posing as universalism on the other. ISCT assumes that there is a broad cross-cultural consensus on some 'hypernorms', such as the right to subsistence ... physical security and well-being, but leaves 'moral free space' within which local economic communities can determine their own local norms. In relation to finance, for example, the strict Islamic law of shariah prohibits gambling, the charging of interest on loans, and contracts that fail to specify in tangible detail the services or goods that are to be sold (Esty 2000).

According to ISTC, where two or more economic communities are in contact and find that some local norms clash, value conflicts are resolved by applying priority rules, paraphrased below:

- Let transactions and practices that are located within a single community, and have no significant negative impact on outside stakeholders, be governed by local community norms
- The more extensive or more global the community, the greater priority should be given to its norms
- Norms that are necessary to maintain the local economic environment should be prioritized over norms that may damage it
- If there are multiple conflicting norms, patterns of consistency provide the basis for prioritization
- Well-defined norms have priority over less precise norms.

There are still strong hints of pro-Western bias in these rules, but at least they leave some room for dialogue. Jürgen Habermas (1984, 1987), the contemporary German philosopher and advocate of critical modern ethics, suggests an alternative perspective, envisaging morality that allows, encourages and arises from the 'ideal speech situation', in which people make themselves understood without fear, coercion, defensiveness or distortion. While Habermas regards this as the medium in which universal ethics emerges, we need not assume that. If dialogue gives rise to agreement on norms that are more just, less damaging and so on in the circumstances, this will do. The next time, we might arrive at something better or different, as circumstances change. Moral traditions at both organizational and societal levels are alive and in flux, with constant room for reform and revision. According to Boston College's Richard Nielsen (1996), who derives much of his thought from postmodern philosophy, tradition building and organizational learning proceeds through dialogue and self-questioning. If the dominant parties are ready, dialogue can serve to reconstruct traditions and disentangle them from that which is revealed to be corrupt and unjust. In ideal form, dialogue entails 'a suspension of thoughts, impulses, judgements, opinions, (and) assumptions' (Cayer 1997: 48). These hang in space (Bohm 1990: 11; Cayer 1997: 49), so that thought becomes aware of itself, its own incoherence, inadequacy and bias (Cayer 1997: 58–9). Nielsen admits, however, that in organizations, 'in large part because of the lack of protected civic space, dialog of any form is unusual' (Nielsen 1996: 216). Nothing is learned, however, if there is only conformity to that which happens to be dominant, and if dominant parties see no compelling reason to question their own assumptions. If dialogue is not possible, there are other options for the ethically minded manager, which I consider later in this chapter.

Bribes, commissions and gifts

Anti-bribery probably qualifies as a hypernorm, in ISCT. Bribery is widely acknowledged to be procedurally and distributively unjust, and fares poorly in utilitarian assessments, because it has extremely damaging, even devastating, social and economic consequences (Andrews 1988; Klitgaard 2000). The narrow expediency of bribe giving is 'role distortion for the firm' (Waters 1988: 183). Host governments in every corner of the globe have made it illegal on their own soil (Wambold 1977; Alpern 1993: 57). Nonetheless, bribery is widespread because, like other crime, it is concealed, sometimes by the very people who have made it illegal. When discovered in high places, during the 1990s, it precipitated the fall of governments in Japan, India, Italy, Indonesia and South Korea. 'Sleaze' became a political issue in the 1997 UK general election, with a very safe Conservative seat falling to an independent candidate Martin Bell, and continues to embarrass the current 'New Labour' government.

A famous bribery case involved Lockheed, which in the 1970s was discovered to have paid out around US$25 million in bribes in connection with sales of its Tristar L-1011 aircraft in Japan (Boulton, 1978). The resulting public outrage led to the Foreign Corrupt Practices Act (FCPA), making the USA the first nation to prohibit bribery abroad (Greanis and Windsor 1982). As summarized by Linda Treviño and Catherine Nelson (1995: 274), the FCPA prohibits the offering of bribes to politicians or government officials in order to sway their judgement and get or hold on to business. It allows 'grease payments' to persuade officials to do their job more swiftly or thoroughly, so long as the final outcome of such work is not distorted. Extortion payments, such as ransoms paid to free a hostage manager, are also allowed. Despite these loopholes, USA businesspeople complained that the FCPA made them suffer competitive disadvantage (Pastin and Hooker 1980). Indeed, other countries in the Organization for Economic Cooperation and Development (OECD), including the UK, implicitly encouraged overseas bribery, by allowing it to be tax deductible (Blackhurst, 1999). The FCPA nevertheless survived the Reagan administration and, after strong opposition from European business lobbies, the OECD's 'Convention on Combating Bribery of Foreign Public Officials' was signed by 34 countries on 17 December, 1997, and came into force on 15 February 1999 (see OECD 2000). International Chamber of Commerce rules, which represent voluntary self-regulation, prohibit international bribery

within the private sector, which the OECD convention does not address (see ICC 2000).

Transparency International (TI) publishes two league tables annually. The 1999 *Bribe Payers Index* (TI 2000a) ranks 19 leading exporting nations, according to their corporations' propensity to bribe senior public officials. Surveys were conducted in 14 emerging market countries, including the Philippines, Argentina, Hungary and Morocco, of perceptions among over 770 senior executives in major companies, professional firms, chambers of commerce, major commercial banks and law firms of the integrity of visiting businesspeople from developed countries. The 'cleanest' businesspeople operating abroad were perceived to be those from Sweden, Australia and Canada. Of European businesspeople, those perceived to be most inclined to offer bribes were from Italy.

Transparency International's 1999 *Corruption Perceptions Index* (TI 2000a, 2000b, 2000c) is based on 17 polls, carried out during 1997 to 1999. These involved a total of more than 20,000 international businesspeople and commentators rating various countries, and around 74,000 members of the general public around the world rating their own countries. This index focuses on the perceived incidence of bribery within the borders of particular countries. Out of 99 nations ranked in the 1999 league table, Denmark, Finland, New Zealand and Sweden were perceived to be the least corrupt locations (that is, ranked 1–4), and Cameroon, Nigeria, Indonesia and Azerbaijan the most corrupt (that is, ranked 96–9). Among European countries, the former Soviet bloc tended to be perceived as more corrupt. Gift giving may go hand in hand with developing business relationships in places like China (ranked equal 58th) and South Korea (ranked equal 50th), and was, according to Confucian tradition, a sign of respect and trust building rather than an instrumental means to personal advantage. Given the difficulty, however, of drawing a line between gifts and bribes, as evident in the mediocre rankings of these countries, companies doing business there, and indeed anywhere, are advised to develop codes of practice specifying limits to what may be given and received, and requiring all gifts to be reported (Snell and Tseng 2001).

Nepotism

Nepotism entails a particular type of favouritism, through which a decision maker's relatives or close friends, or those of an influential stakeholder, are appointed to core positions of influence or perhaps sinecures (token positions to which attractive benefits are attached). Nepotism is normally associated with inefficiency and bureau-pathology. For example, in mainland China, private businesses (Wank 1995:

166–7) and even Western-invested joint venture companies (Snell and Tseng 2000) are routinely pressurized to appoint the relatives of government officials to attractive positions, simply in order to be allowed to grow without bureaucratic harassment. In Indonesia, raging forest fires and the crony relationship, stretching over 40 years, between President Suharto and Bob Hasan, symbolized the evils of Suharto's corrupt regime. Hasan was made head of four associations involved in the regulation of forestry and related trade, and his timber, shipping and insurance businesses thrived on concessions (Dauvergne 1998; Thoenes 1998; Robertson-Snape 1999).

The problem of nepotism is by no means confined to developing or transitional economies. All 20 commissioners of the European Commission resigned after a special audit committee uncovered six cases of 'fraud, mismanagement and nepotism'. Among these was a scandal involving Edith Cresson, then head of the European Union's science, research and development directorate. She was accused of having improperly appointed and remunerated her septuagenarian dentist friend Ron Berthelot from the same home town as a 'special advisor' on research priorities into AIDS, cancer and technological innovation (see Bates 1999; Serbanescu 2000). One month into the contract, during which Berthelot's work output comprised a single three-line document, he became seriously ill and could not continue. He received ten months' salary, on Cresson's insistence. Berthelot did have various medical and legal qualifications beyond his dentistry specialism, but as a member of the European Parliament's research committee commented: 'There's nothing wrong with awarding a contract to someone you know who is qualified, but if it is a personal friend, then it is a different matter. It looks like cronyism' (Williams 1998: 215). That procedures are seen to be scrupulously followed and operators of the system are seen to be above suspicion, are essential attributes of procedural justice.

There are, however, special contexts where nepotism could perhaps be defended. For example, overseas Chinese small businesses are typically run by an inner circle of family members, a practice that they may justify on the grounds of ensured loyalty through Confucian bonds of obligation (Redding 1990; Tu 1998). Nepotism is, however, becoming less acceptable among Chinese managers in Taiwan (Hempel and Chang 2000) and Singapore (Tan 2000).

Ethics and human rights

It is natural and understandable for employers to be concerned about the work ethics of employees, and for them to expect that the workforce will meet basic standards of punctuality, accuracy, truth telling and respect for company property. Annual losses due to employee theft in the USA are estimated to be around $200 billion (Niehoff and Paul 2000), potentially a massive distributive injustice, although it is possible that these figures could also represent a myriad of egotistic reactions to and attempted idiosyncratic and anarchic corrections of pre-existing distributive injustice, that is, perceived exploitation of the workforce.

There are, accordingly, employers who violate employees' rights. For example, Anita Chan (1998) notes that workers in China and elsewhere in the developing world suffer rights abuse, and calls for international agreements on occupational health and safety, maximum working hours, rest periods and banning workplace corporal punishment (as mentioned above, a problem of taking retributive justice into one's own hands). A third type of problem entails the violation of employee rights by other employees, as in sexual harassment. As the case below reveals, abuse can involve quite bizarre acts of violation.

This case might be a somewhat unusual example of the violation of employees' human rights, and the fear

CASE EXAMPLE

One example of rights abuse came to light in May 1995, when Albert Yeung, head of the Emperor group of companies (and owner of Hong Kong's most expensive car licence plate at approximately US$1.6 million), was tried in Hong Kong on two counts of false imprisonment and criminal intimidation towards former employee, Michael Lam. The *Eastern Express* (25 May 1995) reported how Lam was alleged to have undergone a humiliating ordeal on the night of 9–10 December 1994 (after he had left the company and begun work for a possible competitor). This entailed being

made to go down on his hands and knees to serve tea to another employee, being told by Yeung that the most junior employee would slap him in the face to make him smart, and being scolded by Yeung in front of other employees for about 15 minutes. Yeung also allegedly threatened to break Lam's left leg over a 'business dispute'. The *Sunday Hong Kong Standard* (28 May 1995) recorded that the magistrate said that he 'cannot declare justice has been done', on acquitting Yeung after five witnesses, including Lam, refused to give evidence and said that they could not recall what had happened. The newspaper described Yeung as 'a good friend of some of the most respected and well-known people in Hong Kong'.

associated with it, but there is a second general ethical problem that lurks behind it: the extortion of labour. Coercion need not be physical, as it was in the Albert Yeung case. When employees feel economically vulnerable (for example face 'negative equity' on home mortgages), fear loss of livelihood, and lack union protection, employers merely need to insist that employees meet targets by a certain deadline, and keep up with the workflow.

A survey of 400 companies, between them employing more than eight million employees in 17 European countries, revealed that job security declined substantially between 1985 and 1995 (ISR 1995). Looking back at the 1990s, Cary Cooper (1999: 115) characterizes the early part by such weasel words as 'downsizing', 'delayering', 'flattening' and 'rightsizing': 'the hard reality experienced by many was year-on-year redundancy, constant restructuring and substantial organisational change'. The legacy of this has been 'fewer people doing more and feeling much less secure'. A former personnel director from the UK put it this way: 'Once management ever gets its act together, labour doesn't have a cat in hell's chance' (Snell 1993a: 136), but managers and other professionals have not been spared. Cooper notes that a 1997 survey of UK managers found that more than three quarters regularly exceeded weekly contracted hours, more than half reported working every evening, and more than a third regularly worked at weekends. He also reports a 1998 survey, which revealed that a majority of managers regarded such excessive working hours to have adversely affected morale, productivity, health and family relationships (Cooper 1999). Not exactly getting one's act together, then. The 3000-hour year and the 60-hour week are now common in the West (Handy 1995: 179), not only in white-collar sweatshops housed in Hong Kong's high-rises and campuses.

On the surface, this phenomenon may appear to reflect contemporary 'reality', that is, objective necessity. Logic calls for it. If competitors re-engineer and downsize, so must we. If their managerial and professional staff work unofficial 60+, 70+, 80+ hour weeks, so must we, otherwise we lose competitiveness, market share, our jobs. There may even be indirect coercion to use one's own time to enrol in 'post-compulsory' qualification programmes (MacFarlane 2000), so as not to fall behind. Some 'high-fliers' might enjoy this life but, in the struggle, many others risk losing the time needed to 'get a life' of their choosing. Hence my earlier point, when discussing stakeholder approaches, that learning organizations would provide time off for such programmes.

Thus, unofficial working hours escalation is a free-market version of a nuclear arms race that can, in some sense, wipe out lives. Matts Alvesson and Hugh Willmott (1996) point out that colonization of the life world by managerial rationality is addressable and perhaps containable through political processes, which themselves are open to democratic influence. While collective corrective action is being taken to reduce *official* working hours to 48 hours per week in European countries (Walsh 1998), the problem of unofficial working hours' escalation may remain a problem that only open, intimate dialogue between individuals and 'close ones' can begin to address. Bjørn Kjonstad and Hugh Willmott (1995) consider a cognate case dilemma example (a husband attracted by a proposed job posting overseas, a wife with misgivings about relocation), and argue that engaging in dialogue, by drawing on the higher Kohlberg stages of moral reasoning (which I discuss later in the chapter), allows partners (perhaps also their children) to develop their relationship while facing up to such dilemmas.

Ethics and 'green' concerns

There are a number of arguments for and against taking deliberate measures to protect our physical environment by restricting economic development (Donaldson and Werhane 1993: 379–80).

The arguments against are:

- economic growth enhances human life by providing us with more of what we want
- Third World economies must be given room to develop, not held back
- new technologies will inevitably be developed to repair earlier damage
- if recycled products, national parks, a clean environment, and so on are such important preferences, then consumers will choose to pay for them directly.

Arguments in favour are:

- we face the disaster of wiping out our natural resources
- future generations of human beings have the right to a livable environment
- clean air, the preservation of rare animal species and virgin forests and so on are valued by us as non-market resources despite their economic costs
- the 'environment' itself has intrinsic moral standing as an inherent part of the natural order.

Such arguments, for and against, can be illustrated by the following case example of environmental pollution in Hong Kong, where the business community and the government, at least until recently, wholeheartedly adopted the 'against' position.

CASE EXAMPLE

After the opening of Hong Kong's first container port at Kwai Chung in 1972, and the adoption of new economic policies in China in the late 1970s, a 'tidal wave' of steel flowed up from Kwai Chung towards the border with China. While most of the land was officially zoned for agricultural purposes, and the Hong Kong government convicted a company called Melhado in 1982 for wrongful use of land, the owner, a local politician, won the appeal, sweeping aside the requirement for planning permission and precipitating a rush to industrialization that destroyed much of the area. Many farmers laid concrete over their fields and became millionaires by leasing the space for container storage, charging US$250 per container per day in early 1994. Some storage areas have held up to 800 containers, yielding US$200 000 per day. Other farmers used their land for scrapyards. New legislation followed, but between 1991 and 1993, out of 174 cases of unauthorized development of rural land, only 11 landlords and operators were convicted, with fines as low at US$1000.

The government blamed the illegal change of land use for causing traffic jams and, more importantly, widespread flooding during a typhoon in September 1993, which damaged one-third of the remaining farmland. In October 1993, Governor Chris Patten announced further legislation and the setting up of a special task force. The chairman of the Private Sector Committee on the Environment said that he spoke for '65 per cent of the Hang Seng Index', in supporting these measures. Rural leaders, however, accused the government of stripping them of their right to use their own land. A government official who was leading the task force then admitted that since there was no statutory plan in the affected areas, the new legislation had no teeth – nothing would be achieved without cooperation with the landowners. Some local politicians reported that many appointed members of local governing boards had direct or indirect interests in the converted farmland, and had power and 'face' in the localities affected. A compromise solution was reached, under which operators would be issued with temporary licences for two to three years and required to plant trees around the land, pending the relocation of the container parks to designated areas. The understanding for the longer term appeared to be that former container parks would be used for housing rather than restored to farmland or open countryside. Since transition of sovereignty to China in 1997, government policy on this matter has not been revoked. By the middle of 2000, however, there had been no discernible beautification of the areas or indeed any change in the status quo. Indeed, the author of this chapter can see a large container park from his study window.

Source: Drawn from various items in the *South China Morning Post* (13 October 1993, 26 October 1993, 25 November 1993, 28 April 1994, 12 July 1994, 18 October 1994) and from an article in *Window* (15 October 1993).

Is the operator's role in the continued environmental despoliation morally justifiable? From a deontological point of view, the answer is a clear-cut 'no'. The integrity and dignity of the physical environment (of which we are all stewards) has a much stronger moral claim than serving the owners' rights. Applying utilitarianism and stakeholder analysis, the issues are more complex, but still broadly implicate the operators and owners.

One line of utilitarian argument supports their actions. Parks for empty containers play a necessary role within a successful wealth- and benefit-generating system. The growth in container traffic through Hong Kong reflects China's economic development and its increased involvement in international trade. Western consumers get more of what they want, Hong Kong trading companies thrive as 'go-betweens', and the access to overseas markets promises pathways out of grinding poverty for the emerging mainland Chinese manufacturing labour force. Just about everybody is happy with things as they are, and if finding alternative container park sites is too much of a problem it is not the operators' fault.

On the other hand, it can be argued that the owners and operators should take account of the overall well-being of Hong Kong society, jeopardized by the insidious and irreversible loss of natural beauty and the extra inconvenience caused to travelling in the countryside. These might even be considered as threatened market resources, because there are now calls on the Special Administrative Region (SAR) government to promote ecotourism (Ng 2000) and the European Union Minister of Environmental Protection, Jo Leinen, has warned that further environmental deterioration may deter investors from locating regional offices in Hong Kong (Wan 2000). The container park owners and operators imply that market forces could settle the issue, putting the onus on those who feel the problem most acutely to buy their land and change its usage. That would set up an unfair and unjust 'bidding game', in which those relatively few Hong Kong citizens who actively recognize the value of natural beauty would be hopelessly pitted against a multitude of international consumers in the rest of the world, each of whom ultimately pays an infinitesimal share of the rental charges for container storage, but may know nothing about the effects on the countryside. No group of citizens could afford to pay what would amount to a huge 'ransom' to keep containers off the land.

On top of the aesthetic decline, the operators' actions have resulted in the loss of farmland. Consequently, Hong Kong imports more food, mostly from China, where there are already concerns that there may soon be insufficient arable land to sustain the mainland population. It appears that no constructive attempt has been made to resolve the problems of container storage, scrap disposal and changed land use. Representatives of Hong Kong's big business community offered lip-service to the former governor's plans, but seem to have given little else in return for their share of the benefits arising from the operation of the container system as a whole.

Ethical dilemmas and organizational dynamics

So far, in illustrating the conceptual application of business ethics principles, the chapter has analysed a small selection of issues from an 'armchair critic' perspective. It is appropriate now to consider the practical challenges involved in facing organizational pressures and solving ethical dilemmas arising in day-to-day managerial work.

Ethical dilemmas and moral responsibility

Middle managers' everyday ethical dilemmas are typically much 'greyer' than the headline-grabbing issues discussed above (Toffler 1986). Maclagan (1995: 174) quotes from Chapter Five of John Steinbeck's novel *The Grapes of Wrath* in which the spokesmen of a bank, which owned land, have the following dialogue with the tenant farmers whom they have been sent to evict:

'We're sorry. It's not us. It's the monster. The bank isn't like a man.'
'Yes, but the bank is only made of men.'
'No you're wrong there – quite wrong there. The bank is something else than men. It happens that every man in the bank hates what the bank does, and yet the bank does it. The bank is something more than men. I tell you. It's the monster. Men made it, but they can't control it.'

Maclagan (1995: 174) poses a number of questions about the case:

Who is responsible? Can we identify individuals? Most importantly, can we criticize those sent to evict the farmers? Here we can recognize the conflict between ... those who gave the orders to oust the tenants ... and their spokesmen. But is the reaction of the latter based on reasoned thought, or is it emotive? Does it reflect a concern for justice, or a sympathetic reaction to the plight of particular people in a personal encounter?

Similar questions, suitably adapted for the context, would apply to most kinds of managerial dilemma, but perhaps the central theme in this particular case is the apparent mightiness of embedded systems that, on the surface at least, seem to override the will and judgement of individual functionaries, who feel dwarfed, yet somehow responsible. The implied, and niggling, sense of guilt, the very need to offer excuses, suggests a shadowy recognition that while we cannot be purely independent, rational, sovereign actors, we are rarely, if ever, *forced* by transcendent structural arrangements. Rather, we are trapped by the webs of meaning that we ourselves have been spinning in collaboration with others (Barnes 1988).

Barbara Toffler (1986), in her interview study of US managers' dilemmas, found that these were difficult to encapsulate, and involved many contrasting and possibly competing values, along with a variety of organizational pressures and demands. She also found that the managers usually wanted to do 'the right thing', but were uncertain of their responsibilities, unsure about what to do and often felt unable to put their preferred solutions into practice. Two-thirds of the dilemmas reported to Toffler related to the management of relationships. Another study found that 36 per cent of dilemmas concerned line employees, and 6 per cent concerned peers or superiors, while 22 per cent involved customers and 19 per cent suppliers (Waters et al. 1986). Analysing the source of 126 dilemmas reported by 39 managers in six Hong Kong companies, Snell et al. (1996) found that they typically stemmed from being asked to do something that was wrong or mistaken, or from noticing behaviour that was wrong or incompetent (see Table 8.1).

The five bodies of ethical thought introduced in the first half of this chapter are reference points to help managers to appraise ethical problems from various angles, but they may often not yield unequivocal solutions. Turning them into action tends to be the most difficult aspect of typical middle managerial dilemmas such as the one faced by Steinbeck's bank spokesmen, and by Simon in our opening case. There are 10 possible ways in which subordinate managers can respond to such situations where they observe or are involved in wrongdoing (Nielsen 1987):

1. Don't think about it.
2. Quietly, but knowingly, get on with it, conform.

Table 8.1 Sources of dilemmas reported by interviewees

Sources of dilemma	% Incidence
Subordinates' perceived deceit, incompetence or disobedience	18
Policy, or request by superior, that is mistaken	25
Policy, or request by superior, that is ethically suspicious, exploitative or unfair	13
Improper, suspicious or unfair request from client, supplier or colleague	6
Conflicting instructions, decisions or directives from above	9
Caught in the middle in a direct conflict between other parties	5
Direct dispute with another party	6
Aware of other's misconduct, neglect or unfairness, but not directly responsible	8
Other	10

Source: Adapted from Robin Snell, Almaz Chak and Keith Taylor (1996) 'The impact of moral ethos on how ethical dilemmas are experienced and resolved in six Hong Kong companies', *Management Research News*, **19**(9), p. 81.

3. Do it under protest, reluctantly comply.
4. Conscientiously object, refuse to play an active part, let others do it instead.
5. Quit the job.
6. Secretly (anonymously) blow the whistle (report it to the press, the police and so on).
7. Publicly blow the whistle.
8. Secretly threaten to blow the whistle (for example anonymous letter to the CEO).
9. Sabotage (make the action impossible).
10. Negotiate and build consensus for change in the behaviour or policy.

Nielsen (1987) advises against option 6, because it may feel like betrayal and lead to distrust and suspicion. Regarding option 7, review of research on whistle-blowing supports the popular impression that such actions are likely to provoke dire retribution from employers, and may result in court cases, bankruptcy and possibly imprisonment (Vinten 1992). During the 1980s, whistle-blowing British civil servant Clive Ponting narrowly escaped gaol (Ponting 1986), but Sarah Tisdale (who tried option 6) was less fortunate.

While the development and improvement of moral traditions may depend on the radical courage of whistle-blowers, Nielsen recommends option 10, that is, negotiate and build consensus, wherever possible. How realistic is this for Simon in the Chinese context?

Dissenting options (Nielsen's 3, 4 and 10) may be most viable in countries where there are stronger aspirations to egalitarianism, flat hierarchies and individual human rights (for example some Western democracies). Even so, Robert Jackall (1988) found, in three US companies, that disagreeing with the boss was said to be tantamount to 'putting your head between

your legs and kissing your ass goodbye'. The prospect of dissent may be even more daunting in societies characterized by *high power distance* (see Hofstede 1980; Chapter 3), where it is taken for granted that power is distributed and used unequally, and by *high collectivism*, where consensus is valued more than self-expression, and conformity provided in exchange for protection. In a special study of eight dilemmas reported by Hong Kong Chinese managers, arising from requests by a boss or supervisor to do something they knew to be wrong, the following four options were discovered (Snell 1999a):

1. 'Little potato' obedience (quiet, fearful, humble, deferential conformity).
2. Token obedience (following orders half-heartedly and semi-incompetently).
3. Covert or undercover disobedience (only pretending to obey, and keeping disobedience hidden).
4. Open disobedience (conscientious objection).

In line with Jackall's finding, *open disobedience* was chosen only in the two cases where there was either an explicit and official right to dissent or where line authority was not direct, that is, the manager in question was not dissenting or disobeying an immediate 'supervisor'. The reasons why this might be the case are revealed when we look at the phenomenon of whistle-blowing.

Whistle-blowing

Marcia Miceli and Janet Near (1991) have seen the act of whistle-blowing as a practice that directly challenges managerial authority and power. A review of whistle-blower case studies (Perrucci et al. 1980; Near and Jensen 1983; Near and Miceli 1987; Glazer and Glazer 1989; Miceli and Near 1991) suggests that whistle-blowing and retaliation are not a discrete pair of stimulus–response events, but tend to involve a sequence of episodes triggered by an initial event. The triggering event is usually associated with an awareness of initial wrongdoing with regard to illegal, immoral or illegitimate organizational processes and practices. After pre-whistle-blowing decision-making processes have occurred, the actor reviews the choice of actions (or no action) available.

Generally, it has been shown that most whistle-blowers face some form of retaliation unless organizations who have suffered (loss of any kind), and have set in place internal mechanisms to take account of a whistle-blower's allegations, view a whistle-blower not as a dissident but as a reformer (Frith, 1994).

Near and Jensen (1983) also argue that a whistle-blower who stands alone without support is seen as powerless in the organization and can expect greater retaliation from the organization. This could be someone who has no or very few power resources, has strong power dependency relationships and can be easily replaced (Mechanic 1962; Kanter 1979; Conger and Kanungo, 1988; Luthans et al. 1988). These people might expect greater retaliation from the organization. Conversely, they argue, a whistle-blower who has many power resources, that is, is seen as irreplaceable, has others dependent on him or her, has influential networks and a strong case, namely the claims of wrongdoing (that is, can generate public support), might be less vulnerable to retaliation from the organization. They go

on to argue 'that there is a possibility that the organization's pattern of retaliation against whistle-blowers is simply random. In this case the organization may be reacting to a set of unique and unpredictable variables' (Near and Jensen 1983: 8). The abbreviated case study below illustrates how whistle-blowing can surface in an organization and the type of retaliation that can ensue from a whistle-blowing event.

The organization in the case study developed certain rituals of fear, intimidation and power to manage the wrongdoing and the retaliation was not random. It remains to be seen, in the case of the UK, whether the Public Interest Disclosure Act, pioneering legislation enacted in 1998 to protect whistle-blowers, will reduce the number of cases of apparent injustice to them and help to improve moral standards at work (Weale 2000). The signs are promising. On 10 July , 2000, Toni Fernandes, former accountant at Netcom Consultants, of Reading, who had been dismissed after reporting to the board that the company's chief executive had made £371,000 in false claims, was awarded £293,441 compensation (Shaw et al. 2000).

In the case study, the excuse given to Edward by Nigel that receiving kickbacks 'is a part of the game of business' raises wider questions about moral responsibility. As Sims et al. (1993: 59–60) argue, many organizations, indeed probably every organization, has a 'hidden economy' in which it is accepted that individuals can 'profit' and engage in some form of *fiddling* – bending rules, pilfering (for example taking extra pens, short-changing or overcharging, making unauthorized phone calls and so on). Fiddlers often see their fiddling as an added 'perk' or 'entitlement' of the job and some-

CASE EXAMPLE

Edward Farkas was given the position of acting purchasing officer for his company when Felix Shivers went on long service leave. One week into the job, Edward was surprised when one of the company's subcontractors approached him about a forthcoming tender and intimated that he expected that it was 'business as usual'. Despite often being the highest tender, Edward had heard that the subcontractor had been awarded a substantial number of contracts.

Edward was convinced that Felix had been accepting 'kickbacks' from this subcontractor. He decided to take up the issue with his immediate superior, Nigel Walpole, director of finance. Nigel warned Edward that his allegations were very serious and that unless he had more conclusive evidence, he should drop the matter. Edward was dismayed by this response, and recommended that

another contractor be awarded the tender. The subcontractor in question was awarded the contract. Edward's work was now being constantly criticized by Nigel. In retaliation, Edward went to Nigel and threatened to 'blow the whistle' on the tendering racket, having discovered yet another subcontractor receiving preferential treatment. Nigel said: 'It is part of the game of business, and everyone does it!'

Several weeks later, Edward was summoned to the CEO's office and told that several subcontractors had alleged that he had asked for 'kickbacks' on tenders. Nigel accused Edward of having asked subcontractors to deliberately inflate their tender prices to pay their 'kickbacks'. Edward was summarily dismissed and escorted from the premises.

Source: Modified from Robin Snell (1999b) 'Managing ethically', in Liz Fulop and Stephen Linstead (eds) *Management: A Critical Text*, Melbourne: Macmillan Business, p. 349.

thing that others do as well. In effect, many organizations develop a 'zone of indifference' with regard to fiddling, and might even cost these 'activities' into their operational expenses. In other words, it becomes a part of embedded practice, is taken for granted, and is usually more costly to police than to eradicate. Fiddling rarely gives rise to whistle-blowing, for the wrongdoing that triggers whistle blowing is normally of a magnitude that brings into starker relief and conflict for the whistle-blower, such as Toni Fernandes, the brand of morality practised in the organization, the public image the organization tries to present to the outside world, and the moral standards he or she tries to live by outside the organization (Sims et al. 1993: 60).

Fiddling and other distortions can get out of hand, however, as revealed in Westley's (1990) study of the 'lying, stealing, cheating culture' at an automobile factory. Gross-Schaefer et al. (2000: 91) warn that 'a totally lax attitude [to fiddling] will signal that employee theft is acceptable, which is absolutely the wrong message'. They argue (p. 94) that, rather than emphasizing controls and surveillance, a more effective anti-theft strategy would aim to build a moral climate within which justice is seen to be done and where rewards are seen to be fair. Edward Sieh (1987) showed that petty theft at a garment factory was often triggered by episodes of perceived injustice on the part of management. If those at the top are not corrupt, and can demonstrate an open and constructive attitude in relation to justice, they may lead Nielsen's option 10, in relation to 'fiddling', and support corporate training that encourages ethical sensitivity and self-restraint, in relation to 'fiddling'.

Moral reasoning, moral motivations and care

No critical account of business ethics is complete without examining the controversial model of stages of moral reasoning development proposed by Lawrence Kohlberg (1927–87). Kohlberg's attempt to represent the deep structures behind critical reasoning is of special relevance to critical management studies, since conceptual 'tools', as described in the foundations of business ethics (see Table 8.2) are of little use unless people possess the competence to use them. Kohlberg explored the conditions under which the ability to engage in critical moral reasoning may grow and develop.

Kohlberg's own intellectual concern with moral issues was fuelled by a passion for social justice. At the age of 18 he was arrested and interned by British authorities when working to smuggle Jews into British-occupied Palestine (Hunt 1993). Later, he was active in educational reforms, for example playing a leading role in school democracy projects in Germany (Lind 1997)

and the USA (Kohlberg 1985). These aimed to foster capabilities for critical thinking through open dialogue conducted in the spirit of equality, rather than through didactic instruction.

In his 1958 doctoral dissertation, Kohlberg investigated how schoolboys explained their reasons for judging 'right' and 'wrong' decisions in a series of hypothetical ethical dilemmas that involved issues of justice, fairness and welfare. He rejected the cultural relativist notion, popular at the time, that moral behaviour was exclusively a matter of conformity to social norms, and claimed to have discovered a parallel between the boys' *moral* development and psychologist Jean Piaget's theory of *intellectual* development. Piaget assumed that children develop through stages by constructing progressively more complex cognitive structures as they interact with their environment (Crain 1992: 103). Kohlberg assumed, similarly, that the development of moral thought entailed progression through a fixed sequence of stages and proceeds by exposure to the cognitive challenges posed by moral dilemmas, rather than through socialization into particular moral values. Kohlberg died in 1987, and his final formulation of the model, published posthumously, is summarized in Table 8.2.

According to proponents of the model, at stages one and two, morality is confined to the *preconventional*. Typically, the individual operates from pure self-interest and expediency, and is concerned only about personal gain or loss: 'What's in it for me?' 'Why should I bother to help?' 'Who's in charge?' Social norms and conventions are obeyed only if there is a direct payoff. Stages three and four represent *conventional* morality, where conformity is valued for its own sake. At stage three, the concern is to please close friends, family and associates by meeting their expectations. At stage four, professional integrity and lawful pursuit of corporate-minded goals becomes an important end in itself. Morality at stage five and beyond is *postconventional*. At this level, rules or goals are seen to be invalid unless founded on a concern for social justice and collective well-being. Another way of describing the moral motive at stage five, for example, is 'striving to be reasonable, consistent and purposeful in pursuit of principles that are good for the community' (Snell 1997: 189). Stage five is counter to mainstream culture in all societies. Kohlbergian researchers claim to have found that less than one-fifth of adults reach stage five (Hersh et al. 1979; Treviño 1986; Treviño and Youngblood, 1990; Weber 1990), and stages six and seven are rare (Colby et al. 1983: 60)

A common misconception of the Kohlberg stages model concerns what happens when progressing through the moral stages. It is sometimes claimed that Kohlberg believed that as a person progressed to higher stages, they were no longer influenced by the earlier

Table 8.2 Stages in moral development

Stage	Orientation	Moral motives	Principles of what is 'right'	Typical social concerns
Zero	Impulsive and amoral	None	Right is whatever I want at any time, regardless of the consequences	None at all
One	Obedient; punishment-avoiding	Irrational dread of punishment; fear of those in authority	People in authority, and the rules that they set, must be obeyed exactly, so that punishment or disaster is avoided	Self-preservation is all-important. One is preoccupied with what those in power want and how to avoid causing them anger
Two	Personal benefits and rewards; getting a good deal for oneself	How to get the most pleasure and gain for oneself; calculating the personal risks and payoffs of an action	It is human nature to want to get the best for oneself, making deals with other people if necessary	Dealings are governed purely by self-interest. If cooperation with others is an absolute necessity, it is done through 'give and take' bargaining. If cooperation is not necessary, then other people's needs are ignored
Three	Conforming to social expectations; gaining approval	Avoiding disapproval by associates and close ones; wanting to be praised, liked and admired, rather than shamed	One must be nice to others and not hurt their feelings, be loyal to partners and live up to others' expectations	The capacity for empathy with the feelings of those in one's immediate circle is developed. Approval and liking by others comes to be valued for its own sake, and affects self-image. Shared commitments come to be more important than narrow self-interest
Four	Protecting law and order; maintaining the existing system of official social arrangements	Performing formal duties and responsibilities. Meeting official standards, working for the best interests of an institution	One must perform one's duty to society by upholding its law and order, and contributing to the good of the social institutions operating within it	Special effort is made to act consistently with official roles, duties and standards, and properly laid down rules and procedures. One aims to serve the needs and goals of the institution as a whole
Five	Promoting justice and welfare within the wider community, as defined in open and reasonable debate	Following principles that serve the best interests of the great majority. Striving to be reasonable, just and purposeful in one's actions	For the betterment of society as a whole, the underlying spirit of basic democratic and contractual rights must be acknowledged and upheld, even if existing institutions do not protect them	Over and above institutional needs, concern develops for the 'greater good', the wider public interest. Principles of basic justice and human rights are followed, rather than only what is laid down by existing laws or formal roles and rules
Six	Defending everyone's right to justice and welfare, universally applied	Applying well-thought-out principles, being ready to share and debate these openly and non-defensively with others	Everyone's basic human rights must be respected without exception; everyone has basic moral responsibilities from which no one is exempted	There is principled concern and respect for other persons because they are ends in themselves, and not mere instruments to meet others' purposes. One adopts a reflexive, self-critical approach in ethical decision making, so that the consistency of one's decisions is constantly under review
Seven	Respecting the cosmos as an integral whole, a oneness extending well beyond humanity	Respecting the intrinsic value of the cosmos, with its wider harmonies and paradoxes	Rights extend beyond what is immediately useful or interesting to humanity, e.g. to animal species and ecological systems regardless of their social utility	The integrity of 'the environment' and other systems making up the universe, regardless of their immediate importance for *Homo sapiens*, is valued for its own sake

Source: Model adapted from Lawrence Kohlberg (1981) *Essays on Moral Development, Volume One: The Philosophy of Moral Development*, San Francisco: Harper and Row, pp. 121–2, 128 and 409–12, and from Lawrence Kohlberg and Robert Ryncarz (1990) 'Beyond justice reasoning: Moral development and consideration of a seventh stage', in C.N. Alexander, and E.J. Langer, (eds) *Higher Stages of Human Development*, Oxford: Oxford University Press, pp. 193–5.

stages. Not so! The stages hierarchy is a model of the development of moral reasoning *capacity*, which means that if a manager becomes able to reason at, say, stage four, she or he still retains the ability to assess a situation from the point of view of stages zero, one, two and three, and may respond to a moral situation primarily from the lower stages (Elm and Weber 1994: 343). Kohlbergian analysis still entertains the possibility that certain situations, such as those involving distorted perception (Bersoff 1999), temptation, stress and 'bad mood', can alter people's moral predispositions. It follows, according to the model, that corruption spreads not only among people deemed to be 'retarded' in their moral development and who are thus incapable of stage four or above, but can also involve those who, for whatever reason, fail to apply their full moral reasoning capability.

Gendering ethics

Kohlberg identified Martin Luther King (1929–68) and Mahatma Gandhi (1869–1948) as role models of postconventional moral reasoning, perhaps adding fuel to criticism (see Gilligan 1982) that the original 100 per cent male sample cut a theoretical groove exclusively oriented towards social justice. Carol Gilligan, a former student of Kohlberg, sought to correct Kohlberg's relative neglect of care-based morality, a powerful moral force. Kohlberg modified his position in response to Gilligan's criticism, and in a final work (Kohlberg and Ryncarz 1990) elaborated and widened his definitions of postconventional morality, especially at the seventh stage, moving towards Gilligan to encompass the capacity for mercy, compassion, empathy and care, extending to all humanity and beyond.

However, several problems remain with Kohlberg's theory, and similar developmental theories, which Gilligan's criticism initiated, and Kohlberg's response is regarded, particularly by feminists, as inadequate. The criticisms could be summarized as follows.

Male evidence versus female evidence

Not only was Kohlberg's original sample entirely male, but this was a characteristic of much of the other empirical work on which the developmental approach was based. Accordingly the model developed from the assumption that the individual follows a path of development which involves increasing differentiation of the self from the other, until finally the autonomous self stands alone, free of the influence of others and contextual influences. This conception of the self, however, stems from a particularly *Western male experience* and is neither gender nor cross-culturally sensitive. Indeed, given that their moral position is privileged in society (as clerics, lawgivers, lawmakers

and so on), men might be said to have a vested interest in reproducing moral arguments that will justify this privilege, and thus their evidence, regarding moral reasoning, might be regarded as suspect. Women, then, as in much post-Freudian psychology, are inadequate or insufficiently developed males. For Kohlberg, they are arrested at level three, although potentially capable of freeing themselves from the bonds of emotionality that restrict them if given sufficiently challenging moral decisions to make.

Rationality versus emotionality

Owen Flanagan and Jonathan Adler (1983, cited in Held 1997: 636) have criticized the 'adequacy thesis' of Kohlberg's model, which assumes that the more a moral decision is based on formal rationality, the better it is. Since the time of the Greeks, rationality was favoured over other modes of response to the world, and this was traditionally seen as the preserve of men working in public life. So, historically long-held male assumptions were reproduced in the model's preference for the rational and formal in moral choices – such as enlightened self-interest or respect for moral law, rather than situational factors such as care, consideration and empathy. Indeed, certain biological differences, such as sexuality, have been held to define women as 'more emotional' than men and hence less capable of making higher moral judgements. Here theory, in the form of an articulated end point of 'more perfect' decision making, imposes itself on particular experiences and relegates decisions based on or displaying emotional criteria such as caring or nurturing to the immediate context of family and friends. When Kohlberg introduces the caring dimension at the highest level, it is a universal and diffuse version of caring that is presented, not the sort of caring a mother does for her children.

Differentiation versus connectedness

Accordingly, the model also emphasizes the individual 'self' as developing morally in relation to the universal, or to a generalized 'other', free of contextual constraints, especially in level seven. However, the idea of a self which is always defined in relation to, and entwined in, particular others, which gives it its defining characteristics and shape its decisions, is more appropriate to understanding both feminine ethics and non-Western conceptions of the self, particularly in East Asia. Here selves are always connected to other selves and are never independent.

Male moral experience versus female moral experience

If the self is regarded as itself being relational and

embedded, that is to say, the context is inseparable from the selves that develop within it, then the appropriateness of the developmental model is thrown into question. As Virginia Held (1997) points out, the actual experiences of people in making moral choices – their *moral experience* – is important in shaping the kind of judgements made and the criteria used for making them. Most women, for example, because of their relative absence from public life historically, and contemporary barriers such as the 'glass ceiling', have comparatively much less experience than men of dealing with the moral problems of governing, leading, exercising power over others and physical conflict. Many men, on the other hand, have little experience of the moral problems of family life, the relations between adults and children, motherhood and nurturance. However, the theory does not reflect this variety of experience, and men's experience is privileged and counts for more in the scheme.

The point which feminist theorists make is that women's different moral experiences arising from their different social roles need to be taken into account when theory is being developed, and not just incorporated as an afterthought. Indeed, when it is suggested that perhaps the most important of all human social relationships is that between mother or nurturer and child, and that this might provide a better model for social relations than, for example, the fair contract in a free market, it is hard to disagree. It is also hard to disagree with the ideals that relationships need not be dominated by self-interest or egotism, and that the principle of protecting individuals from caprice or domination is a basic human characteristic that should inform any moral schema. Where moral schemes, such as those imported into social relations and organizational life tend implicitly to favour a moral ethos derived from market capitalism and the power of the law backed by military force, an ethics of care, such as feminist ethics, might offer an important means of re-evaluation.

Corporate culture and moral ethos

In this section I will examine the impact on moral reasoning of corporate culture or *moral ethos*: implicit, unwritten, informal codes of conduct within organizations. In the subsequent section, I shall go on to discuss the possible merits and limitations of official, written company codes of conduct.

Moral ethos may be defined as the force field of tacit norms, values, beliefs, expectations and prohibitions, which influence ethical conduct in work settings. This set of pressures and inducements may differ from those in other walks of life. As Treviño (1992: 450) observed, 'individuals play highly differentiated roles that allow them to accept different values, norms and behaviours in different life domains (for example work and home)'.

Commentators argue that moral ethos at work matters, and that it may either be 'good' or 'bad'. Some assume that the typical moral ethos predisposes individuals to act amorally: 'Organization culture may influence perceptions of instrumentalities for motivation to engage in unethical behaviours' (Knouse and Giacalone 1992: 373); 'There is no cause for optimism in the idea that a solitary individual may withstand the organization's blandishments and maintain a strong moral sense. For, while some rare individuals will do so, many will not' (Schwartz 1990: 44). Hannah Arendt's (1963) classic account of the trial of Adolf Eichmann cast the latter as a hollow, bureaucrat-technician, a dull organization man, who was no different from countless others, and whose self-effacing obedience happened to be applied to implementing the Nazi Holocaust programme. If we, like Eichmann, are desensitized by the moral rhetoric of our own organization, how do we know that we are not also just obeying orders, but unluckily find ourselves in the wrong place, at the wrong time? Others argue that 'company tradition' (Ryan 1994) or 'corporate culture' (Schlegelmilch and Houston 1990) can be a force for high ethical standards.

One obvious explanation for such divergent viewpoints is that moral ethos varies considerably from one organization to the next (and even between different parts of the same company). Some theorists (Lavoie and Culbert 1978; Petrick and Wagley, 1992) have speculated that a moral ethos is located at one or other of the Kohlberg moral reasoning stages. Initially, I shared that view (see Snell 1993a), but more recently (Snell 2000: 276) I have argued that moral ethos is better characterized by a *profile*, indicating the relative strength of the various Kohlberg stages, with the mode or peak representing the most prevalent and powerful stage within the moral ethos. A further point about the Kohlberg stages in moral ethos is that, unlike at the individual level of analysis, they represent powerful emotions, not only ways of reasoning. Moral 'stages' (a term that can be misleading when applied to individual adults, and which is an unfortunate misnomer at the organizational level of analysis) involved in moral ethos may nevertheless be heuristically described as:

- stage one: fear, coercion and punishment
- stage two: greed, instrumentality and manipulation
- stage three: conformity to 'inner-circle' group norms and prejudices
- stage four: dutiful accountability to quasi-legal standards set by higher authority
- stage five: passionate stewardship, social responsibility, democratic standards addressing stakeholder needs
- stage six: compassionate community of moral enquiry seeking to balance competing moral principles.

I have hypothesized (Snell 2000) that companies perceived by employees to emphasize the higher moral ethos stages are likely also to be perceived to have higher levels of honesty, environmental awareness, accuracy of records, responsibility and fairness to customers. I have also collaborated in designing a Moral Ethos Questionnaire (MEQ) to assess the relative emphasis within organizations (not individuals) of the Kohlberg stages 1–6 (Snell et al. 1996; 1997; 1999). Items in the MEQ cover perceptions of various aspects of organizational behaviour:

- how information is used
- how opinions are expressed
- how performance is judged
- how rewards are obtained
- relationships with customers
- overall impact on employees' mindsets
- the use of power
- reasons for following rules
- how agreement is reached.

Twenty-one Hong Kong-based companies were assessed anonymously by at least eight of their randomly selected employees, using the MEQ. Findings as yet unpublished were that moral ethos profiles ranged from those emphasizing stages four, five and six, to those emphasizing stages one, two and three, and supported the above mentioned hypotheses.

The dynamics of moral ethos are complex and emotion-laden, and may be influenced by the leadership, the nature of organizational systems adopted to develop and enforce standards of conduct, the extent to which authority resides in domination or trust, whether a stakeholder approach is embraced at strategic levels, and whether critical self-reflection is discouraged or encouraged (Snell 2000). The character of one's immediate 'boss' may mediate the influence of wider moral ethos. While the relationship between moral ethos and an individual employee's actual ethical conduct is a complex one, moral ethos is likely to have a substantial impact on how employees, such as our Simon, experience their working environment and how they construe and tackle the moral dilemmas arising there. If Simon is expected to defer to and obey his boss without question, his scope for independent moral thought and action is limited.

Stephen Fineman (1997: 19) points out that ethical judgements are influenced by emotions such as shame, guilt, embarrassment and fear. Emotions are socially defined and are important for exerting social control in society. Organizations mirror elements of wider forms of emotional control, but in their moral ethos they define for members what is 'right' and acceptable, and give emotional charge to this. In a moral ethos oriented toward Kohlbergian moral ethos stages 1–3, moral behaviour may be influenced more by punitive emotions such as fear of dismissal, humiliation or public disapproval, than by higher moral ideals or concern for the social good. Thus, it is not individual moral reasoning alone, but also emotions and social pressures in the moral ethos that can affect ethical judgements, and might well explain lapses in moral behaviour.

Explicit and formal organization-based approaches to improving business ethics

Three possible means for improving ethical conduct within organizations have emerged in the literature: *corporate codes of conduct, 'moral leadership' from the top*, and *ethical democracy*.

Corporate codes of conduct

These are written documents, ranging from a single paragraph to more than 50 pages, stating explicitly what is desired by a corporation regarding employee behaviour (Stevens 1994). The great majority of large US companies have such codes and their popularity has spread to Europe (Weaver 1993). In Hong Kong, within little more than one year of Governor Chris Patten lamenting that only 20 out of 182 listed companies had codes of conduct (ICAC 1994), a majority of companies had formally adopted their various versions (ICAC 1995). Early studies of typical themes in codes of conduct (Chatov 1980; White and Montgomery 1980; Sanderson and Warner 1984) identified the following common topics:

- dealing with extortion or kickbacks
- conflicts of interest between employee and employer
- the use of insider information by employees for personal advantage
- the accuracy of accounting records
- the misuse of company assets
- moonlighting
- fraud and deception.

This list has not changed significantly over the years, and critics have noted that the motivation behind the inclusion of such items appears to be mainly concerned with maintaining profits (Cressey and Moore 1983) and protecting the company itself against legal liability (Warren 1993; Stevens 1994), rather than with the pursuit of wider social responsibilities and values. This is not to say that these items are ethically unimportant – much depends upon the spirit in which the codes are applied.

According to Simon Webley (1993), areas that codes have tended to neglect include the following:

- the needs and rights of suppliers
- environmental protection and related green issues
- avoiding discrimination against and harassment of minority groups
- duties to local communities
- labour relations
- safety for employees and customers
- fair remuneration
- due process in enforcing and monitoring the code itself.

Some libertarian-minded theorists (for example Donaldson 1989) are very sceptical about the whole idea of codes of conduct and regard them as an imposition that does not respect employees' ability to engage in autonomous moral reasoning. A forbidding legalistic or parental 'don't, don't, don't, must, must, must' style may foster preconventional, risk-aversive ethical reasoning (Warren 1993). Top-down, imposed codes may overlook real concerns at the grass roots, and may neglect the needs of the least powerful stakeholders. Some codes may even represent 'conspiracies against the layman', smokescreens which boost the image of a profession, without actually improving its practices (Mitchell et al. 1994).

Against this, as part of a business ethics development programme, codes of conduct may represent an important first rung of a ladder. In the run-up to transition of sovereignty in 1997, many Hong Kong-based organizations introduced codes of conduct, in response to a government-sponsored campaign to prevent corruption. Many of these codes were imposed top-down, without consultation, and with a bare minimum of training and development. A study of 17 companies suggested that, as might be expected, the mere introduction of codes did not improve the balance of stages in the moral ethos, but they may have helped to prevent a decline in moral conduct (Snell and Herndon 2000).

Denis Collins and Thomas O'Rourke (1993) have suggested the following step-by-step procedure for preparing codes of ethical conduct:

1. Form small discussion groups based on common work tasks. Each group will then work independently through the next seven steps.
2. Identify and list the group's stakeholders.
3. Develop and list ideal standards for the group's own conduct, based, as far as possible, on creating the greatest good to the greatest number and maintaining respect for each and every stakeholder.
4. Reflect on and identify a truthful account of the group's actual, current relationships with each stakeholder.
5. Discuss and resolve what the group must do in order to close the gap between 'ideal' relationships (identified at step three) and 'actual' relationships (identified at step four).
6. Develop a formal policy statement setting down each ideal standard (from step three) and how each of these will be attained, monitored and rewarded (from step five).
7. Annually review the code (created at step six), paying special attention to its practicality and relevance and to how new or ongoing problems may be resolved.
8. While keeping the ideal standards, make necessary modifications within the code as to how these will be attained, monitored and rewarded.

Codes developed in this way, based on members' genuine ideas and concerns, rather than on the imposition of rules from above, and supported by training and development may be of more practical use in guiding members' actual conduct, and helpful to the development of a stakeholder-oriented approach. The process itself presupposes a democratic tradition within the corporation, which may not be so readily entertained in companies with a moral ethos oriented to the preconventional moral stages, and/or where cultural traditions allow only for authoritarian rule.

The Business Roundtable (Keough 1988), a US-based association founded in 1972 to advise on corporate responsibility and ethics, prescribes a somewhat different code development procedure, still based on participative approaches, which ideally entails the following. Staff at all levels are interviewed by senior managers about ethical matters. Ethics programmes, reflecting top management commitment, then 'cascade' from the top. Related development programmes are run in order to build greater openness and trust. There is as much emphasis on education as on regulation. An ethics committee is set up, and compiles, clarifies, monitors, updates, disseminates and promulgates the corporate code of ethics, and investigates and mediates in ethical problem cases. Such committees need to steer a course between becoming at one extreme a peripheral sideshow, or at the other extreme the 'experts' upon whom everyone else should depend. Related alleged 'good practices' include confidential ethical dilemma telephone hotlines or counselling services, and specialist ethical ombudsman posts. Such arrangements are fairly common in US corporations (Edwards 1995). Industrial chaplains have performed similar duties among paternalistic companies in the UK.

Conflict of interest

One topic, *conflict of interest*, is particularly important in relation to procedural justice, and may require some explanation. Michael McDonald (1995) defines conflict of interest as 'a situation in which a person, such as a public official, an employee, or a professional, has a private or personal interest sufficient to appear to influence the objective exercise of his or her official duties'. Although McDonald takes an appropriately wide view of what this phenomenon can entail, it can refer, specifically, to those situations in which an employee has, or is closely associated with, outside commercial interests that directly impinge upon his or her employer's interests. For example, in the case example that began this chapter, Simon's boss may be a partner in a private side business (independent of Sunny) that provides cleaning services for office buildings. Dismissing the 'quite old' cleaning lady from Sunny may present an opportunity for Simon's boss to expand his private side business. If that were the case, his primary, and possibly concealed, motive would be to serve his own extramural business interests, rather than consider those of Sunny, his own employer. In a variation on this conflict of interest scenario, Simon's boss might, as landlord, own a flat that is rented by the cleaning lady, and perhaps there has been a prior dispute between them about the state of repair of the internal fabric of the flat, or the state of maintenance of the appliances. The dismissal may be prompted more by his anger about this extramural dispute, than by the cleaning lady's work performance at Sunny.

To identify when such conflicts of interest are likely to distort managerial decisions, McDonald (1995) suggests the 'trust test': 'Would relevant others [my employer, my clients, professional colleagues, or the general public] trust my judgment if they knew I was in this situation?' He advises managers to 'get out of the situation, or, if you can't, make known to all affected parties your private interest'. One 'escape' option for Simon's boss would be to delegate the decision about whether to continue employing the old woman to Simon, but if Simon knows about the conflict of interest, would that remove its influence?

Moral leadership and democracy

Whatever the outside pressure on a company to 'clean up its act', significant improvement is unlikely to take place in the absence of moral leadership from within. Open meetings to discuss moral issues of concern to the company, and encouragement for transparency in all decisions, are likely to enhance the moral conduct of an organization (Treviño and McCabe 1994). The 'philosopher ruler', who ensures employees' civil liberties and freedom of speech, builds trust and sets up high-quality dialogue, is probably ideal for such activities (Starkey 1998: 544).

Again, cognitive sociomoral development theory is a potential source of insights regarding the qualities of moral leadership. In their research, William Torbert and his co-workers prefer an eight-stage developmental model (Rooke and Torbert 2000) that derives from Robert Kegan (1994) and diverges, at least in terms of emphasis, from that of Kohlberg. Their model characterizes the highest stages by openness to multiple voices and paradigms, a sense of irony and a preference for power that is exercised dialogically, in the spirit of mutuality and awareness-enhancement, rather than unilaterally. They include a woman among their role models: actress/performer/author Shirley MacLaine (see http://www.shirleymaclaine.com). For instrumentation, they use an adapted version of Loevinger's (1985) Sentence Completion Test (see Rooke and Torbert 2000: 23–5, footnote 1), in which sentence fragments are presented to the subject, and are intended, when completed, to reflect that person's processes of reasoning and thinking in relation to others. Out of 497 managers assessed, their research categorized '0 per cent' as having reached the highest two stages (Torbert 1994: 58).

Torbert and his co-workers thus imply that 'late stage' leaders, whom they regard as potentially most likely to be effective in bringing about transformation without also giving rise to evil, are extraordinarily rare, almost to the point of being non-existent. Such leaders may need to keep their brilliance carefully masked, in order to prevent mindless devotion among their followers (Lichtenstein et al. 1995: 108–11). If leaders are not quite at the very highest developmental stages, an attitude of servant leadership (Greenleaf 1977) may suffice. The qualities of leadership that foster the development of virtuous organizations may match those required to build learning organizations (see Kofman and Senge 1993; Snell 2001) – but beware: building learning organizations, despite all the hyperbole, is a formidable and perhaps impossible challenge. At the other end of the spectrum, some types of leaders, who appeal to calculative self-interest (stage two) or fearful obedience (stage one) may reduce the scope for virtuous action (Graham 1995). As Lichtenstein et al. (1995: 102–3) note, leaders who have not progressed beyond the preconventional stages are likely to create a sour, defensive and treacherous atmosphere.

Many leaders, in developmental terms, are probably somewhere in between these benchmark points, and whatever their shortcomings, can still, in their own ways, help to improve moral ethos, and thus indirectly contribute to there being less pollution, less corruption, safer products, less exploitative advertising, more charitable giving and so on (Snell 2000). The benevolent and paternalistic despot, who lays down the moral law somewhat unilaterally and idiosyncratically, might be able to 'sell' ethical values with conviction. Leaders who are charismatic or benevolently autocratic, rather than democratic, can learn from adversity and turn adversity into moral lessons. While adversity might strengthen them, it is also likely to teach them that they are not infallible, as the two following examples illustrate.

The Body Shop's Anita Roddick is, at least in her own view, a charismatic, somewhat abrasive, liberal-minded female role model (Roddick 1991). The extent to which her company practised the deontological principles of basic honesty and unexploitative sourcing, and promoted distributive justice in trade, was questioned during 1994–95 by maverick critic and journalist John Entine. Entine (1994, 1995) claimed that the company's products and human resource policies were not all that they seemed. After some initial defensiveness, Roddick, and The Body Shop, responded positively to at least some of the criticisms by initiating a social, environmental and animal protection audit (Hanson 1995). Such openness helped the company to survive the attack. The Body Shop also won a court case against Channel 4 for libel and damages in respect of its core values, and Roddick reports of various attempts to falsely discredit her company (Roddick 2000: 215–32).

Since Anita and Gordon Roddick stepped down from their co-chair positions, to become non-executive directors in February 2002, the company has continued to espouse a stakeholder-orientation, and in June 2002, celebrated Dame Anita Roddick's award, in honour of her contributions to retailing, charity and the environment. When accessed in June 2003, however, the latest values report available on the company's UK website was dated 1997 (The Body Shop 1997). This raises the question of how rigorously the company has been re-examining its values and their application in the areas of social responsibility, environmental sustainability and animal protection. Before stepping down, the Roddick's claimed that these values were central to the company's transparency and accountability (Roddick 2000: 68–9), despite the challenges of restructuring in the late 1990s when the company laid off staff for the first time in history (Roddick 2000: 259–60). The company's success, or otherwise, as a learning organization, is likely to depend on its willingness to review its values critically by drawing on the perspectives of various stakeholders in relation to tough experiences.

Winston Lo, of the Hong Kong-based soya milk company Vitasoy, has a more conservative image but radiates strong social commitment. Vitasoy's ethical claims are utilitarian, to 'produce and promote high-quality, nutritious and wholesome products that can be purchased anywhere, any time, and at a price that everyone can afford'. Lo adds, 'Vitasoy was founded by my father some 50 years ago … He saw the value of soya protein in order to alleviate the malnutrition among the locals during the war' (Kwong 1996). Lo weathered a crisis in confidence about the company's products (a sour-milk scandal) by a total product recall that cost the company approximately US$10 million: 'at the peak of the crisis, we all shared and felt the pressure. We worked closely on the committee … we learnt a lot about ourselves and about each other.'

Lifelong learning and business ethics

The various ideas discussed in this chapter do not provide correct answers or truths, even when that might be claimed or implied by their originators. Accordingly, in this chapter, I have argued in favour of there being moral dialogue informed by ongoing moral judgement rather than the handing down of imposed moral judgement, however 'expert' or 'authoritative' this may be presented as. As Stephen Linstead and Andrew Chan (1994) demonstrate, with reference to Elias Canetti (1987), commands, however 'morally justified', which are imposed by authorities over subordinates, set up the potentiality for a 'sting', a deferred act of vengeance motivated by resentment, lying in wait for a suitable 'payback' opportunity. Business ethics may be more usefully regarded as a humble, ongoing, mutual learning process, than as a set of technologies for arriving at zero-defect moral decisions.

Self-development strategies in relation to ethics are given in more detail elsewhere (see Snell 1993a: 222–8). Here, just two of these are identified: 'avoiding hubris' and 'holding onto the hot potato'.

Hubris, the fatal delusion that 'my way is always the only right way', is counterbalanced by inviting criticism, looking for disconfirmation, admitting when plans are not working, respecting other points of view and entertaining possible futures rather than a single dream.

The *hot potato* injunction was noted by Eric Berne (1975) as a dysfunctional vehicle for perpetuating domestic violence and alcoholism from one generation to the next. In time, the abused child becomes child abuser, and the adult child of alcoholics becomes an alcoholic parent. It is as if the victim must throw the 'hot potato' to the next victim or remain forever burdened. Something analogous may happen between bosses, subordinates and their subordinates in the workplace (Snell 1993b). To counterbalance this tendency, the golden rule in its negative, Confucian formulation (Allinson 1995: 30) reads: 'Do not impose on others what you yourself do not desire.' Being on the receiving end of cruelty, abuse, neglect, deceit or other forms of poor treatment is of course an unjust state of affairs, but it need not trigger the hot potato syndrome, although history shows that it often does (Bauman 1993). I realize, from experience, how much easier it is to recommend the following sequence than to follow it, but holding onto the hot potato hurts.

- Why am I so upset, angry, aggrieved and so on?
- What ethical principle has been violated?

- How can I follow, rather than breach, the principle that has been violated?
- What would support me in following the principle?
- How can I develop the positive lessons from this experience, rather than their negative shadows?

Conclusion

It is time to return to the introductory questions, along with the initial case about Simon's ethical dilemma.

Answers to questions about business ethics

1 **Does ethics have anything to do with business?** I believe so. Many managers besides Simon have faced workplace ethical dilemmas. They are an inherent aspect of business; lives are affected by managerial decisions and sometimes livelihoods are at stake in them.

2 **Should business decisions be governed by profitability alone?** I don't think so. The previous answer advises managers to be sensitive to ethical considerations. In Simon's case, the dismissal of the cleaning woman may breach some ethical principles. From a utilitarian perspective, the sacking brings little apparent benefit to anyone, unless Simon's boss has a private agenda, a 'conflict of interest', which should not be allowed to interfere with the decision here. Prospect theory would suggest that minutely small gains for the shareholders (if any) are outweighed by great misery for the woman and her dependents. Treating the woman as if she is merely an exhausted resource, to be discarded because she no longer serves the interests of 'the company', is also questionable from the point of view of deontology, which is founded upon respect for persons, their dignity and their human rights. Simon may believe that the woman is too physically weak to complete all the job tasks, but might procedural justice be better served by making some alterations to the facilities, so as to help to overcome whatever physical disability or handicap she may have? Such alterations might better honour the spirit of the Universal Declaration of Human Rights, and help others who are working at or visiting the premises. To Simon, his boss's tone and manner may appear 'high-handed', and he tries to convey a more acceptable image of intentional justice. However, his care for and about the cleaning lady is limited to Kohlbergian stage three. If he really cared, he might draw upon postconventional moral reasoning when discussing the case in the company.

3 **Is there a 'third way', between serving the needs of staff and corporate profitability?** Simon's boss might argue that replacing the woman with a younger, stronger cleaning worker may lead to a healthier working environment, better for the workforce, as well as using money more effectively. A genuine 'third way' would, however, involve doing a thorough stakeholder analysis, asking who is affected by the decision and considering what do they want and need. This would, of course, include discussing the situation with the woman herself. Simon assumes that this has not been done and that the decision is 'surely … a shock'. She has had no opportunity to

Answers continued

discuss the situation, and how to resolve any problem amicably, with her dependents, whose needs have been completely ignored. Colleagues may not have been consulted. After 20 years, it is more than likely that she would be seen as part of the surroundings, and there would be sympathy for her, and a desire to keep her on, perhaps even under a compromise solution of employing an extra part-timer to tackle the heavier tasks. The additional cost would be small, and may have a payback in better workplace morale and an increased sense of care, and justice, within the office moral ethos.

4 **Should managers conform to local rules, customs and etiquette, or are there universal ethical standards to follow?** A cultural relativist solution to the problem would be to 'do what the Hong Kong employers tend to do'. Part of the problem of taking such an approach here is the considerable diversity in Hong Kong practice. In some traditional Chinese companies, there is a social contract of (literal) lifelong employment in return for loyalty. In one chain of jewellery shops that I have studied, for example, staff who are well past their sixties continue selling, or generally stay around HQ or in the shops and help out some ways. Such arrangements compensate for the relative absence of formal social security and benefits entitlements in Hong Kong. On the other hand, Hong Kong employment law tends not to protect employees' rights as fully as do laws in the European Community. Employers have relative freedom to hire and fire at will, and some take advantage of this, as many new mothers discover. In Hong Kong, as in Japan, the cleaning lady may be considered by many employers to be a 'peripheral worker'. Thus, if Simon were to consider applying integrative social contracts theory, the cleaning woman's fate hinges on whether hypernorms favour her retention. They might well do in this case. The right to subsistence of the woman and her dependents is under threat. But is the company responsible? Is Simon's boss responsible? Is Simon responsible? Look at the woman's face, Simon.

5 **What are the options for managers facing moral dilemmas?** Simon's actual conduct was a hybrid of little potato obedience and undercover disobedience. Simon can hardly secretly threaten to blow the whistle, for he would be readily identified. Whistle-blowing of any kind may be futile anyway, for newspapers might not be interested in such a 'kitchen-sink' affair, and in Hong Kong whistle-blowers (and those associated with them) tend to get fired. He might instead try token obedience, such as writing an extremely off-putting job advertisement and then saying 'we have to re-employ her, for no one else will take up the job'. Or he might draw upon the highest moral stage available to him (stage four), for example, offering an accurate translation of the boss's words, along with a message of personal sympathy: 'My boss says that … but I personally feel …'. That would be a kind of 'do it under protest, reluctantly comply' response. But would it help? Another option for Simon would have entailed negotiating and building consensus for change. He could try to buy time, suggesting, for example, that he (Simon) could investigate the case further and make proposals to Mr X, rather than going ahead immediately and dismissing her right away. If granted this reprieve, he might then arrive, after discussion with the woman and with colleagues, at ways

Answers continued

around the problem. Given the complexity of ethical problems, buying time is sometimes necessary.

6 **What aspects of an organization's culture help managers to make the best ethical decisions?** While there is room to manoeuvre in most circumstances, Simon would have more chance of arriving at a just and caring outcome, if his superiors were not to assume that their word was law, and that the questioning of managerial decisions was not construed as mutiny. I believe (perhaps at the risk of tautology) that a moral ethos characterized by critical enquiry, compassion, due process and other attributes of the higher Kohlberg stages is more conducive to good quality ethical decisions, than one dominated by fear, coercion, punishment, greed, instrumentality and manipulation and 'inner-circle' prejudice.

7 **How valuable are codes of ethical conduct in business?** The usefulness of a code of conduct depends on its content and coverage, the manner in which it is developed and the extent to which it is supported by training and development and appropriate grievance and disciplinary procedures. Many codes of conduct are imposed top-down and serve to protect the narrow company interest in a somewhat one-sided manner. Codes that are developed consensually, and after much refection and dialogue across various organizational levels, represent organizational learning and stakeholder considerations, and may provide support for good quality ethical decisions in cases such as this.

8 **To whom should managers look for moral leadership?** Ideally, there is moral leadership at all levels in an organization. Many managers like Simon, do not, however, find themselves in that ideal situation. Simon is responsible, but perhaps he is alone. Like it or not, it is his inescapable right to lead, and it is to his conscience that he looks, and perhaps he follows it, if not this time, then next time.

9 **Is it possible to change a manager's ethical predisposition?** Moral development, both in terms of character and moral reasoning, can continue well into adulthood; indeed there is no reason to regard it as anything less than a lifelong process. Ethical sensitivity can, I believe, be fostered through feedback and 'consciousness raising'. However, just as managers are realizing that corporate cultures uncontrollably unfold, stagnate, twist and fragment according to their own unique histories, so may the ethical predispositions (one could say 'biases') of the individual manager follow their own course. A concerned senior manager may try to enhance junior staff members' moral development through mentoring, counselling, careful exposure, and opportunities to reflect on and talk about problems and experiences, but people, in the end, decide for themselves. Kohlberg believed that there was a tendency, at the higher stages, for people's moral judgements to converge, but I wonder if he was mistaken. Perhaps one of the most developmental experiences is to disagree passionately about an ethical dilemma case, while maintaining respect for and friendship with other parties in the discussion and encourage dialogue.

References

Allen, R.E. and Lucero, M.A. (1996) 'Beyond resentment: Exploring organizationally targeted insider murder', *Journal of Management Inquiry* 5: 86–103.

Allen, R.E. and Lucero, M.A. (1998) 'Subordinate aggression against managers: Empirical analyses of published arbitration decisions', *International Journal of Conflict Management*; 9(3): 234–57.

Allinson, R.E. (1995) 'Ethical values as part of the concept of business enterprise', in Stewart, S. and Donleavy, G. (eds), *Whose Business Values? Some Asian and Cross-cultural Perspectives,* Hong Kong: Hong Kong University Press, pp. 19–40.

Alpern, K.D. (1993) 'Moral dimensions of the Foreign Corrupt Practices Act: Comments on Pastin and Hooker', in Donaldson, T. and Werhane, P.H. (eds), *Ethical Issues in Business: A Philosophical Approach* (4th edn), Englewood Cliffs, NJ: Prentice Hall.

Alvesson, M. and Willmott, H. (1996) *Making Sense of Management: A Critical Introduction*, London: Sage.

Andrews, J. (1988) 'Survey: The Philippines', *Economist* 7 May: S3–18.

Arendt, H. (1963) *Eichmann in Jerusalem: A Report on the Banality of Evil*, London: Faber.

Aristotle (1952) *Aristotle in 23 Volumes,* Vol. 20, trans. by H. Rackham, London: Heinemann.

Baddeley, S. and James, K. (1987) 'Owl, fox, donkey or sheep: Political skills for managers', *Management Education and Development,* 18(1): 3–19.

Barnes, B. (1988) *The Nature of Power*, Cambridge: Polity Press.

Bates, S. (1999) 'The faceless ones are in a flap', *New Statesman* 12(546): 20–1.

Batson, C.D., Bowers, M.J., Leonard, E.A. and Smith, E.C. (2000) 'Does personal morality exacerbate or restrain retaliation after being harmed?' *Personality and Social Psychology Bulletin,* 26(1): 35–45.

Bauman, Z. (1993) *Postmodern Ethics*. Oxford: Blackwell.

Beauchamp, T.L. (1988) 'Ethical theory and its application to business', in Beauchamp, T.L and Bowie, N.E. (eds), *Ethical Theory and Business* (3rd edn), Englewood Cliffs, NJ: Prentice Hall.

Berne, E. (1975) *What Do You Say After You Say Hello?*, London: Corgi.

Bersoff; D.M. (1999) 'Explaining unethical behaviour among people motivated to act prosocially', *Journal of Moral Education,* 28(4): 413–28.

Bies, R.J. and Moag, J.S. (1986) 'Interactional justice: Communication criteria of fairness', in Lewicki, R.J., Sheppard, B.H. and Bazerman, M.H. (eds) *Research on Negotiation in Organizations*, Greenwich, CT: JAI Press.

Blackhurst, C. (1999) 'Blackhurst's diary', *Management Today*, May, pp. 22–4.

Boatright, J.R. (1993) *Ethics and the Conduct of Business*, Englewood Cliffs, NJ: Prentice Hall.

Bohatá, M. (1997) 'Business ethics in Central and Eastern Europe with special focus on the Czech Republic', *Journal of Business Ethics,* 16(14): 1571–7.

Bohm, D. (1990) *David Bohm: On Dialogue*, Ojia, CA: David Bohm Seminars.

Boje, D.M. (1998) 'Nike, Greek goddess of victory or cruelty? Women's stories of Asian factory life', *Journal of Organizational Change Management,* 11(6): 461–80. (Also available at http://cbae.nmsu.edu/mgt/jpub/boje/vnwomennike/index.html, last accessed 11 July 2000.)

Boulton, D. (1978) *The Grease Machine*, New York: Harper & Row.

Bowie, N.E. (1988) 'Fair Markets', *Journal of Business Ethics,* 7(2): 89–98.

Burgoyne, J.G. (1994) 'Stakeholder analysis', in Cassell, C. and Symon, G. (eds), *Organizational Research: A Practical Guide*, London: Sage.

Business Ethics Magazine (1995) 'CAUX Roundtable Principles', Minneapolis, MN (also available in the Ethical Business directory on the Internet at http://www.bath.ac.uk/Centres/Ethical/Papers).

Canetti, E. (1987) *Crowds and Power*, London: Penguin.

Carlton, J.M. and Kurland, N.B. (1996) 'A theory of stakeholder enabling: Giving voice to an emerging postmodern praxis of organizational discourse', in D.M. Boje, R.P. Gephart and T.J. Thatchenkery (eds) *Postmodern Management and Organization Theory* Thousand Oaks, CA: Sage, pp. 154–77.

Carr, A.Z. (1993) 'Is business bluffing ethical?', in Donaldson, T. and Werhane, P.H. (eds), *Ethical Issues in Business: A Philosophical* Approach (4th edn), Englewood Cliffs, NJ: Prentice Hall.

Cayer, M. (1997) 'Bohm's dialogue and action science: Two different approaches', *Journal of Humanistic Psychology,* 37(2): 41–66.

Chan, A. (1998) 'Labor standards and human rights: the case of Chinese workers under market socialism', *Human Rights Quarterly,* 20(4): 886–904.

Chan, A. and Senser, R.A. (1997) 'China's troubled workers', *Foreign Affairs* 76(2): 104–17. (Available on the Internet http://www.senser.com/prclambs.htm, last accessed 11 July 2000.)

Chatov, R. (1980) 'What corporate ethics statements say', *California Management Review,* 22(4): 20–9.

Colby, A., Kohlberg, L., Gibbs, J. and Lieberman, M. (1983) 'A longitudinal study of moral development', *Monographs of the Society for Research in Child Development, Series 200,* 48(1,2): 1–107.

Collins, D. and O'Rourke, T. (1993) *Ethical Dilemmas in Business*, Cincinnati, OH: South Western.

Conger, J.A. and Kanungo, R.N. (1988) 'The empowerment process: Integrating theory and practice', *Academy of Management Review,* **13**(3): 471–82.

Cooper, C.L. (1999) 'The changing psychological contract at work', *European Business Journal,* **11**(3): 115–18.

Crain, W. (1992) *Theories of Development: Concepts and Applications* (3rd edn), London: Prentice Hall.

Cressey, D. and Moore, C.A. (1983) 'Managerial values and corporate codes of ethics', *California Management Review,* **25**: 53–77.

Dauvergne, P. (1998) 'The political economy of Indonesia's 1997 forest fires', *Australian Journal of International Affairs,* **52**(1): 13–17.

De George, R.T. (1995) *Business Ethics* (4th edn), Englewood Cliffs, NJ: Prentice Hall.

Ding, G. (1999) 'China: Party official maps out "spiritual civilization" work for 2000'. *BBC Monitoring Asia Pacific*. London. 30 December.

Dirlik, A. (1989) 'Revolutionary hegemony and the language of revolution: Chinese socialism between present and future', in Dirlik, A. and Meisner, M. (eds), *Marxism and the Chinese experience*. Armonk, NY: M. E. Sharpe, pp. 27–39.

Donaldson, J. (1989) *Key Issues in Business Ethics*, London: Academic Press.

Donaldson, T. (1999) 'Making stakeholder theory whole', *Academy of Management Review,* **24**(2): 237–41.

Donaldson, T. and Dunfee, T.W. (1999) 'When ethics travel: The promise and peril of global business ethics', *California Management Review,* **41**(4): 45–63.

Donaldson, T. and Werhane, P.H. (eds) (1993) *Ethical Issues in Business: A Philosophical Approach* (4th edn), Englewood Cliffs, NJ: Prentice Hall.

Ebrey, P.B. (1993) 'Lei Feng, Chairman Mao's good fighter: Inspirational anecdotes about a model worker and soldier, devoted to aiding the people', in Ebrey, P.B. (ed.), *Chinese Civilization: A Sourcebook*, (2nd edn), New York: Free Press, pp. 442–6.

Edwards, G. (1995) 'Beyond the code: The implementation of corporate ethics', *Ethics in Practice 2*, Hong Kong: Ethics Development Centre.

Ehrenberg, R. (1989) 'Empirical consequences of comparable worth', in Hill, M.A. and Killingsworth, M.R. (eds), *Comparable Worth: Analysis and Evidence*, Cornell, NY: ILR Press, pp. 90–106.

Elm, D.R. and Weber, J. (1994) 'Measuring moral judgment: The moral judgment interview or the defining issues test?' *Journal of Business Ethics,* **13**(5): 341.

Entine, J. (1994) 'Shattered image: Is The Body Shop too good to be true?' *Business Ethics Magazine,* **8**(5): 3–28.

Entine, J. (1995) 'When rainforest ice cream melts: The messy reality of socially responsible business', *Electronic Journal of Radical Organisation Theory*

1(1), http://www.mngt.waikato.ac.nz/ejrot/, last accessed 23 July 2000.

Esty, B.C. (2000) 'The equate project: An introduction to Islamic project finance', *Journal of Project Finance,* **5**(4): 7–20.

Filatov, A. (1994) 'Unethical business behavior in post-Communist Russia: Origins and trends', *Business Ethics Quarterly,* **41**(1): 11–15.

Fineman, S. (1997) 'Emotion and management learning', *Management Learning,* **28**(1): 13–25.

Flam, H. (1993) 'Fear, loyalty and greedy organizations', in Fineman, S. (ed.), *Emotion in Organizations*, London: Sage.

Flanagan, Jnr O.J. and Adler, J.E. (1983) 'Impartiality and particularity', *Social Research,* **50**(3): 576–96.

Frank, R.H. (1988) *Passion with Reason: The Strategic Role of the Emotions*, New York: W.W. Norton.

Frankena, W.K. (ed.) (1963) *Ethics*, Englewood Cliffs, NJ: Prentice Hall.

Frederick, W.C. (1995) *Values, Nature, and Culture in thc American Corporation*, New York: Oxford University Press.

Freeman, R.E. (1998) 'A stakeholder theory of the modern corporation', in Hartman, L.P. (ed.), *Perspectives in Business Ethics*, Chicago: McGraw-Hill, pp. 171–81.

Friedman, M. (1970) 'The social responsibility of business is to increase its profits', *New York Times Magazine,* 13 September.

Frith, F. (1994) 'Crime and punishment: Whistleblowing and intimidation rituals', *Employment Relations: Theory and Practice,* **3**: 641–59.

Gilligan, C. (1982) *In a Different Voice: Psychological Theory and Women's Development*, Cambridge, MA: Harvard University Press.

Glazer, M.P. and Glazer, P.M. (1989), *The Whistle-Blowers: Exposing Corruption in Government and Industry*, New York: Basic Books.

Goodpaster, K.E. (1984) *Ethics in Management*, Boston: Harvard Business School.

Graham, J.W. (1995) 'Leadership, moral development, and citizenship behaviour', *Business Ethics Quarterly,* **5**(1): 43–54.

Greanis, G. and Windsor, D. (1982) *The Foreign Corrupt Practices Act: Anatomy of a Statute*, Lexington, MA: Lexington Books.

Green, R.M. (1994) *The Ethical Manager: A New Method For Business Ethics*, New York: Maxwell Macmillan.

Greenleaf, R.K. (1977) *Servant Leadership*, New York: Paulist Press.

Gross-Schaefer, A., Trigilio, J., Negus, J. and Ro, C-S. (2000) 'Ethics education in the workplace: An effective tool to combat employee theft', *Journal of Business Ethics,* **26**(2): 89–100.

Habermas, J. (1984) *The Theory of Communicative*

Action Volume 1: Reason and the Rationalization of Society, London: Heinemann.

Habermas, J. (1987) *The Theory of Communicative Action Volume 2: Lifeworld and System: A Critique of Functionalist Reason.* London: Heinemann.

Hall, D.T. and Moss, J.E. (1998) 'The new protean career contract: Helping organizations and employees adapt', *Organizational Dynamics,* **26**(3): 22–37.

Handy, C. (1995) *The Empty Raincoat: Making Sense of the Future,* London: Arrow.

Hanson, K.O. (1995) 'The Body Shop International Social Evaluation, 1995', in Hartman, L.P. (ed.), *Perspectives in Business Ethics*, Chicago: McGraw-Hill, pp. 559–65.

Hao, Y. (1999) 'From rule of man to rule of law: An unintended consequence of corruption in China in the 1990s', *Journal of Contemporary China,* **8**(22): 405–23.

Hartman, L.P. (ed.) (1998) *Perspectives in Business Ethics*, Chicago: McGraw-Hill.

Hauserman, N. (1999) 'New values, new conflicts: A response to William Frederick's *Values, Nature, and Culture in the American Corporation*', *Business and Society,* **38**(2): 212–16.

Held, V. (1997) 'Feminism and moral theory' in Meyers, D.T. (ed.), *Feminist Social Thought: A Reader*, New York and London: Routledge.

Hempel, P.S. and Chang, C.Y.D. (2000) 'Reconciling traditional Chinese management with high technology business', paper under journal review, Department of Management, City University of Hong Kong.

Herman, R. (2000) 'The human factor', *Harvard Public Health Review,* Fall: 25–31.

Hersh, R.H., Paolitto, D.P. and Reimer, J. (1979) *Promoting Moral Growth, From Piaget to Kohlberg* (2nd edn), New York: Longman.

Hofstede, G. (1980) *Culture's Consequences: International Differences in Work Related Values*, Beverley Hills, CA: Sage.

Höpfl, H. (1992) 'The making of the corporate acolyte: Some thoughts on charismatic leadership and the reality of organizational commitment', *Journal of Management Studies,* **29**(1): 23–33.

Hosmer, L.T. (1987) *The Ethics of Management*, Boston, MA: Irwin.

Hosmer, L.T. (1991) *The Ethics of Management* (2nd edn), Boston, MA: Irwin.

Hua, S. (1995) *Scientism and Humanism: Two Cultures in post-Mao China (1978–1989),* New York: State University of New York Press.

Hultin, M. and Szulkin, R. (1999) 'Wages and unequal access to organizational power: An empirical test of gender discrimination', *Administrative Science Quarterly,* **44**(3): 453–72.

Hunt, M. (1993) *The Story of Psychology*, New York: Doubleday.

ICAC (Independent Commission Against Corruption) (1994) Conference on Business Ethics, Hong Kong Convention Centre, 4 May.

ICAC (Independent Commission Against Corruption) (1995) Conference on the Opening of the Business Ethics Resource Centre, Hong Kong Convention Centre, 2 May.

ICAC (Independent Commission Against Corruption) (1996) Report on a Survey of Young People's Attitude Towards Work Ethics, Hong Kong: ICAC Community Relations Department.

ICC (International Chamber of Commerce) (2000) 'Extortion and Bribery in International Business Transactions: ICC Rules of Conduct'. 1999 revised version. http://www.iccwbo.org/home/statements_rules/rules/1999/briberydoc99.asp, last accessed 18 July 2000.

Internet Encyclopedia of Philosophy (2000a) 'Categorical Imperative', see http://www.utm.edu/research/ iep/c/catimper.htm, accessed on 9 July 2000.

Internet Encyclopedia of Philosophy (2000b) 'Rule utilitarianism', see http://www.utm.edu/research/iep/r/ruleutil.htm, accessed on 9 July 2000.

Internet Encyclopedia of Philosophy (2000c) 'Rights', see http://www.utm.edu/research/iep/r/rights.htm, accessed on 11 July 2000.

ISR (1995) *Employee Satisfaction: Tracking European Trends*. London: ISR.

Ivanhoe, P.J. (2000) *Confucian Moral Self-Cultivation* (second edition), Indianapolis, IN: Hackett.

Jackall, R. (1988) *Moral Mazes: The World of Corporate Managers*, Oxford: Oxford University Press.

Jones, T.M. (1995) 'Instrumental stakeholder theory: A synthesis of ethics and economics', *Academy of Management Review,* **20**(2): 404–37.

Kanter, R.M. (1979) 'Power failure in management circuits', *Harvard Business Review,* **57**(4): 65–75.

Kanungo, R.N. and Conger, J.A. (1993) 'Promoting altruism as a corporate goal', *Academy of Management Executive,* **7**(3): 37–48.

Kegan, R. (1994) *In Over Our Heads: The Mental Demands of Modern Life*, Cambridge, MA: Harvard University Press.

Keough, J. (ed.) (1998) *Corporate Ethics: A Prime Business Asset*, New York: The Business Roundtable.

Kjonstad, B. and Willmott, H. (1995) 'Business ethics: Restrictive or empowering?' *Journal of Business Ethics,* **14**(6): 445–64.

Klitgaard, R. (2000) 'Subverting corruption', *Finance and Development,* **37**(2): 2–5.

Knouse, S.B. and Giacalone, R.A. (1992) 'Ethical decision-making in business: Behavioural issues and concerns', *Journal of Business Ethics,* **11**: 369–77.

Kofman, F. and Senge, P.M. (1993) 'Communities of commitment: The heart of learning organizations', *Organizational Dynamics,* **22**(2): 5–23.

Kohlberg, L. (1981) *Essays on Moral Development, Volume One*: *The Philosophy of Moral Development*, San Francisco: Harper & Row.

Kohlberg, L. (1984) *Essays in Moral Development, Volume Two*: *The Psychology of Moral Development*, New York: Harper & Row.

Kohlberg, L. (1985) 'The just community approach to moral education in theory and practice', in Berkowitz, M. and Oser, F. (eds), *Moral Education: Theory and Application*, Hillsdale, NJ: Erlbaum Associates.

Kohlberg, L. (1986) 'A current statement on some theoretical issues', in Modgil, S. and Modgil, C. (eds), *Lawrence Kohlberg: Consensus and Controversy*, Lewes: Falmer Press.

Kohlberg, L. and Ryncarz, R.A. (1990) 'Beyond justice reasoning: Moral development and consideration of a seventh stage', in Alexander, C.N. and Langer, E.J. (eds), *Higher Stages of Human Development*, Oxford: Oxford University Press.

Kohlberg, L., Levine, C. and Hewer, A. (1983) *Moral Stages: A Current Formulation and a Response to Critics*, New York: Karger.

Kwong, K. (1996) 'Purity over profit', *Sunday Morning Post, Agenda Section,* 18 February: 2.

Lavoie, D. and Culbert, S.A. (1978) 'Stages of organization and development', *Human Relations, 31*(5): 417–38.

Lee, C.K. (1999) 'From organized dependence to disorganized despotism: Changing labour regimes in Chinese factories', *China Quarterly,* **157**: 44–71.

Leisinger, K.M. (1995) 'Corporate ethics and international business: Some basic issues', in Stewart, S. and Donleavy, G. (eds), *Whose Business Values? Some Asian and Cross-cultural Perspectives,* Hong Kong: Hong Kong University Press, pp. 165–202.

Leung, K. (1988) 'Theoretical advances in justice behavior: Some cross-cultural inputs', in Bond, M.H. (ed.), *The Cross-cultural Challenge to Social Psychology*, Newbury Park, CA: Sage.

Lichtenstein, B.M., Smith, B.A. and Torbert, W.R. (1995) 'Leadership and ethical development: Balancing light and shadow', *Business Ethics Quarterly, 5*(1): 97–116.

Lim, K.S. (1994) *Inner Peace: A Source of Chinese Philosophic Meditative Practice*, Selangor Darul Ehsan, Malaysia: Pelanduk.

Lind, G. (1997) 'The optimal age for moral education: A review of intervention studies and an experimental test of the dual-aspect theory of moral development and education', University of Konstanz, Department of Psychology, 78434 Konstanz, Germany. (Article also available in the Internet, http://www.uni-konstanz.de/ag-moral/optimal.htm, last accessed 1 October, 2000.)

Linstead, S. and Chan, A. (1994) 'The sting of organization: Command, reciprocity and change management', *Journal of Organizational Change Management, 7*(5): 4–19.

Locke, J. (1986) *The Second Treatise on Civil Government*, New York: Prometheus Books. See also www.mind-trek.com/treatise/jl-ccg/.

Loevinger, J. (1985) 'Revision of the Sentence Completion Test for ego development', *Journal of Personality and Social Psychology, 48*(2): 420–7.

Luthans, F., Hodgetts, R.M. and Rosenkrantz, S.A. (1988) *Real Managers*, Cambridge, MA: Ballinger.

McDonald, G.M. (1994) 'Value modification strategies on a national scale: The activities of the Independent Commission Against Corruption in Hong Kong', in Hoffman, W.M., Kam, J.B., Frederick, R.E. and Petry, E.S. (eds), *Emerging Glocal Business Ethics,* Westport, CO: Quorum Books, pp. 14–35.

McDonald, M. (1995) 'Ethics and conflict of interest', http://www.compliance.co.za/documents/ethicsandconflictofinterest2.htm.

MacFarlane, B. (2000) 'Inside the corporate classroom', *Teaching in Higher Education, 5*(1): 51–60.

MacIntyre, A. (1977) 'Utilitarianism and cost-benefit analysis: An essay on the relevance of moral philosophy to bureaucratic theory', in Sayre, K. (ed.) *Values in the Electric Power industry.* Notre Dame, IN: University of Notre Dame Press, pp. 217–37.

MacIntyre, A. (1988) *Whose Justice? Which Rationality?* Notre Dame, IN: University of Notre Dame Press.

McKenna, R. (1999) *New Management*, Roseville, NSW: McGraw-Hill.

Maclagan, P. (1995) 'Ethical thinking in organizations: Implications for management education', *Management Learning, 26*(2): 159–77.

Maclagan, P. (1998) *Management and Morality*, London: Sage.

Mao, Z. (1990) 'In memory of Norman Bethune', *Beijing Review 33*(9): 40. (Article also available in the Internet, http://www.maoism.org/msw/vol2/ mswv2_25.htm, last accessed 23 July, 2000.

Marcic, D. (1997) *Managing with the Wisdom of Love: Uncovering Virtue in People and Organizations*, San Francisco: Jossey-Bass.

Mechanic, D. (1962) 'Sources of power of lower participants in complex organizations', *Administrative Science Quarterly, 7*: 349–64.

Miceli, M.P. and Near, J.P. (1991) 'Whistleblowing as an organizational process', in Bacharach, S.B (ed.), *Research in the Sociology of Organizations 9*: 139–200, Greenwich, CT: JAI Press.

Midgley, M. (1984) *Wickedness: A Philosophical Essay*, London: Routledge & Kegan Paul.

Mill, J.S. (1998) 'Utilitarianism', in Hartman, L.P. (ed.), *Perspectives in Business Ethics,* Chicago: McGraw-Hill.

Mitchell, A., Puxty, T., Sikka, P. and Willmott, H. (1994) 'Ethical statements as smokescreens for sectional interests: The case of the UK accountancy profession', *Journal of Business Ethics,* **13**(1): 39–51.

Mitchell, T.R. and Scott, W.G. (1990) 'America's problems and needed reforms: Confronting the ethic of personal advantage', *Academy of Management Executive,* **4**(3): 23–35.

Morris, T. (1997) *If Aristotle Ran General Motors: The New Soul of Business.* New York: Henry Holt.

Near, J.P. and Jensen, T.C. (1983) 'The whistleblowing process: Retaliation and perceived effectiveness', *Work and Occupations,* **10**(1): 3–28.

Near, J.P. and Miceli, M.P. (1987) 'Whistleblowers in organizations: Dissidents or reformers?', in Staw, B.M. and Cummings, L.L. (eds), *Research in Organizational Behaviour* **9**: 321–68, Greenwich, CT: JAI Press.

Ng, K.C. (2000) 'Green pledge on countryside', *South China Morning Post*, Hong Kong; 25 May, p. 8.

Niehoff, B.P. and Paul, R.J. (2000) 'Causes of employee theft and strategies that HR managers can use for prevention', *Human Resource Management,* **39**(1): 51–6.

Nielsen, R.P. (1987) 'What can managers do about unethical management?', *Journal of Business Ethics,* **6**: 309–20.

Nielsen, R.P. (1996) *The Politics of Ethics: Methods for Acting, Learning, and sometimes Fighting with Others in Addressing Ethics Problems in Organizational Life,* New York: Oxford University Press.

OECD (Organization for Economic Cooperation and Development) (2000) 'Combating Bribery of Foreign Public Officials in International Business Transactions – Text of the Convention', http://www.oecd.org/daf/nocorruption/20nov1e.htm, last accessed 18 July 2000.

Overell, S. (1998) 'Tribunal opens floodgate for equal value awards', *People Management,* **4**(2): 14.

Pastin, M. and Hooker, M. (1980) 'Ethics and the Foreign Corrupt Practices Act', *Business Horizons,* December: 43–7.

Pataki, G. (2000) 'Book reviews: Patrick Maclagan: Management and morality: A developmental perspective', *Organization Studies*, **21**(4): 836–41.

Perrucci, R., Anderson, R.M., Schendel, D.E. and Trachtman, E. (1980) 'Whistleblowing: Professionals' resistance to organizational authority', *Social Problems,* **28**: 149–64.

Petrick, J.A. and Wagley, R.A. (1992) 'Enhancing the responsible strategic management of organizations', *Journal of Management Development,* **11**(4): 57–72.

Pincus, L.B. (1998) 'A free market approach to comparable worth', in Hartman, L.P. (ed.), *Perspectives in Business Ethics*, Chicago: McGraw-Hill, pp. 454–7.

Plantenga, J. and Hansen, J. (1999) 'Assessing equal opportunities in the European Union', *International Labour Review,* **138**(4): 351–79.

Ponting, C. (1986) *Whitehall: Tragedy and Farce*, London: Hamish Hamilton.

Raphael, D.D. (1994) *Moral Philosophy,* (2nd edn), Oxford: Oxford University Press.

Rawls, J. (1971) *A Theory of Justice*, Cambridge, MA: Harvard University Press.

Redding, G. (1990) *The Spirit of Chinese Capitalism*, Berlin: de Gruyter.

Robertson-Snape, F. (1999) 'Corruption, collusion and nepotism in Indonesia', *Third World Quarterly,* **20**(3): 589–602

Roddick, A. (1991) *Body and Soul*, London: Vermillion.

Roddick, A. (2000) *Business As Usual: The Triumph of Anita Roddick: The Body Shop*, London: Thorsons.

Rooke, D. and Torbert, W.R. (2000) 'Organizational transformation as a function of CEOs' developmental stage', available via William Torbert's web page, and at http://www2.bc.edu/~torbert/8_rooke_wrt95.html, last accessed 4 October 2000.

Ryan, L.V. (1994) 'Ethics codes in British companies', *Business Ethics: A European Review,* **3**(1): 54–64.

Sanderson, R. and Warner, I.I. (1994) 'What's wrong with corporate codes of conduct?', *Management Accounting,* **66**: 28–35.

Schlegelmilch, B.B. and Houston, J.E. (1990) 'Corporate codes of ethics', *Management Decision,* **28**(7): 38–43.

Schor, J.B. (1992) *The Overworked American*, New York: Basic Books.

Schwartz, H. (1990) *Narcissistic Process and Corporate Decay*, New York: New York University Press.

Sennett, R. (2000) *The Corrosion of Character: The Personal Consequences of Work in the New Capitalism*, New York: W.W. Norton.

Serbanescu, I. (2000) 'Deficient democracy', *Harvard International Review,* **22**(2): 10–11.

Shaw, T, Legal Correspondent, and Demetriou, D. (2000) 'News: £293,000 awarded to whistleblower who was dismissed', *Daily Telegraph*, London (UK), 11 July, p. 6.

Sieh, E.W. (1987) 'Garment workers: Perceptions of inequity and employee theft', *British Journal of Criminology,* **27**(2): 174–90.

Sims, D., Fineman, S. and Gabriel, Y. (1993) *Organizing and Organizations: An Introduction*, London: Sage.

Singer, P. (ed.) (1991) *A Companion to Ethics*, Oxford: Blackwell.

Smith, A. (1937) *An Enquiry Into the Nature and Causes of the Wealth of Nations*, Cannan, E. (ed.), New York: Modern Library.

Smith, A. (2001) *The Theory of Moral Sentiments*, Haakonussen, K. (ed.), New York: Cambridge University Press.

Snell, R.S. (1993a) *Developing Skills for Ethical Management*, London: Chapman & Hall.

Snell, R.S. (1993b) 'More than meets the eye:

Adopting a management style through modelling', *Leadership and Organization Development Journal,* **14**(5): 3–11.

Snell, R.S. (1997) 'Management learning perspectives on business ethics', in Burgoyne, J.G. and Reynolds, P.M. (eds), *Management Learning: Integrating Perspectives in Theory and Practice*, London: Sage, pp. 182–98.

Snell, R.S. (1999a) 'Obedience to authority and ethical dilemmas in Hong Kong companies', *Business Ethics Quarterly,* **9**(3): 507–26.

Snell, R.S. (1999b) 'Managing ethically', in Fulop, L. and Linstead, S. (eds), *Management: A Critical Text*, Melbourne: Macmillan Business.

Snell, R.S. (2000) 'Studying moral ethos, using an adapted Kohlbergian model', *Organization Studies,* **21**(1): 267–95.

Snell, R.S. (2001) 'Moral foundations of the learning organisation', *Human Relations,* **54**(3): 339-62.

Snell, R.S. and Herndon, N.C. Jr (2000) 'An evaluation of Hong Kong's corporate code of ethics initiative', *Asia Pacific Journal of Management,* **17**(3): 493–518.

Snell, R.S. and Tseng, C.S. (2000) 'Moral atmosphere and moral influence under China's network capitalism', *Organization Studies*, **23**(3): 449–78.

Snell, R.S. and Tseng, C.S. (2001) 'From innocence to experience, From guanxi to corruption: Ethical dilemmas of relationship building in China business', *Thunderbird International Business Review*, **43**(2): 169–98.

Snell, R.S., Chak, A.M.K. and Taylor, K.F. (1996) 'The impact of moral ethos on how ethical dilemmas are experienced and resolved in six Hong Kong companies', *Management Research News,* **19**(9): 72–91.

Snell, R.S., Taylor, K.F. and Chak, A.M.K. (1997) 'Ethical dilemmas and ethical reasoning: A study in Hong Kong', *Human Resource Management Journal,* **7**(3): 19–30.

Snell, R.S., Taylor, K.F., Chu, J.W-H. and Drummond, D. (1999), 'A study of the validity of the moral ethos questionnaire and its transferability to a Chinese context', *Teaching Business Ethics,* **3**(4): 361–81.

Starkey, K. (1998) 'What can we learn from the learning organization?' *Human Relations,* **51**(4): 531–46.

Steidlmeier, P. (1992) *People and Profits: The Ethics of Capitalism*, Englewood Cliffs, NJ: Prentice Hall.

Steidlmeier, P. (1999) 'Gift giving, bribery and corruption: Ethical management of business relationships in China', *Journal of Business Ethics,* **20**(2): 121–32.

Stevens, B. (1994) 'An analysis of corporate ethical code studies: "Where do we go from here?"', *Journal of Business Ethics,* **13**: 63–9.

Storey, J. (1999) 'Equal opportunities in retrospect and prospect', *Human Resource Management Journal,* **9**(1): 5–8.

Tan, D. (2000) Draft PhD thesis, Department of Management Learning, Lancaster University, UK.

Ten Bos, R. (1997) 'Essai: Business ethics and Bauman ethics', *Organization Studies,* **18**(6): 997–1014.

The Body Shop (1997) 'The 1997 Body Shop Values Report', Body Shop International PLC, http://www.uk.the-body-shop.com/aboutus/values.html, last accessed July 22 2000.

The Body Shop (2000) 'Annual Report and Accounts 2000', Body Shop International PLC, http://www.uk.the-body-shop.com/aboutus/report.html, last accessed July 22 2000.

Thoenes, S. (1998) 'Suharto's old friend takes up his portfolio', *Financial Times*, London, 17 March, p. 8.

TI (Transparency International) (2000a) '1999 Bribe Payers Index, 1999 Corruption Perceptions Index', http://www.transparency.de/documents/cpi/index.html, last accessed 18 July 2000.

TI (Transparency International) (2000b) 'The Transparency International Corruption Perceptions Index 1999 – Framework Document', http://www.transparency.de/documents/cpi/cpi_framework.html, last accessed 18 July 2000.

TI (Transparency International) (2000c) 'Sources for the 1999 CPI', http://www.transparency.de/documents/cpi/sources.html, last accessed 18 July 2000.

Toffler, B.L. (1986) *Tough Choices: Managers Talk Ethics*, Chichester: John Wiley.

Torbert, W.R. (1994) 'Managerial learning, organizational learning: A potentially powerful redundancy', *Management Learning,* **25**(1): 57–70.

Treviño, L.K. (1986) 'Ethical decision making in organizations: A person–situation interactionist model', *Academy of Management Review,* **11**(3): 601–17.

Treviño, L.K. (1992) 'Moral reasoning and business ethics: Implications for research, education and management', *Journal of Business Ethics,* **11**: 445–59.

Treviño, L.K. and McCabe, D. (1994) 'Meta-learning about business ethics: Building honorable business school communities', *Journal of Business Ethics,* **13**: 405–16.

Treviño, L.K. and Nelson, K.A. (1995) *Managing Business Ethics: Straight Talk About How to do it Right*, New York: John Wiley.

Treviño, L.K. and Youngblood, S.A. (1990) 'Bad apples in bad barrels: A causal analysis of ethical decision-making behavior', *Journal of Applied Psychology,* **75**(4): 378–85.

Tu, W.M. (1998) 'Probing the "three bonds" and "five relationships" in Confucian humanism', in Slote, W.H. and DeVos, G.A. (eds) *Confucianism and the Family in an Interdisciplinary Comparative Context*, Albany, NY: State University of New York Press, pp. 121–36.

Velasquez, M.G. (1992) *Business Ethics: Concepts and Cases* (3rd edn), Englewood Cliffs, NJ: Prentice Hall.

Vinten, G. (1992) 'Whistle blowing: Corporate help or hindrance?', *Management Decision,* **30**(1): 44–8.

Walker, S. (1992) '"Greed is good"... or is it? Economic ideology and moral tension in a graduate school of business', *Journal of Business Ethics,* **11**(4): 273–83.

Wall Street Journal (1993) 'Ratners posts 1st-half loss, adopts new name of Signet', European edn, p. 5, Brussels, 13 September.

Walsh, J. (1998) 'UK companies forced to comply with 48-hour rule', *People Management,* **4**(8): 12–13.

Wambold, J.J. (1977) 'Prohibiting foreign bribes: Criminal sanctions for corporate payments abroad', *Cornell International Law Journal,* **10**: 235–7.

Wan, C. (2000) 'Pollution warning', *South China Morning Post*, Hong Kong; 3 June, p.2.

Wank, D.L. (1995) 'Bureaucratic patronage and private business: Changing networks of power in urban China', in Walder, A.G. (ed.), *The Waning of the Communist State*, Berkeley: University of California Press, pp. 153–83.

Warren, R. (1993) 'Codes of ethics: Bricks without straw', *Business Ethics: A European Review,* **2**(4): 185–91.

Waters, J. (1988) 'Integrity management: Learning and implementing ethical principles in the workplace', in Srivasta, S. (ed.), *Executive Integrity: The Search for High Human Values in Organizational Life*, San Francisco: Jossey-Bass.

Waters, J., Bird, F. and Chant, P.D. (1986) 'Everyday moral issues experienced by managers', *Journal of Business Ethics,* **5**(5): 373–84.

Weale, S. (2000) 'Law: Is it safe to speak out?: It's a year since new legislation was passed to protect whistleblowers at work. Sally asks if it's working', *The Guardian*, Manchester (UK), 3 July, p. 8.

Weaver, G.R. (1993) 'Corporate codes of ethics: Purpose, process and content issues', *Business and Society,* **32**(1): 44–58.

Weber, J. (1990) 'Managers' moral reasoning: Assessing their responses to three moral dilemmas', *Human Relations,* **43**(7): 687–702.

Webley, S. (1993) *Codes of Business Ethics – Why Companies Should Develop Them*, London: Institute of Business Ethics.

Weiss, J.W. (1994) *Business Ethics: A Managerial, Stakeholder Approach*, Belmont, CA: Wadsworth.

Wellman, C. (1963) 'The ethical implications of cultural relativity', *Journal of Philosophy,* **60**(7): 169–84.

Westley, F.R. (1990) 'The eye of a needle: Cultural and personal transformation in a traditional organization', *Human Relations,* **43**(3): 273–93.

White, B.J. and Montgomery, R. (1980) 'Corporate codes of conduct', *California Management Review,* **23**(2): 80–7.

Whysall, P. (2000) 'Stakeholder mismanagement in retailing: A British perspective', *Journal of Business Ethics,* **23**(1): 19–28.

Williams, G.J. (1992) *Ethics in Modern Management*, New York: Quorum Books.

Williams, N. (1998) 'Cresson told to explain questioned contracts', *Science,* **282**(5387): 215.

Part II

Management Processes

9

Motivation and meaning

Liz Fulop and Stephen Linstead

Questions about motivation and meaning

1 Why do people work?

2 Are people motivated in the same ways?

3 Is how we work affected by how we feel?

4 Can one person motivate another?

5 Is the way a job is designed important for motivation?

6 Does motivation vary from culture to culture?

7 How is motivation different between men and women?

COMMITMENT IN CHESTER

The scene is a hotel room in Chester, UK. It is a cold February night and ten senior managers are gathered around a table having eaten and drunk a great deal. Ostensibly they are here for a strategy meeting scheduled for the next day; occasionally these so-called away days are used to deal with difficulties between members of the group. More often than not, this dealing with consists of joking, scapegoating and other attempts to cut the victims down to size. On this occasion, Graham, the manager of a business unit, has raised some issues about the role that Eric, the managing director, and Steve, the personnel director, are playing in his business [unit]. Several attempts have been made to cut him down to size:

Eric: (to the waiter) And we'll need some more brandy. Bring another bottle. Right. Where were we before we were so rudely interrupted? Ah, yes. The question of commitment, Graham?

Graham: I was not talking about commitment, I was talking about Personnel's right to shift people around without consultation.

Eric: But the rest of us were talking about commitment, Graham.

Colin: My people are committed to plan, Graham, are yours?

Graham: You might have been happy to join in, Colin, for reasons best known to yourself, but I was not talking about commitment, I was talking about poaching my people.

Roger: But your people are not committed, I've heard them say it themselves.

Graham: Roger, I do not give a toss what you claim to have heard. I am not talking about plans or commitment! I am talking about poaching!

Tony: (drunkenly) He's right! He's right! That's what we started talking about. That's what the boy started on about. I distinctly remember.

Roger: You're too pissed to remember anything ...

Eric: Get it off your chest. Tell us what the issue is and then we'll talk about commitment.

Graham: Eric, I've told you what I think the issue is and I don't want to talk about commitment, as you keep calling it, now or later. Either I am running my unit or I am not. I deeply resent Steve telling me that he is moving one of my better – no, my best man – and giving him to Roger.

Steve: It wasn't like that, Graham, and you know it. I talked to you about it ...

Graham: You talked to me about it AFTER ... AFTER you had decided – with Eric no doubt and probably Roger – what you were going to do. He is my man, in my unit, working for me.

Eric: And for the good of the team as a whole, we decided that we needed his contribution elsewhere.

Graham: Cant! Sheer bloody unadulterated cant! 'For the good of the team.' What bloody team? This lot? Us? Look at us! Senior managers in a public company, pissed as newts, debating nonsense – commitment, the good of the team! Working together, contributing to the company. It's all wind! Bloody hypocrisy. Tripe. We make bloody biscuits and crisps, and snacks and pizzas. What's all this crap about commitment and team spirit? It's not life or death, is it? It's no big deal. Biscuits, crisps, toffee bars, stuff everyone can do without. What is all this crap about commitment and team spirit? We are not supposed to be a bloody religious order. We are not on some crusade to save the world! Commitment, for

God's sake. Who cares if we make a few more Nut Surprises? Sell a few more Dream Delights? A handful of shareholders, that's who cares? We have to ask ourselves what all this is about. What is the point of pouring huge amounts of energy into making more and more things that are of no use to anyone? Dream Delights, for God's sake! What's it all come down to? What's it all about? We throw ourselves into this nonsense as if it mattered. As if we were working to free the world from cholera or something. We are riding a monster. Production profit, grind it out. Push it on. Where is it all leading? I'll tell you where – bloody nowhere! It is not progress making more and more biscuits, more and more crisps, the biggest pizza in the world. We go on about being committed as though a few thousand quid either way will make a difference. Right, if you want to know, I am not committed, as you put it. I do not spend every waking hour thinking about Nut Surprises or Dream Delights. I do not want to spend my life thinking about Nut Surprises or Dream Delights. I question the sanity of anyone who does. I don't want to be in the office at seven in the morning and leave nine or ten at night. I do not want to spend time here. Now. Listening to this twaddle about commitment. Arguing about who works for whom. You are welcome to my staff, Roger – all of them. I'd rather be at home. What do you want from me? Blood? I work to live, not the other way round. And so do most of the rest of you – if you don't, you are mad. I work hard not because I am committed. I work to support my wife and family. There is life beyond this company, and I am sick of pretending otherwise. You can have me from nine to five, beyond that I am my own man …

Silence. No one moves. No one catches anyone else's eye. Something has been put asunder, a disjuncture has occurred; one senses a space, a void, a crack opening up, a rush of stale air being expelled; something starkly, rudely present. The door opens and the waiter enters.

Source: Iain Mangham (1996) 'Beyond Goffman', in P. Jeffcutt, R. Grafton Small and S. Linstead (eds) *Organization and Theatre*, special issue of *Studies in Cultures, Organizations, and Societies* **2**(1): 33–5.

QUESTIONS ABOUT THE CASE

1 How many different views of commitment are evident in the case?
2 How could Graham's real or apparent 'lack of commitment' be handled? Does it need to be addressed?
3 What has precipitated the 'blow-up' at Chester?
4 Would the meeting have been different if some of the managers were women?

Introduction

Although we have raised a number of very important questions at the beginning of this chapter, perhaps the most important one is: does motivation matter at all in organizations? Richard McKenna (1999: 301) has argued that the topic of motivation has lost its relevance and needs to be replaced with concepts such as 'sense making', 'identity' and 'diversity'. In fact, he says it doesn't make sense to say that managers can manage the motivation of their employees because to do so implies manipulation and control. Roy Jacques (1996: 160–1) goes further and questions the value of motivation theory at all. He views it as a remnant of the factory system (assembly line technology) in the US and the strong Protestant work ethic of the founding fathers that made a virtue of service to the higher ideals of work and, naturally, capitalism. Jacques actually argues that there are categories of workers who do not need motivation, citing among them many professionals and knowledge workers who are usually more career and professionally oriented. He sees the future of work in terms of removing barriers

that hinder performance rather than focusing on inducing effort through motivational techniques. If we accept the premise that relational management has become important in many workplaces, then we should question how 'motivation' has also changed, both in its meanings and application in management. We can't easily drop the word 'motivation' from the management lexicon but as the chapter unfolds, you will see that it makes more sense to talk about 'motivation and meaning' as two inseparable aspects of working with people. However, it is important to appreciate why organizational behaviour (OB) and management scholars have focused on the topic of motivation, and why it is still a popular theme in many management theories and texts.

Motivation theories have been dominated by two approaches to application, neither of which is entirely separable from the other: (i) developing individual performance-based schemes to reward organizational members and (ii) designing work to increase performance outcomes for the organization and, hopefully, the benefit of the individual. Job design and redesign have a long history in OB and management, gaining prominence with the emergence of Taylorism (see Chapters 2 and 11). Since the 1960s job redesign emphasized making jobs more interesting, satisfying and challenging. By the 1970s worker participation and democracy in the workplace had been included in many Western countries. In the 1980s and early 1990s teamwork, culture, empowerment, total quality management (TQM) and business re-engineering (BR) were fashionable, successfully reinventing earlier theories of motivation. As we begin the new millennium, learning organizations, intellectual capital and knowledge management are the new fads, although we have questioned elsewhere how 'new' these ideas really are (see Introduction and Chapter 1). Many of these fads and fashions have arisen as part of the rise of the so-called 'new economy' that, as we said in the Introduction, supposedly heralds a new 'golden age' of the highly individualistic, young, techno-savvy, worker – 'the millennials' as some refer to them (see Howe 1997). However, one of the key messages of this chapter is that no one categorization of the employee actually works in reality.

Job design was initially aimed at reversing the negative effects of scientific management, particularly in shop-floor and routine jobs, such as clerical work. Management theorists in the 1960s saw motivation as largely about satisfying the needs of people, needs that could only ever really be satisfied through work. These *needs deficiency theories* of motivation helped propagate a belief that if managers could identify the needs of employees, managers could also manipulate or influence these needs, making it easier for employees to improve their performances. The needs-based approach to motivation has left a profound legacy in OB and management studies and it has not been dispelled in many of the popular fads and fashions prevalent in the management marketplace today. In this chapter we examine some of the more popular approaches to job redesign put forward since the time of Taylor and Mayo and the motivation theories behind each of them. Many approaches to job redesign have been premised on a homogeneous view of employees and their needs – usually male needs, as already mentioned in Chapter 2. Motivation theories have dealt with a narrow range of needs and while the focus on diversity has grown in importance during the 1990s, the views espoused in this literature are also conservative, as noted in Chapter 2, often reinforcing normative views of 'good' corporate behaviour.

A more sociologically oriented view of motivation suggests that 'needs' emerge and are constituted in social activities and experiences that shape our identities or the 'social self' and give meaning to work. Identities in the work context are not without their limitations and constraints and are socially structured and enacted within the context of different knowledge and power relations. A more critical view of motivation examines how strategies of job redesign, for example, reproduce certain motivational discourses that are embedded in power relations and give rise to particular disciplinary practices, such as techniques of surveillance. Culture and gender are important in how we define ourselves and who we think we are, yet both are often neglected in studies of motivation. We take the notion of *commitment* and examine its gendered nature and the ramifications for management. At the core of motivation theory (and commitment) is the notion of *trust* and we explore its traditional as well as its contemporary meanings, including its influence on individual identity in an increasingly virtual world of 'identity theft'.

Job redesign post-Taylor

Most early job redesign strategies were concerned with reversing the negative effects of scientific management, effects relating to rigid, overspecialized and inflexibly designed jobs, in order to find new ways of improving worker performance. Under scientific management and Fordism (the latter initiated and perfected mass production through assembly line technology), many jobs were deskilled, reducing the value of labour, making labour less costly and easier to replace. Boring, repetitive and rigidly structured jobs produced inhumane working conditions in which workers suffered extensive psychological trauma and a poor quality of work life. Taylorism acknowledged the messiness of organizations and the factors that contribute to this messiness – individual characteristics, collective consciousness, uneven distribution of knowledge about tasks and gender. The manager under scientific management needed to impose the principles that control and regulate such diversity. This regulation was an integral part of Taylor's work as a response to the persistence of the craft model in industry, which was rife with non-standardized methods, such as individual workers being responsible for setting their own work targets, patterns and hours, and often working with their own different sets of tools and producing varying outputs (see Chapter 11).

A key principle in Taylorism was the notion of *economic man* – a theory of motivation to cover all workers. Taylor, and many theorists after him, believed that the basic motivating principle for workers was money or wages. Workers were assumed to be motivated by personal interest and gain, and capable of being satisfied principally by monetary rewards. Taylor saw this as a very rational type of behaviour supporting the principle of hard work or a Protestant work ethic. Taylor had been raised in a Quaker family and believed that everyone could succeed through hard work and enterprising values. He also believed that poor managers deprived workers of the opportunity to satisfy their economic needs and from reaching their highest possible rewards (Bendix 1956: 256–7).

In the 1960s and 70s, high employment and tight labour markets in countries such as the USA and the UK saw employers turn a critical eye to the effects of deskilling, especially in the wake of declining productivity, increased absenteeism, poor morale, rising rates of labour turnover and increased incidences of industrial sabotage and strikes (Emery and Phillips 1976; Strauss 1976: 23; Child 1984: 31). It is probably this last aspect of deskilling which has most concerned managers because of the obvious impact these problems can have on the overall performance of the organization. Job redesign became one solution for overcoming the problems caused by deskilling. Many job redesign strategies focused on improving the job satisfaction of employees (that is, their motivation to work or their feelings about work), while also hoping to extract greater economic benefits for employers.

George Strauss (1976) suggests that the growing interest in job redesign in the 1970s also reflected concerns relating to managing and motivating a diverse workforce. He points out that the baby boomers (the large number of children born after the Second World War or 1945–1960) who entered the workforce were more resistant to, and challenging of, authority and less afraid of economic insecurity, having grown up in the postwar boom. They were more inclined to value self-fulfilment, agreeable lifestyles, doing meaningful work and controlling their own destinies. Moreover, many women who were also entering the workforce at this period were less likely to measure success in terms of the traditional economic goals of Taylor's economic man. He points out that factors such as Women's Lib, civil rights agitation in the USA and student activism of the 1960s affected how satisfaction was being thought of in many quarters (Strauss 1976: 21–4). These views are echoed by Kelly Goski and Mary Belfry (1991: 215–16) who add that the next generation – the 'baby busters' – were even more focused on entitlements and less accepting of authority. This 'next generation', often referred to as 'generation X' (based on US cultural experience), was supposedly less committed to lifelong employment with one firm (as their parents might have been) and was more prepared to take risks and be occupational nomads. The generation X prototype was also brought up in more diverse ways (for example childcare, single-parent families) than previous generations and 'motivating' them, it was argued, would entail different types of strategies. The recognition that workplaces constitute generations of workers, with very different social values and identity reference points, poses a major challenge for motivation theories because all were premised on a homogeneous (white Anglo-Saxon male, North American) view of workers and their purported universal needs.

Job enrichment and the hierarchy of needs

Many job redesign strategies have their origins in the 1960s. *Job enrichment theory* has had a profound impact on job redesign and theories of motivation. The theoretical basis underpinning this job redesign strategy came from the school known as Neo-Human Relations which revisited the work of Mayo and the Human Relations School. Elton Mayo's research (see Chapters 2 and 11) had encouraged a view that saw management's role include the development of 'good human relations' between itself and workers and between co-workers – a situation that was thought to motivate employees to work together productively, cooperatively and with economic, psychological and social satisfaction. Human relations theory, however, stopped at the conditions under which the work was done and the relationships between people at work and thus never contradicted or challenged the assumptions of Tayloristic approaches to the organization of work and task specialization.

However, unlike Taylor, who saw workers as being rational and calculating individuals, Mayo did not believe this to be the case (see Chapters 2 and 11). On the contrary, he argued that people were motivated by personal sentiments and emotions and craved social routine. He believed that logical thinking only occurred when workers were pressed to solve problems. Logical thinking, and hence the pursuit of self-interest (that is, economic man), was something Mayo thought was a measure 'of the last resort' on the part of workers (Bendix 1956: 313–14). Instead Mayo proposed a *social man* view of behaviour and motivation. He was concerned about the excessive emphasis placed on individualism and self-interest in society in general, and argued instead that people had a need for belonging to a community or having a sense of community as well as order and conformity. Small supportive work groups in organizations would fill the need of workers for social cohesiveness and social conformity. The forming of informal groups (that is, the informal organization that Taylor rejected) was, he argued, natural to workers, but managers could gain control of employees by paying attention to their social needs and facilitating group cohesion (Bendix 1956: 316–17; Rose 1975: 120–1).

Maslow's hierarchy of needs

While not denying that this school was important, during the 1950s and 60s researchers from the developing area

Exhibit 9.1 Maslow's hierarchy of needs

Higher order needs

Self-actualization needs
(Need to reach one's full potential)

Self-esteem needs
(Need for recognition and a belief in one's self)

Social acceptance needs
(Need to be able to form satisfactory affective and support relations)

Lower order needs

Safety and security needs
(Need to feel safe, and free of fear)

Basic physiological needs
(Need for food, warmth, shelter, clothing)

Source: Adapted from Maslow, A.H. (1943) 'A theory of human motivation', *Psychological Review*, **50**(4): 370–96.

of behavioural science began to extend the psychological dimension of human relations. Psychological well-being, it was argued, required not only good work conditions but also a meaningful job over which the individual worker had control. Abraham Maslow's (1943) hierarchy of human needs (see Chapter 2) provides the basis for this school of thought. He developed a classification of human needs that he considered to be a more or less sequential development from 'lower order' to 'higher order' needs. It is usually asserted that Maslow assumed that these needs applied universally to all individuals. The hierarchy is described in Exhibit 9.1.

Since the physiological needs are classified as primary (or even primitive), they are given first priority. If a person is starving, only food occupies his or her mind. However, once this need is substantially satisfied, the person becomes concerned with a need that was formerly of less salience, safety and security. According to Maslow, people are motivated by unsatisfied needs: a person is never completely satisfied on any need level, but a reasonable amount of gratification with basic needs must be felt before he or she proceeds up the hierarchy. Maslow's model has been used to argue that with growing economic security and affluence in society generally, and rising educational levels, the workforce would increasingly be motivated only by the higher order needs of self-esteem and self-actualization. This was not quite Maslow's analysis: Maslow in fact took the view that people were either self-actualizers or they were not, and society's problem was creating the conditions for those who were self-actualizers to self-

actualize, rather than being reactive to circumstances. The economic man needs of Taylor and the social man needs of Mayo were thus given low priority in Maslow's *complex man* approach – in fact, Maslow was concerned with those elite individuals he called *self-actualizers*, and in giving advice as to the sort of social and educational systems that should be developed for them. While he held onto a vision of a self-actualizing society, a less emphasized aspect of his theory was that not everyone was able to self-actualize because of their nature, and many people would remain caught at the lower motivational levels.

However, it should be noted that Maslow himself did not intend his model to be an all-embracing theory of motivation and was aware of some of its shortcomings (Aungles and Parker 1988: 13–17). In fact, he was critical of the fact that so many OB and management theorists had adapted his work but no one had bothered to test and develop it. This work was not done until the 1960s, after Maslow himself did his one and only piece of organizational investigation – an informal summer spent in a technology company in 1962 which he wrote up as a journal (Maslow 1965; for a critique see Linstead 2002). We have critiqued the gender suppression in Maslow's work (see Chapter 2), and despite its massive and evident shortcomings as an evolutionary theory of needs, it remains a standard approach used to explain motivation even today (see Cullen 2000; Usher 2000).

Herzberg and job enrichment

Frederick Herzberg (1966, 1987) could be said to have taken Maslow's ideas one step further by identifying the job or work itself as the substantive source of motivation. Herzberg denied that his theory was based on Maslow's work, but subsequent commentators have noted the similarities. Herzberg's theory grew out of research directed at ascertaining factors that lead to greater employee satisfaction. Studies undertaken prior to Herzberg's assessed employee satisfaction using a multiplicity of factors, such as the work itself, pay, status, working conditions and so on. The underlying assumption was that there was a single continuum ranging from job satisfaction at one end to job dissatisfaction at the other. The Herzberg theory proposed that there were in fact two different continua, as follows (Herzberg 1966: 71–91):

- One class of factors, *hygiene factors*, makes up a continuum ranging from dissatisfaction to no dissatisfaction. Examples of these factors are pay, interpersonal relations, supervision, company policy, working conditions, job security and so on. Herzberg argued that these factors do not serve to promote job satisfaction. Their absence, however, can create job dissatisfaction. Their presence can only serve to eliminate dissatisfaction. These hygiene aspects were often referred to as the 'context of work'.

■ The second class of factors, *motivation factors*, makes up a continuum leading from no satisfaction to satisfaction. Examples of motivators are the job itself being challenging, gaining recognition and scope for achievement, with the possibilities for growth, advancement and greater responsibility. If the worker is to be truly motivated, the job itself must be the source of that motivation (that is, the 'job content'). All hygiene factors can do is eliminate dissatisfaction by cleaning up the environment.

Herzberg's approach to employee satisfaction rested on two assumptions about the nature of people: the need to avoid pain and the need to grow. Hygiene factors prevent dissatisfaction and pain by providing a good environment or work context. Motivation factors enable growth towards self-actualization. He arrived at these conclusions by surveying 200 engineers and accountants, but not operative or shop-floor workers. His methodology, that is, asking middle-class employees to report satisfaction or dissatisfaction with their job, and who were likely to attribute success to their own initiative (motivation factors), has also been criticized (Fincham and Rhodes 1992: 112–13). However, given the two continua of hygiene and motivation needs found in the research, Herzberg argued that out of this we can discern two complementary continua based on, first, *mental health* and, second, *mental illness*.

There were four categories on the mentally healthy continuum, and three on the mentally ill one (Herzberg 1966: 83–8).

In terms of a mentally healthy approach, Herzberg argued that self-fulfilment was found in all personal growth experiences, including both work and non-work experiences. In Herzberg's approach, a mentally healthy person was a motivation seeker who has a fixed set of needs at the higher level of the hierarchy – this was unchangeable (Herzberg 1966: 81–91). Herzberg argued that mental health requires a balance of both motivation and hygiene factors. Hygiene seekers were put in the mental illness category because they could never become motivation seekers, and vice versa. Figure 9.1 summarizes Herzberg's arguments.

Herzberg did not believe that all jobs were capable of being enriched or for that matter required enrichment. It was possible that hygiene seekers could be quite productive and satisfied in their jobs even if they were monotonous and deskilled ones (Herzberg 1987: 117). However, in the case of motivation seekers, Herzberg believed that the principle of *vertical loading* (that is, discretion) had to be an integral part of their job content. Vertical (job) loading means designing jobs that increase motivation factors and allow for the psychological or personal growth of the employee (that is, achieve higher order needs).

In order to develop the job content of motivation seekers, Herzberg proposed *job enrichment*, which would increase basic skills on the horizontal level and autonomy and responsibility on the vertical one. Job

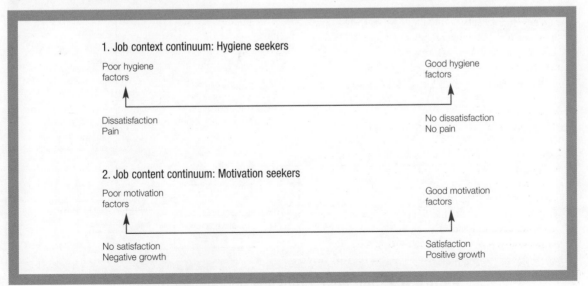

Figure 9.1 Herzberg's needs typology

Source: Liz Fulop and Dennis Mortimer (1992) 'Job redesign strategies' in Fulop, L. with Frith, F. and Hayward, H. (eds) *Management for Australian Business: A Critical Text*, Melbourne: Macmillan, p. 83.

enrichment involves giving whole tasks to individuals that require more complex skills and greater expertise. Through vertical job loading, employees were given more responsibility, recognition, growth, achievement, challenge and advancement. Herzberg was not particularly interested in looking at the effects of horizontal specialization, especially in relationship to unskilled work on assembly lines (Herzberg 1987: 114, 116). This is not surprising because he based his job enrichment theory on the study of professional workers (that is, engineers and accountants) who were not deskilled in terms of horizontal specialization. The jobs Herzberg analysed were highly amenable to increases in discretion (that is, problem solving or planning) (Child 1984: 36).

The Hackman and Oldham model

Herzberg's approach to job enrichment was improved upon and made popular by Hackman et al., who developed the *job characteristics enrichment model* described in Figure 9.2 (hereafter called the *Hackman model*). In this model, needs are treated as a hierarchy and not two separate continua, as they were by Herzberg. The Hackman model suggests that in order to create job enrichment and job satisfaction, tasks have to be interesting and *meaningful*, entail *responsibility* for outcomes and provide *feedback* or knowledge about outcomes. These three components were the critical factors for high motivation, satisfaction and performance (Hackman and Oldham 1975: 162: see Figure 9.2). There are five core dimensions of a job and each of these impacts differently on job redesign. The first three, *combining tasks*, *forming natural work units* or teams and *establishing client relations*, make work meaningful, but not enriched. The remaining two, *vertical loading* (that is, responsibility) and *feedback*,

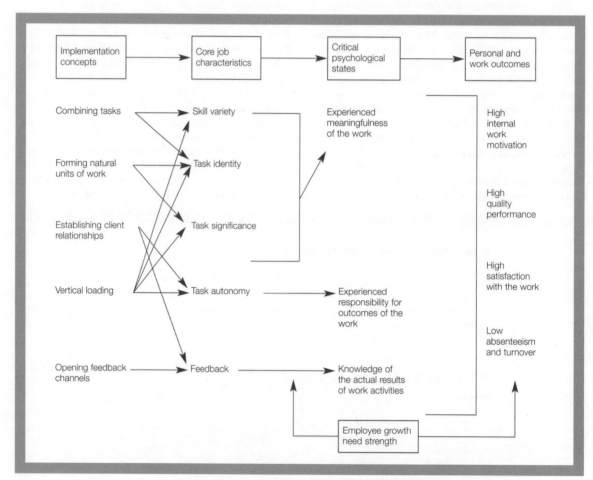

Figure 9.2 Job characteristics enrichment model

Source: J. Richard Hackman, Greg Oldham, Robert Janson and Kenneth Purdy 'A new strategy for job enrichment'. Copyright © 1975, by The Regents of the University of California. Reprinted from the *California Management Review*, **17**(4): 58, by permission of The Regents.

are the most important. Both of these relate to increasing discretion in a job and mean removing supervisory controls. The vertical loading in Figure 9.2 is the core aspect of job enrichment. 'Personal and work outcomes' describe the expected benefits of job enrichment for the individual and the organization and satisfy growth needs.

Hackman and Oldham (1980: 82–8) state that individuals must have the knowledge and skills to perform their new tasks or jobs, otherwise frustration, stress and resentment will prevail. This might require training to allow success at an enriched job. According to the model, individuals whose jobs are to be enriched must have strong needs or desires for self-direction, learning and achievement or challenge. They must be intrinsically self-motivated. In Herzberg's term, they must be motivation seekers, but in Hackman and Oldham's, they must have high scores on *strength of growth needs*, a measure of commitment and the drive to succeed. According to the latter, studies show that high individual scores on the 'strength of growth needs' measure was strongly correlated with the attainment of job satisfaction from the enrichment of jobs, whereas low scores resulted in no satisfaction among workers even though their jobs had been enriched. Consistent with Herzberg and Maslow, Hackman's model of job enrichment suggests that lower order needs (that is, hygiene factors) must be satisfied if job enrichment is to be successful. However, the fact that the Hackman model introduced the notion of individual differences and needs puts it into a slightly more acceptable form than Herzberg's original proposal, although those with high-growth needs are still the only ones being targeted for enrichment (Lansbury and Spillane 1983: 184; Child 1984: 36). Moreover, in the model any failure to display the 'appropriate' need drives is an individual failure or weakness.

Job enrichment has been widely criticized for a number of reasons:

1. It seems more appropriate to professional jobs, where limits on skill variety, task identity and task significance are more readily redressed.
2. It seems to be suited to individual rather than group tasks.
3. It presumes universal, fixed needs for all workers and cannot explain or accommodate changing needs or wants, except as deviant behaviour or mental illness.
4. It fails to address the influence of contextual factors (for example unions, technology, wages, salaries and supervisory levels) in redesigning work; the moderators identified in Hackman's model relate to individual factors only.
5. It is managerialist since ideas for redesign are based on management's perceptions of the need for the strategies.
6. It presumes that motivation seekers will always need and welcome job enrichment, and thus assumes a continuous consensus between management and workers regarding job redesign.
7. It pays little attention to allowing worker participation in the job redesign strategy, and clearly rejects unions as a factor in improving job redesign (Strauss 1976; Buchanan 1979: 46–52; Kelly 1982: 68–70; Fincham and Rhodes 1992: 126–30).

A dynamic view of needs

David McClelland (1961) proposed a different view of motivation – one that included not only personality factors but social influences as well. Although this was not a theory of job redesign, it offered a valuable corrective on the hierarchy of needs approach. McClelland did not subscribe to the view that people had a hierarchy of needs, but rather that needs varied based on the importance individuals attached to them. Needs can be significantly reordered in terms of priorities. McClelland (1961; McClelland and Burnham 1976) identified three basic needs of individuals: *need to achieve*, *need for power* and *need to affiliate*.

Need for achievement

The need to achieve is most closely related to business success. Persons with a high need to achieve react well to challenges while those with a low need to achieve are more likely to seek less stimulating and challenging work in order to avoid failure and risk taking. McClelland believed that the need for achievement, and the associated learning that supports this, is established early in life and is not easily changed. Ironically, McClelland noted that families who sought to instil self-control, high standards, individual initiative and independence were setting patterns for high need achievement. Yet in contrast, families who emphasized compliance, dependence, a collective orientation and getting on with others produced children with low need achievement (Fincham and Rhodes 1992: 73). Compliance, collective orientations and getting on with others (especially in teamwork) have often been cited as the basis of good management. McClelland believed that the need to achieve can be increased by training, which differs from Herzberg's view of fixed psychological needs. The need to achieve is measured by a Thematic Apperception Test (TAT) (see below).

McClelland argued that high achievers set their own goals, are selective about the goals they pursue, tend to be independent in the choices they make and realistic about the likely success of these choices. High achievers seek immediate feedback. In McClelland's approach, people with high need achievement seek jobs that are already highly paid (thus not discrediting Herzberg) and offering them more pay has to be linked to some form of incentive for success by way of feedback.

The need to achieve seems to correlate positively with success among entrepreneurs, especially in small and medium-sized enterprises (SMEs). High achievers tend to seek careers in business and related areas, but do not necessarily make good managers because they tend to feel that they are the most competent person and will be reluctant to delegate (Petzall et al. 1991: 62; Fincham and Rhodes 1992: 83). One interesting aspect of McClelland's work was his attempt to show that the general level of achievement in individuals was linked with economic and technological growth in society (Fincham and Rhodes 1992: 73). Again, this emphasized a social dimension in explaining needs rather than seeing them as purely behavioural and innate.

Need for power

According to McClelland and Burnham (1976), by including the dimensions of need for power and need for affiliation, it was possible to see how each of the three variables affected management's performance. McClelland and Boyatzis (1982, cited in Fincham and Rhodes 1992: 83) found that effective or successful managers had a higher need for power than a need for affinity. In short, they enjoy the exercise of power more than they enjoy being liked by colleagues or subordinates (Fincham and Rhodes 1992: 83). McClelland's concept of need for power also implied that there were two types of need for power. *Negative power* was used to dominate or exert undue influence over others and was the basis of corrupt and unsocialized forms of behaviour, such as using brute force to dominate subordinates. In contrast, *positive* or *socialized use of power* was associated with healthy competition, persuasion and interpersonal influence. The person who had a positive need for power was likely to excite and inspire followers to achieve higher goals and outcomes (Petzall et al. 1991: 62–3).

Need for affiliation

The need for affiliation is similar to the social man theory of Mayo, and in McClelland's approach it is generally not associated with becoming a successful manager or achieving high performance in the workplace. It is important, however, to balance the excessive need for power in its negative form. McClelland believed that there was only a moderate need for affiliation because of all the unpopular decisions a manager has to make. This might not hold true across all cultural groupings; for example Japanese managers have had a strong need for affiliation encouraged in the workplace.

McClelland's work has been criticized on a number of counts, and was certainly not as popular as Herzberg's work. The method for establishing needs (that is, the TAT test) is especially open to criticism. McClelland did not establish any sure way of measuring the needs he talked about. The TAT test is administered by an instructor and is based on subjects writing a story about a notional person seen in an image. Subjects usually project their own personalities and meanings onto the image or figure. Analysing the 'stories' to select the various dimensions of needs was difficult to replicate. McClelland claimed that needs, especially the need for achievement, can be learnt but many others would reject this view, especially those psychoanalysts who believe that personality traits are established in childhood and are difficult to change (Petzall et al. 1991: 64). The theory is also presented as being culturally neutral and therefore hardly explains needs in different cultures, despite the fact that McClelland conducted several cross-cultural studies. Nor does McClelland's theory recognize the importance of individual differences such as gender or age in defining various needs.

Nevertheless, researchers have used McClelland's ideas in trying to account for why women score lower on need achievement (using the TAT) than men. One popular theory was that women who want to achieve also acquire a fear of success (Fincham and Rhodes 1992: 75, citing Horner 1972). The theory states that stress, anxiety and tension accompany this conflict in women with a high need for achievement and it can only be addressed by radical changes in the type of social learning that they are exposed to in early childhood. McClelland's theory at least supports early views that women's failure to achieve was at least as much explained by social factors as by individual predispositions (Wilson 1995: 297–301). However, McClelland gave only a crude indication of what constitutes factors important for high performance, because his approach ignored a range of other factors that might also contribute to success and achievement in one's job, for example adequate resources to do the job or mentoring. Moreover, his focus was only on managers, as opposed to workers or other professionals, limiting his concept of 'needs' and thus exhibiting a bias similar to that found in Herzberg's work.

Motivation theory itself continued to produce other variants: *equity theory* (which proposed that individuals have an idea of what a 'fair' reward for their efforts is, and are affected adversely by either being paid too much or too little); *expectancy theory* (which argued that individuals are motivated according to whether they expect that they will be successful and whether the associated reward is valued); and various attempts to provide a motivational calculus to combine the two. We do not wish to dwell further on the specifics of motivation theory here, because our argument is that both job design and motivation have moved on, under the influence of other disciplines such as systems theory, and the key current issues relating to both are now being addressed in literature which does not always appear to be about either motivation or the technical specifics of job design. In the next section we look at a classic attempt to move beyond simple job design principles, *sociotechnical systems*, then we look at some more recent developments in the redesign of work, and follow that by looking at new ideas which relate to and, we argue, change considerably our understanding of motivational issues and why the whole approach needs rethinking.

Sociotechnical systems (STS)

Some of the limitations of the job enrichment model(s) and needs theory were partially overcome in the emergence of the *sociotechnical systems* approach to job redesign (see also Chapter 11). There are four critical factors in the STS approach as far as motivation theories are concerned:

1. analysis was switched from individuals to work groups
2. small-group theory was integrated with systems theory, thus broadening the factors involved in redesign
3. three systems were identified as being critical in job redesign (the technological, the social and the economic systems)
4. the creation of cohesive, self-regulating, autonomous work groups became the 'one best way' for redesigning jobs.

At its simplest level, the STS approach can be said to involve making a group autonomous and responsible for a whole task(s) in which the integration of technical and social aspects of work take precedence (Buchanan 1979: 98–114; Dunphy 1981: 47–9, 163, 196–7; Lansbury and Spillane 1983: 122–31; Child 1984: 34–5; Dawson 1986: 67–9). Attention to the group nature of work was the focus of the Tavistock Institute of Human Relations in London and researchers such as Eric Trist and Kenneth Bamforth (1951), Fred Emery (1969) and Eric Miller and Albert Rice (1967). Their work stated that organizations consisted of interdependent social and technical systems, operating in an economic environment. It was argued that managers had a degree of choice in the way they structured or designed work, and that the best design was the one which aimed for joint optimization of both social and technical systems (Lupton 1971: 66–70).

This approach was first developed in the context of a study of the effects of mechanization in British coal mining (Trist and Bamforth 1951: 3–38). The advent of coal-cutters and mechanical conveyors had made possible the working of a single long face in place of a series of short coal faces. In 'shortwall working', the focus was on a small group consisting of a skilled man and his mate, assisted by several labourers. The new 'longwall' method was organized around a coal face group of 40–50 men with task specialization according to shift, very specific job roles and different methods of payment per shift. It therefore took on the characteristics of a small factory system that broke down the previous system of autonomous small groups. This breakdown led to manifestations of the miners' isolation and frustrations, such as different shifts blaming each other for failures, petty deceptions with regard to timekeeping and reporting for work, and informal cliques developing across small parts of the workplace, leaving some workers isolated. The reduced autonomy involved in the new process also made it virtually impossible for management to pinpoint the source of the problem.

Trist and Bamforth found that an alternative system, known as the 'composite longwall method', was possible within the same technological and economic constraints. This involved the reintroduction of work groups responsible for the whole task. Within each group, members allocated themselves to shifts and jobs and were paid according to a group bonus. Instead of perpetuating blame across shifts, the new system led to situations where members of a group who finished their tasks early would stay on to undertake the next activity in the sequence to help group members on the next shift. This system was better geared to the workers' social and psychological needs for greater job autonomy and close working relationships, and therefore led to greater productivity, job satisfaction and reduced absenteeism (Pugh et al. 1983: 84–6).

Trist and Bamforth's study showed the importance of the *semi-autonomous group* aspects of work, as well as viewing the role of work from the perspective of those actually undertaking it, rather than on the basis of an imposed perspective, such as that of Maslow and Herzberg. This study led Trist and Bamforth to the conclusion that working groups were neither technical nor social systems, but interdependent ones. The *technical system* referred to equipment layout, work flows, interdependence of tasks and task uncertainty (that is, whether a task is routine or not). The *social system* referred to the social and psychological characteristics of workers. Later work by members of the Tavistock Institute, such as that of Miller and Rice (1967), however, became prescriptive in assuming workers' needs, especially affiliation and security needs (Buchanan 1979: 95, 109, 131; Honour and Mainwaring 1982: 82).

Even though the STS approach expanded the

strategies for job redesign, its human relations origins made it compatible with job enrichment strategies. Thus many of its underlying assumptions, especially relating to the needs of workers, the role of management and external groups (that is, unions) remained the same as in job enrichment (Honour and Mainwaring 1982: 82). However, STS departed from job enrichment in a number of ways: the level of worker participation in the design of tasks; the importance of group work or teams; incentive schemes (the economic man concept); and the flexibility in setting standards. The STS approach principally departed from job enrichment principles with the creation of semi-autonomous work groups or self-managing work teams. Both these concepts are still relevant today, although now people are also focusing on virtual teams and knowledge workers as well (see Chapter 11).

Reinventing motivation through TQM

During the 1980s, the success of Japanese car manufacturers, especially in terms of high levels of quality (for example fewer product defects) and productivity, led to a new wave of interest in job redesign focused on quality principles and practices (Womack et al. 1990). Just as Taylor before them, the new engineering gurus of *total quality management* (TQM), such as W. Edwards Deming (1986), Joseph Juran (1988, 1989) and Phillip Crosby (1979), set out to create a 'new mental revolution' in management. This new mental revolution was, in its most optimistic form, supposed to undo or reverse some of the most negative aspects of Taylorism, while at the same time incorporating the more progressive and humanistic elements of job enrichment and STS. Its underlying philosophy was *continuous improvement* as discussed in Chapter 11.

As David Boje and Robert Winsor (1993) argue, TQM went far beyond other job redesign strategies because it sought to establish a carefully integrated programme of social and psychological engineering. In the late 1980s and early 1990s, TQM was seen as one of the main organizational strategies for regaining competitive advantage and restoring the pride and integrity of US manufacturing (Boje and Winsor 1993: 57–8). Of course TQM was not confined to the manufacturing sector and in many Western countries it was also introduced into the public sector as well. Many organizations still compete for quality awards based on TQM principles and, as we shall see, the quality movement keeps being reinvented.

Both in theory and practice, the TQM gurus sought to transform the entire work culture or ethic of Western business to mirror the values, norms and attitudes (that is, culture) of Japanese workplaces, especially instilling

loyalty, trust and commitment through a strong collective orientation to continuous improvement (see Chapter 11). The origins of TQM are disputed, but once taken out of the Japanese context, both its ethos and implementation in Western businesses have been problematical and achieved uneven success. As Boje and Winsor (1993) suggest, the view favoured in the USA was that TQM had been pioneered in Japanese business through the transfer of American management know-how, and that it was logical to attribute the success of Japanese manufacturing, at least in equal part, to American ingenuity.

However, many commentaries on TQM, and Japanese management practices, point out that even before Deming arrived in Japan, lean production, using Fordist methods, and Taylorism had already been incorporated into Japanese manufacturing in firms such as Toyota. So too had the now well-documented practices of lifetime employment (supported by employee contributions to retirement funds); apprenticeship training; company festivals and celebrations; school programmes emphasizing factory loyalty and the virtues of the efficiency of workers (that is, the work ethic); company housing; company welfare and health services; and the company-funded education of employees' children to adopt appropriate work attitudes and behaviour, such as emphasizing maths and science in curricula. This was tantamount to what Jacques describes as treating the family as part of the supplier partnership (Jacques 1996: 168). Boje and Winsor (1993: 59), along with others, noted that the aforementioned practices were the pillars of building loyalty, commitment and a collective work ethic that was peculiar to Japanese factories, and rarely if ever replicated in the West. They argue that these changes were entrenched in Japanese businesses by the 1920s and were reinforced by appeals to the samurai tradition of constant learning and training to achieve perfection, along with other principles of mutual help and self-effacing contentment in helping others.

Later work practices, such as on the job training, involving both reskilling (learning new work roles that are similar) and multiskilling (learning new and varied tasks and skills), job rotation, seniority-based wage and promotion systems, were also introduced in large companies. The seniority system meant that length of service, and hence loyalty to the organization, was valued and rewarded above merit. Enterprise unions and bargaining (based and supported by the company) were also introduced. A relatively homogeneous and masculine workforce, in the ranks of executives, engineers and supervisors in the large companies, helped to create an image of extreme industrial harmony, happiness and contentment of the workforce and their families. These images have been shattered today as people question the ability of Japanese business to transform itself to be more globally competitive and adaptive.

The concept of *kaizen* or continuous improvement formed the guiding philosophy or framework for quality programmes such as TQM. *Kaizen* encompassed deeply entrenched norms and values aimed at building a strong culture of meticulous, detailed and incremental improvements. It also incorporated a set of tools and strategies used to reinforce quality practices. TQM led to the widespread use of statistical control methods and, in many respects, brought back to many workplaces the inflexibility and control elements so prevalent in Taylorism. Although opinions vary, the core principles of TQM are described in Exhibit 9.2.

In terms of job redesign and motivation, TQM programmes embraced a number of subtle changes to how job satisfaction was addressed. One key element was the degree to which knowledge sharing became a key part of the worker's role – the very group of workers who Taylor thought should 'park their brains at the door' or be deskilled, so that managers would be the knowledge workers (also see Chapter 11). It also deviated from the principles of specialization and division of labour, instead focusing on new scientific

tools and methods which, through training, were to be used by teams of employees to improve performance across all work processes. Building on sociotechnical systems theories, teams became the important units of production.

More importantly, proponents of TQM argued that too many Western organizations were dominated by specialists, notably in middle management, employed in narrow 'functional silos', such as marketing, accountancy and information systems, who looked inward to their departments and only cooperated when tasks straddled functional areas. In developing this cooperation, they often created new layers of management to coordinate these tasks, thereby creating more hierarchies in the organization and layers of supervisors and managers. Both approaches argued that to redesign procedures or processes, which would produce or supply something that customers' value, meant making everyone more outwardly focused. TQM was and is driven by the philosophy of service to customers, using new scientific methods, tools, rules and procedures to deliver value to customers. As Walter Balk (1995: 246) suggests, this brought accountability to external needs or constituents into the job redesign context where previously it had not existed. As Jacques adds, it basically needed the hierarchical divisions and functionally bound 'fiefdoms' of the past to be torn down to work and disempower the very people who stood to benefit from these arrangements. Process-centred authority relationships preached in TQM would require that power shift back to the production level and reverse Taylor and Ford's industrial revolution – an unlikely outcome in Jacques' view (1996: 168).

Exhibit 9.2 Principles of TQM

❏ Top management leadership of quality improvements, akin to heroic leadership or inspirational leadership.

❏ Customer focus (internal and external to organization) – driven by a service to the customer ethos.

❏ No tolerance for errors; prevention of anticipated problems or 'defects' to products or service.

❏ Fact-based decisions using a range of tools and techniques based on statistical quality control and a range of decision science techniques.

❏ Long-term planning and change, with incremental improvements the norm.

❏ Teamwork using different types of teams to produce organization-wide quality practices.

❏ A culture of continuous improvement to help to build trust and eradicate the fear among employees of reporting errors, defects or mistakes in the work process or coming forward with suggestions for improvement – a direct legacy of Taylorism and the 'great mental divide' between managers and workers.

The collective vs the individual under TQM

Under TQM, teams of various sorts replaced individual approaches to work and hence being a team player became important – being individualistic was not seen as a virtue and this clashed with Western values. Collective forms of problem solving and decision making became important. Teams were encouraged to communicate up the hierarchy to improve processes and procedures and hence some degree of delegation of authority was advocated. Self-regulation and self-control were devolved to teams (as discussed in Chapter 11). Steering committees, comprising top management, were still seen as 'the brain of TQM' (Cox 1995: 105), and these top management teams were meant to set goals and objectives to be achieved through TQM programmes and initiate TQM's introduction.

As will be expanded upon in Chapter 11, the team approach used in TQM was claimed to introduce a new form of collective disciplinary control to supplement management's control. A punitive system of peer assessment of errors or mistakes affecting a team's performance, in the form of 'demerits', increased pressures for conformity and surveillance from within teams. These negative aspects of TQM have been particularly evident in Japanese 'transplant' companies where, for example, such things as flashing lights, buzzers and sirens are used regularly when a particular area of the production process is slowed down or an operator has difficulty keeping pace with production (Boje and Winsor 1993: 63). One of the authors visited one of these transplant factories of Nissan in northern England in the early 1990s and even the most committed quality advocates included in the visit were visibly shocked by the harsh and unrelenting pace at which young employees had to work.

TQM, viewed from a strictly Japanese transplant perspective, places little importance on managing differences in teams and places enormous pressure on group conformity. Rigid training espoused by TQM proponents serves to ensure workers' conceptualize, interpret and frame quality problems in similar frameworks, and consensus decision making becomes the norm. There is little regard for the sense-making and creative capacities of individuals who are capable of changing what they know and how they learn (De Cock and Hipkin 1997: 670). As Christian De Cock and Ian Hipkin suggest:

even though TQM ... programmes may provide greater freedom of action than [more] mechanistic management practices, [they] actually may reduce freedom of choice by submitting employees to awareness training designed to create a common frame of reference and to skills training aimed at establishing preferred ways of solving problems and working in teams. (1997: 671, citing Spencer 1994)

As such, TQM adopts a highly disciplinary view of the knowledge worker even though its proponents hailed this approach as a 'new paradigm' for managing.

Even though participation and empowerment are claimed to be the rewards for working in TQM teams, Balk (1995) argues that participation is not necessarily its own reward and after the first 'flush' of enthusiasm has dissipated, team members were likely to look for extrinsic and intrinsic rewards on an individual basis. Some small rewards have been offered under the 'suggestion' system, institutionalized through TQM, as a way of gathering up the knowledge of employees (also see Chapter 11 and the NUMMI example). As the following quote indicates:

a suggestion system implemented at Canon, Inc. yielded suggestions in 1983 alone worth a total of $100 million ... In 1987, about 350 large Japanese companies saved approximately $2 billion from the implementation of employee suggestions ... 'a small ... token of recognition'. The system used by Hewlett-Packard, where, to receive the

maximum reward of $80 (which must be approved by the 'functional manager', which is three levels above the worker), employees are required to make a detailed suggestion which must be graded with perfect scores under five criteria and save the company at least $3,000 in the first year alone. Then, in an annual 'award ceremony', a 'plaque' and a token of appreciation, such as a 'designer watch', are awarded to the *six best suggestions of the year*. In another example, a NUMMI worker's innovative and time-saving suggestion earned him '20 points' in the suggestion programme – equivalent to a bath towel or pair of socks ... Overall, suggestion systems typically yield insignificant awards to the suggester ... while resulting in immense savings to the company. Obviously there is little in these schemes which is of benefit to the employees, other than the increased workloads which frequently result. (abbreviated from Boje and Winsor 1993)

Proponents of TQM assume that team members will be motivated to continually monitor and improve their own performance using statistical and analytical techniques acquired through training. Balk points out that not everyone has the same interest or capacity to absorb such information or interest in using such methods (1995: 252). Others question if such training really leads to organizational learning and promoting innovation and creativity. The training focus of TQM was claimed not to appeal to more educated and skilled workers who were apt to want more autonomy, creativity and control than TQM programmes allow. They were also likely to get bored with such a programmed and mechanistic view of work.

At its extreme, TQM recasts the notion of employee satisfaction to one that depends on a complete subordination of the individual to the collective whole, be it the team, the organization or its culture. This 'subordination' is based on a form of corporate citizenship that demands considerable trust, loyalty and commitment on the part of organizational members. In Chapter 3 we raised concerns about the implications of the notion of a strong culture for managing diversity, change and learning in organizations. We noted that in organizations where there are strong professional groupings, such as in hospitals and universities, it is difficult to create one all-embracing culture, whether it is based on quality or something else. Teams are equally difficult to implement or, if implemented, do not work in the ways envisaged in the TQM literature. In organizations that operate in a crisis mode, the same has been evident.

As stated elsewhere (Halachami and Bouckaert 1995), there have been huge differences between the public and private sectors in respect of implementing TQM programmes. Some large organizations, such as Kodak-Eastman, boasted great success with TQM as a change programme, while other companies who have tried it subsequently abandoned TQM because it was either too costly, time consuming, bureaucratic or achieved few short-term gains. Other businesses have expressed disappointment with results and the general lack of commitment by management to a 10–12-year programme of improvement, which is claimed to be the time frame for creating an organization-wide culture of improvement (see also De Cock and Hipkin 1997: 661).

The 'failures' of TQM programmes, and the critique made of the approach, provide warnings to managers about confusing the popular TQM discourse with the actual difficulties associated with its implementation. The TQM discourse privileges certain forms of knowledge (for example science-based), is silent on other organizational issues, such as politics and power, and marginalizes the positions of some groups in terms of their agency and identities. As David Collins (2000: 189–97) discusses, the eight major gurus of TQM all have significant disagreements on what its tenets should be. This is because one of the most important aspects of fads, such as TQM, is that it becomes the legitimating discourse for a set of practices that management can tout as being something new and at the cutting edge of change. TQM was embraced in many parts of the world and hailed as the next managerial 'revolution'. It provided many managers with the appropriate language and jargon to instil trust and faith in this new method and worry their competitors (Grey and Garsten 2001: 241).

David Knights and Darren McCabe (1999) add another important observation about the TQM discourse. They suggest that most proponents of TQM ran the risk of suggesting that those who introduce these programmes have unbridled power to 'transform the "powerless" individuals into beings who derive their sense of meaning and understandings of the world from the discourses it propagates' (Knights and McCabe 1999: 203). Rather, they point out that the 'self' is constituted through various discourses and interactions and that competing pressures – the hierarchy and power structures in an organization, peer groups, gender and ethnicity, family, education and other such identity-forming effects – intervene to create both compliant and resistant people. They maintain that there is no absolute independent identity or self that can be completely and totally colonized by management practices such as TQM or the like. Social relations, they argue, as we have seen in various sections of this text, happen in formative contexts in which both the disciplining effects of TQM discourses and practices are enacted with varying degrees of compliance, resistance or even plain indifference on the part of those involved. Power, they say, must never be considered as absolutely the property of some privileged group (for example managers) or that identities are fixed in certain ways (see Chapter 2). They contend that there will always be pockets or spaces for resistance and challenge. They do

not discount the likelihood that these sources of resistance and opposition to TQM could emerge from within management groups as well (Knights and McCabe 1999: 219), and this is certainly where Jacques expects to find the greatest resistance to TQM (1996: 168). We will pursue the issue of identity further but, before we do, we will examine how TQM has been recast into new fads of management.

Business re-engineering

The general disenchantment with TQM, or more particularly its focus on incremental or gradual process and systems improvements, led to the more radical job redesign strategy of *business re-engineering* (BR) and *business process re-engineering* (BPR). The most popular proponents of BR and BPR were Michael Hammer and James Champy (1993) and Thomas Davenport (1993). Unlike TQM, which focuses on continuous improvement, BR and BPR advocate radical improvements in costs, quality and service by starting from scratch or with a 'blank' or clean sheet of paper (Hammer and Champy 1993: 21, 134). Three key principles drive the BR and BPR processes – customers, competition and change. Inefficiencies of scientific management (fragmentation of tasks, many supervisory layers, bureaucracy) and other management methods created what Hammer and Champy saw as highly fragmented functional departments, narrowly focused overmanned organizations with many layers of management, and inflexible methods and systems. For Hammer and Champy, the focus of a business is its markets and a 'process' is anything the business produces that is of value to customers.

To improve BR or BPR processes means looking at how things are done in an organization or asking why they are done at all rather than tinkering with existing processes. In Hammer and Champy's view, many processes exist because of historical precedent (that is, 'the way we do it around here') or because of common-sense thinking rather than applying rational methods. BR and BPR depend on developing systems using information technology (IT) and teams that mirror the processes that the business actually works around rather than the functions (for example marketing, finance) used to execute processes (De Cock and Hipkin 1997: 662). Re-engineering, in one form or another, is a continuing feature of many organizations and is now centred on business process modelling and work flow management systems and still draws heavily on IT. Re-engineering is being accelerated by e-commerce and the Internet and is spreading into services as well as knowledge work (Hales 2000; Metters and Vargas 2000).

Hammer, Champy and Davenport's ideas are of course IT-driven (Oliver 1993), and they have built their BR and BPR approaches around an IT revolution occurring in organizations – in a sense similar to Taylor's version of a mental revolution led by the stopwatch! An example of an IT-driven BPR process would be Hewlett-Packard streamlining its purchasing functions by centrally developing block contracts for purchase of goods and using technology to develop a database to disseminate information to everyone in the organization relating to approved suppliers they can use. Many areas of business-to-business (B2B) and business-to-customer (B2C) Internet developments, especially the ability to outsource to Internet service providers (ISPs), continue to fuel the re-engineering agenda, although other words such as 'downsizing' and 'rightsizing' have crept into the lexicon to soften its meaning. These developments achieve two of the early aims of BR and BPR – reducing staff levels and overhead costs (for example levels of inventory, telephone costs) (Hammer 1990, cited in De Cock and Hipkin 1997: 662).

Whereas BR suggests organization-wide change, BPR implies that only certain processes will be targeted for radical change or elimination. Neither Hammer and Champy nor Davenport specify exactly what constitute core processes (Buchanan 1995: 5). Those sympathetic to BR and BPR suggest this ambiguity is not a problem and is to be expected in a new approach. Others less sympathetic to the approach describe re-engineering as a consulting fad and a repacking of old ideas that are sold as a 'fresh start' approach implying all business activities can be up for review (Oliver 1993). The notion of being able to start afresh is questioned by many theorists.

Hammer and Champy stress that radical change or BPR will not make people happy, will mean that some employees will lose their jobs and certainly will not advantage everyone. Even though they make it clear that they are not talking about restructuring or downsizing (which they say is doing less with less), but with doing more with less (Hammer and Champy 1993: 48), a key characteristic of re-engineering is combining or eliminating jobs. For this reason, proponents of BR argue that the leaders of re-engineering have to be visionary, motivators (to build commitment) and 'leg breakers' (Stewart 1994), that is, able to inflict the hardship that BR implies for many employees. Hammer and Champy see the main drive and motivation for change coming from a senior executive who has the clout to turn the organization inside out and upside down (1993: 103).

The BR and BPR approaches espoused by Hammer, Champy and Davenport send confusing messages about job redesign and motivation. For example, cultures take a long time to change or establish; however, by contrast, BR and BPR suggest that radical change or creating a new dynamic culture is possible. David Buchanan (1995: 5) argues that the re-engineering approach adopts a job enrichment approach, coupled with a 1970s view of cultural change in organizations (focusing on changing values, attitudes and beliefs) and empowerment, with its pluralist connotations (see Chapter 6). He says it is premised on the following prescriptions: multiskilled work (job enrichment); activity carried out in cross-functional teams (form of STS); flatter organizational structures; and executives leading and not directing change (as under Taylorism) (Buchanan 1995: 4). Davenport also emphasizes the importance of cross-functional teams and organization culture – a culture that leads to empowerment, participation in decision making and open communication. Participative cultures become a prerequisite for higher productivity and employee satisfaction. Cross-functional teams are certainly not always effective and can become quite unfocused and competitive (Newell and Swan 2000: 1291).

Hammer and Champy (1993: 71–2) believe that employees who are educated (that is, knowledge workers) will form the core of future organizations thereby shifting the emphasis from training to education. These 'brain workers' constitute the 'right' type of employees for the challenges of re-engineering, that is, people who, using McClelland's term, have a high need for achievement. But Hammer and Champy insist that character is important for empowerment. People will be highly rewarded for individual achievements, for self-discipline and so long as they are self-starters and prepared to do everything to serve the customer. Presumably these people will be less in fear of losing their jobs, less inclined to want job security, less stressed by riveting change and be more individualistically oriented employees. As Hammer and Champy argue, old departments, divisions, titles and groups cease to matter. Psychological and political disruptions accompany these changes and without strong leadership the BR or BPR processes can be sabotaged (Hall et al. 1993: 119).

The most common examples given of organizations adopting BR and BPR refer to those experiencing crises, struggling for survival or going through tough economic downturns. Claims about the success for BR and BPR are as common as the claims of its failure. Claims of its success draw mainly on case examples, such as IBM Credit reducing the time to prepare a quote for buying or leasing a computer from seven days to four hours and increasing the number of deals a hundredfold (Hammer and Champy 1993: 38–9). Failures tend to focus on the inability of re-engineering programmes to meet performance targets, such as reducing costs, increasing profits or the value of shares (Hall et al. 1993: 120; Mishra et al. 1998: 84). Stripping the organization of its knowledge repositories (see Chapter 14), and the people needed to undertake tasks when the organization 'turns around', are also seen as the major drawbacks of re-engineering.

De Cock and Hipkin (1997: 662–3) further suggest that studies of BPR show that the methods used to implement it are often simplistic and mechanistic, such as accountants determining the percentage reduction needed to improve bottom-line figures (for example profit, sales, turnover), and then BPR being used to legitimate drastic or radical cutbacks. Indeed, the authors quote studies that reveal that BPR is not a single method but many different approaches that do not in any way make it clear what the long-term successes are. Little is said about managing the human costs or morale and motivation of those left behind or the managers who have to carry out the downsizing exercises. A survey of employees in the USA found only 31 per cent saying that they still trusted their organizations after re-engineering. Survivors generally reduced their commitment if they considered the downsizing process was unfair. It is claimed that managers who have had to implement layoffs 'often become abrasive, narcissistic, withdrawn, alienated, apathetic, or depressed. Many blame themselves for the harm they have caused others' (Mishra et al. 1998: 84). Contrary to the rhetoric of empowerment and being 'coaches' of change, many BPR programmes are extremely dictatorial and hierarchical, that is, determined and pushed through by senior management to improve bottom-line profits and shareholder value (De Cock and Hipkin 1997: 670; Mishra et al. 1998: 84; also Knights and Willmott 2000 for a critical overview). The wave of re-engineering, as well as layoffs, that began in the 1990s was again accelerated in the early 2000s, with the collapse of many Internet or dot.com companies – the so-called 'new economy' businesses that in fact had their managers turning to 'old economy' methods to deal with the crisis!

Softer versions of both TQM and BRP appeared in the mid-1990s under the label of the 'balanced scorecard' (Kaplan and Norton 1992, 1993; Meyer 1994). This approach emphasizes a number of core principles related to the use of financial measures, particularly satisfying shareholders; customer performance incorporating elements that are very similar to TQM. These include operational performance that brings in core ideas of BPR, along with employee satisfaction and training and innovation and learning, which is again very similar to TQM, but recognizes that new product development is also essential to being competitive as well as having a continuous improvement ethos. To implement the balanced scorecard requires five key steps:

1. defining a vision
2. defining key measures
3. developing key performance measures (especially around customer satisfaction)
4. defining operational definitions (for example cost per unit of producing something), and
5. setting stretch targets over different time frames.

The balanced scorecard is very much a senior management tool used to redesign and measure work, and is, as with BPR and TQM, developed as though it is a universally applicable tool, devoid of context and the meanings of those who will employ them, including their power to resist such strategies. It is of course an approach that suits many managers who have been trained in highly quantitative disciplines, such as accounting, engineering and IT, and who look for universal panaceas and 'laws' to govern workplace relations. As Laurence Prusak and Don Cohen (2001: 89) argue, re-engineering, and its progeny, value efficient processes at any cost which they say runs counter to developing trust and cooperation in the workplace.

Cross-cultural issues in motivation and job design

Another dimension that raises questions for the assumptions behind motivation theories, which arose in the TQM movement and job design strategies, is the issue of cultural relativity. As Geert Hofstede (1988: 119) points out, even without carrying out specific studies on motivation, theoretical knowledge of cultural orientations indicates a strong likelihood that existing motivational theories, dominated by a Western and, indeed, American sense of individuality, autonomy and choice, would not apply in many contexts. Indeed Hofstede argues that the USA has a combination of traits – low uncertainty avoidance (that is, willingness to take risks), high masculinity (concern with performance, measurement, quantity), ultra-high individualism and moderate power distance (acceptance of authority) – that make it highly likely that human behaviour would be described or interpreted in terms of self-interest, and that needs-based theories like Maslow's hierarchy of needs and McClelland's approach are a natural consequence of such an orientation.

In looking at how other countries are grouped in terms of significant traits, Hofstede identifies three main groups: countries high in *achievement motivation* (performance and risk); countries high in *security motivation* (performance plus security); and countries high in *social motivation* (quality of life/security; but another variety can combine quality of life with risk). This last category may also be combined with collectivism, especially in Asia.

Hofstede notes that other countries high in achievement motivation scored high on McClelland's measure of achievement need, while countries in the other categories did not. Indeed, he argues that this type

---

Exhibit 9.3 **Cross-cultural views of motivation**

1. McClelland's need for achievement (NAch) can be divided into two subtypes – individual oriented (IOAch) and social oriented (SOAch). This explains the high achievement scores of Chinese communities that are otherwise very different from Anglo-American cultures. Put simply, in these high collectivist cultures, achievement is for the family and not for oneself (Yu 1974; Yang 1982, 1986; Westwood 1992: 299).

2. Sociability, security and status needs are defined by Hsu (1971) as essentially social phenomena. Yang (1981) agrees that 'fitting in' to external social norms can be a strong motivator, with individuals acting to preserve face and avoid punishment, rejection, conflict, blame, embarrassment or ridicule. Bond and Hwang (1986) link this view to that of Snyder (1979) and **social facilitation theory** (Mitchell and Larson 1987), which argues that the mere presence of others is a motivating factor in social action. People perform for others, and in ways that recognize audience, appropriateness and acceptability, being aware that these performances, whether formal or informal, are being evaluated. We seek to look good and avoid looking bad. This aspect of motivation has been, with the possible exception of the work of Erving Goffman, neglected in Western motivation theory, but cross-cultural considerations should cause a reassessment of its importance (see 'Social view of motivation' below).

3. Yu (1991) found, from tests of Herzberg's model, three factors rather than two. He discovered that, as well as motivators and hygiene factors, there were also clear **demotivators** (usually polar opposites of motivators).

4. **Equity theory**, which applies not so much to motivation but to reward, argues that people pay attention to the fairness or equity of the rewards they get for their efforts relative to others, whether overpaid or underpaid, and adjust the quality or quantity of their work accordingly. Most of the research supporting this has been via laboratory experiments, so its applicability to real situations is questionable. However, Yu (1991) noted that people will accept some differences in outcomes, and even inequity, before they feel that they have to make a response or protest (Westwood 1992: 307). Based on research in China, he calls this the **equity difference threshold** – which determines whether a differential is important enough to merit a response. This concept is interesting as it can help to explain to Western managers in particular why feedback on changes in reward remuneration and recognition systems is not as readily forthcoming in Asian countries as it is in the West – and may appear to go smoothly for long periods until it suddenly goes awry (Linstead and Chan 1994).

---

of motivation is found 'exclusively in countries in the Anglo-American group and some of their former colonies' (Hofstede 1988: 121). He also notes that the term 'achievement' is hardly capable of translation into other languages and could not be used in his cross-cultural research questionnaire.

Hofstede also notes, with importance for our consideration of job and work redesign, that the US approach has been predictably towards job enrichment and the restructuring of individual jobs. In contrast, Scandinavian countries have emphasized restructuring into group work. His explanation is that in the USA 'humanization' equates to 'masculinization' – greater opportunity to perform as an individual. In Scandinavia, this means greater 'feminization' – improving interpersonal relationships and reducing personal competitiveness. This reflection would seem to find some support in the differing circumstances of both NUMMI's 'learning bureaucracy' and Uddevalla's 'learning environment' (see Chapters 11 and 1).

Several studies have sought to test some of the classical theories in other cultures, as discussed extensively by Robert Westwood (1992) with regard to Southeast Asia (see Chapter 10). Westwood notes that the picture is confusing, but that studies have led to some significant modifications to theory in these different contexts, which we summarize in Exhibit 9.3.

In summary, there is considerable, if mixed, evidence that motivation does take different forms in different cultures, even if some more general theories can be loosely applied cross-culturally. However, what is most significant is the potential for *defamiliarization* of cross-cultural studies; as the work of the Chinese researchers shows, theory needs modification when 'read back' into Western assumptions and raises some interesting questions about dimensions that may be neglected. In other words, Western individualism may not be a wholly accurate description even of Western human behaviour.

Commitment

The management discourse is dominated by a number

of themes beyond job redesign captured in terms such as: 'organization learning', 'quality management', 'intellectual capital and knowledge management' (for example Sherman 1994; Stewart 1994; Ulrich 1998), 'teamwork' (virtual teams), 'diversity' and 'empowerment'. All these depend on creating a more committed, motivated and diverse workforce. Commitment seems to be at the core of more modernist attempts to redefine motivation and create a more contemporary view of the employee. In motivational terms, commitment has traditionally been studied from two main perspectives: the *attitudinal* and *behavioural*. We will examine these perspectives along with the notion of the *psychological contract*. Much of this literature still focuses on the individual and less on how commitment, as a sociological phenomenon, is embedded in social practices that give rise to differing meanings and interpretations of commitment. As we will show, when the sociological perspective is introduced, the *gendered nature of commitment* emerges as a new area of study and concern for managers.

Attitudinal

From the *attitudinal* perspective, commitment is defined 'as the relative strength of an individual's identification with and involvement in a particular organization' (Oliver 1990: 19–20). The focus is on commitment to the organization, that is, beliefs in the goals of the organization are seen as a strong motivating force. Individual factors, such as personal characteristics, role-related features, work experience, nature of job and organizational structures (for example supervisory levels) are said to affect levels of commitment which affect outcomes such as turnover, productivity and compliance. Commitment is built around an *exchange theory approach* that sees commitment as being directly related to an exchange for rewards or anticipated rewards (Oliver 1990: 20). This approach has subsequently been defined as the *affective attachment approach* to commitment. The basic argument is that people with strong affective attachment stay in an organization because they want to (Allen and Meyer 1990: 2–3).

Behavioural

The *behavioural* perspective of commitment is concerned with how people develop commitment to their own actions rather than to the organization (Oliver 1990: 20). Two different approaches have emerged from within the behavioural school: *side-bets* and *psychological ownership of actions*.

Side-bets (a theory proposed by Becker 1964) argues that concrete investments (time, resources, money) increase commitment by increasing the material cost of

withdrawal from the organization (cost–benefit and exchange theory as mentioned by Turner in Table 9.1). The loss incurred in changing a course of action creates committing actions, even if the course of action chosen is a disastrous one (Oliver 1990: 21). This approach has been labelled by some as the *continuance approach* to commitment, which means people stay in their organizations either because they have invested too much to leave (for example in learning certain skills) or they see no alternatives to leaving, that is, the costs are too high or they have nowhere else to go (Allen and Meyer 1990: 3–4).

Natalie Allen and John Meyer (1990: 3) propose that a *normative approach* to commitment can also be discerned in the literature, which focuses on the *obligations* people feel to their organizations. Although a less common approach, it acknowledges the strong sense of responsibility that some people feel towards their organizations. These people, they say, have 'totally internalized normative pressures' and therefore behave in certain ways that meet organizational goals or interests that they believe constitute the 'right' or 'moral' thing to do. Probably these people would be described as extremely loyal employees. Others label this as a *value commitment* which defines those people who have a strong identification with the organization and are therefore more likely to be cooperative, altruistic and engage in unrewarded, spontaneous citizenship behaviour (Davis et al. 1997: 30).

Allen and Meyer do not see the three approaches as separate approaches to commitment, but rather as components of commitment that any one person could experience to some degree (Allen and Meyer 1990: 3–4). Others suggest that an *investment model* of commitment might be more appropriate, which views a person's commitment to his or her job as an 'additive function of satisfaction (conceived as the rewards the job offers less the cost it entails), investments in the job and alternatives to it' (Oliver 1990: 21). This approach combines elements of the attitudinal and side-bets views of commitment.

Psychological ownership of actions, as proposed by Gerald Salancik (1977), argues that 'individuals become bound by actions and through these actions to beliefs that sustain them' (Salancik 1977: 62, cited in Oliver 1990: 20). In Salancik's view, attitudes are malleable, messy, relatively private and not easily thought-out. Behaviour or action is more public and irrevocable and once someone does something, it is hard to undo it. If it becomes harder to change behaviour or undo one's actions (that is, it has become irrevocable), then people will selectively mobilize to justify or rationalize the behaviour or actions they have taken and this alters their beliefs about commitment to an action (Weick 1995: 156).

Inconsistencies between attitudes and behaviour, that

is, what one says or does, and between actions taken in a particular situation, are likely to cause people to seek reconciliation of these inconsistencies. Therefore, the context in which an action is taken becomes important. In any context four conditions are thought to determine commitment to one's action:

1. *explicitness* (how obvious is the action to others)
2. *revocability* (how difficult is it to reverse the action)
3. *publicity* (how many people know about the action)
4. *volition* (how voluntary is the action).

These determine the level or extent of psychological investment in an action, and hence one's likely commitment to it (Oliver 1990; Weick 1995: 156–7).

Karl Weick believes commitment arises only if an action entails volition (or choice) and is done with few external demands or extrinsic reasons, such as threats, demands, sanctions or fear. It must also involve considerable effort or personal sacrifice. Without these further conditions, he believes people will not recognize or take responsibility for their actions, hence commitment is highly improbable (Weick 1995: 157). One of the main points of Weick's argument is that committed people see the world differently and behave differently. Organizations can alter contexts or situations to encourage commitment. He doubts, however, that bureaucratically designed organizations which encourage formalization and centralization (that is, have high levels of control and limited power sharing) can foster commitment because there are limits in exercising choice, which he sees as a very important condition for making a commitment.

Psychological contracts

A third view of commitment argues that committing is an informal process which involves establishing *psychological contracts*, that is, an unwritten and often largely non verbalized set of expectations and assumptions about the obligations that people ascribe to their organizations (Ring 1997: 137). The shift is to contracting and agreements occurring between individuals, at the expense of collective agreements. According to several theorists (Herriot et al. 1997; Morrison and Robinson 1997), psychological contracts are becoming increasingly difficult to manage as restructuring, downsizing, forced redundancies, the increasing use of temporary workers, the increasing use of specific performance-based schemes, decreasing union power, diversity in the workplace and foreign competition alter the more traditional underpinnings of these 'contracts'. These underpinnings were job security, steady rewards for hard work and promotion opportunities from the organization in exchange for

loyalty, conformity and effort on the part of employees (Herriot et al. 1997: 152; Morrison and Robinson 1997: 226). As a corollary, increasing attention is being paid by researchers to the consequences of organizations breaching and violating their psychological contracts and looking at other forms of contracting such as 'career contracting'. which requires both employees and their managers to plan for career transitions based around 'implacement' or building a stable and flexible workforce around continual changes and transitions within the workplace (Herriot et al. 1998). The notion of psychological contracting has it origins in the US literature on workplace change and reform and is less widely acknowledged or incorporated into the European management lexicon, where there is a stronger tradition of trade unionism and social partnerships between government and business–union stakeholders.

Traditional research on psychological contracts has focused on the nature of reciprocal obligations between employees and their organization, that is, the entitlements and benefits each party can expect to receive from the other, and what each is obliged to give the other in exchange for securing their contribution. Elizabeth Wolfe Morrison and Sandra Robinson (1997: 227–9) point out that employees' beliefs about the nature of reciprocal obligations are not always shared by the agents of the organization, that is, management. Employees usually view the 'contract' as being between themselves and the organization, and not some third-party individual such as a manager. Managers, by contrast, might see their role as reinterpreting such understandings in the light of everyday organizational operations and requirements. For some managers, psychological contracts are merely a form of 'motherhood' statement, relating to ideals that are always subject to the vicissitudes of everyday business. Generally speaking, in most of the research, psychological contracts are considered to be the domain of employees, not supervisors or other parties (Herriot et al. 1997: 151; Morrison and Robinson 1997: 228–9). However, in many workplaces, managers can also be employees, shareholders and even subordinate to others and this is increasingly recognized in research on the topic (see below), although often it is how executives view other's commitments that is the subject of research rather than their own.

Transactional and relational contracts

A further important distinction is drawn between psychological contracts that are largely *transactional* and those that are *relational*. One definition of the transactional contract says it is focused on monetarized values, such as employees taking on longer hours of work and additional roles in exchange for high performance-related pay and job-related training and development. Relational contracts involve socioemotional elements such as reciprocity, loyalty, support and job security (Herriot et al. 1997: 152; Morrison and Robinson 1997: 229, citing Rousseau and McLean Parks 1993). Morrison and Robinson suggest that employees can have both forms of psychological contract, but violations of each have different consequences for employees and their organizations. Herriot et al. (1997: 152–3) argue that because certain aspects of the psychological contract are based on reciprocity (see Chapter 6), this invites opportunities for violation as well as allowing for exceptional generosity.

Herriot et al. undertook research in the UK to ascertain what factors constitute the transactional and relational dimensions of a psychological contract. They selected two groups of 184 people, one comprising employees and the other representatives of organizations. These people were selected from a cross-section of industries, with men and women (though not ethnic or racial groups), different age groups, different lengths of service, public and private sectors and small, medium- and large-sized organizations all being represented. The organization group included supervisors, middle managers and executives while the employee group drew from a wide cross-section of occupations. Each person was asked to recall an incident where an employee and the organization had fallen short of or exceeded expectations of how they might reasonably have been expected to treat the other party – a form of 'critical incident' technique (Herriot et al. 1997: 254).

The results of their findings, in terms of what both employees and organizational representatives considered to be the *organization's obligations* to each party, varied markedly. Employees focused more on transactional relations or what seem to be Herzberg's hygiene factors, such as the work environment, pay, benefits and job security. Organizational representatives focused more on relational elements, most frequently nominating loyalty and good citizenship behaviour. The expectations both groups had for *employee obligations* were less divergent. The three most frequently cited obligations in respect of the employee sample were hours, work and honesty. Organizational representatives also mentioned hours, work and honesty. They also mentioned loyalty and flexibility more often than did employees.

Herriot et al. suggest that the differences in these perceptions between the two groups can be explained by how each group deals with *reciprocity*. They argue that many organizations which have implemented the restructuring changes mentioned earlier, such as removing job security, have broken their side of the bargain and employees reciprocate accordingly by altering or lowering their commitment. What individuals see as being fair to expect from employees – principally transactional obligations – seems to enjoy greater consensus between both groups than does the question of the organization's obligations to employees. Managers in the study mentioned intangibles such as humanity, recognition and benefits more than the employee group. Morrison and Robinson (1997: 238) point out that balance (fairness) and repayment are important elements of fulfilling transactional agreements and are more easily monitored by employees. Herriot et al. (1997: 159–61) believe that it is the mistrust of management which probably accounts for employees preferring transactional relationships that highlight pay and security because the old relationally based psychological contracts have either been, or are very likely to be, broken. They say that until organizations overcome this mistrust, the bases of organizational obligations will be difficult to change, even though many organizations require fewer people to do more, and in many places innovation and risk taking are still important in order to remain competitive (see also Ulrich 1998).

The Herriot et al. study is gender blind in its findings. Although their sample included men and women, the findings on organizational obligation do not differentiate on the basis of gender. While the authors hypothesized a different distribution of perceived obligations between genders, which was not subsequently found (and nor do they question why), they did not examine other relationships, such as the strength of the perception of the obligation, or differential reactions to its violation between men and women. This is particularly important because, as we mention above, one of the key findings of the study was that differing perceptions of obligation between employers and employees were dependent on the notion of reciprocity. As we discuss in Chapter 6, and later in Chapter 16, the concept of reciprocity is widely discussed in the management literature, but it is overwhelmingly based on notions of either transactional equity and fairness (Ring 1997) or gift giving and gaining some power and deference in relationships (Mauss 1990 [1926] cited in Fulop and Linstead 1999). Both approaches are insensitive to how reciprocity might have a gendered dimension to it or that women and men might see and enact their obligations differently in the workplace. We will explore this issue shortly but, before we do, we need to look at the issue of breaches and violations of the psychological contract.

Breaches and violations

Morrison and Robinson (1997: 230–1) also distinguish between contractual breaches and violations. They argue that a *breach* in a psychological contract is cognitive, that is, involving a perceived breach or failure on the part of the organization to fulfil an obligation commensurate with one's contribution. A *violation* is the emotional or affective state or experience that can also accompany one's belief that there has been a failure by the organization to fulfil a psychological contract. Violation, they say, creates deep visceral feelings that:

> involve[s] disappointment, frustration, and distress stemming from the perceived failure to receive something that is both expected and desired … In addition, central to the experience of violation are feelings of anger, resentment, bitterness, indignation, and even outrage that emanate from the perception that one has been betrayed or mistreated. (Morrison and Robinson 1997: 231)

Violation, they suggest, decreases the trust that employees have in their organization as well as the satisfaction they have with their jobs, the organization as a whole, obligations they feel towards their organization and their intention to stay. Some possible outcomes of violating a psychological contract are a reduced contribution from the person violated, unwillingness to take on extra roles (seen as citizenship behaviour) and, in the extreme, seeking retaliation, revenge, sabotage, theft or acts of aggressive behaviour (Morrison and Robinson 1997: 227). It is debatable whether or not we can so neatly separate cognitive (rational actions or behaviour) from emotional ones and we would contend that all forms of breach carry certain feelings and emotions (see Fineman 2000: 10–13).

Morrison and Robinson suggest that there are number of complex reasons why organizations (or their representatives) fail to fulfil a psychological contract and therefore renege on a perceived promise to an employee. These can include the inability of the organization to meet its obligations because its economic circumstances might have changed or the basis of making the promise (for example rapid promotion opportunities) might have been unrealistic. Sometimes the organization might be deliberately unwilling to fulfil an obligation because to do so might cost too much in the form of resources consumed (for example extra benefits for increased performance). It could also be because the employee has little bargaining power, such as expertise, and can be easily replaced. Sometimes employees' behaviour might not be considered appropriate or they may not come up to expectations and are perceived by the organization to have broken the contract, and the organization merely reciprocates (Morrison and Robinson 1997: 233–4). Other times it could be political – someone in a higher position does not like someone for whatever reason and intends to thwart his or her career.

Morrison and Robinson argue that for a person to feel that they have experienced a violation of a psychological contract involves sense-making and subjective interpretations of events as well as a negotiation of meanings and, as a result, people will perceive and react differently to their circumstances. Cultural factors, as well as individual differences related to the propensity to feel aggrieved, are important in explaining different perceptions and reactions to a breach, although gender is not mentioned (see below). Morrison and Robinson suggest that the perceived importance or salience of a violation will also affect how a person experiences or make sense of a breach of a psychological contract. A violation involves employees having to come to terms with the outcomes of a breach, such as failing to gain a promotion, the large office they were promised or the company car, which can also involve loss of status, loss of benefits and low self-esteem. One common strategy for coping with a breach is to find someone to whom one can assign blame or responsibility for the wrongdoing. Coming to terms with a breach can intensify feelings of anger and contempt for the organization and even lead to sabotage and violence. Morrison and Robinson argue that it is in the organization's interest to convince employees that the breach was beyond the organization's control or that it was not a purposeful act (even though it might have been). Employees who are less likely to blame the organization for the breach are likely to remain committed to some degree and not lose complete trust in the organization or its people (Morrison and Robinson 1997: 244). However as we shall discuss below, trust, especially the notion of distrust and betrayal, is much more complex than is suggested by Morrison and Robinson.

Considerable debate also arises in relation to how many types of contract exist and the levels of integration these achieve for employees. Denise Rousseau (1995), for example, uses two dimensions: *level* (individual or group) and *perspective* (within and outside) to identify four different types of contract. The individual contract, derived from *within* the relationship, is identified as a *psychological contract*. However, a group contract, derived from within, becomes a *normative contract*: one that is a shared psychological contract that emerges when members of a group or organization hold common beliefs. Individual contracts perceived from *outside* the relationship are *implied contracts* (interpretations that third parties make of the contractual terms), and group contracts perceived from outside are *social contracts*: broad beliefs and obligations associated with a society's culture. These classifications and characterizations beg the question outlined above about whose perceptions the contracts may be representing and whose expectations they are meeting. It also sheds light on the complexity of the concept when the context is not treated only in terms of what goes on in the organization.

Rousseau's classification fails to distinguish another category of contracting, that between employees and groups external to the organization, such as clients and customers. These very important relationships complicate the question of whose expectations the psychological contract actually meets in the workplace. A study of commitment among a sales team suggested that not only does performance increase with commitment to supervisors (a point Morrison and Robinson would dispute), but that it is also affected by commitment to customers (Siders et al. 2001). Again gender was a factor in the study but did not figure in the final analysis. While performance outcomes vary, the study highlights that it is no longer adequate to talk of only work-based commitments but this discussion must extend to a whole range of stakeholders, including the family (also see Clark 2000), professional groups and a range of 'significant others' ignored in the literature to date. It is not surprising that in recent times there has been a growing questioning of the usefulness of the concept of 'organizational commitment', in favour of the idea of 'work commitment' embracing elements of occupational, professional and career commitment (Blau 2001). Working out where professional and occupational commitment begins and ends for some people, such as professionals in high service areas such as healthcare, is difficult but the focus is shifting away from organizational commitment per se to a more complex view of commitment and identity formation, such as with professional identities (see Dent and Whitehead 2002). We will revisit commitment below.

The social view of motivation

An alternative sociological view to motivation might overcome the problems identified in the more traditional approaches to motivation based on job redesign. One such approach is called the *social constructionist* view, which emphasizes the important role of meanings and interpretations in shaping people's motivations. Social constructionists emphasize the importance of interpretations – how people understand and make sense of their organizational encounters – of events, situations, constraints, opportunities, moments of resistance and so on. Sims et al. (1993: 294–5) argue that:

'Social constructionism' is a philosophy in its own right, and one which puts individuals at the centre of their own universe as architects, more or less, of their own world views and meaning systems.

The social constructionists study motivation from an eclectic point of view and focus on accounts of motivation that are specifically learned, social, interpretative, cultural and context-bound. Jonathan Turner's (1987) model of interactional motivation provides a useful example of the complexities that emerge when a social constructionist approach is used to study motivation, and an attempt made to link it to job redesign. Turner developed his model by studying five main areas of sociological theory from which he distilled a number of key ideas relating to motivation. Table 9.1 outlines Turner's main findings in terms of key theories and concepts he used to develop a social interactionist theory of motivation. Turner's study was not exhaustive and excluded a number of areas such as political sociology and postmodernism. From his study, Turner concluded that there were seven fundamental states of being that people sought from their social interactions, three of which had primary motivational significance for how people thought and acted:

1. the need for a sense of *group inclusion*
2. the need for a sense of *trust*
3. the need for *ontological security*.

Referring to Table 9.1, the need for group inclusion derives from the interaction ritual chains approach and the notions of trust and ontological security from structuration theory. Turner argued that the need for inclusion, trust and security were very strong and absence of these would lead to high anxiety. He also said that the need to maintain or have one's self-concept reaffirmed (for example one's sexual identity) also influenced how the needs for inclusion, trust and security were accomplished (Turner 1987: 24). Needs relating to *symbolic* and *material gratifications* (exchange theory) also influence or are related to how individuals manage their self-concept or develop ways of presenting the 'self' (see below). Similarly, symbolic/material gratifications also relate to achieving group inclusion and affect or influence negotiations and exchanges.

Turner believed his model revealed some of the more complex unconscious (that is, anxiety-reducing) aspects of motivation. The key causes of anxiety were failure to achieve inclusion, trust and security. He also proposed that his model explained some of the more complex reasons why people cooperated (or failed to cooperate) than had previous theories of motivation. Turner's work reaffirmed the importance of sense making, understanding and language to motivational processes. He argued that people's *need for facticity*, or the presumption that they share with others an intersubjective world or have things in common, was directly influenced by the use of *ethnomethods* (see Table 9.1). Facticity, as Turner refers to it, was also influenced by or associated with anxieties (and deprivations) relating to:

1. ontological security (a sense that things are as they appear)
2. trust (actions of others are predictable and reliable)

Table 9.1 Turner's model of interactional motivation

Theoretical perspective	Well-known theorists	Key concepts	Key 'motivational' assumptions
Exchange theory	George Homans (1961) Peter Blau (1996) Richard Emerson (1972)	Central motivational force is to maximize gratification, avoid deprivation or punishments in social interactions. Hierarchies of preferences and values, costs versus benefits, and so on	Key motivating force is needs for power, prestige and approval in social relations. Actors compete for both material and symbolic resources, and impression management is important (save face, etc.)
Social interactionism	Herbert Blumer (1969)	Behavioural capacities to sustain self (image) and cooperate with others. Individuals possess configurations of self-referencing attitudes, dispositions, feelings, definitions and meanings and they seek to reaffirm these configurations with others with whom they interact	Need to adjust, adapt and cooperate with others. Need for sense of identity (who am I?). Pressure to continually construct definitions of and orientations to situations. Need to sustain esteem and consistency in presenting the 'self' to others
Ethnomethodology	Harold Garfinkel (1967)	Actors are motivated to create a sense, even an illusionary sense, of sharing a common universe – to have a common reference point for belonging. Individuals create folk talk (or ethnomethods) to sustain or establish the presumption that they share a common world	Need for a sense of facticity – a presumption that individuals in social interactions share things in common. Conversational exchanges revolve around 'filling in', 'waiting for' or 'glossing over' information to create a common world; giving background information and dealing with unclear messages
Structuration theory	Anthony Giddens (1984)	Efforts to stabilize and/or establish routines and social integration. Reflexive monitoring by giving reasons for one's acts and others' and developing a 'stock of knowledge' that helps us move from one situation to the other – reduces anxiety and eases the process of fitting in	Unconscious need to achieve trust and an unconscious need or drive to achieve ontological security – i.e. matters in the social world are as they appear, i.e. a sense of certainty
Interaction ritual chains	Randall Collins (1975, 1986)	Actors use resources to take advantage of a situation. Emotional energy (positive feelings and sentiments about oneself) and cultural capital (approval, prestige, group membership, control over materials/resources) are utilized in conversational exchanges. Actors monitor situations (work, ceremonial or social) to determine what levels of expenditure of emotional energy and cultural capital are needed	Group membership is the primary force behind expenditure of emotional energy and cultural capital. People seek a sense of group solidarity and have a desire to belong to groups. Extracting emotional and cultural 'profit' or benefits are the main motivations for social interaction

Source: Adapted from Jonathan Turner (1987) 'Toward a sociological theory of motivation', *American Sociological Review*, **52**: 15–27.

3. group inclusion (interactions are part of a common social process being shared by others)
4. concept of 'self' (reactions of others to how you present yourself are sincere and genuine).

Turner suggested that when people use ethnomethods they employ conversational techniques to establish that their respective self-concepts have been sincerely, appropriately or adequately interpreted – that others know what you stand for and who you are. Ethnomethods are also used to establish ontological security – that the situation one finds oneself in is how it appears, that there are no 'traps', 'surprises' or 'shocks' in store. Turner suggests that the successful or unsuccessful use of ethnomethods in negotiations and exchanges determines whether or not facticity is achieved (that is, establishing and sharing common knowledge). Facticity influences how the self and ontological security are achieved and if ethnomethods fail to achieve facticity, then motivational dynamics or processes become arrested (1987: 25). If Turner's last proposition is correct, then the whole idea of motivation and managing complex identity sets takes on new challenges.

The importance of developing a common language and understanding among culturally diverse groups now becomes an important motivational issue (see previous discussion). The potentially negative motivational effects of not addressing identity issues (that is, of the self) relating to gender and sexuality, for example, are also likely to affect the level of facticity that men and women can achieve. Turner was, however, cautious on this point, noting that while individuals strive to sustain group standards, affirm the self (or sexual identity) and cooperate with others (inclusion), these motivational forces need to be reconciled with each other and, indeed, with other basic sex impulses, organic drives and various acquired needs (1987: 20). This reconciliation might prove impossible but, in the end, Turner gave primacy to the learned, social and interpretive elements of motivation over other drives. We will now explore how the sociological influence on motivation theory has helped to redefine the meaning of work.

The meaning of work and identity

If we hark back to the problem of job redesign and motivation, one of the factors affecting the success of such interventions, and similar ones, is the question of what work means to those who actually do it – a question largely ignored by job redesign strategies such as TQM and BPR. Studies on *orientations to work* draw a distinction between workers' needs and wants (Goldthorpe et al. 1968). Instead of accepting that employees all have an inbuilt hierarchy of needs, the orientation to work approach (sometimes referred to as the *social action approach*) proposed that employee attitudes and behaviours should be understood in terms of the realities of a particular situation and based on the employees' own definitions of what work means to them. Whereas self-actualizing theories of behaviour focused on the satisfaction of universal needs, the orientation to work approach claimed that workers have variable wants which are not hierarchically arranged, but shift and change depending on the situation of the worker. Wants are not psychological constants as proposed in the hierarchy of needs; in other words, individuals order their priorities and act accordingly. Thus money and financial rewards may take precedence over career pathing and multiskilling if financial problems beset employees, who may change jobs in order to satisfy this want, even though they have, in Maslow's terms, reached the top of the self-actualizing hierarchy. The employee is not deviant or mentally ill, but rather making a rational choice or even an emotional one based on his or her assessment of priorities and preferences (Rose 1975: 23–42; Lansbury and Spillane 1983: 139–40; Dawson 1986: 11–12).

Some new directions in motivation theory have also linked the psychological treatment of motivation to the idea of the *meaning of work*, which has traditionally been a sociological question. Stephen Fineman (1983), through a study of unemployed executives, argues that studies of people in work can only provide a limited view of what is important to them, as much of what work provides is taken for granted or unconscious and until it is removed the individual is not aware of it. He argues that our individual sense of what it means to be a person implicitly involves the idea of being a working person for many people. Similarly, our position in the social structure and among our circle of friends is affected. Think about what happens when one member of a working couple becomes unemployed, and is transformed from breadwinner or equal partner to dependent husband/wife or failed provider – they experience a loss of identity. It need not be something so drastic – even the move sideways, downwards or to another functional area can destablize a person's identity and sense of self-worth (Herriot et al. 1998). Fineman argues that work is far more important to our late twentieth-century psyche than most studies acknowledge. The implications of this are that changes to the structure of work, increasingly part-time, flexible employment, inevitably affect our view of ourselves as persons – in other words they affect the structure of consciousness as well (Mauss 1990 [1926] in Fulop and Linstead 1999).

Burkard Sievers (1995), in a collection of studies originally written from 1985 onwards, argues that changes in the structure of work have deskilled many jobs and made work more meaningless. Instead of recognizing this, corporations have sought to place the blame on the individual and have treated it as a problem of motivation. They have addressed this through reward structures, but mainly through the development of strong collective corporate cultures and teams with which the individual can identify. This superficial sense of corporate community, he argues, is a mere distraction from the fact that the work remains intrinsically meaningless – motivation as a surrogate for meaning. Think about Disneyland or McDonald's, he argues – behind the powerful family image of the company, both internally and externally, and the importance of team membership, are two highly Tayloristic organizations which studies have demonstrated depend on a high proportion of expendable part-time and contract labour and a punitive control system. George Ritzer (1990) makes similar arguments in a very provocative text on the influence of McDonald's and its processes on society at large. Ritzer argues that society is undergoing a process of 'McDonaldization' – that standardization and control are spreading on a global scale as large corporations acquire the power to dominate and homogenize their markets, which of course drives down the cost of sales. This is coupled with a push to drive down the costs of production and disempower trade unions, which leaves employees in a state of frequently oppressive exploitation, contradicting the image the company projects of wholesome family values and charitable corporate giving. And if the advent of the new economy was going to change all this – think again. Amazon.com, arguably once the flagship of the dot.com 'revolution', employs highly Tayloristic and Fordist principles in its warehouse operations.

Howard Schwartz (1990) looks more deeply at this corporate 'meaning-making' process. He demonstrates that when corporations attempt to make meaning – or at least this rather easy version of meaning – they are usurping what he calls the *ontological function* for individuals, as described by Turner above. In other words, we all need to ask, and know, 'who am I?' When we enter the world, the process of finding the answer is essential to our becoming fully developed individuals. Corporations with strong cultures, or which purport to have them, in effect say, 'you do not need to ask, we'll tell you. Just do as we do, be one of us and the question is irrelevant.' As a result, Schwartz argues, something very dangerous happens. People stop asking important questions, and in significant ways stop thinking for themselves. His interest is in how supposedly excellent corporations can act in reckless and dangerous ways, with little regard for the safety of the rest of the world, while continuing to believe in their own righteousness. He discusses antisocial actions of committed organizational participants – in other words how large numbers of sane and well-meaning people can come to

do things which actually or potentially damage the lives of even larger numbers of others. He uses the example of NASA and the Challenger disaster to illustrate this idea (see Introduction). Because of the way the NASA culture had developed, its members were unwilling to acknowledge that NASA could make mistakes and so denied or covered them up all along the line, while still believing that they were right. Schwartz argues that the Challenger disaster (or some other one) had to happen sooner or later. The members of the organization were in effect addicted to their own organizational rhetoric – a condition Schwartz calls *corporate narcissism* – which fed their fantasy of who they were, and they had to get more and more of it until reality, in the form of a disaster, rudely intervened (see Chapter 10).

Ritzer's more recent work, for example *Enchanting a Disenchanted World* (1999), has engaged with this fantasmic dimension of experience, and has incorporated the work of Jean Baudrillard on consumption and symbolic exchange, alongside his work on changes in the relations of production. Baudrillard was heavily influenced by the writings of Georges Bataille (1993, 1998), and his book *Simulacra and Simulation* (1994a) was featured in the virtual reality film *The Matrix*. Ritzer also employs the ideas of Guy Debord (1994) to enable us to see the narcissistic fantasies of Schwartz's corporate culture on a wider canvas. Ritzer argues that in response to new means of consumption, where people purchase goods electronically by telephone, Internet or TV shopping, or by one-stop shopping where several outlets are located in the same place such as the mall or entertainment centre, retailers and resellers of services have had to focus on new ways to attract customers. It isn't enough to have the best or the cheapest goods, for example in order to get people to make the physical trip to the mall or a hotel in the Nevada desert, you have to create an experience, a spectacle, which primes people for the purchases they will make and entertains them. The worlds of entertainment and shopping *implode* as the boundaries between them blur. Consumers aren't so much motivated to purchase as amused to purchase.

Since the rise of public relations after the First World War, when Edward Bernays (1923, 1952, 1955, 1965) sought to create an applied social science in which psychological insights – drawn from the work of his uncle, Sigmund Freud, on human unconscious drives and the images that can capture them – could be used to mould public opinion, it has been no secret that people can be manipulated as a mass to support specific campaigns or make specific purchases. For Bernays, this was all about identity and the sort of person those people would like to be seen as. Bernays, who influenced the shape of advertising and before his death at the age of 103 in 1995 had influenced the rise of the modern spin doctor – indeed a book (Tye 1995) on

Bernays' life called him 'the father of spin' – felt that if the right symbol were chosen to reflect the underlying psychological desire, then opposition could be turned to enthusiastic support. One such spectacular campaign was the one he organized for American Tobacco (among whose brands was Lucky Strike cigarettes) to get women to find smoking acceptable. Working with the psychological concept of penis envy (need for power) and the social phenomenon of feminism, by organizing demonstrations of beautiful role model debutantes at public events such as the 1929 Easter Parade, where they would light up en masse, he turned smoking into an expression of women's increasing social independence – in lighting a cigarette, they lit up 'torches of freedom'. The campaign was massively successful and its knock-on effects were felt in the UK as well as the US.

The use of the means of consumption and the purchase of particular products was widely recognized as a means of bolstering or constructing a social identity – even to the point of appealing at a subconscious level to the darker sides of human motivation, such as jealousy, greed, envy or fear. The new 'cathedrals of consumption' as Ritzer calls them – hypermalls, casinos, megahotels, theme parks where one can spend a whole vacation, theme restaurants and stores – exploit this but in a more diffused way, selling an array of products in the context of a complex symbolic experience. Consumers are not controlled and exploited in a coercive way, although Ritzer notes that they may be led to spend too much, but 'are quite eager to behave in these ways' (Ritzer 1999: 75). Indeed Ritzer believes that it may be that consumers are in control in their demands for re-enchantment, although this may simply be the success of Bernays' style of public relations, where the opinions of the masses are forged by those who need to remain invisible so that the masses can believe that their opinions are indeed their own. There is a good chance that you had never heard of Bernays before reading this – but *Life* magazine named him one of the 100 most influential people of the twentieth century in 1990 (Ewen 1996).

Ritzer makes a further point that where modern social theory deals with agents making choices, postmodern theory looks more at the settings and processes of consumption and decentres the individual consumer. From the point of view of motivation theory, motivation is firmly about individuals either responding to drives or engaging in a motivational calculus. From the perspective of consumption theory, people express themselves and construct their identity partly through their purchases. From the perspective of the *theory of the spectacle*, the spectacle is put on to obscure the fact that the goods and services are ultimately dissatisfying, and the identities they help to construct therefore alienating. People are outside the spectacle put on for

them, and their critical and imaginative faculties are dulled by it. From the perspective of the simulation, however, events are put on – such as the running show that is Disneyland – which involve the consumer in them, where the consumer takes a part and actively recreates the simulation. They are not dulled, but distracted by these events. The whole interaction has a simulated character, as Ritzer warns us:

Instead of 'real' human interaction with servers in fast food restaurants, with clerks in shopping malls and superstores, with telemarketers, and so on, we can think of these as simulated interactions. Employees follow scripts, and customers counter with recipe response (that is, those routine responses they have developed over time to deal with such scripted behaviour), with the result that authentic interaction rarely, if ever, takes place. In fact, so many of our interactions in these settings (and out) are simulated, and we have become so accustomed to them, that we lose a sense of 'real' interaction. In the end, all we have are the simulated interactions. In fact, the entire distinction between the simulated and the real is lost; simulated interaction *is* the reality. (Ritzer 1999: 116–17)

Philip Hancock (1999), in discussing the work of Baudrillard, makes a similar point – if this is what happens in the process of identity formation, if the real and the fake have imploded, and if the idea of the self-aware and choosing agent is unsustainable, what is the consequence for theories of motivation that were predicated on just these assumptions? As we are also consumers as well as employees, we are aware of how it feels to be on both sides of the production/consumption divide, as the meaning of work and the meaning of consumption come together; indeed, as Paul du Gay (1996) argues, the capacities and predispositions of consumers and employees are increasingly difficult to distinguish. There are no easy answers here, except that when considering the processes of meaning formation and identity construction, we need to be wary of underestimating their complexity, neglecting the operation of cultural forces in the wider context, and overestimating the power of individual agency. The problem of individual agency leads us back to the problem of ontological security and the affect that gender has on this both in terms of meanings and identity formation.

Gendered nature of commitment

As we said above, Turner's work raised important issues about identity, especially in terms of ontological security or knowing who you are and where you stand in relation to others. We can extend the debate about ontological security to women's identity in the workplace. Stephen Whitehead (2001) argues that while there might well be a fundamental commonality between men and women, some aspects of managerial work are unique to women managers, and many of them are caught up in what he terms a 'seductive ontology' (2001: 99). As Whitehead notes (2001: 101), the search for ontological security is not of itself gendered since ontological security is a need of both men and women. What is gendered, however, is the application of these needs or wants in social and cultural contexts. He says one possible way in which men negotiate the quest for ontological security (and trust and group cohesion), and therefore manage their identities, is to concentrate on their public roles as managers, co-workers and mates. By privileging the public role, this automatically signals that the other role – the private one – is the lesser of the two and separate from work (also Trethewey 1999: 426). It is not that men do not do some childcare and domestic work but that it is not presented as their primary role or responsibility. For women managers, many of whom are primary carers by choice or designation, this presents a difficult paradox. They exist, as Whitehead says, in gendered relationships in which being a gendered subject most often means finding ontological security in a world where they have to straddle the symbolic boundaries of both public and private spheres to manage their success. Their very presence in many organizations is also seen as destabilizing because men have been at the centre of these organizations for so long and have dominated in every possible way, right down to how the role of their personal assistant is often defined to help them to balance home and work (Whitehead 2001: 99). Angela Trethewey (1999: 426) goes further and argues that 'women's ability to form their own identities using strategies of "gender management", for example, are undermined, because the professional managerial discourse (reproduced in many textbooks as well) constitutes subjectivity in the corporation's "masculine" image'. Whitehead (2001) argues that, in achieving ontological security, many women no longer search for this anchoring in what has been traditionally carved out by men and women alike as the domain of females or the feminine, where nurturing intimate relationships in the family and among friends is the key to success. Thus professional management presents a seductive ontology to women because it seems as though it is possible for women to achieve their sense of identity through work but in fact this striving places them in a struggle to find a new anchoring that is often more suited to the masculine image of the manager. Citing Silvia Gherardi (1995), Whitehead notes that women 'need to negotiate multiple public and private roles across gendered landscapes where much of male and female remains polarized' (2001: 100).

The effect of the seductive ontology is evident when we look at how men and women differ in the meanings they attach to the notion of commitment across differing contexts. It seems that there is a gendered aspect to commitment and an emotional dimension to it that is also gendered. In a sobering review of labour trends, and the perceptions that many male managers hold of women employees, Catherin Hakim (1995) found that women were represented as less career conscious than men, not staying in their jobs for the long haul, being less interested than men in training and promotion, having higher turnover and levels of absenteeism, and unwilling to place work ahead of domestic demands. She found that labour market trends over several decades had not altered these patterns and concluded that, on balance, women tend to be unstable employees (in terms of job tenure and length of time with a particular employer). She acknowledged that many women are found in casual and part-time work while there is also a small group of women who pursue their careers through education and qualifications, although again not necessarily remaining in the workforce as long as their male counterparts. She draws attention to the conservative attitudes of women who work part time or choose not to work at all even if they have no children, and the equally conservative attitude of their spouses to women in the workforce. Industries that are typically male or female dominated showed no difference in women's employment patterns. Hakim makes a strong case for looking at female orientations to work as the key explanatory factor accounting for these trends that prevail to this day. Her work did not, however, focus on those women who remained in full-time employment and how they were experiencing life in what seems to be workplaces suited more to men than women.

There are surprisingly few studies that actually focus on the meaning that different categories of workers have of commitment, especially along gender lines. One study that specifically set out to discover the meanings that men and women attach to commitment found that there were indeed differences based on gender. The study was a cross-cultural/national study that used matched pairs of male and female engineering managers in the high-tech, male-dominated aerospace industry at the forefront of technological advances and constantly recruiting high calibre graduates (Singh and Vinnicombe 2000). Differences were also found between the various levels of management from executives to senior technologists. Part of the aim of the study was to reveal how in promotion and career progression, masculine constructions of commitment have dominated while female ones have been ignored or studied in such a way that masculine models or factors determine the findings.

Respondents were asked to give their own definitions of commitment, then describe a manager who they thought was committed, and finally rate the importance to them of the various meanings of commitment that were elicited from the first part of the study. The conclusions of the study are interesting in that it was found that career (the authors seem to reduce this to professional commitment) and organizational commitment were quite strong but mainly in terms of affective commitment and hardly at all in terms of continuance commitment. In order to explain their findings along gender lines, different categories of commitment had to be developed. Overwhelmingly, the four most frequent responses to the meaning of commitment were: *task delivery*; *put self out, do extra, do extra, effort*; *involvement* (personal engagement to achieve goals of the organization) and *quality* (doing a good piece of work and so on), with women ranking all but task delivery higher than men (Singh and Vinnicombe 2000: 9). 'Task delivery' was more frequently cited by the Swedish engineers, suggesting a strong cultural influence on this dimension. 'Putting yourself out' was more commonly cited by married respondents, top managers and the British women engineers. Senior managers did not, on the whole, give 'involvement' as a meaning of commitment and more women than men chose this meaning. Senior managers focused on meanings such as being: 'proactive, ready for challenge, creativity and innovation, and added value/business/customer awareness' (Singh and Vinnicombe 2000: 11) as their understandings of what it means to be a committed professional employee.

Figure 9.3 gives a summary of the key findings of the study and introduces some interesting gendered dimensions to commitment, based on the visibility of what one does to attract the attention of managers and individual versus organizational orientation.

Taking each one of the dimensions at a time, we can conclude the following:

- *Gender-shared meanings:* there are certain generic meanings shared by both professional men and women focused on dedication, responsibility and the like that are likely to be found in many other professional groups
- *Vanguard meanings: higher visibility, individual orientation* – encompasses meanings strongly associated with the masculine work ethos and culture (forward-looking, self- and organizational development) and shared by many top men and women managers

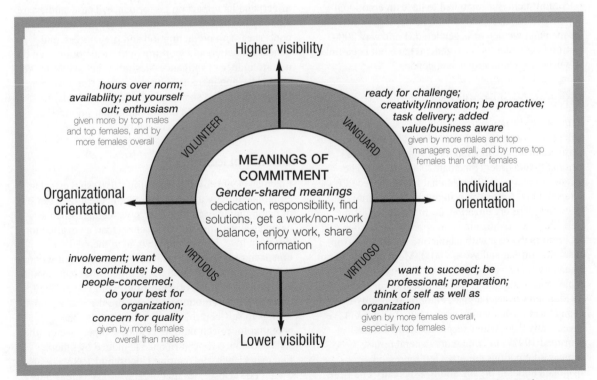

Figure 9.3 Gendered meanings of commitment by visibility and orientation

Source: Val Singh and Susan Vinnicombe (2000) 'The gendered meanings of commitment from high technology engineering managers in the United Kingdom and Sweden', *Gender, Work & Organization,* **7**(1): 15.

- *Volunteer meaning: higher visibility, organizational orientation* – more top males and female managers subscribe to these meanings of commitment and more females overall. Good citizenship behaviour and cooperative behaviour are valued but not often rewarded through normal reward systems and so on
- *Virtuoso meaning: lower visibility, individual orientation* – encompasses meanings that top female managers and most females relate to and value (enhancing the individual career)
- *Virtuous meaning: lower visibility, organizational orientation* – encompassing meanings that women relate to more than men, close to affective commitment which is not seen as something men easily relate to or value.

Val Singh and Susan Vinnicombe conclude that on the whole women gave more volunteer and virtuous meanings and top women gave more virtuoso and vanguard meanings, similar to top men. However, while top male managers shared similar meanings with top women managers, their meanings related most strongly with those of other men. The authors concluded that the traditional measures of commitment which use the instruments and approaches we described above have been insensitive to gender because they were principally masculinist constructs to start with.

Commitment is also argued to have an emotional dimension, involving emotional labour that is different for men and women or is gendered (Franzway 2000). Until recently, emotions in general have not been linked to workplace commitment and gender.

Emotions and identity

In many organizations, managers are charged with the task of removing unpredictable behaviours, particularly those emanating from emotional states, to ensure rationality and order (Fineman 2000: 10–12). The recent fascination with emotional intelligence (EQ) (see Chapter 1) is focused on bringing emotions into the 'service' of the organization as an added part of the 'self' that the organization can appropriate, as has occurred in the past with labour and knowledge (for example Druskat and Wolff 2001). More often than not, managers seek to deny emotional dimensions of behaviour, treating it as problematical or an aberration. As Stephen Linstead argues, emotion is usually treated as an abject phenomenon, denied but ever present, yet never really dealt with except very superficially (Linstead 1997: 1142). In more general terms, unpleasant emotions are often left repressed or unspoken about in organizations, especially emotions that are seen as negative, such as anger (Fitness 2000), cynicism (Dean et al. 1998), envy or greed (Bedeian 1995) or taboos, such as desire (see below). Greed and

envy, for example, are often presented as a natural part of the personality, yet self-aggrandizement, individualism, opportunism and competitiveness are commonly rewarded in many Western businesses. Indeed, depending on the social context or the culture, the notion of greed and envy, for example, might change or might not even exist (Burkitt 1991: 204, citing Lichtman 1982). In other words, certain contexts and situations give rise to these emotions and feelings and others do not. Focusing on individuals' emotions and their flaws in managing these in the workplace disguises the social nature of emotions.

Emotions have been studied from a number of perspectives, ranging from their psychological substates, cognitive antecedents or behavioural outcomes (Fitness 2000) to sociological perspectives (Hochschild 1983; Fineman 1993, 2000). Cynthia Fisher and Neal Ashkanasy (2000) state that there has been a long history in the study of emotions in the workplace but the publication of *The Managed Heart*, by Arlie Hochschild in 1983, accelerated this interest and changed how many scholars studied it. They cite a number of early studies in OB that tested how dispositional affect (or emotions) influence job satisfaction and performance. This initial interest in affect led to studies on trait affectivity (identifying emotional traits) and then to studies of mood (state affect) and its impact on performance. These studies are still popular and dominate much of the literature and are concerned with predicting job and life success, and hence behaviour, and working out how emotions can be used to induce or influence 'desirable' behaviour in the workplace and increase job satisfaction (for example Fisher 2000). The sociological shift in the study of emotions to a focus on emotional labour provided a more critical approach to its study.

Emotional labour

Fineman (1993: 14, citing Collins 1990) suggests that emotional energy is very important in creating a sense of belonging in each of us. He says feelings, such as being accepted, respect, diffidence, fear, awe, affection and even love, help to bind people to their organizational worlds or roles. He contends that without 'socially connected emotions of embarrassment, shame and guilt' (1993: 17) organizations would be difficult to manage. These emotions, he says, are the motivational springs to self-control because they involve the potential for rejection, threats to how others see us (the self) and how our performance is judged by others. Fineman (1993, 1997, citing Hochschild 1983; see also Chapter 3) also argues that organizations increasingly demand various forms of 'emotional labour', but this is not given recognition by the organization or at least its management. 'Emotion management' is also built into the design of many jobs and job training, he says. Not only do people have to deal with their own emotions in a motivational sense, but often have to prove their worth, loyalty and commitment to the organization by engaging continuously and 'successfully' in emotional performances. These performances amount to wearing the company-prescribed 'mask' in whatever form it takes and whatever situation arises, usually to satisfy customers or clients. Fineman draws on Arlie Hochschild's (1983) research on flight attendants and debt collectors to illustrate the dimensions of emotional labour structured into these jobs – flight attendants smiling and being courteous under all circumstances and conditions; debt collectors being dominant in the situation and making the debtor feel guilty and unworthy. Emotional labour is increasingly built into many service-related jobs and can become the 'feeling rules' that are associated with professional training and conduct, for example doctors being seen as 'caring', 'rational', 'scientific' and 'objective' (Fineman 1993: 86). However, emotional self-management can also extend to the self-identity of those with whom the persons interacts, for example, doctors need to manage their patients' identities so that they will follow the prescribed treatment.

Emotional labour has its 'costs' for those who cannot reconcile how they privately feel about the 'public performance' required of them, especially if they feel pressured or coerced into performing the emotional 'act'. They might feel confused and uncomfortable about their self-identity or the self-concept that the performance violates (Fineman 1997: 18, citing Hochschild 1983). Fineman (1993: 21) suggests that ritualized expressions of emotions can also be invoked in situations that are seen as informal but operate through strong (unwritten) rules or obligations to participate. Some of these ritualized expressions include such things as drinking parties, pub crawls, sporting events and various 'bonding' sessions. Fineman (1993, citing Hochschild 1983) points out that while this emotional labour does not cause everyone to feel self-estranged, it can do so for some people. A number of these rituals are, for example, gender-based, and emotional labour carries high 'costs' for many women (and maybe even for some men!) participating in more masculine forms of ritual expressions.

Suzanne Franzway (2000) uses the concept of 'greedy institutions' to study the union movement in Australia and the limited nature of women's representation in unions. Not only does she suggest that union work demands high levels of commitment and loyalty as well as high levels of work but also emotional labour. She found that not only do women interpret commitment differently (often ambivalently because the male meanings of commitment are so powerful in the union) but also emotional labour

associated with their work. Franzway argues that women have to negotiate two greedy institutions – the union movement and the family – that make demands on them which are different from many men. She looked at how specific discourses and practices shape the union movement and, in turn, shape the way women see and represent themselves. Unions, she argues, have created powerful discourses that have the male unionists cast as the normative (good or exemplary) union official while women are represented as problematical and different. In terms of commitment, Franzway found women unionists no less committed than men but less able to find a meaning for commitment in the traditional notion of sacrifice for the organization. Women focused on such dimensions as service to members to broaden their meanings of commitment, including service roles that spell increasing the power and influence of women. Where the concept of service becomes problematical is in its different translation by male and female union members. For males, service is translated most often as defence of wages and conditions, whereas for women service is intimately connected to caring for members (Franzway 2000: 265).

The essence of emotional labour, according to Franzway, is caring for others and producing appropriate feelings in others and this often describes the type of work women are expected to perform. Combative behaviour, hard-nosed negotiations and conflict resolution are also emotionally taxing aspects of union work but, as Franzway suggests, such emotional labour is seen as more appropriately the domain of male and not female officials. The picture Franzway and her interviews paint of the union movement is not static or unchanging but there is a clear 'macho' culture that taxes men and women differently in terms of commitment, workload and emotional labour.

Fineman (2000: 5) argues that emotional labour should be looked at in terms of how it is regulated and how emotions are engineered, and to what extent people tolerate, enjoy or rebel against such measures. He also questions to what extent there is a need for certain degrees of this labour (even if it is inauthentic or faked) to allow for social transactions, and when it crosses the boundary of tolerable to become oppressive. He notes that different occupational settings, where for example the 'wrong sex' occupies the job, such as female firefighters or female construction workers, are also likely to create emotional labour. The gender/emotion stereotypes that prevail in these settings are likely to cause identity crisis for all sorts of people – male and female alike. In more general terms, Fineman (2000: 6–7) believes that the emphasis on self-help, self-development, being in touch with one's self, and a whole range of other interpersonal interventions have focused people more on managing emotions, emotion management and emotional intelligence, thus making the issue of emotional labour appear non-problematical in many organizations. However, he believes this popular discourse disguises other ways in which emotions are exploited. He introduces the idea of the 'emotional body' (2000: 9) to further extend the debate about how emotions shape identities and, in the process, produce insidious forms of control. He cites examples such as having to adorn the body in certain forms of dress and attire, deportment and carriage, and aesthetic demands relating to the body, such as not being overweight, being tall, sexy and so on, generating their own forms of embodied labour (also Witz et al. 2001). Extending this notion of embodied labour, others suggest that many women through the disciplines of diet, make-up and dress are slavishly focused on 'self-modification': 'appearance, looks, bodily comportment, and image' to make themselves more desirable (Trethewey 1999: 425). When this is extended to the workplace, women are required to engage in particular forms of discipline and aesthetic presentation that do not offend, and in fact please the 'other' – the 'masculine connoisseur' (Trethewey 1999: 425) cum colleague or boss. This argument suggests that women's identities are formed around how they are 'seen by another'– the male – and the struggle in the workplace is often a struggle against the male stereotype of the ideal body, where the female body is represented in the popular discourse as embodying weaknesses, nurturing and dependence. The notion of a female identity underscores the claim of emotional labour having gendered aspects.

Desire

We should also mention here that all theories of motivation familiar in organization studies are based around an assumption of *desire*, the force that operates to underpin motivation. In the work of Sigmund Freud, following the German philosopher Georg Frederick Hegel, desire is occasioned by a sense of incompleteness and is fundamentally the desire to be complete. Awareness that there are other people who have different experiences from us may be sufficient to occasion this desire – if they have specific qualities that we envy, we might be more focused in what we desire. If they have possessions, we might transfer our desire to be as handsome or beautiful as they are onto a car or clothes or nice apartment, in the hope that possession of these artefacts might make us as desirable as they are. Indeed, we might wish to become desirable to them, to contain and control them. Whichever way, we are motivated to get those possessions, acquire those artefacts or become worthy in some other way by getting a new job, a promotion or achieving something

on the sports field. For Freud, these operations of transference, or *cathexis*, are at the unconscious level and we do not know that we are doing these things. Indeed, Freud felt that it was too often our baser instincts that drove us to fill these lacks.

Michel Foucault, however, argued that these lacks were not natural as Freud assumed, but were constructed by contemporary discourses to make people feel inadequate. Anorexia in the sixteenth century would have been impossible, as to have a well-rounded figure was thought desirable, but in the twenty-first century, where we are bombarded with magazines full of slim bodies and shelves of diet books, it is easy for a woman to feel freakishly inadequate if she is anything more than a size 8. So, for Foucault, desire was manufactured and artificial, and any approach based on Freud was inadequate. Foucault would have rejected the main organizational theories of motivation. An alternative approach was offered in the 1920s by Georges Bataille, who argued that desire was more free-flowing than this. He argued that human beings were naturally exuberant, and expressed their humanity best not in productive work-based activity, but in wasteful activity such as poetry, art, song, dance, literature and drinking. He argued that the accumulation-based 'restricted economy' operates alongside the spendthrift and symbolic 'general economy' and we define ourselves best in how we spend our excess energies in the latter, rather than how we spend our money in the former (Brewis and Linstead 2000: 174–81). Gilles Deleuze and Felix Guattari (1984) argue, following Bataille, that desire is free-flowing, but where Freud feels that desire is created by discourse and symbols, they argue that discourse just picks up and channels the flow of desire. Motivation then is not something we need to create from scratch, but is already constantly in motion unless stifled by organizational arrangements. The problem, for Deleuze and Guattari, would be how to channel such a nomadic desire without distorting or killing it. The possibility of thinking about motivation in terms of desire is that it becomes much less exchange and interest-based and leaves more scope for recognition of the need for excitement and the space for exuberance, enjoyment or 'fun' in organizations. But, of course, to have fun you need to feel that you won't be made vulnerable by exposing yourself, which is the basis of trust.

The trust dynamic

Turner's work also drew attention to *trust* and we need to consider trust and its relation to motivation and identity. The attention to trust is not a recent development in organization or motivation theory (Costigan et al. 1998), and was treated at length in Alan

Fox's classic text, *Man Mismanagement* (1972). Fox argued that despite the claims of scientific management, it was impossible to specify the nature of a task – partly because of the nature of language, partly because of the nature of work – so tightly as to remove the need for an element of worker discretion, which entailed a degree of trust. Indeed, Taylor recognized this in his emphasis on the abilities and importance of the 'first class man'. Fox argues that the balance of trust and control should be, and needs to be, more even in workplace relations, and that this is in fact more efficient than excessive and ultimately costly control measures. He called for management to 'extend the hand of trust' to employees, rather than tighten regimes of control.

These sentiments were echoed by Richard Walton (1985), whose article, 'From control to commitment in the workplace', spelt out what he considered to be key job design strategies intrinsic to building a committed workforce. Some of the strategies he mentioned included equality of sacrifice, assurance of no job losses if employees take on more responsibilities, priority of training and retaining the existing workforce, flexible definition of duties and a number of others. Other researchers suggest that commitment is contingent upon the organization broadening its perceptions of what employees want from their jobs to include more consideration of such things as family commitments (Ulrich 1998) and diversity issues (see Chapter 3).

Control-oriented systems, as described by Fox and Walton above, are designed to ensure that enduring trust-based relationships do not develop even though some small degree of trust exists in all relationships (Misztal 1996; Ring 1997; McKnight et al. 1998). The degree of trust and the types of trust evident at any given time are variable and differ between employees, managers and colleagues and between individuals, teams and groups (for example Costigan et al. 1998; Williams 2001). 'Extending the hand of trust' in today's work organizations is considered by some theorists to be at the very heart of creating a high-commitment management philosophy essential to knowledge work, teamwork, collaboration and the learning organization. In high-commitment cultures, people are supposed to be no longer inhibited, self-protective and defensive (Costigan et al. 1998; also see Chapter 1). Others believe that trust adds a new dimension to control in organizations that is needed as we move away from more bureaucratic structures to flexible modes of operating, where increasingly people have to depend on others, especially strangers, to build and share knowledge, innovate and learn. It is suggested that 'post-bureaucratic' organizations are unable to build on traditional forms of trust because they are characterized by increasing numbers of temporary employees, workers hired under contracts or on a consultancy basis, people working from home or teleworking, or

constantly changing skills, roles and jobs within the organizations to cope with flexibility (Grey and Garsten 2001: 239; Knights et al. 2001). For many managers today a key issue will be how they manage more impersonal forms of trust as traditional forms decline both at work and in the wider society (Grey and Garsten 2001: 235; Knights et al. 2001).

Dyadic view of trust

Behaviourists, who view trust as something that occurs between two people (a dyad), argue that it is associated with the willingness of a person to make himself/herself vulnerable and to take risks in the context of a particular relationship (Davis et al. 1997: 33; Mayer et al. 1995). This 'relationship' seems to be posited between persons who share like qualities or characteristics. The argument posits, and is very strong in the trust literature, that without trust people will not take risks, be confident enough to learn, experiment, innovate or realize their creative potential. Transactional relationships (principally based on some notion of the rational actor) create a type of trust that Ring (1997: 123–5, drawing on Mayer et al. 1995) describes as *fragile trust* (also see McKnight et al. 1998: 482–3). This form of trust depends on a limited set of judgements being made by individuals about others that predispose the trustor to take some risks and trust the other person who becomes the trustee. It also focuses on a person's abilities (assuming these are all under a person's control), and how these are perceived by others. Abilities include such things as (Mayer et al. 1995; Ring 1997: 123–5):

- competence in one's job
- business sense
- good judgement
- accessibility
- interpersonal competence.

Resilient trust, by contrast, is the basis for developing the relational transactions that are important for building long-term commitments and encouraging risk taking (Ring 1997). The key to this form of trust is a perception that the trustee will behave with:

- integrity (which includes being consistent in actions, communicating credibly about other people)
- a strong sense of justice (being fair and showing discretion)
- benevolence (being a caring person)
- altruism (doing good for others and being selfless)
- loyalty and openness.

Under the behavioural approach, individuals can

cooperate, and even have confidence in someone without trusting them; for example, cooperation can be induced through fear or threats. Confidence can come from being able to predict someone's behaviour, even if the behaviour is undesirable and does not induce trust, for example being able to predict that someone is not trustworthy! Cooperating is not the same as making a commitment to something or someone (Mayer et al. 1995). However a major criticism of this *interpersonal approach* to trust is that it is limited to a dyadic relation between trustor and trustee (that is, the characteristics of individuals and their behaviours) and ignores the fact that trust also develops among groups and organizations, between individuals and groups and within specific contexts or institutional settings. As we will show in Chapter 16, some even believe that trust has a national dimension to it, with certain countries being high in trust-building capacities or national cultures. Moreover, except for some brief mention of the balance of power in relationships affecting trust formation, the behavioural approach deals only with the psychological processes of the trustor and trustee and thus neglects broader social processes (Wekselberg 1996: 333; Jones and George 1998). Its proponents also neglect to mention the consequences to the organization when trust is violated and cooperation on a wider scale is compromised or threatened because two people no longer trust each other or a key person. The behavioural approach sees risk and trust as belonging to the dyadic relationship and not having broader consequences (Wekselberg 1996: 333–5).

Whitener et al. (1998) attempt to remedy this deficiency by not only focusing on the interpersonal factors that lead to trust-based relations but on a number of others that constrain or enhance trust from developing and working over time. Included in this approach are human relations (HR) practices and organizational culture as well as a number of other individual factors not covered in the dyadic approach. The authors conclude, in a similar fashion to Fox and Walton, that low control organizations generate greater potentials for trusting relationships (Whitener et al. 1998: 519).

Trust as a multi-level phenomenon

Most theories of trust adopt a multi-level approach to explaining the phenomenon (Lane 1998: 3; Rousseau et al. 1998: 393, 395) and identify several key conditions that give rise to trust:

1. it must involve risk and uncertainty as typically found in economic exchange where opportunistic behaviour or cheating is a threat
2. it involves the potential of losing from a relationship
3. it involves reciprocal relationships, in the sense of 'gift giving' and notions of fair exchange

4. it means being interdependent on others and thus being made vulnerable in a social relationship.

Where theorists diverge markedly is in how they explain the grounds upon which trust can be built or its social basis, and the views of human nature or the types of social interaction that are used to build their theories, such as seeing people as rational egoists or moral or emotional agents (Lane 1998: 4). Christel Lane suggests that the objects of trust and the context in which they are studied also create a divergence in theories of trust. Trust is also generally viewed as something that is in a dynamic state, ebbing and flowing, even declining and then resurfacing (Rousseau et al. 1998). Lane says that a small group of economists, who have had a significant influence on the debate about trust, particularly interorganizational trust (see Chapter 11), present trust as being largely based on economic calculation and opportunism. By contrast, she suggests that sociologists and organizational theorists have generally focused on the common values, norms and moral orientations to explain trust dynamics. Others would suggest that what has overwhelmingly interested organizational researchers has been institutionalized rather than personalized forms of trust and the concomitant focus on control and regulation (Reed 2001). As Michael Reed suggests, the field has been dominated by a narrow perspective that has been primarily concerned with explaining the integrative functions of trust/control relations and the maintenance of stable and ordered social interactions based on shared obligations and expectations (Reed 2001: 214). Motivations to trust are assumed to be universally the same for everyone and the notion of human agency or choice is hardly acknowledged in much of this theorizing. Reed wants to present a critical realist view (see Introduction) of trust and hence sees the problem in terms of the structure versus action/agency binary. Where Ritzer takes on board postmodern arguments about the implosion of binaries, and problematizes the notion of agency and choice relative to identity, Reed feels that trust cannot be collapsed into a matter of relationships but that there are objective issues outside those relationships which affect the exercise of choice to trust or not to trust, and which may even be causal of trust. While postmodernists would argue that context is already within the relationship because of the implosion of boundaries, and would question the relation of causality, they would nevertheless accept Reed's observation that the field has concentrated on the integrative functions of trust and the maintenance of stability, and would similarly want to give emphasis to contextual factors, without resurrecting the structure/agency binary.

Lane points out that many theorists subscribe to the view that there are stages in the development of trust and it is a multidimensional concept resting on more than one basis. Typologies of trust dominate the literature and usually cover at least three dimensions. Lane identifies some of the most common of these typologies as: *cognitive trust* (rational decision to trust or withhold trust based on various judgements such as dependability and competence) coupled with *value and emotion-based trust* (deep emotional investment in a relationship). As mentioned above, most popular among economists is *calculative trust* which is usually coupled with either moral or cognitive trust but not both. She says some theorists combine all three to come up with *deterrence* (see below), *knowledge* (presupposes prior knowledge and first-hand experience between parties) and *identification-based trust*. The aforementioned approximate with calculative, value-based and cognitive trust (Lane 1998: 4; also Newell and Swan 2000). Others suggest that *personality-based trust,* or the disposition to trust others because of a trusting stance or a general faith in humanity, needs to be added to the typologies of trust (McKnight et al. 1998). Rousseau et al. (1998) also treat trust as a 'meso'-concept and identify four different forms that can be easily subsumed under Lane's categories:

- *deference-based trust* (related to utilitarianism) draws on the notion that costly sanctions are in place to punish breaches of agreements or opportunistic behaviour so that risk taking can occur
- *calculus-based trust* (or rational choice in economic exchanges) involves not only deterrence but also depends on having reliable information about the competence and intentions of the other person that will result in risk taking
- *relational trust* (affective or identity-based trust) involving repeated transactions that lead to predictability and reliability on others and emotional attachment resulting from long-term relationships in which care and reciprocal concerns are paramount
- *institutional-based trust*, such as legal frameworks, guarantees, contracts and so on and reputation-building systems (for example in academia with publications, peer reviews) which allow trust to build into calculative and relational forms.

Trust is rarely dealt with in the literature as a gendered concept, even though it is identified as having a high affective element or emotional dimension. Gareth Jones and Jennifer George (1998: 534), for example, describe emotions and moods as integral to building trust, and cite feelings, impressions and negative moods as impacting on the willingness to trust others. Others cite particular qualities, such as consistency in behaviour, integrity, sharing and delegation, communication (for example accuracy,

openness) and demonstration of concern for others as dimensions of trustworthiness, but no mention is made of gender differences in this respect (Whitener et al. 1998). Other common constructions of trust are gender neutral or more correctly, blind. Hence, in a number of scholarly overviews of different disciplinary approaches to trust (for example Lane 1998; Rousseau et al. 1998; Newell and Swan 2000; Grey and Garsten 2001; Reed 2001), no mention is made of gender or other factors that account for differences in workplaces. There are several exceptions (Kanter 1977; Lorber 1979; Zucker 1986; Costigan et al. 1998; Williams 2001), but on the whole, gender suppression and blindness are the norm. We explore the gendered nature of trust in Chapter 16 as well as some important cross-cultural considerations.

Nonetheless, the typologies described above are by no means exhaustive of what can be found in the literature, there are a plethora of different dimensions used to describe the bases of trust. Nor do theorists agree on which form of trust is the most potent. Some would suggest that affect-based trust is the most enduring (Jones and George 1998; Williams 2001), while others emphasize the institutional and regulative role of trust, de-emphasizing its emotional and cognitive dimensions (Reed 2001: 203). One of the most vexing aspects of these typologies is that they present trust as having inevitable trajectories, in which people have no choice but to conform or go along with what has been determined for them. Chris Grey and Christina Garsten (2001: 230) warn that trust is something that is constructed for and by people in organizations and while it can provide some level of predictability and control it can just as easily have the opposite effects. Distrust and betrayal are 'part and parcel' of all trust-based relations and are two of the key risks involved in trusting another person. As Reed notes, this aspect of trust was identified by Fox over twenty years ago (1972: 67–8) when he made the following statement:

the essential character of all trust relations is their reciprocal nature. Trust tends to evoke trust, distrust to evoke distrust. As trust shrinks, distrust takes over.

Distrust can be analysed from a number of perspectives depending on which typology is invoked (for example Elangovan and Shapiro 1998; Lane 1998: 22–5). However, it is generally agreed that the most common form of distrust is associated with a deliberate and voluntary violation by a trustee of a trustor that involves mutually known pivotal expectations and obligations (Elangovan and Shapiro 1998: 548). Organizational or institutional factors can intercede (such as a high trust culture, codes of conduct and low levels of politics and power struggles) to attenuate acts of betrayal but betrayal is very much about personal relationships that can have organizational consequences. Moreover, it pertains to pivotal expectations that all parties (trustee and trustor) are aware of and these usually relate to tasks or values, such as providing support, keeping secrets, not lying or cheating, harming or abusing the trustor (Elangovan and Shapiro: 1998: 549). Premeditated betrayal is to not accept the pivotal expectations in a relationship but instead use them to gain the trust of someone in order to betray them. Betrayal involves actual acts and must result in harm to the trustor. However, not all acts of betrayal are antisocial, as when exposing the wrongdoings (for example padding expenses) of a colleague who has sought the confidence of the trustee (Elangovan and Shapiro 1998: 550).

There are a number of different modes of betrayal, with *opportunistic betrayal* being the most common, that is, the violation arises when events or circumstances present themselves in an already existing trust-based relationship that leads the trustee to make a calculated (cost–benefit) decision to betray the trustor. The concept of betrayal does not privilege any one group as being more trustworthy, but rather suggests that some people are more predisposed to betrayal (Elangovan and Shapiro 1998). As Grey and Garsten (2001: 235) point out, the popular management literature assumes that managers are trustworthy by definition and are engaged in developing trustworthiness, when in fact the problem is to render managers trustworthy in organizations where the conditions for trust formation are becoming increasingly difficult and more impersonal and betrayal perhaps more common.

When trust diminishes

Some theorists question whether or not certain forms of trust are diminishing in importance. Lynne Zucker (1986; also Shapiro 1987; Knights et al. 2001) believes that increasingly indirect measures (or indicators) are used to 'signal' trust and these are increasingly dependent on institutional forms. Zucker suggests that certain forms of trust are becoming scarce, such as those based on close personal ties or the characteristic mode of trust production, and more impersonal, institutional forms are taking their place. She says that when common background expectations are present – because of some form of homogeneity in vital characteristics (for example gender, ethnicity, family background) – it makes it easier to build trust but without this, it has to be produced and worked at (Lane 1998: 11). Thus Zucker conceives of trust as being increasingly produced through institutions. In her view, even *process-based trust*, which depends on such things as reputations of either individuals or businesses, and the incremental gathering of direct and indirect

information (for example through gossip or hearsay) about how others act in various forms of exchange, is also on the decline. Zucker believes that this mode of trust production is governed by idiosyncratic understandings and rules that are highly specific to particular individuals or brands (Zucker 1986: 62). Rapid change and high turnover of personnel and other factors associated with high instability diminish the salience of reputations or make them harder to establish and maintain. She also argues that diversity in workplaces and the need to work across large geographical areas, are two key reasons why it is hard to achieve homogeneity – the core element of personal trust-based relations (Zucker 1986). Zucker considers that the spread of bureaucratic organizations, the growth in professional credentialism, the rise of the service economy – particularly financial intermediaries, such as banks, insurance companies and government services, and the resort to regulations and legislation – all contribute to the creation of *impersonal* trust-based mechanisms and the production of *institutional* forms of trust. Her arguments suggest an immanent and inevitable decline in certain forms of trust – a view criticized by Reed (2001), as mentioned above, for being far too dismissive of human agency and choice.

Nonetheless Knights et al. (2001), drawing on Zucker's work, discuss how the Internet presents challenges to identity formation, especially how trust production is being redefined in the realm of the virtual (see also Chapter 17). Knights et al. invoke the common punch line used by many Internet enthusiasts that 'on the Internet nobody knows you are a dog'. The virtual realm is, they say, *Janus-faced*. On the one hand, it provides the opportunity to escape the normal constraints of identity ('beat the meat' as they quote) and 'dispose' of all the inscriptions of the body (such as gender, race, age, physical appearance, geographical location and sexuality), and allows its users to engage in various forms of 'consensual hallucinations' about who they are or want to be (Knights et al. 2001: 320). In many workplaces, the development of virtual teams and projects and innovative information networks create the same potential for 'figments of the imagination' to enter into virtual relationships. On the other hand, cyber-relationships, by virtue of the 'faceless' and 'bodiless' nature of these interactions, make it easier to devise ways of being fraudulent and engage in cyber theft, including those of one's identity (see Cohen 2001). Knights et al. (2001: 321) contend that the real risk in cyberspace relationships is the loss of identity or the misappropriation of it. The protection of identity, however, has led to the creation of various forms of biometric surveillance (for example using the cornea for identification) which leads to a form of 'ontological security' in which the potential to monitor and track a person is no less invasive than those used in prisons and so on to control criminal movements (Knights et al. 2001: 326). Thus the nexus between being identifiable and being able to verify or establish one's identity is critical for overcoming uncertainty and risk and building trust into these relationships.

However, the consequence of this form of ontological security (that is, rendering things and persons predictable and stable even when they are 'absent') has both utopian and dystopian potentials in terms of trust and control. New forms of power and domination are immanent in the biometrics of verification, such as undue surveillance as well as theft and abuse mentioned above, while also offering new forms of freedom for the self and access to others. While in many workplaces people are increasingly forming trust-based relations with people they hardly know (McKnight et al. 1998), how people transfer these dynamics into the realm of cyberspace where new uncertainties and complexities arise remains one of the major challenges in management. Indeed, a recent project undertaken for British Telecom in the UK was designed to research how to persuade people involved in complex procurement and installation activities of new and replacement telecommunications exchanges, from salespeople to field engineers, to develop trust in electronic systems which progressed the order/design/installation sequence. The initial problem had been that people at every stage of the process had been customizing the process – for the right reasons – which had resulted in some spectacular breakdowns in understanding, with customers being sold a service which BT could not provide, or unable to go online because of the failure of a particular part to be designated as time-critical. The system had been seen to be an external constraint by those involved in it, when it should have been an enabling factor. The redesigned systems humanized the presentation and storage of information, and the people involved in the different parts of the system were incorporated into it, explaining to the other system users what they needed to do their job and what issues were particularly critical. The system users were introduced to a set of principles that habituated trust into the system – that is, made the system trustworthy – by other users, who became more familiar and trustworthy through this process. The problem of virtual reality was dealt with by injecting more interpersonal reality and subjective identification between users, which could be said to have recognized the 'motivation' of the system and 'motivated' people to use it correctly.

Conclusion

The questions raised at the beginning of the chapter form a nice way to conclude. Before we do, some general comments are warranted. As we have moved from the more traditional views of motivation where needs were presented as fixed and universal and open to managerial manipulation, the concept of motivation becomes more problematic. Should we no longer use this term? It does seem difficult to imagine how motivation works when the focus shifts to managing relationships and differences in the workplace. No matter which theory we examine, whether it has to do with meanings of work, TQM, BPR, commitment, emotional labour or trust, it gets harder to work with the notion of a compliant or even resistant employee or worker who can be easily manipulated or coerced into performing well. Rather, if we accept the concept that people have complex identities and orientations to work, then the challenge becomes one of figuring out how to bring out the best in people by being a better manager of one's own and others. This chapter is written to sensitize managers to the value of being more critical in their approach to what makes people 'tick' and to confront some of limitations in the popular and enduring theories of motivation.

We have all worked for people who have brought out the best in us and with those who have made every day a struggle to get through, making it exceedingly difficult not to take out all the day's problems on friends, family, children or partners. It is far easier to treat people as though they have universal needs and will respond to a range of workplace interventions and job redesign strategies. The performance might always fall below expectations but it is always easy to blame those who fail to be motivated. It is

Conclusion cont'd

harder to accept the view that people are quite different in how they respond to what the workplace has to offer and that their feelings, moods and emotions are just as important in explaining why they work well and are happy, as are things that have been the focus of motivational theorists for a long time. Men, women and people from different cultures or religions might have expectations from their work that are never met or even addressed. To answer the questions posed for this chapter is not easy, but unless managers are prepared to look beyond the conventional wisdom of many texts and approaches to motivation, they are unlikely ever to get the best out of their people or themselves.

Answers to questions about motivation and meaning

1 **Why do people work?** Classical theories of motivation identify that we work because we have needs to satisfy – needs for the basic staples of life like food and shelter – and these are primarily obtained through the wage or salary. Beyond that, we may work to be regarded with affection by our colleagues, to be esteemed or, as Maslow puts it, for self-actualization, to realize our full potential. Of course, we may meet these needs equally well outside work. McClelland identified needs for power, achievement and affiliation as being socially significant, but more recent approaches to wants, as opposed to needs, have taken even more account of the symbolic dimensions, or the ways in which people need to manage meaning. Turner identifies seven basic social needs of which three – group inclusion, trust and ontological security – are most important and particularly relevant to work.

2 **Are people motivated in the same ways?** There are common features to motivation, but what motivates one person rather than another is subject to infinite variation. Life experience, age, physical and psychological make-up will be significant variables, but so also will gender, race and ethnicity – and people may be motivated differently at different times and in different contexts.

3 **Is how we work affected by how we feel?** Emotion is an important and neglected part of work life, and theories of motivation have tended to view motivation as a sort of calculus rather than a form of inspiration. Both approaches have something to offer, but the protracted neglect of the emotional impact on motivation means that we still have much to learn about it. Recent interest in the area of violation of psychological contracts suggests that emotions are an important part of understanding commitment and why people withdraw commitment or seem to lose motivation or interest in their work.

4 **Can one person motivate another?** It is clear from the research that motivation is very complex, having material and deeper psychological and spiritual aspects. The old 'carrot and stick' model, which oscillated between bribery and bullying, has been superseded, and although simple linear relationships between what a manager does and how a worker responds have been discredited, there is still no shortage of effort to improve workplace motivation. These are perhaps better seen as attempts to influence the

Answers continued

motivational context and process, so although one person may have an impact on another's motivation, it is rare that such motivation can be entirely attributed to that person's efforts. As we explore further the notion of self and identity, it also becomes more challenging to bring out the best in people, with the emphasis shifting to being highly sensitive and receptive to differences among people and finding ways to accommodate this so that maximum effort is forthcoming. Studies of breaches and violations of psychological contracts and trust demonstrate that people can withhold their services and even bring organizations down because all that matters is not materially solved. There is also an assumption that to motivate means to be physically present to do but as we increasingly move into virtual relationships, managers will have to devise ways of handling impersonal work relations.

5 **Is the way a job is designed important for motivation?** Not exclusively, but research on job design does indicate that a well-designed job or group of jobs can have an influence. However, efforts that seek to motivate solely through good job design, neglecting other situational factors, such as organizational politics, are unlikely to be successful. Today, aspects of work relating to emotional labour, commitment and trust are also major factors in improving how work gets done, whether this is in teams, virtual reality or the learning organization. People need a lot more in their jobs than has been the focus on job redesign including TQM and BPR.

6 **Does motivation vary from culture to culture?** Despite the fact that very few writers and managers have acknowledged it, the research evidence that it does is extensive. Discovering how it varies, and what impact these variations have in specific situations, will be an increasing challenge as world business globalizes further. There is no evidence that globalization has neutralized national cultures (see Introduction).

7 **How is motivation different between men and women?** Two areas that we have particularly focused on are commitment and emotional labour. When it comes to commitment, it is noteworthy that few studies have actually asked women and men what they believe constitutes commitment in the workplace. When this has occurred, men and women have been found to share some common understandings of commitment, as indeed do top female and male manages. However, by and large, men still identify more strongly with similar meanings associated with commitment than do women. Women still share meanings about commitment that are likely to give them lower visibility and more traditional feminine meanings such as those based on affective commitment. What is clear is that organizational commitment is becoming less meaningful for both men and women but that in some organizations that are defined as 'greedy organizations', such as some trade unions, women's commitment is different to the vast majority of the male membership, posing huge challenges for these women to remain committed and avoid excessive and destructive forms of emotional labour. There are many forms of emotional labour and some forms that entail bodily aspects, such as being beautiful and seductive, impact more harshly on women.

REVISITING
THE CASE STUDY

1 How many different views of commitment are evident in the case?

Colin seems to think that commitment means commitment to a course of action, that is, meeting the targets laid down by the strategic plan for the business unit. Roger seems to regard commitment as an emotional thing which people express verbally from time to time. Eric seems to think that commitment means doing what he and the personnel director decide is best, and accepting disadvantage 'for the good of the team' in a mood of loyal self-sacrifice. Graham does not, he says, want to talk about commitment, but poaching of his staff. Graham's storyline reads very much like the emotional response, the deep visceral feelings described by Morrison and Robinson. Graham has failed to receive something he expected, felt he deserved and is being cheated from having.

It is unclear why the organization has reneged on its promise to Graham but, for him, talk of commitment is all empty rhetoric and hypocrisy. Doing what the company does, selling biscuits and crisps, is not something which is intrinsically motivating, and he questions the sanity of anyone who finds it so. He claims that the company's attempts to claim more and more of his time in the name of commitment, which is used merely as a mask for organizational politics, have gone too far. If that is what it takes, he declares, he is not committed.

2 How could Graham's real or apparent 'lack of commitment' be handled? Does it need to be addressed?

This is a difficult one. Clearly Graham's problem is not adequately expressed in the term 'lack of commitment'. Graham is annoyed that the company plays a political game, playing managers off against each other, forcing them to compete against each other to meet production targets. The competitive and divisive nature is masked by talk of 'commitment' to the team and the plan, when in fact the spirit is not collective but one of masculine aggression – note that the others try to 'cut him down to size'. What Graham is saying is that commitment here is empty, and it is just cut and thrust and power politics.

Graham does not like this, and finally he says so. The silence of the others indicates that he has struck a nerve. For a moment they wonder, what would it be like if we really were a team? If we weren't constantly bickering but helped each other? And perhaps if we brought more of our family values into the workplace? They wonder what life would be like if work were perhaps more meaningful, more cooperative, based on trust rather than gamesmanship.

There is no way of dealing with Graham's lack of commitment at this level, because it would mean radical change. It would entail all the men in the room being able to set aside their political differences and open up about their misgivings about how they work together – and committing to change. In reality, they will stay silent for a while then change the subject; eventually Eric will talk 'man to man' with Graham and the incident will be forgotten. To really deal with the problem would require a different sort of commitment.

3 What has precipitated the 'blow-up' at Chester?

What precipitated the 'blow-up' was the political play which resulted in Graham losing his 'best man', which will affect his department's ability to meet its targets. However, it was also precipitated by the fact that everyone was drunk, and their night away seems as much an escape from the unpleasantness of the realities of work as it is a planning meeting. On this evidence, we might wonder whether any of them is really 'committed' – that is, believes in and values what the company is doing – beyond just working for long hours. Perhaps the problem is that Graham is struggling with the 'emotional performance' that these events extract, including the drinking and the 'rituals' of the annual event.

4 Would the meeting have been different if some of the managers were women?

This is an interesting question, because the dynamics of this meeting are so masculine that it would almost certainly have to be. But the question underlying this is whether women and men are motivated differently, communicate differently, and have different values at work.

Consider what Eric might say to Graham after his outburst:

(a) as a man
(b) if Graham was a woman
(c) if Eric was a woman, and Graham a man
(d) if the group were all women.

References

Allen, N.J. and Meyer, J.P. (1990) 'The measurement and antecedents of affective, continuance and normative commitment to the organization', *Journal of Occupational Psychology,* **63**: 1–18.

Aungles, S.B. and Parker, S.R. (1988) *Work Organisation and Change,* Sydney: Allen & Unwin.

Balk, W.L. (1995) 'Is there life beyond TQM?', in Halachimi, A. and Bouckaert, G. (eds) *Public Productivity Through Quality and Strategic Management*, Amsterdam: IOS Press, and Brussels: International Institute of Administrative Sciences.

Baudrillard, J. (1993) *Symbolic Exchange and Death,* London: Sage

Baudrillard, J. (1994) *The Consumer Society: Myths and Structures,* London: Sage

Baudrillard, J. (1994a) *Simulacra and Simulation,* Ann Arbor: University of Michigan Press.

Becker, H.S. (1964) 'Personal change in adult life', *Sociometry,* **27**: 40–53.

Bedeian, A.G. (1995) 'Workplace envy', *Organizational Dynamics,* **23**(4): 49–56.

Bendix, R. (1956) *Work and Authority in Industry*, New York: Harper.

Bernays, E.L. (1923) *Crystallizing Public Opinion,* New York: Liveright.

Bernays, E.L. (1952) *Public Relations,* Norman, OK: University of Oklahoma Press.

Bernays, E.L. (1955) *The Engineering of Consent,* Norman, OK: University of Oklahoma Press.

Bernays, E.L. (1965) *Biography of an Idea: Memoirs of a Public Relations Counsel,* New York: Simon & Schuster.

Blau, G. (2001) 'On assessing the construct validity of two multi-dimensional constructs: occupational commitment and occupational entrenchment', *Human Resource Management Review,* **11**: 279–98.

Boje, D.M. and Winsor, R.D. (1993) 'The resurrection of Taylorism: Total quality management's hidden agenda', *Journal of Organizational Change Management,* **6**(4): 57–70.

Bond, M.H. and Hwang, K.K. (1986) 'The social psychology of Chinese people', in Bond, M.H. (ed.) *The Psychology of the Chinese People*, Hong Kong: Oxford University Press.

Brewis, J. and Linstead, S. (2000) *Sex, Work and Sex Work,* London: Routledge.

Buchanan, D.A. (1979) *The Development of Job Design Theories and Techniques,* Farnborough: Saxon House.

Buchanan, D. (1995) 'The limitations and opportunities of business process re-engineering in a politicized organizational climate', Human Resource and Change Management Research Group, Loughborough University Business School, Leicestershire (Version: 31 January).

Burkitt, I. (1991) 'Social selves: Theories of the social formation of personality', *Current Sociology,* **23**(3): 1–217.

Child, J. (1984) *Organisation: A Guide to Problems and Practice,* London: Harper & Row.

Clark, C.S. (2000) 'Work/family border theory: A new theory of work/family balance', *Human Relations,* **53**(6): 747–70.

Cohen, A. (2001) 'Internet security', *Times* 2 July: 49–55.

Collins, R. (1975) *Conflict Sociology: Toward an Explanatory Science*, New York: Academic Press.

Collins, R. (1990) 'Stratification, emotional energy, and the transient emotions', in Kemper, T.D. (ed.) *Research Agendas in the Sociology of Emotions*, Albany: State University of New York Press.

Costigan, R.D., Ilter, S.S. and Berman, J.J. (1998) 'A multi-dimensional study of trust in organizations', *Journal of Managerial Issues,* **10**(3): 303–17.

Cox, R.W. (1995) 'Organization development and total quality management: Which is the chicken and which is the egg?', in Halachimi, A. and Bouckaert, G. (eds) *Public Productivity Through Quality and Strategic Management*, Amsterdam: IOS Press, and Brussels: International Institute of Administrative Sciences.

Crosby, P. (1979) *Quality is Free*, New York: New American Library.

Cullen, D. (2000) 'Comment on socioevolutionary theory', *Academy of Management Review,* **25**(4): 696–7 October.

Davenport, T.H. (1993) *Process Innovation: Reengineering Work Through Information Technology*, Harvard: Harvard Business School Press.

Davis, J.H., Schooram, F.D. and Donaldson, L. (1997) 'Toward a stewardship theory of management', *Academy of Management Review,* **22**(1): 20–47.

Dawson, S. (1986) *Analysing Organisations*, London: Macmillan – now Palgrave Macmillan.

Dean, J.W., Brandes, P. and Dharwadka, R. (1998) 'Organizational Cynicism', *Academy of Management Review,* **23**(2): 341–52.

Debord, G. (1994) *The Society of the Spectacle,* New York: Zone Books.

De Cock, C. and Hipkin, I. (1997) 'TQM and BPR: Beyond the myth', *Journal of Management Studies,* **34**(5): 659–75.

Deleuze, G. and Guattari, F. (1984) *Anti-Oedipus: Capitalism and Schizophrenia,* London: Athlone.

Deming, W.E. (1986) *Out of the Crisis: Quality Productivity and the Competitive Position*, Cambridge, MA: MIT Press.

Dent, M. and Whitehead, S. (eds) (2002) *Managing*

Professional Identities: Knowledge, Performativity and the 'New' Professional, London: Routledge.

Druskat, V.U. and Wolff, S.B. (2001) 'Building emotional intelligence for groups', *Harvard Business Review*, March: 81–90.

du Gay, P. (1996) *Consumption and Identity*, London: Sage.

Dunphy, D. (1981) *Organisational Change by Choice*, Sydney: McGraw-Hill.

Elangovan, A.R. and Shapiro, D.L. (1998) 'Betrayal of trust in organizations', *Academy of Management Review*, **23**(3): 547–66.

Emery, F.E. (1969) *Systems Thinking: Selected Readings*, Harmondsworth: Penguin.

Emery, F.E. and Phillips, C.R. (1976) *Living at Work*, Canberra: Australian Government Publishing Service.

Ewen, S. (1996) *PR!: A Social History of Spin*, New York: Basic Books.

Fincham, R. and Rhodes, P.S. (1992) *The Individual, Work and Organization: Behavioural Studies for Business and Management*, London: Weidenfeld & Nicolson.

Fineman, S. (1983) 'Work meanings, non-work and the taken-for-granted', *Journal of Management Studies*, **20**(2): 143–55.

Fineman, S. (1993) 'Organizations as emotional arenas', in Fineman, S. (ed.) *Emotion in Organizations*, London: Sage.

Fineman, S. (1997) 'Emotion and management learning', *Management Learning* **28**(1): 13–25.

Fineman, S. (2000) *Emotion in Organizations* (2nd edn) London: Sage.

Fisher, C.D. (2000) 'Mood and emotions while working: Missing pieces in job satisfaction', *Journal of Organizational Behavior*, **21**: 185–202.

Fisher, C.D. and Ashkanasy, N. (2000) 'The emerging role of emotions in work life: An introduction', *Journal of Organizational Behavior*, **21**: 123–9.

Fitness, J. (2000) 'Anger in the workplace: An emotion script approach to anger episodes between workers and their superiors, co-workers and subordinates', *Journal of Organizational Behavior*, **21**: 47–62.

Fox, A. (1972) *Man Mismanagement*, Oxford: Oxford University Press.

Franzway, S. (2000) 'Women working in a greedy institution: Commitment and emotional labour in the union movement', *Gender, Work & Organization* **7**(4): 258–68.

Fulop, L. and Linstead, S. (1999) 'Managing motivation', in Fulop, L. and Linstead, S. (eds) *Management: A Critical Text*, Melbourne: Macmillan Business.

Fulop, L. and Mortimer, D. (1992) 'Job redesign strategies' in Fulop, L. with Frith, F. and Hayward, H. (eds)

Management for Australian Business: A Critical Text, Melbourne: Macmillan.

Gherardi, S. (1995) *Gender, Symbolism and Organizational Cultures*: London: Sage.

Giddens, A. (1984) *The Constitution of Society: Outline of the Theory of Stratifications*, Berkeley: University of California Press.

Goldthorpe, J., Lockwood, D., Bechofer, F. and Platt, J. (1968) *The Affluent Worker*, Cambridge: Cambridge University Press.

Goski, K.L. and Belfry, M. (1991) 'Achieving competitive advantage through employee participation', *Employment Relations Today*, Summer: 213–20.

Grey, C. and Garsten, C. (2001) 'Trust, control and post-bureaucracy', *Organization Studies: Special Issue: Trust and Control in Organizational Relations*, **22**(2): 229–84.

Hackman, J.R. and Oldham, G. (1975) 'Development of the Job Diagnostic Survey', *Journal of Applied Psychology*, **60**(2): 159–70.

Hackman, J.R. and Oldham, G. (1980) *Work Redesign*, Reading, MA: Addison-Wesley.

Hackman, J.R., Oldham, G., Janson, R. and Purdy, K. (1975) 'A new strategy for job enrichment', *California Management Review*, **17**(4): 57–71.

Hakim, C. (1995) 'Five feminist myths about women's employment', *British Journal of Sociology*, **46**(3): 429–55.

Halachami, A. and Bouckaert, G. (eds) (1995) *Public Productivity Through Quality and Strategic Management*, Amsterdam: IOS Press, and Brussels: International Institute of Administrative Sciences.

Hales, K. (2000) 'Business process modeling and workflow', *Information Management & Technology*, **33**(6): 261–5.

Hall, G., Rosenthal, J. and Wade, J. (1993) 'How to make reengineering really work', *Harvard Business Review*, November–December: 119–31.

Hammer, M. (1990) 'Reeingineering work: Don't automate, obliterate', *Harvard Business Review*, July–August: 104–12.

Hammer, M. and Champy, J. (1993) *Reengineering the Corporation: A Manifesto for Business Revolution*, New York: Harper Business.

Hancock, P. (1999) 'Baudrillard and the metaphysics of motivation: A reappraisal of corporate culturalism in the light of the work and ideas of Jean Baudrillard', *Journal of Management Studies*, **36**(2): 155–75.

Herriot, P., Hirsh, W. and Reilly, P. (1998) *Trust and Transition: Managing Today's Employment Relationship*, Chichester: John Wiley & Sons.

Herriot, P., Manning, N.E.G. and Kidd, J.M. (1997) 'The content of the psychological contract', *British Journal of Management*, **8**: 151–62.

Herzberg, F. (1966) *Work and the Nature of Man*, London: Staples Press.

Herzberg, F. (1987) 'One more time: How do you motivate employees?', *Harvard Business Review,* **46**(1): 109–31.

Hochschild, A.R. (1983) *The Managed Heart*, Berkeley: University of California Press.

Hofstede, G. (1988) 'Motivation, leadership and organisation: Do American theories apply abroad?', *Organizational Dynamics,* **9**: 42–63, reproduced in Lane, H. and di Stefa, J. (eds) *International Management Behaviour: From Policy to Practice*, Scarborough, Ontario: Nelson Canada.

Homans, G.C. (1961) *Social Behavior: Its Elementary Forms*, New York: Harcourt.

Honour, T.F. and Mainwaring, R.M. (1982) *Business and Sociology*, London: Croom Helm.

Horner, M. (1972) 'Toward an understanding of achievement related conflicts in women', *Journal of Social Issues,* **15**: 157–75.

Howe, N. (1997) *The Fourth Turning: An American Prophecy*, New York: Broadway Books.

Hsu, F.L.K. (1971) 'Psychological homeostasis and jen: Conceptual tools of advancing psychological anthropology', *American Anthropologist,* **73**: 23–44.

Jacques, R. (1996) *Manufacturing the Employee: Management Knowledge from the 19th to 21st Centuries*: London: Sage.

Jones, G.R. and George, J.M. (1998) 'The experience and evolution of trust – implications for cooperation and teamwork', *Academy of Management Review,* **23**(3): 531–46.

Juran, J. (1988) *Juran on Planning for Quality*, New York: Collier Macmillan.

Juran, J. (1989) *Juran on Leadership for Quality*, New York: Free Press.

Kanter, R.M. (1977) *Men and Women of the Corporation*, New York: Basic Books.

Kaplan, R.S. and Norton, D.P. (1993) 'The balanced scorecard: Measures that drive performance', *Harvard Business Review,* **70**(1): 71–9.

Kaplan, R.S. and Norton, D.P. (1994) 'Putting the balanced scorecard to work', *Harvard Business Review,* **71**(5): 134–7.

Kelly, J.E. (1982) *Scientific Management, Job Redesign and Work Performance,* London: Academic Press.

Knights, D. and McCabe, D. (1999) '"Are there no limits to authority?" TQM and organizational power', *Organization Studies,* **20**(2): 197–224.

Knights, D. and Willmott, M. (2000) *The Re-engineering Revolution: Critical Studies of Corporate Change*, London: Sage.

Knights, D., Noble, F., Vurdubakis, T. and Willmott, H. (2001) 'Chasing shadows: Control, cirtuality and the production of trust', *Organization Studies: Special Issue: Trust and Control in Organizational Relations,* **22**(2): 311–36.

Lane, C. (1998) 'Introduction: Theories and issues in the study of trust', in Lane, C. and Bachmann, R. (eds) *Trust Within and Between Organizations*. New York: Oxford University Press.

Lansbury, R.D. and Spillane, R. (1983) *Organisational Behaviour in the Australian Context,* Melbourne: Longman Cheshire.

Lichtman, R. (1982) *The Production of Desire: The Integration of Psychoanalysis into Marxism,* New York: Free Press.

Linstead, S.A. (1997) 'Abjection and organization: Men, violence and management', *Human Relations,* **50**(9): 1115–45.

Linstead, S.A. (2002) 'Organizational Kitsch', *Organization,* **9**(4): 657–82.

Linstead, S. and Chan, A. (1994) 'The sting of organization: Command, reciprocity and change management' *Journal of Organization Change Management,* **7**(5): 4–19.

Lorber, J. (1979) 'Trust, loyalty, and the place of women in the informal organization of work', in Freeman, J. (ed.) *Women: A Feminist Perspective* (2nd edn) California: Mayfield Publishing.

Lupton, T. (1971) *Management and the Social Sciences,* Harmondsworth: Penguin.

McClelland, D. (1961) *The Achieving Society*, Princeton: Van Norstrand.

McClelland, D. and Boyatzis, R.E. (1982) 'Leadership motive pattern and long–term success in management', *Journal of Applied Psychology,* **67**: 737–43.

McClelland, D. and Burnham, D.H. (1976) 'Power is the great motivator', *Harvard Business Review,* **54**: 100–10.

McKenna, R. (1999) *New Management*, Sydney: McGraw-Hill.

McKnight, D., Harrison, D., Cummings, L.L. and Chervany, N.L. (1998) 'Initial trust formation in new organizational relationships', *Academy of Management Review,* **23**(3): 473–90.

Mangham, I.L. (1996) 'Beyond Goffman', in Jeffcutt, P., Grafton Small, R. and Linstead, S. (eds) *Organization and Theatre*, special issue of *Studies in Cultures, Organizations, and Societies,* **2**(1): 33–5.

Maslow, A.H. (1943) 'A theory of human motivation', *Psychological Review,* **50**(4): 370–96.

Maslow, A.H. (1965) *Motivation and Personality*, New York: Harper & Row.

Mauss, M. (1990)[1926] *The Gift*, New York: Norton.

Mayer, R.C., Davis, J.H. and Schooram, D.F. (1995) 'An integration model of organizational trust', *Academy of Management Review,* **20**(3): 709–34.

Metters, R. and Vargas, V. (2000) 'Organising work in service firms', *Business Horizons,* **43**(4): 23–33.

Meyer, C. (1994) 'How the right measures help teams excel', *Harvard Business Review,* **72**(3): 95–103.

Miller, E.J. and Rice, A.J. (1967) *Systems of Organ-*

isation: The Control of Tasks and Sentient Boundaries, London: Tavistock.

Mishra, K.E., Spreitzer, G.M. and Mishra, A.K. (1998) 'Preserving employee morale during downsizing', *Sloan Management Review,* Winter: 83–95.

Misztal, B (1996) *Trust in Modern Societies,* Cambridge: Polity Press.

Mitchell, T.R. and Larson, J.R. Jr (1987) *People in Organizations: An Introduction to Organizational Behavior* (3rd edn) New York: McGraw-Hill.

Morrison, W.E. and Robinson, S.L. (1997) 'When employees feel betrayed: A model of how psychological contract violation develops', *Academy of Management Review,* **22**(1): 226–56.

Newell, S. and Swan, J. (2000) 'Trust and inter-organizational networking', *Human Relations,* **53**(10): 1287–320.

Oliver, J. (1993) 'Shocking to the core', *Management Today,* August: 18–21.

Oliver, N. (1990) 'Rewards, investments, alternatives and organizational commitment: Empirical evidence and theoretical development', *Journal of Occupational Psychology,* **63**: 19–31.

Petzall, S.B., Selvarajah, C.T. and Willis, Q.F. (1991) *Management: A Behavioural Approach*, Melbourne: Longman Cheshire.

Prusak, L. and Cohen, D. (2001) 'How to invest in social capital', *Harvard Business Review,* June: 86–93.

Pugh, D.S., Hickson, D.J. and Hinings, C.R. (1983) *Writers on Organizations,* Harmondsworth: Penguin.

Reed, M.I. (2001) 'Organization, trust and contol: Realist analysis', *Organization Studies: Special Issue: Trust and Control in Organizational Relations,* **22**(2): 201–28.

Ring, P.S. (1997) 'Processes facilitating reliance on trust in inter-organizational networks', in Ebers, M. (ed.) *The Formation of Inter-Organizational Networks*, Oxford: Oxford University Press.

Ritzer, G. (1990) *The McDonaldization of Society*, Thousand Oaks, CA: Pine Forge Press.

Ritzer, G. (1999) *Enchanting a Disenchanted World: Revolutionizing the Means of Consumption*, Thousand Oaks, CA: Pine Forge Press.

Rose, M. (1975) *Industrial Behaviour: Theoretical Development Since Taylor,* London: Allen Lane.

Rousseau, D. (1995) *Psychological Contracts in Organization*, London: Sage.

Rousseau, D.H. and McLean Parks, J. (1993) 'The contracts of individuals and organizations', in Cummings, L.L. and Staw, B.M. (eds) *Research in Organizational Behavior*, **15**: 1–47, Greenwich, CT: JAI Press.

Rousseau, D.M., Sitkin, S.B., Burt, R.S. and Camerer, C. (1998) 'Introduction to special topic forum: Not so different after all: A cross-discipline view of trust', *Academy of Management Review,* **23**(3): 393–404.

Salancik, G.R. (1977) 'Commitment and the control of organizational behaviour and belief', in Staw, B.M. and Salancik, G.R. (eds) *New Directions in Organizational Behaviour*, Chicago: St Clair Press.

Schwartz, H.S. (1990) *Narcissistic Process and Corporate Decay*, New York: New York University Press.

Shapiro, S.P. (1987) 'The social control of impersonal trust', *American Journal of Sociology,* **93**(3): 623–58.

Sherman, S. (1994) 'Leaders learn to heed the voice within', *Fortune*, August 22: 72–8.

Siders, M.A., George, G. and Dharwadkar, R. (2001) 'The relationship of internal and external commitment foci to objective job performance', *Academy of Management Review* **44**(3): 570–9.

Sievers, B. (1995) *Work, Death and Life Itself*, Berlin: Walter de Gruyter.

Sims, D., Fineman, S. and Gabriel, Y. (1993) *Organizing and Organizations: An Introduction*, London: Sage.

Singh, V, and Vinnicombe, S. (2000) 'Gendered meanings of commitment from high technology engineering managers in the United Kingdom and Sweden', *Gender, Work & Organization*, **7**(1): 1–19.

Snyder, M. (1979) 'Self–monitoring processes', in Berkowitz, L. (ed.) *Advances in Experimental Social Psychology* 12, New York: Academic Press.

Spencer, B.A. (1994) 'Models of organization and total quality management: A comparison and critical evaluation', *Academy of Management Review*, **19**(3): 446–71.

Stewart, T.A. (1994) 'Your company's most valuable asset: Intellectual capital', *Fortune,* 3 October: 34–6, 40–2.

Strauss, G. (1976) 'Job satisfaction, motivation, and job redesign', in Strauss, G., Miles, R.E., Snow, C.C. and Tannenbaum, A.S. (eds) *Organizational Behavior: Research and Issues*, Belmont, CA: Wadsworth.

Trethewey, A. (1999) 'Disciplined bodies: women's embodied identities at work', *Organization Studies,* **20**(3): 423–50.

Trist, E.L. and Bamforth, K.W. (1951) 'Some social and psychological consequences of the long-wall method of coal-mining', *Human Relations,* **4**(1): 3–38.

Turner, J.H. (1987) 'Toward a sociological theory of motivation', *American Sociological Review,* **52**: 15–27.

Tye, L. (1995) *The Father of Spin: Edward L. Bernays And The Birth Of Public Relations,* New York: Crown Publishers.

Ulrich, D. (1998) 'Intellectual capital = competence × commitment', *Sloan Management Review,* winter: 15–26.

Usher J.M. (2000) 'Dust in the Wind: A Lesson from Maslow's Monkeys', *Academy of Management Review,* **25**(4): 700–1 October.

Walton, R.E. (1985) 'From control to commitment in the workplace', *Harvard Business Review,* March–April: 76–84.

Weick, K.E. (1995) *Sensemaking in Organizations*, London: Sage.

Wekselberg, V. (1996) 'Reduced "social" in a new model of organizational trust', *Academy of Management Review,* **21**(2): 333–5.

Westwood, R. (1992) *Organizational Behaviour: South-East Asian Perspectives*, Hong Kong: Longman.

Whitehead, S. (2001) 'Woman as manager: A seductive ontology', *Gender, Work & Organization,* **8**(1): 84–107.

Whitener, E.M., Brodt, S.E., Korsgaard, M.A. and Werner, J.M. (1998) 'Managers as initiators of trust: An exchange relationship framework for understanding managerial trustworthy behavior', *Academy of Management Review* **23**(3): 513–30.

Williams, M. (2001) 'In whom we trust: Group membership as an affective context for trust development', *Academy of Management Review,* **26**(3): 377–98.

Wilson, F. (1995) *Organisational Behaviour and Gender*, London: McGraw-Hill.

Witz, A., Warhurst, C. and Nickson, D. (2001) 'The labour of aesthetics and the aesthetics of organisation', paper presented at the Critical Management Studies Conference, University of Manchester, Manchester, UK, 11–13 July.

Womack, J.P., Jones, D.T. and Roos, D. (1990) *The Massachusetts Institute of Technology 5 Million Dollar 5 Year Study on the Future of the Automobile Industry*, New York: Rawson Associates.

Yang, K.S. (1981) 'Social orientation and individual modernity amongst Chinese students in Taiwan', *Journal of Social Psychology,* **113**: 159–70.

Yang, K.S. (1982) 'The Sinicization of psychological research in a Chinese society: Directions and issues', in Yang, K.S. and Wen, C.I. (eds) *The Sinicization of Social and Behavioural Science Research in China*, Taipei: Institute of Ethnology, Academic Sinica.

Yang, K.S. (1986) 'Chinese personality and its change', in Bond, M.H. (ed.) *The Psychology of the Chinese People,* Hong Kong: Oxford University Press.

Yu, E.S.H. (1974) 'Achievement motive, familism, and Hsiao: A replication of McClelland-Winterbottom Studies', *Dissertation Abstracts International*, **35**, 593A, University Microfilms, 74–14, 942.

Yu, W. (1991) 'Motivational and demotivational factors in enterprises', *Chinese Journal of Applied Psychology,* **6**(1): 5–14.

Zucker, L.G. (1986) 'Production of trust; institutional sources of economic structure, 1840–1920', *Research in Organizational Behavior,* **8**: 60–111.

CHAPTER 10

Leading and managing

Liz Fulop, Stephen Linstead and Richard Dunford

Questions about leadership

1 What is a leader?
2 Are all managers leaders?
3 Are women and men different as leaders?
4 Can leaders change their styles or behaviours?
5 Do we need leaders?

THE FLYING DUTCHMAN

Ruud Gullit was one of the most successful European footballers ever, having led with great skill the Dutch team which brought 'total football' to its peak in the 1980s and being recognized as Europe's Player of the Year. A popular and attractive figure, stylish and articulate, he was made for media celebrity. He took over as manager of Newcastle United Football Club (NUFC) at the beginning of the 1998–99 season, following two successful years in charge as player-manager at Chelsea. During his time in London he steered the Blues to victory in the FA Cup and a sixth place finish in the Premier League – this at a club which had achieved little for some twenty years. NUFC, likewise, had flirted with success over the previous decade in particular, but at the time of Gullit's arrival had not won any trophies since the Inter-Cities Fairs' Cup (now the UEFA Cup) in 1969:

> Yes there were the ups of the Nineties, the romance of the Kevin Keegan (former manager) years, the coup of signing Alan Shearer and the mass blubfests after losing vital games to Manchester United and Liverpool, but the trophy cupboard has been bare for 30 years. (Wilson 1999a: 4)

Moreover, this flirtation had been achieved at an extraordinary financial cost, mostly involving massive cash injections by the Hall family who were the major shareholders. The pressure for Gullit to deliver clear-cut success was therefore enormous – and was made worse by NUFC's entry on to the alternative investment market of the stock exchange.

Gullit's achievements and standing as a player are a matter of record and at Chelsea his skills had been regularly displayed for an English football audience, not just highlighted in the occasional international match for Holland or AC Milan. This made him very different from the previous two Newcastle managers (Kevin Keegan and Kenny Dalglish). Although both still enjoy legendary status among the English football-watching public – and their counterparts elsewhere in the world – Keegan and Dalglish's playing careers were very definitely in the past. Gullit was also decidedly different in terms of his race, his background and his ability to market himself:

> The dreadlocked figure of Ruud Gullit disembarked from an Amsterdam flight promising the return of 'sexy football' to Tyneside. Whatever the future held, it would not be dull. (Hutchinson 1997: 240)

> Black, Dutch and the epitome of cool, Gullit is a master of six languages … he wasn't slow to appreciate his marketing appeal. Utterly at home in front of the camera, with discreet good tailoring and a relaxed, intelligent manner, Gullit knocked the spots off cliché ridden football commentary. (Lindsey 1998: 7)

But by August 1999 – just 366 days into his tenure – it was all over for Gullit and NUFC: he resigned. What exactly had gone so badly wrong?

At both Chelsea and Newcastle, Gullit introduced a system of squad rotation – a system which other clubs have used but in the UK only Manchester United appear to practise with complete success. He argued that it kept players' legs and minds fresh and that, given the number of matches which Premier League clubs face – the domestic league, two domestic cups and (for some) European competitions, as well as international commitments for many players – rotation was particularly important in order to rest players and have slack in the system to cover for the inevitable injuries. But squad rotation is unpopular with many players and if a player is to be dropped for a specific game, then a careful and sensitive approach by the manager is required. Many managers insist on being the one to tell a player that he has been left out and explaining why, especially because of the very real danger that this may pose to the player's career, their chance of international recognition and so on. Every football game – in the top flight in particular – is a chance for players to perform – literally and metaphorically. Players view games as self-marketing opportunities; to prove their worth to their club and/or other clubs, especially now that international transfers are so commonplace. So if a player does not play (or if he does not play well), then ultimately his tenure at a club, as well as his opportunities to move elsewhere and command higher wages and more prestige as a result, are at risk.

But Gullit did not explain to his players why they had been dropped. He did not even tell them himself when he left them out. Instead, at Chelsea and then again at NUFC, he left them to find out by reading the team sheet, expecting them to work it out for themselves. He also intimated to his players that, if they did not like his system, then they could request a transfer. Gullit's treatment of Gianluca Vialli in particular (who, ironically, replaced him as manager) attracted critical attention during his reign at Stamford Bridge, and he repeated the pattern at St James' Park. In an interview, former NUFC captain Robert Lee said:

> I wasn't one of Ruud's lovely boys ... [but] we didn't have a massive row. We had disagreements rather than rows. The problem was that, because I was the captain, I was the one player he really talked to. At the start, I thought Ruud liked me, we seemed to get on, but he didn't like being disagreed with and, as captain, my job was to put forward the players' viewpoint. By the end, he didn't speak to me at all. He didn't want me anywhere near the training ground. (Taylor 2000: 3)

As Lee himself testifies, the stripping of his captaincy and Gullit's subsequent refusal to give him a squad number served to unite public opinion against the manager. Also evident in his comments is the way in which Gullit behaved towards Alan Shearer, the local boy who was the club's star player and the England captain:

> Ruud didn't realize that I'd played for Newcastle for seven years, and that counted for something ... I think he wanted the supporters to love him more than Alan [Shearer], but he didn't realise the exceptional support Alan has here ... in the end they showed they loved Alan more ... He wanted the fans to love him more than any player. He couldn't accept that Alan was a local hero. (Taylor 2000: 3)

Shearer, a lifelong NUFC devotee, brought back to his northeast origins by Gullit's predecessor Kevin Keegan, is hero-worshipped in the region. He succeeded Lee as club captain. Moreover, Shearer had established himself at club and national levels to such an extent that he was regarded as an automatic selection both for NUFC and England. But before Gullit even joined NUFC, he publicly criticized their expensive purchase of Shearer – which at the time set a national record of £15 million – as being 'a crazy price, a waste of money' (Walker 1998: 1). He went on to describe Shearer as follows in his first press conference at the club:

> Shearer's an out-and-out goalscorer but he doesn't seem to get any joy from the game if he fails to hit the target. I prefer players who contribute in other areas and have a sense of fun ... Alan is the captain of the national team and scores a lot of goals ... he is important but a whole lot of players are important for the team. Nobody is more important than anybody else. (Walker 1998: 1)

Gullit went on to drop Shearer. Eventually he dropped him for a rainswept derby against hated local rivals Sunderland – the fervent rivalry between the two cities is legendary inside and outside football and dates back to the English Civil War in the seventeenth century – brought him on with only minutes of the match to go and then blamed Shearer and his fellow substitute Duncan Ferguson for the subsequent defeat. This was, furthermore, only one in a disastrous series of results which had seen NUFC slip to one place above the bottom of the Premier League, having taken just a single point from a possible fifteen. The bitter pill was made even harsher by the fact that Sunderland's star striker, Kevin Phillips, who scored the winning goal in the game, had been the apprentice who cleaned Shearer's boots when they were both at Southampton. As if to add insult to injury, Gullit had also suggested that the derby game wasn't even a proper derby because Sunderland fans and Newcastle fans live and work in different cities.

Gullit was also a 'semi-detached' manager. He never settled in the northeast and instead commuted to St James' Park from Amsterdam on a regular basis. In a climate where club support still runs broadly speaking along geographical lines, and especially in a football-obsessed area like Newcastle, this could be seen as a serious tactical error on his part: English managers are expected, by both fans and players, to be totally focused on their work, to literally sleep, breathe and eat football. Instead Gullit left his NUFC charges 'home alone'. Moreover, his implied criticism of the area in not relocating there – apparently his partner did not like Newcastle – went down badly with the fans, who are very proud of their town and its heritage, and indeed its more recent stylishness. He had been subject to censure at Chelsea for similar reasons:

> word leaked from the [Stamford] Bridge [Chelsea's headquarters] that he really wasn't that involved, [Graham] Rix and the backroom boys did everything; Gullit was just a figurehead. Again most of the lads in the stand would hardly have accepted that as sufficient grounds for a P45 [tax statement given on termination of employment, usually indicating the sack]; if he had done nothing else it was his presence which had delivered [Gianluca] Vialli, [Gianfranco] Zola and [Roberto] Di Matteo. But then came the crunch ... Gullit didn't care enough. He was only interested in the club as a vehicle for his own ego ... For the fan this is a crime deserving of punishment much greater than redundancy. Not caring about the club: that is the charge levelled at those asset strippers of Brighton and Doncaster [clubs who have now left the football league]. (White 1998: 25)

> Ammunition for the criticism that Ruud Gullit is a 'semi-detached' manager of Newcastle has been supplied a day after the club's stormy annual meeting with the Dutchman on a seven-day family break in Amsterdam. (Thomas 1998: 22)

the Dutchman's managerial reputation is in tatters [after his resig-nation from NUFC], with the same accusations of aloofness, complacency and poor man-management pursuing him from both his English clubs. (Wilson 1999b: 9)

So in the August of 1999, Gullit was manager of a team which was staring relegation in the face after only a handful of games. He had also managed to alienate two local heroes as well as other fans' favourites such as Dietmar Hamann, David Batty and Keith Gillespie, who all moved to play for other competing big-name clubs (Walker 1999). Furthermore, the signings he made – the big injury-prone Scottish striker Duncan Ferguson and moody Croatian inter-national midfielder Silvio Maric, for example – had failed to match those he had attracted at Chelsea or perform with any consistency. Moreover, he had few laurels to rest on: NUFC had finished a disappointing thirteenth in the league

the previous season and, despite reaching the FA Cup final for the second year in succession, had been humiliated at Wembley by a rampant Manchester United. Scarcely surprising, then, that he jumped rather than being pushed just three days after the ill-fated derby, that he was not given the traditional training ground farewell by the players and that he was subsequently replaced by 'Uncle Bobby' – local lad Bobby Robson, former NUFC player and England manager, and another lifelong fan of the Magpies. By Christmas 2001 they were heading the Premiership once more, at the end of 2001–2 season finished 4th with a place in European competition and heading the top scorers in the Premiership was the veteran Shearer.

Source: Adapted from Sarah Gilmore (2001) 'Mothers, babies and football managers', paper presented to 2nd Conference on Critical Management Studies, University of Manchester.

QUESTIONS ABOUT THE CASE

1 How would you characterize Ruud Gullit's leadership style?
2 What considerations seem to be most important to Gullit?
3 What kind of relationships would you expect Gullit to have with
   (a) his players?
   (b) the fans?
   (c) the board of directors?
4 How do you think Gullit would think that it is appropriate to develop future football managers?
5 How would you characterize the leadership approach at NUFC?
6 What culture or gender influences could have been operating in this situation?

Introduction

It is worth reflecting on the fascination we have with the quest for great leaders. All societies look for great leaders or at least often like to think of their history in terms of how leadership played an important part, especially in times of war and crisis. However, the media increasingly draw attention to the failures and follies of our once most respected leaders, so much so that finding a truly great leader seems impossible. Early theories of leadership assumed that the qualities which made great military, social and political leaders were also those which would make great industrial leaders, forgetting that business leaders were often singularly focused on profit regardless of the other consequences of their actions. The thinking on leadership seems to change almost every decade and, increasingly, the concept has become contested with leadership associated with both negative and positive behaviours. 'Good' or 'bad' leadership means different things to different people. Cruel and despotic behaviour can characterize the leadership style of one individual while another leader may develop a style based on kindness

and benevolence. In either case, the leader is able to influence and persuade others to follow them. The contemporary spectacle of corporate failures and the fallout of corporate greed and excess, particularly in the US, has seen some of the hero CEOs of the 1990s facing public outrage, government scrutiny and even imprisonment, as the legacy of their era of massive salaries and benefits, the often illusory pursuit of shareholder value and questionable ethical practices.

Often, leadership is associated with great political figures who inspire others because of their extraordinary vision or commitment to high ideals. These leaders seem to embody the most desirable and sought-after characteristics: they are people who are able to command loyalty, commitment, trust, dedication, respect, obedience, love or even worship from their followers. In the extreme, some followers are prepared to lay down their lives for their leader or the leader's cause. This quality of leadership seems far removed from many workplaces. Yet one of the most significant claims of the human relations movement (see Chapters 2 and 11) was that leadership at the supervisory level was the single most important factor in motivating employees and improving productivity. Early leadership studies focused attention on finding a 'one best way' style of leadership appropriate for shop-floor or supervisory conditions. A major aim of these studies was the development of training programmes to assist managers to become good or effective leaders. However, once leadership studies moved beyond supervisory levels, a more complex picture emerged, one in which leadership became associated with communication, influence and visionary qualities. In fact, leadership is a fundamental component of many theories of organization and management.

This chapter presents an overview of the way leadership has been analysed and assesses its relevance to claims about managerial performance, beginning with some very early, but nonetheless influential theories, and moving on to studies questioning the role of leadership in organizations. The 'dark' side of leadership – a topic often omitted from management texts – is also examined in the context of the narcissistic leader. We also include gender and cross-cultural considerations of leadership, carrying on themes developed in our earlier chapters.

The trait approach

The most basic approach to understanding leadership began from the assumption that good leadership resides in the innate abilities of certain individuals who are considered to be born leaders – usually 'great men' of history such as Bonaparte, Churchill, Gandhi and so on. Often, however, leadership qualities were simply associated with being very rich, famous and powerful, and in the US management literature they were made synonymous with great industrialists such as Dale Carnegie, Henry Ford, and Alfred Sloan (of GM). As the practice of industrial psychology developed, greater emphasis was placed on identifying the very specific characteristics or traits that constitute the behaviour of good leaders, and examining the common factors. *Trait theory*, as it became known, was particularly popular because it offered ways to measure the strength of leadership qualities. However, it was bedevilled by the fact that it is not easy to define traits or qualities of leadership that are actually those which people are born with as distinct from those they acquire or, for that matter, those which are applicable in all situations (that is, are universal). The traits mentioned in Exhibit 10.1 below are qualities which research has indicated can be associated with good leadership, although none of these are necessarily those with which leaders are born. The trait approaches are decidedly masculine and heroic in their assumptions, often glorifying quite brutal, uncaring behaviour, such as in the 'strong man' model described below.

One of the attractions of the approach was that it promised that good leadership would be guaranteed by selecting individuals with the appropriate positive traits for the role, but it also assumed that leaders are born more than they are made. But when transferred into the management context, the notion of the 'born leader' is difficult to put into practice. Fundamentally, trait theory assumes that we cannot train managers to be leaders and the concept of leadership and management are inextricably separate activities, entailing different qualities. In many organizations, it also disguises how founders, who are often entrepreneurs, rise to lead companies using qualities that are far from those associated with great political leaders. As noted by Liz Fulop et al. (1999: 162; see also Dunford 1992: 57):

The interest in leadership traits developed as part of the personnel testing movement in the period immediately following the First World War. Wartime use of psychological testing for the selection of military personnel was followed by industrial applications of similar techniques. Leadership research developed as part of this (Stogdill 1974a). However, there is a notable lack of evidence for a certain trait or set of traits being universally appropriate in all situations (Stogdill 1974b; Spillane 1984). Even if it was accepted, for example, that Gandhi, the charismatic leader from India who in the 1940s led the independence movement, was a born leader, it is impossible to establish that his qualities would create effective leadership in another culture or society.

However, Shelley Kirkpatrick and Edwin Locke (1991), in reviewing recent research on traits, found that certain traits do appear to have a consistent impact on leader effectiveness. These traits include those listed in Exhibit 10.1. Nevertheless, there is no fixed set of traits that constitutes good leadership. The traits in Exhibit 10.1 can be found in a variety of mixes in effective leaders in practice and it is difficult to distinguish between some of them and acquired skills or behaviours. Are we born with all these traits or are some of them attained through learning, experience and relationships?

Charles Manz and Henry Sims (1992: 310–11) suggested that a variation on the 'great man' model of leadership was the 'strong man' one. Deliberately masculine in its assumptions, this form of leadership was reserved for males. It glorified the tough, head-kicking image of authority in which the leader had superior strengths, skills and the courage to size up the situation, take decisive action and command the troops. Reprimands (head-kicking or 'kick-ass') and punishment followed non-compliance by subordinates. The authors suggested that while this leadership approach might seem out of favour, there was still much evidence of it in corporate America (and no doubt elsewhere).

Exhibit 10.1 **Common leader traits**

❏ **Drive**
- high desire for achievement
- ambition to get ahead in work and career
- high level of energy
- tenacity or persistence in the right things
- initiative to change things and make things happen

❏ **Leadership motivation**
- the desire to lead
- the willingness to assume responsibility
- the seeking of power as a means to achieve desired goals (*socialized power motive*) rather than as an end in itself (*personalized power motive*)

❏ **Honesty and integrity**
- the correspondence between word and deed
- being trustworthy
- the foundation to attract and retain followers through gaining their trust

❏ **Self-confidence**
- needed to withstand setbacks, persevere through hard times and lead others in new directions
- the ability to take hard decisions and stand by them
- managing the perceptions of others on self-confidence, and commanding their respect
- emotionally stable

❏ **Cognitive ability**
- above-average intelligence to analyse situations accurately, solve problems effectively, and make suitable decisions
- not necessarily a genius, usually not
- managing the perceptions of others on intelligence

❏ **Knowledge of the business**
- able to gather and assimilate extensive information about the company and industry
- necessary for developing suitable visions, strategies and business plans

Source: Shelley Kirkpatrick and Edwin A. Locke (1991) 'Leadership: Do traits matter?', *Academy of Management Executive,* **5**(2), pp. 48–60.

Leadership style – it's not what you do, it's the way that you do it

Although there was some agreement by researchers on the broad family of traits that leaders were likely to possess, there was no stable group of traits which could be identified as characteristic of all leaders. If successful leaders could not therefore be identified through testing for traits, then research needed to focus on what leaders did and how, to determine desired leadership behaviours. Being a leader then became not a question of the leader's personal qualities, but how leaders act.

Much of the research which took place between and after the two world wars showed a concern with whether leaders were dictatorial, exclusive and authoritarian in their approach, or consultative, inclusive and democratic/participative in style. While it is easy to oversimplify, authoritarian approaches were frequently associated with scientific management and the work-measurement approaches to management, while the human relations movement was often associated with the more participative styles of leadership because of its emphasis on interpersonal relations. Both cases are probably overstated, as more recent work on the labour process under both Taylorism and human relations regimes would suggest (see

Chapters 2 and 11). Researchers in either camp were capable of assuming that one or the other style was the best, regardless of the circumstances. This tendency to dualistic thinking is not confined to management thought, but this either/or logic has proved seductive to both scholars and practitioners, often to the detriment of theories which were not originally intended to be as black and white as they were interpreted. The style theory we will discuss next is a typical example.

McGregor's Theory X and Theory Y

Building on the work of Maslow (see Chapter 9) on motivation theory and self-actualization, Douglas McGregor (1960) argued that managers tended to hold one of two sets of assumptions about work and employees which were implicit in their leadership behaviours. McGregor argued that one could infer from certain managers' treatment of their employees that they believed that:

- The average human being has an inherent dislike of work and will avoid it if possible.
- Because of this most people must be coerced, controlled, directed and threatened with punishment

to put adequate effort into the achievement of organizational objectives.

- The average human being prefers to be directed, wishes to avoid responsibility, has relatively little ambition and wants security above all (McGregor 1960: 33–4).

Clearly, managers who held these beliefs could have little understanding of even the lower levels of Maslow's theory of motivation. Indeed, their actions were likely to become self-fulfilling and remove all possibility of change, as workers treated in this way would be quite likely to acquire appropriate behaviours and beliefs themselves. Workers who were managed as though they were irresponsible, and thus never given any opportunity to exercise responsibility, would be likely to assume that taking responsibility was not rewarded or even permissible, and would therefore display no signs of wishing to assume it. This set of assumptions, which McGregor termed *Theory X*, was, he believed, one of the major problems with US management practices of the time. By treating them as uncooperative, lacking in initiative, unimaginative and irresponsible, McGregor felt that US management was producing a workforce which was indeed uncooperative, lacking in initiative, unimaginative and irresponsible.

While McGregor acknowledged that Theory X might be acceptable in times of economic crisis and recession, he felt it was always a regressive style, and that, under conditions of anything less than duress, management styles needed to display an awareness that workers wanted and needed more than wages, benefits and security and sought recognition and opportunities for self-improvement in their work. He termed the more progressive style *Theory Y* (McGregor 1960: 47–8):

- Work is as natural as rest or play.
- External control and threat of punishment are not the only means for bringing about effort towards organizational objectives. People will exercise self-direction and self-control in the service of objectives to which they are committed.
- Commitment to objectives is a function of the rewards associated with their achievement.
- The average human being learns under proper conditions not only to accept but to seek responsibility.
- The capacity to exercise a relatively high degree of imagination, ingenuity and creativity in the solution of organizational problems is widely, not narrowly, distributed in the population.
- In most work organizations, the abilities of most employees are only partially utilized.

Theory Y implies that problems of a lazy uncooperative workforce are not the problems of the workforce, which is what Theory X assumed, but the problems of management, and the management practices which made the workers that way. A Theory Y regime would be consultative with employees, seek and value their opinions and might even explore various forms of participative decision making. Rather than tight, external and measured controls, self-direction, autonomy and group control were recommended. McGregor was clear that a style of mutuality, which was participative, consultative and democratic was the one best way to manage in almost all circumstances. As noted by Fulop et al. (1999: 165; also Dunford 1992: 59):

The validity of McGregor's approach is rather difficult to assess, however, because it is more a philosophical stance than a coherent set of conclusions drawn from specific research data. Stephen Robbins (1988) claims that there is a lack of evidence that actions consistent with Theory Y assumptions lead to more motivated workers, a view shared by Tony Watson (1986), although the latter does argue that McGregor's work is beneficial to the extent that it invites managers to think about the behavioural assumptions they make in their dealings with subordinates.

Still, many managers easily identify with the Theory X and Y distinction and its normative view of 'good' and 'bad' leadership.

The Ohio State studies

Where McGregor's position was more of a moral and philosophical one, empirically grounded studies of leadership style have focused, in one way or another, on whether leaders behave as though they are concerned more with *task accomplishment* (often associated with Theory X) and *concern for subordinates* (often associated with Theory Y) rather than questioning leaders' motivational assumptions.

During the 1940s, pioneering research was undertaken at Ohio State University, Columbus, in the USA. Subordinates' assessments of their leaders' behaviour were analysed and deemed to be reducible to two core dimensions. The first, *consideration*, refers to the extent to which an individual is likely to encourage and develop job relationships characterized by mutual trust, respect for subordinates' ideas and concern for their feelings. The second, *initiating structure*, refers to the extent to which leaders are likely to define and structure their role and those of subordinates towards the attainment of formal organizational goals (Fleishman and Peters 1962; Stogdill 1974b: 128–41).

The Ohio State researchers argued that:

- High 'consideration' was associated with higher subordinate satisfaction.

- High 'initiating structure' was associated with greater effectiveness, higher grievance levels and higher absenteeism.
- Leaders could be rated high or low on both dimensions. When a leader was rated high on both, the high grievance levels did not occur.

The Ohio results were interpreted as indicating that the ideal leader would be high on both dimensions, although subsequently critics have argued against this interpretation (Korman, 1966). A complementary set of studies based around research at the University of Michigan in the USA differentiated *production-centred* and *employee-centred* managers. The former were characterized by rigid work standards, detailed task organization and close supervision; the latter involved the encouragement of participation in workplace practices, trust and respect (Likert 1961). Very similar in orientation to the Ohio studies, its findings were much the same, with a high ranking on both criteria being seen as ideal.

Subsequent studies have tended to confirm the conclusions of the Ohio State and Michigan University studies, although with slight variations on the themes and variables examined (Vecchio et al. 1996: 481–6).

Blake's grid

A widely used approach (in more arenas than simply work performance), which focuses on style and uses an extended version of the production–employee-centred theme, is the *leadership grid approach* developed initially by Robert Blake and Jane Mouton (1978). This

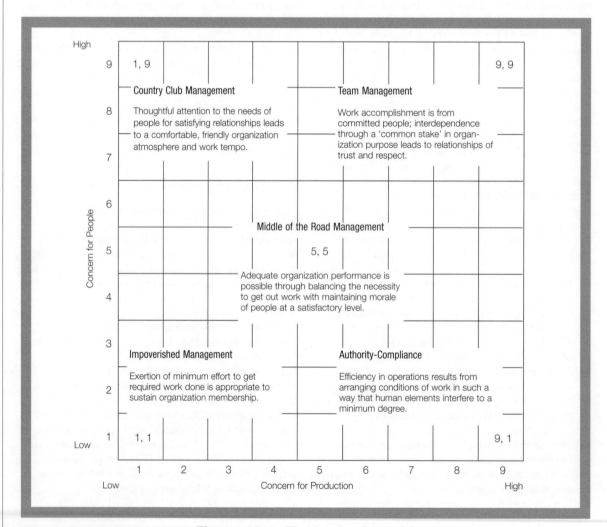

Figure 10.1 The leadership grid

Source: Robert R. Blake and Anne Adams McCanse (1991) *Leadership Dilemmas – Grid Solutions*, Houston: Gulf, p. 29. Copyright © 1991, by Scientific Methods, Inc. Reproduced by permission of the owners.

was subsequently refined by Blake and Anne McCanse (1991). It was devised with management training in mind and easily adapted to take them through a series of stages towards the most effective leadership style. This style (9, 9 in Figure 10.1) involves maximizing concern for both production and people, with these two factors being seen as interdependent, rather than being treated as independent (or as separate dimensions), as they were in the Ohio studies and Theory X and Theory Y.

Blake and Mouton's management grid, originally developed in the 1960s, identified four factors, while the Blake and McCanse version identifies five basic combinations of concern for people and concern for production, using a scale of 1–9 for each factor. These five factors are described in Figure 10.1 above.

The leadership grid approach, with its arguments in favour of the team management style, fitted in well with the human relations notion that productivity and satisfaction could be mutually optimized. However, empirical support for the universal application of their model is at best mixed (see for example Larson et al. 1976; Bryman 1986). Furthermore, Blake and Mouton, in advocating a preferred leadership style in all situations, also espoused 'one best way' to manage or lead.

Likert's System 4 approach

The *System 4 approach* developed by Rensis Likert (1961, 1967, 1979) is based on four kinds of management systems, as described below:

- *System 1 Exploitative authoritative*: where leadership is autocratic, incorporating punishment-centred motivation, minimal delegation, minimal information provision to subordinates and decision making by edict.
- *System 2 Benevolent authoritative*: use of rewards to motivate but no less centralization of decision making than in System 1.
- *System 3 Consultative*: subordinates are consulted over decisions; some trust and teamwork exist.
- *System 4 Participative*: high level of trust and confidence; decision making through participation; communication/information flows upwards, downwards and laterally.

Likert developed his model by surveying over two hundred organizations in an attempt to isolate their performance characteristics. Later he used his classification to look at a broad range of organizational activities, including leadership, motivation, communication, interaction and influence, decision making, goal setting and control processes. Likert surveyed several hundred managers and claimed to have found that the least productive departments or

units equated with systems 1 and 2, and the more productive with systems 3 and 4. A participative style of leadership (that is, system 4) was found to be superior in terms of high productivity and quality and fostering loyalty and cooperation among subordinates (Mullins 1985: 149). System 4 is another version of the 'one best way' approach to leadership and is very similar in concept to Theory Y. Systems 1 and 2 leadership bear some relationship to Theory X.

Contingency approaches: from best way to best fit

The approaches we have discussed so far are problematic insofar as they concentrate to the point of obsession on variations in the styles of leaders – and these variations are seen as being atemporal. Thus they fail to take into account the possibility of the significance of the *situation* or *context* in which the leader is operating. In attempting to overcome this inadequacy, contingency approaches to leadership seek to systematize the relationship between situation and leadership style. That is, they attempt to identify particular contextual situations and determine the style of leadership most appropriate for each. Nevertheless, *contingency theory* is normative, as it is based on the assumption that for a given situation there will be one identifiably best leadership style.

Matching leader and situation

The classic contingency study is that of Fred Fiedler (1967, 1974). His contingency theory involves the identification of leaders as either *relationship-centred* or *task-centred*, thus continuing the duality of styles present in the previous style studies. However, in Fiedler's schema no style is best under all circumstances, and he adopted a controversial methodology to explore it. An individual's leadership style is assessed on the basis of the *Least-preferred Co-worker* (LPC) scale or coefficient. This involves the individual thinking of the person that he or she least enjoyed working with and then characterizing him or her in terms of a set of bipolar adjectives, for example 'pleasant–unpleasant', 'friendly–unfriendly'. On the basis of an individual's answers on the LPC scale, he or she is characterized as relationship- or task-oriented. An individual who has a high score (64 and above) is strongly relationship-oriented, while a person with a low score (57 or below) will be task-oriented.

Fiedler argued that a low LPC score, for example, indicated that the person, when given the choice, would opt for getting the job done rather than worrying about developing good interpersonal relations. A relationship-motivated or high LPC leader accomplishes tasks through good interpersonal relations and in situations that involve a whole group performing tasks. The relationship-motivated leader may perform poorly under pressure or stress because of his or her propensity to pay attention to interpersonal relations rather than the task. Alternatively, the task-motivated or low LPC leader is strongly committed to completing the task through adopting clear, standardized procedures and a no-nonsense attitude to getting the job done. Under pressure or when the situation is out of control, the task-motivated leader will put the task ahead of the group's feelings and pursue its accomplishment at all costs (Fiedler et al. 1976: 6–11).

The situation determining leadership style is analysed in terms of three aspects: *leader–member relations*, *task structure* and *leader's position power*. Leader–member relations refers to how well leaders get on with their subordinates, how well they are respected or trusted. Task structure is a measure of how clearly the task is specified (for example highly structured and detailed). The leader's position power is a measure of the formal authority of leaders and their capacity to exercise authority through rewards or punishments. Collectively,

these three factors are termed the 'favourability of the situation'. In the most favourable situations there is little need for relationship-focused activities, since relationships are already good. In this situation, the task-centred leader performs best. On the other hand, in an unfavourable situation, the relationship-centred leader may give insufficient attention to task-related problems. In this situation, the task-motivated leader also comes to the fore. The task-oriented leader operates best at these extremes. In the 'middle', that is, where the situation is moderately favourable and the external pressures are not so pronounced, the skills of the relationship-centred leader come into their own in providing the drive and energy for action through activating the personal motivations of the group (see Figure 10.2).

An example of situation 1 leadership in Figure 10.2 would be a popular squad leader in the army. The member–leader relations are good, especially because expertise and experience are highly regarded, the task is structured and position power is very strong. In this situation, Fiedler's model suggests that a task-oriented leader would be most effective. Situation 5 leadership is

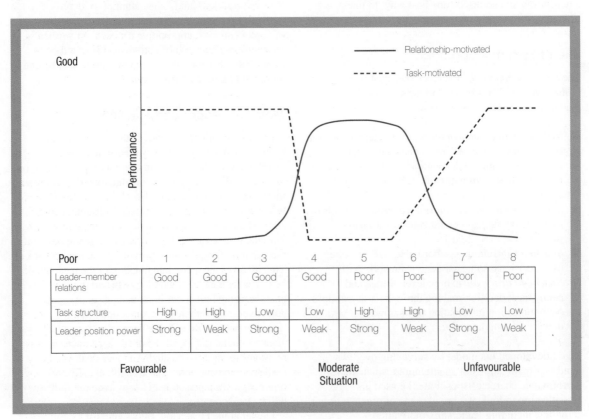

	1	2	3	4	5	6	7	8
Leader–member relations	Good	Good	Good	Good	Poor	Poor	Poor	Poor
Task structure	High	High	Low	Low	High	High	Low	Low
Leader position power	Strong	Weak	Strong	Weak	Strong	Weak	Strong	Weak

Favourable   Moderate   Unfavourable
                                   Situation

Figure 10.2 The performance of relationship- and task-motivated leaders in different situational-favourable conditions

Source: Fred E. Fiedler (1974) 'The contingency model – new directions for leadership utilisation', *Journal of Contemporary Business*, **3**, Autumn, p. 71.

where a person occupies an unpopular position, such as a shop-floor supervisor, and while authority can be wielded it will not often succeed in gaining cooperation. In this situation, the relationship-oriented leader is likely to achieve continuous support and compliance (Duncan 1978: 232–3).

Unlike the stance taken by theorists such as Likert or Blake and Mouton, Fiedler is not confident that a person's leadership style can be changed by training. In effect, if you have to change the task, you are more likely to get results by also changing the leader or the situational conditions (Fiedler et al. 1976). Leader–member relations might, for example, be changed through such things as increasing informal or social interaction with subordinates or showing greater appreciation for their efforts. Task structure might be modified by such things as delegating more (or less) decision making to subordinates. Position power can be altered by such strategies as giving more (or less) authority to subordinates or by increasing (or decreasing) subordinates' access to information.

Despite its classic status, Fiedler's study has been subject to considerable criticism. This includes the claims that the LPC measure corresponds poorly with subordinates' accounts of leader behaviour; that the LPC score for an individual often varies over time; and that there has been a failure to replicate results (Bryman 1985, 1986). However, Fiedler disputes these criticisms, arguing that the LPC score is 'a highly reliable and surprisingly stable measure' (Fiedler and Garcia 1987: 79) and that the weight of evidence clearly attests to the validity of the model (Fiedler and Garcia 1987: 86–93). Some organizational behaviour texts do note that there has been some dispute over the validity of Fiedler's approach (Stoner et al. 1985; Hellriegel et al. 1986), but others simply treat it as an uncontested classic study (Hunsaker and Cook 1986).

Path–goal theory

Path–goal theory, developed by Robert House (1971) and others (Evans 1970), proposes that leaders can affect the job satisfaction, motivation and performance of group members by their actions. One way is to make rewards dependent on the meeting of performance goals, but the leader can also help the subordinates to achieve these goals by outlining the paths towards the goals and by removing obstacles in their way. This may entail the leader adopting different styles of leadership according to the situation. The theory identifies four different types of behaviour:

1. *Directive leadership* – giving specific guidance to subordinates and asking them to follow standard rules and regulations. Shows low consideration for people, but high regard for task and structure.

2. *Supportive leadership* – includes being friendly to subordinates and sensitive to their needs. Shows high consideration for people and low regard for task and structure.
3. *Participative leadership* – involves sharing information with subordinates and consulting with them before making decisions. Shows high concern for both structure and consideration.
4. *Achievement-oriented leadership* – entails setting challenging goals and emphasizing excellence while simultaneously showing confidence that subordinates will perform well. It does not really involve subordinates, so it is not that high on consideration in that sense – in fact, it has some similarities with the more positive features of scientific management.

House argues that all four styles can be, and often are, used by a leader in varying situations, or as a situation unfolds, and among his research subjects have been US presidents, who have to influence a wide variety of people. The theory has put forward a number of propositions on what behaviours suit what type of situation, including:

- *Ambiguous situations* benefit from *directive behaviour*. Subordinates appreciate their superior's help in increasing the probability that they will be able to attain the desired reward. Where situations have greater clarity in the nature of the task or the goal, this will be less necessary.
- *Stressful situations* benefit from *supportive leader behaviour* which alleviates subordinate tension and dissatisfaction.

The existing research on path–goal theory tends to support these propositions, which are clearly consistent with earlier theories and, one might add, with common sense. It has been argued that one of the strengths of this theory is its attempt to link leader behaviour with theories of motivation. Indeed, much of this behaviour would be familiar to a coach trying to get the best out of a team. Yet much of what is implicit in the theory relies on taken-for-granted assumptions about power and organizational politics. For example, sharing information under participative leadership might not occur for political reasons rather than because of a style issue. Even when it is shared, the information may even be misinformation or partial information for precisely the same reasons. Given that much of House's research was conducted in the White House, events in both the 1970s (Watergate) and the 1990s (Monica Lewinsky) suggest that leader behaviour may serve a number of simultaneous purposes – and events of the 1980s (the Iran-Contra scandal) suggest that when they do communicate they may not actually remember what they said nor why!

Leader–member exchange theory

Originally called the *vertical dyad linkage model of leadership*, this theory was developed by George Graen and his colleagues (Dansereau et al. 1975; Graen and Schiemann 1978; Liden and Graen 1980). Graen et al. question the conventional view that leaders display the same style and behaviours towards all their subordinates. On the contrary, they argue, there is no 'average' leadership style. Just take your own experience of work or school – can you think of one boss or teacher that everyone liked, or by whom everyone felt that they were treated the same? Such equitable treatment is hard to achieve, and leaders are only human – the nature of their tasks and their own personal preferences will mean that they interact with some people more than others. Graen et al. argue that leaders behave somewhat differently towards *each* subordinate, and the resulting linkages or relationships between the leader and a subordinate (the *dyad*) are likely to differ in quality. The same superior might have poor interpersonal relations with some subordinates but fairly open and trusting relations with others. Graen et al. argue that these patterns of relations fall into two groups, being dependent on whether the subordinate is 'in' or 'out'. Members of the *in-group* are invited to share in decision making and are given added responsibility, and are often taken into the manager's confidence. Members of the *out-group*, however, are supervised within the narrow terms of their formal employment contract, and managed on a 'need-to-know' basis. The trusted 'right hands' in the in-group tend to find their jobs enriched and their personal development accelerated, while the 'hired hands' in the out-group have limited opportunities and display low satisfaction and higher turnover.

Leaders and in-group members tend to believe that competence is the major reason why they are members of that group, but out-group members argue that it is ingratiation, favouritism and politics (Aktouf 1996). Interpersonal attraction certainly must be important, and research has demonstrated that in-group members tend to see problems in the same way as their leader. This may be an indication that leaders prefer people to be like them, which has its own dangers of 'groupthink' and the 'yes-man' mentality. As initially indicated by the Hawthorne Studies, once people are separated into high-performing and low-performing groups, this tends to become a self-fulfilling prophecy, and people become high or low performing accordingly, but favouritism can also lead to people being promoted beyond their competence. Omar Aktouf (1996), in a study conducted on both capitalist and communist workplace relations, argues that although supervisors report *competence* as a criterion for promotion and preferment, it is impression-management that seems to be most important in practice.

Graen et al. have undertaken research on the model in Confucian cultures, where society is based on concentric circles of intimacy and favouritism from the family outwards. Despite the social background of several circles, in practice the in-group/out-group dualism is common where the patriarchal leadership style prevails. Research has not yet been done on the gender dimensions of this theory, but one would expect it to display close links to the 'glass ceiling' concept of limits to women's progress in organizations (see Chapter 2).

Leaders and followers: Hersey and Blanchard's situational leadership

One characteristic of an effective leader is, according to Warren Bennis (1985), the ability to *manage* and *communicate meaning* to ensure that those leading can capture the imaginations of others and align these behind the organizational goals and priorities. Paul Hersey and Kenneth Blanchard (1996; Hersey 1985) developed their *situational leadership model* to enable a better understanding of how to achieve this, focusing on the 'actual behaviour' of leaders rather than their 'values or orientations', as in other approaches. Their approach to leadership has two basic assumptions:

1. *What leaders do to people is more important than what they intend to do*, that is, leaders are judged and assessed by others on their behaviours not their attitudes (for this reason, it is important to explore the various behaviours that leaders can adopt).
2. *What leaders do to others must be task-specific*, that is, leadership effectiveness depends on the ability to influence individuals and what they are doing.

Let us consider the implications of both of these assumptions for leadership effectiveness. The first part of the discussion relates to the behaviours which leaders can adopt when attempting to influence the performance of others. Hersey and Blanchard suggest that there are two distinctive sets of behaviours which you use when leading others – *directive* and *supportive behaviour*.

Directive behaviour

This behaviour relates to the extent to which leaders show or tell people what to do, how to do it and where and when to do it, and then closely supervise those people's performance. A leader has a choice, in any given situation, to use a lot or very little of this behaviour. For example, *highly* directive: 'I want you to take the hammer in the right hand, hold the nail with the left hand, and when I nod my head, hit it with the hammer with all your might' – in which case the instructions must be clear and non-ambiguous – or *low* directive: 'You decide what will work best in this situation to achieve the given objective.'

Supportive behaviour

This represents the extent to which you encourage and praise people and facilitate involvement in problem solving and decision making by seeking their ideas and opinions and listening actively to their responses. A leader, again, has a choice as to how much support is offered. For example, *highly* supportive: 'What do you need to tackle this problem – how can I help you get the best result?', or *low* supportive: 'Just get it right, or else.'

Hersey and Blanchard subsequently defined four leadership styles which are the combinations of high and low directive and supportive behaviours as described in Figure 10.3.

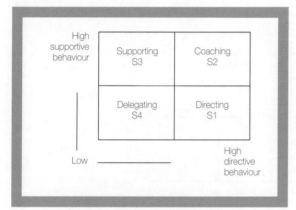

Figure 10.3 Hersey and Blanchard's leadership styles

Source: Adapted from Blanchard et al. (1985). Reprinted by permission of HarperCollins Publishers Ltd. Copyright © Kenneth Blanchard, Patricia Zigarmi and Drea Zigarmi 1985.

They labelled these styles S1 to S4 and suggested that whenever leaders encountered situations where it was necessary to influence another's performance, they always had four possible approaches (Blanchard et al. 1985: 56). These approaches are:

- *S1 directing* – providing structure and control
- *S2 coaching* – providing direction and support
- *S3 supporting* – praising, listening and facilitating
- *S4 delegating* – turning over responsibility for day-to-day decision making.

Task specificity

The skill of effective leadership is to know the characteristics of the situation wherein the various styles are likely to work most effectively. Hersey and Blanchard also concluded that two critical aspects of the follower (the person being influenced) are important determinants of leadership effectiveness and that for all followers, these characteristics are task-specific. They coined the term *development level* and suggested that it has two elements:

1. *competence* – the extent to which the person, for a particular task, possesses the knowledge and skills which could be gained from education, training and/or experience
2. *commitment* – the extent to which the person possesses the confidence and motivation to do the task.

Hersey and Blanchard suggested that the four leadership styles relate to four different development levels, being various combinations of competence and commitment, which they defined as:

- *Dl Enthusiastic beginners* Characteristic of people who lack competence, but are enthusiastic and committed. The authors suggested that such people need direction and supervision to get them going (S1).
- *D2 Disillusioned learners* Characteristic of people who have some competence but lack commitment (having become disillusioned about their ability to achieve outcomes). The authors suggested that such people need direction for their lack of total competence but also support to rebuild their enthusiasm and self-esteem (S2).
- *D3 Reluctant contributors* Characteristic of people who actually have the competence to do a task but lack confidence and/or motivation actually to attempt the task. It is suggested that rather than needing to be told how to perform, these people need support and encouragement to raise their flagging commitment (S3).
- *D4 Peak performer* Characteristic of people who are both competent and committed to achieving a particular task. Such people need only the opportunity to perform (S4).

The resulting model is illustrated in Figure 10.4 (Blanchard et al. 1985). It suggests several important things:

- individuals' development levels change in a more or less 'typical' pattern which follows the increase in levels of competence
- for different tasks people may or will have different levels of development
- effective leaders match their leadership, for each task, to the development level of their followers
- effective leaders recognize the 'development cycle of individuals learning a task' and therefore vary their leadership style to meet the followers' need.

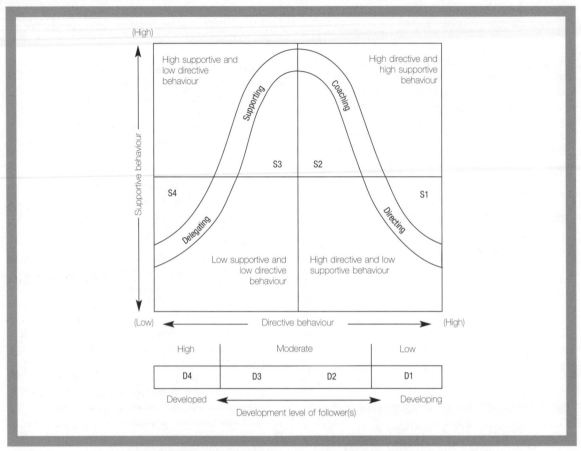

Figure 10.4 The four leadership styles

Source: Kenneth Blanchard, Patricia Zigarmi and Drea Zigarmi (1985) *Leadership and the One-Minute Manager*, London: HarperCollins, p. 69.

The management of meaning for the leader becomes a task of understanding:

■ what goal is to be achieved
■ what tasks must be undertaken to achieve this goal
■ who will be undertaking these tasks
■ what their development level is for each task
■ what leadership style is thus appropriate.

The main features of the contingency approaches we have discussed are summarized in Table 10.1. The importance of these theories was to show the variability and complexity of leadership situations and the problems of adopting a 'one best way' to lead or manage.

Contingency theorists have been criticized on a number of points, there being two main criticisms. First, the theories do not present a cumulative set of ideas, with each one seeming to choose different variables (or contingency factors) to explain or build the theory. Often the choice of the variables, such as 'supportive' and 'directive' behaviour, as in the case of Hersey and Blanchard, is not sufficiently well explained or justified. Contingency theorists seem to amass a range of factors that can leave the manager overwhelmed and unclear about which factors are the important ones to consider (Barrett and Sutcliffe 1992: 12). Second, the contingency factors are not related to or explained in terms of such things as organization structure, technology, size or other dimensions that are also likely to impact on leadership processes (Barrett and Sutcliffe 1992: 12).

Leadership substitutes

Contingency approaches assume that there is no one right style for all situations, but they also assume that there is a right one for a particular situation: it is assumed that leadership style is important. This is

Table 10.1 Comparison of major contingency leadership models

Model	Leader behaviour	Situational variables	Outcomes/criteria
Fiedler's contingency model	Task-oriented (low LPC) Relationship-oriented (high LPC)	Leader–member relations Task structure Position power	Performance
Path–goal theory	Directive Supportive Participative Achievement-oriented	Task structure Subordinate characteristics	Satisfaction Motivation Performance
Vertical dyad linkage	Differential treatment of subordinates (in-group or out-group)	Subordinate competence Subordinate loyalty	Satisfaction Performance Turnover
Hersey–Blanchard's situational leadership	Concern for people (directive or supportive) Concern for task (competence and commitment)	Developmental levels of subordinates (D1, D2, D3, D4)	Effectiveness

Source: Modified from Robert Vecchio, Greg Hearn and Greg Southey (1996) *Organizational Behaviour*, Sydney: Harcourt Brace, p. 497.

questioned by Steven Kerr and John Jermier (1978), who argue that leadership is sometimes not important because of the existence of *leadership substitutes* or *neutralizers*. Table 10.2 summarizes the Kerr and Jermier model based on subsequent research by Jon Howell et al. (1990) whose model included the concept of *enhancers*.

A *leadership substitute* is something that by its presence makes the behaviour unnecessary: for example employees with a strong attachment to a profession are likely to develop horizontal relationships inside and/or outside their organization, thereby making any leadership style less relevant. Highly trained and educated individuals are more likely to be self-directed and seek autonomy, minimizing the importance of leadership. Experience on the job can also reduce the need for leadership. To the extent that professional peer assessment is important, such as in professions like medicine, the significance of the organizational leader's role is reduced, if not removed in some circumstances.

A *leadership neutralizer* is something that by its absence prevents the leadership behaviour from being important: for example, to the extent that the employee is indifferent towards the rewards that the organization is able to provide, any type of leader loses significance. On the other hand, organizations might look for leadership substitutes if they believe leaders are not performing well and cannot be retrained, removed, transferred or their position redefined. This could be the situation, for example, facing organizations in which a family member has been appointed to management. Leadership neutralizers include such things as removing rewards from the control of leaders or managers so that promotion and so on is not influenced by them. Others are listed in Table 10.2.

Leadership *enhancers* amplify the impact a leader has on employees, such as altering reward systems. Leadership enhancers increase the influence of leaders, while neutralizers are deliberate strategies used to create 'power vacuums' (Howell et al. 1990: 30–4). Leadership substitutes are difficult to overcome and often lie outside the control of management yet are recognized as important influences on the changing role of leadership in organizations.

Kerr and Jermier see their approach as 'a true situational theory of leadership' (1978: 401), in that it is based on the argument that in some situations the role of the leader is replaced by alternative mechanisms. Effective leadership is correspondingly treated as 'the ability to supply subordinates with needed guidance and good feelings which are not being supplied by other sources' (Kerr and Jermier 1978: 400). One of the criticisms made against Kerr and Jermier's approach is that rather than acting as substitutes or neutralizers, such factors are supplements to leadership, that is, they coexist, 'filling in for one another as the situation dictates' (Howell and Dorfman 1981: 728). Thus the point is made that leadership is merely one factor at play in the determination of organizational outcomes.

Leadership as political influence

One of the main limitations of leadership studies is the predominant focus on supervisory style. Whether it be in terms of democratic versus autocratic or task-oriented versus people-oriented, leadership studies have primarily focused on the way in which leaders have treated their subordinates in a supervisory sense. This

Table 10.2 Leadership substitutes, neutralizers and enhancers: eleven managerial leadership problems and effective coping strategies*		
Leadership problems	Enhancer/Neutralizer	Substitutes
Leader doesn't keep on top of details in the department; coordination among subordinates is difficult	Not useful	Develop self-managed work teams; encourage team members to interact within and across departments
Competent leadership is resisted through non-compliance or passive resistance	**Enhancers:** increase employees' dependence on leader through greater leader control of rewards/resources; increase their perception of leader's influence outside of work group	Develop collegial systems of guidance for decision making
Leader doesn't provide support or recognition for jobs well done	Not useful	Develop a reward system that operates independently of the leader. Enrich jobs to make them inherently satisfying
Leader doesn't set targets or goals, or clarify roles for employees	Not useful	Emphasize experience and ability in selecting subordinates. Establish group goal-setting. Develop an organizational culture that stresses high performance expectations
A leader behaves inconsistently over time	**Enhancers:** these are dysfunctional **Neutralizer:** remove rewards from leader's control	Develop group goal-setting and group rewards
An upper-level manager regularly bypasses a leader in dealing with employees, or countermands the leader's directions	**Enhancers:** increase leader's control over rewards and resources; build leader's image via in-house champion or visible 'important' responsibilities **Neutralizer:** physically distance subordinates from upper-level managers	Increase the professionalization of employees
A unit is in disarray or out of control	Not useful	Develop highly formalized plans, goals, routines and areas of responsibility
Leadership is brutal, autocratic	**Enhancers:** these are dysfunctional. **Neutralizers:** physically distance subordinates; remove rewards from leader's control	Establish group goal-setting and peer performance appraisal
There is inconsistency across different organizational units	Not useful	Increase formalization. Set up a behaviourally focused reward system
Leadership is unstable over time, leaders are rotated and/or leave office frequently	Not useful	Establish competent advisory staff units. Increase professionalism of employees
Incumbent management is poor; there's no heir apparent	**Enhancers:** these are dysfunctional. **Neutralizer:** assign non-leader duties to problem managers	Emphasize experience and ability in selecting employees. Give employees more training

Source: Howell et al. (1990) 'Substitutes for leadership: Effective alternatives to ineffective leadership', *Organizational Dynamics,* Summer, pp. 28–9.

* The suggested solutions are examples of many possibilities for each problem.

has led to a relative lack of attention to the actions of those in leadership positions designated as *organizational networkers*. In the late 1940s, Donald Pelz (1952) attempted to identify the attitudes and behaviours that lead to greater employee satisfaction. To his surprise, he discovered that there was no

significant difference in this regard between the leaders of 'high-satisfaction' and 'low-satisfaction' groups. The key explanatory factor seemed to be not the leader's style, but rather the extent to which he or she had influence outside the group, in the broader organizational milieu. Pelz found that:

If a supervisor (or any group leader) has considerable influence within his organization, then when he behaves so as to help employees towards their goals, he will achieve concrete benefits for them … Not his good intentions, but his actual accomplishments are what pay dividends in employee satisfaction. (Pelz 1952: 213)

In fact, well-meaning, democratic leaders without influence may actually reduce satisfaction because they might arouse expectations which they are subsequently unable to meet (Pelz 1952). This 'lost tradition' in leadership research was resurrected by theorists such as Rosabeth Moss Kanter (1977, 1979, 1983) who argued that what was important was the leader's ability to get a good share of available resources, opportunities (for promotion and so on) and rewards for his or her subordinates. Leadership thus had more to do with developing lateral and vertical contacts (or connections) than with the supervisory style of the leader. The role of leader is likely to be predominantly one of acting strategically within an established network of connections. This is what the employees in Pelz's study were referring to when they asserted the importance of the leader having 'influence'. It was not influence over them that concerned them; it was the ability of leaders successfully – in terms of their subordinates'

Exhibit 10.2 Some common symbols of a manager's organizational power (influence upward, influence outward)

To what extent a manager can intercede favourably on behalf of someone in trouble with top management:

❏ Get a good placement for a talented subordinate

❏ Get approval for expenditures beyond the budget

❏ Get above-average salary increases for subordinates

❏ Get important items on the agenda at various meetings

❏ Get fast access to top management

❏ Get regular, frequent access to top management

❏ Get early information about important decisions and major changes to policy

Source: Adapted and reprinted by permission of *Harvard Business Review* from 'Power failure in management circuits' by Rosabeth Moss Kanter, July/August 1979, p. 67. Copyright © 1979 by Harvard Business School of Publishing Corporation. All rights reserved.

---

expectations of what they can do for them – to operate in or be influential in the broader organizational networks (Bolman and Deal 1991: 437–9). Exhibit 10.2 identifies some indicators of a manager's influence within an organization. The political and power implications of this approach were discussed in Chapter 6, but are also discussed below.

Leadership as strategic influence

The view of leadership that emerges from the recognition of the limitations of the style perspective is centred on the strategic influence of particular individuals. When we talk of leadership, what we are referring to is the notion that in any collectivity it is likely that specific individuals play a dominant role in structuring activities and creating interpretations for others that come to hold sway or influence. Linda Smircich and Gareth Morgan (1982: 255) express this perspective on leadership when they claim that individuals:

emerge as leaders because of their role in framing experience in a way that provides a viable basis for action, for example, by mobilising meaning, articulating and defining what has previously remained implicit and unsaid, by inventing images and meanings that provide a focus for new attention and by consolidating or changing prevailing wisdom.

From this perspective, leadership is fundamentally a matter of providing a clear sense of purpose, of 'what are we doing and why are we doing it' (Pondy 1978). Sometimes this is referred to as providing a clear 'vision'. In particular, the management literature of the 1980s and early 1990s argued for the virtues of *transformational leadership*, which gives a high priority to this aspect of visionary leadership (Bass 1985; Tichy and Devanna 1986; Kouzes and Posner 1989). Transformational leadership involves a focus on change and the importance of developing a sense of direction and commitment. Exhibit 10.3 presents a summary of the characteristics of transformational leadership.

Transformational leadership is typically contrasted with *transactional leadership,* which focuses on leadership being essentially a matter of supporting, directing and coordinating work or effort towards a known goal or purpose. Transactional leadership is not focused on initiating radical or dramatic change but rather fine-tuning what goes on in the organization. In an effort to evangelize the virtues of the transformational leader, the transformation/transaction difference tends to suggest that only transformational leaders create meanings that organizations should value. It can be argued, however, that all leadership activity involves the establishment of meaning, even if it is

Exhibit 10.3 Transformational leadership

1. **Visioning a new corporate future**

   ❏ creating the new vision
   ❏ breaking the old frame
   ❏ demonstrating personal commitment to the vision

2. **Communicating the vision**

   ❏ communicating and dramatizing the vision
   ❏ focusing on people
   ❏ seizing the moment

3. **Implementing the vision**

   ❏ building an effective top team
   ❏ reorganizing
   ❏ building a new culture

Source: Dexter Dunphy and Doug Stace (1990) *Under New Management: Australian Organisations in Transition,* Sydney: McGraw-Hill, p. 155.

these levels and institutionalize the changes on these levels so that there is no turning back. The revitalized organization finds new energy, stops replaying old scripts and embraces new ones. Thus the key skills of transformational leaders are not just in visioning, but in making things happen at all levels, and at times it can require close hands-on involvement to drive through. The transformational leadership approach is often said to be needed in situations of organizational crisis.

Criticisms of the transformational leadership approach have focused on such things as the excessive, almost evangelical role accorded the transformational leader, who almost single-handedly has the vision to steer (as a captain would) the organization through turbulent change and crisis. Transformational leadership theorists have also propagated the view, or at least reinforced it, that leadership and management are separate activities. Thus they have indirectly reaffirmed the trait theory of leadership. To 'qualify' as a transformational leader is to be equivalent to the 'great man' model that was edified by the early trait theorists. Whereas the leadership-style theorists subscribed to a view that managers could be trained as leaders, and contingency theorists argued that situations determined appropriate leadership approaches, the transformational leadership approach has presented an elitist view of leadership. This heroic form of leadership can only be the attribute of a few dynamic, charismatic and no doubt highly remunerated individuals (Barrett and Sutcliffe 1993: 22).

The transformational leadership approach has principally drawn support for its claims from data collected through the interview method, based on the perceptions that followers have of the attributes of the leader. Research has found that the ratings transformational leaders give of their attributes tend to correlate with those given by their subordinates or followers (for example Hater and Bass 1988). John Coopey says that if we substitute the words 'transformational leadership' with 'a drive or need for power', then these findings on transformational leadership can be seen in a very different light. He says that research using projective tests (special tests to determine dimensions of personality) suggests that people in leadership positions crave power or have a higher need for power than do others (Coopey 1995: 207, citing Shackleton and Fletcher 1984). Those who have a strong, lifelong desire for power, which is reinforced through their socialization (that is, how they learn and behave in school, the family and the wider community), usually also have a strong lifelong hunger for acceptance and confirmation (Coopey 1995: 207, citing Kets de Vries 1991). Whatever other skills, attributes or abilities these people have, it is their high need for power that sets them apart. Conversely, followers oblige this type of leader by a process of

unconscious and possibly negative, as can be the case even with transformational leadership (Pondy 1978, Smircich and Morgan 1982). Transformational leadership is most closely related at its roots, however, to the image of great political leaders and heroic leadership, and thus focuses on visionary leadership, creating a vision, communicating it and finding the symbols and experiences to support it (Bolman and Deal 1991: 439–45).

In Figure 10.5 Noel Tichy and David Ulrich (1987: 299) illustrate how transactional leadership can stop short of what an organization needs in attempting to change. Moving along from the trigger events on the diagram, the bottom half represents the emotional reactions to what is happening in the top half. Once there is a perceived need for change, which could be a marked decline in sales, for example, key leaders will try to initiate change and will encounter resistant forces; technical obstacles, political obstacles from powerful pressure groups within the organization and cultural obstacles where people cannot think differently. Emotionally, they are disengaged and disenchanted because the old ways have to end. When they move into the transition state, transactional leaders tend to stick with technical solutions to problems or incremental change because they have no alternative vision. However, what the organization needs is not just death and disintegration, but a way of seeing endings as new beginnings, a vision to enable rebirth. Transformational leaders are able to create a new technical, political and cultural vision, mobilize commitment to the vision on

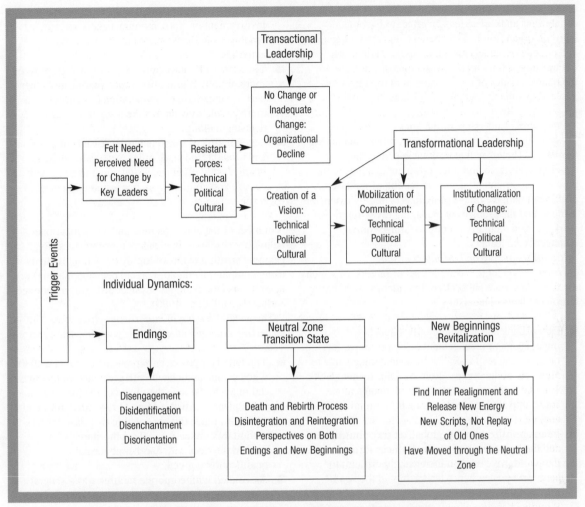

Figure 10.5 Transformational leadership

Source: Noel Tichy and David Ulrich (1987) 'The leadership challenge: A call for the transformational leader', in A.D. Timpe (ed.) *Leadership*, New York: Facts on File Publications, p. 29.

'idealized transference', in which the followers make every effort to please the leader to compensate for their own sense of helplessness and vulnerability. Coopey adds that unless leaders of this type are sufficiently self-reflexive and able to distance themselves from this adulation, they are likely to mirror the adulation and come to believe in their own 'greatness' (Coopey 1995: 207). It is not surprising then that there are strong correlations between the perceptions of followers and transformational leaders about the latter's attributes and qualities.

Post-heroic leadership

Post-heroic leadership became popular in the 1990s as a reaction to a number of noticeable trends (discussed

below). However, its origins date back to the work of David Bradford and Allan Cohen (1984). Bradford and Cohen identified a new form of leadership, which is associated with transformational leadership but has a much greater emphasis on managers developing their subordinates. There is a tendency for transformational leaders still to display, and be expected to display, heroic characteristics, to be either the super *technician* who can do everything in the organization as well as or better than the next person, or the super *conductor* who sits on top of the organization directing the players with a 'wave of the baton'. In neither of these situations is responsibility shared; nor are employees empowered, and they do not develop into new and emerging roles. Bradford and Cohen argue that the *post-heroic* leader is the manager as *developer*, who approaches every situation as an opportunity for him or her, his or her employees or the organization to develop their capabilities and capacities – in effect to become a learning organization. They believe that the technician and conductor models have their uses, but that the circumstances for which they were most fitted are not the characteristics of most postmodern organizations. Table 10.3 summarizes the three leadership styles proposed by Bradford and Cohen.

Post-heroic leadership, or the questioning of the image of the transformational leader, intensified during the 1990s. Three key factors contributed to this development: rapid and often turbulent changes in the business environment; a general feeling of malaise or discontent with the image of managers and by extension leaders; and the problem of managing diversity in the workplace, particularly accommodating women managers cum leaders.

Rapidly changing and turbulent business environments refer to a complex set of factors, of which the following were particularly important in debunking notions of heroic leadership:

■ Downsizing and flattening of businesses led to many layers of management being removed, forcing or allocating responsibility for managing change to all levels of the organization. As John Kotter (1990: 104) says, 'More change always demands more leadership' and leadership is focused on initiating change.
■ Internationalization and globalization of businesses, and the burgeoning of regional offices throughout the world, have made it increasingly difficult to centralize power, hence leadership, in the head office of the organization.
■ Rapidly changing, highly sophisticated, integrated networked technologies have allowed for more

information dissemination and exchange and the involvement of many more managers and employees in decision-making and strategic activities.
■ The increasing number of executive and employee share option programmes, profit sharing and other performance-based remuneration has encouraged more people to want to have a say in strategic decision making.
■ Deregulation of markets has increased competition and brought into stark relief inefficient business practices that often necessitate organization-wide change and commitment, not just at the senior levels.

A number of the above factors, and some mentioned below, are similar to the leadership substitutes (for example creating teams of highly trained individuals, using computer technology to aid decision making) or neutralizers (for example physical distance) mentioned earlier (Howell et al. 1990).

The general *feeling of malaise and discontent* with leadership emerged again from a complex set of factors:

■ The failed corporate entrepreneurs of the late 1980s, who became associated with greed and ruthlessness, did much to damage the image of the lone, heroic (male) leader. Alistair Mant (1994, cited in Caulkin 1993: 40) made the observation that most leaders who fit this image are male authoritarians, of stunted intellect with another abnormal qualification – greed.
■ Associated with corporate failures was a general questioning of how leadership actually contributed to wealth creation in organizations.
■ The general trend of running companies through

		Technician	Conductor	Post-heroic
Table 10.3 Appellation				
1.	Subordinates work independently	×		
2.	Subordinates do simple tasks	×		
3.	Environment is stable	×	×	
4.	Subordinates have low technical knowledge compared to boss	×	×	
5.	Subordinate commitment not needed	×	×	
6.	Subordinates do complex tasks		×	×
7.	Subordinates require considerable coordination		×	×
8.	Environment is changing			×
9.	Subordinates have high technical knowledge			×
10.	Subordinate commitment necessary for excellence			×

Table 10.3 Appropriate leadership styles

Source: David Bradford and Allan Cohen (1984) *Managing for Excellence*, New York: John Wiley, p. 56.

committees and boards tended to diminish the idea that a single leader was setting the direction and vision for the organization.

- The rise to CEO positions of functional specialists in accounting and finance, who were less concerned with, and often less skilled in, leadership (for example visioning, motivating, communicating, building cultures for change) and who placed a greater focus on 'bottom-line' issues, such as cost cutting, shedding labour and return on investment, led to the downgrading of the leadership factor in management (Caulkin 1993: 41; Haigh 1994: 14).

- Research has found, not surprisingly, that leaders have followers, and sometimes the followers are just as capable as the leaders of providing leadership (Nutt 1995: 68, citing Kelley 1992). This trend might be expected whenever you have a professional and highly educated workforce often being managed by an older generation of less qualified and educated managers.

- Research in the USA also found that at least 50 per cent of followers surveyed, or people being led, expressed deep dissatisfaction with their leaders (often managers), citing the fact that few of their leaders provided positive role models and even fewer instilled trust (Nutt 1995: 68, citing Kelley 1992). This has been supported by observations made by Andrew Campbell, who argues that leaders 'can equally well be saints or complete bastards, simple and sane or rampant schizophrenics' (quoted in Caulkin 1993: 40). (Also see discussion on the narcissistic leader below.)

- The recognition that the time has long gone when a company could rely on a single leader to do the thinking (strategic or otherwise), while the followers 'parked their brains at the door', added to discontent with leadership theories (Caulkin 1993: 40).

- It was also thought that followers, especially if empowered, which presumes post-heroic leadership, were more likely to be able to provide checks and balances in an organization. Powerless employees have little opportunity, other than through, say, whistle-blowing, of keeping those at the 'top' accountable for their actions (Caulkin 1993: 41).

- As John Huey (1994: 26) states, post-heroic leadership works where organizations are trying to gain competitive advantage from creating intellectual capital and attracting knowledge workers (see Chapter 8) who do not readily respond to the highly controlled mode of leadership found under the transformational approach or the heroic activities of a single leader (see also Crawford 1991).

- Pressures for lifelong learning (see Kotter 1995), and the need to promote radical innovations and change, are increasingly seen to be dependent on employees' willingness to change – forceful and remote leadership is seen as counterproductive to this.

- The pressure for ordinary managers to invent, push and implement radical change, and encourage more teamwork, has also brought into question the relevance of heroic leadership (Sherman 1994: 73; also Chapters 9 and 11).

- Organizations are always experimenting with new ways of gaining competitive advantage, and one of these is to tap the 'spiritual' or deeper emotional sides of people's personalities. The 'macho' transformational heroic leader image does not sit well with efforts to tap the tacit (or personal) knowledge of employees for sources of creativity and innovation (Sherman 1994: 74; Cavaleri and Fearon 1996: 363–74; and Chapter 11).

- As organizations also become more involved in networks and interorganizational relations (IOR) with suppliers, customers and competitors, different styles of leadership will be required to share information and build trust. We pursue these issues further in Chapter 16, but, suffice it to say, the leadership skills a manager might use effectively within the organization are not always likely to translate to successful leadership practices outside the organization.

The problems of *managing diversity* were discussed in Chapter 2. Leadership, particularly in relation to women managers, remains an area of considerable debate and controversy. Managing diversity has raised concerns about how men and women manage and has again brought into question the gender stereotyping associated with heroic leadership. A growing body of literature (for example Rosener 1990; Denmark 1993) has suggested that women do lead differently, even in terms of the transformational variables, that is, women are more likely to adopt empowering strategies and develop followers. Even though some of these gender assumptions have been questioned in Chapter 2, the issue of women in management, and women achieving senior or top management positions, has helped to raise concerns about gender stereotyping and the dominance of heroic images of leadership (see discussion later in 'Gender and leadership').

Research by Robert Kelley (cited in Nutt 1995: 69 and Caulkin 1993: 41) suggests that many organizations do not need heroic leaders because they are already well endowed with *exemplary followers*. These exemplary followers challenge the very idea of leadership. He states that many leaders feel threatened by their subordinates, yet exemplary followers are crucial to the success of an organization because they are vital to designing and carrying out plans. Exemplary followers are active, independent and critical thinkers. They also tend to have strong values and are what Kelley calls the *courageous conscience* of the organization (Nutt 1995: 69, citing Kelley 1992). However, according to Kelley, leaders cannot 'create' exemplary followers. They can, however, use a number of strategies to ensure that exemplary followers and leaders form partnerships and that the CEO (strategic leader) ensures that exemplary followers succeed and are productive. This can be achieved in several ways:

- Information sharing with exemplary followers.
- Involving exemplary followers in the co-determination of major strategies.
- Sharing the risks and rewards with exemplary followers – including the 'glory' of success.
- Making sure these people have the resources to do their jobs.
- Letting them shine – allowing exemplary followers to lead teams and share the limelight when there is success.

To quote:

To be a post-heroic leader requires very different qualities to that of the heroic leader, post-heroic leaders do not expect to solve all the problems themselves. They realise no one person can deal with the emerging colliding tyrannies of speed, quality, customer satisfaction, innovation, diversity and technology. Virtual leaders just say no to their egos (Huey 1994: 26).

Power has been omitted from many theories of leadership, including consideration of the legal and proprietorial rights that CEOs and top managers enjoy, and against which they are judged, and which also help them to gain wealth within companies. The 'heroic image' goes with this power (Coopey 1995: 195). Many CEOs or senior managers might not wish to embrace the idea of post-heroic leadership (as described in the quote above), as they might perceive it as threatening their status, power, prestige and public standing. Take, for example, one of the key elements of providing support for exemplary followers mentioned earlier, that is, sharing in risks and rewards. According to Kelley (cited in Nutt 1995: 69), this means that leaders must, when times get tough, such as when there is downsizing or layoffs, demonstrate that they are willing to share the loss with their followers. Kelley gives an example of the CEO of Firestone (a large multinational based in the USA) who accepted a huge bonus at a time when his company was halving its workforce. He also describes how, by contrast, Perot, a vice-president on the board of General Motors, resigned from the board in the 1980s in protest at increased executive bonuses at a time when plants were being closed. Another example

comes from the UK, where, in 1998, the chief executive of Goodyear sacrificed his annual salary in an attempt to impress upon employees the need to think carefully about the company's position before demanding a wage rise.

A number of different versions of the post-heroic leadership approach have emerged in the management literature (see for example Manz and Sims 1992 on self-leadership). One approach developed by Ronald Heifetz and Donald Laurie (1997) encapsulates many elements of the post-heroic agenda. The authors argue that changes in societies such as: markets being more open; customers being more demanding, diverse and international; increased competition and collaboration through networks and alliances; and technological advances require a serious rethinking of what leadership might mean in many organizations. They believe that the leader's work is focused now more than ever on coping with a *multiplicity of adaptive challenges* rather than one major crisis. Instead of focusing on styles or contingencies, they argue that leadership is now the work of many people in an organization. They believe (as do many other theorists) that organizations have to rethink their values, develop new strategies and learn new ways of operating to meet adaptive challenges. Leaders have to be able to mobilize (that is, influence) people to adopt new behaviours and, in the process, change their own behaviours, especially the tendency to provide solutions, solve problems and take responsibility for driving change (that is, the transformational leader with the 'vision' in hand).

Heifetz and Laurie identify subtle changes in leadership and followership as a result of having to face adaptive challenges. Adaptive challenges mean leaders must figure out how to harness the collective intelligence of the organization through building new relationships within, across and outside the organization. They say this requires: 'Leaders from above or below, with or without authority – [engaging] people in confronting the [adaptive] challenges, adjusting their values, changing perspectives, and learning new habits' (Heifetz and Laurie 1997: 134). Solutions are discovered or learned and are no longer 'handed down' or 'given out' by leaders, as envisaged in heroic approaches to leadership.

The authors note that the adaptive challenges are also distressing because they make demands on people to take on new roles, relationships, values, work practices and behaviours (Heifetz and Laurie 1997: 124). All these changes can involve pain, a sense of loss and fears about the future, and leaders need the sensitivity, skills and knowledge to manage the emotional labour involved in such change (see Chapter 9).

Heifetz and Laurie propose six principles as guides to the work of leading to meet adaptive challenges:

1. Getting on the balcony

■ Leaders (or leadership teams) need to be able to stand back and reflect on the need for change. They no longer 'helicopter' over the organization seeing the 'big picture' as in the transformational leadership approaches. Rather, the leader (or leaders) needs to be able to create or see the context for change, and then impart this need for change in a compelling story or narrative that allows others to let go of the past, embrace the need for change, and accept responsibility for shaping a new future. There is no all-embracing vision but rather a direction for change that is negotiated through confronting issues and challenges. An example of how this might work is discussed below in the case study on KPMG Netherlands. Richard Hackman (1992: 156–9) notes that the voluminous literature on leadership and management includes little on the direction-setting activities of managers. He notes that in trying to create a self-managing unit, leaders walk a very fine line between being too directive and not being directive enough. Hackman uses the metaphor of climbing a mountain to make his point. He says that in many circumstances the choice of the mountain to climb (direction) might be non-negotiable, but how to climb it might be left open to negotiation and choice. Hackman believes a direction has to be set to orient members toward common objectives, energize them by giving new purpose and meaning and provide some tangible criterion for working out alternatives to follow.

■ Although leaders, metaphorically speaking, stand on a balcony to take a broader view of what is happening in the organization, they must come down to the field of action or the minutiae of the change process to see where power struggles and resistance to change are occurring or amassing. Leaders must be able to devise strategies with others to deal with the 'normal' resistance to change.

2. Identifying adaptive challenges

■ Leaders must develop trust among colleagues so that people learn to collaborate and develop a collective sense of responsibility for change (Heifetz and Laurie 1997: 126). We discussed the issue of trust in Chapter 9, but point out here that creating trust is far more complex than suggested by Heifetz and Laurie. It is extremely difficult to develop trust across a whole organization, yet trust is a key factor in many aspects of knowledge work and building intellectual capital in an organization.

■ Leaders need to be able to differentiate between technical challenges (identified as basic routines) and adaptive challenges which require learning new ways of doing business, developing new competencies and the need to work collectively (Heifetz and Laurie 1997: 126).

■ Conflicts are clues for adaptive challenges and leaders must dig deep to unearth the root causes of conflicts. Often conflicts appear to be over technical issues (for example procedures, schedules) but usually go deeper to values, norms and politics, and leaders must push to have these deeper issues addressed.

■ Leaders must hold up a 'mirror' to see how they, as leaders of change, are also a part of the adaptive challenge. They need to ask in what ways is the executive team dysfunctional (see Chapter 11) and how might its members develop insights to help them better understand their roles in confronting adaptive challenges (Heifetz and Laurie 1997: 126) (that is, how they can develop reflective practice, as mentioned in Chapter 1).

3. Regulating distress

■ Leaders need to strike a delicate balance between having people feel the need for change and at the same time not allowing them to be overwhelmed by it, yet all the while keeping up the momentum for change (Heifetz and Laurie 1997: 127).

■ Leaders take responsibility for the direction of change: they articulate key adaptive challenges by framing key questions and issues; they offer protection so that the pressure for change does not become intolerable for people; they have to challenge those roles that need to change, but resist the pressure to define new roles too quickly; they expose conflict and see it as important to creativity and learning; they help to challenge norms that need to change and protect those that must endure (Heifetz and Laurie 1997: 127–8).

■ Leaders have to have the emotional capacity to endure uncertainty, frustration and pain and understand fears, stresses and sacrifices, yet the poise and steadiness to instil confidence.

4. Disciplining attention

■ Leaders build on diversity, multiple views, realities and perspectives in order to encourage innovation and learning. To do this leaders (or managers) must deal with, and bring out into the open, all forms of work avoidance, such as scapegoating, denial, stereotyping, focusing on technical issues, blaming others, attacking individual perspectives and so on. Leaders need strategies that enable them to get people to refocus on building dialogue, problem solving and creativity (see Chapter 1).

5. *Giving work back to people*

■ Leaders share the responsibility, pain and need for change by learning to support rather than control employees, who will often need to learn how to take responsibility for success and failures (Heifetz and Laurie 1997: 129). 'Give work back to people' is a short-cut term for 'empowerment'. Empowering can involve such things as sharing information (extensively), including opening up the company's books to employees and exposing sensitive information (Quinn and Spreitzer 1997: 39). This was also mentioned by Kelley (1992) in followership strategies. Robert Quinn and Gretchen Spreitzer point out that empowerment is not a set of specific management practices but rather a reflection of a person's beliefs or feelings about their work. Empowered people have a strong sense of self-determination, that is, they feel relatively free to choose how they do their work; they care about their work, or it means something important to them; they feel competent, or confident about their ability to perform; and they have a sense of impact (that is, they feel they have influence and others listen to their ideas (Quinn and Spreitzer 1997: 41; also Chapter 6). These views echo the sentiments of Peter F. Drucker (quoted in Harris 1993: 122) who has said: 'It is not a great step forward to take power out at the top and put it at the bottom. It's still power. To build achieving organizations, you must replace power with responsibility.'

Ironically, rewards (monetary or others) are not mentioned by Heifetz and Laurie, but are considered important by others as compensation for people taking more risks and responsibilities, and being held more accountable for outcomes (Quinn and Spreitzer 1997: 40). This is certainly a criticism of many approaches to leadership that have ignored monetary reward, almost as an excessive reaction to Taylorism.

6. *Protecting voices of leadership from below*

■ Heifetz and Laurie (1997: 729) say that it is important to give a 'voice' to all people in the organization and that this giving of voice is key to encouraging experimentation and learning (see also Chapter 1). Yet they note that whistle-blowers, creative deviants and other original thinkers often have their voices smashed or routinely silenced because organizations and their managers (leaders) want equilibrium, harmony and consensus, and

often seek affirmation of their views and support for their pet projects. Teamwork or being a team player, and other 'unifying' or 'conforming' strategies, are often used to bring dissenting voices into check (see Chapter 11). The reasons why leaders often do not listen to the 'voices of leadership from below' are much more complex than Heifetz and Laurie suggest. They believe that people who speak beyond their authority are apt to be self-conscious and generate too much passion about their cause, and are likely to pick the wrong place, time and person to open up to. They exhort leaders to see these people as valuable sources of information, insight and leadership and not persons to be silenced (Heifetz and Laurie 1997: 129–30).

In Chapter 8 we discussed in greater detail the ethical reasons why managers as leaders are likely to silence and victimize the very actions that Heifetz and Laurie want to 'normalize' as a part of post-heroic leadership. In the next section of this chapter, we also explore why some managers, described as narcissistic leaders, could never undertake the work of leadership associated with post-heroic leadership or the leadership approach outlined by Heifetz and Laurie. But the question inevitably arises: how does the post-heroic agenda, outlined above, work in practice?

The KPMG case example describes how one organization studied by Heifetz and Laurie encapsulates what they see as the work of leadership within the context of meeting adaptive challenges. Huey (1994: 28) summarizes in a nutshell what adaptive challenges constitute for managers: getting people from diverse backgrounds to pull in the same direction when they have to.

The case represents only one possible approach to post-heroic leadership. Other organizations, such as SEMCO in Brazil (Semler 1993) and W.L. Gore and Associates in the USA (Huey 1994; Skipper and Manz 1994), are regularly cited as examples of post-heroic leadership in practice. Both these organizations have developed a post-heroic, or even craft-style approach to leadership (Mintzberg 1997: 14) by working on the principles of trust and commitment to spread the work of leadership to as many people as possible. In the case of SEMCO, this has involved shop-floor employees or relatively unskilled workers taking on leadership roles and rotating leadership positions at the executive level. W.L. Gore and Associates is a high-tech company employing highly professional people, whereas SEMCO is principally a manufacturer of pumps, mixer valves and other industrial equipment. Neither firms' owners portray themselves as leaders (Ricardo Semler of SEMCO sees himself as a 'counsellor') and both shirk titles and many symbols of status in the workplace, such as a large office. SEMCO has built its system of trust to include a package of monetary

CASE EXAMPLE

KPMG NETHERLANDS
(Leaders in auditing, consulting and tax preparation)

Ruud Koedijk, the chairperson of the company, recognized in 1994 that although the KPMG partnership was the industry leader in the Netherlands and was highly profitable, the growth potential for its services was limited. New opportunities for growth had to be found. The chair and his board had the strategic skills to reposition the organization but they were less certain they could gain commitment to strategic change from the firm's partners. The partners had a history of resisting change, having been successful for so many years and also having built the organization of 300 around small fiefdoms of power and control. Profitability of individual units was the sole criterion of success. Independence, unit autonomy and minimizing conflict was the norm. Change was not overtly resisted, partners would just work on the idea of 'say yes, do no'. Directors and partners rewarded other professionals for not making mistakes and for delivering a high number of billable hours per week. Innovation and creativity were not rewarded. Koedijk's approach to leadership was to do the following:

1. He called a meeting of 300 partners to review KPMG's history, current business position and future issues. He asked questions about how to go about changing the firm rather than offering a direction. Beginning a dialogue rather than pronouncing 'edicts' (as leaders often do in the media and so on) was Koedijk's only real strategy.

2. One hundred partners and non-partners were released for 60 per cent of their time for four months to work on strategic challenges. Twelve senior partners formed a strategic integration team to work with the 100 professionals. Four task forces were set up covering three areas: gauging future trends and discontinuities; defining core competence; and

grappling with adaptive challenges. 'The 100' (as they were called) were housed on a separate floor, unencumbered by the rules and protocols of the rest of the organization. They had a project manager, KPMG's director of marketing and communications. Many non-partner members who had never been involved in strategy processes were included.

3. Inertia and dysfunctions emerged as 'the 100' tried to do strategy work confined by a 'culture' perceived of as fostering opposing views (that is, individualism and unit loyalty), demand for perfection and conflict avoidance. Producing an alternative view of a desired culture became the focus of the teams. This also became a part of individual adaptive challenges; everyone had to examine attitudes, behaviours and habits that needed change and actions had to be devised to make the change happen. The alternative new culture that was identified subsequently had three key characteristics: opportunity for self-fulfilment; developing a caring environment; and maintaining trusting relations with colleagues.

4. Stress levels in 'the 100' were often high, and various forums with the board, including theatrics (for example a board member standing on a table during a breakfast meeting) were used to push for more creativity and change, yet allowing for venting of frustrations, fears and even anger.

5. Dress rules were relaxed, new symbols were created, games were used to encourage fun at work and rules were developed to encourage listening and understanding other people's perspectives.

6. KPMG identified $50–60 million worth of new business opportunities and in the process changed the services it offered to clients – one being to teach others how to use adaptive challenges to change and to use leadership as a learning strategy.

Source: Reprinted by permission of *Harvard Business Review.* From 'The work of leadership' by Ronald Heifetz and Donald Laurie, December 2001. Copyright © 2001 by Harvard Business School of Publishing Corporation. All rights reserved.

rewards, including profit sharing and incentives. Semler has now become a celebrated management guru, and another guru, former Stanford academic Jim Collins, has popularized the idea of humility being a necessary factor in a style of twenty-first century leadership which will see the demise of the heroic leader. On the basis of large-scale research conducted by his self-funded research 'lab', Collins (2001; Collins and Porras 1994, see also www.jimcollins.com) argues that leadership has five levels: level 1 is individual ability; level 2 is team skills; level 3 is managerial capability; level 4 is

leadership as traditionally conceived, emphasizing heroism, performance and the 'celebrity CEO'; and level 5 is what Collins calls the 'extra dimension' – a blend of *personal humility* (putting the long-term good of the company and the contributions of others above personal credit or ego) and *professional will* (commitment, staying power, willingness to make tough decisions if they are right). For Collins, their ambition is not for themselves but for their institution, to make it great. Over five years, Collins' researchers studied companies who had consistently outperformed the stock market by more than three times and discovered CEOs who few people had ever heard of like Darwin Smith who headed Kimberley Clark for over twenty years and never stopped trying to be 'qualified for the job' and David Maxwell, who, having turned Fannie Mae from a lossmaker into a company beating the stock market by seven times, gave a third of his retirement bonus to charity lest he damage the company reputation by appearing greedy – who had successes far in excess of those of the media stars such as Lee Iacocca or Al Dunlap. Collins argues that level 5 leadership is the antithesis of egocentric celebrity, which displays the symptoms of what has been called *narcissism*.

The narcissistic leader

The most powerful critical responses to the rhetoric of the transformational leaders recognize the tendency toward superficiality in the advocacy of 'visionary' leadership. Indeed, despite the advocacy of the 'post-heroic' leadership style, heroic behaviours, celebrity images and virtual cult followings still seem to be very much in evidence. But the vision which many managers have is not of the organization, or the future, but of *themselves*, and they seek to remake the world in their image (see Fineman 1993: 25–7). Many are suffering from narcissism – which has been defined as the most common behavioural disease of the late twentieth century (Callaghan 1997).

Narcissism was first identified by Freud, but its extent and social impact was not mapped until Christopher Lasch's 1979 book, *The Culture of Narcissism*. Coming as it did at the end of the 'me' decade, it was at first interpreted as a review of the 1970s, but Lasch insisted that it was a warning, and was as prophetic as it was documentary. In 1980 narcissism was officially given a diagnosis and set of symptoms in the *Diagnostic and Statistical Manual of Mental Disorders* (see Task Force on DSM IV 2000)

and several books have since developed the subject (for example Symington 1993). Howard Schwartz (1990) applied the concept to organizational cultures, as we discussed in Chapter 3; Adrian Carr (1994, 1998) has applied the concept to individuals establishing identity within organizational relationships; Andrew Brown (1997) has considered its impact at individual, group and organizational levels; and Alan Downs (1997) has applied the concept specifically to managers.

The narcissist, as a result of experiences in childhood, is driven by an anxiety, an inner feeling of lack of self-worth. This anxiety develops as a form of self-absorption or self-obsession which can appear as the opposite of this – as arrogance, overconfidence, disdain or contempt for others and a ruthless determination to stop at nothing to get what they want. Narcissists learn three basic lessons:

1. They must be something more than they are.
2. Their value as people is dependent upon the image they project.
3. Other people are objects who must be manipulated to get the validation that narcissists need.

As Downs (1997) argues, narcissistic behaviour produces a dearth of values, careful image management, an absence of empathy, loyalty or any deep emotion, and an obsession with personal gain. The narcissist, as leader, creates problems for organizations. For them, organizations should word their value statements carefully so that they can be easily discarded or twisted. Wrongdoing is sanctioned not by ethics but by such things as the legal liability faced by the company. Loyalty to employees, caring for customers or altruistic philanthropy (that is, anything not geared to making more money) is considered weakness. The Al Dunlap case example illustrates a narcissistic leader displaying many of the qualities and behaviour associated with this form of leadership.

CASE EXAMPLE

MEMO TO AL DUNLAP: YOU'RE FIRED!

In 1994 Al Dunlap took over as chairman and chief executive officer of Scott Paper to the acclaim of all those who believed that what mattered most in company management was enhancing shareholder value. Scott Paper had become, like so many other sclerotic companies, slow to move, bloated and bleed-ing money. Dunlap, a man who enters a room as though he has just rappelled down the side of the build-ing, immediately took a chainsaw to the business, cut-

ting employees by the thousands, closing plants, and even reneging on commitments made to charities by his predecessor. He reportedly looked at a shelf of binders containing the company's strategic plans from previous years and ordered that they all be eliminated, sniffing, 'I don't read fiction.'

Dunlap hacked away at employees and facilities over the next 18 months, and then negotiated a takeover by Kimberly-Clark at a price that was more than twice what the stock was worth when he arrived at the company. Wall Street was ecstatic, but others weren't quite so sure. Kimberly-Clark executives learned after the fact that Dunlap all but eliminated major plant and equipment maintenance, slashed R&D expenses, and found other ways to borrow from the future in order to inflate the present bottom line. That was Dunlap's modus operandi, however. As Byrne puts it, 'Dunlap ran Scott's factories and drove people as if the company were going out of business.'

Even as Kimberly-Clark executives spent hundreds of millions of dollars to clean up the mess Dunlap had created, Scott investors were singing his praises for enriching them. At the same time, a new breed of activist investors was beginning to target underperforming companies, not for hostile takeovers, but for drastic makeovers. Michael Price and Michael Steinhardt were among those investors who had enormous sums at their disposal. They had locked their sights on Sunbeam and in 1996 engineered Dunlap's appointment as chairman and CEO, ostensibly to turn the company around. Dunlap took the position, with everyone quite convinced that it was going to be another Scott. The stock market reacted in kind and within two months boosted the stock price from 12 to 24. It continued to move up to a high of 52 before Dunlap and the company began to unravel.

Dunlap was not a master of turnarounds and restructurings, but of tantrums, abusive behaviour, dissembling and subterfuge. He implemented cuts arbitrarily, based on his own whims and recommendations from his right-hand man, Donald Burnham, a senior partner at Coopers & Lybrand. Swarms of accountants descended on Sunbeam operations looking only for ways to cut costs, not for ways to improve operations or profitability. Burnham's recommendations were often misguided, revealing a lack of understanding of the company's basic businesses. A recommendation to outsource the company's computer operations, for example, resulted in months of downtime and higher costs. The draconian cuts encouraged Sunbeam's more able employees to head for the exits as quickly as possible. Dunlap quickly became a hated man among the employees of the company and eventually bought a bullet-proof vest and a gun – and charged them both to the company.

Donald Uzzi, a manufacturing executive in the firm, questioned the wisdom of closing a particular plant. His projections showed that closing the plant would save about $200,000 in annual transportation costs, but cost the company more than $10 million to consolidate the plant's operations with another plant some 40 miles away. Uzzi suspected that the decision was a trick. 'I thought Al was trying to see if I knew what I was doing.' But when he raised the issue with Dunlap, the CEO refused to discuss it. He had made his mind up that the plant was to be closed, period. Indeed, in his first week, Dunlap, with no real information to base his decision on, told his senior executive team that the company would eventually have just 4 or 5 plants operating, down from the current 26.

As the company's stock price went up, Dunlap realized that the 'Dunlap premium' was working against him because the company was becoming too expensive for any other company to acquire. Meanwhile Dunlap and his cronies resorted to a growing number of questionable accounting practices to 'make the numbers' each quarter. The most notorious was 'inventory-stuffing': selling customers far more product than they needed, but offering them considerable financial inducements to take the products. Such short-term tricks pump up the sales figures for a quarter or two, but come back to haunt the company when the customer refuses to buy any more product for months.

Duinlap's was an all-too-familiar story: a person with an enormous ego begins to believe his own press clippings. Investors flock to him, showering him with power and wealth, but failing to create any system of accountability. Hubris and greed dominate this story, but Dunlap was humiliated when he was fired and Michael Price watched his more than $600 million profit in Sunbeam stock evaporate. Both are, however, still extraordinarily wealthy men today. Never mind the long-term effects of their actions on thousands of individuals, the impact on communities, or the wisdom of such short-term thinking. Dunlap's so-called turnaround of Sunbeam in 1997 was little more than a manufactured illusion based on improper accounting moves, but for too many in the investment community, the response is 'who cares as long as I can make money on the stock.'

Source: Adapted from an anonymous review of John Byrne (1999) *Chainsaw: The Notorious Career of Al Dunlap in the Era of Profit-At-Any-Price,* New York: HarperCollins on Knowledge@Wharton 10 December 1999, http://knowledge. wharton.upenn.edu/articles.cfm?articleid=105, accessed 12 February 2003.

The problem is that as one or two ruthless managers start to be successful, the message spreads and the behaviour develops into a situation of epidemic proportions. Eventually, corporate cultures succumb, and everyone must play by the narcissist's rules – 'kill or be killed'. Downs sees this as a major sickness of corporate America but Lasch sees it as one of American society as a whole, and according to Callaghan it is not confined to the borders of the USA. If this is true, the malaise is deeper than Downs thinks. We can think of several examples of narcissistic leaders we have worked for – our only hope is to recognize them for what they are and try to handle them appropriately.

Brown (1997) has attempted to specify both the basic

features of narcissism and how they impact at different levels of the organization, on individual behaviour, group process and organizational culture. The traits are: *denial* (of unacceptable facts about narcissists or their situation); *rationalization* (where action or fact has to be acknowledged, it is explained away); *self-aggrandizement* (self-flattery, fantasies of omnipotence and control); *attributional egotism* (blaming others for the narcissist's own personal problems); *self-entitlement* (exploiting others for personal gain); and basic *anxiety* (a constant striving for certainty and struggling for self-worth). These dimensions are explained in Table 10.4.

Downs points out that narcissistic behaviour and cultures are difficult to change. Once managers have reached a position of authority, they have probably had a couple of decades or more of reinforcement of their narcissism. The underlying problem cannot be fixed easily, and it requires the narcissist to want to change. Cultures in which narcissistic behaviour is widespread and has become the norm need top management commitment to change and that commitment has to be towards openness, trust and a respect for the truth. However, Downs tends to take the approach that cultures are basically a collection of individuals, and underemphasizes the extent to which structures – of power, political groupings, coalitions of interests,

Table 10.4 Narcissism in organizations

| Narcissistic traits | Level of analysis | | |
	Individual	Group	Organization
Denial	Individuals deny the reality of market demands and resource constraints, facts about themselves and features of past occurrences	Groups deny facts under the influence of groupthink and through denial myths	Organizations deny facts about themselves through spokes-people, propaganda campaigns, annual reports and myths
Rationalization	Individuals rationalize action, inaction, policies and decisions	Groups offer collective rationalizations for their activities, their structures and behaviour, their decisions and their status	Organizations provide rationalizations that structure thought and *post hoc* justify their actions, inaction and responsibility
Self-aggrandizement	Individuals engage in fantasies of omnipotence and control, exhibit grandiosity and exhibitionism, create cultures in their own image, narrate stories that flatter themselves, make nonsensical acquisitions, engage in ego-boosting rituals, and write immodest autobiographies	Groups use myth and humour to exaggerate their sense of worth, have fantasies of unlimited ability when under stress, and engage in exhibitionistic social cohesion ceremonies	Organizations endow themselves with rightness, make claims to uniqueness, commission corporate histories, and deploy their office layouts and architecture as expressions of status, prestige and vanity
Attributional egotism	Individuals blame external authority for their personal plight and narrate stories that contain self-enhancing explanations	Collectivities attribute the failure of their decisions to external factors	Organizations (or management groups) use annual reports to blame unfavourable results on external factors and attribute positive outcomes to themselves
Sense of entitlement	Individuals are exploitive, lack empathy, engage in social relationships that lack depth and favour their interests over shareholders	Groups use songs and humour and ceremonies to express a sense of entitlement	Organizations are structured according to a principle of entitlement to exploit. Organizations assume entitlement to continued successful existence
Anxiety	Individuals suffer internally, need stability and certainty, experience deprivation and emptiness, are paralysed by personal anxiety and tension, and struggle to maintain a sense of their self-worth	Management groups are prone to anxiety. Groups such as nurses and social care workers suffer from particularly high levels of anxiety	Organizations suffer from anomie and alienation, requiring shared culture, moral order, a common sense of purpose; leadership attempts to secure commitment, and the broader distribution of work responsibilities

Source: Adapted from Andrew D. Brown (1997) 'Narcissism, identity and legitimacy', *Academy of Management Review*, **22**(3), pp. 643–6, 652–3.

resource control and flow of information – may severely restrict what individuals can achieve. Downs does acknowledge that, in reality, change may not be possible, and suggests ways of living with a narcissistic colleague or manager.

For Downs, the first step to dealing with a narcissist is always to know your own motivation and what you need from the narcissist. No one is immune to narcissistic behaviour and sometimes we can contribute to the problem. Problems most often occur with narcissist leaders when we are trying to serve the same needs, primarily for power and recognition, as they are. The three most common difficulties arising from this are competition, conflict and incompatibility. The latter occurs when one party is focused on internal motivations like personal satisfaction and the other on external ones like monetary reward. Table 10.5 shows the methods suggested by Downs for coping with these difficulties.

However, it would be a mistake to think that narcissism does not affect other approaches to leadership. Daniel Sankowsky (1995) has examined how narcissism can also be found in those who are identified as being charismatic or transformational leaders. He says that these types of leader possess great symbolic power because their followers often come to idolize them and perceive them as someone they can profoundly trust. In turn narcissistic charismatic leaders expect to be idolized by their loyal followers. Followers tend to idolize charismatic leaders because of all or one of the following:

1. omnipotent archetype (the leader will nurture and guide them)
2. leader as mystic (knows the way and has the answers)
3. heroic stereotype (can move mountains)
4. the value-driven virtuous leader (looks after the collective good and is empowering) (Sankowsky 1995: 64).

Sankowsky suggests that when charisma and the pathology of narcissism are combined, leaders often promote visions that reflect their own sense of grandiosity, sweeping others up in their grand plans. They often approach ventures based on their own sureness of self rather than their command of information or clarity of insight (Sankowsky 1995: 65). They expect people to defer to them, to accept blindly their view of reality. Sankowsky (1995: 67) gives examples of a number of leaders who might qualify as narcissistic charismatic leaders, for example Steve Jobs (creator of Apple and NeXT), whose followers often spoke of him in terms of his perfection and high expectations and how they, as followers, could never be as good as him. One important aspect of charismatic/narcissistic leaders' influence is their ability to diminish the self-worth of others or make this totally dependent on their approval.

Finally, Carr (1998: 86) points out that to see narcissism as a disorder with *only* negative effects is to neglect its 'Janus-like nature'. He reminds us that Freud considered that narcissism was ubiquitous and a necessary element in loving relationships, and cites Alford's observation that 'narcissism may serve as a stimulus for the achievement of the highest ideals' (Alford 1988: 27 cited in Carr 1998: 86). The source of the narcissists' anxiety and feeling of inferiority is the demands of an image of an ideal self that they find impossible to satisfy, but the pursuit of this ideal may lead to socially valued activities and goals as well as undesirable ones. Although Downs is probably correct in saying that the negative aspects of narcissism have reached epidemic proportions, we should not neglect its positive possibilities. Nor should we neglect the fact that narcissism is a quality or behaviour that not only plagues managers and leaders but can manifest in subordinates and peers as well, resulting in distinct problems for handling this behaviour in the workplace (Diamond and Allcorn 1990).

Table 10.5	Suggestions for handling narcissist leaders	
Competition	**Conflict**	**Incompatibility**
1. Create a clear division of labour without overlap	1. Create a clear division of responsibilities without 'turf' overlap	1. Recognize that their motivations may be different from yours, but you can coexist
2. Show them how your success will support them	2. Keep talking at the highest level of agreement. Do not get bogged down in conflict over details	2. Scan each situation for what will motivate them (extrinsic rewards)
3. Do not be greedy. Share the spotlight	3. Assure the leader of your agreement over larger objectives; request control over small areas within this	3. Make decisions based on what will bring them the extrinsic satisfaction they need, while meeting your intrinsic needs

Source: Adapted from Alan Downs (1997) *Beyond the Looking Glass*, New York: Amacom, pp. 168–74.

Gender and leadership

The existing research on women and leadership has been aptly summarized by Fiona Wilson (1995: 172–8). She points out that the study of leadership (or power) has rarely included sex or sex roles as organizationally significant variables. Leaders seem to be not only male, but quite masculine with it, and where women and leadership is a topic in texts on leadership, it is usually treated as a separate chapter. In other words, women are not integrated into the mainstream theorizing of leadership. This is hardly surprising, given the fact that most theories of leadership have ignored gender (see the discussion in Chapter 2).

Judy Rosener, in researching prominent women leaders and men across a number of countries, found men tend to describe themselves in ways consistent with 'transactional' leadership. They viewed their performance as a series of transactions with subordinates involving rewards and punishment or what are really exchange relationships. Women in the study described themselves in ways consistent with transformational leadership (Rosener 1990: 120), although with different emphases from the masculine heroic image. Among the transformational qualities women favoured were: interactive leadership or participation; making people feel important and energized; sharing information and power; and placing less emphasis on formal authority (that is, status, position). A similar study in the UK found that women reported themselves as catalyst or visionary leaders, while the men were traditionalist leaders (see Wilson 1995). In a US study, Florence Denmark (1993) also found that women were perceived to be more democratic than men, that is, they encouraged more participation in decision making. Denmark also found that when women behaved autocratically (or like many male managers might), they were viewed more negatively by both men and women. Women who occupied leadership positions traditionally held by men were more devalued by male evaluators. Yet men rated women superiors higher in leadership qualities than did women (Denmark 1993: 353–5).

But the differences are less clear when we look at how subordinates perceive men and women leaders. Wilson noted that other women subordinates responded differently to the same behaviour, depending on whether it was displayed by a man or a woman. Wilson also noted that consideration behaviours displayed by a woman leader tended to be more favourably evaluated, and women subordinates preferred a more democratic style of leadership and sought greater involvement in decision making (Wilson 1995:173). Exhibit 10.4 summarizes some findings on research on female leaders.

Interestingly, women appear to perceive power

Exhibit 10.4 Characteristics of female leaders

Research has found female leaders to be:

❏ accommodative or affiliative (close to those people they interact with)
❏ less self-enhancing
❏ more self-disclosing
❏ more vulnerable
❏ willing to admit to lack of self-confidence
❏ willing to express emotions
❏ more positive in giving encouragement, support and information
❏ less assertive
❏ better communicators
❏ better at reading non-verbal behaviour
❏ more sensitive and socially objective
❏ more cooperative and democratic
❏ better group facilitators and consultants.

Source: Adapted from Fiona Wilson (1995) *Organizational Behaviour and Gender*, London: McGraw-Hill, pp. 173–6.

(hence influence) differently from men, seeing it as a liberating force in the community (that is, capacity, competence and energy) rather than as a means of controlling and dominating others, and therefore they tend to be non-aggressive and more concerned for the welfare of others (Huxham 1996: 22, citing Hartsock 1985). Men, on the other hand, are more likely to seek to maintain distance from their subordinates in order to maintain status, to be instrumental and task-oriented, and more dominant, self-assured, directive, precise and quick to challenge others. These views are echoed by Judith Pringle (1994: 136–7) who cites research from the USA (Helgesen 1990 and Astin and Leland 1991) which supports the view that women do interpret and represent their leadership styles as being different from those often portrayed as being masculine, particularly in terms of power. Women, she says, describe a leader as someone who plays a catalytic empowering role, and who works to create a collective effort to improve the quality of life of those who work for them. There are also men who would identify with this more 'feminine' version of leadership.

Much of the research, however, does appear to indicate that there may be considerable pressure on both men and women to conform to stereotypes held by subordinates. Richard Scase and Robert Goffee (1990) also argued that the reportedly preferred managerial styles of both men and women are influenced by prevailing fads and fashions about effective management. In a study carried out in the 1980s, when assertiveness became popularly valued, 88 per cent of women managers surveyed claimed to be tough, aggressive, firm and assertive, while less than 50 per cent mentioned being open, cooperative and consultative. Additionally, how people look and their appearance is important to the way in which people respond to them as leaders and it is an advantage to look mature rather than glamorous or even 'sexy'. This may have affected the power-dressing fashion of the 1980s (Brewis et al. 1997).

It seems clear, though, that however difficult it may be to determine a feminine or a definitively masculine managerial style of leadership, women do display skills and behaviours that complement, and sometimes challenge, those traditionally displayed by men. It is quite possible that as organizations change in style and structure, even the concept of 'leader' may change. But before this happens there will need to be more serious critical analysis of the masculinist domination of the discourse about leadership, as Marta Calás and Linda Smircich (1995) reveal (see also Chapter 2). We might well ask: why have leadership studies neglected gender issues or sought to represent the differences between men and women as a 'negative difference' for women in management (Sinclair 1998)?

At beginning of the chapter we asked the question: 'Are women and men different as leaders?' This question is really about how the differences between men and women are constructed or represented in the first place, and how these differences have influenced leadership theories. If men dominate leadership positions, as we have already established in Chapter 2, then women are always the subordinate term in the leadership equation, and their rise to leadership assumes doing as well as, if not better, than men to succeed. To be able to lead often means women outperforming male leaders.

None of the theories of leadership examined in this chapter, with the possible exception of post-heroic leadership, were ever intended to be inclusive of women. Even contingency theorists treated the context or the situation as unproblematic in terms of diversity because 'leaders' were all the same in each category, irrespective of gender or sexuality. Leadership theories have pretended gender neutrality or displayed gender blindness but have inevitably imported male values and characteristics as the norm, and have been 'phallocentric' – viewing the world implicitly from a masculine point of view.

Studies such as those of Rosener or Denmark simply reaffirm that differences in leadership styles arise from special feminine qualities, excluding men from possessing such qualities or feeling legitimate in displaying them. They also support the view that these qualities are somehow 'inferior' and can never appear adequate when measured, consciously or unconsciously, against a masculine yardstick. In the heroic genre of leadership theories, women always stand to lose, given the representations of leadership traits and qualities that prevail, unless they adopt heroic traits that will always be precariously valued by men and would be seen as 'unnatural' for women.

For the concept of leadership to have a more inclusive meaning, it would require seriously questioning the assumptions behind how differences are presented and represented in everyday organizations, especially by critiquing the cult of leadership that is so ingrained in much thinking about organizations. It would mean seriously considering how to be more inclusive of women's experiences of themselves, both in terms of their gender and sexuality, as well as of those men who no longer identify with the popular imagery of leadership or masculinity. It would also mean developing concepts of leadership that do not implicitly set men against women as natural or normative opposites based on biological differences, socially developed notions of superiority and inferiority or socialization (see Chapter 2). New approaches to leadership have to emphasize how men and women can and do work side by side, complementing, strengthening and elevating each other to achieve as leaders, facilitators or counsellors and how leadership occurs as a social practice rather than an individual quality. Women will fail or succeed as leaders and it is important to look at how such achievements or failures arise and whether and how gender figures in them. We need to learn more about how organizations and the people in them 'do' gender.

Cross-cultural dimensions of leadership

Another neglected dimension of leadership – and most other dimensions of organization theory – is its culture boundedness. As argued in Chapter 2, the knowledge project in which early management theorists were engaged was about the identification of universal principles which were context-free – thus gender was suppressed and so was culture. At a technical level, at which much of scientific management was involved, some of these principles were readily adaptable to other countries, including the USSR and Japan. In fact, Akio Morita, the former president of Sony Corporation, said: 'US and Japanese management are 95 per cent the same, and differ in all important respects.' What he meant was that culture was the 5 per cent difference, the rest was methods, technology and structure.

Leadership then falls into the 5 per cent, and as Geert Hofstede (1992) argues, the very theories which purport to be universalistic are in fact shaped significantly by the fact that they were developed by US theorists in the USA. He also argues that if we want to know whether US theories apply abroad, there is no need to test them before we can reach a view – looking at the key characteristics of different cultures according to his model will predict whether there will be difficulties and what those difficulties are likely to be.

As mentioned in Chapter 3, Hofstede developed a measure of culture on four dimensions and, later, with Michael Bond, added a fifth. These were power distance, uncertainty avoidance, masculinity/feminitiy, individualism/collectivism, and long-term/short-term orientation. Differences in these dimensions will affect the way leaders see their role and also the way subordinates perceive it – in fact, the differences in subordinate perception are most significant because it is these assumptions that will make it difficult for a manager from a different culture to operate in a new one.

Most of the US leadership theories tend to advocate, implicitly or explicitly, participation by subordinates in decision making, but the initiative in extending participation is the manager's (Hofstede 1992). This is consistent with a medium power distance culture such as the USA. In a high power distance culture, such as Hong Kong, the manager's authority would not be shared, and in a low power distance culture, such as Scandinavia, participation would be seen as the norm, not a managerial option (see Chapter 11). Another dimension that affects this is uncertainty avoidance – in a low uncertainty avoidance country, such as Sweden,

local experiments in democracy are encouraged and if successful become regulations, but in a high uncertainty avoidance country, such as Germany, the regulatory framework (laws, and so on) has to come first.

Hofstede (1992: 113–18) discusses the problems in imposing management techniques associated with leadership styles which have an implicit cultural bias. An example might be the case of self-managed work teams (see Chapter 11), which assumes medium power distance (negotiations are meaningful, employees not too weak), weak uncertainty avoidance (that is, willing to take risks) and high masculinity (performance orientation). Hofstede also notes the difficulties of operating with subordinates with differing cultural biases from the manager, pointing out that often subordinates from high power distance cultures, such as those in Asia, prefer autocratic Theory X leadership. David McClelland (1961) found variations on the need for achievement, an important factor in leadership style, between Turkey (3.62) and Belgium (0.43) (see Chapter 9). Such a wide variation across cultures questions whether we can meaningfully use the same term for 'leadership' in Turkey and Belgium. The more complex combinations of cultural factors may require that the concept of leadership be replaced altogether with a different concept, such as 'influence'. However, we need to keep in mind that there will always be variations within nations regarding these cultural dimensions and, as stated in Chapter 3, a whole range of experiences might predispose a manager to act or behave outside cultural expectations and norms (see Triandis 1995).

Robert Westwood (1992) identifies one particularly common alternative model to the Western leadership

---

Exhibit 10.5 Paternal leadership style

- **Dependence orientation of subordinates** The acceptance of hierarchy and the concept of filial piety lead to the cultural norm of conforming to headship and dependence on the patriarch.

- **Personalism** Personal relationships play a more important role in governing behaviour than formal systems and rules.

- **Moral leadership** The leader is assumed to possess virtues such as humanity and integrity as a requirement in his role. He must act as a model and be worthy of respect.

- **Harmony building** Part of the leadership role is to build and maintain harmony. He should be sensitive to the feelings of subordinates.

- **Conflict diffusion** The leader needs to make sure that conflicts are prevented from happening.

- **Social distance** The leader tends to stay at a social distance from the subordinates to preserve his father-like authority.

- **Didactic leadership** The leader is assumed to be the master who possesses the necessary knowledge and information and is expected to act like a teacher.

- **Dialogue ideal** A subtle and informal communication is expected so that the leader can signal his intentions and be aware of the sentiments and views of the subordinate.

Source: Robert Westwood (1992) *Organizational Behaviour*, Hong Kong: Longmans Group (FE), pp. 121–41.

Exhibit 10.6 Paternal leadership tactics

❏ **Centralization** The leader, as part of the autocratic elements of his leadership, will not allow much involvement of subordinates in the decision-making process.

❏ **Non-specific intentions** The leader will not be explicit in revealing his intentions and expectations.

❏ **Secrecy** The leader will always keep certain information or knowledge to himself.

❏ **Avoidance of formality** The leader will avoid turning the way of doing things through relations into formal procedures.

❏ **Protection of dominance** The leader will seek to protect his authority position through playing down the importance of the subordinates, altering the responsibility requirements at will,

making subjective evaluation of subordinate performance, and so on.

❏ **Patronage and nepotism** The leader will use his position power and the resources at his disposal to do selective favours to the subordinates. Family members or those linked to the leader are often appointed to key positions.

❏ **Non-emotional ties** The leader will avoid emotional bonds with the subordinates to shield his dignity and to evade obligations.

❏ **Political manipulation** The leader controls the group through differential treatment of the individuals.

❏ **Reputation building** The leader will be very concerned about building and protecting his reputation, especially in external ties with business associates.

Source: Robert Westwood (1992) *Organizational Behaviour*, Hong Kong: Longmans Group (FE), pp. 121–41.

model in the East. This is the model of headship or paternalism. The paternalistic leadership style characteristic of Southeast Asia, especially in small businesses, is derived from cultures with a high level of power distance, and hence tends to be more directive and autocratic. It has the combination of characteristics shown in Exhibit 10.5.

The adoption of this style also leads to the use of some very specific behaviours and tactics which keep the father figure leader – and you will notice that we

deliberately use the pronoun 'he' throughout this section when referring to the leader – in unchallenged authority, as described in Exhibit 10.6.

Now, it might be useful to pause a moment to consider this question: In what ways is the 'paternalistic style of leadership' commonly demonstrated by small business owners in Southeast Asia different from the 'autocratic' style discussed in the Western world? You should be able to answer this question by reviewing the above material.

Conclusion

Leadership is widely regarded as a central determinant of organizational performance but it is a difficult concept to tie down. Trait and style approaches have proven limited in utility, while the contingency perspective threatens to become paralysed by the volume of possible contingent factors, although the latter approach has value in establishing that there is no 'one best way' to lead in all situations. These approaches tend to focus on leadership as supervisory style. An alternative approach is to see leadership as political and strategic *influence,* centred on such activities as building and maintaining networks, creating and perpetuating a sense of purpose, enabling and empowering followers and basically sharing the power and glory of leadership. Post-heroic leadership questions the importance of leadership as something that belongs to a lone hero manager.

Nonetheless, most leadership training still focuses on the concept of style within a contingency/situational framework. As such it is subject to an extremely basic criticism: that style is simply one aspect of leadership. Perhaps such training is relatively harmless, but the focus on styles as manifest in leadership training may have its darker side. Underlying the style perspective is a perspective on organizations which assumes that once the most appropriate styles of leadership are known, first, selections will take place guided by this knowledge and, second, leadership styles will be changed as a result of training. This ignores some fundamental aspects of organizational life.

The selection of leaders is embedded in the complex politics of organizational life and the qualification of having an appropriate leadership style as designated by current theory constitutes merely one claim for selection. Embedded commitments and established images of the 'right sort' are likely to be more formidable bases for selection. The rules of the organizational world, as presumed in leadership training, are often at odds with the reality of organizational practice. Second, leaders are not merely free agents who can choose to change their leadership style as a result of training-based 'enlightenment'. Enmeshed in the organization, the individual leader is constrained both positively and negatively. Pressures to conform to the expectations of peers, subordinates and superiors are likely to affect the actual behaviour of leaders (Pfeffer 1978: 20). This applies equally to men and women.

One implication of this chapter for leadership training would seem to be the utility of reorientating it so that it focuses on the activity of leaders as networkers, strategic actors, influencers in the organizational network. A central part of this should involve an ability to analyse the leadership implications of the organizational culture, since this can be a significant influence on how a leader is received. Steven Feldman (1986) notes the response of senior managers to a new CEO who had a quite different style of leadership from his predecessors. The executives were used to non-ambiguous, directive CEOs. They complained of a 'lack of direction' and an absence of 'presence of command'. The established organizational culture revolved around a 'strong' CEO. In view of this kind of finding, perhaps it is the organization which needs training not the leader. But certainly explicit attention needs to be given to issues like follower maturity related to gender and diversity issues if women and other minorities are to break through the glass ceiling into leadership positions – it is not enough simply to regard this as a problem for training individuals.

We have also identified a post-heroic leadership agenda for organizations and their managers. There is a tendency in the popular literature to suggest that post-heroic leadership is 'one best way' for managing or leading in the new age of the knowledge or brain worker. However, we would argue that key elements of the approach, such as the role of trust in organizations, have not been examined in sufficient depth for us to have confidence in the broad applicability of the approach. Our discussion of the narcissistic leader also illustrates the point that managers as leaders do not 'park their emotions at the door' when they come to work, including their egos. As Huey (1994) and Collins (2001) remind us, much of the post-heroic leadership agenda requires that many managers say 'no' to their egos. A narcissistic leader could never do this.

Answers to questions about leadership

1 What is a leader? This has changed over the years, particularly as leadership ideas have been adapted to changes in organizations. One of the dominant themes in the leadership research has been the role played by heredity and traits in the shaping of leadership qualities, particularly the drive or need for power. Views tend to polarize around the 'born leader' versus the trained or 'made leader'. Certainly, the popularity of the transformational leadership image of the 1980s lent support to the trait theory. Conversely, as organizations change – and not necessarily in uniform ways – the idea of post-heroic leadership has become ever more popular. The post-heroic leadership idea supports leadership teams, rotating leadership positions and generally sharing power and spreading it around. Yet many large companies seem less able to embrace the idea of post-heroic leadership. These very large companies, with major shareholders, boards and committees, have governance structures that still seem to favour 'the captain of industry' model of leadership – 'the great man' of the trait theorists and the absolute power of the leader this entails.

The essence of leadership is not something that can be agreed to, especially as issues of diversity no longer make it sensible to subscribe to one dominant model of leadership. Many leadership approaches have also been gender or culture-blind. Leadership is very much a product of the society in which organizations operate, and these are now becoming international or global societies (see Chapter 3). Cultural variables will affect how managers from different cultural backgrounds manage in expatriate or foreign cultures and with culturally diverse groups. Leadership is also a product or is defined in terms of the problems or circumstances facing an organization. We suggest that leadership, or the role of the leader, is most appropriately thought of as predominantly concerned with *influence* and the form of influence that is used has to be seen as legitimate by a wide group of interests within any organization. The particular form of leadership influence chosen or practised by leaders or leadership teams should relate to, and be judged as part of, enhancing the performance of any organization.

2 Are all managers leaders? The answer to this question depends on which school of leadership thought one subscribes to. Early theories of leadership were definitely focused on selecting the born leader and nurturing him to greatness. Then again, the style and contingency theorists had strong views on the malleability or adaptability of leadership styles. In their views, all managers had leadership potential, even if in some cases it was, say, Theory X leadership. The post-heroic leadership literature has tried to dispel the notion of a single heroic leader running the organization and has proposed instead more broad leadership development across the organization. The performance of organizations adopting a post-heroic style or approach to leadership needs to be evaluated further as the number of post-heroic leadership organizations grow.

Answers continued

3 Are women and men different as leaders? When it comes to the question of gender and leadership, research lends support to the idea that men and women are different as leaders. However, on close examination of this evidence, there is no clear indication as to why this should be, and the idea of there being a masculine style versus a feminine style is very difficult to support. Even the idea of the androgynous leader who has both male and female characteristics is rather superficial, and further problems occur when we recognize that perceived behaviour reported by managers varies from that reported by subordinates, and female managers are just as influenced by fads and the need to appear to be doing the right thing as anyone else. What this means is that there are differences, and we need more studies of actual women leaders at work, in context, rather than more surveys, in order to understand better the field of interacting forces in which they operate.

4 Can leaders change their styles or behaviours? This is one of the most vexing questions in leadership. It is unlikely that narcissistic leaders can change their style, and the reality is that organizations can promote this form of leadership. Cultural aspects of leadership are also likely to be highly resistant to change. However, crises or major upheavals have been known to precipitate change in leadership approaches. This might involve altering or attenuating aspects of leadership style or bringing in a new leader or leadership team. Organizations reward certain styles of leadership and politically it is often these styles that ensure career success. Our view is that adopting post-heroic leadership styles for many managers, or even Theory Y for the narcissistic leader, is very difficult. Politics, power and certain predispositions suggest that the training of managers to adopt particular leadership styles only works to a degree, and only if their organizations genuinely reward or encourage a particular approach.

5 Do we need leaders? This is perhaps the hardest question to answer. Leadership substitute theories seem to suggest there are ways and circumstances in which leadership is not necessary. Post-heroic leadership theories do not subscribe to the abolition of leadership, but to a radical rethinking of it, often using leadership substitutes and neutralizers or ideas drawn from the organization learning literature. Others propose that leadership is the work of every one if adaptive challenges become the focus of this work. We are also reminded that many of the qualities of post-heroic leadership are often nothing more than the qualities needed to do everyday work (Sashkin 1992: 155). In organizations of all kinds, the question of whether leadership is important or needed, and the type of leadership that is championed, is determined by those who wield power and have vested political and personal interests in favouring a particular rhetoric and approach to leadership. To change the leadership practices in an organization usually requires leadership from somewhere at the top levels. On this point alone, it is clear that there will always be organizations that claim they need strong, visionary leaders, heroic or otherwise, and will not subscribe in practice to any post-heroic agenda. There will also be those organizations that will adopt the 'post-heroic' discourse, but their leadership practices might stay relatively heroic.

REVISITING
THE CASE STUDY

1 How would you characterize Ruud Gullit's leadership style?

He seems to be very task- and structure-oriented so, in Blake and Mouton's terms, he would rate high on this factor and probably low to medium on people, given that he seemed to be driving some of his players away, making it an authority-compliance basic style. In Likert's terms, he would be somewhere between S1 and S2, but Fiedler would suggest that this style was appropriate for the 'crisis' which NUFC was arguably facing. Of course, whether this style is appropriate for a CEO every day is questionable. Hersey and Blanchard would categorize the behaviour as S1 or S2, but the followers in this case are highly skilled and experienced professionals.

2 What considerations seem to be most important to Gullit?

Clearly, bringing things under his own personal control seems to be at the centre of his plan. His own personal style seems to be an issue, and to that extent his approach seems to be narcissistic. Those theories which suggest that leaders need to change styles imply that leadership is a performance, but they tend to underestimate the wider audience for that performance – in this case the supporters, shareholders and directors. Gullit seems to divorce the football club from its wider context and only engages with footballing matters.

3 What kind of relationships would you expect Gullit to have with:

(a) his players?

Gullit seems to have difficult relations with some of his players, but these seem to stem from his own inflexibility and his requirement for the players to be flexible. He seems somewhat intolerant of players who do not have the skills which he had and the ability to play 'total football' in any position. He spends little time communicating, and doesn't help them to understand why they are not in the team or what they need to do to get back into it. He has a firm idea of what players should do, and he seems not to be able to get the best out of a squad. He

splits the squad, as LMX (leader-member exchange) theory might recognize, by having his in-group of 'lovely boys'. Indeed he seems quite intimidatory in the way he almost writes people off and manages some of them by 'Theory F' where the 'F' is for fear (see Linstead and Chan 1994).

(b) the fans?

His relationship with the fans, who were prepared to hero-worship him, was spoiled by his inability to understand and respect their history and background. They expected total commitment to the club and the region, but got an absentee manager who had no affection for the city or the region, and indeed was unable to understand the centuries of rivalry between Newcastle and Sunderland which stretched back to the English Civil War in the seventeenth century. Gullit's focus on the task rather than the culture badly affected these relationships.

(c) the board of directors?

Gullit's arrogance would not necessarily affect a board of directors as long as he was bringing them success – Newcastle was one of the world's richest clubs, and a business success, but had not had much success on the field of play in recent years. Shareholders, sponsors and supporters alike expected him to deliver. This became much more of a problem when he spent large amounts of the club's money only to bring in players who seemed unable to fit in – or who he failed to blend as a team.

4 How do you think Gullit would think that it is appropriate to develop future football managers?

Gullit seems unable to take a developmental approach, and to help players to improve – if they don't make the grade in his eyes, he rejects them, even players who left to become star players at big clubs like Leeds and Liverpool and to win international caps for England, Germany and Ireland. He seems to have little patience and one might expect that his 'you can do it or you can't' approach to managing to make the idea of developing the next manager redundant. When the club made it known that they expected Shearer to one day become manager, there were clear tensions.

5 How would you characterize the leadership approach at NUFC?

Is Gullit a transactional or transformational leader? He sees himself as driving change, even being radical, but with a rather fixed set of views about what players should do and how they should relate to their manager. However, he is more than transactional as he is breaking up the routines, although it seems that at Chelsea he became transactional when he lost interest. He is certainly charismatic, and a little whimsical. At times he seems to combine styles, such as conservative transformational or radical transactional, where change is an extreme reassertion of older, perhaps forgotten principles. Certainly he seems as though he wants to be heroic, but can't quite get people to love him enough, perhaps because he is insufficiently post-heroic to relax his principles and involve them in his plans.

6 What culture or gender influences could have been operating in this situation?

Football, although it is a masculine game, is a game of egos as much as bodies, and confidence is as important as ability and fitness. Often, a manager needs to be capable of bullying and cajoling at times, and at others to be encouraging and supporting, displaying both tough masculine and softer, more motherly qualities to get the best out of all his squad at all times and in all situations, public and private, pressured or relaxed. Gullit's sexy football idea was based on some quite rigid masculine values, and he seemed to be unable to display the soft skills necessary to keep the confidence of his team high when things were not going well, and he was too ready to blame them for their position. Culturally, it is possible that Gullit's Dutch pragmatism, and tendency to go straight to the point without ceremony, which English people often find abrasive, also contributed to his failure to communicate with or understand his team, fans and bosses.

References

Aktouf, O. (1996) 'Competence, symbolic activity and promotability', in Linstead, S., Grafton Small, R. and Jeffcutt, P. (eds) *Understanding Management*, London: Sage.

Alford, C. (1988) *Narcissism: Socrates, the Frankfurt School, and Psychoanalytic Theory,* New Haven, CT: Yale University Press.

Astin, H. and Leland, C. (1991) *Women of Influence, Women of Vision: A Cross-Generational Study of Leaders of Change*, San Francisco: Jossey-Bass.

Barrett, M. and Sutcliffe, P. (1992) 'Incorporating a critical perspective into management: The case of leadership models', paper presented to 1992 ANZAM Conference Penrith, 6–9 December, University of Western Sydney: 1–29.

Barrett, M. and Sutcliffe, P. (1993) 'Leadership theories: A critique and its implications for management education', *Queensland University of Technology, Faculty of Business, Key Centre in Strategic Management, Working Paper Series, No. 24*, Brisbane: Queensland University of Technology.

Bass, B. (1985) *Leadership and Performance Beyond Expectations*, New York: Free Press.

Bennis, W.G. (1985) *Leaders: Strategies for Taking Charge*, New York: Harper & Row.

Blake, R. and McCanse, A.A. (1991) *Leadership Dilemmas – Grid Solutions*, Houston: Gulf.

Blake, R. and Mouton, J. (1978) *The New Managerial Grid*, Houston: Gulf.

Blanchard, K., Zigarmi, P. and Zigarmi, D. (1985) *Leadership and the One-Minute Manager*, London: HarperCollins.

Bolman, L.G. and Deal, T.E. (1991) *Reframing Organizations: Artistry, Choice and Leadership*, San Francisco and Oxford: Jossey-Bass.

Bradford, D. and Cohen, A. (1984) *Managing for Excellence*, New York: John Wiley.

Brewis, J., Hampton, M. and Linstead, S. (1997) 'Unpacking Priscilla: Subjectivity and identity in the organization of gendered appearance', *Human Relations* **50**(10): 1275–304.

Brown, A.D. (1997) 'Narcissism, identity and legitimacy', *Academy of Management Review* **22**(3): 643–86.

Bryman, A. (1985) 'Leadership' in Elliot, K. and Lawrence, P. (eds) *Introducing Management*, Harmondsworth: Penguin.

Bryman, A. (1986) *Leadership and Organizations*, London: Routledge & Kegan Paul.

Calás, M.B. and Smircich L. (1995) 'Dangerous liaisons: The "feminine-in management" meets "globalization"', in P. Frost, V. Mitchell and W. Nord (eds) *Managerial Reality*, New York: HarperCollins.

Callaghan, G. (1997) 'Here's looking at me, kid', *The Australian Magazine,* 25–26 October: 12–17.

Carr, A. (1994) 'For self or others? The quest for narcissism and the ego-ideal in work organizations', *Administrative Theory and Praxis,* **16**(2): 208–22.

Carr, A. (1998) 'Identity, compliance and dissent in organizations: A psychoanalytic perspective', *Organization,* **5**(1): 81–99.

Caulkin, S. (1993) 'The lust for leadership', *Management Today,* November, **38**: 40–3.

Cavaleri, S. and Fearon, D. (eds) (1996) *Managing in Organizations that Learn,* Cambridge, MA: Blackwell Business.

Collins, J. (2001) *Good to Great: Why Some Companies Make the Leap and Others Don't,* New York: HarperCollins.

Collins, J. and Porras, J.I. (1994) *Built to Last: Successful Habits of Visionary Companies,* New York: Harper Buisness.

Coopey, J. (1995) 'The learning organization: Power, politics and ideology', *Management Learning* **26**(2): 193–213.

Crawford, R. (1991) *In the Era of Human Capital: The Emergence of Talent, Intelligence, and Knowledge as a Worldwide Economic Force and What it Means to Managers and Investors,* New York: Harper Business.

Dansereau, F., Graen, G. and Haga, W.J. (1975) 'A vertical dyad linkage approach to leadership within formal organizations: A longitudinal investigation of the role-making process', *Organizational Behaviour and Human Performance,* **15**: 46–78.

Denmark, F.L. (1993) 'Women, leadership, and empowerment', *Psychology of Women Quarterly,* **17**: 343–56.

Diamond, M.A. and Allcorn, S. (1990) 'The Freudian factor', *Personnel Journal,* March: 54–65.

Downs, A. (1997) *Beyond the Looking Glass,* New York: Amacom.

Duncan, W.J. (1978) *Organizational Behavior,* Boston, MA: Houghton Mifflin.

Dunford, R. (1992) *Organisational Behaviour: An Organisational Analysis Perspective,* Sydney: Addison-Wesley Business Series.

Dunphy, D. and Stace, D. (1990) *Under New Management: Australian Organizations in Transition,* Sydney: McGraw-Hill.

Evans, M.G. (1970) 'The effects of supervisory behaviour on the path-goal relationship', *Organizational Behaviour and Human Performance* **5**: 277–98.

Feldman, S.P. (1986) 'Culture, charisma – and the CEO: An essay on the meaning of high office', *Human Relations,* **39**: 211–28.

Fiedler, F.E. (1967) *A Theory of Leadership Effectiveness,* New York: McGraw-Hill.

Fiedler, F.E. (1974) 'The contingency model – New directions for leadership utilization', *Journal of Contemporary Business,* **3**: 65–79.

Fiedler, F.E. and Garcia, J.E. (1987) *New Approaches to Effective Leadership,* New York: John Wiley.

Fiedler, F.E., Chemers, M.M. and Mahar, L. (1976) *Improving Leadership Effectiveness,* New York: John Wiley.

Fineman, S. (1993) 'Organizations as emotional arenas', in Fineman, S. (ed.) *Emotion in Organizations,* London: Sage.

Fleishman, E.A. and Peters, D.R. (1962) 'International values, leadership attitudes and managerial success', *Personnel Psychology,* **15**: 127–43.

Fulop, L., Linstead, S. and Dunford, R. (1999) 'Leading and Managing', in Fulop, L. and Linstead, S. (eds) *Management: A Critical Text,* Melbourne: Macmillan.

Gilmore, S. (2001) 'Mothers, babies and football managers' paper presented to 2nd Conference on Critical Management Studies, University of Manchester.

Graen, G. and Hui, C. (1999) 'Transcultural global leadership in the twenty-first century: Challenges and implications for development', in Mobley, W.H., Arnold, V. and Gessner, M. (eds) *Advances in Global Leadership,* Vol. 1, Stamford, CT: JAI Press, pp. 9–26.

Graen, G. and Schiemann, W. (1978) 'Leader–member agreement: A vertical dyad linkage approach', *Journal of Applied Psychology,* **63**: 206–12.

Graen, G. and Uhl-Bien, M. (1995) 'Development of leader-member exchange (LMX) theory of leadership over 25 years: Applying a multi-level-multi-domain perspective', *Leadership Quarterly,* **6**(2): 219–47.

Graen, G. and Wakabayashi, M. (1994) 'Cross-cultural leadership-making: Bridging American and Japanese diversity for team advantage', in Dunnette, M.D., Hough, M. and Triandis, H. (eds) *Handbook of Industrial and Organizational Psychology,* Vol. 4, New York: Consulting Psychologists Press, pp. 415–46.

Graen, G. and Zalsny, M. (1994) 'Exchange theory in leadership revisited: Same actors, different plot and location', in Kieser, A., Reber, G. and Wunderer, R. (eds) *Handbook of Leadership,* 2nd edn, Stuttgart: Poeschl Verlag, pp. 714–27.

Hackman, R.J. (1992) 'The psychology of self-management in organizations', in Glaser, R. (ed.) *Classic Readings in Self-Managing Teamwork,* King of Prussia, PA: Organization Design and Development Inc.

Haigh, G. (1994) 'Power without glory', *The Australian Magazine,* 25–26 June: 13–16, 20.

Harris, T.G. (1993) 'The post-capitalist executive: An interview with Peter F. Drucker', *Harvard Business Review,* May–June: 115–22.

Hartsock, N.C.M. (1985) *Money, Sex and Power: Toward a Feminist Historical Materialism,* New York: Simon & Schuster.

Hater, J.J. and Bass, B.M. (1988) 'Superiors' evaluations and subordinates' perceptions of transformational and transactional leadership', *Journal of Applied Psychology, 37*(4): 695–702.

Heifetz, R.A. and Laurie, D.L. (1997) 'The work of leadership', *Harvard Business Review,* January–February: 124–34.

Helgesen, S. (1990) *The Female Advantage: Women's Ways of Leadership*, New York: Doubleday.

Hellreigel, D.J., Slocum, W. and Woodman, W. (1986) *Organizational Behaviour*, St Paul: West Publishing.

Hersey, P. (1985) *The Situational Leader*, New York: Warner Books.

Hersey, P. and Blanchard, K. (1996) *Management of Organizational Behavior: Utilizing Human Resources*, Englewood Cliffs, NJ: Prentice Hall.

Hofstede, G. (1980/1992) 'Motivation, leadership and organization; Do American theories apply abroad', in Lane, H.W. and DiStefano, J.J. (eds) *International Management Behavior*, Boston: PWS/Kent.

House, R. (1971) 'A path–goal theory of leader effectiveness', *Administrative Science Quarterly,* **16**: 321–38.

Howell, J.P. and Dorfman, P.W. (1981) 'Substitutes for leadership: Test of a construct', *Academy of Management Journal,* **24**: 714–28.

Howell, J.P., Bowen, D.E., Dorfman, P.W., Kerr, S. and Podsakoff, P.M. (1990) 'Substitutes for leadership: Effective alternatives to ineffective leadership', *Organizational Dynamics,* Summer: 20–38.

Huey, J. (1994) 'The new post-heroic leadership', *Fortune,* 21 February: 24–8.

Hunsaker, P.L. and Cook, C.W. (1986) *Managing Organizational Behavior,* Reading, MA: Addison-Wesley.

Hutchinson, R. (1997) *The Toon: A Complete History of Newcastle United Football Club*, Edinburgh: Mainstream.

Huxham, C. (ed.) (1996) *Creating Collaborative Advantage*, London: Sage.

Kanter, R.M. (1977) *Men and Women of the Corporation*, New York: Basic Books.

Kanter, R.M. (1979) 'Power failure in management circuits', *Harvard Business Review, 57*(4): 65–75.

Kanter, R.M. (1983) The *Change Masters: Innovations for Productivity in American Corporations*, New York: Simon & Schuster.

Kelley, R. (1992) *The Power of Followership*, New York: Doubleday.

Kerr, S. and Jermier, J.M. (1978) 'Substitutes for leadership: Their meaning and measurement', *Organizational Behaviour and Human Performance,* **22**: 375–403.

Kets de Vries, M. (1991) 'Whatever happened to the philosopher king? The leader's addiction to power', *Journal of Management Studies, 28*(4): 339–51.

Kirkpatrick, S. and Locke, E.A. (1991) 'Leadership: Do traits matter?', *Academy of Management Executive,* **5**(2): 48–60.

Korman, A.K. (1966) '"Consideration", "initiating structure" and organizational criteria – a review', *Personnel Psychology,* **19**: 349–61.

Kotter, J. (1990) 'What leaders really do', *Harvard Business Review,* May–June: 103–11.

Kotter, J. (1995) *The New Rules: How to Succeed in Today's Post-Corporate World*, New York: Free Press.

Kouzes, J.M. and Posner, B.Z. (1989) *The Leadership Challenge,* San Francisco: Jossey-Bass.

Larson, L., Hunt, J.G. and Osborn, R.N. (1976) 'The great hi-hi leader behaviour myth: A lesson from Occam's Razor', *Academy of Management Journal,* **19**: 628–41.

Lasch, C. (1979) *The Culture of Narcissism – American Life in an Age of Diminishing Expectations*, New York: W.W. Norton.

Liden, R.C. and Graen, G. (1980) 'Generalizability of the vertical dyad model of leadership', *Academy of Management Journal,* **23**: 451–65.

Likert, R. (1961) *New Patterns of Management*, New York: McGraw-Hill.

Likert, R. (1967) *The Human Organization: Its Management and Value*, New York: McGraw-Hill.

Likert, R. (1979) 'From production and employee-centredness to systems 1–4', *Journal of Management,* **5**: 147–56.

Lindsey, E. (1998) 'Funky "dread" who put Chelsea back on the map', *Observer,* 15 February: 7.

Linstead, S. and Chan, A. (1994) 'The sting of organization: Command, reciprocity and change management', *Journal of Organizational Change Management, 7*(5): 4–19.

McClelland, D. (1961) *The Achieving Society*, Princeton, NJ: Van Nostrand.

McGregor, D. (1960) *The Human Side of Enterprise*, New York: McGraw-Hill.

Mant, A. (1994) *Leaders We Deserve* (2nd edn) Melbourne: Currency Production.

Manz, C.C. and Sims, H.P. Jr (1992) 'Becoming a super leader', in Glaser, R. (ed.) *Classic Readings in Self-Managing Teamwork*, King of Prussia, PA: Organization Design and Development Inc.

Maslow, A.H. (1987) *Motivation and Personality*, New York: Harper & Row.

Mintzberg, H. (1997) 'Toward healthier hospitals', *Health Care Management Review,* **22**(4): 9–18.

Mullins, L.J. (1985) *Management and Organizational Behaviour*, London: Pitman.

Nutt, P.C. (1995) 'Transforming public organizations with strategic leadership', in Halachmi, A. and Bouckaert, G. (eds) *Public Productivity Through Quality and Strategic Management*, Amsterdam: IOS Press.

Pelz, D. (1952) 'Influence: A key to effective leadership in the first line supervisor', *Personnel, 29*: 209–17.

Pfeffer, J. (1978) 'The ambiguity of leadership', in McCall, M.W. Jr and Lombardo, M.M. (eds) *Leadership: Where Else Can We Go?* Durham: Duke University Press.

Pondy, R. (1978) 'Leadership is a language game', in McCall, M.W. Jr and Lombardo, M.M. (eds) *Leadership: Where Else Can We Go?*, Durham: Duke University Press.

Pringle, J. (1994) 'Feminism and management: Critique and contribution', in Kouzmin, A., Still, L.V. and Clarke, R. (eds) *New Directions in Management*, Sydney: McGraw-Hill.

Quinn, R.E. and Spreitzer, G.M. (1997) 'The road to empowerment: Seven questions every leader should consider', *Organizational Dynamics,* Autumn: 37–44.

Robbins, S. (1988) *Essentials of Organizational Behavior*, Englewood Cliffs, NJ: Prentice Hall.

Rosener, J. (1990) 'Ways women lead', *Harvard Business Review*, November–December: 119–25.

Sankowsky, D. (1995) 'The charismatic leader as narcissist: Understanding the abuse of power', *Organizational Dynamics,* Spring: 57–72.

Sashkin, M. (1992) 'Strategic leadership competencies', in Phillips, R.L. and Hunt, J.G. (eds) *Strategic Leadership: A Multiorganizational-Level Perspective*, Wesport, CT: Quorum Books.

Scase, R. and Goffee, R. (1990) 'Women in management: Towards a research agenda', *International Journal of Human Resource Management, 1*(1): 107–25.

Schwartz, H. (1990) *Narcissistic Process and Corporate Decay*, New York: NYU Press.

Semler, R. (1993) *Maverick: The Success Story Behind the World's Most Unusual Workplace*, London: Century.

Shackleton, V. and Fletcher, C. (1984) *Individual Differences: Theories and Applications*, London: Methuen.

Sherman, S. (1994) 'Leaders learn to heed the voice within', *Fortune,* 22 August: 72–8.

Sinclair, A. (1998) *Doing Leadership Differently: Gender, Power and Sexuality in a Changing Business Culture*, Melbourne: Melbourne University Press.

Skipper, F. and Manz, C.C. (1994) 'W.L. Gore & Associates Inc.', in Rowe, A.J., Mason, R.O., Dickel, K.E., Mann, R.B. and Mockler, R.J. (eds) *Strategic Management: A Methodological Approach* (4th edn) Reading, MA: Addison-Wesley.

Smircich, L. and Morgan, G. (1982) 'Leadership: The management of meaning', *Journal of Applied Behavioural Science, 18*(3): 257–73.

Spillane, R. (1984) *Achieving Peak Performance*, Sydney: Harper & Row.

Sproull, R. and Stevens, M. (1997) *The Australian*, 1 October: 25–6.

Stogdill, R.M. (1974a) 'Historical trends in leadership theory and research', *Journal of Contemporary Business, 3*: 1–17.

Stogdill, R.M. (1974b) *Handbook of Leadership*, New York: Free Press.

Stoner, J.A., Collins, R.R. and Yetton, P.W. (1985) *Management in Australia*, Sydney: Prentice Hall.

Symington, N. (1993) *Narcissism*, London: Karnak Books.

Task Force on DSM IV (2000) *Diagnostic and Statistical Manual of Mental Disorders*, 4th edn, Text revision (DSM-IV-TR), Washington, DC: American Psychiatric Association.

Taylor, L. (2000) 'Lee back from the wilderness,' *Sunday Times*, 2 January: 3.

Thomas, R. (1998) 'Absentee Gullit in Amsterdam for a week,' *Guardian*, 23 December: 22.

Tichy, N.M. and Devanna, M.A. (1986) *The Transformational Leader*, New York: John Wiley.

Tichy, N.M. and Ulrich, D. (1987) 'The leadership challenge: A call for the transformational leader', in Timpe, D.A. (ed.) *Leadership*, New York: Facts on File Publications.

Triandis, H.C. (1995) *Individualism and Collectivism*, Boulder, CO: Westview.

Vecchio, R.P., Hearn, G. and Southey, G. (1996) *Organizational Behaviour*, Sydney: Harcourt Brace.

Walker, M. (1998) 'Dutch and go for Geordie nation: Gullit brings "sexy football" back to barren Tyneside', *Guardian*, 29 August: 1.

Walker, M. (1999) 'The Ruud, the bad and the ugly', *Guardian*, 30 August: 2.

Watson, T.J. (1986) *Management, Organization and Employment Strategy*, London: Routledge & Kegan Paul.

Westwood, R. (1992) *Organizational Behaviour,* Hong Kong: Longmans Group (FE).

White, J. (1998) 'Gullit's blue period gets Stalinesque reworking as the Bridge spin doctors play "didn't care enough" trump card', *Guardian*, 17 February: 25.

Wilson, F.M. (1995) *Organizational Behaviour and Gender*, London: McGraw-Hill.

Wilson, P. (1999a) 'Cool Ruud says it for the underdogs,' *Observer*, 16 May: 4.

Wilson, P. (1999b) 'Ruud farewell: Newcastle can't afford third error', *Observer*, 29 August: 6.

Managing teams

11

Stephen Procter, Liz Fulop, Stephen Linstead,
Frank Mueller and Graham Sewell

Questions about teams

1 What is a team?

2 What needs and whose needs can a team serve?

3 Do managers need to manage differently in a team situation?

4 Are there different ideas of what a team is and does?

5 How do teams develop?

WOMBAT MANUFACTURING – PART 1

Wombat Manufacturing, a maker of automotive components, was an organization in which change was being driven by a theoretical framework advanced by one of its managers, Norman Stone. Stone promoted a principle called 'process intent', where the overall objectives of production processes should be understood clearly by everyone concerned. This principle would allow Wombat managers to innovate and change specific work processes as long as the integrity of the intent (that is, the purpose and objectives) of the process was maintained. Such change was to be achieved through: (1) a quality focus on statistical process control (where monitoring the frequency and magnitude of production errors guides improvement); (2) an emphasis on participative management with shop-floor team involvement in the process; and (3) the achievement of productivity gains, which involved taking a look at cost effectiveness throughout the whole production 'value-chain', reaching from suppliers through to delivery to the manufacturers.

Wombat Manufacturing, as an academic researcher found it, was undergoing an intensive process of participative redesign of their traditional work systems. The plant's personnel were, the academic wrote, '... not only pioneering a new shop floor-driven approach to productivity and efficiency, but a new theory of organizational change to go with it'. This exciting prospect seemed substantive, for the '... employee involvement programme is not a shop-window programme, all appearance and no substance. It does encourage genuine involvement, and it does lead to some shop-floor improvements,' which were supported by documentation. Taking a look at the process of change, the researcher noted that the company was '... now engaging directly with the establishment of genuine self-managing teams or semi-autonomous work groups', a process involving the 'painstaking reintegration of fragmented shop-floor tasks and devolution of production authority'. The researcher noted 'the dogged determination the groups have shown in identifying problems, and manoeuvring their way around obstacles lying in the path of a solution'.

What then were the key factors contributing to successful change? First of all, the change process was built on the back of an earlier Employee Involvement Programme, under which various cross-functional groups (combining workers with different tasks and specialities) had been established. In addition, a more recent firm-based, quality accreditation programme, which also employed cross-functional teams (but with less shop-floor involvement than the earlier initiative), was established to address production problems. The result of these developments was a major improvement in production quality (as measured by defect rates). Stories circulated about how one of the teams succeeded in solving what had previously been an intractable quality control problem with one of the mountings of a dashboard component. Second, an industrial relations and skill development package had been put in place that involved not only a payment agreement (the usual industrial relations outcome), but also the establishment both of a career development path and competency-based training for unskilled shop-floor employees (an innovation in this arena). Third, process management within Wombat was improved via a greater emphasis on shop-floor responsibility and through the introduction of more effective systems in the areas of production scheduling (with the introduction of a Japanese-type kanban production control system), quality control (through a greater emphasis on inspection by operators backed up by a periodic, quality audit procedure) and performance management (through a focused, performance measurement system administered by the shop-floor work groups). Fourth, teams were introduced throughout the plant with the establishment of work area groups, which were supported at a supervisory level by a team of managers acting as production and team coordinators and 'blockage removers'.

Source: Richard Badham, Paul Couchman and Stephen Linstead (1995) 'Power tools: Narrating the factory of the future', Annual Conference on the Labour Process, Blackpool, University of Central Lancashire, April.

QUESTIONS ABOUT THE CASE

1 How important is the theory behind the practice in Wombat?
2 What impact have the changes had?
3 How far are teams involved in setting their own performance levels?

Introduction: teamworking in perspective

We trained hard – but it seemed that every time we were beginning to form up into teams, we would be reorganized. I was to learn later in life that we tend to meet any new situation by reorganizing, and a wonderful method it can be for creating the illusion of progress while producing confusion, inefficiency and demoralization. (attributed to Caius Petronius Arbiter AD 66 – see Davis 1994: 248)

The current wave of teamworking

Recent years have seen organizations of all kinds adopt some form of teamworking for their employees. As early as 1990, almost half of the largest US companies reported using self-managed work teams for at least some employees (Cohen et al. 1996). In the UK figures compiled by the Industrial Society (1995) show 40 per cent of personnel managers reporting that their organization used some self-managed teams, of which around 65 per cent were no more than three years old. A survey of manufacturing companies undertaken by the Institute of Work Psychology found team-based working being used to some extent by 70 per cent of respondents (Waterson et al. 1997), and this was backed up by the most recent survey, the fourth in the authoritative Workplace Employee Relations Survey (WERS) series, which found 65 per cent of workplaces reporting the use of team-based working for at least some employees (Cully et al. 1998).

While illustrative of the enormous surge of interest in teams and teamworking, these figures on their own tell us little about such questions as what rationales organizations may have for introducing teamworking, how teams are managed within organizations, how teams are experienced by employees, and whether in fact teams have a positive impact on the performance of an organization and the well-being of individuals within it. In order to answer these and other questions, this chapter takes two broad perspectives on issues surrounding the management of teams:

■ Teamworking as a management strategy for the organization of work. The analysis from this perspective is conducted at the level of the organization as a whole and is concerned with management rationale and performance impact.

■ The formation, development and operation of teams. The analysis here is more at the level of the team itself, and we are concerned with the roles that individuals take on and how they interact with one another.

With this distinction in mind, the chapter divides into four main parts. In the remainder of this introductory section we attempt to place the current wave of interest in teamworking into historical perspective. This is achieved by an examination of two major currents of thought on how work should be organized: scientific management and human relations.

Building on this historical perspective, the second part of the chapter looks at the two main traditions on which the current wave of teamworking draws more directly: the example of Japanese industry, and the idea of autonomous working groups (AWGs) which has its origins in sociotechnical systems theory (STS).

The third part of the chapter looks at how we can understand teamworking today. The key point is that it needs to be seen in the context of the broader restructuring of organizations and work. Teamworking here can be portrayed as a way of harnessing organizational knowledge and encouraging innovation, although the alternative critical perspective would see it as the means by which organizations extend control over their employees.

We turn finally to an examination of what goes on inside teams. Our concerns here are such things as how individuals behave within a team, how they interact with one another, how teams develop over time and how they might best be led and managed. An area of particular interest here is the operation of teams in different national and regional cultures.

We turn first, therefore, to a consideration of the historical perspective in which teams and teamworking must be set. The quote at the head of this chapter indicates that teams have been a feature of human organization for several centuries, and that they have encountered difficulties for just as long, while as Paul Thompson and Terry Wallace (1996) point out, how groups of people work together is an issue which has been of long-standing interest in organizational and management thought. A reversion to historical sources in order to bolster the appeal of teams is also a common feature of popular management literature. This reflects a significant theme: that collective organization resembling teams is somehow the natural way to organize human effort. Perhaps the most sophisticated representation of this position is contained in Jon Katzenbach and Douglas Smith's book, *The Wisdom of Teams* (1993). Here, the authors allude to an idealized period of pre-industrial manufacturing where production was undertaken by independent craftworkers operating in loosely governed, cooperative groups. This type of image attracts managers in modern organizations to teams as representative of an ideal of autonomous and collaborative 'empowered' workers.

Frederick Taylor and scientific management

Although we can trace the history of job or work design back to Adam Smith's (1776) enunciation of the benefits of a highly developed division of labour, it is only really since the end of the nineteenth century that these and other ideas have been applied systematically in organizations. According to Buchanan's (1994: 85) account, we can divide this more recent history very roughly into three phases:

- the period up to around 1950, which was dominated by the ideas of scientific management.
- the period from the middle of the century to around 1980, which, in reaction against scientific management, saw a concern to design jobs with workers' motivation and satisfaction in mind.
- the period since the late 1970s/early 1980s, in which we saw the emergence of what Buchanan describes as team-based 'high performance work systems'.

The first of Buchanan's three periods centres on the development and influence of the ideas of Frederick Winslow Taylor (1903, 1911, 1964), who is widely considered to be the founding father of *scientific management*. Whereas before scientific management, even under large-scale factory organization, the responsibility for both the conception and execution of work might have rested with fairly autonomous groups of craftworkers, there was now a scientific rationale for breaking this convention. Given that, under scientific management, work was designed to be repetitive, was synchronized by stopwatches and therefore precisely measured, and also involved high levels of division of labour, it was no surprise that workers had little responsibility and discretion. According to Taylor, it was the scientifically trained manager's duty to understand the workers' expertise and management's prerogative as to how it was used.

Taylor's work – indeed, his life – is best understood in terms of the pursuit of efficiency (Rose 1975; Kanigel 1997). While inefficiency on the side of management could be attributed to simple incompetence, of key importance on the workers' side

was the phenomenon of 'soldiering'. This could take two forms: 'First, from the natural instinct and tendency of men to take it easy, which may be called natural soldiering. Second, from more intricate second thought and reasoning caused by their relations with other men, which may be called systematic soldiering' (Taylor 1947: 19). As Rose (1975: 33) makes clear, it was this latter form of soldiering that Taylor was most concerned with identifying and eliminating. Taylor recognized that, in the circumstances in which they worked, it was perfectly rational for workers to collude in order to restrict their output. Under conditions of piecework, for example, increased production by workers was likely to be met by a reduction in the amount they were paid for each unit they produced. They would then be in the position of working harder for the same level of income. For Taylor, however, if workers would give up control of production to management, the application of scientific principles would allow both management and workers to benefit from large increases in productivity.

Although not always introduced with this commonality of interest in mind, Taylorism had very definite practical implications in the area of industrial organization and beyond. Many followers of Taylor, (for example Gilbreth 1914; Gilbreth and Gilbreth 1917) applied the principles of scientific management to many work settings, including the office. Taylorism's impact in terms of politics and ideology was equally as important. The initial interest in scientific management was significant enough to initiate an inquiry by the United States Congress, where Taylor gave a famous testimony in 1912 before an investigating committee. The generally favourable outcome of the senate inquiry went a long way to legitimizing scientific management as an approach to the organization of work, and it was adopted widely in the USA and elsewhere. Nevertheless, a study of the development of US manufacturing shows that enthusiasm for Taylorism was by no means universal among corporate leaders or employees, a position echoed by others (Hounshell 1985).

Some authors have argued that Taylorism's real impact was more political than practical, and that its significance in furthering a managerial ideology of domination and control was far greater than its role in instigating a wholesale transformation across manufacturing industry. Much of this debate has centred around Harry Braverman's (1974) 'deskilling thesis', which was based on Marxist ideas of the 'labour process'. In this account Taylor's ideas had proved overwhelmingly to be the dominant force in the organization and control of work since the beginning of the century. Its fragmentation and the removal of worker responsibility for its organization had thus led to work being progressively deskilled or degraded.

Although much subsequent research has sought to modify the work of Braverman (for example Friedman 1977), his basic thesis remains a powerful one.

One particular problem associated with Taylorism – the isolating and repetitive nature of work tasks – stands out on both sides of what has become the classical Marxist debate. For workers and their advocates in the trade union movement, it was seen as the ultimate dehumanizing and alienating approach to work. Managers, too, found that the demotivating effect of the endless monotony of the factory was likely to emerge in the long run.

Human relations

In the second of Buchanan's (1994) eras of work organization, we observe moves away from at least some of the worst excesses of Tayloristic organization and control. Many of these moves had their origins in a school of thought that has become known as *human relations*. In fact, it was as early as the 1920s that it had became evident that the more optimistic claims of increased efficiency were difficult to obtain in practice. As a result of this, researchers and managers began to examine other factors that might play a role in productivity (see Chapter 2). The famous Hawthorne Studies (named after the suburb of Chicago where the plant under study was located) were undertaken between 1924 and 1932 to examine such factors. The Hawthorne Studies were run by the Western Electric Company managers, but with the effective academic direction after 1926 of Elton Mayo, an expatriate Australian who, before moving to the USA, had been the inaugural chair of philosophy at the University of Queensland.

The studies were intended to establish the effect of the work environment on productivity, with the initial focus being on lighting levels. It soon became obvious to the researchers that the physical organization of production also had to be compatible with its social organization. Furthermore, alongside the formal social organization of the plant there exists a set of *informal social relationships* – perhaps based on kinship groups, ethnic background, personal friendships, sentiment and emotion (Bendix 1956: 313–17; Rose 1975: 120–2). Although these informal relationships could have a positive impact on productivity, the Hawthorne Studies found that there was an unofficial and, in the eyes of Mayo, a distinctly negative code of behaviour, which exerted a strong influence on members of informal groups. This code of behaviour can be expressed as follows:

■ Do not work too hard. If you do you will 'show up' other members, and you will receive the disapproval of your peers by being identified as a 'rate buster'.

■ Do not take it too easy. If you do, you run the risk of 'letting the side down', and you will receive the disapproval of your peers by being identified as a 'chiseller'.

■ Do not tell anybody in a supervisory position anything that might expose your peers to disapproval. If you do, then you are a 'squealer'.

It was here that Mayo (1933, 1945) had identified the strong peer group pressure that operates on individuals to conform to certain norms within the workplace. Two main implications emerge from taking this position. First, regardless of whether they have any previous affiliations, no collection of people can be in contact for any length of time at work without informal groupings emerging. Second, because of their resilient nature, it would be futile, and even unwise, to try and break up such groupings. Rather, management should seek to establish a convergence of interests between the organization and its employees and design work practices that are compatible with informal associations at work. If this design is effective, at worst, informal groupings should have a neutral effect on productivity and, at best, they should prove to be positively beneficial. Here, we see a possible confluence between Taylorist drives for efficiency and the potential of teamwork.

Although Mayo's work is often presented as being quite progressive in its attitudes towards issues such as the quality of work life (QWL) and the psychological impact of work, he was ideologically motivated by a desire to reduce the likelihood of workplace unrest. It must be remembered that at the time of the Hawthorne Studies, the Russian Revolution was a recent and sobering memory, and there were real concerns that it might be repeated in the USA and other liberal democracies. In this sense, Mayo was intent on making minor concessions rather than bringing about significant change. The responsibility for studying work practices and designing new approaches still lay with professional technocrat-managers rather than with the workers themselves. Moreover, work was still to be analysed and organized on an individualized basis, with the informal groupings identified by the Hawthorne Studies merely being 'taken into account' in any design process. Thus two main points emerge:

1. Mayo's work did little to reverse Taylorism's emphasis on the individual as the focus for standardizing and formalizing work tasks.
2. Mayo's work did nothing to undermine managers' control over the determination of work tasks. The separation between the conception and execution of work was maintained.

Nevertheless, Mayo's work has continued to be

influential, not least because it seems to promise a rationale for addressing some problems associated with scientific management. The human relations movement also had an impact on a number of subsequent management approaches, including the QWL movement, job enrichment schemes and quality circles (Waring 1991; see below and Chapter 9). While these approaches all entail greater involvement of the workforce in task design and general decision making, none challenges the fundamental tenets of scientific management. Waring (1991: 164) rather uncharitably describes them as an attempt to 'hide the excesses of Taylorism behind chintz curtains'.

This raises the question of whether teamworking should be seen in the same way. To help to address this question, we return to our case study of Wombat Manufacturing, and examine how it went about trying to introduce changes to the organization.

WOMBAT MANUFACTURING – THE PROJECT – PART 2

Following the enthusiastic reports of developments in team-work and participative management at Wombat, another team of researchers were attached to the company to support the introduction of a new production process in part of the plant. The new process was to be designed and put in place to assemble a new version of the main dashboard component (the design of which had been more or less finalized). The project – to introduce a new assembly process employing in some way teams or 'cells' of workers – was initiated with a brainstorming session of all managers, supervisors and engineers (but not shop-floor personnel) at the plant. This session clarified the features of the new component and identified a set of broad objectives (covering both production and people issues) for the design of the assembly process. Following this, a cross-functional design team, with shop-floor representation, was established to implement the objectives. The team, facilitated by the researchers, met regularly over a four-month period and explored various options for cell-based and conventional assembly processes in order to meet the project objectives within the set time frame. There was considerable debate and conflict within the team, as the disparate team members sought to gain a common understanding both of the production design challenges and of the constraints on any solution to it (for example two major constraints were, first, the product design was fixed and, second, only limited funds were available for new production facilities). The researchers contributed to this debate with suggestions and specific analyses (for example using a computer simulation programme, a study was carried out of how quickly production could resume after a stoppage for two configurations, workers clustered in cells versus workers strung out along assembly-lines).

The cross-functional design team was forged through a difficult process as the group pursued the project's goal of moving beyond what were seen by the 'Fordist' (meaning roughly that they favoured production lines) engineers as conventional solutions to production system design. It was widely agreed that the whole group were all on a very steep learning curve. The researchers also had to deal with a number of crises. These were brought to a head when a meeting was convened between the project's research managers and the senior managers in the plant in order to ensure a clear understanding of the project's goals and to reinforce management commitment toward these goals.

Progress towards an agreed solution was being made, however, until the team design process was brought to a premature conclusion by the plant's engineering manager. He imposed his own solution (which appeared to have been developed separately from the team's activities), much to the consternation of the team members. The imposed solution was a compromise between the team-based cell concept and a conventional assembly-line. Assembly was to be split into three distinct stages: a team would be responsible for each of these stages, which were to be managed as cells, and 'buffer' stocks were to be accumulated between each stage to achieve the desired effect of uncoupling production so as to permit it to work in three segments, versions of the original cell idea.

Shortly after this pronouncement, even that solution was cancelled as a result of an engineering failure in another area of the plant. The existing assembly-line was retained (although a small experimental cell was later set up to assemble a small number of the old-model components, as 'carry-over' products, alongside production of the new models). The engineering manager also selected another team to modify the main production line so that it could be used for the new product, and by excluding the researchers from this, effectively brought the project to a halt.

MORE QUESTIONS ABOUT THE CASE

4 How effective was the involvement process?
5 What were its problems?
6 How significant was the engineering manager's management style?
7 How would you characterize the plant culture at this stage?
8 How would Taylor or Mayo interpret what happened at Wombat?

Teamworking: two traditions

While an examination of scientific management and human relations is essential in mapping out the territory of work organization within which the idea of teamworking can be located, the current wave of interest in teamworking draws more directly on two more specific traditions (Benders and Van Hootegem 1999). The first of these, perhaps the less well-defined from a theoretical standpoint, is the example offered by Japanese industry; the second is sociotechnical systems (STS) theory and, in particular, its idea of autonomous work groups (AWGs). We shall look at each of them in turn.

Teamworking in Japanese industry

With regard to Japanese industry the situation is complicated first of all by the fact that the idea of teams or teamworking can take a variety of forms. As Benders and Van Hootegem (2000) claim, there are three with which we should primarily be concerned. The first of these is the idea that the company or organization *as a whole* constitutes a team and that this carries with it responsibilities for each individual. This seems to be what Peter Wickens, UK personnel director of the Japanese automotive company, Nissan, had in mind when referring to teamwork in his company's newly established British operation (Wickens 1987).

Of more pertinence for our purposes is the second form of teamworking, the use of 'off-line' teams. In their search for the source of Japanese industry's competitive advantage in the late 1970s and early 1980s, many commentators seized on its use of *quality circles*. The idea here was that workers would meet in small groups on a regular and voluntary basis in order to discuss, propose and implement improvements to the production process in their work area. Although widely adopted in the US, the UK and elsewhere, their use tended to be short-lived. For Hill (1991) and others, the problem lay in 'organizational dualism': rather than providing the basic unit of organization, quality circles were grafted onto and cut across existing structures.

It is the third definition of teamworking in Japanese industry that interests us most. This overcomes the problem of organizational dualism by identifying the basic work group as a team. In its most recent guise, the archetypal Japanese production system is described as *lean production* (Womack et al. 1990). Although the emphasis is very much on the advantages of running production with the lowest possible level of inventories – on a 'just-in-time' or JIT basis – it is also claimed that 'it is the dynamic work team that emerges as the heart of the lean factory' (Womack et al. 1990: 99].

The nature of this type of Japanese production team is investigated by Benders and Van Hootegem (2000). Drawing on Dore's (1973) and Cole's (1971) classic studies, the key characteristics of the Japanese model are identified as: the focal position of foremen; the minute description and rigorous regulation of work through standard operating procedures (SOPs); and the use of continuous improvement (*kaizen*) techniques to effect marginal improvement in these SOPs rather than more radical innovation. This is a picture backed up by more recent research. Delbridge et al. (2000) examined managerial perceptions of employee roles and responsibilities in 'lean' plants in the automotive components manufacturing sector worldwide. Their main findings were that the role of production workers was quite limited in the areas of maintenance and production management, and that significant responsibility had been vested in the position of team leader.

One of the most detailed accounts of attempts to adopt Japanese practice in these areas is provided by the work of Paul Adler (Adler 1993a, 1993b; Adler and Borys 1996). Adler's depiction of NUMMI (New United Motor Manufacturing Inc.) – the General Motors–Toyota joint venture assembly plant in Fremont, California – provides a vivid representation of the problems and possibilities posed by teamwork. He shows how a plant can combine many of the features of orthodox organization with the use of teams in order to pursue continuous improvement.

The General Motors (GM) assembly plant that predated NUMMI was described by one of its managers as 'the worst plant in the world' (Adler 1993a: 98). Organized on Taylorist and Fordist principles, the plant had the lowest productivity of any GM plant, quality was abysmal, drug and alcohol abuse were rampant, absenteeism was high, the union was militant, and between 1963 and 1982 wildcat strikes and lockouts occurred on several occasions. The plant was closed in 1982 at about the same time that Toyota and GM had begun discussions on a joint venture. NUMMI resulted from the joint venture agreement which saw GM take responsibility for marketing and sales and Toyota for product design, engineering and daily operations. The new production system was based on Toyota's methods.

Despite their extensive use of teams, Adler uses terms like 'regimentation' and 'standardization' to characterize NUMMI's principles of organization. He suggests that, in this case at least, teams under conditions of routinization are not a paradox. Management at the plant insisted that teams should seek to improve upon standardized work on the basis that standards set minimum performance criteria. The role of the team was seen as a vehicle for establishing new standards on the basis of improvements made on the shop floor. This approach reflects an acknowledgement of the inability of managers to come up with a perfectly standardized and continuously improving programme of work. Planning is no longer left solely to the manager, as Taylor had originally conceived. The team assists in work planning but in a restricted way. It concentrates its problem-solving energies very tightly around existing routines and standards set primarily by managers.

The continuous improvement programme (or the gathering up of the knowledge of workers) at NUMMI is described by Adler (1993a: 102–3) as including:

- a very aggressive suggestion system, with special teams designated to examine individual suggestions and carry out improvements
- continual refinement of procedures
- the design of every machine and process to detect malfunctions, missing parts or incorrect assembly
- careful analysis and design of jobs
- rotating workers
- cross-training workers in all team assignments
- tight scheduling of production, including quotas and so on.

As Adler (1993a: 103) states, 'team members themselves hold the stopwatch' and must learn the techniques of work analysis, description and improvement – part of the 'brain work' Taylor sought to remove from the worker's discretion or decision making.

This continuous improvement is used to increase standardization in the way jobs are performed in teams. Thus team members at NUMMI time one another using stopwatches; establish the most efficient pace of work; break down tasks to explore how they can improve performance; compare and analyse results from other teams on various shifts doing the same task and then write detailed specifications for how team members doing that job will carry out the task. As Adler (1993a: 103) states, all workers are 'industrial engineers'.

Although the amount of autonomy afforded to workers in teams at NUMMI is limited, management must still ensure that any innovations made in the production process are both revealed and operationalized. This is the 'double-bind of discretion' (Sewell 1998): teams need to be managed in order to concentrate their efforts on solving problems that benefit the organization as a whole, yet they need to be given the autonomy to exercise their learning capabilities to the extent that such problems are actually solved. Adler suggests that the team's discretion in being able to make changes to its work process is sufficient to motivate members to seek continuous improvement.

What we see here is an attempt to retain the standardizing benefits of Taylorism while at the same time incorporating the knowledge-finding and motivating possibilities of teamwork (see Chapter 9). The experience of NUMMI can be seen as a partial reversal of some of the tendencies of Taylorism – especially the separation of the planning and execution of work. The workers are now also responsible for gathering up the knowledge of craftspeople and workers under the banner of continuous improvement. Yet irrespective of such continuous improvement, the NUMMI plant is also typified by intense machine pacing (for example 60 seconds to complete tasks on the assembly line), rigid production quotas, close surveillance, regimentation, the sacrificing of safety standards (Berggren et al. 1994), and hard-driving management practices.

The sociotechnical tradition

The way in which teams operate in Japanese or Japanese-influenced settings is only part of the story. A second major influence on current practice is the *sociotechnical systems* approach (STS) (see Chapter 9), in which the work of the London-based Tavistock Institute was of key importance. The principles of researchers from the Tavistock, based on the idea of the 'joint optimization' of the social and technical subsystems in organizations, gave rise to their proposing the development of autonomous working groups (AWGs) of employees. Trist and Bamforth's (1951) study of the postwar British coal-mining industry, for example, showed how automation had brought with it the introduction of a version of scientific management, the 'longwall' method, which displaced the autonomous multiskilled groups which had operated under the old 'hand-got' system. Later work (Trist et al. 1963) revealed the development of a compromise 'composite shortwall' method, based on multiskilled, self-selecting groups, responsible on one shift for the whole of the coal-getting cycle.

As Buchanan (2000) points out, it is interesting that, in this and other cases, the AWGs were the spontaneous, intuitive response of the workers themselves to certain working conditions. In contrast to more recent management innovations such as business process re-engineering (BPR) (see Chapter 9), teamworking was thus not something invented by consultants and imposed upon organizations. Because it emerged from quite fundamental considerations about the way in which work should be organized, argues Buchanan, its value is likely to be much more longlasting. In his words, teamworking is subject to an 'eager and enduring embrace' (2000: 25).

Sociotechnical ideas were picked up and developed or modified in several countries. In the Netherlands, for example, an expert-oriented form of sociotechnical theory, *modern sociotechnology*, was worked out (Benders and Van Hootegem 1999). In Germany, although industry never developed its own sociotechnical approach, the period from the mid-1970s saw substantial official interest in the humanization of work. Experiments in this spirit were based on dividing up production lines into *production islands* (Harvey and von Behr 1994). In the US the idea of teams was an important part of the QWL movement of the 1970s (Parker and Slaughter 1988; Benders and Van Hootegem 1999; Buchanan 2000). Rediscovered in the 1980s, such thinking has formed part of a number of different sets of ideas (Buchanan 2000): the emerging rhetoric of human resource management (HRM), for example, as well as high involvement or high performance work systems (HPWS) (Lawler 1986, 1992). In the UK, cellular manufacturing has been important in reintroducing AWGs to the country in which they were first identified (Benders and Van Hootegem 1999). The two ideas have long enjoyed what Buchanan (2000: 31) describes as an 'ambiguous romance'.

It is Scandinavia, however, that is most closely associated with the use of AWGs. It is here that we find their most celebrated and controversial appearance: in the automotive manufacturer, Volvo. Volvo has had a tradition of progressive job design and work group autonomy at its Kalmar car plant since the 1970s. Thompson and Wallace (1995, 1996) found that Volvo used teams not as a move towards shop-floor democratization but as a response to production requirements (see also Fincham and Rhodes 1992: 212). At Kalmar, workers were responsible for clusters of tasks with variations on the production line concept. Christian Berggren (1989) argues that Kalmar still involved centralized control, and teams or semi-autonomous work groups were limited (see Chapter 9). Uddevalla, however, Volvo's most team-oriented plant, represented a more socialized form of production, with a massive automated materials handling centre around which operated 51 independent assembly workshops.

Paul Bernstein (1992: 355–6) examined the team experiments that Volvo began in 1966 with what was termed the 'spontaneous trial period'. The aim then was to address problems of absenteeism, high turnover, recruitment costs, ergonomic problems and changed work expectations. A range of team-based approaches was employed, and this culminated in the radical approach used at Uddevalla, where the emphasis was on building a learning environment through teamwork. In 1985, when Uddevalla was being planned, Volvo had already introduced its Dialog programme to encourage and support change and learning. Dialog embraced the Volvo culture: 'quality, care, competence, communication, development and involvement' (Bernstein 1992: 368). Uddevalla was closed in 1993 as a result of a drop in sales, excess capacity and cash-flow problems (Carmona and Grönlund 1998: 22), and the production moved to a plant that was not designed around teams. This suggests that teams are something Swedish firms, such as Volvo, embraced when it was economically viable to do so, but are not so deeply embedded in the culture and institutions of Swedish

society as some theorists claim (Carmona and Grönlund 1998: 22).

Based on their studies of Volvo, Thompson and Wallace suggest that the essential factors affecting the success of teams can be grouped into three categories: technical, governance and normative (Thompson and Wallace 1996; see also Findlay et al. 2000). This can be seen in diagrammatic form in Figure 11.1. The *technical* dimension has to do with the team's ability to offer degrees of 'flexibility and self-regulation' that one could not get from a production line of individuals. Two important *support systems* that help to develop these team-based competencies are the type of industrial relations system in the organization and the selection methods, reward and performance appraisal systems used. In terms of *governance*, direct supervision can shift from one manager overseeing a hundred employees on a production line to a team leader with six team members. Governance also includes the role of managers and experts in the team process. Even with a team structure, though, the question remains of where decisions are made. A critical support system here is how organizational decision making processes work – are they hierarchical or decentralized or a combination of the two? Finally, the *normative* dimension involves aligning individuals' goals with the goals of the organization to boost productivity via a more coherent focus. The main support system helping this happen is training and staff development.

As noted above, the technical dimension persuaded management at various Volvo sites to engage teams. In terms of governance, Thompson and Wallace suggest that the team structure seemed to take hold more readily in Volvo's Swedish plants, where the history of industrial relations had a more cooperative flavour than in the UK and Belgium. According to Robin Fincham and Peter Rhodes, Volvo admits that hard economic motives had driven its job reforms mainly because 'you cannot get Swedes to work on assembly lines' (1992: 213), especially given that unions and the Swedish employers' federation have both actively pursued job redesign. Because of these cultural differences, Thompson and Wallace argue that a stronger normative effort is likely to be required in the UK and Belgium to build the concept of a 'team player' than was evident at Uddevalla. Other contextual factors also affect the success of teamwork. These factors include the local history of the plant in question, product market concerns, the type of leadership in the plant, and the role of specialists in teams. The result of this mix of factors means that the approach and responses to teamwork at each site have differed even within Volvo (Thompson and Wallace 1996).

Thompson and Wallace's assessment of the Volvo 'experiment' also demonstrates the importance of *knowledge gathering*. At Uddevalla, for example,

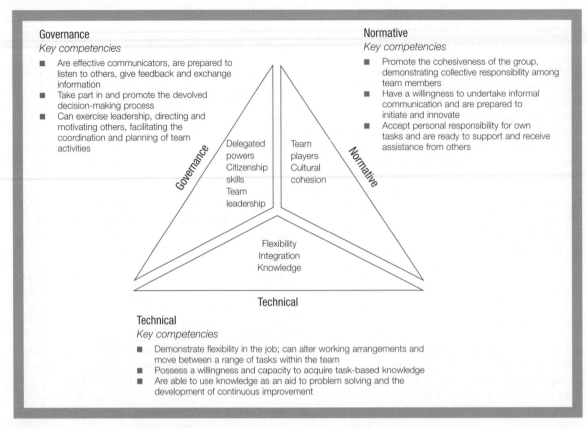

Figure 11.1 Dimensions of teamwork competencies

Source: Adapted from Abigail Marks, Patricia Findlay, James Hine, Alan McKinlay and Paul Thompson (1997) 'Whisky galore: Teamworking and workplace transformation in the Scottish spirits industry', 15th Annual Labour Process Conference, March, Edinburgh (Appendices 1 and 2).

management used two interrelated concepts to encourage learning: the *holistic principle* and the *reflective principle* (Berggren et al. 1994). In the case of the former, this meant that employees had to understand the whole process of car assembly and the interdependence of all tasks. With respect to the latter, workers in the plant were not only asked to perform complex tasks, but had to have a detailed and articulated intellectual understanding of the processes of car assembly. These two principles resulted in, for example, cost and time reductions in the introduction of new models of cars. Assembly teams implemented changes for new car models, including redesigning their work patterns. They were skilled at analysing the requirements for new product design, including anticipated faults and problems, and were able also to incorporate continuous improvements without the 'lean production' system at NUMMI.

One of the very early problems faced at Uddevalla was that many manufacturing and industrial engineers did not know how to fit into this new team approach, preferring

instead to keep the old, hierarchical ways (Berggren et al. 1994). Engineers did not want to surrender the status and power that they enjoyed in the old system. For a time the assembly teams on the shop floor had a decentralized structure, while the management structure remained hierarchical and management was located in a separate building. Later a new plant manager changed all this by creating two hierarchies – shop-floor and plant management. Managers and engineers had to work in assembly teams and were relocated closer to the shop floor (Berggren et al. 1994).

Understanding teamworking today

Teamworking and the restructuring of organizations and work

We can see from the previous section that there are considerable differences between the lean teams of the Japanese model and the AWGs of the sociotechnical tradition. In particular, the autonomy that in some sense

Table 11.1 Summary of recent perspectives on organizational restructuring

Nominal approach	Exemplary texts	Diagnosis of existing forms	Prescription	Organizational implications
Total quality management	Deming (1986)	Orthodox mass production creates a consciousness where the responsibility for quality does not reside at the point of production. Problems are the fault of poor management rather than a defective or recalcitrant workforce	Deming's 'fourteen points' focusing on training, quality assurance techniques, continuous improvement, communication between management and hourly-paid workers, and the 'ownership' of quality problems. Acknowledges the contribution workers can make to continuous improvement. Workers must be 'trusted' to take responsibility for quality problems and devise solutions themselves	Dismantle the traditional division of labour and reorganize using teams as the fundamental unit of production. Teams provide the main forum for identifying and resolving quality problems
The 'network' firm	Lipnack and Stamps (1994)	Traditional hierarchical approaches to organization are not responsive enough to cope with today's dynamic business environment	Dismantle hierarchy and facilitate intra- and inter-organizational communication through information technology	Dismantle 'hierarchy/bureaucracy' and install 'team-networks' – i.e. cross-functional groupings which incorporate individuals within and between organizations
Organizational learning	Senge (1990)	Organizations are 'prisoners' of outmoded approaches to environmental adaptation	Senge's five disciplines of 'Systems Thinking'; 'Personal Mastery'; 'Mental Models'; 'Building a Shared Vision'; and 'Team Learning'	Reduce the complexity of organizations to encourage flexibility and openness. 'Localize' authority by investing 'real' decision-making power in devolved teams
Lean production	Womack et al. (1990)	Taylorized/Fordist mass production perpetuates sub-optimal use of productive resources to protect against the uncertainty of demand, labour supply, etc. Problems are the fault of poor management rather than a defective or recalcitrant workforce	Institute Just-in-Time production, shorten time to market of new products through 'concurrent' engineering, utilize flexible productive technology	Radical restructuring of the physical layout of manufacturing plants. Augment dedicated product and continuous-flow (i.e. Fordist) production lines with flexible and multiskilled teams
Business process re-engineering (BPR)	Hammer and Champy (1993)	Hierarchy and the minute division of labour cannot respond to the demands of fragmented markets. Problems are the fault of poor management rather than a defective or recalcitrant workforce	Reject '200 years' of orthodox organizational thinking and adopt 'discontinuous thinking' to embrace BPR in a series of incremental steps. However, BPR must break from the past in being a fundamental, radical, and dramatic change in business processes. Use information technology to facilitate change to achieve flexibility in responsiveness. Visionary leadership essential	Wholesale dismantling of discrete functions of an organization and a reintegration to eliminate waste. Interesting tension between team-oriented restructuring and the desire to rationalize in order to reduce duplication and unnecessary complexity

Source: Graham Sewell (1998) 'How the giraffe got its neck: An organizational "Just-So" story', in S. Clegg, E. Ibarra and L. Bueno (eds) *Theories of the Management Process: Making Sense Through Difference*, London: Sage.

defines the latter appears to be largely absent in the former. One way out of this (Benders and Van Hootegem 2000) is to avoid exclusive definitions, to accept as a team anything that is called a team, but to make clear case by case what precisely the term covers. While this approach does have some merit, it carries with it the danger that teamworking will lose meaning. We argue here that the characteristics of the current wave of teamworking are such that what brings our two traditions together is more important than what separates them.

For one thing, teamworking can be seen as a move beyond the prescriptions of the simpler notions of scientific management and human relations. In the former approach, the implication is that any form of group working – either formal or informal – is inconsistent with basic principles and is likely to lead to the erosion of the necessary separation between mental and manual labour. In the latter approach, while it is acknowledged that informal groups will have a significant impact on efficiency and that any formal organization of work must take this into account, this is not taken to imply that formal organization itself should be undertaken on a group basis (Mouzelis 1975: 102–3).

What we also see in the current wave of interest in teamworking is a difference in what management is using it for. With the rising living standards and tight labour markets of the postwar world, firms were faced with the problems of absenteeism and high rates of labour turnover. The objective in introducing team-working was to address these issues by improving the quality of working life (Buchanan 1994; Jenkins 1994). In the more straitened economic circumstances which have persisted since the late 1970s, work design has come to have as its concern the way in which organiz-ations deal with their customers and their competitors (Buchanan 1994; Jenkins 1994). The objectives, in other words, are strategic rather than operational.

Just examine the popular approaches to management described in Table 11.1. Not only is teamwork a central pillar of each one, but each is seen as a radical departure from ways of organizing that have dominated the twentieth century. This leads to a major implication of modern visions of teams: that it is absolutely imperative for the formal organization of work to revolve around a *collective form*, unlike the extreme individualism of Taylorism or even its more moderated version found in human relations. Rather than breaking down tasks to their most minute elements, as Taylor suggested, tasks should only be broadly specified. The team is then able to exercise its collective wisdom in order to establish how a particular task should be executed. The team should be 'empowered' to undertake this task along the lines that it has itself devised. Management and supervisory roles are invariably seen as centring on 'coaching' or 'facilitating' rather than 'directing' activities.

Teamworking and performance

What the strategic nature of teamworking – and work design more generally – does is to put it in a much more direct relationship with organizational performance. In Mueller's (1994) terms, management's objectives in introducing teamworking are moving from the social to the economic. From a sociotechnical perspective, the link between teamworking and performance can be explained by the self-regulation provided to employees by the more structural properties of teams, but as Cohen and Ledford (1994) point out, because the kinds of jobs such teams give rise to – high in variety, autonomy, identity, significance and feedback – are similar to those advocated by the job characteristics model of Hackman and Oldham (1976, 1980), a single channel of influence is difficult to identify.

Another issue is what precisely is meant by performance. Dunphy and Bryant (1996), for example, identify three forms of teams, each of which is most suited to the pursuit of a particular aspect of performance. While simple, multiskilled teams are thus likely to impact most heavily on an organization's costs, self-managed teams will have their main effects on value, and self-led teams on innovation. In a similar vein Cohen and Ledford (1994) found that while the introduction of self-managed teams in a telecommunications company had resulted in significant improvements, this was restricted to those aspects of performance to which the intervention was most directly related.

What complicates the situation further is that teamworking is often taken to be just one part of human resource management (HRM) or the high performance work systems (HPWS) we referred to above. Although a relatively small part of HRM which has been the focus of attention in the UK (Guest 1997), teamworking has emerged as a key part of US debates (Becker and Gerhart 1996; Ichniowski et al. 1996). On the one hand this has the effect of making the impact of teamworking more difficult to isolate; on the other, it does mean that greater attention is paid to the circumstances in which teamworking operates. As Ichniowski et al. (1996) argue, it shows that the effect of what they call 'innovative work practices', as well as through making workers work harder or more efficiently, can come through the broader organizational changes with which they are associated.

Teams and organizational knowledge

One way of approaching the strategic nature of teamworking and its relationship with organizational performance is to look at these issues in terms of *organizational knowledge*. In going beyond scientific management and human relations, the implication of recent writings on teamworking is that the separation of mental and manual labour ignores the rich resources of expertise, experience and knowledge held by workers, which can be exploited to the benefit of employers. Although Taylor acknowledged that workers possessed these qualities, he was worried that they would rarely be exercised to the benefit of the company. Bearing in mind this risk, he claimed that it was better to pursue a strategy of close scrutiny and control through formalization and standardization.

An almost complete reversal of this position appears to have taken place. In the TQM movement, for example (see Table 11.1 and Chapters 7 and 9), employees are seen as the most knowledgeable and insightful about how to do their jobs, although they will not necessarily exercise their insights in the cause of knowledge. This belief leads to calls for workers to take responsibility, or 'ownership', of problems on the shop floor, exercise their discretion and participate in problem-solving activities, although at the same time necessarily being policed by formal reporting systems. Above all, it is claimed, workers must be 'empowered' to act on their own initiative. How is the ingenuity of the workforce best captured? The answer is, of course, through teams. As Jon Katzenbach and Douglas Smith (1993: 15) claim:

teams – real teams, not just groups that management call 'teams' – should be the basic unit of performance for most organizations, regardless of size. In any situation requiring the real-time combination of multiple skills, experiences, and judgements, a team inevitably gets better results than a collection of individuals operating within confined job roles and responsibilities.

If we return to the principles of scientific management, it is evident that what Taylor was interested in was revealing workers' knowledge of the work process and pressing that into the service of the organization. Although this was an acknowledgment that workers often know more about their work than their managers, this was balanced by the recognition that workers would use this for their own rather than organizational ends. Taylor's fear of systematic soldiering meant that his controlling instincts won out over any inclination to allow workers the autonomy and discretion to exercise this knowledge. Thus Taylorism has meant initially gathering and analysing the knowledge of workers on a once-and-for-all basis to design procedures to use as the benchmark for subsequent work behaviour. Any transgression of these rules, even if it might lead to improvements in productivity, would be seen as a threat to the managerial prerogative to determine work tasks. Of course, this attitude would effectively preclude ideas from workers that could contribute to what today we would call *continuous improvement*.

A link between this search for continuous improvement and the need to reveal organizational knowledge is explained by Sidney Winter (1994). He identifies three interdependent elements of this relationship:

1. *corporate knowledge* in an organization, which is embedded in
2. *organizational routines*, and needs to be revealed through a process of
3. *organizational learning*.

Firms improve when managers and workers scrutinize existing routines and identify and select new routines, such as new assembly methods. These new routines do not come from some universal technical handbook. Rather, they derive from examining the idiosyncrasies of processes that have grown from unique aspects of an individual firm's history. For Winter, the crucial element in this process of learning is the elicitation and representation of the knowledge embedded in these organizational routines and patterns of work.

Knowledge embedded in routines is commonly unearthed by the use of teams. In the current wave of interest in teams, an early example of this use of teams as a source of knowledge for continuous improvement was the popularity of quality circles in the 1980s. Quality circles provided a means of focusing the workforce's problem-solving capabilities on specific issues within the workplace. As we have already seen, however, the use of quality circles in many American and British organizations did not represent any systematic change in the way in which production and work were organized. Like the teams of the human relations movement before them, quality circles represent provisional committees that are meant to reflect on procedures rather than teams used as the basic unit of industrial organization. Nevertheless, they are often presented as a staging post on the way to the creation of 'true' teamworking conditions, and they do represent an attempt to reveal organizational knowledge in pursuit of continuous improvement.

Teams and innovation

We can take this a stage further by looking at how, in the longer term, teams can contribute to innovation within organizations. Teams, in their contemporary sense, need to effect the move from *people management* (and control) to *knowledge management* (and dissemination). They are a critical element in ensuring that individual learning is transmitted to organizational activities, and are also a source of innovation if they are able to achieve a fluid collective process (Bell et al. 1997). If this is to happen, teams must not be drawn or forced into competing with each other, and structural arrangements must facilitate cross-functional communications. Bell et al. (1997) argue that there are four types of innovation (see Exhibit 11.1), and that these types affect the nature and form of teams required.

Teams involved in innovation are important in providing the right amount of support in conditions of uncertainty and change, and in enabling this chaos to stimulate creativity rather than collapse. Teams can improve the capacity and ability of staff in learning skills, questioning, considering, communicating, modelling, improvising and reconstructing ideas. Pilkington, for example, developed 'virtual teams' to work across sites and disciplines by means of video conferencing and intranet technology (Bell et al. 1997). Percy Barnevik, head of ABB (Asea Brown Boveri), has spent $US800 million a year on ABB's global network technology linking 70,000 people. This, he argues, makes it 'possible to design a piece of equipment in the US, manufacture it in Brazil and sell it in Kazakhstan' (McLachlan 1997: 12). Teams can also prove significant in facilitating the type of restructuring they require to be effective, developing a sense of community, empowerment and collective problem solving (Bell et al. 1997: 59).

Along similar lines Jessica Lipnack and Jeffrey Stamps (1994; see also Lipnack and Stamps 1997) define 'teamnets' as including clusters of organizations connected in a kind of social network which allows

Exhibit 11.1 Types of innovation

❏ **Normal innovation** includes the kind of incremental developments that are part of everyday working and is a sort of base camp for more complex innovation.

❏ **Domain innovation** is significant development within a specialism or subspecialism, such as image engineering, and requires its expert or group of experts.

❏ **Boundary innovation** is significant development that arises from cooperation and coordination across specialisms. Here open-mindedness and dialogue, and cultures and working practices that support this, are necessary.

❏ **Radical innovation** is development that is both significant scientifically – that is, an important advancement in knowledge – and across disciplines. Yet while some 'super-scientists' or 'hero innovators' may work in this area, it is equally important that these innovations are diffused and the general capacity of the organization to innovate is increased (Bell et al. 1997: 59).

team members to serve customers better than any one company could. Lipnack and Stamps point to the VISA credit card corporation with 23,000 collaborating financial institutions and 11 million merchants in 250 countries and territories (1994: 90). They focus on the spirit of – and the conditions for – collaboration that should infuse interactions between team members.

Teams as surveillance and control

There is another way of looking at all of this. Although we have looked at teamworking within the context of the employment relationship – and thus with the employer in the main having the upper hand – it has so far been portrayed, broadly speaking, as a liberating experience for employees. Looking at the same developments from a different perspective, however, allows them to be seen as the means by which surveillance and control over employees is extended. Notable among those taking this view have been Mike Parker and Jane Slaughter (1988) and Guillermo Grenier (1989). These authors associate teams with a managerial agenda of intensification of effort, increased control and anti-trade union industrial relations.

Teams can descend into various exploitative practices where the teams themselves take on many of the disciplinary and controlling roles previously associated with managerial supervision (Barker 1993). Teams may be viewed as an unobtrusive or 'invisible' form of control, one that enables managers to give workers a sense of autonomy.

From this perspective it is the group dynamics of the team that create the disciplinary force that keeps its objectives and actions in line with those of the organization (Sewell and Wilkinson 1992a, 1992b; Barker 1993; Sewell 1998; also see Heterick and Boje 1992; Steingard and Fitzgibbons 1993). Traditionally, surveillance has been associated with establishing obedience and maintaining order. Surveillance, in the form of workplace performance monitoring, can always identify those who fail to match the required standards. This is particularly suited to Taylorized work roles, where obedience involves carefully following work procedures planned by managers. However, as shown in the NUMMI case, such restriction does not fit well with expectations of 'continuous improvement' through the extraction and use of workers' knowledge. The systems of surveillance that identify workers who fail to reach management targets, however, can also reveal those who exceed them. This also applies to the team performance: surveillance of a team can identify those members who are outperforming their peers. Here the team takes on the disciplinary role identified by James Barker (1993). It provides a means whereby the expected performance of each member is based on the standards set by the highest performing individual in the group. In this sense, working 'smarter' by one person is working harder for all. Team members boost their productive capacity, which means that their ingenuity and potential have been used to pursue organizational objectives alone. This process can give rise to all kinds of coercive peer group pressures and petty tyrannies that are far away from the vision of teams that most management texts contain.

One particular phenomenon that has been observed is that as group size increases, there is a tendency for the effort put in by the group to be less than the combined effort that would be put in if group members were individually engaged in the same task. This is described as the *free-rider problem*, where the collective nature of the 'contract' obscures the fact of individual members failing to honour their own parts of it (Albanese and Van Fleet 1985). Organizational psychologists tend to view this problem as one of *social loafing* and typically define it as one where everyone puts in a little less effort (Gabrenya et al. 1981).

Attempts to identify the reasons for social loafing have not proved conclusive. One possibility is that an individual perceives that others in the group are not pulling their own weight, and so reduces his or her own effort; but this would hardly explain the widespread nature of the phenomenon and would tend to force itself into a downward spiral that would need to be constantly checked and readjusted to by the group. It is also possible that where the contribution of individuals is not visible or attributable in terms of outputs, and hence of rewards, then they see no benefit in putting in the maximum effort.

What this lack of conclusiveness also demonstrates is that in order to understand teamworking fully we should not confine ourselves to seeing it as a management strategy at the level of the organization. As indicated in the introductory section of this chapter, we must also be concerned at the level of the individual teams. To put it another way, we are interested in what goes on inside the team, and it is to the issues raised by this perspective that we now turn.

Inside the team

How teams develop

The first of these issues is how teams develop over time. The most common form of representing the basic stages of group development was developed by Bruce Tuckman (1965) (stages 1–4), and more recently four new stages have been added by Gersick (1988, 1989). These stages are shown in Exhibit 11.2.

Connie Gersick (1988, 1989) noted that teams tend to evolve in a sequence of abrupt jumps rather than by making a smooth transition between stages. She observed two teams of students as part of a project to test a team effectiveness model. In the course of the study, however, Gersick became interested in team evolution and she observed two further teams going through a complete project lifecycle. Her conclusions were that all four teams had made an abrupt transition midway through their project. She likened the shift to a 'midlife transition', a concept developed by Dan Levinson (1978), as all the teams seemed to experience a crisis at a point halfway between their inception and their delivery deadline, *regardless of the length of time of the project*.

Exhibit 11.2 **Stages of group formation**

1. **Forming** Team members getting to know each other and trying to comprehend their task.

2. **Conforming** Team members fall into an easy consensus in order to feel as though they are really working together.

3. **Storming** Frustration emerges over differences and conflicts that have been suppressed, with arguments about who leads, what goals and procedures should be and so on; personalities clash.

4. **Norming** The group sets standards and agrees on goals; patterns of acceptable behaviour take root.

5. **Reforming** The group checks and operates the new norms, reorienting itself to the new standards in practice and correcting problems.

6. **Performing** Members get down to work at full effectiveness.

7. **Adjourning** The process of signalling completion and deciding that the task is completed. In its positive mode this involves a rational letting go; in its negative mode it involves a reluctance to conclude, with much reminiscing and congratulating or blaming.

8. **Mourning** The individual and collective processing of sadness of parting from compatriots can become nostalgic. When group members are involved in new projects, they constantly try to recreate the old project in a new form, often saying things like 'we always did it this way in my old project team, company and so on.' This prolongs the reluctance to move on and learn new things.

Gersick then observed an additional four teams – at a community agency, bank, hospital and mental health treatment facility – to show how group focus shifted over time. It seemed that up to the halfway point, roughly conforming to the forming, storming and norming stages, low performance was observed and options were only infrequently re-examined. However, the midpoint 'wake-up alarm' plunged the team into a reassessment of its goals, and this usually resulted in some sort of a change of direction. It appeared that insufficient or even missing storming/conflict in the early stages has its effects on the group later on, and that these suppressed differences need to be addressed before the group can produce effectively. The final stages then are high performing, pressured activity and adjourning. Gersick explained the pattern of development by borrowing, from biology and social studies of science, the concept of *punctuated equilibrium*: stable periods of steady progress interrupted by abrupt transitions to new states in which steady progress resumes.

Team roles

In looking at the questions of what roles individuals take on as members of teams and, perhaps more importantly,

what combinations of roles are associated with successful teams, the most widely used typology has been that developed by Meredith Belbin (1981, 1993). Although originally identifying eight team roles, Belbin (1993) later extended this to include a ninth. These roles are described in Table 11.2. They show key contributions to be made by all team members, and the allowable weaknesses of people filling these roles. It should be noted that Belbin's model does not preclude overlap in these functions, and more than one role may be performed by a person, especially in a small group, but the important consideration is balance. Additionally, where much of the work on teams emphasizes flexibility and multiskilling, Belbin's work emphasizes interpersonal multiskilling but still leaves room for technical expertise to be drawn upon by the group in the ninth role of 'specialist'.

An important message in Belbin's (1981) work was that, while balance was important in team roles, successful teams tended to have persons with coordinating strengths being appointed as chairpersons. At least one person who could fill the 'plant role' was also included in winning teams. Belbin did not consider 'shapers' to be generally good team leaders and too many of them in any one team was found to cause problems. This imbalance of

Table 11.2 Belbin's team roles	
Roles and descriptions – team-role contribution	**Allowable weaknesses**
Plant: Creative, imaginative, unorthodox. Solves difficult problems.	Ignores details. Too preoccupied to communicate effectively.
Resource investigator: Extrovert, enthusiastic, communicative. Explores opportunities. Develops contacts.	Overoptimistic. Loses interest once initial enthusiasm has passed.
Co-ordinator: Mature, confident, a good chairperson. Clarifies goals, promotes decision-making, delegates well.	Can be seen as manipulative. Delegates personal work.
Shaper: Challenging, dynamic, thrives on pressure. Has the drive and courage to overcome obstacles.	Can provoke others. Hurts people's feelings.
Monitor evaluator: Sober, strategic and discerning. Sees all options. Judges accurately.	Lacks drive and ability to inspire others. Overly critical.
Teamworker: Cooperative, mild, perceptive and diplomatic. Listens, builds, averts friction, calms the waters.	Indecisive in crunch situations. Can be easily influenced.
Implementer: Disciplined, reliable, conservative and efficient. Turns ideas into practical actions.	Somewhat inflexible. Slow to respond to new possibilities.
Completer: Painstaking, conscientious, anxious. Searches out errors and omissions. Delivers on time.	Inclined to worry unduly. Reluctant to delegate. Can be a nit-picker.
Specialist: Single-minded, self-starting, dedicated. Provides knowledge and skills in rare supply.	Contributes on only a narrow front. Dwells on technicalities. Overlooks the 'big picture'.

Source: R. Meredith Belbin (1993) *Team Roles at Work*, London: Butterworth/Heinemann, p. 23.

Note: Strength of contribution in any one of the roles is commonly associated with particular weaknesses. These are called 'allowable weaknesses'. Executives are seldom strong in all nine team roles.

'shapers' in team situations is likely to be noticeable among professional groups such as academics, lawyers and doctors.

Team behaviours

Behaviours in groups, which ultimately affect the behaviours *of* groups, can be classified in the following way:

- *Task behaviours* involve initiating structure, communicating, establishing consensus and advancing the problem-solving process.
- *Group maintenance* involves gatekeeping, harmonizing, supporting, setting standards and improving the process of interpersonal interaction.
- *Self-oriented behaviour* is concerned with the individual's own needs and not those of the group.

Whenever people form into groups, they have to address questions about their identity. They find that things they would normally be aware of are not always present, especially if the group members are not known to each other or normal hierarchies do not apply. There are four *vacuums* present in leaderless, newly formed groups, but these vacuums remain as a threat even as groups develop. The four vacuums are:

- *The structure vacuum:* expressed in terms of who has authority, who will play what role, what role will I play, can I be who I want to be?
- *The knowledge vacuum:* who has the key information, knowledge, skills, expertise?
- *The emotional vacuum:* how do I feel about the people in this group, how do they feel about me, will I be liked or feared, accepted or rejected?
- *The power vacuum:* who controls the group, who has most influence, who are potential allies/enemies, what are my interests and those of others, will there be conflict?

Groups and individuals will gradually fill these vacuums as roles are assigned, created or seized, although this will usually not be without its problems. The process may involve attacking or defending, blocking others, withdrawing from interaction, appealing for sympathy from others, or dominating by overcontributing or 'point scoring'.

One type of self-oriented behaviour that often makes a team task difficult is *defensive behaviour*. Basic types of defensive behaviour were identified by the British psychologist, Wilfred Bion, before and during the Second World War. From studies of therapy groups of servicemen, he concluded that pressure makes members of groups revert to primitive types of defensive behaviour (Bion 1959). Pressure is that which threatens

the individual's perceived identity, and what counts as 'pressure' depends on the individual. It might include an imminent deadline, possible retrenchment, a domineering colleague or a potentially positive change that challenges firmly held beliefs, such as switching from 'the boss will always tell us what to do' to 'we need to set our own production goals'.

Humans react to psychological threat in much the same way as animals react to physical threat – by fighting back or running away. Bion (1959) identified primitive defences as:

- *fight or flight* behaviour: arguing or withdrawal, where groups may become extremely combative among themselves, or engage in diversions from the task like joking to avoid confrontation
- *dependency* on authority replacing individual initiative
- *pairing* among individuals, a move towards strength in numbers (see also Stacey 1993).

Josh MacNeish and Tony Richardson (1994), Australian management consultants, have characterized each defence as a step towards group cohesion in response to a threat or learning opportunity. Individual feuding is followed, in turn, by dependency on the manager, by possible counterdependency as a reaction to the inevitable failure of authority to solve all the problems, and by pairing. Eventually, however, group members can achieve productive interdependence. Of course, all the stages other than interdependence are dysfunctional, and Ralph Stacey (1993: 198, citing Turquet 1974) suggests that this is because of a false sense of oneness. Typically a group that forms to create a powerful force or union can allow its members to feel that there is overwhelming unity even though this might not be so. This sense of oneness can render members passive to the actions of the group.

Because self-oriented behaviour is emotional in its origins, the style adopted by self-oriented individuals depends on whether their emotional orientation is affectionate, hostile or neutral towards others. These three basic orientations were developed into archetypes, identified by Kolb and colleagues (1984: 133), as shown in Table 11.3. They are:

- *friendly helper* – who strives for harmony at all costs
- *tough battler* – who sees all decisions as a contest or conflict
- *logical thinker* – who strives for order and reason.

Archetypes do not refer to individuals in explicit roles but to basic, often unquestioned, emotional dispositions that compel people to behave in a particular way. Archetypes are often unconsciously supported by others

Table 11.3 Three bests of all possible worlds		
1. Friendly helper	**2. Tough battler**	**3. Logical thinker**
A world of mutual love, affection, tenderness, sympathy	A world of conflict, fight, power, assertiveness	A world of understanding, logic, systems, knowledge
Task-maintenance behaviour Harmonizing Compromising Gatekeeping by concern Encouraging Expressing warmth	Initiating Coordinating Pressing for results Pressing for consensus Exploring differences Gatekeeping by command	Gathering information Clarifying ideas and words Systematizing procedures Evaluating the logic of proposals
Constructs used in evaluating others Who is warm and who is hostile? Who helps and who hurts others?	Who is strong and who is weak? Who is winning and who is losing?	Who is bright and who is stupid? Who is accurate and who is inaccurate? Who thinks clearly and who is fuzzy?
Methods of influence Appeasing Appealing to pity	Giving orders Offering challenges Threatening	Appealing to rules and regulations Appealing to logic Referring to 'facts' and overwhelming knowledge
Personal threats That he or she will not be loved That he or she will be overwhelmed by feelings of hostility	That he or she will lose his or her ability to fight (power) That he or she will become 'soft' and 'sentimental'	That his or her world is not ordered That he or she will be overwhelmed by love or hate

Source: Organizational Psychology: An Experiential Approach (2nd edn) by Kolb/Ruben/McIntyre, ©. Reprinted by permission of Pearson Education, Inc., Upper Saddle River, NJ.

and society by the persistence of myths and strong images, such as the dominant aggressive male and the submissive caring female (see Chapter 2). Most people will exhibit a combination of behaviours from each of the archetypes, and some of the most effective group performers are those who know how to behave caringly, confrontingly or logically as the need arises. The difference between them and those who conform to one archetype consistently is that behaviour changes in accordance with what they think is necessary to get the task completed.

It is possible to associate both positive and negative influences with specific types of behavioural concern in groups, as shown in Figure 11.2. For example, there is a need to integrate the actions of various members if a group is to function effectively. However, it is possible that instead of organizing action towards a group goal, an individual could use other calculating, manipulating and using actions to further their own interests. In organizations it is not unknown for managers to make things happen so that they look good in the short term. They might take credit for the work of others so as to ensure that they get a promotion and thus move on, leaving others to tidy up the long-term mess that they have created. Figure 11.2 summarizes essential actions for group functioning in the inner circle, helpful

behaviours related to these actions in the middle circle and unhelpful behaviours in the outer circle.

Leadership of teams

An important factor in the way in which people behave in teams is the way in which the leadership of those teams is exercised. Rollin Glaser (1992) has proposed a four-stage model of facilitative leadership (shown in Figure 11.3 below) in which he describes how empowerment switches over time from team facilitators' control to group members' control. Glaser's approach focuses on leadership that helps to create self-managing work teams and how this role might change over time. Self-managing work teams usually include elements of the following: they manage themselves; control and monitor their work; assign jobs to members; control work schedules, the pace of work and goals to be achieved; make decisions about inventory, quality, work stoppages, repairs and so on; and take actions to remedy problems (Kirkman and Shapiro 1997: 731). Based on this description, Uddevalla would be considered to have embraced many of the attributes of self-managing work teams, while NUMMI would be classified as a less developed example.

Figure 11.3 shows that in stage 1 of Glaser's model,

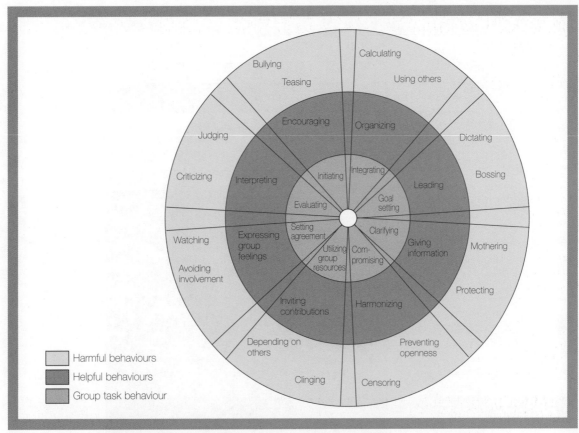

Figure 11.2 Helpful and unhelpful behaviours in groups

there is no empowerment of the team but the leader consciously uses traditional hierarchical forms of control to try to get the team to direct itself. In stages 2 and 3, there is increasing evidence of the empowerment of group members. In stage 2 the leader as facilitator tries to open up communications and discussion; while in stage 3 the team becomes involved in meaningful problem solving, decision making and critical reflection. In stage 4, the group members are substantially empowered and no longer need a leader or coach. By empowering others, the superleader has theoretically freed himself or herself to allow others to accomplish tasks through self-leadership, meaning that the collective output of both the 'leader' and the team improves. This is similar to post-heroic leadership described in Chapter 10.

Glaser develops his idea of superleadership based on the basis of the notion of followership (see Manz and Sims 1992; Manz 1992). Superleaders have the capacity to help their followers develop self-leadership so they can all contribute more fully to their organization's efforts. Team facilitators have to be empowered in order to empower teams. Empowerment for Glaser is measured along the dimensions of the power profile described in Chapter 6.

Glaser's notion of stages in team development is supported by Kozlowski et al. (1996), who also suggest some general principles and guidelines for team leaders, focusing on how different leadership skills are needed at different stages of team evolution. The authors contend that training in team leadership is often too simplistic, and that the team leader's training role should evolve as the team evolves. The authors maintain that during *formation*, a team is often a team in name only and that the leader needs to model appropriate 'team' behaviour or bonding and act as a *mentor*. What comes after formation is a *novice* stage, where the leader acts as a technical *instructor* in guiding task development and knowledge. Then comes the first part of the *refinement* stage where the leader acts as a *coach*, blending task work with teamwork in what are now seen as *expert teams*. The second part of the refinement stage is where the leader is a *facilitator* of what is really supposed to be *reflective practice* for a self-leading team (see Introduction and Chapter 1).

Ralph Stacey (1993: 243, 349–56) suggests that for innovation and learning to occur, organizations and their managers need to think beyond ideas such as self-managing work teams, self-leading teams and to

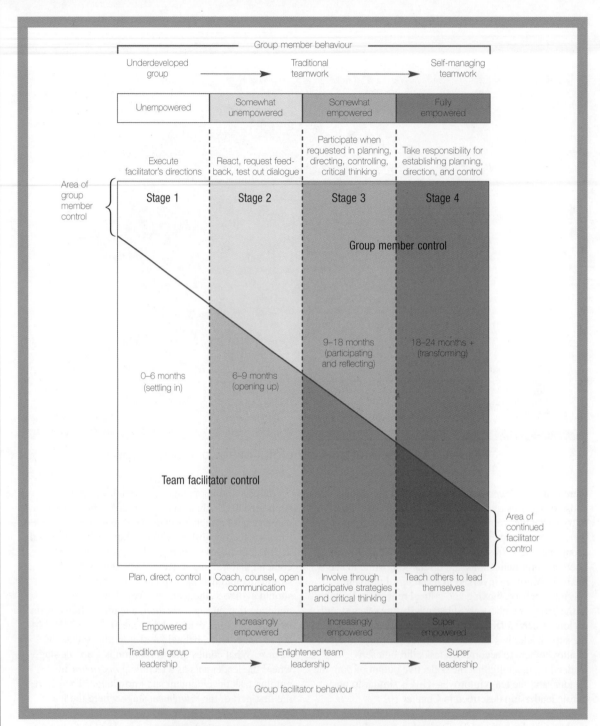

Figure 11.3 Facilitative leadership model

Source: Rollin Glaser (1992) *Moving Your Team Toward Self-Management*,
King of Prussia, PA: Organisation Design and Development Inc., p. 9.

embrace *extraordinary leadership*. He says managers need to encourage more *self-organization* through informal groups. Self-organization, he says, is one of the most important ways in which managers can create new knowledge by allowing small groups of people to develop spontaneously. These self-organizing networks need not be democratic but can be highly political, diverse or homogeneous (Stacey 1993: 353). Self-organization as a concept means management does not 'authorize' these networks of informal members to meet or form. Self-organizing networks are not permanent structures in the manner of self-managing work teams, but Stacey believes that organizations need to develop greater flexibility to cope with rapid and turbulent change. One important aspect of self-organization is that it does not presuppose a need for a strong culture. The self-organization concept does, however, raise questions about how much innovation, knowledge sharing and learning is possible in self-managed work teams. These more informal groups can provide emotional and intellectual support outside the hierarchy or formal team structures (Ulrich 1998: 23).

Internal politics

Teams are often presented as developing processes that will help to minimize power and eliminate organizational politics. A team is often assumed to be based on consensus and conformity to group norms and expectations. These pressures can discourage diversity of views and opinions and can stifle open debate and dialogue (also see Rifkin and Fulop 1997: 140). Much of the empowerment literature propagates the view that 'real' teams are somehow non-political and that politics and conflict do not have positive benefits.

Rosabeth Moss Kanter (1983: 260–2) suggests that politics within teams arises from a number of factors. For one thing, while teams are meant to ensure democracy and participation, it is difficult to eliminate internal competition or jockeying for status. Individuals have self-interest and different outcomes they want from the team, such as impressing those who reward and promote them. Few people completely subordinate their self-interest to the benefit of the team. This self-interest can be more pronounced in teams when the organization is divisive and uncooperative and can, for example, encourage departmental rivalry.

Teams which have to compete for scarce external resources and rewards, moreover, are likely to generate internal conflicts and competition. Teams where members are representing a department, unit or function are likely to be more political in protecting their 'turf' than where team members participate as individuals. It is difficult for 'representative' members to support a team decision that disadvantages their 'constituents' or colleagues. Kanter argues that individual representation is superior to other forms in many team situations.

Teams can become arenas for 'flexing muscles' and politicizing agendas. This can occur if a few members come to dominate the team and behave like 'oligarchies'. For example, Kanter cites a factory in which participative practices were encouraged but team members feared ostracism by a clique in the team. Peer pressure is a mechanism for group control upon which management often depends in trying to keep teams performing. Teams can also become politicized when there are historical tensions between them. Many management and labour (or union-based) teams simply amplify conflicts and hostilities, and members never reach or agree on mutual problem-solving strategies. Kanter says it is naive to expect that in all cases historical combatants will set aside their differences for the good of the team.

Cross-cultural issues

Bradley Kirkman and Debra Shapiro (1997) argue that self-managing work teams produce a number of substantial benefits when they are working successfully. These benefits include some of the following: greater levels of team productivity; higher quality; greater customer satisfaction; higher levels of safety; and lower levels of costs. Individually, team members in self-managing work teams report greater job satisfaction and commitment to the organization (Kirkman and Shapiro 1997: 731–2). Kirkman and Shapiro suggest that cross-cultural factors will influence whether or not self-managing work teams – a Western business concept – can be successfully introduced in non-Western cultures. They suggest that self-managing work teams comprise two critical dynamics or processes: *self-management* and *teamwork*.

Self-management

Self-management relates to the degree to which a team has discretionary decisions over such things as hiring and firing co-workers and being able to procure raw materials and services. Resistance to self-management in teams can manifest itself in overt actions such as sabotage, protests and other forms of disruptive behaviour. Resistance can also impact attitudinally and can include withdrawal from the organization through avoidance of co-workers, refusal to cooperate and a general lack of commitment to the job, evident in such things as absenteeism, lateness and substandard work (Kirkman and Shapiro 1997: 732–3).

Borrowing from Hofstede (see Chapter 3) and others, Kirkman and Shapiro argue that self-managing work teams in non-Western countries, which they term *globalized self-managed work teams*, are affected by three key cultural variables that influence acceptance or resistance to self-management: *power distance* (PD), *doing or being orientation* (DBO) and *determinism* (DE). These three cultural variables are claimed by the authors to vary more across cultures than within them. The authors note that the culture within an organization can moderate the influence of these broader cultural variables, as indeed do a number of others, including those mentioned by Marks et al. (1997). Nonetheless, the authors believe that cultural variables provide useful predictors of potential success or failure in globalized self-managing work teams. The following summary is drawn from Kirkman and Shapiro (1997: 737–9).

- *Power distance:* In countries that have low power distance cultures (see Chapter 3), it is acceptable to bypass one's boss or superior to get work done. Status, formality and titles are not expected to be conformed to and people are generally comfortable with accepting higher levels of responsibility in their jobs than is defined in their titles. Countries such as the USA, Australia and Canada have low power distance cultures. Malaysia, by contrast, provides an example of a high power distance society where individuals do not accept delegated responsibility or authority very easily and are usually poor at developing these skills in others. Bypassing a boss or a superior is considered insubordinate. Autonomy and responsibility are likely to be resisted or not well handled in high power distance cultures, suggesting that globalized self-managing work teams are likely to face resistance. Kirkman and Shapiro suggest that Japanese society's high power distance accounts for the absence of innovation in many of their team approaches.
- *Doing versus being orientation:* This relates to the extent to which individuals in a society value work (doing) versus non-work (being) activities. Dominant doing-oriented cultures stress hard work and accomplishment through work. Dominant being-oriented cultures see work as second to enjoying life away from work. People from dominant 'doing' cultures are more comfortable and willing to set their own goals and respond to goal-directed behaviour. Both these attributes are important in self-management. The authors cite countries such as Mexico and Malaysia as having dominant being-oriented cultures in which self-management is likely to flounder as part of a team strategy.
- *Determinism versus free will:* Cultures that have a strong element of determinism create a sense or feeling among people that many things are beyond their control and governed by external forces. The Muslim faith has strong elements of this. Dominant

'free-will' cultures such as the USA stress people having control over events and actions and their destinies. Self-management requires making changes within the team that often mean altering strategies, plans and even directions, and establishing new standards of performance or outcomes. A deterministic world view would not easily support these aspects of self-management.

Teamwork

Kirkman and Shapiro's second critical process, *teamwork*, focuses on how groups work interdependently to solve problems and accomplish tasks (1997: 739). Katzenbach (1997) and others suggest that teamwork depends on such things as communication, collaboration, cooperation and compromise. Interdependency varies among teams, and high interdependency means team members can only successfully accomplish their tasks collectively and thus have frequent encounters with each other for such activities as exchanging materials and information. Kirkman and Shapiro (1997: 739–40) suggest that resistance to teamwork is resistance to the interdependence that is necessary for highly effective self-managing work teams. They point out that people might accept greater responsibility for tasks (which is a self-management aspect) but may not want to share that responsibility (which is a teamwork aspect) in self-managing work teams.

Collectivism and *individualism* are the variables that most affect the success or failure of teamwork across cultures (see Chapter 3). People from collectivist cultures tend to identify with group interests, put aside self-interest and are thus more willing to rely on group decisions. This can also mean that individual performance differences can be disregarded when giving employees rewards. Shame and loss of face can also be associated with behaviour that contravenes group norms. Pursuing individual agendas (usually politically) is publicly frowned upon. By contrast, individualistic cultures promote the interest of the individual over the welfare of the group (Kirkman and Shapiro 1997: 740).

In support of this, a study of managerial trainees from the USA and the People's Republic of China found the social loafing effect in the American but not in the Chinese sample. The study by Christopher Earley (1989) suggests that people from a culture such as China's will more readily throw themselves into work for collective goals than will those from a highly individualistic culture. It might also be added that where the individual's sense of self depends very much on the groups of which they are a member, they will not feel themselves to be *fully* themselves unless working in a group situation and may feel uncomfortable working in a very large group where they feel isolated.

Individualistic cultures produce a sense of self which is not realized collectively by immersion in and playing one's part in the group, but rather by differentiating and asserting one's attitudes as an individual. People from individualistic cultures are less likely to accept teamwork in self-managing work teams where interdependence requires members to focus on the welfare of the group and not the individual.

There may be a tendency in more collectivist cultures to romanticize the condition of group harmony and undervalue creative conflict. It is also important to note that while collectivist cultures may not display the mechanisms of group surveillance and control as visibly as individualist cultures, there are often sets of overt and covert forces – social expectations, sanctions and benefits – working outside the group that serve to discipline group members before they enter the group (Kondo 1990; Yamamoto 1990; Sewell 1992).

Kirkman and Shapiro (1997: 741) note that people from individualistic cultures prefer equity-based rewards, where team members are differentially paid according to performance. In collectivist cultures,

equality-based pay, where each team member is paid the same, is often accepted and serves to reduce status differences. Not surprisingly, these two aspects relate to perceptions of fairness of pay and suggest that team-based pay is very likely to be more acceptable in collectivist cultures.

The authors also argue (Kirkman and Shapiro 1997: 745–6) that among the moderators of all these cultural influences, diversity is a very strong one. The diversity of a group affects the level of resistance to, and success of, self-managing work teams. Diversity within a team tends to increase turnover and therefore limit opportunities for long-term influence. Diverse teams also have less scope for cohesiveness along cultural lines, and consensus is more difficult to achieve. Resisters simply have a more difficult task of influencing others in a diverse group. Minority views usually find it more difficult to influence majority views in diverse teams, so resistance is again more difficult. Team leaders, however, can have undue influence over teams in resisting either self-management or teamwork.

Conclusion

Given the pervasiveness of teams across popular and academic management texts, it should come as no surprise that an emerging critical backlash can be identified. Take, for example, Stanley Herman's *A Force of Ones* (1994) or Lyman Ketchum and Eric Trist's *All Teams Are Not Created Equal* (1992). These authors see themselves as reeling in some of the more excessive claims that are made in support of teams. At the same time there is a long and well-developed tradition of workplace democratization that emanates from Northern Europe. This movement sees teamwork as an important component of efforts to increase self-determination and genuine democracy at work.

Democracy at work, though, is far removed from the highly normative and instrumental approaches to teamwork that are currently associated with management fads, fashions and the North American 'management gurus', which simply see teamwork as a means of increasing traditional benchmarks like profitability, competitive advantage, capital utilization or productive efficiency. This is not to say that teamwork, in any of its incarnations, is an unattractive proposition for organizations and their employees. Rather, we should be sceptical of the claims made for teamwork, subjecting them to critical scrutiny in order to establish whether they create conditions of mutual benefit or perpetuate or even develop new forms of organizational asymmetry. This critical perspective will enable us to make informed choices about important organizational changes, rather than blindly following the exhortations of the latest management guru.

Answers to questions about teams

1 **What is a team?** We can see that although there are many possible definitions of a team, the lowest common denominator is the idea of a group

Answers continued

working towards a defined or shared set of objectives. Where definitions may diverge is around the degree of specificity of the roles played within the team by individuals, the degree of empowerment and autonomy of the members and the extent of the hierarchy.

2 What needs and whose needs can a team serve? Within some teams, job design considerations may lead to higher motivation and job satisfaction for workers, whose needs may appear to be better satisfied than in other forms of organizing. However, teams can also be stressful places where members are expected to police themselves and work both harder and smarter in the service of managerial ends.

3 Do managers need to manage differently in a team situation? Managers, and particularly those at supervisory level, do need to manage differently in a teamwork situation, but the nature and type of leadership skills they need to exercise will vary according to the type of team they are in, its stage of development and whether they are aiming for self-managing work teams and self-leadership principles.

4 Are there different ideas of what a team is and does? Furthermore, there are clearly different ideas of what a team is and does, and the success or failure of a team depends on its relationship with its context as well as its internal characteristics.

5 How do teams develop? Teams develop, and succeed or fail, in context (Mueller et al. 2000). Teams may work well in one company and not in another. They might be broadly embraced and effective in one national culture and not in another. The shape of teams will therefore be affected by contextual forces which constrain or enable them. Nevertheless, this is likely to take place following patterns of development, stages, periods of activity and inertia, which have been identified by recent research. Teams might not be the universal panacea which some popular treatments claim, but they do have some common features and properties, knowledge of which can help us both to manage some teams and be a useful member of others.

REVISITING
THE CASE STUDY

1 How important is the theory behind the practice in Wombat?

The theory behind the practice seems to be very important in this case, and the basic principles have been thoroughly worked out by the manager, Norman Stone. Indeed, these principles seem sound and well understood.

2 What impact have the changes had?

They have had considerable impact on performance in the short term, although the process is still in its initial stages, and several significant gains seem to have been experienced.

3 How far are teams involved in setting their own performance levels?

The employees are not heavily involved as yet in setting their own standards and the groups are, at best, at stage 2 of Glaser's model of facilitative leadership, with operators being used as inspectors rather than anything more creative. But problem solving has occurred and progress seems exceptionally good at the end of the first part of the case.

4 How effective was the involvement process?

In the second part of the case, some problems emerge. First, the involvement of the teams in the design process was limited, and the resources they were given were rather limited, which meant that they were working under severe constraints. While the researchers were able to help and facilitate the groups, it appears that the engineering managers did not fully understand their role in the team project, and the researchers were not receiving information. The engineering manager's management style here seems very different from that of Norman Stone, and the theory outlined in the first part of the case is not being put into practice. Essentially, the engineers want to develop another production line and are reluctant to design anything jointly with the operators that will give them control over their own work. The plant culture seems to be hierarchical and task- and function-dominated, with some evidence of a thinly veiled power struggle which the engineers want to win, and by the end of this section the operators would be very dispirited and disillusioned.

How could the outcome described earlier have happened, given the first researchers' story about the plant? Contrary to the innovative, participatory change process coordinated by a supportive management team, there was a tense industrial relations climate (exacerbated by broader conflicts within the industry), with little trust between shop-floor workers and management. The management structure at the plant was confusing to workers (and constantly changing), and there was poor coordination across management functions. While there had been some notable team successes in solving production problems (as the earlier study illustrated), there was in fact very little diffusion of effective teamwork throughout the plant. The successes were transitional phenomena restricted to only limited areas. The work area 'teams' existed more in name than in any substantive meaning of the term. The only 'team activity' engaged in by these groups was a weekly

problem-solving session when the line was stopped during normal production time to allow for it. Wombat's much-vaunted 'employee involvement' programme proved to be more a token gesture than a form of meaningful participation. Top managers, as described, overruled recommendations of employee teams.

5 What were its problems?

This situation was a result of two main problems. The first was that the processes for team problem solving were inadequately developed, and no specific plant-wide training was provided for teamwork (although the company did provide other, widely praised, competency-based training programmes for its shop-floor employees). The second problem was that the production process at the plant remained dominated by conventional industrial engineering. Thus the organization of work followed Taylorist/Fordist principles, with extensive task fragmentation, short task cycles (of around 60 seconds), machines setting the pace of work, very little shop-floor autonomy and responsibility, and traditional supervision and control mechanisms.

6 How significant was the engineering manager's management style?

Within this unfavourable climate, three other factors contributed to the team/cell project's outcome. First, most of the plant's management 'team' and engineers had not been involved in the establishment of the project, and so were neither adequately prepared for nor fully committed to it. The project had been developed in negotiation with the original manager (Norman Stone) and his senior manager responsible for new business. Although the other managers had been informed about the project, they had had little other preparation and no chance for consultation on the project's details. Second, and exacerbating the first factor, Norman Stone retired before the project actually began. He was replaced by another manager who was not sympathetic to the project and its aims. As an industrial engineer, the new plant manager was much more technocratic (at one stage he commented: 'We have tried the team approach, and as far as I am concerned it has not worked') and so was more committed to introducing technical solutions to solve problems at the plant. Third, the management and engineering teams were excessively 'lean', with relatively small numbers of salaried employees responsible not only for managing existing processes but also for the development and introduction of new products and their manufacturing processes. This lean structure allowed little time for innovative projects and put considerable pressure on the assembly process design team.

7 How would you characterize the plant culture at this stage?

There was far less senior management commitment to change than was originally claimed, a far greater climate of distrust and suspicion among the workforce, far less extensive teamwork, and a less innovative organizational culture.

8 How would Taylor or Mayo interpret what happened at Wombat?

Taylor would not have seen the project as mistaken, but mishandled – he would not have approved of the efficiency losses or the lack of clarity of procedures, but he would also not have approved of the loss of esprit de corps. Mayo would have seen the earlier phases as a necessary part of letting the workers get things out of their

system, and would have castigated the managers for not listening to the workers' concerns more closely. However, he would have advocated greater training and support for the supervisory role within the existing structure rather than a new structure.

The failure of teams at Wombat arose from the fact that several situational factors were not favourable. The tense climate and lack of trust, the engineers' lack of understanding of the project and lack of commitment to it, the loss of Stone's leadership, which was central to putting the theory into practice, and failure to diffuse successes across the organization all meant that early changes were not sustainable. What seems to be important here is the need to educate on a wide basis all those who need to understand the proposed changes, to persuade them of the value of the changes, to continue to communicate from the top while allowing the teams considerable autonomy, and attention to breaking down existing political obstacles. If teams are to be successful in the future, they need to be linked to the culture of the organization, which may necessitate change on a broad scale, and will necessitate sustained top management support and leadership over a number of years.

References

Adler, P.S. (1993a) 'Time-and-motion regained', *Harvard Business Review,* **71**(1): 97–108.

Adler, P.S. (1993b) 'The "learning bureaucracy": New United Motor Manufacturing, Inc', *Research in Organizational Behaviour,* **15**: 111–94.

Adler, P.S. and Borys, B. (1996) 'Two types of bureaucracy: Enabling and coercive', *Administrative Science Quarterly,* **41**(1): 61–89.

Albanese, R. and Van Fleet, D.D. (1985) 'Rational behaviour in groups: The free-riding tendency', *Academy of Management Review,* **10**(2): 244–55.

Badham, R., Couchman, P. and Linstead, S.A. (1995) 'Power tools: Narrating the factory of the future', Annual Conference on the Labour Process, Blackpool, University of Central Lancashire, April.

Barker, J.R. (1993) 'Tightening the iron cage: Concertive control in self-managing teams', *Administrative Science Quarterly,* **38**(3): 408–37.

Becker, B. and Gerhart, B. (1996) 'The impact of human resource management on organizational performance: Progress and prospects', *Academy of Management Journal,* **39**(4): 779–801.

Belbin, R.M. (1981) *Management Teams: Why They Succeed or Fail*, London: Butterworth Heinemann.

Belbin, R.M. (1993) *Team Roles at Work*, London: Butterworth Heinemann.

Bell, L., Blackler, F. and Crump, N. (1997) 'Look smart', *People Management,* **23**: 56–9.

Benders, J. and Van Hootegem, G. (1999) 'Teams and their context: Moving the team discussion beyond dichotomies', *Journal of Management Studies,* **36**(5): 609–28.

Benders, J. and Van Hootegem, G. (2000) 'How the Japanese got teams', in Procter, S. and Mueller, F. (eds) *Teamworking*, Basingstoke: Macmillan – now Palgrave Macmillan.

Bendix, R. (1956) *Work and Authority in Industry*, New York: Harper.

Berggren, C. (1989) 'New production concepts in final assembly: The Swedish experience', in Wood, S. (ed.) *The Transformation of Work?*, London: Unwin.

Berggren, C., Adler, P.S. and Cole, Robert E. (1994)

'NUMMI vs Uddevalla; Rejoinder', *Sloan Management Review,* **35**(2): 37–9.

Bernstein, P. (1992) 'The learning curve at Volvo', in Glaser, R. (ed.) *Classic Readings in Self-Managing Teamwork*, King of Prussia, PA: Organization Design and Development Inc.

Bion, W. (1959) *Experiences in Groups*, New York: Basic Books.

Braverman, H. (1974) *Labor and Monopoly Capital: The Degradation of Work in the Twentieth Century*, New York: Monthly Review Press.

Buchanan, D. (1994) 'Principles and practice in work design', in Sisson, K. (ed.) *Personnel Management: A Comprehensive Guide to Theory and Practice in Britain* (2nd edn) Oxford: Blackwell.

Buchanan, D. (2000) 'An eager and enduring embrace: The ongoing rediscovery of teamworking as a management idea', in Procter, S. and Mueller, F. (eds) *Teamworking*, Basingstoke: Macmillan – now Palgrave Macmillan.

Carmona, S. and Grönlund, A. (1998) 'Learning from forgetting: An experimental study of two European car manufacturers', *Management Learning,* **29**(1): 21–38.

Cohen, S. and Ledford, G. (1994) 'The effectiveness of self-managing teams: A quasi-experiment', *Human Relations,* **47**(1): 13–42.

Cohen, S., Ledford, G. and Spreitzer, G. (1996) 'A predictive model of self-managing work team effectiveness', *Human Relations,* **49**(5): 643–76.

Cole, R. (1971) *Japanese Blue Collar: the Changing Tradition*, Berkeley/Los Angeles/London: University of California Press.

Cully, M., Woodland, S., O'Reilly, A. and Dix, G. (1998) *The 1998 Workplace Employee Relations Survey: First Findings*, London: DTI.

Davis, G. (1994) 'Research note: The stubborn silence of Petronius Arbiter', *Australian Journal of Public Administration,* **53**(2): 248–51.

Delbridge, R., Lowe, J. and Oliver, N. (2000) 'Worker autonomy in lean teams: Evidence from the world automotive components industry', in Procter, S. and Mueller, F. (eds) *Teamworking*, Basingstoke: Macmillan – now Palgrave Macmillan.

Dore, R. (1973) *British Factory – Japanese Factory*, London: Allen & Unwin.

Dunphy, D. and Bryant, B. (1996) 'Teams: panaceas or prescriptions for improved performance?', *Human Relations,* **49**(5): 677–99.

Earley, P.C. (1989) 'Social loafing and collectivism: A comparison of the United States and the People's Republic of China', *Administrative Science Quarterly,* **34**(4): 565–81.

Fincham, R. and Rhodes, P.S. (1992) *The Individual, Work and Organization: Behaviour Studies for Business and Management* (2nd edn), London: Weidenfeld & Nicolson.

Findlay, P., McKinlay, A., Marks, A. and Thompson, P. (2000) '"Flexible when it suits them": The use and abuse of teamwork skills', in Procter, S. and Mueller, F. (eds) *Teamworking*, Basingstoke: Macmillan – now Palgrave Macmillan.

Friedman, A. (1977) *Industry and Labour*, Basingstoke: Macmillan – now Palgrave Macmillan.

Gabrenya, W.K., Latane, B. and Wang, Y.E. (1981) 'Social loafing in a cross-cultural perspective', *Journal of Cross-Cultural Psychology,* **14**: 368–84.

Gersick, C. (1988) 'Time and transition in work teams: Toward a new model of group development', *Academy of Management Journal,* **31**(1): 9–41.

Gersick, C. (1989) 'Marking time: Predictable transitions in task groups', *Academy of Management Journal,* **32**(2): 274–309.

Gilbreth, F.B. and Gilbreth, L.M. (1917) *Applied Motion Study: A Collection of Papers on the Efficient Method to Industrial Preparedness*, New York: Sturgis & Walton.

Gilbreth, L.M. (1914) *Psychology of Management*, New York: Sturgis & Walton.

Glaser, R. (1992) *Moving Your Team Toward Self-management*, King of Prussia, PA: Organisation Design and Development Inc.

Grenier, G. (1989) *Inhuman Relations: Quality Circles and Anti-Unionism in American Industry*, Philadelphia: Temple University Press.

Guest, D. (1997) 'Human resource management and performance: A review and research agenda', *International Journal of Human Resource Management,* **8**(3): 263–76.

Hackman, J. and Oldham, G. (1976) 'Motivation through the design of work: Test of a theory', *Organizational Behavior and Human Performance,* **16**: 250–79.

Hackman, J. and Oldham, G. (1980) *Work Redesign*, Reading, MA: Addison-Wesley.

Harvey, N. and von Behr, M. (1994) 'Group work in the American and German nonautomotive metal manufacturing industry', *International Journal of Human Factors in Manufacturing,* **4**(4): 345–60.

Herman, S.M. (1994) *A Force of Ones: Reclaiming Individual Power in a Time of Teams, Work Groups, and Other Crowds*, San Francisco: Jossey-Bass.

Heterick, W.P. and Boje, D.M. (1992) 'Organization and the body: Post-Fordist dimensions', *Journal of Organizational Change Management,* **5**(1): 48–57.

Hill, S. (1991) 'Why quality circles failed but total quality might succeed', *British Journal of Industrial Relations,* **29**(4): 541–68.

Hounshell, D. (1985) *From the American System to Mass Production, 1800–1932: The Development of*

Manufacturing Technology in the United States, Baltimore, MD: Johns Hopkins University Press.

Ichniowski, C., Kochan, T., Levine, D., Olson, C. and Strauss, G. (1996) 'What works at work: Overview and assessment', *Industrial Relations,* **35**(3): 299–333.

Industrial Society (1995) *Self-managed Teams* London: Industrial Society.

Jenkins, A. (1994) 'Teams: from "ideology" to analysis', *Organization Studies,* **15**(6): 849–60.

Kanigel, R. (1997) *The One Best Way: Frederick Winslow Taylor and the Enigma of Efficiency*, London: Little, Brown.

Kanter, R.M. (1983) *The Change Masters: Innovations for Productivity in the American Corporation*, New York: Simon & Schuster.

Katzenbach, J.R. (1997) 'The myth of the top management team', *Harvard Business Review*, November–December: 83–91.

Katzenbach, J.R. and Smith, D.K. (1993) *The Wisdom of Teams*, Boston, MA: Harvard Business School Press.

Ketchum, L.D. and Trist, E. (1992) *All Teams Are Not Created Equal: How Employee Empowerment Really Works*, Newbury Park: Sage.

Kirkman, B.L. and Shapiro, D.L. (1997) 'The impact of cultural values on employee resistance to teams: Toward a model of globalized self-managing work team effectiveness', *Academy of Management Review,* **22**(3): 730–57.

Kolb, D.A., Rubin, I.M. and McIntyre, J.M. (1984) *Organizational Psychology: An Experiential Approach to Organizational Behavior*, Englewood Cliffs, NJ: Prentice Hall.

Kondo, D.K. (1990) *Crafting Selves*, Chicago: Chicago University Press.

Kozlowski, S.W.J., Gully, S.M., Salas, E. and Cannon-Bowers, J.A. (1996) 'Team leadership and development: Theory, principles, and guidelines for training leaders and teams', *Advances in Interdisciplinary Studies of Work Teams* 3: 253–91, Greenwich, CT: JAI Press.

Lawler, E. (1986) *High Involvement Management*, San Francisco: Jossey-Bass.

Lawler, E. (1992) *The Ultimate Advantage: Creating the High Involvement Organization*, San Francisco: Jossey-Bass.

Levinson, D. (1978) *The Seasons of a Man's Life*, New York: Alfred A. Knopf.

Lipnack, J. and Stamps, J. (1994) *The Age of the Network: Organizing Principles for the 21st Century*, Essex Junction, VT: Oliver Wight Publications.

Lipnack, J. and Stamps, J. (1997) *Virtual Teams: Reaching Across Space, Time and Organizations with Technology*, New York: John Wiley.

McLachlan, R. (1997) 'Harrogate Report, 3: Knowledge

management – Porter fails to focus on employees', *People Management,* **6**: 11–12.

MacNeish, J. and Richardson, T. (1994) *The Choice: Either Change the System or Polish the Fruit – A Pictorial Guide to Creating Productive Workplaces*, Sydney: Don't Press.

Manz, C.C. (1992) 'Beyond self-managing work teams: Toward self-leading teams in the workplace', in Glaser, R. (ed.) *Classic Readings in Self-Managing Teamwork*, King of Prussia, PA: Organization Design and Development Inc.

Manz, C.C. and Sims, H.P. (1992) 'Becoming a super-leader', in Glaser, R. (ed.) *Classic Readings in Self-Managing Teamwork*, King of Prussia, PA: Organization Design and Development Inc.

Marks, A., Findlay, P., Hine, J., McKinlay, A. and Thompson, P. (1997) 'Whisky galore: Teamworking and workplace transformation in the Scottish spirits industry', paper presented to the 15th Annual Labour Process Conference, March, Edinburgh.

Mayo, E. (1933) *The Human Problems of an Industrial Civilization*, New York: Macmillan.

Mayo, E. (1945) *The Social Problems of an Industrial Civilization*, Boston, MA.: Division of Research, Graduate School of Business Administration, Harvard University.

Mouzelis, N. (1975) *Organisation and Bureaucracy*, London: Routledge & Kegan Paul.

Mueller, F. (1994) 'Teams between hierarchy and commitment: Change strategies and the "internal environment"', *Journal of Management Studies,* **31**(3): 383–403.

Mueller, F., Procter, S. and Buchanan, D. (2000) 'Teamworking in its context(s): Antecedents, nature and dimensions', *Human Relations,* **53**(11): 1387–424.

Parker, M. and Slaughter, J. (1988) *Choosing Sides: Unions and the Team Concept*, Boston: South End Press.

Rifkin, W. and Fulop, L. (1997) 'A review and case study of learning organizations', *The Learning Organization: An International Journal,* **4**(4): 135–48.

Rose, M. (1975) *Industrial Behaviour* (2nd edn) Harmondsworth: Penguin.

Sewell, G. (1992) 'In (In)formation we trust?', paper presented to MERIT 10th Anniversary Conference, 10–12 December, Maastricht, the Netherlands.

Sewell, G. (1998) 'How the giraffe got its neck: An organisational 'Just-So' story', in Clegg, S., Ibarra, E. and Bueno, L. (eds) *Theories of the Management Process: Making Sense Through Difference*, London: Sage.

Sewell, G. and Wilkinson, B. (1992a) 'Someone to watch over me: Surveillance, discipline and the just-in-time labour process', *Sociology,* **26**: 271–89.

Sewell, G. and Wilkinson, B. (1992b) 'Empowerment or emasculation: Shopfloor surveillance in a total quality organisation', in Blyton, P. and Turnbull, P. (eds) *Reassessing Human Resource Management*, London: Sage.

Smith, A. (1776) *An Inquiry into the Nature and Causes of the Wealth of Nations*, Dublin: Whitestone.

Stacey, R.D. (1993) *Strategic Management and Organizational Dynamics*, London: Pitman Publishing.

Steingard, D.S. and Fitzgibbons, D.E. (1993) 'A postmodern deconstruction of total quality management (TQM)', *Journal of Organizational Change Management*, **6**(4): 27–42.

Taylor, F.W. (1903) *Shop Management*, revised 1947 and republished 1964 as *Scientific Management*, New York: Harper & Row.

Taylor, F.W. (1911) *The Principles of Scientific Management*, revised 1947 and republished 1964 as *Scientific Management*, New York: Harper & Row.

Taylor, F.W. (1912) 'Testimony before the Special House Committee', revised 1947 and republished 1964 in *Scientific Management*, New York: Harper & Row.

Taylor, F.W. (1947) *Scientific Management: Comprising Shop Management, The Principles of Scientific Management and Testimony Before the Special House Committee*, New York; Harper.

Taylor, F.W. (1964) *Scientific Management*, New York: Harper & Row.

Thompson, P. and Wallace, T. (1995) 'Teamworking: Lean machine or dream machine?', 13th International Labour Process Conference, University of Central Lancashire: Blackpool.

Thompson, P. and Wallace, T. (1996) 'Redesigning production through teamworking: Case studies from the Volvo Truck Corporation', *International Journal of Operations and Production Management*, **16**(2): 103–18.

Trist, E. and Bamforth, K.W. (1951) 'Some social and psychological consequences of the long wall method of coal getting', *Human Relations*, **4**: 3–38.

Trist, E., Higgin, G., Murray, H. and Pollock, A. (1963) *Organizational Choice: Capabilities of Groups at the Coal Face under Changing Technologies: The Loss, Rediscovery and Transformation of a Work Tradition*, London: Tavistock.

Tuckman, B.W. (1965) 'Developmental sequences in small groups', *Psychological Bulletin*, **63**(6): 384–99.

Turquet, P. (1974) 'Leadership: The individual and the group', in Gibbard, G.S., Hartman, J.J. and Mann, R.D. (eds) *Analysis of Groups*, San Francisco: Jossey-Bass.

Ulrich, D. (1998) 'Intellectual capital = competence × commitment', *Sloan Management Review*, Winter: 15–26.

Waring, S.P. (1991) *Taylorism Transformed: Scientific Management Theory Since 1945*, Chapel Hill: University of North Carolina Press.

Waterson, P., Clegg, C., Bolden, R., Pepper, K., Warr, P. and Wall, T. (1997) *The Use and Effectiveness of Modern Manufacturing Practices in the United Kingdom*, Sheffield: Institute of Work Psychology.

Wickens, P. (1987) *The Road to Nissan: Flexibility, Quality, Teamwork*, Basingstoke: Macmillan – now Palgrave Macmillan.

Winter, S.G. (1994) 'Organizing for continuous improvement: Evolutionary theory meets the quality revolution', in Baum, J.A.C. and Singh, J. (eds) *Evolutionary Dynamics of Organizations*, Oxford: Oxford University Press.

Womack, J.P., Jones, D.T. and Roos, D. (1990) *The Machine that Changed the World*, New York: Rawson Associates.

Yamamoto, K. (1990) 'Japanese style industrial relations and an "informal" employee organization: A case study of the Ohgi-Kai at T', *Electric Institute of Social Science Occasional Paper* No. 8, Tokyo: University of Tokyo.

CHAPTER 12

Managing conflict and negotiation

Stephen Linstead, Jonathan Gosling, Liz Fulop, Anne-marie Greene and David S. Richards

Questions about conflict

1 Can all conflict be negotiated to a win–win solution?
2 What happens when people really enjoy the conflict?
3 Is there ever a final resolution to a conflict or rather is it just a stage in a relationship?
4 Are conflicts a break in normal relationships or part of them?

ANNUAL PAY NEGOTIATIONS AT METALCO

It was 9 pm and Mark James looked up from his cup of coffee to see Peter Green walking in through the entrance of the motorway services towards him. 'Good to see you Pete', said Mark, standing up to shake his hand, checking at the same time that he recognized no one from the firm in the vicinity, 'Let's get down to business!' While the members wanted a 4.5 per cent rise in pay, Mark recognized that this was an impossible demand. But there had to be some give: after the massive redundancies at the sister firm, members were scared and wanted some reassurance that the union could get things done, and Mark and Peter both agreed that productivity had increased beyond all expectations. On the other hand, Peter was facing immense pressure from the managing director to be tough on the union and they both knew the meagre level of influence he had over the new senior management team. He was the one remaining token manager from the old regime, and the insistence on meeting the bottom line by the new owners meant that a long-term view on human resource issues was not an option. Eventually Mark, the union convenor, and Peter, the personnel director, came to a compromise agreement: the union would suggest acceptance of a 3 per cent pay rise, with improved sick pay provision and guaranteed overtime rates. The union would also agree to begin discussing the implementation of the first stages of the restructuring proposal. Three hours later, Mark James began his drive home. He was satisfied that they were prepared for the negotiations tomorrow and knew what the game plan would be.

As he walked into the factory the next morning, Mark James reflected on how hard the last year had been at MetalCo. This was a small town, everyone knew someone who worked at one of the factories and most employees lived within walking distance. Families had three or four generations working in 'metal-bashing' – sons and daughters following fathers and mothers. This was a town and an industry built on long-embedded, traditional ways of doing things; there had been incredible continuity in work organization and management strategy for the last 50 years. This had all changed with the takeover of MetalCo and the second largest firm in the town last year by a US multinational – Security Inc. At the other firm, they had seen dramatic restructuring in the name of becoming a 'world class manufacturing firm' – the introduction of teamworking, abolition of piecework pay, breakdown of traditional job demarcations and, most disheartening of all, redundancies amounting to two-thirds of the workforce.

Security Inc. was now beginning to introduce a process of restructuring at MetalCo, potentially threatening the 950-strong workforce. What could the union do to ameliorate the impact of the restructuring? How could Mark maintain the faith and confidence of the membership that the union could do something? Everything had to be planned carefully and attended to constantly. Mark knew what the opinion was of the union at the other firm: suddenly people at the other firm were leaving the union when they had always maintained near 100 per cent membership density at the two firms. The union convenor there was seen as powerless, secretive and 'in management's pocket'. While he did not believe this was the case, Mark did not share the views of his counterpart convenor in the other firm on either the nature of the restructuring or how to lead shop-floor union organization. While his counterpart felt that the changes would yield gains in the long term, Mark doubted that the restructuring would be predominantly beneficial for members and was keen to fight against some elements of the change programme.

Unlike his counterpart, who had never been good at delegating duties and had developed no mechanisms for communication of members' views, Mark had always been concerned to canvass the views of the shop floor. This took a long time, walking around and talking to people but was worth it in the end: he did feel that he 'had the ear' of the membership. His style had always been to emphasize to the 17 shop stewards that they must be seen as accountable to the membership. Mark recognized that members were very anxious about the proposed changes and worried for their jobs but the message for the shop stewards was that they had to retain a united front and instil confidence by remaining optimistic. Despite the depressing state of affairs recently, Mark was pleased that shop steward meetings were generally upbeat, not because they were any happier about the proposals for restructuring, but because they felt that the union could and would fight for the best interests of members.

This was not to say that Mark did not have views on the need for some change. The industry was in a beleaguered state, orders were down and profit margins had fallen, largely because of the increased threat of cheaper foreign imports. Something had to be done and this would inevitably mean bad news for at least some of the members. This was a traditional firm and people did not like change – especially when it happened too fast. What was important was that as far as possible, Mark had to demonstrate that he and the shop stewards were doing all they could to protect the interests of employees and could make some demonstrable gains. Then, hopefully, the members would stick by the union even if the company still managed to introduce sweeping change and some 'unavoidable' redundancies.

In a firm like MetalCo, a lot was done by custom and practice – there were very few formal written procedures determining the way in which the union interacted with management. This could be problematic, particularly if you did not 'know the ropes', but Mark had a good relationship with the Personnel Director Peter Green, built up carefully over twenty years and they had come to a pragmatic understanding about what was and was not possible. Personally, Mark liked him – they shared a lot of interests and found conversation easy. Peter was someone Mark felt he could negotiate with and Mark was keen that they should have a cooperative relationship with management. Generally Mark trusted Peter, but at the end of the day, he was still management. Mark knew that Peter himself felt threatened by the new management and would be less inclined now than ever to make concessions to the union.

In the face of tougher management over the last few months, it had been even more important than usual for Mark to publicly demonstrate opposition to management. 'Notice-board wars' had become a regular feature at the factory, with letters posted between himself and Peter and other managers, sometimes involving quite personal attacks. Mark had also made a deliberate decision to begin challenging managers on issues as they were walking around the factory, rather than arranging meetings in their offices. Last month a member had praised him for 'having a good old go' at Peter Green, as they stood arguing by assembly line D. In reality, Mark reflected that it was more of a heated discussion, and he probably had been a bit more vocal than he needed to have been, but the impression produced was very useful in its own way. In addition, militancy on a wider basis had been required on occasion, if the union was to have any credibility, with either the members or management, as a viable threat. Three months ago, management changed the piecework values on a line without consultation with the union. In response, the women assemblers had rallied around Mark, refused to work to the new values and dropped to basic productivity levels, even suffering a drop in earnings by reverting to un-measured pay. Management had been forced to completely reverse their policy and reinstate the old values.

So far, allowing a degree of cooperation while also maintaining a clear opposition to management appeared to have been successful. Unlike at the sister firm, Mark knew that he had been kept informed at most stages along the change process, usually through Peter (and where he had not, the company had met united action). Often, Mark heard about an initiative or proposal before some of the middle managers. Mark had also been able to force the addition of training and education clauses to the work organization proposals and established the right of the union to be 'meaningfully consulted' by a new management team with a history of 'union-bashing' tactics in the US. In order to retain the support of his shop stewards, Mark had also been careful to demand the presence of the senior shop stewards at key meetings, refusing managers' demands for personal face-to-face meetings. He had also resisted unreasonable demands for joint meetings at an inconvenient place or time, or where the given notice had been too short for adequate preparation. This preparation was essential: the union had to be seen in the right light from both management and membership sides and he and his shop stewards had to rehearse their positions to provide a united front – one independent militant could upset the whole situation. It was a daily battle to get the balance between cooperation and opposition right.

The battle of the annual round of pay negotiations began in the boardroom at 10 am. It played itself out within the usual ritualistic boundaries. The union offered the membership demand of a rise of 4.5 per cent, the management refused. Voices were raised, sections of rules were deliberated upon, accusations of unreasonableness were made, and fists were banged on tables. By the time it came to break for lunch, no agreement had been reached. The shop stewards reported back to the shop floor that the union was still holding out for demands but might have to offer some concessions. The negotiating committee reconvened and finally reached the compromise agreement four hours later: the union would agree to a 3 per cent pay rise, in exchange for improved sick pay provision and guaranteed overtime rates. The union would also agree to begin discussing the implementation of the first stages of the restructuring proposal. At the mass meeting on the car park at 6 pm, the deal was overwhelming accepted by members.

Note: MetalCo is a real company. The case study was developed by Anne-marie Greene and is based on material from a research project conducted by the author at the company.

QUESTIONS ON THE CASE

1 Which individuals or groups of individuals can be identified as stakeholders in the pay negotiations at MetalCo?

2 What vested interests did each of these stakeholders have in the outcome of the negotiations?

3 In what ways did Mark James manage the processes of interaction between the different stakeholders before and during the pay negotiations?

4 Would you consider that Mark James was acting in the best interests of his members?

Introduction

A normal corollary of organizational diversity – of interests, or simply expressed as differences between members – is conflict. All the fundamental distinctions relevant to management may be understood to imply conflict of some sort, and this conflict may be seen to have a necessary function in the maintenance and development of business and organization (see Table 12.1). This chapter is particularly concerned with explicit disagreements between people and groups and how these are dealt with in organized ways, although we will also consider some broader views of the nature of conflict.

In all the cases in Table 12.1, *social institutions* of various kinds act to mediate the differing interests of the parties, containing specific conflicts and leveraging the outcomes for the benefit of society at large. If we zoom in from this institutional level to the interactions between parties, we become concerned with a host of techniques, some of which are to do with *tactics* (offers and counteroffers, bluffs and counterbluffs and so on) and some to do with *skills* – managing emotions, evaluating tradeoffs, constituency interests and so forth.

This level of detail is usually discussed as *the art of negotiation*. A lot has been written about negotiations and how to conduct them successfully. However, when we come to the problems of conflict within organizations, there are both advantages and disadvantages to approaching them in this way. The principal advantages are that if the causes of conflict can be stated clearly, they can be treated as a set of negotiations. The disadvantages arise because many conflicts in organizations are not so easily reduced and clarified. This chapter suggests an alternative way of approaching conflicts – as part of a narrative process – that can open up a broader range of approaches for anyone intervening in conflicts.

First, we explore theories of conflict at different levels and some strategies that have been proposed for dealing with them, including different conflict management styles. We go on to describe the processes of negotiation, and then expose some of the underlying assumptions about the structure of relationships, identity and progress. Using a narrative approach consistent with our arguments about postmodern approaches in other chapters in this book, we examine how these assumptions can explain why conflict resolution is so often structured as if it followed a rather common, and somewhat predictable, pattern – we use the metaphor of a five-act play. In contrast to this, we show how organizational life is actually more like a soap opera than a stage play. Taking up this metaphor, we examine the assumptions underlying the production of soap

Table 12.1 A functionalist view of the social purposes of conflict	
Conflict	**Normative function**
Between buyer and seller	Normal way to fix prices
Between competitors	Maintain market efficiency
Between free-market agents and regulatory authorities	Distinguish roles of government and business
Between potential investment projects	Exercise executive decision making
Between shareholders, employees and customers	The motor of (shareholder models of) capitalist enterprise
Between candidates for a job	Labour market efficacy
Between responsibility to the company and the environment	Defines the moral boundaries of enterprise and where regulation is needed
Between demands of the job and family	Clarifies priorities, psychological defences and narcissistic desires

operas, and extract from that a paradigm to set against that of negotiation. We conclude with some suggestions for what this might mean in practice for those responsible for responding to conflicts in organizations.

Conflict

Conflict in organizations is not always obvious. Very often it may be *latent* where differing interests between people and groups exist but are not acted upon, or it may be *manifest*, where people begin to actualize their different aims and aspirations and often openly disagree with each other. Analysts often distinguish between *perceived conflict* where parties see a clear divergence of interest; *felt conflict* where parties experience tension, fear, hostility, mistrust and anger but don't necessarily see a conflict of interest; and *behavioural conflict* where people act to advance or defend their interests in ways that may range from passive resistance and cynicism (cold conflict) to outright hostility (hot conflict) through shades of manoeuvring in between. Although personal factors may contribute to the existence of conflict, more often than not it is a product of tensions surrounding the organizational situation such as:

■ scarcity of financial resources produces conflict over budgets
■ differentiation of tasks and roles places people in win–lose situations

■ hierarchical relations create conflicts around control and the reaction to control
■ status differences create barriers to communication or feelings of inequity and resentment
■ patterns of interdependence may make one group dependent on another where priorities are not shared
■ scheduling priorities may be at variance
■ roles and objectives may conflict
■ elements of a person's role may be internally inconsistent (for example discipline/counselling).

Additionally, conflict episodes in an organization may mean that the aftermath of one conflict just sets the scene for the next. Particular events may form a series, or annual events, such as wage bargaining or appraisal, may become either the source or the focus of conflict. In the case example below, the recently popular practice of appraisal ranking is described and it is suggested that although it can breed a culture of talent, this also becomes one of arrogance, greed and selfishness, coupled with individualism, lack of teamwork, suspicion and the withholding of help, cooperation or information from others. It is perhaps no accident that Enron, the company held up as exemplary in this article, was the first of the major US corporations to crash after falsifying its financial reports (as we discuss in Chapter 17). In a company which drives the necessity to look good in order to survive above all else into its managers at an individual level, we might not be surprised to find such organizational effects.

However, conflict is not always or simply problematic, as it may also, as we noted at the

---

CASE EXAMPLE

RANK AND FIRE: WHEN APPRAISAL MEANS CONFLICT

June is nail-biting time at Enron Corp., a Texas energy and trading giant, at which managers assemble twice a year to evaluate and cull employees as if they were head of cattle. Wrangling behind closed doors for up to two days at a time, the bosses compare and contrast the performance of workers over the prior six months and rate them on a five-point scale, with the top 5 per cent designated 'superior' and the bottom 15 per cent labelled 'needs improvement'. In between are 'excellent' (30 per cent), 'strong' (30 per cent) and 'satisfactory' (20 per cent). You don't want to be in the cellar: anyone described as needing improvement has six months to either get up to standard or scram. Evaluations have always been one of the more conflicted aspects of organizational behaviour. Employees fear

getting bad ones, and many managers have a hard time handing out negative news, which deprives the subjects of a candid appraisal. Best-to-worst forced-ranking systems are the latest attempts by corporations to take a systematic, long-term approach to evaluations. The goal: a continually improving workforce.

Whether they're fair or not, bell curve-like rating systems, which many employees now call rank and yank, have spread in recent years to some 20 per cent of US companies, including Ford, Microsoft and Sun Microsystems, and the trend is growing. They're particularly handy during periods of economic slowdown like the present one, when employees tend to cling to their jobs rather than retire or change positions. That lowers the normal rate of departures through attrition, which can run as high as 20 per cent of a corporate workforce when people feel like job hopping, just when companies are seeking to cut their costs to satisfy Wall Street. Many companies were just as fond of ranking and yanking when times were good, since the threat of poor ratings and their consequences help to concentrate the minds of workers. Or as Michael Loeb, a San Francisco expert in employment law, puts it, 'You don't want companies where everyone's completely comfortable.'

Ranking and yanking is nothing new at Enron, which launched the system among its fiercely competitive wholesale energy traders a decade ago and has since expanded it to cover all the Houston-based company's 18,000 employees. In a typically intense session, as many as 25 managers may gather around a conference table in a windowless room, with a computer screen filled with employee rankings projected on one wall. Each participant comes armed with notebooks bulging with job reviews. As the discussion proceeds, the managers may shift people from one ranking to another, deciding their fate with the click of a computer mouse.

What makes this process less Star Chamber-like is that workers can turn in self-assessments and choose up to seven colleagues and clients to write evaluations on their behalf. Moreover, anyone in the company can voluntarily submit a review of anyone else's performance. What it does depend on is the willingness of managers to fight for valued employees during what can swiftly become a brutal horse-trading session. Surprisingly, it's the employees in the middle rather than at the bottom of the scale who may feel the most demoralized by the forced-evaluation rankings. People don't like to be considered average and to boost their sagging

morale management must reassure those in the middle group that they meet the high standards which the company expects.

For those who ace their evaluations, the rankings can swell their self-esteem and wallets, a prospect that makes Enron a hotbed of overachievers. (And profitable too: Enron has reported increased earnings in each of the past four years.) The ranking system 'attracts hard drivers', Enron says. 'The proof is in the pudding. Our employees are very talented, and they're glad to be working here.' In its 2001 ranking of the world's most admired companies, *Fortune* rated Enron No. 1 in innovativeness and No. 2 in getting and keeping talent.

If competitive systems like Enron's have a weakness, it's that they can stir suspicion and discourage teamwork. 'If I help you, you'll get a better rank than I will.' John Challenger, CEO of the Challenger, Gray & Christmas outplacement firm, tells of a manager who recently had to rank all his people in preparation for a 10 per cent workforce reduction. 'It was agonizing', Challenger says, 'because everyone in his department played a unique role.' When such choices arise, he adds, 'all the relationships instantly become strained'.

Source: Adapted from John Greenwald (2001) 'Rank and fire – Attrition isn't working, so best-to-worst grading is gaining – and those on the bottom get the boot', *Time Magazine*, 18 June, www.time.com/time/magazine/article/ 0,9171,1101010618-129915,00.html.

beginning of the chapter, have some positive functions for an organization from a managerial point of view. It can:

■ energize action
■ encourage self-evaluation
■ stimulate adaptation
■ stimulate innovation
■ improve the quality of decision making
■ serve as a release valve and maintain the status quo.

Organizations may, of course, experience too much conflict, which can result in paralysis of decision making, demotivation of members, lack of trust and communication and the sorts of behaviours we observed in Company T in Chapter 3 which disrupted cultural commonality. Alternatively, there might be not enough conflict if members are constrained not to 'rock the boat' and a diversity of views and opinions are not heard. Conflict of interest will not always be manifested in open disagreement, since existing power relationships may be such that conflicts are never openly aired. Conflict may not manifest itself in terms of *overt conflict* where there is knowledge of the

issues over which there is conflict between interested parties, and all parties press their own interests. There are also degrees of *covertness of conflict* where the knowledge of the issues may differ between interested parties and the choice of action in pressing their own interests is variable.

How a particular instance of conflict is viewed, whether by managers, employees or theorists, is influenced by the frame of reference or general perspective on conflict to which they subscribe. There are three main common perspectives – *unitarist*, *pluralist* and *radical* – as identified by Burrell and Morgan (1979) and which we discussed from the perspective of power in Chapter 6. They are summarized in Table 12.2.

The three perspectives

Unitarists do not talk of interests, but rather of organizational goals and objectives, generally making the assumption that they are able to identify a social level – society, organization, group – under which everyone's interests may be subsumed and assumed to be served – as with Alfred Sloan's dictum that 'What's

Table 12.2 Three approaches to conflict and power

	Unitarist	Pluralist	Radical
Interests	Places emphasis on the achievement of common objectives. The organization is viewed as being united under the umbrella of commongoals and striving towards their achievement in the manner of a well-integrated team	Places emphasis on the diversity of individual and group interests. The organization is regarded as a loose coalition which has only a passing interest in the formal goals of the organization	Places emphasis on the oppositional nature of 'class' and sectional interests. Organization is viewed as a battleground where rival forces (e.g. management and unions) strive for the achievement of largely incompatible ends
Conflict	Regards conflict as a rare and transient phenomenon that can be removed through appropriate managerial action. Where it does arise, it is usually attributed to the activities of deviants and troublemakers	Regards conflict as an inherent and ineradicable characteristic of organizational affairs and stresses its potentially positive or functional aspects	Regards organizational conflict as inevitable and part of wider conflicts in society. It is recognized that conflicts may be suppressed and thus often exist as latent rather than manifest characteristics of both organizations and society
Power	Largely ignores the role of power in organizational life. Concepts such as authority, leadership and control tend to be preferred means of describing the managerial prerogative of guiding the organization towards the achievement of common interests	Regards power as a crucial variable. Power is the medium through which conflicts of interest are alleviated and resolved. The organization is viewed as a plurality of power holders drawing their power from a variety of sources	Regards power as a key feature of an organization. Power is unequally distributed and viewed as a reflection of power relations in society at large, and closely linked to wider processes of social control, e.g. control of economic power, the legal system and education. Power is seen as a form of manipulation and suppression

Source: Adapted from Gibson Burrell and Gareth Morgan (1979) *Sociological Paradigms and Organizational Analysis* London: Heinemann pp. 204, 388.

Key: ▨ Not normally mentioned

good for General Motors is good for the USA'. Nor do they pay much attention to the concept of power, rejecting it in favour of emphasizing authority and the management prerogative – management's 'right to manage'. The unitary approach to conflict has enjoyed prominence in management and, to a lesser extent, organizational behaviour literature for most of the last century and this resulted in a growth industry in conflict management methods and techniques. Unitarists focus on the need to control conflict by either minimizing it or eliminating it altogether. The main source of conflict is usually considered to be an individual troublemaker or deviant who can be either 'reformed', that is, treated with some form of retraining, counselling or soft therapy, or dismissed.

Pluralists, as one might expect, represent a highly diverse group of views, but they share certain common assumptions, the most important one being that organizations are not viewed as reified entities or structures but rather as multiple stakeholders who pursue diverse interests and make differing claims upon an organization's resources. Although pluralists treat

power, conflict and interests as interrelated phenomena, in the management and organizational behaviour literature, and in pluralist practice, the tendency has been to give prominence to the processes of conflict management and resolution, while relegating power issues to a residual role.

The *radical* view is also diverse in its theoretical origins, rooted in the work of Marx, Weber and critical theory and, more recently, in what might be called *critical postmodernism*. Nevertheless it stresses that organizations reproduce many of the systems of domination and exploitation that are apparent in the wider society. Thus, many organizational and management practices are claimed to serve the interests of the rich, powerful and/or the owners of capital. Criticizing pluralist approaches in general, the radical view draws attention to the unobtrusive but nonetheless insidious methods of control used in organizations to ensure that power, authority and control remain in the hands of managerial groups who represent the interests of capital. Conflict, in the radical view, is necessary for change, but the resolution of conflict is likely to be skewed in favour of management and capital by, on the one hand, asymmetries of power, and, on the other, the ability of the agents of capital to control or affect the ways in which the issues about which there is conflict come to be framed and overtly understood. Each of these approaches will now be considered in greater detail.

The unitary approach to conflict

This has some of its origins in scientific management, human relations and leadership theories, as discussed in previous chapters, but could also be seen to have roots in nineteenth-century social theories such as social Darwinism or moral/religious principles such as the Protestant work ethic. Although these theories dealt with broader management and organizational issues than simply conflict, they shared several assumptions about the nature of conflict that stressed its negative and disruptive dysfunctional impact on the otherwise smooth running of an organization. Unitarists make no necessary connections between conflict and power, or inequality. They operate within a consensus ideology derived from the assumptions made about the universal needs, interests and motivations of workers. In scientific management, the consensus between management and workers was presumed to be, in the end, inevitable because of their common interests in the pursuit of monetary or economic goals. The concept of 'economic man' was driven by the dominant beliefs and values that surrounded the Protestant work ethic, particularly the emphases placed on hard work and material accumulation. The principles of scientific management were considered to promote the economic well-being of *all* involved in an organization, albeit not equally, but they would be self-reinforcing in terms of further concretizing the assumptions of common goals and purposes.

In contrast, but nevertheless in support of the overall view of common goals, the consensus ideology of human relations and leadership theories sprang from different assumptions. Elton Mayo (1933) placed great stress on the possibilities of 'social man' and the importance of leadership, considerate supervision and paternalism in the workplace to meet the social as well as economic needs of the workers. Leadership and motivation theorists went further with the 'complex man' concept of behaviour, which proposed that self-actualization was the highest level of human potential and only fully achievable through work. Workers who possessed higher order needs sought more responsibility, challenge and creativity and logically cooperated and supported management. Self-actualizers were healthy, hard-working people who would not threaten or challenge management's prerogative. Workers with dominant lower order needs, or low growth ones, were problematic (in terms of consensus) but were ultimately amenable to cooption so long as monetary and other rewards (for example hygiene factors) were maintained. Conflict inevitably sprang from the failure of individuals to adapt their behaviours to fit in with organizations which already served everyone's self-interest, or almost every one.

Mayo and the human relations theorists laid the foundations of the emphasis on teamwork and group behaviour as a major technique of managerial control, although the emphasis remained on the individual *in* the team rather than on the collective itself. Not surprisingly, the unitary view of conflict presents the organization as a team in which members are assumed to be striving towards common objectives. These objectives are defined by management, and although consultation may be undertaken, this will be with a sense of *noblesse oblige* rather than any idea of power sharing. Conflict, when it occurs, is seen as pathological because it upsets the harmony of the team and the organization. In the unitary approach, emphasis is placed on developing supportive leadership practices in order to integrate and maintain happy work groups which are striving to achieve management's objectives. Goals are not considered to be a problem in the unitary approach because they are presumed to be supported by all.

Mayo's work concentrated on understanding emotionally oriented, irrational behaviour among workers. However, the definition of rationality taken was implicitly that of management, and worker behaviour was only to be regarded as rational insofar as it was congruent with management's goals and policies (Child 1973: 186). This is characteristic of the unitary approach, which reinforces management's right to manage, because the pursuit of managerial goals is the only rational strategy that it will allow. Rationality here then is in fact *rhetoric*, a tool of persuasion. According to this approach, if management's and workers' goals are, or should be, identical, then to challenge the managerial pursuit of what is in everybody's interests is simply irrational. Management's power is therefore *legitimate*.

In the unitary approach, collective worker organizations, such as trade unions, are viewed by management as illegitimate intrusions into the otherwise unified command and control structure of the workplace. They are seen as competitors for the loyalty and commitment of employees and thus as not having any legitimate place in the organization – the source of the 'us' and 'them' mentality. It is interesting to note that although Taylor is usually given as one of the main sources of these ideas, towards the end of his life he actually changed his views and came to accept that unions could play a positive role in organizations – representing worker views and suggesting improvements to the workplace – without being seen as solely oppositional, a view which is closer to contemporary managerial views in the wake of the widespread Japanization of industry. However, the pure unitary perspective denies the validity of conflict in organizations: conflict is unnatural and distracts from the sense of a common purpose and prevailing harmony. When conflict does occur, it is attributed to the personal failings of individuals. Two main sources of conflict are identified in this approach:

- interpersonal problems and personality clashes: poor communication; failure to understand how managerial and employee interests coincide
- trouble made by troublemakers: the work of agitators and *agents provocateurs* who are usually seen as having personal problems rather than political issues; if they are recognized as political, they are regarded as 'the enemy within'.

Unitarists would generally concede some other sources of conflict, such as poor or inappropriate leadership style and the absence of hygiene factors, but these would not be considered major ones. Conflict in the unitary model is therefore signified by the breakdown of normal, healthy interaction among individuals or groups and is considered harmful both to the organization and employees themselves. Some of the common techniques used to manage and resolve conflict from a unitary perspective are shown in Table

12.3. These techniques are consistent with the various schools of thought from which the unitary approach has sprung. They imply that individuals need to change or adapt to the existing system and that a consensus between management and workers (although not necessarily a negotiated consensus) is the desirable norm, even where there are valid and compelling reasons for conflict such as poor remuneration or working conditions.

Where managers do work from a unitary perspective, they tend to see conflict as not being inevitable and may be more likely to pursue outflanking strategies to remove this aberration. Unitarism has moved on from its origins in the early management literature, where it tended to reinforce the right of the master to demand unquestioning obedience from the workers, an ideology of control enshrined in the employment contract. Outside influences such as unions or even arbitration are only accepted as a last resort and are seen as an intrusion into the domesticity of the organization, where management performs a patriarchal role in which, however enlightened, it has the right to control through discipline, punishment, penalties and coercion. Nevertheless, although it rests upon managers seeking 'to persuade their employees and the public at large that industry is a harmony of cooperation which only fools and knaves choose to disrupt' (Fox 1974: 250), modern unitarism has evolved more subtle forms of persuasion,

Table 12.3 Common methods of conflict resolution from a unitary perspective	
Methods	Outcome
Increase diagnostic skills	Increased interpersonal awareness and sensitivity
Rules and regulations	Affirm authority and managerial prerogatives
Team building	Reinforces sense of belonging to organization and commitment to goals
Problem-solving sessions	Development of mutual trust relationships, makes individual/groups aware of pathological systems accompanying conflict
Third party or change agent	Increases interpersonal awareness; reappraisal of viewpoints; submission to judgement of third party (usually a management consultant)
Forcing, by the use of authority or managerial prerogative	Suppression of conflict
Communication	Increased interpersonal contact, feedback and flow of information, notice-boards, suggestion boxes and in-house journals
Avoidance	Ignoring the existence of conflict situations
Smoothing	Minimizing the extent and importance of conflict
Majority rule	Resolving conflict by majority rule
Leadership training	Improving morale and commitment
Job redesign	Increasing job satisfaction
Improve job context	Providing better working conditions

Source: Adapted from *Managing Organizational Conflict: A Non-traditional Approach* by Robbins, S.P., ©. Reprinted by permission of Pearson Education, Inc., Upper Saddle River, NJ.

as we have argued in Chapters 3 and 11, with varieties of limited trade union involvement such as single union deals and no-strike agreements. Unitarism therefore has both simple and sophisticated varieties, and continues to evolve.

Pluralist approaches to conflict

Pluralists generally question the proposition that the goals of the organization are implicitly understood and agreed with by all participants, and thus for them conflict is a naturally occurring phenomenon due to different perspectives and interests. In all organizations there are varying goals and objectives which different individuals, departments or subunits may pursue and these may not all or always reflect the stated goals of top management. It is almost impossible, pluralists say, to establish an overall set of goals or objectives for an organization, because of the diversity of stakeholders and multiple interests and objectives they pursue. These stakeholders have different interpretations of an organization's purpose, goals and objectives and conflicts occur as a result of the pursuit of competing claims and demands (Westerlund and Sjøstrand 1979: 33–42; Dawson 1986: 18–22, 31–3).

For pluralists, conflict is multifaceted and emerges from different pressure points both within and outside the organization. Employers, employees, shareholders, unions, government, collaborators in networks, partners and even customers all have different goals and allegiances and seek to press their interests or the interests of those they represent. Pluralist management then involves understanding the complex sets of tensions that arise from these competing claims and enabling all stakeholders to achieve some degree of success.

Table 12.4 shows the major sources of conflict identified by pluralist thinkers. While pluralists would not advocate 'one best way' for managing conflict, they have nevertheless expended much energy on diagnosing conflict and devising strategies to resolve it. There is still room in the pluralist approach for 'pragmatic pluralist' managers to concentrate on interpersonal sources of conflict while ignoring many others, particularly political ones (Kelly 1982: 173). Conflict in the pluralist scheme can be beneficial for an organization: if it can be properly institutionalized so that different points of view can be expressed openly; disagreement does not indicate disloyalty; and individual and group aspirations and goals can be accommodated within properly established managerial frameworks, such as joint consultation structures or confrontation sessions. In some cases, conflict is viewed as an essential part of creative and innovative group decision making (Stoner et al. 1985: 509–11).

Pluralists accept that in a conflict situation there are usually a number of different parties involved, making the resolution of individual or group claims extremely difficult. Conflicts can be intrapersonal (where an individual is conflicted over goals); interpersonal (between two or more individuals); intragroup (between various members of a group or clique); intergroup (across two or more groups); intraorganizational

Table 12.4 Sources of conflict in the pluralist approach	
Structural conflict	Relating to design or administrative changes affecting the workplace, task interdependence, job reclassifications
Conflict over economic resources	Distribution of profit, sources of finance, debts and borrowings
Conflict over nature of work	Standards in the industry, specialization, technology, safety standards, productivity, quality
Interpersonal	Communication, leadership, organizational culture
Conflict over scarce resources in the workplace	Promotions, superannuation, award payments, bonuses, staffing levels
Conflict over goals	Company vs personal goals, professional goals, departmental goals, unofficial or taboo goals, changing goals
Conflict over different value systems	Managerialism, equal employment opportunity, democratic vs autocratic styles of leadership
Conflict over symbolic items	Size of office, type of company car, titles and jobs, organizational charts, listings in reports etc
Conflict over role of external groups	Unions, government, arbitration and conciliation, consumer groups, media
Individual	Different needs and wants: job satisfaction

Source: Adapted from T. Lupton (1978) *Management and the Social Sciences*, London: Penguin, pp. 81–8, S. Dawson (1986) *Analysing Organisations*, London: Macmillan – now Palgrave Macmillan, pp. 18–36.

(between horizontal or vertical levels such as line/staff); and interorganizational (between different branches, divisions, partners or outside groups). From a pluralist view, each one of these situations would be seen to demand a different strategy or response. Given that several different categories of stakeholders can be involved in any one conflict situation, the repertoire of interventions necessary will need to be varied.

Conflicts are also seen as having knock-on effects, in other words, they are never finally settled because the solution of one conflict episode may give rise to conflicts elsewhere, especially if win–win situations cannot be created, and one group ends up losing out in the resolution. We will look more closely at conflicts as episodic and serial in the second half of the chapter.

Among the various competing perspectives which pluralism subsumes, *managerial pluralism* is the most popular. Under managerial pluralism, emphasis is placed on developing and increasing mutual interests and trust between managers and employees, while also promoting greater individuality (for example rewarding performance) and establishing flexible work practices. It is a form of collective (as opposed to individual) self-improvement, which is coordinated by management with the consultation of employees. Enterprise unions are an important part of this strategy. Managerial pluralism implies that conflict can be contained and used to mutual benefit, as long as management and employees can get together and draw up their own agreements and rules relating to work practices. This is possible because mutual trust and common interests allow consensus to develop. Managerial pluralism acknowledges unions as stakeholders and the employees' rights to membership of these organizations but only as long as they operate according to company policies, procedures and goals (Watson 1995: 286–9).

Historically, at least up to the 1980s, unions and labour organizations have adopted what is loosely identified as a *radical* approach to conflict, the so-called *adversarial* model in which the 'them versus us' ideology still dominates (see Table 12.5). Workers and management are considered to be pursuing quite different, often irreconcilable goals, an analysis often based on Marx's view of capitalism in which management, as the agents of the owners of capital, bought labour (which has *use value*) to create their products or services which they sell for their *exchange value*. The difference between exchange and use value is *surplus value* which the owners of capital appropriate and accumulate. The contradictions of capitalism arise from the fact that capital needs the willing cooperation of the workforce in order to create surplus value, to actualize the advantages it gets through the ownership of the means of production (and, more extensively, of distribution and exchange – markets and financial institutions). Yet labour is seen only as selling its labour, while capital has, in its own interests, to keep the price of labour low and the price of goods high. Labour, on the other hand, needs to seek a greater share of surplus value and secure its redistribution rather than concentration and accumulation in the hands of the few. In Marx's analysis, the logic of capitalism ultimately tears it apart and the *dialectical movement* between capital and labour leads to a revolutionary reversal of the positions and a new form of political economy emerges (Nichols 1980; Watson 1995; Hatch 1997; Thompson and McHugh 2002). Following Hegel, conflict is considered to be inevitable, as this dialectical movement is the engine of history which moved humanity from slavery to feudalism to modernity. Conflict is not only potentially but necessarily disruptive – it is necessary for social change and progress to occur. Strikes, for example, are simply strategies thought to advance labour's position relative

Table 12.5 A comparison of radicalism and managerial pluralism	
Radical view	Managerial pluralism
Conflict inevitable and the only way to change	Emphasis on mutual interests
Low trust	Increased trust in limited field
Central control/coordination of bargaining /negotiation/representation	Individualism
Equity/equality/uniformity	Flexibility
Industrial democracy/participation	Participation to secure commitment
Self-management and autonomy	Cooperation with unions/stakeholders
Unions have role as key decision makers	Collective bargaining as last resort

Source: Adapted from Table 9.3 in Liz Fulop, Faye Frith and Harold Hayward (1992) *Management for Australian Business: A Critical Text*, p. 221; adapted from 'Report to the Business Council of Australia' Industrial Relations Study Commission 1 July 1989 and J.E. Kelly (1982) *Scientific Management, Job Redesign and Performance*, London and New York: Academic Press, p. 173.

Table 12.6 Common pluralist techniques for conflict resolution	
Techniques	Outcome
Grievances or appeal procedures, internal dispute mechanisms	Allow parties involved in conflict to have equal power bases and not allow unfair advantages to occur
Negotiation, bargaining and participation	Allow parties involved to be part of this process; establish consultative committees or informal process
Industrial negotiations and collective bargaining relations system	Resort to arbitration and conciliation through the industrial
Counter-planning and confrontation meetings	Allow for 'choice' in any planning or decision making; encourage innovation and novelty
Structural change	Create new or autonomous departments; establish integrative functions or units (coordinating committees); restructure the organization (flatten the hierarchy)

Note: Techniques from the unitary approach may also be used by pluralists
Source: Liz Fulop, Faye Frith and Harold Hayward (1992) *Management for Australian Business: A Critical Text*, Melbourne: Macmillan.

to management. Low trust between management and workers is considered to be the norm, as harmony is engendered by false consciousness of labour's class position, manipulated by ideologies which legitimize managerial domination. There is no strong support or acceptance of enterprise unions here. On the contrary, central bodies such as conciliation and arbitration courts are favoured. Individuality and flexibility are seen as ways of institutionalizing inequalities that have been fought against through such things as industry awards, agreements and centralized wage-fixing processes. Table 12.5 summarizes the two approaches.

Some common techniques used to manage conflict resolution from a pluralist approach are shown in Table 12.6. Managerial pluralism supports collective bargaining but probably as a last resort, looking to solve conflicts internally through grievance procedures or outflanking. Radicals would reject many of these techniques, viewing them as managerially controlled. They would be seeking strategies to shift power to workers and their unions.

The radical approach has not been popular with management because it seeks to institutionalize resistance and challenge management prerogative in the workplace, especially management's control over the labour process in general. Radicals are particularly concerned by the use of technology to accelerate the process of deskilling of jobs identified by Braverman (1974), which erodes worker power by rendering them easily replaceable; and also by the processes of stratification which have created a dual labour market, where a core of workers central to the organization are very well treated while a periphery of lower status workers are paid less, given short-term or part-time contracts and rendered replaceable. This model, radicals argue, is replicated at the level of social structure, not just at organizational levels, as the privileged few become more entrenched while the

existence of the periphery becomes more and more parlous (Hatch 1997).

Nevertheless, with such things as award restructuring and enterprise agreements, a form of managerial pluralism has already taken hold in many organizations. Managerial pluralism still supports a bargaining view of the organization, in which it is generally recognized that checks and balances are needed to accommodate inevitable conflicts. Management's role is still seen as one of maintaining equilibrium among various competing groups. Pluralists, however, believe that power is relatively equally balanced in organizations and do not consider power differentials, exploitation and domination issues to be significant. For pluralists, conflict becomes an instrument for accommodation, social change and dynamism, rather than a symptom of breakdown: part of the everyday occurrences in any organization. A manager working from a pluralist approach to conflict would acknowledge it as inevitable and therefore would be more open to understanding and decreasing conflictual situations.

In the pluralist approach, conflict is controlled through continuous negotiation, concession and compromise. Some pluralists would, however, also resort to quite conventional methods, such as job enrichment, job redesign, team building and leadership training to resolve or stabilize conflict (see Table 12.5). However, even within this approach, management might only identify one or two reasons for conflict occurring and would still protect its managerial prerogative at all costs, however subtly. Thus, decision-making processes would still be seen as top-down and managerial goals would very rarely be bargained away.

Conflict interventions

Whatever their ideological position, managers who

Table 12.7 Strategies for increasing or decreasing conflict

Area of concern	General issue	Strategies for too much conflict	Strategies for too little conflict
Attitudes	Clarifies differences and similarities Increased sophistication about intergroup relations Change feelings and perceptions	Emphasize interdependencies Clarify dynamics and costs of escalation Share perceptions to depolarize stereotypes	Emphasize conflict of interest Clarify costs and dynamics of collusion Consciousness raising about group and others
Behaviour	Modify within-group behaviour Train group representative to be more effective Monitor between-group behaviour	Increase expression of within-group differences Expand skills to include cooperative strategies Third-party peacemaking	Increase within-group cohesion and consensus Expand skills to include assertive, confrontive strategies Third-party process consultation
Structure	Invoke larger system interventions Develop regulatory contexts Create new interface mechanisms Redefine group boundaries and goals	Refer to common hierarchy Impose rules on interaction that limit conflict Develop integrating roles of groups Redesign organization to emphasize task	Hierarchical pressure for better performance De-emphasise rules that stifle conflict Create devil's advocate or ombudsmen Clarify group boundaries and goals to increase differentiation

want to intervene in organizations to alter the level of conflict can attempt do this in three main ways:

1. *By changing perceptions/attitudes:*
   - the use of symbolism and the management of meaning
   - redefining interests, developing a new superordinate goal or new patterns of rivalry or internal competition
   - changing understandings of interdependencies and relationships
   - influencing feelings, stereotypes and processes of enactment.

2. *By changing behaviours:*
   - manipulating patterns of reward and punishment
   - training individuals to recognize and deal with conflict resolution, improving bargaining, negotiating and team-building skills
   - changing interpersonal dynamics.

3. *By changing structures:*
   - redesigning roles and interdependencies
   - creating rules that set new contexts for conflict resolution or arbitration
   - by introducing third parties as mediators or process consultants
   - by creating integrating roles or new interface mechanisms
   - by establishing consultative groups and other early warning systems (see Brown 1983).

These interventions can be further classified according to the objectives related to the specific area of concern regarding attitudes, behaviour or structure, and typical interventions targeted at increasing or decreasing the levels of conflict can be associated with particular general issues, as outlined in Table 12.7.

Kenneth Thomas (1977, 1992) classifies a range of possible conflict approaches using the dimensions of *cooperativeness* (attempting to satisfy others' concerns) and *assertiveness* (attempting to satisfy one's own concerns) and identifies five conflict handling styles (Figure 12.1).

In Thomas's research (cf Thomas 1992: 266), the five modes are defined as follows:

1. Avoiding (unassertive, uncooperative):
   - ignoring conflicts and hoping they'll go away
   - putting problems under consideration or on hold
   - invoking slow procedures to stifle the conflict (for example cooling off periods)
   - using secrecy to avoid confrontation
   - appealing to bureaucratic rules as a source of conflict resolution.

2. Compromising (medium assertive, medium cooperative):
   - negotiation
   - looking for deals and tradeoffs to find satisfactory or acceptable solutions.

3. Competition (assertive, uncooperative):
   - creation of win–lose situations
   - use of rivalry
   - use of power plays to achieve one's ends
   - forcing submission.

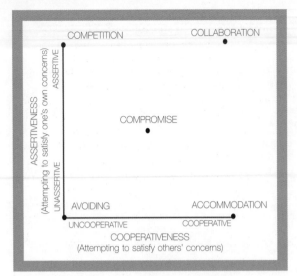

Figure 12.1 Two-dimensional model of conflict-handling modes

Source: Adapted from Kenneth W. Thomas and Ralph H. Kilman (1974) *Thomas–Kilman Conflict Mode Instrument,* Tuxedo, NY: Xicom, Inc., p 11 by Kenneth W. Thomas (1992) 'Conflict and conflict management: Reflections and update', *Journal of Organizational Behaviour,* 13: 266. Copyright © 1992 John Wiley & Sons. Reprinted with permission.

4. Accommodation (unassertive, cooperative) :
■ giving way
■ submission and compliance.

5. Collaboration (assertive, cooperative) means:
■ joint problem solving
■ confronting differences and sharing ideas and information

■ search for integrative solutions
■ finding situations where we all can win
■ seeing problems and conflicts as challenging.

Thomas (1977) studied 28 chief executives who indicated when they would expect to employ the five conflict-handling modes. It is interesting to note that all the modes were reported to have their place in the CEO's repertoire – the successful chief executive is not necessarily the hard-driving competitor or even the collaborator, but someone who knows how to use all the options available appropriately (Thomas 1977: 193.).

Blake et al. (see Figure 12.2) similarly employ an active–passive dimension in the analysis but also take into account whether the stakes are perceived to be high for the parties, and whether there is the possibility of either avoiding conflict or reaching agreement, according to the context and content of the problem. We can note here again that, in contrast to pluralist approaches, bargaining, collectively or otherwise, is a middle range solution and not an optimal one. This form of psychologically based research has been used by managerialists and managers alike, especially in the UK, to justify resistance to trade union pressure to extend the scope of collective bargaining in organizations into arenas wider than wage and salary negotiations including corporate governance.

In a later paper, Thomas (1992) compares the *process model* of conflict, designed to explain discrete conflict episodes, with the *structural model* of conflict. The structural model, he argues, assists our understanding of those parameters which apply across conflict episodes. It attempts to identify four factors which affect dyadic interaction in conflict (Thomas 1992: 267–8):

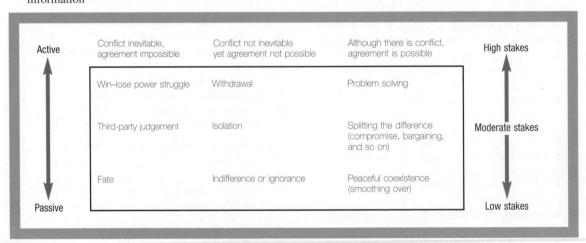

Figure 12.2 Three basic assumptions toward intergroup disagreements and their management

Source: Blake, Robert R., Shepherd, Harold A., and Mouton, Jane S. (1964) *Managing Inter-Group Conflict in Industry,* Houston: Gulf Publishing Company.

1. the individual predispositions of each party in the conflict
2. the social pressures on each party in the conflict
3. the incentive structure and degree of conflict of interest between the parties in dispute
4. the framework of rules and procedures which governs or limits each party's conflict behaviour.

Thomas stresses that it is important to recognize that trying to cope with some system of forces and constraints is not the whole answer to conflict management. There is the issue of trying to 'change the system', those structural variables that result in suboptimal processes and outcomes. Over time, successful management seems to require that organizational leaders engage in both *pragmatic coping* and *visionary improvement* (Thomas 1992: 271).

One of the classes of variables identified by Thomas relating to the rules and procedures, or constraints upon the interaction process, such as decision rules or negotiating procedures for mediating or arbitrating a dispute, is *bargaining*. Bargaining may be of two types – *distributive* or *integrative*. Distributive bargaining is where finite resources exist and essentially the parties are in a win–lose situation. The more that one party gains, the less is left for the other party. Behaviours of groups in this situation may involve game playing, walkouts, making demands, selective release of information, rewards and punishments, side deals, offensive behaviour, domination or attempting to control the agenda of what is discussed and so on. In the industrial struggles common in the UK and Australia in the 1980s, several meetings were held simply to agree on the agenda of the meetings.

Integrative bargaining is where both parties try to seek a solution that will be optimal for both sides, a win–win process. Parties here will state their preferences as considerations, not demands; share information about these preferences and why they are important; ask questions to learn more about others' preferences; willingly contribute to the search process; help to test solution options to see if they meet the needs of all parties and are practical and implementable; and determine whether there are any objective standards for selecting among options. A third option to integrative or distributive bargaining would be to attempt coalition building, which we discussed in Chapter 6 (Lewicki 1985).

Gender issues in conflict and negotiation

As Menkel-Meadow (2000) observes, empirical evidence and theory frequently present conflicting observations about what role, if any, gender plays in negotiation. Often, for example, because of structural power imbalances between males and females, it proves impossible to separate the effects of power from the effects of gender. Much research has concentrated on trying to establish what the differences are between male and female styles of negotiation, and under what conditions these may be expected to emerge but findings are often inconsistent. One problem has been that most studies are not with managers, and the negotiations are not genuine negotiations in work settings but lab-based interactions among students. Gender stereotypes are often used as benchmarks in research, but interestingly Kray et al. (2001) found that gender stereotypes only work effectively when they are implicit; once they are surfaced, the parties specifically react against them. This work supports the ideas of Deborah Kolb, who develops most fully the idea of the 'shadow' negotiation in her joint work with Judith Williams (Kolb and Williams 2000). Kolb and Williams (2000: 23) argue that 'any negotiation is caught in a web of influence, social values and informal codes of conduct' which influences expectations about what women should and can do. What appears to be a level playing field, because of this shadow side of negotiation, may well disadvantage women. Kolb (2000) further argues that rather than put effort into identifying male and female styles, it would be more useful to look at gender as a performative product emergent in the negotiating process itself, where examining how gender relations are performed illuminates the shadow side of negotiation. Lab studies would find it difficult to open up this shadow side, as they are decontextualized to such a great extent. In short, beyond observing such commonplaces that women often tend to undervalue themselves when entering into negotiations, in the absence of enough of the right kind of empirical material it is difficult to draw any conclusions about the impact of gender on negotiations.

Conflict and negotiation across cultures

Cultural differences

Cross-cultural conflicts, disputes and negotiations are increasingly important for a number of reasons: societies are becoming more multicultural; businesses more global; and international conflicts apparently more intractable. In these circumstances some appreciation of what we currently know about dispute processing within and across cultures is important. Leung and Wu (1990) categorize cross-cultural differences in conflict as based on the subjective incompatibility of goals and interference or blocking behaviour. Values, norms and beliefs influence the definitions of what are incompatible goals (for example wealth and happiness, risk and uncertainty).

Similarly, culture affects the interpretation of behaviour as interference in or blocking of the achievement of goals. For example North Americans value contracts, the Japanese do not. Contracts are necessary only when both parties are trying to maximize their own interest without considering the interest of the other party, which Americans are likely to do but the Japanese are not, since they value kindness and goodwill (Leung and Wu 1996: 212). North American negotiators are usually argumentative but impersonal, whereas 'Malays see a much stronger association between a person and his or her position on an issue. Rejection of a position is often seen as rejection of the person and can often create significant interpersonal conflict' (pp. 211–12).

In an illuminating study of intercultural conflict styles, Stella Ting-Toomey (1998) defines conflict as occurring in problematic circumstances in which two interdependent parties perceive or have incompatible needs or goals. She ties this to the management of 'face' (or self-image), that is, the processes of managing the self in social interaction. It is clear that there are particular differences between Asian and Western countries in perceptions of face and its enhancement (Bond and Hwang 1986). Face is grounded, Ting-Toomey (1988) argues, in webs of interpersonal and sociocultural variability. These are, in turn, embedded in differences in the preference for and value of relationships and connectedness between people (Fulop and Richards 2002). One important distinction is between *individualistic* and *collectivist* cultures. It is the most reliable of the dimensions studied by Hofstede (1991), has frequently been used to contrast Asian and Western cultural behaviours and is considered to be a core cultural dimension (Triandis 1995; Earley 1997; Trompenaars and Hampden-Turner 1997).

In an individualistic society (for example the USA), the people have a strong self-orientation, and are more concerned about their own needs, interests and goals than those of others. Here *face-work* focuses more on maintaining one's personal identity, with little concern about helping others to protect theirs. In contrast, people in a more collectivist culture (for example China) are more concerned about the groups' interests than their own and are willing to sacrifice personal interests for those of the group. Thus, face-work is strongly concerned with how to protect or enhance both their own *and others'* face (Ting-Toomey 1988). In an individualistic society, face-work establishes a positive image by demonstrating abilities, appropriate feelings and personal qualities. By comparison, the face-work efforts made by members of a collectivist society strengthen connections and status within fixed hierarchical relationships (Bond and Hwang 1986). Bond and Hwang argue that face-work is frequently used in Chinese society for enhancing one's influence over others (1986: 225). Thus, one engages in *impression management* so as to give the most positive impression to others. Members of collectivist or high-context cultures attend more to face-work and look upon conflict from a social rather than a task perspective, avoiding conflict if at all possible (Ting-Toomey 1988).

Conflict management styles

Studies of communication processes suggest that 'conflict management styles are linked closely to one's concern for face' (Gao et al. 1996: 291). Three face concerns have been identified by Ting-Toomey (1988): *self-face*, *other face* and *mutual face*. She argues that people in collectivist cultures are more concerned with other face than are those in individualistic cultures. 'Concern for other face often leads to a non-confrontational style of conflict management such as avoiding, obliging and compromising' (Gao et al. 1996: 291). In societies that stress collectivism, face is closely associated with 'shame', or the 'loss of face'. Both are strongly associated with people from the East, who stress harmony but 'are none the less assertive' (Yuen 1992: 374). Relating this to the Thomas–Kilman classification of conflict management styles (Thomas 1983) reveals that these preferences lead to *compromising* and *avoiding* as the preferred conflict management styles. Reluctance to confront the conflicting part leads to avoiding and a desire to save face leads to compromising. A *collaborating* style is also used but the individualistic preference for the *competing* style, often found in the West, is not usually acceptable because it may result in one party losing face. Giving others face requires one not to argue or disagree openly with others in public, since 'meanings in messages cannot be negotiated in public' (Gao et al. 1996: 291). Negotiating meanings in such a way questions, and therefore undermines, authority and interpersonal harmony. Unassertiveness and indirectness in negotiations is preferred, together with space being left for private negotiations. Truth may also be less important than meeting the requirements of face saving and face negotiating: 'providing the appropriate information at the appropriate time and context with the appropriate persons is a more desirable process than is honest and truthful communication' (Gao et al. 1996: 291).

Western styles of conflict resolution generally emphasize directness and clarity and the attainment of tangible outcomes. In collectivist societies, such as in Asia, there is a much greater preference for indirectness and ambiguity, for example in the use of intermediaries, or third-party intervention, where there is a risk of one party losing face. This allows the parties concerned not to have to face each other and avoids the direct approach favoured by Westerners (Bond and Wang 1986). There is, however, a reluctance to use legal or procedural means to achieve settlements (Yuen 1992). Intangible outcomes such as trust, suspicion, loss of face and the level of perceived comfort in future relations are important in Asian cultures, sometimes more important than any tangible outcome.

Negotiations

Researchers generally agree that there are 'significant cross-cultural differences in a number of negotiation behaviours' (Leung and Wu 1990: 224). Leung and Wu categorize these as:

- *Persuasion styles* – such as rational argument (North Americans) or affective, based on feelings (Arabs)
- *Confrontation vs. avoidance* – confrontation in France and the US, avoidance in Japan or among Malays
- *Initial positions* – extreme for Russians, Arabs, Chinese and Japanese, moderate for North Americans
- *Concession patterns* – reluctant to make concession (Russians) compared with likely to do so (Norwegians, North Americans, Arabs and Malays)
- *Non-verbal behaviour* – silence used most by the Japanese, least by Brazilians, touching used most by Brazilians, least by the Japanese.

Negotiations in Asia often exhibit compromising behaviour. In business negotiations, a proposal–counter-proposal style is avoided (Hellweg et al. 1991). This is because in many Asian countries, for example China, 'argumentative and confrontational modes of communication are avoided at all costs' (Gao et al. 1996: 282). Shenkar and Ronen (1987) proposed that three categories of norms guide Chinese negotiations. Norms involving communication patterns include: emotional restraint and self-control; careful conformity to politeness ceremonials; and avoidance of methods of aggressive persuasion. Generally in Asia, negotiation intentions will be articulated in an indirect manner and room will be left for negotiations in private. This creates a pleasant climate for future cooperation and negotiation. Both parties will start off apparently far apart, with greatly inflated positions which, however, are intended to give very wide margins for compromise. During negotiation both sides give in gradually until a compromise position is reached. Thus neither side appears to be the outright winner or loser. Conflict is sidestepped by avoidance strategies and compromise (Shi and Westwood, 2000). This contrasts with the view of compromise in Anglo cultures, where it is seen as suboptimal, requiring the making of concessions (Kirkbride et al. 1991). However, since behaviour in

collectivist cultures towards out-groups can be very different from that towards in-groups, the competing style can be used 'when dealing with outsiders or when a party perceives that the other side did not give it face' (Yuen 1992: 374).

Need for training

These extensive and significant differences in negotiation and dispute processing behaviour create cultural barriers that can make cross-cultural negotiation very difficult. Thus 'negotiators who are unfamiliar with these barriers are likely to leave the bargaining table confused, frustrated, and even upset, and unnecessary delays, deadlocks, and escalation of the conflict will follow' (Leung and Wu 1990: 227). Negotiators must therefore be trained in cross-cultural negotiation to reduce the impact of barriers 'such as biased perception, stereotypes, prejudice, misattribution, misunderstanding, and communication breakdown' (Leung and Wu 1990: 227). The knowledge, understanding and skills generated by such training can help multinational corporations and organizations and national governments to develop effective strategies and appropriate behaviours for intercultural and international negotiations.

From negotiation to narrative

Negotiation may be defined as a structured set of interactions in which parties weigh up alternative courses of action, each of which may have different consequences, both for the parties themselves and others in their social, political or commercial constituency. Negotiations don't always lead to decisions or agreements. Other outcomes can include softening or hardening of position, personal understanding between negotiators and symbolic messages sent to the rest of the stakeholder community. For example, the CEOs of competing companies may meet to discuss a merger; whatever the outcome, the 'fact' of the meeting will have an impact on how others foresee the future.

Perhaps the most influential and useful account of negotiation has been that of Roger Fisher and William Urry – *Getting to Yes: Negotiating Agreement Without Giving In* (1981). At the heart of their message lies the distinction between 'interests' and 'positions'. Parties to a conflict have interests that they want to pursue, and as they enter negotiations they take up positions that they hope will protect or further their interests. It is all too easy to launch into a process of bargaining about positions, trading offers and demands. But often these positions really *are* contradictory and can be settled only by a 'zero-sum' outcome: one part wins, the other loses.

However, it is almost always the case that, stepping back from the positions people have taken, one finds that their underlying interests could be met by some other arrangement. The art of negotiation, therefore, is to shift the discussion first towards what would meet the interests of each party, and only then to what positions or outcomes each could reach that would accommodate all their interests – at least for the time being. This is the route to the so-called *win–win* outcome.

This approach has been found valuable by negotiators in many situations, but it relies on the parties being able to articulate their interests. Indeed, facing a negotiation like this can be an excellent prompt to think this through. A crucial aspect – as in most formal approaches to negotiation – is the combination of two kinds of rationality. Firstly, there is the idea that the imposition of rational procedures channels interactions in a certain way; and secondly there is an attempt to contain emotions by expressing desires and fears as 'interests'.

Responsibility for designing and operating these rational processes may lie with the parties (as in most sales negotiations) or with a third party. In some situations a manager can also act as arbitrator – taking the authority to decide the outcome of a conflict and imposing a solution with legal or constitutional sanctions. But this is comparatively rare, and much more often managers act as mediators, which takes us into a much more subtle and delicate area.

Mediation

Mediation occurs where someone not directly involved as a party to a conflict acts to help them to resolve it. What mediators actually do varies tremendously, ranging from very informal discussions with all, one or more parties, to conducting quite formal negotiations. In fact, negotiation is often a subset of mediation – and sometimes mediation (by a third party) can be a part of a negotiation process. In a world where new forms of organizations, such as virtual and networked, are developing; where traditional organizations are becoming involved in new forms of relationship and partnership with customers, collaborators, cooperatives and even competitors; where transnational and cross-cultural activities are increasing and where risk and trust between parties are commonly identified as among the most important factors in the success or failure of such new ventures, mediation has enormous potential to help diverse interests to work together in productive mutuality.

Figure 12.3 graphically represents the process of mediation, and the way in which it is supposed to enable parties to get into a state of mind in which they can begin to work rationally on resolving their dispute. In this model, mediation is put forward as a kind of

facilitated negotiation. Parties are helped, by the skilled presence of the mediator, to escape a cycle of anger and defensiveness, to focus on the issues at stake.

The practice of mediation has been developed in a number of situations: usually as a way of handling disputes without the expensive and inflammatory involvement of law courts (for example divorce); as a means to empower communities to deal with their own problems (it is also used in schools for this purpose); and in international and communal conflicts, where settlement depends on the cooperation of all parties. The field in which it is most highly developed is as a response to neighbour disputes (which may involve individuals, associations, corporations and authorities). This is also where we will find some of the more useful analogies for our own organizational agenda. So we will briefly examine neighbour mediation services as a model for such roles.

The past 20 years has seen the growth of organizations set up explicitly to work with and hopefully resolve conflicts in 'the community' – currently there are 139 such schemes in the UK, and many hundreds in the USA. The aims and working processes of these organizations have almost invariably been expressed in what might be termed a 'negotiating' paradigm of social exchange. The emphasis has been on defining the 'parties', and training quasi-professional mediators to facilitate negotiations between them (Miller 1987).

The work itself arises when one or more people present themselves as involved in a conflict of some sort, and request the intervention of 'mediators'. These latter are usually working under the auspices of an organization, and describe their stance as 'neutral' or 'impartial' in respect of the claims of the various conflicting parties. The service they offer therefore is not advocacy, and consists of advice only insofar as it pertains to how to manage oneself in a conflict-resolving process.

The process of mediation gets the parties to speak to and listen to each other, and hopefully reach some agreement about future actions. The ideal is generally that parties should meet face to face to do this, but 'shuttle diplomacy' is also often accepted as a way of working.

So people involved in a conflict present themselves as 'disputants'. They enter the system as a complainant, are recorded as 'case s' and processed along the following lines:

1. The main characters are introduced, a series of events is described, explaining and justifying their arrival on stage, and we are told what issues we will be confronted with as the process unfolds.
2. A series of negotiations take place, aiming to get the parties to discuss their conflict face to face. Various conditions are laid down, other people are consulted

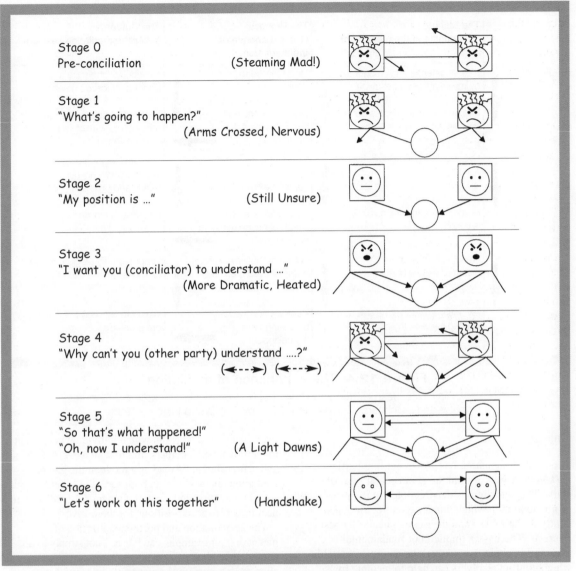

Figure 12.3 Stages in the resolution of conflict

Source: Conflict Handling, San Francisco: San Francisco Community Boards, 1986.

and the differences in power and potential gains become evident.

3. A meeting either takes place or doesn't – in either case this is a moment full of expectations and the opportunity for the mediators to perform their skills and techniques. If the mediation does not take place, the process goes straight on to the fifth stage.

4. The mediation session proceeds, encapsulating the kinds of changes of mood and temper characterized in Figure 12.3. All the issues presented so far are either dealt with or avoided – in either case this segment leads to a kind of denouement, signing an agreement in which each character is faced with the consequences of their involvement in the process.

5. The parties leave, the case file is closed, sometimes after some 'follow-up' in which the ramifications of the mediation are recorded.

Figure 12.4 shows how the experience of participating in a mediation session both resolves the presenting issues and leads to a reconciliation with the wider community. In this process, resolving a conflict does more than simply settle the matters in dispute – it realigns and empowers the parties.

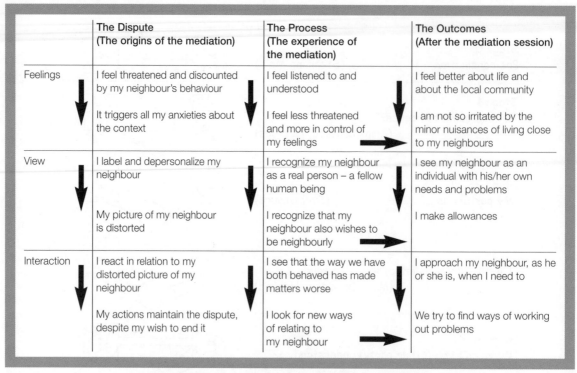

	The Dispute (The origins of the mediation)	The Process (The experience of the mediation)	The Outcomes (After the mediation session)
Feelings	I feel threatened and discounted by my neighbour's behaviour It triggers all my anxieties about the context	I feel listened to and understood I feel less threatened and more in control of my feelings	I feel better about life and about the local community I am not so irritated by the minor nuisances of living close to my neighbours
View	I label and depersonalize my neighbour My picture of my neighbour is distorted	I recognize my neighbour as a real person – a fellow human being I recognize that my neighbour also wishes to be neighbourly	I see my neighbour as an individual with his/her own needs and problems I make allowances
Interaction	I react in relation to my distorted picture of my neighbour My actions maintain the dispute, despite my wish to end it	I see that the way we have both behaved has made matters worse I look for new ways of relating to my neighbour	I approach my neighbour, as he or she is, when I need to We try to find ways of working out problems

Figure 12.4 The experience of mediation

Source: Colin Quine, Jean Hutton and Bruce Reed, 'Community Mediation of Disputes between Neighbours', Table 4. Published by The Grubb Institute 1988.

Critique

The field of mediation has grown out of a particular paradigm or way of thinking about social relationships. This paradigm is deeply rooted in the processes of negotiation in which human agents act independently in their own (and their constituencies') best interests. There is an implicit but fundamental assumption about the competitive nature of social life, which conflict resolvers can help to mediate by seeking 'win–win solutions'.

The ethics of mediation are concerned largely with issues of power imbalance between the parties and parties' ignorance of their rights. Both are seen as potential hindrances to a rational model of negotiation. Taken together, one can see that a negotiation paradigm for mediation is consistent with the notion of society as a marketplace in which rational actors exchange perceived benefits. It is no surprise therefore that the countries with least ambivalence towards market capitalism are at the forefront of the development of mediation.

This is pertinent for understanding current moves to accredit community mediation projects in the UK and 'professional' mediators in the USA. The expert status implied by the negotiation paradigm connects mediation with the greater political scheme in which power is brokered and control of resources is wrangled over. As this is a world in which individual people act in their own best interests, and in which every utterance and action should be read as a move in the game, mediation qua negotiation both serves as a field for such social interaction and is itself a means for mediators to negotiate enhanced positions for themselves.

The accreditation and professionalization of mediators, for example, can be seen not simply as an attempt to achieve effectiveness, but rather as a means to align mediators with the powerful, the adjudicators, those who construct and approve the dominant account of events. In fairness, this is often explicitly stated in the promotional literature of mediation schemes: serving as a volunteer mediator is a means to gain useful skills and, crucially, an elevated position in relation to disputants. Mediators gain membership of the class of service providers as distinct from the class of clients or patients. A corollary of this is that they become involved in the paraphernalia of service provision: case notes, client files, written records of meetings and agreements, expense claims and so on. Thus they become co-authors of an official textual account that, in spite of initially only referring to specific events and experiences, comes to act as the authoritative representation of those events. In other words, authority is equivalent to authorship of the official record.

To summarize, there are two principal effects of

basing our understanding of mediation on a paradigm of negotiation:

1. It affirms the independence of the human subject.
2. It allies mediators with the powerful as
   (a) the authors of the official account of conflict and its resolution, and
   (b) incorporated into the dominant political modes of practice and language.

But closer scrutiny of the mediation process seen as the construction of a story reveals ways in which this apparent alliance of mediation with 'power' may be undermined by internal contradictions.

Storytelling

An alternative paradigm to that of negotiation arises from taking a different view of mediation sessions (Rifkin and Cobb 1991). Instead of focusing on the bargaining process, parties are seen to be each telling their own story. Negotiation or bargaining is just one of the ways in which they are working out the plot, developing their characterizations of themselves and each other.

Janet Rifkin and Sarah Cobb (1991) argue that there are two aspects of narrative construction that are relevant here:

1. First, the account given by each speaker consists of three elements:
   - *Plot*: a sequence of events linked by a chain of cause and effect, although not necessarily in a linear fashion. Plots can link events like a network or web.
   - *Characters*: in stories of conflicts as told by the protagonists, characters tend to be divided into good guys and bad guys.
   - *Themes*: the real core of any story, values such as 'safety', 'well-being', 'community spirit' and so on. These seem to oblige the characters to act in certain ways, and constitute the second order meaning of their actions and characterizations.

2. Each person's story is interdependent with those of others. They do not make sense unless linked. For example, every victim requires an offender to fill the role assigned by the story. If the characterization of the offender is changed through mediation, the victim's identity (as a victim) in his or her own story is threatened.

Stories are accomplished by interactions with others rather than in isolation. That is, people argue with adversaries, talk over their experiences with family, friends, advisors and in their own minds. They select events for the plot, build characterizations of the parties and generally rehearse the telling of the story.

Hence the authorial stance is crucial to any story: whose point of view is dominant? Thus mediation may be viewed as an opportunity to tell and hear various stories (or the same basic story from different perspectives) and construct a new, blended story.

Mediation sessions and the case discussions and reports that lie behind them are occasions for retelling and extending the 'original' stories, which then, because of the new interpretative context, constitute 'new' stories. The mediator's role in these sessions is to clarify and reframe the stories. They do this by drawing out the logic (plots), characters and themes, and looking for opportunities for reinterpretation whereby their meaning can be shifted. In other words, mediators deconstruct the narratives as told by the parties and, together with them, identify at least a common 'theme' for a new narrative – such as mutual well-being. The new one gives both parties positive characterizations, if possible.

This can be difficult to do. The whole point of a good story is that it constructs meanings and interpretations around events to appear entirely coherent and sufficient. A good opening story explains everything. This does not mean, however, that it is the only interpretation that can be put on the events. This is exactly the problem mediators often face: to convince the parties that another story could be equally plausible and coherent.

Indeed, the first party's story is often so coherent that it can be difficult to listen openly to the second and following accounts. The latter become defensive statements or justifications by the party who has been characterized as the bad guy in the first telling. There are ways of dealing with this. Experienced disputants often respond by telling a completely different story, so that the listeners are obliged to start afresh. One solution is for the mediator to hear the initial stories separately, in private sessions.

In any case the mediator's stance needs to be one of critical analysis: to identify the elements and structure of the story and destabilize its coherence by looking for ways in which it could be reinterpreted. For example, mediators focus on alternative hypotheses about the motivation of belligerents (claims by a neighbour that the people next door 'make the kids cry just to annoy me' may not be the only interpretation of events!); or look for evidence that belies the characterization of an actor as either 'victim' or 'offender'.

Thus the attempt to reframe the conflict story offers the opportunity to undermine adversarial good/bad narratives. Paradoxically, the written form of this new narrative, the agreement signed by all parties, is often couched in terms of the original framing of the dispute. The shared experience of working together on the construction of a public story is denied prominence in the public memorial to that experience, and participants must learn to integrate the experience into the personal. In these cases there is a systematic reconstitution of the subject as the centre of experience and consciousness. It may only be by foregoing the written account that the story of mediation can survive; or, to put this another way, mediation eludes the written account.

This consideration of mediation as storytelling suggests that the process aims to construct a new consensus, a new 'blended story' in which the characters can see themselves and each other in constructive interrelationships. It also provides a helpful formulation of the role of people working with conflicts, especially where shared assumptions about social and cultural relationships have broken down. Engaging in mediation can be a way to clarify and articulate 'where we are at now'. Conflicts emerge as episodes in stories, with functions to perform in service both of the plot and the main themes. Mediation itself is not a bargaining process, but a collective sense-making ritual, an opportunity to integrate the past, as we remember it, with the present.

Mediation as discourse

To say that mediation works for the production of consensus is to distinguish the emergence of a common semantic framework from the settlement of a dispute. In other words, we are not talking here about agreement on the issues presented as the basis of the conflict; instead we are exposing the development of shared interpretations and meanings of words, phrases and signs among all those taking part in the mediation session. Of course it is not just any old meaning that is attributable: very specific selections of the many possible definitions and interpretations of words and actions are used. In many ways it is the mediators' job to summarize and edit the various accounts that are offered, in a manner that excludes some possible meanings, in particular, as far as possible, ambiguity and aporia.

As Sarah Cobb and Janet Rifkin put it:

The location for struggle and conflict is not only differences in interest: the location for struggle is also over meaning … mediation is a hegemonic process precisely because it generates a dominant ideology (a dominant story) by creating a web of shared meanings, a web created out of the available stories/myths and their engendered forms of practices. The dominant ideology 'dominates' not by coercion (mediators do not tell disputants what to say) but by consent (disputants *use* this web of meaning, co-constructed with mediators, as grounds both to affirm *and* to contest). (Cobb and Rifkin 1991: 61)

The wider 'community' context in which this takes place is also important. The mediation process itself relies on being able to assert its right to inclusion in the stories of those involved.

At a local level, where individual and panel mediators 'hammer out' an agreement between disputants, they effectively construct an episode in their own narrative, in which they feature as heroic figures. The episode can then be inserted as a new chapter in the annals not only of that mediation programme, but in the grand narrative of mediation itself.

Thus it is important for the survival of mediation programmes, and for the continued coherence of mediators' own stories, that the 'fact of mediation' be included in the important stories of the community. One means of doing this is to create recognizable artefacts that symbolize the shared experience of having found meaning in the act of mediating. This is the function served by the written agreement. A contract or treaty is a most potent and pervasive symbol of shared meaning in all types of negotiation. Agreements are artefacts that serve as reminders or fetishes of shared interpretations, of a common story, of a demand for continued attention to a specific collection of 'facts'. One might even propose that a community benefits from the presence of such symbols of shared meaning, together with the reassurance they provide of rationality and stability over time.

Thus mediation is the process of critical analysis of stories or 'texts', and a simultaneous process of textualization, writing, storytelling itself; and the enactment of a social and political discourse of power. However, although we have tried here to distinguish between 'negotiating' and 'narrative' frames of reference, it is certainly more complex. For a start, each framework may be employed in the service of the other. For example, if we treat accounts of conflicts as just that – interim statements of balances and flows – we can see that the stories people tell us are sense-making tools used to further the teller's interests in a bargaining situation. Furthermore, the process of telling these stories in a mediation context is simply another episode in the stories. It may well be that the stories are changed first and adapted to accommodate the kind of negotiation themes that their tellers believe will be of interest to mediators.

This has important implications for the way we would work with conflicts. We might not, for example, want to set up adversarial meetings between complainant and respondent, but instead concentrate on collaborative research and inquiry. As mediators we might ally ourselves with educators rather than lawyers (which is not to say that the production and dissemination of knowledge is any less of a hegemonic process than the production of 'rights'!).

Traditional approaches

This proposition is not entirely far-fetched. Many mediation projects explain themselves with reference to traditional means of dealing with disputes: by priests, elders, neighbourhood shopkeepers. These august individuals and institutions are claimed as ancestors of the mediation programme. But, for example, assisting negotiations between individuals is a rather sparse description of a priest's role that might be understood better as enabling people to explore the meanings and values they attach to events and relationships within the community.

Resolutions to conflicts might well happen as a result of the priestly task or other community institutions, but not as a result of the provision of conflict resolution services per se. The same can be said of managers in organizations of all kinds. The common medium for all these activities is that of 'talk', rather than simply language, and the ways in which the exploration and and reconstruction of meanings and values commonly takes place is, as we have argued, through narrative rather than the statement and rebuttal of propositions (Boden 1994; Gabriel 2000; Boje 2001). Indeed, priests, elders and even managers tend to be most effective when they adopt the skills and approaches of the *storyteller* to enhance their role.

So let us turn now to a more specific tradition of storytelling, examine its processes and norms and the methods by which it constructs, develops and evolves meanings for its protagonists and its broader audience.

Soap opera

First a brief justification for the approach. Compare these two statements :

A soap opera is a continuing fictional dramatic television programme, presented in multiple serial instalments each week, through a narrative composed of interlocking storylines that focus on the relationships within a specific community of characters. (Mumford 1995: 18)

An organization is a continuing dramatic programme, presented in multiple serial instalments each week, through a narrative composed of interlocking storylines that focus on the relationships within a specific community of characters. (adapted from Mumford 1995: 18)

From the point of view of organization members and observers, organization life is pretty much like this. Before proceeding to the implications for conflict resolution, we will look a little more deeply into the qualities and production norms of soap opera, as these will be the source of our proposals.

Soap opera forms and norms

■ *Soap operas are never-ending.* They are not

working towards a final climax and closure – in fact, each apparent climax (such as a wedding) always prompts events that propel the plot into a new theme (in-laws fight, the bride's ex-lover turns up and so on). In this way they are much like office parties, the closure of a big deal or even a merger: the seeds of future trouble are already germinating.

Furthermore, soap opera audiences are always being projected into the future via the expectations aroused by long familiarity with the characters, the ability to see the convergence of events from different parts of the plot, and the breaks between episodes, which provide opportunities for speculation and anticipation. These three features that punctuate the never-endingness – familiarity/continuity; multiple plot lines; and episodic timing – also characterize life in work organizations, and serve to tie their members into expectations about the future.

It has been argued that the way in which soap operas undermine climactic moments, and manage instead to hold on to a constant rise and fall of tension, marks them out as a feminine genre (Kilbarn 1992; Mumford 1995). Certainly women make up the majority of the audiences, and a good deal of the pleasure that people derive from soaps is because they provide a vehicle for talking about feelings (Brown 1994) – supposedly a more feminine form. Furthermore, when soaps started to be programmed in evening prime-time slots (starting with *Dallas* in 1978), climactic events became more prominent, aiming at a mixed-gender audience. Similar distinctions are found in conversational networks in organizations; it is relevant here because formal processes of mediation are structured very much around the meeting of the parties, reaching their apotheosis in the signing of an agreement. The way in which soap operas subvert and contextualize climactic events alerts us to the wider narrative context in which conflicts exist – in other words, to a more conversational, feminine form of engagement.

■ *They are daily occurrences.* Soaps are produced on a relentless schedule, day after day, which requires real discipline on the part of all those involved, but it also makes it impossible for producers to police them in the way they can a stage play or short tele-drama. Actors can discover new nuances of character, and new vectors in the plot, but must stay within the bounds of a coherent aesthetic (Nochimson 1992). Similarly, work organizations occur with relentless daily regularity, depend on a degree of improvisation, but also require members to act within a common aesthetic.

- *Multiple plots are developing simultaneously.* We have already referred to how the existence of several plot lines adds to the flexibility of soap operas, and constructs a tension as we see events unfolding in parallel, sometimes converging towards an anticipated crisis. In the same way, members of work organizations are aware of events unfolding in different spheres, both inside firms and in their relations with customers, regulators, competitors and so on.

- *The text unfolds.* Although the soap opera plots are written in advance of their performance, and producers decide on themes to bring to the foreground over a given period (the arrival of a homosexual couple in a conservative community, the arrest of a minister's son on drugs charges and so on), these are subject to a certain amount of improvisation as episodes are written and recorded. More importantly, though, is the way the storylines and the characters unfold over time for the audience. They grow up together, and thus soap operas provide a part of the social context. Current and anticipated events become the subject of conversations which serve to identify audience members, their attachments, loyalties and so on. People who don't follow the same soap, for example, can't join in the conversation, in much the same way as people who don't follow the progress of the football league can't join in football talk. The same can be said for 'shop talk' in and about organizations. The lives of audiences develop alongside, and are intimately interwoven with, the events in these adjacent worlds.

- *Cliffhangers and teases.* Any story with episodes has the opportunity to keep people hanging on to see what will happen. The same applies when the outcome is not visible or is in the hands of one group of characters alone: one never quite knows what the other parties will do. These features contribute an emotional force to the continuity of the narrative, a frisson that makes it intriguing to see what will happen next (Kilbarn 1992). Managing expectations is just as important in work organizations, and every leader knows the importance of timing an announcement or holding some information back for the right moment.

- *Soap operas have a central core of about 20 characters.* This is a significant feature of soap operas – there seem to be very few people involved and endless extraordinary permutations of what they can get up to together (Kilbarn 1992). Similarly, most people in work organizations relate regularly to a relatively small number of colleagues or customers, and find their place in the venture as a whole through membership of this particular subset of the full cast of characters.

In both work organizations and soap operas, individual characters are expendable. However apparently central, key people can disappear abruptly, and in spite of the turbulence this may cause, it hardly ever stops the flow altogether. Indeed, an important feature of soap opera communities is that death can come at any moment. This often occurs when an actor becomes ill, or pushes too hard in negotiating higher fees. Producers have been known to radically rewrite parts of the storyline to eliminate an awkward actor. Sometimes they can simply switch attention to a subsidiary plot line – another feature that has implications for flexibility in firms. Underlying this is the fact that while individual characters come and go, and individual members of the audience (customers) change, the key focus for producers, like strategic managers, must be the relationship with the audience as whole.

- *Character flaws in one sphere are the basis of success in another.* Because we see characters in soap operas over many years in several situations, we can see how what makes them fail in some circumstances prove to be strengths in others. Thus a violent husband is seen to be an effective and focused manager. In organizational life we seldom see all sides of a person, yet we know they exist. In fact many companies have tried to list the characteristics that they require in their employees – so-called 'behavioural values' or 'competence frameworks' – only to be frustrated to find that some people can be social pigs but high achievers.

- *Mergers.* This is a prominent feature of corporate life, and likewise soap operas have also got caught up in the process. In the USA, characters from one soap (*Corinth*) have appeared on another (*All My Children*), and in one case this led to intermarriage and a full merger (Mumford 1995: 133). But it is almost more important to note why mergers don't take place more often. Principally this is because soap operas are commercial enterprises that are justified by attracting viewers, winning their trust and transferring that trust to the sponsors and advertisers. Brand identity and customer loyalty is so crucial to the commercial viability of soap operas that they will mess around with it only reluctantly. But as deregulated TV networks proliferate the number of soaps, the market will become saturated, and competition for viewers will produce the same pressures for consolidation as we see in other industries.

- *Conflict of family and emotional needs.* Soap opera

characters become apparently real because we are aware of them as individuals and also as embedded in their social setting. This is commonly expressed in conflicts between the emotional needs of individuals and the demands made on them by their families or friends. In real life it is unusual to see these dilemmas presented so visibly and starkly; but it is nonetheless reassuring to see it because it reaffirms one of the central themes of social life – the tension between 'being-for-oneself' and 'being-for-others', as Sartre put it. Much of the talk about soap characters centres around how they will react to social pressures, and what effects their personal actions will have on the community. In work organizations we are acutely aware of the same tensions, in ourselves and others. What this indicates is the probability that there are underlying causes to the way we see people respond to events; it suggests that behaviour is symptomatic of existential and emotional concerns as well as desired outcomes, and the problems we are presented with may not in fact be the ones about which people are most exercised.

So there are many features of organizational life that are similar to soap operas (Table 12.8). Mainstream organization theory tends to describe interactions as negotiations between independent self-interested individuals; on the other hand, a metaphor of soap opera shows interactions and interdependence to be more fundamental than individuals, and highlights features such as never-endingness and the wider social context.

But what does this mean for purposeful interventions in conflicts? Against a background of emerging interrelated and multistranded reality, what can an individual do to affect the outcome of specific conflicts? The answer is in two parts: first, by conceiving the situation as a kind of soap opera, certain dynamics are revealed, involving the putative intervener as well as other actors; second, specific interventions are indicated. The next section shows what these might be.

Implications for interventions in conflict situations

■ *Explore plot and character developments.* Find out how those involved see events unfolding, and the options for how the 'plot' might develop in the future. What shifts in character would have to take place for each of these? There are numerous ways to help people to develop other sides of their characters – usually by changing how they perceive others and are perceived by them, for example behaving in ways to defy expectations and prejudices. But be patient – it takes time to come to terms with the fact that someone we have seen as an all-round rotter turns out to have a soft side.

■ *Use thematic periodization as time/space structure for actions.* This point has two aspects, one at the level of the overall 'themes', and one in terms of interventions. If you can figure what themes, at a fairly general level, are being worked out, it becomes possible to see the overall shape of the issue and its likely time frames. For example, in a dispute about delivery reliability for a new piece of software, an underlying theme might be one of status. A customer feels that the young software engineers are really simple technicians who should look up to him, both as more experienced and as the customer, but he may at the same time feel somewhat in awe of the language of code and the equally foreign culture of youth. The engineers may look at him as both an uninteresting paymaster but also as a hint of what they may become. Thus the 'theme' behind the overt conflict is one of ageing and identity. While it may be easy to resolve a dispute about delivery of a specific product, that will turn out to be just one episode in a series which express concerns about the passage of time, and what will become of each of us.

This perspective might suggest a series of interventions to broaden the relationships between

Table 12.8 Summary of the two paradigms	
Negotiating	**Soap opera**
■ Exchange outcomes	■ Unfolding
■ Time used for progress, accumulation of benefits	■ Time marked by episodes within a continuity
■ Climactic	■ Multiplot context
■ Causal predictability	■ Emphasizing the interdependent subjective construction of characters
■ Winning justice	
■ Emphasizes independent self-interested individuals	

the parties – to allow them to see a bit behind the appearances of age and youth, to see a little more of each other as complex characters, each more nuanced and contingent than the immediate roles of customer and engineer might suggest. So discussions preceded by a tour of the software labs and a chance to share some personal history could help.

But 'big' themes like this take a while to unfold and resolve. They actually need several episodes of conflict in order to proceed. So it may be better to plan for this. We can find some clues in the way themes are scheduled in soap operas (see Figure 12.5). Here a number of plot lines are being worked on simultaneously, all in relation to the current dominant theme. While attention is on one such plot line, others are progressing 'off-screen', so that next time we return to them we do so not just to continue where we left off, but to witness the consequences of whatever we saw previously. Each such return to a plot line is called a 'beat'. By the end of the episode all three lines have been progressed and the theme further illuminated in a number of ways.

Interventions in conflict situations can follow this. An underlying theme will find expression in a range of 'plot lines', all of which need several 'beats'. So an effective intervention might also extend to a number of plot lines. In our example above, both the customer and the engineers can be steered into other encounters (not necessarily with each other) that allow them to work on the theme of ageing and identity.

- *Extend focus either side of climaxes.* Engage in relationships beyond the presentation of conflict, and help the parties to maintain a focus on the other things going on in their relationship, past and future.

- *Explore multiplots and long-term interconnections.* Find out what else is going on in the parties' lives, and whether changes in these other 'plots' would affect the presenting conflict – in contrast to narrowing the focus onto the immediate claims.

- *Conversational opportunities for gossip, speculation, fantasy, anticipation.* These reveal the pleasure that people take in the characterizations they have given themselves and others. Conflicts, however painful, can also be reassuring (for example that we know good from evil). Gossip is a means for people to explore different permutations of an otherwise rigid and fixed story. It is also a means for those on the sidelines to participate in events – as well as influencing how others act, gossip can diffuse the focus from central figures to those on the margins, allowing all manner of permutations on the account given by the main protagonists.

- *Seek repetition and return as well as change.* Although conflicts often lead to changes, they also belong within a continuing relatedness (even if the parties no longer have direct relationships). Many things need to remain the same and be confirmed by familiar patterns of interaction. After pay negotiations, management and employees continue to work together; neighbours go on living next door after a dispute is settled. In soap operas we see the same patterns of behaviour in characters, and view changes of behaviour, living arrangements and so on as somewhat fragile and uncertain. It is the continuity of personality, demonstrated in behaviour, that shows we are still part of the same story, and that it makes sense. Conflicts may emphasize the need for change, but the context in which they exist (as an episode) is more marked by repetitious patterns of behaviour. When intervening in a conflict situation, we need to pay attention to these, viewing changes as permutations rather than radical discontinuities.

- *Value empathy and partiality.* Most conflict management approaches emphasize the need for impartiality and emotional distance from the protagonists. Of course a degree of stability is important, but the soap opera metaphor helps us to see

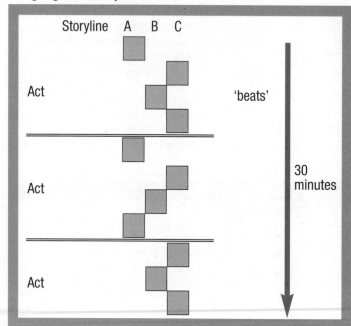

Figure 12.5 The periodization of themes in a soap opera episode

how problematic this can be – both difficult to attain, and not entirely true to reality. A judge may be impartial 'within the law', but the law is itself a partial framework set up to protect certain rights such as property and privacy, which in turn favour some people over others – that is, those with private wealth or secrets to hide from their fellow citizens. A soap opera is powerful precisely because it encourages its audience to feel involved. Empathy with the characters allows an audience to express their own reactions to similar situations and their preferences and political positions.

Without this kind of involvement, an audience simply sees a more or less meaningless chain of events. Empathy and partiality are integral to understanding the characters, the choices they make, the themes that engross them. Anyone intervening in a conflict must be prepared to step empathetically into the characters, to side with them, at least in the imagination. Let us turn now to the questions with which the chapter began.

Conclusion

In this chapter we have taken a much broader view of the issues of conflict and negotiation than is customary in most texts. As we have seen, our views here are borne out by recent research across the areas of industrial relations and conflict mediation, and have relevance wherever conflict may occur – between individuals, families, work colleagues, suppliers and customers, political groups, or in war and peace between nations and groups. Conflict is to some degree inevitable in human activity and it may be argued to have some positive social effects. What recent research has emphasized is that the important foundations laid by earlier work on the behavioural and psychological dimensions of conflict and negotiation need to be extended; similarly the work informed by industrial sociology and political economy which has given rise to analysis in terms of varieties of unitarism, pluralism and radicalism also has its limitations. Approaches based on a view of human sense-making as discursive, a form of narrative or storytelling, sees conflict and negotiation as a process in which psychological and ideological issues play their part as they are worked out in an interaction of emerging storylines. Rather than seeing conflict and negotiation in terms of individual episodes or a connected series of episodes, an approach which views them in terms of a wider set of overlapping issues, or a lamination of plots and sub-plots, in a process which never reaches any definitive conclusion, is more useful for conveying the complexity of conflict. Viewing things in this way, the traditional mix of vested interests of the parties can be seen to be much more fluid and interactionally formed, and the question of diversity of approaches and concerns arising from gendered or cross-cultural perspectives can be more readily incorporated into the analysis – indeed the process comes to resemble more closely the richness of real-life negotiation.

? Answers to questions about conflict

1 **Can all conflict be negotiated to a win–win solution?** No, because some conflicts are rooted in real inequalities and injustices that can't be done away with. For example, an employer might agree to allow his staff to work a flexible rota. That might seem like a fair resolution to a conflict about working hours; but only if the employees accept that they have to be subject to the dictates of the employment relationship. Also, the idea of 'win–win' only makes sense if you see each party as an independent negotiating unit. Partners in an alliance might find that while one maximizes production capacity the other extends

Answers cont'd

market reach. They both 'win' in the sense that the explicit interests of each of them are expressed in the alliance, but this only remains a reality as their relationship continues, which involves many other tacit aspects, not to do with 'winning' but with shared 'themes' and 'plots'.

2 What happens when people really enjoy the conflict? They are getting something from it that they may not get elsewhere. Sometimes it's a lot of attention, or confirmation that others are out to get them. Interventions that simply try to resolve the surface disputes are bound to fail. But an intervention that recasts the characters in a new light forces them all to think of themselves differently and find their pleasures in new ways!

3 Is there ever really a final resolution to a conflict or is it just a stage in a relationship? Some specific issues may be resolved, and if that's all there is to a relationship, yes, some things might be finally resolved. But even these temporary transactions live on in the memories and therefore the expectations of the parties, and affect their approach to future conflicts. So the answer to this question depends on the frame we bring to it. If it is short in time and shallow in depth, the answer may be 'yes'; otherwise – probably not!

4 Are conflicts a break in normal relationships or part of them? They may lead to a break, but, in themselves, conflicts are intrinsically linked to the unfolding plot lines by which characters develop themselves.

REVISITING
THE CASE STUDY

1 Which individuals or groups of individuals can be identified as stakeholders in the pay negotiations at MetalCo?

At MetalCo, much of the daily interaction between managers and union representatives was based on informal personal relationships between the different parties. There were few long-established formal procedures and this fact holds with it the possible danger that Mark James and Peter Green (union representative and management) may be seen to be 'in cahoots'. Currently within both academic and practitioner debates, there is a lot of criticism of modern partnership agreements between unions and employers, where there is a view that management–union cooperation simply means that the union is rendered weak and has to bend to the will of the union. However, this case study demonstrates the more complex subtleties of interaction between parties who are ultimately in conflict with one another. In particular the case study indicates how the terms of any cooperation and conflict need to be carefully formulated if the vested interests of different stakeholders and their constituencies are to be maintained. The stakehol-ders here extend well beyond the bounds of this pair however – union representatives are accountable to shop stewards, who in turn have to report to union members who have families and relatives depending on them. The personnel director reports to his manager who has to report to a senior management team responding to demands of the new US parent to become 'world class'. Somewhere, too, there are customers whose demands are contributing to the volatility of the industry.

2 What vested interests did each of these stakeholders have in the outcome of the negotiations?

Members want to be rewarded for their productivity but also want to keep their jobs – security is important as a sister company has been downsized. They want to know that their efforts will bring continued employment. Senior management need 'restructuring' to gain greater efficiencies to help the company survive and attract further investment in a turbulent environment. The families and the community, and the town itself, depend on the company's survival for their own well-being. Mark James, Peter Green, the managing director and the shop stewards all have to operate between parties – demonstrating their abilities to get things done, to make a difference and wield influence – in order to keep their own jobs.

The terms of the engagement between conflicting parties, such as the union convenor and the personnel director, therefore need to be managed carefully. Management was probably the more powerful party within the employment relationship at MetalCo and, as management was determined to introduce the restructuring programme, Mark James and the wider union membership at the factory may have had very little room for manoeuvre, particularly as the changes were seen as necessary for the survival of the firm. However, 'necessity' can be seen as socially defined, where the views of the different stakeholders can be moderated within their interactions with one another. This process of definition partly determines what is possible, or desirable, in particular circumstances. Therefore, a certain level of cooperation with management was a prerequisite if the union was to have any influence on the way that the restructuring was to be brought about.

3 In what ways did Mark James manage the processes of interaction between the different stakeholders before and during the pay negotiations?

Recent social attitude surveys (in Britain and the US at least) indicate that most workers still feel that there are conflicts of interest between workers and management. Mark James as the union representative had to be seen to recognise and demonstrate this conflict if he was not to be perceived as 'in management's pocket'. He was therefore very careful to retain the drama of being in opposition with management, and the case study indicates a number of these instances over a long period of time. Drawing on the dramaturgical metaphor, the 'performance' of the relationship between union and management had to be carefully played out. The existence of public conflict between managers and the union was seen as a positive aspect of the relationship – thus Mark James related how the member had praised him for his 'argument' with the manager on the shop floor. The most prominent example of Mark James (and arguably also Peter Green the personnel manager) 'playing out' this public presentation of the relationship between parties who are supposed to be in conflict with one another, was the clandestine meeting at the

motorway services. Clearly, it was at this meeting that the pay negotiations were really decided, and not at the official negotiations event. One view of Mark James's behaviour is that he was essentially 'tricking' his members, which may lead one to question whether he really is acting in their best interests. However, such a view may be a very simplistic and idealistic view of the relationship between management and union representatives.

4 Would you consider that Mark James was acting in the best interests of his members?

We have to consider whether Mark James was only concerned with his own self-interest. Certainly there must be some element of self-interest: if the union loses support, Mark may be out of a job. However there does appear to be more behind Mark's behaviour that relates to wider concerns of the local community in which Mark lives and works. In particular, he did seem concerned to get the best deal possible for the members within the context of a situation where, inevitably, some of his members would be negatively affected. Unlike at the other firm, Mark had been able to demand certain concessions within the proposals for change. Mark appears to have demonstrated a far more participatory and collectivist style than his counterpart at the other firm. While we can only surmise here, given the snapshot of time at MetalCo offered by the case study, through Mark's efforts to involve them, it was likely that the workers at the factory would be able to have some kind of input into policy and might be able to place some limitations on the autonomy of the convenor than they would have been able to at the other firm. Members certainly seemed to be willing to rally around in support of the union, as demonstrated by the overwhelming acceptance by the workforce of the proposal for restructuring at the mass meeting after the pay negotiations. They also seemed willing to make a stand against management when necessary in terms of taking industrial action.

We have to weigh up the different pressures and influences Mark James faced in his position as union convenor. On the one hand, he knew that the members expected him to make a stand and demonstrate his opposition to management. On the other hand, members would not have supported unnecessary conflict, simply for the sake of it, there were also expectations of a certain level of cooperation with management.

Indeed, because an essential part of the union role is to bargain for the best deal for members, unions have to discuss management proposals, thus embedding the management proposals and the management role with some legitimacy. In other words, it is likely that workers would want the company to survive so they could keep their jobs and so would be willing to support a level of restructuring that would require the union's cooperation. However, they also wanted to be convinced that the union was acting in their best interests in opposing the most detrimental aspects of that restructuring. People have shifting frames of reference between conflict and cooperation, which may inevitably be ambivalent.

An analysis such as the one presented so far may be seen to support a view of negotiations as being like the 'five-part play', with a set pattern for performance, that is concluded in line with what was set out at the beginning of the play. As was discussed earlier in this chapter, such a view does not highlight adequately the 'never-endingness' of negotiation processes and the importance of the wider social context. However, such ongoing

processes are clear from the MetalCo case, in which the negotiation processes demonstrated are not only delimited to this particular event (or 'play') of the annual pay negotiations. The employment relationship is in a constant process of negotiation, not just at particular moments of wage demands or grievance disputes. Thus, Mark James had to take action to 'frame', 'script' and 'perform' over a much longer period of time (twenty years in this case), taking into consideration deeply embedded views, opinions and traditions of context. It is this everyday management of relations between the stakeholders that is perhaps more important than the specific and more formal moments of engagement and interaction. An analysis of negotiation processes which is firmly rooted in the specific organizational (and local community) context of MetalCo is very important here, supporting the critique of 'best practice' or 'one way' models of negotiation practice. For Mark James and Peter Green, the daily playing out of the soap opera of MetalCo was an inherent part of the processes and outcome of the annual pay negotiation.

References

Blake, R.R., Shepherd, H.A., and Mouton, J.S. (1964) *Managing Intergroup Conflict in Industry,* Houston: Gulf Publishing Company.

Boden, D. (1994) *The Business of Talk,* London: Sage.

Boje, D.M. (2001) *Narrative Methods for Organization and Communication Research,* London: Sage.

Bond, M.H. and Hwang, K. (1986) 'The social psychology of the Chinese people', in M.H. Bond (ed.) *The Psychology of the Chinese People,* Hong Kong, Oxford University Press, pp. 213–66.

Braverman, H. (1974) *Labour and Monopoly Capital: The Degradation of Work in the Twentieth Century,* New York: Monthly Review Press.

Brown, L.D. (1983) 'Managing conflict among groups' in D. Kolb, I.M. Rubin and J. McIntyre (eds) *Organizational Psychology,* Englewood Cliffs, NJ: Prentice Hall, pp. 225–37.

Brown, M.E. (1994) *Soap Opera and Women's Talk: The Pleasure of Resistance,* London: Sage.

Burrell, G. and Morgan, G. (1979) *Sociological Paradigms and Organizational Analysis,* London: Heinemann, pp. 204, 388.

Child, J. (ed.) (1973) *Man and Organizations: The Search for Explanation and Social Relevance,* London: Allen & Unwin.

Cobb, S. and Rifkin, J. (1991) 'Practice and paradox: Deconstructing neutrality in mediation' *Law and Social Enquiry,* Journal of the American Bar Foundation, **16**(1): 35–62.

Dawson, S. (1986) *Analysing Organizations,* London: Macmillan Education.

Earley, P.C. (1997) *Face, Harmony and Social Structure,* New York, Oxford University Press.

Fisher, R. and Urry, W. (1981) 'Getting to Yes: Negotiating Agreement Without Giving in', London: Century Hutchinson.

Fox, A. (1974) *Beyond Contract: Work, Power and Trust Relations,* London: Faber and Faber.

Fulop, L. and Richards, D. (2002) 'Connections, culture and context: Business relationships and networks in the Asia Pacific region', in C. Harvie and B.C. Lee (eds) Globalisation and Small and Medium Sized Enterprises in East Asia, Cheltenham: Edward Elgar, pp. 273–96.

Fulop, L., Frith, F. and Hayward, H. (1992) *Management for Australian Business: A Critical Text,* p. 221; adapted from 'Report to the Business Council of Australia' Industrial Relations Study Commission 1 July 1989.

Gabriel, Y. (2000) *Storytelling in Organizations: Facts, Fictions and Fantasies,* Oxford: Oxford University Press.

Gao, G., Ting-Toomey, S. and Gudykunst, W.B. (1996) 'Chinese communication processes', in M.H. Bond (ed.) *The Handbook of Chinese Psychology,* Hong Kong: Oxford University Press, pp. 280–93.

Greenwald, J (2001) 'Rank And Fire – Attrition isn't working, so best-to-worst grading is gaining – and those on the bottom get the boot', *Time Magazine,* 18 June www.time.com/time/magazine/article/0,9171, 1101010618-129915,00.html.

Hatch, M.J. (1997) *Organization Theory: Modern, Symbolic and Postmodern Perspectives,* Oxford: Oxford University Press.

Hellweg, S.A., Samovar, L.A. and Skow, L. (1991) 'Cultural variations in negotiating styles', in L.A. Samovar and R.E. Porter (eds) *Intercultural Communication: A Reader* (6th edn), Belmont, CA: Wadsworth, pp. 185–92.

Hofstede, G. (1991) *Cultures and Organizations: Software of the Mind,* London: McGraw-Hill.

Hutton, J. and Quine, C. (1988) *Evaluation of Southwark Mediation Scheme,* London: Grubb Institute.

Kelly, J.E. (1982) *Scientific Management, Job Redesign and Work Performance,* London and New York: Academic Press, p. 173.

Kilbarn, R. (1992) *Television Soaps,* Batsford, London.

Kirkbride, P.S., Tang, S.F.Y. and Westwood, R.I. (1991) 'Chinese conflict preferences and negotiating behaviour: Cultural and psychological influences', *Organizational Studies,* **12**: 365–86.

Kolb, D.M. (2000) More than just a footnote: constructing a theoretical framework for teaching about gender in negotiation, *Negotiation Journal,* **16**(4): 347–56.

Kolb, D.M. and Williams, J. (2000) *The Shadow Negotiation,* New York: Simon & Schuster.

Kray, L.J., Thompson, L. and Galinsky, A. (2001) 'Battle of the sexes: Gender stereotype confirmation and reactance in negotiations', *Journal of Personality and Social Psychology,* **80**(6): 942–58.

Leung, K. and Wu, P.G. (1990) 'Dispute processing: A cross-cultural analysis', in R.W. Brislin (ed.) *Applied Cross-cultural Psychology*, Newbury Park, CA: Sage, pp. 209–31.

Lewicki, R. (1985) *Decision-making in Conflict Situations,* Washington, DC: National Institute for Dispute Resolution.

Mayo, E. (1933) *The Human Problems of an Industrial Civilisation*, New York: Macmillan.

Menkel-Meadow, C. (2000) 'Teaching about gender and negotiation: sex, truths, and videotape', *Negotiation Journal,* **16**(4): 357–76.

Miller, E. (1987) *Conflict,* London: Tavistock Institute of Human Relations, Occasional Paper No. 9.

Mumford, L.S. (1995) *Love and Ideology in the Afternoon: Soap Opera, Women and a TV Genre,* Bloomington: Indiana University Press.

Nichols, T. (ed.) (1980) *Capital and Labour: A Marxist Primer,* London: Fontana.

Nochimson, M. (1992) *No End to Her: Soap Opera and the Female Subject,* Berkeley, CA: University of California Press.

Rifkin, J. and Cobb, S. (1991) 'Toward a new discourse for mediation: A critique of neutrality', in *Mediation Quarterly,* **9**(2): 151–67.

Robbins, S. (1974) *Managing Organizational Conflict: A Non-Traditional Approach*, Englewood Cliffs, NJ: Prentice Hall, p. 99.

San Franciso Community Boards (1986) *Concilliation Skills,* San Francisco: San Francisco Community Boards.

Shenkar, O. and Ronen, S. (1987) 'The structure and importance of work goals among managers in the People's Republic of China', *Academy of Management Journal,* **30**(3): 564–76.

Shi, X. and Westwood, R. (2000) 'International business negotiations in the Chinese context', in J.T. Li, A.S. Tsui and E. Weldon, *Management and Organizations in the Chinese Context,* Basingstoke: Macmillan – now Palgrave Macmillan, pp. 185–224.

Stoner, J.A.F., Collins, R.R. and Yetton, P. (1985) *Management in Australia,* Melbourne: Prentice Hall.

Thomas, K.W. (1977) 'Toward multi-dimensional values in teaching: The example of conflict behaviours', *Academy of Management Review,* **12**(4): 484–90.

Thomas, K.W. (1983) 'Conflict and conflict management', in M.D. Dunnette (ed.) *Handbook of Industrial and Organizational Psychology* (2nd edn), Chicago: Rand McNally.

Thomas, K.W. (1992) 'Conflict and conflict management: Reflections and update', *Journal of Organizational Behaviour,* **13**: 265–74.

Thomas, K.W. and Kilman, R.H. (1974) *Thomas–Kilman Conflict Mode Instrument* Tuxedo NY: Xicom, Inc p. 11 by Kenneth W. Thomas (1992) 'Conflict and conflict management: Reflections and update' *Journal of Organizational Behaviour,* **13**: 266.

Thompson, P. and McHugh, D. (2002) *Work Organisations: A Critical Introduction,* Basingstoke: Palgrave Macmillan.

Ting-Toomey, S. (1988) 'Intercultural conflict styles: A face-negotiation theory', in Y.Y. Kim and A.B. Gudykunst (eds) *Theories in Intercultural Communication*, Newbury Park, CA: Sage, pp. 213–35.

Triandis, H.C. (1995) *Individualism and Collectivism*, Boulder, CO: Westview.

Trompenaars, F. and Hampden-Turner, C. (1997) *Riding the Waves of Culture: Understanding Cultural Diversity in Global Business* (2nd edn), London: Nicholas Brealey.

Watson, T. (1995) *Sociology, Work and Industry,* London: Routledge.

Westerlund, G. and Sjøstrand, S.E. (1979) *Organizational Myths,* New York: Harper & Row.

Yuen, E. (1992) 'Conflict handling processes', in R.I. Westwood (ed.) *Organisational Behaviour: Southeast Asian Perspectives*. Hong Kong: Longman.

CHAPTER

13 Managing change

*Stephen Linstead and Alison Linstead**

Questions about change

1 What are the reasons why organizations change?

2 Is resistance to change inevitable?

3 Should change be top-down or bottom-up?

4 How is our understanding of change changing?

MORGAN MOTOR COMPANY – 1

The Morgan Motor Company was founded in Malvern, on the borders of England and Wales, in 1909 by the legendary H.F.S. Morgan, and is still a family company. In the late 1980s H.F.S. Morgan's son Peter ran the company with the assistance of his son Charles, a former news cameraman, and four of the seven directors were family. The company's fortunes were founded on an economical three-wheeler car, which enjoyed tremendous success up to the middle of the 1920s, and remained popular into the 1950s. The original factory, which is still in use in 2002, managed to turn out 2300 cars a year, more than five times the number it was producing in 1989. In 1935 a four-wheel model was introduced, on which the main product in 1989 was still based. The top of the range model by that time boasted a 3.5 litre V8 engine, but in many respects was recognizably the same vehicle, substantially hand-made.

Morgan declared at the time that the waiting list for a car was 4/5 years, but no one seemed to know the real answer and it was rumoured that the truth was closer to 10 years. Peter Morgan was worried about the waiting list, as it was off-putting to potential customers, but he remembered his father telling him always to make sure that demand is slightly ahead of supply. Morgan survived as a small car manufacturer against all the odds, through the kind of peaks and troughs of demand which forced most of their contemporaries out of business or had them – like MG or Triumph, taken over by the big mass-production firms. The memories of bad times had affected the development of the company deeply.

After the Second World War, during which time the company made munitions, they began making cars again, but were only able to survive because of the international demand for the car. By 1959 85 per cent of all Morgans were going to the United States, but stiff emission control regulations in the late 1960s caused the US market to collapse. Fortunately the UK market had by that time recovered. Indeed, with such high demand for the car, people began to speculate on the Morgan waiting list and it was not unknown for people to trade their place in the queue. Morgan discouraged the practice by making only for the customer named on the list and insisting that the car is not delivered until it has been registered in that customer's name, but they are often sold with delivery-only mileage for 20 per cent more than the list price.

In 1989, Morgan was making money but there were questions as to whether it was making enough to guarantee its survival. As a manufacturer of a luxury good, Morgan was making only 5–9 per cent profit rather than the 20 per cent which might be expected to grow and develop the business. The company knew it ought to increase production, and set themselves the modest aim of upping the number of cars produced each week from 9 to 10. The reluctant workforce agreed to produce 10 cars a week on a three-week trial basis. They were promised extra money if they succeeded, but no one knew exactly how much. Previous attempts foundered because not all the shops involved were capable of sustaining the increased level of production for more than a few weeks at a time, and they slipped back into a level with which they were comfortable. While management were united in public, there were latent disagreements about the long-term direction of the company.

In summary, in 1989, the car had a tremendously enthusiastic following, an enormous global waiting list and exported half its production. But there was no direction or growth and profits appeared insufficient. Labour costs, because of the method of production, were high and a high proportion of the car's cost. Inevitably, such a product would eventually become uneconomic and the company would decline if the problems were not addressed. One visitor observed:

> A tour of the factory is like a visit to Santa's workshop. The louvres in the bonnet are stamped out by hand using a fly-press. The wings are beaten over what looks like a tree stump. The door panels are trimmed with tin snips until they fit. Cars in various stages of completion, with a build ticket bearing the customer's name, are pushed from one shed to the next.

Sir John Harvey-Jones visited the factory in 1989 to advise Morgan, and noted the following:

---

* *Authors' note:* We are grateful for the provision of the section on cross-cultural approaches to change by David S. Richards.

Production

The factory gives the impression of being run by a bunch of enthusiastic amateurs. Mark Aston, the works manager, has been with Morgan thirteen years, but it seems like thirty. He does see the need for some change to the way the car is made, but basically likes the way things are at the moment: it is almost as if Morgan blood ran through his veins. So lacking in flexibility, he got his job at Morgan not because he is a trained engineer, but simply because he loves everything about the car. There is no logical flow of production through the factory, and very little production planning. The machine shop, where bought-in castings are worked, is antique, badly undercapitalized and in need of some fresh investment – so many ancient machines. The layout of the factory is historic, and apparently hasn't changed much since 1919 when the original factory was extended. There are plans to amalgamate the wiring and wing-fitting shop … but this falls a long way short of the complete overhaul that the whole factory really needs.

Sales and marketing

Derek Day, the sales director, finds it hard to think of making beyond 450–500 cars a year. In fact, he hasn't actually had to sell a car for twenty years and is effectively Morgan's customer liaison man. Morgan's sales department is production led. They don't think in terms of how many they can sell, but how many they can produce. The company is introducing a clean-burn engine which would meet United States regulations, but is doing this without any idea of how many cars they could sell over there. They export to Germany and Japan, but have no idea what would happen there if they put the price up – although the second-hand market is so healthy that you can sell a Morgan for more than you paid for it. The company has absolutely no idea what the demand for the car is.

Information technology

There is no computer in the stockroom (or the company) and the average stock level is between three and four months' supply. But no one is sitting down and working out what the optimum level of stock ought to be. Stock levels are probably higher than they need to be, with the result that the company has far too much money tied up in stock.

Human resources

The shop-floor workers are paid a basic wage, and a production bonus which generally accounts for around half their weekly wage. However, the bonus doesn't work as an incentive, as hiccups in the production flow often slow things up somewhere else in the process of making the completed car. The foremen are paid more but they aren't paid anything extra if their workers increase production so they have no incentive to exhort them to work harder.

Design development and technology

Maurice Owen, the chief development engineer, is not the youngest member of the Morgan management team. But he is one of the few people working at Morgan with any clear sense of what is wrong with the company and any sort of vision of what it could become. The design philosophy behind Morgan is to redefine and improve the mechanics while maintaining the shape of the body. The last four or five years have been spent adapting the mechanics of the car to meet new legislation. Morgan drivers, those who are fanatical about the car, are a conservative lot and worrying about the reaction of Morgan owners can be a big restraint on management thinking. Apparently it took him eleven or twelve years to persuade the company to go over to rack and pinion steering which now makes the car very firm and responsive to drive. He thinks the way the car is made is wrong. At the moment the engines are put on the chassis at the beginning, the bodywork is then fitted on to the chassis, and the wiring is put in last. On one model, this last operation involves the fitters in wild contortions to get the wiring in place. He is convinced the factory could be better organized. He would like to build the body and chassis separately. The body could be sprayed and even wired and the engine wouldn't need to be put in until the end; avoiding the current situation whereby expensive engines sit around on the chassis for three or four months while the cars are completed. He would like all the cars to have the same chassis and the same basic body. Apparently he has been saying this for years, and he is still working on the problem. Whenever the subject is mentioned the instant reaction is always the same: the customers like the car made the way it is, and it is this antiquated way of doing things that actually sells the car. The ethos of the company is very risk averse, except that they seem to have no idea they are actually steering the most risky course of all when they fail to face up to change.

Change aversion

Complacency is a big problem. From their point of view they are doing so well at the moment that they can see no need to change and none of them are really aware of the dangers they face. When you go round the factory, there's hardly a shop which couldn't do with new investment: Morgan seems dedicated to making things in the most expensive way. Everybody defends their own corner and there is this iron-strong belief that any change of any sort will alter the attraction of the car. The company is in real peril unless it can accept the need for change.

An article in *Esquire* shortly after said:

> from a Harvard Business School point of view, the company has done almost nothing right in its 83 years of existence. It has for the most part failed to automate or expand, failed to diversify, failed to change its product line, failed to turn to the stock market for new capital … It has, in short failed to do everything but succeed.

Source: Adapted from the Morgan Motor Company case in John Harvey-Jones (1990) *Troubleshooter,* London: Penguin Books, pp. 99–126, and subsequent material from John Harvey-Jones (1993) *Troubleshooter 2,* London: Penguin Books, pp. 202–4. The company website (http://www.morgan-motor.co.uk; http://autozine.kyul.net/html/Morgan.htm, accessed 26 February 2003; and BBCi reports).

QUESTIONS ABOUT THE CASE

1 How ready is the Morgan Motor Company for change?
2 What seem to be the main obstacles to change?
3 How could a change agent try to persuade them to change?

Introduction

Change has become a defining feature of contemporary organizations and change and its management pose key challenges for all sorts of organizations, private, public and voluntary. Whether it is true or not that organizations are changing faster than ever before, it seems that every generation not only claims this but feels it to be true. It is certainly a truism among management writers that organizational change is a fact of life, but it is often an uncomfortable one. Les Worall and Cary Cooper (1997) state that the most common forms of change experienced across industry sectors are cost reduction, redundancies, culture change and performance improvement. Their findings also suggested that 61 per cent of managers at that time had been affected by an organizational change programme. The term *organizational change* usually refers to modifications in an organization's structure, goals, technology and work tasks, but since the 1980s can also include changes in attitudes and cultural values. Organizational change affects working conditions, structural features, roles, jobs and behaviours; it can be introduced deliberately and in a planned way, imposed by policy change, or arise through external pressure. An externally driven view of change argues that the external climate is determined by economic conditions, government interventions, changes in technology, political pressures and global competition, and to survive organizations must be responsive to change and foster attitudes of flexibility and dynamism to manage the external demands placed upon them. Most managers, then, are in a situation where they are affected by pressures to change which are not of their own making and are not under their control.

Change can also emanate from within an organization, primarily because organizations go through processes of ageing (including buildings, machinery, workforce), and strategies for renewal and development are therefore necessary at every level, from the individual to the complete physical relocation of the organization. Thus, a change in an organization can refer to any alteration in activities or tasks, such as minor changes in procedures and operations, or large-scale transformational changes brought about by rapid restructuring (Kanter 1991). Understanding, responding to and managing change are primary skills increasingly required of managers. However, change is reciprocal – the changes that managers make to their organizations also can affect the nature of managerial work. Rosemary Stewart (1991) describes how changes in organizations affect the kinds of jobs that managers have to do amid the shifting nature of their lives and careers. These changes include:

- Wider networking
- Flatter hierarchies of authority
- Reduced middle management cohorts with more responsible roles
- Less predictable career paths
- Greater choices in their work and careers.

Recently emphasis has been placed on the continuing process of change rather than a sequence of 'step' changes required for organizations to be successful (Collins 1998). Tom Peters (1987) comments that change should be treated as a norm rather than a series of one-off exercises as 'the only constant thing today is change'. The 'new wave' writers (such as Waterman 1988) emphasize reviewing and renewing organizational structures and processes, and focusing on creativity, innovation and leadership for managing change constantly.

There are many claims and counterclaims in the general debate about what change means and the influences on the organization, and these claims are often based on little empirical evidence (Dawson and Webb 1989). The popular literature on change in the 1980s still treated change in a unitarist fashion as a matter of developing and communicating top management vision (see Chapter 12), although by this period research had begun to acknowledge the contingent factors that influence the nature of change and how individuals manage and cope with it. Pettigrew and Whipp (1991) drew attention to the conditioning factors that help to explain the degree of openness of an organization to its environment, and its responsiveness to the changes in its environment. The factors they identified were:

- The extent to which there are key actors within the firm who are prepared to champion assessment techniques which increase the openness of the organization
- The structural and cultural characteristics of the company

Exhibit 13.1 Eight habitual paradoxes of successful change

1. Enduring long-term policy versus exciting 'play on the day'

A crisis is good for getting people to pull together. Making sacrifices for the survival of the company is a stirring and motivating experience. However, many organizations who are good at coping with crises do not know what to do to maintain this momentum without engineering the next crisis, and find it difficult to make enduring plans, and particularly commitments to their workforce (Hampden-Turner 1990: 94–5).

2. Cynicism as a product of successful change

When the crisis is over, many companies or other organizations are unable to deliver any benefits to those who made the sacrifices, often benefits promised, and may even find themselves forced to contract or restructure rather than reward. Employees come to see culture change as having no altruistic or humanistic content, but simply as an expedient rhetoric to enable needed business modifications to take place. The 'bottom line' is paramount after all.

3. Lack of internal care

Often the key people in the management of change become left out. In British Airways, flight crew were asked to give extra care to the customer while being handled in a disciplinarian fashion (Höpfl and Linstead 1993), as were crew in Cathay Pacific Airways (Linstead 1995). Anthony (1989) notes the dislocation of middle management in culture change, where they are often left as the only ones believing in it. Senior management are manipulative, first-line management and workers cynical, and the burden of convincing others and carrying through the change falls on middle management.

4. Disillusionment with the quick fix

When rapid change follows rapid change, the value of these changes is thrown into question. The failure of speed and decisiveness to solve problems once and for all produces an acknowledgment of the value of time and patience in the management of change. Nevertheless, often the organization is unable to put these virtues into practice.

5. Commitment versus motivation

Companies require, and frequently get, commitment from their staff without making tremendous efforts to reward this commitment. It is not motivation for advancement, improved conditions or improved salary which keeps managers in many companies at their desks well into the evening six or seven days a week. It is a combination of professionalism, concern for their jobs and the company, and a kind of resignation in the face of the inevitable (Höpfl 1993). Commitment can occur, paradoxically, in the absence of motivation or morale.

6. High productivity can occur with low morale

Long hours and high achievement do not necessarily indicate high morale. In fact, increasingly they seem to occur in the company of low morale. Two of the companies in which we worked were among the most profitable and successful in their field, in the UK and worldwide, and managers consistently reported this to us in our discussions with them (see also Thomas and Linstead 2001; Linstead and Thomas 2002).

7. Bureaucracy and politics subvert empowerment

As suggested above, old habits die hard. But simultaneously, bureaucracy and politics seek to colonize empowerment for their own purposes, which was a major factor in the failure of a TQM initiative in a large specialist shipbuilder we worked with (see also Hampden-Turner 1990).

8. The CEO: energizer or distraction?

This occurs when the CEO becomes locked into symbolic action to drive change. The energizing function of symbolic management which often emphasizes detail, and is effective early in change initiatives (Johnson 1992), can become a distraction when the full nature and impact of the change becomes well known to those involved in it, and demands more complex and subtle responses, which are often not available to the CEO who is cut off from this level of learning. The changing reception of a famous story circulated within British Airways (Bruce 1987) illustrates this. Sir Colin Marshall, at the relaunch of the super-shuttle service, turned up at the terminal to greet passengers and ended up checking them in, to emphasize to supervisors that when the need was customer service, rank and job descriptions did not matter. Nevertheless, in sessions held with managers some years after this event, they voiced a fear that this was indicative of overattention to detail which they saw as a personal quality of the CEO, and a problem which pervaded the organization, the CEO's attitude having been invoked to justify the blocking of creative initiatives.

Source: Adapted from Stephen Linstead and Andrew Chan (1994) 'The sting of organization: Command, reciprocity and change management', *Journal of Organizational Change Management,* **7**(5): 4–19.

- The extent to which environmental pressures are recognized
- The degree to which assessment occurs as a multifunction activity which is not viewed as an end in itself but is then linked to the central operations of the business.

Nevertheless, despite the guidelines which research-led commentators like Pettigrew and Whipp discerned, the complexities of change continue to present situations where interventions have unintended consequences, producing both the intended effect and its exact opposite, and where change seems to unravel more quickly than ever regardless of how well it has been planned and executed. In Exhibit 13.1, Linstead and Chan (1994) identify eight paradoxes of organizational change which capture the flavour of this way of life for contemporary managers.

Philosophies of change

Even acknowledging the paradoxical nature of change, it might seem odd that if change is the norm rather than the exception, we should have difficulties not only in dealing with it, but even in talking about it – finding the right language to express it. The problem seems to lie in whether we approach the world as though stability and fixity are the norm, and change is a deviance from the norm, or whether we see change as the norm and stability some vain attempt to arrest its process. Taking one or other of these views has been common since the pre-Socratic philosophers of ancient Greece: if we take the first, like the followers of Parmenides, we will view change as difficult, requiring energy to be generated to overcome inertia and resistance, force to be exerted to keep the change in motion until it is completed, and control put in place to prevent decay or slippage back into the pre-change state (see Stacey et al. 2000: Ch. 2 and Appendix 1; Chia 1999). Further change requires further forceful intervention. This view conforms to the view taken in most of the existing change literature. However, if we take the second view, like the followers of Heraclitus, change requires intervention into an ongoing process in which the energy and movement are already present and only require channelling or influencing. Change has its own momentum. The difficulty here is that the change never fully stabilizes, but that need not be a problem in a system which is self-aware and self-monitoring and can respond appropriately. This second view aligns more closely with postmodern approaches, including those from the new sciences which draw on complexity theory and chaos theory.

Most modern change theory, as we have said, is grounded in a stability view of change rather than a

Table 13.1 Four themes distinguishing modern and postmodern theories

Modern post-industrial theory	Postmodern post-industrial theory
Polar oppositions	Perpetual transformation
Depoliticized view of organizations	Politicized view of organizations
Theory based on market and economic assumptions	Theory based on linguistic assumptions
Universal theorizing	Diversity/local theorizing

Source: Robert F. White and Roy Jacques (1995) 'Operationalizing the postmodernity construct for efficient organizational change management', *Journal of Organizational Change Management*, **8**(2): 45–71.

process view, and the contrast between the two is simply captured by White and Jacques in Table 13.1. As they put it, modern theories tend to prioritize stability of concepts, things and states, and this is characterized by tendency to treat ideas and processes as things, operationlized in an either/or logic – we change *from* this *to* that, do this *or* that, rather than being in a state with elements of both. Postmodern approaches emphasize instability, the fact that the future is always emerging in the present, and that at any moment a state contains elements both of what was and what is coming to be. In a state of transformation, reality can only be grasped by thinking in terms of both/and logic – we are *both* a little of this *and* a little of that at any one time. Where modernism emphasizes stability, it favours the idea of absolute qualities which do not change over time and are not subject to human construction. Thus many modern theories argue that there is only one answer to a problem, or one best answer to a problem, and, like Taylorism in organizations, refuse to acknowledge power as a factor, only 'science' based on facts. Postmodernism recognizes that in a system which is unstable and transformative, stability is not evidence of what is naturally fixed and true, but is evidence of human intervention to create categories which *appear* fixed and true – and powerful groups have the opportunity to stabilize those conditions which are most favourable to them and get the less powerful to accept them as truth. Modernism tends to treat politics as irrelevant or, where present, as aberrant behaviour caused by psychological dysfunction or deeper problems elsewhere in the system; postmodernism regards politics as the very means of constructing organized life. Accordingly, modernist approaches to management and organization have a tendency to look outside the organization for determining forces such as the market or economic conditions, which restrict the possibilities of micro-behaviour, while postmodern approaches argue for the importance of the medium through which the interpretation and construction of those conditions occurs, most particularly language, arguing that micro-political conditions in communication affect the ways in which markets and economies are created and change. Finally, while modernists seek universal theories of change which can apply to all or, at least, most situations, postmodernists argue that different situations create different realities, and that the rules can change accordingly as micro-differences accumulate. Change management then is a matter of sensitivity to diversity and responsiveness to local factors, rather than the application of predetermined methods and practices in all situations.

Of course, not all theories conform to the modern or postmodern stereotypes, and some theories overlap considerably – largely because change theorists are usually oriented towards practice as much as pure theory. Postmodern approaches, although often grounded in some quite impenetrable theorizing, are attractive to managers because they capture the sense of continuing contradiction and paradox which seems to characterize contemporary change management, as we identified earlier (see Exhibit 13.1). In the next sections we will take a critical look at how the frames of reference approach discussed in Chapter 12 is useful in understanding change, then at Van de Ven and Poole's (1995) attempt to build philosophically based accounts

of possible paradigms of change grounded in modernist thought but attempting not to be confined within modernism by incorporating a political dimension. We will then look at recent attempts to build bridges between philosophy, recent theories of complexity and organizational change theory.

Frames of reference in change

David Collins (1998) builds on the work of Burrell and Morgan (1979) to consider how the *unitary*, *pluralist*, *radical* and *Marxist* frames of reference can be elaborated in terms of their approaches to, and explanations of, organizational and social change processes. From the *unitary* point of view (see Tables 13.2, 13.3), the efficient and effective functioning of the organization is paramount, and change is about improvement and adaptation to improve this. Conflict is seen as a problem and a hindrance to task accomplishment and the organization therefore has no proper provisions for dealing with it – harmony is emphasized above all, and conflict is constantly attributed to the individual level rather than the collective, and dealt with as an individual problem of maladjustment. As there are no legitimate grounds for dissent, change management becomes a matter of communication. Managing change is about the effective communication of managerial goals to all levels of the

Table 13.2 Unitary and pluralist perspectives on change

	Focus	Limitations	Implications for change management
Unitarist frame of reference	Organizational effectiveness and adaptation. Avoidance of conflict	Focus upon harmony to exclusion of consideration of conflict except in limited psychological terms. Inability to rationalize group conflict. No credibility accorded to serious expressions of discontent. No real role for people, their orientations or problems	Since there can be no real or credible grounds for opposition to management, change management becomes management of communications. Dominant strategy for change management revolves around communication of objectives of management to workers. Resistance to change rationalized as being due to fear or/and poor communications
Pluralist frame of reference	Organizational effectiveness and adaptation. Management of order through management of conflict. Maintenance of social stability	Limited view of conflict, narrow range of factors considered. Conflict viewed as having, predominantly, psychological roots. Limited view of context; assumption that state plays disinterested role in regulating the workplace and the economy	Pluralism allows for expression of valid and credible opposition, so process of change management becomes more complex. Ideally, pluralist models of the change process would tend to portray change management as a process where individuals and groups pursuing different drivers and aims must negotiate to reach some form of compromise regarding the ends and processes of change

Source: David Collins (1998) *Organizational Change: Sociological Perspectives*, London: Routledge, p. 153.

organization, with feedback welcomed as a matter of fine-tuning only. Problems and resistance are regarded as misunderstandings and failures of communication, or attributed to irrational fears of the unknown.

The *pluralist* or *liberal pluralist* point of view (see Table 13.2) has its emphasis on organizational effectiveness and adaptation, but recognizes conflict as a reality and therefore makes the management of conflict central to organizational activity. Social and organizational order cannot be taken for granted, and stability must be maintained by the proper management of differences. Conflict, however, is viewed in a limited way, mostly as having psychological roots. The state as a regulator of the economy and work is assumed to be disinterested and objective, and the role of context in producing and shaping conflict outcomes is minimized. Nevertheless, because conflict and the expression of difference are viewed as legitimate, change becomes more complex and a more drawn out process. Managers must seek to reconcile differences, build support, consult and negotiate in order to achieve agreement on the goals and outcomes of change, as far as possible.

The *radical* or *radical pluralist* perspective sees the need for root changes in society, and the workplace is one important arena for developing participation and accountability. Context then permeates the workplace, and participation in workplace decision-making is seen as a means to increasing the politicization of society as a whole. However, various forms of participation and bargaining seem to be the only mechanisms acknowledged for achieving this change, and gains are easily reversible. As with the discourse on empowerment, management can incorporate or hijack

participatory discourse for unitary ends. Change management calls for open and equal participation in reforming modes of production and distribution, but there is little evidence that management has involved itself in such agendas. Evidence is small and contradictory, but companies like The Body Shop may be argued to have taken some steps on this road.

For *Marxists*, the workplace is the key site of control and domination in society, and the economic base of society determines the political options available for the superstructure, rather than the reverse (see Table 13.3). One of the difficulties with this approach is that structural and big picture arguments tend to dominate, making accommodation problematic, and management's role can be demonized, making collaboration and trust relations difficult to develop. The focus on 'change' as a management topic, and even as a chapter in this book, and management's continuing inability to resolve problems of change, are seen merely as symptoms of deeper problems in the structure of capitalist social relations of production. There is thus a tendency to devalue any change efforts which do not entail or at least address such large-scale issues of structural inequality.

From these perspectives there is considerable conflict between focus of the maintenance of order and stability, or the energising of appropriate mechanisms of change; change as an individual or local matter or change as deeply embedded in social context and structure. Collins (1998:167–79) discusses the possibility of working simultaneously from more than one of these perspectives and notes that there is considerable disagreement on whether these perspectives, and the intellectual research paradigms which have been

Table 13.3 Radical and Marxist perspectives on change			
	Focus	Limitations	Implications for change management
Radical frame of reference	Root changes in nature of work organizations. To facilitate changes at work, changes must take place in the wider society. Wider participation in civic and industrial decision-making promoted. Participation is promoted as a means to politicize the population	No apparent mechanism to secure lasting change. Gains won through increased participation seem fairly easily reversible. Management may hijack rhetoric of participation and empowerment only to harness this to unitarist ends and processes	Radical agenda for change. Management calls for more open, equal and democratic forms of production and distribution. Little evidence, however, of any managerial commitment to this agenda
Marxist frame of reference	Workplace as a key site of control and domination. The economic base of society, in large measure, dictates the political superstructure erected in society	Structural arguments tend to predominate. Marxist arguments demonize management	Management's focus upon change and management's inability to 'solve' change management problems is indicative of structural problems which define capitalist social relations of production

Source: David Collins (1998) *Organizational Change: Sociological Perspectives*, London: Routledge, p. 168.

developed from them, can be compatible in specific circumstances – that is, it may be possible to embrace a unitary approach on certain tasks while agreeing to debate and discuss others, or to work longer term on lobbying for political change while dealing pragmatically with issues of company survival. Collins sketches a broad field of orientations to social and organizational change usefully, but Andrew Van de Ven and Marshall Scott Poole (1995), with a similar interest in whether and how change drivers or motors can be combined, develop their typology with a specific focus on the organizational level and make specific observations on combinatory possibilities.

Van de Ven and Poole: motorizing frames of reference

Van de Ven and Poole (1995) undertook a wide-ranging study of theoretical approaches to change management and developed a four-fold typology of *lifecycle, teleological, dialectical* and *evolutionary approaches*, shown diagrammatically in Figure 13.1. Boddy (2002) uses a similar but much less elaborated typology of lifecycle, emergent, participatory and political, where emergent seems to equate to evolutionary, participatory to teleological and political to dialectical. *Lifecycle approaches* are based around the assumption of organic growth, and consequent decline, impelled by an *immanent programme* or rule determined by nature, logic or social institution. The basic metaphor here is, of course, the lifecycle of biological organisms in which the programme unfolds through a prefigured sequence with compliant adaptation, is linear and irreversible (such as ageing) as potentials present at the beginning unfold into actuality. This change is prescribed for the organism or organization – they cannot affect its course in any significant way. Pioneers of this approach were early sociologists such as Comte and Spencer, or developmentalists such as Piaget, and key applied approaches in organizations involve stage, step and cyclical models, attempts to determine the nature of the firm and control deviance 'off-message', the viewing of change as metamorphosis or passage from one stage to the next, product lifecycle approaches and various means of prolonging the lifecycle of the organization by instigating new and additional lifecycles of products, technology and people. Lifecycles may thus be augmented or renewed, but not rejuvenated. Lifecycle approaches typically focus on one entity, be it group or organization, and not on interactions between entities or between components of an entity – so conflict between organizational members would be viewed as irrelevant, and environmental effects minor. These views would be compatible with many of the unitary assumptions, if more sophisticated.

Teleological approaches are based around the assumption of purposeful cooperation and enactment impelled by an *envisioned end state*, consensus on the means of goal achievement and recognition of synergies. Here the organization or entity acts discretely but reflexively self-monitors its actions, taking part in a process of socially constructing visioned end states, discontinuously resetting goals accordingly, implementing consequent actions and adapting means to ends (equifinality) in order to reach the desired end state. Organizational approaches here include planning, goal setting and social constructionism, which may seem to rely on a rather restricted if not idiosyncratic reading of those traditions. Indeed, while their citation of Herbert Simon as a pioneer of this approach may be unsurprising, Max Weber and George Herbert Mead are perhaps at best the result of one-sided interpretations of their work. Teleological approaches would normally emphasize causality rather than consensus, although falling short of the determinism of lifecycle approaches. Teleology, although still operating at the level of the single entity and minimizing the significance of interaction beyond the organization in the setting of goals, allows for change to be internally driven but *constructive* rather than prescribed as in the lifecycle approach. Van de Ven and Poole argue that goals change and are reinterpreted, so an organization does not remain in equilibrium once it has attained a goal; they also note that the environment places some constraints on what it can accomplish, which might mean that goals have to be readdressed. The management of change here *can* make a difference and goal setting and monitoring processes are important.

Dialectical theories assume opposition and conflict as a normal state of affairs, as colliding forces, contradictory values and events 'compete with each other for domination and control'. The driving motor here is *conflict and confrontation* between opposing forces, interests or classes operating through a logic of opposition between thesis, antithesis and achieved synthesis. Such conflict occasions are discontinuous and recurrent, and one confrontation may take a substantial amount of time to resolve into a productive synthesis – indeed, for Hegel, it may necessitate revolution if the 'thesis' acquires sufficient power to become hegemonic and resist the dialectic. Again Van de Ven and Poole seem to collapse some uncomfortable bedfellows together – Hegel, Marx and Freud being seen as the pioneers – and movements as diverse as social conflict theory, dialectical materialism (Marxism), pluralism and collective action being included. As we saw in Collins' discussion, pluralism, radicalism and Marxism are quite different in their approaches, once the analysis gets beyond the common recognition of conflict as a social norm. This model of change differs from the lifecycle and teleological models in that it locates change as something that happens as a result of interaction between entities, rather than solely the entity following its own decision tracks – change is rooted on conflict and bargaining rather than being hindered or facilitated by them. Furthermore, the interaction takes place between a multiplicity of entities, and the change rules, if any, emerge from dialectical interplay and nothing more.

The fourth approach in their model is that of *evolutionary theory*. These theories assume a situation of competitive survival working through a logic of natural selection within a similar (or species) population or organizations, driven by *population scarcity*, commensality (the need to coexist from the same resources) and competition for the best available resources. The population level may be drawn across communities, industries or society at large, and is sometimes termed *population ecology*. Here change proceeds through a cycle of variation, selection of best behaviours or performers, and retention of the successful characteristics. *Variation*, the emergence of new or novel forms, is often viewed to emerge by chance, and the processes of innovation are generally inadequately theorized from this perspective. *Selection* is a combination of competition for scarce resources and the

influence of the environment on the number and type of organizations a niche can support. *Retention* also involves inertia and persistence, so the process of evolutionary change involves a recurrent and cumulative interaction between the three. Whether this evolution is gradual, imperceptible and intergenerational (Darwinian) or incorporates learning and imitation that can lead to intragenerational step changes (Lamarckian) is a subject of considerable debate among organizational scholars. Some have argued for a form of saltation theory known as *punctuated equilibrium*, which has been applied at group, organization and population levels, in which entities remain fairly stable and static for long periods, move into periods of rapid and often unpredictable change, then settle into long periods of stability again. This approach includes the biologists Darwin, Lamarck, Mendel and Gould among its pioneers and in organization theory one would include Howard Aldrich. Although evolutionary theory operates through multiple entities who interact to produce change, this change is largely *prescribed* within the niche of the population itself, in parallel with the prescribed changes of lifecycle theory. Indeed, evolutionary and lifecycle theories address *first-order change*, or variations on a theme,

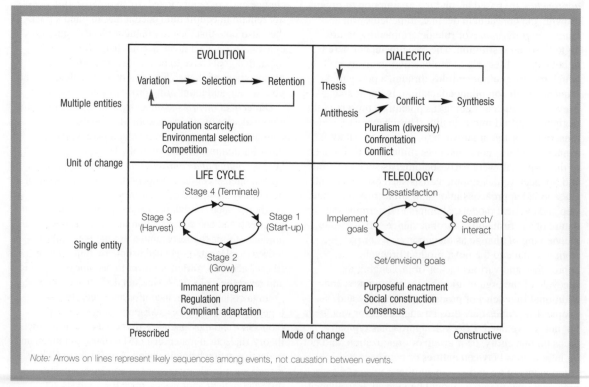

Note: Arrows on lines represent likely sequences among events, not causation between events.

Figure 13.1 Process theories of organizational development and change
Source: Andrew Van de Ven and Marshall Scott Poole (1995) 'Explaining development and change in organizations', *Academy of Management Review*, **20**(3): 520.

while dialectical and teleological theories address *second-order change*, or a break with past assumptions or frameworks (Watzlawick et al. 1974).

Van de Ven and Poole (1995: 533–6) in summarizing what has become quite a laborious argument, note the importance of identifying how all the different motors of change may be operating in any change situation, both at the same level and where these motors are 'nested', or different motors operate at different levels. On one dimension, this could be taken as an argument for political, cultural, economic and institutional embeddedness for which more sociologically informed analysts such as Granovetter (1985), Pettigrew (1985) and Clegg (1990) argue. On another, however, the edifice which Van de Ven and Poole build seems to be resting on shaky theoretical understandings of pluralism, dialectics and teleology, for example, and the claims they make for their framework must therefore be questioned. In order to fit their framework, they collapse very different approaches into one another and simplify concepts. If, for example the concept of teleology is unpacked from its origins in Aristotle, it can be seen to have five possible variants (Stacey et al. 2000, especially Chapters 2 and 3 and pp. 195–8). Stacey et al. identify what they call *secular natural law teleology* (that is, uncovering natural laws and truths about reality and repeating the best way to deal with them) which corresponds to scientific management in organizations, a perspective which Van de Ven and Poole miss, a change approach whose objective is to kill change. *Rationalist teleology* corresponds to the approach which Van de Ven and Poole call simply teleology– choice and purposeful pursuit of goals. *Formative teleology* implies a movement towards maturity and corresponds to the lifecycle approach. *Adaptionist teleology* corresponds to evolutionary approaches. Here Van de Ven and Poole and Stacey et al. part company. Partly because of their emphasis on cause and effect, Stacey et al. neglect dialectical models, which are usually not considered to be telelogical as is the case in Van de Ven and Poole. Conflict of goals or evolutionary paths is not emphasized in Stacey et al.'s model. However, they do add a dimension which goes beyond Van de Ven and Poole's understanding and introduces the idea of *transformative teleology* – where the future is under perpetual construction by the process of movement itself, where micro-interaction constitutes transformative cause. In this view the tensions between identity and difference, continuity and transformation, the known and the unknown are perpetually simultaneously present, with paradoxical effects. It is this transformative understanding of teleology which underpins the efforts of complexity theory to build more subtle and sensitive forms of systems theory in order to explain the same sorts of problem with which Van de Ven and Poole struggle (for a diagrammatic summary of the typology see Stacey et al. 2000: 52–3).

We could therefore expand Van de Ven and Poole's model to include six approaches to the change process – scientific or natural law approaches; formative approaches; adaptationist approaches; rational choice approaches; dialectical approaches; and transformative/ postmodern approaches. This disrupts the workings of the Van de Ven and Poole two-by-two matrix, but represents the main narratives of change more comprehensively and takes into account the more philosophically informed arguments of Stacey et al.

In the next section we will discuss the development of systems theory, and look at how complex adaptive systems theory and chaos theory have developed in relation to it.

From systems and causes to complexity and chaos

Open systems theory

Before going any further, it is necessary to look at the incorporation of *open systems theory* into organization theory, another importation from biology originated by Ludwig von Bertallanfy and developed into the form of a general systems theory which could apply to a variety of models. Where mechanical or machine-based models of organization had tended to see the organization operating in terms of the best way to perform a particular function, without the method or the function being moderated by or in interaction with the environment, the biological or organismic model saw the system as being open, both internally and externally. An open system therefore was constantly in transaction with its environment, with inputs from the environment undergoing transformation processes and being produced as outputs back into the environment, upon which they had an impact which affected the next set of environmental inputs into the organization. The internal parts of the organization were also inputting into each others' activities, and adjusting to them as necessary. An open system has several characteristics:

- *Embeddedness* – any system is located within a wider system and alongside other subsystems, much as the human body has an immune system, digestive system and so on. Each subsystem forms part of the internal environment for the other systems. In organizations, for example, the human resources subsystem interfaces with all the other subsystems, while parts of a production line may only interface with those systems feeding product into them and those into which they feed product which has been further processed.
- *Negative entropy* – there is normally a finite amount of energy in any system and this is gradually used up in the system's normal operations, so the system

must transact with the environment in order to replace this energy and obtain additional resources to grow. Transactions are not without cost or risk, however, and most organisms are vulnerable when they seek to take in resources (feeding) or reproduce (change). Survival depends on the transactions with the environment being favourable.

■ *Homeostasis* – or equilibrium seeking. This means that the system, rather like the human system which regulates temperature, when finding deviant conditions affecting one part of the system can make changes in other parts to restore the balance of the system as a whole. The system thus preserves a steady state over time while accommodating partial change.

■ *Boundedness* – systems are defined by boundaries, both internal and external. Internal boundaries regulate the components of the system and differentiate them from each other, while the external boundary or boundaries differentiate the organization from the larger environment and filter and regulate the flow of information, energy and materials between the two. The functions which operate the boundary, scanning it and responding to it, act as a 'maintenance envelope' (see Figure 13.2).

■ *Feedback* – specific loops of information relate to the quality and quantity of outputs into the environment and enable adjustments to be made to inputs (which may be of the wrong quality) and transformation processes (which may display error).

■ *Equifinality* – systems may reach the same end by a variety of means, and different configurations are possible. There may even be parallel subsystems in operation – some animals like the clown-fish of Australia's Great Barrier Reef are capable of changing sex repeatedly when necessary according to the needs of the species population.

■ *Cyclical* – many actions of systems are repetitive and patterned, and tend to occur in sequences of input, throughput (transformation) and output. Revenues from the production of outputs need to be collected and recycled to make purchases to fund further production of outputs and payment of costs; system maintenance needs to be regularly scheduled; wider environmental cycles (for example summer holidays) need to be accommodated.

Figure 13.2 shows an organization as a simplified open system. Note that the systems are not necessarily the functional or departmental configurations which

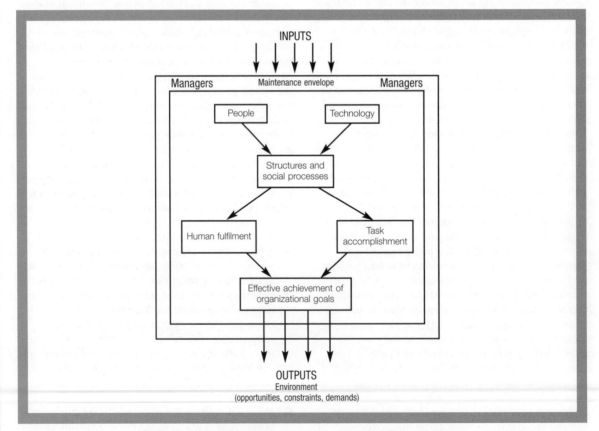

Figure 13.2 The organization as an open system

Source: Roger Plant (1987) *Managing Change and Making it Stick,* London: Fontana Collins, p. 99.

may be represented on the organization chart, but are often better represented in terms of the process characteristics of cognate groupings – people, technology, structures and so on. Seeing the organization in systems terms, even in such a simplified form as this, influenced the development of contingency theories, which we will discuss later in this chapter, and had an impact on organization development. Indeed, for both practitioners and academics, the idea of an open system, although not necessarily in all its ramifications, had become common sense by the 1990s. After the Gulf War, even the US military declared that the battlefield was an 'open system'.

Complex adaptive systems theory

A development of general systems theory, pioneered by Walter Buckley (1968; see also Morgan 1986) and drawing on cybernetics and information theory, complex adaptive systems theory looked at the working of systems which appeared to be able to change their character, often radically, in order to survive. In the sciences, the examination of the behaviour of organisms and systems which had moved far from equilibrium, to a point where homeostasis was no longer possible, offered some relevant insights into the behaviour of organizations that could completely change their character and sphere of operations in order to perpetuate themselves. In the social sciences, the work of Thomas Kuhn (1962) on scientific revolutions and paradigm shifts also had some relevance, and the idea that neither incremental progression nor cyclical shifts fully accounted for the varieties of change found in organizations was increasingly accommodated.

Buckley's (1968) complex adaptive systems have certain characteristics, or abilities, that distinguish them from more simple open systems:

- *Plasticity or irritability* – the system is constantly in motion, carrying on an interchange with environmental events, both acting on and reacting to them.
- *Requisite variety* – a source of mechanism for variety, to act as a potential pool of adaptive variability to meet the problem of mapping new or more detailed variety and constraints as the environment changes. According to Ashby's law of 'requisite variety', the variety within a system must

be at least as great as the environmental variety against which it is attempting to regulate itself, as only variety can regulate variety. This involves the inculcation and toleration of non-pathological deviance – error and chance – to generate variety. Error and variety are key elements in evolutionary change and hierarchical systems need to deliver freedom in order for them to work.

- *Selection criteria* – for choosing between those elements in the 'variety pool' that most closely map the environment and those that do not. This requires greater and greater flexibility of structure, what Weick calls 'loose–tight' properties, as the more rigid, traditionalistic means of addressing problems and seeking goals are replaced by mechanisms which monitor and adjust only to error (that is, cybernetic processes of control). This essentially requires *a new view of hierarchy*, where hierarchies emerge from the properties of power order systems in order to regulate pathological error, rather than being imposed in advance and top-down.
- *Learning* – or an arrangement for preserving and propagating the most successful mappings.
- *Autopoeisis* – in particular, Buckley notes that complex adaptive systems are not just open to the environment but are internally open, with feedback loops between their parts. Interchange among their components may result in significant changes in the nature of the components themselves. True feedback control loops make possible not only self-regulation, but *self-direction* or autopoeisis. Greater refinement and accuracy in mapping, decoding and encoding the external environment and the systems' own internal characteristics deliver greater independence from the physical environment.
- *Morphogenesis* – in adaptation to changing environments, the system may change or elaborate its structure as a condition of survival or viability – it may change its shape completely. An organism must not be identified with any one of its particular structural arrangements at any point in time, and therefore as well as structure-maintaining elements it also requires a *structure-elaborating* element. This involves a greater elaboration of self-regulating substructures in order to restructure purposely the system without destroying it, rather than simply restoring lost equilibrium (Exhibit 13.2).

Exhibit 13.2 **Simple yet complex**

Look up into the sky any spring day and complexity theory is easy to understand. A single bird on its own behaves simply, following basic rules such as when and where to eat. But when birds form a group their behaviour becomes different. As individual birds

interact, complex, unpredictable and creative behaviours emerge naturally.

We all know that the classic V-formation enables a flock of birds to cover great distances faster than any individual, and it is an efficient formation for jet fighters. Such a flock is a complex adaptive system. Three simple rules apply to becoming and remaining a member of a flock – avoid colliding with others; avoid falling behind; and stay close together laterally. Following these rules leads to a complicated group of birds flying with the cohesion of a single bird – with the sort of speed and precision that aerobatics groups such as the US Navy's Blue Angels and the RAF's Red Arrows can only strive to emulate.

What can managers learn when complexity theory is applied to organizations? Creativity and efficiency – terms often seen as opposites (creativity involves waste) – emerge together naturally in organizations. There is therefore no need for managers to control or impose models and methods on their employees. Given some basic ground rules, managers should encourage interaction, communication and learning among their employees. Solutions will then emerge, but managers won't know in advance what they will be – an approach that offends 'planners'. But just as the performance of a flock of birds is more than the sum of its parts, so is the performance of a group of enthusiastically interacting people.

The current climate of business in which Internet-enabled business ecosystems and the landscapes within them are changing rapidly is ripe for complexity theory, according to Roger Lewin and Birute Regine (see Santosus 1998). Despite the fact that there is no simple definition of complexity theory, it can be defined as the opposite of the mechanistic, linear, simple cause and effect way which is typical of the traditional business view of the world – one which offered predictability. Complexity theory, on the contrary, regards these systems as organic, non-linear and holistic and guided by three simple rules:

1. Managers should attend to relationships at all levels within their organizations.
2. Small changes can have large effects (for better or worse).
3. Interesting and unpredictable properties can be expected to emerge from a system, so it is hard to implement a strategic plan for anything but the short term. A desired direction can be set but not the ultimate goal (Lewin in Santosus 1998).

It is sometimes felt that complexity theory subordinates human relationships to mathematical models, but this is not the case. As Regine argues, underlying principles found in nature, such as emergence, apply to human organizations.

In computer models based on complexity theory, when autonomous agents interact and mutually affect one another, patterns will emerge – an intrinsic order just waiting to unfold. But it comes about in a non-linear way, so the order can't be predicted. When we translate computer models into human terms, the autonomous agents are people and the interactions among them are relationships. Complexity theory underscores the importance of *relationships* (Regine in Santosus 1998).

In other words, how people relate to one another affects what emerges in the organization – culture, creativity, productivity, efficiency and so on. The relational level is paramount for a growing and creative organization, which will depend on the answers to such questions as: Can people be honest with one another? Is there enough trust? Do people acknowledge each other and credit the good work they do? Where relationships are the bottom line, care and connection are palpable. Where these qualities are not simulated 'people are more willing to change and are more adaptable because they feel they're not alone and that together they can manage almost anything' (Regine in Santosus 1998).

Lewin and Regine argue that the traditional model of business is upside down. It is more effective 'to allow solutions to problems to emerge from the people close to the problem rather than to impose them from higher up' (Lewin in Santosus 1998). Indeed control cannot be imposed from higher up in such a system because rather than the macro-level being dominant, in complexity theory 'the most powerful processes happen at the micro-level – the people, relationship dimension' (Regine in Santosus 1998).

In order to kick-start these creative processes, Lewin and Regine recommend that managers start small, experiment, include others and promote a 'just try it' environment.

In short, set up a few simple rules, then let go. Small successes will encourage other people to start pilot projects, and a comfort with change will catch on.

Complex adaptive systems can work in three states:

1. *the stable zone:* here the company is in a state of inertia, not responding to opportunities or adapting to changes. But stability is not something to seek because it leads to an unresponsive system.
2. *the chaotic zone:* here the organization is bouncing off the walls, haphazard, led by events rather than choices and overreacting.
3. *the creative zone:* the place to be – not so stable that very little changes, nor so unstable that everything falls apart. Here there is much fluctuation – highs and lows keep occurring and paradoxes keep emerging. But paradox is the stuff of modern manangement, for as Lewin says:

'Leaders in complex adaptive systems need to be strong and have vision, yet they also need to be comfortable managing with a hands-off approach. Also, companies may know the direction in which they're moving, but they don't know exactly where they will end up. Creativity emerges from tolerating such ambiguity.'

From complexity to conversations

Complex adaptive systems theory and complexity theory are often associated with another approach which emphasizes the non-linear development of systems, that of *chaos theory* or *chaordics* (Fitzgerald 2002; Fitzgerald and Van Eijnatten 2002). The differences in approach between chaos and complexity have been summarized by Goldberg and Markóczy (2000) in Table 13.4. In summary, it might be said that complexity theory looks at the order and pattern emerging from complexity and apparent disorder; chaos theory looks at the tendency of all simply ordered systems to cumulate, recombine and break down in complex ways. Put together, there is a picture of the simple emerging from the complex, and the complex emerging from the simple, in constant change.

All types of systems theory, even complex adaptive systems, have problems in defining what the systems' boundaries are and this can lead to a tendency to reify the system. This is more of a problem when applied to social systems, in that issues such as free will and individuality tend to become system properties rather than individual properties. Social systems are living systems and as a result include what systems theory would call *hierarchical control programmes*, which in this case would include political, cultural and ethnic systems. These proscribe and delimit the areas into which behaviour, both creative and adaptive, will be allowed to evolve. Such cultural change then is never adequately dealt with by systems theories of any sort. Nevertheless, approaches to change based on chaos and complexity theory come much closer to recognizing this than earlier theories. It is in the study of the kinds of creative variety or novelty that are allowed or even cultivated by cultural, social or organizational systems, where clues to the future shape of organizations may be found (Chia and King 1998). For Robert Chia (1999) this approach is a *rhizomics* of change, following the work of philosopher Gilles Deleuze; Pat Kane

(forthcoming; http://www.theplayethic.com accessed 1 March 2003), another commentator influenced by Deleuze, thinks of it as the *play* which the system allows – which he argues requires the move from a work ethic to a play ethic.

Louise Fitzgerald (2002) identifies five principles of chaos thinking which differentiate it from the common assumptions of materialism, reductionism, determinism, mechanism and conservatism (maintenance of equilibrium) in scientific approaches to social and organizational change. *Consciousness*, which is also stressed by Stacey et al. (2000) and Hugo Letiche (2000) in his *phenomenal complexity theory*, argues that mind, rather than matter, represents the fundamental ground state of the universe – which is to say that meaning should be sought in the organization and relationships between elements of the universe or in their awareness of each other, rather than their physical properties. *Connectivity* emphasizes that no thing or event can exist independently of any other, and that holistic approaches need to be taken to events, paying attention to how characteristics of the whole system are inscribed in and can be generated from micro-interactions (holons). *Indeterminacy* observes that the universe is so dynamically complex that links between cause and effect are instantly obscured, meaning that outcomes of such relations are unknowable in advance and error is the norm, rather than the exception. *Emergence* notes that the trajectory of being is towards ascending orders of differentiation, coherence and complexity but that this leads to *dissipation* – the cycle of falling apart and recombination in new and novel ways which break with past forms of organization. Surrendering to emergence and falling apart 'gracefully' are traditionally what organizational systems are set against, and are now what they must learn to do (Fitzgerald 2002: 355).

Stacey et al. (2000) develop these insights to assess the connections between abstract relationships and concrete change in organizations. They come up with

Table 13.4 Chaos and complexity compared	
Chaos	Complexity
How complex things arise from simple systems	How simple things arise from complex systems
Simple non-linear systems lead to extremely complicated behaviour	Simple interactions of many things (often repeated) lead to higher level patterns
How to recognize, describe and make meaningful predictions from systems that exhibit that property	How a system that is complicated can lead to surprising patterns when the system is looked at as a whole
Uses reductionist analysis, explaining phenomena in terms of simpler entities or things already explained and the interactions between them	Uses reductionist analysis explaining macro-level phenomena directly in terms of the most basic elements without resource to intermediate levels
Source: After Jeffrey Goldberg and Livia Markóczy (2000) 'Complex rhetoric and simple games', *Emergence*, **2**(1): 72–100.	

some practically useful observations which we will summarize here. First, abstract relationships may display *different kinds of dynamic quality in different conditions*. Dynamics are 'patterns of repetitive interaction in which people get "stuck" and patterns of spontaneous, creative relationship in which the possibility of transformation arises' (Stacey et al. 2000: 192). Second, abstract relationships appear to have an intrinsic capacity for self-organization and produce emergent patterns of coherence, independent of external intervention. In other words, *order arises in organizational life without the reliance on top-down planning or strategic intent*. Third, abstract relationships produce novelty only when these relationships are between diverse entities and in the presence of fluctuations. Although success is most often associated with uniformity and consistency, *diversity and irregularity are not the enemies of success but the source of innovation and creative evolution* (see for example Calori 2002; Linstead 2002; O'Shea 2002; Wood 2002). Fluctuations in the environment should therefore be sought out as the source of change rather than screened out as interference so that future developments can be anticipated. Fourth, abstract relationships produce change that is *inherently paradoxical*, being both predictable and unpredictable, known and unknown, stable and unstable, capable of measurement and immeasurable at the same time. Finally, as abstract relationships produce emergent change that is radically unpredictable – novelty – *people in organizations must continue to act although the best they can hope for is to come to know and discover what they are doing*.

What emerges from this is that this process of coming to know proceeds through dialogue, communication and conversation as relationships configure (Ford and Ford 1995; Ford et al. 2002). It assumes that human action is best understood from within that action and participation in the change process. Interventions in change therefore involve recognition of the various voices in conversation, the metaphors and symbols in use and the narratives and stories unfolding, bringing these qualities into awareness and widening their diversity so as to enrich the conversation and increase its potential for generating novelty (see Boje 2000 for an example of the application of phenomenal complexity theory and narrative analysis to the Disney organization). This approach should recognize that formal models do not generate action in conformance, and that language does not communicate pre-organized thought, but that organization and thought take place in language and symbols, in the very back and forth, side to side, rhizomatic movement of the process of a multi-voiced conversation. It should also, as Stacey et al. (2000: 175–6) point out, recognize that this communicative process also involves the signalling and formation of power relationships. Language, in orienting users towards the world, also expresses the social configurations of power. Thinking, as a product of the engagement with the concrete world in language, is therefore always already embedded in and partially formed by power relations. Opening up these relations through widening the range and scope of language and conversation is essential if change is to avoid their hidden determining capacity. This has much in common with the narrative approaches we have associated with postmodernism throughout this book.

MORGAN MOTOR COMPANY – 2

In the late 1980s the Morgan Motor Company was the oldest privately owned car manufacturer still in existence in the world, and the roles of Peter Morgan, the founder's son, and his son Charles were therefore critical to the company's development. John Harvey-Jones formed the opinion that the company needed to determine the demand for the car in its various markets, stop being production-led, and think about the consequences of the US market opening up if their clean-burn emission control modifications were successful. Second, they needed to think about the quality of information flow in the company, particularly with regard to the high levels of stock (and hence money) they had tied up in the operation. Finally he suggested that they needed to do a thorough re-evaluation of the way the car was made, with the involvement of a consultant to show them how the most modern technology could help them. Overall, he suggested that they needed to go for radical change, to double production, rather than their plans for incrementally increasing production, and one rationale for that was that attitudes and culture would be so hard to change that any level of change would be problematic, and the company might as well grasp the nettle.

The relationship between Peter and Charles was critical, and seemed to change. Peter's experiences of empty order books and the company almost going out of business in the 1960s made him cautious. Charles was more ambitious for the company but nevertheless ambivalent: on the one hand, he wanted to capitalize on demand, thought the company could double in size, had plans to bring in air tools and computerized stock control, wanted more R&D on the car and had ideas to market Morgan-branded clothing and accessories; on the other, he was still feeling his way and was reluctant to confront his father – for whom he had great and genuine respect – on resolving the dilemmas the company faced, such as new versus old methods, comput-erization versus the personal touch, the waiting list as unsatisfied demand versus the waiting list as insurance policy. Above all, Peter seemed to dominate Charles at times and reminded him that the head of the Porsche car company had said that fathers found businesses which are consolidated by their sons and ruined by their grandsons, which clearly worried him. They didn't seem to discuss ideas of strategy together at other times, and neither seemed to want to say anything that would upset the other one.

Harvey-Jones was pugnacious in his challenges to the company, and they reacted defensively. Indeed Charles became most conservative and defensive of his father's company. They rejected the idea that demand was much of a problem by arguing that it is cyclical not consistent; but they didn't know the features of the cycle as it was a hunch. They had a keen and loyal workforce but everyone was very conservative and change-averse, and as the main bottleneck was in the sheet metal shop where it takes four years to train a new recruit, any change to production

would be medium to long term. Peter Morgan, however, argued that it was space that was the constraint, not the use of space – but they rejected any advice on how space might be used better. In the end, they rejected, prevaricated or temporized over Harvey-Jones's views and his offers to broker specialist advice for them. Peter Morgan retired as managing director on the Friday of his 70th birthday, but was back at his desk on the following Monday as chairman and chief executive. Charles remained production director.

Source: Adapted from the Morgan Motor Car Co. case in John Harvey-Jones (1990) *Troubleshooter,* London: Penguin Books, pp. 99–126, and subsequent material from John Harvey-Jones (1993) *Troubleshooter 2,* London: Penguin Books, pp. 202–4. The company website (http://www.morgan-motor.co.uk, http://autozine.kyul.net/html/Morgan.htm, accessed 26 February 2003; and BBCi reports).

MORE QUESTIONS ON THE CASE

4 Will Morgan ever change? Where do you see potential pressures coming from?

5 Are there any potential leverage points in the company that might energize change?

Contingency theories

These offer an adaptation of systems theory to organizational change, which emphasizes choice and internal factors in the organization and argue that the best way to organize depends on the circumstances. Contingency theories set themselves the objective of identifying as many relevant internal and external variables as possible, and achieving 'best fit' between organization and environment so that all the elements are aligned, or congruent. Contingency theory emphasized the nature of the task, the structure of the organization, the human factors and the technology involved, but within these broad categories there was much work done to classify features. Environments were also similarly classified. The classic work of Burns and Stalker (1961) on mechanistic and organic forms, for example, indicated the importance of organizational design to a firm's ability to innovate and adapt to a turbulent environment. At Harvard, Paul Lawrence and Jay Lorsch (1967) pioneered the investigation of integrating and differentiating functions within the organization, and the extent to which organizations could either be too well integrated to respond to the environment, or too differentiated to pull together coherently when the environment became more diverse. Contingency theory was associated with systems theory, and placed emphasis on environmental scanning processes, boundary spanning and management, and alignment of organizational subsystems with different parts of the environment. In

the UK the Aston theorists, who included Derek Pugh, David Hickson, John Child, Bob Hinings, Royston Greenwood, Diana Pheysey and Lex Donaldson at different times from the mid-1960s to the mid-1980s, made, inter alia, an important contribution in introducing the concept of power to contingency models through the consideration of the means of determining the relative power of organizational subunits, and the extent to which contingencies were as much a matter of strategic choice exercised within environmental constraints as of 'best fit' determined by constraints. Currently, the Burke–Litwin contingency model, which has been used very publicly with major corporations such as British Airways and the BBC, shown as Figure 13.3 and discussed extensively and applied by John Hayes (2002), embodies the typical strengths and weaknesses of the approach.

Burke and Litwin (1992) locate their model within and in interaction with an environment characterized as in a dynamic relation with individual and organizational performance (output). They argue that feedback from the environment (input) does not directly affect the whole organization, at least not at first, but works through a series of causal links and chains, beginning with its impact on leadership, mission and strategy, and organizational culture. Burke and Litwin incorporate the distinction between transformation and transaction that we saw in Chapter 10 on leadership. Indeed, the tight link between these three factors in relation to the environment and organizational performance makes them the *transformative* factors. Change in the other

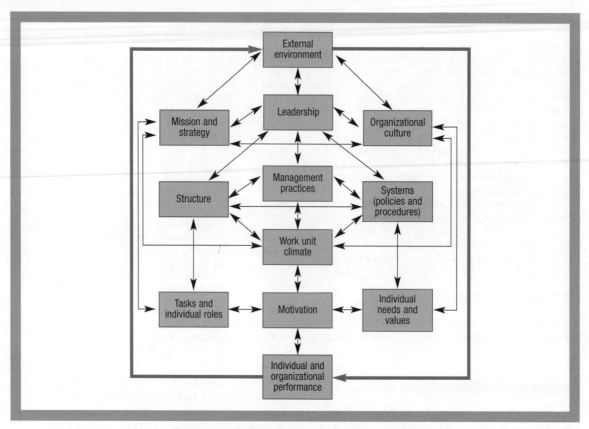

Figure 13.3 The Burke–Litwin model

Source: Reprinted from *Journal of Management* **18**(3): 528, Warner Burke and G.H. Litwin (1992) 'A causal model of organizational performance'. Copyright, with permission from Elsevier.

levels may be necessary to carry through change fully, but without change in these three factors, major system transformation will not be possible. As the links are followed, influence is two-way, but there is a hierarchy in place which can be summarized as 'don't start at the bottom to change the top'. Similarly, Figure 13.3 reveals that changing the structure of the organization would not be a good way to change the culture, and that structure is not transformative but *transactional*; but we noted in Chapter 3 how often theorists and practitioners mistake structural elements for culture ones and change the wrong things!

Contingency models have been popular with organizational development (OD) practitioners as they tend to generate questionnaire items corresponding to the boxes and items they contain, which provides a means of collecting initial data in the diagnosis phase of a change initiative. Hayes (2002: 98) gives an example of data collected with the Burke–Litwin model from the BBC which enabled the identification of problem areas with leadership, structure and motivation, and issues to be dealt with under task, climate, culture, management

actions and responsiveness to the environment. However, the model does not include, for example, specific areas of concentration on information systems (or information and knowledge management) or organizational politics, except where these are reduced to properties of individual behaviour. It may be countered that these variables have not been established in the way that the others have, and of which Burke and Litwin give a comprehensive account of the literature, to be causally related to the other variables. This then tends to reinforce the scepticism with which such models might be approached – not only are managers concerned about these issues, but across the social sciences, power and knowledge are recognized as being at the very heart of social organization, and an approach to organizations which ignores or decentres these issues can hardly perform a critical function; neither can it analyse organizational change in any great depth, nor with much sense of the reality of managers' lives.

The problems identified with contingency approaches typically include the fact that they do not tackle the historical and political dimensions of change, as we have seen, and indeed may incorporate a hidden unitary ideology. Second, despite the fact that contingency theories urge choice on the organization, they make no attempt to provide a typology of change *strategies* and conditions for their use during the actual process of organizational change. In what follows, we will backtrack a little to look at some of the foundational approaches to the practice and process of organizational change itself; we will then move on to see how the problems of politics and history are addressed by approaches known as *contextual* and *processual approaches*; finally considering how that of typology has been addressed by Dexter Dunphy and Doug Stace (1990) in their consideration of change strategies and their appropriateness to different change situations.

Managing the change process

Sources of change

While we have emphasized earlier that recent theories of change have argued that it is continuous and clear beginnings and ends are easily identified, traditional approaches to change have found it useful to recognize particular sources of change.

External forces of change may include:

- *social* – rising levels of education, an ageing population, changing expectations and roles of women, consumer preferences, work/life balance
- *economic* – changes in oil prices, interest rates, recession, failure of financial markets, exchange rate fluctuations, IMF policies
- *technological* – computing advances, robotics, manufacturing systems, networking improvements, faster communications (for example broadband), ability to access and process more information (knowledge acquisition and management)
- *market* – competition, new products, pricing policies, changing tastes, globalization of markets, politics (for example WTO, wars)
- *political/legislative* – privatization of the public sector, public–private partnerships, industrial relations reform, tariff policies and changes, deregulation of banks and financial markets, policies on affirmative action.

Internal forces which often trigger change include:

- increasing operational costs, waste or rework
- increasing absences, sickness reports or accidents
- increased employee turnover
- employee discontent manifest in grievances or industrial action
- loss of orders or declining sales
- missed delivery dates

- customer complaints
- appointments not kept, messages not received or returned
- tasks incomplete or agreed actions not followed up
- decisions postponed or never made
- suppliers not paid, invoices not issued or concerns raised by financial or quality audits
- failure to meet performance targets.

More broadly, change could be seen to be an effect of the natural lifecycle of an organization, or as a result of pressures for growth. The lifecycle view tends to see the organization as subject to natural forces of growth and decline, moving through stages. The growth approach argues that as the passage from stage to stage occurs, it involves responding to crises which stimulate negentropic growth and thus renew the life of the organization against decline. A simple lifecycle would involve *infancy* (fast-paced start-up, aggressive and entrepreneurial; non-hierarchical, informal and dominated by founder's personality; few procedures and rules); *adolescence* (too big for direct control by founder; professional managers appointed; systems introduced; conflict between subsystems begins to emerge, but pace still fast); *maturity* (end of relative stability and fast growth; sales and profits stabilize; goals shift to long term; plans understood and accepted); *middle-age* (focus shifts to how people do things, process; rituals become important; organizational politics emerge to the forefront as managers struggle with each other, not their competitors; personal survival paramount as scapegoats are sought for failure); *old age* systems become the end not the means; analysis paralysis; reactive or inert rather than proactive; defensive, fatalistic; no one takes risks or responsibility). Of course, in reality it may be that different lifecycles are operating in different parts of a complex organization, even across different products.

The classic approach to phases of growth and change was developed by Larry Greiner (1972/1998), as depicted in Figure 13.4 which relates in part to the traditional lifecycle model but identifies means of reversing it. The phases of growth are:

- *Growth through creativity* – The early growth of an organization is driven by the creative energies of its founder or founders. Procedures tend to be informal and organizational structure loose. This growth phase may come to an end when the founders find themselves unable to handle the requirements (for example operations or personnel) of a growing company (see Eric Flamholtz's excellent *Growing Pains* for a study of this phenomenon). This results in a *crisis of leadership*.
- *Growth through direction* – This crisis can be resolved by introducing greater formalization

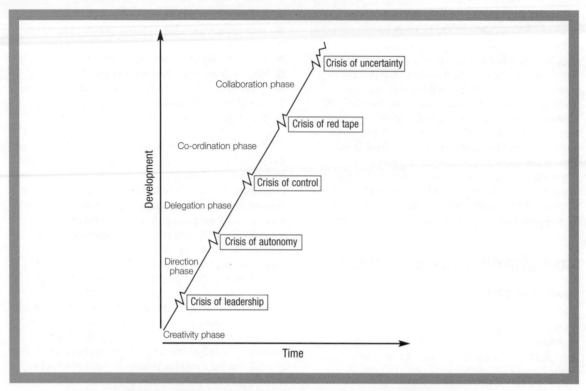

Figure 13.4 Larry Greiner's growth cycles approach

Source: Adapted and reprinted by permission of *Harvard Business Review*. From 'Evolution and revolution as organizations grow' by L.E. Greiner, May/June 1998, p. 58. Copyright © 1998 by Harvard Business School of Publishing Corporation. All rights reserved.

through the appointment of professional administrators/managers and consequent restructuring. This results in the creation of more bureaucracy, programmes, divisions and structure into the organization, creating a new phase of growth. Whether this growth is efficient and effective depends on the quality of its management. Eventually, however, such managers may demand greater self-direction in the form of more control over their operations or divisions. If resisted, this can result in a *crisis of autonomy*.

■ *Growth through delegation* – This crisis can be resolved by delegating powers to lower level managers in the organization, freeing senior managers to concentrate on longer range planning, and inducing a new phase of organizational growth, often via further restructuring. However, this may result in different sections of the organization pulling in different directions and threatening the unity and cohesion of the company, resulting in a *crisis of control*.

■ *Growth through coordination* – This crisis can be resolved by establishing links between different sections and departments of the organization to improve communication and coordination, via

committees, projects, knowledge and information management initiatives and so on. However, the resulting growth may eventually be choked by a proliferation of coordinating mechanisms and programmes, resulting in a *crisis of red tape*.

■ *Growth through collaboration* – This crisis can be resolved by attempts at simplifying formal structures and teaching managers how to cope with situations and create synergies without creating structure, thus managing in conditions of greater ambiguity. Growth can occur in this phase as managers learn how to collaborate by placing greater reliance on informality, social norms and self-control instead of formal structures. As this works out and new opportunities emerge, the *crisis is emergent, but uncertain*.

The point here is that initiatives to deal with organizational sclerosis have the capacity to revitalize the organization and inject greater efficiency and pace, but they always come with a downside which cumulatively leads to the next sclerotic condition which needs to be tackled when it reaches crisis proportions. The point of specific change initiatives therefore could be to identify and anticipate the need for change before it becomes critical, which is the main reason why planned approaches to organizational change developed.

Planned change

Planned change is a deliberately designed movement occurring from one organizational state to another that has a commitment to producing a specified outcome. Most planned organizational change is triggered by the need to respond to new challenges or opportunities presented by the external environment, or in anticipation of the need to cope with potential future problems, for example legislation, new product development by a competitor or technological improvements. Planned change represents the intention to systematically and stepwise improve the operational effectiveness of the organization. Managing change involves two fundamental objectives:

1. modifying the behaviour of individuals within the organization
2. improving the ability of the organization to cope with changes in its environment.

Stages in a planned change programme

There are almost as many models of the stages in a planned change process as there are commentators on it. Earlier models ignored or downplayed the need to develop enthusiasm for the changes and pay attention to the human issues, but more recent attempts have attempted to remedy this. A composite representation of stages, drawing on several current models, looks like this:

1. Recognize the need for change (internal and external scanning)
2. Diagnose organizational readiness for change and likely effects (+ and –) on the organization's affected parts
3. Identify likely sources of resistance
4. Set overall goals and vision for change
5. Educate and enthuse people about the change, giving special emphasis to (3)
6. Get involvement
7. Identify specific change targets
8. Clarify and decide on specific change approaches/techniques
9. Implement change
10. Support change (pick up the disaffected early, re-energize the change agents)
11. Evaluate change.

The idea that change can move systematically from stage to stage is very difficult to achieve smoothly in practice, especially in complex and diverse organizations. Some groups and individuals will lag behind others, others may resist firmly for whatever reasons, some may require greater persuasion, education or support than others. A less specific and more flexible approach is grounded in a three stage approach based on force-field analysis, which could be said to be the basis of modern change management as it has developed over the past fifty to sixty years.

Force-field analysis

Force-field analysis is a diagnostic technique developed by Kurt Lewin (1947). Lewin (1951) developed a three-phase model of change, based on the premise that an understanding of the critical steps in the change process will increase the likelihood of the successful management of change. The steps in the process are:

■ *Unfreezing* – Recognizing the need for change, action is taken to unfreeze existing attitudes and behaviour, which is essential for supporting employees and minimizing resistance. Lewin's force-field analysis states that there are two forces in operation in any social system, those driving change, and those attempting to maintain the status quo, as illustrated in Figure 13.5. If these forces are of equal strength, they are in a state of equilibrium; to bring about change an organization needs to either increase the strength of the driving forces, decrease the strength of the resisting forces or ideally work on both simultaneously. If successful the organization moves into the next state of:

■ *Changing* – Moving the organization to the desired state involves the actual implementation of new systems of operation. This may involve experimentation, modification of systems or patterns of behaviour, technology or systems; may also be where people need to leave or new people join the company as the full nature of the transition emerges. Once the changes appear to have reached equilibrium once more, it is time for the process of:

■ *Refreezing* – The positive reinforcement of desired outcomes to promote the internalization of new attitudes and behaviours. An appraisal of the change programme becomes necessary at this stage – although not too soon – to ensure that the new way of operating becomes a matter of habit rather than regulation. In addition, if the change is proving successful, it will be reinforced by widely communicating the evaluation results.

Dawson (1994) observes that although Lewin's model is still used widely, there are some weaknesses with the approach. Augmenting Dawson, we could say that:

■ the model is a simple representation and, although

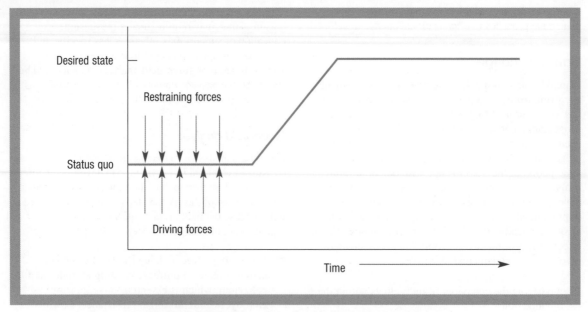

Figure 13.5 Kurt Lewin's force-field analysis

this can be a strength, presents a unidirectional, single path model of change.

■ there is emphasis on a stable state of refreezing, and therefore elements of complexity and change as a dynamic process are avoided.

■ structures and cultures may be formed that are not conducive to continuous change.

■ the change process is represented as rather mechanistic, something done to the organization rather than part of a learning process which may be facilitated, but is part of the normal process of organizing.

■ where the rapidly changing environment is a factor that requires a continuous acceptance and attitude for change, the planned model seems to be inappropriate. Contingency models are more appropriate for analysing change to 'understand the relationships among variables to deal effectively with different kinds and rates of environmental change' (Dawson 1986: 22).

Organization development (OD) as planned change

This approach is described by Morten Huse (1982: 555) as the 'application of behavioural science knowledge in a long-range effort to improve an organization's ability to cope with changes in its external environment and increase its internal problem-solving capabilities'. Based on the human relations perspective (see Chapter 11) which stresses collaborative management, Wendell

French and Cecil Bell (1983: 15) state that, the approach is 'a long-range effort to improve an organisation's problem solving and renewal processes – with the assistance of a change agent or catalyst and the use of the theory and technology of applied behavioural science'.

The features of the approach, as discussed by French and Bell (1983), can be summarized as:

■ The goal is to improve an organization's health and effectiveness.

■ The focus of the change effort is on the whole system (such as a division or organization).

■ Change is introduced systematically as a planned intervention.

■ Top-down strategies are applied, that is, change starts at the top of the organization and is gradually implemented downwards throughout the organization.

■ Employees at all organizational levels must be committed to the change.

■ Change is made slowly, allowing for continual assessment of change strategies.

■ Specialist change agents usually guide change programmes.

■ The organization development approach is interdisciplinary.

■ The objective is to achieve lasting rather than temporary change within an organization.

■ The approach can be used on 'healthy' and 'unhealthy' organizations.

As a systematic approach to managing the change process successfully, the process involves:

1. identifying the need for change
2. selecting an intervention technique
3. gaining top management support
4. planning the change process
5. overcoming resistance to change
6. evaluating the change process

which is a variant of the expanded model introduced earlier. The problem with this approach is that as an explicitly normative approach, it assumes that there is one best way to manage change that will increase organizational effectiveness and simultaneously achieve the well-being of employees. The approach does not account for revolutionary change, which is, according to Dunphy and Stace (1990), best managed by top-down coercive strategies of change (see later in this chapter).

Contextual and processual approaches

A *contexualist approach* acknowledges change as a dynamic process, and examines the context, content and process of change as being central to explanations of organizational transition (Clark et al. 1988; Pettigrew 1987). This approach moves away from the limitations of the systems and contingency approaches to change and:

- examines the processes of change within a historical and organizational context (Johnson 1987)
- has a multidisciplinary approach, drawing on a range of perspectives (Whipp et al. 1987; Clark et al. 1988)
- explores the processes of organizational transition (Child and Smith 1987), focusing on longitudinal qualitative data as a strategy and methodology (Pettigrew 1990) for understanding the complex and dynamic processes of change.

A weakness of the contexualist approach stems from the richness and complexity of a multi-level analysis, which can create barriers for the manager who seeks practical tools of action as well as for researchers seeking access (Buchanan and Boddy 1992). In order to address this weakness, Dawson (1994) develops a *processual* framework for analysing change that classifies the major determinants of change and locates these within a temporal framework moving from conception through transition to operation (see Figure 13.6). The determinants are:

- *The substance of change* – the type and scale of organizational change such as JIT, TQM and management information systems.
- *The politics of change* – the political activity of consultation, negotiation, conflict and resistance that occurs at various levels within and outside an organization during the process of managing change, such as government pressure, competitor alliance, shop-floor negotiations and so on. These influence decision making and the setting of agendas.
- *The context of change* – the past and present external and internal operating environments as well as the influence of future projections and expectations on current operating practice environments. Both internal and external contextual factors apply.

As Collins (1998: 75) points out, Dawson draws attention to the role which trade unions may play in change processes, which is hardly emphasized at all in the US literature but is more important in the UK, Europe, Australia and Canada, although variable in the rest of the world. However, Collins also argues that Dawson does not deliver what he promises, as in his attempts to translate and codify change factors for practitioners and managers, he loses the inherent complexity of these matters, and ends up producing a checklist of learning points which sounds very much like the guru-speak upon which his analysis was intended to advance.

Andrew Pettigrew and Richard Whipp (1993), with a similar intent to deliver practical relevance from the innate complexity of contextualism without oversimplification, identify five empirically derived central factors for managing change successfully (see Figure 13.7):

1. *Environmental assessment* – Organizations are required to become 'open learning systems', that is, strategies emerge from the way the company at all levels processes information about its environment.
2. *Leading change* – There are no clear rules, and leadership is sensitive to context. Leadership tasks are incremental and less dramatic than business press images, and involve linking action by people at all levels of the organization.
3. *Linking strategic and operational change* – Intentions are implemented and transformed over time. The cumulative effect of separate acts of implementation may be immensely powerful, and may supply a new context for future strategic action.
4. *Human resources as assets and liabilities* – A long-term learning process that requires ongoing positive development cycles of human resource management.
5. *Coherence in the management of change* – The coherence arises from the demands of the other

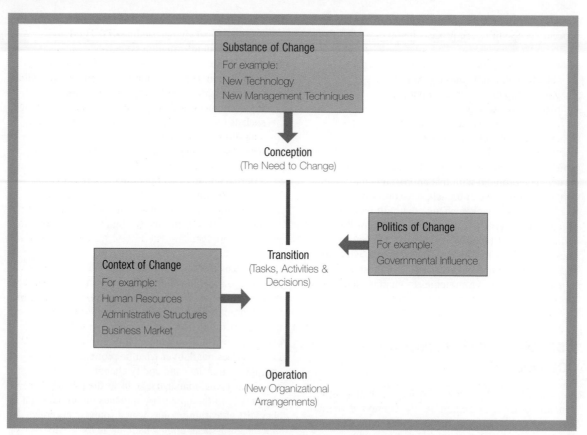

Figure 13.6 Organizational change – a processual framework

Source: Reprinted by permission of Sage Publications Ltd from Patrick Dawson,
Organizational Change, copyright © Sage Ltd 1994.

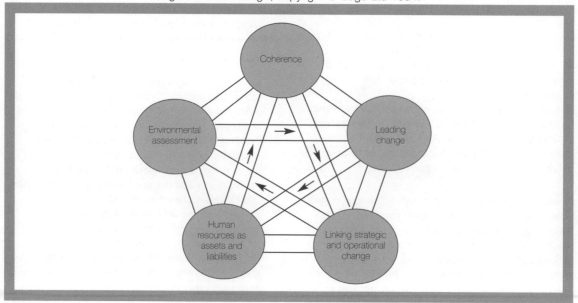

Figure 13.7 Managing change for competitive success: the five central factors

Source: Andrew Pettigrew and Richard Whipp (1993) *Managing Change
for Competitive Success*, Oxford: Blackwell, p. 6.

factors. Primary conditioning factors require reinforcing by a complementary set of mechanisms; these features react to the formation of strategy such as the consistency of goals, adaptive responses to the environment, maintenance for competitive advantage and feasibility so that insoluble problems are not created.

Contextualist approaches then have maintained the importance of internal and external environment found in contingency theory, but have problematized the concepts of both 'best fit' and 'choice'. Nevertheless, it is probably fair to see them as advancements in contingency theory rather than breaks from it. In a similar spirit of extending contingency theory, Dexter Dunphy and Doug Stace (1990) have attempted to explore the change process in terms of how organizations go about addressing the problem of adjusting to their environment, the styles available and the styles commonly in use.

They developed a matrix of possible change styles which varies according to the degree of collaborative involvement of those affected by change, or the style of change on the one hand, and the scale of the change initiative on the other (see Figure 13.8). Styles of change include coercive, directive, consultative and collaborative, while change encompasses fine-tuning, incremental adjustment, modular transformation and corporate transformation. The terms generate 16 possible combinations but Dunphy and Stace consider that these fall into four families or types of change approach – participative evolution, charismatic transformation, forced evolution or dictatorial transformation. Participative evolution would be typical of extensive collective bargaining arrangements as found in parts of Europe; charismatic transformation is characteristic of the large-scale 'culture change' models of the 1980s and 90s; forced evolution is typically entrepreneurial; and dictatorial transformation would be characteristic of crisis and turnaround.

Stace and Dunphy (1994) developed and related their model to specific and common types of change approach and conducted empirical research in Australia to explore which approaches were most common or experienced as most viable in the current environment and the directions of any changes in approach (see Figure 13.9).

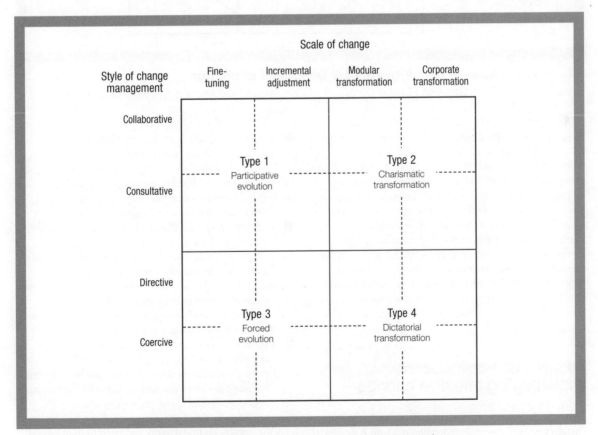

Figure 13.8 Four types of change strategies

Source: Dexter Dunphy and Doug Stace (1990) *Under New Management,* Sydney: McGraw-Hill, p. 82.

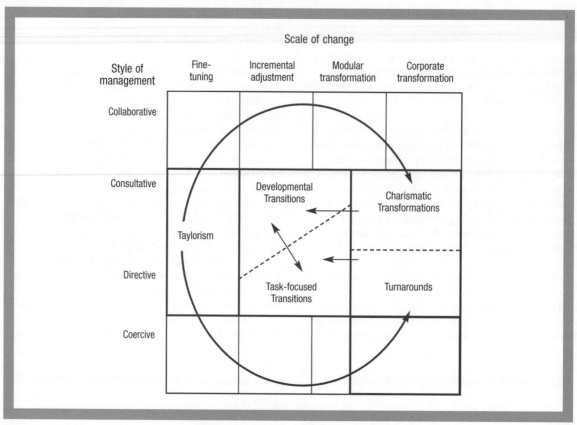

Figure 13.9 Directions of change

Source: Doug Stace and Dexter Dunphy (1994) *Beyond the Boundaries,* Sydney: McGraw-Hill.

First, they found that change styles concentrated along the two middle bands of directive and consultative, therefore being hybrid rather than paradigmatic, with the exception of turnarounds. Directive/consultative fine-tuning was targeted at bringing lower performers up to the mark, typical of Taylorism; directive/consultative incremental adjustment shaded into modular transformation and was targeted at medium to high performers, aiming to maintain alignment with or shape the competitive environment. The more consultative approaches would be developmental, process-oriented transitions, while the more directive ones would be task-focused transitions but both would be characterized by constant change.

Barriers and resistance to implementing effective change

There are two common barriers that influence the change process – *organizational inertia* and *hostility*. Adams (1987) outlines the following blocks to change caused by *inertia*:

- *Emotional blocks* occur when people feel threatened by change and fear the uncertainty associated with it. Avoidance behaviour and evasion are common when the need for changed is not acknowledged. Group-think encourages complacency and impairs people from evaluating their individual circumstances.
- *Cultural blocks* are the subtle ways in which our culture may be hostile to change. The ways of thought that promote effective change often involve factors like insight and irreverence towards the organization. Factors like humour can be helpful in disturbing the existing pattern, yet these may be regarded as frivolous and may be frowned upon in normal organizational exchanges.
- *Cognitive blocks* are the inability to use correct information and language. The nature of information transmitted to people who are affected by change is very important in terms of explaining the change processes to employees in an organization. Change managers require the qualities of empathy and flexibility, and need to explain the change in a clear and accessible manner.
- *Perceptual blocks* comprise people defining

problems narrowly; having an inability to see problems from more than one perspective; an inability to distinguish relevant information from all the information that is available; memories of bad experiences in previous change situations; while selective perception can mislead people into not being able to take in the relevant information about the problems which have acted as triggers to change.

■ *Environmental blocks* include lack of support and managers not accepting and acting on criticisms. In change circumstances, people are more likely to trust change managers if everybody can become involved and help to shape decisions.

Hostility occurs when individuals or groups of individuals fail to take on the change initiative, or some element of the change programme, and actively work to frustrate it. Despite the potentially positive outcomes, change is often resisted at both the individual and organizational level (Greiner 1992). Resistance to change, or the thought of the possible negative implications of the change, appears to be a common issue in change initiatives, since people are naturally suspicious of the unfamiliar. *Resistance* to change may take many forms. There are *overt* symptoms such as strikes, output restrictions and falling productivity, quality and so on, and sabotage of the change process. *Covert* forms include lateness, absence, falling morale, higher accident rate, loss of goodwill, lack of commitment and loss of creativity. Lewin identified two major psychological obstacles to change:

1. people are either unwilling or unable to alter attitudes or behaviour
2. people often revert to their traditional pattern of behaviour, so change only lasts a short time.

Resistance exists at both organizational and individual levels and needs to be worked through, not dismissed or defeated. The consequences of this suggest that change which is likely to be sustainable needs to be prepared carefully, with those affected being involved at the earliest stage possible, in order to give them time not only to adjust to but also to influence and own the change. Those who may be affected adversely by change need to be provided with some positive benefits, or helped to see some future advantages which the change will eventually deliver. If a win–win situation cannot be engineered, then losses for those who will suffer should generally be minimized. Communicating the change often and consistently is important but not enough. The second point indicates that change needs to be supported – the people affected need support, and the required resources need to be adequate, in order to make sure that the change is appropriate and sustainable in practice.

Resistance at an organizational level is often a result of the lack of an integrated approach to change. Many change initiatives fail to consider the simultaneous impact of change at all levels – organizational, group and individual. Even relatively small changes can have knock-on or symbolic effects far greater than any change intended, and surprising resistance can be produced. Indeed the emergence of OD, and the later culture change initiatives and complexity approaches, is a recognition of the existence of complex and difficult-to-capture chains of resistance, which need to be addressed holistically in order for their impact to be properly discerned. These resistances, although holistically based in such things as values and attitudes, may surface in different arenas according to the circumstances of change initiatives. Markus (1983, cited in Rollinson et al. 1998: 620) identifies four broad classes of resistance to change:

1. *People-focused* resistance that resides in individuals, due to their psychological differences such as attitudes, values and perceptions.
2. *System-focused* resistance arises because new systems can be complex and unfriendly to the user. If these are introduced without appropriate training and induction, users will be reticent about using them and hold onto the old systems.
3. *Organization-focused* resistance often occurs because new systems do not integrate well with the organization's structure, culture or technology, and one or other of these three organizational variables acts as an obstacle to change.
4. *Politics-focused* resistance emerges from the organization's power structure and also those external power structures in which the organization is embedded. Politics and power issues are an inevitable part of everyday working life, and if an individual or group is in danger of losing its power due to the introduction of new systems, there can be a great deal of resistance to change.

Psychological or *people-focused* resistance may occur at the individual or group levels, and at any hierarchical level in the organization. Essentially, when people experience change, even where there is a sense of positive expectation and anticipation, they experience loss – at its most rudimentary, a loss of the familiar, right through to the loss of something important or in which they believed. This loss will be experienced as shock, in its mildest form a sense of disorientation and in more extreme cases complete personal dysfunctionality. It may be expressed as a blow to one's personal competence, which may or may not be job-related, but is our sense of security and confidence in knowing what to do next in any set of circumstances. If circumstances change, our situational

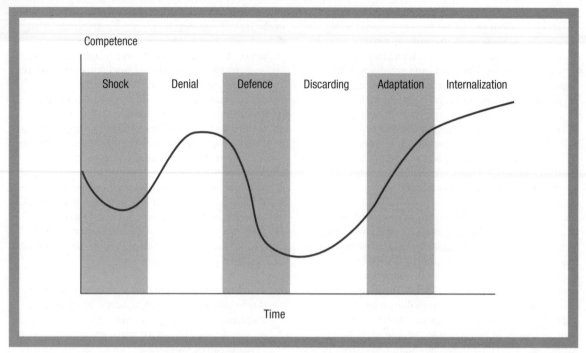

Figure 13.10 Stages of coping with trauma

competence is affected until we work out, discover or are told what to do next and learn how to act accordingly. This may also include our feelings and values – we don't know what to feel about changed relationships or how much to value them, as we may not be sure whether they will turn out to be the right ones or endure. Such psychological and emotional reactions do tend to follow a pattern familiar in studies of grieving and mourning, and although there is no predetermined period for each stage or the process overall, the typical stages are identified in Figure 13.10 and summarized below, although people will experience these stages with differing degrees of intensity:

- *Shock* or surprise, disbelief and, in extreme cases, panic and immobilization; a sense of being over-whelmed and an inability to act and feel normally.
- *Denial* of the need for change or validity of new ideas; group cohesiveness may increase, even evoking euphoria.
- *Defence* in relation to jobs, territory, practices, behaviour, norms etc; feelings of frustration and depression; articulations of ritualistic behaviours; provides the effect of creating time and 'space' to allow people to come to terms with the changes.
- *Discarding* or the process of letting go of the past: a gradual process of perception, starting with recognition; awareness that change is necessary or inevitable; understanding of existing 'incompet-

encies'; acceptance of new realities; awakening sense that present anxieties are too much to bear or the future not as forbidding as it first seemed; creates tensions; people feel disoriented and upset.
- *Adaptation* is when individuals begin to test the new system, experimenting with new behaviours, skills, standards; search for meaning, understanding and knowledge; practice phase; learning occurs; trying to do things differently; feedback of results; successes and failures; feelings of frustration, sometimes anger.
- *Internalization* means that once people go through the cognitive process of making sense of what has happened the new behaviour becomes part of 'normal' behaviour.

System and *organization-focused resistance* centres on the technical aspects of the change, and clashes with what exists in the present, but this type of resistance is also very much affected by the characteristics of the change process itself. The three characteristics most directly affecting resistance are:

1. *Pace of change:* The slower the process, the longer the time for questions to be asked and problems acknowledged, solutions negotiated, reassurances given and training provided. Radical changes may be accepted initially because of the pressure of a crisis, but resistance and resentment may appear

later as the change becomes consolidated. Timing is crucial and sensitivity to incidents may indicate that the time isn't right, even if the change itself is.

2. *Manner of change:* The need for change must be communicated clearly and fears must be confronted and if possible calmed. The creation of an appropriate atmosphere for change, the readying and motivation of individuals to accept the changes is essential. Acknowledging and discussing resistance is critical, as is the circulation of information and the communication of expectations, attitudes and behaviour.

3. *Scope of change:* the extent of the change will have a different impact on individuals, and whether the organization has sufficient awareness of the inevitable hidden and unintended changes requires consideration.

Politics-focused resistance emerges from the organization's power structure. Issues of power and political influence are an inevitable part of everyday organizational life, a consequence of differing interests and objectives. Where individuals or groups are in danger of losing power due to the introduction of new systems, or feel that new arrangements may put them at a material disadvantage, then resistance will emerge. In some cases it will be visible and collective, and may find its outlet through formal channels. Often this sort of resistance can emerge in advance of any threat, as groups jockey for position in order to be able to influence the direction of any change in their favour. Before implementation, resistors may stall with excessive fault finding or requests for further information, argue that the change has been tried before and did not work, attempt to link the discussion of change with pay or other matters or boycott meetings to discuss the project. When implementation occurs, resistors may refuse to use new systems, make no effort to learn how to perform under the new system or operate new machinery, use older systems whenever possible, refuse to release staff for training or cover for them, sabotage or misuse the system. Overt, covert or tacit political resistance similarly is not always in the form of management versus workers, as in most cases other departments and units have the opportunity to make suggestions and become involved on the particular form of implementation of the change. David Boddy (2002: 344–5) discusses the views of Peter Keen (1981) on *counterimplementation*. Keen argues that overt resistance may be risky and managers who want to subvert the implementation process have a number of options to do it more surreptitiously. These involve:

- diverting resources away from the change project, such as splitting the budget across other projects,

seconding key staff elsewhere, moving or sharing equipment
- exploiting inertia may involve suggesting that everyone wait for a key person's views or opinion or until everyone has made a response, or wait for evaluations of other projects
- goals can be kept vague or complex, generalized, grandiose or multidimensional
- lack of organizational awareness can be exploited, such as suggesting that certain issues can be left until later, knowing that these will be critical
- suggesting that the change is a good one and worth doing properly will involve so many people that the differing views or conflicting interests will never be sorted out or reconciled
- energies can be dissipated in conducting surveys, excessive data gathering, studies of other change events, report production or convening special meetings
- where change has a champion, then rumour and gossip can be used to damage his or her credibility
- finally, resistors can often work better by keeping a low profile and not presenting an easy target to those driving change.

David Buchanan (1999) argues that ongoing political action and strategies emerge from two interacting 'loops' of behaviour. Contextual factors involve organizational features, such as:

- falling margins in old business necessitating a change of strategy into new business areas
- stakeholder influence, including views of other managers and directors, salespeople, professional service people and team members
- and the narrator or initiator (champion) of change and his or her formal management responsibility for implementing the strategic change agenda.

These interactions produce a tacit warrant for political behaviour based on the subversive tactics of others. When this is put into action, what emerges is a formal warrant for the strategic change agenda, in other words, some agreement about what will really happen. As an outcome of ongoing change behaviours, there are *organizational outcomes* of implementing the change agenda and the successful or unsuccessful development of new business, and *personal outcomes* for those involved in accounting for action, where they become able to justify to themselves and others that political behaviour is reasonable and necessary in the context. In combination, these lead to the development of *reputation*, where the manager is seen to be effective, as one who gets things done and as a political player. Buchanan and Boddy (1992) and Buchanan and Badham (1999) explore in more detail the necessities of political behaviour in managing change, particularly for change agents, using many examples of actual change practices.

Managing and overcoming resistance to change

There are several specific approaches that management can consider when anticipating and responding to resistance to change (see Table 13.5). These include:

- *Education, support and training* – Training programmes need to be organized to provide knowledge, and allow employees to learn the new skills which are necessary for new systems. Counselling programmes may be necessary to help employees to cope with the stress created by change (especially those individuals whose jobs will change or those made redundant).
- *Participation and involvement* – Involvement and participation can be used to gain acceptance of change in organizations, to outflank resistance (see

Chapter 12) rather than using them only to deal with resistance to change (McCalman and Paton 1992).

- *Negotiation and agreement* – Negotiation helps management to establish change as a win–win process, rather than a win–lose process, and for employees to know what specific benefits change could bring to them. It is essential that those affected by change should not perceive the change processes as a 'give' and then 'give a bit more' situation on their part. It is important to avoid imposed solutions that only suit managers and to search for those solutions that are agreed and accepted by most employees – even those affected adversely should be helped to cope with the situation and not demoralized by it.
- *Manipulation and cooptation* – Manipulation implies distortion of information by emphasizing the advantages of change and disregarding its disadvantages. Cooptation refers to involving people who are key resistors in the decision-making process and making them part of the change decisions so that they alter their approach to change.

Table 13.5 Methods for dealing with resistance to change				
Approach	Involves	Commonly used when...	Advantages	Disadvantages
1 Education + communication	Explaining the need for and logic of change to individuals, groups, and even entire organizations	There is a lack of information or inaccurate information and analysis	Once persuaded, people will often help implement the change	Can be very time-consuming if many people are involved
2 Participation + involvement	Asking members of organization to help design the change	The initiators do not have all the information they need to design the change, and others have considerable power to resist	People who participate will be committed to implementing change, and any relevant information they have will be integrated into the change plan	Can be very time-consuming if participators design an inappropriate change
3 Facilitation + support	Offering retraining programs, time off, emotional support and understanding to people affected by the change	People are resisting because of adjustment problems	No other approach works as well with adjustment problems	Can be time-consuming, expensive, and still fail
4 Negotiation + agreement	Negotiating with potential resisters; even soliciting written letters of understanding	Some person or group with considerable power to resist will clearly lose out in a change	Sometimes it is a relatively easy way to avoid major resistance	Can be too expensive if it alerts others to negotiate for compliance
5 Manipulation + cooptation	Giving key persons a desirable role in designing or implementing change process	Other tactics will not work or are too expensive	It can be a relatively quick and inexpensive solution to resistance problems	Can lead to future problems if people feel manipulated
6 Explicit + implicit coercion	Threatening job loss or transfer, lack of promotion etc	Speed is essential, and the change initiators possess considerable power	It is speedy and can overcome any kind of resistance	Can be risky if it leaves people angry with the initiators

Source: Adapted and reprinted by permission of *Harvard Business Review*. From 'Choosing strategies for change' by John P. Kotter and Leonard A. Schlesinger, March/April 1979, p. 111. Copyright © 1979 by Harvard Business School of Publishing Corporation. All rights reserved.

- *Explicit and implicit coercion* – Sometimes management decides not to look for consensus, it simply makes decisions regarding change and announces the probability that redundancies or transfers will occur for those who cannot deal with change.

Making change durable

It would be unusual for an organization to embark on change without considering whether the change was likely to have long-term impact. Not all changes, of course, do this, as some are necessary to cope with short-term changes in the environment, such as peaks or troughs in sales. However, where the changes are likely to involve long-term changes in behaviour or attitude if they are to be considered successful, then it is important that change is not successfully resisted at an early stage, or rolled back easily by behaviours decaying or falling back into previous ways of working before the change has become the new norm. That is not to say that the questioning of the status quo at any time is not important, but that inertia should not constantly inhibit or subvert new initiatives.

In Figure 13.11 we consider the likelihood of change being durable at the overall system level which includes the political dimension; of behaviour change being sustained at an individual level; and of resistance occurring, plotted against the degree and timing of involvement in change and the motivational level to change associated with it. Of course, resistance to change may occur at any point in the process, partly because change initiatives and employment relations have a history which shapes people's attitudes and expectations; partly because the future is unknown. Even with early involvement and the best of goodwill, it cannot be guaranteed that there will be no resistance. However, Figure 13.11 is a useful indicator of how likely it is that resistance will definitely occur, how serious that resistance might be and how deeply embraced any change intervention might become. We have also made the assumption here that there is a difference between resistance and opposition – opposition being the expression of views dissenting from the change, which are at least open to discussion when overt. The overt resistance we incorporate in Figure 13.11 indicates when the willingness of those affected by change to entertain it as a possibility has evaporated and they act openly to challenge, oppose and derail it, for example in industrial action and strikes.

The top line of the continuum refers to the attitudes of those affected by the change, where particularly those driving the change and inspiring others to be committed to it need to be involved at its inception, while those responsible for carrying it through into implementation need to be involved, at the latest, shortly after. Beyond this point, the level of inspiration

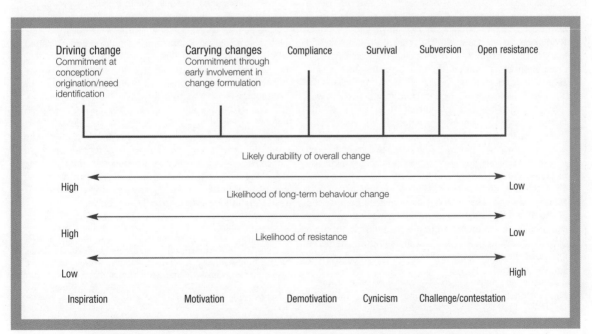

Figure 13.11 Involvement, motivation and durability of change

Source: Original but incorporating some elements of diagram in Roger Plant (1987) *Managing Change and Making it Stick,* London: Fontana/Collins, p. 23.

or motivation to change is likely to fall. With less involvement, ownership of the change diminishes and a neutral, compliant approach emerges, which may include a sense of 'doing what is necessary to survive'. If greater disaffection sets in, actual hostility to the change may take over, from subversion to open opposition. Motivationally, demotivation begins to set in with the compliance mentality, followed by cynicism, challenge and finally contestation. Moving from left to right, the likelihood of system change and behavioural change being durable diminishes, while the likelihood of resistance increases.

MORGAN MOTOR COMPANY – 3

In 2000, the new 160mph Aero 8 model stole the show in its class at several motor shows. John Harvey-Jones and his *Troubleshooter* production team revisited the factory and proclaimed it to be an outstanding success. *Autocar* magazine voted the Morgan Motor Car Company 'Specialist Manufacturer of the Year', saying: 'Morgan has transformed not only its product but, in the process, its business too.' In 2001, the company passed the milestone of 14 cars per week and its production was greater than at any time since the 1920s. By 2002, the company announced that waiting lists were down to 18 months and even resumed racing at Le Mans against the world's best, doing creditably although having to retire. What could have happened to the sleepy, old-fashioned company?

Before Harvey-Jones' last follow-up visit to the company, developments in the approval process for the clean-burn engine for the US market meant that Morgan looked likely to get approval, and although they would have a two-year probation period to devise better restraints or airbags, they had to anticipate greater demand. This seemed to galvanize Charles into some action. He enrolled for an evening course at Worcester Technical College to find out about modern manufacturing techniques and visit advanced factories. Production did not rise to a full ten cars a week, but he and Maurice Owen began to work on a plan that would increase production by a quarter by changing the layout and sequence, although Pete was still committed to incremental change. In 1992, when a second *Troubleshooter* series was made, Morgan refused to let Harvey-Jones revisit the factory. Morgan's own history notes of the visit that it 'caused quite a stir ... his conclusions were significantly at odds with the views held by the Morgan family, who said so ... [but the] programme had the effect of including hundreds of orders into the factory, and ironically is one of the principal reasons behind the extensive waiting list'. Peter Morgan has said that he spent three or four days on the phone after the programme was aired taking orders – every line into the company was busy! He continued to throw himself into his work – in 2000, at the age of 80, he had a hip replacement operation and was back at his desk only two weeks later.

Change was beginning to take place, however. Charles had introduced a manufacturing resource planning computer system into the factory, as he had intimated earlier, and enrolled on a course at Coventry University in modern manufacturing, leading to an MBA. Prices had begun to rise slightly in advance of inflation. On the technical side, engines were updated and new developments were trialled on the race track with the collaboration of a Morgan dealer, including an aluminium chassis. Aerodynamics emerged as a major limiting factor, and Charles went to the drawing board himself – or, by now, an impressive CAD/CAM system – and personally helped to design the shape of what was to be the new model. New aluminium superform wings were introduced as were airbags, all making the car more marketable. Production improvements also included a new paint shop, a major investment which used water-based paints. Output reached 11 cars per week from February 1999, when the yearly output of the factory had not been greater since before the war. With the arrival of a standard European Whole Vehicle Approval System, much work was undertaken to ensure all Morgan's cars complied. Most small manufacturers used, and still have to this day, a low volume exemption. With their reliance on export markets (approx. 50 per cent of sales), Morgan felt that they could not rely on this as a solution. As Morgan put it, the expertise gained in this development of the +8 model for the federal US market and the racing programme provided the backbone to the launch and development of the most exciting new product in the company's history – the award-winning, BMW-powered, aerodynamic sensation the Aero 8, which had 550 orders in its first six months. The production of this car required its own production line, the trim shop was extended, the repair shop modernized to free up more space, and the whole factory seemed transformed. They even had a website where you could find out about the company, buy Morgan merchandise, and even order your new Morgan for delivery – in only 18 months.

Source: Adapted from the Morgan Motor Car Co. case in John Harvey-Jones (1990) *Troubleshooter,* London: Penguin Books, pp. 99–126, and subsequent material from John Harvey-Jones (1993) *Troubleshooter 2,* London: Penguin Books, pp. 202–4. The company website (http://www.morgan-motor.co.uk, http://autozine.kyul.net/html/Morgan.htm, accessed 26 February 2003; and BBCi reports).

ANOTHER QUESTION ON THE CASE

6 Why and how did Morgan change?

Gender and change

In 1990, Eagly and Johnson identified that, according to existing leadership studies, the democratic and participative styles which were increasingly being advocated among commentators such as Handy and Kanter were more commonly found among women rather than men (see Chapter 2 for discussion). Nevertheless, studies of women's approaches to change or women involved in the management of change remain few. Colgan and Ledwith (1996a) draw on Baddeley and James (1987) to classify the political skills which women need in acting as change agents in organizations. *Reading* is the ability to read an organization, both formal and informal, to identify its decision processes, appropriate power bases inside and outside the organization, the extent of the change agent's own power bases, the organization's culture and management styles, its purpose and direction and the importance of politics in this, overt and hidden agendas (Colgan and Ledwith 1996a: 31). The reading of the informal structure of male power is often problematic both for internal and external female change agents. Job segregation may prevent women internals from gaining access and developing the appropriate reading skills. Even training courses may assume informal tacit knowledge which women are prevented from possessing. Homosociability, with its social networks outside the organization such as freemasonry, golf or rugby clubs, again may mean that change issues may be negotiated and settled outside the workplace where women have no access. All this exclusion from symbolic and tacit information networks poses problems for women when they need to take action to promote change.

The second dimension is *carrying*, as in the carrying of a role relative to one's personal life. This may be done with integrity, or by operating with ego defences to the fore. Key elements here are the woman's awareness of who she is, and her own identity, her organizational credibility and image, and her presentation of self. Additionally, she must be able to win the respect of colleagues (which may be given for a man who is capable of giving out simple signals) and demonstrate a capacity for leadership, which often provokes resistance. One advantage, however, is that having experience of being marginalized, women often find it easier to innovate and cross traditional boundaries. At present the awareness that innovation comes from the margins is one of the hot topics in management (see Chapter 17) and the value of women for disrupting traditional structures which oppress creativity is increasingly being recognized (Colgan and Ledwith 1996b: 298). Women may act politically in a 'wise' way – a combination of reading the organization well and maintaining one's integrity, building and using networks of alliances; a 'clever' way – which involves behaving opportunistically to further personal ends, behaving so as to display and draw attention to themselves, often with the sponsorship of a senior male. These women seem either unaware of the risky nature of political shifts or are prepared to take the risk. Inept behaviour which arises from prioritizing personal needs and misreading the politics, game playing and unawareness of power issues can get both oneself and others into difficulties. Particularly, women run the risk of being stereotyped by males into one of the four deviant roles – 'Queen Bee', 'token woman', 'seductress' or 'man-hater' (Kanter 1977; Morgan 1986). Innocent behaviour is more of a blindness than a perspective. It means following the rules and appealing only to formal behaviour, pretending that there is no informal organization or that it is irrelevant. Avoiding conflict, such people, which especially includes women, often drift into technical or administrative jobs where they can blend into the background and have no need to confront the existence of a shadow organization. Unfortunately, if the informal system isn't acknowledged, then it can't be changed, and political incompetence results. Buchanan and Badham (1999) and Buchanan and Boddy (1992) emphasize at length the importance of political behaviour for successful change agency.

Su Maddock (1999: 5), in a study of the UK public sector, found that radically innovative women, grounded in a strong 'user' focus, adopted:

- A process approach to change and new relationships
- A people approach not a systems approach
- Confidence in the social values of the organization
- A local connectedness or social awareness
- Confidence that those who are on the margins or challengers were instrumental in social transformation
- A confidence in the community and the workforce that inspired trusting relationships.

Maddock also argues that many of the frustrations and experiences encountered in the public sector were shared by women in the private sector. Those women who were most insistent on the need for change in their sector, to improve delivery to the end user, showed:

- Confidence in alternatives based on social values
- Ability to handle diversity, ambiguity and change
- Experience in developing organizations where social objectives determined work – plans, programmes and indicators
- An awareness of diversity and gender cultures
- A capacity to be critically aware and capable of trusting others
- A desire to develop a collaborative culture.

This combines with the ability to listen, adapt to and communicate with others, personal readiness to collaborate, to think holistically, to promote social and egalitarian relations, to break boundaries and readjust, and to think strategically in achieving improvements, to embody the more feminized authority that some commentators have argued is necessary for transformational organizational change (Maddock 1999: 43).

In recent studies of women in the US involved in the field of organizational development and acting as external consultants, Waclawski et al. (1995) identified two sets of values – those that were important at the present time, and those towards which the women felt the field should move. The picture was not as positive as Maddock's. They found that:

It appears as although women today are relying less on the traditional social psychologically based methods of OD consulting (eg Gestalt methods, T-groups and sociotechnical interventions) and are focusing their efforts instead on helping organizations achieve their desired future states through a combination of approaches including management development programmes – once the exclusive realm of HR and T&D departments – systemic efforts to achieve long-term change, and enhancing group goal-setting skills. (Waclawski et al. 1995: 16)

This, they suggested, supports the idea of a general move in the field towards more business-oriented interventions than the traditional 'touchy-feely' approaches, and an emphasis on process and problem solving. They also suggested that:

The primary values of women practitioners in the field today focus on achieving organizational effectiveness and efficiency … the important values for tomorrow focus on more humanistic concerns (ie creating openness in communication and empowering employees to act) as humanistic issues are given prominence in social and organizational development efforts. (Waclawski et al. 1995: 20)

Women change agents, then, appear to continue to harbour a different, more relational vision of the future, and their methods contain elements of a more socially oriented nature, but the effects of the simple pragmatism of the client relationship and the persistence of patriarchal cultures in organizations mean that they still work in constrained ways. One consultant interviewed by Kaplan (1995: 65), whose study on the voices of women change agents is perhaps the most thorough review of the issues, did believe that there was a major change in orientation of OD under way and the women were making a difference, because traditional OD methods involved:

Kind of stripping people of their defenses and making them feel bad. I think I've managed to contribute something to that whole movement, I would call it the awareness development or training movement, which has now become a big business … we're doing much better today in many organizations understanding what these issues really mean to people as a result of that early work.

Women, with their greater mentoring skills, notwithstanding the fact that women's problems in organizations often stem from other women, are better placed to help organizations to grow, and men to attend to things that they have not been historically trained to attend to, rather than to plan and instruct or challenge them to do these things. Nevertheless, much more research needs to be done in this area before we understand how men and women both cope with and drive change (Covin and Harris 1995).

Cross-cultural aspects of organizational change

Kenichi Ohmae, perhaps the best-known Japanese management consultant, argued in the mid-1980s that from then on all major companies in America and Japan had to plan and implement their strategies globally (Ohmae 1985). This, he argued, would require, probably simultaneously, both competition and cooperation, selfishness and reciprocity. It seems no accident that Ohmae should propose an argument so apparently contradictory. In East Asia, unlike in the West and North of the world, notions such as this are common-place. 'In order to compete, and here lies the irony, companies need to co-operate' (Lessem 1998). In the same way that ideas of competition and cooperation are deeply embedded within cultural assumptions and values, so are notions such as 'the management of organizational change'. Each element: management, organizations and change means something different to people from different cultures.

This can be examined through the idea of 'two major cultural polarities' that provide change, the East–West divide (Lessem 1998: 44). Lessem bases his arguments on the work of Hampden-Turner and Trompenaars (1997) in which they highlight the differences in business approaches between the East (Asian tigers) and the West (Anglo-Saxons). The foundation for the work of Hampden-Turner and Trompenaars is the results from their survey of cultural values (Trompenaars and Hampden-Turner 1997). Here they measured values by means of a Dilemma Questionnaire, which contrasts values like competing with others like cooperating and presents alternative responses to a series of dilemmas from which respondents choose one. Trompenaars and Hampden-

Table 13.6 Competing cultural values	
Specific criteria (eg profitability)	Diffuse criteria (eg knowledge)
Winning/compromising	Negotiating consensus
Individualism (eg competing)	Communitarianism (eg cooperating)
Inner-directed (steered from within)	Outer-directed (steered from without)
Status achieved (success is good)	Status ascribed (the good should succeed)
Universalism (rule by laws)	Particularism (unique and exceptional)
Sequential time (time as a race)	Synchronous (time as a dance)

Turner provide a sophisticated system of categorizing results, which are ranged along a series of seven dimensions (Table 13.6).

The research results show that on all their seven dimensions 'North American and most West European managers prefer the left-hand column and most East Asian managers prefer the right-hand column' (Hampden-Turner and Trompenaars 1997: viii). Although this is the preference of East Asian managers, they can *include* the left-hand column, because they have learnt Western values in international trade and in working for and with multinational and joint venture companies. 'Unfortunately', Hampden-Turner and Trompenaars say, 'the same cannot be said for many Westerners ... (who) ... champion the left column but tend to dismiss the right column as inferior' (Hampden-Turner and Trompenaars 1997: viii). This results in Westerners finding themselves playing 'Finite Games in which individuals win or lose by specific criteria in universal contests' (Hampden-Turner and Trompenaars 1997: viii). Easterners, in contrast, play 'Infinite Games with rules which are adapted by the exceptions they encounter, with contests from which all players learn co-operatively' (Hampden-Turner and Trompenaars 1997: viii), a view stemming from ancient traditions in the East that seek unity in diversity and complexity. Hampden-Turner and Trompenaars (1997: ix) argue that this deficiency will result in disaster for Western business and that they must rapidly learn what has been learnt in the East 'before it is too late'.

Understanding the cross-cultural aspects of change is helped by the notion of the infinite game. 'Infinite games are preferred by cultures which dislike confrontation, prefer conversation to debate, are shy and respond indirectly to questions and believe in the values of harmony. This includes China, Japan, Indonesia,

Thailand and most of the economies managed by the Chinese' (Lessem 1998: 51). In such countries the mutual relationship comes before, and takes precedence over, the contract and its terms. *Wa* (harmony), *guanxi* and dynamic reciprocity, where favours escalate on both sides, are more important than contract terms. 'Where changing circumstances render contract terms onerous to one or both parties, let the terms be changed'. The mutual relationship, that made the contract initially, takes precedence over the terms negotiated (Hampden-Turner and Trompenaars 1997: 178). A relationship is long term, a contract is not and is only like a banister on stairs, Hampden-Turner and Trompenaars (1997: 181) say, 'to be gripped only in emergencies'.

These contrasts described by Hampden-Turner and Trompenaars provide many similarities to Morgan's (1986) metaphors of change. He argues that stability is a surface appearance of the 'explicate' world around us, underpinned by the deeper dynamic logic of 'implicate' constant transformation. Hampden-Turner and Trompenaars contrast the nature of knowledge in East and West, essentially a difference between the *linear* and the *circle* or *spiral*. In the West early scientific thinking was influenced by the philosopher Descartes, who argued for a split between mind and body (Cartesian dualism). 'The mind did the seeing. The body or bodies *were seen*' (Hampden-Turner and Trompenaars 1997: 13, emphasis in original). The mind was the seat of the soul and therefore a religious matter, whereas scientific investigation involved the mundane accumulation of facts, of which our bodies were examples. In the East the dominant way of thinking is 'The Way of Complementarity', which is 'a framework not so much for accumulating facts but for elevating human nature, a far more ambitious project' (Hampden-Turner and Trompenaars 1997: 13). In the East people are busy weaving values together, whereas 'westerners pile one value on top of another, a heap of 'goods' (good things) 'added' to each other' (Lessem, 1998: 46).

The complementarity paradigm derives from Taoism, originated by the Chinese thinker Lao Tzu in the sixth century BC. The Tao means 'The Way of the Universe' and is most famously symbolized in the Tai Chi, or Diagram of the Supreme Ultimate (Figure 13.12).

Figure 13.12 The Tai Chi

The importance of the Tai Chi is partly in its subtlety. It shows that every extreme or polarity contains the seed of its opposite, so that 'paradox lies in the heart of the universe … (and) … opposites are complementary and potentially reconcilable through harmony' (Hampden-Turner and Trompenaars 1997: 14). 'In short', Hampden-Turner and Trompenaars go on to say, 'East Asian cultures have an ancient framework for comprehending the complementarity of values, which most Western culture lack' (Hampden-Turner and Trompenaars 1997: 17).

Hampden-Turner and Trompenaars' metaphor of the infinite game shares with Morgan's dialectical change metaphor the assumption 'that the tension between opposites reveals the logic of systems and change that is the central tenet of Taoist philosophy … The underlying assumption of Taoism is of a holistic and non-linear universe within which everything changes to change everything else in an unending circularity' (Lowe 2002: 29). Lessem describes this as *synchronicity* and compares it to Western notions of creativity as being the interaction of single ideas within one mind; whereas Hampden-Turner and Trompenaars maintain that the Japanese view creativity as the interaction of many ideas within a team, especially one which crosses disciplines and other boundaries (Lessem 1998, 66; Hampden-Turner and Trompenaars 1997: 111–17).

Interventions to help managers and organizations manage change often reflect a Western approach that is linear, task-focused, convergent and goal-directed. We should investigate development initiatives based on the principles of the infinite game, metaphorically centred in organic networks, where clusters beget clusters and knowledge passes from one to another. Lessem recommends that:

A consensus orientation, ultimately is vital to the building of the clusters, in which victory in one game contributes to victories in clusters of games or one infinite game. These are typically joined by horizontal technologies which act as catalysts … Clustering also greatly increases the chance of fortuitous and creative connections, combining competition with co-operation. (Lessem 1998: 55–6)

The use of such organic forms will be vital in creating and sustaining international business, particularly in the Asia-Pacific region.

Conclusion

Change is complex at whatever level it is considered – philosophically or practically. On the one hand, change is a natural part of growth and decay in life, an ongoing process, yet on the other, it is often imposed by adverse conditions in the environment as a discrete event. In this chapter we have considered a variety of philosophical arguments on the nature of change and have looked at some of the approaches which have explicitly derived from a set of philosophical concerns, including varieties of evolutionary theory, contingency theory, systems, complexity and chaos theories. We have considered popular frames of reference and the political dimensions of change in unitary, pluralist, radical and liberal approaches, which link to our consideration of conflict and negotiation, and we have seen that language and narrative can play a significant role in change as a conversation. We have considered a range of practical approaches to managing change, including planned change and organizational development (OD) and, in particular, psychological dimensions of change. Resistance to change, both psychological and political, was also considered, as well as the practical challenges of managing and overcoming it. Change is never entirely controllable and always depends to some measure on the unexpected, chance and serendipity, but embarking on change without some conceptual framework as a guide to what might be expected is like setting out to sea without a map. But when considering change, we must always be prepared for the eventuality that we might have to tear the map up as our journey proceeds.

Answers to questions about change

1 What are the reasons why organizations change? Organizations change for a variety of reasons, both external and internal. External reasons often include changes in the competitive position of the organization relative to others in the field. Technological change in manufacturing methods, design technology or information management may also initiate change. Changes in the labour market and the availability of skills may also cause adaptations. Crises may also be prompted by political and financial factors. Internal factors may be political, the result of innovative or visionary individuals or simply due to an ongoing review of business processes seeking to maintain or improve efficiency and quality, or respond to customers needs more quickly.

2 Is resistance to change inevitable? Yes, there will always be people who do not support something different, and they may have a point. But it doesn't always have to be downright opposition. It is important, therefore, to recognize and involve at an early stage all those people who might contribute to, or be affected by, the change. It is also important, when the change is under way, to continue to deal with objections and also help those affected to cope with the changes.

3 Should change be top-down or bottom-up? Idealistically, it would be desirable if change were bottom-up, and this would fit in with more recent systems arguments about hierarchy. However, even OD was pragmatic enough to recognize that, without top management involvement and ownership, change was unlikely to happen. OD practitioners felt that norms should be changed at the top, and then filtered down, and the Burke–Litwin model retains that assumption. There are signs that some organizations, and some change agents, are beginning to move in a more democratic direction.

4 How is our understanding of change changing? Briefly, we have changes at the theoretical level, with complexity theory and postmodern ideas arguing for change to be seen as flow, rather than a sequence of disparate events which are planned ahead of time. Also the tendency to universalize has been challenged severely by feminist approaches, by diversity approaches which consider race, ethnicity and disability, and by more global considerations of different cultural approaches to change. In short, change is broader and more holistic in its construction and more hands-off than controlling. In addition, power and politics are now accepted as part of the change agent's remit, and the social context of the organization is coming to be recognized over the psychological conditions of managing.

REVISITING
THE CASE STUDY

1 How ready is the Morgan Motor Company for change?

Not really ready at all. Talk of change shows evidence of little real enthusiasm for the challenges, and a perception of any obstacle as being a huge one. This conservatism runs right through the organization.

2 What seem to be the main obstacles to change?

It would perhaps be easier to list those factors that are not obstacles. The complex customized nature of the cars, the layout of the factory and the systems of work all require systemic change; the conservatism and inertia of the workforce, along with the power they have because of their skills, mean that they can't move too quickly. The recent history of the company, which barely survived the 1960s, and the immense influence and power of Peter Morgan effectively hold Charles back. The lack of information in so many areas, on stock, sales and market conditions, all mean that there is little leverage from knowledge and no hard evidence from their environment to signal the need for change. They are comfortable with their myths.

3 How could a change agent try to persuade them to change?

By pressuring the organization, Harvey-Jones caused them to withdraw into their shell, but their determination to do things their way released the creative spirit that had founded the company. Harvey-Jones, for various reasons, hit them hard, but there are other styles of consulting which probe more gently and specifically, rather like judo, finding the momentum within the organization and accelerating it into a new direction. Oddly enough, by producing a position which was extreme enough for them to reject, Harvey-Jones let them give themselves permission to change slowly, and paradoxically energized the change process.

4 Will Morgan ever change? Where do you see potential pressures coming from?

At this point it seems most unlikely. External market pressures will either cause a collapse, or more likely the company will gradually slide into an economic crisis. If demand increases, the

company will have to act drastically to meet it. But the technical developments which are downplayed in the case have the potential to open up new markets and this will have knock-on effects. Also, although they want to improve things slowly and don't readily embrace the need for change, the management are willing to learn – at their own pace.

5 Are there any potential leverage points in the company that might energize change?

The vision of the chief engineer, the mindset of Charles and his confidence increasing as he gains more experience, the willingness of the people in the company to keep going, their love of the product and the customer loyalty.

6 Why and how did Morgan change?

First, after the TV programme aired, the waiting list trebled. Then the company was successful in getting its emission-control system up to standard for the US market, a result of its own vision. They could at this point raise prices. These increases in demand could not be ignored. Then the chief engineer and Charles studied new manufacturing methods, and built their own capability to a point where they could design and manage changes in the way the product was made and the systems and equipment used, including up-to-date information systems. This enabled them to increase production. Peter took more of a back seat. Charles, in the Morgan tradition, began a racing programme for testing purposes which led to the development of the Aero 8, which won Car of the Year Awards, as did the company as a manufacturer. The changes are still ongoing, and the question remains as to whether Morgan have done enough to increase supply, although the waiting list is now down to 18 months for the older designs.

How did they change? They changed themselves. On the lines of autopoesis, the complex structure was changed by small initiatives in different areas in line with an overall general orientation, some planning, some responses to unforeseen events, surprises and some good luck.

References

Adams J.L. (1987) *Conceptual Blockbusting*, Harmondsworth, Penguin.

Anthony, P. (1989) 'The paradox of the management of culture, or "He who leads is lost"', *Personnel Review*, **19**(4): 3–8.

Baddeley, S. and James, K. (1987) 'Owl, fox, donkey or

sheep: Political skills for managers', *Management Education and Development,* **18**(1): 3–19.

Boddy, D. (2002) *Management: An Introduction,* London: Financial Times.

Boje, D.M. (2000) 'Phenomenal complexity theory and change at Disney: Response to Letiche', *Journal of Organizational Change Management,* **13**(6): 558–66.

Bruce, M. (1987) 'Managing people first – Bringing the service concept to British Airways', *Industrial and Commercial Training,* March/April, pp. 21–6.

Buchanan, D. (1999) 'The logic of political action: An experiment with the epistemology of the particular', *British Journal of Management,* **10**: S73–S88.

Buchanan, D. and Badham, R. (1999) *Power Politics and Organizational Change: Winning the Turf Game,* London: Sage.

Buchanan, D. and Boddy, D. (1992) *The Expertise of the Change Agent: Public Performance and Backstage Activity,* London: Prentice Hall.

Buckley, W.F. (1968) *Modern Systems Research for the Behavioral Scientist,* Chicago: Aldine.

Burke, W.W. and Litwin, G.H. (1992) 'A causal model of organizational performance', *Journal of Management,* **18**(3): 528.

Burns, T. and Stalker, G.M. (1961) *The Management of Innovation,* London: Tavistock.

Burrell, G. and Morgan, G. (1979) *Sociological Paradigms and Organizational Analysis,* London: Heinemann.

Calori, R. (2002) 'Organizational development and the ontology of creative dialectical evolution', *Organization,* **9**(1): 127–50.

Chia, R. (1999) 'A "Rhizomic" model of organizational change and transformation: Perspective from a metaphysics of change', *British Journal of Management,* **10**: 209–27.

Chia, R. and King, I. (1998) 'The organizational structuring of novelty', *Organization,* **5**(4): 461–78.

Child, T. and Smith, C. (1987) 'The context and process of organisational transformation', *Journal of Management Studies,* **24**(6): 565–93.

Clark, J., McLoughlin, I., Rose, A. and King, R. (1988) *The Process of Technological Change: New Technology and Social Change in the Workplace,* Cambridge: Cambridge University Press.

Clegg, S. (1990) *Modern Organizations,* London: Sage.

Colgan, F. and Ledwith, S. (1996a) 'Women as organizational change agents', in S. Ledwith and F. Colgan *Women in Organizations: Challenging Gender Politics,* Basingstoke: Macmillan – now Palgrave Macmillan, pp. 1–43.

Colgan, F. and Ledwith, S. (1996b) 'Movers and shakers: Creating organizational change', in S. Ledwith and F. Colgan *Women in Organizations: Challenging Gender Politics,* Basingstoke: Macmillan – now Palgrave Macmillan, pp. 278–300.

Collins, D. (1998) *Organizational Change: Sociological Perspectives,* London: Routledge.

Covin, T.J. and Harris, M.E. (1995) 'Viewpoint: Perspectives on women in consulting', *Journal of Organizational Change Management,* **8**(1): 7–11.

Dawson, P. (1994) *Organisational Change: A Processual Approach,* London: Paul Chapman.

Dawson, P. and Webb, J. (1989) 'New production arrangements: The totally flexible cage?', *Work, Employment and Society,* **3**(2): 22–38.

Dawson, S. (1986) *Analysing Organizations,* Basingstoke: Macmillan – now Palgrave Macmillan.

Dunphy, D. and Stace, D. (1990) *Under New Management: Australian Organisations in Transition,* Sydney: McGraw-Hill.

Eagly, A.H. and Johnson, B.T. (1990) 'Gender and leadership style: a meta-analysis', *Psychological Bulletin,* **108**(2): 233–56.

Fitzgerald, L.A. (2002) 'Chaos: The lens that transcends', *Journal of Organizational Change Management,* **15**(4): 339–58.

Fitzgerald, L.A. and Van Eijnatten, F.M. (2002) 'Reflections: Chaos in organizational change', *Journal of Organizational Change Management,* **15**(4): 402–11.

Flamholtz, E. and Randle, Y. (2000) *Growing Pains: Transitioning from an Entrepreneurship to a Professionally Managed Firm* (3rd edn), San Francisco: Jossey-Bass.

Ford, J.D. and Ford, L.W. (1995) 'The roles of conversations in producing intentional change', *Academy of Management Review,* **20**(3): 541–70.

Ford, J.D., Ford, L.W. and McNamara, R.T. (2002) 'Resistance and the background conversations of change', *Journal of Organizational Change Management,* **15**(2): 105–21.

French, W. and Bell, C. (1983) *Organisation Development: Behavioural Science Interventions for Organisation Improvement,* Englewood Cliffs, NJ: Prentice Hall.

Goldberg, J. and Markóczy, L. (2000) 'Complex rhetoric and simple games', *Emergence,* **2**(1): 72–100.

Granovetter, M. (1985) 'Economic action and social structure: The problem of embeddedness', *American Journal of Sociology,* **91**: 481–510.

Greiner, L.E. (1972/1998) 'Evolution and revolution as organizations grow,' *Harvard Business Review,* July–August, 1972. Also commentary and revision, *Harvard Business Review,* May–June, 1998, pp. 3–11.

Greiner, L.E. (1992) 'Resistance to change during restructuring,' *Journal of Management Inquiry,* **1**(1).

Hampden-Turner, C. (1990) *Corporate Cultures: from Vicious to Virtuous Circles,* London: Hutchinson/Economist Books.

Hampden-Turner, C. and Trompenaars, F. (1997) *Mastering the Infinite Game*, Oxford: Capstone.

Harvey-Jones J. (1990) *Troubleshooter,* London: Penguin Books.

Harvey-Jones J. (1993) *Troubleshooter 2,* London: Penguin Books.

Hayes, J. (2002) *The Theory and Practice of Change Management,* London: Palgrave Macmillan.

Höpfl, H.J. (1993) 'Culture and commitment: British Airways', in Gowler, D., Legge, K. and Clegg, C. (eds) *Cases in Organizational Behaviour and Human Resource Management*, London: Paul Chapman, pp. 117–25.

Höpfl, H.J., and Linstead, S.A. (1993) 'Passion and performance: Suffering and the carrying of organizational roles', in Fineman, S. (ed.) *Emotion in Organizations*, London: Sage, pp. 76–93.

Huse, M.F. (1982) *Management*, New York: West.

Johnson, G. (1992) 'Managing strategic change – strategy, culture and action', *Long Range Planning*, **25**(1): 28–36.

Kane, P. (forthcoming) *The Play Ethic,* London: Palgrave Macmillan.

Kanter, R. (1977) *Men and Women of the Corporation*, New York: Basic Books.

Kanter, R.M. (1991) 'Transcending business boundaries: 12,000 world managers view change', *Harvard Business Review*, May–June, 151–64.

Kaplan, K.L. (1995) 'Women's voices in organizational development: questions, stories and implications', *Journal of Organizational Change Management,* **8**(1): 52–80.

Keen, P. (1981) 'Information systems and organization change', in E. Rhodeas and D. Weild (eds) *Implementing New Technologies,* Oxford: Blackwell/Open University Press.

Kotter, J.P. and Schlesinger, L.A. (1979) 'Choosing Strategies for Change', *Harvard Business Review,* March–April.

Kuhn, T. (1962) *The Structure of Scientific Revolutions,* Chicago: University of Chicago Press.

Lawrence, P. and Lorsch, J. (1967) *Organization and Environment,* Boston, MA: Harvard Business School Press.

Lessem, R. (1998) *Management Development through Cultural Diversity*, London: Routledge.

Letiche, H. (2000) 'Phenomenal complexity theory as informed by Bergson', *Journal of Organizational Change Management*, **13**(6): 545–57.

Lewin, K. (1947) 'Frontiers of group dynamics, *Human Relations*, **1**: 5–42.

Lewin, K. (1951) *Field Theory in Social Science*, New York: Harper & Row.

Linstead, A. and Thomas, R. (2002) 'What do you want from me? A poststructuralist feminist reading of middle managers' identities', *Culture and Organization, 8*(1): 1–20.

Linstead, S.A. (1995) 'Averting the gaze: Power and gender on the perfumed picket line', *Gender, Work and Organizations*, **2**(4): 192–206.

Linstead, S.A. (2002) 'Organization as reply: Henri Bergson and casual organization theory', *Organization, 9*(1): 95–111.

Linstead, S.A. and Chan, A. (1994) 'The sting of organization: Command, reciprocity and change management', *Journal of Organizational Change Management,* **7**(5): 4–19.

Lowe, S. (2002) 'The shadows of cross cultural research', *Culture and Organization*, **8**(1): 21–34.

McCalman, J. and Paton, R.A. (1992) *Change Management: A Guide to Effective Implementation*, London: Paul Chapman.

Maddock, S. (1999) *Challenging Women*: *Gender, Culture and Organization*, London: Sage.

Markus, M.L. (1983) 'Power, politics and MIS implementation', *Communications of the ACM*, **26**(6): 430–44.

Morgan, G. (1986) *Images of Organization*, London: Sage.

Ohmae, K. (1985) *Triad Power*, New York: Free Press.

O'Shea, A. (2002) 'The (R)evolution of new product innovation', *Organization, 9*(1): 113–25.

Peters, T. (1987) *Thriving on Chaos*, Basingstoke: Macmillan – now Palgrave Macmillan.

Pettigrew, A. (1985) *The Awakening Giant,* Oxford: Blackwell.

Pettigrew, A. (ed.) (1987) *The Management of Strategic Change*, Oxford: Blackwell.

Pettigrew, A. (1990) 'Longitudinal field research on change: Theory and practice', *Organisation Science*, **1**(3): 267–92.

Pettigrew, A. and Whipp, R. (1993) *Managing Change for Competitive Success*, Oxford: Blackwell.

Plant, R. (1987) *Managing Change and Making it Stick,* London: Fontana Collins.

Rollinson, D., Broadfield, A. and Edwards, D.J. (1998) *Organisational Behaviour and Analysis*, Harlow: Addison-Wesley.

Santosus, M. (1998) 'Simple yet complex – How complexity theory can help business management' (an interview with Roger Lewin and Birute Regine), *CIO Enterprise Magazine,* April 15 http://www.cio.com/archive/enterprise/041598_qanda.html.

Stace, D. and Dunphy, D. (1994) *Beyond the Boundaries,* Sydney: McGraw-Hill.

Stacey, R., Griffin, D. and Shaw, P. (2000) *Complexity and Management: Fad or Radical Challenge to Systems Thinking,* London: Routledge.

Stewart, R. (1991) *Managing Today and Tomorrow*, Basingstoke: Macmillan – now Palgrave Macmillan.

Thomas, R. and Linstead, A. (2001) 'Losing the plot?

Middle managers and identity', *Organization,* **9**(1): 71–93.

Trompenaars, F. and Hampden-Turner, C. (1997) *Riding the Waves of Culture: Understanding Cultural Diversity in Global Business* (2nd edn), London: Nicholas Brealey.

Van de Ven, A. and Poole, M.S. (1995) 'Explaining development and change in organizations', *Academy of Management Review,* **20**(3): 510–40.

Waclawski, J., Church, A.H. and Burke, W.W. (1995) 'Women in organization development: A profile of the intervention styles and values of today's practitioners', *Journal of Organizational Change Management,* **8**(1): 12–22.

Waterman, R.H. (1988) *The Renewal Factor: How the Best Get and Keep the Competitive Edge*, New York: Bantam.

Watzlawick, P. Weakland, J.H. and Fisch, R. (1974) *Change: Principles of Problem Formation and Problem Resolution*, New York: W.W. Norton.

Whipp, R., Rosenfeld, R. and Pettigrew, A. (1987) 'Understanding strategic change processes: Some preliminary British findings', in Pettigrew, A. (ed.) *The Management of Strategic Change*, Oxford: Blackwell.

White, R.F. and Jacques, R. (1995) 'Operationalizing the postmodernity construct for efficient organizational change management', *Journal of Organizational Change Management,* **8**(2): 45–71.

Wood, M. (2002) 'Mind the gap? A processual reconsideration of organizational knowledge', *Organization,* **9**(1): 151–71.

Worall, L. and Cooper, C.L. (1997) *The Quality of Working Life*, Corby: Institute of Management.

14

Decision making in organizations

Liz Fulop, Stephen Linstead, Simon Lilley
and Rodney J. Clarke

Questions about decision making

1 What is a 'decision'?

2 Why is the decision-making process important in organizations?

3 What kind of choices do decision makers have?

4 How does the behaviour of organizational participants affect decision making?

5 How are knowledge, information and power related in decision making?

THE MORAL MAZE OF DECISION MAKING

Note: This 'case', adapted from Robert Jackall's (1988) masterful *Moral Mazes*, differs in form to those utilized in other chapters in that it includes interview data from, and commentary on decision making in, a number of US organizations, rather than material from just one enterprise. This breadth facilitates consideration of a range of different aspects of decision making in the 'real world'.

The study of decision making is complicated by the difficulties of assessing to what extent rational devices actually are used in making decisions, particularly by higher-ups. The CEO of Covenant Corporation (pseudonym for a large US conglomerate), for instance, sold the sporting goods business from one of his operating companies to the president of that company and some associates in a leveraged buyout. The sale surprised many people since at the time the business was the only profitable operation in that particular operating company and there were strong expectations for its long-term growth. Most likely, according to some managers, the corporation was just not big enough to hold two egos as large and bruising as those of the president and the CEO. However, the official reason was that sporting goods, being a consumer business, did not fit the 'strategic profile' of the corporation as a whole. Similarly, Covenant's CEO sold large tracts of land with valuable minerals at dumbfoundingly low prices. The CEO and his aides said that Covenant simply did not have the experience to mine these minerals efficiently, a self-evident fact from the low profit rate of the business. In all likelihood, according to a manager close to the situation, the CEO, a man with a financial bent and a ready eye for the quick paper deal, felt so uncomfortable with the exigencies of mining these minerals that he ignored the fact that the prices the corporation was getting for the minerals had been negotiated 40 years earlier. Such impulsiveness and indeed, one might say from a certain perspective, irra-

tionality is of course always justified in rational and reasonable terms. It is so commonplace in the corporate world that many managers expect whatever ordered processes they do erect to be subverted or overturned by executive fiat, masquerading, of course, as an established bureaucratic procedure or considered judgement.

Looking up and around

Despite such capriciousness and the ambiguity it creates, many managerial decisions are routine ones based on well-established and generally agreed-upon procedures. For the most part, these kinds of decisions do not pose problems for managers. But, whenever non-routine matters, or problems for which there are no specified procedures or questions that involve evaluative judgements are at issue, managers' behaviour and perspective change markedly. In such cases, managers' essential problem is how to make things turn out the way they are supposed to, that is, as defined or expected by their bosses.

A middle-level designer in Weft Corporation's (pseudonym for a US company) fashion business provides a rudimentary but instructive example of this dynamic at work. She says:

> You know that old saying: 'Success has many parents; failure is an orphan'? Well, that describes decision making. A lot of people don't want to make a commitment, at least publicly. This is a widespread problem. They can't make judgements. They stand around and wait for everybody else's reactions. Let me tell you a story which perfectly illustrates this. There was a [museum] collection coming, the [Arctic] collection, and there was a great deal of interest among designers in [Arctic] things. My own feeling was that it wouldn't sell but I also recognized that everybody wanted to do it. But in this case, [our] design department was spared the trouble. There was an independent designer who had access to our president and he showed him a collection of [Arctic]

designs. There were two things wrong: (1) it was too early because the collection hadn't hit town yet; (2) more important, the designs themselves were horrible. Anyway, [the collection] was shown in a room with everything spread out on a large table. I was called down to this room which was crowded with about nine people from the company who had seen the designs. I looked at this display and instantly hated them. I was asked what I thought but before I could open my mouth, people were jumping up and down clapping the designer on the back and so on. They had already decided to do it because the president had loved it. Of course, the whole affair was a total failure. The point is that in making decisions, people look up and look around. They rely on others, not because of inexperience, but because of fear of failure. They look up and look to others before they take any plunges.

Gut decisions

Looking up and looking around becomes particularly crucial when managers face what they call 'gut decisions', that is, decisions that involve big money, public exposure or significant effects on one's organization. The term probably derives from the gut-wrenching anxiety that such troublesome decisions cause. At all but the highest levels of both Covenant Corporation and Weft Corporation, and frequently there as well, the actual rules for making gut decisions were quite different from managerial theories or rhetoric about decision making. (Note: Some readers may not initially recognize this rendering of 'gut decision'. In the UK, at least, the phrase is more usually associated with those decisions taken on 'gut instinct' or 'feeling', that is, on the basis of a visceral or intuitive sense of rectitude rather than one resulting from 'rational' analysis. However, the two usages are not that different, as the case illustrates – decisions made on so-called 'gut feeling' are likely to be 'gut-wrenching', not only because they are significant and exposing but also precisely because they lack a formally sanctioned and demonstrable rationale.) An upper-middle level manager explains:

There's a tremendous emphasis put on decision making here and in business in general, but decision making is not an individual process. We have training programs to teach people how to manage, we have courses, and all the guys know the rhetoric and they know they have to repeat it. But all these things have no relationship to the way they actually manage or make decisions. The basic principles of decision making in this organization and probably any organization are: (1) avoid making any decision if at all possible; (2) if a decision has to be made, involve as many people as you can so that, if things go south, you're able to point in as many directions as possible.

Decision-making paralysis is, predictably enough, most common at the middle levels. A lawyer talks about the difficulty he has in extracting decisions from the managers he advises:

It's tough for people to make decisions. Like today, I needed a decision from a business guy involving $200000 and he just didn't want to make the decision. It involved a claim from another company. They claimed that a certain clause in the contract that we have with them is unfair to a partner of theirs and that it is costing them money and that to be equitable we owed them 200 grand [thousand dollars]. I reviewed the contract and checked with a couple of other lawyers and decided that we didn't owe them a dime. It was a pretty straightforward case in our view. But it's not our decision to make so we went to the proper business guy and he didn't want to decide. So we said we need a decision and we would have to go to the next highest guy, his boss, and get it. He said: 'No, no, don't do that, because he'll send it back to me.' And he wanted us to send it to some other guy, a counterpart of his in a business area that isn't even related. He felt uncomfortable about making the decision because of the amount of money involved. Also, he was afraid of making a mistake. And he was afraid of impacting on others in areas he couldn't even see. Now, clearly, he should have just taken the decision up to his boss. But people don't want to do that. People have a very hard time making decisions and there's no question that this guy had the authority to make this decision. You see this sort of thing all the time. If you just walk around and look at people's desks, you'll see them piled with paper and that's an indication of their paralysis.

Senior managers are generally better at making decisions precisely because their positions allow them to establish the evaluative frameworks against which their choices will be measured. But even they evince the same kind of paralysis if they sense trouble or if their purported autonomy is really a mirage. For example, a financial planning manager, in discussing one of the cycles of financial commitment making in Alchemy Inc. (a subsidiary of Covenant Corporation) describes how even very high-ranking managers look up and look around:

People are fearful to make decisions on their own, and that goes all the way up to [the president] ... People try to cover themselves. They avoid putting things clearly in writing. They try to make group decisions so that responsibility is not always clearly defined. This is obvious to me in the planning process; and all the plans end up on my desk.

There's a lot of it [fear and anxiety]. To a large degree it's because people are more honest with themselves than you might believe. People know their own shortcomings. They know when they're in over their heads. A lot of people are sitting in jobs that they know are bigger than they should be in. But they can't admit that in public and, at still another level, to themselves. The organizational push for advancement produces many people who get in over their heads and don't know what they are doing. And they are very fearful of making a mistake and this leads to all sorts of personal disloyalty. But people know their capabilities and know that they are on thin ice. And they know that if they make mistakes, it will cost them dearly. So there's no honesty in our daily interaction and there's doubt about our abilities. The two go together.

Of course, one must never betray such uncertainty to others. Here the premium on self-control comes into play and many a manager's life becomes a struggle to keep one's nerve and appear calm and cool into the bargain. Making a decision, or standing by a decision once made, exposes carefully nurtured images of competence and know-how to the judgements of others, particularly one's superiors. As a result, many managers become extremely adept at sidestepping decisions altogether and shrugging off responsibility, all the while projecting an air of command, authority and decisiveness, leaving those who actually do decide to carry the ball alone in the open field.

Source: Modified from Robert Jackall (1988) *Moral Mazes: The World of Corporate Managers*, Oxford: Oxford University Press, pp. 76–80 (excerpts from Robert Jackall 1988).

QUESTIONS ABOUT THE CASE

1 What criteria do people apply when making decisions in the companies described?
2 Why are people afraid to make decisions?

Introduction

Decision making is generally considered by managers, and the academic discipline of management, to be central to organizational activity. There are several reasons why decision making is considered to be so crucial. There is the need to formalize and codify management work, promote communication between managers and others in organizations, and be able to justify a selected course of action from a range of likely or perceived options. There is also the very real disciplinary imperative to distinguish management work from other types of work in organizations. Describing management work as decision making seems so obvious and natural that it is hard to conceive of an alternative to it. In this chapter we will critically evaluate some of the assumptions behind traditional decision-making studies, including the notions of 'choice' and 'decision', drawing on traditions which normally lie outside the management discipline and its decision-making literature. We will then examine some major difficulties associated with these traditional management decision-making theories. In the last part of the chapter a postmodern, textual process model of organizations (Clarke 1991, 1992; Linstead 1985, 1999) is introduced which addresses some of the concerns raised in our evaluation of the traditional decision-making literature.

Despite the fact that managers are often expected to be and appear 'decisive', and frequently report themselves to be 'decision makers', actually defining a 'decision' and identifying when it has been made is extremely difficult (Miller et al. 1996). The process of decision making often seems to resist reduction to discrete decisions taken, or choices avoided or suppressed.

The scientific management approach, which we have discussed in previous chapters, even reduced the idea of the decision itself to the point of disappearance, implying that management was a process of applying and following abstract principles. Decision making was, at best, a matter which was tightly constrained by

evidence gathered through scientific methods on the optimal way of accomplishing a task. It was Chester Barnard (1938), in *The Functions of the Executive*, who contested these assumptions and argued that managers have a range of possible actions over which they can exercise discretion and *choice*. Decision making for Barnard is rational, purposeful and intentional, and these characteristics have dominated subsequent approaches.

Many writers on decision making have emphasized the rational aspect of decision making, seeing causes and effects and assuming that all actions have clear and identifiable antecedents and consequences. The theorists tend to assume that decision makers are fully aware of what they are doing, and that they look for the best or optimum outcome in all circumstances. There is also a tendency to regard decisions as being made at specific moments in time, perhaps at meetings specially called for the purpose. Several pieces of research, which we will discuss later, have demonstrated that all these assumptions can be questioned.

We will examine in more detail the following approaches to decision making: the *rational model* of decision making, the *administrative or bureaucratic model* (which questions whether managers are capable of making rational decisions), the *garbage can model* of decision making (which tries to introduce the idea that decisions are really problems looking for solutions), and the *political model* of decision making (which includes discussion of the role of powerful decision-making groups called 'dominant coalitions' and why many decisions are really 'non-decisions'). Before we examine these models, however, we need to consider what might constitute a 'decision'.

What is a 'decision'?

We discuss the developments associated with later versions of the rational decision-making model later in the chapter, but what concerns us now is how the assumptions of this model have led people to define a 'decision' as a *product* of decision-making *processes*. In fact, the process of identifying a decision is often problematic, as Mintzberg et al. (1990: 2) argue, because decisions are 'difficult to track down' and, as the cases above illustrate, managers often seek to avoid making decisions or obscure them. For Mintzberg et al., because decisions may unfold rather than be explicitly made at one point in time, the important thing is *action* – once actions are observed, then patterns can be observed, and the role of the decision in determining these actions can be inferred by looking for a point where consensus emerges before the action. In effect, they say that 'decision' is too slippery a concept to work with and displace it in favour of action, although they infer that decision is a necessary prior condition for action. An alternative approach sees decisions as occurring in a flow of smaller decisional acts. For example, when a manager chooses to pay attention to balance sheet figures rather than customer complaints, that is a kind of decision, but a very restricted one. This we can call a *decisional act*.

Think of a manager who at the beginning of the day sets priorities on several tasks, regarding some as more important, some less, and orders them accordingly. Some tasks may not be very important in themselves, such as putting more paper in the office printer, but may need to be done first, so the tasks need to be sequenced. Sometimes the tasks may be grouped or divided. Additionally, the manager will have to consider whose advice to take, and whose to ignore, whose interests to respect and whose to take lightly, effectively placing some things at the centre of the day and others at the margins. As events unfold, some commitments may need to be cancelled or erased, some 'pencilled in' for the future. Indeed, in ordering, sequencing, dividing up, centring, marginalizing, planning and erasing the day in this way, managers could be said to be *writing* their world – because these are exactly the same things that we do when we write something. This is no mere metaphorical mapping. Many of these tasks will literally be achieved through the '*writing*' of words on paper, disk and screen (Kallinikos 1996; Lennie 2001; Ezzamel et al. forthcoming).

Little decisional acts pile up on each other, as managers and others are constantly making them, and form what can be called a *text*. Decision processes produce not decisions as products, but texts – particular patterns of organizational experience that people come to accept as being relatively true or authoritative. For example, consider the idea of a decision support system. The simplest of these is the coin which can be tossed in the air and determines, for example, which side bats first in a cricket match. However, the situation must already be carved up into a dualism, so that it can be expressed in the form 'heads is yes, tails is no' or something similar. So a range of possibilities is suppressed, condensed or discarded so that two alternatives can be carved out of the moment and a decision can be made. A slightly more elaborate device, which incorporates more variety, is the die, as exemplified in Luke Rhinehart's novel *The Dice Man*. Here the hero, or anti-hero, develops a system for running his whole life based on the principle that all decisions (no matter how small or large, important or unimportant) can be divided into six optional courses of action, *one of which has to be unacceptable to the decision maker*. This element of challenge and risk adds excitement to the process – the possibility that the randomization of decision upon decision in this way as each day unfolds and presents its possibilities for action could lead to either a highly conservative outcome or a wildly unpredictable one. The decision maker never knows what is going to happen, and has only the responsibility of making the *range* of possible choices, never the choice itself, and feels a sense of being unburdened! The point here is that the die imposes a set of decision rules, which are appropriate to its technology (a six-sided cube), and also to its genre, or the style of its use, that of a game which one can win or lose. The rules, technology and genre of the decision system, especially with more complex systems, unfold to create a pattern of inclusion and exclusion which we can regard as a text. To pursue Rhinehart's example, the dice-man is included as a definer of alternatives but excluded as a chooser between these alternatives, although he has, of course, already taken another choice, that of having his life run by the die according to the self-imposed rules of his game. One unfolding of a life ordered in this way is the text of *The Dice Man*.

At the end of this chapter we will look more closely at what a textual approach to decision making looks like. However, we will now take a look at what traditional theories of decision making have to say about 'choice'.

Traditional decision-making theories and 'choice'

Decision making is a complex process which can be seen to involve many different stages or events before an actual decision is taken. Despite what we have just argued, managers *do* have to make decisions, under varying circumstances, pressures and constraints. These have naturally led to competing explanations of decision making in organizations. There is strong evidence among traditional theories of a polarization between unitary and pluralist approaches to decision making. *Unitary approaches* to decision making posit a general agreement about goals and the best means to achieve them. *Pluralist approaches* to decision making emphasize conflict and power struggles between individual coalitions in organizations in circumstances in which participants have substantial knowledge and information.

The basis of most of the traditional models of decision making, as we have observed, is choice. Decision making in this approach can be defined as *a response to a situation requiring a choice*. This is made after an evaluation of the alternatives on the basis of relevant choice criteria. Examples of such criteria could be 'maximum contribution to profitability', 'must complement existing product range' or 'must have an engine capacity of two litres'. In practice, however, as we have also noted, decision making is not always as objective and rational as this suggests. It may be influenced by values and institutional arrangements which bias data collection and evaluation, and affect the formulation of choice criteria (March 1987). Parties to a decision process may be unaware of the influence of these factors or may be outflanked because of their ignorance (see Chapter 6). If one accepts that organizational participants pursue objectives, then the question of choice inevitably arises because there will not always be agreement about goals or the means to achieve them. Even if there is agreement on these things, the constrained nature of organizational resources is such that there will always be a weighing of pros and cons about particular courses of action. Decision situations in organizations range from relatively simple 'within policy' matters of staffing and operations to more open-ended concerns about goals, missions and strategic direction.

Some approaches to decision making focus on identifying the types of choices available to managers. These are: *clear choice*, competing choice, choice avoidance and choice suppression. An example of a relatively clear choice would be that between which of two new products to adopt, A or B. This type of choice is straightforward because the same decision-making methodologies can be applied to each alternative. If the choice criterion to be applied in this case is 'maximum contribution to profitability', it should be a relatively simple matter to estimate the expected returns for each alternative and calculate the contribution to profitability. This example assumes that agreement has already been reached that there should be a new product, and that choice is limited to determining the best one financially. An example of a *competing choice* would be the alternatives of improving profitability by either launching a new product or upgrading computing facilities in order to improve bad debt collection. This type of choice is more open-ended than the previous example, and although it is still possible to evaluate each alternative in terms of profitability, it involves different assumptions and affects different interests within the organization. It might therefore be more

problematical and conflict-ridden. *Choice avoidance* occurs when issues arise requiring resolution but this does not occur. Non-action in this situation is itself a decision. *Choice suppression* is when information is distorted or suppressed in such a way that any decision made on an issue entails a predetermined outcome. This is a form of non-decision making (see Chapter 6) or, to put it another way, the decision is prefabricated so that, as Margaret Thatcher, the former British prime minister, was fond of saying: 'There is no alternative.'

Other approaches to decision making have sought to identify or categorize decisions into various types. One advantage of looking at decisions in this way is that it helps to highlight the varying complexity of decisions that managers have to deal with. It also overcomes the tendency to simplify this aspect of decision making. Later, when we examine various models of decision making, it will become apparent that many of these focus on certain types of decision to the exclusion of others. In doing so, they tend to simplify the decision-making aspect of management by focusing upon only those types of decision that can be explained by the particular theory being posited.

Decision types

In the largest study of decisions to date (undertaken by Hickson et al. 1986) the researchers found it necessary to describe the processes of decision making by categorizing decisions. The Bradford researchers (from Bradford University in the UK) argued that the categorization was related to the content of the decision. They identified three types of categorization for decisions: sporadic, fluid or constricted, and these are illustrated in Figure 14.1.

Sporadic decision processes are those which are informal and will suffer from delays through being impeded by all sorts of things from waiting for information to overcoming resistance or opposition. There is often a variability in information because it is gathered from various sources of expertise, some better than others. As a result, information sources are not usually regarded with confidence and more information may be requested. There will usually be scope for negotiation which takes place informally through personal contacts. The decision will take a long time to make (between one and a half and three years) and will eventually be made at the highest level. Political activity may well come to the fore in these decisions, and managers often find themselves involved in more than one of these processes at any one time. An example may be a decision to purchase a stake in a supplier, where there is uncertainty about the future of the market. This kind of decision does not happen on a routine basis and tends to entail weighty and

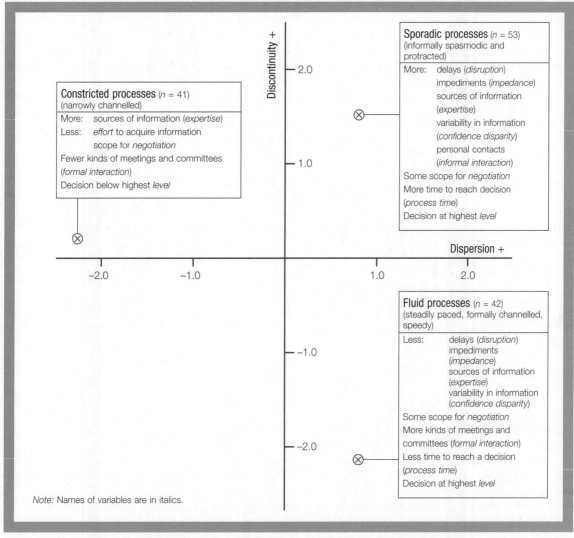

Figure 14.1 Three ways of making decisions

Source: David J. Hickson, Richard J. Butler, David Cray, Geoffrey R. Mallory and David C. Wilson *Top Decisions: Strategic Decision Making in Organizations*. Copyright © 1986 D.J. Hickson, R.J. Butler, D. Cray, G.R. Mallory and D.C. Wilson. This material is used by permission of John Wiley & Sons Inc.

controversial considerations, what Hickson et al. call *vortex matters*.

Fluid decision processes, in contrast and as their name suggests, flow. They are formally channelled, and relatively speedy and predictable. Sources of information are fewer, more familiar and seen to be reliable. Consequently, there are fewer delays. There will be some, but not much, negotiation, more formal meetings, but, as with the sporadic type, the decision will eventually be made at the highest level. An example given by Hickson et al. (1986: 120–1) is the decision of a metropolitan authority to launch a lottery, which went through all the necessary committees very smoothly. The smoothness of passage of the decision in this example is likely to depend on the degree of political support it has and the majority of the dominant party. In other, less formally political situations the known sponsorship of a dominant coalition can help to ensure that the process runs smoothly, if all other things are equal. Decision processes will be fluid when confronting unusual, but non-controversial *tractable matters*.

Constricted decision processes are narrowly channelled. There is a need for more sources of information, but this is usually technical and there is less effort needed to acquire it as it is readily available. There is scope for negotiation but there are fewer meetings, and the decision can usually be made at the local level or at least at a lower level than the top of the

Table 14.1 Overview of five organizational decision-making models

Dimension	Rational (unitary)	Bureaucratic (unitary)	Garbage can (pluralist)	Political power (pluralist)	Postmodern (textual)
Preferences and goals	Consistent among participants	Reasonably consistent	Unclear, ambiguous, may be constructed afterwards to legitimize actions	Inconsistent, diverse or conflicting goals and preferences	Goals and preferences become coherent according to the discourses which position them
Power and control	Focuses on hierarchical authority	Less centralized but still legitimate authority	Very decentralized, anarchic; power is also recognized	Shifting coalitions and interest groups who have power but not necessarily authority	Discourses and the institutions and practices which support them create compliant or oppositional 'social subjects' in decision making
Decision process	Orderly, rational	Procedural rationality embodied in programmes and standard operating procedures	Ad hoc	Disorderly, characterized by push and pull of interest groups	Fragmented, networked and shifts historically as discourse changes. Context and genre may produce unusual forms
Expected results and outcomes	Maximization and optimization	Follow from 'satisficing' mode	Unclear, ambiguous	Power and stabilization of demands	A simulation of order; a coherent 'text'
Information requirements	Extensive and systematic information gathering	Reduced by the use of rules and procedures information	Haphazard collection and use of	Information used and withheld strategically	Information flows and is held widely. Knowledge is distributed and needs to be shared; is often tacit and symbolic
Rationale	Efficiency and effectiveness in achieving agreed-to performance criteria	Stability, fairness	Playfulness	Conflict and power struggles among relatively equal opponents	Speed of change; complexity of environment; diversity of representations of reality

Source: Modified from Jeffrey Pfeffer (1981) *Power in Organizations*, London: Pitman, p. 31.

hierarchy. An example given by Hickson et al. is that of an insurance company which wanted to modernize its processes. These kind of decisions deal with *familiar matters*.

The attempt by Hickson et al. to typologize decisions according to their characteristics yielded some useful insights into the differences between decisions, and the conditions under which organizational politics were likely to have more impact. The next section examines various models of decision making. Each of these makes different assumptions about various aspects of decision making such as: the preferences and goals of participants; the types of conditions with which different styles and processes of decision making are associated; the nature of power and authority implicit in them; expected results and outcomes; the nature of the technology employed; and the underlying values, beliefs and dominant rationale. Table 14.1 summarizes the key dimensions on which these approaches vary. Different types of choice criteria are implicit in each model. We also include in Table 14.1 what we have termed the *postmodern (textual)* approach to decision making, which was not originally mentioned by Jeffrey Pfeffer (1981), whose work forms the basis of Table 14.1.

The rational decision model

Under the *rational model* of decision making, the assumption is made that participants have agreed in advance that making a decision is the right process to follow and that the rules and language of decision making are understood by all. The rational model aims at making optimal decisions on the basis of a careful evaluation of alternative courses of action. Depending on the complexity of the problem, computational or quantitative techniques may be used to assist this process. The model is claimed to be the basis of much decision making in private and commercial life and is effective under the conditions it assumes: a finite choice situation; relevant and unproblematic data; and clear and uncontroversial choice criteria. The model views the decision-making process as a sequential series of activities leading from an initial recognition of a problem, through the delineation and evaluation of alternative courses of action, and the selection of the preferred alternative to the implementation of action (Dawson 1986: 182; Minkes 1987: 37–8). This sequential process is depicted in Figure 14.2.

Consider the decision processes involved in the choice about which of two new products should be launched. If the agreed objective was profitability, rationalists would say that it is a relatively straightforward procedure to estimate incomes and expenditures associated with both proposed products

and determine the preferred alternative. In these circumstances, decision making becomes largely a matter of technical expertise. Where there are adequate information, clear choice criteria and agreed goals, then the rational model is said to work well. However, not all decision situations are as clear-cut as the example suggests, and the assumptions indicated above cannot always be presumed.

One major assumption is that the rational approach provides 'one best way' to reach decisions. However, the advocates of the rational approach pay little heed to the organizational context of decision making. As pointed out by Hickson et al. (1986), this context influences the way problems are defined, information gathered and choice criteria formulated. The use of logical frameworks and quantitative techniques do not of themselves make a decision rational. It would be better to regard such techniques as one input into a process which is influenced by the preferences and interests of key organizational participants (Pfeffer 1981: 31). For

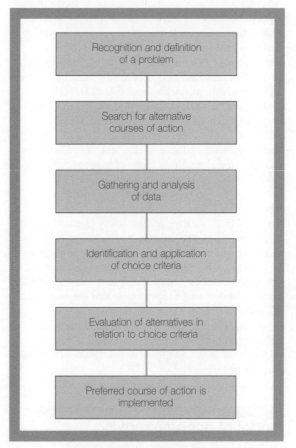

Figure 14.2 The rational decision process

Source: Adapted from Anthony Hopwood (1974) *Accounting and Human Behaviour,* London: Accountancy Age Books, p. 124.

example, in the case of the product decision previously discussed, it would be illuminating to know how the organizational agenda was set to allow the emergence of the choice situation, that is, what events led to the decision to offer a new product. Which other potential products did not make it into the final pair of alternatives? What other profit-making alternatives were eliminated or overlooked in the process leading up to the choice situation (that is, the competing choices)? Which organizational participants stand to gain or lose by the decision? Who supplied the information and to what extent have biases or values influenced the information-gathering process? What groups were not represented in the decision process (that is, choice suppression)? Thus every organizational decision is influenced by a history, a social context and anticipated consequences for organizational participants.

The rational model has been greatly influenced by classical management and economic theory, especially in terms of the notion of a world populated by individuals 'rationally' seeking the best rewards, using the best methods to achieve them: that is, profit or 'utility' maximization through choice optimization, as per 'economic man'. However, in practice, time and cost frequently rule out the search for optimal solutions, and profit maximization is not the only criterion applied to choice situations (Hopwood 1974: 125). More fundamentally, what 'rationality' might be, and who might decide on this question, is seldom, if ever, explicated in the work of proponents of the rational model. Within the context of classical theory, decision making assumes a unitary frame of reference and a stable or predictable environment (Dessler 1976: 313–14), although there is seldom agreement in organizations about goals and the means to achieve them, and environments are frequently characterized by uncertainty. In mathematics, a 'rational number' is one which is expressible as a ratio of integers, as a relation between two whole numbers. The world in which we live, however, is not always easily divisible into whole, discrete entities, and it is even rarer that the magnitude of such entities is ascertainable on a common or consistent scale. In such circumstances, there is no incontrovertibly largest or smallest to be selected as evidently the best, and thus little possibility of 'rational' decision making.

The bureaucratic or administrative model of decision making

In reaction to the unrealistic assumptions of the rational model, Herbert Simon (1960) sought to develop a model of decision making based on the actual behaviour of decision makers. This approach has come to be known as the *bureaucratic* or *administrative*

model (see Table 14.1). Simon recognized that the human animal has a limited capacity for processing information, and thus there are cognitive or mental limits to human rationality. These limits or constraints on individuals mean that decision making is governed, according to Simon, by *bounded rationality*. Seemingly suboptimal efforts to reach decisions (Mouzelis 1967: 124; Minkes 1987: 70–3) in everyday life also result from the influence of non-rational, emotional and unconscious elements in human thinking and behaviour, for example poor work habits, limited skills and pressure of time. Group pressures are also likely to limit the optimizing behaviour so central to the rational model of decision making. Furthermore, perfect information (on which to make decisions) is not always available, and there are time and cost considerations attached to information gathering and evaluation (Williamson 1975). The sheer amount of information to be processed and the necessity to meet deadlines frequently rule out optimal decisions.

While ideally organizational arrangements should be set up to enhance decision making, which Simon sees as a primary management function, in practice the conditions for perfectly rational decisions will seldom, if ever, be attained. Thus, in lieu of the optimizing 'economic man' of the rational model, Simon proposes an 'administrative man' who 'satisfices'. *Satisficing* is a term he coined to describe a 'best in the circumstances' decision. The metaphor suggested is that of 'looking for a needle in a haystack'. If one discovers a blunt or rusty needle that will more or less do the job required, it is unlikely one will keep searching until the perfect needle is discovered – there may not even be one! Thus a satisficing decision is one which broadly satisfies the parameters of a problem. To continue to search for an ideal or optimal solution may not only exceed the information-processing capacity of the decision maker, it may also involve a cost which must be offset against the advantage of a quicker, near-enough or satisficing decision: hence the bounded rationality of decisions (March and Simon 1958; Perrow 1972: 154–6; Minkes 1987: 71–5).

In addressing the question of what needs to be done to enhance organizational decision making, Simon (1984) distinguishes between two types of decisions: programmed and non-programmed. *Programmed decisions* are not novel in nature and evolve from policies, precedents and guidelines. These decisions deal with repetitive and procedural events and could include such things as decisions about salary payments, customer orders, inventory restocking and so on (that is, they appear as clear choice criteria). In larger organizations, procedure manuals and precedents often set the direction for a programmed decision. This type of decision making is very amenable to bureaucratization ('red tape' and rules) and computerization (Weeks 1980). By contrast, a *non-programmed decision* involves finding solutions to problems which are novel or unstructured. Examples would be a decision to diversify, relocate, acquire a new business or initiate a range of staff redundancies for the first time. Usually there is little in the way of precedent or procedure to guide such decisions. This distinction can be related back to the typology of Hickson et al. (1986) that we considered earlier. Sporadic decisions are similar to what Simon terms non-programmed decisions, while fluid and constricted decisions may be seen as examples of programmed decisions, although fluid decisions tend to have a greater element of uncertainty than a limited reading of 'programmed' would imply.

The distinction between programmed and non-programmed decision making is important because they not only require different methods of problem solving but also involve different modes of managing and organizing. The implications and characteristics of the two decision-making modes are set out in Table 14.2. Programmable decisions lend themselves readily to operations research techniques and are compatible with mechanistic organizational structures. In a modernist view, non-programmable decisions are best approached heuristically (that is, using predictive models, including informal ones, to answer 'what if?' questions) and are compatible with more organic (that is, non-bureaucratic or flexible) organizations. Simon believed that the decision-making activities of the middle and lower-level groups within an organization were more amenable to programmable decisions, while the upper levels were to deal more regularly with non-programmable decisions. Indeed, the bounded rationality of human beings is frequently used to account for, and thus also to naturalize, the existence of the hierarchical structures we see in organizations. The argument runs something like this: if each of us can only process a limited amount of information, then to deal with complex matters that involve processing amounts of information that exceed these limits, we must organize ourselves in ways that enhance our collective information-processing powers.

Hierarchy provides just such a form of organization. It ensures that the information-processing powers of senior decision makers are not overloaded by making subordinates both summarize information, passing only its most salient aspects to those above, and apply pre-programmed rules to familiar problems, so that they only need to pass up exceptional cases (Galbraith 1974; see also Schotter 1981). Within such moves, the 'problem' of limited human information-processing capacity is recognized and represented in the form of a 'solution': that of a formally organized hierarchy (Cooper 1992). But there is no such thing as a free lunch! Rules begin to take precedence over what they are intended to achieve and hierarchical position becomes more important than level of competence, as we saw in the cases above. Furthermore, questions concerning who 'passes' (Munro 2001) what to whom

Table 14.2 Traditional, modern and postmodern techniques of decision making

Types of decision	Traditional decision-making techniques	Modern decision-making techniques	Postmodern decision-making techniques
1. *Programmed* Routine, repetitive decisions; organization develops specific processes for handling them. Low uncertainty and ambiguity	(a) Habit (b) Clerical routine: standard operating procedures, policies and manuals (c) Organization structure: know your place (d) System of subgoals (e) Well-defined informational channels	(a) Operations research: mathematical analysis, models, computer simulations (b) Electronic data processing (c) Management information systems	(a) Decision devolved to 'empowered' teams *but* these teams are self-inspecting and policing (surveillance) (b) Manipulation of culture, myth and symbols to control decision outcomes and limit options (simulate contexts: simulacra)
2. *Non-programmed* One-shot, ill-structured novel policy decisions. Handled by general non-routine problem-solving processes. High uncertainty and ambiguity	(a) Judgement, intuition, and creativity (b) Rule of thumb (by top management)	Heuristic (problem-solving) techniques applied to: (a) constructing computer models (b) brainstorming (c) counter-planning (d) simulation	Risk taking encouraged but within: (a) the context of learning environments (b) fast flow of knowledge and information through virtual dissemination (c) flat flexible structures which can temporarily realign to support decision makers

Source: Modified from 'Decision-making and organizational design', p. 208 from *Organizational Theory: Selected Readings* edited by Derek S. Pugh (Penguin Books 1971, 4th edn 1997). Introduction and notes copyright © D.S. Pugh 1971, 1984, 1990, 1997.

become ever more pressing, as we shall see in our later consideration of the political model. Nevertheless, Simon hoped that through the application of sophisticated organizational design many decisions would become programmable and subject to more control and predictability.

In the postmodern context, programmable decisions operate through various forms of self-discipline and control, as shown in Chapter 11 with teamwork and culture in Chapter 3. Non-programmable decisions are associated with the virtual or teamnet-type organization mentioned in Chapters 11 and 16. In these organizations, creating knowledge (intellectual capital) and learning are seen as critical to innovation and change (see Ulrich 1998). Simon did not include postmodern techniques of decision making in his typology, but these have been added to help to draw comparisons between techniques of decision making.

In terms of postmodern decision making, two forms of knowledge have become particularly important for creating *intellectual capital*: tacit knowledge and understanding (Wikström et al. 1994: 10–12). *Tacit knowledge* is described by many theorists as being embodied in individuals as informal knowledge, skills and know-how. This form of knowledge is vital to organizations so that problems can be solved, questions answered about how things should or ought to be done, and decisions made based on lessons learnt from the past (Wikström et al. 1994: 11). Tacit knowledge has always been seen as important to efficiency and cooperation in workplaces (Manwaring and Wood 1985; Davenport et al. 1998). As a source of intellectual capital, tacit knowledge is considered vital to gaining a competitive advantage by exploiting the brain power of individuals and using the diversity of individual talent and know-how to create a winning edge. Tacit knowledge, as described here, draws on experience and skills *already* learnt in solving problems and getting the job done, and often by exceeding the demands of the job. *Understanding*, which is also embedded in individuals as informal knowledge, develops through interpretations of meanings, sense making (as discussed in Chapter 1) and, most importantly, reflection or self-reflexive practice (see Introduction).

Understanding builds from cognitive (judgements, intuition and awareness), emotional, spiritual and visceral (instinctive) experiences. The knowledge repositories from which people draw to develop understanding in organizations were described in Chapter 1 under the six different types of knowledge. Understanding leads to new insights, new frameworks of meaning, and new mental 'maps' through which people learn to be creative and innovative. Understanding allows people to identify or make new connections, come up with novel solutions to problems or discover new patterns of thought that are unique to them

(Wikström et al. 1994: 12; Davenport at el. 1998: 43). Understanding and its corollary, learning, are hard to capture, measure, calculate or put a dollar value on, both individually and organizationally (see Stewart 1994).

Along with that which is tacit, there is knowledge which is *explicit*. Explicit knowledge is public and can be further divided into *information* and *explanatory knowledge*, both of which are important resources for the construction of various knowledge repositories such as expert systems and, at the extreme, artificial intelligence (Davenport et al. 1998). Information and explanatory knowledge have been used extensively in organizations to aid decision making and problem solving, as described in Table 14.2. So-called virtual organizations and/or teamnets thrive on rapid and frequent exchanges of information in electronic forms, and in some situations this flow of information can radically alter how decisions are made and the structure of organizations in which they are made. For example, Thomas Malone (1997) has used the term 'cyber cowboys' to describe those people whose decision making will become increasingly autonomous (that is, not referred back to a head office or does not go through a hierarchy), but is dependent on vast amounts of information accessed from remote sites through electronic means. This fast flow of information is what is commonly associated with the information revolution of the 1980s and 90s, or the information age (Wikström et al. 1994: 13). However, we must be careful when we talk about information, and any age or revolution associated with it, for it is a very slippery concept.

Information is partly processed, organized or categorized data that has the potential to be informative but it cannot contribute to knowledge unless it is connectable in some way with what is already known. There already has to be some knowledge, some pre-existing representation, or model, of the world (MacKay 1969) for the information to strengthen or undermine if it is to have any meaning or make any sense. Information can be used to develop skills and know-how as well as 'triggering' new forms of understanding, often through disrupting old ones. And in this sense, we can see that:

The essence of information is revealed to us in its name. Information is an inward-forming. It is the change in a person from an encounter with data. It is a change in the knowledge, beliefs, values or behavior of that person. The in-forming could be part of a general 'sense-making' process and be found in the distinctive way a person has come to understand the world, or it could be the way a particular situation has come to be defined. (Boland 1987: 363)

On its own, however, information does nothing and cannot be the the source of innovation or learning. It is used by people to answer questions relating to the 'what', 'where', 'who', 'how' or 'when' of something that is of concern to them (Wikström et al. 1994: 11), something about which, through an existing repesentation or viewpoint, they already know. As Robert Cooper (1992: 255) elegantly notes: 'information is that which augments or reduces the power of a representation'. Such a view challenges somewhat the notion of information as solely explicit or public. However, since 'inward-forming ... is not readily available for observation' (Boland, 1987: 363), that which produced our 'in-formation', the symbols and sounds that we pass between ourselves, is substituted for the meaning generation or sense-making process it engenders. Since these symbols and sounds *are* visible and audible, they stand in for in-formation, enabling it to become a noun rather than a verb, a thing rather than a process. Information can then be *treated as if it were public* or explicit knowledge, because it seems as though it is able to be shared, can be bought or exchanged, has a definable value and is programmable, as described by Simon. But confronting two individuals with the same set of symbols will not necessarily produce the same 'in-forming' in both of them – it depends on how they interpret or make sense of it, which depends upon their previous experience and pre-existing representations or models of the world.

Explanatory knowledge is important to the development of tacit knowledge and understanding, but it is not the same as either. Explanatory knowledge is usually equated with positivistic scientific knowledge which is used to solve problems and render solutions to processes or events that are predictable or potentially programmable. This knowledge, like information, was at one time person-based or embedded in the individual, but has become public or explicit knowledge through documentation and dissemination (Wikström et al. 1994: 13). Journals, conference papers, textbooks, manuals, reports, websites and other electronic methods of information dissemination are commonly used to make this knowledge explicit and commodified, in the sense that commercial values can be attached to it. Explanatory knowledge forms the rules that constitute the navigational map followed by the inference engines that process data and/or information in expert systems. But as Harry Collins (1987), among others, has noted, such systems still require *some* expertise or knowledge on the part of the user, if they are to be useable. Just as information must be interpreted in order to 'in-form', rules too must be interpreted if they are to be successfully applied; as no set of rules can contain the rules of its own application, unless it is infinite in size.

To illustrate his point, Collins (1987) provides the delightful example of an expert system called 'pick-up', designed to determine who one should take home from a bar! Its 'if-then' logic works fine when one can

assume some intelligence and cultural competence on the part of the user, but as one tries to build more of this into the programme itself, so that a less informed user could benefit from the system, the number of rules begins to expand monstrously. For example, a particular subject may be willing to come home with you if they have a fleeting smile and maintain prolonged eye contact. But how long does a 'fleeting smile' last? Is it the same as a tic? Does eye contact involve direct contact between the eyeballs? And is it okay to measure the length of a fleeting smile with a stopwatch? In the absence of the assumption of some common sense and understanding of the situation on the part of the user, the list of potentially necessary clarifications is endless. Just as the problems of bureaucracy are usually the result of a role incumbent not knowing which particular rule to apply or how to apply it in a given, specific situation, or not being sufficiently empowered to feel able to make such decisions, additional knowledge is always required to both appropriately shape the input to an expert system and interpret its output.

Rule-based explanatory knowledge that promises to help solve problems in a standardized and seemingly rational way, in order to produce the optimal solution, can be highly valued or even overvalued by organizations because it is produced in a technical or scientific form (Wikström et al. 1994: 12–13). And although other forms of explicit knowledge also exist, for example descriptive knowledge that comprises such things as organizational texts, stories, myths and metaphors, since their form does not afford the same opportunities for becoming programmable and their relationship to problem solving is often more difficult to establish, they tend to be less highly valued, at least formally.

In fact, organizations have a number of knowledge repositories that they develop, but the greatest challenge remains accessing the tacit knowledge and understanding of people in the organization who usually have some control over how they use these forms of knowledge, although it is not clear that people can ever be fully aware of their knowledge repositories. While judgement, intuition and creativity were also acknowledged by Simon as traditional techniques of decision making (see Table 14.2), he said that these were only applicable to situations of high uncertainty and ambiguity, and only applied to novel, one-off situations. For postmodernists many situations are novel and one-off and high uncertainty and ambiguity are the norm, as organizations have to deal with diversity within the organization and complex relationships in their environments. Simon's idea of programmable decisions was central to the information revolution, yet increasingly the area of non-programmable decision making is taking centre stage in discussions about competitiveness, intellectual capital, knowledge management and decision making. Risk taking, innovation and learning have become synonymous with spreading non-programmable decision-making capacities across the whole organization. Simon's concerns about satisficing have been recast to concerns about maximizing the output in areas of non-programmable (virtual) decision-making, where there are many different forms of knowledge and some we might never tap. Peter Drucker puts it another way: 'knowledge is taking the place of capital – the flow of things has been replaced by the flow of information – knowledge becomes power' (cited in Harris 1993: 120). Simon was a unitarist and so he was silent on the issue of power and politics.

Disjointed incrementalism

Simon's approach to decision making was criticized for its neglect of the power or political dimensions of decision making (see below), for example for failing to take account of the diversity of interests in an organization and the role of powerful groups in shaping decision-making agendas (see Pettigrew 1972). This was partially remedied in the work of Charles Lindblom, who also sought to highlight the limitations of the rational model of decision making and, through an examination of decision making in public administration, introduced the concept of politics. Lindblom described decision making in public administration as being characterized by a process of 'muddling through' or *disjointed incrementalism*. He suggests that many policy decisions are so complex that they cannot be handled by the rational model of decision making, which he calls the 'root' method. Instead, Lindblom argues that policy decisions are made through the 'branch' method (Lindblom 1990: 278–82; Minkes 1987: 57–61). Policy decisions, such as where to locate new welfare housing or decrease unemployment benefits, are difficult if not impossible to deal with under any rational approach.

According to Lindblom, in incrementalism the decision maker does not attempt to root out all possible alternatives or objectives before tackling a problem, but rather places limits on the alternatives to be considered, based on the current state of knowledge, and solves the problem through making small and gradual changes. Incrementalism reflects the troublesome character of decision-making processes arising from the competing interests and values that are brought into play in complex decision-making situations. Lindblom suggests that successful policy making proceeds by a process of 'mutual partisan adjustment', not some prior ordering of objectives and goals as advocated by the 'root' method. Decision makers simplify the choices between competing policies by identifying the margins by which

circumstances or outcomes – if altered – will differ (Pugh and Hickson 1989: 130). Thus the only prior values that interest the policy maker are the increments by which two policies might differ. Lindblom argues that objectives can be fitted to policies and vice versa, since the process of decision making involves continual adjustments, modifications and reinterpretations of values and preferences. The 'science of muddling through' is a sophisticated problem-solving strategy which does not reject the rational approach but sees it as a form of 'simple-minded inadequacy'.

Lindblom is not, however, suggesting that policy makers simply make decisions on the basis of politics or intuition alone. Rather, he intends to expose the qualitative and politically motivated behaviours which lead to successful decision making in some situations. He does not support a 'one best way' approach to decision making, but he does subscribe to the concept of bounded rationality in terms of the limits on information search evident in the branch method. The model of disjointed incrementalism describes the type of decision making that is likely to occur in that 'grey area' between programmed and non-programmed decisions (Minkes 1987: 52). Moreover, because the choice criteria are marginal, the likelihood of conflict is considered to be minimal; changes are incremental and mutually adjusted. Logical incrementalism is moving closer to a pluralist view of decision making and thus avoids some of the obvious criticisms of the administrative model of decision making, which had little to say on politics and power.

The garbage can model of decision making

So far in this chapter several approaches to organizational decision making have been considered: the rational approach, which assumed that objectives and the means of achieving them could be clearly identified; the administrative one, proposing that organizational decision making is a product of bounded rationality; and incrementalism, introducing the notion of mutual adjustment and gradual change.

These approaches assume a clear linkage between goals, people and solutions. Cohen et al. (1972) argue that this cannot always be assumed and some organizations display characteristics of what they call *organized anarchy*. The characteristics of organized anarchy are problematic goals, unclear technology (all sorts of methods are likely to be used to make decisions) and fluid (member) participation (see Table 14.1). Cohen et al. have noted that under such conditions, where clear criteria of choice are absent, extraneous matters tend to get lumped into the decision-making process, and solutions often bear little relation to problems. They have appropriately labelled this phenomenon the *garbage can model* of organization decision making.

Under conditions of organized anarchy, it is not clear when an issue arises whether it is a problem or a solution to a problem. A collection of such issues is what Cohen et al. refer to as the *garbage can*. Through a process of jumbled decision making, problems and solutions become linked together so that a problem in one area becomes a solution in another. For example, a university administration was moving to new premises elsewhere in the city and the question arose of what was to be done about the vacated premises. Ostensibly, this was a problem for the university. Elsewhere within the university, there were moves to establish a new school of technology. One of the objections to this proposal had been the lack of suitable premises. After some discussion, it was decided that the new school would be established and that it would be located in the vacated premises.

While this decision seems superficially sensible, in the absence of clear choice criteria such as 'will it add to our surplus (profit)?', it was neither optimizing (as in the rational model) nor satisficing (as in the bureaucratic model). It was a reaction to circumstances by those who happened at that time to be on key committees (that is, in fluid membership). No one asked critical questions, such as whether or not the new school was really required, whether the old premises were the best location for the proposed school or what the effect would be on the budget.

These two issues, that is, the vacant premises and the proposed new school, were simultaneously problems and solutions. The decision was made by turning each of the issues into a solution for the other. According to the garbage can theory of decision making, therefore, the factors that influence decision making in organizations are the range of issues cum solutions cum problems that happen to be in the garbage can at a particular time and the total demands upon the decision makers at that time. In comparison with the rational and administrative models of decision making, the garbage can model could be said to be based on 'circumstantial' rationality.

A noticeable difficulty with the model is its failure to account for the political activity of participants who encourage conditions of organized anarchy, or who exploit them for particular advantage. However, the approach does help us to appreciate why decisions in organizations are not always 'rational' in an absolute or objective sense. In fact, Gunnar Westerlund and Sven-Erik Sjøstrand (1979) believe that the garbage can approach to decision making exposes one of the most popular myths in organizations, that of the *rational organization*. They suggest that the rational process of decision making (that is, the step by step sequential process outlined earlier in Figure 14.2) clouds the fact that the choice of problems and methods of handling them are largely influenced by the personal preferences, values and expectations of decision makers. What is often thought of as 'rational' simply depends on for whom it has to appear as being such (Westerlund and Sjøstrand 1979: 90–6).

The garbage can model also highlights *ritualistic* decision-making activities. For example, research has shown that not all problems lead to efforts to reach decisions that might solve them. Decision making often has to be forced on individuals who actively seek to avoid handling a problem, as shown in the cases cited at the beginning of the chapter. Even though decisions are made, they may not be executed because someone may feel uncomfortable with the decision or it can be safely deferred (Westerlund and Sjøstrand 1979: 99). March (1984, 1987, 1988) has expanded on the ritualistic nature of decision making by proposing that much of what we observe about it is not so much concerned with how choices are made but how individuals interpret and justify their choices to others. He argues that most decision making is only incidentally about weighing up and evaluating choice criteria. Rather, decision-making sessions are often about how decision makers define the virtues and correctness of their choices, trying to make sense of what they have done and justifying future actions (see also Jackall 1988). The prime resource they mobilize to accomplish this is the imagery of rationality derived from the rational model and its antecedents in classical management and economic theory.

Decision-making events can also provide arenas for apportioning glory and blame. They create opportunities for reaffirming old alliances, friendships, antagonisms and power and status differences. March believes that these ritualistic aspects of decision making are useful for 'training' or 'educating' new recruits into the ways of the company. Furthermore, he says, decision-making processes can be a source of enjoyment and a way of having a good time while one learns the meanings of organizational life (March 1984: 96).

There is another sense in which the garbage can approach has had a profound effect on the ways in which decision making is considered. March (1976) continued his criticisms of the rational model, but from a slightly different angle than is found in the garbage can approach. March entered a plea for incorporating what he calls *playfulness* and *sensible foolishness* into decision-making processes. He wanted to see organizations encouraging untried or novel ideas and using intuition to address problems and make decisions (somewhat akin to Edward De Bono's (1990) notion of 'lateral thinking'). These propositions were taken up by Tom Peters and Robert Waterman

(1982/84) who argued that entrepreneurship and innovation could only occur on a grand scale if organizational leaders loosened up their control and coordination mechanisms, thereby encouraging experimentation and risk taking, that is, playfulness and foolishness (Peters and Waterman 1984: 29–54, 101). However, March, along with Peters and Waterman, recognized that more playful organizations were only feasible if widely held misconceptions or myths about rational decision making were tackled by senior managers.

The political model of decision making

In the discussion of the rational model, it was noted that there will not always be agreement between organizational participants over organizational goals and how they are to be achieved. Such disagreements may occur not because such participants are bloody-minded and/or 'difficult to get on with', but because of fundamental differences over values and preferences and the perceptions of various choice criteria. Disagreements may also occur because of the existence of structural arrangements such as divisions, departments or cost and profit centres, and the demands made by participants in these subunits on the scarce resources of the organization. The well-known tension that exists between the marketing and production functions in organizations may simply reflect that these groups have different roles to perform, which sometimes bring them into conflict; that is, marketing is concerned with the adaptation of existing activities, while production is concerned with their maintenance. However, it is also true that subunits in organizations may develop goals related to their activities that are important to the group and its priorities, but are hard to reconcile with the goals of other subunits or the 'official' goals of the organization (that is, competing choices) (Perrow 1972: 158).

The view that recognizes the role of conflict and conflict resolution in the decision-making process is, as we have described, the political model. This view was first proposed by Cyert and March (1963) who argued that organizations should be understood as consisting of shifting coalitions that form and reform around issues of concern to them. Coalition members will not all be drawn from the organization and could include suppliers, customers, shareholders and external interest groups. Because of the shifting nature of coalitions, it is difficult to draw strict boundaries around them, although fairly consistent alignments will emerge over some matters, for example during budget time, department members will usually close ranks and support each other to get more resources.

By contrast with the unitary frame of the rational model, the political approach is pluralistic in nature, recognizing the role of various stakeholders in affecting and shaping matters of significance to the organization. In this view, what are commonly referred to as the 'goals of the organization' are in fact the goals of coalitions (Lupton 1971: 119). Implicit in this is the possibility that these goals will be challenged by other coalitions or that another dominant coalition may some day emerge. Decision making is thus about reconciling the interests of different stakeholders. Organizations are portrayed as systems adapting and learning to cope with a variety of internal and external constraints.

Once we accept the idea of coalitions, we are by definition recognizing that different groups have different goals and strategies for pursuing their interests (Weeks 1980: 196). Cyert and March (1963) are not unduly worried about the fact that coalitions may be chasing diverse or multiple goals. As long as an organization is not operating in a turbulent or hostile environment and has surplus resources, that is, slack, then conflict and power struggles will not be overly harmful. Moreover, they believe that organizations have mechanisms by which they can stabilize power struggles and conflicts. *Side-payments* was a term used to describe the ways in which organizational slack is transformed into different forms of reward for coalition members. Side-payments can be such things as monetary rewards, preferential treatment, increased authority (status) or benefits from various policies. Cyert and March (1963) believe that side-payments of a monetary kind are not satisfactory methods of resolving conflict or buying loyalty from coalition members. Thus while side-payments of a monetary kind (overtime payments, leave loading and so on) are considered important, side-payments which involve policy commitments to employees are thought to be more beneficial. These include employment contracts, retirement and superannuation schemes, workers' compensation arrangements, systems of annual review, promotional structures or equal employment opportunity provisions. They are likely to minimize political activity and win the long-term support and loyalty of individual coalition members.

While side-payments tend to be associated with rewards to management, it has to be recognized that they need not be limited to this group alone: profit sharing can act to stall or neutralize conflict and political activity at all levels of an organization. Rewards such as bonuses for achieving or increasing targets for various managers and other personnel are an increasingly popular way of using the budgetary process to control the demands of coalition members, while also ensuring that decisions are not being constantly challenged (see also Curwen 1963: 144).

Dominant coalitions and non-decision making

The pluralist view of decision making provides an important critique of the unitary perspective, particularly the rational model. However, the pluralist approach does not go far enough in mapping out or explaining how decisions can be made or avoided in organizations because of the influence or pressure of external groups who may form part of a dominant coalition. Furthermore, the pluralist approach presumes that conflict and power struggles occur under circumstances in which all participants have substantial knowledge and information about such things as organizational slack and have access to decision-making arenas.

Cyert and March's approach to decision making, for example, could not explain how very powerful individuals from a wide spectrum of interests (for example banking, media, legal, political) form coalitions which negotiate and bargain among themselves to influence and shape decisions not just in a single business but across whole sections of an economy or industry. The failure to account for the influence of these types of dominant coalitions was considered a serious flaw by John Child, who has been the major proponent of the strategic choice view of decision making (Child 1972: 1–11). He has sought to further explain decision-making processes by emphasizing the role that dominant coalitions play in the choice of strategies made by organizations, choices which can impact on every individual and dramatically affect such things as side-payments and slack.

According to Child, the *dominant coalition* does not necessarily refer only to formal authority holders (those with legitimate authority in an organization) but to a collection of individuals who hold power over a particular decision-making period and are in positions to have input into policy initiation and implementation. Coalition members can draw their support from a wide range of key or strategically placed individuals. Important strategic decisions (mergers, takeovers, moving off-shore and so on) are often the result of negotiations and bargains between coalition members and not necessarily the result of some well-thought-out rational method of decision making. Decisions about such things as mergers, for example, are not necessarily made because there are laws, principles, facts or figures which support this strategy. A choice to merge may be made because a powerful person owes a favour, has cross-board membership or is locked into a struggle to defeat a third party and so on (see the Convenant Corporation case study).

Dominant coalitions can be so powerful that their members have opportunities to select the types of environments in which they will operate rather than passively responding to external threats and pressures. For example, some company leaders and their backers may simply choose to pull out of a particular strategy if it proves too hostile, or they may wait to enter a new market when conditions improve. However, the striking feature of dominant coalitions is that they can produce such awesome concentrations of power and influence that they can totally reshape the environment in which they are operating, and a few key decision makers can effectively monopolize control within and across whole industries such as brewing, television, computer software, banking or the media. Dominant coalitions may face significant barriers in their environments, such as accusations of anti-competitive behaviour, but the point is that they do not see themselves as passive in the face of their environments. The scale of their potential influence means that they can actively shape the environment in the image of their desires.

Child (1972) tends to counter the notion that all actors have the opportunity to engage in coalitions that will be of benefit to them. Dominant coalitions are not accessible to all because the nature of organizations is such that inequity and disadvantage are generic features: there are always the powerful and the powerless. Thus dominant coalitions are usually made up of managerial elites who are relatively unfettered in circumventing, breaking or modifying the bounds of decision making, and therefore determining what counts as a relevant decision topic for various groups (Wilson et al. 1986: 310, 328–9). This does not suggest that lower participants are entirely powerless in decision making (for example information filtering from members in various locations, such as sales staff, branch managers and so on). However, Child points out that there is a sharp distinction between those who initiate a decision in regard to major organizational choices and those who are 'marginal' to these decision-making processes.

This last point leads into the second criticism of the pluralist approach. It would be misleading to believe that all organizational participants can form coalitions and act politically to influence major decisions affecting their rights and benefits. The pluralist view fails to account for the ways in which many important decisions are removed from decision-making processes or are suffocated and never become decision topics. Lukes uses the term *non-decision making* to describe how powerful individuals can use their authority and influence to ensure that sensitive or potentially harmful information can be neutralized, suppressed or hidden. Non-decision making involves considerable resources, effort and skill because certain individuals and groups have to be censured and kept in check or else they may force power holders to make revelations and be held accountable (see Chapter 6).

The essential feature of non-decision making is that it

draws attention to the many ways in which powerful groups or individuals can structure organizational agendas to their advantage (Lukes 1974: 18–19). Once information is selectively filtered, suppressed or delayed from being made public, the outcome of certain decisions becomes a foregone conclusion, hence non-decision making. For many years the occupational health and safety of workers was an issue which was ignored and sensitive information was withheld at the cost of endangering the lives of workers. Often it was too costly to institute proper safety measures while maintaining profits (at least, unilaterally), so safety issues were not incorporated into company policies or practices by key decision makers. The dangers of asbestos are a case in point. Its harmful effects have been known since about 1907, but many governments and businesses throughout the world mined the ore without providing proper protection for workers, thus causing many deaths and illnesses from asbestos-related cancers. Through non-decision making, managers were able to control outcomes and suffocate opposition.

While Lukes is concerned with how potential issues are turned into non-decision events by the very powerful, in many large organizations the pressures and competition for scarce resources (salaries and so on) and rewards (promotion and so on) can encourage all sorts of individuals and groups to consciously and deliberately manipulate information, bend rules, policies and procedures in order to gain a distinct advantage or benefit from certain decisions. There are many instances of non-decision making in organizations. A quality control department which fails to implement proper tests and studies but lends support to the release of a new product without revealing the shortcomings of its findings is creating a non-decision-making situation.

Perhaps because of pressures from other divisions and the need to be seen as efficient and competitive, some key staff in quality control may choose to allow others to make decisions about a product's safety while suppressing negative or unwelcome results or, for that matter, concealing the fact that adequate testing was not undertaken. Many organizations become involved in costly litigation and bad media exposure because they are caught violating codes, standards and regulations applying to their industry. Often the decisions which lead to these situations can only be explained as outcomes of non-decision-making processes (Pfeffer 1981: 146–54; Stephenson 1985: 153–4).

The whole area of non-decision making raises many important issues about the ethical conduct of organizational participants and the exercise of power (see Chapter 6). Those who control major resources and activities are positioned more strategically to engage in effective non-decision making. In other words, it is easier to bend rules if you are in a position to make the rules or interpret them for others. Some recent decision theorists view non-decision making as being the most relevant of the traditional management decision-making models, especially in terms of describing the activities of powerful and dominant coalitions (see Chapter 6). Nonetheless, non-decision making is itself a problematic approach to decision making. Robert Chia (1996: 200–1), for example, proposes that 'obscured activity' better describes the processes of non-decision making, and advocates of the model are oblivious to the 'formative nature' of the non-decision-making process. At the very heart of any non-decision making are 'decisional acts' of inclusion and exclusion, and such 'non-activity' is ultimately productive of social reality. This point is illustrated in the case study below.

CASE EXAMPLE

NON-DECISIONS

Decisions involving huge outlays of capital are almost always classic gut decisions; they involve risky, inherently ambiguous judgements between unclear alternatives. In mature industries, like textiles and chemicals, managers are regularly faced with troubling reinvestment decisions.

Alchemy Inc.'s non-decision

Numerical measures and other seemingly sophisticated analytical tools can only be 'guideposts' in making such choices. Satisfactory rates of return are socially determined; they vary from industry to industry, indeed, from

firm to firm, and involve complicated assessments of competitors' strategies, actual, possible, or pending regulation, possible alternative investments and, most important, key managers' determinations of what levels of return are desirable, acceptable and defensible. Since credit flows up and details get pushed down in corporate hierarchies, managers at the middle and upper-middle levels are often left to sort out extremely complicated questions about technology, investment and their bosses' desires and intentions.

Consider, for instance, the case of a large coking plant. Coke making requires a gigantic battery to cook the coke slowly and evenly for long periods; the battery is the most important piece of capital equipment in a coking plant. In 1975, Alchemy's battery showed signs of weakening and certain managers at corporate headquarters had to decide whether to invest $6 million to restore the battery to top form. Clearly, because of the amount of money involved, this was a gut decision.

No decision was made. The CEO had sent the word out to defer all unnecessary capital expenditures to give the corporation cash reserves for other investments. So the managers allocated small amounts of money to patch the battery up until 1979, when it collapsed entirely. This brought the company into a breach of contract with a steel producer and into violation of various Environmental Protection Agency (EPA) pollution regulations. The total bill, including lawsuits and now federally mandated repairs to the battery, exceeded $100 million. I have heard figures as high as $150 million, but because of 'creative accounting', no one is sure of the exact amount.

This simple but very typical example gets to the heart of how decision making is intertwined with a company's authority structure and advancement patterns. As Alchemy managers see it, the decisions facing them in 1975 and 1979 were crucially different. Had they acted decisively in 1975 – in hindsight, the only substantively rational course – they would have salvaged the battery and saved their corporation millions of dollars in the long run.

In the short run, however, since even seemingly rational decisions are subject to widely varying interpretations, particularly decisions that run counter to a CEO's stated objectives, they would have been taking serious personal risks in restoring the battery. What is more, their political networks might have unravelled, leaving them vulnerable to attack. They chose short-term [personal] safety over long-term [organizational] gain.

This goes to the heart of the problem. Managers think in the short run because they are evaluated by both their superiors and peers on their short-term results. Those who are not seen to be producing requisite short-run gains come to be thought of as embarrassing liabilities. Of course, past work gets downgraded in such a process. The old saw, still heard frequently today, 'I know what you did for me yesterday, but what have you done for me lately?' is more than a tired garment district salesman's joke. It accurately reflects the widespread amnesia among managers about others' past accomplishments, however notable, and points to the probationary crucibles at the core of managerial life. Managers feel that if they do not survive the short run, the long run hardly matters, and one can only buy time for the future by attending to short-term goals. As one manager says: 'Our horizon is today's lunch.'

Within such a context, managers know that even farsighted, correct decisions can shorten promising careers. A manager at Weft Corporation reflects:

> People are always calculating how others will see the decisions that they make. They are always asking: 'What are the consequences of this decision?' They know that they have to gauge not just the external ... market consequences of a decision, but the internal political consequences. And sometimes you can make the right market decision, but it can be the wrong political decision.
>
> Decisions are made only when they are inevitable. To make a decision ahead of the time it has to be made risks political catastrophe. People can always interpret the decision as an unwise one even if it seems to be correct on other grounds.

When a decision is inevitable, managers say, 'The decision made itself.' Diffusion of responsibility, in the case of the coke battery by procrastinating until total crisis voided real choices, is intrinsic to organizational life because the real issue in most gut decisions is: Who is going to get blamed if things go wrong?

Note: Alchemy Inc. is a subsidiary of Covenant Corporation.

Source: Modified from Robert Jackall (1988) *Moral Mazes: The World of Corporate Managers*, Oxford: Oxford University Press, pp. 80–2, 84–5.

The above case illustrates that although knowledge is extremely important in organizational decision making, organizational members will draw on a much wider variety of knowledge than decision theory is customarily able to recognize. The postmodern organization increasingly relies on the quality of its information for making critical decisions quickly but, as Robert Jackall (1988) notes, these are often still 'gut decisions' rather than calculated ones. Put simply, this arises because all knowledge is about the past, and all decisions are about the future, so there is always an element of incommensurability to them – they do not quite fit together. Knowledge is often not shared between managers and groups of managers for political reasons, despite the furious networking they may do, *until* it looks as though their project may need some help to avoid failure. So here, in a real sense, knowledge is power, and is realized through both action and non-action, informed by information which ranges from, say, the president's body language to three feet of printout from scenario planning software.

Groupthink

Many decisions may also be affected by the effectiveness of group behaviour, and ironically, successful groups may be affected by these problems as much as unsuccessful ones. In the case of successful groups, a phenomenon which can lead to the escalation of bad decisions to the point of debacle is referred to as *groupthink*. Irving Janis, in his 1972 book *Victims of Groupthink,* identified it as the 'deterioration of mental efficiency, reality testing and moral judgment that results from in-group pressures' (see also Janis 1982). Here a group with a track history of success gets carried away with its own cohesiveness and triumphs, and members become reluctant to criticize – poor decisions are not challenged and can become fiascos, such as the decision of the US to invade Cuba at the Bay of Pigs or the increasing military commitment of the US in Vietnam.

The hubris of groupthink, according to Janis, may be a characteristic of any type of group but is particularly prevalent where the group is talented and successful, on the principle of 'the bigger they come, the harder they fall'. It has several symptoms:

- an illusion of invulnerability, with excessive optimism and risk taking as the group begins to behave as though it cannot make a bad decision.
- Pressures on individual members to conform and reach consensus mean that unpopular ideas may be suppressed. Members who oppose the group, even with gentle dissension, are stereotyped as weak, evil or stupid.
- The continuing search for group consensus can result in collective rationalization by members, which leads them to discount warnings and negative information. As they feed off each other's energies, what emerges is an illusion of unanimity and self-censorship of any deviation from group norms or apparent group consensus. Privately, everyone with doubts thinks that they are the only one with negative thoughts and suppresses them.
- An unquestioned belief in the inherent morality of the group which leads members to be convinced of the logical correctness of what they are doing and ignore the ethical or moral consequences of decisions. They appear to think, 'we could never make a bad decision because we are such good and clever people'.

The primary condition for groupthink is group cohesion, underwritten by a history of individual and group success. Strong bonds in a group can be positive or negative influences on decision making, but where a group is isolated from the rest of the organization, or for security reasons is working in secret, a sense of unreality can emerge. In these cases, the better the group get along together, the greater the problem can be. The leader of the group, if there is one, may steer the group unwittingly by setting agendas, expressing preferences or pressuring the group to make decisions.

With groupthink, members' striving for unanimity, their need for consensus, overrides their motivation to realistically appraise alternative courses of action.

Groupthink can be avoided with some effort. Groups should try not to work without interaction with other groups unless absolutely necessary and should stay in touch with the rest of the organization. Consultants or others should be invited in, with licence to challenge the group with alternatives, question their methods and reflect back bad processes to the group as they occur. Leaders need to be sufficiently reflexive so as to be able to assess their own behaviour and stay impartial unless it becomes impossible to do so. Groups can also be directed deliberately to develop alternative plans, create different decision stories and adopt multiple perspectives, such as putting them-selves in the place of stakeholders or those whom the decision will affect.

Cross-cultural issues in decision making

Miller et al. (1996) note with alarm that virtually all the major studies of decision making have been American, British or Scandinavian. They note that the existing studies do display some evidence of differences between the different varieties of Western culture, but that on the whole such cultures consistently engender decision making which is 'pluralistic, bluntly competitive and impersonal' (Miller et al. 1996: 308). Elsewhere in the world, approaches may be more person-centred, where loyalty is owed to the person not the job, higher authority may be greatly venerated and harmony and consideration for others may offset the drive for achievement by the individual. As Miller et al. (1996: 309) suggest, these processes may not be adequately accounted for by such concepts as 'satisficing search, incrementalism, rationality and politicality, recycling, sporadic or fluid or constricted movement, or coinciding garbage'.

Decision making in the Arab Middle East tends to be centralized, with authority having high status, especially where it is family-based. There is a certain *noblesse oblige* to consult subordinates, but this is not the Western sense of participation and has no impact on the decision-making process. In Latin America decision making is centralized and personal, and in Brazil particular decisions are made almost hastily and informally. In Africa, decision making is likely to be more authoritarian and politicized. Concepts such as political sporadic processes, or the garbage can model, seem unlikely in these settings.

But of course what Miller et al. (1996) describe are the elements of different discourses which shape the decisional text, in regions where social subjectivity varies widely. Their puzzlement, which arises from an almost nostalgic feeling that earlier decision-making studies might have been engaging with a knowledge that was universal and not local, and that their own theories might have been caught up in that process, would not be perplexing when viewed from the textual approach which we outline later in this chapter. Nevertheless, Miller et al. (1996) have moved a considerable distance from Anglo-American-centred universalistic discourse, and they cautiously argue for greater global research on decision-making processes, while observing that even in relatively open societies like the West managers do not readily open their doors to scrutiny of high-level decision making. In more authoritarian or familial cultures, problems associated with access for research would become enormous – but it should still be noted that theories which depend on Anglo-American data neglect a huge proportion of humankind.

Critique of 'decision' and 'choice'

The management decision-making schools reviewed above develop their theories of decision making by making specific reference to the inherent capabilities of individual decision makers, especially their capabilities for rational thinking. They often also make assumptions that are essentialist in nature, that is, they assume decision makers have commonly held aspirations, goals or universal experiences. Historically, the use of 'choice' as an explanation for decision making has been crucial as a move away from the determinism of management science, with its *normative* models of decision making. Peter Keen and Michael Scott Morton (1978: 62) point out that the emphasis had been 'on how managers *should* act rather than on observing how they actually behave'. Choice is such a compelling concept in decision-making theory that it has attained the status of 'common sense' (Belsey 1980). Common-sense categories are rarely challenged and, as a consequence, will tend to organize research directions, agendas and questions within a field. But common sense is as much sensible because it is common, as it is common because it is sensible. By recognizing that the idea of choice has become a common-sense category, our responsibility becomes one of questioning the prevailing assumptions implied by it. The common-sense category of choice, in the context of management decision making, organizes the field so as to view the function, status and value of management work in terms of purposefulness and reason (that is, as rational).

There have been recent developments, as pointed out earlier, which recognize some of the limitations of traditional decision-making literature and have led to a shift away from 'decisions' to other concerns such as

'action' (Mintzberg et al. 1990); from 'choice' to that of 'change' in the context of decision making (Pettigrew 1990) or to the interpretation of 'action' (March 1988). These revisions acknowledge that the concept of a decision is problematic and managers are not always faced with clear-cut rational choices. March (1988) in fact argues that reality is messy and decision makers often *value* ambiguity (see also Munro 1995) – it means that they do not have to commit themselves to potentially risky courses of action until it is absolutely necessary. It also means that they can see how events unfold and influence interpretations of them so that they can look good and avoid blame, as the managers in Covenant and Weft Corporations sought to do. However, in many respects 'actions', 'change' and 'interpretation' function simply as aliases for traditional categories. Underlying these new concepts are the same kinds of assumptions concerning the individual, rationalist intentionality of management action, 'reinforced by a predisposition towards the use of linear causal thinking in the explanatory scheme of things and towards a subtle privileging of the conscious over the unconscious in accounting for decisional "events"' (Chia 1996: 193). A significant theoretical problem for most accounts of management decision making is the use of the psychological subject, that is, the individual person, as the formative unit, where groups are theorized as collections of individuals and group characteristics are the sum of individual characteristics. Group activities then are seen to be primarily shaped by psychological forces rather than, for example, social, anthropological, political or linguistic ones.

What these approaches fail to acknowledge is what we have termed, following Chia, the flow of *decisional acts* that contribute to the decision-making process. In their everyday lives managers are ordering their world, constantly redrawing boundaries, and Mintzberg et al. and March are, at the level of theory, doing the same thing. Making a 'decision' is a matter of making distinctions between things, actions and events, which leads us to perceive the world in a particular way. To view 'decision' as choice, change, action or interpretation is to fail to pay attention to other alternatives, and also to see that this in itself is a decision. In fact, as Chia argues, making decisions, or decisional acts, is an inescapable condition of being human, not just a special activity undertaken by decision makers at specific decision-making events.

Mintzberg et al. (1990), Pettigrew (1972) and March (1988) do make some attempt to counteract the rationalist tendency in decision making and produce a more fully *descriptive* and *analytical* rather than a *prescriptive* model of managerial decision making. However, they do not go far enough in addressing what such a model might require. We would suggest that its attributes would include:

- the replacement of the mentalist, rational concept of 'decision' with an explicitly social theory of *communicative action*
- a social theory of *subjectivity* and *agency* to replace the individualism of rationalist models of management decision making
- a *contextual approach* to decision making where context includes an account of both the broader disciplinary and institutional contexts, given that disciplines act to discipline and control their practitioners (Lenoir 1993: 70–102), and the immediate situational contexts which inform specific decision-making occasions
- a *descriptive* and *textual* model based on a discursive (see definition below) theory of human communication, in order to describe under which organizational circumstances specific 'choices' become available or unavailable, permissible or not permissible, or thinkable or unthinkable for groups of managers.

Retheorizing decision making

In light of the criticisms provided in the previous section, this chapter proposes an account of decision making based on the *textual process model of organizations* (Clarke 1991, 1992). In order to build this model, we draw from theories of communication which have been developed in critical theory, communications and cultural studies, psychoanalysis, social semiotics and feminist studies. Much of this literature is generally unfamiliar to students of management, although you will find theory relating to its elements used in other chapters of this text (see for example Chapters 2, 3, 6 and 15). Retheorizing decision making using a textual process model, means in this instance that the analytical emphasis is placed on understanding the practices involved in communication in specific organizational contexts. Elements of the model (discourse, text, genre and social subjectivity) are described in turn in order to simplify the discussion and introduce the necessary concepts.

Discourse

Knowledge is intimately related to power, as many commentators have noted. As such, knowledge is never neutral, since any account or knowledge of the world embodies particular ways of viewing the world, and any way of viewing the world privileges the interests of certain groups rather than others. To give a simple example, knowledge of the world predicated upon mathematics privileges the numerate. A key vehicle for the construction and dissemination of knowledge is 'discourse' and the role of discursive

knowledge in the construction and change of societal institutions, and those who are subject to them, has been extensively investigated by the French social theorist, philosopher and historian, Michel Foucault (1972, 1980). Discourse refers to the ways in which language and practices intertwine and coalesce into specific resources that enable us to see and speak of the world in particular ways. This coalescence of ways of speaking and seeing in particular institutions, such as religion, science, government, business and education, creates a sense of belonging for each of the discourse publics posited by each of the institutions, and a limited range of specific identities that can be adopted by those who share that sense of belonging. Anyone who is subject to a particular religious orthodoxy, a particular educational or economic system, or who is part of a particular cultural, ethnic or indigenous group, is a 'member' of a particular discourse public. Such 'membership' carries with it various opportunities and restrictions, unwritten rules about which ideas are acceptable for debate or discussion and which ones taboo. Prohibitions and permissions permeate the discourse of institutions and determine what can be said, seen, heard and visualized by members. We can only meaningfully speak, hear, visualize and see through the language and modes of interpretation given to us by discourse, through the particular framework for knowledge that a particular discourse provides. As such, discourse provides the ground, the basic resources, through which we are able to 'read' particular arrangements of words as sensible and appropriate, and 'see' particular arrangements of objects as meaningful and coherent visual scenes. According to Kress (1985: 6–7):

Discourses are systematically-organised sets of statements which give expression to the meanings and values of an institution. Beyond that they define, describe and delimit what it is possible to say and not possible to say (and by extension – what it is possible to do or not to do) with respect to the area of concern of that institution, whether marginally or centrally. A discourse provides a set of possible statements about a given area, and organises and gives structure to the manner in which a particular topic, object, process is to be talked about. In that it provides descriptions, rules, permissions and prohibitions of social and individual actions.

As we noted above, however, discourses do not only work through written statements, they also work through the ways in which the world is pictured and seen in the visual realm (see Ezzamel et al. forthcoming), a facet of their operation that is too often ignored when the role of language in discourse is appreciated too narrowly. For example, in a closely argued reading of IT consultancy reports, Brian Bloomfield and Theo Vurdubakis (1994) convincingly demonstrate the ways in which particular forms of visualization and diagramming dominate thought and action in the field of systems design. They note that a particular aesthetic holds sway in this work which partially determines the way in which problems of information and decision are thought about and acted upon, with perhaps the most obvious instance being the 'decision tree' which informs and organizes much of the work of decision support systems designers. Just as particular formations of words provide a particular account of the world which privileges certain positions and readings over others, so does a particular way of picturing the world construct a particular view, which also privileges certain positions and possibilities over others. But the visual and verbal aspects of discourse can also intertwine. For example, Dick Boland (1987) demonstrates the way in which

the imagery of 'decision space' in Simon's work has led to a certain view of the appropriate role of information systems designers, something we also touched upon in our account of the bureaucratic/administrative model of decision making. By constructing the way in which the world is seen and said, discourses embody the power that is associated with knowledge, by providing the very language with which we see and describe the world. Take a look at the case study below on the discourse of 'enterprise', which has been common since the 1980s; 100 years ago the discourse of 'progress' might have performed the same role in mobilizing society. The important thing to remember here is that language and power are inseparably connected in discourse and have a much broader influence than simply the things we say.

CASE EXAMPLE

ENTERPRISE CULTURE IN THE UK

During the 1980s, the Conservative government of the UK led by Margaret Thatcher determined that it would change the social structures which had underpinned the welfare state – regulation of business practices by the state, high levels of taxation, relatively militant trade unionism, high levels of welfare benefits paid. Along with this, they wanted to change the expectations of the people who, Thatcher believed, had become too dependent on the state and were insufficiently entrepreneurial, profit-oriented and business and competition minded.

> I used to have a nightmare for the first six years in office that, when I had got the finances right, when I had got the law right, the deregulation and so on, that the British sense of enterprise and initiative would have been killed by socialism. I was really afraid that when I had got it all ready to spring back, it would no longer be there and it would not come back. (Thatcher, *Sunday Times,* 8 May 1988)

The project of economic reconstruction clearly went much further – 'Economics are the method. The object is to change the soul' (Thatcher, *Sunday Times,* 7 May 1989); 'fighting and changing the culture and psychology of two generations … changing psychology to change the business culture' (Lawson 1984). Although the overall project of Thatcherism was not completely cohesive, it involved the combined efforts of 'think-tanks' such as the Centre for Policy Studies, who produced papers on economic, political and legal issues associated with fiscal policy and deregulation; policy advisers such as Keith Josephs and Brian Griffiths

who developed moral and ethical arguments; businessmen/politicians such as David Young who developed and applied the language of managerialism – competition, customers, enterprise, markets, niches, competitive advantage, distinctive competence, strategic positioning, quality, process control, cost, profit and loss and so on – to all areas of the state including health and education; marketing specialists and advertising geniuses such as Saatchi and Saatchi who promoted and publicized the ideology; a minor military victory in the Falklands which provided the inspiration for the carefully orchestrated campaign against the 'enemy within' to break the power of the trade unions; support of the media, cemented by refranchising the independent TV and radio stations and reforming the BBC; redrawing of electoral boundaries which reduced the impact of the opposition vote (that is, the effective expression of dissension) in marginal seats; and of course the well-documented economic and legal strategies followed by the government. This complex web of speeches, books, articles, TV programmes, legislation, political stratagems and practical actions was designed to change not only the way people lived their lives but how they thought about themselves, and allowed room for no alternatives to the vision of personal independence, individual enterprise and self-responsibility. The very meanings of such words as enterprise and quality were redefined in a way which fitted the political and ideological programme, and predisposed individuals and businesses to a certain type of action. This, in its entirety, was the *enterprise discourse.*

Note: See Russell Keat and Nicholas Abercrombie (1991) *Enterprise Culture,* London: Routledge, for an extensive treatment of how this discourse was constructed.

To apply the concept of discourse to a management decision-making situation, consider the following hypothetical example: the strategic managers of UK corporatized public service company are faced with a continuing slump in profits due to the deregulation of the market in which they operate. The short-term decision-making prospects seem to be limited to a small range of 'tried and true' choices including management restructuring, corporate downsizing and outsourcing of 'non-core' activities. What dictates this particular set of options? Discourse theory suggests that the choices have already been partly preordained by what is currently considered to be efficient private sector best practice, since current economic and management discourses dictate that public sector entities should operate in the same fashion as private sector entities. Thus the strategic managers within the company will probably be locked into specific courses of action which are already in part predetermined by the fact that these managers see themselves as managers through frameworks of understanding provided by discourses which *assume* the equivalence of public and private sector entities and their members – discourses like that of 'enterprise'. In effect discourse theory says that these managers will already be actively involved in a kind of 'collective' and unacknowledged blindness to entire courses of action. This collective blindness is inscribed in the discourses which circulate within organizations predisposing, but in no way entirely determining, what constitutes effective and efficient management decision making. It is important to note here that discourses never directly operate on managers or others. Discourses inform texts (see below) which in turn are 'read' by managers or others in specific organizational contexts and discourses themselves are carried by their members' reading of texts. Discourses neither exist in isolation nor determine finally what members will think and do, they must have participants in order to function and those participants must have some freedom to interpret the discourse according to the particularities of their own specific situations.

In a large number of modern 'scientific' disciplines, including modern management science, and its related disciplines of information systems and accounting, the psychological individual is viewed as the origin of meaning in social and cultural practices. In the previous section, we described decision-making theory as having attained the status of 'common sense' (Belsey 1980; Garfinkel 1987). This is possible because particular types of discourse, such as *liberal-humanist discourse*, operate throughout Western culture. The effect of these types of discourse is to *naturalize*, that is, to allow to operate unchallenged, the view that individuals are single, unified originators of meanings. In turn, liberal-humanist discourse has influenced academics and practitioners to reproduce uncritically these discourses as 'common sense' when creating theories of decision making. As these traditional models pass into the literature and are adopted and enacted by practitioners, the common-sense nature of the individual decision maker, unproblematically choosing from a range of options, becomes reproduced. Within the field of decision making, the literature simply assumes that managers are readily able to evaluate a 'full range' of potential choices, differentiate between competing choices, select a clear favourite or avoid or suppress choice altogether. Yet, as we have already noted, even studies informed by these assumptions uncover anomalous findings which they struggle to explain.

Furthermore, theorizing or presenting speakers (managers) as the originators of meanings (decisions) favours those who are allowed or authorized to speak in specific circumstances. Similarly, issues of power and control tend to be discussed from just such an individualist standpoint. Power in organizations is often treated as if it were a commodity – the possession of individuals, rather than a relational product of the ways in which language allocates different positions, rights, responsibilities and opportunities to the range of individuals it differentiates. This individualism obscures the way that organizations operate as a product of various influences, such as markets, technology and so on and processes such as discrimination and exploitation.

Gender as a discourse

To illustrate our point about the importance of discourse, and who is allowed to speak and in what way, let us take the example of gender. Men and women have never been viewed as or treated as equals in the workplace. Jobs have been differentiated and even whole occupations, especially those in service industries, have been designated 'women's work'. Fewer than 20 per cent of all managerial posts are held by women, and at more senior levels this falls to 10 per cent (see Chapter 2). Men are often seen to be rational, calculating and resilient, whereas women are seen as being emotional, changeable and lacking resolution, and the work of Deborah Tannen (1995) (also mentioned in Chapter 2) indicates that this background of cultural presumptions results in men and women actually *talking* differently and thus communicating different things when they speak. As Tannen argues, women tend to learn styles of speaking which make them appear less confident and self-assured than they really are, and as a result they lose out on those organizational issues – like promotion – that depend on appearing confident. They also tend to be called upon less to speak in decision-making processes, and if they are, are less likely to be regarded as being persuasive or credible.

The Harvard feminist scholar Carol Cohn (1987) notes an even more startling outcome of adopting a gendered (and, in this case, militaristic) way of talking in her account of her experience of the discourse of nuclear doctrine as a participant observer within a university centre for defence technology and arms control. While initially 'aghast, but morbidly fascinated … by the extraordinary abstraction' that the (almost exclusively white male) defence intellectuals used to discuss their subject, she found that as she learned the language of her temporary colleagues – the language which allows 'defense intellectuals to think and act as they do' (1987: 690), to think and act in ways that Cohn clearly found not only gendered but also abhorrent – she 'became more and more engaged with their information and their arguments' (p. 688). Indeed as she became further inured in the language of defence, she began to find 'that talking about nuclear weapons is fun' (p. 704)! Talking this language reduced Cohn's fear of nuclear war but she had joined the programme to question the rationale surrounding nuclear doctrine, not to come to accept it. As such, she tried to challenge the logics of her colleagues but in doing so she confronted a seemingly insurmountable divide. When she sought to express her initial concerns in 'English rather than expert jargon', the men responded as though she were 'ignorant, simpleminded or both' (p. 708). Yet when she strove to avoid being patronized in this way and adapted her 'everyday speech to the vocabulary of strategic analysis' (p. 708), she found it increasingly impossible to express her own ideas and values and, worse still, she began to find it hard even to keep these ideas and values in her head! In short, she could either be heard, or she could say what she wanted to, but she could not do both.

Learning to speak the language of defense intellectuals is not a conscious, cold-blooded decision to ignore the effects of nuclear weapons on real live human beings, to ignore the sensory, the emotional experience, the human impact. It is simply learning a new language, but by the time you are through, the content of what you can talk about is monumentally different, as is the perspective from which you speak. (Cohn 1987: 705)

Returning to our central concern in this chapter, in their study on the decision-making experiences of women and people of colour, Priscilla Elsass and Laura Graves (1997: 954–5) found evidence which confirmed that women contribute to group tasks at the lower end, make fewer attempts to influence the group, are less often chosen as leaders and are generally less committed to group outcomes. In terms of communication style, and echoing Tannen's comments in Chapter 2, Elsass and Graves noted that white male behaviour is typically the norm by which other groups are judged. In the context of decision making, the open-ended free-wheeling decision-making environment in many Western organizations is likely to intimidate those not comfortable with this style. In some cultures, speaking aggressively or interrupting others might also be seen as rude, whether done by men or women.

In an interesting experiment, Elizabeth Mapstone (cited in Powell 1998; also see Mapstone 1998) sorted 72 men and women into an equal number of pairs comprising man–man, man–woman and woman–woman. Each participant was given a detective story to read with a number of possible solutions. Once the story was read, each person was asked to discuss his or her decisions with his or her partners. While some men were able to convince their male partners to change their minds about the correct solution to the mystery, and the same occurred with women-only pairs, the men who had women partners were not influenced to change their minds. Mapstone concludes, as do Elsass and Graves, that there are so many stereotypes drawn upon when women seek to argue with or influence male colleagues that, more often than not, women's views are more easily discounted or not listened to. One corollary of this is that women often avoid arguing because of both the discomfort this causes the men around them and the negative stereotypes (hostile, aggressive, hysterical) that may be applied to them if they do engage in such behaviour. The conclusion from these various studies suggests that powerful people, which usually means men, are more likely to reward and listen to people with similar language styles.

Language styles can affect the type and richness of information that we receive in the process of linguistic exchange. A restricted style can mean a restricted input of information, less fruitful discussion and a failure to achieve smooth implementation, as not all the relevant dimensions of the problem were available for consideration. This must seriously impact on the quality of decision making under conditions of diversity. So what people say and how they say it can be different depending on their gender, and this may both open and close doors to them and may enrich or impoverish the process of organizational decision making. An organization which only rewards one communicative style is losing its ability to hear a wide range of information, share knowledge and increase the flexibility of its actions.

Texts

Any specific utterance or document mobilized in a social setting, including discussions between managers involved in decision-making occasions, can be referred to as a *text*. Following our discursive vein, the term 'text' is used to indicate that decision making involves language. According to this approach, texts are made intelligible through reference to *genres* that provide a set of expectations in light of which the text can be read, as another example of a familiar story. The plural form, texts, is generally used to signify two important aspects of the theory:

1. Decision-making occasions, along with most other organizational practices, generally produce *more than one text*. If we were studying a specific decision-making occasion, we might use a tape recorder to make a record of what managers were saying (one text), which we might subsequently use to produce a transcript of what transpired during the meeting (another text), while also collecting associated written texts which would help understand what took place (agendas, minutes and attachments).

2. Meaning-making occasions are 'processes'. To consider a text as simply a document would be ignoring the fact that while a text can be defined as 'a structure of messages or messages traces which has a socially ascribed unity' (Hodge and Kress 1988: 6), its constituent messages, and consequently the text itself, can *never have a single, fixed meaning*.

This last point requires further consideration. Catherine Belsey (1980: 26) states that while language provides the possibility of meaning, any text exhibits multiple meanings because meanings never remain static. This is easily demonstrated by the extent to which people in meetings disagree with the minutes of a previous meeting. Participants may agree that the same decisions were made (although that is certainly not always the case), but those same decisions may carry different meanings for the different people involved. Not everyone 'reads' a text in the same way. This does not, however, mean that anything goes. The person or people who produce a particular text usually have a view or perspective on what that text should mean or, to put it another way, specific texts are embedded in specific discourses (Belsey 1980: 19–20). The meaning of a text depends on the reading position one adopts to 'make sense' of it, and generally a text will be (more) intelligible from one particular position. If readers recognize the correct discursive underpinnings of a text, they will adopt the appropriate position to make sense of it as the producer intended. One particular meaning is thus privileged by the text and its context, but there is always the possibility for others to be read in from different positions and, indeed, many jokes turn on the division between two possible readings of text. To give but one example, a number of new signs have recently appeared at the side of a road in the UK, each of them boldly pointing to an apparently 'secret bunker'! Now the idea of a sign pointing to a *secret* bunker is clearly

somewhat oxymoronic, to say the least, and it is not how the text of the sign is intended to be read. But it is certainly an intelligible reading, albeit a somewhat destructive one for our normal notions of 'secret' and 'sign'. However, the signs do make perfect sense when one adds the necessary extra information needed to ascertain their official meaning. The locations of bunkers to which the signs point *were* secret during the Cold War. They were the sites where it was hoped that government would continue in the wake of a nuclear strike. However, since the end of the Cold War and the recession of the nuclear threat, these bunkers have found a new function, one which requires that their locations be anything but secret. They are being rebranded as revenue-generating, historical attractions for tourists who wish to experience an unrealized potential future for governance in the UK, mapped out in the paranoia of the post war era.

Genre

Apart from being simultaneously a product and a process, a text will also possess a specific staging, referred to as its *genre*. As the example above makes clear, knowing the purpose that a text serves in a particular social setting enables us to anticipate to a surprising degree of accuracy both the overall text structure and also its internal organization of messages, or meanings. In a typical decision-making occasion, we would expect to be involved in a spoken text which conforms to the generic structure of a meeting, as opposed, for example, to a birthday party, a wedding or Holy Communion. If the meeting were preceded by the exchange of gifts, a request to all those who knew of any just cause or impediment to say why the meeting should not proceed or communal confession, then we would be very puzzled indeed, just as we would be if asked to participate in a secret ballot on what games to play at a party, to present a report on the previous year's birthday party or to seek forgiveness for any bad things we may have done at other parties before being allowed to take part in the current one. All these situations would violate the conventions of the genre. A familiarity with the genres associated with a decision-making circumstance in a given organization helps managers to 'understand' the meanings being negotiated with the text, for example the weight to be given to the views of the chairperson or the importance of 'looking good and avoiding blame' as a tactic to pursue in meetings (remember our initial case). Participants understand texts in social contexts because they have prior experience of them and read them as examples of identifiable genres in, and of, specific social contexts. As a part of our lived experience within institutions (Martin 1992), we learn to ascribe certain kinds of meanings to certain kinds of texts.

Genres assist in constructing or reinforcing some of the meaning of the text – comic, tragic, epic, ironic – or how it is to be 'read', identifying the agent(s) of the text (the heroes and possibly villains) and specifying the audience. Belsey (1980: 26) points out that meanings in texts are conventional, requiring familiarity not intuition. But more than one convention can be carried or read into a text, and they need not necessarily be in harmony with each other. Indeed, it is the conflict and contradiction in a text which makes it possible for participants to read the text in different ways. It is also possible for the same participants to read in different meanings from the same text at different times and on different social occasions. In this way texts are 'implicated in social processes of development and change' and can be reconstructed and reinterpreted over time (Hodge and Kress 1988: 6).

Social subjectivity

Having defined the concept of discourse, and seen that managers and others in decision-making contexts negotiate specific sets of meanings (texts) on specific social occasions (genres), we turn our attention to the final major concept used in the textual process model of organizations, that of the *social subject* (Clarke 1991). In society, at work, at home and at play, we are all social subjects. Rather than inviolable free agents or atomistic individuals, we are social beings, the product of social influences that create our sense of individuality and self-awareness. These social influences operate through language and communication, hence the centrality of discourse, texts and genres to social subjectivity. *Subjectivity*, simultaneously the condition of 'individuality' and one's self-awareness of that condition, is continually formed and reformed under changing social, economic and historical circumstances (Henriques et al. 1984). In the context of decision-making theory, using the social subjectivity concept to look at managers and others in organizations prevents us from adopting the rationalism identified in many of the traditional decision-making models reviewed in the first section of this chapter. It is often the case that readers encountering this concept for the first time recoil in horror at the thought that they are socially constituted and not individual free agents. This effect is discursively produced! It is the result of the operation of a liberal-humanist discourse that constructs the subject of psychology known as the 'individual' as a subject position which is not happy to accept that the way in which it thinks and acts may not be entirely under its own control. However, such 'individuals' should not be too afraid because, as already noted, discourses never operate directly on those who are subject to them, rather they are 'read', in the form of

'texts', by those subjects in specific organizational contexts. And to be 'read' rather than automatically obeyed or enacted, there is a necessity for at least some freedom of interpretation on the part of the reader. Discourses must have social subjects who enjoy some freedom to 'choose', in order to exist. For, rather than being determined by mere discourses, we are social subjects *because* of them (Dore 1995: 151–76). Discourses, although simultaneously constraining, are also the source of our freedom. It is the *multiple* nature of discourses that frees us from the singularity of instinct, from merely following the one and only programme, because it is discourse that, through language, carves out a range of possibilities of how to be, a range of positions we can adopt and forces us to reflect upon them. Bound up then with the concepts of discourse, text and social subjectivity is the concept of *positioning*.

Social subjects are positioned (with respect to themselves and others) through, and in relation to, particular discourses and practices. As we noted above, texts appear coherent when parts of the text work together to shape a particular meaning. But the ability to read that meaning depends upon the reader adopting a particular *reading position* (or discursive subject position) which informs the subject 'who, what, and how to be in a given social situation, occasion, interaction' (Kress 1985: 39; Linstead 1985) and what to think about themselves. A reading position is the dominant position from which a specific text appears meaningful and usually coherent. In adopting the reading position of the text, the subject accepts the position constructed for it in the discourse(s) carried by the text, and is referred to as a *compliant subject*. In adopting or 'occupying the reading position', the subject is defined and described by, and may identify with, the discourses of the text. The idea of social subjects is based on Louis Althusser's (1971) idea of the *interpellated subject*, where subjects are called to a particular way of being by the text, and are invited to recognize themselves through the adoption of a particular identity.

Reading positions can operate in very curious ways and it is not only the position of persons that texts can call upon us to adopt or use to position us. Many works of fiction utilize this technique to produce their novel effects, with perhaps the most famous example being Anna Sewell's *Black Beauty*, a story told from the perspective of the eponymous horse. However, it is not only in fiction that such tricks are played; in many texts mobilized in organizations, we, as readers, have to accept a position subject to the whims of a hero or villain that is anything but human, such as the seemingly ubiquitous and universal impersonal forces of 'globalization' and 'the market', or that more local intransigent character of action, 'the computer system'.

Such entities function as the central subjects of many texts in which employees and managers alike are forced to take positions as extras, or bit part players, as nothing more than a supporting cast. One of the most vivid examples of this phenomenon, however, comes not from the field of management, but the discourse of nuclear doctrine which we encountered earlier. Cohn, whose work we have already alluded to, describes a particular defence scenario in which stability is seemingly assured because neither side has any incentive to strike first. This claim is founded on the following argument:

Since it takes roughly two warheads to destroy one enemy silo, an attacker must expend two of his missiles to destroy one of the enemy's. A first strike disarms the attacker. The aggressor ends up worse off than the aggressed.
(Krauthammer 1985, cited in Cohn 1987: 710)

Not surprisingly, Cohn struggles to make sense of this logic. How can it be that the 'aggressor ends up worse off than the aggressed' when the 'homeland of "the aggressed" has just been devastated by the explosions of, say, a thousand nuclear bombs, each likely to be ten to one hundred times more powerful than the bomb dropped on Hiroshima' while the homeland of the aggressor is 'still untouched'? (Cohn 1987: 710–11). Indeed it is impossible to accept this account of winners and losers until one understands who (or what) the *subject* of this particular discourse is. And the answer?:

In technostrategic discourse, the reference point is not white men, it is not human beings at all; it is the weapons themselves.

The aggressor thus ends up worse off than the aggressed because he has fewer weapons left; human factors are irrelevant to the calculus of gain and loss. (Cohn 1987: 711)

Compliant subjects are positioned by the text so that they do not see any contradictions it may contain. For example, the only way to comply with the text that Cohn considers above, to make sense of it, is to accept that technostrategic discourse is about weapons themselves and to forget about any human casualities that might be involved, for doing so makes the contradiction that presents itself to a naive reader disappear. Compliant subjects in organizations are sometimes socially rewarded so that it becomes against their material interest to draw attention to any contradictions they might notice. When subjects resist the obvious reading position encoded in the text, or refuse to accept the role offered to them by the organization, they are referred to as a *resisting* or *oppositional subject* (Linstead 1985). Because subjects are socially and discursively formed, each will bring to the decision-making situations different sets of institutional and linguistic experiences (Kress 1988: 127). It is possible for those who share similar institutional experiences (for example workplaces, schools, churches) and similar linguistic experiences (nationality, class and culture) to appear to comply quite naturally with specific discourses in decision-making contexts. However, as no two subjects will share absolutely identical discursive histories, it is unlikely that they will consistently share the same meanings, and people who agree may come to disagree in time without any obvious conflict.

Conclusion

As decision-making activities are often viewed as one of the distinguishing characteristics of management work, there has been sustained interest in theorizing and building models in order to understand it. Choice has proved to be a significant and enduring category in traditional decision-making theories and models. It is extremely difficult to presume that only unitary models of decision making (for example rational and administrative approaches) accurately capture decision-making activities. In reaction to unitary models, other models of decision making have been developed including the garbage can, political, dominant coalitions and non-decision-making models. These models at least critique the assumption that decisions are entirely predictable, neutral and objective, although these critiques often rest on dubious claims concerning the influence of 'subjective choices' and the 'preferences' of those participating in the decision making.

There have been developments which recognize the limitations of traditional decision-making literature. Alternatives proposed have included shifts to 'action' and

Conclusion cont'd

'choice'. However, these have been shown to function simply as aliases for traditional categories, while still relying upon the same kinds of assumptions concerning individual decision makers. In an attempt to retheorize decision making in a way which does not reproduce these assumptions, this chapter has proposed a new model of decision making. This model, referred to as the textual process model of organizations, employs the concepts of discourse, text, genre and social subjectivity to place the analytical emphasis on understanding decision making as communicative processes operating in specific organizational contexts.

? Answers to questions about decision making

1 **What is a 'decision'?** A decision is not as straightforward to define as we might think. It can be regarded as a commitment to a course of action, but from that point views diverge. It is often difficult to pinpoint or 'track down' when a decision is actually made or reached, although many managers try to represent themselves as the key decision makers in their organizations, especially of the good decisions – the bad ones are another story. At best, any decision that is 'announced' or 'made' usually involves lots of decisional acts that accumulate into what is often described as 'the' decision. Even a major decision to close a subsidiary or issue dividends comes from many decisional acts taken at different times and places and by different people and these acts accumulate into a 'decision'. Decisions are also considered by some to be associated with actions taken and as the preconditions for an action to occur, including inaction. Decisions accumulate in very messy and unpredictable ways and it is problematic to think of managers as decision makers, although many popular texts propagate such a view as indeed do managers themselves.

2 **Why is the decision-making process important in organizations?** It is important because the quality of decisions is important, and if irrational and whimsical actions are successfully presented as rational and ordered, then the organization ultimately suffers, as the case study material illustrates. As we have argued, decisional processes are the particular patterns of organizational experiences that are drawn upon to justify, lend truth to or legitimate the rules, tools and technologies that are used to make decisions. Decision processes are constituted as texts which people draw upon to exclude, include or marginalize certain options for action or for making sense of what is happening. In some organizations you will see prominence given to the idea of rational decision models and these are accompanied by textual interpretations that have particular genres, including particulars that are invoked by technologies and their associated tools and methods. Never is it the case that there is only one text in circulation but the dominant form of discourse can circumscribe what people are prepared to share or discuss. As we illustrate in the case of *The Dice Man*, there are any number of ways the game can be played but the die limits certain possibilities as far as the game is concerned (for example the number of possible outcomes of a throw, how the throw can be made and so on) and the decisions that can be

Answers continued

made. *The Dice Man* also sets the rules for the game in a particular way that precludes other games being played but is unable to change certain parameters once the die is chosen as the medium for taking a decision. The decision process is no more or less than the texts that are created to make the rules, tools and the technology work in particular ways. The textual possibilities for the game (a genre that is based on gambling and winning and losing) are limited because to play the game involves discarding other possibilities, options and ideas.

3 **What kind of choices do decision makers have?** We looked at the issue of choice, and the ways decision-making behaviour can be said to be constrained by it, and indeed critiqued the concept of choice for preserving the 'mentalism' of the decision-making self, rather than seeing the actor acting within a field of influences and constraints as described above. As we observed, the greatest myth in management is that of the rational decision maker that is part of popular management discourse that gives substantial power and influence to certain elite people in organizations and disproportionately rewards the few, so-called 'key' decision makers (to the tune of millions). We have argued that such a representation makes little sense but those with power to change, our senior corporate leaders, seem to have a collective blindness to this possibility, at least so far.

4 **How does the behaviour of organizational participants affect decision making?** Decision making can be affected by the behaviour of the participants in many ways, as they may preserve defensive routines which delay or stop a decision altogether, and cover up the inconsistencies in the organization's processes, become inward-looking and self-censoring, or improve the process by reflexive critical engagement with it, recognizing the limits of decision-making theories and working to change how managers think and speak about decisions and about how they are made.

5 **How are knowledge, information and power related in decision making?** The analysis of the case studies has explored the links between knowledge, information and power in decision making. Information is an inward-forming activity that we all engage in, in very different ways. No two people process information in exactly the same way or make the same sense of it. Information is only useful if it is connected to knowledge of some sort such as a particular theory or pre-existing representation (such as the rational manager) and information strengthens or undermines pre-existing knowledge. Knowledge and power are intimately connected in how we frame the world and make decisions and we all draw on a much wider variety of knowledge sources to make decisions than any theory can account for. Managers also use knowledge strategically and politically, withholding, manipulating and circulating misinformation. Certain forms of managerial discourse also serve to privilege some groups over others and increase the power and currency of certain forms of knowledge and expertise. Texts and genres are the 'stuff' that create powerful forms of discourse and the possibility for oppositional and counter-readings are many and varied.

REVISITING
THE CASE STUDY

Let us now see how the analysis in our conclusion could be applied to the case study at the beginning of the chapter to illustrate the textual approach to decision making.

1 What criteria do people apply in making decisions in the companies described?

First, in Covenant, they use rational vocabularies to disguise decisions which are essentially impulsive and irrational, made by those in power. In Weft Corporation, when non-routine decisions have to be made, they look up and around, to see what indications the powerful are giving about how they should act, and they do what they think is expected of them. When big decisions have to be made, they avoid them for as long as possible, then try to involve as many people as possible so that if the decision goes badly, they can pass or share the blame. They sidestep decisions where possible, and they try to avoid being seen to make a mistake.

2 Why are they afraid to make decisions?

Partly because they know that any order they put in place could be, and frequently is, swept away by the fiat of one of the senior managers. This is partly because several of them have gone beyond their level of competence and are afraid of being found out. The culture of the company pushes them to grab for advancement, but they then doubt their abilities when they reach their limits and try at all costs not to let their uncertainties be exposed.

Looking at these companies as a text then, since the dilemmas of decision making that we witness seem to be similar in all three of them, what discourse can we see at work? First there are clearly aspects of a discourse of hierarchical, and probably patriarchal, power. This discourse indicates that the powerful can do whatever they like as long as they can make it look rational. Although the overt discourse here is one of rational management, the subtext is clearly one of power. Taken together, these two aspects of the text entail a notion of careerism, because the higher you climb up the hierarchy, the less likely you are to be subverted or have your decisions overturned. Power is thus not untrammelled here, it involves accommodation on the part of the

powerful, if they are to maintain their roles. The text intertwines the overt discourse and its subtext. For example, one must mange the appearance of competence to maintain one's elevated status because hierarchy also implies fitness for position and ability. So the discourse operating is one of survival, by looking rational and competent, avoiding blame, mistakes and being found out.

The particular strategies which managers use in these companies – collective involvement, putting decisions off and avoiding them if possible – are all reported as part of the text. The behaviour at the unveiling of the designer collection indicated that there was more than one text in operation, but that most people were buying into the one which they thought the president supported. The very fact, however, that managers had to do a lot of collective interpretative work to 'define' the collection as a success indicates that even dominant texts do not have a fixed and final meaning, they have to be sustained.

In terms of genre, a majority of the managers 'read' the viewing of the collection as though it were a public affirmation of the president's good taste and power, rather than a critical appraisal of the commercial potential of a set of designs. They viewed it, in short, as a ceremonial, a ritual, and not as a working meeting. This helped them all to act together in praising the collection, as they all understood what they thought was required of them. Cultures which set up ritual events may find that this produces solidarity as it did here, but it does not produce good decisions, as we also saw.

In this case, the evidence of the awfulness of the collection was effectively denied, but only for so long; eventually the market redefined it as a failure. At that point, we would expect people to begin to rewrite history to try to distance themselves from the failure, saying, for example, that they had never liked it in the first place, as indeed does the middle-level designer from Weft who provides our account of the unveiling. No account or text is disinterested and, consequently, completely unchallenged, and much can be read between the lines. For example, at one level, our designer's account of the behaviour of other managers at the unveiling describes a performance that evidences the power element of the dominant discourse that had these managers acting, as they believed, to reflect the views of the powerful back to them, *and thus reduce the risk of becoming unacceptable. However, at another level, the telling of this story is also a performance in itself, one in which the designer indicates that she is different to the other managers who she describes, that she is not really a member of the 'they' who cause such failures. Her telling of the tale tells us that she is not stupid, that she is somehow better than the other characters in the scene. Not only did her superior judgement tell her in advance that the collection would not succeed (or at least that is what she would have us believe now, after the fact!), it also prevented her from publicly going against the grain at the time of the unveiling: 'before I could open my mouth, people were jumping up and down clapping the designer on the back'. By rendering events in this way, she indicates that she understands both the market and the hierarchy of the firm, and thus performs a text in which the reader is encouraged to see her as being particularly competent in the context of the company and thus an obvious choice for a senior role!*

Where managers accept the need to preserve the appearance of being competent, the myth of the rational manager, they are acting as compliant subjects in the terms specified by the corporate discourse. Some of the managers who commented, like the middle-level designer in Weft, show signs of being resisting or oppositional subjects, but they appear relatively inactive rather than rebellious. So without (totally) accepting the imperatives of the corporation to be dishonest, they are nevertheless not fighting to overturn them. In this situation, then, decisions are not likely to be made on the evidence or treated according to their merits, but in a decisional flow which looks simultaneously forward to identify what action will gain merit, and backward to erase any mistakes or blemishes from the record. Whether this can be altered is largely dependent on these organizations addressing these issues of hypocrisy for themselves, learning to read their own 'texts', developing greater language and analytic skills in their managers which, as far as possible within the power structure, would allow suppressed virtues to re-emerge and a new discourse – perhaps of a flat hierarchy where communication was open and managers supported and trusted rather than blamed each other – to develop and take root. Finally, our use of the text model illustrates how knowledge, information and power are closely connected through the concept of discourse.

References

Althusser, L. (1971) *Lenin and Philosophy and Other Essays*, London: New Left Books.

Barnard, C.I. (1938) *The Functions of the Executive*, Cambridge, MA: Harvard University Press.

Belsey, C. (1980) *Critical Practice*, London: Methuen.

Bloomfield, B.P. and Vurdubakis, T. (1994) 'Representing technology: IT consultancy reports as textual reality constructions', *Sociology*, **28**(2).

Boland, R.J. Jr (1987) 'The in-formation of information systems', in Boland, R.J. Jr and Hirschheim R.A. (eds), *Critical Issues in Information Systems Research*, New York: John Wiley.

Chia, R. (1996) *Organizational Analysis as Deconstructive Practice*, Berlin: Walter de Gruyter.

Child, J. (1972) 'The role of strategic choice', *Sociology*, **6**: 1–22.

Clarke, R.J. (1991) 'Discourses in systems development failure', in Aungles, S. (ed.), *Information Technology in Australia: Transforming Organisational Structure and Culture*, Sydney: University of New South Wales Press.

Clarke, R.J. (1992) 'Some applications of social semiotics in information systems discipline and practice', in MacGregor, R., Clarke, R.J., Little, S., Gould, T. and Ang, A. (eds), *Information Systems as Organisational Processes – ISOP '92: Proceedings of the Third Australian Conference on Information Systems*, Department of Business Systems, University of Wollongong, 5–8 October.

Cohen, M.D., March, T.J. and Olsen, J.P. (1972) 'A garbage can model of organizational choice', *Administrative Science Quarterly*, **17**: 1–25.

Cohn, C. (1987) 'Sex and death in the rational world of defense intellectuals', *Signs: Journal of Women in Culture and Society*, **12**(4): 687–718.

Collins, H.M. (1987) 'Expert systems, artificial intelligence and the behavioural co-ordinates of skill', in Bloomfield, B.P. (ed.), *The Question of Artificial Intelligence*, London: Croom Helm.

Cooper, R. (1992) 'Formal organization as representation: Remote control, displacement and abbreviation', in Reed, M. and Hughes, M. (eds) *Rethinking Organization: New Directions in Organization Theory and Analysis*, London: Sage.

Curwen, C.J. (1963) *Theory of the Firm*, Basingstoke: Macmillan – now Palgrave Macmillan.

Cyert, R. and March, J.G. (1963) *A Behavioural Theory of the Firm*, Englewood Cliffs, NJ: Prentice Hall.

Davenport, T.H., De Long, D.W. and Beers, M.C. (1998) 'Successful knowledge management projects', *Sloan Management Review,* Winter: 43–57.

Dawson, S. (1986) *Analysing Organisations*, Basingstoke: Macmillan – now Palgrave Macmillan.

De Bono, E. (1990) *Lateral Thinking: Creativity Step-by-Step*, New York: HarperCollins.

Dessler, G. (1976) *Organisation and Management: A Contingency Approach*, Englewood Cliffs, NJ: Prentice Hall.

Dore, J. (1995) 'The emergence of language from dialogue', in Mandelker, A. (ed.), *Bakhtin in Contexts: Across the Disciplines*, Evanston, IL: Northwestern University Press.

Elsass, P.M. and Graves, L.A. (1997) 'Demographic diversity in decision-making groups: The experiences of women and people of color', *Academy of Management Review,* **22**(4): 946–73.

Ezzamel, M., Lilley, S. and Willmott, H. (forthcoming) 'Accounting, representation and the road to commercial salvation', *Accounting, Organizations and Society.*

Foucault, M. (1972) *The Archaeology of Knowledge*, trans. Shendon Smith, A.M., London: Tavistock.

Foucault, M. (1980) *Power/Knowledge,* Brighton: Harvester.

Galbraith, J. (1974) 'Organization design: An information processing view', *Interface,* **4**(3): 28–36.

Garfinkel, H. (1987) *Studies in Ethnomethodology,* Oxford: Polity Press.

Harris, G.T. (1993) 'The post-capitalist executive: An interview with Peter F. Drucker', *Harvard Business Review,* May–June: 115–22.

Henriques, J., Hollway, W., Urwin, C., Venn, C. and Walkerdine V. (1984) *Changing the Subject: Psychology, Social Regulation and Subjectivity*, London and New York: Methuen.

Hickson, D.J., Butler, R.J., Cray, D., Mallory, G.R. and Wilson, D.C. (1986) *Top Decisions: Strategic Decision Making in Organizations*, San Francisco: Jossey-Bass.

Hodge, R. and Kress, G. (1988) *Social Semiotics,* Oxford: Polity Press.

Hopwood, A. (1974) *Accounting and Human Behaviour*, London: Accountancy Age Books.

Jackall, R. (1988) *Moral Mazes: The World of Corporate Managers*, New York: Oxford University Press.

Janis, I.L. (1972) *Victims of Groupthink,* Boston: Hougton Mifflin.

Janis, I.L. (1982) *Groupthink: Psychological Studies of Policy Decisions and Fiascoes,* Boston: Houghton Mifflin.

Kallinikos, J. (1996) 'Predictable worlds: On writing, accountability and other things', *Scandanavian Journal of Management,* **12**(1), reprinted as Chapter 2 in Kallinikos, J. (1996) *Technology and Society: Interdisciplinary Studies in Formal Organization*, Munich: Accedo.

Keat, R. and Abercrombie, N. (1991) *Enterprise Culture,* London: Routledge.

Keen, P.G. and Scott Morton, M.S. (1978) *Decision Support Systems: An Organizational Perspective,* Reading, MA: Addison-Wesley.

Krauthammer, C. (1985) 'Will star wars kill arms control?', *New Republic,* **3**(653): 12–16.

Kress, G. (1985) *Linguistic Processes in Sociocultural Practice*, ECS806 Sociocultural aspects of language and education, Waurn Ponds, Victoria: Deakin University.

Lawson, N. (1984) *The British Experiment*, Fifth Mais Lecture, HM Treasury.

Lennie, I. (2001) 'Language that organizes: Plans and lists', in Westwood, R. and Linstead, S. (eds) *The Language of Organization*, London: Sage.

Lindblom, C.E. (1990) 'The science of muddling through' in Pugh, D.S. (ed.), *Organization Theory, Selected Readings*, Harmondsworth: Penguin.

Linstead, S.A. (1985) 'Organizational induction: The re-creation of order and the re-reading of discourse', *Personnel Review,* **14**(1): 3–11.

Linstead, S.A. (1999) 'An introduction to the textuality of organization', in Linstead, S. (ed.) *The Textuality of Organization* (1) *Reading the Research Text,* special issue of *Studies in Cultures, Organizations and Societies,* **5**(1).

Lukes, S. (1974) *Power: A Radical View*, Basingstoke: Macmillan – now Palgrave Macmillan.

Lupton, T. (1971) *Management and the Social Sciences*, Harmondsworth: Penguin.

MacKay, D.M. (1969) *Information, Mechanism and Meaning*, Cambridge, MA: Harvard University Press.

Malone, T.W. (1997) 'Is empowerment just a fad? Control, decision making and IT', *Sloan Management Review,* Winter: 23–35.

Manwaring, T. and Wood, S. (1985) 'The ghost in the labour process', in Knight, D., Willmott, H. and Collinson, D. (eds), *Job Redesign*, Aldershot: Gower.

Mapstone, E. (1998) *War of Words: Women and Men Arguing*, London: Chatto & Windus.

March, J.G. (1976) 'The technology of foolishness', in March, J.G. and Olsen, J.P. (eds), *Ambiguity and Choice in Organizations*, Bergen, Norway: Univeritiets Forlaget.

March, J.G. (1984) 'Theories of choice and making

decisions', in Paton, R. and Brown, S. (eds) *Organizations: Cases, Issues and Concepts*, London: Harper & Row/Open University.

March, J.G. (1987) 'Ambiguity and accounting: The elusive link between information and decision making', *Accounting, Organizations and Society*, **12**(2): 153–68.

March, J.G. (1988) *Decisions and Organizations*, Oxford: Blackwell.

March, J.G. and Simon, H.A. (1958) *Organizations*, New York: John Wiley.

Martin, J.R. (1992) *English Text: System and Structure*, Philadelphia/Amsterdam: John Benjamins.

Miller, S.J., Hickson, D.J. and Wilson, D.C. (1996) 'Decision-making in organizations', in Clegg, S.R., Hardy, C. and Nord, W.R. (eds) *Handbook of Organizational Studies*, London: Sage.

Minkes, A.L. (1987) *The Entrepreneurial Manager: Decisions, Goals and Business Ideas*, Harmondsworth: Penguin.

Mintzberg, H., Waters, J., Pettigrew, A.M. and Butler, R. (1990) 'Studying deciding: An exchange of views between Mintzberg and Waters, Pettigrew and Butler', *Organization Studies*, **11**(1): 1–16.

Mouzelis, N.P. (1967) *Organizations and Bureaucracy: An Analysis of Modern Theories*, London: Routledge & Kegan Paul.

Munro, R. (1995) 'Managing by ambiguity: An archaeology of the social in the absence of management accounting', *Critical Perspectives on Accounting*, **6**: 433–82.

Munro, R. (2001) 'After knowledge: The language of information', in Westwood, R. and Linstead, S. (eds), *The Language of Organization*, London: Sage.

Perrow, C. (1972) *Complex Organizations: A Critical Essay*, Glenview, IL: Scott, Foresman.

Peters, T.J. and Waterman, R.H. (1984) *In Search of Excellence*, New York: Harper & Row.

Pettigrew, A.M. (1972) *The Politics of Organizational Decision Making*, London: Tavistock.

Pettigrew, A.M. (1990) 'Studying deciding: An exchange of views between Mintzberg and Waters, Pettigrew and Butler', *Organization Studies*, **11**(1): 1–16.

Pfeffer, J. (1981) *Power in Organizations*, London: Pitman.

Powell, S. (1998) 'Nice girls do argue: Why do women almost never win arguments with men, even when they're right?', *The Australian*, 4 May: 15.

Pugh, D.S. (ed.) (1997) *Organizational Theory: Selected Readings*, 4th edn, Harmondsworth: Penguin.

Pugh, D.S. and Hickson, J. (1989) *Writers on Organizations*, Harmondsworth: Penguin.

Rhinehart, L. (1971) *The Dice Man*, London: Talmy, Franklin Ltd.

Schotter, A. (1981) *The Economic Theory of Social Institutions*, Cambridge: Cambridge University Press.

Sewell, A. (1900) *Black Beauty*, Chicago: W.B. Conkey.

Simon, H. (1960) *Administrative Behavior*, New York: Macmillan.

Stephenson, T. (1985) *Management: A Political Activity*, Basingstoke: Macmillan – now Palgrave Macmillan.

Stewart, T.A. (1994) 'Your company's most valuable asset: Intellectual capital', *Fortune*, October (2): 34–6.

Tannen, D. (1995) 'The power of talk', *Harvard Business Review*, September–October: 138–48.

Ulrich, D. (1998) 'Intellectual capital = competence × commitment', *Sloan Management Review*, Winter: 15–26.

Weeks, D.K. (1980) 'Organizations and decision making', in Thompson, K. and Salaman, G. (eds) *Control and Ideology in Organizations*, Milton Keynes: Open University Press.

Westerlund, G. and Sjøstrand, S.E. (1979) *Organisational Myths*, London: Harper & Row.

Wikström, S., Normann, R., Anell, B., Ekvall, G., Forslin, J. and Skärvad, P.H. (1994) *Knowledge & Value: A New Perspective on Corporate Transformation*, London: Routledge.

Williamson, O.E. (1975) *The Theory of Social and Economic Organization*, Glencoe, IL: Free Press.

Wilson, D.C., Butler, R.J., Cray, D., Hickson, D.J., Mallory, G.R. (1986) 'Breaking the bounds of organization in strategic decision making', *Human Relations*, **39**(4): 309–32.

Managing strategically

CHAPTER

15

Bobby Banerjee, Michael Browne, Liz Fulop, Simon Lilley and Stephen Linstead

Questions about managing strategically

1 What is a strategy?

2 How are strategies formulated?

3 What is the value of strategic planning?

4 Why do some firms outperform others?

5 Do all organizations need a strategy?

THE SPORTS SHOE SAGA

Dick Foster was a worried man. As vice-president of production of Image Inc., the sixth-largest sports shoe manufacturer in the world, his cup of sorrow (not water!) was overflowing. His primary producing markets were in a shambles. The Asian currency crisis had hit them hard, particularly in Indonesia, Malaysia and Thailand. Their major sports endorsee, the first pick in last year's US National Basketball Association (NBA) draft, a rookie already of superstar status, died of a heroin overdose eight months after signing a $70 million endorsement deal with the company. They had signed him up for everything: running shoes, casual shoes, socks, shirts, shorts, wristbands, thighbands, earrings, nose-rings, watches, lotions and whatever else their new product development people could think of. As Dan Flintstone, their R&D director frequently reminded his colleagues, 'we literally own his ass: he's got our logo tattooed right there, or so I've been told'. Labour costs all over were increasing and so was labour unrest: last month there were four demonstrations outside their Korean plant. The last one was particularly bad, one worker was killed by the police and several others injured. Jae Sae Kim, the local activist, a highly respected lawyer and a thorn in the side for transnational corporations, was jailed for her part in the demonstrations. Within hours, the international media had descended on the plains of Pusan. Both *48 hours* and *60 Minutes* did a story, and neither was remotely flattering to the company. After the story broke in the US and European markets, there was bad press everywhere. It was easing off a bit now, but for a while it had seemed like there was a reference to their company, mostly negative, every day. Wall St was jittery. Production was still suffering and there was talk of more trouble in the plant. The subcontractor threatened to shut down the plant if demonstrations continued. Their expansion plans in the Asia-Pacific region, a $3 billion investment, were put on hold by the executive board. The CEO had called the firm's directors from every region in the world for a series of strategy meetings over the next few days. And Dick Foster was going to be in the spotlight. They were his subcontractors, it was his region. With their annual shareholder meeting less than six weeks away, it wasn't going to be an easy time. Sighing resignedly, as he manoeuvred his car through the heavy midtown Manhattan traffic, Dick thought about the time when he was first put in charge of international production nearly twenty years ago. Could they have known this was going to happen? What was he going to recommend to his boss? Continue with their expansion plans in the region? Replace the subcontractors? Relocate? How could he ensure smooth production over the next few years? He needed to prepare a medium-term plan fairly quickly.

Jae Sae sat in her cell and contemplated her next move. The demonstration had gone off well, several of her colleagues were interviewed by both local and foreign media. Greenpeace announced its support for the Korean workers. In an interview with CNN some hours ago, the CEO of Image Inc. said he would be visiting Korean government officials and businesspeople next week for talks on how to resolve the issue. She hoped they wouldn't be able to just shut down the plant. Things were bad enough as it was, and the last thing she wanted was to put people out of work in these hard times. The last few decades had seen phenomenal economic growth in the Asia-Pacific region, with annual GNP growth of 8–10 per cent. Rapid industrial development resulted in higher wages in South Korea and neighbouring countries, but was accompanied by social and environmental problems. Labour unrest became common in South Korea as the government's authoritarian control over the workplace diminished somewhat in the 1980s.

The global sports shoe market is a multibillion dollar industry employing over 100,000 people in the Asian region, with manufacturing operations in South Korea, Thailand, Malaysia, Vietnam, China, the Philippines, Taiwan and

Indonesia. Reebok, Nike, Hi-Tec, Adidas and Puma are the market leaders, with Reebok having the highest sales value and Hi-Tec the highest volume sales. The biggest export market is the USA, accounting for 65 per cent of the market by value, followed by Germany, the UK and France. Over 90 per cent of branded athletic footwear production is located in Asia. In the late 1970s and early 1980s, Pusan, South Korea was the sneaker capital of the world. Cheap land, labour and raw materials were the chief sources of attraction for manufacturers of athletic footwear and low production costs more than offset the higher shipping costs. 'Manufacturers' is a misleading term: none of the major firms actually make their products. Instead, all production is subcontracted out to local contractors in the region. This practice, pioneered by Nike in the 1970s, was soon adopted by the other transnational corporations and is the norm in the industry. Competition over brand names became more fierce, with $250 million annual advertising budgets being common. After a period of extraordinary growth in the 1980s, the market unexpectedly began to stagnate. The attractiveness of South Korea and Taiwan as cheap labour markets declined as labour costs rose and competition became tougher and in the mid-1980s companies began to develop subcontractors in neighbouring regions, especially in Indonesia, Thailand, China and Vietnam. Declining growth rates now threatened to diminish even more in the wake of the financial crisis sweeping over the region.

Footwear manufacturing is a labour-intensive process requiring little machinery but a large number of raw materials, especially volatile organic compounds. Strict environmental regulation covered the use and disposal of these materials in North America and Europe. Such is not the case in several Asian countries. Hourly wages of $9 and higher in North American and European markets could not compete with rates of 23 cents per hour and 37 cents per hour which were the norm in China and the Philippines. While it is difficult to calculate a precise breakdown of costs, estimates of labour costs range from 10–12 per cent. Raw materials account for 70 per cent of the cost. The labour component of a typical product with a retail price of $US60 at the store (including development, marketing and shipping costs, retailing costs and profits) ranges from $0.46 to $1.50 per pair of shoes.

The major companies in the industry were mainly involved in design, distribution and marketing. Nike's pioneering 100 per cent outsourcing strategy became a norm in the industry. Competition among subcontractors was fierce as a result of an industry strategy of pitting one subcontractor against another and awarding the cheapest subcontractor the largest share of production. It was not uncommon for one subcontractor to manufacture products for Nike, Reebok and Adidas, all made in the same plant. Most subcontractors were locally owned and controlled and regularly negotiated short-term production contracts with the transnational corporations.

Global branding was followed by all the major corporations. Richard Donahue, vice-chairman of Nike, described their strategy in the following terms: 'the commitment is to be a global company – one management, one theme, one value, one ethic throughout the world'. High advertising and promotion costs also characterized this market with huge sponsorship deals involving the world's top athletes. Many corporations shifted their subcontracting operations from South Korea and Taiwan to countries like Vietnam, Thailand and China to take advantage of cheaper labour costs. The low end of the market was crowded and Nike and Reebok were already looking to shift their focus to the higher end of the market, with an emphasis on product innovation and quality.

News stories about labour practices in Asia highlighted many problems: forced overtime, minimum wages, hire and fire policies, the hiring of predominantly casual labour and refugees, discrimination against trade unions, inadequate safety standards and, in some cases, physical coercion and surveillance and the sexual harassment of women. In the *48 hours* news story, an employee of Image Inc.'s Thailand subcontractor was interviewed who claimed they were being paid half the normal rate and that she was fired when she complained. Her sister, who worked in the same plant, was fired after she became pregnant: over 85 per cent of the subcontractor's workforce were female, the company hired single women only and no maternity benefits were provided. Subsequently, Dick Foster had met with the subcontractor and threatened to discontinue the relationship if work practices were not improved. The company was now working on a global code of conduct for subcontracting operations.

The companies' responses to these criticisms mainly revolved around issues of ownership. They claimed no local laws were broken and the minimum wage paid was in accordance with local customs. They had no financial or legal ties with the subcontractors and did not own the companies operating in Asia. As David Taylor of Reebok put it, 'we don't pay anybody at the factories and we don't set policy within the factories. It is their business to run'.

Note: This case was developed by Bobby Banerjee. Image Inc. is a fictitious company. Figures cited and other material were gleaned from a variety of articles in the business press and a case study conducted by Bethan Brookes and Peter Madden from a research project commissioned by the Christian Aid Foundation.

QUESTIONS ABOUT THE CASE

1 What is Image Inc.'s product?
2 How did the outsourcing strategy emerge?
3 What factors were considered in the decision to outsource?
4 Where is Image Inc.'s strategy headed?

Introduction

The idea of knowing the central purpose of one's activity and referring back to this as a guide in all matters of decision is not a modern one, as the existence of grand projects throughout history attests. To take but one example, while the exact details of how the Egyptian pyramids were built remain a mystery, structures of this scale and complexity of construction are simply inconceivable without some capacity to articulate, record and disseminate both the intended outcome of the project and the components that will be combined to achieve it. In short, large-scale projects of this sort are unthinkable in the absence of an analysis of what will be required to achieve them, followed by synthesis of the constituent parts and tasks so identified.

Indeed, it is exactly this sort of *rational planning* that was identified as a major function of top management by the classical management theorists. Henri Fayol (1841–1925), one of the early classical management theorists, whose book *General and Industrial Management* was only translated into English in 1949, advocated that forecasting and planning were essential management functions in ensuring that an organization attained its objectives (Fayol 1949: 50). He also added control to the functions of management in order to ensure that plans were monitored and appropriate steps taken to correct performance. Similarly, Frederick Winslow Taylor argued that managers were to be the forward-looking 'planners' and controllers of activities, while the workers on the shop floor were to be the 'doers' (see Chapter 11). For Taylor, humanity could be systematically divided into two classes. A small number were seen to have the capacity to act as 'minds', 'scientifically' conceiving of production processes and improvements to them, while the majority would merely play out, as 'hands', the roles written for them by the 'minds'. Industrial planning appears here to be dependent upon prior assumptions about people, leadership and hierarchy (see Chapter 4), and particularly about the seeming essentialness of the latter in the complex conditions that surround large-scale projects (see Blaug 1999).

The notion of *strategy,* as it first appears in the modern management literature, draws heavily on these understandings and is easily seen as merely some sort of upward extension of operational planning. Indeed 'strategy' can often appear to be little more than a term reserved for the grandest of plans. This modern notion of *strategic planning* in business dates from the work of Igor Ansoff (1965), whose book *Corporate Strategy*, written in the USA, helped to establish what became known as the *Planning School* approach to strategy. But this is certainly not the first time that the Western world had mobilized the idea of strategy. The term itself has a very long history indeed.

The most cited ancient text on strategy, and a continuing favourite of those who work in one of the most hypercompetitive arenas of contemporary economic life – financial and commodity derivatives trading (see for example Lewis 1989) – is Sun Tzu's *The Art of War* (Wing 1984). This series of contemplations on the essence of maintaining and defending a territory or state was first published over 2000 years ago, apparently on a series of animal hides. It is taken by many commentators as the origin of a line of thought on military strategy which continues to the present day. Yet it seems only from the 1950s and 60s that we begin to see explicit reflection on business strategy, notwithstanding business historian Alfred Chandler's (1962) efforts to impute 'strategy' to earlier industrial leaders. Why should this be the case? And why should only those aspects of the military strategic cannon associated with planning be adopted?

According to commentators such as David Knights and Glenn Morgan (1990, 1991), some of the answers to these questions lie in an analysis of the conduct of, and significance attributed to, the Second World War. This war was seen to be markedly different from those that had preceded it, although many of these differences can already be seen in less developed forms in the First World War. While the wars of the eighteenth and nineteenth centuries, and indeed the majority of earlier conflicts, had tended to be settled by showpiece battles between the military classes of each of the protagonists, the great wars of the twentieth century were much more about the total mobilization of a state or, more accurately, an alliance of states, against another equally, totally mobilized opponent. Rather than war as a series of battles which could continue, to some extent, alongside 'normal' life, we witness war as a process of attrition between opponents who focus all the activities and resources of their society towards the total degradation of the other's capacity to continue. Such wars, with their total alignment towards a concerted, organized and enduring objective, containing various sub-objectives, were seen to require planning and coordination of activities on a hitherto unprecedented scale. The victory of the allies, particularly in the Second World War, differences in resources notwithstanding, was seen by many commentators to be attributable to the superiority of their efforts in planning. To put it bluntly, during the latter stages of the conflict at least, they were seen to have planned bigger and better than their opponents.

For businesses involved in the war effort – and given the scale and scope of the new version of war, there were few that were not – plans emanating from the state had become part and parcel of the normal processes of organizing. And while 'the state' did not continue to intervene in the affairs of business at this detailed level after the cessation of hostilities, at least not in the West, the confidence placed in planning resulting from the experience of the war did result in states of all sorts engaging in various forms of corporatist coordination. Indeed, the Cold War that ensued in this period continued to encourage coordinated competition between large blocs of humanity. This 'organizational society' (Presthus 1979) entailed extensive coordination between firms as a result of state planning and, within the firm, some businesses continued to conduct their affairs using the practices of planning that had been imposed upon them during the war.

The chapter proceeds by providing an overview of key approaches to strategy, and the ways in which they can be categorized, before exploring in a little more detail the key ingredients of what we have termed the *Extended Design School* model, which remains the most common form for articulating strategy in business enterprises. We also compare and contrast approaches which focus on the environment in which the business finds itself, such as Michael Porter's 'competitive strategy', with those that focus on the assets of the enterprise itself, such as Wernerfelt's 'resource-based view'. We then begin to unpick the prescriptions of these various accounts by looking at 'reconfigurationist approaches', which emphasize the ways in which the politics of organizational life ensure that in practice the formulation and implementation of strategy is seldom, if ever, as rational and predictable as the prescriptions suggest. We consider the ways in which these ideas have led to renewed emphasis on *strategic thinking* and the *crafting* of strategy in dynamic accounts of practice, as opposed to the somewhat static pictures offered by the theorists previously considered. However, we also note the limitations of the reconfigurist approach, in terms of both the problems of strategic drift and its related silence on the matter of how new insights into new directions can be created. We develop this critique through consideration of imaginative techniques such as *scenario planning* which allow us subsequently to introduce a *postmodernist approach* to strategy as a way of explaining how the dominant modes of strategy that are adopted in enterprises sustain themselves. Through this critique we are able to see both how certain, key, privileged positions, such as that of the white, male strategist, are constructed through the strategy literature's adoption of certain literary styles or genres, and how those positions and their associated privileges are made to appear 'natural' and *un*constructed. A subsequent brief consideration of a cross-cultural view of strategy emphasizes again that strategy is not universal, but rendered in different ways, in different times and places. We conclude by answering the questions and analysing the case provided at the beginning of the chapter in the light of the different lenses we have introduced as ways of viewing the strategy process.

Overview of key approaches to strategy

Out of the complex of influences described in the introduction, the central ideas of the *Planning School* were developed in the 1950s and 60s, a period of steady economic growth and stability in world markets. But they did not take universal root at this time, at least not within the majority of firms. Somewhat ironically, it was only in the 1970s, a period of unprecedented economic instability and stagnation, that the Planning School, as a supposedly useful approach for individual businesses, became popular throughout the West.

Another influential approach to strategic planning, which emerged at around the same time, also in the USA, was the *Design School,* with its focus on analysing the strengths and weaknesses, opportunities and threats (SWOT) of organizations. This approach was, if not inaugurated, then certainly formalized by the publication, also in 1965, of Learned et al.'s seminal book, *Business Policy: Text and Cases*, based upon the work of Professor Kenneth Andrews and his team of associates at the Harvard Business School. SWOT analysis is still used by many managers in their planning processes. If we consider that strategy concerns the controlled movement of an organization from A to B, we may see that the SWOT analysis of the Design School provided an account of A in terms of both the organization (SW) and the environment (OT), while the Planning School held out the promise of the structure required to engage in an orderly progression to B. But as Pearson (1999) notes, neither approach offered any guidance in identifying which of all the range of possible Bs is the most desirable one to aim for. Both approaches placed great faith in the virtues of rational planning and the scientific rationalist approach to strategy formulation. The implicit assumption in these approaches was that the environments in which planners operated were sufficiently knowable and stable to allow for the development of strategies and the formulation and implementation of detailed plans, often spanning 10 or 20 years.

In the 1980s strategy fell under the influence of the *Entrepreneurial School* and the *Positioning School*, again both originating in the USA. The former was associated with the works of Tom Peters and Robert Waterman (1982) and Terrence Deal and Allan Kennedy (1982), who were more cynical about the virtues of rational planning and more concerned with energizing and mobilizing planning efforts around turbulent environments, using ideas such as corporate culture, vision, mission and transformational leadership. In short, they sought to delineate how interesting Bs could be identified and aimed for in a climate in which the assumptions of the Planning and Design Schools, concerning the knowability of the environment, were seen to be increasingly untenable. However, this scepticism with regard to the capacity to plan was certainly not total, even within the Entrepreneurial School and, indeed, the notion of planning received renewed impetus from the other major development of strategy of the time. The Positioning School, with its origins in the work of Michael Porter of the Harvard Business School (Porter 1980, 1985), gave an enhanced role to economics as the basis for strategic planning, with a noticeable shift to industry analysis as a key determinant of strategy. The Extended Design School also became popular in this period and its principles were, and still are, found in many texts throughout the world. Incorporating and refining earlier principles of rational decision making, including their elaborations by Porter, and borrowing key insights from the Entrepreneurial School, the Extended Design School model sought to combine the best elements of previous approaches into a package that would hopefully avoid importation of the limitations of its sources. It attempted to deliver an economically sound basis for a form of planning that was both more modest than its predecessors, in terms of the detail of its prescriptions, and more energizing and motivational, in terms of its exhortatory aims.

The Extended Design School remains the most popular prescriptive model of the process of strategy formulation. The prescriptiveness of its account enables us to characterize it as a *rationalist model* (see Chapter 14) of strategy, a status it shares most obviously with the Planning, Design and Positioning aspects of its antecedents. However, although the most popular model of strategy formulation, it is not the only one in existence in the academic literature. An alternative view of strategy formulation, influenced by 'political' and 'learning' school perspectives, which we term the *reconfigurationist approach*, emphasizes the key role of 'strategic thinking' in opposition to the prescriptions of planning. But this model itself has also been subjected to sustained critique, resulting in a recently emergent appreciation of strategy, which we term the *postmodernist approach*. This approach treats strategy as a discourse, and principally as a textual flow of ideas, meanings and justifications (see also Chapter 14). The notions of *genre* and *social subjectivity* are introduced here to render an account of how organizations develop their strategic *texts* or stories and how these texts become the 'official' strategy of the organization. This approach deconstructs how the 'official strategies' of managers and their organizations mirror dominant strategic discourses and the knowledge and power relations that are embedded in these discourses.

Table 15.1 describes the key differences between the three approaches to strategy discussed above. The remainder of the chapter examines how these three approaches have emerged and what substantive claims they make about strategy.

Strategic management, as a field of study, encompasses a wide variety of perspectives and approaches. Indeed, according to Mintzberg (1990), thirteen years ago there were no less than ten 'schools of

Table 15.1 Three approaches to strategy		
The rationalist model	**The reconfigurationist model**	**The postmodernist approach**
Mission and vision: a unitarist view of the organization	Multiple stakeholders: a pluralist view of the organization as consisting of different stakeholders with different interests. Objectives determined by *mutual partisan adjustment* (negotiation)	Objectives are written into the narratives of strategy. The players are encouraged/coerced to adopt suitable roles. Vision moves into three, four and five dimensions
Legitimate authority: managers have the power to command the activities of the enterprise	Multiple sources of power are distributed throughout organizations; the power of managers is limited	Power–knowledge relations are supported by the strategic narrative
Comprehensive rational analysis	Bounded rationality	Bounded emotionality; intuition; creativity
Evaluation of all possible alternatives	Limited, successive comparisons	Textual criticism; how the story is unfolding; subtexts and contexts
Explicit strategies and detailed plans	Strategies emerge over time, developing incrementally, 'grass roots' strategies	The story is told, retold and modified, contested and added to
Objectivity	Subjectivity and selectivity: different actors pay attention to different aspects of the organization and its environment leading to different interpretations of the situation	Intersubjectivity and intertextuality. There is more than one story and they all simultaneously compete and coexist
Source: Liz Fulop and Stephen Linstead (1999) *Management: A Critical Text*, South Yarra: Macmillan.		

thought' discernable in strategy formulation. For our purposes here, however, the threefold distinction given above is more than adequate, for it succinctly captures the key differences in approach between the plethora of individual models and accounts that vie for attention in an extremely crowded and lucrative marketplace, although we will consider some of the more important of these in more detail later in the chapter. The *rationalist model* is the term we use to describe what are essentially *prescriptive* schools of thought, that is, approaches which are primarily normative or focused on how the enterprise should approach strategy formation. These prescriptive approaches are based on applying rationalist models and theories to strategy. The *reconfigurationist model* refers to *descriptive* schools of thought, less concerned with prescribing how strategy should be formulated than with the description and explanation of how enterprise strategies are actually formed in practice. Consideration of the *postmodernist approach*, closes our chapter as it attempts to account for the existence and appeal of the preceding two models.

It is worth noting at the outset that elements of reconfigurationist model and particularly the postmodernist approach will probably be unfamiliar to most readers. This is because the rationalist approach has dominated strategic discourse and contains the majority of the key elements that many managers would either identify or be taught to consider as universally applicable ways to go about formulating strategy. We thus consider it first. Its three key elements are: the hierarchy of plans that has its origins in Ansoff's seminal work; the SWOT analysis that derives from the Design School as mentioned above, and the strategic planning model that has its origins in the Extended Design School model.

Rationalist approaches

The hierarchy of plans

As a number of prominent writers on planning (for example Ackoff 1970; Chandler 1977; Ansoff 1979) have suggested, it is hard, if not impossible, to conceive of a formally organized end being achieved if one cannot first articulate and organize the contributory elements, or means, required to achieve that end. In other words, in order to achieve an overall planned goal, one needs to construct a planning hierarchy within which overarching aims are accomplished through the careful consideration and organization of more basic activities. This hierarchy of plans should ensure that each superordinate activity is supplied with appropriate inputs from its subordinate activities. Different types of planning, considering different key elements and criteria, will consequently be required at different levels of organization. Given an overall aim, the hierarchy

provides answers to the what, where, how and when questions required to accomplish that aim. An activity's position in the hierarchy can be determined in a variety of ways, for example the level of management involved or the duration of the activity (or activity cycle), but lower level activities are always seen to fulfil the needs of higher level ones. Or, to put it another way, the scope of the higher level is always greater than that of the lower (or at least this is the claim made by those who inhabit the tops of such hierarchies and are able to command the rewards associated with such elevated positions – Summa 1992). Figure 15.1 describes a typical hierarchy of plans.

Charles Hofer and Dan Schendel (1978), and virtually every text on strategic management since, propose four hierarchical levels of strategy, which in many ways mirror the 'hierarchy of needs' associated with the work of Abraham Maslow (see Chapter 9). These are enterprise strategy at the top, followed by corporate, business and functional strategies. It is important here to note, however, that not all business entities have formally articulated strategies at each of these levels. Sometimes one or more of these strategic levels will not be furnished with any formally articulated strategy, on any piece of paper, anywhere in the organization. Many such 'strategies' are merely the result of imputation by various stakeholders and observers of the firm. Indeed, if one were being cynical, one might even venture that the majority of these so-called strategies exist only in the heads of business academics! Nevertheless, the existence of such a hierarchy of strategies, whether imputed or written down, is seen as essential for the rationalist model and it is thus worth paying the different levels a little more attention.

Enterprise strategy is the broadest level of strategy that articulates the role that the business entity plays in society. It should answer the questions: Why does this enterprise exist? What purpose does it serve for society? However, it is not only the function of the enterprise that should be addressed at this level, but also its appropriate form (including ownership structure) and mode of governance. In contemporary business argot, it seeks to provide the *mission* and *vision* of the enterprise as a whole. This level of strategy should describe the overarching ethos which guides all the organization's activities. For example, being a responsible corporate citizen, increasing shareholder value and providing customer satisfaction are considered as acceptable goals for any business firm and their inclusion in a viable enterprise strategy is one way of conferring institutional legitimacy upon that enterprise. Few organizations, however, consistently meet the demands that literal interpretation of such a 'strategy' would entail. As always the devil is in the detail, and enterprise strategies seldom, if ever, articulate exactly how responsible the enterprise must be, how much its shareholder value should grow or indeed how satisfied its customers should be. As we noted in Chapter 8, it is all too easy for such high level strategies and statements of intent to degenerate into the empty rhetoric and hubris of self-justification or a belief that one does indeed command one's destiny. This, of course, is enterprise strategy at its worst. At its best it provides something of a soul for the corporation and a set of ideals to which all decisions should be subject.

Corporate strategy involves identifying the kind of businesses that the enterprise should be in to meet its enterprise strategy goals. It answers the overarching question: What sorts of businesses can serve the purpose articulated in the enterprise strategy? Sociopolitical and cultural factors are considered further at this level of strategy, although at the corporate strategy level the focus tends to be upon the influence of these factors at the industry level rather than at the broader societal level. Key sub-questions to be answered at this level of specificity include: What product markets is the corporation interested in? What technologies will be used to compete within them? Of vital importance at this level is the balance between the competing demands that various business strategies will place upon the corporate centre, a need to which the notions of 'balanced portfolio' and 'balanced scorecard', provided by the Boston Consulting Group (1968a, 1968b), respond.

An enterprise's *business strategy* seeks to ensure that the business allocates its available resources in such a way that it can serve its customers better than any other competing business. It answers the question: How are we going to meet *our* customers needs? A successful business strategy will not merely mimic the activities of others in the industry; instead it will provide the business with a distinctive offering that precisely satisfies the complex desires of its customers in the field in which it has chosen to operate. In the process, this level of strategy also integrates the variety of functional areas which contribute to the organization's business processes, such as accounting and marketing, into a coherent whole.

At the bottom of the hierarchy, *functional strategy* is something of a misnomer in our contemporary business environment. Originally the notion was intended to capture the integration of sub-functional areas into functional wholes, so that, for example, accounting staff supporting the production arena adopted similar policies to those accounting staff supporting and recording the activities of the sales department. However, it is increasingly the case that business processes dominate what are now seen to be narrow and parochial functional concerns and thus the view that functional strategy should ensure the integration of sub-functions is seen by many to be woefully outdated. Coordination of activities *across* functions is now seen to be the key focus of strategy at this lower level, for example ensuring that the advertising plan for a new product launch is coordinated with personal selling and sales promotions, a set of tasks potentially requiring input from marketing, accounting and operational functions. In the contemporary world, the challenge seems to be much more about maintaining some, indeed any, coherence for functionally oriented career paths in the face of an increasingly cross-functional, process-oriented business world. Many businesses have given up on this notion entirely, preferring their hierarchy to reflect only a process-oriented model of the world. Yet they are often still keen to recruit suitably rounded, functional specialists as key components of their process teams; thus the issues that functional strategy originally sought to address are certainly still with us, albeit in a very confused form.

It is important to realize that these strategy levels are hierarchical and each level of strategy is constrained by the one above it. For instance, a functional strategy

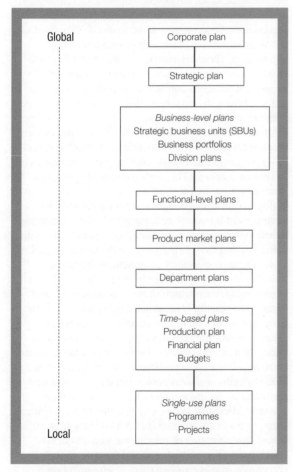

Global

Corporate plan

Strategic plan

Business-level plans
Strategic business units (SBUs)
Business portfolios
Division plans

Functional-level plans

Product market plans

Department plans

Time-based plans
Production plan
Financial plan
Budgets

Single-use plans
Programmes
Projects

Local

Figure 15.1 Hierarchy of plans

Source: Liz Fulop and Stephen Linstead (1999) *Management: A Critical Text*, South Yarra: Macmillan, p. 372.

would be constrained by a firm's business strategy, which in turn is constrained by corporate and enterprise strategy. From this hierarchical structure, it follows that for a firm the enterprise strategy is the most important level of strategy which drives the other levels. However, it is also important to note that the strategy process is not unidirectional, despite the hierarchical structure that is advocated by the Planning School approach.

Lower levels of strategy can and do influence corporate strategy. Consider, for example, the convergence and cross-selling of utilities such as gas, electricity, water and even telephony services that has recently occurred in many Western economies. In the past each of these services represented separate industries, populated by separate companies, many of them state-owned monopolies formed through nationalization and/or agglomeration of diverse regional operations. However, in the wake of the privatizations and deregulation imposed by governments in the 1980s and 90s, these organizations found themselves having to satisfy both the demands of shareholders for returns and the strictures of competition. As a result of prior functional strategies which aimed to facilitate the billing of customers through construction and maintenance of sophisticated computerized databases, many of these organizations had considerable competence and infrastrucure devoted to data management. The existence of these functional assets led some of these organizations aggressively to pursue corporate strategies of diversification into the management of the supply of other utility services, a practice facilitated by the fact that the prior monopoly suppliers of those services were now facing competition in their core businesses and needed innovative ways to shift their product in order to maximize their use of their fixed assets. Here we witness competencies and assets, resulting from functional strategies derived from the support of existing business strategies, being exploited in new corporate diversification strategies, which in turn led a number of utility suppliers to assert new enterprise strategies, emphasizing excellence of customer service, as a way of reintegrating the diversity of activities that their actions had created. However, the success of these moves on the part of some utility players prompted virtually all the others to pursue similar policies, resulting in the distinctive policies of the few becoming the norm for all, in a new, increasingly global industry of multi-utility players – a consequence which removed the uniqueness of the practice and thus its capacity to act as a strategic source of sustainable competitive advantage.

What is clear is that although many graphic descriptions of the planning process tend to give an impression of precision and simplicity (Westerlund and Sjøstrand 1979: 23), the neatness and tidiness implied is questionable to say the least, as critics such as Mintzberg

(1973) and John Kotter (1982) have noted. Their behavioural studies left both far from convinced that planning occurred in any ordered sequence or entailed a precise and predictable process. Practice seemed unamenable to description in the terms advocated by the prescriptions of the hierarchy of plans approach.

SWOT analysis

The *Design School* is the term that Mintzberg gave to the approach to strategy formulation pioneered by Professor Kenneth Andrews of the Harvard Business School. The core of this approach is a simple and eminently reasonable proposition: that strategy is concerned with identifying opportunities in the enterprise's external environment which it is better qualified to exploit than its competitors. Thus, in formulating strategy, managers should conduct an audit of both their external environment, to identify opportunities and threats, and their internal environment, to identify the strengths and weaknesses of the enterprise. The acronym SWOT (strengths, weaknesses, opportunities and threats) is often used as a shorthand summary of the approach. Ideally, the organization should pursue those opportunities in the external environment that are uniquely exploitable by its internal strengths, while simultaneously guarding against those external threats that are likely to impinge upon its internal weaknesses.

On the surface, SWOT analysis seems to provide an entirely sensible approach to strategy formulation and its apparent simplicity and rationality explains much of its immense appeal. The analysis typically involves 'brainstorming' by teams of managers who attempt to divide the constituents of the organization and the environment into the four categories before attempting to match them across the internal/external divide, with particular emphasis being given to the threat–weakness and strength–opportunity conjunctions. In practice, however, the approach is far from simple and clear-cut. Questions such as 'which strength is strongest?' and 'which opportunity is most inviting?' are far from easy to answer, with attempts to quantify elements more often degenerating into arguments about technique rather than insights into competitive advantage. Indeed, many aspects of an organization can even appear as both strengths *and* weaknesses, depending upon how the future of the environment has been defined (for example Microsoft's dominant position in the software industry may be a strength, but is also the source of the unwelcome attention of the competition authorities which had temporarily threatened the split of the company). And even when there is agreement on both the identity of the key elements in each category and their most salient conjunctions, the technique, as we noted in the introduction, offers nothing that would ensure consensus over the appropriate strategic direction to be pursued.

The objectivity that SWOT holds out in its prescriptions turns into a chimera in practice. A moment's reflection reveals that what we are dealing with here is not the organization or environment 'in itself'; rather we are attempting to extract and combine the perceptions of these entities that exist in the minds of managers. And managers, being humans, are wont to disagree. The strengths, weaknesses, opportunities and threats assembled by the analysis are not attributes of an enterprise or its environment, they are *judgements* about the attributes of an enterprise and its environment. Strengths and weaknesses do not exist in organizations, they exist only as constructions of reality by those doing the analysis; likewise opportunities and threats. As the saying has it: 'one person's meat is another's poison.' In the light of this revision of the process, we can see the arguments about technique that we encountered above as arguments about the *criteria* that are to be employed when judgements are made. The development of an appropriate SWOT analysis would thus seem to depend upon the development of relatively objective and consistent criteria to overcome subjective bias (Andrews 1988: 47). But why should it be any easier to gain agreement on criteria than it is to gain agreement on judgements? The search for 'objective' criteria does not solve the problem of subjectivity in judgement, it merely moves it to another level. While there are tools or techniques developed for assessing strengths and weaknesses (for example a company capability profile, vulnerability analysis; see Rowe et al. 1987), the scoring of the elements that these tools delineate and their relative weightings is ultimately influenced by managerial judgement, level of experience and political interests (Bowman and Asch 1987: 87). They are operationalized by people and thus remain essentially subjective.

The expectation that objectivity could be found in managerial reflections upon strategy relies upon an essentially bloodless view of organizational life. For example, one of the great difficulties with internal audit (SW) is that it requires review and scrutiny of management competencies and few, if any, managers are keen on describing themselves as incompetent and/or redundant in the light of current circumstances. Unsurprisingly, therefore,what we often witness in practice is internal weaknesses being captured by fairly arbitrary, intuitive methods (for example rules of thumb, opinions and so on), while more 'objective', quantifiable and historically based data (for example budgets) are used to measure strengths. But even these data, and indeed those concerning the external environment, are selected by managers and emphasized or downplayed as a result of their experience, which is

probably no bad thing. If we did not view this experience as important, we would not emphasize it when attempting to recruit and mentor individuals to fill managerial roles. A key part of this experience is related to the ability to survive and prosper in managerial hierarchies, an ability which is heavily dependent on political skill and expediency (Watson 1994, 1996). A strategist who is not capable of managing his or her own career up the slippery pole of an organizational hierarchy is unlikely to deliver sustainable advantage to an organization in a competitive external environment (see also Chapter 4).

The strategic planning model

The approach to strategy formulation that is currently prevalent in most organizations that have attempted to formalize the process arguably retains the central proposition of the Design School as its core. However, the model has been successively augmented through importation of key elements from other perspectives, resulting in an increasingly elaborate body of prescription. Key contributions from the Entrepreneurial and Planning Schools have been integrated into what we have termed the *Extended Design School* model of strategy formulation. Figure 15.2 outlines the key elements of the Extended Design School model.

The key contribution from the Entrepreneurial School was that enterprises should be infused with a sense of 'mission', a singular and common sense of purpose, intended to provide a common source of motivation for all members of the enterprise and to which all the enterprise's decisions should be ultimately referenced. This quasi-religious conception of organizational life saw the notion of 'culture' move to the centre of the organizational stage (see Chapter 3). Coinciding with, and contributing to, the 1980s valorization of all things commercial, the corporate culture movement, popularized by best-selling texts such as Peters and Waterman's (1982) *In Search of Excellence* and Deal and Kennedy's (1982) *Corporate Cultures*, captured much of the managerial mood of the moment. Often associated with the contemporary rise of a new form of personnel practice, or human resource management, the Entrepreneurial School sought to capitalize upon the untapped enthusiasm and creativity of all staff in a somewhat optimistic view of the potential togetherness of organizational life. The conflicts of interest delineated by earlier accounts of managerial practice were to be eliminated through the elaboration of a strong organizational culture, a set of strong common values and a common purpose (see Chapter 3). Based on observations of a number of very successful enterprises of the time, the prescription for organizational paradise was a simple one – emulate

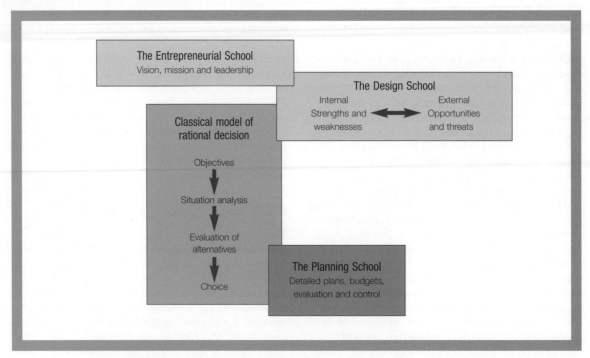

Figure 15.2 Components of the Extended Design School model

Source: Liz Fulop and Stephen Linstead (1999) *Management: A Critical Text*, South Yarra: Macmillan, p. 375.

these successful enterprises. Conflict was not, however, to be got rid of by a removal of the difference in status between leaders and followers. Rather, the role of the leader was enhanced. The role of managers, particularly senior managers, was no longer seen as involving the detailed control of the activities of subordinates and thus employees were 'empowered' to release their full initiative in a new happy organizational family. But in order to allow this to happen, the father figures (they were, and remain, predominantly male) of corporate life had to ensure that values were shared by all, values determined by senior managers as most congruent with organizational success. If an enterprise was not infused with a common sense of purpose, a strong culture, the solution was leadership: the articulation by management of a 'vision' for the enterprise, a common destiny in which all the organization's members could share (see also Chapter 10). In the development of the Extended Design School Model of strategy formulation, 'vision' and 'mission' were appended to the model as superordinate to the definition of more specific goals and objectives, the B to the A provided by SWOT. And while the corporate evangelists advocated a new 'freedom' for employees in the haven of the shared culture, in practice, although enterprises tended to adopt a very general and even ambiguous statement of mission (the almost ubiquitous 'mission statement') as the ultimate reference point for strategic decisions, more specific objectives, and even precise targets or

goals as the focus of particular strategies, were still often articulated from on high.

The Entrepreneurial School clearly embodies a 'unitarist' view of organizations – that of the organization as a team, unified by a common managerially defined purpose. Exceptionally, this may indeed be the case. However, identifying that some successful companies exhibit a high degree of consensus and a strong sense of common purpose is one thing. Deducing, without examining other possible explanations, that a sense of common purpose is the determining cause of the organization's success is quite another. It requires a further quantum leap in logic, and indeed the advocation of a quasi-totalitarian approach to values, to then offer the prescription that organizations without such characteristics could and should obtain them simply by the exercise of management leadership. Although these prescriptions were enthusiastically embraced by managers, the notion that an organization's culture was a variable amenable to management control is an arrogant assumption. Subsequent research has cast much doubt on the validity of this assumption, both in terms of its instrumental effectives (Furnham and Gunter 1993: 255) and indeed the ethical desirability of the managerial manipulations it sustains (Willmott 1993). Numerous criticisms of this unificatory approach to the management of diversity have also been raised throughout other chapters in this text.

The Planning School provided detailed articulation of strategies in specific action plans, budgets and so on. Planning of this nature is inherently hierarchical and, given prior determination of the organization's overall strategy, is concerned fundamentally with the allocation of responsibilities, tasks and resources necessary to operationalize that strategy. As we noted earlier, the Planning School provides the link between the formulation of strategy and its implementation, the road map from A to B. Detailed plans are not only designed to govern the implementation of the strategy, they also provide a tangible set of reference points, or milestones, to enable evaluation and control of the strategy's implementation.

Together these influences constitute the textbook approach to strategy formulation: the Extended Design School model summarized in Figure 15.3. The dominance of the Extended Design School model can probably be accounted for by its simplicity and practical appeal – for practising managers the Design School promises a systematic, comprehensive and ostensibly practical approach to formulating strategy. Ironically, however, the Extended Design School model is not derived from practical experience! Indeed, it is almost entirely a theoretical construct. At its core, the classical model of rational decision making relies not on experience but on purely abstract ideas as to what constitutes rationality. We specify our objectives, analyse the situation and evaluate all possible alternatives before making a decision, not because this has been the lesson of experience, but because we understand it is rational to do so (see Chapter 14). Similarly, the proposition that success is to be achieved by exploiting opportunities in the external environment, for which the organization is better qualified by its strengths than its rivals, has an intuitive appeal. But is this simple idea a sufficient basis on which to determine a strategy when the environment the organization faces is complex and uncertain? And how reliable in practice are the prescriptions that the Entrepreneurial and Planning Schools have lent to the model? Although the Extended Design School model has considerable appeal, through seeming both rational and practical, we need to look more closely at its underlying assumptions and the likely circumstances of its application in practice before we can be confident of its practicality.

The Extended Design School model prescribes, but often treats unproblematically, the analysis of the strategic circumstances of the organization. But the analysis of a strategic situation is by no means a simple and straightforward task; there are a number of considerations which may tend to make the task fraught with uncertainty and indeterminacy. Among these considerations are:

1. the diversity and complexity of both the internal and external environments
2. the natural limits to the cognitive capacities of managers (bounded rationality) and, consequently,
3. the subjective bias or selectivity that these necessarily introduce into the exercise.

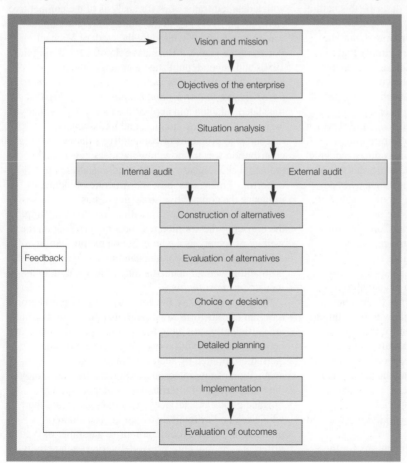

Figure 15.3 The Extended Design School model

Source: John Forster and Michael Browne (1996) *Principles of Strategic Management*, Melbourne: Macmillan, p. 168.

First are the issues of *diversity* and *complexity*. Strategic management is concerned with the management of organizations in the context of their economic relationships with customers and other organizations (as competitors, strategic allies, suppliers or joint ventures and so on). It should be borne in mind that the phenomena with which strategy is concerned have been subject to extraordinary reinvention and change. Indeed, much of this reinvention and change has itself been the result of organizational strategies: economic relationships between organizations have been, and continue to be, the subject of deliberate strategies to re-engineer them in the interests of the various enterprises involved. Consequently, the external environments which face organizations are likely to be diverse, complex and dynamic. That is, they are subject to change and uncertainty.

Second, in the face of this diversity and complexity, managers are constrained by the natural limits of their cognitive ability. *Bounded rationality,* as mentioned in Chapter 14, was the term coined by Herbert Simon (1976: 135; see also Simon 1979) to describe this natural condition of all decision makers. Taken together, the diversity and complexity of the environment, and the bounded rationality of decision makers imply that, except in very simple situations, managers are unable to deal comprehensively and objectively with their external environments. Rather, they must deal *selectively* and *subjectively* with the external environment, paying attention only to those aspects of the environment which they judge to be crucial to the task of formulating strategy. This selectivity, inevitably, introduces a degree of subjective bias into the tasks of strategic analysis and strategy formulation. For not only must managers pay selective attention to aspects of their environment, but different managers within the enterprise may pay selective attention to different aspects. Consider, for example, the problem of the specialist–generalist dimension or professional demarcations in organizations. Human resource specialists, marketing managers and finance directors each pay attention to quite different aspects of the enterprise. Even where their interests do intersect they are likely to have quite different emphases and interpretations of the circumstances. Consequently, the specialist managers may reach quite varying conclusions about the situation at hand, the nature of the problem and the appropriate strategy to deal with the circumstances. This can be compounded if organizations have specialist professional groups such as those found in hospitals and universities (see Chapter 3).

These issues have significant implications for the application of the Extended Design School model in practice. With subjectivity and selectivity, the possibility of a lack of consensus regarding the salience for strategy of various aspects of the environment, their implications and appropriate solutions, compounded by the possibilities of plural interests and the lack of a unifying common purpose, the purported rationality of the Extended Design School model (which was one of its primary intuitive appeals) starts to look shaky indeed.

Competitive strategy and the Positioning School

As its name suggests, at the core of the Extended Design School model of strategy formulation lies the Design School's central emphasis upon SWOT analysis, the explicit attempt to search out those opportunities in the enterprise's environment for which the enterprise is better qualified by its capabilities (or strengths) to exploit than are its actual or potential rivals. The presence of 'rivals' in this account alerts us to the essential role of competition in this definition of strategy but, somewhat ironically, the Design School did not furnish strategists with a detailed framework for analysis of the competitive environment. This gap in the strategy literature market was comprehensively filled by the work of Michael Porter, of the Harvard Business School, who, during the 1980s and beyond, published a number of texts, including his classic *Competitive Strategy: Techniques for Analyzing Industries and Competitors* (1980), that translated, adapted and applied the theory and deductive logic of industrial economics, and its associated discourse, to problems of competitive strategy. Porter's contribution was to show how the ideas generated by industrial economists could be used to address the concerns of managers: how the structure of industries influence the competitive strategies of business enterprises (and vice versa), with a view to evaluating the impact of these structures and strategies, not on the welfare of society as a whole, but on the profitability of enterprises. The key to understanding an organization's profitability was an understanding of its location in its industry, its *positioning*.

'Industries' here are the entire systems of production required to transform raw materials into products which are sufficiently satisfying to consumers for the latter to be willing to part with money in exchange for them. Activities entailed by such systems include the acquisition of raw materials and production technology, the manufacture of intermediate (component) and finished goods and services, their packaging and their wholesale and/or retail distribution. The chain of production involved could comprise a number of different, separate enterprises delivering each activity, or the entire process could be managed by a single, vertically integrated enterprise. More usually, however, the chain will be of neither extreme, with a range of different enterprises of differing scope combining to connect raw materials to consumers. At the end of the chain (and also potentially at various points along it) markets exist where various products are made available to end (and intermediary) consumers. 'Markets' are systems of exchange in which competing goods are presented by suppliers to buyers: they are points at which intermediate or finished goods are exchanged for money in the form of cash or credit.

The five forces

Reflecting the emphasis upon 'industry' and 'market' outlined above, there are two dimensions to Porter's analytical framework. The vertical dimension connects raw materials to consumers, or suppliers to buyers, while the horizontal dimension reflects competing ways in which this connection can be made. These two dimensions are graphically depicted in the famous *five forces model* (Figure 15.4). The two dimensions of the model intersect in existing *competitive rivalry*.

Enterprises compete with existing rivals upstream, to obtain supplies (for example of raw materials, labour, capital, fuel, finance) and downstream, to obtain customers; and the central premise of Porter's approach is that the profitability of an enterprise is determined by the bargaining power it enjoys in negotiating prices or the terms of exchange with its suppliers and customers. Porter suggests that an enterprise in a strong bargaining position can negotiate low prices from its suppliers thus reducing the enterprise's costs. This is likely to be the case when competition among suppliers is high, that is, when there are many supplying organizations and few buying organizations, or existing rivals. An enterprise in a strong bargaining position with respect to its customers can negotiate higher prices, higher revenues

and consequently higher profits. This strong bargaining position will most likely be enjoyed when there are many buyers, but few supplying organizations, or existing rivals. Porter's contribution to strategic planning was to translate the theory of industry economics in such a way as to explain how elements of the economic structure of markets determine the bargaining power of enterprises. He also went on to explain how the strategies of enterprises could change the economic structure of markets, with critical consequences for the prospective profitability of the enterprise. The essence of Porter's advice is that profitability is highest when competition is lowest, because competition erodes profits. To maximize profits one should seek to position one's organization so as to avoid competition. The avoidance of competition affords power to the enterprise to negotiate the terms of exchange, and thus market structures which tend to a monopoly of downstream markets and monopsony in upstream markets will ensure the greatest profits.

However, market positions in which there is little competition are likely to prove attractive to others and so Porter adds in to the horizontal dimension of his model two important constraints on the ability of enterprises to exploit relatively uncompetitive market situations: the *threat of entry* and *threat of substitution* (see Figure 15.4). According to Porter, new entrants are most likely to be attracted when existing rivals engage in collusive activities to sustain high prices and high profitability, reflecting his unshakeable belief in the virtues of competition for the consumer. They are most likely to act upon this attraction when there are minimal barriers to entry to the market, for example low capital requirements and widely available production technology. Markets exhibiting these characteristics are

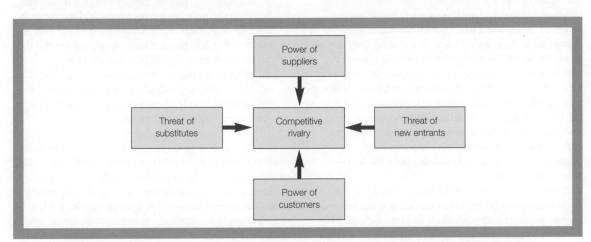

Figure 15.4 Elements of industry structure: Porter's five forces model

seen as easily contestable. High barriers of entry, on the other hand, render markets relatively incontestable and shield incumbent firms from potential new entrants, thus increasing their power over prices. Even with high barriers to entry, however, the behaviour of enterprises in a market with high levels of concentration (that is, few competing firms), may still be constrained by the threat of new entrants. For example, incumbent firms might (collusively?) adopt a strategy of 'limit pricing' where short-term profits are forgone in order to limit the attractiveness of the market to potential new competitors, because if profits rise too fast, then barriers to entry can begin to appear relatively small when compared to the rewards available for climbing them. They may also seek to raise the barriers to entry further, for example by forming expensive and relatively exclusive trade associations entailing minimal agreed standards to offer reassurance to consumers, or by investing in costly information systems for use by selling agents, in an attempt to monopolize key distribution channels. The potential and actuality of such moves on the part of enterprises emphasizes Porter's contention that the enterprise is not necessarily powerless in the face of given competitive conditions. Enterprises can and do adopt strategies which can change the competitive structures of the markets in which they are active.

The threat of substitution also impacts on the power of enterprises to determine the terms of exchange. Porter says a distinction needs to be made between rivalry and substitution, although the distinction is a matter of degree rather than essence. The term *rivalry* is normally used to describe competition between enterprises which are providing very similar, if not identical, goods and services in the marketplace. Thus the airlines British Airways and Virgin Atlantic are rivals on the north Atlantic air routes. *Substitution*, however, refers to products which are not in direct competition. Thus transatlantic cruise ships may not be rivals for British Airways, Virgin Atlantic and other transatlantic airlines, but for some customers they may be a substitute. The significance of substitution is that it qualifies the bargaining power of customers. Porter says the bargaining power of selling firms to set the terms of exchange, in particular prices, will be limited by the extent to which customers have the power and the propensity to shift their purchasing decision to a substitute product.

Porter not only provided advice on how firms can maximize profits through maintaining or changing fundamental industry structures, he also elucidated ways in which an enterprise can achieve higher than average profitability without fundamentally altering the industry in which they operate, although again in practice this distinction is likely to be one of degree rather than kind. Porter again utilizes two dimensions to organize his analysis, with two positions available for adoption on each. The four resulting positions are perhaps also best understood as different types of competition avoidance. On the first dimension an enterprise can choose to be either a *cost leader* or a *differentiator*.

1. *Cost leadership* entails directing all efforts to ensuring that the organization is the lowest cost producer in the industry. Keeping cost down delivers above-average profitability if the market price is still obtained for the product, but is most successful if combined with a price leadership position due to the benefits of economies of scale and experience (see later section 'The resource-based view'). If price leadership is to be pursued, the firm needs to ensure that the difference between its cost position and the industry average is greater than the difference between its price position and the industry average. Since there can, by definition, only be one cost leader, the enterprise adopting such a position is inevitably in a monopoly position with regard to the supply of products to (cost-sensitive) consumers. However, there will often be much competition with rivals to attain this position.

2. *Differentiation* entails the provision of products which are perceived to be sufficiently different from those of other competing suppliers to command a premium price. The basis of differentiation must be one that is valued by the consumer, rendering the product sufficiently superior in the consumer's eyes to merit a premium price. For above-average profitability to result from the adoption of this provision, the difference between the increased price commandable for the product and its increased production cost must be greater than the difference between the industry average price and the industry average cost. Here the differentiation of the product ensures that it is not perfectly substitutable with the products of other suppliers, resulting in the differentiated producer being a monopoly supplier of that *particular* product. Indeed, viewed from this perspective, cost leadership is simply a particular (cost-based) form of differentiation.

The second dimension on which a firm can position itself to exploit one of Porter's generic strategies is that of *scope* or *focus*. An enterprise can choose to be a cost leader or differentiator for the entire market or merely a particular market segment. A focused cost leadership strategy would concentrate on meeting the lower level needs of a particularly cost-conscious market segment. A focused differentiation strategy would concentrate upon meeting the higher level needs of a particularly cost-insensitive market segment. This is to ensure, once again, that the revenue loss incurred in the provision of a cost-leading product or the extra cost incurred in the provision of a differentiated product still leaves a margin that is greater than the industry average, because the aim of Porter's prescriptions is the attainment of above-average profitability. The essence of Porter's advice for both narrowly and broadly competing enterprises and for both cost leaders and differentiators is buy low, sell high.

Porter's writing creates the illusion that the generic strategies are derived from the much more impressive industry analysis that precedes them in his classic text, but the effect is achieved by adjacency rather than logical implication. Porter's industry analysis is derived from the (deeply questionable) laws of neoclassical economics concerning the relationship between price and competition, while Porter's generic strategies are merely the obvious result of considering the possibilities for enhancing profit from attention to either the cost or the price aspect of the equation: profit = price – cost. The only thing that relates the neoclassical economics of price and competition and the profit, price, cost equation is the inclusion of both in a bestselling text and the subsequent attribution of Porter's name to the prescriptive notions that are separately derived from them.

The value chain

Regardless of the analytical problems alluded to above, the publication of *Competitive Strategy* in 1980 certainly captured the attention of both strategic management academics and practitioners and Porter soon capitalized on this success with the publication, in 1985, of *Competitive Advantage: Creating and Sustaining Superior Performance*. While in the earlier work Porter focused on the strategic analysis of the external competitive conditions which enterprises faced in their industry, *Competitive Advantage* shifted his attention to address the internal dimensions of strategy. At the centre of his analysis was the concept of the *value chain*, a description of the internal processes of production and/or service delivery within an enterprise. However, to realize the strategic importance of analysing the internal value chain of the enterprise (that is, as a technique for analysing sources of competitive advantage), Porter argued that it was necessary to consider the broader *industry value chain* of which the enterprise forms a part. The industry value chain encompasses all the activities required to turn raw materials into a product or service that can be purchased by an end consumer, and, as we noted above, a particular organization's value chain may encompass all, or only a small part, of this overall industry value chain.

However, by conceptualizing or describing this chain of production as a 'value chain', Porter drew attention to the way in which the successive processes involved

in transforming raw materials into finished goods and services for end consumption can be represented as value-adding activities. As in the previous discussion of generic strategies, Porter argues that the ability of an enterprise to generate profits depends on its ability to realize added value, its ability to derive revenues in its downstream markets in excess of its costs of production (Porter 1985: 38).

Porter's market-based approach to industrial organization presents an archetypal picture of an industry as a chain of successive value-adding processes coordinated through a set of vertically related markets. Yet this archetype does little to reflect the realities of a huge swathe of commercial activity, both today and historically. Many successive processes of production are coordinated *within* enterprises by management, rather than *between* enterprises, by markets. A past pre-eminent example is the integrated steel mills of BHP at Port Kembla and Newcastle in Australia, where successive stages in the production of steel products – mining of iron ore and coal; production of coking coal; transportation by rail and ship to the steel mills; production of electricity for the plant; smelting of iron; production of steel and stainless steel; its rolling into plate and wire and a multitude of other forms; production of finished products such as specially coated roofing materials and their transportation and distribution – are all coordinated internally within the corporation. Historical examples include the vertical integrations of Rockefeller's Standard Oil Company and indeed Ford's Motor Company, the latter giving rise to the term Fordism, frequently used to describe, and increasingly to deride, such all-encompassing arrangements.

While particular examples may have particular explanations (for example Blackmur 1997), a general theoretical account of the emergence of organizational forms of coordination was provided by Ronald Coase (1937), who argued that markets are not necessarily the most efficient form of industrial coordination. In particular, he argued that market transactions are not costless. *Transaction costs* include the time and expense of market search and the negotiating, writing and enforcing of contracts as well as the risks of default and opportunistic behaviour on the part of suppliers (Williamson 1975; Oster 1994; Besanko et al. 1996: 93). Thus successive stages of industrial production may be coordinated within vertically integrated enterprises in circumstances where it is a more cost-efficient form of coordination than the mediation of market-based transactions (see Chapter 16).

Porter's generic value chain of the enterprise is represented graphically in Figure 15.5. The figure describes the enterprise as a chain of production represented by the primary activities of inbound logistics, operations, outbound logistics, marketing and

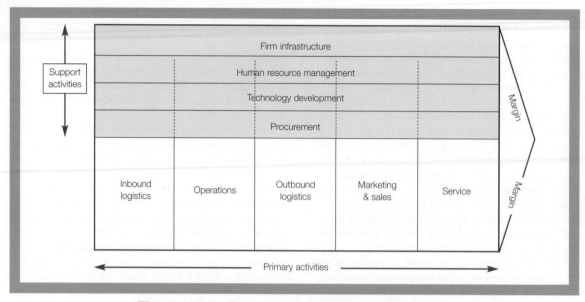

Figure 15.5 The generic (intrafirm) value chain

Source: Reprinted by permission of The Free Press, a Division of Simon & Schuster Adult Publishing Group, from *Competitive Advantage: Creating and Sustaining Superior Performance* by Michael E. Porter. Copyright © 1985, 1998 by Michael E. Porter. All rights reserved.

sales and service, which, as we noted above can, in their entirety, comprise either the whole production process from raw material to consumable product, or merely a small part of this overall industry chain. Each of these primary activities is described in more detail in Exhibit 15.1. Also incorporated in Porter's generic value chain is a set of support activities: the infrastructure of the firm, the human resource management function, technology development and procurement. This representation is of course extremely general, and for any particular enterprise a much more detailed and specific representation of the processes of production can be produced.

The purpose of this categorization is to draw attention to the specific activities of the enterprise so that they can be investigated for their actual or potential contribution to the competitive advantage of the enterprise as a whole. Porter's analysis of competitive advantage is referenced to the broader framework which he had already supplied in *Competitive Strategy*. That is, the sources of competitive advantage which are uncovered in an analysis of the enterprise's internal microsystem of production and value adding are referenced to the generic strategies of cost leadership and differentiation. Notably, Porter believes, it is not sufficient that the enterprise's activities contribute added value (the difference between the costs of production and the revenues realized by sales in the marketplace). This may be achieved without having either a competitive advantage or superior performance.

Rather, Porter says the route to superior performance requires the identification of actual or potential capabilities that constitute sources of advantage over the competition – the ability to produce comparable products more efficiently (cost leadership) or to produce products that better serve the needs of relatively price insensitive, target customers (differentiation). Thus for Porter the strategic analysis of the enterprise's sources of competitive advantage demands external reference to both the enterprise's customers and its competitors.

This particular notion of competitive advantage reflects Porter's assertion that strategy is about choices and tradeoffs, as much about choosing what *not* to do as what *to* do. Porter claims, with some justification, that to derive a real (sustainable) competitive advantage an enterprise's offering to the market must be unique, echoing the incompatibility between competition and superior profitability we encountered earlier. Porter claims that enterprises must choose and sustain their position in an industry through adoption of only one of the four generic strategies identified above. Not to do so is to be 'stuck in the middle' and condemned to both strategic and economic mediocrity. This choice is key since it is seen to guide all subsequent choices made when considering the value chain. However, it is not hard to think of counterexamples, companies who pursue both cost leadership *and* differentiation to great success. Phillip Morris have among the lowest production costs in the tobacco industry, while their

Exhibit 15.1 Primary activities in Porter's generic value chain

❑ **Inbound logistics** Activities associated with receiving, storing, and disseminating inputs to the product, such as materials handling, warehousing, inventory control, vehicle scheduling and returns to suppliers.

❑ **Operations** Activities associated with transforming inputs into the final product form, such as machining, packaging, assembly, equipment maintenance, testing, printing and facility operations.

❑ **Outbound logistics** Activities associated with collecting, storing and physically distributing the product to buyers, such as finished goods warehousing, material handling, delivery vehicle operation, order processing and scheduling.

❑ **Marketing and sales** Activities associated with providing a means by which buyers can purchase the product and inducing them to do so, such as advertising, promotion, salesforce, quoting, channel selection, channel relations and pricing.

❑ **Service** Activities associated with providing services to enhance or maintain the value of the product, such as installation, repair, training, parts supply and product adjustment.

Source: Reprinted by permission of The Free Press, a Division of Simon & Schuster Adult Publishing Group, from *Competitive Advantage: Creating and Sustaining Superior Performance* by Michael E. Porter. Copyright © 1985, 1998 by Michael E. Porter. All rights reserved.

brands command premium prices; certain chains of supermarkets position themselves as both cost-focused and differentiated in a 'best of both worlds' approach; and much of the Japanese car industry during the late 1970s, 80s and much of the 90s offered differentiated products at low cost. While Porter (1996) has tried to address these troubling empirical glitches, the fact that new ones keep appearing only serves to emphasize the inadequacy of any simplifying theory in the face of a diverse, complex and dynamic business reality.

Much of this diversity, complexity and dynamism is of course the result of the impact of strategists acting on the basis of models such as Porter's. The analysis of the enterprise value chain is obviously intended to raise questions about the activities which comprise it, including decisions regarding the addition of new value-adding activities or the retirement of existing activities which no longer contribute to the enterprise's competitive advantage. Choices made here are not,

however, simply the result of dispassionate analysis, and may reflect not only the personal and parochial concerns of individual managers but also the dictates of fashion. For example, many large enterprises have recently reconsidered the relative economies of managerial and market forms of coordination. Whereas market forms of coordination may be associated with search and transaction costs and the risks of default in supply contracts or access to essential supplies, management forms of coordination are not costless either. Particularly in industries characterized by rapid technological change or changes in market needs and expectations, investments in vertically integrated systems of production not only represent high fixed costs but may also leave the enterprise with a reduced ability to respond flexibly and efficiently. Consequently, many formerly highly vertically integrated enterprises have moved towards outsourcing those aspects of the production system which can be obtained at less cost or in higher quality from external suppliers than the enterprise is capable of producing itself. However, the number of firms adopting such policies suggests not merely a realization of inappropriate arrangements in the face of new circumstances but also a bandwagon effect caused by intense academic and journalistic prescriptive commentary based upon pastiche representations of forms of industrial production that have emerged in Japan (see Chapter 16).

Although in strategic terms, enterprises adopting such an approach can be described as focusing their energies on their 'core competencies' (Pralahad and Hamel 1990) – those activities in which they are able to maintain a distinctive competitive advantage against their competitors – in rather more cynical terms, and particularly in less technologically dynamic sectors, they can be seen as limiting their responsibilities and liabilities in the absence of any more creative response to underutilized assets. Even where there are good 'strategic' reasons for outsourcing, other costs need to be borne in mind, such as those associated with developing enhanced capabilities in negotiating and managing contractual relationships with suppliers. As Porter reminds us, it's all about choices.

The resource-based view

As we noted above, *Competitive Advantage* shifted Porter's focus from the external dimensions of enterprise strategy (the structural characteristics of the industry in which the enterprise competes) to the internal determinants of competitive advantage. But Porter was not alone in instigating this shift. Birger Wernerfelt's article, 'A resource-based view of the firm', published in 1984, provided a banner for what has since become one of the most active research agendas in the field, one which, in the opinion of a number of commentators and contributors, shows promise of redefining the field (Mahoney and Pandian 1992; Barney and Zajac 1994; Schendel 1994; Foss 1997).

This was not, however, the first time that the 'resources' of the enterprise had been considered as significant in consideration of matters strategic. Attention to the 'strengths' and 'weaknesses' aspects of SWOT analysis obviously involves consideration of internal aspects of the enterprise, but perhaps the most famous early mobilization of strategic consideration of the firm's resources is to be found in the work of the Boston Consulting Group (BCG) (1968a, 1968b). For the BCG, the key resource of a firm, was its *experience*. This group investigated the costs incurred in the production and sale of a range of commodity products and uncovered a relationship which was, somewhat surprisingly, consistent across different products and industries, between these costs and total production and sales. The BCG investigated 24 different products and by mapping unit cost against the total volume of product produced and sold, it introduced the *experience curve* to the world of strategic management. The smoothness of the cost/total volume curve, total volume being the proxy for 'experience', suggested a stable relationship. Indeed, on the basis of its research and analyses, the BCG was able to assert that unit costs reduced by between 20 and 30 per cent every time experience, or total volume of production, doubled, a finding that has since been replicated and confirmed by other studies (for example Abell and Hammond 1979). The experience curve is represented in Figure 15.6.

In a new product market, a doubling of total experience for a firm might not take very long, but in a mature product market such an increase in total production would probably take many, many years to accrue. Thus, in younger product markets one would expect prices to fall, as a result of the experience effect, more rapidly than in more mature ones. The trick, for a firm of consultants attempting to sell its advice to strategic managers, was to devise a way of exploiting this finding. Since the fall in costs was attributable to increase in experience, the best way to gain a relative cost advantage would be to increase your experience faster than your competitors could increase theirs or, to put it another way, to ensure that your production grew faster than that of your competitors. Now most businesses try to expand faster than their competitors in most industries. The insight that the BCG offered was that this was particularly important in new markets and that the advantages gained by early growth in production and consequent increase in relative experience could produce a cost advantage gap that competitors would find very hard subsequently to close. The scale of that advantage would depend upon the extent to which the experience of the most experienced firm exceeded that of its nearest competitor. On the basis of the finding that, during the growth phase of a market, returns from growth in market share are particularly high since they can produce a widening experience and thus cost gap, the BCG was able to offer its now famous portfolio matrix as advice for corporate managers on where and why they should direct their (limited) resources.

In the matrix, businesses are divided into four quadrants according to two dimensions: their relative

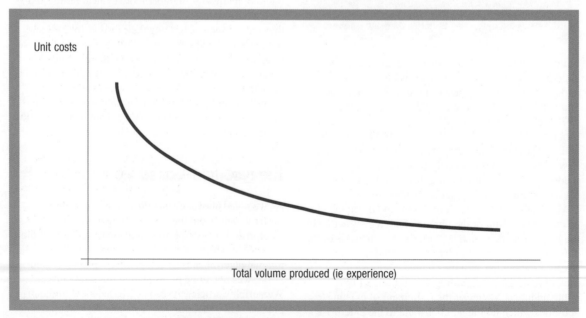

Figure 15.6 The experience curve

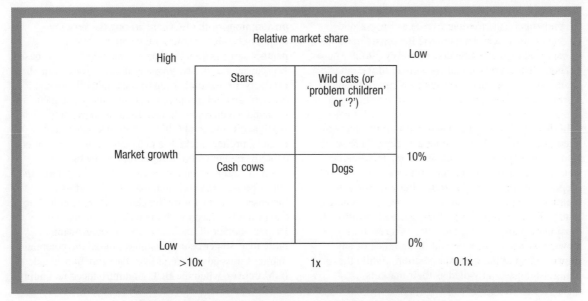

Figure 15.7 The Boston matrix (or Boston box)

share of the market in which they operate and the extent of growth of that market as a whole. A business's relative market share was expressed as a proportion of its largest competitor's market share, with the break between 'high' and 'low' being equality of market share with the leading competitor. Relative market share acted as a proxy for experience, or rather relative experience, since a business with a high market share almost certainly had a higher total production and thus greater experience than a firm with a low market share. Market growth was included since it was only in rapidly growing markets that experience-based, advantageous cost reductions were likely to be significant. Market growth of above 10 per cent per annum was deemed to be 'high'.

Strategists at the corporate level are enjoined to place each of the businesses for which they are responsible in a quadrant, determined by analysis of their relative market share and the growth of the markets in which they operate. According to the BCG, the inhabitants of each of the quadrants have different business characteristics:

■ *Stars*, with high shares of fast-growing markets, have the benefits of high relative experience and consequently low relative costs. They should thus be the highest profit generators in the markets in which they operate. They may nevertheless consume cash, since growth is often costly in terms of the set-up of new production facilities and increased working capital demands (for example Pfizer's Viagra in the fast-growing market for treatments for erectile dysfunction).

■ *Cash cows*, who have high market shares of low growth markets, are likely to be profitable as a result of their high relative market shares and the economies of scale and experience-derived cost advantages that come with them. Better still, in cash flow terms, the lack of growth in the markets they serve means that they do not require cash to fund expansion. They generate surplus cash that can be invested elsewhere in the business (for example Microsoft Windows in the relatively mature market for operating systems).

■ *Dogs* is the name given to low growth businesses with low market share. Their low market share means that they are unlikely to be very profitable, if at all, but the lack of growth in their market means that they are also unlikely to require investment to fund growth (for example Red Hat Linux would be rendered a dog of the operating systems market by the BCG).

■ *Wild cats* (or 'problem children' or 'question marks') are businesses with a low share in a fast-growing market. They again are unlikely to be very profitable due to their relatively small market share and worse still, in cash flow terms, they are likely to require significant investment merely to maintain that share and their market position as the market grows (for example Abbott's Uprima, another oral treatment for erectile dysfunction. However, differences in its mode of operation would mean that, strictly speaking, Uprima is not a direct commodity competitor for Pfizer's market leader, although expected offerings from both Glaxo and

Bayer look likely to be based upon the same preparation and treatment route as Viagra, and would thus meet strict criteria for consideration as wild cat market contenders (Godfrey 2002). These complexities reveal that, as with all of the other prescriptive models we have considered, the devil is in the detail of application).

In the absence of careful and explicit management attention and activity to counteract them, there were also felt to be natural tendencies at work, whereby stars gradually became either wild cats or cash cows (depending upon whether or not they were able to maintain their market share), cash cows and wild cats gradually degenerated into dogs (the former through erosion of market share, the latter as a result of slowing of market growth and the absence of any improvement in their market position), while the mangiest dogs simply died as their markets disappeared. Such outcomes are particularly likely in a cost-cutting culture, as stars and cash cows lose their leading positions in a disinvestment spiral that eventually results in a portfolio entirely made up of dogs.

From these characterizations of businesses, their account of 'natural' business tendencies and their insights into the experience curve, the BCG came up with the following prescriptions to manage cash flow so as to counteract unwelcome tendencies to decline and maintain a 'balanced portfolio' at the corporate level – one which ensured that today's cash flows were invested in the best possible way to ensure tomorrow's:

■ *Stars:* Invest to fund growth, maintain market share and ensure that today's star becomes tomorrow's cash cow. Keep prices up, reducing them only if it becomes necessary to do so to maintain market share.
■ *Cash cows:* Ration new investment. Again keep prices up where possible. Reduce them only to prevent new entrants to the market. Use cash flow surpluses to fund growth of stars and promising wild cats.
■ *Wild cats:* Since the BCG analysis suggests that the value of increased market share is at its highest when markets are growing fast, if possible investment should be made to fund growth in order to convert these businesses into stars, even though this may prove extremely costly in the short term. If such a strategy appears to be prohibitively expensive, or otherwise unlikely to succeed (for example if the market leader is simply too far ahead), the BCG advised withdrawing on the most advantageous terms, by progressively pricing out of the market.
■ *Dogs:* Manage carefully for cash and withdraw.

It is important to note that while the analyses and prescriptions of the BCG are among the very few empirically supportable findings in the strategy pantheon, the original research upon which it was based was carried out in fast-growing markets for commodity products (for example transistors, crude oil, diodes, ethylene and polypropylene), as was the subsequent research which replicated its findings (for example Abell and Hammond (1979), examined integrated circuits, broiler chickens and steam turbine generators). Moreover, many who have mobilized the original portfolio and its derivatives have fudged or relaxed the cutoff points in the original matrix in an effort to increase its applicability. Indeed the BCG itself did so early on when faced with the recognition that the limited number of markets in the world growing at more than 10 per cent per annum limited the potential market for its advice, or at least the more upbeat side of it. Moreover, when the BCG first introduced its findings on experience, it clearly indicated that the data it was presenting was based solely on commodity products, but when it presented its portfolio, it seemingly recognized this potentional commercial limitation in the market for its services and provided no caveats to restrict the claims and prescriptions of the model to commodities. It was sold as a consultancy package to the major multinationals who were almost universally into branding, the main purpose of which was to avoid competing on price. Perhaps this explains why marketeers have suggested using the Boston portfolio for controlling mature branded products – which seems to be the main application of the model today (Pearson, personal communication). Nevertheless, if the product under consideration is not a commodity, that is, is a differentiated offering, or the market in which it is sold is not growing quickly, then the BCG's experience/cost relationship may well not hold true and the advice derived from it, via matrix categorizations, may well prove inappropriate.

Even in fast-growing commodity markets, despite the robustness of the empirical findings, it is unlikely that cost decline happens automatically. It is much more likely, at least in part, to result from competent management actively driving costs down as volume increases. If, however, one bears in mind the constraints of the model in terms of its limited applicability, it may well prove to be a useful heuristic when considering the deployment of limited resources across a number of competing businesses beneath one overarching corporate umbrella. Since, by definition, there can only be one non-dog in virtually all mature industries, the advice for the majority of businesses to simply withdraw from the market does seem a little fatalistic and is certainly not what we tend to witness in practice. The BCG matrix and prescriptions may provide useful advice to those with high market shares in fast-growing commodity markets, but it has little to offer the rest, indeed the majority, of existing enterprises.

The reinvigoration of a resource-based view, following the publication of Wernerfelt's article in the mid-1980s, spawned a significant and ongoing research agenda, one that sought for 'resources' within the business that managers could manipulate more directly than the clearly, partially externally determined resource of 'experience'. But throughout its revival, the resource-based view has been bedevilled by problems of terminology. In 1980, Lenz complained that the terms used in investigating these issues were vague and ambiguous, and that there was great inconsistency in the frames of reference within which the terms were used. Eight years later, complaints about the 'welter of overlapping meanings of competitive advantage' (Day and Wensley 1988: 2) were still being voiced. And as recently as 1997, both Wernerfelt (1997: xvii) and Nicolai Foss (1997: 8) were still pointing to problems of terminology. Nevertheless, as Wernerfelt goes on to explain, 'the resource-based view is a puzzle under construction' and that, in spite of differences in terminology, a large degree of consensus has emerged that 'sustainable competitive advantages are conferred by resources which are hard to imitate and scarce relative to their economic value' (Wernerfelt 1997: xvii).

As is often the case, the resource-based view's agenda has been significantly conditioned by its status as a riposte to the perceived overemphasis on external industry-structural factors in some of Porter's account of enterprise profitability. Other accounts suggest that part of the attraction of the resource-based perspective lies in the perceived failure of strategies for growth based on acquisitions and diversification which were characteristic of the 1960s and 70s (Sterne 1992). It is certainly true that a narrow reading of Porter would suggest that the primary strategic choice is which industry or industries an enterprise should engage in and that subsequent choices are largely determined by that context (Schendel 1994: 1–2), just as a narrow reading of the BCGs advice would be that the only determinants of strategy are market share and market growth. But neither of these readings is accurate or fair. Industry choice and positioning and buy, hold or sell decisions are clearly important parts of strategy but they are not the whole story, just as the resources of a firm be they experiential (BCG, 1968a), financial, physical, human, organizational or technological (Lenz 1980: 225; Grant, 1991: 160) cannot alone explain an enterprise's fortunes. Rather, as even simple models like the Boston matrix and SWOT analysis make clear, the determinants of success are to be found in the interaction of internal resources and external circumstances. Just as one does not play a successful pass in soccer, basketball, hockey, or rugby without looking at the positions of both one's own teammates and those of one's opponents, and indeed their relative attributes and the ways in which these combine into oppositional capabilities (Grant 1991: 158), one cannot meaningfully engage in strategic action without considering both the inside and outside of the enterprise.

Attempts to empirically test the relative importance of external, particularly industry-specific factors and internal, 'resource'-type factors on profitability have been beset both by the definitional problems we have already alluded to and the consequent difficulties of operationalizing notions such as 'resource' and indeed 'success'. They have had, not surprisingly, mixed results. For example, while Richard Schmalensee (1985) found that industry factors were strong compared to corporate and market share effects in explaining enterprise profitability, a subsequent study concluded that:

if our findings of the relative importance can be generalised, it would suggest that the critical issue in firm success and development is not primarily the selection of growth industries or product niches, but it is the building of an effective, directed, human organisation in the selected industries. (Hansen and Wernerfelt 1989: 409)

Hansen and Wernerfelt's findings were supported by a later study in which Richard Rumelt (1991) found small stable industry effects and very large effects at the business unit level. Although this rather specious argument is far from settled in the academy, it is clear that the so-called resource-based view was always likely to prevail in practice. For the average practising manager, even the average practising 'strategic' manager, shifting the entire organization to a secluded niche in an attractive industry sector is either impractical, unthinkable or both. The pursuit of such a seemingly ideal location is simply not often an option in the real world and thus the hunger of practising managers for potential solutions to immediate strategic problems has increased demand for practical prescriptions, prescriptions which thus almost inevitably tend to focus upon those factors that are felt to be under managerial control, namely the 'resources' of the firm. Largely following the publication of Prahalad and Hamel's (1990) article, 'The core competence of the corporation' in the *Harvard Business Review*, the ideas of 'core competencies', 'capabilities' and 'sustainable competitive advantage' have quickly become part of the language of corporate management, although it is worthwhile noting that the authors of this vehicle for the popularization of the resource-based perspective do not themselves consider that they are ploughing a resource-based furrow. As, if not more, important to Pralahad and Hamel's account of the determinants of success is the motivating role of *strategic intent*, which Hamel and Pralahad articulated in an earlier *Harvard Business Review* article (1989). As Pearson (1999: 315) summarizes: 'Successful competitors begin with crazy ambitions – an obsession with winning at all levels of the organization and a 10–20 year quest for global leadership. This is referred to as *strategic intent*'. This visionary aim is clearly partly predicated upon external considerations – 'It is vital to understand the resolution, stamina and inventiveness of potential competitors' (Pearson 1999: 315) – and it is seemingly crucial to enabling the integration of resources into the meaningful 'capability' or 'core competence' that constitutes the firm's uniqueness and value in the marketplace.

Those entities claimed as resources by those who do admit their membership of the resource-based perspective are admirably broad and thus the natures and qualities of these resources are complex and diverse. According to Forster and Browne (1996: 127), resources may be internally generated or externally acquired; they may be durable or consumed in production; they may be tangible or intangible; and they may transcend the borders of the enterprise via relationships with other enterprises through alliances or via customers in terms of reputation and loyalty. All of which reminds us yet again, that a distinction between internal and external and between resources and the environments in which they are deployed is often more obfuscating than clarifying. There does seem to be some agreement, however, over the fact that resources alone are not enough. The competitive advantage of Grant's (1991: 158) capabilities is seen to derive from the unique ways in which more or less unique resources have been combined, just as Prahalad and Hamel's 'core competence' of the organization resides in its 'collective learning … especially how to coordinate diverse production skills and integrate multiple streams of technologies' (1990: 82). The notion of competitive advantage here once more reminds us that a resource-based view can no more ignore the environment of the organization than any other meaningful account of strategy. Indeed, for any *sustainable* competitive advantage to be built, an enterprise's resources, and/or the capabilities formed by them, must be either scarce, and therefore unavailable to competitors, inimitable, unsubstitutable or imperfectly mobile. That is, they must be relatively specific to the firm (see Foss 1997: 10), a judgement of which can only be made through consideration of the competitive environment, or industry, in which the firm finds itself or wishes to position itself. Indeed, for Dan Schendel (1994: 1), the way in which a broad reading of 'resources' can cut across arbitrary distinctions – such as those between the external and internal foci, between formulation and implementation and between content and process – and

demonstrate the interdependence of these facets of strategy is one of the keys to its recent success.

Reconfigurationist approaches

The Positioning School is particularly silent on the issue of implementing strategies. By contrast, the Extended Design School model made the tacit assumption that senior managers, who have primary responsibility for the formulation of strategy, automatically enjoy the authority to command its implementation. The model, therefore, takes for granted a unitarist view of organizations, one which recognizes managerial authority as the only source of legitimate power to command the activities of the enterprise. The rationalist approaches to strategy focused on the mechanics of developing a strategic plan and getting the steps or stages of the strategic process 'right'. All the approaches examined under the rationalist approach assumed a top-down view of strategy making, presenting the planning process very much as edicts or directives issued by those in authority to be implemented unquestionably throughout all levels of the organization. Resistance or defiance were not considered problems.

An alternative view, however, is that in practice managerial authority is not the only source of power in organizations, and indeed that both official and unofficial sources of power and influence are distributed throughout organizations (see Chapter 6). In these circumstances, it cannot be assumed that strategies formulated by senior managers will be implemented automatically and remain unchanged by organizational stakeholders and those responsible for their implementation. The relationship between formulation and implementation of strategies is not as unproblematic as the Extended Design School model might lead one to suppose.

The reconfigurationist approaches question the wisdom and viability of the unitarist approach to planning, suggesting a number of improvements to ensure the success of strategies. One of these was the increased focus during the 1980s on the implementation of strategies. An important development was the realization that while senior managers could formulate strategies, to work in practice a strategy would require many people's commitment to and ownership of it. An important part of understanding how the implementation of a particular strategy might be supported or resisted occurred with the adoption of a more pluralist view of strategy making. Increasingly it became apparent that strategy had to include more devolved and participatory methods to ensure that all levels of the organization could contribute to the strategy process and identify with the plan if this much-needed ownership and commitment were to materialize. Implementation became as important as the formulation of strategy, hence the term *strategic management* replaced strategic planning.

Attention became focused on the constraints and opportunities impacting upon or affecting the implementation of strategy, that is, on the sorts of things that were likely to frustrate or impede the organization's capacity to carry out its strategies. As we discussed in Chapters 6, 7 and 8, this entailed recognizing that organizations comprise multiple and diverse stakeholders who are likely to view any new strategic direction or plan as potentially affecting their power, influence and control over valued or scarce resources. Pluralists agree that stakeholders, or coalitions of them, probably view any new strategy in terms of its costs and benefits to them personally. Strategic change was recognized as involving the threat or real loss of power, influence and control over traditional resources and often placed new restrictions on people's ability to act independently. Resistance became identified as an inevitable consequence of implementing new plans. The organization's stakeholders were considered most likely to evaluate the costs and benefits of any proposed strategy with respect to their underlying assumptions, preferences, interests and values. In other words, the strategy had to be made to 'fit' the contours of these interests, as well as the resource and structural considerations of the organization vis-à-vis its competitive position. This contingency approach to strategy emphasized the importance of achieving *fit* between the company's structure, culture, strategy and environment. The better the fit, the smoother the implementation of any strategy, or so the argument went.

Incrementalism

For some theorists, the accommodation of interests required to achieve this strategic 'fit' has less to do with rational behaviour and more to do with political negotiation and bargaining, as discussed in Chapters 6 and 14. This was evident in the work of Charles Lindblom (1959) on *incrementalism* in decision making. Lindblom's ideas, derived from the public policy context, have nevertheless resonated with several writers in the field of private sector strategy formulation. For example, the conclusion that the processes of decision making in the organizational context are likely to be characterized by political rather than comprehensively rational processes is shared by a number of theorists (for example Jemison 1981: 604; Brunnson 1982: 30; Narayanan and Fahey 1982; Piercy 1989: 27). But Lindblom's ideas have been taken up most forcibly by James Brian Quinn (1980) who argued that *logical incrementalism* is a more apt description for strategic decision making.

Logical incrementalism is a process for making decisions in the context of an uncertain environment. Arguably, most strategic decisions are indeed incremental as are their implementations. Take, for example, the marketing strategies an enterprise might employ. On relatively rare occasions – such as the launching of a new product – marketing strategy formulation may take the form of a marketing plan specified in detail prior to implementation. But this does not describe the vast majority of marketing decisions. Most decisions in marketing strategy are taken in the context where a strategy is already in place and a product is already active in the market. The decisions taken under these circumstances will be incremental – small piecemeal changes to the strategy already in place: a discount on prices; some further advertising; the negotiation of an extension to a distribution contract. These changes are taken in response to new opportunities. In the process, the enterprise learns a great deal: how consumers respond to the enterprise's initiatives; the reaction of competitors; the reliability of the distribution system; and the flexibility of the enterprise's own production team. Thus strategies do not derive from a rational planning process fully specified and ready for implementation. Rather strategies emerge incrementally over time and incrementalism is not 'muddling through' but 'is a purposeful, effective, proactive management technique for improving and integrating both the analytical and behavioural aspects of strategy formulation' (Quinn 1978: 8).

In reality the rational consensus model of strategy implementation is distorted by conflicting goals, bargaining and negotiation of interests, leading to the creation of dominant/dependent coalitions within an organization's various domains of operation. In Quinn's terms, the whole strategy implementation process becomes fragmented and evolutionary, that is, it follows a path of 'logical incrementalism' (Quinn 1978). Decisions are taken incrementally and opportunistically as a result of communicating assumptions, integrating corporate and divisional plans and resolving political differences.

Each aspect of a strategy's implementation that involves the acquisition, reorganization and redistribution of scarce resources is contested by individual stakeholders when their expectations are threatened. The resolution of negotiations between stakeholders with differential bases of power produces a temporarily structured order within the company, so that, according to Anselm Strauss (1978), strategic outcomes are the result of a process of 'negotiated order', not the product of a rational/analytic planning process.

Organizational environments can be structured by the actions of key players operating in those arenas which provide them with the greatest strategic advantage (see Chapter 6). Strategic planners and managers will hold multiple roles within their organization, thereby enabling them to select the most propitious arenas in order to promote and pursue their agendas for strategic implementation. In this way strategy is continuously moulded and fashioned by the actions of key players. Strategy formulation is a political process involving various groups and individuals pursuing their interests, using power and influence and various tactics to devise actions which can at times go against other major corporate players (Byrt 1973: 2). We have critiqued this view of action in Chapter 14.

The problem of strategic 'drift'

Not all commentators on strategy believe that it is possible to change an organization incrementally or otherwise, except in very specific circumstances, because human beings do not naturally work in that way. Mindsets, or cultures, only change slowly and often under extreme pressure, to the extent that some researchers question whether it is realistic to talk about changing the culture to facilitate a strategic change. Gerry Johnson (1992) argues, as does Peter Anthony (1994), that in the context of the organization or company, it is the change of behaviour which matters most, and really the idea that managers can engineer change in belief systems is rather fanciful. Johnson suggests that the organization is embedded in a cultural web of stories and myths, rituals and routines, symbols, power structures, control systems, organizational structures, and all of these shape the *paradigm*. A paradigm is basically a formula for what the organization is and what it does and what the people in the organization think are the recipes for its success or otherwise. Figure 15.8 describes the key elements of such a *cultural web*. The paradigm is at the heart of the web and is sustained by its other elements.

This paradigm can make the organization insensitive to change and produce the situation of *strategic drift,* as described in Figure 15.9. Johnson gives several examples of this from manufacturing and service industries. The effect of strategic drift is that the organization (or its management) gets further and further out of step with its environment, while believing that it is doing everything possible to keep up. Incremental change is attenuated by the biased perception that the organization has of its environment, and the modifications it makes are too little because of its cultural filter. When crisis approaches, the organization abandons its incremental progression and tries out a number of responses, but again none of them are radical enough by now and the organization is so confused that it often goes backwards and undoes some of the progress it has made. Eventually, radical change is necessary to enable the organization to survive, as in many of the corporate 'turnaround' stories of the 1980s. Johnson offers some advice on how to avoid strategic drift, which includes creating an open and communicative culture where challenge of the status quo is encouraged; frequent use of external consultants and outsider input to challenge established mindsets; and the constant deployment of symbols of change rather than tradition.

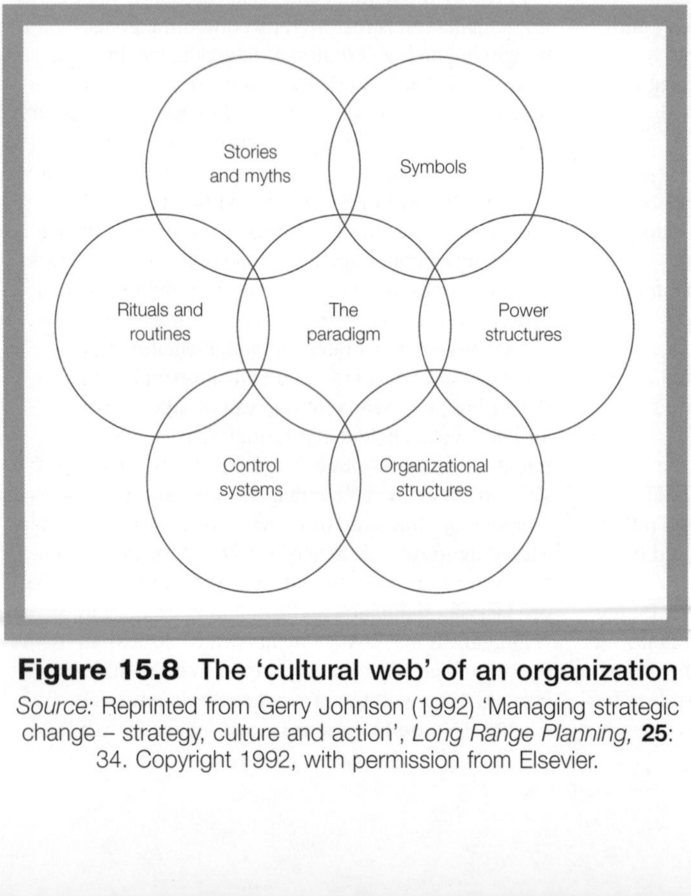

Mintzberg (1987: 71–3) also contended that many organizations are incapable of major shifts in strategic orientation. He maintained that organizations adopt different forms of strategic behaviour at different times. Strategic change often involves perfecting a given approach (for example retailing) and doing more of the same, but perhaps in a better way, for example pursuing continuous improvement in the firm's distinctive competencies. However, he noted that in pursuing this incremental approach, the environment of the business could change, even to the point of putting the organization's strategic orientation way out of synchronization with its environment. Mintzberg believed that a strategic revolution needs to take place to realign the organization and re-establish a 'fit' with its environment. In Johnson's terms, the paradigm has to be challenged and changed.

Mintzberg was optimistic about the

Figure 15.8 The 'cultural web' of an organization
Source: Reprinted from Gerry Johnson (1992) 'Managing strategic change – strategy, culture and action', *Long Range Planning,* **25**: 34. Copyright 1992, with permission from Elsevier.

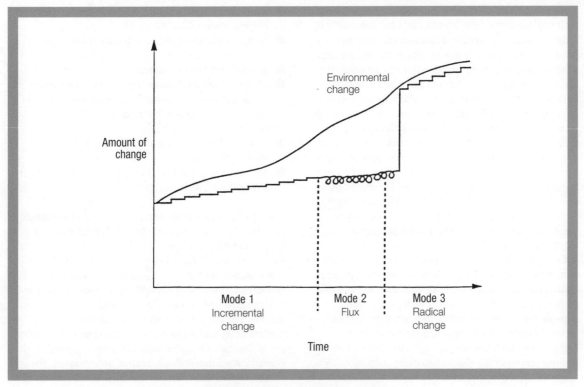

Figure 15.9 Strategic drift

Source: Reprinted from Gerry Johnson (1992) 'Managing strategic change – strategy, culture and action', *Long Range Planning,* **25**: 34. Copyright 1992, with permission from Elsevier.

potential for a radical turnaround of organizations in such turmoil. Organizations, he said, always have both deliberately planned and emergent strategies coexisting. He believed that many large-scale mass production organizations can be typified by incrementalism, but noted that some organizations are designed and operate to institutionalize change and encourage both emergent and deliberate strategies. For Mintzberg, managing incremental change is the predominant and normal strategic role for most managers and those who are concerned with 'crafting strategy'.

Crafting strategy

Mintzberg drew a distinction between planning strategy and crafting strategy. He said:

Imagine someone planning strategy. What most likely springs to mind is an image of orderly thinking: a senior manager or a group of them, sitting in an office formulating courses of action that everyone else will implement on schedule. The keynote is reason – rational control, the systematic analysis of competitors and markets, of company strengths and weaknesses, the combination of these analyses producing clear, explicit, full-blown strategies. (Mintzberg 1987: 58)

Mintzberg has criticized the view that the making of strategy somehow reflects senior management's intentions alone. This view, espoused by many managers, creates an image of tidiness and purpose and conceals the complexity and confusion – the many meetings, debates, dead ends and diverse ideas – that drive the organization forward (Mintzberg 1987: 67–8). He preferred instead to describe planning as *crafting strategy* and deliberately used the crafting metaphor to distance his concept of planning from the mechanistic or mechanical models of formal planning – to infuse it with the ideas of creativity, uncertainty, feeling involved and the fusion of design and implementation (1987: 66). Crafting strategy is more like a fluid learning process in which formulation and implementation merge to produce effective and creative strategies (Mintzberg 1987: 66). Not only did Mintzberg advocate that senior managers abandon top-down planning in favour of a more negotiated or interactive style, but he also argued that the concept of strategy had to incorporate the emergent and more dynamic ways in which planning actually happens.

Crafting strategy involves managing the differences between *emergent* and *deliberate* (or intentional) *strategy making*. Mintzberg proposed that senior managers could develop an 'umbrella strategy' within their organizations, which would involve them only in setting broad guidelines or goals (for example to produce only high-margin products at the cutting edge of technology), leaving the specifics (for example the choice of products) to others in the organization. An umbrella strategy would allow scope for substrategy development within departments, units or divisions, that is, a portfolio of plans coordinated at the centre (Mintzberg 1987: 70–1). Mintzberg believed that the implementers of plans (the 'grass-roots' people) had to become the formulators of plans as well or have a more significant role in devising strategies. He argued that senior managers should focus on strategy formation, rather than formulation, and involve the grass roots of the organization, particularly middle managers (Mintzberg 1987: 70–1).

Crafting strategy was considered especially important in adhocracies (see Chapter 4) or in post-entrepreneurial organizations, which have been characterized by quite complex cross-functional relationships between departments, teams, divisions and suppliers and more turbulent environments (see Kanter 1989: 89–90; Chapter 4). The focus on learning and strategy has become an important element in more contemporary views of strategy, particularly strategic thinking. Mintzberg's singular message in the use of the crafting metaphor was to argue that grass-roots strategies emerge or take root whenever people have the capacity or opportunity to learn. This opportunity to learn depends on a strategic framework or context that is deliberate, but not so inflexible that it leaves no room for experimentation, innovation or creativity (Mintzberg 1987: 69–71).

Strategic thinking

According to Lenz, 'most strategic planning processes do not facilitate the self-reflective learning that is necessary for organizations to adapt to changing competitive conditions' because of the 'paralysis of analysis' (1987: 34–9; see also Pearson, 1999). Following this path avoids strategic thinking because it is crowded out by the mechanics of strategic planning (Rowe et al. 1986: 36). Rational thinking alone tends to preclude the use of dialogue, argument and debate, so that entrepreneurial creativity in strategic planning is stifled, and the process becomes mechanistic. Lenz (1987: 39) suggests several steps to ensure a self-reflective strategic planning process:

- Make it the job of the strategic planner to be concerned with facilitating organizational learning.
- Keep the process as simple as possible.
- Avoid routinized behaviour and processes.
- Emphasize logical arguments; use numbers as backup material.
- Simplify planning reviews; focus on action, not theatricals.
- Stimulate thinking and action.
- Do not allow analytic techniques to oversimplify the situation: use them instead to illuminate problems.
- Strategic planning is good; strategic thinking is better.
- Base evaluation on insights provided, not techniques used.
- Manage the evolution of the planning process so it becomes self-learning.

A similar sentiment is expressed by Kenichi Ohmae (1983), who also criticized strategy formulation for being too rational or formal and obsessed with facts and figures. Ohmae believed very firmly in the virtues of analysis, but not the sort of analysis that merely produces rational or predictable responses to problems. In a sense, much of what Porter describes as competitive advantage rests on the market's predictability and logic operating in certain industries, while Ohmae argues that strategic thinking requires going beyond the obvious, beyond appearances, beyond proven logics, to search out the truly novel sources of competitive advantage. For Ohmae, strategic thinking means seeking a clear understanding of the elements of a problem or situation and the important underlying relationships, then restructuring or reconfiguring these relationships in the most advantageous way (1983: 12–15). Ohmae suggests that rational analysis has to be combined with imaginative reintegration if strategic thinking is to produce a competitive edge.

For Ohmae, the most important part of strategic thinking is the ability to identify critical issues and solutions – to abandon preconceived ideas and preconceptions. Ohmae suggests a number of steps that managers can follow to develop their strategic thinking capabilities, as well as devising an issues diagram to identify issues and solutions-oriented questions. The issues diagram is similar to a decision tree, a rational method of decision making used to list a number of alternative possibilities to an issue, with 'yes' and 'no' alternatives identified to guide possible actions. Ohmae drew on his engineering background to develop the issue diagram by using value engineering and value analysis to determine or identify the critical issues that managers need to ask about their competing products (1983: 23). The former refers to quality and reliability issues relating to a product, the latter to the cost and price of products. Analysis for Ohmae, and the focus on quality, was deeply rooted in his Japanese origins (see Chapter 9).

Ohmae suggests that strategic thinking, and the development of an issues diagram, require four main processes:

1. identifying all the key factors in a business that put it at a disadvantage relative to its competitors
2. grouping the factors based on some common denominator or principle
3. evaluating each underlying relationship within the categories identified to try to find the critical issues
4. asking solution-oriented questions for each critical issue, with the ultimate aim being to prioritize actions.

As mentioned above, Ohmae draws concepts from engineering to identify critical issues. Ohmae's approach is less formula-driven or based on a specific model. It is far more dependent on managers developing or mastering strategic thinking, which in the end means having the superior 'battle plan' (Ohmae 1983: 37–8, 240–1).

Scenario planning

Strategic thinking has been considerably refined in the area of *scenario planning*, which is not focused on detailed predictions about the current environment of an organization but rather on learning and gaining insights through challenging assumptions and thinking creatively about the future of an industry. Scenario planning embraces the key elements of emergent and intended strategy, as described by Mintzberg in his crafting strategy metaphor, but also builds on the notion of strategy as learning – looking at or to the future and breaking paradigms (as per Johnson). It also goes much further than previous approaches by using narratives and stories as a way of breaking new ground in strategic thinking and questioning assumptions. In fact scenarios are treated as myths about the future (Schwartz 1996: 39). Scenario planning comes close to what might be described as a *postmodern* concept of strategy.

Scenario planning did not originate in the USA, nor is it derived from the corporate experience of that country. Rather, Peter Schwartz, its key proponent, learnt about scenario planning after joining the Royal Dutch Shell Company and working with some of the architects of the method, such as Pierre Wack (1985a, 1985b). Wack was responsible for Shell being emotionally prepared for the 'oil crisis' of 1973. Shell emerged from this crisis to become a market leader and the most profitable oil company among its competitors. Wack had presented a scenario to Shell's directors of an impending oil crisis that meant they had to rethink their business dramatically (Schwartz 1996: 7–9). However, it is important to note that many oil companies had envisioned similar possible future scenarios, the price of oil having been amazingly, indeed unnaturally, consistent over the preceding century, given that it is a finite commodity. It seems, however, that the mindset of 'business as usual' prevented those in the other major oil companies and indeed the major US car manufacturers (Halberstam 1987) from really seeing, and thus preparing for, the impact of the shock.

Scenarios, as developed by Schwartz and his team at Global Business Networks (see Ogilvy 1998), are most typically developed by a multidisciplinary team comprising members from cross-functional areas or drawing on people external to the organization. Indeed, the application of scenario planning is not restricted to enterprise-based activities. For example, Weston and Hodgson (1996) conducted a scenario-planning exercise involving a number of entrepreneurs and researchers in an attempt to predict alternative manufacturing futures (Hodgson et al. 1998). When conducted for a particular enterprise, the senior management of the organization usually define the strategic issue for which scenario planning is to be used, but in doing so they will not be in control of the outcomes – they direct them. Figure 15.10 presents the eight key elements of a scenario-planning process as developed by Global Business Networks (Schwartz 1996; Ogilvy 1998). Each step will be examined below:

1. *Focal issue* The first step in the scenario-planning process requires the team to think about the issue for which they must develop sets of scenario logics. The team is confronted with the challenge of exploring the future of a particular issue for which a strategic choice needs to be made, for example should we enter a new market, should we broaden our product range and so on. There has to be sufficient uncertainty about the future, in particular the external environment, for scenario planning to be considered.

2. *Key factors* This step helps to identify the critical uncertainties that relate to the focal issue. Key factors tend to be issues over which the organization has some or would hope to have some future influence. Key factors usually relate to the industry(ies) within which the organization operates. These factors could be both internal and external factors, the key point being that the organization's management must believe they can influence these factors, for example size of market, competition, customer base, suppliers, employees and partners.

3. *Environmental forces* This step relates to the previous one, whereby the team is looking to establish the critical uncertainties over which the organization has little or no influence. The team develops a list of key factors and environmental forces through a brainstorming process, for example social forces, technological changes and

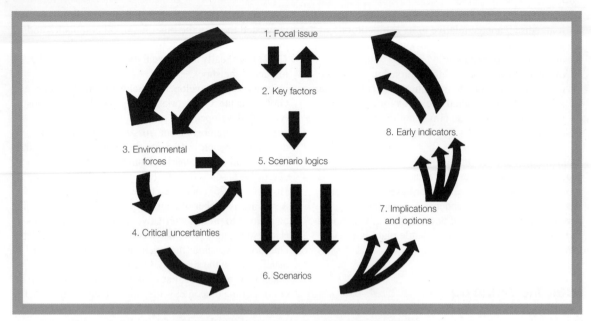

Figure 15.10 Developing scenarios

Source: Jay Ogilvy (1998) 'Learning scenario planning – an introduction to scenario thinking – a four day simulation course', 1–5 February, presented by Australian Business Network and Global Business Networks (Sydney).

organizational competencies. These are not categorized as in a SWOT analysis. This process is by no means highly structured nor does it result in an ordered set of factors.

In order to undertake steps 1, 2 and 3, additional research might be required. The team needs to have sufficient knowledge within the group to identify as many potential issues as possible, although, given the inherent unknowability of the future, no list can ever be exhaustive. Nevertheless, as a result of steps 1, 2 and 3, the team would hope to produce a fairly comprehensive list of the key factors and environmental forces that relate to the focal issue. There is a possibility that the focal issue might need to be reframed as a result of going through steps 1–3. For example, senior management might have seen the focal issue to be one of expanding the current business through expanding the services offered by the organization. However, as a result of steps 1–3, the focal issue might change to examine the sustainability of core services rather than expansion. Alternatively, other focal issues might emerge after having gone through all eight steps.

4. *Critical uncertainties* In this step the team tries to identify what are both critical and highly uncertain issues in relation to the focal issue. Issues need to be gradually eliminated so that the team arrives at

the two most important and uncertain issues. Failure to achieve such a culling results in an exponential problem. Too many dimensions create too many futures for any of them to be seriously considered. Focusing on the most salient issues is best achieved by a stepped process of elimination (for example a voting system). In the process of elimination there is usually a strong element of distress in the team as issues, which were identified as important and/or uncertain, are eliminated by the voting process. This is referred to as 'the zone of terror'. The eliminated issues are in fact revisited in a later stage of the process. Issues have to be clustered in the elimination process and this in itself can cause distress. Scoring dictates the elimination of issues, whereby points or scores are allocated only on the most critical and uncertain issues.

In scenario planning, a person called a 'lateral poppy' or 'remarkable person' (see Schwartz 1996) can be used to assist the team in breaking mental models or fixed frames of references (see Chapter 1). The remarkable person need not be a person who is an expert or familiar with the focal issue. These people challenge the assumptions made about the five or so clustered issues. The five issues are filtered down to the two most important and uncertain ones. The final choice of issues is a negotiated process.

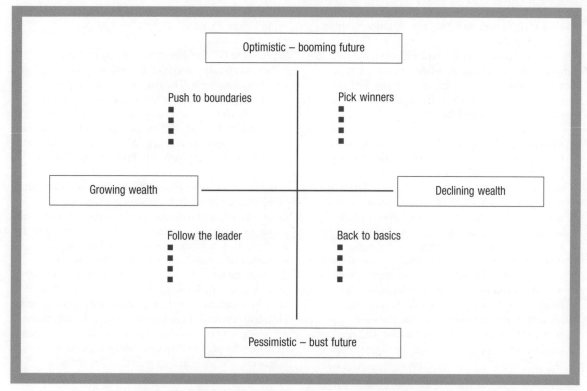

Figure 15.11 An example of a scenario matrix

The two issues selected are matrixed, one on a vertical axis and one on a horizontal axis. These are two bipolar axes that cannot be overly dependent on each other, for example you could not have the structure of the market on one axis and distribution channels on the other, as these are dependent variables (Figure 15.11).

5. *Scenario logics* At this stage the team now has a scenario matrix with four separate quadrants, each one representing what is best described as a version of the future. The purpose of this step is to create a meaning, that is, a theme or a story for each of the four quadrants; for example a healthy economy that is also outward-looking is an environment for change and reinvention. Each quadrant should represent a theme and creative names are preferred to encourage frame breaking, but engaging themes that are able to create new connections and new ways of seeing things are also encouraged. This stage is really where new understandings can begin to develop.

6. *Scenarios* This step involves developing the scenario logic into a story about the future. Any form of storyline would be helpful but some basic elements need to be captured in the story: it needs to be in line with the logic of the scenario, it needs to start today and move gradually to the end state (that is, typically a 10-year time line) and it should have a beginning, middle and end. As the team develops a story, it might be useful to discuss and capture what this scenario looks like two years from now (beginning), five years from now (middle) and 10 years from now (at the end). The purpose of this approach is to assist the audience (that is, management group) who receive the scenarios and findings to be able to relate to the scenarios and be 'led' to the end state. Schwartz (1996: 136–55) actually describes the story as being somewhat akin to writing a movie script with plots that have storylines often around themes such as winners and losers, revolution, cycles or infinite possibilities. Stories should focus on the external environment of the organization and not describe the organization's strategies, activities or results. The story is outward-looking and does not deal with how the organization would yet respond. This is explored under step 7.

Once the four stories are developed for each scenario, it becomes important to identify which one of these scenarios the organization and its management believe best represents the organization's current environment and supports their current strategy. At this point in time, this would be described as the organization's *official scenario*. The point of doing this is to provide some relevance or a frame of reference for managers to recognize where the current strategy fits among these various scenarios.

In making up the story for each scenario, the eliminated key issues are revisited and some are selectively woven into the text of the story. The story then might overcome some of the distress felt in 'the zone of terror' mentioned earlier.

7. *Implications and options* Having constructed the four stories, the team then develops the implications for the industry and the organization of each scenario. Once the scenarios have been developed, ideally the implications of each scenario are further explored to develop strategic options for each scenario. So the team ends up with four sets of implications and strategic options. A number of different decision-making techniques can be used to order and prioritize options, for example identifying a robust scenario might mean eliminating 'no brainers' or those options within each scenario that are common to all four. Given the possible scenarios, senior management and/or the team can explore which options best suit the organization's

future strategy orientation. Some of these are listed in Figure 15.12.

8. *Early indicators* The team has completed the scenario matrix and all the implications and options of each scenario. The purpose of this step is to identify early warning signs of change that support a particular scenario story. An example of this might be falling sales of McDonald's products in China as an early warning indicator of social dissatisfaction with Western capitalism or business methods.

Issues are likely to arise in the political environment of the organization when the team attempts to disseminate scenario outcomes. For a variety of reasons, scenarios can be unacceptable to senior management, for example the results might not support the current strategy, and senior management are usually the dominant coalition in the organization and the defenders of the status quo. Scenarios have to be worked through the power structures at the top end of the organization to have any potential impact or acceptance. Unacceptable scenarios can even result in the dismissal or disciplining of those who present unacceptable or unpopular scenarios. The team and its members can often be viewed as having a dissenting voice from the accepted strategy of the organization. A scenario might represent a major problem if it does not fit easily into the accepted discourse of strategy development that senior managers articulate for the organization. That is, it does not fit with the chosen storyline(s) of key strategists. However, scenario planning obviously provides no guarantee of a safe future.

In the mediated aftermath of the horrific events in New York, Washington and near Pittsburgh of 11 September 2001, it became clear that the use of planes as flying bombs was clearly a scenario that had been considered by the defence and intelligence communities, but such consideration alone was unable to prevent such a scenario being realized. The likelihood and consequences of scenarios must be mentally accepted by those in positions of power if the organization is to be mobilized to either ensure or prevent their realization. Their mere existence achieves nothing. Indeed, in the wake of 11 September, many organizations operating in, for example, the airline industry, may themselves be forced into some form of scenario planning in an effort to deal with the extreme uncertainty and crisis which confronts them.

Although not exactly pushing a scenario-planning approach, Hamel (1996) uses a similar approach to strategic thinking. Unlike Mintzberg, Hamel does not believe that incrementalism – whether it is in the form of continuous improvement programmes, looking at market share or following what competitors or the industry are doing – is a recipe for future strategic

Given a set of alternative scenarios, what are the possible strategic responses?

Pick one scenario and bet the company

Hedge across all scenarios

Rank strategic options by risks and rewards

Modify existing strategy

?

Pursue least regret (Pascal's Wager)*

Reframe the industry

Become a learning organization

Identify predetermined elements

Look for vulnerabilities and bottlenecks

Note: *Pascal's Wager refers to a seventeenth-century French mathematician who developed a four-quadrant matrix that identified the options available to a person trying to identify a limited number of choices.

Figure 15.12 Strategic responses

Source: Jay Ogilvy (1998) 'Learning scenario planning – an introduction to scenario thinking – a four day simulation course', 1–5 February, presented by Australian Business Network and Global Business Networks (Sydney).

success in our rapidly changing world. *Strategizing*, he says, means adopting the posture of revolutionary change. He sets out 10 principles for developing revolutionary strategies and these are described in Exhibit 15.2. These 10 principles have a strong underlying message – that there are deeply entrenched political forces at the top of many organizations intent upon ensuring that 'official strategies' are not challenged and that incrementalism remains the norm.

Hamel's 10 principles, and the discussion on strategic thinking, move us into the last part of the chapter where we discuss how managers might consider strategy as a set of competing discourses. Viewing the various schools of thought as competing

---

Exhibit 15.2 Hamel's 10 principles of revolutionary strategy

1. **Strategic planning isn't strategic** Strategy making works from today forward, not from the future back, thus assuming that the future will be more or less the same as the present. Planning is elitist, using a limited amount of the organization's creative capacity. Planning is the curse of incrementalism – strategizing is about discovery and a quest.

2. **Strategy making must be subversive** Creators of strategy must cast off industry conventions and look for new ways of thinking. Be rule breakers and try to redefine the industry rather than seeing it as a given.

3. **The bottleneck is at the top of the bottle** Senior managers are the most powerful defenders of orthodoxy – orthodoxy that protects their privileges and status. This group has the least diversity of views, invests heavily in the past and often represents industry dogma. Senior managers have to question their own limitations or capacities to change.

4. **Revolutionaries exist in every company** Most revolutionaries are in middle management but are constrained by orthodoxy. Senior managers have to look for 'revolutionaries' outside their own ranks.

5. **Change is not the problem; engagement is** Senior managers often assume people (especially middle managers) are against change and that only hero-led change (see Chapter 5) can force an organization forward. Senior managers adopt epic storylines to portray themselves as dragging their organizations into the future. Senior managers often talk of change as fear-induced or something nasty (for example downsizing). They often fail to give people responsibility for managing change and taking some control of their destinies. They do not create a dialogue about the future, but rather make directives and pronouncements.

6. **Strategy making must be democratic** Senior managers rely on others for operational improvements (for example continuous improvement programmes – see Chapter 6), but not for strategic improvements. Executives tend to want to 'learn' from each other, not recognizing that creativity is spread throughout an organization. The hierarchy of experience (position, status) must coexist with a hierarchy of imagination. Many potentially creative people (young people, new employees, employees in remote sites) are often automatically excluded from strategy making.

7. **Anyone can be a strategy activist** Senior managers are reluctant to give up their monopoly on strategy. Activists (revolutionaries) are needed because senior managers are often distracted or too busy protecting the past. Senior managers should see activists (challengers of the status quo) as good corporate citizens and not as anarchists.

8. **Perspective is worth 50 IQ points** Companies have to break their paradigms, reframe, invent new futures (as per scenario planning), identify and challenge unshakeable beliefs, search for discontinuities (for example in technology), develop a deep understanding of core competencies and use all the company's knowledge to identify unconventional ideas.

9. **Top-down and bottom-up are not the alternatives** Strategy activists who fail to win the political support of top management achieve very little. Many senior managers still operate from the view that planners are at the top and doers at the bottom. Many people must endorse and be committed to a strategizing process to achieve diversity of input and unity of purpose (top management support).

10. **You can't see the end from the beginning** Strategizing can involve surprises (as we saw in scenario planning) and many senior managers are afraid of open-ended, inclusive processes. New voices and perspectives must come into the strategy-making process.

discourses opens up the opportunity for new discourses to emerge or at least challenge the dominant or popular ones. In many respects, Hamel (1996), and the scenario-planning approach, already hint at the need to consider alternative ways of looking at and practising strategy.

A postmodernist approach to strategy

In the second millennium it is claimed that strategic challenges will be different for organizations than they have been in the past. David Barry and Michael Elmes (1997: 442), for example, argue that the strategic needs of organizations are shifting because of accelerating changes in information technology, shifts in global politics and the rise in knowledge-based competition between and within organizations. The pace and rate of change are speeding up and, while opportunities for creating competitive advantage will be more fleeting, the opportunities will also multiply by virtue of the information revolution. Quick-thinking, knowledgeable employees who are capable of innovation and working in paradoxical relationships, such as teamnets and virtual organizations and through networks and interorganizational relations (IORs), will be more important for gaining strategic advantage than in the past. Barry and Elmes believe that the question of 'who knows what' or intellectual capital (see Chapter 14) will become a key part of strategy. The reliance on the printed word, on one strategic model or plan and familiar strategic discourses will simply have less advantage in a world where knowledge is rapidly changing and information is becoming more accessible to customers, clients and consumers. They believe that diverse strategic narratives or texts are likely to proliferate in organizations, posing challenges as to how strategy is managed.

In Chapter 14 we introduced the notion of *discourse* – the complex nest of ideas, linguistic expressions, assumptions, justifications, defences, social institutions and practical actions that constitute a cohesive way of approaching the world. Postmodernism rejects modernistic representations of 'reality' through conventional scientific methods and focuses instead on the central role of language in constituting 'reality'. Consequently, if all knowledge is constituted by language, and (as we have seen in Chapter 6) knowledge is an important dimension of power, all language embodies power relationships. Barry and Elmes (1997) advocate looking at strategy as a type of narrative or story (or multiple narratives and many stories). One example of a broader strategic narrative, or meta-narrative (one which explains several more specific narratives, such as individual company strategies), is the narrative of 'globalization', popularly represented by the

injunction to 'think global, act local'. Our case study at the beginning of this chapter illustrates this discourse.

Globalization is one of the buzz-words of the 1990s and 2000s: we live in a 'global' village, we consume 'global' brands, corporations have to be competitive in a 'global' marketplace and governments have to be responsive to the needs of the 'global' economy. Companies are expected to achieve overall worldwide objectives by adapting to local conditions in several countries. In some cases this may mean tailoring products for national markets, in others paying exceptionally low rates for labour because it is the local norm. In the developed world, executives and government officials often claim that globalization is responsible for the dismantling of social institutions, layoffs or plant closures. The globalization discourse is captivating. It can be used by its champions to promise a leaner, more efficient economy, one that will ensure growth and be beneficial to all the nations of the world.

When we begin to consider the research data available on globalization, it becomes evident that the 'benefits' of globalization are unevenly distributed, accruing primarily to large Western corporations (Renner 1997; Rodrik 1997). Indeed, globalization emerges as a strategic narrative, a gloss put on the explanation of a complex and disturbing reality which suppresses the consideration of some of its more perplexing aspects. In fact, many of the values, interests, ways of thinking, political, social and economic systems of the Western economies are often privileged in this narrative, while alternative perspectives and interests of marginalized cultures are ignored or suppressed. This is perhaps most obvious in the difference of treatments that capital and labour receive in a 'globalized' world. While the West, through various intermediaries, actively strives to open national borders to remove restrictions on the flow of money, it seeks to close them with just as much vigour when so-called 'economic migrants' or supposedly 'bogus' asylum seekers attempt to follow the money with their labouring bodies.

Taking a view of strategy as narrative enables us to focus critically on the elements which any particular formulation of the strategic storyline may leave out. Elements of the globalization 'story' we have told above may serve to place the individual globalizing strategies of particular companies, or even countries, into a perspective that is quite different from how they are more commonly portrayed and is one that, we would argue, needs to be taken fully into account in strategic analysis.

A number of the theories discussed in this chapter are embedded in what some writers call the *modernist* project (Parker 1992). The core of modernity is rationalism – the belief that science and reason can enable humans to understand nature and things 'out there' and that our capacity to generate knowledge about the world we live in, especially laws and principles, is related to achieving progress. Dominant theories of strategy are embedded in this context and 'accurate' representations of the business environment overwhelmingly use 'rational' criteria like sales, market share, return on assets and profitability. The narrative of modernism is a belief in science as progress and this world view, which assumes its own validity, is called a 'meta-narrative' (Lyotard 1984; Rosenau 1992; Kilduff and Mehra 1997). As we have seen in Chapter 14, looking at strategy as sets of discourses helps the manager to focus on paradox and enables a critique of the underlying assumptions of all theoretical perspectives.

Traditional views of strategy do not explicitly address the role of language in strategy development. A narrative view of strategy would focus on how language (rather than unexamined notions of, for example, globalization, or 'fitting into external environments') is used to construct meaning and how this meaning (which is far from necessarily 'truth') then creates a discourse that positions people in an organization. This fictional view of strategy can be applied to all schools of strategy; and, as Barry and Elmes (1997: 432–3) point out, emergent strategies are also fictional in the sense that future stories are constructed (organization actions are labelled as 'strategic') and the past is interpreted as other stories. The strength of the story is manifested by its degree of acceptance by readers and the extent to which organization members take on the roles of the characters in the story. In other words, the effectiveness of a strategy is less to do with its inherent 'truth' and more to do with its acceptance and approval by organization members and the extent of their participation in the story, as we saw in scenario planning.

Taking this approach highlights the importance of language in the strategy discourse and allows the questioning of constructs like 'market' or 'competition', which go unchallenged in traditional approaches to strategy. Barry and Elmes (1997) argue that a narrative approach to strategy is more effective in revealing the politics of strategy because of the type of questions that can be asked: Who gets to write and read strategy? How are reading and writing linked to power? Who is marginalized in the writing/reading process? (Barry and Elmes 1997: 430).

The notion of *genre*, which we have discussed in Chapter 14, is also useful in postmodern analysis. All texts are developed in a specific setting and narratives of strategy are no exception. The genres of strategy assist in constructing and reinforcing the meanings of narratives, including who reads them, how they should be read and who are the 'heroes' and 'villains'. Mintzberg's schools of strategy are all genres containing narratives with specific structures and content. For instance, Barry and Elmes (1997) described how Mintzberg's Design School is an 'epic genre', where organizations following a SWOT model 'become epic journeyers', systematically navigating towards

opportunities and success. This 'epic' genre faded away after producing an initial burst of narratives as managers identified several problems with the model (for example How are strengths and weaknesses identified? How are they evaluated? Who evaluates them?).

Epic genres are constituted by appealing to the familiar: we all know stories of the handsome stranger (inevitably white, male and heterosexual) who gets rid of the bad guys and cleans up the town. The hero fights his enemies and wins. This genre can be seen in some strategy narratives: if we employ the right 'weapons' (for example SWOT analysis) we can win the war. Thus the manager fighting a battle in the market becomes a hero when the enemy is defeated (a book detailing the Coke–Pepsi 'wars' is entitled *The Other Guy Blinked*).

Barry and Elmes (1997: 437–8) also describe how a plot could be romantic. Companies facing hard times and engaging in significant downsizing as a result often follow a romantic plot. ('We need to do some soul searching about who we really are and where we want to go. Then we will return to our position as market leader.') A range of the company's stakeholders may be implicated in this romantic revival: shareholders must make do with less return, employees with fewer rewards, although this rarely means that CEOs will make do with less (a point also raised by Hamel 1996).

Another characteristic of the narrative process is *defamiliarization* (Barry and Elmes 1997: 439). Defamiliarization refers to the novelty of a narrative and how new ways of looking at things make the story more effective. Maintaining novelty over a period of time is not easy, as the initial excitement wanes and we become familiar with the story. Barry and Elmes argue that different strategic frameworks were developed precisely because the novelty of each preceding one wore off and people were ready for a new method. Thus different schools of strategy emerged, each within its own genre. For instance, Barry and Elmes (1997: 440) describe the emergence and wide acceptance of the 'purist genre' as exemplified by the works of Miles and Snow (1978) and Porter (1980). It provided distinct identities and categories ('cost leadership' or 'differentiation' or 'defenders') and showed how companies could 'succeed' in competitive markets. Heavily character-based, the purist genre appealed to managers by reframing market and organizational conditions as personalities – 'leaders', 'defenders', 'prospectors', 'differentiators', 'focusers', 'reactors' or 'muddlers'). The novelty of this narrative, however, appears to be waning as managers found the typologies difficult to operationalize and other frameworks emerged (Barry and Elmes 1997). Novelty is an important part of explaining why fads or new genres keep proliferating in the strategy discourse. Managers are 'happy' to embrace new ideas, even those which are really only theoretical constructs, repackaged in a dominant discourse such as the Extended Design School model. Being able to talk the new strategy language, drop words such as 'competitive advantage', 'core competence' and so on can give managers a sense of power over the unknown and often unpredictable nature of their organizations. Talking strategy gives the semblance of taking control or at least making managers feel that they have control. In talking about strategy, attending strategic-planning days, drawing up strategic plans, posting mission statements and so on, some managers will adopt a compliant reading position and 'buy' into the rhetoric and language of particular forms of discourse. Others will adopt a resistant reading position – these people will probably be the new breed of managers, responsible for creating new competing forms of strategic discourse. Exhibit 15.3 gives but one example of the new discourse being used in Silicon Valley, the 'hub' of the Internet 'revolution'. The 'geeks' of Silicon Valley's start-ups (new Internet companies) are developing a new form of business discourse, dubbed here as 'Valley speak'. The strategies that flow from this discourse will not sit comfortably with many of the strategies we have examined in this chapter and perhaps suggest why many of these companies came to grief in the late 1990s and early 2000s.

Looking at strategy as discourse uncovers new dimensions of power relationships that remain hidden in the meta-narratives of 'efficiency'. Narratives of strategy arose not from a meta-narrative of scientific progress but from a peculiar set of local conditions in postwar North America. These include changes in corporate ownership relations and changes in international market conditions after the Second World War (Knights and Morgan 1991; Knights 1992), along with the other aspects of military influence we considered in the introduction. 'True' representations of markets and environments, and accounts of the effects of strategies on markets and environments, were constructed within the dominant science of the day, that is, rational economic models, without widespread questioning of the assumptions behind these theories. Concepts like 'strategy', 'cost leadership', 'flexible specialization' or 'niche marketing' emerged not through a scientific, ordered progression of thoughts and ideas but as products of power relations between corporations, governments and educational institutions (Knights 1992). Strategy is not therefore simply a body of knowledge but a mechanism of power. These power effects have important consequences: as David Knights and Glenn Morgan point out, they 'provide managers in organizations with a rationalization of their successes and failures, while generating a sense of personal and organizational security for managers' (1991: 262).

In Chapter 14 we also introduced the notion of *social subjectivity*, as the sense of individuality and socially positioned self-awareness, which is continually formed and reformed under changing social, economic and historical conditions. By engaging in strategic discourse in an organization,

---

Exhibit 15.3 Dubbing: a glossary of Valley speak

CLICKS AND MORTAR	A bricks-and-mortar company that goes online
DUB-DUB-DUB	Shorthand for www
FIRST-MOVER ADVANTAGE	What you get when you start your website before they do
GRAY-HAIRS	Experienced execs hired to run the day-to-day operations of a start-up
HALO EFFECT	The phenomenon of having people take you seriously because of your big-name venture capitalist
NDA	Non-disclosure agreement; binds the signatory to secrecy so you can negotiate
OPM	Other people's money; why you shouldn't be worried too much about failing
OPEN THE KIMONO	To reveal your business idea, normally after demanding that the other person sign an NDA
PLANE MONEY	Signing bonus for execs; sometimes enough to buy a plane
STEALTH MODE	Keeping your business idea a secret, often using a STEALTH NAME
VEST IN PEACE	Having sold your start-up to a big company, you quietly wait for your stock options to vest; then you can quit time as big. As in, 'We're going to be amazon.com3X'
YACC	Yet another calendar company, the most overused idea of the summer

Source: 'Silicon Valley's Second Name: Get Rich.com', *Time*, 4 October 1999, p. 58. © 1999 Time Inc. Reprinted by permission.

using the language of markets and competition and the methodological tools of the particular discourse, organizational members constitute their sense of reality in organizational practice. This process allows the emergence of selected 'experts' within and outside the organization who continue to engage in the strategy discourse and construct representations of the different realities that their organization must face, while attempting to bring under control the complex relations between a business and its environment through a 'rational' process. Thus the discourse presents to the outside world and to itself 'rational' managerial actions without a representation of the power relations underlying the discourse, thereby facilitating and legitimizing the exercise of power (Knights and Morgan 1991).

Challenging dominant forms of representation in the strategy discourse makes explicit the embedded power relations. Conceptions of rationality that have dominated the strategy discourse are based on a primarily masculine model – control (of the external environment), assertiveness and aggressiveness are typically 'masculine' traits (Knights and Morgan 1991). Conventional strategy discourse fits in conveniently with other masculine identities of managers, aggressive salesmen and the like (for instance organizations need to 'penetrate' markets) and tends to promote masculinist conceptions of power (Knights and Morgan 1991).

The rationale behind strategic planning is based on the assumptions of rationality in neoclassical economics and strategy. Historical analysis of the use of the term 'strategy' in language indicates that its origins were located in descriptions of eighteenth-century battles (Knights and Morgan 1991; Whipp 1996) and indeed in the earlier accounts of warfare that we considered in the introduction. The transition from military battles to competitive battles in the marketplace is still transparent in some of the business jargon we use today: 'rival firm', 'winning or losing (market share)', 'offensive and defensive strategies', 'attacking' a competitor's market or 'defending' one's market share, 'surrendering' market position, 'leader' or 'follower' and 'first-mover advantage' strategies. The marketplace is the modern battlefield, the managers the generals. The battle and war metaphors pervade the language of strategy across many cultures (see below).

Using a postmodern framework to analyse Porter's model of strategy, Knights (1992) shows how the rules of formation of strategy are linked to power and knowledge. He describes how notions of 'cost leadership' and 'differentiation' are constructed by Porter without any attempt to problematize them in terms of power. Instead, the dominant scientific method of the day – neoclassical economics – is used to construct these categories and establish relationships between them. Assumptions underlying positive models

of science do not take into account the behaviour of individual organizational members in the process of achieving competitive advantage. Rather, the language of strategy transforms the individuals into subjects who constitute their sense of reality and individuality through the discourse by making sense of the representations. Managers in an organization will engage in practices that support notions of 'competitive advantage', 'cost leadership' and 'niche marketing'.

Through this process, the status of 'expert' knowledge is not questioned, rather subjectivity is constituted to meet the needs of the knowledge produced. This does not mean that all members behave in the same way or follow similar strategies to 'get there'. As the descriptive school of strategy suggests, managers do not automatically follow a strategy prescribed by top management – internal politics could result in a wide range of behaviours. However, as Knights (1992) points out, the diversity of behaviours is still enclosed within the representation of 'official strategy'. This is an example of the power effects of strategy discourse (Knights and Morgan 1991). Strategy is used to rationalize 'success' and 'failures' – in Porter's model, companies that are neither cost leaders nor niche players are doomed to fail – a self-fulfilling prophecy that is determined by the conditions of the production of these categories in the first place. Thus the 'truth effects' of Porter's model remain entrenched, regardless of whether organizations are able to apply these strategies successfully or not. The fact that the knowledge produced by Porter is unreliable can only be exposed through an analysis of the discourse of knowledge production, with a particular emphasis on subjectivity (or in this case, how knowledge production ignores subjectivity). Thinking that we find 'strategy' and indeed 'strategists' when we find behaviours and individuals who comply with our prescriptive ingredients of, and recipes for, business success risks putting the cart before the horse. It may just be that individuals behave in these ways and think of themselves in these terms in order to be seen to be acting appropriately, to fit in with the expectations that both they and others hold of senior positions in the organizational hierarchy, to fulfil the often spurious expectations that result from the wide dissemination of prescriptive models of business strategy in our contemporary discursive climate. To 'do' management increasingly means to 'do' strategy. And in such circumstances, it matters much less whether what we do in the name of 'strategy' is organizationally, or indeed societally, beneficial, and much more that we are seen to play the part properly, to present ourselves as in control. Such performance not only protects us from the existential dread of accepting that we are not certain who we are or what we are doing, but also seems sufficient to garner significant material awards.

A postmodernist approach would take into account

and make explicit the conditions that made it possible for our knowledge of strategy to develop, thus exposing its fragile nature. By confronting the power–knowledge relationship, a postmodernist approach to strategy does not produce truths; rather it perceives truth as an effect of these relations (Knights 1992). It attempts to disrupt universal knowledge by exposing the subjective conditions in which such knowledge, deemed rational or 'objective', and whose underlying assumptions remain unchallenged, is produced.

A postmodernist approach to strategy, then, reminds us that the categories which other perspectives on strategy treat as unproblematic – competence, the environment, competitiveness, rationality – are themselves all constructs, not things in themselves. The meaning of these constructs shifts according to the ways in which they are positioned in strategic narratives, relative to each other. These meanings are always affected by the interconnections of knowledge and power from which they arise. The idea of strategy itself, not just of which strategies emerge under what conditions, is always under critical scrutiny from a postmodern perspective. Importantly, from taking such a perspective, we become acutely aware of the deeper influences of culture on strategy, and it is these we will consider in the next section.

A cross-cultural view of strategy

Strategy will have different meanings for different national and cultural groups, and our discussions of the cultural relativity of basic theories such as leadership (which underpins strategic implementation) in other chapters reinforce this. During the 1980s, however, there was considerable interest in cultural difference in strategy formulation and implementation. This was closely related to the intense interest in Japanese economic success, and focused on two ancient books which were widely held to be the foundational texts for Japanese business strategists – *The Book of Five Rings* by the samurai Miyamoto Musashi and *The Art of War* by the Chinese military genius Sun Tzu, which we encountered in our Introduction. Rosalie Tung (1994) summarizes these and two other books – *The Three Kingdoms* by the fourteenth-century author Lo Kuan-Chung (which is issued to all Sony executives on promotion to senior management) and *Lure the Tiger out of the Mountains* by Gao Yuan (which is based on the I Ching, or the *Book of Changes*, and the thirty-six stratagems). Tung identifies 12 themes or principles running through these texts, as shown in Exhibit 15.4.

The importance of strategies, the first point, emphasizes strategy as a means of avoiding perhaps costly and damaging warfare – on the principle that the supreme victory is to subdue the enemy without

---

Exhibit 15.4 Strategy and culture

- ❏ The importance of strategies
- ❏ Transforming an enemy's strength into weakness
- ❏ Engaging in deception to gain a strategic advantage
- ❏ Understanding contradictions and using them to gain an advantage
- ❏ Compromising
- ❏ Striving for total victory
- ❏ Taking advantage of an adversary's or competitor's misfortune
- ❏ Flexibility
- ❏ Gathering intelligence and information
- ❏ Grasping the interdependent relationship of situations
- ❏ Patience
- ❏ Avoiding strong emotions

Source: Rosalie Tung (1994) 'Strategic management thought in East Asia', *Organizational Dynamics*, Spring, pp. 58–9.

---

fighting. To this end, Tung notes, East Asians tend to play mind games, trying to find hidden meanings and strategies behind communications. Game playing here is considered an asset, not a distraction as in the West. Turning the opponent's strength into a weakness (or its converse, your weakness into a strength) teaches that it is unwise to be complacent, because fortunes and misfortunes are reversible, times and situations change in cycles and preparation should be made for these changes. Deception, which might be considered immoral or amoral in other cultures, is a way of life in East Asia, where it is important to look as prosperous as possible even in hard times, and weakness is conversely often feigned to make the opponent complacent. This adds a cautionary note to the later point about taking advantage of an adversary's misfortune – it may not always be easy to tell when misfortune is genuine or not. A useful point to remember is that it is necessary to think like the other person thinks in order to understand him or her, and not operate out of one's own cultural suppositions.

Understanding contradictions means to see every situation in terms of its light and dark aspects, positive and negative sides, and exploit it accordingly. Compromise implies an ongoing relationship, and may involve sacrifice, bribery, gift giving and lavish entertainment in order to secure greater rewards later in the piece. Striving for total victory emphasizes again the need not to be complacent even when winning as long as there is opposition able to act – if there is an opponent, then their next move must be anticipated. Taking advantage of an adversary's misfortune may seem to be unsporting to Westerners, but it is an entirely pragmatic issue to the East Asians. If the opponent is down, then they are there to be eliminated. Where the Japanese are taught that it is courageous to face death, the Chinese believe it is better to run away and live to fight another day, and as a result may be harder to eliminate in the long term. Flexibility is a related principle – there are times when it is advisable to attack, and others when it is advisable to flee.

An interesting misunderstanding between Eastern and Western views of strategy is exemplified in Porter's 1996 article in the *Harvard Business Review*, 'What is strategy?' The article argues that the essence of strategy is distinctiveness and that this basis of superior performance must be clearly delineated from other aspects of merely good practice, what Porter refers to as 'operational effectiveness'. Porter intimates that the preceding success of particularly Japanese businesses resulted from improvements in operational effectiveness that were unlikely to form the basis of a sustainable competitive advantage, since they lacked the distinctiveness that Porter sees as the hallmark of strategy, the 'daring to be different'. However, in our discussions with Japanese students concerning the suggestion that Japanese businesses do not have 'strategies', an interesting point emerged. The ideogram representing strategy is apparently indistinguishable from that representing war and as a consequence of the experience of the 1930s and 40s is deemed an inappropriate symbol for description of business policy. In such circumstances, Porter's account looks to be as much the product of mistranslation predicated upon limited cultural understanding as of any substantive analysis, and thus the chauvinism and complacency which his argument may engender seems woefully misplaced.

Although the preceding example appears to be merely the consequence of accident, gathering intelligence and information, or using spies, is a normal part of business life in East Asia and includes the spreading of misinformation. This issue is of particular consequence in relation to global partnerships and alliances, where partners who are expected to share information often do not, but steal the partner's know-how only to set up independently in competition. East Asian businesses spend a long time developing relationships and gathering information to prevent such problems occurring in a world where competition and cooperation may be part of the same relationship. Indeed, grasping the interdependence of relationships, taking a holistic view, is important enough in its own right, as in the long-term things that seem to be unrelated may indeed be related. Patience and the avoidance of strong emotions are similar aspects of the need to take a very

long-term view and not to let one's perspective become distorted by powerful feelings or passions.

Tung (1994) argues that these cultural dimensions are important shapers of the ways in which East Asians develop strategies, yet commentators such as Richard Whitley (1992) and Monir Tayeb (1988) have argued that cultural dimensions of strategy are not as important as the social, political and economic institutions which constrain and enable business relationships, such as the *chaebol* in Korea, to exist. The *chaebol* are amazingly concentrated, conglomorate organizations, comprising many companies holding shares in each other, with the parent company usually controlled by one family. In the case of Japan, both Whitley and Tayeb suggest that it is Japanese financial organizations and the Ministry of International Trade and Industry (MITI) which have engineered Japanese economic success more than the Japanese character. As Tayeb states:

The term 'culture' is very narrow in scope and it should give way to 'nation'. We perhaps should be talking about cross-national as opposed to cross-cultural studies of organisations. Organisations are influenced by other national institutions besides culture (understood as a set of learned, shared values and ideas). The term 'nation' not only refers to culture but also to other societal, economic and political institutions which have bearings on the nature of organisations located in particular countries. (Tayeb 1988: 154)

Barry Wilkinson (1996) takes a slightly different view, arguing for the relevance of culture but noting that both cultural and institutional theorists tend to overstate their position. Wilkinson argues for an approach which focuses more on the specific contextual factors that affect particular groups of actors, saying, in effect, that strategy formation needs to be studied as the product of the actions of identifiable groups of actors embedded in identifiable social, institutional, political and economic contexts, and needs to be researched in an appropriate way.

Although strategy has its effects across cultures, causing companies to operate in and withdraw from markets and producing areas, it is itself also a cultural construct. As Tung (1994) points out, Western strategists would not think in the same ways as Asian ones, and would therefore be unlikely to produce the same decisions consistently. However, one of the problems with the cultural approach she exemplifies is that it tends to draw on literature which is about personal or organized combat, usually in a medieval setting. This is too removed from contemporary business and can therefore only apply metaphorically. Precisely how particular cultural assumptions work in reality (rather than hypothetically) to give rise to the specific decision patterns of actual decision makers and strategies of real businesses is not clear. Yet it is a factor that cannot be dismissed.

Conclusion

To conclude, let us take a look at the questions with which we began the chapter. Remember there are no absolutely right answers and you may have different views of your own – the important thing is to know why views differ and what to do about this difference, which is also a challenge for strategic thinking itself.

? Answers to questions about managing strategically

1 **What is a strategy?** As we have seen, there are many possible answers to this question. A strategy is a general view of what sort of 'business' the enterprise is or should be in, and entails some planned and systematic consideration of how to remain or become successful in that business, addressing factors internal to the organization, such as its structure and people, and external factors, such as its customers and competitors. It may well operate through a hierarchy of plans, but arguably it is just as likely to have elements which emerge through the action of people involved in making decisions and carrying them out, as Mintzberg suggests. An alternative view of strategy is that it is a story, or narrative, which attempts to 'write' or account for a whole series of disconnected and emergent elements as though they were a unified whole – but more than one such story is possible. These stories then act as guides to action.

2 **How are strategies formulated?** Strategies may be formulated in a variety of ways, from the simple, rule-of-thumb approach of the SWOT analysis (which may become more complex in itself), through fairly disciplined and calculated planning approaches, to the blue-sky anticipatory exercises involved in scenario planning. Yet the influence of cultural and cross-cultural elements should not be discounted, even in the most calculative of formative processes.

3 **What is the value of strategic planning?** Strategic planning helps the organization to place its resources where they are likely to be of most benefit, to identify and remedy what appears to be weaknesses in its resourcing, skills, product offering, service support and so on, especially relative to its competitors. It also enables the big picture to be identified, so that focused operational developments can maximize their coordinated contribution to the long-term development and success of the enterprise. It enables the organization to anticipate the actions of its competitors and be proactive rather than responding to the initiatives of others. This of course entails a calculated risk, but if the risk is controlled and properly attenuated, it can be fully exploited if it pays off. Viewed as narrative, the value of a strategic plan lies as much in its buttressing of the identities and privileges of senior managers as in any direct 'business benefit'.

4 **Why do some firms outperform others?** There is no answer to this question which is good for all situations at all times – sometimes the answer is good luck, or being in the right place at the right time, and political, social and economic positioning often limits the effects of even the best managerial practices. But firms which acquire and create knowledge, and are able through critical self-reflection and analysis of their relationships with different

Answers continued

parts of their environment, and investment in their own development, to strengthen and change these relationships, are more likely to be able to convert this into sustainable competitive advantage over the long term. In other words, they will develop and implement strategies to become learning organizations.

5 **Do all organizations need a strategy?** Strategy, like structure and culture, is something which happens as a result of processes which will emerge whether managers like them or not. Although structures, cultures and strategies may be more or less formal and visible, they will always be present, always in change and flux. The question therefore is not whether organizations need a strategy, as they will have one whether they like it or not, but whether the strategy they have – the strategic story that they are implicitly or explicitly acting out – is the one they really want. This can only be determined by the sort of critical self-reflection we have been arguing for throughout this book.

REVISITING
THE CASE STUDY

1 What is Image Inc.'s product?

The answer to this question is less obvious than it appears. After all, what is their product? Sports shoes? What about their other lines: clothing, perfume, soft drinks, healthcare products? Or do we consider Image Inc. to be a consumer products company? What is becoming more apparent in this industry is the power of the brand. One could argue that Nike's product is the 'swoosh' which now adorns shoes, T-shirts, socks, wrist bands, watches, personal care products (and even the Australian cricketer Shane Warne's ears). Image Inc.'s product is really its brand – in the postmodern world we live in, the brand has become the product and the product has become the brand, regardless of whether the product is a shoe or clothing item or a piece of jewellery.

2 How did the outsourcing strategy emerge?

The case can be analysed at different levels with differing results and outcomes. For instance, if we take the rationalist approach, we can understand how the outsourcing strategy emerged. In a highly competitive market, with high advertising and promotion costs and a constant emphasis on product innovation, companies can secure a competitive advantage through product differentiation or cost leadership. The market

leaders did differentiate their products from their competitors through strong branding strategies. However, the battle of market shares at the top end of the market meant that firms needed to be more competitive. The major players in the market all offered premium products; competitive advantage in this part of the market meant lower costs. The strategy these firms developed was to lower production costs, the rationale being that, in a consumer market, marketing costs could not be reduced. Thus the 'rational' strategy was to reduce production costs in an attempt to be more competitive in the market. It is worth noting here that the strategy adopted by many in this industry may appear to present a successful example of being 'stuck in the middle', challenging Porter's claim that such a position is a recipe for strategic mediocrity and below-average returns. For Porter, however, differentiation only matters if it matters to the customer – thus for as long as the customer perceives quality to be an aspect of the good and its advertising and not of its means of production, the strategy can be represented as appropriately positioned in Porter's terms.

3 What factors were considered in the decision to outsource?

Image Inc. followed this strategy, looking at the success of outsourcing strategies developed by Nike and Reebok. It was certainly not 'daring to be different' in this regard. Reducing production costs meant finding cheaper sources of labour and cheaper raw materials. Obviously European and North American labour costs were many times higher than the labour costs in developing countries. In fact, the cost differentials were more than made up for by the higher shipping costs. It can be argued that the labour component of sports shoe manufacturing is not significantly high (10–12 per cent), so why should the companies concentrate so much on finding sources of cheap labour? There could be several reasons why outsourcing remains such a popular option. First, even if the labour component is not significantly high, wage rates are still considerably higher in European and North American markets. One could argue that the reason why the labour component is small is because of the low wage rates in the developing countries. Second, and probably considerably more importantly, other production costs were also significantly lower in developing countries which provided cheap raw materials. Companies did not face strict regulation relating to the disposal of chemicals in developing countries and as a result found it easier and cheaper to produce in these regions. Third, the outsourcing strategy meant that very few resources needed to be deployed by companies. Here the discourse of globalization we mentioned earlier was useful to managers, who could present their actions as being necessitated by global business logics, and distance themselves from the less admirable consequences of their actions – sweatshop conditions, health and safety violations, subsistence wages, discrimination and failure to feed back any profit into the community.

4 Where is Image Inc.'s strategy headed?

Thus the rational strategy for Image Inc. is to continue to focus on reducing costs in order to stay competitive. The other option is to enhance its presence at the high end of the market and focus on producing premium products. These strategies would lead to different outcomes: in the first instance, the company's efforts would be directed at developing new production centres and regions that offer cheaper labour and raw materials. A premium product strategy would focus on innovation and design (differentiation) and, while production costs are important, they would not drive the strategy. As we noted above, however, it is not unusual in this industry sector for some organizations to follow both these routes simultaneously, because

as we also noted earlier, it is, in rational business terms, only worth differentiating if the customer values the differentiation.

A reconfigurationalist approach in this case implies that the company should acknowledge the needs of multiple stakeholders. Image Inc.'s argument that it is not 'its business' how factories are run is questionable if we take a stakeholder approach: the labour force may be employed by subcontractors, however, they are stakeholders of the company as well because the company's action has a direct impact on the lives of these people. Different stakeholders have different interests and the task of the company is to balance these interests and develop objectives that would meet the needs of all stakeholders. Is it possible for a company to do this? Stakeholders in this case could include subcontractors, factory workers, labour activists, environmental agencies, governments and neighbouring communities apart from the company's employees, customers and shareholders. How can Image Inc. accommodate everyone's interest? Whose interest should be given first priority? Who will argue for the legitimacy of stakeholders who do not command sufficient resources to be heard? Fear of public boycotts and a negative company image might compel Image Inc. to take a broader perspective of the situation, as 'quality' of production conditions comes to be seen as part of the product and thus a relevant aspect of (marketing) strategy. Developing a universal code of conduct that all subcontractors must follow is one way by which Image Inc. can address stakeholder interests. However, labour reform by subcontractors could mean higher costs for the company which means it could lose its competitive position, especially if consumers are not concerned about the backstage, unpleasant consequences of their purchases and their competitors do not change their practices and continue to enjoy cheap wage rates. Unless all players in the industry are compelled to change labour practices, it is not in the financial interest of Image Inc. to do so, at least not in the absence of demands for 'ethical' practice on the part of consumers, the meeting of which can be used to enhance differentiation. Even small public boycotts and a negative image can harm the company's financial position, and may provide a rationale for changing current practices.

While such a pluralist view of the organization might address these issues, it is important to realize that the process by which these issues are resolved remains embedded in the power relations between different stakeholders. The process of negotiating stakeholder relations operates within the economic paradigm of markets, profits and cost leadership and these criteria continue to direct the rationale behind strategies. A postmodernist approach to the case can highlight the power relations that drive the negotiation process in an emergent strategy.

For instance, if we look at strategy as a narrative we can see how the narrative supports power–knowledge relations. In this case, the strategy narrative is one that frames market share and profitability as its objectives. Within this framework, different actors in the organization take on (either by encouragement or coercion) different roles and perform actions that the script allows. Dick Foster is worried because his performance will not look good if labour unrest continues or customers boycott his company's products. The story of his company's strategy is the story of leveraging a dominant position in the market. As this story unfolds in different locations, other stories are created and more characters emerge and are manipulated within the text. Dick Foster's role is interpellated in this strategic text; his role as vice-president of production is positioned in the narrative and the narrative also specifies the range of possible actions he can take. In other words, the text constructs Dick Foster's reading position and he can make sense of the situation by being a part of the discourse – in this case by solving the company's current production problems – or reject it by refusing to be read in this way by resigning.

Even the stakeholder approach is part of the discourse of strategy. The overall objective in this case of acquiring a competitive position in the market, thus enhancing profitability and shareholder value, seems to have an undesirable consequence: abusive labour practices are apparently giving the company its advantage. A traditional strategy discourse would frame stakeholder interests within the dominant market discourse without interrogating power–knowledge relations. The narrative supports the kind of knowledge that supports the dominance of the organization or industry. Thus, Dick Foster would have to show that he is an 'international production expert' by solving the company's problems. Concepts such as 'flexible specialization' or 'relationship building' are constructed and deployed within the strategy narratives of market share and profitability. Other narratives like the abuse of workers in the factories are positioned as 'problems' that need to be solved, often problems created by 'them' and not 'us' and part of 'going global'. Obviously, strategy gets written by 'us', those of us employed in organizations; the extent of the influence of other stakeholders emerges only in situations of conflict such as the one in which Image Inc. finds itself.

The situation described in the case could have several outcomes: the company could change the subcontractors' labour policies, the foreign governments could pass new labour and environmental laws, the subcontractors could relocate to other 'less problematic' regions, media interest could wane and the subcontractors could return to their old ways of doing things. A postmodern view would be less concerned about the 'truth' of the different actions; rather it would reveal how these truths were arrived at.

References

Abell, D.F. and Hammond, J.S. (1979) *Strategic Market Planning: Problems and Analytical Approaches?*, Englewood Cliffs, NJ: Prentice Hall.

Ackoff, R.L. (1970) *A Concept of Corporate Planning*, New York: Wiley Interscience.

Andrews, K.R. (1988) 'The concept of corporate strategy', in Quinn, J.B., Mintzberg, H. and James, R.M. (eds) *The Strategy Process: Concepts Contexts, Cases*, Englewood Cliffs, NJ: Prentice Hall.

Ansoff, H.I. (1965) *Corporate Strategy* (revised edn 1987), London: Penguin.

Ansoff, H.I. (1979) *Strategic Management*, Basingstoke: Macmillan – now Palgrave Macmillan.

Anthony, P. (1994) *Managing Culture*, Buckingham: Open University Press.

Barney, J.B. and Zajac, E.J. (1994) 'Competitive organisational behaviour: Toward an organisationally-based theory of competitive advantage', *Strategic Management Journal,* **15**: 5–9.

Barry, D. and Elmes, M. (1997) 'Strategy retold: Toward a narrative view of strategic discourse', *Academy of Management Review,* **22**(2): 429–52.

Besanko, D., Danove, D. and Shanley, M. (1996) *The Economics of Strategy*, New York: John Wiley.

Blackmur, D. (1997) 'Determinants of organisational size: BHP and vertical integration', *Journal of the Australian and New Zealand Academy of Management,* **3**(1): 15–29.

Blaug, R. (1999) 'The tyranny of the visible: Problems in the evaluation of anti-institutional radicalism', *Organization*, **6**(1): 33–56.

Boston Consulting Group (1968a) *Perspectives on Experience*, Boston, MA: BCG.

Boston Consulting Group (1968b) *Growth and Financial Strategies*, Boston, MA: BCG.

Bowman, C. and Asch, D. (1987) *Strategic Management*, Basingstoke: Macmillan – now Palgrave Macmillan.

Brunnson, N. (1982) 'The irrationality of action and action rationality: Decisions, ideologies and organisational actions', *Journal of Management Studies,* **19**(1): 29–44.

Byrt, W.J. (1973) *Theories of Organisation*, Sydney: McGraw-Hill.

Chandler, A.D. Jr (1962) *Strategy and Structure: Chapters in the History of Industrial Enterprise*, Cambridge, MA: MIT Press.

Chandler, A.D. Jr (1977) *The Visible Hand – The Managerial Revolution in American Business*, Cambridge, MA: The Belknap Press of Harvard University Press.

Coase, R. (1937) 'The nature of the firm', *Economica,* **4**: 386–405.

Day, G.S. and Wensley, R. (1988) 'Assessing advantage: A framework for diagnosing competitive superiority', *Journal of Marketing,* **52** (April): 1–20.

Deal, T.W. and Kennedy, A.A. (1982) *Corporate Cultures*, Reading, MA: Addison-Wesley.

Enrico, R. and Kornbluth, J. (1986) *The Other Guy Blinked: How Pepsi Won the Cola Wars*, New York: Bantam.

Fayol, H. (1949) *General and Industrial Management*, London: Pitman.

Forster, J. and Browne, M. (1996) *Principles of Strategic Management*, Melbourne: Macmillan.

Foss, N.J. (ed.) (1997) *Resource, Firms and Industries: A Reader in the Resource-Based Perspective*, New York: Oxford University Press.

Fulop, L. and Linstead, S. (1999) *Management: A Critical Text*, South Yarra: Macmillan.

Furnham, A. and Gunter, B. (1993) 'Corporate culture: Definition, diagnosis and change', in Cooper, C.L. and Robertson, I.T. (eds) *International Review of Industrial and Organisational Psychology*, Vol. 8, London: John Wiley.

Godfrey, R. (2002) Stiff Competition for Viagra. Unpublished MBA dissertation, Keele University.

Grant, R.M. (1991) 'Analyzing resources and capabilities', extract from Grant, R.M., *Contemporary Strategic Analysis: Concepts, Techniques and Applications*, Cambridge, MA: Blackwell, reprinted in Lewis, G., Morkel, A. and Hubbard, G. (1993) *Australian Strategic Management: Concepts, Contexts and Cases*, Sydney: Prentice Hall.

Halberstam, D. (1987) *The Reckoning*, London: Bantam.

Hamel, G. (1996) 'Strategy as revolution', *Harvard Business Review,* July–August: 69–80.

Hamel, G. and Pralahad, C. K. (1989) 'Strategic intent', *Harvard Business Review*, May–June: 63–76.

Hansen, G.S. and Wernerfelt, B. (1989) 'Determinants of firm performance: The relative importance of economic and organisational factors', *Strategic Management Journal,* **10**: 399–411.

Hodgson, A., Li, G. and Weston, R.H. (1998) 'Manufacturing strategies and next century enterprises', *International Journal of Business Performance Management*, **1**(1): 90–109.

Hofer, C.W. and Schendel, D.E. (1978) *Strategy Formulation: Analytical Concepts*, St Paul, MN: West Publishing.

Jemison, D.B. (1981) 'The importance of an integrative approach to strategic management research', *Academy of Management Review,* **6**(4): 601–8.

Johnson, G. (1992) 'Managing strategic change – strategy, culture and action', *Long Range Planning,* **25**(1): 28–36.

Kanter, R.M. (1989) 'The new managerial work', *Harvard Business Review,* November–December: 85–92.

Kilduff, M. and Mehra, A. (1997) 'Postmodernism and organizational research', *Academy of Management Review,* **22**(2): 453–81.

Knights, D. (1992) 'Changing spaces: The disruptive impact of a new epistemological location for the study of management', *Academy of Management Review,* **17**(3): 514–36.

Knights, D. and Morgan, G. (1990) 'The concept of strategy in sociology: A note of dissent', *Sociology,* **24**(3): 475–83.

Knights, D. and Morgan, G. (1991) 'Strategic discourse and subjectivity: Towards a critical analysis of corporate strategy in organizations', *Organization Studies,* **12**(2): 251–73.

Kotter, J. (1982) *The General Manager*, New York: Free Press.

Learned, E.P., Christensen, C.R., Andrews, K.R. and

Guth, W.D. (1965) *Business Policy: Text and Cases*, Homewood, IL: Irwin.

Lenz, R.T. (1980) 'Strategic capabilities: A concept and framework for analysis', *Academy of Management Review,* **5**(2): 225–34.

Lenz, R.T. (1987) 'Managing the evolution of the strategic planning process', *Business Horizons*, January–February: 34–9.

Lewis, M. (1989) *Liar's Poker*, London: Corgi.

Lindblom, C. (1959) 'The science of "muddling through"', *Public Administration Review,* **19**(2): 79–88.

Lyotard, J.F. (1984) *The Post-Modern Condition: A Report on Knowledge*, Minneapolis: University of Minnesota Press.

Mahoney, J.T. and Pandian, J.R. (1992) 'The resource-based view within the conversation of strategic management', *Strategic Management Journal,* **13**: 363–80.

Miles, R.E. and Snow, C.C. (1978) *Organizational Strategy, Structure and Process*, New York: McGraw-Hill.

Mintzberg, H. (1973) *The Nature of Managerial Work*, New York: Harper & Row.

Mintzberg, H. (1987) 'Crafting strategy', *Harvard Business Review,* July–August: 67–81.

Mintzberg, H. (1990) 'Strategy formation: Schools of thought', in Frederickson, J.W. (ed.) *Perspective on Strategic Management*, New York: Harper Business.

Narayanan, V.K. and Fahey, L. (1982) 'The micro-politics of strategy formulation', *Academy of Management Review,* **7**(1): 25–34.

Ogilvy, J. (1998) 'Learning scenario planning – an introduction to scenario thinking – a four day simulation course', 1–5 February presented by Australian Business Network and Global Business Networks (Sydney).

Ohmae, K. (1983) *The Mind of the Strategist: Business Planning for Competitive Advantage*, New York: Penguin.

Oster, S. (1994) *Modern Competitive Analysis*, New York: Oxford University Press.

Parker, M. (1992) 'Post-modern organizations or postmodern organization theory', *Organization Studies,* **13**(1): 1–17.

Pearson, G. (1999) *Strategy in Action*, London: Prentice Hall.

Peters, T. and Waterman, R. (1982) *In Search of Excellence,* New York: Addison-Wesley.

Pettigrew, A.M. (1985) *The Awakening Giant: Continuity and Change in Imperial Chemical Industries*, Oxford: Blackwell.

Piercy, N. (1989) 'Marketing concepts and actions: Implementing marketing-led strategic change', *European Journal of Marketing,* **24**(2): 24–42.

Porter, M.E. (1980) *Competitive Strategy: Techniques for Analyzing Industries and Competitors*, New York: Free Press.

Porter, M.E. (1985) *Competitive Advantage: Creating and Sustaining Superior Performance*, New York: Free Press.

Porter, M.E. (1996) 'What is strategy?', *Harvard Business Review*, November–December: 61–78.

Prahalad, C.K. and Hamel, G. (1990) 'The core competence of the corporation', *Harvard Business Review,* May–June: 79–91.

Presthus, R.A. (1979) *The Organizational Society*, Basingstoke: Macmillan – now Palgrave Macmillan.

Quinn, J.B. (1978) 'Strategic change: "Logical incrementalism"', *Sloan Management Review,* Fall: 1–21.

Quinn, J.B. (1980) *Strategies for Change: Logical Incrementalism*, Homewood, IL: Irwin.

Renner, M. (1997) *Fighting for Survival: Environmental Decline, Social Conflict and the New Age of Insecurity*, London: Earthscan.

Rodrik, D. (1997) 'Has globalization gone too far?', *California Management Review,* **39**(3): 29–53.

Rosenau, P.M. (1992) *Post-Modernism and the Social Sciences: Insights, Inroads, and Intrusions*, Princeton, NJ: Princeton University Press.

Rowe, A.J., Mason, R.O. and Dickel, K.E. (1986) *Strategic Management: A Methodological Approach*, Reading, MA: Addison-Wesley.

Rowe, A.J., Mason, R.O., Dickel, K.E. and Westcott, P.A. (1987) *Computer Models for Strategic Management*, Reading, MA: Addison-Wesley.

Rumelt, R.P. (1991) 'How much does industry matter', *Strategic Management Journal,* **12**: 167–85.

Schendel, D. (1994) 'Competitive organisational behaviour: Toward an organisationally-based theory of competitive advantage', *Strategic Management Journal,* **15**: 1–5.

Schmalensee, R. (1985) 'Do markets differ much?', *American Economic Review,* **75** (June): 341–51.

Schwartz, P. (1996) *The Art of the Long View: Paths to Strategic Insight for Yourself and Your Company,* New York: Currency/Doubleday.

Simon, H.A. (1976) 'From substantive to procedural rationality', in Latsis, S.J. (ed.) *Method and Appraisal in Economics*, Cambridge: Cambridge University Press.

Simon, H.A. (1979) 'Rational decision making in business organisations', *American Economic Review,* **69** (September): 493–512.

Sterne, D. (1992) 'Core competencies: The key to corporate advantage', *Multinational Business,* **3** (Summer): 13–20.

Strauss, A. (1978) *Negotiations: Varieties, Contexts, Processes and Social Order*, London: Jossey-Bass.

Summa, H. (1992) 'The rhetoric of efficiency: Applied social science as depoliticization', in R. H. Brown (ed.) *Writing the Social Text: Poetics and Politics in Social Science Discourse*, New York: Aldine de Gruyter.

Tayeb, M.H. (1988) *Organisations and National Culture*, London: Sage.

Time 'Silicon Valley's Second Name: Get Rich.com', 4 October, 1999, p. 58.

Tung, R.L. (1994) 'Strategic management thought in East Asia', *Organizational Dynamics,* Spring: 55–65.

Wack, P. (1985a) 'The gentle art of reperceiving', *Harvard Business Review,* September–October (1): 73–89.

Wack, P. (1985b) 'Scenarios – shooting up the rapids', *Harvard Business Review*, November–December (2): 139–50.

Watson, T.J (1994) *In Search of Management: Culture, Chaos and Control in Managerial Work*, London: Routledge.

Watson, T.J. (1996) 'How do managers think? – morality and pragmatism in theory and practice', *Management Learning*, **27**: 323–41.

Wernerfelt, B. (1984) 'A resource-based view of the firm', *Strategic Management Journal,* **5**(2): 171–80.

Wernerfelt, B. (1997) 'Foreword' in Foss, N.J. (ed.) *Resource, Firms and Industries: A Reader in the Resource-Based Perspective*, New York: Oxford University Press.

Westerlund, G. and Sjøstrand, S.E. (1979) *Organisational Myths*, London: Harper & Row.

Weston, R.H. and Hodgson, A. (1996) *Report on Scenario Planning Exercise*, Loughborough University: MSI Research Institute Publications.

Whipp, R. (1996) 'Creative deconstruction: Strategy and organizations', in Clegg, S.R., Hardy, C. and Nord, W.R. (eds) *Handbook of Organization Studies,* London: Sage.

Whitley, R. (1992) *Business Systems in East Asia: Firms, Markets and Societies*, London: Sage.

Wilkinson, B. (1996) 'Culture, institutions and business in East Asia', *Organization Studies,* **17**(3): 421–47.

Williamson, O.E. (1975) *Markets and Hierarchies*, New York: Free Press.

Willmott, H.C. (1993) 'Strength is ignorance; slavery is freedom: Managing culture in modern organizations', *Journal of Management Studies*, **30**(4): 515–52.

Wing, L. (1984) *The Art of Strategy – A Translation of Sun Tzu's 'The Art of War'*, London: Doubleday.

Interorganizational networking

Liz Fulop

16

Questions about networking

1 Why do organizations enter into interorganizational relations?
2 What types of cooperation and/or collaboration are possible?
3 What common problems face organizations wanting to cooperate or collaborate?
4 What problems are associated with networking across cultures?

WEB WONDER LOOKS FOR PARTNERS

Web Wonder is an Internet service provider (ISP) based in the United Kingdom with sites or centres in ten countries on the Continent. It employs some 400 people, with 80 of them in its head office in London. Web Wonder has specialized in offering connectivity to corporate and retail customers offering e-consulting and solutions principally in the form of website design and hosting. It has been in this market since 1997 and has so far funded its growth through cash flow. In the last two years it has added a range of services to its portfolio, one of which was a virtual supermarket for selling goods and services online. This venture has not lived up to expectations, as has been the case with other ISPs trying to capitalize on e-commerce through selling to customers online. Web Wonder is in a highly competitive market, with other providers in Asia, notably India, providing stiff competition. Its owner-founder, Sue Hguina, has had extensive experience in retailing, particularly in the area of purchasing and procurement, as well as having been managing director of a major retail outlet before launching her own dot.com company. She is still the majority shareholder in Web Wonder, which is an unlisted company, but has a board of directors comprising private sector investors from several European countries.

Web Wonder is at a crossroads. The revolution in online selling has lagged behind the more profitable online buying in business-to-business (B2B) transactions. The retail market has struggled with the business-to-customer (B2C) selling on the net, with many e-marketplaces, along with their websites and providers, having gone out of business since the first crash in 'new economy' stock in March 2000. The NASDAQ stock market broke the 5,000 barrier mark on 9 March, 2000 and then plummeted within two days, creating the first wave of dot.com collapses, the so-called 'dot-bombers'. The index had dropped by 49 per cent by the end of 2000. Even though subscribers to Web Wonder have grown rapidly, just on 100 per cent in its last quarter,

and now number 50,000, the board has been reluctant to float the company, fearing that the volatility of the high-tech market could lead to an artificially low market capitalization of the company. Web Wonder has just over 60 regular clients in various areas of retailing.

Web Wonder is considering embarking on a strategy that, if it succeeds, will make it more viable in the longer term and a more attractive float prospect. It has decided to pursue two simultaneous growth strategies, and in order to do this, it will have to form strategic alliances with other Internet companies, one of which will be in Asia, as well as some old economy businesses. It has decided to strengthen its B2B operations by developing its e-procurement capacity, which means pooling the buying needs of large companies under a new business managed by one of Wonder Web's new strategic alliances. Large companies will be able to negotiate better prices and identify best buys, offering potentially substantial savings to them as well as allowing them to outsource their procurement operations. The board is therefore considering forming an alliance with two other Internet companies that are leading developments in this area, one in Australia and the other on the Continent. E-procurement will attract both buyers and sellers, hopefully on a global scale. However, Web Wonder, along with other e-procurers, faces the challenge of potential anti-trust regulators stepping in if the strategic alliance acts to freeze out new market entrants and other competitors. This had already occurred, with the European Commission stepping in to prevent a B2B aircraft component joint venture. Other risks are also involved, such as e-procurement diluting innovation by eliminating product differentiation and eventually forcing members to leave. Web Wonder's new strategic alliance business will have the large companies as paying members and also floating the company with special non-voting share options for participating businesses.

Wonder Web also wants to expand its B2C services

through developing stronger 'clicks and mortar' websites that are supported by large retailers or chains, as opposed to creating pure e-tail ventures, such as cyber malls. Web Wonder wants to serve a particular niche in the 'clicks and mortar' market and is considering forming a strategic alliance to back this new strategy. Costs are anticipated to increase as more sites will be needed for both ventures. High labour costs involved in running their European operations have made Asia an attractive place to concentrate some of the core servicing work for the new ventures. Thus, Web Wonder is looking to form an alliance with a leading ISP in Asia, but is concerned about a number of issues relating to internationalizing its operations. Web Wonder does not have any personal relationships with any of these potential business partners, and there will be a need to share intellectual property (IP) and new strategies with some of them. In the e-procurement venture, the IP resides with the Australian and European businesses, with the former having taken out a patent on its business processes and methods. In the 'clicks and mortar' venture, Web Wonder has developed considerable IP that it wishes to protect at all costs. The Asian partnership will involve limited IP exposure.

Note: This case study draws on a number of articles on Internet companies and businesses.

QUESTIONS ABOUT THE CASE

1 What would you do in the place of Web Wonder's board and management about the two proposed strategic alliances?

2 If you were the manager of the e-procurement company in Australia, how would you react to Web Wonder's proposal?

3 How might a potential Asian ISP respond to Web Wonder's approach?

Introduction

The term 'interorganizational networking' refers to a number of different forms of cooperation and collaboration occurring among organizations and some of these include, 'strategic alliances', 'business networks', 'consortia,' 'joint ventures', 'clusters' and 'linkages'. Some argue that the sheer growth in the number of interorganizational relations (IORs) in the 1990s was part of a large-scale social experiment occurring between organizations, industries and governments to find the appropriate design and operation of businesses (James 1994: 56, citing Mitroff and Linstone 1993). However, networking ought not to be romanticized as a new era for businesses because, as Roy Jacques (1996: 6) aptly notes, early US industrialists, such as Carneige and Rockefeller, identified the advent of the industrial era with the decline of open competition and the shift to industry-wide cooperation among employers. This form of 'cooperation' might well be called 'collusion' but, as Jacques says, it was not competitive in nature. Even today networking is very much about cooperating to compete but networks are formed for a variety of reasons with associated costs and benefits. It is not just businesses, however, that are engaged in IORs. Public sector organizations and non-government organizations (NGOs), such as neighbourhood centres, refuges, major aid organizations and charities, also provide ample evidence of IORs and indeed, in some cases, long histories of leading in this area of management. Many aid agencies would be a case in point. Moreover, it is increasingly common to find cross-sector collaborations, such as those occurring between universities and businesses, as the private sector increasingly looks to shift costly R&D to other areas of the economy. The focus of this chapter is predominantly on IORs in the private sector that have encouraged the growth of networking activities. We use the term *networking* to describe a range of IORs.

The term *interorganizational* means activities that go on between organizations, as opposed to those within them. Indeed, organizations enter into IORs for many different reasons and these forms of connectedness can include very simple forms of cooperation to more sophisticated levels of collaboration. For example, *cooperation* might be for the purpose of sharing information, premises or some equipment that is useful to several parties, but does not threaten any of their competitive positions. *Collaboration*, on the other hand, as we use it here, refers to the sharing of a significant aspect of each partner's core competence and organizational intelligence. As we shall discuss, the sharing of knowledge that affects a core competency of an organization poses the greatest challenge for IORs. Such forms of collaboration involve risks associated with sharing highly valued forms of intellectual property or capital.

All who work in organizations need to understand the benefits that can be gained from entering into various forms of cooperation and collaboration, and to what extent these might be damaging to their organizations. There are quite destructive and exploitative forms of IORs. Entering into a networking arrangement is not recommended for all businesses and nor is it inevitable that all business will need to develop such relationships. Some forms of networking also arise accidentally and not through any intended strategy of management.

A starting point for understanding the contingent nature of networking is to unravel why organizations, or at least those who work in them, enter into IORs in the first place and what choices, if any, they have with respect to the types of relationship they forge. Those who put a positive slant on IORs talk of organizations having to develop *collaborative advantage* as an imperative or necessity for success (see Huxham 1993, 1996; Kanter 1994). Managers need to understand what collaborative advantage actually entails in practical terms, and how, if needs be, they can foster it across different industries, organizations and cultures. In this chapter we examine the different ways theorists have sought to explain how organizations develop IORs, and what distinguishes these relationships from other ways of doing business. We examine some common ways of describing IORs as well as the major costs and benefits of networking, especially those associated with building trust in and across different industry sectors. The gendered nature of the interorganizational networking literature will be considered as well as the cross-cultural dimensions of IORs.

The rise of networking

If we were to summarize why networking has increased over the last decade, several key trends emerge:

■ *Globalization* – Almost everyone acknowledges that many organizations are operating in a global environment and that the basis of competition has shifted. Building strategic alliances, networks and other forms of cooperation and collaboration have helped many organizations to go global and operate in many countries and across national borders. To a large extent, Internet technology has further opened up opportunities for new forms of 'connectivity' and communication, giving additional opportunities for operating in a more global way through networking.

■ *Information technology and the knowledge age* – With the combination of growth in more expensive information-based and knowledge-intensive modes of production, typified by high costs of R&D in many areas, such as genetic engineering, partnerships have grown to spread the high risks as well as harnessing and exploiting the knowledge required in these ventures. The unrelenting demand for high-quality customized products and services makes it difficult to 'go it alone' in many ventures because of the pressure to be innovative and get products to market quickly (Alter and Hage 1993: 21; Lane 1998: 1; Buttery 1999: 417–18). In the early 1990s, Catherine Alter and Gerald Hage observed that alliances were being formed

predominantly in industry sectors where the cost of product development was high or the speed of product development was rapid. They also noted (citing Pollack 1992) that there were discernible industry trends, with biotechnology, for example, leading the field in the rate at which overseas or cross-border alliances were formed. Similar trends were noted in other industries in the USA, such as information technology, new materials manufacture (especially in the steel industry). These trends are persisting and extend to include telecommunications, healthcare and hospitality, to name a few. The Internet has added to the twin pressures of IT and knowledge management and forced the integration of more traditional ways of doing business with the use of the Internet. This has created many new inter-organizational partnerships, often of a virtual kind and some more enduring than others (Porter 2001).

■ *Robotics* – Another leap in technology, robotics, coupled with computer-aided design (CAD) and production (computer-aided manufacturing – CAM), injected a new potential flexibility into the production arena. Long production runs brought about by the need to undertake costly retooling were no longer the deciding factor in production. Robotics took over particularly in areas such as manufacturing, stevedoring and other areas of heavy engineering, shortening product lifecycles and allowing for more customized models or products to be introduced into markets more rapidly. Even the workforce changed from being dominated by semi-skilled workers to having greater numbers of technicians and scientists, with fewer of them required for production. The growth of middle management positions associated with managing production workers also declined. We also witnessed the development of concurrent engineering (a systematic, integrated approach to the design of products and their related processes, including manufacturing and support) and just-in-time (JIT) production systems (having inventory delivered from suppliers when needed for production) that all led to the outsourcing of various facets of the manufacturing process and the necessity to build new partnerships, particularly with suppliers and customers (Buttery et al. 1999: 419–20) (also see Chapter 11).

■ *Anti-merger strategies* – Traditionally growth of organizations has been via either internal R&D developments in production and marketing or acquiring new products, services or markets through merger and acquisition. Horizontal and vertical integration always led to larger organizations and introduced the possibilities of economies of scale.

Exhibit 16.1 Triggers for networking

Market entry and positioning

❏ tailor products to local markets

❏ lack of resources for marketing products and services to best advantage

❏ limited essential expertise and knowledge in foreign markets and cultures

❏ realization that market opportunities cannot be exploited solo

❏ overcoming prejudice in the market by joining with an indigenous partner

❏ overcoming pressure generated by customers in the marketplace

❏ finding a means to replace the market mechanism (that is, rather than trading in a market setting, the firm enters into a longer term networking arrangement which effectively supersedes the market)

Scarce resources

❏ limited finance for development

❏ limited technological know-how

❏ limited management expertise/desire to 'buy in' management talent

❏ realization that partner can produce a good more efficiently

Scale, scope and complementarity

❏ prevent or reduce excess capacity – scale

❏ share fixed costs (technology, plant and equipment, facilities, distribution, brand name) – scale

❏ achieve efficiency in volume of production and unit of production – scale

❏ improve utilization of resources with different applications – scope

❏ achieve benefits of complementary competence and resources – complementarity

❏ create varied sources of learning and monitoring to reduce uncertainty – complementarity

❏ swap product or market combinations – complementarity

Strategic and political goals

❏ share and diversify risks, including political ones

❏ collecting information about a competitor

❏ pre-empt competition

❏ avoid having to defensively attack a competitor through a merger

❏ offensively attack a competitor at their home base by collaborating with a local partner

❏ collude on price or set up entry barriers to markets

❏ increase speed of lodging patents

❏ government encouragement, for example grants, allowances, subsidies

❏ regional policy to lift the game of a depressed region

❏ taking advantage of a naturally occurring phenomenon, for example the opportunity to regenerate an area or region following fire, flood and so on

❏ spreading business risk by diversifying out of a single economy

❏ generating national or global flexibility by being able to join and leave networks

Source: Adapted from Ewa Buttery and Alan Buttery (1995) *The Dynamics of the Network Situation*, Canberra: AusIndustry Business Networks Program, pp. 16–18; and Bart Nooteboom (1997) *Design of Inter-Firm Relations: Goals, Conditions, Problems and Solutions*, Paper for the EGOS Colloquium, Sub-Theme 2, Budapest, 3–5 July, pp. 5–6.

Exhibit 16.2 Triggers for networking in the new economy

❏ To innovate

❏ To outsource non-core activities, such as R&D

❏ To develop intellectual property (IP) and tacit knowledge

❏ To reinvent the business

❏ To be adaptive and responsive to rapid changes

❏ To develop virtual relationships

❏ To shift risks of R&D to other sectors of the economy

Often integration strategies were motivated by the urge to own or dominate a market or segment through increasing an organization's scope of offerings. During the late 1980s and into the 1990s, downsizing of vertically integrated businesses became a feature across a number of industry sectors, such as automotives, engineering and other heavy industries. What this revealed was that the vertically integrated business was not always the most competitive way of organizing a business (Buttery et al. 1999: 418). These trends have not been attenuated in the late 1990s and early 2000s, with major mergers occurring in areas such as telecommunication, banking and finance, Internet and web-based businesses, airlines and many other sectors of the economy. The pressure for this remains the same – global market domination of not only traditional markets but also new ones in countries such as China and India.

■ Competition from low-wage countries – Severe price competition from low-wage countries, including the trend for many multinational corporations (MNCs) to move their operations off shore to new industrializing countries (NICs), has made it critical for many businesses to forge new partnerships in foreign countries that can help them to produce cheaper products (Lane 1998: 1). Thus, as Ewa and Alan Buttery* say:

It was far more important to develop and own brands and be able to manage marketing than production. This has led us now to a world where production can be separated from marketing, marketing can be described as global, that is, managed on a global basis, but it recognizes local requirements and cultures. Brand names exchange for billions of dollars and managers are willing to look around the world to see where it is best (and cheapest) to produce various parts of the product, how to market on a global basis and how to finance the deals globally. (Buttery et al. 1999: 420)

Added to this has been the rise in outsourcing of many peripheral business operations to countries such as India, where cheap labour can be found for many routine and repetitive tasks, such as billing customers and filling and dispatching orders, which can be handled via the Internet, at significantly lower labour costs, overheads and regulations than in many Western countries. These countries have become the sweatshops and even 'sex shops' (for example sexual exploitation of child labour) of global production,

although the former can be found in all countries, although the scale will vary (see Chapter 5).

The growth of networking has coincided with the decline or transformation in traditional forms of manufacturing and the rise of the 'new economy' of information-based technologies, the Internet and knowledge and information as additional factors in competition and growth (Porter 2001). The 'old economy' of manufacturing (as described in the Introduction) was based on developments that encouraged growth through horizontal and vertical integration and mergers, which are the antithesis of networking strategies. This is not to say that old economy businesses are not adopting the new economy technologies, such as the Internet, and turning to networking as a means of driving change in their organizations. However, it is also true to say that many dot.coms are learning that they cannot ignore the sound business principles and methods of the old economy and invent new organizations out of 'thin air' (Porter 2001).

Buttery and Buttery (1995) and Bart Nooteboom (1997) separately undertook an extensive literature review and identified a number of key internal and external triggers for organizations, or at least the people in them, to network. These are summarized in Exhibit 16.1.

If we consider why businesses might network in terms of the new economy, and the push to high-tech, Internet and knowledge-based businesses, then the factors mentioned in Exhibit 16.2 are likely to be more important.

Network typologies and taxonomies

A number of different classification systems have emerged in the networking literature and some of the more common ones are listed in Exhibit 16.3. We refer

---

Exhibit 16.3 Classification of network types

❑ Vertical and horizontal networks

❑ Pooled and complementary networks

❑ Product, service and learning networks

❑ Number of firms in the network

❑ Strategic focus

Source: Adapted from Ewa Buttery, Liz Fulop and Alan Buttery (1999) 'Networks and interorganizational relations', in Fulop, L. and Linstead, S. (eds) *Management: A Critical Text*, Melbourne: Macmillan Business, p. 428. (This exhibit was prepared by Buttery and Buttery.)

---

* *Author's note:* In the previously published version of this chapter, the authorship of the material was acknowledged in terms of individual author contributions and this is being reflected in this significantly revised chapter.

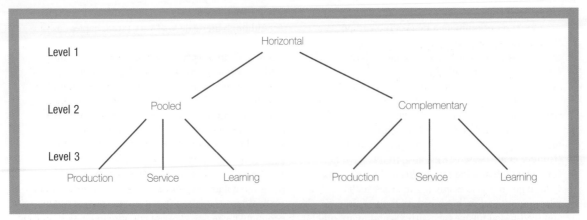

Figure 16.1 Hierarchy of networks classification of horizontal relations

Source: Ewa Buttery, Liz Fulop and Alan Buttery (1999) 'Networks and interorganizational relations', in Fulop, L. and Linstead, S. (eds) *Management: A Critical Text*, Melbourne: Macmillan Business, p. 429. (This figure was prepared by Buttery and Buttery.)

to these typologies as a way of giving a 'snapshot' view of the types of relationships being debated in the literature.

Drawing on the work of Buttery and Buttery (Buttery et al. 1999: 428–34), we can start by categorizing the different levels of cooperation shown in Exhibit 16.3. Three levels of classification are most commonly used in the literature and these correspond with the first three

items listed in Exhibit 16.3. A useful way of presenting this is shown in Figure 16.1, which illustrates how each level relates to the other and how they are distinguished from each other, at least in theory. Figure 16.1 shows the nature of *horizontal network relationships*. Exhibit 16.4 provides an explanation for how the classification system works and examples of the network types are shown in Exhibit 16.5.

Exhibit 16.4 Description of horizontal networks

Level 1 – *the value chain* – horizontal systems or arrangements that continue at the same stage of the value-adding chain.

Level 2 – this second-level classification relates to the idea of competitive domain overlap (Borys and Jemison 1989) and two specific forms of overlap:

a. *Pooled network* – partners compete head on and share common opportunities and threats, belong to the same strategic group because they share a similar past, and are from the same industry sector.

b. *Complementary network* – partners do not compete, perhaps even come from differing industries, in which case the participants may seek to combine differing strengths. These mutually beneficial networks are likely to enjoy longevity beyond a few years.

Level 3 – relates to the tangibility of the cooperative benefit and draws on the work of Joe Burke (1990):

a. One subclassification measures if all partners are involved in operating together on one or more projects to create a tangible product; if this is the case, the *production network* emerges.

b. If partners simply jointly buy or provide a service (for example marketing) that does not result in the joint ownership of anything, the *service network* emerges.

c. A competitive advantage may be derived from a third type of collaboration, the *learning network*, where firms seek out national and international partners who provide leading-edge expertise in areas of core competence.

Source: Adapted from Ewa Buttery, Liz Fulop and Alan Buttery (1999) 'Networks and interorganizational relations', in Fulop, L. and Linstead, S. (eds) *Management: A Critical Text*, Melbourne: Macmillan Business, pp. 427–9. (This material was prepared by Buttery and Buttery.)

Exhibit 16.5 Examples of different types of horizontal networks

- ❏ **Pooled production network:** a group of growers who set up a joint sorting and packing operation.

- ❏ **Complementary production network:** Kentucky Fried Chicken (KFC) combining its operational skills and store format with Mitsubishi's site selection skills in Japan to establish a KFC chain in Japan.

- ❏ **Pooled service network:** a number of hotels pooling advertising dollars to promote the region's tourist attractions.

- ❏ **Complementary service network:** a selection of enterprises in education, manufacturing or tourism pooling advertising dollars to promote an entire region.

- ❏ **Complementary learning network:** the forging of an alliance between Siemens, with its strength in global telecommunications and cable manufacturing technology, and Corning, with its technological expertise in optical fibres and glass, to create leading-edge technology in fibreoptics.

- ❏ **Pooled learning network:** a number of dental laboratories combining to develop state-of-the-art dental implant technology.

Source: Ewa Buttery, Liz Fulop and Alan Buttery (1999) 'Networks and interorganizational relations', in Fulop, L. and Linstead, S. (eds) *Management: A Critical Text*, Melbourne: Macmillan Business, p. 429. (This material was prepared by Buttery and Buttery.)

Vertical networks

At the broadest level, networks can also be classified according to whether or not they are *vertical* systems that extend along the value-adding chain (see Chapter 15), as in buyer and supplier relationships (for example the Toyota network of component suppliers) and franchises. The value-added chain is concerned with showing how value is added at each stage of producing and distributing a product.

Size of networks

Alter and Hage (1993: 23) introduce another important distinction based on the *number of firms* in a network. They argue that the term 'interorganizational relations' refers principally to dyadic relations, where only two parties (organizations) are involved. They would cite many joint ventures as examples of dyadic relations.

They would reserve the term *network* for multiple relationships involving at least three or more parties or partners, sometimes even competitors. In fact, they argue that when the relationships between multiple partners are aggregated, then a network emerges (Alter and Hage 1993: 23). Alter and Hage believe these *multi-organizational* or *partnered networks* are the really interesting new developments in the field of cooperation and collaboration. They argue that networks with many members find it harder to cooperate or collaborate than do those with dyadic or triadic membership (three organizations).

In the networking situation, one often reads that the ideal size of the group is four to six members. Once a group gets too large for an individual to weigh up trust and the aims and preferences of colleagues, and cope with different personalities, the group can become less cohesive and more prone to opportunistic behaviour. For some theorists, the very notion of social exchange implies a limited number of partners to ensure better communication and coordination so that there is stability of membership and a more focused use of resources (Ring 1997a: 115). But, more importantly, many theories of trust have been based on studies of the dyadic relationship, that is, how trust develops between two people on a personal level and not among a group of people, and particularly people who are strangers and might even be competitors. We will pursue the issue of trust later in the chapter, but suffice it to say that it is a key concept in theories of interorganizational networking.

For the purposes of this chapter, we are interested in distinguishing networking from other forms of cooperation (for example mergers, takeovers and acquisitions which are forms of vertical integration), on the basis that a network arrangement only exists while the majority of participating members or organizations remain *separate legal entities*. One of the reasons why organizations enter into network arrangements is to avoid the problems, particularly the power struggles, legal battles, bad publicity and so on, that often come with takeovers and mergers. The fact that some organizations merge does not exclude their having other networking relationships with other partners. In other words, we are signalling that ownership is an important part of distinguishing networks from other forms of cooperation and collaboration, as are the contractual relationships they enter into (Oliver and Ebers 1998: 575–6).

Strategic foci

According to Buttery and Buttery (Buttery et al. 1999: 430–4), both vertical and horizontal networks, and the various subclassifications under them (see Figure 16.1), can be further categorized. They argue that to gain a competitive edge, organizations might consider several broad categories of cooperative and collaborative strategies, each of which is described in more detail in Exhibit 16.6, and include the following:

- licensing
- franchising
- joint venture
- supplier–buyer relationships in the value-added chain
- consortium
- strategic alliances along the whole value-added chain
- cluster.

Exhibit 16.6 Strategic foci of networks

Licensing

Description: An unsophisticated, yet potent form of cooperation, especially in the service sector, which involves the purchase of the right to use an asset for a particular time, and offers rapid access to new products, technologies or innovations (Borys and Jemison 1989).

Benefits: The pursuit of a licensing strategy permits a firm to control product image and quality while requiring little financial investment. Licensors must, however, secure substantial training, set adequate standards of performance and define compensation; their lack can represent a serious threat to the licensing arrangements. The major benefits of licensing include the ability to reach large, often unexploited markets quickly, and permit expansion where local laws hinder direct foreign investment.

Risks: Licensing arrangements, as a rule, are enforceable by contract, but the strategy is not without risks, and the risks are magnified if the licensor transfers core competence technology, or if the transfer occurs across frontiers where licensing arrangements are sometimes hard to enforce.

Franchising

Description: Franchising is used to improve control without a takeover or merger. Trademarks, management assistance and know-how are granted in return for lump-sum payments, royalties and compliance with the rules and procedures of the franchiser.

Benefits: The speed at which expansion can take place, including global expansion, owing to the spread of costs and opportunities among many individuals.

Risks: If brand names and products are changed through mergers and takeovers, the franchisee can lose market share very rapidly and become subject to the politics that surround such strategies.

Supplier–buyer relationships

Description: Also referred to as 'sequential' or 'vertical alliances', they are based on contracts where one business's output is purchased by another. Buyers must ensure that suppliers' processes, capacity and inputs meet their quantitative and qualitative requirements in a timely manner, while the supplier designs a product that meets the appropriate technical standards and delivery schedules of the purchaser.

Benefits: As the relationship proves beneficial, it is likely to be converted into a single sourcing arrangement, and ultimately the supplier becomes an important part of the buyer's product and marketing process, leading to significant financial benefits to both parties.

Risks: The buyer finds the supplier an unreliable source and the supplier gets locked into the pricing and other policies of the buyer and can be squeezed hard on prices.

Joint venture

Description: Refers to two or more organizations forming a business for cooperative purposes, often also described as a 'strategic alliance' or, when involving mainly SMEs, a 'business network'. Within the business, partners of the joint venture decide strategy and make key decisions. Joint ventures are often formed to gain economies of scale, especially in mature industries, such as steel production and car manufacture or for R&D purposes. More often, though, joint ventures are struck to learn new technological, production or marketing skills through R&D and new product or process developments.

Benefits: While the management burden of restructuring joint ventures can be heavy, the benefits can more than outstrip the efforts. According to Joel Bleeke and David Ernst (1995), disguised sales partnerships, such as mergers, rarely last more than five years. In the area of R&D they offer opportunities to rapidly develop new products and processes.

Risks: Joint ventures have high failure rates. For example, Asian companies as a rule have benefited more from joint ventures in the past, often because the Asian partner assists the market entry into the Asian market, while the Western company provides technical expertise. The former is frequently founded in personal relationships between the Asian business and the Asian market, and therefore cannot be transferred, while the technical expertise, once transferred, can be enjoyed by the Asian business and used against joint venture partners.

Consortium

Description: Involves a number of businesses pooling their resources into an integrated, new organization, leading to economies of scale and the efficient use of specialist equipment and resources. Often a consortium represents the only means of avoiding duplication of projects within a national economy or in developing large, complex projects.

Benefits: Increases the competitiveness of high-tech industries such as microelectronics and semi-conductors. Brings together critical mass in R&D technology and marketing. Associated with this feature is cost reduction for individual businesses, risk diversification and increased economies of scale and scope, often underpinned by close supplier–buyer relationships.

Risks: Market concentration and dominance can lead to anti-competitive practices.

Strategic alliances along the entire value-added chain

Description: Alliances along the value-added chain involve a 'set of independent companies that work closely together to manage the flow of goods and services along the entire value-added chain (Johnston and Lawrence 1988: 94). The chain is concerned with what value is added at each stage from supply of raw materials, manufacture and distribution of the product to retailers and customers.

Benefits: Increases flexibility by allowing organizations to outsource those aspects of production that can be obtained at lower cost and higher quality from external suppliers. Allows an organization to focus on core competence and increase its distinctive competitive advantage.

Risks: Need to develop superior capabilities in negotiating contracts and managing contractual relations that depend on a strong culture of supplier commitment to the value-added concept.

Cluster

Description: Usually comprises dense horizontal relations. One of the most famous is in the Emilia-Romagna region of Italy, where small manufactures have used geographical proximity to create a critical mass of value-adding businesses and institutional support (for example chambers of commerce), allowing them to dominate market sectors. Another is Silicon Valley in the USA where high-tech firms have co-located and developed new Internet products, R&D ventures and other spinoffs associated with such things as communications and information technology. Clusters can emerge through government intervention or spontaneously and can involve complex cross-membership arrangements.

Benefits: Similar to those of a consortium but, for governments, clusters are a way of encouraging the competitiveness of a region, especially one in decline, to create critical mass to compete globally or avoid duplication in high-cost industry developments, such as those involving R&D.

Disadvantage: If the region or cluster declines, then all businesses suffer and lose value and market share. The level of interdependence developed among suppliers and buyers makes it hard to move out of the region even if better opportunities present themselves. It can become a case of 'irreversible lock-in'.

Source: Adapted from Ewa Buttery, Liz Fulop and Alan Buttery (1999) 'Networks and interorganizational relations', in Fulop, L. and Linstead, S. (eds) *Management: A Critical Text*, Melbourne: Macmillan Business, pp. 430–4. (This material was initially prepared by Buttery and Buttery and modified by Fulop for this publication.)

Examples can be readily found for each of the aforementioned IORs. For example, Buttery and Buttery identify how *licensing* was adopted by Sun Microsystems to develop its innovative systems (microchips) by using Philip's production and distribution expertise (Buttery et al. 1999: 431). *Franchising* is probably one of the most recognized forms of networking with common examples being McDonald's and KFC. Moving on, recent changes to The Body Shop's operations have forced the organization to create strong *buyer–supplier relationships*. The Body Shop now outsources all its manufacturing, and its relationship with its suppliers is governed by the principle of 'due diligence' to maintain high ethical standards in product testing. The Body Shop does not enter into a supplier relationship until the manufacturer undertakes a full social, animal and environmental audit (Roddick 2000: 254–3). However, *joint ventures* are probably still the most common form of strategic alliance and dominate many network strategies. One of the most well-known examples of a joint venture was between Ericsson, with its techno-logical strengths in telecommunications, and Hewlett-Packard, with its expertise in computer and software, which created a significant presence in the network management systems area (Buttery et al. 1999: 432).

Consortia are common in large-scale projects, such as constructing dams, railways, mining and mineral exploration, car and aircraft manufacture, telecommunications, information technology and aerospace. Buttery and Buttery (Buttery et al. 1999: 433) cite the Airbus consortium in Europe as a good example of a major success in networking. An example of strategic alliances along the extended *buyer-supplier* value chain is commonly found in the healthcare sector where health insurers provide a range of services from general practice, specialist services (for example imaging, physiotherapy), health and fitness products and services, to hospital and ambulatory care as well as aged care and other specialist services. Exhibit 16.6 describes two famous *clusters* found in Europe and the USA.

A number of major criticisms can be made about network typologies. They are heavily influenced by Western approaches to IORs and thus are insensitive to cross-cultural factors (we discuss cross-cultural aspects of networking later in the chapter). Neither are they particularly sensitive to local or national variations, except perhaps in the discussion of clusters. Nor do they tell us much about how networking differs from other forms of organizing and what specific management challenges are posed by networking relationships. Perhaps a useful way of starting to consider these challenges is to look at some of the costs and benefits of networking.

Costs and benefits of networking

Mark Ebers and Anna Grandori (1997: 273, 274) believe that research on networks has generally focused on the benefits of these forms of cooperation and collaboration to the individual firm to the exclusion of considering undesirable costs. They believe that joint ventures, consortia, franchising and a range of other forms of association can create negative effects for organizations excluded from the networks. Entry barriers based on reciprocal cooperation are often used to exclude competitors. Ebers and Grandori (1997) cite a study of coalitions of construction and engineering businesses forming joint ventures or consortia to bid for job assignments. These businesses sign contracts among themselves and only include businesses that have close informal links and have cooperated in the past. These potential negative costs of networks warrant attention because they reveal how various forms of cooperation and collaboration can stifle competition and act as costs to a whole range of excluded groups. Consumers, for example, often find their choices limited, prices fixed and efficiency not guaranteed, once these exclusionary consortia or joint venture arrangements come into play.

The costs and benefits of networking have been generally defined in terms of economic exchange and therefore other costs or benefits of networking that are not purely economic have been excluded. Negative or destructive costs of networks are also often overlooked as many authors present the network as a panacea or 'one best way' to organize (Ebers and Grandori 1997:

273). While there is sufficient evidence to suggest that networking is on the rise (see earlier discussion), there is also ample evidence to suggest that many who enter networks report lack of success or that their expectations were not met by the network experience.

Paul de Laat (1997: 147–8; also Child 1998) reminds us that networks are fraught with risk, particularly in joint ventures, and that many attempts to set up networks actually fail. Moreover, he cites research showing that once an alliance or network is formed only 30 per cent (based on a sample of 92) thrive in the long run, while other studies report up to 45 per cent success rate (based on a sample of 895 alliances, and mainly joint ventures). Alan Buttery, Liz Fulop and Ewa Buttery (1999: 444–5) have studied, between them, some 50 networks and over 200 businesses in Australia. Their studies covered a range of network types, comprising mainly small businesses, and they found that only about 20 per cent of these networks were successful. They used a range of indicators to measure success, including evaluations made by network members. Of those that had reported success, the majority were in complementary operations networks with a small percentage of pooled operations networks also succeeding (see above). The pooled operations networks (of competitors) succeeded for one of the following reasons: a major crisis in the industry made the network a viable option for dealing with the crisis; the network sought new markets and products that did not threaten the existing markets or products of members; or a separate company was established and managed by the network that did not compete with any member's business. The greatest frustrations, disappointments and failures were found in service networks where core operations were not significantly affected by the network's activities.

Networking is not easy and sometimes the costs far outweigh the benefits. Some of the common costs and benefits associated with networking are described in Table 16.1, which is based on research by Alter and Hage (1993: 35–8) who drew on an extensive list of authors to identify what they considered to be the 'calculus of interorganizational collaboration'. They did not suggest that their list of costs and benefits was exhaustive; however, they did note that costs and benefits cover a wide range of motivations and perceptions relating to the risks associated with cooperation and collaboration. Benefits are usually associated with opportunities to gain access to information, know-how and expertise or create new niche markets in areas that require a great number of specializations, especially where product development is both costly and lengthy. Minimizing risk and uncertainty are two prime benefits of cooperation. Alter and Hage also noted that risk and uncertainty rise dramatically when organizations try to enter foreign

Costs	Benefits

Table 16.1 Calculus of interorganizational collaboration

Costs	Benefits
Loss of technological superiority; risk of losing competitive position	Opportunities to learn and to adapt, develop competencies or jointly develop new products
Loss of resources – time, money, information, raw materials, legitimacy, status, etc	Gain of resources – time, money, information, raw materials, legitimacy, status, etc. utilization of unused plant capacity
Being linked with failure; sharing the costs of failing such as loss of reputation, status, and financial position	Sharing the cost of product development and associated risks (such as failure to develop new products quickly enough and with enough quality), risks associated with commercial acceptance, and risks associated with size of market share
Loss of autonomy and ability to unilaterally control outcomes; goal displacement; loss of control	Gain of influence over domain; ability to penetrate new markets; competitive positioning and access to foreign markets; need for global products
Loss of stability, certainty, and known time-tested technology; feelings of dislocation	Ability to manage uncertainty, solve invisible and complex problems, ability to specialize or diversify; ability to fend off competitors
Delays in solutions due to problems in coordination	Rapid responses to changing market demands; less delay in use of new technologies
Government intrusion, regulation, and so on	Gaining acceptance from foreign governments for participation in the country

Source: Modified from Catherine Alter and Gerald Hage (1993) *Organizations Working Together*, Newbury Park, CA: Sage, pp. 36–7. Reproduced in Ewa Buttery, Liz Fulop and Alan Buttery (1999) 'Networks and interorganizational relations', in Fulop, L. and Linstead, S. (eds) *Management: A Critical Text*, Melbourne: Macmillan Business, p. 446. (This table was developed by L. Fulop.)

markets, and cooperation and collaboration are often sought with foreign partners in order to reduce this risk and uncertainty. Sometimes governments, such as in the People's Republic of China (PRC), require that firms develop a cooperative venture of some sort in order to enter the country in the first instance (Alter and Hage 1993: 37–8). The 'calculus of interorganizational collaboration' has to be read as every cost is also a potential benefit and vice versa.

Table 16.1 reveals some of the inherent complexities that networking can create for organizations and their managers. It is probably true that not all managers embrace networking willingly or by choice. Often pressures outside the control of managers (as described above) force organizations to experiment with forming IORs without a great deal of understanding of what is at stake or being asked of the organization. We now turn to a discussion of some of the theoretical perspectives that help to shed further light on the networking phenomenon, and to a more critical assessment of IORs.

Theories of networks

It is not easy to do justice to the many theoretical perspectives that have influenced the study of interorganizational networking, however, as Amalya

Oliver and Ebers (citing Nohria 1992: 3), state: 'Anyone reading what purports to be network literature will readily perceive the analogy between it and a "terminology jungle in which any newcomer may plant a tree"' (1998: 549). Oliver and Ebers undertook a content analysis of a number of major management journals and discovered 17 approaches being used in this literature. After further analysis, they were able to distil four substantive configurations of research endeavour around which interorganizational network theorists have coalesced (see also Grandori and Soda 1995; Johannisson and Mønsted 1996 for different analyses of the literature). Table 16.2 describes these four areas, which are: *social network, power and control, institutionalism*, and *institutional economics and strategy*. These four configurations led the authors to conclude that theories drawing on network, political power and resource dependence perspectives were most commonly invoked to explain IORs and networking. They found that the most common outcomes sought from networking were: power and control, prevalence (or precedence) and success.

The most common antecedent conditions that helped to explain network relations focused on:

■ *the need to acquire resources*, both material (money, stocks, facilities and so on) and

Table 16.2 Four substantive configurations within research on interorganizational networking			
Configuration	Social network	Power and control	Institutionalism	Institutional economics and strategy
Theories	network	political power, resource dependence, exchange	institutionalism	transaction cost, strategy
Ties	political, horizontal	political	social	dyadic, vertical, ownership, contractual
Levels of analysis	individual	region/industry	societal, groups of individuals	organizational
Antecedents	network position	goal congruence, dependence, conflict	organizational density, trust	market constraints, material resources, stability, resource munificence, asset specificity
Outcomes		power/control, centrality, stability, political participation	density, conflict, legitimacy, extinction, persistence, commitment, trust, size	success, take-over, cost/price, make-or-buy, opportunism

Source: Amanda L. Oliver and Mark Ebers (1998) 'Networking network studies: An analysis of conceptual configurations in the study of inter-organizational relationships', *Organization Studies,* **19**(4), p. 564. Reprinted by permission of Sage Publications Ltd. Copyright © Sage Publications 1998.

immaterial ones (power, information, knowledge and so on)

- *dependence* (what situations make one party dependent on another)
- *network position* (where an organization fits in the web of relations)
- *goal congruence* (degree of harmony and agreement between members)
- *resource munificence* (scarcity or generosity of resource endowment of members).

Although not mentioned in Table 16.2, intentions and motivations were also raised in a number of studies. Oliver and Ebers also discovered that the variable of 'trust' did not figure significantly in accounts of how network relationships worked, despite its importance in some theoretical perspectives. They believed one possible explanation for this was the difficulty of studying the concept and the fact that if other key factors, such as common goals, were present in networks, then trust seemed to lose its explanatory relevance (Oliver and Ebers 1998: 565–6).

However, in order to understand the significance of some of the configurations mentioned above, we first examine the *power and control* perspective to introduce some of the more problematical aspects of networking from the perspective of SMEs. We then examine some very influential writers in the field who

belong to the *social network* and *institutionalism* perspectives and the *transaction cost* approaches, which come under *institutional economics and strategy*. From there we will look at how trust figures in discussions of networking. We will also consider how *strategy* has influenced networking theory and specifically the notion of *interorganizational learning* (IOL) and the relational challenges this form of networking present for managers. However, as Table 11.2 and the discussion above suggests, very few theorists study networking from a single perspective and multi-perspective approaches dominate the field.

Power dimensions of networks and SMEs

Perhaps one of the most widely cited works on power in networks, which appeared in *Harvard Business Review* in 1990, was the study by Robert Howard, who specifically focused on small businesses and networking relationships. He argued that networking was creating new forms of organization that would give small businesses a significant role to play in creating competitive nations. The article is interesting because the power dynamics it describes are still highly relevant to discussions of networking today. The economic importance of small businesses in the twenty-first century remains an open question, but Howard was convinced that they were growing in importance and would do so throughout the 1990s. Yet we note that one of the most noticeable trends in the late 1990s and early 2000s has been the rise of the 'giga-corporations'. These comprise companies that have used mergers to form corporate entities whose market capitalization is larger than many nations, for example General Electrics (US) is ranked twelfth ahead of Australia and just behind Spain on such a measure (Sheehan 2001: 32). Networking and SME partnerships pale in importance against the might and power of these merged entities. These are not alliances of giants but mergers in which global market concentration or domination is the sole aim.

Howard presents four arguments for why he thinks small businesses would become central to the changing economy of countries in the Organization for Economic Cooperation and Development (OECD), such as the USA, Australia, Canada and Germany. His arguments are still plausible today, but they coexist alongside other trends, such as the rise of giga-corporations and global mergers. First, he identifies how small businesses (employing fewer than 500 employees in the USA) have a significant role to play in making major manufacturers more competitive, especially by reducing costs associated with purchases from small-scale suppliers. Second, he argues that size is no longer the critical issue for competitiveness, but instead what is needed is an industrial organization that combines the efficiency of large-scale organizations with the flexibility associated with small businesses. On this point, Howard could well be challenged, but the reality is that many businesses that do not become giga-corporations will have to continue to find ways of being more competitive. Networking is likely to remain a popular option. Howard contends that for the new industrial organization to become a reality, decentralized networks of companies have to be created. Third, along with others, Howard proffers the view that a country's capacity to build strong production or industrial networks is the basis of future competitive advantage (see Chapter 15 and the work of Michael Porter). Howard did not of course have the foresight to anticipate the rise of new economy stock and the bust and boom associated with these businesses in the late 1990s and early 2000s. Nonetheless, Howard merely supports views expressed by others before him (for example Sabel 1990), that collaboration affects other social institutions, such as universities, trade and professional associations, creating a vital and dynamic economy around industrial clusters. This occurs because small businesses generally need assistance with R&D, staff training and technological support for these production networks to work and this gave rise to changes in social institutions (Howard 1990: 88–9, 94; see also Porter 1990; Powell 1996). Fourth, power

relationships are an integral part of explaining a variety of network forms found in different countries involving small businesses.

Supporting these claims, Howard cites an International Labour Organization (ILO) study in 1990 which found that small businesses were becoming increasingly important to new forms of industrial organization. The study discovered that there was a uniform growth in employment in the small business sector in manufacturing in the industrialized world during the mid-1980s, while at the same time there was a corresponding decline in employment growth in large businesses (Sengenberger et al. 1990; also previous discussion). In this vein, it is possible that giga-corporations are not necessarily employment generators, given the ways in which technology is transforming many workplaces and outsourcing grows in importance. Small businesses at the lower end of the 'technology tree' are still likely to be more labour-intensive than large corporations, and this trend is also likely to continue in the twenty-first century. Howard concludes that a new 'economic space' is being created, comprising those small businesses that are close to their markets, technologically dynamic and linked to other companies through networks of production. He found evidence that these network types display differing power relations. The ILO study identifies two dominant forms of power relations, to which Howard adds a third. These are the *kingdom* and *republic* networks (see Sengenberger et al. 1990) and the hybrid network introduced by Howard (1990: 94). Howard designated the Japanese supplier group system as a classical example of the kingdom network, the industrial districts of Europe as republics and Silicon Valley in the US as an example of the hybrid form. He also suggests that networks could be transformed from one form to another.

Kingdom network

A *kingdom network* ties 'small suppliers to a large corporate customer in a vertical supplier chain, under the strategic direction of the large company' (Howard 1990: 94), often called a 'lead company'. The Toyota production system, commonly referred to as a *keiretsu*, involves several tiers of differing degrees of power and dependency in supplier and buyer relationships. The Toyota production system, linking at one time 10,000 subcontractors, has been the most famous example of the *keiretsu* (Buttery et al. 1999: 443). At the top or in the 'first tier' is a 'parent company' responsible for final assembly and below can be found several different levels of specialist subcontractors. Howard (1990: 94) reported that one survey of Japanese subcontractors found that 68 per cent had never changed their 'parent', and 53 per cent had been doing business with the same 'parent' for 15 years or more.

Howard (1990: 94) notes that most studies of the supplier group system present it as little more than a way for big, powerful companies to take advantage of weaker ones, in what often amount to grossly unequal dependency relationships. In these relationships, the smaller businesses are almost totally dependent on 'the parent' who can force their smaller and weaker partners to bear the cost of downturns as well as prioritizing the connections at the various levels to favour those that show the most compliance and long-term commitment. Howard identifies the key defining features of this system as involving the sharing of detailed information about production, costs and techniques between customers and suppliers, joint agreements about sharing savings from cost reductions, and agreed productivity improvements prior to undertaking a job.

Studies cited in Howard's article by the Massachusetts Institute of Technology (MIT) (Womack et al. 1990b; see also 1990a) and the US Congress's Office of Technology Assessment (OTA) (1990) found that kingdom networks were by no means free of problems. Key among these are the 'parent' organization insisting on high quality and continual price reductions that can be enforced because the 'parent' has multiple sources of supply. It can punish suppliers who fail to meet these aforementioned demands by cutting their share of sales in favour of a more compliant competitor. This is confirmed in studies that have found that while relations are supposed to be based on long-term commitments by each partner, they are also dictated by short-term contracts that often require price reductions for renewal (also Hagen and Choe 1998: 4). Mark Scher 1997: 10–11) found in a subsequent study that usually two suppliers are pitted against each other for every component and are expected to absorb the additional costs of production. The MIT and OTA studies also found that wages in the lower tiers of the pyramid were frequently at least 25 per cent below those received by employees of the lead company, where job security for core workers was also higher.

Nonetheless, Howard points out how both studies also found that small businesses benefited from these simultaneously competitive and cooperative relationships. Principally, they gain access to reliable, long-term markets; parent companies lend expensive state-of-the-art equipment to suppliers and often provided financial assistance to purchase such equipment; they provide experts to train staff in small companies to use the equipment; and risks of innovation are spread throughout the system as small companies become more adept at technological adoption (Howard 1990: 96). Howard emphasizes that the Japanese government also had provided a complex array of financial support to small businesses as well financing a national system of innovation that gave

small businesses access to free, public technology extension services, such as testing and research centres, all of which helped to support this form of industrial organization. The *keiretsu* is only one dimension of this system, albeit a significant one.

As Scher (1997) further points out, the *keiretsu*, which is based on feudal and asymmetrical power relations, is dominated at another level by the clan form of cooperation found in the *kigyo shudan*. The latter comprises large businesses that are no longer owned by a holding company, as was the case in pre-World War II with the *zaibatsu*. In the *kigyo shudan,* relations are based on a system of collegial, non-competitive, synergistic behaviours. Three of the biggest of these are Mitsui, Sumitomo and Mitsubishi and, until recently, the *kigyo shudan* heavily depended on the group's trading company or bank to help to develop joint ventures (Scher 1997: 9–10). Some authors still refer to this grouping as a *keiretsu* (Powell 1996; *The Economist* 2000). With the financial crisis continuing in Japan into the early 2000s, considerable restructuring within these powerful networks is supposedly occurring, potentially freeing up companies within them to act more strategically and independently (*The Economist* 2000: 118). These vertically organized groups rotate staff and used to share a strong belief in *kaisha*, the dogma of long-term growth rather than short-term profitability (Scher 1997: 9–10). These beliefs are now contested at least publicly if not privately. The *keiretsu* is an extension of this higher level set of relationships and comprises the vertical agglomeration under the umbrella of a major manufacturer from within the *kigyo shudan* (Scher 1997: 9–10).

The kingdom form of network is not something unique to Japan and has been exported in various forms to other countries, such as the UK and the US. Car manufacturers, such as Nissan for example, had set up a greenfield site in the early 1990s in Newcastle upon Tyne in northern England and created supplier systems similar to those found in Japan. Although there were sharp cultural variations, Nissan specifically favoured the site in Newcastle upon Tyne because the economy was depressed, with high unemployment, *inter alia*, ensuring the ready compliance on the part of small businesses with the new supplier networks, and employees with a strict quality-driven regime of production. However, John Humphrey (1998: 225) notes that in a more volatile market, even Japanese companies have been rethinking the extent to which they want to create strong dependency relationships with their suppliers. He gives an example of how a leading Japanese electrical company operating in Malaysia has deliberately eschewed a preferred supplier strategy, allowing it the freedom to switch to low-cost suppliers if the need arises. Nor does this company encourage its suppliers to go offshore on the basis of long-term contracts because this entails obligations the 'parent' can no longer afford as it increasingly forges 'close enough' relations to replace those involving long-term, high levels of commitment.

Republic network

Howard describes the *republic network* as 'horizontal connections between specialty producers that work together to produce complete components and finished goods (1990: 96). No large organization dominates in terms of giving strategic direction, but rather a 'broker' or 'third-party' agent from a public institution or association provides services and coordination for the network. The key benefits of the republic-type network are that it allows for multiple forms of partnerships, which is discouraged in the kingdom form, and it allows members to cope with rapid change in technology and markets. Where they have been formed with government assistance, such as in Emilia-Romagna, small businesses have been given access to R&D assistance through centres that help with such things as market forecasting, design research and access to new technologies (Howard 1990: 96–7). Howard describes how, in the early 1990s, Emilia-Romagna, a region of north-central Italy, had an economy dominated by 90,000 small manufacturing businesses (that is, employing less than 50 people) linked into a complex web of overlapping networking relationships. These networks are used to build the critical mass needed to expand into world markets and revitalize the industrial base of the region, which even today is highly successful in terms of export performance and wealth creation. Others have observed how, alongside these areas of wealth, impoverished small businesses are also created that are not geographically or socially included in the 'republic' (Powell 1996).

However, Howard notes that, with success, challenges arose to the decentralized structures that characterize the earlier networking arrangements in various industrial districts. The OTA study, for example, found that large companies were coming into industrial regions in Italy, and while decentralized networking persisted, many networks were increasingly coming under the control or influence of these large organizations. Howard concludes that republics could become kingdoms and vice versa (Howard 1990: 100). In terms of the last point, Howard notes that in Tokyo's industrial district of Ota-ku, about 1000 innovative small businesses, employing less than 30 people, were no longer tied to a single parent company. Through government assistance, these small businesses were being encouraged to form cooperative associations to replace their vertical ties with big companies. These

networks, Howard notes, work together on R&D, share knowledge and expertise covering a range of areas, including marketing, and, in the process, substitute a number of the benefits that might once have only been possible from belonging to a kingdom network (Howard 1990: 100). However, as Buttery and Buttery note: 'there is ample evidence in the network literature to suggest that weaker partners (e.g. firms smaller in size, capital or share in network) can be exploited by stronger partners who deliberately set out to dominate the relationship' (Buttery et al. 1999: 442). De Laat also draws attention to how some large firms in the UK have deliberately drawn small businesses into R&D alliances so that they can behave in a 'predatory manner' (de Laat 1997: 168).

The hybrid network

Howard argues that 'new hybrids are growing that explode the distinction between kingdom and republics altogether' (1990: 100). Silicon Valley in the US and particularly successful second-generation small businesses in the semiconductor industry provided Howard with examples of *hybrid networks*. A key defining feature of hybrid networks is that they deal with dominant companies, but these companies do not become 'parents' because tight integration and becoming too dependent on any one business are avoided. Howard suggests that, unlike suppliers in the Japanese supplier networks, the small innovative Silicon Valley businesses have room to manoeuvre because of their technological expertise and capacity to deal with a range of competitors of large companies. He cites the example of Weitek, which employs 230 people and collaborates with Hewlett-Packard (HP) who manufactures Weitek's high-performance chips that can, under agreement, be sold to HP's competitors. Howard argues that this system 'allows businesses to share costs and the risks of innovation' (Howard 1990: 102).

He also notes that while government assistance has not been used to develop this form of networking, regional institutions have played a major part in providing the 'glue' that holds together such a complex competitive and cooperative system. These institutions provide venture capital, market research, PR and consulting. Howard argues that there are national differences that account for these developments and that some countries have programmes and policies, such as Germany, that are likely to encourage more extensive forms of networking, while countries such as the US lag behind. Indeed, during the 1990s, a number of OECD countries introduced networking policies to try to encourage Silicon Valley-type developments, and clustering in particular. Howard's paper points to the fact that power is an integral part of explaining network dynamics and there are quite substantial costs and benefits of networking for all organizations. We need to explore further the complexities of networking and how they differ from other types of business arrangements.

The network as a 'new' organization or institutional form

Walter W. Powell, writing from the *social network* and *institutionalism* perspectives, sought to establish that the network is a distinct organizational form and very different from other organizations, such as those based on markets or hierarchies (or the integrated firm). Networks, he claims, have distinct characteristics or 'traits' and thus represent a unique way of doing business. These forms were based on 'peer group joint decision-making, reciprocal, preferential, mutually supportive actions, trust and informal, extra-contractual agreements' (Ebers and Grandori 1997: 266). We will contrast Powell's perspective with that of Oliver Williamson (1985), who, drawing heavily on *institutional economics* and the *transaction cost* approach, treats the network as an intermediate or

hybrid organizational form in which one is likely to find elements of both markets and hierarchies, but nothing uniquely different, such as a network. From this latter perspective, many forms of cooperation can be included under the term 'network' (Ebers and Grandori 1997: 266).

Powell (1990) is one of the best-known proponents of the view that the network should be treated as a unique organizational form. He basically asks the question: if firms were exchanging things such as know-how, pooling strategically important resources and their relations were long term and recurrent did it still make sense to speak of these entities as separate organizations operating competitively and opportunistically, as the market generally dictates (1990: 301)? Moreover, if these entities are 'held together' by other dynamics, such as obligation, indebtedness, reputation and trust, and their interdependence or reliance on each is so embedded, could these entities still be treated the same as organizations that are under one common ownership (for example the single firm) or legal agreement? Powell argues that the term 'network' is a more appropriate concept for describing relationships that

---

Table 16.3 Powell's comparison of forms of economic organization

Key features	FORMS		
	Market	Hierarchy (vertically integrated firm)	Network
Normative basis	Drive the hardest bargain Contracts – classical and spot Property rights Legal sanctions	Employment relationship One's position in the hierarchy matters most Career mobility Personal advancement	Synergistic strengths Relational contract
Means of communication	Formal, limited within context of exchange	Routines/policies/procedures	Open, relational ties Open communication within the boundaries of the network
Methods of conflict resolution	Haggling – resort to courts for enforcement	Administrative – resort to procedures for solution	Norm of reciprocity – reputational concerns
Degree of flexibility	High – anyone can enter or leave at will	Low, very rigid structure	Medium
Amount of commitment among the parties	Low, individual self-interest, non-cooperative, opportunism	Medium to high	Medium to high
Tone or climate	Precision and/or suspicion	Formal, bureaucratic	Open-ended, mutual benefits
Actor preferences or choices	Independent (arm's length)	Dependent	Interdependent

were not merely the old forms of cooperation, such as many joint ventures, but represented new forms of collaboration (1990: 301; also Bradach and Eccles 1989). Powell is keen to show that the network is a new type of organization with its own form of governance.

In developing the network concept, Powell sought to differentiate it from markets and hierarchies. While he actually never believed there was such a thing as a pure or perfect market or hierarchy, he believes that the activities in networks are sufficiently unique to differentiate them from more traditional forms of business operation. Table 16.3 provides an adapted version of Powell's now famous distinctions between *market*, *hierarchy* and *network*.

The market

Powell (1990: 302) depicts the *market* as a place where opportunistic behaviour and self-interest are the norm, and while this form of behaviour is a key to success in the market, it would not work the same way in networks. In fact, he asserts that those who prosper in markets might well be seen as 'untrustworthy shysters' in the network context. Powell considers the market as a distinct form of business transaction and therefore network relations were unlikely to emerge from market-based relations. In markets, the preferred strategy is to drive a hard bargain, the benefits of the transaction are clear, no trust is required, and the bargain is supported by legal sanctions (Powell 1990: 302). Market transactions are depicted as entailing very limited personal commitment. While the market is open to any player, there are no future attachments necessary, no bonds, just choice, opportunity and flexibility. Communication is simple, price alone decides production and exchange (Powell 1990: 302). In the market situation, Powell says that managers or owners of businesses exercise choice as to when they enter or leave the market, enjoy the flexibility to run their businesses how they see fit, and they are not dependent on others in developing their strategies.

In markets, the classical and spot contracts represent a longer term agreement that determines the actions of both parties as events unfold. These contracts are legally binding and often follow a period of intense negotiation. Typical classical contracts include leasing agreements, works contracts and bank finance agreements. Spot contracts represent the vast majority of contracts used in the business world; they take place at market prices, are based on standard terms and do not require protracted negotiation. However, organizations also engage in spot contracts for their least important expenditure, for example the purchase of stationery. There are numerous situations, however, where the spot

contract is not appropriate and long-term relationships are obligatory, as Powell suggests.

The hierarchy

Hierarchies, on the other hand, emerge when the organization stretches its boundaries and internalizes transactions hitherto conducted in the marketplace, for example canners taking over farming organizations. As Powell puts it, 'the visible hand of management supplants the invisible hand of the market' (1990: 303). In the hierarchy (or integrated firm), the employment contract becomes the basis of stability in relations and so careers are important. Relationships are shaped by previous interactions between players. Interorganizational communication is conducted between players familiar with the business and each other; the parties become dependent on each other. The main characteristics of hierarchical relations, as described by Powell, are shown in Table 16.3. One of the key characteristics of the hierarchy is that people relate to each other in terms of their status and roles or in terms of their positions in the hierarchy. Rewards in this organization flow from the ability to act in predictable and routine ways.

Powell argues, as have many other theorists, that the hierarchical organization was well suited to the demands of mass production and mass distribution, where high volume, standardization and price were critical to economic success (see Chapter 7). Large, vertically integrated organizations, created to control their markets, in order to obtain both resources and distribution, depended on the hierarchical form. It was and is also a highly impersonal form of organization, dominated by rules, regulations and policies.

Inflexibility was and is one of the key features of hierarchies. Most importantly though, this system of administration is seen to be efficient because it is designed to measure and monitor how resources are consumed by the development of controls using complex and detailed systems of reporting and accountability. What is evident from this description is that the hierarchical form of organization (in terms of the integrated firm) is not well suited to conditions of rapid change or sharp fluctuations in markets (Powell 1990: 303). This image of the hierarchical organization, and the one presented in the transaction cost approach discussed below, fails to acknowledge the political and power dimensions present in *all* organizations (see Chapter 6). Mark Granovetter (1985: 504), for example, suggests that the personal desire of CEOs for self-aggrandizement might just as much motivate the acquisition of another firm (that is, a takeover or merger) in a hierarchy, while 'efficiency' is merely the language used to justify such actions.

The network

Powell argues that the *network* involves people looking outside their organization, beyond its boundaries, to form new relationships with other firms in order to secure critical resources. Many traditional theories of the firm (and strategy) had developed from the view that the prime unit of economic activity was the stand-alone business, organized in particular ways (for example monopoly, oligopoly) to dominate its markets. In the network situation, by contrast, standard behaviour is to create long-term obligations through *relational contracts*. Relational contracts are 'tacit agreements between the parties which are enforced not through legal processes, but through the shared needs of the parties to go on doing business with each other' (Kay 1993: 55). The parties agree to forgo the right to pursue their own interest at the expense of the other partner. Powell said it takes time to establish and sustain networks and, as time goes on, knowledge about the partner assists problem solving, while benefits and encumbrances are shared. In short, the 'entangling strings' of reputation, friendship, inter-dependence and altruism become integral parts of the relationship (Powell 1990: 304, citing Macneil 1985). But if ever problems do occur, the strategy is to apply normative rather than legal sanctions, for example threatening to reveal the dishonest behaviour of a partner rather than resorting to legal actions. Ulti-mately, the best insurance against opportunism, according to Powell, is the belief that both parties need a long-term perspective in their relationship and must keep doing business with each other.

Networks, Powell claims, involve 'reciprocal, preferential, mutually supportive actions' (Powell 1990: 304). Powell argues that, in network relations, *dependency* is high on the list of resources of another organization or person, but the advantages of pooling resources are equally high. Once this form of inter-dependence develops, which occurs over a period of time, parties are unable to act on the basis ofself-interest alone or opportunistically. Interdependence also means that they no longer control their own destinies as a stand-alone organization might. Powell believes that the complementary needs of organ-izations provide a solid basis for developing successful production networks (see below). He is less enthusiastic about the long-term viability of competitor networks.

Powell (1990) also believes that networks provide unique opportunities to be competitive because they are more flexible and much more effective in the exchange of 'commodities' whose values are difficult to measure, such as know-how, enhancing technological capabilities or transfer, fostering innovation or experimentation, and sharing valuable information that is not traded readily in the markets or is difficult to extract in hierarchies. He says that networks are best suited to transmitting and learning new knowledge and skills. Powell (1990: 304) suggests that the type of information that is most valued for transmitting and learning new knowledge is more easily accomplished in networks, where personal relations are important and trust is a key factor in how business is conducted. Later he asserted that trust was not something that was chosen or embedded but learned and reinforced through interaction, discussion, debate and dialogue (Powell 1996: 63). In effect, this approach was concerned with what sorts of governance mechanisms were likely to work best under certain conditions of uncertainty and constraint (Oliver and Ebers 1998: 568–9).

'Intermediate' or 'hybrid' form of the network

Transaction costs are associated with an economic exchange, such as the costs of monitoring and enforcing contractual agreements. These 'costs' have been termed *transaction costs* by Williamson (1985). They arise from the fear of opportunism that results when firms specialize in order to capitalize on what they do best and enhance their performance. Three key terms are used by transaction cost theorists: asset specificity; governance structure; and efficiency.

Asset specificity

Transaction cost theorists argue that the fundamentals of economic exchange are built around the costs and benefits that accrue to the owner of a specialized resource. In theory, the benefit to an owner of any specialized resource derives from the fact that he or she should be able to charge more for its use than for a less specialized resource, and this is what leads firms to pursue specialization. However, the more specialized a resource becomes (that is, the greater *asset specificity* it has), the fewer alternative uses it generally has. Asset specificity refers to such things as investment in dedicated equipment or a specialized labour force. Thus the buyer of the specialist resource has a degree of 'hold' over the owner or seller of the specialist resource, who cannot easily change its use or application; for example, IBM had computer chips produced in the Philippines, but the only customer for such specialized chips was IBM. The Philippine workforce and the equipment to produce those chips were totally specialized. The fear of opportunism becomes the cost of such a transaction, which, if uncontrolled, can be destabilizing for the owner of specialized assets. Therefore transaction cost theorists argue that some form of control is called for to provide, at a minimum cost, the mechanisms necessary for parties to believe that engaging or doing business with others in an exchange relationship will make them better off (Williamson 1985).

Governance

In terms of these exchanges, market exchanges can be considered at one end of a continuum, while transaction costs within hierarchies can be considered at the other end of the continuum. According to transaction cost theorists, exchanges that are easy, straightforward or non-repetitive and require no transaction-specific investments are likely to take place in markets (for example leasing agreements, work contracts, finance agreements). This requires hardly any relationships, only very clearly defined, detailed contracts that reduce the flexibility of each party so that they cannot 'cheat' on the other. Transactions that are repetitive, involve uncertainty and are complex, thus requiring transaction-specific investments, are internalized, for example power station design and building. This type of relationship requires the kinds of administrative relationships that exist in hierarchical organizations. As the conditions that favour internalization build up, there is a movement away from markets to internalization within a hierarchy.

According to transaction cost theory, when asset specificity is low, then *market governance* through spot and classical contracts is judged to be the most efficient means of conducting business. The sale of general stationery is conducted via a spot contract, and setting up a loan with a bank is conducted by a classical contract. In these cases, buyers and sellers have alternative options. Conversely, when asset specificity and environmental uncertainty are deemed to be high, organizations ideally operate through the hierarchy (for example a unique, but critical input to a specialized machine, using outsourcing arrangements, however well protected contractually, may still represent a risk the organization is unable to take). Networks fall somewhere in between, but are not uniquely different. Therefore what theorists such as Williamson (1985) are saying is that the degree of asset specificity and levels of uncertainty will determine the most efficient governance structure.

Efficiency

The key to *efficiency* in the transaction cost approach is to match a governance structure with the level of asset specificity and uncertainty. If an organization fails to do this it can be costly (Hennart 1988). Examples of costs are loss of market discipline where a business pays too much for a component part, or being cheated because the business has not contractually safeguarded its transaction. Transaction cost theory is built around the assumption that competitive economic behaviour is based on the pursuit of self-interest, but also opportunism, guile and deceit. Individuals are portrayed as subtle and devious creatures operating in predictable, rational ways. According to Williamson's views (1985), *malfeasance* is portrayed as the norm in the marketplace. Indeed, one of the key assumptions in the transaction cost approach is that decision makers have limited information (bounded rationality) and might pursue their self-interest with incomplete or misleading information disclosure (that is, engage in opportunism) (see also Chapter 14).

Transaction cost theorists view hierarchies as an efficient, impersonal means by which to curb malfeasance and opportunism beyond market transactions. Hierarchies are deemed efficient in curbing opportunism because management is in control of all decision making. These theorists see no significant role for personal or social relations either in helping to build trust or curbing malfeasance and opportunism, even in networks (Granovetter 1985: 490–1). While Williamson (1991, 1993) has acknowledged that trustworthy behaviour can extend into market relations, and such things as a business's reputation for fairness might be an important asset, he maintains that transactions based on personal relations are the exception rather than the rule in the way business is or ought to be conducted. In such explanations, trust does not figure because it is either subsumed by calculated self-interest or, if it is present, it is usually in the form of blind trust that does not guarantee survival in the market or hierarchy (Lane 1998: 6–10; Nooteboom, 2000: 919). This view of behaviour is referred to as an 'undersocialized view' that is in stark contrast to a more socially embedded view of behaviour (Lane 1998: 6).

Embeddedness of networks

Transaction cost theory has been heavily criticized for presenting the behaviour of markets and hierarchies as though social aspects of relationships, and the contexts in which they occur, have no part to play in explaining business and organizational practices. Therefore, personal relations are seen as irrational forms of behaviour, while self-interest and opportunism are 'plainly' more sensible and prevalent (Granovetter 1985: 506). Mark Granovetter argues that the transaction cost approach ignores the *embeddedness* of these forms of economic activity in social and cultural milieux (Granovetter 1985: 490; Powell 1990: 299; Grabher 1993; Nooteboom 2000: 919). Granovetter's work is important in focusing on the concepts of sociability and social capital (Portes 1998) in networking theory. He emphasizes the role of friendly association and the pleasure people derive from social interaction as important for building trust in economic exchanges. Thus, while transaction cost approaches would argue that one incentive in the marketplace for not cheating is the cost of damage this might cause one's reputation, the embeddedness approach suggests that we establish the reputation of a person or business not just on the basis of some general economic motive (for example an owner of a business not cheating because it will damage his or her reputation), but also through social processes (as also mentioned by Powell above). For example, this might occur by what some trusted person might have to say about his or her experiences with the person or business in question, or preferably, our past dealings with the business in question.

In other words, Granovetter contends that social relations create strong expectations and knowledge about trust and helps to curb opportunistic behaviour in dealings with others (Granovetter 1985: 490–1). Granovetter, who is a staunch critic of the transaction cost approach, asserts that the social or more personal nature of trust-based relations also creates opportunities for malfeasance, such as cheating, confidence rackets, fraud, kickbacks and so on (Granovetter 1985: 493). However, unlike transaction cost theory, the embeddedness approach does not suggest that malfeasance is the norm – context and social relations play an important part in explaining all transactions (see Introduction). In other words, the relational dimension of networking is important in explaining how risks are managed in networking by the development of social capital and particularly trust. We now turn to the topic of social capital and trust dynamics to explore further the issues of embeddedness.

Social capital and trust dynamics

There are very specific problems facing those networks in which knowledge, which comprises one or all of the partners' core competencies (see Chapter 15), is traded or exchanged. Broadly speaking, many networks involve different forms of learning (see Levinson and Asahi 1995), but the focus on the *learning network* is on the trading of tacit knowledge (also see Chapter 14) and particular forms of intellectual capital. Powell's work has already alluded to the importance of *social capital*, with his emphasis on networks being most useful for transmitting and learning new knowledge and trading sensitive information. Powell (1990: 304) suggests that the type of information that is most valued for transmitting and learning new knowledge is more easily accomplished in networks, where personal relations are important and trust is a key factor in how business is conducted. Granovetter raised the importance of the embeddedness of network relations and the social basis of these interactions. We now want to explore more closely the link between social capital

and the learning network and how interorganizational learning can enhance an organization's *core competence* (Doz 1989; Hamel 1991; Parkhe 1991; Levinson and Asahi 1995; Dyer and Singh 1996, 1997; Lei 1997; Lütz 1997; Nahapiet and Ghoshal 1998; Nooteboom 2000). To do this we need to explore in more detail the notion of social capital. There are four key ideas invoked in discussions of social capital and networking: sociability; reputation; reciprocity; and trust.

Sociability

The distinguished sociologist Alejandro Portes makes the claim that there is nothing new about the concept of *social capital*, and the notion of *sociability* from whence it derives (Portes 1998: 1; also Gray 1999). He argues that sociologists have long studied it in their efforts to understand how involvement in groups can have both positive and negative consequences for individuals and communities. However, according to Portes, what is distinctive about the repackaging of the concept in the 1990s is the almost exclusive focus on the positive outcomes of sociability, ignoring its negative consequences. In terms of networking theory, the concept has been extended to explain how non-monetary forms of exchange, which are intangible and based on social relations, can be important in building human capital and gaining a sustainable advantage over competitors (for example Nahapiet and Ghoshal 1998). According to Portes, it has also been applied inappropriately to explain a whole range of social problems within capitalist societies when the concept was never meant to be used in such a general way, but restricted to community and familial associations (Portes 1998, citing Putnam 1993; but also see Fukuyama 1995; and more recently OECD 2001).

In Portes's view, three theorists in particular have profoundly influenced contemporary debates about social capital and sociability, and these we contend also apply to networking theory. He credits Pierre Bourdieu (1985) with having produced one of the most theoretically refined approaches to the topic (Portes 1998: 1–2). Bourdieu (1985: 248) described social capital as 'the aggregate of actual and potential resources which are linked to possession of a durable network of more or less institutionalized relationships of mutual acquaintance or recognition'. In this context, Bourdieu is referring to institutions such as the family, schools and those formed through bonds of friendship rather than those found within businesses or other economic organizations. Thus, for Bourdieu, two elements define social capital: social relationships that give access to resources and the quality of those resources. Both of these he felt constitute the major benefits of participating in a group and constructing sociability. Bourdieu also acknowledges that transactions involving social capital involve many uncertainties and unknowns, such as unspecified obligations that cannot be easily measured, uncertain time horizons for repaying favours and potential violations of reciprocity. When contrasted against economic exchanges, where money and other hard assets are traded, there is a distinct lack of clarity in respect of how one builds social capital and sociability in general (Portes 1998: 2).

Portes believes that Glen Loury (1977, 1981), an economist, provides another important dimension to understanding social capital by showing that social connections and different contexts add another layer to how sociability limits opportunities and access to resources that can change a person's life chances. Loury did not specifically deal with the concept of social capital but his studies on the effects of race, on access to important social connections affecting intergenerational social mobility, were taken up by other theorists. Portes credits Loury with paving the way for James Coleman's (1988, 1990) exposition of the relationship between social and human capital.

According to Portes, Coleman is responsible 'for relabelling of a number of different and even contradictory processes as social capital' (Portes 1998: 2). Coleman's definition of social capital is broad, positing the latter as entailing a variety of entities that are embodied in social structures and facilitate certain actions by actors (Coleman 1988: S98; Coleman 1990: 302). In Portes's view (1998: 2), this rather vague definition allowed Coleman to define social capital in a number of ways, such as: *mechanisms* that generate social capital (reciprocity, expectations, enforcement of norms); *consequences* of possessing social capital (for example privileged access to information); and the *appropriable social organization* that provides the context for both the sources and consequences to materialize. The term 'appropriable' refers to networks being created for one purpose turning out to serve another, as might a professional network in giving not only status but also openings to, say, political office, as in the case certain professions. Portes, however, finds Coleman's approach weak, inasmuch as it obscures the difference between resources themselves and the ability to obtain them through membership in different social structures, as highlighted by Bordieu and Loury. For Portes, it is also important to differentiate between the motives of those who seek to gain valuable resources through relationships mediated by social capital and those of the donors who are prepared to enter into these more indeterminate forms of exchange.

Strength of strong ties and strength of weak ties

Portes suggests that where Coleman really advances the concept of social capital is by pointing out how its development is contingent upon the *strength of ties* between members of a social grouping (Portes 1998: 3). Coleman uses the term *closure* to describe the existence of sufficiently dense ties between certain people to guarantee that the norms of reciprocity and sanctions against violations would minimize malfeasance and reduce the need for legal contracts in facilitating certain transactions (Coleman 1988: S99, cited in Portes 1998: 3). As Portes points out, the debate about social capital has led to two competing views regarding the nature of closure. The first position, as championed by Coleman and indirectly by Loury, suggests that dense networks that can enforce normative control and sanctions are necessary for the emergence of social capital and are important as a resource (Portes 1998: 3,6). This view had been dubbed *the strength of strong ties* position in earlier studies. Opposing this view are theorists such as Ronald Burt (1992, cited in Portes 1998: 3, 6) and Granovetter who argue that weak network ties are critical for building social capital. Burt coins the term *structural holes* to capture this aspect of social capital formation by stressing that dense networks are more tradition and rule-bound, while networks showing a relative paucity of ties allow for new sources of knowledge and resources to become available and are therefore likely to be more innovative and better able to promote social mobility. Granovetter (1974, cited in Portes 1998: 6) introduces the term *strength of weak ties* to argue that informal relationships outside the family and close friends provide valuable sources of access and opportunities, such as employment referrals or business leads, and are just as important in terms of social capital formation. These two contested views of social capital formation reveal how sociability can create pressures for integration and control that can be of benefit but can also act to stifle innovation and flexibility and reduce the capacity to forge new ties. It very much captures the notion of the inclusive and exclusiveness of groups and the rules they develop to enforce or minimize closure.

Portes identifies four negative consequences of social capital, and at least three of these can be extended to IORs and networking. Each of the negatives can also be cast in terms of benefits as well, hence his claim that sociability is a 'mixed blessing'. First, he cites the problem of exclusion of outsiders (especially when ties are strong) and this is evidenced in networks that are formed along ethnic or cultural lines, such as shown above with the Japanese *keiretsu*, which excludes many businesses from joining, but also makes it hard for new ideas or practices to be adopted. Second, closure or strong ties might also lead to excessive claims on group members, so that in cases where family or clan-based relations, for example, are the basis of network formation, as found in China, the network might have to provide all sorts of 'social welfare' and other support to extended family members at the expense of growing a successful business. Third, strong ties can create pressures for conformity and exert strong social controls on members, restricting autonomy and privacy and, in the process, quelling innovation and change.

Fourth, going beyond these network forms to clusters, Portes (1998: 9–10) criticizes the celebratory versions of social capital, particularly how some theorists have applied the term to the development of 'civicness' or civil society in towns, cities and even nations (Portes citing Putnam 1993). Portes complains that not only have theorists taken the concept out of its original theoretical groundings, but have used it to explain civic virtue in terms of its effects rather than causes or what gives rise to it. Thus, towns or cities that display civic virtues and a stock of social capital, such as Emilia-Romagna described above, are described as having certain social institutions in place that lead to civicness, but these institutions and their functions are also invoked to explain the outcomes of civicness. Portes's analysis and exposition of the theories of social capital provides valuable insights into the theoretical tradition in which notions of social capital, and associated concepts such as reciprocity and trust, have emerged in networking theories.

Reciprocity and trust

Portes notes that the undersocialized view of human behaviour found in economics presents social capital in terms of the 'accumulation of obligations from others according to the norms of reciprocity' (Coleman 1990; Lane 1998; Portes 1998: 4). The notion of *reciprocity* is a complex one and Portes links it to the concept of *enforceable trust*. There are two senses in which enforceable trust can give a meaning to the idea of reciprocity. First, enforceable trust arises when transactions are embedded in common social structures where a collectivity, rather than individuals, allows for donors of gifts (for example benefactors donating scholarships to, say, indigenous high school students) to receive returns from others in the form of status, honour or approval (for example some public form of recognition). Second, the collectivity also acts as the 'policing force' by providing 'guarantees' (for example sanctions, threats of ostracism and so on) that debts (in this case, meeting the conditions of the scholarship) are honoured by the recipient (Portes 1998: 4). It is the social embeddedness of actors which allows enforceable trust to become a valuable source of social capital formation and reciprocity to work in the place of more formal mechanisms such as classical legal contracts. These same concepts are also used in network theories.

According to Powell (1990, 1996), reciprocity and trust actually define networks as distinct forms of organization (Powell 1990: 304). For Powell, however, reciprocity involves notions of *indebtedness* and *obligation*, rather than enforceable trust as described above. Drawing on the work of Marcel Mauss (1967/1925; also see Chapter 6; also Zucker 1986: 61) on 'gift giving', Powell identifies reciprocity as the basis of creating long-term commitments in network relations between individuals. The obligations to give, receive and return are important in creating a sense of mutual interest and setting standards of behaviour that disavow self-interest or opportunism and build trust. There is a sense here in which trust and sociability are in a circular relationship, one feeding off the other. Long-term commitments, he says, help to bring a sense of security and stability into relations that will facilitate the sharing of proprietary knowledge, sensitive or confidential information and make partners more open and better able to learn from each other so that new opportunities can be exploited (also Lane 1998: 20). Powell believes that in other, more instrumental or calculating relations, such as those found in markets and hierarchies, reciprocity is based on obligations that involved rough equivalents or notions of *equivalent exchange* – 'returning ill for ill and good for good' (Powell 1990: 304) – and making sure that one's self-interest is protected.

One major area of debate surrounds how trust develops in relationships that have to be created between strangers and/or people from different parts of the world, and perhaps where these relations are brokered by consultants, banks or legal organizations (Shapiro 1987; Lane 1998). In grappling with these issues, Peter Smith Ring (1997a) has drawn a distinction between *fragile trust* and *resilient trust*. Both concepts are associated with the willingness to take risks and make oneself vulnerable in a relationship but the former assumes low levels of embeddedness while resilient trust, which encourages the highest level of risk taking and learning, assumes high levels of social embeddedness. An underlying assumption is that trust is not something that develops only among friends or is based on personal relations (that is, always socially embedded), but can grow from a very fragile base through repeated encounters (also Lane 1998: 21).

Fragile trust

Ring maintains that fragile trust can be present in networking relations, especially in the early stages of setting up a network, and has been evident in more traditional forms of cooperation, such as joint ventures where certain forms of sensitive information must be revealed, even the fact that a businesses is looking for a new partner. Fragile trust (or *calculative trust* in some approaches) is found in many economic exchanges (for example relying on classical contracts, non-disclosure agreements), and is not deeply embedded in social relations where a hand shake or one's word might be good enough for trusting someone. It involves the underlying assumption that people will act opportunistically and in self-interested ways (Ring and Van de Ven 1994; de Laat 1997; Ring 1997a: 120), and where revealing or transferring sensitive information or secrets to a partner must be done in a protective and formal way. However, it does not preclude people moving on from relationships based solely on fragile trust to those based on more resilient forms of trust, where, over time, with repeated transactions and encounters, reputations are developed for complying with norms, rules and contracts and track records of performance are built up in gradual stages (de Laat 1997; Lane 1998: 21; Ring 1997a: 127). Nor does it exclude the fact that fragile trust can invite political behaviour and power plays because opportunism and struggles to control or limit dependency remain important.

Fragile trust typically relies on such things as formal contractual agreements, hedging bets with guarantees and safeguards, including recourse to courts, mediators and arbitrators to settle the terms of an exchange. De Laat (1997) also maintains the distinction between fragile and resilient trust and suggests that when organizations conduct their network business on the basis of classical contracts alone they are really signalling distrust that can end up spiralling into greater distrust (also Lane 1998: 23). He argues that organizations that enter into classical contractual agreements do so to specify in minute detail all the conditions of the exchange, with the aim of trying to control completely the partner or partners. He says this usually encourages partners to find 'loopholes' or breach the contract in any way because it is so restrictive that its terms and conditions are hard to meet (de Laat 1997: 163–4). So while these types of contracts might signal some form of trust, they are inherently biased towards creating distrust.

The notion of fragile trust recognizes that many business transactions are not socially embedded and social capital formation is weak, hence enforceable trust mechanisms are absent and other trust-based mechanisms need to be developed. Ring argues that economic exchanges are usually imbued with elements of fragile trust, while social exchanges, which are important in networks, depend more on resilient trust. He suggests that economic actors rely on more than one form of trust and it is erroneous to assume that market-based relations cannot transform into network ones, although he sees this as a very difficult thing to achieve. He argues that in all transactions there are three distinct formal phases: negotiation, transactions (for example laying out expectations and obligations, revealing strategies and sharing sensitive information and so on)

and administration (monitoring how obligations and so on are honoured) (also Child 1998). The formal processes are mediated by informal processes that either help to build social capital or make it very difficult to do so. Resilient trust presupposes social exchange as the basis of networking.

Resilient trust

The processes that create both fragile and resilient trust are embedded in *informal social processes,* which Ring says are universal in nature. These are, first, basic human motivations (also described in Chapter 9 as the search for identity, facticity and inclusion), second, sense making and forming new identities that give rise to different modes of learning, third, developing new forms of understandings (including ways of communicating), and lastly, committing or establishing psychological contracts (Ring 1997a: 134–8). Resilient trust, as defined by Ring (1997a: 121–2), specifically identifies social capital, and the strength of strong ties, as being highly conducive for such forms of trust to emerge (Ring 1997a: 127). His approach does not acknowledge the 'negative' sides of social capital outlined by Portes, but he does point out some of the problems such forms of sociability create for networking across different ethnic and cultural groups, countries and regions (also see below). Ring believes that it is far more difficult to engage in sense making and learning, understanding and committing when large networks are formed with people from different cultures, nation states or industries because so much more has to be made sense of, learnt and understood before trust alone influences the conduct of business. He does not mention how this might have a gender dimension as well. In other words, trust is highly contingent and contextual. He believes that trust of varying sorts can develop in networks that lack high levels of social capital but that this will not easily translate into resilient trust (Zucker 1986: 63; Ring 1997a: 136–8). However, between fragile and resilient trust are a whole range of other forms of trust-based relations and mechanisms used to 'oil' relationships and, as Christel Lane (1998: 4, 21, 23) points out, there is really no agreement on whether trust can be intentionally created or whether it is socially embedded. What generally emerges are various combinations of trust, and very different levels of explanation, with the social side often reduced in importance (Wekselberg 1996).

For Ring, the notion of resilient trust is based on the experiences a person has of having successfully completed transactions in the past with others, and how successful these were in establishing norms of equity and reciprocity (1997a: 128). Equity or fairness in this context means cooperating or collaborating on the basis that some time in the future proportional benefits from the exchange will be received.

Reciprocity, in the context of resilient trust, means that there is an accepted and demonstrated moral obligation on the part of those involved in a network to give back to all members some fair return for the investment they have made. It is based on the assumption that goodwill or the moral integrity of others counts when greater risks and sacrifices are being sought and the network form is where these types of relationships can be best transacted (Lane 1998: 22). This comes closer to Portes' notion of enforceable trust but in Ring's approach, dyadic relations or those between two individuals is the main level of analysis and hence builds on the concept of *personal trust*.

Elsewhere, Ring (1997b), as well as others (see Lane 1998; Rousseau et al. 1998), acknowledges that the dominance of the transaction cost approach in networking has meant that the more *affective* and *emotional* aspects of IORs have been played down or underemphasized, yet these also help to create trusting relations (also Lewis and Weigert 1985; Misztal 1996; Lane 1998: 6). For example, he says that the sheer fact that people actually come to like or even love each other, and care for others in a network relationship, can go a long way in building deeper commitments than those based on resilient or fragile trust (Ring 1997b: 9). He also says that this strong emotional connection is likely to lead to very different types of learning occurring than is traditionally discussed in network theory. It is likely to be based on greater empathy for others and developing a better understanding of oneself as well as the values, ideas, fears and concerns of others. In Chapter 1 we associated this type of learning with reflexive practice. Ring gives an example of a joint venture between NASA in the USA and 3M, both of whom had had no prior business involvements but built their IORs on the emotional bonds between people (all males) rather than trust as a prerequisite. The project was focused on the commercial use of outer space. It was the genuine liking and bonding between two of the key players from the respective organizations that eventually pushed the project and the joint venture ahead, even when there was opposition to it in both organizations at the very highest levels. Barbara Misztal (1996: 19–21) actually argues that sociability is only one way of forming trust relations and intimacy or civility are two others, but that all social relationships are imbued with different degrees and types of trust, including distrust (see Chapter 9 for a more extended discussion of dimensions of trust).

Trust and power

Personal trust and emotional bonds are often claimed to be the foundations for building sound networks (for example Buttery and Buttery 1994). But the reality is more complicated because many IORs in the West bring together complete strangers. Often networks involve people from different backgrounds, cultures and genders, who have no history of positive or prior interactions (Hardy et al. 1996: 9, 1998: 70). Moreover, the length of time involved in establishing networks also means that different people become involved at different stages of development or leave during the life of a joint project or venture. In network arrangements that have few partners (that is, are dyadic or triadic) this might not be a problem, but in international consortia, for example, relying on personal trust is unlikely to be possible and other forms of trust are likely to emerge (Zucker 1986; Shapiro 1987).

Theorists from within the neo-institutionalism perspective (an offshoot of institutionalism described in Table 16.2) place a much greater emphasis on power in explaining the nature of trust-based relations. Instead of looking at trust and sociability in terms of its integrative or regulative functions, they contend that trust needs to be differentiated from façades of trust where power and conflict can 'stimulate or simulate 'high trust' relations' (Reed 2001, citing Hardy et al. 1998: 65; also 1996). In fact, they claim that any notion of trust that does not draw this distinction will fail to account for how people take risks when they trust in someone or feel they have no choice but to do so because of unequal dependency relations. Power relations, they say, vary across different contexts and situations (Hardy et al. 1996: 4–5, 1998: 67) and there is a significant difference between 'cooperation achieved through power differentials that render some partners unable to engage in opportunistic behaviour, and a willingness to voluntarily sacrifice the benefits of opportunistic behaviour in order to cooperate with a trusted partner' (Hardy et al. 1996: 6).

Hardy et al. (1996, 1998) argue that trust is based on developing shared meanings between partners about what trust stands for. This form of trust is based on reciprocal communication that disavows any form of communication used to create unequal dependency relations or exploit a power position (Hardy et al. 1998: 71). In a similar vein to Ring, they argue that meanings are established in language, and the conversation and the talk that goes on between different actors provide the ritual contexts for developing shared understandings and a common language to make sense of the world. Hardy et al. (1996: 10, 1998) believe that trust arises by people trying to invoke a sense of a common or shared reality that creates a level of predictability and provides opportunities for participation in communicative processes that help to build goodwill and reciprocity. Trust is a myth created by people to signal some common understandings about membership of a group and the protocols and practices acceptable to them. The myth of trust only works for those who accept or share the meanings of the group and it facilitates information sharing, informal interactions and other forms of social actions that can be 'read' as signalling trust. Predictability and goodwill are not, however, without problems.

Creating common myths or identities is complicated when symbolic meanings (or symbols used to signal trust) are not shared or trust itself has no significant meaning to a group, such as in cross-cultural networking (Zucker 1986; Child 1998). And there is no guarantee that when actors try to create common meanings, this process will not be dominated or 'hijacked' by those who can manipulate meanings for their own vested interests, with the intention of consolidating the power of one person or group over another (Hardy et al. 1996: 13, 1998). Hardy et al. (1996, 1998) describe situations in which manipulation occurs where truth and sincerity are deliberately distorted so that what is communicated by one partner to another involves deceptions that hide one partner's attempt at consolidating power. In so doing, the manipulator tries to ensure predictability and the 'guarantee' of a desired outcome. He or she eliminates the risk of developing goodwill in a relationship and genuine synergies in order to ensure that a calculated (highly predictable) outcome is achieved. Manipulation reduces risks for the manipulator and allows asymmetrical power relationships to form the bases of cooperation (Hardy et al. 1998: 81–3). Thus, meanings are deliberately distorted to weaken another, making it hard to assume one ever knows who is truly trustworthy. The authors identify other façades of trust. The discussion of power and manipulation brings us back to Granovetter's earlier point that the belief in trust opens up enormous opportunities for people to manipulate it for their own ends. Indeed, studies have identified instances where apparent trust-based relationships, rather than being enhanced over time, have eroded, only to be replaced by abuse of power and intense distrust (de Laat 1997). We take up the problem of trust in more detail in relation to the idea of the learning network and explore further how power is likely to be a factor in most forms of IORs involving highly competitive situations.

Interorganizational learning (IOL)

The impetus for engaging in IOL varies among organizations and, as Larsson et al. (1998: 285) point out, the majority of the literature on the topic focuses on how organizations either can be 'good partners' or 'race to outlearn' their partners and exploit them in the process. They suggest that these two dilemmas are played out in varying degrees across strategic alliances (their focus of study) and give rise to a number of different possibilities from outright competition to genuine collaboration. However, they believe that the key to understanding IOL is to recognize that these forms of IORs are all potentially affected by several key factors: partners' lack of motivation to fully commit to this type of partnership; the inability to absorb or communicate knowledge between partners; and the potential for power, opportunism and suspicion to dominate exchanges. These build distrust and impede collective knowledge development and information transfer. Citing a number of classic studies in the field (for example Hamel 1991; Doz 1996), Larsson et al. (1998) point to the inherent dangers of 'good partner' strategies in IOL and the high risk of being cheated on by others. They identify competitive intent, low transparency (openness) and receptivity (potential to absorb new knowledge) as significantly affecting how collective learning and knowledge sharing occurs among partners, and help to a large extent to account for less successful experiences in IOL. In order to explore the dynamics of IOL further, we will look more closely at several key ideas introduced earlier in the text, starting with the notion of *strategy* and *core competence*, *tacit* and *explicit knowledge*, as well as introducing the concept of *credible commitments*.

Core competence

In Chapter 15 we introduced the resource-based view of strategy and the argument that in order to maintain competitive advantage, different types of organization-specific resources, such as skills and capabilities, particularly know-how, can be enhanced through, *inter alia*, cooperation and collaboration across organizations (Lei 1997: 209). In the case of SMEs and micro-businesses, knowledge acquisition and transfer, which is often taken for granted in many large organizations, is only possible through cooperation and collaboration, and the network becomes a rare source of knowledge diffusion for these small businesses (Reve 1995: 10). David Lei (citing Prahalad and Hamel 1990) suggests that all organizations can build or enhance their core competence by working across the boundaries of the organization. In very simple terms, core competencies are 'a bundle of firm-specific knowledge, skills, technological capabilities and an organization that form the basis of the firm's ability to create value in ways that other competitors cannot do easily' (Lei 1997: 211). As Lei points out, core competencies are dependent on different types and forms of knowledge being learnt by people over many years as they enhance their skills, adapt to change, experiment with new technologies and applications or gather information and organizational intelligence. Core competencies are interwoven into the 'social fabric' of the organization, where they are largely 'invisible' and 'embedded' in the daily routines and practices of the organization and the complex social relations of people who work in it (Lei 1997: 211). In effect, an organization's core competence is *context-specific*, or embedded, and is therefore hard to imitate or even fully communicate.

Core competence can be both the source of advantage over competitors as well as a disadvantage for the organization. Lei (1997: 211–12) argues that because knowledge accumulation occurs over long periods of time, an organization's capabilities, and hence its future directions, are constrained by what it has done and learnt in the past. Management is constrained by the types of information and knowledge it has invested in over the years, including the people employed to build an organization's core competence. Each organization also develops a unique core competence, whether this turns out to be adequate or inadequate to sustain a competitive advantage. In effect, core competencies are *idiosyncratic* because they are built through unique organizational relations, practices, routines and discourses. In this sense, every organization has to live with its own history, culture, politics, past decisions and circumstances, which collectively 'act' as an 'irreversible' investment in the future. No organization can totally reinvent itself or start over again from scratch.

'Lock in' and 'lock out'

In developing their core competencies, organizations can gain advantage from 'lock in', which means they have learnt skills and knowledge that are usually highly specialized, likely to be sustainable for a while and are also untradable. Something that is untradable is hard to value in dollar terms, difficult to sell and often indecipherable to outsiders. The intellectual capital of an organization comprises what many would describe as an untradable 'asset'. To understand what constitutes another organization's core competence, an outsider would have to understand fully, and have 'access' to, the whole repertoire of skills and knowledge embedded in an organization's dynamic routines, practices, politics, culture and the multiple and complex relations that bind people to the organization (Levinson and Asahi 1995; Lei 1997: 212). Without the capacity to learn and change, an organization and its people are unable to get ahead of competitors or even keep up with them and thus become incapable of influencing the environment in which they have to compete or operate (Lei 1997: 212). 'Lock in' gives an organization the advantage of being able to search out and find new ways of building or redefining its competencies and knowledge base.

However, the downside of developing an organization's core competence is that it also creates the potential danger of 'lock out'. Lei argues that this happens when an organization is unable to change and/or build new competencies because it has become so dependent on what it has done in the past, usually very successfully, and has invested heavily in certain resources, routines and practices that lock it into a hopeless future. An organization and its management can become incapable of redeploying or reacquiring highly specialized and non-tradable 'assets'. Lei gives the example of the US consumer electronics industry in the 1970s which failed to invest in new skills and technologies, such as miniaturization and automated production (for example CAD/CAM and robotics), that became the bases of the next generation of televisions, VCRs, multimedia equipment and compact disc technologies (Lei 1997: 213).

Organizations therefore need to develop both an organization-specific core competence (that is, they need to 'lock in') as well as ensuring that they avoid the traps of being 'locked out' to such an extent that they lose all their capacity to assimilate new technologies, knowledge and skills in their field. One way of trying to protect against 'lock out' is to enter into cooperative and collaborative arrangements with other organizations through a process of IOL. While an organization's management can invest in their own R&D and undertake a whole range of activities, such as continuous improvement, poaching employees from competitors and developing new products and processes, the evidence from the literature suggests that most innovations in products, processes and technology emerge from sources external to the organization. By copying or importing ideas and practices learnt from suppliers, competitors and customers, for example, many organizations are able to innovate in their own right (Dyer and Singh 1996, 1997: 9; Lei 1997). However, networking is a way of trying to develop superior interorganizational knowledge-sharing routines and practices that can help to accelerate the innovation process, reduce costs and speed up the commercialization of products (Dyer and Singh 1996, 1997: 10; de Laat 1997; Lei 1997: 215).

Despite evidence indicating that most innovations come from external influences, and not from internal R&D and intellectual capital, the fact remains that organizations are reluctant to cooperate or collaborate in areas that are strategically important to them in developing what they define as their core competence and their distinct competitive advantage (Lütz 1997: 222). Those organizations that do so, qualify as learning networks, but not necessarily successful ones. For organizations that operate under conditions of uncertainty (for example rapidly changing markets, technology or customer demand) and have complex, knowledge-intensive products (for example large numbers of interdependent components, functions or processes), there is high value and urgency associated with 'non-contractible' activities such as innovation, flexibility, responsiveness and knowledge sharing. These organizations in particular have to find ways of sharing and acquiring knowledge through relational exchanges and IOL (Dyer and Singh 1996, 1997: 30–1; see also Powell 1990).

Tacit and explicit knowledge

Networking involves two key strategies that can enhance an organization's core competence in the context of IOL, and this occurs principally through knowledge sharing and building up complementary resource endowments, as described above in the discussion of complementary networks (Dyer and Singh 1996, 1997). As we mentioned in Chapter 14, there are two kinds of knowledge that are seen as having strategic importance in organizations: *tacit knowledge* (those things which are incommunicable) and *explicit knowledge* (those things which are or can be codified), and managers are most reluctant to trade or exchange tacit knowledge (Polanyi 1967; Boisot 1995). These two forms of knowledge are described in Exhibit 16.7. This categorization is one of several, with a more recent one including four dimensions (see Chapter 14), with a specific focus on social tacit knowledge and social explicit knowledge in order to differentiate between the type of knowledge and intellectual capital that individuals possess as distinct from that which is socially embedded in what becomes viewed as

collective knowledge (Nahapiet and Ghoshal 1998). When considering the issue of IOL and enhancing core competence, organizations are likely to try to trade in all forms of knowledge sharing and building of intellectual capital, but the hardest of these would be those knowledge routines and practices that are embedded.

As mentioned in Chapter 14, tacit knowledge refers to know-how, while explicit knowledge is said to embody information that is written down, encoded, explained and understandable by any one with some expertise in a specific field. Tacit knowledge, by contrast, is 'sticky', complex and difficult to codify, interpret and understand (see Dyer and Singh 1996, 1997: 10–11; Lei 1997: 213–14). Moreover, tacit knowledge is context-specific or embedded in organizational routines, practices and relationships, and is part of sense making that draws on various forms of knowledge and experiences (see Chapters 1 and 14). When Apple Computers, for example, was designing the first Macintosh computer, one of the metaphors that drove the design team was that the computer was to make people feel 'warm and fuzzy'. The Macintosh design team flew the 'Jolly Roger' pirate flag over its building to symbolize that they were the 'bad kids' of the company who were allowed to break rules. They were also incredibly selective in who they allowed into the team and in a sense created extremely powerful social tacit knowledge that was dependent on the collectivity and its unique social dynamics (Spender 1996 cited in Nahapiet and Ghoshal 1998).

Tacit knowledge is embodied or captured in organizational discourses and, as we described in

---

Exhibit 16.7 Tacit and explicit knowledge

Tacit knowledge	Explicit knowledge
❏ Unwritten know-how	❏ Blueprints for design
❏ Ways of solving problems	❏ All forms of formulae
❏ Imagination, creativity	❏ Technical specifications
❏ Craftsmanship	❏ Training manuals
❏ Artisan-like skills	❏ Circuit patterns
❏ Metaphors	❏ Steps in a manufacturing process
❏ Myths and stories	❏ Specifications
❏ Symbols	❏ Best practice benchmarks
❏ Discourses	❏ Industry standards

Source: Adapted and modified from David Lei (1997) 'Competence-building, technology fusion and competitive advantage: The key roles of organizational learning and strategic alliances', *International Journal of Technology Management,* **14**(2/3/4), p. 213.

Chapter 14, these provide the descriptions, rules, permissions and limits of actions of groups, such as a project team, and individuals. In other words, discourses give expression and meaning to power in particular contexts and actions. It is no surprise then that there is considerable debate in the management literature as to whether or not tacit knowledge is something organizations can 'manage', control or direct in any purposeful way. Knowledge, whether described as tacit or explicit, individual or social, is not neutral and is influenced by power, and what is defined as tradable or shareable, or even valued as knowledge, depends on how particular discourses operate across different organizations.

Tacit knowledge is context-specific and comprises different texts and genres (see Chapter 14), and is therefore difficult to learn, copy or imitate in arm's length relationships. So organizations look to networks and strategic alliances to achieve these ends. Lei maintains that core competencies rest on organizations developing both forms of knowledge, but it is tacit knowledge that gives an organization its dynamic routines and practices, both of which are so important to innovation and change. Indeed, he says that managers who build their core competence on explicit knowledge are not building a sustainable core competence (Lei 1997: 215; see also Chapter 14). Irrespective of patents, almost everything involving explicit knowledge can be copied.

Networks and alliances formed principally to trade in explicit knowledge do not often require close interaction and are largely based on contractual relations, which are also more likely to encourage opportunism (Lei 1997: 215; also see de Laat 1997). In joint ventures, in particular, the trading or sharing of explicit knowledge often means that another organization, with a strong intent to learn and a comparable knowledge base, is able to acquire this knowledge, be it technological, marketing or production related, and eventually decode and recombine it into their own core competence. Disloyal partners can start competing with their alliance partner and make the partner dependent on them for future components and even the next generation of new products. Alternatively, they can 'go it alone' and become direct competitors of the joint venture or alliance partner (de Laat 1997: 150; Lei 1997: 215). This had been particularly evident in the strategic alliances formed between Japanese and US and European companies, with the Japanese partner often becoming a competitor against its alliance partner or the joint venture firm (Lei 1997: 215). For these reasons, the cooperation within this form of networking is usually very limited and remains largely based on classical contractual arrangements that are often detailed and highly codified. This form of contracting encourages limited commitment and so will usually invite the risk of opportunism, such as cheating, stealing secrets, partners meeting only minimal obligations, starving the alliance of resources and not committing the best people to the venture (de Laat 1997: 149–56; Ring 1997a: 120).

When it comes to sharing tacit knowledge in IORs, organizations cannot hope to achieve this in an arm's length relationship, but must enter into an 'apprenticeship' relationship or some form of relationship that involves 'long term, dense social interactions' (Dyer and Singh 1996, 1997: 11; Lei 1997: 216). Staff might have to be exchanged, premises opened up or even combined and secrets shared. As already mentioned in Chapter14, know-how is typically transferred or learnt in direct, intimate relationships and with extensive face-to-face exposure. Individuals or small groups sharing know-how have to develop their own unique language and discourse to transmit complex forms of 'sticky' knowledge (Dyer and Singh 1996, 1997: 12, citing Kogurt and Zander 1988: 389).

However, one of the great risks of sharing tacit knowledge is, as de Laat notes (as do others), the problem of *inequity*. Rarely are partners on equal terms and the stronger partner can, if it is technologically superior, 'outlearn' the other partner (de Laat 1997: 167). Lei also suggests that differential learning rates (or the absorptive capacity of organizations) will significantly affect the bargaining power of alliance partners. He says that 'disparities in organizational receptivity to learning, knowledge embeddedness and strategic intent will work to favour one partner's 'outlearning' the other in absorbing and internalizing the skills over time' (Lei 1997: 216). In a similar vein, others argue that the ability to learn in the interorganizational context is related to the 'absorptive capacity' of an organization or its managers and this means having the ability to unpackage, assimilate and act upon new knowledge and know-how. It also means being able to create, for example, the necessary dialogue, communication and language to achieve this, or, in other words, a new network discourse (Levinson and Asahi 1995: 58–60; Dyer and Singh 1996, 1997: 13–14; Powell 1996). This capacity is not equally distributed in many IORs and, as stated above, learning networks are often used as races to 'outlearn' a partner or become a 'competition for competence' (Lei 1997: 216).

Credible commitments

De Laat (1997: 167) also warns that inequity in resources, for example the superior market or financial position of one partner over another, is also an incentive for organizations to 'run off' with jointly developed projects or results. The incentives for knowledge sharing (transferring) and knowledge acquisition (receiving) are inherently unequal in many instances and mutual benefits are difficult to achieve (see discussion above on power). De Laat (1997: 151) suggests that this is why, in the case of R&D, a separate research company or consortium is favoured over joint ventures. In the consortium or separate company situation, cooperation or collaboration is non-competitive and the hazards of knowledge abuse are greatly reduced because results are incorporated into a differentiated product from those of the alliance partners or destined for different markets. For example, the alliance between Philips and Siemens in the 1980s to develop integrated circuits saw Philips focus on SRAMs and Siemens on DRAMs. The memory chips were for different applications in different markets: SRAMs in telecommunication equipment in professional markets and DRAMs for the upgrade of electronic products for consumers. In this arrangement, both parties had agreed to exchange all relevant knowledge (de Laat 1997: 151).

De Laat describes a number of elaborate forms of *credible commitments* (also Sydow 1998: 39) that organizations use, either in the form of contracts or other forms of pledging, to make it possible to share know-how. Expressions of commitment represent an explicit or implicit pledge of relational continuity between partners (Dwyer et al. 1987). Some examples of credible commitments include agreements that involve 'phased commitments' of a minimalist kind where partners agree to share knowledge as the alliance unfolds and not upfront. Another more powerful one is 'mutual commitments' where partners agree to suspend or limit their own independent research while participating in the alliance. Exhibit 16.8 describes a number of other forms of credible commitments and includes a distinction between those of a minimalist kind, such as sharing some proprietary knowledge and facilities, or optimum ones, such as adopting systemic procedures, offering cross-share holdings and charging entry fees. De Laat says that when firms are willing to negotiate credible commitments, they actually provide tangible proof or watertight guarantees that they will faithfully execute the agreement and if they renege, the nature of these agreements is such that losses will affect all concerned (1997: 156–60). He also suggests that as credible commitments are built up and executed, trust of a very resilient kind emerges (de Laat 1997: 163–5). Learning networks would have to be more dependent on credible commitments than classical contracts alone in order to facilitate the sharing of tacit knowledge.

De Laat (1997: 164) points out that in making credible commitments and therefore showing more resilient trust, network members actually signal a willingness to take risks. However, de Laat makes it clear that networks are likely to use both classical contracts and credible commitments, which can also be in the form of contracts or other forms of agreement, but that neither is a substitute for the other – they imply different types of trust (de Laat 1997: 164). A classical contract between two network members might, in fact, be necessary to satisfy the demands of the network's customers but have no bearing on the relationship between the network partners who might well have developed some very strong signals of trust.

There are some interesting case studies on how tacit knowledge can lead to learning networks, but they often involve a third party or intermediary, such as a university research body or publicly funded research institute, neither of which is a direct competitor of a business partner (for example Lütz 1997). Such third party entities and *cross-sector collaborations* are becoming important to R&D especially in biotechnology and pharmaceuticals (Cohen et al. 2002; Macmillan et al. 2000). Some have gone so far as to predict that the new face of corporate America will be typified by companies shedding their laboratories and in-house R&D in favour of cross-sector collaborations so that they can spend more time on product development and design (Drucker 2001; Buderi 2000).

Exhibit 16.8 Examples of credible commitments

❑ Levels of investment proportionate to size or wealth of partners

❑ Taking monetary shares or having cross-share holdings in partners' businesses

❑ Giving guarantees to purchase components produced by network

❑ Bundling agreements so there is no stand-alone joint venture

❑ Phased commitments – commit to share knowledge or know-how in stages as project unfolds

❑ Advance commitments – asking for investment in production from larger partner before R&D completed

❑ Eliminate independent research for duration of project

❑ Set entry fees that are non-refundable

❑ Joint equity in joint venture held by all or only some partners

Source: Adapted from Paul de Laat (1997) 'Research and development alliances: Ensuring trust by mutual commitments', in Ebers, M. (ed.) *The Formation of Inter-Organizational Networks*, New York: Oxford University Press, pp. 146–73.

CASE EXAMPLE

THE 'SEE3' CONTACT LENS PROJECT

This case study describes a cross-sector collaboration involving three organizations: the Co-operative Research Centre for Eye Research and Technology (CRCERT),* Australia's major national public sector research agency (CSIRO), and the company Ciba Vision (CV), which is a division of the Swiss-based multinational corporation Novartis AG. The project involved collaboration among scientists, engineers, clinicians and other product development specialists based in four different locations in three countries. It was formally initiated in 1993 and one of its major aims was to develop a commercially viable contact lens which could be worn continuously for a period of up to 30 days. This was achieved and, in November 1998, CV publicly announced a breakthrough new high-oxygen soft contact lens material called lotrafilcon A, at the same time also indicating that the new lenses were to be test marketed in Mexico.

The central participant in CRCERT is the Cornea and Contact Lens Research Unit (CCLRU) (located in the School of Optometry at the University of New South Wales) which has developed an international reputation for contact lens research, most notably in the field of clinical evaluation. Indeed, the CCLRU has claimed that it is the largest centre in the world devoted to cornea and contact lens research. CSIRO is a statutory agency of the Commonwealth Government. It is Australia's largest R&D organization. The particular division that collaborated on the 'See3' project was the Melbourne-based Division of Chemicals and Polymers whose aim is to contribute to the development of industries in the chemicals and plastics sector (47% of the division's research effort is devoted to this) and the pharmaceutical and human health sector (43%). Following CSIRO policy and directions, the Division is committed to collaborating with external partners to produce commercializable outcomes.

CV was established in 1980 as a result of diversification by the US Pharmaceutical Division of the Swiss multinational Ciba-Geigy. In 1996, Ciba-Geigy merged with another Swiss multinational, Sandoz, to form Novartis AG, which has its core business in healthcare, agribusiness and nutritional products, with CV becoming the eye care unit of Novartis. In 2002, and at the time of compiling this case study, CV had two main strategic business units: Ciba Vision Optics, responsible for contact lens and lens care products and based in Atlanta, Georgia, USA (also the worldwide headquarters for CV), and Ciba Vision Opthalmics, responsible for the development and production of ophthalmic pharmaceuticals, based in Bülach, Switzerland.

Although the first practical contact lenses (made of glass and covering the whole eye) were invented in the late 19th century, it was not until 1948 that a hard plastic lens (made from poly [methyl methacrylate], or PMMA) covering only the cornea was introduced. These lenses could be worn comfortably for 6–10 hours and provided the desired visual correction after an adaptation period. But the contact lens industry did not really flourish until the 1970s, following the introduction by Bausch and Lomb of soft 'hydrogel' lenses (made from poly [hydroxyethyl methacrylate] or HEMA) that could be used for daily wear. Soft lenses were very comfortable and required minimal adaptation, a significant advantage over the hard PMMA lenses. However, despite their popularity and advantages, soft lenses do have a number of significant problems, including: they are prone to the build up of deposits which can create discomfort with extended wear; they are harder to keep clean; they are more difficult to handle; and they have poor durability. The contact lens market is a multibillion one and competition is fierce to bring new products to market.

The success of the hydrogel lenses led to the search for new materials for an 'extended wear' contact lens which could be worn continuously for many days, thereby making lens wearing simpler and more convenient by reducing the daily routine for conventional lense users. But the development of a suitable material has been no trivial task because the extended wear lens has to satisfy stringent design requirements to make it safe and comfortable to wear without causing eye damage. Two main approaches were pursued from the 1980s to develop soft lenses: the introduction of very thin HEMA lenses with higher oxygen permeability (for example Ciba-Geigy's 'Cibathin' and Bausch and Lomb's 'Soflens O Series'), and high water content hydrogel lenses (for example Johnson & Johnson's 'Accuvue').

Developing a lens material which was capable of transmitting sufficient oxygen to the cornea when the eye is closed at night has been the major barrier to successful extended wear contact lenses. Given that modified hydrogel lenses had proven to be unsuitable for this, a search began for new materials and researchers began to focus on combining hydrogels with silicone-containing polymers which offered the benefit of high-oxygen permeability. The major problem faced in the development of these new materials was that of achieving an optimum surface chemistry with high biocompatibility and good wetting characteristics. In the early 1990s all the major companies were pursuing this approach but, by the mid-1990s, no silicone hydrogel contact lenses were commercially available.

In the early 1990s, the head of CV's R&D and marketing activities began reorganizing the company's research effort by reducing the number of projects pursued. One of the selected projects was the extended wear contact lens. At around the same time, two people who knew of the fledgling CRC (an ex-employee of the CCLRU and another acquaintance) suggested to the CV executive that this was a group that had much to offer the company. As a result, the CV executive met with the CRC's Director, Professor Brien Holden (an eminent scientist who had established the optimum oxygen permeability required of a contact lens) and in 1993 an R&D collaboration contract was negotiated for a seven-year period. Under the contract, the company agreed to provide substantial funding for the R&D project (initially a sum of 5 million Swiss francs over three years was committed) and this was to be matched by the CRC with equivalent resources, largely in-kind contributions of CRC partner research time. The 'See3' project was set up under the CRC's biomaterials programme, and different participants in the Centre were assigned responsibility for specific elements of the project's work. For example, the CCLRU assumed responsibility for the clinical trials of the developed products while parallel R&D and product development work was also carried out within two units of CV.

The R&D project was substantial, involving 70 scientists (around 100 people in total) working in teams at four sites. The key tasks of the project were: to develop a contact lens which could be worn continuously for up to 30 days, to manage the intellectual property created by the project, to test the effectiveness and safety of the new lens in clinical trials, to obtain regulatory approval for the final product, and to develop a commercially viable manufacturing process. By 1997, the new lenses, made from an entirely new revolutionary material called lotrafilcon A, had been produced and successfully trialled in a six-month pilot study. They were then subject to US Food and Drug Administration trials (conducted in three countries) and were subsequently approved in the following year. In November 1998 test marketing of the new lens, branded Focus® NIGHT and DAY™, began in Mexico and at the same time CV publicly announced the breakthrough new material in the CV news release of 24 November 1998. Full launch of the product began in Spain in January 1999, with limited release in Australia and New Zealand in May of that year.

Examples of credible commitments that emerged in the collaboration included: the allocation of material resources (in accordance with the role and stake in the project of each of the parties, which for the public sector agencies meant committed facilities and the dedicated time of researchers, while for the company it also included an advanced commitment of capital (5 million Swiss francs) in the expectation of a return on the investment); the free sharing of project information (with an explicit commitment to have no secrets or hidden agendas); and the joint assignation of intellectual property rights resulting from the project. This ensured that, for the CRC and CSIRO, there would be a flow of royalties if the project was successful and this would be a material return for their participation and contributions to the development process. Through these commitments, a situation of spiralling trust, based on 'self-amplifying reciprocity', did emerge as the project progressed. Proof of this is to be found in the decision by the company to continue its collaborative R&D relationship with the CRC. The largest partner also carried the greatest financial risk.

A central element of the project was that 'critical tasks' (such as polymer synthesis, surface chemistry and clinical assessment) were placed on 'parallel tracks', that is, were conducted at several sites simultaneously. This was important in terms of balancing the power relationships in the project by not allowing any one group to become too central to the process. Phased commitments ensured that knowledge was shared as the project unfolded. It also created healthy rivalry. For example, the polymer synthesis laboratory work was carried out concurrently at CSIRO, CV USA and CV Switzerland; the three teams had the same goals, but used differing and complementary approaches. This lead to 'friendly competition', with the teams benchmarking each other, and ensured that the project was rarely brought to a halt because of technical problems at one site. Also, with different teams working in parallel on the same problem, more options could be explored and tested in the time available. A number of protocols and computer technologies were developed for information dissemination and to ensure intellectual property was protected, but with the free flow of ideas where possible.

Source: Adapted from Paul Couchman and Liz Fulop (2001) 'Risk in cross-sector R&D collaboration', a paper presented to the R&D Management Conference, Leveraging Research and Technology, Victoria University of Wellington, Wellington NZ, February 8–9.

* In Australia, Co-operative Research Centres (CRCs) are publicly funded research consortia made up of universities, the private sector and other agencies, depending on the nature of the project. The CRCERT differs from most other CRCs in that it has no partners from the business sector (a result of the derivative nature of the eye care products industry in Australia, which is mostly sales focused, with few companies involved in manufacture and R&D) but, like all the CRCs in the medical science and technology sector, its core participants include other medical research institutes.

The See3 collaboration is one that led to a breakthrough new product being brought to market. The case study shows how a cross-sector collaboration developed around the learning network concept, two of the three partners being publicly funded research entities. Credible commitments were used to develop trust and knowledge-sharing protocols, although contracting also occurred early in the project and would have been required by the CRC and CSIRO. Commercialization of R&D is a complex form of IORs, involving very different organizational cultures. Cross-sector collaborations cause all partners to change how they operate. In the case of the publicly funded body or third party, how they change will depend on whether they are involved in order to solve a common problem, share knowledge with their other partners, or achieve a commercializable outcome through developing IP (Cyert and Goodman 1997; Robertson et al. 1997; Liebeskind and Oliver 1998; Prahbu 1999; Hagedoon et al. 2000; Okubu and Sjöberg 2000). There are different kinds of risks for each partner (see Couchman and Fulop 2001) and, in the See3 case, there was litigation over patents and extensive and costly delays in getting Federal Drug Administration (FDA) approval in the US.

Gender and networking theory

The theories and concepts discussed so far show a glaring omission, already noted in many areas of management, that can either be a case of gender blindness (ignoring gender difference as a matter of fact) or gender suppression (being aware of gender differences but deliberately ignoring them) (see Chapter 2). Some areas of networking theory have adopted a less masculinist language than is found in other areas of management, particularly in strategic management, where war metaphors are frequently adopted (for example 'defensive move', 'fighting for market share', 'market penetration'). In the *relational view* of networking, words such as 'sharing', 'trust', 'loyalty', 'benevolence', 'altruism', 'fair dealings' and 'equity' are common. In the *affective view* proposed by Ring (1997b), words such as 'love' and 'caring' are also introduced. Yet the content and meanings of these terms, including trust, are established in discourses or the discursive practices of managers who are largely presumed to be male. Networking discourses exist alongside others in organizations, such as the competitive strategy discourse described in Chapter 15 and others we have identified throughout this text, as being gendered in favour of masculinist constructs. In many organizations, the underlying language games are so deeply rooted in various ideas of rationality, competitiveness, control and self-interest that notions of trust, even in the network discourse, cannot carry substantially new or different meanings, let alone less masculinist ones. Networking, and the language used to theorize it, including trust, remains inherently bound up with masculinist ideals, practices and linguistic constructs.

Critiques offered in our earlier chapters on ethics (8) and gender (2) apply here and these are:

- male evidence versus female evidence
- rationality versus emotionality
- differentiation versus connectedness
- male networking experience versus female experience.

Male evidence versus female evidence

Much of the network literature draws on empirical evidence dominated entirely by male samples, and is characteristic of much of the other empirical work from which IORs and networking draws its theories. Reading the network literature, one gets the distinct impression that it is about how men do business and, for many researchers, the absence of women in these studies does not even merit attention. We can conclude that as with many management approaches, the literature on networking is dominated by assumptions based on Western male experiences and is therefore gender-blind in most instances. Indeed, as we said earlier, given the dominance of male managers in privileged and powerful positions in society and business, men might be said to have a vested interest in reproducing certain networking rituals and practices that will justify this privilege, and relegate women managers to the realms of marginalized 'others' in the networking stakes. The current masculinist construction of networking relations, including sociability, fails to acknowledge the female experience and, in effect, excludes female evidence. In so doing, it also misses the feminine in many male experiences of sociability and bonding that could entail other feelings, such as warmth, intimacy, nurturing, protecting and sacrificing. An underlying premise, for example, in the notion of trust and social capital is the importance of friendships and close associations, but the literature focuses on male evidence to the exclusion of female evidence. In her now famous study, Zucker (1986: 60–1; also Chapter 9) identifies what she terms *characteristic-based trust*, evolving on the basis of family background, ethnicity and gender. She goes on to argue that this form of trust is 'free trust' because it is 'earned' on the basis of ascription or societal processes that assign certain expectations to particular characteristics, such as being a woman. This insight seems to have been lost in much of the literature, although Zucker's typology is widely cited and extensively used in the literature (see Lane 1998). The obvious gender blindness in much of this literature shows up elsewhere, excluding female evidence where it might be most relevant, such as in discussions of trust.

Rationality versus emotionality

As we stated in Chapter 8, since the time of the Greeks, rationality was favoured over other modes of response to the world, and this was traditionally seen as the preserve of men working in public life. Historically, long-held male assumptions were reproduced in classical and scientific managements' preference for the rational and formal rather than emotional factors such as care, consideration and empathy. In IOR and networking, the overwhelming problems of a relational kind are principally defined in terms of fear of opportunism and risk taking that can be managed by developing certain forms of trust. No mention is made in this literature of how men and women might relate differently to the notion of trust and networking in general and, in this regard, most of the constructs are homogenizing in the extreme. As we have already said, words such as 'sharing', 'trust', 'loyalty', 'benevolence', 'altruism', 'fair dealings' and 'equity' are common in the literature dealing with trust and networking but what other ones are missing? One very obvious example is the extensive research that has been undertaken to address the relationship between personal factors, such as gender and gender roles, on behaviours relating to self-disclosure and trusting individuals (Foubert and Sholley 1996). Self-disclosure is strongly related to people displaying strong feminine roles, including androgynous males. In the affective view of trust proposed by Ring (1997b), words such as 'love' and 'caring' are introduced, but not revealing oneself to another or other aspects related to self-disclosure are not mentioned in terms of potential gender differences. One engages in gender suppression when one assumes that the content and meanings of words, such as 'care' and 'love', can be established in discourses or the discursive practices of only male managers. Even though Ring writes about how affection and caring for others can foster trust and collaboration, his conclusions are based solely on relationships between senior male executives. In many organizations, the underlying language games are so deeply rooted in various ideas of rationality, competitiveness, control and self-interest that notions of trust rarely carry new or different meanings, let alone more gender-inclusive ones.

Differentiation versus 'connectedness'

We argued earlier that one of the dominant ways in which management theory has developed in the West is with its emphasis on individual achievements, competitiveness and self-interest, often glorified in notions of the entrepreneur as the supreme risk taker and aggressor (Couchman and Fulop 2000). As with the notion of moral development, where the emphasis is on the individual 'self' developing morally in relation to

the universal or a generalized 'other', free of contextual constraints, the network literature also struggles to establish the notion of sociability in the business context. The notion of 'strength of weak ties' or 'strength of strong ties', as suggested above, emerges from a deep ambivalence in Western business towards notions of connectedness. As we argued in Chapter 8, the idea of 'self', which is always defined in relation to, and entwined in, particular 'others', giving it its defining characteristics and shaping its identity and being, is more appropriate to understanding both feminine ethics and non-Western conceptions of the 'self', particularly in East Asia. Here 'selves' are always connected to other 'selves' and are never independent. Much of what happens in terms of networking appears contrived in the West compared to other parts of the world (Fulop and Richards 2002). More importantly, the notion of embeddedness that pervades the network literature is distinctly insensitive to sociability as a gendered concept. In other words, it is constructed around the way in which men do business and build bonds and enduring relations, often somewhat akin to a 'boys' club', and are visibly insensitive to how women (and other groups) might enrich social capital. Indeed, Fukuyama's (1995) entire argument about trust-based societies makes no concession to the absence of women from business and public life in Japanese society, upon which he bases his main arguments, and their exclusion from the sociability discourse.

Male experience versus female experience

As we have already argued, if the 'self' is regarded as itself being relational and embedded, that is, the context is inseparable from the 'selves' that develop within it, then the appropriateness of any theory that fails to acknowledge gender differences is thrown into question. As we mentioned in Chapter 8, the actual experience of people in making moral choices – their *moral experience* – is important in shaping the kinds of judgements made and the criteria used for making them. We went on to say that most women, because of their relative absence from public life historically and contemporary barriers such as the glass ceiling, have comparatively much less experience than men of dealing with the moral problems of governing, leading, exercising power over others and physical conflict. Many men, on the other hand, have little experience of the moral problems of family life, the relations between adults and children, motherhood and nurturance and, if they do, are not asked to compromise or choose between them in their careers. Most management theories do not reflect this variety of experience, and men's experience is privileged and underplays the emotional and affective elements. The argument might well be made by many theorists that if women could be more attuned to how men network, could free themselves from the bonds of emotionality that restrict them from being more accomplished organizational players, then they would be included in networking studies. This sort of gender stereotyping is reflected in, for example, a conceptual taxonomy being developed to study the affect of culture on the formation of trust (Doney et al. 1998). This taxonomy draws heavily on Hofstede's work (see Chapter 3) and has femininity associated with trust but mainly in the context of social psychological and sociological factors. Thus, women are seen as more predictable, their behaviours geared towards others and more likely to honour obligations. Men, on the other hand, are presented as being influenced by economic and calculative motives, such as opportunistic behaviour and maximizing self-interest as well as being more focused on capabilities. While this recognizes the female experience, it stereotypes it as a 'domesticated' one and creates a binary in which women are cast as the 'soft side' of trusting behaviour while men are portrayed as being hard and geared to the tough world of business (see Chapter 2). Such binaries leave no room for men and women to be both or neither.

Differences in men's and women's experiences of trust are likely to be much more problematic than is even remotely recognized in the network literature, even though the highly emotive nature of trust is regularly mentioned. Some hints of this can be found in Judith Lorber's (1979) article, 'Trust, loyalty, and the place of women in the informal organization of work', a feminist analysis of the topic. Lorber proposes that men cannot trust women for a number of reasons, and she suggests that different rules operate implicitly for men and women in the informal organization. This has clear ramifications for networking, which is by and large an informal process and depends on certain forms of sociability. She notes that the colleague/peer group culture in many organizations is male-dominated, fostering fierce competitiveness, individualism and often bitter rivalries, and many colleague groups mirror these expectations and behaviours, even in teamwork contexts. In such groups, women are 'natural' outsiders who must be either 'docile handmaidens', 'sexual prizes' or 'trophies' for men, but never equals. The 'band of brothers', as she refers to them, that form in workplaces through informal groups, build trust-based relations in which favours are exchanged for deeds that largely exclude women, and where loyalty is given to those who bestow sponsorship and patronage, neither of which generally come from women (see Chapter 6).

Lorber believes that women cannot become fully fledged members of 'the band', instead they will have tokenistic gestures bestowed upon them, ensuring that sociability is kept to a minimum. Lorber believes that trust cannot develop along gender lines because men trust those who are like them and, mainly as consensually joined 'brother breakers of moral codes' (such as womanizing on business trips as part of the entertaining ritual), they learn to look the other way in many transgressions and come to trust in each other's discretion. Women, she says, are often seen as the 'other' or opposite to this – the moral entrepreneurs who will not look the other way unless they are subordinates or dependent in other ways. Lorber concludes that there are primary loyalties and they are gendered in highly masculinist ways and enacted in informal organizations, irrespective of what is formally proscribed. Even if Lorber's arguments are not empirically tested, they begin to challenge the assumption that men and women execute trust-based relationships in similar ways. Moreover, if Lorber's arguments are followed through, it would seem that women are at a relative disadvantage if they assume that trust will work for them in some neutral, non-gendered way, whether this is in the workplace or in networking relationships (see also Kanter 1997).

As we said earlier, the point that feminist and post-feminist theorists are making is that women's different experiences, arising from their different social roles, need to be taken into account when theory is being developed, and not just incorporated as an afterthought. In the case of networking theory, even the afterthought has not been evident.

Dynamics of cross-cultural networking

Business structures and relationships are influenced significantly by culture and key institutions in society that mirror and sustain cultural practices (see Chapter 3). As Fulop and Richards (2002)* note, different forms of networking arise because of cultural influences and the institutional arrangements that reinforce cultural differences between nations (see Chapter 3). The literature on cross-cultural studies is heavily influenced by Western paradigms in which binaries dominate. In Chapter 3 we introduced the work of Hofstede (1980, 1991) and his five continua that differentiate societies on the basis of presumed shared meanings and relativities which underpin organiza-tional life based on notions of national culture. We also mentioned the other ways in which national culture is differentiated, one of the most common being to distinguish between high- and low-context cultures.

---

* *Author's note:* Although sharing joint authorship, the first part of this section and the first and second paragraphs of the second part, are based on D. Richards' contribution and his area of expertise. The remainder of this section is based largely on L. Fulop's contribution.

Following the work of Hall (1976), in high-context cultures, the external environment is very important, many things are hidden and meaning is conveyed indirectly and great importance is placed on who is speaking rather than what is said. Criticism of speech in high-context societies can be taken as a criticism of the speaker. In low-context countries the environment is less important, things are made more explicit and meaning is often conveyed directly so that what is being said is rather more important than who says it. Criticism of speech in such cultures is seen as an attack on the content and meaning and not the speaker per se. Fulop and Richards (2002) note that although Hall does not clearly place different countries within his model, others (Hofstede 1991, 1993; Mead 1998; and Chapter 3) have done so.

Typically, high-context cultures include China, Japan, Korea, Vietnam and other Asian countries, countries around the Mediterranean and in the Middle East. As noted by many theorists, high-context cultures are characterized by: longlasting relationships; implicit, shared and indirect communication codes; personal authority, with loyalty to superiors and subordinates; spoken (rather than written) agreements; clear distinctions between insiders and outsiders; and cultural patterns that are slow to change (Fulop and Richards 2002). By contrast, low-context cultures include the Anglo-Saxon countries (Australia, the UK, Canada, New Zealand and the USA), Scandinavia and Germany. These cultures are characterized by short-term relationships; explicit, logical and direct communication codes; bureaucratic and diffuse authority with impersonal relationships; written (rather than spoken) agreements based on legal systems; imprecise distinctions between insiders and outsiders; and cultural patterns which are more adaptable to change (Fulop and Richards 2002). Legal forms of contracting are costly and inflexible and do little to foster trust (see discussion above). Fulop and Richards (2002; also Child 1998) claim that this is particularly true in the high-context cultures of Asia, where agreements between people are based on deep, personal forms of trust and relationship are 'spoken' rather than 'written'. After a contract has been signed in China or Japan, the partner may request further changes. This, Hall point outs, causes Western indignation, particularly in Americans who 'regard a contract as binding, a stable element in a changing and uncertain world' (Hall 1987: 128–9).

Fulop and Richards (2002) also contend, as have many others, that while trust is generally thought to be all-important between business partners, particularly in networking and relationships in international and cross-cultural contexts, the reality is that people from different cultures are more or less willing to trust in a negotiation or relationship and are more or less suspicious of the other. For example, they cite a study of the perceptions of transaction costs in partners of American companies in 38 countries in which it was found that cultures high in Hofstede's power distance and uncertainty avoidance had low degrees of interpersonal trust (Shane 1993). These are cultures in which people strongly distinguish between 'we' and 'they' and thus find trust impossible in hierarchical relationships. Since trust is low in high power distance cultures, then partners need greater control, are afraid of paying higher transaction costs, and prefer to be on their own or with their families. Relatives are much more trustworthy. Conversely, the study found evidence that partners from low power distance cultures were much more likely to trust in joint venture partnerships (Shane 1993).

As Fulop and Richards (2002) point out, other researchers have come to similar conclusions about culture. For example, Fons Trompenaars and Charles Hampden-Turner found that in universalist cultures, where behaviour is based on universal and abstract rules and principles (as in Anglo-Saxon cultures, Germany and Switzerland) 'a trustworthy person is one who honours their word or contract' (1997: 45). However, they argue that in particularist cultures, where judgements are made according to the nature of the particular relationship between people, a trustworthy person is one who respects the demands of the relationship. This resonates with the high-context and low-context distinctions. Southeast and East Asian cultures are characterized by such *relational personalism* that typically will judge trust in this way. Indeed, in such cultures, the demand for written contracts is a sign of mistrust, since they are only necessary when both parties are trying to maximize their own advantage at the expense of the other (Fulop and Richards 2002). To explore these issues further, we now consider networking in China as an example of how institutional and cultural factors come into play to shape networking relations that are particularly problematical in terms of building cross-cultural relationships based on trust. We suggest that all societies have institutional and cultural factors that make it hard for persons from different parts of the world to 'fit in' and build certain types of relationships.

Institutions and trust in cross-cultural contexts

One of the reasons why the People's Republic of China is a focus of this section is that, as John Child (1998: 241) points out, it is by far the largest developing country hosting foreign direct investment (FDI), and indeed was the second largest recipient in the world of FDI in 1998. Child describes how the developed countries that form a 'triad', comprising North America, Europe and Japan, invest heavily in newly industrializing countries (NICs), such as Taiwan, Korea and Singapore as well as in the so-called 'emerging economies', such as China and India. As Child also notes, in many of the emerging economies, and particularly China, international joint ventures have been the most common approach to establishing business relationships and this has been strongly sanctioned by government policy. In the case of China, the development of an international strategic alliance occurs in an institutional context that Child characterizes as having two aspects: *crude complexity* and *effective complexity*. He describes these two elements of the institutional context as being a product of particular historical legacies that have created very low forms of trust in Chinese institutions, but paradoxically led to the strong collectivist nature of Chinese society, and the preference to use personal relations to conduct business.

The collective nature of Chinese society results in a preference for getting things done through interpersonal relationships, or *guanxi*. People are linked in complex networks of *guanxi*, through which they navigate their social worlds. *Guanxi*, as well as meaning personal or informal relationships, can also be translated as 'connections'. (Fulop and Richards 2002; see also Redding 1990: 66; Boisot and Child 1996; Child 1998: 257)

Child believes that the institutional context in China, and the cultural underpinnings of how trust-based relations are formed leave Western businesses with two options for developing their international strategic alliances – a high-trust versus low-trust strategy.

Crude and effective complexity

Child (but also Redding 1990) describes how the institutional environment in China has been renowned for providing few guarantees against the betrayal of trust (1998: 254). He cites the legal system as being far from independent, being deeply ensconced in the state, and the political manipulations this has allowed. The absence of codified commercial laws subject all involved in commerce to the vicissitudes of an arbitrary taxation system, licensing fees, restrictions on trade and travel and the unbridled influence and power of imperial officials. Corruption, bribery and secret commissions are part and parcel of doing business in China. Child notes that despite continued legal reforms since 1979, and the emergence of some legal rules and institutions, the law in China remains a tool of the state, still lacking independence, and always within reach of the Chinese Communist Party. This has created an environment in which there are limited institutional guarantors for economic transactions, and hence many transactions are not bound by codified agreements but rather implicit and tacit conditions (Child 1998: 255, 257). He believes that the institutional context creates huge complexities and uncertainties for international strategic alliances.

Child identifies *crude complexity* as largely derived from the existence of different business systems (state-controlled, collective and private businesses), with different levels of marketization or degrees of free markets evident across these sectors (Child 1998: 255). Added to this are differences between regions, some more progressive and liberalized than others, such as the trading zones, and even generational differences among managers and potential partners heavily influenced by different cultural revolutions and shifts in the ideologies of successive Chinese leadership. Child believes that the more problematical aspects of complexity are those relating to *effective complexity*. He identifies three key elements here: the close involvement of government agencies in business and commercial affairs; political uncertainties; and the persistence of resource limitations in all areas of business development (Child 1998: 255).

We have alluded to the problem of state ownership, but Child argues that the heavy involvement of central governmental bodies in a wide range of areas, such as banking, licensing and labour regulation, means that centrally determined laws and policies have to be administered at the local level, leaving it difficult to work out who is really 'the government'. This ambiguity is exacerbated by the proliferation of state-owned enterprises, especially ownership rights over assets, and this is particularly evident in areas such as working capital and enforcement of transactions that can affect the joint ventures being formed by Chinese businesses and MNCs (Child 1998: 256). Uncertainty principally arises in relation to three key factors (Child 1998: 255–6):

1. The lack of transparency and/or enforcement of laws
2. The influential but highly unaccountable role of local government agencies in interpreting regulations, imposing taxes and issuing licences, which creates ample opportunities for corruption and arbitrary practices to which there is often no recourse to higher authorities for adjudication
3. The different ways in which agreements are interpreted, often influenced by relations between local authorities and higher level officials, and the lack of enforcement of signed contracts that can be 'broken' if the local authority chooses not to act on them for political or other reasons.

Resource scarcity, mainly in domestic working capital and high-quality, well-trained managers, reduces the potential to develop the business and build a loyal workforce. When this is coupled with poor infrastructure, particularly in transport, the climate is ripe for opportunism in the form of unethical behaviour and corruption. Child cites the example of product and 'brand piracy' – the illegal use of a foreign partner's name – and embezzlement, as common examples of opportunism. In concluding, Child argues that both forms of complexity, coupled with Chinese Confucianism and its emphasis on filial loyalty and family relations, has led to the family being the primary source of trust in Chinese business and society (Child 1998: 257). Child cites Redding (1990: 66) to explain how connections work within Chinese society, where connections between family and other units, which are based on a shared identity (or characteristic-based trust), are the primary forms of sociability and survival and prosperity. It is from these forms of trust-based relations that *guanxi* has developed as the 'strength of strong ties' typifying other network relations that are more clan-based and extensive.

Child sees the family-based system underpinning Chinese business and society as being dependent on group loyalty and identity based on blood ties and upbringing, where identification and affect form the basis of trust. Network relations are, by contrast, more clan-like and extensive (see also Pearce and Robinson 2000) and trust is based on *guanxi,* where credits, doing favours and reciprocity are critical. These are deeply embedded forms of social capital in which the dynamics of enforceable trust (see above) are particularly strong and highly effective from the insider's point of view. As Fulop and Richards (2002) argue, because these social networks are relatively permanent, they are characterized by the importance and enforceability of the Chinese conceptions of *reciprocity* and *retribution* (*bao*). Western societies emphasize short-term, symmetrical reciprocation in exchange relationships, while people in Confucian societies believe that relationships are for the long term and will extend into the unforeseeable future. The concept of *bao* covers both positive and negative events and therefore either reciprocity or retribution may extend into the very long term. They go on to describe how the development of networks of *guanxi* requires the presence of intermediaries. They cite research that has found that there are four common methods of establishing *guanxi* with another (Chang and Holt 1991):

- appealing to kin relations
- pointing to a previous association
- using in-group connections or mediators
- social interaction requiring social skills (such as the ability to play the *renguing* (favour) game).

Low- and high-trust options for alliances

Child concludes that it is extremely difficult for foreign companies to build trust-based relations in either the family or clan-based systems. He suggests that organizations have two options. The first is to adopt what he terms the 'low-trust' option that entails imposing Western business routines and standards on the Chinese partners, by both external and internal means. Under the external route, he mentions such things as lobbying foreign governments to pressure China to develop a more codified environment through legislation to create enforceable laws and regulations. Child believes that MNCs have the clout to change Chinese attitudes to foreign investment and create higher levels of tolerance as well as using the Chinese need for foreign investment, especially in technology, to lever changes. In terms of internal measures, these largely revolve around standardizing and controlling internal operations and procedures to mirror the head office's policies, procedures and practices (Child 1998: 259). It involves having expatriates run the venture in its early phases and later replacing them with 'home-grown' Chinese managers, usually drawn from young recruits. As Child notes, the basis upon which relations are developed are on calculative trust, and as such are unlikely to lead to enduring trust-based relations that would make it is easier to replace expatriate managers. Favourable rewards and calculated exchanges for both partners (for example technology transfers, dividends) and individual employees (for example high personal income and some added benefits) are unlikely, in Child's view, to create long-term commitments. Many foreign managers, Child notes, complain about the consequences of adopting the low-trust strategy option, which creates an instrumental orientation in their partners and this gives rise to various forms of opportunism (see above) proliferating in the venture (Child 1998: 259). However as Child points out, the MNC's strategy in this approach is to dominate its local partners and markets, most evident in car manufacturing, and seek to create kingdom-type relationships, with all the associated asymmetrical forms of control and power (Child 1998: 261). As Child says, and for much the same reasons we noted above in respect of kingdom networks, the Chinese partners are willing to relinquish control because of the reputation of the foreign partner, especially its global span and size, the perceived competence of its management and technological expertise and the prospect of earning favourable profits from the venture (Child 1998: 262–3).

The high-trust strategy, by contrast, relies on using 'local' Chinese capabilities to absorb the complexities and here again Child notes that there are both external and internal strategies. In respect of the former, this usually entails choosing partners who are well connected and adept at dealing with officials and government administration in order to eliminate the arbitrariness of the institutional context. In terms of internal strategies, this is likely to entail the involve-ment of Chinese partners in decision making and operations affecting the venture or its subsidiaries in order to build a more collective identity; adapting procedures and practices to suit the local context, although maintaining standard reporting procedures and ensuring that long-term relationships are built through frequent visits, long-term assignments and stressing cultural sensitivity through extensive training. Included in this strategy is the use of intermediaries or third parties who work to span the cultural gap between the two systems of management (Child 1998: 259–60; 264–8). However, as we noted in our discussion of façades of trust, the abuse of trust could be very high if intermediaries are not well chosen and cultivated. Child identifies various stages through which relationships proceed (see above discussion by Ring) and he sees the potential for normative trust and cognitive trust (sharing each other's common understandings and world views) as only possible if both the internal and external complexities are carefully managed over a long period. Below is an example of a successful high trust-based strategy identified by Child involving a major glass manufacturer.

Child uses a typical Western typology to explain what are inherently cross-cultural processes. It would seem that theorists from the West work hard at reproducing the Western cultural logic in discussions of trust. This is aptly revealed by the following observations made about how trust is considered in Japanese business relationships. The notion of what a business relationship means is very different in Japan and, as Mark Scher (1997: 11–12) suggests, many Western commentators fail to appreciate the very limited or non-existent meaning that trust has in Japanese business. He says the word 'relationship' in Japan comes from two words: *kan*, meaning barrier or gate, and *kei*, meaning duty to the familial or clan group. Access, he says, in Japanese business is not about opening doors, but controlling entry and determining who is allowed past the barrier gates. He cites examples of the Japanese exclusionary system of *dango*, which entails a collusive, rigged bidding or tendering system that has roots in the guild system. *Dango* is used to afford access to a chosen group of contractors, no matter what. Scher says that long-term relationships among Japanese businesses are often portrayed as being based on trust, but this is not a word commonly used by the Japanese to describe their transactions. The right of 'access' provided to *keiretsu* relationships is seen as a franchise or license to do business, while trust refers to credit,

CASE EXAMPLE

This international strategic alliance was established after several years of negotiation. Two foreign partners took up a 25 per cent equity share (the minimum permitted by Chinese joint-venture regulations), although only one was an active partner. The active foreign partner supplied its advanced glass-making technology on a royalty basis; it also provided the first joint-venture general manager and a considerable amount of technical and managerial training. The Chinese partner provided the rest of the management, and the venture today is wholly Chinese-managed. The initial calculus was that the active foreign partner would benefit from technology transfer with minimum investment risk exposure, while relying on the main Chinese partner to develop the market. Since the technology royalty was based on sales, there would be a direct gain from market development. The Chinese partners, who were a mix of government investment trust, construction industry bureau and state enterprise, would through the joint venture promote the technological upgrading of the domestic glass industry and benefit from the construction boom in their country.

The main foreign and Chinese partners have maintained close relations, which were augmented by extensive training provided by the foreign side. The foreign partner has never sought to dominate the joint venture, and when the first foreign general manager had completed his first term of office, he was succeeded by the then Chinese deputy general manager who continues to head the joint venture. The Chinese management team have been highly successful in developing both the domestic Chinese market as well as sales in other East Asian markets which the foreign company considered too difficult to enter … Another indication of the trust which has developed is the fact that this joint venture has joined its foreign parent in forming further joint ventures in China. The relationship has deepened, on a knowledge-sharing basis, through the continued technological support offered by the foreign partner and through full access to the joint venture which the majority Chinese partners have always accorded to it. It has also become highly personalized over the course of some ten years, through a close bond between the original general manager and his then deputy, who are also directors of the joint venture. Interestingly, this bond developed despite the fact that neither has a good command of the other's language.

Source: John Child (1998) 'Trust in international strategic alliances: The case of sino-foreign joint ventures', in Christel Lane and Reinhard Bachmann (eds) *Trust Within and Between Organizations*, Oxford: Oxford University Press, pp. 241–72.

credit associations, trust companies, trust funds and trust agreements and the like (Scher 1997: 12).

It is not that trust is absent in Japanese culture, but rather it is not translated into the business context to mean loyalty, obligation, integrity and so on. In Japanese businesses, transactions are based on the 'insider–outsider' status. The *keiretsu* is an extremely complex system based on the general expectation that decisions will be made (even though they might not be commercially sound) and discretion used to service long-term relationships (Scher 1997: 15). This form of reliance is not built on personal trust or the type of bonding we favour in the West, but rather on uncodified ground rules of behaviour. These are deeply embedded in traditional power relations of inclusion and exclusion that are known, accepted and codified by the group (Scher 1997: 16).

George Brenkert (1998; also Humphrey 1998) argues that doing business in the international context creates its own versions of trust and morality and that context determines how each form operates. He also develops a three-dimensional approach to trust – *basic trust*, *guarded trust* and *extended trust* – that differs from Child's typology. *Basic trust* assumes impersonal, systematic relations as the basis of interaction in business, which means that people trust those who have a commonality of motives, values and ends and who behave consistently (Brenkert 1998: 286). Brenkert distinguishes basic trust from 'goodwill trust' – a category introduced in other studies of international IORs – that is premised on the assumption that a person is capable of high discretion, and is dependable and comes close to the notion of building trust based on one's reputation. There might well be elements of basic trust in even the low-trust strategies mentioned by Child but not goodwill trust. *Guarded trust* is premised on a commonality of motives and consistent behaviour as well as knowledge of the competence of another partner. This form of trust is required in contracting to cover the lack of clarity and uncertainty that all contracts entail because not everything can be specified. Guarded trust does not prevent broken promises or breaches of trust. Nor does it suggest that other forms of morality are excluded in contracting, but it is considered an essential element in market-based and contractual forms of governance because, as we noted earlier, to specify everything via contracts leads to distrust and invites breaches. Guarded trust involves limitations on transactions and provides various forms of monitoring devices (as is common in low-trust strategies and the early stages of high-trust ones). *Extended trust* presupposes both of the above and involves acting in ways that go beyond basic and guarded trust and allows for contracts and monitoring devices to be relaxed. A key element in this is openness, which can involve opening up one's plant or even books to others or involving partners in decision making (Brenkert 1998: 287). In Brenkert's approach, Child is actually describing forms of goodwill and extended trust that do not assume normative or even cognitive forms of trust.

Brenkert (1998: 289) suggests that basic trust can be enhanced by such things as regular contact, guarded trust by better governance devices and extended trust through such things as intermediaries and extended periods working in the host country. Many of these strategies might be available to MNCs, but not to SMEs.

Suzana Rodrigues (1995, also cited in Fulop and Richards 2002) suggests that most SMEs, without the clout of MNCs, seek to internationalize their operations, usually by adopting a gradualist approach, such as employing an overseas agent, rather than 'leapfrogging' and forming a partnership, such as a joint venture or non-equity strategic alliance (Rodrigues, 1995: 12). Moreover, SMEs lack the resources to collect the relevant interbusiness and intercountry knowledge and information that Rodrigues (1995: 13–14) says creates huge problems for them in their negotiations with overseas partners, especially in countries such as China. These obstacles tend to enlarge differences in interests and culture by introducing high levels of uncertainty and ambiguity into negotiations (see above). This lack of knowledge also often means that critical information about a partner's capabilities, reputation, financial strength and competitiveness is not obtained by SMEs, resulting in financially risky ventures. This lack of knowledge also affects the selection of suitable agents and intermediaries and points of access to markets (for example trade fairs versus direct marketing). In her study of how Brazilian SMEs sought entry into China, Rodrigues found that the intricacies of institutional and bureaucratic systems and the collective dimensions embedded in complex and dispersed systems of decision making (crude and effective complexity) were poorly understood. These SMEs relied on intermediaries, such as consultants, foreign agents or Hong Kong trading companies to deal with these complexities, but then found that the costs of such services were prohibitive. The competitiveness of the foreign investor was also a critical factor and included not only the ability of the SME to compete on price, which was and is vital in Asia, but also having experience in managing large contracts involving subcontracting arrangements. This also entailed having knowledge of how bids and contracts were won, including the role of governments in these processes, as well as being able to access and influence the bidding and tendering processes, which again was costly for SMEs and involved unaffordable commissions and bribes as a part of the routine practice of doing business in China (Rodrigues 1995: 17). The inability to maintain a high presence overseas made SMEs easy victims of the complexities mentioned above and only able to entertain low-trust, arm's length strategies.

Conclusion

A number of generic triggers for networking have been identified in the literature to which we added such things as the Internet, new communication systems and the rise of the new economy. However, there is nothing inevitable about networking. It represents a choice or option to try something different in some cases, while in others it might be a necessity or an unplanned event. Throughout this text we have been emphasizing that the world of work is changing, although the change has been gradual and occurring for a long time (see Introduction), from standardization and automation, to flexibility in production, communications and organizational architecture. In some facets of business, intense competition has given way to various cooperative and collaborative arrangements, but not always with beneficial results. We have stressed the virtues and vices of cooperation and collaboration and the different scales at which they occur. However, networking ought not to be seen as the 'new age of business' because it is simply one of a number of strategic options that managers pursue to justify a whole range of motives and interests. Nor is it, as once thought, a counterforce against powerful forms of concentration arising from mergers among MNCs. We mentioned how giga-corporations are significantly reshaping the global landscape and dictating the terms and conditions under which many business relationships, including networking ones, will be conducted.

In this chapter we have focused on organizations and their interorganizational relations, but 'it is people and their relationships who stand at the centre of networks. Society, culture, economics, politics, aspirations and greed are all reflected in our attempt at explaining what networking is about' (Buttery et al. 1999: 457). In explaining what networking is about, we have moved from a relatively descriptive account of network types and relationships to consideration of the more complex relational dimensions of this phenomenon. For example we have, where possible, highlighted the political dimensions of networking relationships, especially how these affect SMEs and their relationship with MNCs. In examining network theories, we have paid particular attention to social capital formation and the complex aspects of trust and distrust. Attention was drawn to how trust is a highly problematical concept around which opinions diverge in terms of how it contributes to the relational dimensions of networking, including how it might be seen as a mythical construct used in some cases to create façades of trust.

This chapter is probably the first to consider how gender has been written out of the literature and identify the masculinist bias in how relationships are dealt with in networking theories. We also examined the concept of the learning network and IOL, and suggested that this network presents the greatest opportunities for enhancing an organization and is people's core competence, but also carries the greatest risks in terms of opportunism. It was suggested that the learning network depends on building credible commitments and the language and dialogue to create an environment of trust where sharing know-how is possible and resilient trust is paramount. The whole area of IOL holds out the most promise in terms of benefits from networking and perhaps best exemplifies the limits and boundaries of the relational dimensions of networking.

We concluded by examining the cross-cultural dimensions of networking and the interplay of cultural and institutional factors on IORs. To highlight the relational

Conclusion cont'd

dimension, we specifically focused on how trust might emerge in such relationships and chose China as a focus. A noticeable pattern in cross-cultural studies is to consider trust from a Western perspective, and we finished off by questioning the integrity of this form of ethnocentrism. To pursue some of the above points further, we now turn to the questions at the beginning of the chapter.

? Answers to questions about networking

1 **Why do organizations enter into interorganizational relations?** We identified a number of factors that account for the rise of networking as well as describing a number of internal and external triggers for networking. Key among these were such factors as gaining economies of scale and scope, gaining market entry, particularly foreign markets, improving learning capabilities, spreading the risks of R&D, dominating markets on a global scale, complying with foreign regulations and so on. As has been noted previously, 'some organizations [or the people in them] form networks to exploit others, dominate their markets or industry and to generally create entry barriers to competitors. Some organizations are more prone or pressured into networking because their environments are volatile and their technologies change rapidly, as do their customers' demands' (Buttery et al. 1999: 457). As we point out, there are identifiable costs and benefits associated with networking, and for every plus there is usually a minus. Drawing on various theoretical perspectives, we sought to explain the complexity of networking from a number of vantage points. For example, we have examined what happens when managers allow their organizations to enter into IORs to enhance their people's core competence and the specific risks that this entails, especially when tacit forms of knowledge are being traded or shared. Overseas joint ventures or international strategic alliances were also examined from the vantage point of describing why they arise and how they unfold in particular contexts, such as China.

2 **What types of cooperation and/or collaboration are possible?** There is an enormous variety and complexity of network types, and the types of cooperation and/or collaboration found among them. We have noted, for example, that networks comprising large firms and SMEs, for example, can follow the pattern of a kingdom, republic or hybrid networks, with differing concentrations of power and/or dependency and interdependency within them. We noted that these network forms can change over time and that they can be heavily influenced by what governments choose to do to help SMEs in particular. Using various typologies, we also described six different types of networks using labels such as 'pooled', 'complementary', 'production', 'service' and 'learning'. Networks or IORs can have different strategic foci, with licensing and franchising involving the least commitment to developing strong relational ties. Joint ventures seem to carry highest risks when R&D or the sharing of tacit knowledge is involved because they invite particular forms of opportunism, especially outlearning one's partner and becoming a competitor. Consortia or separate companies offer more protection and less scope for

Answers continued

opportunism when tacit knowledge sharing is an issue for network partners. As we noted, the learning networks present the greatest opportunities for organizational members to enhance their core competence, but the risks are also the greatest. The chapter also introduced issues relating to social capital and the strength of strong ties versus weak ties. This chapter has focused on networking as an embedded activity in which trust plays an important part in determining what types of collaboration are possible and, who are likely to be chosen over others. In this vein, the discussion of gender and networking is particularly important because it suggests that, for women, much of what is understood as networking in the Western business context largely excludes consideration of them and supports highly masculinist constructions of IORs.

3 **What common problems face organizations wanting to cooperate or collaborate?** As we outlined in Table 16.1, networking entails fairly well-documented costs and benefits. Major benefits include: gaining access to new information, know-how and expertise; product development opportunities; and access to new markets, especially foreign ones. However, major 'costs' or the negatives of networking include: loss of control or autonomy; loss of secrets; having to contribute resources that could have been better deployed elsewhere, perhaps more successfully, and ultimately receiving no mutual benefit. We cite research that shows the high failure rate among joint ventures and, in terms of SMEs, the major difficulties they face in terms of power discrepancies in IORs.

We have given a great deal of attention to the issues of sociability, social capital and the development of trust as key factors in Western approaches to networking. Several negative aspects of social capital were introduced, focusing on the high levels of control and conformity such processes can engender, often restricting innovation and change as well as supporting nepotism and favouritism. We described how hard it is to develop resilient forms of trust, and proposed that trust can act as a myth created by network members to sustain their relationships, often in order to dominate others. Networks often 'hang together', not because of trust but because of the power and pressure exerted on parties to cooperate against their better judgement or interests.

4 **What problems are associated with networking across cultures?** Networking has been principally described as involving relational exchanges and, more recently, even affective or emotional exchanges. Cultural as well as institutional factors play a large part in explaining the numerous conflicts and tensions that arise in cross-border networks. Clashes occur at the basic cultural level in terms of what cooperation and collaboration constitute in different settings. We gave the example of international strategic alliances and the different forms of complexity that come into play in various forms of cooperation and collaboration. We noted that taken-for-granted assumptions, even about what trust means from one culture to another, are dangerous. We discussed how, for very good reasons, in some cultures, such as China, relations with outsiders are not easily built into the conduct of business. Relationships are differentially valued across cultures and embedded in

Answers continued

different institutional forms, for example in Japan it is more 'access' that defines the boundaries of IORs than the Western concept of 'trust' or even contracts. Similarly, in China, being connected by third parties 'oils' relationships, defines who can be trusted and what forms of reciprocity and retribution are used to build IORs that work differently for insider and outsiders.

We identified different forms of internal and external strategies that can be used to manage different forms of networking, specifically in terms of China, where the different forms of complexity that were identified would hold in many emerging economies. We have suggested various approaches to cross-cultural management, highlighting the differences between high- and low-context cultures. While we in the West tend to divide the world into such binaries, particularly to understand culture at the national or macro-level, the reality is that there are enormous subtleties that are played out in the institutional context and at other more personal and individual levels. It is at these more dense and intimate levels that the discourse of networking is given substance and meaning.

REVISITING
THE CASE STUDY

1 What would you do in the place of Web Wonder's board of management about the two proposed strategic alliances?

At the core of this case, and indeed in most forms of IORs, is the issue of trust. Web Wonder has three fundamental needs: (i) finding a suitable partner in Australia and Europe to pursue its B2B e-procurement strategy, and in this instance there are already two recognized market leaders; (ii) finding suitable retailing giants to support its 'clicks and mortar' strategy; and (iii) finding suitable ISPs in Asia that have a reputation for being reliable and cheap providers. Two overarching concerns arise in respect of both (i) and (ii) and these are: the issue of sharing IP and the degree of control that Web Wonder is willing to relinquish in entering into these alliances. Web Wonder does not wish to be absorbed by any of the new ventures and is seeking partnerships that will allow it to remain a separate business. Remember, it is not the board but the CEO who is the main shareholder and who in the end will have to be convinced that her position, wealth and future are also secure.

In terms of the B2B strategy, Web Wonder is seeking a partnership with two other Internet

businesses that have the IP it needs and the board and CEO will have to convince its future partners that it is a credible operator. A key strategy for Web Wonder is to work out before it approaches its potential partners how the IP issue can be best dealt with and, in so doing, work out some very visible ways in which it can signal that it is willing to enter into a fairly resilient form of trust-based relation. Web Wonder might think through the forms of credible commitments that might make this venture work and be careful about how much it is willing to rely on contracting out to establish the relationship. Failing this, and if the alliance does not work out, Web Wonder might seek out a research institute or university partner to help it to develop the IP it needs to launch its own e-procurement strategy, and perhaps invite a new partner to join the new business who does not have significant IP in this area and who will also be subject to various forms of credible commitments.

In terms of the B2C strategy, Web Wonder faces the inevitable problem of finding itself in a kingdom-type partnership with large retailers who might exploit the relationship to their own advantage, and even use Web Wonder to establish a competing business. One option for the board and CEO is to consider a hybrid strategy and deal with a number of companies that are competitors. This will give Web Wonder flexibility and avoid overdependence on any one retailing giant. Because of the IP component in this venture, Web Wonder will have to work out what forms of credible commitments are needed to ensure that breaches and violations are punished in ways that will hurt all partners.

In terms of finding an ISP partner in Asia to carry out what is commonly referred to as 'back-office work', Web Wonder has to decide if it will go to an emerging economy country, such as India, or the more high labour cost countries that form the NICs. Costs are likely to drive Web Wonder to the emerging economy choice and, whichever country is chosen, the board and CEO will have to work out which forms of crude and effective complexity are likely to most impact on IORs. India has a reputation for becoming highly competitive in this field and Web Wonder might start by seeking out ISPs that have offices in London or Europe so that closer ties can be forged. Alternatively, it can 'piggyback' onto ISPs that are being used in Asia by MNCs for their back-office work by outsourcing its customer services operations to countries such as India. Web Wonder will be best served by a gradualist strategy and should start off with a modest operation based and built on a guarded form of trust. Ultimately, it will need to find an ISP that has the management and technological capacities to build more extensive service support. Who negotiates the contracts and establishes the venture will be an issue for the board because the CEO is a woman and she might find it difficult to deal with her male counterpart in some Asian countries. Web Wonder is a new player in this arena and will probably have to rely on intermediaries if it goes to certain countries.

2 If you were the manager of the e-procurement company in Australia, how would you react to Web Wonder's proposal?

The manager would have to be very careful about Web Wonder in terms of the problems associated with IOL. She might well avoid a joint venture and look to establishing a stand-alone company for the new venture. Web Wonder would have to be assessed for its potential as a 'good partner' in terms of its level of commitment and its potential to 'outlearn' its partner and become a future competitor. The manager would have to think seriously about whether being a 'good partner' might expose her business to the risks of being cheated on, not only by Web Wonder but by the

European partners. The manager might be very happy to deal with a woman CEO, being one herself, and be a bit sceptical about the European partner, who is a male and might not fit in. The fact that Sue is a majority shareholder also makes a difference because haggling with a board is the last thing the manager wants. The manager recognizes that she is the stronger partner and can dictate the terms. She should be ensuring that the forms of credible commitments extracted in the early phase of the partnership, should it proceed, entail optimum ones, such as in the case of Web Wonder, making it put in a disproportionately higher amount of venture capital and the European partner being made to agree to some phased commitments as it will also be exposed to high risks with IP. Both the new partners' reputations and credibility will need to be checked out.

3 How might a potential Asian ISP respond to Web Wonder's approach?

It would be highly ethnocentric to assume that an ISP in an emerging economy would automatically see Web Wonder as a useful partner in a new networking arrangement that could involve others as well. Essentially, Web Wonder is proposing to treat the ISP as a peripheral partner. It would also be unwise to assume that ISPs in Asia are somehow lesser entities than their Western counterparts. India hosts a number of successful Internet companies (as noted in the case) and ISPs. And while it might be true that many of these countries lack knowledge workers who are competitive in global markets, the same can be said of many of the dot.bombers. Given that Web Wonder is looking principally to outsource some of its most routine tasks to a back-office arrangement, and include the ISP in the new venture as a non-equity partner, then the Asian ISP is likely to see the venture as being typical of the 'low wage country' strategy adopted by many Western businesses. A more profitable and highly regarded ISP that has MNC clients might not even wish to take on Web Wonder and its new partners. This would mean that Web Wonder would have to 'go down-market' and endure all the risks and problems that come from operating a low-trust strategy with less reliable and reputable partners. However, unlike MNCs, Web Wonder and its partners will not have the resources to invest in the external and internal strategies needed to keep such partnerships on

track, unless of course they find someone who
is based in Europe as well. For the Asian ISP,
Web Wonder and its partners might well invite
opportunistic behaviour, as indeed would be
the case with similar Western partners. It would
be highly fortuitous if Sue Hguina had family
and clan connections in Asia that could help
Web Wonder to build relationships with an
Asian ISP.

References

Alter, C. and Hage, G. (1993) *Organizations Working Together*, Newbury Park, CA: Sage.

Anderson, J. and Narus, J. (1990) 'Model of distributor firm and manufacturer working partnership', *Journal of Marketing,* January: 42–58.

Bleeke, J. and Ernst, D. (1995) 'Is your strategic alliance really a sale', *Harvard Business Review,* January–February: 97–105.

Boisot, M. (1995) *Information Space: A Framework for Learning in Organisations, Institutions and Cultures*, London: Routledge.

Boisot, M. and Child, J. (1996) 'From fiefs to clans and network capitalism: Explaining China's emerging economic order', *Administrative Science Quarterly*, 41: 600–28.

Borys, B. and Jemison, D. (1989) 'Hybrid arrangements as strategic alliances: Theoretical issues in organizational combinations', *Academy of Management Review*, 14(2): 234–49.

Bourdieu, P. (1985) 'The forms of capital', in Richardson, J.G. (ed.) *Handbook of Theory and Research for the Sociology of Education*, New York: Greenwood, pp. 242–58.

Bradach, J.L. and Eccles, R.G. (1989) 'Price, authority, and trust: From ideal types to plural forms', *Annual Review of Sociology*, 15: 97–118.

Brenkert, G.G. (1998) 'Trust, morality and international business', in Lane, C. and Bachmann, R. (eds) *Trust Within and Between Organizations*, New York: Oxford University Press.

Buderi, R. (2000) *Engines of Tomorrow: How the World's Best Companies are Using their Research Labs to Win the Future*, New York: Simon & Schuster.

Burke, J. (1990) 'Networking', a discussion paper for the Australian Manufacturing Council, March.

Burt, R.S. (1992) *Structural Holes: The Social Structure of Competition*, Cambridge, MA: Harvard University Press.

Buttery, E. and Buttery, A. (1994) *Business Networks,* Melbourne: Longman Business & Professional.

Buttery, E. and Buttery, A. (1995) *The Dynamics of the Network Situation*, Canberra AusIndustry Business Networks Program.

Buttery, E., Fulop, L. and Buttery, A. (1999) 'Networks and interorganizational relations', in Fulop, L. and Linstead, S. (eds) *Management: A Critical Text*, Melbourne: Macmillan Business.

Chang, H. and Holt, G.R. (1991) 'More than relationship: Chinese interaction and the principle of Kuan-hsi', *Communication Quarterly*, 39: 251–71.

Child, J. (1998) 'Trust in international strategic alliances: The case of Sino-foreign joint ventures', in Lane, C. and Bachmann, R. (eds) *Trust Within and Between Organizations*, New York: Oxford University Press.

Cohen, W.M., Nelson, R.R. and Walsh, J.P. (2002) 'Links and impacts: the influence of public research on industrial R&D', *Management Science*, 48(1): 1–23.

Coleman, S.J. (1988) 'Social capital in the creation of human capital', *American Journal of Sociology,* 94: S95–121.

Coleman, S.J. (1990) *Foundations of Social Theory,* Cambridge, MA: Belknap Press of Harvard University Press.

Couchman, P. and Fulop, L. (2000) 'Discourses of risk and management practice: Making sense of risk in an interorganizational collaboration', paper presented at the Asia Pacific Researchers in Organizations Studies (APROS) 2000: Organizing Knowledge Economies and Societies, University of Technology, Sydney, 14–17 December. http:/www.bus.uts.edu.au/apros2000/index.html.

Couchman. P. and Fulop, L. (2001) 'Risk in cross-sector R&D collaboration', paper presented at The R&D Management Conference, Leveraging Research and Technology, Victoria University of Wellington, New Zealand, 8–9 February.

Cyert, R.M. and Goodman, P.S. (1997) 'Creating effective university-industry alliances: An organizational learning perspective', *Organizational Dynamics,* Spring: 45–57.

de Laat, P. (1997) 'Research and development alliances: Ensuring trust by mutual commitments', in Ebers, M. (ed.) *The Formation of Inter-Organizational Networks*, New York: Oxford University Press, pp. 146–73.

Doney, P.M., Cannon, J. and Mullen, M.F. (1998) 'Understanding the influence of national culture', *Academy of Management Review*, 28(3): 601–23.

Doz, Y. (1996) 'The evolution of cooperation in strategic alliances: Initial conditions or learning processes', *Strategic Management Journal,* 17: 55–83.

Doz, Y., Hamel, G. and Prahalad, C. (1989) ' Collaborate with your competitors and win', *Harvard Business Review,* January–February: 133–9.

Drucker, P. (2001) 'The next society – a survey of the near future', *The Economist*, 33 November: 3–22.

Dwyer, R., Schurr, P. and Oh, S. (1987) 'Developing buyer-seller relationships', *Journal of Marketing,* **51**: 11–27.

Dyer, J.H. (1996) 'Does governance matter? Keiretsu alliances and asset specificity as sources of Japanese competitive advantage', *Organizational Science,* **7**(6): 649–66.

Dyer, J.H. and Singh, H. (1997) 'The relational view: Cooperative strategy and sources of interorganizational competitive advantage', *Academy of Management Review*, **23**(4): 660–79.

Ebers, M. and Grandori, A. (1997) 'The forms, costs and development dynamics of inter-organizational networking', in Ebers, M. (ed.) *The Formation of Inter-Organizational Networks*, New York: Oxford University Press.

Economist, The (2000) 'Japan's *keiretsu* regrouping', 25 November, p.118.

Foubert, J.D.and Sholley, B.K, (1996) 'Effects of gender, gender role, and individualized trust on self-disclosure', *Journal of Social Behaviour and Personality* (Handbook of gender research – special issue), **11**(5): 277–88.

Fukuyama, F. (1995) *Trust: Social Virtues and the Creation of Prosperity*, London: Hamish Hamilton.

Fulop, L. and Richards, D. (2002) 'Connections, culture and context: Business relationships and networks in the Asia Pacific region', in Harvie, C. and Lee, B.C. (eds) *Globalisation and SMEs in East Asia: Studies of small and medium-sized enterprises in East Asia* (Vol 1), Cheltenham: Edward Elgar.

Grabher, G. (1993) 'Rediscovering the social in the economics of interfirm relations', in Grabher, G. (ed.) *The Embedded Firm: On the Socioeconomics of Industrial Networks,* London and New York: Routledge.

Grandori, A. and Soda, G. (1995) 'Inter-firm networks: Antecedents, mechanisms and forms', *Organization Studies,* **16**(2): 183–214.

Granovetter, M. (1974) *Getting a Job: A Study of Contacts and Careers*, Cambridge, MA: Harvard University Press.

Granovetter, M. (1985) 'Economic action and social structure: The problem of embeddedness', *American Journal of Sociology,* **91**(3): 481–510.

Gray, B. (1999) 'Theoretical perspectives on collaboration over the last decade: Looking back and looking forward'. A paper presented to the Colloquium on Collaboration Research Practice: Academic and Executive Perspectives, Collaboration Research Group, University of Technology Sydney, 7 May.

Hagedoon, J., Link, A.N. and Vonortas, N.S. (2000) 'Research partnerships', *Research Policy,* **29**: 567–86.

Hagen, J.M. and Choe, S. (1998) 'Trust in Japanese interfirm relations: Institutional sanctions matter', *Academy of Management Review (Special Topic Forum on Trust in and Between Organizations)* **23**(3): 589–601.

Hall, E.T. (1976) *Beyond Culture*. New York: Anchor Press/Doubleday.

Hall, E.T. (1987) *Hidden Differences.* New York: Anchor Press/Doubleday.

Hamel, G. (1991) 'Competition for competence and life-partner learning within international strategic alliances', *Strategic Management Journal*, **12**: 83–103.

Hampden-Turner, C. and Trompenaars, F. (1997) *Mastering the Infinite Game.* Oxford: Capstone.

Hardy, C., Phillips, N. and Lawrence, T. (1996) 'Forms and façades of trust: Distinguishing trust and power in interorganisational relations', paper presented at 'Diversity & Change: Challenges for Management into the 21st Century', Australian and New Zealand Academy of Management Conference, Wollongong, NSW, 4–7 December.

Hardy, C., Phillips, N. and Lawrence, T. (1998) 'Distinguishing trust and power in interorganisational relations: Forms and façades of trust', in Lane, C. and Bachmann, R. (eds) *Trust Within and Between Organizations*, New York: Oxford University Press.

Hennart, J. (1988) 'A transaction cost theory of equity joint ventures', *Strategic Management Journal,* **9**: 361–74.

Hofstede, G. (1980) *Culture's Consequences: International Differences in Work-related Values*. London: Sage.

Hofstede, G. (1991) *Cultures and Organizations: Software for the Mind*. London: McGraw-Hill.

Hofstede, G. (1993) 'Cultural constraints in management theories', *Academy of Management Executive,* **7**(1): 81–94.

Howard, R. (1990) 'Can small business help countries compete?', *Harvard Business Review,* November–December: 88–103.

Humphrey, J. (1998) 'Trust and the transformation of supplier relations in Indian industry', in Lane, C. and Bachmann, R. (eds) *Trust Within and Between Organizations*, New York: Oxford University Press.

Huxham, C. (1993) 'Collaborative capability: An intra-organizational perspective on collaborative advantage', *Public Money and Management,* July–September: 21–28.

Huxham, C. (1996) *Creating Collaborative Advantage*, London: Sage.

Jacques, R. (1996) *Manufacturing the Employee:*

Management Knowledge from the 19th to 21st Centuries, London: Sage.

James, D. (1994) 'The struggle to make sense of a world beyond ideology', *Business Review Weekly,* 31 January: 57–8.

Johannisson, B. and Mønsted, M. (1996) 'Networking in context – SMEs and networks in Scandinavia', Plenary Presentation of the 9th Nordic Small Business Conference, Lillehamer, Norway, 29–31 May.

Johnston, R. and Lawrence, P. (1988) 'Beyond vertical integration: The rise of the value-adding partnership', *Harvard Business Review,* July–August: 94–101.

Kanter, R.M. (1977) *Men and Women of the Corporation*, New York: Basic Books.

Kanter, R.M. (1994) 'Collaborative advantage: The art of alliances', *Harvard Business Review,* July–August: 96–112.

Kay, J.A. (1993) *Foundations of Corporate Success: How Business Strategies Add Value*, Oxford: Oxford University Press.

Kogurt, B. and Zander, U. (1988) 'Knowledge of the firm, combinative capabilities, and the replication of technology', *Organization Science,* 3(3): 383–97.

Kreiner, K. and Schultz, M. (1993) 'Informal collaboration in R&D: The formation of networks across organizations', *Organization Studies,* 14(2): 189–209.

Lane, C. (1998) 'Introduction: Theories and issues in the study of trust', in Lane, C. and Bachmann, R. (eds) *Trust Within and Between Organizations*, New York: Oxford University Press.

Larsson, R., Bengtsson, L., Henriksson, K. and Sparks, J. (1998) 'The interorganizational learning dilemma: Collective knowledge development in strategic alliances', *Organization Science,* 9(3): 285–305.

Lei, D.T. (1997) 'Competence-building, technology fusion and competitive advantage: The key roles of organizational learning and strategic alliances', *International Journal of Technology Management,* 14(2/3/4): 208–37.

Levinson, N. and Asahi, M. (1995) 'Cross national alliances and interorganisational learning', *Organizational Dynamics,* Autumn: 50–63.

Lewis, J.D. and Weigert, A. (1985) 'Trust as social reality', *Social Forces,* 63(4): 967–84.

Liebeskind, J.P. and Oliver, A.L. (1998) 'From handshake to contract: Intellectual property, trust, and the social structure of academic research', in Lane, C. and Bachmann, R. (eds) *Trust Within and Between Organizations*, New York: Oxford University Press, pp. 118–45.

Lorber, J. (1979) 'Trust, loyalty, and the place of women in the informal organization of work', in Freeman, J. (ed.) *Women: A Feminist Perspective* (2nd edn), Palo Alto, CA: Mayfield.

Loury, G.C. (1977) 'A dynamic theory of racial income differences', in Wallace, P.A. and La Mond, A.M. (eds) *Women. Minorities, and Employment Discrimination*, Lexington, MA.: Heath, pp. 153–86.

Loury, G.C. (1981) 'Interorganisational transfers and distribution of earnings', *Econometrica*, 49: 843–67.

Lütz, S. (1997) 'Learning through intermediaries: The case of inter-company research collaboration', in Ebers, M. (ed.) *The Formation of Inter-Organizational Networks*, New York: Oxford University Press, pp. 222–37.

Macmillan, G.S., Narin, F. and Deeds, D.L. (2000) 'An analysis of the critical role of public science in innovation: The case of biotechnology', *Research Policy,* 29: 1–8.

Macneil, I.R. (1985) 'Relational contracts: What we do and do not know', *Wisconsin Law Review,* 3: 483–526.

Mauss, M. (1967[1925]) *The Gift*, New York: Norton.

Mead, R. (1998) *International Management: Cross-cultural Dimensions* (2nd edn), Oxford: Blackwell.

Misztal, B. (1996) *Trust in Modern Societies*, Cambridge: Polity Press.

Mitroff, I. and Linstone, H.A. (1993) *The Unbounded Mind: Breaking the Chains of Traditional Business Thinking*, New York: Oxford University Press.

Nahapiet, J. and Ghoshal, S. (1998) 'Social capital, intellectual capital, and the organizational advantage', *Academy of Management Review,* 23(2): 242–66.

Nohria, N. (1992) 'Is a network perspective a useful way of studying organizations?', in Nohria, N. and Eccles, R.G. (eds) *Networks and Organizations: Structure, Form and Action*, Boston, MA: Harvard Business School Press.

Nooteboom, B. (1997) 'Design of inter-firm relations: goals, conditions, problems and solutions'. Paper presented at 13th EGOS Colloquium: Organizational Responses to Radical Environmental Changes: Sub-theme 2: Inter-Organizational Networks and Radical Environmental Change, Budapest University of Economic Sciences: Budapest, 3–5 July.

Nooteboom, B. (2000) 'Institutions and forms of co-ordination in innovation systems', *Organization Studies;* Special issue on *The Institutional Dynamics of Innovation Systems,* 21(5): 915–40.

Office of Technology Assessment (1990) *Making Things Better: Competing in Manufacturing, A Report of the Office of Technology Assessment, US Congress,* Washington DC: Government Printing Office.

Okubu, Y. and Sjöberg, C. (2000) 'The changing pattern of industrial scientific collaboration in Sweden', *Research Policy,* **29**: 81–98.

Oliver, A.L. and Ebers, M. (1998) 'Networking network studies: An analysis of conceptualization configurations in the study of inter-organizational relationships', *Organization Studies,* **19**(4): 549–83.

Organization for Economic Development (OECD) (2001) *The Well-Being of Nations: The Role of Human and Social Capital*, Paris, 10 May.

Parkhe, A. (1991) 'Interfirm diversity, organization learning and longevity in strategic alliances', *Journal of International Business Studies,* **22**(4): 579–601.

Pearce II, J.A. and Robinson, Jr R.R. (2000) 'Cultivating gaunxi as a foreign investor strategy', *Business Horizon*, Jan–Feb: 31–8.

Polanyi, M. (1967) *The Tacit Dimension*, London: Routledge and Kegan. (First published 1966).

Pollack, A. (1992) 'Technology without borders raises big questions for US', *The New York Times* 1 January: 1.

Porter, M. (1990) *The Competitive Advantage of Nations*, London: Macmillan – now Palgrave Macmillan.

Porter, M. (2001) 'Strategy after the net', *Harvard Business Review*, March: 62–80.

Portes, A. (1998) 'Social capital: Its origins and applications in modern sociology', *Annual Review of Sociology,* **24**(1): 1–24.

Powell, W.W. (1990) 'Neither market nor hierarchy: Network forms of organization', *Research in Organisational Behaviour,* **12**: 295–336, Greenwich, CT: JAI Press.

Powell, W.W. (1996) 'Trust-based forms of governance', in Tyler, T. and Kramer, R. (eds) *Trust in Organizations; Frontiers in Theory and Research*, Thousand Oaks, CA: Sage, pp. 51–67.

Prabhu, G.N. (1999) 'Implementing university-industry joint product innovation projects', *Technovation,* **19**(8): 495–505.

Prahalad, C.K. and Hamel, G. (1990) 'The core competence of the corporation', *Harvard Business Review,* **68**(3): 79–93.

Putnam, R.D. (1993) 'The prosperous community: social capital and public life', *American Prospect,* **13**: 35–42.

Redding, S.G. (1990) *The Spirit of Chinese Capitalism*. Berlin and New York: de Gruyter.

Reed, M. (2001) 'Organization, trust and control: A realist analysis', *Organization Studies*, **22**(2): 201–28.

Reve, T. (1995) 'Networks – the Norwegian way: An evaluation of the Norwegian Business Network Program', *Network News*, Issue 3 (December): 10–12 (Canberra: AusIndustry Business Network Program).

Ring, P.S. (1997a) 'Process facilitating reliance in trust in inter-organizational networks', in Ebers, M. (ed.) *The Formation of Inter-Organizational Networks*, New York: Oxford University Press.

Ring, P.S. (1997b) 'Transacting in the state of exchange governed by convergent interests', *Journal of Management Studies,* **34**(1): 1–25.

Ring, P.S. and Van de Ven, A.H. (1994) 'Developmental processes of cooperative inter-organizational relationships', *Academy of Management Review* **19**(1): 90–118.

Robertson, M., Scarbrough, H. and Swan, J. (1997) 'Innovation, knowledge and networking: A comparative study of the role of inter- and intra-organizational networks in innovation processes'. Paper presented at 13th EGOS Colloquium: Organisational Responses to Radical Environmental Changes, Budapest University of Economic Sciences, Budapest, 3–5 July, (www.cd-klub.hu/pccd).

Roddick, A. (2000) *Business as Unusual: The Triumph of Anita Roddick*, London: Thorsons.

Rodrigues, S.B. (1995) 'Negotiations for strategic alliances: Brazillian firms entering the Chinese market', paper presented at the European Group for Organizational Studies Colloquium, workshop on local vs global rationality, Istanbul, Turkey, 6–8 July.

Rousseau, D.M., Sitkin, S.B., Burt, R.S. and Camerer, C. (1998) 'Introduction to special topic forum: Not so different after all: A cross-discipline view of trust', *Academy of Management Review,* **23**(3): 393–404.

Sabel, C. (1990) 'Skills Without a Place: The Reorganization of the Corporation and the Experience of Work'. An address to the plenary session of the British Sociological Association, April 2.

Scher, M.J. (1997) 'The limitations of "trust-based" theories in Japan's inter-organizational networks in the era of globalization', paper presented at 13th EGOS Colloquium*: Sub-theme 2: Inter-organizational Networks and Radical Environmental Change*, Budapest, 3–5 July.

Sengenberger, W., Loveman, G. and Piore, M. (1990) 'The re-emergence of small enterprise: Industrial restructuring', in *Industrialised Economies*, Geneva: International Labour Organisation.

Shane, S. (1993) 'The effect of cultural differences in perception of transaction costs on national differences in the preference for international joint ventures', *Asia-Pacific Journal of Management*, **10**(1): 57–69.

Shapiro, S.P. (1987) 'The social control of impersonal trust', *American Journal of Sociology,* **93**(3): 623–58.

Sheehan, P. (2001) 'Global warning', *The Sydney Morning Herald – News Review*, Saturday, 31 March, p. 32.

Spender, J.C. (1996) 'Making knowledge the basis of a dynamic theory of the firm', *Strategic Management Journal,* **17**(S2): 45–62.

Sydow, J. (1998) 'Understanding the constitution of interorganizational trust', in Lane, C. and Bachmann, R. (eds) *Trust Within and Between Organizations*, New York: Oxford University Press.

Trompenaars, F. and Hampden-Turner, C. (1997) *Riding the Waves of Culture.* London: Nicholas Brealey.

Wekselberg, V. (1996) 'Reduced "social" in a new model of organizational trust', *Academy of Management Review,* **21**(2): 333–5.

Williamson, O. (1985) *The Economic Institutions of Capitalism: Firms, Markets and Relational Contracting,* New York: Free Press.

Williamson, O. (1991) 'Strategizing, economizing and economic organization', *Strategic Management Journal,* **2**: 75–94.

Williamson, O. (1993) 'Calculativeness, trust, and economic organization', *Journal of Law and Economics*, **36**: 453–86.

Womack, J.P., Jones, D.T. and Roos, D. (1990a) *The Machine That Changed the World,* New York: Rawson Associates.

Womack, J.P., Jones, D.T. and Roos, D. (1990b) *The Massachusetts Institute of Technology 5 Million Dollar 5 Year Study on the Future of the Automobile Industry*, New York: Rawson Associates.

Zucker, L.G. (1986) 'Production of trust: Institutional sources of economic structure, 1840–1920', in Straws, B.M. and Cummings, L.L. (eds), *Research in Organizational Behaviour*, **8**: 53–111. Greenwich, CT: JAI Press.

Zucker, L., Brewer, M. and Peng, Y. (1986) 'Organizational boundaries as trust production', in Kramer, R. and Tyler, T. (eds) *Trust in Organizations: Frontiers of Theory and Research*, Thousand Oaks, CA: Sage.

Zucker, L.G., Darby, M.R., Brewer, M.B. and Peng, Y. (1995) 'Collaboration structure and information dilemmas in biotechnology: Organizational boundaries as trust production', Working Paper No. 5199, Cambridge, US: National Bureau of Economic Research.

Part III
Conclusion

17

Managing in a virtual world

Stephen Linstead and Simon Lilley

Introduction: brave new virtual world?

To bring our book to a close we consider contemporary changes in the organization of work that are seen by many to either herald or follow the advent of a *virtual world*. In doing so we adopt a slightly different style in the presentation of our thoughts on the matter, because consideration of the notion of managing in a virtual world gives us a welcome opportunity to look back and reflect upon our own practices in the production of this text. So this chapter represents an extended attempt to highlight what managing in a virtual world might be like, both by consideration of the production of this book and a look at some other pertinent examples that shed some light on the potential future of work for managers and employees alike. As such, it does not follow the basic structure – questions, questions on a case – adopted in other chapters, instead it represents an extended questioning and answering of a number of cases and propositions about contemporary and future circumstances. It examines the nature of the virtual world, its history and its consequences for accountability. It looks at the present and the future of both office and factory work and concludes with a discussion of the implications for identity of life in a virtual world. We begin, however, with some facts about the present case.

MANAGEMENT AND ORGANIZATION: A CRITICAL TEXT – A VIRTUAL PRODUCT?

This book has had two titles during its production. The three main authors, from two different continents, have, between them, worked in seven different organizations during its production (four in the UK, two in different states in Australia, one in Hungary). Our associates, who contributed much of the specialist content of the text, are currently based in, or have emerged from, at least three different continents and have passed through the doors of innumerable institutions during the production of the text. The name of the imprint has changed once and the identity of the commissioning editor at the publishers, working with us on the text, has changed three times. In short, little or nothing around the text has stayed fixed during its production. Most of the production of the text was electronically mediated. We swapped versions of chapters by attaching them to emails (using a number of different accounts). We frequently commented on each other's contributions using facilities such as MS Review. Many of the case materials and illustrative examples were downloaded from the Web, and the draft versions of the text (and the reviewers' comments on them), along with the final version to be sent to the publisher, were all transmitted using electronic means. At any given time, many different fragments of the text, in many different forms, existed simultaneously in a number of different electronic receptacles and pathways. But now the text is produced as a commodity for sale, it parades its integrity, as a *product*, that belies much of this detail concerning the unstable circumstances of its production. However, as we note in the Preface, this is a product that, along with the supporting web-based materials, can be consumed in myriad different ways. It exhibits considerable *interpretive flexibility* (Pinch and Bijker 1987). As such, both in terms of its production and in its form as a product, this book is avowedly a constituent of a virtual world.

Having concluded our statement of facts with such a claim, before going any further we need to correct a couple of potential misunderstandings to which such a statement can give rise. The first concerns the implicit ascription of *newness* to the virtual world, because there is nothing necessarily new about virtuality. Ever since we have been able to record and disseminate text in symbolic form (see for example Ong 1982; Goody 1986, 1987; McArthur 1986) and trade in other representative tokens, we can be said to have conducted part of our existence in virtuality (see for example Heidegger 1977; Barker 1984; Cooper 1991; Kallinikos 1995). Money is perhaps the most obvious example here, an example that not only indicates the lack of newness of virtuality, but also its incompleteness as a metaphor for understanding the totality of our condition: 'No matter how virtual the subject may become, there is always a body attached' (Stone 1991).

Money … is not the thing itself. Over time we can come to think of money as wealth … but in truth, this is sloppy abstract thinking. It has allowed its focus of attention to wander from the bun to the penny which symbolizes the bun. In effect we've had an information economy ever since we invented money. But we still haven't learnt to digest copper. (Bey 1996: 372)

Neither then is the associated notion of a *virtual community* a new one. A geographical region within which certain coins or notes consistently stand for agreed amounts of value can certainly be seen to constitute the location of a virtual community. And as Stone (1991) notes, the 'community of gentlemen' that was assembled by the scientist Robert Boyle to assist during his debates with the political scientist Thomas Hobbes, in the seventeenth century, can easily be construed as an early example of a 'textual' virtual community. So virtuality is not new, nor is it capable of providing us with a complete account of our existence – we cannot eat virtual food! And while we *do* need to consider what has happened to us and our managing in the face of a *partially* virtual world (more of this later), we should be wary here of the second potential misunderstanding that consideration of matters virtual throws up. That is, the extent of (access to) the virtual world. For if we understand virtuality in more conventional terms, as signalled by the existence of a (computer-mediated) 'information economy' (Porat 1977; see also Castells 1993, 2000a, 2000b, 2000c), then it is a mode of existence experienced by very few. For while even in 1990 over 40 per cent of the populations of the US, the UK, France and West Germany 'were engaged in information processing activities … and the proportion continues to rise over time' (Castells 1993), the same cannot be said for the world as a whole.

Exclusive technology – is the Internet for the elite?

If we take the Internet as our exemplar of virtuality, this becomes clear. As David Trend (2001: 182) points out, 'little more than a decade ago admission to cyberspace required membership of an elite community: the university'. And as he further notes, although a figure of 200 million Internet users, worldwide (a figure available of course, at his time of writing, and one about which we should take considerable care, given the difficulties in accurately stating Internet usage and the variability in the figures offered by different commentators – see Jordan 1999; Bell 2001), sounds impressive, 'it is important to recognize that Internet users represent less than four per cent of the world's 6 billion people' (Trend 2001: 124).

On many levels the vast expansion of information technology has created what the US Commerce Department has termed a 'digital divide.' Reports indicate that households with incomes under $25,000 were 20 times less likely to have Internet access than those with high incomes, and people with little education were 25 per cent less likely to be netizens than college graduates … Consolidation of commercial and residential capital into such technology-rich centers as Boston, Silicon Valley, and Seattle continues, while simultaneously producing growing transient or ghettoized populations in less fortunate regions or in the nations of the developing world that produce the majority of the world's silicon chips. (Trend 2001: 124)

Jordan [1999] writes that in July 1998, the US had 65 per cent of all Internet hosts; Slevin (2000: 40) states that 'almost 99 per cent of all Internet connections were in North America, Western Europe and Japan' by the late 1990s … Striking concentrations and inequalities are also revealed elsewhere: of the 145,000 hosts in sub-Saharan Africa in 1998, more than 96 per cent were in South Africa – take away South Africa, and the stats for sub-Saharan Africa show only one user per 5,000 people. More than three-quarters of the 115,000 hosts in the Middle East and North Africa in 1998 were in Israel. The cost of Internet access in Vietnam in 1999 was one third of the average annual salary. In Indonesia, Internet access costs twelve times more than it does in the US. Moreover, between one third and one half of the world's population lives more than two hours from the nearest public telephone. And so on – the pattern that emerges is of huge disparities globally, all of them exacerbating what Sean Cubbitt (1998: 149) calls, in a telling phrase 'the excommunication of the developing world' (see also Holderness 1998). (Bell 2001: 17; see also various contributions to Bell and Kennedy 2000)

More worrying than these brute figures is the direction of the future development of the Web, delineated by many commentators. For example, Arthur Kroker and Michael Weinstein (1994/2001) suggest that much of the 'virtual class', directing this future, can best be conceived of as 'the post-historical successor to the early bourgeoisie of primitive capitalism', as a class that 'only wants to subordinate digital reality to the will of capitalism' (2001: 153). And, as such, we can expect little in the way of amelioration of extant inequalities to come from the virtual revolution of the information economy. Instead we should expect an exacerbation of these disparities. As the popular book *Netocracy* declaims on its cover: 'Those who can harness global networks of information and master new forms of communication will inherit the power. They are the Netocrats' (Bard and Söderqvist 2002).

Popular technology: Is the Internet for everyone?

The power of the Web is in its universality. Access by everyone regardless of disability is an essential aspect. (Berners-Lee 2003)

But things are not all bad! For, as Kroker and Weinstein also note (1994/2001: 151): 'Dedicated flesh rebels against the virtual class' and acts as 'the Internet equivalent of the Paris Commune: anarchistic, utopian, and in full revolt against the suppression of the general (tele-)human possibilities of the Net in favour of the specific (monetary) interests of the virtual class' (2001: 153). The virtual future is still open. Consider the following case example.

CASE EXAMPLE

MARILLION CHALLENGE THE MUSIC INDUSTRY WITH FAN POWER

In what is believed to be an unprecedented venture which could revolutionize the music industry, Marillion fans have financed the making of the band's 2001 album, *Anoraknophobia*, after an Internet campaign raised over £100,000 – conclusive proof of the power of the Internet for artists and record companies alike.

Marillion, who have been writing and recording for almost 20 years, approached their database of over 30,000 fans via email, as an alternative to taking up the deals they were being offered from established record companies. The response was overwhelmingly positive: within three weeks fans offered to prepay for the album, to the tune of 5 per cent of total worldwide expected sales, providing enough money to cover the costs of making their 12th studio album. In doing so, a record company advance was rendered redundant and the band retained the rights to their new music. This groundbreaking idea enabled the band to return to EMI Records who agreed to license the album for a world-wide marketing and distribution deal. The album was released in spring 2001 through their Liberty label: 12,647 pre-orders were manufactured and fulfilled by Marillion's own Internet mail-order company, Racket Records, and shipped on the week of release. The 8,000 fans pre-ordering albums within an initial limited period of one month were thanked personally in the sleeve notes of the special first edition of the album. Marillion then ceased manufacture and sale of the pre-ordered version upon the album release, after which the album became available only at retail. The scheme led to a number of copycat initiatives from other well-known bands, including Dodgy and The Levellers.

Commenting on the initiative, Lucy Jordache, Marillion's marketing manager, said:

> We were being offered deals from various record companies, but what the guys really wanted, was to have total control of their music, yet still be able to utilize the expertise and distribution facilities of a major record label. This could only be achieved if we obtained the capital to record an album from another source, and then took the finished product to a label. This is a real testament to the loyal support of Marillion's fans, old and new. It also demonstrates the power of the Internet and what it has to offer both artists and the record industry as a whole. 95 per cent of the band's market still remains beyond the scope of the pre-order idea, so retailers should see no noticeable loss in potential sales. Indeed, an upturn is expected as Marillion return to their original EMI stable.

EMI Liberty's co-director Peter Duckworth added: 'We were very impressed with this venture which we believe breaks new ground in the industry. We are all in a win–win situation, EMI are happy, retail is happy, the band are happy and the fans are extremely happy.'

Marillion are no strangers to harnessing the power of the Internet. They were one of the first groups in the UK to set up a website ('http://www.marillion.com') in the mid-1990s to communicate with and sell Marillion products to their fans – fans from as far and wide as Brazil to Japan and Australia to Iceland. They now have an active database of over 30,000 fans who visit their website on an average weekly basis. UK fans, objecting to a chance remark by Simon Mayo on Radio 1 last summer, brought the radio station's computer system to a standstill when they emailed to complain and demanded he play a Marillion track. He subsequently interviewed keyboard-player Mark Kelly on air in an attempt to understand and appease the phenomenal passion of Marillion's audience. Back in 1997 American fans underwrote an entire US tour to the tune of $60,000, with donations following an Internet campaign – an idea conceived and managed by the fans before any involvement by the band. Lead singer Steve 'h' Hogarth added: 'It's not just about the money – the Internet allows us to communicate directly to our fans worldwide in a way that's spontaneous and instant. It's a two-way communication process that's changed everything for us – the fans feel like a worldwide family now. Faith moves mountains, so watch out.'

Subsequently the band challenged standard music industry practices with the release of their double A side single 'Between you and me/Map of the world'. In another unprecedented project, fans buying the single from their popular website, www.marillion.com, were given a free copy for each single bought. The fans then sent the free copy (along with a letter and band biography provided by Marillion) to their local radio station to encourage its airplay. Over 10,000 copies were posted to local radio stations worldwide, and the band's exposure was massively enhanced. Hogarth urged, 'Look around, listen around. Surely the music business has to change. How do REAL bands compete with the Hear'Say/Britney Spears astronomical marketing/promotion spend? This experiment enables us to plough any profits straight into promotion AND to mobilize our legendary fans to raise a concerted voice to radio and, to a lesser extent, the media. On balance, we decided our own independent release is the way to go. It's great that EMI have the vision to let us run with this. There's been a lot of indifference to us at radio. Now we're in a position to let everyone know we're alive and well with the best weapons we have – our music and our fans.' As well as much press and media interest, this venture has also seen the band appear on the recent BBC2 documentary *The Future Just Happened,* explaining how the concept of Internet self-financing worked for them. With the innovative single release, Marillion once again proved that the combination of faithful fans, the Internet and radical thinking can ensure the continued success of both their business and their contemporary music.

Source: Adapted from press releases issued by the band, archived at http://www.marillion.com/news/2000/1606.html, accessed 27 February 2003.

There is even a new word for this – *devox* – coined by futurists Ryan Mathews and Watts Wacker to represent the voice or spirit of deviant ideas, people and products. According to Wacker (Tucker 2002: 66), the devox starts:

way out on the Fringe. It then moves to the Edge, then to the Realm of the Cool and then becomes the Next Big Thing. Then it turns into Social Convention. From there it can go into Cliché, Icon, Archetype or Oblivion.

Wacker may well simply be using trendy terms to track the process of paradigm shifting that social scientists have been familiar with since Kuhn, but his point is that corporations need to be able to pick their winners much earlier in the fast-moving, Internet-enabled, competitive environment of today, and identify which deviant ideas are the ones which will create new markets. It is a risky business, but the rewards can be immense – Bill Gates and the Microsoft team were all deviants when they set out on the high-tech fringe (see Bell 2001: 11), but now Gates is the icon of the monopoly capitalist. Las Vegas began as a desert gambling den for laundering mob money, became cool with Sinatra and Martin, moved into social convention as other states and even other countries began to copy its methods and now, as cliché, is a place where the whole family can holiday without ever gambling (Tucker 2002).

Marillion, despite their early popularity in the 1980s, were still out on the 'fringe', a cultish band with deviant appeal. But their cultural deviance led them to think deviantly about their business affairs, and they created a successful model, using the information technology at their and their fans' disposal, to shift both their creative and economic power base. They are now certainly 'cool' in that respect – the question remains open as to whether other bands will turn their ideas into 'social convention'. So one consequence of the advent of the virtual world could be increased emancipation, greater empowerment of producers as distributed capital in the hands of consumers can be mobilized sufficiently quickly and in sufficient volume to short-circuit the need for large amounts of invested and accumulated capital. However, the communication and information-rich world may also offer quite different prospects, as our previous warnings from Kroker and Weinstein suggest. We take up these themes with reference to the shifting ways in which accountability is realized in the virtual world.

No time for accountability? Living in a scandalous world

One of the things that the virtual world of the information economy has effected is a radical increase in the compression of time and space (Harvey 1989), a change that had already been inaugurated by the mechanical and informational products of the industrial age. As a result, time has increasingly become a competitive issue.

Increased competitive pressure has sharpened what has always been a point of difference between companies, namely time, into a strategic issue. Time appears in the business world in many guises: time-to-market, down-time, real time, customer-facing time, fee-earning time, on-time. Some companies realize that these terms are part of a business shift from economies of scale to economies of time. It is the speed and responsiveness of an organization that now gives it a comparative advantage … It is no longer good enough to have the right product at the right price. It also has to be in the right place at the right time. All factors have to be present to satisfy customers. This changes the rules of the game. (Kreitzman 1999: 121–2)

Customers now evaluate manufacturers and service providers according to the changing rules of a world 'which has speeded up so as to make, as the saying has it "twenty-four hours a very long time"' (Harvey 1989: 285). Indeed, so complex is this world that the most successful and talented are made long-term ill by conditions such as 'yuppie flu' or myalgic encephalitis (ME), otherwise known as chronic fatigue syndrome, the Epstein–Barr virus and other forms of long-term fatigue. Why should this happen, and why do managers nevertheless seem so willing to engage in practices which sustain it, even while expressing sentiments like Kreitzman's (1999: 134) respondent 'Mike Dollar's children will not go into the same business as him. At least, not if he can help it'?

Harvey's (1989) view is that the phenomena which Kreitzman observes are the result of the latest and perhaps most spectacular phase of historical time–space compression, where the acceleration of the development of technological and informational systems has added a new dimension to capitalism's historical and paradoxical need for growth and further accumulation, even in conditions of overaccumulation and post-scarcity, which produces the need to find new forms of *flexible accumulation* and therefore new 'spaces' – geographical and cultural – to exploit. Speed of manufacturing production, speed of information flow to and from markets, speed of flow of capital through deregulated financial and trading systems, speed of transportation which takes advantage of distributing manufacturing around the world and

establishing localized partial assembly functions to put together products with flexible features have had spectacular results in increasing the availability and reducing the cost of products, with short time-to-market and rapid modification and monitoring of customers' needs and preferences. Economies are economies of time and space, not just of material value. Furthermore, as Lash and Urry (1993: 10–11) note, the rapid flow of information cannot be fully organized because there is not time to screen and evaluate all information. As Paul Virilio, perhaps the foremost theorist of speed, puts it: 'The twin phenomena of immediacy and of instantaneity are presently one of the most pressing problems confronting [us]' (1995; see also Virilio 2000). Virilio sees this not so much as the result of the forces of capitalism, favoured as explanation by Harvey, but rather as the result of military imperatives. Such a view foregrounds, to take one pertinent example, the role of the military in the construction of the antecedents of the Internet (see Bell 2001: 11–14, for an account of these antecedents, along with some welcome unpacking of the mythology that has grown up around it). The racing of information through its new circuits and the problems associated with such racing, Virilio terms *dromology*. Taking a less pessimistic and, indeed, less nostalgic and conservative line than that adopted by Virilio (Kellner 1999, particularly 103), we may note that the more information and knowledge flow, the more problems, paradoxes and unforeseen consequences occur, and the more such a system depends on individuals who are *reflexive*, aware of emerging problems and committed to coming up with at least partial solutions to them. *Disorganized capitalism* is sustained by *reflexive accumulation*. As Harvey notes, this entails a good deal of risk:

Time-space compression always exacts a toll on our capacity to grapple with the realities unfolding around us. Under stress, for example, it becomes harder and harder to react to events … the world's financial markets are on the boil in ways that make a snap judgement here, an unconsidered word there and a gut reaction somewhere else the slip that can unravel the whole skein of fictitious capital formation and of interdependency. (Harvey 1989: 306)

In a world where unforeseen problems are thrown up constantly and there is rarely time to respond to them in a considered way, how can it be possible to hold people *accountable*? How can rational procedures be followed to the letter when there is no time to follow rational evaluation procedures? This goes beyond Simon's 'satisficing' (see Chapter 14) because even though Simon (1960) recognized that rationality is bounded, and we often settle for the best decision that can be made in circumstances of imperfect information, the problem often is one of too much information, some of which may be contradictory, none of which is stable, all of which is likely to change rapidly, and where the degree and extensiveness of *interconnection* and *interconnectedness*, familiar from chaos and complexity theories, can mean that a small change in one part of the nexus – including this decision – could produce changes elsewhere which might transform the whole. Oddly, this decision might be the right one in terms of all we know before it is made, but its existence might have unforeseen effects which make it the wrong one as soon as it has been made. Sounds familiar? Did you ever have that feeling that you couldn't do anything right? In these circumstances, when can *achievement* be unequivocally demonstrated and performance properly evaluated?

We would expect then that there would be, at one level, a proliferation of ever-changing performance measurement and evaluation systems, in many cases a modernist act of faith, but also that organizations would need to be able to know that they had managers who were *reflexive* and *committed* to trying to solve

unanticipated problems quickly and in the right way, with insufficient time to do so. In a world where time and space are compressed, competence may have to mean not achievement but commitment, signalled by availability – 24/7 in some cases in Kreitzman's 24-hour society. Accountability may mean not following rules and procedures, but having the right values and mindset to respond in the right way, to be a good corporate citizen even in deviating and transgressing existing norms. We should also note, accordingly, that the new compressed economies of time and space need to be sustained symbolically, and responsible participation in and commitment to them consolidated, as far as such things can be, by economies of signs, cultural developments where identities can be formed and commitment can be seduced into being (see Lash and Urry 1993; Baudrillard 1981: 90). That said, in many cases, the speed of information seems to combine with ever-shifting, transitory, 'structures' of (ir)responsibility in such a way that accountability simply breaks down. Consider the following recent cases in point.

CASE EXAMPLES

CAPITALISM IN CRISIS?: UNCLE SAM'S SCANDALS AT A GLANCE

An unprecedented wave of corporate scandals has engulfed Wall Street and unnerved investors. Share prices have fallen 40 per cent since the start of the year on both sides of the Atlantic. The September 11 terrorist attacks dealt a blow to investor confidence but the fraud and December bankruptcy at energy trader Enron really set the sell-off rolling. Since then there has been a steady stream of corporate scandals. Cooking the books at Enron cost investors $67bn (£42bn). World-Com lost telecoms shareholders $175bn while the Tyco conglomerate was desperately reassuring the market last night that it was not on the verge of bankruptcy.

The Securities and Exchange Commission (SEC) in the US opened 63 investigations into financial reporting irregularities in the first three months of 2002 alone. This may be more than the tip of the iceberg, but it is unlikely to be the whole of it.

ENRON *(power and energy trading)*

Enron, the seventh largest corporation in the US at the beginning of 2001, started the corporate crisis in America by announcing on October 16 2001 that it would take a $1bn special charge and write down shareholders' funds by a further $1.2bn. This followed losses arising from a private equity operation run by

chief financial officer Andrew Fastow. Within a week the SEC had started a fraud probe and by the end of the month Enron shares had fallen 50 per cent. It filed for bankruptcy in December, having wiped out $67bn of shareholder funds. One of its VPs resigned and committed suicide. Its auditor Arthur Andersen admitted shredding documents on the case, while Enron's links with the White House have tarnished the Bush administration.

WORLDCOM *(telecoms, Internet)*

Internal audit at WorldCom, the world's biggest telecommunications supplier, showed more than $3.8bn in expenses had been fraudulently disguised over five quarters dating back to January 2001. The SEC filed civil fraud charges and the Justice Department began a criminal investigation. The stock had peaked at $64.50 in 1999 but was suspended on July 2 2002 at 83 cents when the company filed for bankruptcy in order to buy time to restructure.

GLOBAL CROSSING *(telecoms)*

Global Crossing sought protection from its creditors at the end of January. On February 8 it revealed that the SEC had started an official inquiry into the collapse and had subpoenaed documents relating to claims by a former employee that the company had used creative accounting to inflate its earnings. The investigation was further bad news for accountancy firm Arthur Andersen which audited Global Crossing as well as Enron.

TYCO (Industrial conglomerate)

Tyco's former chairman Dennis Kozlowski was indicted in early June on tax evasion charges over art purchases worth £13m. He has also been charged with tampering with evidence. Prosecutors said they would reopen an investigation into the $2.5m sale of former Conservative Party treasurer Lord Ashcroft's Florida home to a senior executive of Tyco. Lord Ashcroft is a board member at heavily indebted Tyco whose debt has been downgraded to junk status. The company yesterday denied bankruptcy rumours.

XEROX (office machines)

Xerox restated $6.4bn of revenues dating back to 1997. It reached agreement with the SEC three months ago over the way it booked as revenues the long-term leases of copiers but the figures were three times larger than investors expected. The stock lost 13 per cent of its value in one day in July 2002.

BRISTOL-MYERS SQUIBB (pharmaceuticals)

Bristol-Myers Squibb was charged with illegal attempts to block generic rivals to its top-selling breast cancer drug, Taxol. Twenty-nine American states led by Ohio have filed a lawsuit in the US district court of Columbia saying the company profited unfairly from its monopoly and was depriving consumers of less expensive versions of the treatment.

AOL TIME WARNER (Internet and media)

AOL revealed that its accounts were under investigation by the SEC. It is the second time within a month that the financial regulator has looked at the company's books. The company's share price has been on the slide since AOL joined with Time Warner in a merger worth $165bn but the latest allegations of creative book keeping have further damaged its standing. Chief executive Richard Parsons said the inquiry was just a 'fact finding' mission inevitable in the current volatile atmosphere.

ADELPHIA (cable operator)

John Rigas, the 77-year-old founder, his two sons plus two other former executives were arrested and charged with 'looting Adelphia on a massive scale'. These are the first criminal charges to be bought in the recent spate of corporate scandals. Adelphia, the US's sixth largest cable operator, is also facing civil charges from the SEC. The company filed for Chapter 11 protection from creditors in summer 2002.

JOHNSON & JOHNSON (drugs and household products)

Johnson & Johnson, maker of Band Aid, admitted it was under US criminal investigation over allegations that it made errors in drug manufacturing and then tried to cover them up. Former employee Hector Arce claims in a wrongful dismissal suit that he was pressured into changing key data to hide mistakes in making anaemia drug Exprex at a factory in Puerto Rico. News of the investigation prompted a dramatic fall in Johnson & Johnson's share price.

HALLIBURTON (engineering)

Halliburton admitted in May 2002 that the engineering and oil services group was being investigated by the SEC over accounting practices when it was run by US vice president Dick Cheney between 1995 and 2000. The legal pressure group Judicial Watch is suing Mr Cheney and the firm, alleging they defrauded shareholders by overstating company revenues by $450m. The company and the White House have denied this.

QWEST (telecoms)

Qwest Communications was already under investigation by the SEC for its accounting practices when it disclosed that it had incorrectly accounted for more than $1bn of revenue over three years. The company's new management – appointed in June 2002 – also said it might make further accounting revisions after the SEC and its own auditors completed their investigations. Qwest had booked hundreds of millions of dollars of revenue at the end of its quarterly reporting which should have been delayed until the next quarter. Like many telecom companies, Qwest was under intense pressure to meet quarterly revenue and profit targets.

Source: Adapted from The Guardian Unlimited
http://www.guardian.co.uk, Monday 29 July 2002,
© Guardian Newspapers Limited 2002.

So what seems to be going wrong? Various theories have been put forward, from the need to emphasize ethics more in the MBA curriculum (many of the officers involved have Ivy League MBAs), to corporate culture, to the need for greater regulation by the state, to gender issues (the whistle-blower at Enron was the only woman VP). However, we can draw on what we have already covered in the book to glean some insights. If we turn to Chapter 3, we will see that Deal and Kennedy (1982) proposed that the two dimensions of corporate culture were *risk* and *speed of feedback*. If we interpret speed of feedback to be information flow, then it is clear that Deal and Kennedy stumbled upon what are two of the most important concepts in contemporary social science, *risk* and *information*, especially in a network society (Castells, 2000a). Thus the important tasks for contemporary management are risk management and knowledge/information management.

In a world economy which has seen sustained long-term growth over the last ten years in the West, a bull market, pressures to maintain growth and profits to shareholders tend to become intense. In companies like Enron, high growth comes through riskier projects, often with long-term payoffs like pipelines for example, promising only slow feedback. Enron employed an army of mathematicians and accountants to deal with these risk management problems, hedging risk by setting up companies – partnerships which were not included on its balance sheet – in which investors would insure them against risk and Enron would prop them up with its own shares. In other words, beneath the complex deals in which some Enron senior managers would make millions, the company was guaranteeing itself against its own losses. Then, through sophisticated accounting measures, it was able to report as profit in the current year (on which dividends were paid) projected profits from projects only just signed up, such as pipelines not yet built, in order to impress the stock markets and shore up its share price, which was necessary to underwrite the off-balance sheet partnerships. For example, Enron invested in a high-risk Internet company whose share price inflated to give a $300 million paper profit. Enron declared that profit and then insured itself against the fall of the price of the Internet stock. As long as everyone continued to believe the emperor had clothes, as long as they were kept moving fast enough that they did not have time to look, or there was no outside disaster to cause the stock market to fall to a point at which they could not cover their debt, they could get away with it. But they were living on borrowed time, and the crash of share prices after 11 September 2001 triggered disaster. For speed seems to be as effective in bringing the pile of cards down as it is in sustaining its construction. This is Virilio's *information bomb* (2000).

Clearly, companies have been misreporting expenses as capital (for example WorldCom), evading tax on a massive scale, and manipulating information in order to give investors apparently accurate and early feedback that products and performance, which may in fact be problematic, are in rude health, in order to encourage further investment and artificially shore up the share price. Misinformation, indeed lies and fraudulent information, have been superabundant. What is perturbing is that the accountants, particularly one firm, Arthur Andersen, who appear to have been involved in almost all the major scandals, including their indictment for shredding evidence in the Enron case, appear to

have colluded and abetted in these practices. As one investor has said, investors have to trust *something*, and it is usually the figures. If you can't trust the accountants who produce the figures, you can't trust the figures. Thus until the market finds something to trust in the system again, investment will rein itself in.

As we noted in Chapter 7, the accountancy profession has a huge presence in and influence over all forms of corporate life. Its involvement in auditing all aspects of business activity acted as a foot in the door of the major corporations, facilitating the growth of huge business consultancy practices associated with accounting firms, from an investor's perspective a network organization of the worst possible sort. In the case of Enron, for example, Andersen had offices for its auditors in the Enron building and its consultants gave advice on the setting up and operation of the improper partnerships, which its own auditors were auditing. Not only was Andersen auditing itself, it was legitimating Enron, effectively guaranteeing its own profits. Here we witness a different form of the *digital divide*, the construction of an information loop in which the goods stay on the *inside*, since no one from outside can see in to witness their misappropriation. This hermetic circle was energized by the fact that every transaction, profitable in reality or not, was generating huge fees and bonuses for both the accountants and the Enron employees involved. Personal greed and corporate interest thus fed off each other to create a situation which the parties involved felt they could justify because they only had to justify it to each other, at least until the charmed circle broke. A network of accountability was constructed in which accountability was only owed to those who stood to benefit from the continuation of malpractice, never to those who might suffer from its consequences. Perhaps the most disillusioning spectacle has been of Arthur Andersen's corporate lawyers arguing that shredding roomfuls of documentation in an exercise which involved their employing additional shredding capacity, at a time when they knew that an investigation by the Securities and Exchange Commission (SEC) was likely, was merely normal practice and that as such any company in America could face the same charges. As Prem Sikka (2002) notes in the following case study, this situation is not limited to the US.

What Sikka could have also noted is that, on both sides of the Atlantic, the profits generated in these transactions have been used to fund the activities of the major political parties, whether on the left, centre or right. Indeed, the list above of the US corporate scandals includes several of the main campaign funders of the Republican Party – for example, during the Florida recount in the 2000 elections, George W. Bush flew around the state in an Enron helicopter. Such scenes illuminate vividly and horrifically the powers of

CASE EXAMPLE

HOW ACCOUNTANTS HELP THEMSELVES

Hardly a week passes without revelations of some shortcomings in accounting and auditing. In each case, the companies concerned employed and remunerated accountants to massage their accounts. In accordance with carefully developed plans, large amounts of cash were siphoned off. Audit firms did not notice anything because in some cases, in their capacity as consultants, they created many of the transactions and opaque corporate structures. Auditors collected fat audit and consultancy fees and blamed everyone else for their own failures. Ordinary people lost their jobs, homes, investments, savings and pensions.

Rather than developing alternative modes of accountability and institutions of democracy, failed auditing and accounting technology has been extended to almost all walks of life. The expertise of accountancy firms has been used to sell off public assets, promote the private finance initiative and restructure the NHS. With 250,000 qualified accountants, Britain has more accountants than the rest of the EU put together and one of the highest numbers of accountants per capita in the world. This unparalleled investment in economic surveillance has failed to deliver better corporate governance, company accounts, audits and freedom from frauds or scandals. Yet the ranks of accountants continue to swell.

Company auditors have more rights than the police. They have access to all company records, files and documents. They have a statutory right of information and explanation from any officer or employee of the company. Yet this private police force of capitalism has always failed and will continue to fail. The basic model of auditing is flawed. It expects a bunch of capitalist entrepreneurs (accountancy firms) to invigilate and regulate another bunch of capitalist entrepreneurs (company directors). Profits, market share and the number of clients measure the success and failure of both. Doing anything for the public is not part of the equation.

Accountancy firms enjoy a state-guaranteed monopoly of auditing. This provides the basis for selling consultancy and generates a double-digit growth in profits. Auditors are regulated by professional accountancy bodies who have no independence from the auditing industry. Audit firms are not required to publish any information about the conduct of an audit. No scandal has ever come to light because of audit firms or the professional accountancy bodies.

The practices of auditing firms encourage audit failures. Partners are given bonuses for selling consultancy services to audit clients. The prime concern of audit firms is to appease company directors. The same partners want to squeeze more productivity from the trainees doing company audits. They are expected to work evenings and weekends for free. Most find the work boring and resent the exploitation. More than 50 per cent admit to falsifying audit work.

The legal pressures for delivering good audits are weak. Auditors only owe a 'duty of care' to the company they audit, not to any individual shareholder, creditor or employee, no matter how negligent they are. In the wake of audit failures, most lawsuits are by one accountancy firm, acting as a receiver or liquidator, against another. Win or lose, they do very nicely out of it. Ordinary stakeholders rarely do.

On some occasions the Department of Trade and Industry (DTI) appoints inspectors. This provides nice fees for accountancy firms, as one of the inspectors is usually a partner from a major accountancy firm. Inspectors ensure that uncomfortable questions are avoided. Many DTI inspectors' reports never see the light of day. Some, like the Maxwell report, are published some 10 years after the event.

The DTI does not prosecute audit firms for delivering poor audits or for colluding with companies. That task is delegated to the accountancy bodies. The disciplinary processes are under the control of big firms, with their partners occupying key positions within the accountancy bodies. Any benchmarks with fines, firm closures and disqualification will come back to haunt them. So a feather-duster approach is institutionalized. With weak legal and institutional structures and the profit motive of accountancy firms, audit failures are institutionalized too. But accountants make money at every stage. More Enrons are inevitable, although the scale might differ. Greater reforms are needed but unlikely as major firms have close links with government departments, senior civil servants and political parties.

Source: Adapted from Prem Sikka 'We are a nation of accountants but it does us no good when the industry remains so self-serving', *Guardian,* Wednesday 20 February 2002, © Prem Sikka 2002.

the dominant coalitions we considered in Chapter 14, emphasizing again that many virtual worlds are far from inclusive, with those that are excluded frequently footing the bill. Since the fall of the Berlin Wall and the collapse of communism, some commentators have argued that the triumph of capitalism, and its necessary political corollary, liberal democracy, is now complete. Apparently there are no longer any viable alternatives, and even the People's Republic of China is moving towards a moderated capitalist form. The growth of the

Internet has accelerated this triumphalism, this hyper-reality, which has fed off its own image and rhetoric and has led to the development of corporate cultures where highly talented technicians – economists, mathematicians, lawyers and IT specialists and so on – with the help of public relations spin doctors, market researchers, advertising agencies and highly active political lobbyists have bought into the illusion that they can do anything and get away with it. It seems like a modern, technologically mediated version of the gangster capitalism of the mob in the 1920s and 30s and that corruption should arise is hardly surprising. The kleptocratic culture that seems to have gripped Enron extends beyond the US. Some major banks, accountants and lawyers, including Swiss bank UBS, French oil company Elf Aquitaine and former German Chancellor Helmut Kohl, are now involved in investigations into the moving and rendering invisible of countless billions squirrelled away by ruthless mega-rich dictators of some of the poorest and most embattled countries on earth – including Marcos of the Philippines, Salinas of Mexico, Suharto of Indonesia, Abacha of Nigeria, Milosevic of Yugoslavia and Karadzic of Bosnia – and those with connections with organized crime, especially in Russia where the presidents of Russia, the Ukraine and Kazakhstan have also been implicated (see http://www.marcosbillions.com/ marcos/dictators.htm, accessed 2 February 2003, for links and further information).

So which of our two scenarios is the real future? The increasing empowerment of the fringe, the opening up of capitalism to the grass roots? Or the increasing corruption of big business, with its growing capacity to hide its fraud and keep its secrets? Well, the answer is likely to be 'both and neither' and thus the question becomes: What can managers do to manage in the space between and how will their lives be affected?

Too much time on protecting accountability? The new office

Obviously, the key site to which information

technology has been applied up to now is the office, the white-collar paper mills in which most managers spend most of their time. In a study conducted under the auspices of the UK's Economic and Social Research Council's 'Virtual Society?' programme, Steve Brown and Geoff Lightfoot (see Brown and Lightfoot 1998, 2002; Brown et al. 2001) have made considerable inroads into the task of articulating the consequences of this application of technology. Of particular interest to them has been that field of applications collectively known as 'groupware':

The term broadly refers to a range of office organization software based on local and wide area computer networks. Such networks typically consist of a large number of personal computers distributed throughout the organization (clients), which are all connected to a smaller number of server systems. Clients are then able to access information stored on central servers as well as pass information by way of these servers to other clients. Common groupware activities include supporting workflow (for example receiving and processing customer orders), allowing access to common databases, facilitating computerized conferencing and offering email or document sharing protocols. (Brown and Lightfoot, http://www.regard.ac.uk/research_findings/L132251042/report.pdf, accessed 25 February 2003)

Brown and Lightfoot note that the initial appeal of groupware, and the ways in which it has been sold to organizations, seems to be considerably at odds with much of the detail of its operation in practice. These differences turn particularly around issues of accountability, as shown in the case example below.

What are we to make of all this? While not everyone agrees with Brown and Lightfoot's account of the use of email in organizations (see for example Lee 1996; Shortis 2001), for many readers who have worked in electronically mediated workplaces much of their account will be familiar. Two points seem particularly noteworthy. First is *the disparity between the cyberenthusiasm of early proponents of groupware and the findings of the study* (Trend 2001: 2). This disparity turns around the distinction between the

CASE EXAMPLE

GROUPWARE AND ACCOUNTABILITY

Since the late 1970s, a vision of how modern organizations could be radically reshaped by the power of networked information communication technologies has been widely disseminated. In their influential thesis, *The Network Nation*, Hiltz and Turoff (1978) argued that

over the next two decades, computer-mediated communication would come to have a profoundly democratizing effect on organizational structures, resulting in decentralized, flatter or 'virtual' organizations built around open exchanges between dispersed groups of individuals with common interests. Geographical and hierarchical barriers would be overcome in this organization of the future through common use of computerized conferencing and electronic messaging facilities. Such media would, it was claimed, not only supersede much routine face-to-face interaction, but would also come to replace a whole range of communication tools, like postal services, fax and voice telephony. In the organizational heartlands of the network nation, computer-mediated communication would be the norm.

Perhaps unsurprisingly, the reality of the contemporary 'virtual organization' is somewhat different. There is, for example, little evidence to suggest that computerized conferencing is as yet allowing organizations to dispense with more traditional face-to-face meetings. Despite its ubiquitous presence, email also seems to have expanded upon rather than dominated the range of potential communications tools available to modern organizations (Sproull and Kiesler, 1998). The crucial questions to be posed around the impact of computerized communication technologies are then not around what is gained and lost in the shift towards virtual organization, but instead how electronic and traditional media mutually shape one another in the context of what might be called 'semi' or 'partly' virtual organizations.

Proponents of groupware emphasize the ability it affords to integrate the storage and retrieval of information with computer-mediated communication occurring across different places and times. Meetings may, for example, be held between participants dispersed across a number of sites using either video or text-based services. Alternatively, much of the work which was previously routinely achieved at meetings (for example communicating schedules, consultation, assigning tasks) can be performed through emails sent to specific groups of individuals (that is, members of a department or work groups). A further advantage here is that electronic communication can generate a continuous record of any exchange, providing a far more detailed account of what transpires than traditional minutes of meetings. In this way groupware can effectively support 'organizational memory' (Khoshafian and Buckiewicz 1995), that is, the ability of an organization to retain and archive its own history.

Previous research into the introduction of groupware systems has concentrated on their impact on interpersonal relations between users (Rice and Love 1987; Schmitz and Fulk 1991) or directly on organizational efficiency. Vogel and Nunamaker (1990), for example, list a whole range of benefits, including improved meeting efficiency, increased quality of input by participants and the creation of more complete records. These studies tend, however, to assume that the availability of and access to increased amounts of information is an unalloyed good. They do not explore, for example, the uses which might be made of these more complete

records by managers and others, or the content of computer-mediated interactions between users. There is also an idealized view of how meetings operate contained in these studies. Meetings are treated as though they were sites where information is exchanged and decisions duly generated.

We take a very different view of meetings. They are exchanges where participants struggle to establish their own version of past events, while simultaneously guarding their own accountability. Although decisions are often retrospectively attributed to meetings, they often occur outside the formal agenda. The relationship between the formal record of a meeting and what actually happened is often ambiguous and can sometimes be subject to multiple interpretations by participants. Meetings can then be highly strategic affairs, with participants engaged in skilled rhetorical performances to secure their own objectives.

This approach to meetings is informed by ethnographic and discourse analytic studies of organizational life (Drew and Heritage 1992; Law 1994; Watson 1994). One of the major concerns here is how participants in meetings formulate matters at hand in rhetorically persuasive ways. In this sense recollections of past events by participants are treated as accounts which are structured in accord with the speaker's current interests and objectives. Groupware thoroughly impacts upon the ability of participants to generate accounts in this way. The potential to provide a more complete record of the meeting, for example, makes it increasingly difficult for participants to provide alternative interpretations of what actually happened. A clear implication here is that the content of meetings may be substantially affected by participants' prior concerns with how the meeting will be subsequently recorded. Furthermore, when the work previously done at meetings is performed instead through the exchange of emails, an entirely different range of rhetorical skills is required to manage the interaction. Participants in such exchanges are faced with a unique set of problems. The entire dialogue may be edited or archived by either participant. It may also be forwarded throughout the organization, possibly in a truncated form. This means that participants must rapidly acquire skills for the strategic use of the medium.

Our findings confirm that the adoption of groupware is highly variable. Users point to a number of problems, ranging from the purely technical (poor quality of some conferencing facilities) through to perceptions that groupware creates excessive demands on managerial time. More importantly, users tend to experience the electronic communication offered by groupware as a *highly formal* and *politicized medium* [emphasis added]. Users perceive that their personal standing within the organization could be enhanced or diminished by the quality of their electronic communications. Such communications were not seen as ephemeral, but as highly durable records which required careful crafting, since they could be archived, forwarded throughout the organization and retrieved at some future date, to the potential cost of the sender. In response, users describe a range of strategies they adopted to manage electronic communication. These include attempts to prolong debate in order to expose potential flaws in prior parts of the exchange and the strategic mobilization of possible allies through the copying in of superiors and interested parties.

At the same time, we found evidence that while the implementation of groupware has actually tended to increase rather than reduce the number of face-to-face meetings held by the two participant organizations (additional meetings are now held to resolve disputes emerging from groupware communication), there has been some impact on the formal nature of meetings. Managers reported that less meetings are now formally minuted, especially at senior levels. This is due to two unexpected consequences. First, that email is being used to distribute brief action points generated by meetings in place of formal minutes, and second that much of the rhetorical work previously performed by managers at meetings – ensuring that particular state-ments are 'on record' – is now more easily done through electronic media, which managers are more-over able to archive themselves.

More generally, managers are tending to routinely store colossal numbers of emails and other electronic documents, sometimes stretching back five years or more. Such archives are strategically used by managers to rapidly produce persuasive evidence in their favour when their own actions are questioned, or to reintroduce potentially damaging past exchanges opportunely to challenge the current actions of rivals. Managers also use of a range of tactics to gather information for their own archiving practices. These include 'lurking' on exchanges which are becoming increasingly hostile, provoking others to produce complex accounts of the past by sending innocuous looking suggestions about current strategies and routinely copying in particular individuals who are known to 'keep everything'. Organizational memory is then not the simple preservation of information, but rather a strategic process of archiving, editing and reintroducing selection from masses of past electronic communications.

Source: Adapted from http://www.regard.ac.uk/ research_findings/L132251042/report.pdf, accessed 25 February 2003.

rather bloodless view of organizational life of proponents of technological solutions to 'communications' and 'memory' problems and the rather more realistic and subtle approach adopted by Brown and Lightfoot. As we noted in Chapter 15, discourses of strategic conduct are consumed by individuals as much as by organizations, and as the oft-heard phrase 'my career strategy' attests, individuals are more than capable of acting strategically in their own interests, and potentially against those of their co-workers. Contrary to the simplifications of the cyberenthusiasts, the experience of email described by Brown and Lightfoot is just what we should expect when it is deployed within hierarchical organizations, as Chapters 4 and 7 have already alerted us. Brown and Lightfoot's account is a description of a virtual world completely different from that envisaged by system designers. The incorporation of system features such as blind copying, continuous voting and auto-copying, seen as innocuous tools in providing the grail of greater, *better* information for everyone, become ambiguous and contestable weapons when put in a management setting. Revealing the strategic or 'political' dimension to groupware use also helps to put our knowledge of different kinds of information communication

technologies on a new footing. Previously, many theorists have used a distinction between 'task-oriented' and 'relationship-oriented' activities to focus on the impacts of communication technologies and the development of the virtual organization. Yet it seems more likely that running between this distinction is a whole series of strategic activities aimed at sustaining accountability and reconstructing the past. These activities lead to the creation of formal and informal communication networks, based not on common interests but on common *antagonisms*, people allying against a particular project, individual or coalition, as much as for anything. This facet of virtual community building is also reflected on and around the wider Internet (see for example Brown et al. 1998), a theme to which we return in our concluding section 'Community and identity in a virtual world'. The impact, then, of the virtual organisation has been to provide *a new set of resources in which managers can re-enact the work of managing*, as they define it, rather than a democratization of the workplace.

The second key point to emerge from the study is that *the virtual organization is only part of the organization as a whole*, with electronically mediated organizational life going on alongside other aspects of organizational existence, rather than replacing it. We live, those of us lucky enough to be among the four per cent that Trend (2001) identifies, in a partially virtual world. Indeed, we can go much further and note that the infrastructure on which the virtual world depends and much of the content that sustains it is far from virtual in its production and maintenance. This world…

has an immense material base underpinning its operations, which depend upon complex wired and wireless systems of transmission via microwave towers, communications satellites, fibreoptic networks and on line services. (Luke 1999: 31)

The cyberspatial resources of global computer nets permit virtual enterprises to employ thousands of poor women in Jamaica, Mauritius or the Philippines in low-paid, tedious data entry or word-processing jobs for firms in London, Paris or San Diego. (Luke 1999: 37)

Luke calls this political economy of the control (capital) and maintenance (labour) behind cyberspace, drawing on Virilio, as characterized by *dromoeconomics* and it is all too easily overlooked in the glib discussions and techno-boosterism that fill many of the column inches that are apparently devoted to understanding the future of work. It is also a facet of the darker side of the factory of the future that we go on to consider in the next section.

We should not, however, be too surprised by the ways in which new technology has failed radically to alter the office and its existing structures; for the language of techno-boosterism is slippery stuff and the changes associated with technologies are, even when apparent, complex and often far from unidirectional. As Bell (2001: 38) notes with regard to the impact of the use of email on interactivity at his place of work:

Email has certainly reconfigured the way we talk to each other at work. In some cases, it's diminished social contact – it's quicker to send an email than go to someone's office for a chat (they might not be in, for one thing). But it's also enlarged the sphere of 'public' communication within our workplace – I am the recipient of far more emails that I was a participant in 'RL' [real life] discussions at work.

Language is obviously most at risk, however, when we enter the realm of marketing and promotion. For example, although 'interactive' digital television is certainly more 'interactive' on one level than merely sitting in front of a standard analogue broadcast as a recipient, it is considerably less interactive than, say, going to the pub. Or, indeed, talking to our co-watchers in the lounge – a practice that may itself be increasingly unlikely if one watcher is 'interacting' with the programme. As the British journalist Suzanne Moore commented during the third and last episode of UK Channel Four's excellent series *Visions of Heaven and Hell* (1994), exploring potential futures of our virtual world:

I get as excited as everybody else by the visions of the future that are conjured up. That we'll all be united in this global village which will all work on behalf of … the greater good. But I think we can look at the past and see what other technology has done for us. I mean when video first started it was going to … free us from huge media conglomerations, because we were going to make our own films. It was going to be a two way process … It was going to revolutionalise our lives. And we ended up with Jeremy Beadle! [Jeremy Beadle was the original presenter of the UK's leading amusing home video clips show *You've Been Framed!*, a genre of programming well represented throughout the world.] We ended up with a machine that just fits into the domestic set up and doesn't really disrupt very much. So I am a bit sceptical about it because it's a question of who owns it and whether they are gong to work on behalf of 'the public' … or work for themselves. I mean this idea that we all actually own it is a lovely utopian idea. But we don't.

The Internet and the factory of the future?

So who is the Internet for? In the case example opposite, Jack Welch, the retiring CEO of one of the world's biggest corporations offers some reflections that the Internet is the way of the future not just for the fringe, not just for the frauds, but for the big and old corporations – in other words, *the places where the norms of management tend to be most obviously found.*

For Welch, the Internet offers excitement to all workers, who are increasingly becoming knowledge workers rather than just hands. If you do the job, you know about it, and GE wants to put that knowledge to use. But significantly Welch argues that it is not just the obvious selling and procuring functions that the Internet enables, although these functions will not be any less important, but the 'make' functions. Unfortunately, in this interview he does not expand on that. Nevertheless, we can get an idea of what the factory of the future may look like from the case example of an uncelebrated Chicago company who has found itself competing with GE and Cisco Systems to develop the means of making such a factory possible.

Corrugated paper's blueprint for a factory linked to its customers and suppliers, capable of rapid responses to customer demand and quick customization, may be the model for other industries or it may not. However, the likelihood is that with the research and development efforts being put in by so many major players, sooner or later models for all industries will be in place. Whether there will be a practical means of creating a brokerage

CASE EXAMPLE

Jack Welch, former CEO of the giant General Electric Corporation in the US and *Fortune's* Manager of the Century, commented on how the Internet had affected its way of doing business shortly before he retired.

'We laugh at bureaucracy, we laugh at bureaucrats,' he says. 'It really is the corner family grocery store and we treat it that way. The corporate leader of tomorrow', he says firmly, 'is the person who understands that it's necessary to search everywhere for the best idea and share it with others. One who can go out and excite an organization to look outside itself, to engage every person in the place, to let no mind be quiet, to get rid of any pomposity, to rid itself of layers because everyone is going to have the same information,' he says.

Optimism obviously comes naturally to Welch. Even so, his enthusiasm for the Net and the gains for companies like GE and the entire world economy is extraordinary. It's made him one of the messiahs of e-commerce and GE a leader in it. Welch believes that the productivity surge is only just beginning because what he calls the 'make' side of a business – as opposed to the buying and selling – is only now beginning to benefit from the efficiency and the possibilities of the Internet.

'The Internet makes the company transparent so the old command and control structure [that came] after the war and that we all built on is a dead duck,' he says. And then repeats slowly for emphasis. 'A dead duck.' But what seems to have him even more enthused is the changes it will create in people's work by getting rid of all the 'mind-numbingly dull jobs' – chasing down the orders, doing the paperwork, filing the bills, following the process.

'We replace them with knowledge workers,' he says. 'So there's another gain. You can't believe it when you see people coming to meetings now totally energized. I remember sitting at our long-range planning review in

July ... for these people in the widget business, basically our dullest industrial business. It's worth $US7 billion and it sells switches, that sort of thing. They were standing on the table practically they were so excited about the issue because they basically have got a way to change the atmosphere in their business.

'Everything will be online, all the information will be available, they will deal with their customers – they are in their customer's shops, they are looking right at suppliers. Running an auction is more fun than you can imagine. It's like going to the track.'

Not that he concedes there is any such thing as a new economy/old economy division, grumbling that it's a dumb journalistic invention. 'The Internet belongs to the big and the old,' he says. 'Every advantage accrues to the big and the old. Brand is important, fulfilment is important, loyalty is important on the Net. We all copied dot.coms because we all thought it was Nobel Prize work – particularly people my age, probably 50 and above. We all went after auctions for purchasing and procurement. We all had our little dot.com *sell* model but we missed the biggest opportunity of all which is the *'make'* part.' And Welch of all people understands just how important that 'make part' is.

'Twenty years ago, you didn't go hanging around with a bunch of factory guys and ask them for their best ideas,' he says. 'We didn't send factory guys out to buy machine tools. We sent kids who had just gotten a degree and gave them a purchasing pad and told them to go buy a machine tool. They'd never seen a machine tool and they're making the buy. So now we send factory workers out. The people who use it, do it.'

'The important thing is not to predict what is going to happen,' he says. 'It's to be agile enough to capitalize on what does happen. That means massive, constant, change and values that promote informality and good communication and lack of hierarchy.'

Source: Adapted from Jennifer Hewett 'This quick Jack is Net nimble', *Sydney Morning Herald,* 23 September 2000, pp. 21, 24.

---

for manufacturing capacity so that demand can be diverted from one factory to another, creating a global factory through the cooperation of various suppliers to an industry seems to be a question that will outstrip the ability of technology to achieve it and is more likely to rest upon the abilities of corporate lawyers and politicians to remove the barriers to it. But with the contracting out of manufacturing capacity already the norm in industries like the athletic apparel industry, where one factory may be making designs for Nike, Reebok or Adidas, or where the same shoe is capable of

being manufactured in India, Thailand or Mexico, the principle is already in place. For companies with several plants worldwide, the ability to shift capacity and use it more effectively will be a godsend. This is already happening in the field of informational content, as we noted earlier in our citing of Luke (1999). It is also increasingly the case with the information and technology-rich call centres we considered in Chapter 7, which are ever more likely to be found in the cheap labour markets of the developing world. The likelihood for the future is that there will be fewer workers in the

CASE EXAMPLE

SUPERPLANT – THE WEB-READY FACTORY

In 1998, Rick Van Horne, owner of Chicago's Corrugated paper decided to remake the factory. Actually, he decided to hook up his Chicago plant to cyberspace, to test whether the much-touted Internet really could transform big, groaning meta-industries like his into nimble paragons of technological efficiency. In Van Horne's vision, all his plant's machinery – trimmers, slitters, giant corrugators, everything on the factory floor – would feed data to the Internet, and to the rest of the company and the outside world. Corrugated would give its customers a password so they could peek into the plant's innards anytime. Customers – and customers' customers – would call up Corrugated's production schedules on the Internet to see exactly where their orders were on the factory floor and whether they would arrive on time. No more little white lies that an order was on its way. Suppliers would be able to tap the system to manage their own inventory – not just inventory they were selling to Corrugated but material they were storing at Corrugated's plant to sell to someone else. Here's the capper: Van Horne decided that he wouldn't just figure out a way to Webify his own plant. He imagined creating a seamless, replicable system that could bring the full power of the Internet to any manufacturing operation, anywhere in the world. And then he would sell it.

Not that factories aren't computerized. Manufacturers spent vast amounts of money installing computer-driven machinery during the 1990s. But very little of that massive info-tech spending had anything to do with the Internet. If anything, plant managers have tended to play it safe and to keep their production machinery away from the Web. Most computer-driven machinery installed in recent years runs on proprietary software; trying to hook those machines together – with outside customers and suppliers, or even with a company's own far-flung operations – often produces a tech Tower of Babel. Many factory managers who tried including production equipment in their computer networks discovered that Ethernet switches couldn't handle more than one packet of information at a time. When there was trouble and a dozen machines sent bursts of messages at once, they collided and the system slowed down or crashed. In an office network, such glitches are mostly irritations. But if an assembly line can't be shut down instantaneously in an emergency, million-dollar machinery is trashed or someone is maimed or killed.

Imagine taking all that wonderfully efficient automation on the factory floor and linking it to the Web. The potential for even more productivity gains is enormous.

The challenge lies in devising a network that can handle both internal and external demands. Ford, for example, wants a Web-based system that would let customers tap in design preferences for cars. The information would be shared with Ford suppliers that design car parts as well as with Ford's factories. In effect, hooking up the assembly line to the Internet would give a Ford customer direct input as his car moves down the assembly line, sort of just-in-time designing, replacing inventory with information. Software agents could be sent out by machines onto the Internet as brokers, matching machines with excess capacity to others seeking more production capacity, producing a 'global factory floor'.

Van Horne didn't have a clue about any of this when he decided to turn his plant into an Internet proving ground. Indeed, Corrugated's 80,000 square-foot production floor was a perfect example of why plant managers shun the Web. The machines are huge, complicated, noisy, dirty, and dangerous, and they require constant babying. Corrugated had a website that customers could use to place orders, but most of them preferred ordering the old-fashioned way, by fax or phone. In 1998, Corrugated's half-dozen customer service reps handled as many as 300 orders a day, mostly by hand. To check the status of an order, a rep had to drop the phone, run next door to the plant, and hope someone could find it. Thirty per cent of orders were late.

But improving order fulfilment wasn't what drew Van Horne to the Internet. At first, he saw it as a terrific new marketing tool. Marketing is vital in the corrugated-paper business; it's about the only way for a company like Van Horne's to differentiate itself from its 125 competitors. But building one of the world's first completed Web-based production plants from scratch is a lot more demanding. Van Horne realized that there are no systems-in-a-box for converting a plant to an Internet factory.

Cutting corrugated paper for boxes is a little like laying out sewing patterns on rolls of fabric. The idea is to get as many pieces as possible out of a single roll. On Corrugated's plant floor, people called schedulers arrange each order, which may involve anywhere from 50,000 boxes to just a few dozen, to be cut from pasted-together layers of paper spooling through the corrugator. On a single 25,000-foot roll, the schedulers may lay out dozens of orders, each a different size, shape, and quantity. One of the main objectives is to leave as little left-over paper to be trimmed away as possible. Wasted paper is wasted money.

How could Internet technology help? A group of software programmers began a total rewrite of the company's computer code to produce graphically intuitive and easy-to-use Web interfaces to control what customers would see when they dialed up the Corrugated site. All this would be tied into a single database; the idea being to make the system available to everyone, from the machinists on the plant floor to customers off-site, in real time, with no delay. Running on a wireless network, even the forklifts (which have dashboard PCs) have instant access to the database.

Customers are key in the Corrugated equation. Many of Corrugated's customers don't have their own inventory tracking systems, so Corrugated hopes to supply its main customers with wireless networks – linked to Corrugated's database – and bar code scanners so that the company will know when its product arrives. This makes the customer more efficient with the idea that the customer and Corrugated can work together to pinpoint exactly what happened if a shipment goes wrong. Corrugated even has a full-time employee who introduces customers to Corrugated's Web system.

Here's how the whole thing is supposed to work: Say you make computers and you need corrugated paper for your shipping boxes. You want the paper cut to order so you can fold it into boxes, put your computers in, and move them out. You call up Corrugated's website and punch in an order for corrugated paper precisely cut and folded for 10,000 computer boxes. Off goes the order. The order lands in Corrugated's computers, which come up with a suggestion on how best to blend in your order with others. A scheduler looks over the computer's plan on one of the numerous computer screens scattered around the plant; they're all linked. If it looks OK, the scheduler hits the Send button. Software then directs the big corrugators on when and how to fill the order. If you've indicated that it's a rush job, the computer will adjust. The machines start doing their thing, spewing out corrugated paper at 800 feet per minute, slicing and dic-

ing it to fit your order. Computer-controlled conveyor belts take your custom-cut box paper toward the loading dock. A wireless PC on a forklift instructs the forklift operator to take your load to a specific truck trailer. Truckers pull in and log on to the network. They're told by computer which trailer they're supposed to haul to maximize their trip's efficiency. And they're off. Your order usually is delivered by the next day.

The system already is generating productivity gains. Corrugated's sales have climbed to $70 million from $40 million three years ago, and are expected to hit $100 million this year. Paper waste, one of the plant's major costs, has been cut by about 35 per cent with the new technology. Turnaround time on orders has fallen from an average of 2.5 days to 18 hours. Customer service has dropped to three employees from six, but they are handling as many as 800 orders daily – more than double the previous volume. About 70 per cent of the orders now come in by Internet and are routed electronically to the plant floor. No more reps running invoices back and forth with little notes spelling out special-order details.

Van Horne estimates that about 90 per cent of his customers don't yet quite understand that the Internet can link their factory floor and Corrugated's factory floor into one virtual box-making operation. Van Horne boasts that his company will be able to build a comparable factory from the ground up, incorporating the new technology system, for less than $30 million – and could manage it with significantly fewer people than anyone else. 'It doesn't make sense to do it just once,' he says.

Source: Reprinted by permission of *Fortune* magazine from Bill Richards (2000) 'Superplant', *Ecompany Now*, November, pp. 182–96. Copyright © 2000 Time Inc. All rights reserved.

headquarters of organizations operating in this way and that those who remain will manage information rather than anything else. Will the new order affect the lives of people working in Third World factories for the better? No one seems to think so – the factory of the future seems to be leaner and meaner in the advanced economies, but simply mean in the less developed ones. And many commentators have noted the power of the technology to introduce new forms of surveillance to further ensure compliance and control (see Chapter 7) both within the factory (Zuboff 1988; Rosen and Baroudi 1992; Sewell and Wilkinson 1992a, 1992b) and beyond (Dandeker 1990; Lyon 2001). But information technology is not the only way in which manufacturing is likely to be revolutionized in the not-too-distant future, as shown in the following case study.

The machine tool industry is one of the standard indices for the economic health of manufacturing industry in any country. The kind of radical change which the powder press could bring about could enable companies to retool cheaply and rapidly, and may even help small firms to stay in business. So although it may seem to have the potential to reduce staff at the tool manufacturers, it may, by enabling growth elsewhere in the manufacturing sector, create sufficient growth in tool manufacturing to offset this. When considered in combination with the Internet factory capability we saw in the case of the Chicago superplant, it would seem as if manufacturing in the twenty-first century is going to be a very different phenomenon from manufacturing in the last decade. Nevertheless, we should continue to exercise caution here, because we

NEW MANUFACTURING FOR A NEW AGE

If you own a manufacturing business, you might want to pay a visit to West Lebanon, New Hampshire. What's going on there may forever change the way you do business – or perhaps put you out of it altogether. Tucked away in an unremarkable industrial building on the outskirts of town is a little machine about the size of a three-drawer filing cabinet. Feed a bit of metal powder into its maw, and after a moment of whirring and digesting, it spits out, say, a valve for a diesel engine or a gear for a car transmission or a pump component for a hot tub. It's an odd bit of industrial alchemy to watch – mere dust transforming itself into highly refined hardware.

The little machine in West Lebanon is known as a 'powder metallurgy press', and to most manufacturers, there ought to be nothing especially new about it. Powder presses have been around for 70 years, stamping out everything from truck-motor parts to medical equipment. Remarkably common though they are, these machines are remarkably crude. Most power presses are great, loud, chugging things, about the size and shape of a tractor trailer and demanding the ministrations of at least 200 people to keep them running through a workweek. Retooling the presses to switch from making one component to another can take days. And any parts the machines do produce are coarse at best, requiring up to a dozen refinements and improvements before they're ready for use.

The West Lebanon machine, developed by Mii Technologies LLC, is a whole different industrial beast. It's part of a new manufacturing system that is fast, portable or computerized. It can be shipped wherever it's needed and easily reconfigured to make just about any part for just about any manufacturer. While the machine the West Lebanon inventors are giving the world is not quite the personal computer, it could become to twenty-first-century manufacturers what the cotton gin was to the farmer or the loom to the miller. 'If these guys have the materials and can automate the manufacturing process,' says Kevin Prouty, an industry analyst with AMR Research in Boston, 'that's moving toward a new level – toward a manufacturing renaissance.'

By any measure, a renaissance in manufacturing is long overdue. Traditional powder presses are not the only low-tech way parts have been built over the years; stamping machines, casting machines and forging machines are used to melt or muscle metal into shape. Not only are these machines imprecise, they are also fantastically expensive and hard to come by. Mii's powder press may change all that, turning American industry on its head, reinventing not just products and components but the factory itself – creating a readily available and mobile digital manufacturing system for the New Economy with the kind of near-zero-tolerance quality needed in industrial manufacturing.

The cabinet-size press is an astonishingly economical piece of engineering – and an astonishingly powerful one. A traditional 935-cu.ft press generates about 440,000 lbs of force to compress its metal dust. The new 16-cu.ft press generates a whopping 920,000 lbs. Four built-in computerized control systems run the press's robotics, monitoring quality and minimizing work-stopping breakdowns. This helps reduce the team of 200 workers normally required to run such a machine to just three. What's more, by keeping quality high and eliminating the extra finishing steps needed by parts produced by cruder processes, the new press can complete a job up to 50 per cent faster which means it can lower costs by 30 per cent to 50 per cent.

It's Mii's powder as much as its machine that makes this kind of radical improvement possible, as they bond together differently and reduce the likelihood of clotting – and the ruination of a batch – to zero. And Mii's robotic presses can not only be shipped around the world, they can also be remotely operated. Thus a supervisor at a computer console in, say, Singapore can monitor a press in, say, Seattle, trouble-shooting any problems that come up. 'This is like the airplane or copying machine in previous eras,' say Jay Agarwal, an analyst with Charles River Associates 'How long it takes the market to form will depend on how long it takes manufacturers to change the way they think about their businesses and the laws of physics.' If the new press can really deliver on its promise, the laws of economics will probably have something to say about it too.

Source: Adapted from Jeffrey Kluger (2000) 'A new factory for a new age', *Time Magazine*, pp. 75–7.

have heard before stories of revolution in the machine tool industry – and this previous story was one of information revolution! Numerical control (NC) of machine tools (see Noble 1985, 1986), which allowed the modifiable specification of workpiece dimensions, was first introduced commercially in the USA in 1955 and its diffusion has carried on steadily since then. The system allowed one to control the path of a cutting tool by inputting a reprogrammable description of required tool movements. In his investigation of these changes, David Noble draws specific attention to the choices that were available, and those that were taken, in the design of automatically controlled machine tools. These choices are understood in terms of the social relations of capitalist production. According to Noble (1985: 109), the introduction of NC and computer numerically controlled (CNC) machines led to a reorganization of the production process in metal-working 'in the direction of greater managerial control'. He identifies changes in both horizontal and vertical relations of production within metalworking. The former has seen a shift towards concentration in the industry, resulting in a small number of large firms, with a large number of small firms falling by the wayside. The latter entails 'a dramatic transfer of planning and control from the shop floor to the office'. To expect some sort of decentralization and democratization of manufacturing arrangements from the powder press, in the face of such historical precedents, might therefore seem a little naive. As Noble asks of the preceding information revolution in machine tooling:

Is it just a coincidence that the technology tends to strengthen the market position of these firms and enhance managerial authority in the [machine] shop? Why did this new technology take the form that it did, a form which seems to have rendered it accessible to only some firms, and why only this technology? Is there any other way to automate machine tools, a technology, for example, which would lend itself less to managerial control? (1985: 109–10)

To answer these questions, we need a little more detail on the history of the information revolution that was effected in the machine tool industry. Prior to this intervention, machine tools had traditionally been controlled by machinists, skilled craftsmen who transmitted their 'skill and purpose to the machine by means of cranks, levers, and handles'. The task involves complex and ongoing decision making about how the work should proceed to achieve the end product, which must itself be visualized by the machinist. A range of highly developed skills is involved, with tacit knowledge built up through a lengthy apprenticeship, with experience being of particular importance. During the 1930s and 40s, 'tracer technology' was developed. This allowed a recording of the movements of a skilled machinist via use of a sensor. This trace could then be 'played back' to control the machine to cut a similar piece on its own. Since machine tools are general-purpose machines that are used to cut a huge variety of parts, a separate trace was required for each new part and the source of this trace remained the skilled, tacit knowledge and abilities of a machinist. In the late 1940s an alternative mode of automation emerged, supported by the US Air Force and the Massachusetts Institute of Technology. This was the numerical control, (NC) system, a digital alternative to the analogue record playback. In this system:

The specifications for a part – the information contained in an engineering blueprint – are first broken down into a mathematical representation of the part, then into a mathematical description of the desired path of the cutting tool along up to five axes, and finally into hundreds or thousands of discrete instructions, translated for economy into a numerical code, which is read and translated into electrical signals for the machine controls. The N/C tape, in short, is a means of formally circumventing the role of the machinist as the source of intelligence of production. (Noble 1985: 111)

The key question to be answered is why NC technology was developed in favour of record playback technology. Noble notes that between 1949 and 1959, when the US air force ceased its formal support of the development of NC software, the military spent at least $62 million on the research, development and transfer of NC. Only one commercial company put their own money into this research. In 1955 the air force:

undertook to pay for the purchase, installation, and maintenance of over 100 N/C machines in factories of prime subcontractors; the contractors, aircraft manufacturers, and their suppliers would also be paid to learn to use the new technology. In short, the air force created a market for N/C. (Noble 1985: 113)

Noble's key point here is that the air force support that made the development of NC possible 'also helped determine the shape the technology would take'. The software for controlling these machines turned out to be the biggest problem that needed solving. Noble notes that various sites had differing levels of success in their attempts to make the transformation from embodied skill to disembodied digital instructions, with a variety of simple 'higher level' computer languages being invented for this purpose at a local level. Eventually, however, a standard, but complex, software system, APT (automatically programmed tools), was developed that usurped locally developed languages. It was flexible and made up of very basic fundamental 'skeletons' of shapes of actions that were fleshed out for each particular case. This fleshing out required complex programming skills (not generally possessed by current workers) and large computers. Despite these problems, the:

air force loved APT ... it seemed to allow for rapid mobilization, for rapid design change, and for interchangeability between machines within a plant, between users and vendors, and between contractors and subcontractors throughout the country (presumably of 'strategic importance' in case of enemy attack). (Noble 1985: 114)

This usurping of local, simpler, but less generic and hence less widely applicable, computer languages was initially resisted, but resistance was eventually overcome by 'higher level management, who had come to believe it necessary to learn how to use the new system for "business reasons" (cost-plus contracts with the air force)' (1985: 114). There were still huge problems with APT for all concerned, but these problems were most apparent for small manufacturers. Standardization retarded the development of simpler, alternative languages (which would have favoured smaller firms) and forced those who wanted to use NC into dependence upon the controllers of APT development, large computers and mathematically sophisticated programmers. Problems could be overcome by the large manufacturers receiving air force subsidy because of the resources at their disposal. Smaller, commercial users were not so fortunate. Any company that wanted military contracts had to use APT and together we can see how these changes served, over time, to concentrate the industry into a small number of large firms. As Noble (1985: 115) notes: 'APT served the air force and the aircraft industry well, but at the expense of less well endowed competitors.'

It would seem that record playback would have been a better bet for small manufacturers, yet it was abandoned by their large competitors and small companies never even got to see it. The company producing the system was bought out by one of the major NC manufacturers, who promptly shelved record playback in order to continue its focus on NC systems. NC represented the computer age and the advent of the brave new world. Perhaps most importantly, it furthered an ideology that sought to remove control from unpredictable and belligerent workers and place it in the hands of the far more trustworthy and dependable management. It provided an automated route to the Taylorist goal of complete *management* control. And management were the ones taking the decision, with the support of the air force, to go for this technology. As Peter Drucker (1967: 26) once observed: 'What is today called automation is conceptually a logical extension of Taylor's scientific management.'

A desire for control of the workforce and work clearly drove NC and its successor CNC. For example, control panels on machines on the floor were frequently disabled, allowing only remote programming from a central office, a practice which also served to ensure that the potentially 'subversive' (because of their unionization) machinists could not learn the new skills and reassert their power. And we should not forget that the introduction of C/NC had the added bonus of providing management with more of the essential thing that it requires to undertake its task and justify its existence: *information*. Managers generally do not work directly on the world of materials, they work on and through information, and in this sense we might say that

management has always been an activity carried out in a (partially) *virtual world.*

However, as Noble notes, *a desire for control on the part of management is seldom entirely satisfied.* In the C/NC case, tacit craft skills are still frequently required to moderate the execution of programmes. Use of 'cheap', unskilled staff was resisted by well-organized unions and, even when it could be deployed, unskilled labour proved costly, in particular, when machine reliability was not 100 per cent (which it never was) and errors could lead to the 'smash-up' of a very expensive machine. It proved very difficult to replace completely the tacit, craft skills of the operators with mathematically derived, logical instructions. This is a problem we may see repeated with the powder press when it is in numerous different locations without extensive, skilled, on-site support. In this case, then, existing powers of the military and concentrated capital strengthened their position in the face of opportunities for flexible distributed manufacture and we would be foolish not to consider the possibilities of such an occurrence in the factories of the virtual future. Having looked at how managing might be affected by the move to a (partially) virtual world, we conclude our book with a brief examination of how we ourselves might be affected by such moves. Consideration of these matters allows us to finish where we started, with consideration of both the *relationality* of the virtual world and its implications for *identity*, particularly those dimensions of identity associated with gender.

Community and identity in a virtual world

Who lives in the virtual parts of our partly virtual world and how do they relate to each other?

users are white [or about 90% of them are], have professional or managerial occupations, higher than average incomes and are likely to be located in the developed world. (Jordan, 1999: 53–4)

As Jordan also notes, the age profile of users is relatively stable, with the majority being in their early to mid-thirties and while the gender breakdown of users can be seen to be slowly equalizing, the virtual world is still predominantly male. It is to this gendering of the virtual world and its implications for the identities lived out within it that we devote most of our concluding thoughts. As we have already noted, many proponents of the virtual world suggest that it is a place where we can leave all our problematic distinctions, the bases for the invoking of prejudices by others, behind. Trend (2001: 183) illustrates this naive belief with a recent

MCI WorldCom ad, which 'typifies the boosterism that posits the Net as colorless, carefree, and democratic':

There is no race. There is no gender. There is no age. There are no infirmities. There are only minds. Utopia? No, Internet.

But, as our statistics above suggest, this is simply not the case, and MCI WorldCom know this as well as anyone. What is clearly being referred to in the quote is the way in which one's disembodied presence on the Internet allows one to hide, deny or invent anew one's actual embodied materiality. If you're a boy, you can say you're a girl. If you are white, you can say you are black, in an endless masked parade of identities. But this does not mean that one's bodily identity is so easily dispensed with and matters little if the environment online is generally tolerant of material that would offend those of colour, women and those whose sexual persuasion is other than straight:

In any visit to an online chat room one will observe voluminous anti-Semitic, racist, homophobic, and especially sexist speech, giving the lie to the myth of a disembodied or colorless cyberspace. (Trend 2001: 184)

Indeed, in such circumstances, non-whites, non-male, non-heterosexual users who have chosen to perform their identity online as other than it bodily/materially is will feel their 'real' identities intensely as they are simultaneously self-erased. Such a *life on screen* (Turkle 1996) is far from utopian. As indeed is much of the 'community' formed online (see Brown et al. 1998). 'Community' is one of Raymond Williams' keywords. He uses its references to common interests and remarks that it is a:

'warmly persuasive' word, whether used to describe existing or alternative relationships: what is more important, perhaps, is that unlike other terms of social organisation (state, nation, society etc) it never seems to be used unfavourably and never to be given any positive opposing or distinguishing term. (Williams 1976: 66)

Despite such usage, one can witness online communities as being formed not so much by a coming together over shared likes but more over shared *dislikes*, antagonisms, as we witnessed earlier in our groupware case. And thus the anti-Semitism, racism, homophobia and sexism signalled by Trend may perhaps unfortunately be seen as emblematic of a particular mode of community formation, in which the 'other' functions as a scapegoat (Burke 1969) who ritually accepts all the iniquities of the community formers as they coalesce around their enmity for their shared victim. Consider the following less extreme form of the process and its interrogation (or for an even more extreme version see Aycock and Buchignani 1995).

John Seabrook's dismay as his past writings for the *New Yorker* are served up in an online community for public disapproval.

The community in question is WELL – Whole Earth 'lectronic Link. For more on virtual communities, see Turkle (1984 and 1996) and Stone (1995).

Topic 748 [media]: The New Yorker

#145: The Sweat of Fear Smells Disgusting (rbr)

Well, good! So here we can turn our attentions to the travails of John Seabrook, who, in a remarkable impression of Ved Mehta, gets ten pages out of one e-mail message.

This piece reminded me a little of Bill Clinton's address to the 1988 Democratic National Convention. Seabrook touches all of the bases, and speaks to many of the points that need to be spoken to, and it's encouraging to see someone speaking to these 5 points under the national spotlight. And yet, he rambles, stumbles over the complexity of the issues, and ends up talking for a very long time for all the actual information he manages to impart.

Then Jon Carroll, the *Chronicle* columnist, posted:

#152· One word: rostrum

heh. veteran readers will remember seabrook as the author of the 'he likes me! he really likes me!' article about Bill Gates. This article seemed to consist of the author creating a persona that he believed would be attractive but was in fact intolerable. I found myself rooting for the flamer [Seabrook's article included both an interview with Bill Gates and an account of a subsequent 'flaming' from an author of an earlier book on Gates who considered that Seabrook had 'ripped off' their work.], altho I'm not a flaming kind of guy. Put this animal out of its misery, I thought, although that was an uncharitable and wrong thought.

#160· One word: rostrum

I'm sorry; I hate flamewars as much as anyone and more

than some. I have no idea why seabrook makes me think evil thoughts. It's just so darn passive aggressive.

#161: Kathleen Creighton (casey)

Sounds like he's a chucklehead and will be rightfully driven from the net. In fact, I'd like his e-mail address *right now* myself. I've got this pent-up hostility – oh, 45 years' worth – I'd like to do something with :-). (Seabrook, 1997: 168–71)

Seabrook eventually responds in the following way and also seeks some information on scapegoating from the archive:

Put yourself in my position. It's kind of scary. It wasn't that long ago that I was tremblingly showing my overwritten manuscripts to editors and feeling that sick feeling in the pit of my stomach when their voice came onto the phone with that sympathetic tone in it saying, 'It's really well written but …' Now, I'm listening to people call my writing/me 'intolerable' (jrc); a 'chucklehead' (casey); 'painfully uninteresting' (rbr); 'a specialty writer' (kj); 'not a specialty writer' (mnemonic); and 'aggressively and dangerously stupid' (hlr) … But perhaps the cruellest cut of all was to compare me to Ved Mehta (rbr).

#229: Howard Rheingold (hlr)[1]

It's an initiation ritual, John Seabrook. Stick around and help us dump on the next guy. ;-)

Another poster said:
Welcome to (if I may say it) the real world.' (ibid., p. 177)

Topic 173 [archives]: System Scapegoat – does the WELL always need one?
Started by: Stewart Brand (sbb)

This is a topic for public discussion of my shortcomings and how they are the source of all problems on the WELL.;

The purpose is to determine what is the proper behavior toward whoever is the current System Scapegoat, and how the goat should best behave.

#15: well's cargo (dlee)

Maybe it's because I don't frequent the 'right' conferences, but it seems pretty rare to see an sbb posting. I have great respect for his accomplishments, and like Howard says, it seems fairly natural to be both fascinated and intimidated by Stewart. But Howard's description of him as 'aloof' and paternal fits what little I've seen of his postings, and it seems like Stewart's happy enough being aloof and intimidating.

It fits the pattern that he would open this topic, and with the words he used. I didn't see that, by WELL standards, he's been flamed that much, but he seems mightily annoyed that people would be so low class as to question him at all. Scapegoat?

Hardly, Stewart; you flatter yourself.

If you're content to rest on your laurels, then fine, Stewart. Go away. That's not what the WELL's about. We're all peers here, dude. If you think you're being treated unfairly then tell us why, and tell us what IS going on. Give us something more than 'wise' terseness. If you really care about us, and the ongoing health and viability of the WELL, then be a part of it and us. Otherwise it's easy to think that you see the WELL more as another nice item for your biography.

#36: Stewart Brand (sbb)

Who actually does the hard work of scapegoating?

Judging by mine, they are volunteers, not paid, self-appointed, not elected or otherwise appointed, and energetic. Unrelentingness is part of the profile. If the scapegoat's behavior is not changing as demanded, hit harder and more often. Sometimes a Tormenter goes so over the top that he or she flips into the Scapegoat role, for over-reaching and thus endangering the system. Gans has been there, I believe. Tormenters never get to be the System Darling, who is the mirror of the System Scapegoat. I've been the Darling a time or two. Last time I checked Cliff Figallo was sort of it, but John Coate is carrying the main burden, this week. Darlinghood is limited because you're only allowed to say adorable things on line, same as the Goat is only allowed to say defensive things on-line (if he or she says something adorable, it must be attacked).

I've learned there are only two viable responses to Scapegoathood – defensiveness, and defiance. This topic represents my changing gears from the one to other. That I'm having a good time with the experiment is driving my Tormenters crazy, as it is intended to.

#43: Stewart Brand (sbb)

Now a tricky moral question.

Do Scapegoats feel pain?

Of course not. A Scapegoat is a chimaeric entity, a projection, and therefore incapable of pain.

Well then, do Tormenters intend to inflict pain?

Yes, and it apparently gives them pleasure to do so, but that may be my biased perspective. However, they know that a chimaeric entity feels no pain after all, so they are absolved from feeling bad.

This is a demonstration of a fundamental truth, quickly and harshly learned, of Scapegoathood. Never show blood in a flock of chickens.

#57: Mouthy Scorp (axon)

well, heaven forfend that i should bully saint stewart. i'm afraid this latest exercise in obfuscation fails to sustain my interest. it's just a lot of handwaving.

now that i've been branded a Torturer i suppose i can die happy. but it isn't true that my intention is to inflict pain. far from it. my only intention is to help. you took it wrong, and my apologies to all. if my rhetoric offends. but it seems to have gotten your attention, at least, and i'm willing to be 'the bad guy' (new well cultural icon; alongside The Scapegoat, The Tormentor and The Darling) if it will give you a safe way to gauge the depth of user resentment without sacrificing your own ego needs. (Seabrook, 1997: 158–61)

How are we to make sense of this? In J.G. Ballard's recent novel *Cocaine Nights*, it is suggested that this is always how communities form, in response to a perceived outside threat. In the novel, crime is the threat that delivers the inspiration for community formation. As one of the protagonists puts it:

'Burglary fills you with anger, even a self-righteous rage. The police are useless, fobbing you off with vague promises, and that generates a sense of injustice, a feeling that you're surrounded by a world without shame. Everything around you, the paintings and silverware you've taken for granted, fit into this new moral framework. You're more aware of yourself. Dormant areas of your mind that you haven't visited for years become important again. You begin to reassess yourself …' 'Exactly.' Crawford patted my arm, happy to welcome me to his flock. 'We form watch committees, elect a local council, take pride in our neighbourhoods, join sports clubs and local history societies, rediscover the everyday world we once took for granted. We know that it's more important to be a third rate painter than to watch a CD ROM on the Renaissance. Together we begin to thrive, and at last find our full potential as individuals and as a community.' (1996: 244–5)

For others the issue is more related to the specificity of the virtual environment, particularly the potential anonymity we considered earlier:

Because people cannot see or hear others laugh, wince, or indicate other immediate reactions to their performances they become less socially inhibited and more likely to be rude (or, as it is called, within the CMC subculture, to 'flame') … The upshot of these findings for the social potential is well summarised by Baron (1984) who writes that 'Computer Mediated Communication – at least as currently used – is ill suited for such 'social' uses of language (p. 136). (Baym 1995: 140)

Indeed, Seabrook notes down a conversation with Eugene Spafford, a self-professed Usenet old-timer attempting to 'get people to act with "decency" on Usenet':

What I see is new users getting on-line, promptly getting flamed by the older users, and then saying to themselves, hey let's get down and dirty and go for it. In any other kind of medium, the reality of the two people talking would prevent a lot of ugliness from happening, but with nothing but bits between them, people feel they can say anything they like – it's not a human you're talking to, it's just a machine. (Seabrook 1997: 119)

But it may not just be the anonymity of the medium, or a consequence of the lack of cues associated with the screening that the system provides, but also because our vantage point on our virtual world is one which, despite the rhetoric of virtual reality, is separate and separates us out as a viewing self, distinct from the virtual environment, not a part of it. We look *at* the virtual world, move *forward* through it (Bailey 1996). We accept a Cartesian, rational viewing point that 'permits the world to be constructed as something to be examined, manipulated, or owned' (Trend 2001: 184), positioning the viewer as 'male, white, straight, able bodied and dominant classed (Bailey 1996, cited in Trend 2001: 184), as indeed our statistics suggest they are. This is not a welcoming world for those who do not fit the bill.

Or so some say! It is nice to finish on a positive note and that is what we try to do. Other commentators have seen the form of page linking that exists on the Internet, 'hypertext', as a veritable embodiment of the postmodernist/poststructuralist modes of critical thinking that we have frequently valorized throughout this text (see, particularly, Landow 1991). Landow draws on the literary theorist Roland Barthes's distinction between writerly and readerly texts. The former can only be read by following the prescribed lines of the author. The author produces; the reader merely consumes (in the most impoverished sense of the term). In the latter, readerly case, the 'reader is no longer a consumer, but a producer of the text' (Barthes 1974: 4). In the opportunities it gives 'readers' to produce their own texts by creating their own pathways through the bringing together of different chunks of text from different sources, hypertext is, for Landow, a readerly text. Even though a book is 'a linear thing, decidedly non-hypertexty' (Bell 2001: 1), we hope that the eclectic mix of chapters and themes produced here in this text, along with our varying

treatments of them and our accounts of the variety of ways in which they might be used, constitutes something of a readerly text itself. That's what we've tried to make possible – a *virtuality* whose realization is down to you!

References

Aycock, A. and Buchignani, N. (1995) 'The e-mail Murders: Reflections on dead letters' in S.G. Jones (ed.) *Cybersociety: Computer Mediated Communication and Community,* Thousand Oaks, CA: Sage.

Bailey, C. (1996) 'Virtual skin: Articulating race in cyberspace', in A. Moser and D. MacLead (eds) *Immersed in Technology: Art and Visual Environments*, Cambridge: MIT Press.

Ballard, J.G. (1996) *Cocaine Nights,* Flamingo: London.

Bard A. and Söderqvist J. (2002) *Netocracy,* tr. Neil Smith, London: Pearson Education.

Barker, F. (1984) *The Tremulous Private Body: Essays in Subjection*, London: Methuen.

Baron, N.S. (1984) 'Computer mediated communication as a force in language change', *Visible Language*, **18**(2): 118–41.

Barthes, R. (1974) *S/Z*, tr. R. Miller, New York: Hill and Wang.

Baudrillard, J. (1981/90) *Seduction*, Basingstoke: Palgrave Macmillan.

Baym, N.K. (1995) 'The emergence of community in computer mediated community' in S.G. Jones (ed.) *Cybersociety: Computer Mediated Communication and Community,* Thousand Oaks, CA: Sage.

Bell, D. (2001) *An Introduction to Cybercultures*, London: Routledge.

Bell, D. and Kennedy, B. (2000) *The Cybercultures Reader*, London: Routledge.

Berners-Lee, T. (2003) W3C director and inventor of the World Wide Web (W3C Web Accessibility Initiative – http://www.w3.org/WAI/ accessed 27 February).

Bey, H. (1996) 'The information war' in T. Druckery (ed.), *Electronic Culture: Technology and Visual Representation*, New York: Aperture: 369–75.

Brown, S.D. and Lightfoot, G.M. (1998) 'Insistent emplacement: Heidegger on the technologies of informing', *Information Technology & People*, **11**(4): 290–304.

Brown, S.D. and Lightfoot, G. (2002) 'Presence, absence and accountability: E-mail and the mediation of organisational memory' in S. Woolgar (ed.) *Virtual Society?: Technology, Cyberbole, Reality*, Oxford: Oxford University Press.

Brown, S.D., Lilley, S. and Lightfoot, G. (1998) 'Crime, Cohesion and (Virtual) Community', paper presented at the European Association for the Study of Science and Technology, Lisbon.

Brown, S.D., Middleton, D. and Lightfoot, G. (2001) 'Performing the past in electronic archives: Interdepencies in the discursive and non-discursive organisation of institutional rememberings' *Culture & Psychology,* **7**(2): 123–44.

Burke, K. (1969) *A Grammar of Motives*, Berkeley: University of California Press.

Castells, M. (1993) 'The new informational economy in the new international division of labour', in M. Carnoy, M. Castells, S. Cohen and F. Cardoso (eds), *The New Global Economy in the Information Age*, University Park, PA: Pennsylvania State University Press

Castells, M. (2000a) *The Information Age: Economy, Society and Culture – Volume I: The Rise of the Network Society*, Oxford: Blackwell.

Castells, M. (2000b) *The Information Age: Economy, Society and Culture – Volume II: The Power of Identity*, Oxford: Blackwell.

Castells, M. (2000c) *The Information Age: Economy, Society and Culture – Volume III: End of Millennium*, Oxford: Blackwell.

Cooper,. R. (1991) 'Formal organizations and representation: Remote control, displacement, abbreviation', in M. Redd and M. Hughes (eds) *Rethinking Organization: New Directions in Organization Theory and Analysis*, London: Sage.

Cubitt, S. (1998) *Digital Aesthetics*, London: Sage.

Dandeker, C. (1990) *Surveillance, Power and Modernity*, Cambridge: Cambridge University Press.

Deal, T.E. and Kennedy, A.A. (1982) *Corporate Cultures: The Rites and Rituals of Corporate Life*, New York: Addison-Wesley.

Drew, P. and Heritage, J.C. (1992) *Talk at Work: Interaction in Institutional Settings,* Cambridge: Cambridge University Press.

Drucker, P. (1967) 'Technology and Society in the Twentieth Century', in M. Kranzberg and C.W. Pursell (eds), *Technology in Western Civilization*, New York: Oxford University Press.

Goody, J. (1986) *The Logic of Writing and the Organization of Society*, Cambridge: Cambridge University Press.

Goody, J. (1987) *The Interface Between the Written and the Oral*, Cambridge, Cambridge University Press.

Harvey, D. (1989) *The Condition of Postmodernity*, Oxford: Blackwell.

Heidegger, M. (1977) *The Question Concerning Technology and Other Essays*, New York: Harper & Row.

Hewett, J. (2000) 'This quick Jack is Net nimble', *Sydney Morning Herald*, 23 September, pp. 21, 24.

Hiltz, S.R. and Turoff, M. (1978) *The Network Nation: Human Communication via Computer*, Cambridge, MA: MIT Press.

Holderness, M. (1998) 'Who are the world's information-poor?', in B. Loader (ed.) *Cyberspace Divide: Equality, Agency and Policy in the Information Society*, London: Routledge.

Jordan, T. (1999) *Cyberpower: The Culture and Politics of Cyberspace and the Internet*, London: Routledge.

Kallinikos, J. (1995) 'The architecture of the invisible', *Organization*, 2(1): 117–40.

Kellner, D. (1999) 'Virilio, war and technology: some critical reflections', *Theory, Culture and Society*, 16(5–6): 103–26.

Khoshafian, S. and Buckiewicz, M. (1995) *Introduction to Groupware, Workflow and Workgroup Computing*, New York: John Wiley.

Kluger, J. (2000) 'A new factory for a new age', *Time Magazine*, pp. 75–7.

Kreitzman, L. (1999) *The 24 Hour Society*, London: Profile Books.

Kroker, A. and Weinstein, M.A. (1994) 'The theory of the virtual class', in A. Kroker and M.A. Weinstein, *Data Trash: The Theory of the Virtual Class*, New York: St Martin's Press: 4–26; partially reproduced in Trend (2001: 144–53).

Landow, G. (1991) *Hypertext: The Convergence of Contemporary Critical Theory and Technology*, London: John Hopkins University Press.

Lash, S. and Urry, J. (1993) *Economies of Signs and Space*, London: Sage.

Law, J. (1994) *Organising Modernity*, Oxford: Blackwell.

Lee, J.Y. (1996) 'Charting the codes of cyberspace: A rhetoric of electronic mail', in L. Strate, R. Jacobson and S. Gibson (eds) *Communication and Cyberspace: Social Interaction in an Electronic Environment*, Cresskill, NJ: Hampton Press.

Luke, T. (1999) 'Simulated sovereignty, telematic territory: the political economy of cyberspace', in M. Featherstone and S. Lash (eds) *Spaces of Culture: City, Nation, World*, London: Sage.

Lyon, D. (2001) *Surveillance Society: Monitory Everyday Life*, Buckingham: Open University Press.

McArthur, T. (1986) *Worlds of Reference: Lexicography, Learning and Language From the Clay Tablet to the Computer*, Cambridge: Cambridge University Press.

Mathews, R. and Wacker, W. (2002) *The Deviant's Advantage; How Fringe Ideas Create Mass Markets*, New York: Crown.

Noble, D. (1985) 'Social choice in machine design: The case of automatically controlled machine tools', in D. MacKenzie and J. Wajcman (eds.) *The Social Shaping of Technology*, Milton Keynes: Open University Press.

Noble, D. (1986) *Forces of Production*, Oxford University Press.

Ong, W. (1982) *Orality and Literacy*, London: Methuen.

Pinch, T.J. and Bijker, W.E. (1987) 'The social construction of facts and artefacts: Or how the sociology of science and the sociology of technology might benefit each other', in W.E. Bijker, T.P. Hughes and T.J. Pinch (eds) *The Social Construction of Technological Systems: New Directions in the Sociology and History of Technology*, Cambridge, MA: MIT Press.

Porat, M. (1977) *The Information Economy: Definition and Measurement*, Special Publication 77-12(1), Washington, DC: US Department of Commerce, Office of Telecommunications.

Rice, R. and Love, G. (1987) 'Electronic emotion: Socioemotional content in a computer mediated communication network', *Communication Research*, 4(1): 85–103.

Richards, B. (2000) 'Superplant', www.company.com, November, pp. 182–96.

Rosen, M. and Baroudi, J. (1992) 'Computer based technology and the emergence of new forms of managerial control', in A. Sturdy, D. Knights and H. Willmott (eds) *Skill and Consent: Contemporary Studies in the Labour Process*, London: Routledge.

Schmitz, J. and Fulk, J. (1991) 'Organizational colleagues, media richness and electronic mail: A test of the social influence model of technology use', *Communication Research*, 18(4): 487–523.

Seabrook, J. (1997) *Deeper: My Two Year Odyssey in Cyberspace*, London: Faber and Faber.

Sewell, G. and Wilkinson, B. (1992a) 'Someone to watch over me: Surveillance, discipline and the just-in-time labour process', *Sociology*, 26(2): 271–89.

Sewell, G. and Wilkinson, B. (1992b) 'Empowerment or emasculation: A tale of shopfloor surveillance in a total quality organization' in Blyton, P. and Turnbull, P. (eds) *New Perspectives on Human Resource Management*, London: Sage.

Shortis, T. (2001) *The Language of ICT: Information and Communication Technology*, London: Routledge.

Sikka, P. (2002) 'We are a nation of accountants But it does us no good when the industry remains so self-serving', *Guardian* Wednesday 20 February.

Simon, H. (1960) *Administrative Behavior*, New York: Macmillan.

Slevin, J. (2000) *The Internet and Society*, Cambridge: Polity Press.

Sproull, L. and Kiesler, S. (1998) *Connections: New Ways of Working in the Networked Organization*, 6th edn, Cambridge, MA: MIT Press.

Stone, A.E. (1995) *The War of Desire and Technology at the Close of the Mechanical Age,* Cambridge, MA: MIT Press.

Stone, A.R. (S.) (1991) 'Will the real body please stand up? Boundary stories about virtual cultures', in M. Benedikt (ed.), *Cyberspace: First Steps*, Cambridge, MA: MIT Press.

Trend, D. (ed.) (2001) *Reading Digital Culture*, Oxford: Blackwell.

Tucker, C. (2002) Managing the Edge, *American Way,* 15 August, pp. 66–9.

Turkle, S. (1984) *The Second Self: Computers and the Human Spirit,* New York: Simon & Schuster.

Turkle, S. (1996) *Life on the Screen,* London: Weidenfield & Nicholson.

Virilio, P. (1995) 'Speed and information: Cyberspace alarm!', *Le Monde Diplomatique*, August, tr. P. Riemens and included in Trend (2001: 23–7).

Virilio, P. (2000) *The Information Bomb*, London: Verso.

Visions of Heaven and Hell III: The Virtual Wastelands, written by Mark Harrison, produced and directed by Mark Harrison and Leanne Klein, 1994, Channel Four Television.

Vogel, D. and Nunamaker, J. (1990) 'Group decision support system impact: Multi-methodological exploration', *Information and Management*, Winter 15–28.

Watson, T.J. (1994) *In Search of Management*, London: Routledge.

Williams, R. (1976) *Keywords,* London: Penguin

Zuboff, S. (1988) *In the Age of the Smart Machine: The Future of Work and Power*, New York: Basic Books.